Domestic Violence Against Male Same-Sex Partners
in the EU with Special Reference to Refugee
and Migrant Gay Men in Germany

Yeshwant Naik

Domestic Violence Against Male Same-Sex Partners in the EU with Special Reference to Refugee and Migrant Gay Men in Germany

 Springer

Yeshwant Naik
Institute for International and Comparative Public Law
Westfälische Wilhelms-Universität Münster
Münster, Germany

ISBN 978-3-030-86809-3   ISBN 978-3-030-86807-9   (eBook)
https://doi.org/10.1007/978-3-030-86807-9

This Springer imprint is published by the registered company Springer Nature Switzerland AG.
The registered company address is: Gewerbestrasse 11, 6330 Cham, Switzerland

Acknowledgement

This book would have been impossible without the support of the Fritz Thyssen Stiftung, and the Westfälische Wilhelms-Universität Münster. I would like to thank all those who helped me throughout the process of this project.

5.10   Positive Judicial Findings   94
5.11   From Persecution to Acceptance: LGBT Rights in Germany . . .   97
5.12   Conclusion   99
References   100

6   **Domestic Violence Among German, Refugee, and Migrant Gay
    Men in Germany**   103
6.1   Sexual Racism   103
6.2   Gay Refugees and Migrants in Germany   104
6.3   Overt Discrimination on Gay Chat Websites   106
6.4   Queer Refugee Activism   107
6.5   Sexual Abuse Among Gay Men   108
6.6   Implications, Policy, and Research   111
6.7   NGO Reports on Domestic Violence   113
6.8   Conclusion   115
References   116

7   **Epilogue: Domestic Violence and Happiness**   121
References   125

Table of Cases   127

Abbreviations and Acronyms

ACHPR	Protocol to the African Charter on Human and Peoples' Rights
ACHR	American Convention on Human Rights
African Charter	African Charter on Human and People's Rights
African Commission	The African Commission on Human and Peoples Rights
CAT	UN Committee Against Torture
CEDAW	UN Convention on the Elimination of All Forms of Discrimination Against Women
CESCR	The Committee on Economic, Social and Cultural Rights
CFR	Charter of Fundamental Rights of the European Union
CJEU	Court of Justice of the European Union
CoE	Council of Europe
ECHR	European Convention for the Protection of Human Rights and Fundamental Freedoms
ECJ	The European Court of Justice
ECtHR	European Court of Human Rights
EEC	European Economic Community
ESC	European Social Charter
HASC	Home Affairs Select Committee
HRC	The Human Rights Committee
IACHR	Inter-American Commission on Human Rights
IAOtHR	Inter-American Court of Human Rights
ICCPR	The International Covenant on Civil and Political Rights
ICESCR	The International Covenant on Economic, Social and Cultural Rights
ICJ	International Court of Justice
NPIA	The National Police Improvement Agency
OHCHR	UN High Commissioner for Human Rights
UDHR	Universal Declaration of Human Rights

UNHRC	UN Human Rights Council
VAW	Violence Against Women
WHO	World Health Organization

Chapter 1
An Introduction to Sexual Abuse and Domestic Violence in Germany

Much has been written about sexual racism among gay men, e.g., white gay men stereotype Asian men as feminine and desexualized and Black men as hypersexual;[1] Asian men discriminate against or ignore Arabs, Latinos, Blacks, and vice-versa; and Arabs, Asians, Latinos, and Blacks have shown a preference for gay white men, according to reports. In the gay community, whiteness has always been an acceptable norm, and non-whiteness the exception,[2] which merely reflects racist power hierarchies.[3] Most white men hesitate to defend these facts and simply disguise their discrimination as "preferences" or "choices."[4] In the present day, racial preference has become a very common criteria on gay dating sites, although citing user ethnicity is "voluntary" on such sites: especially white men expect non-white men to disclose their ethnicity and origin.[5] The Britain-based "LGBT Fact Site" conducted a survey and found that "[m]ore than two-thirds of the men from Black, Asian and other minority ethnic backgrounds had personally experienced racism on the gay scene."[6] Sexual racism was even evident during Pride Month in Philadelphia, when a gay bar responded to racist allegations by adding black and brown to the rainbow flag.[7] In Germany, the refugee crisis has had a striking impact on the gay scene. Unlike in Britain and the United States, the German gay community appears to be tolerant and liberal toward refugees and migrants; however, this tolerance is only superficial and the reality of racist power hierarchies is not much different. Whereas British and

---

[1] See Hoang (1999), pp. 235–253.

[2] Hoang (1999).

[3] Callander et al. (2012).

[4] Paul (2010).

[5] Paul (2010).

[6] Haggas (2017).

[7] Flores (2017).

Y. Naik, *Domestic Violence Against Male Same-Sex Partners in the EU with Special Reference to Refugee and Migrant Gay Men in Germany*, https://doi.org/10.1007/978-3-030-86807-9_1

1

American white gay men spew offensive or racial comments about non-white men,[8] German gay men silently distance themselves from them.

The problem is compounded by the European migration crisis. Among the large number of persons from non-European countries who have entered Germany through the Balkan and Mediterranean routes are many gay men. They have arrived in Germany only to realize that they would have to face the same people they feared in their home country, as migrators have brought along with them the same conservative views about homosexuality.[9] Many are still living in the closet and would not consider coming out. They suppress their sexuality in refugee shelters. Many feel ashamed and are afraid of being attacked if they disclose their orientation. There have been reports of an attack on a Syrian gay couple seeking asylum in Germany, and of refugees suffering from physical assaults and verbal threats by other refugees because of their sexuality. On account of such incidents, gay rights activists have opened shelters for gay refugees in cities like Berlin and Cologne, among others.[10] Most refugees have a tough time convincing immigration authorities of their sexual orientation. "Straight-acting" gay men are often mistaken as heterosexual by authorities. Also, some straight-acting bisexual men claim to be gay. To take advantage of this situation, some heterosexual men also claim to be gay. Since newly arrived refugees merely resume the social scenario of corruption existing in their home country in Germany, which includes bribing the authorities, they indeed create a challenge to the European Court of Justice, which banned sexuality "tests" for asylum seekers.[11] Activists allege that immigration authorities have been asking gay refugees embarrassing questions;[12] that the decision makers are not trained in LGBT issues; and that gays are victimized.[13]

Beside these structural and institutional hardships, it is also significant to note how German gay men discriminate against refugee and migrant gay men.[14] Discrimination is invisible to the mainstream public, but it is a well-known fact among gay men. German gay men are divided in their approach toward the refugees and migrants. Some like them, whereas others do not. In both cases, though, abuse is a common factor. Similar to Britain and the United States, the most common place for refugee and migrant men to experience sexual abuse and racism in Germany is on gay chat websites like "Planet Romeo" or "Gay Royal," where most contacts among gay men are made. German gay men usually defend themselves in their profile texts by claiming that they have been fooled or cheated by refugees or migrants, either for money or for the purpose of obtaining a visa or passport. On the other hand, some young refugees and migrants are forced to use drugs or alcohol to enable unwanted

---

[8] See Allen (2015).

[9] Dammers (2016).

[10] See *Berlin opens Germany's first major gay refugee centre* (2016).

[11] See Judgment of the Court (Grand Chamber) of December 2, 2014.

[12] Lowe (2017).

[13] Hauswedell (2017).

[14] Hauswedell (2017).

sex practices, especially for high or long duration sex performance.[15] Young refugees from war zones are popular for offering sex for money. Berlin's *Tiergarten* is a noted destination for young male refugee prostitution.[16]

Despite the sexual racism and abuse experienced by some gay men, studies on LGBT sexual abuse in Germany are mostly conducted on lesbian women.[17] Generally speaking, there are a plethora of studies on the experiences and treatment of women exposed to intimate partner violence.[18] Far fewer studies exist pertaining to sexual abuse among gay men. In some of the studies that have been conducted, researchers found evidence of a higher percentage of violence in gay relationships as opposed to heterosexual ones. These studies typically employ a very small sample group; they found that percentages of violence within homosexual relationships range between 15–50%.[19]

Research findings reveal that most abuse experienced in homosexual relationships is similar to that in heterosexual relationships, the only difference being that it is less talked about and hence "invisible."[20] It is all too often assumed that men can't be victims of sexual abuse because they are supposed to be stronger and aggressive. Or, due to the myth that most gay men are promiscuous and have a high sex drive,[21] the general awareness of sexual abuse among adult men is only a recent development in medical, psychological, and sociological literature. Most of the early literature focused on male children rather than adults.[22] The National Crime Victimization Survey conducted by the United States Bureau of Justice Statistics found that 11% of total sexual assault victims are male.[23] England and Wales reported that male rape comprises 7.5% of all rape reported to criminal authorities.[24] The invisibility of same-sex domestic violence is evidenced by the general lack of statistics on its prevalence in states throughout the world. The UN Secretary-General's database on violence against women includes reports submitted by each of the 192 member states of the United Nations on documented cases of violence against women, including statistics for opposite-sex domestic violence. However, no similar database exists for the prevalence of same-sex domestic violence in any of these states.[25]

Lara Stemple describes the lack of awareness of sexual abuse and assault among gay men in the following words: "Despite the grave and widespread nature of sexual

---

[15] Deimel et al. (2016).

[16] See Bückmann and Schaible (2017).

[17] See Brückner (2002), Curtis (1999), Frenznick and Müller (2002), Ohms and Müller (2001), Ohms (2008), and Hagemann-White (1997).

[18] Larsen et al. (2014).

[19] Losehand (2012).

[20] Walby and Allen (2004).

[21] See Stemple (2009).

[22] Tewksbury (2007), pp. 22–23.

[23] Stemple (2009), p. 607.

[24] Stemple (2009), p. 607.

[25] Serra (2013), p. 598.

violence against men and boys, the current international human rights framework is inadequate for addressing this problem . . . The international instruments that contain the most comprehensive and meaningful definitions of sexual violence exclude men on their face, reflecting and embedding the assumption that sexual violence is a phenomenon relevant only to women and girls."[26]

Unlike heterosexual and lesbian relationships, problems of domestic and sexual violence usually go unreported; gay victims see these problems as private affairs and do not believe they will receive a supportive response.[27] Also, most gay men never realize the seriousness of the abuse. Several reports reveal that sexual abuse victims (both men and children) are less likely to report their victimization than female victims due to the social biases against them.[28] The stigma attached to their sexuality incites fear that they might be doubted.[29] These reasons obviously keep refugees and migrants from complaining about abuse. Due to the misconceptions of instability revolving around gay relationships, the public does not realize the seriousness of this problem. Very few services exist for gay men who are abused by other gay men. According to Jeffery Weeks, even the public agencies lack education and awareness on the subject and hence are not able to respond effectively.[30] In order to overcome the ongoing stress and anxiety, many have resorted to alcohol, drugs, medications,[31] and unsafe sex practices leading to STDs.[32]

1.1   Book's Aim

In November 2018, I set out to acquire knowledge about sexual racism and domestic violence among gay men, especially among refugees and migrants living in Germany, phenomena which have been either largely ignored or silenced socially and politically. Given the sensitive and controversial character of domestic violence among gay men—something which concerns their *most* private lives—it was a challenge for me to obtain significant data from them because trust was required, which can only be built over time. This book was written in the three-year span of a research stipend provided by the Fritz Thyssen Foundation. The project had an interdisciplinary nature, uniquely combining methods of jurisprudence and ethnology, which is reflected in this work.

---

[26] Stemple (2009), p. 619.
[27] Donovan et al. (2006).
[28] Stemple and Meyer (2014).
[29] Stemple and Meyer (2014).
[30] See Donovan et al. (2001).
[31] Donovan et al. (2001), p. 29.
[32] Donovan et al. (2001), p. 28.

The research during this period was analytical and empirical; it was designed to deepen our knowledge and understanding of the nature of domestic violence,[33] and sexual abuse among male same-sex partners and dating violence.[34] The analytical component involved looking at the causes of violence and how violence is manifested in male same-sex partnerships. A comprehensive literature review was done on topics relating to domestic violence: the concept itself, including its historical background, evolution, and its determinants in the East and West; court decisions concerning domestic violence; and domestic violence among gay men (refugee and migrant) in Germany and the EU. The literature review informed of the state of the art of knowledge, revealed the gap in current literature, and indicated what needs to be done to advance knowledge about the topic.

We found that German studies on LGBT domestic violence is most strongly emphasized in the context of lesbian women.[35] This situation is not limited to Germany, but applies to other jurisdictions, e.g., the US, UK, Australia, and Canada. While there are many studies on the experiences and treatment of women exposed to domestic violence,[36] we only found a few studies pertaining to violence among consenting gay men. Many studies found that there is a higher percentage of violence in gay relationships as opposed to heterosexual ones. But these studies typically employ a very small sample group.[37]

Research findings also showed that most abuse experienced in homosexual relationships is similar to that in heterosexual relationships, the only difference being that it is less talked about and hence "invisible."[38] The invisibility of same-sex violence is evidenced by the general lack of statistics on its prevalence in states throughout the world, as mentioned above. In summary, domestic violence usually goes unreported because gay victims see this as a private affair and do not believe they will receive a supportive response.[39] The stigma attached to their sexuality incites fear, and this fear, when coupled with the fact of xenophobia, especially discourages refugees and migrants from complaining about abuse.

Literature obviously exists on justice in divorce cases involving domestic violence against women and how the judicial justice system has dealt with such problems. Judicial responses to domestic violence and intimate partner violence across countries (e.g., Canada, UK, Australia, Europe, etc.) typically involve only women and children.[40] When domestic violence was examined in the context of

---

[33] I.e., physical, mental, and verbal abuse.

[34] E.g., the acts of dominating, forcing, or pressuring unwanted specific sex acts.

[35] Brückner (2002), Curtis (1999), Frenznick and Müller (2002), Ohms and Müller (2001), Ohms (2008), and Hagemann-White (1997).

[36] Larsen et al. (2014).

[37] Losehand (2012).

[38] Walby and Allen (2004).

[39] Donovan et al. (2006).

[40] See Arcidiacono and Crocitti (2015), Erez (2002), Maxwell et al. (2001), and Keith (1988).

immigration and asylum, only women were taken into consideration as victims.[41] There is very limited research on domestic violence in the context of immigration in which gay refugee and migrant men are victims.[42] On the whole, data on same-sex intimate partner violence is sparse due to a lack of awareness, taboo, and the stigmatization of homosexuality. Sensitizing this issue on local, national, and international levels can help to promote awareness, and policy research can help fill in the current research gap.

In this book, good practices in place in the EU are analysed, as well as the agencies and institutions mandated to tackle domestic and dating violence. I respond to the measures taken by European legislators to prevent domestic violence. My research falls within the scope of Resolution 1582 (2007), to combat domestic violence against women; Resolution 1697 (2009), to consider the special risk of domestic violence against migrant women, and the Committee of Ministers' Recommendation Rec(2002)5, to protect women against violence.[43] It argues that the provisions of these Conventions and domestic laws should be extended to male same-sex relationships.

The empirical or ethnological component of this project involved extensive data collection, which I gathered using participant observation and other ethnographic practices, such as formal and informal interviews, individual or focus group interviews, questionnaires, discussions, in-depth case studies, orally told stories, and informal conversations.[44] Snowball sampling and purpose sampling were used.[45] Expert interviews were conducted with people who possessed specific knowledge about social facts, such as scholars, government officials working with refugees, lawyers, social workers, and the refugees themselves. Some of the refugees I interviewed were networked through NGOs. I would like to thank the NGOs LSVD (The Lesbian and Gay Federation in Germany), Rosa Strippe, Bochum, Queer Refugee Café, Muenster, Rainbow refugees (Dresden and Munich) for helping me to network and collect data.

1.2   Summary of Chapters

In Chap. 2, "A Legal Historical Overview of Domestic Violence," I examine the definition of domestic violence, as well as the ancient, medieval, and modern legal history of domestic violence. Historically, when abuse inflicted on males by females was made public, it caused men disgrace, and this attitude did not even alter in the

---

[41] See Thiara et al. (2011) and Gonçalves and Matos (2016).

[42] Huntley et al. (2019), Oliveira Araujo et al. (2019), Schrijver et al. (2018), Regan et al. (2012), and Robert Wood Johnson Foundation (2009).

[43] See Viggiani (2016).

[44] Blommaert and Dong (2010), pp. 62–65.

[45] Blommaert and Dong (2010), pp. 62–65.

1970s, with the emergence of women's and men's rights movements. Since the 1970s, scholars have focused on violence against women and have ignored the fact that violence transcends gender. To avoid debasing themselves, men have failed to report victimization. Due to a data shortage, policymakers, law enforcement bodies, the LGBT community, and psychoanalysts have failed to obtain a clear impression of the problem, which directly affects policies and services allotted to the LGBT community. In conclusion, I consider domestic violence from a broader perspective and ask why do humans practice abusive or violent behavior. In response, I refer to the Indian philosophy of Sri Aurobindo.

In Chap. 3, I describe the development of international law on domestic violence in heterosexual relationships, and argue that it can be used as a model for international law on same-sex domestic violence. International organizations, national governments, domestic violence agencies, and LGBT communities are finding it difficult to integrate the problem of same-sex domestic violence into international deliberation. But the rate of same-sex domestic violence victims is at least equal to the 25% of the heterosexual women who experience domestic violence during their lifetimes. Chapter 3 therefore emphasizes equality before the law and non-discrimination as two crucial principles for accessing legal remedies against same-sex domestic violence. The judicial interpretation and role of human rights defenders are also summarized.

Chapter 4 examines the legal framework in the EU for preventing or combating domestic violence and dating violence among male same-sex partners. Globally, the norms to tackle domestic violence have evolved through the medium of law and jurisprudence. Since the scope of this study is limited to the European Union, this chapter provides an overview of the formation, composition, jurisdiction, and the activism of the Court of Justice and the European Court of Human Rights on LGBT family rights. Concerning the protection and promotion of LGBT rights, we find that the courts have developed a more elaborate concept to reduce discrimination with the help of the EU legislature, which has indirectly influenced the member states to adopt effective directives. Furthermore, fundamental rights and collective action have been more enhanced by the ECtHR than the ECJ.

Relying on landmark judgments, Chap. 5 looks at the public and private dichotomy of domestic violence. With the help of provisions of the ECHR, the chapter affirms state obligations to protect women from domestic violence, and claims the obligations should be extended to the LGBT community. Domestic violence law in the jurisprudence of the European and German Courts is elaborated. Even though domestic violence has gained attention at the international level in recent years, especially from international bodies like the United Nations, LGBT domestic violence has hardly been addressed. Against this backdrop, the chapter assesses the legal history and evolution of LGBT rights in Germany.

In Chap. 6, I propose that LGBT access to domestic violence remedies can be improved by incorporating same-sex domestic violence into the emerging international doctrine on LGBT human rights as well as into domestic laws. In this chapter, the problem of sexual racism is considered in light of the increase of queer refugees and migrants in Germany. Through direct interviews with queer refugees, victims of domestic violence, and members of the German gay community, the queer refugee experience of living in Germany is captured. Additionally, this chapter examines the situation of sexual exploitation among queer refugees and Germans, which is surprisingly practiced by both. Finally, the work and knowledge of various European NGOs are taken into account, as well as implications for practice, policy, and future research.

1.3 Conclusion

International discourse on domestic violence had its earliest roots in the Convention on the Elimination of All Forms of Discrimination against Women, which was adopted by the UN General Assembly in 1979 and entered into force in 1981.[46] The General Assembly adopted a resolution specifically seeking the "elimination of domestic violence against women" in 2004.[47] However, these guidelines have not yet been extended to same-sex domestic violence survivors. In 2007, a group of experts from twenty-five states released the Yogyakarta Principles on the Application of Human Rights Law in Relation to Sexual Orientation and Gender Identity,[48] but these principles do to address issues pertaining to domestic violence in same-sex households. The first UN resolution on LGBT human rights was brought into effect in 2011. It provided recommendations for member states to address abuses against LGBT people,[49] but did not specifically provide for eliminating domestic violence among intimate partners.

Domestic violence encroaches upon the fundamental human rights of its survivors. Like the survivors in opposite-sex relationships, LGBT survivors experience a violation of the human right to life and to their dignity and bodily integrity when they are abused by partners. Hence, same-sex domestic violence must be incorporated into the international discourse on LGBT human rights.[50] The omission amounts to the failure of states to offer survivors access to national domestic violence

---

[46] See Convention on the Elimination of All Forms of Discrimination Against Women (December 18, 1979).

[47] See Elimination of Domestic Violence Against Women, G.A. Res. 58/147, U.N. Doc. A/RES/58/147 (February 19, 2004).

[48] See *An Activist's Guide to The Yogyakarta Principles* (2010). For human rights defenders, see Gross (2008), pp. 235–253.

[49] *Discrimination on Grounds of Sexual Orientation and Gender Identity in Europe*, Council of Europe, Strasbourg, June 2011, p. 52; see, *Homophobia, Transphobia and Discrimination on Grounds of Sexual Orientation and Gender Identity in the EU Member States: Summary of Findings, Trends, Challenges and Promising Practices*, European Union Agency for Fundamental Rights, Vienna, 2011, p. 13.

[50] See *The United Nations Speaks Out: Tackling discrimination on grounds of sexual orientation and gender identity* (n.d.).

remedies,[51] presents a clear instance of state-sanctioned discrimination, and makes LGBT communities especially vulnerable to domestic violence. Existing international law on domestic violence against women can serve as a model for drafting guidelines to prevent same-sex domestic violence.[52]

References

Allen S (2015) 'No Blacks' is not a sexual preference. It's racism. Daily Beast. Retrieved November 20, 2017 from https://www.thedailybeast.com/no-blacks-is-not-a-sexual-preference-its-racism

An Activist's Guide to The Yogyakarta Principles (2010). Retrieved March 27, 2017 from www.yogyakartaprinciples.org

Arcidiacono D, Crocitti S (2015) Criminal justice system responses to intimate partner violence: the Italian case. Criminol Crim Justice 15(5):613–632. https://doi.org/10.1177/1748895815586271

Berlin opens Germany's first major gay refugee centre (2016) The Local. Retrieved November 19, 2017 from http://www.newnownext.com/serbia-refugee-camp-germany-attack/07/2017/

Blommaert J, Dong J (2010) Ethnographic fieldwork: a beginner's guide. Multilingual Matters, Bristol

Brückner M (2002) Gewalt im Geschlechterverhältnis – Möglichkeiten und Grenzen eines geschlechtertheoretischen Ansatzes zur Analyse häuslicher Gewalt. In: Göttert M, Walser K (eds) Gender und soziale Praxis. Helmer, Königsstein im Taunus, pp 55–68

Bückmann AK, Schaible I (2017) 'It's about survival': why young male refugees are turning to prostitution. The Local. Retrieved November 23, 2017 from https://www.thelocal.de/20170522/its-about-survival-why-young-male-refugees-are-turning-to-prostitution

Callander D, Holt M, Newman C (2012) Just a preference: racialised language in the sex-seeking profiles of gay and bisexual me. Cult Health Sex 14(9):1049–1063. https://doi.org/10.1080/13691058.2012.714799

Curtis F (1999) Gestalt-Paartherapie mit lesbischen Paaren: Anwendung von Theorie und Praxis auf die lesbische Erfahrung. In: Wheeler G, Beckmann S (eds) Gestalttherapie mit Paaren. Peter Hammer Verlag, Cologne

Dammers T (2016) This is what it's like to be a gay refugee in Germany. Vice. Retrieved November 20, 2017 from https://www.vice.com/en_us/article/yvxjgg/gay-refugees-germany-876

Deimel D, Stöver H, Hößelbarth S, Dichtl A, Graf N, Gebhardt V (2016) Drug use and health behaviour among German men who have sex with men: results of a qualitative, multi-centre study. Harm Reduct J 13(36). https://doi.org/10.1186/s12954-016-0125-y

Discrimination on Grounds of Sexual Orientation and Gender Identity in Europe (2011) Council of Europe, Strasbourg. Retrieved March 27, 2017 from https://rm.coe.int/discrimination-on-grounds-of-sexual-orientation-and-gender-identity-in/16809079e2

Donovan C, Heaphy B, Weeks J (2001) Same sex intimacies: families of choice and other life experiments. Routledge, London and New York

Donovan C, Hester M, Holmes J, McCarry M (2006) Comparing domestic abuse in same sex and heterosexual relationships. University of Sunderland and University of Bristol. Retrieved November 27, 2017 from http://www.equation.org.uk/wp-content/uploads/2012/12/Comparing-Domestic-Abuse-in-Same-Sex-and-Heterosexual-relationships.pdf

Erez E (2002) Domestic violence and the criminal justice system: an overview. Online J Issues Nurs 7(1). Retrieved November 27, 2017 from https://ojin.nursingworld.org/MainMenuCategories/

---

[51] Stemple (2009).
[52] Stemple (2009).

ANAMarketplace/ANAPeriodicals/OJIN/TableofContents/Volume72002/No1Jan2002/
DomesticViolenceandCriminalJustice.aspx

Flores AR (2017) Yes, there's racism in the LGBT community. But there's more outside it. The
Washington Post. Retrieved November 18, 2017 from https://www.washingtonpost.com/news/
monkey-cage/wp/2017/07/07/yes-there-is-racism-in-the-lgbtq-community-but-not-as-much-as-
outside-it/?utm_term=.3bfd583845dd

Frenznick M, Müller K (2002) Psychosoziale Beratung bei Gewalt in lesbischen Beziehungen. In:
Ohms C (ed) Gegen Gewalt – Ein Leitfaden für Beratungsstellen und Polizei zum Umgang mit
Gewalt in lesbischen Beziehungen. Anti-Gewalt-Projekt der Lesben Informations- und
Beratungsstelle Frankfurt

Gonçalves M, Matos M (2016) Prevalence of violence against immigrant women: a systematic
review of the literature. J Fam Violence 31:697–710

Gross AM (2008) Sex, love, and marriage: questioning gender and sexuality rights in international
law. Leiden J Int Law 21(01):235–253. https://doi.org/10.1017/S0922156507004839

Hagemann-White C, Kavemann B, Ohl D (eds) (1997) Parteilichkeit und Solidarität –
Praxiserfahrungen und Streitfragen zur Gewalt im Geschlechterverhältnis. USP International,
Bielefeld

Haggas S (2017) Racism and the gay scene. GMFA. Retrieved June 24, 2021 from https://www.
gmfa.org.uk/fs148-racism-and-the-gay-scene

Hauswedell C (2017) Hostile environment for homosexual refugees. DW. Retrieved November
18, 2017 from https://www.dw.com/en/hostile-environment-for-homosexual-refugees/
a-39673732

Hoang NT (1999) The resurrection of Brandon Lee: the making of a gay Asian American Porn Star.
In: Larry PG, Woods JD (eds) The Columbia reader on lesbians and gay men in media, society,
and politics. Between men—between women. Columbia University Press, New York, pp
235–253

Homophobia, Transphobia and Discrimination on Grounds of Sexual Orientation and Gender
Identity in the EU Member States: Summary of Findings, Trends, Challenges and Promising
Practices (2011) European Union Agency for Fundamental Rights, Vienna. Retrieved March
27, 2017 from https://op.europa.eu/en/publication-detail/-/publication/38227f8f-b0ad-4740-
a1bc-0d772541aabd/language-en

Huntley AL, Potter L, Williamson E, Malpass A, Szilassy E, Feder G (2019) Help-seeking by male
victims of domestic violence and abuse (DVA): a systematic review and qualitative evidence
synthesis. BMJ Open. https://doi.org/10.1136/bmjopen-2018-021960

Keith P (1988) The police response to domestic violence incidents. MTAS Publications. Retrieved
November 27, 2017 from https://trace.tennessee.edu/utk_mtaspubs/262

Larsen M, Krohn J, Püschel K, Seifert D (2014) Experiences of health and health care among
women exposed to intimate partner violence: qualitative findings from Germany. Health Care
Women Int 35(4):359–379. https://doi.org/10.1080/07399332.2012.738264

Losehand J (2012) Gewalt Zwischen Homosexuellen Männern. Zentrum QWIEN. Retrieved
November 18, 2017 from http://www.qwien.at/QWIEN_Gewalt_2012.pdf

Lowe J (2017) Refugees in Europe: German authorities question gay refugees on their sex lives.
Newsweek. Retrieved November 19, 2017 from http://www.newsweek.com/germany-eu-
refugees-crisis-gay-aylum-seekers-635334

Maxwell CD, Garner JH, Fagan JA (2001) The effects of arrest on intimate partner violence: new
evidence from spouse assault replication program. National Institute of Justice. Retrieved
November 27, 2017 from https://www.ojp.gov/ncjrs/virtual-library/abstracts/effects-arrest-
intimate-partner-violence-new-evidence-spouse

Ohms C (2008) Das Fremde in mir – Gewaltdynamiken in Liebesbeziehungen zwischen Frauen.
Soziologische Perspektiven auf ein Tabuthema. Transcript Verlag, Bielefeld

Ohms C, Müller K (eds) (2001) Gut aufgehoben? Zur psychosozialen Versorgung lesbischer Frauen
mit Gewalt- und/oder Diskriminierungserfahrungen im europäischen Vergleich. Anti-Gewalt-
Projekt der Lesben Informations- und Beratungsstelle Frankfurt

Oliveira Araujo J, de Souza FM, Proenca R, Bastos ML, Trajman A, Faerstein E (2019) Prevalence of sexual violence among refugees: a systematic review. Rev Saude Publica 53:78. https://doi.org/10.11606/s1518-8787.2019053001081

Paul JP, Ayala G, Choi KH (2010) Internet sex ads for MSM and partner selection criteria: the potency of race/ethnicity online. J Sex Res 47(6):528–538. https://doi.org/10.1080/00224490903244575

Regan L, Coulter M, Chantler K, Davenport R, Green L (2012) Exploring the service and support needs of male, lesbian, gay, bi-sexual and transgendered and black and other minority ethnic victims of domestic and sexual violence. Home Office SRG/06/017, Bristol. Retrieved November 27, 2017 from https://research-information.bris.ac.uk/en/publications/exploring-the-service-and-support-needs-of-male-lesbian-gay-bi-se

Robert Wood Johnson Foundation (2009) Intimate partner violence in immigrant and refugee communities: challenges, promising practices and recommendations. Retrieved November 19, 2017 from https://www.futureswithoutviolence.org/userfiles/file/ImmigrantWomen/IPV_Report_March_2009.pdf

Schrijver L, Beken TV, Krahe B, Keygnaert I (2018) Prevalence of sexual violence in migrants, applicants for international protection, and refugees in Europe: a critical interpretive synthesis of the evidence. Int J Environ Res Public Health 15(9):1979. https://doi.org/10.3390/ijerph15091979

Serra NE (2013) Queering international human rights: LGBT access to domestic violence remedies. J Gender Soc Policy Law 21(3):583–607

Stemple L (2009) Male rape and human rights. Hast Law J 60:605–647

Stemple L, Meyer I (2014) The sexual victimization of men in America: new data challenge old assumptions. Am J Public Health 104(6):19–26. https://doi.org/10.2105/AJPH.2014.301946

Tewksbury R (2007) Effects of sexual assault on men: physical, mental and sexual consequences. Int J Men's Health 6(1):22–35. https://doi.org/10.3149/jmh.0601.22

The United Nations Speaks Out: Tackling discrimination on grounds of sexual orientation and gender identity (n.d.) Retrieved March 27, 2017 from http://www.ohchr.org/Documents/Issues/Discrimination/LGBT_discrimination_A4.pdf

Thiara RK, Condon SA, Schröttle M (2011) Violence against women and ethnicity: commonalities and differences across Europe. Verlag Barbara Budrich, Leverkusen

Viggiani G (2016) Domestic and dating violence against LBT women in the EU. ILGA-Europe. Retrieved November 18, 2017 from https://www.ilga-europe.org/sites/default/files/research-book-eng.pdf

Walby S, Allen J (2004) Domestic violence, sexual assault and stalking: findings from the British Crime Survey. Home Office Research Study 276. Retrieved November 27, 2017 from http://citeseerx.ist.psu.edu/viewdoc/download?doi=10.1.1.477.2558&rep=rep1&type=pdf

Chapter 2
A Legal Historical Overview of Domestic Violence

2.1 Definitions

Domestic violence, also known as intimate partner violence (IPV), domestic abuse, dating violence, spousal abuse, and intimate partner abuse is any form of illtreatment that takes place in a heterosexual or homosexual passionate relationship between adults or adolescents. Women are often presumed to be the only victims of domestic violence.[1] Domestic violence has been defined as a pattern of assaultive, coercive behaviours involving physical, sexual, or psychological attacks and economic coercion among adults or adolescents against their spouses and intimate partners.[2]

Webster's New Collegiate Dictionary defines "violence" as the exertion of any physical force, for instance, violent treatment or procedure, infringement, outrage assault, strength, energy, activity displayed or exerted, forcible or destructive action or force. It further describes violence as the excessive or unjustifiable use of force.[3] *The Oxford Dictionary* defines violence as behavior involving physical force intended to hurt, damage, or kill.[4] According to the *Encyclopedia of Crime and Justice*, "violence is a general term referring to all types of behavior, either threatened or actual, that result in the damage or destruction of property or the injury or death of an individual." In general, the definition covers behavior that is generally considered as violent, including crimes such as criminal homicide, forcible rape, child abuse, aggravated assault, and most kinds of collective violence.[5] According to *Black's Law Dictionary*, "violence means unjust or unwarranted use of force usually accompanied by fury, vehemence, or outrage, physical force unlawfully exercised

---

[1] Ganley (2008), pp. 16, 17.
[2] Ganley (2008), pp. 18–21.
[3] See *Webster's New Collegiate Dictionary* (1981), p. 952.
[4] See *Oxford Dictionary & Thesaurus, South Asian Edition* (2005), p. 1021.
[5] See *Encyclopedia of Crime and Justice* (1983), pp. 1618–1619.

with the intent to harm." And, domestic violence is "violence between members of a household, usually spouses, an assault or other violent act committed by one member of a household against another."[6] The 1993 Home Affairs Select Committee (HASC) Report defined domestic violence as "any form of physical, sexual or emotional abuse which takes place within the context of a close relationship. In most cases, the relationship will be between partners (married, cohabiting, or otherwise) or ex-partners."[7] In the *Morris Dictionary*, the phrase "domestic violence" denotes that the victim has been subjected to a criminal act, but often conceals who is the perpetrator and who is the victim. Domestic violence is obviously not a new problem, though it has only attracted attention recently. Documentation of domestic violence originated in Western Europe, North America, Australia, and New Zealand; it has now been documented across nations and worldwide.[8]

2.2 Scope of Domestic Violence

According to the World Health Organization (WHO), domestic violence is related to any behaviour between a couple that involves acts of physical and sexual violence, emotional and psychological abuse, and controlling behaviour.[9] The National Police Improvement Agency (NPIA) claims, "Domestic violence includes any incident of threatening behaviour, violence or abuse (psychological, physical, sexual, financial or emotional) between adults, aged 18 and over, who are or have been intimate partners or family members, regardless of gender and sexuality."[10]

Perpetrator and victim are often referred to with masculine and feminine pronouns, respectively; however, the perpetrator and victim could be dating, cohabiting, married, divorced, or separated. They could be heterosexual, gay, lesbian, or transgender.[11] The U.S. Department of Justice estimates that 95% of reported assaults on spouses or ex-spouses are committed by men against women.[12] However, Buttell and Cannon[13] stated that domestic violence was not about gender, "but more about

---

[6]See *Black's Law Dictionary* (1999), p. 1564.

[7]Kury and Smartt (2006), p. 395.

[8]Kaur (2004).

[9]Rollè et al. (2018), p. 1.

[10]This is the definition of domestic violence according to the National Police Improvement agency (NPIA), the shared Association of Chief Police Officers (ACPO), Crown Prosecution Service (CPS), and Government; see National Policing Improvement Agency's Guidance on Investigating Domestic Abuse (2008).

[11]Ganley (2008), p. 17.

[12]Ganley (2008), p. 17. See Douglas (1991), pp. 525–535.

[13]Buttell and Cannon (2015), pp. 65–77.

power and control dynamics," and that to apply gender related stereotypes to treat such violence is pointless.[14]

Domestic violence is not an individual or isolated event but rather a pattern of perpetrator behaviour against a victim which could involve physical abuse,[15] emotional abuse,[16] sexual abuse,[17] psychological abuse,[18] or economic coercion.[19] Sometimes children are also victimized, or acts are directed toward them.[20] Economic abuse would involve perpetrators controlling the victim's access to family resources, questioning how the finances are spent, or making all of the financial decisions alone to maintain control. Many factors contribute and influence domestic violence behaviour, especially behaviours learned through observation or interaction, which are reinforced by societal institutions (e.g., familial, social, legal, religious, educational, mental health, medical, entertainment or the media). Besides, cultural factors, immigrant status, and language skills can influence identification, assessment, and intervention. For instance, wife beating was culturally acceptable in the past.[21] Laws did not consider violence against intimates as a crime; rather, medical and mental health systems blamed victims for provoking the violence.[22]

As mentioned, the social construction of gender is crucial to understanding domestic violence. Historically, men were expected to dominate women when necessary. The stronger party dominates the weaker one. Dominance is determined by the physical, emotional, and mental strength of a person. While "mutual battering" among gay and lesbian partners is presumed to be rare, this is only the case because less cases are reported. Even though gay and lesbian partners share the same gender, and have a comparable size and weight, a primary aggressor usually creates the atmosphere of fear and intimidation that characterizes abusive relationships. Male violence is more serious than female violence. Women use physical force against partners for self-defence, whereas men use force for control and to display power. In the case of same-sex domestic violence, the gender pattern is

---

[14] Brown (2008).

[15] Physical abuse may include spitting, scratching, biting, grabbing, shaking, shoving, pushing, restraining, throwing, twisting, slapping, punching, choking, burning, and/or use of weapons (e.g., household objects, knives, guns, etc.) against the victim.

[16] Emotional abuse may include verbal attacks against the victim and isolation.

[17] Sexual abuse may include being pressured to have sex when the victim does not want to, coerced sex by manipulation or threat, physically forced sex, or sexual assault accompanied by violence.

[18] Psychological abuse includes threats of violence and suicide threats.

[19] Ganley (2008), pp. 18–21.

[20] Ganley (2008), p. 21. Acts directed against children involve not paying child support, requiring the children to spy, requiring that at least one child always be in the company of the victim, threatening to take children away from her, involving her in long legal fights over custody, or kidnapping or taking the children hostage.

[21] Ganley (2008), pp. 21, 26.

[22] Ganley (2008), p. 24.

different.[23] Gay victims may have difficulty accepting themselves as victims because to be a victim is a sign that one lacks masculinity.

2.3   Legal History of Domestic Violence

Wife beating has been condoned throughout history. The first written laws (ca. 2500 BC) provided that the name of a woman who verbally abused her husband to be engraved on a brick, which was then to be used to dash out her teeth.[24] Hammurabi's Code, a collection of 282 rules governing ancient Babylon from 1792 to 1750 BC, contains the oldest written law on domestic violence. In Hammurabi's Code, the husband was expected to punish family members if he felt they deserved it. In ancient civilisations, wives and children were the husband's property, and in cases of adultery, a wife was to be drowned by her husband, and the son's hands were cut off if he tried to stop his father.[25] In antiquity, Aristotle and later Galen developed ideologies confirming men as more perfect than women, which lasted until the seventeenth century. According to the Roman "Code of Paterfamilias," men were the heads of the family. They had absolute authority over their family members. They could put them into slavery or even kill or sell them. Men could decide the future of a new-born baby, whether it was to be cared for or abandoned and left to die. In nineteenth century British law books, it is stated that "the husband had by law 'power and dominion over his wife', but, in a progressive measure, introduced 'the rule of thumb' whereby the husband could beat his wife only with a stick 'no thicker than his thumb', not in a 'cruel or violent manner.'"[26] Even Napoleon believed that women must be treated as "lifelong, irresponsible minors" and "legislated women into a position where they were victims of whatever abuse their husbands meted out and wrote no law to protect them."[27]

Historical accounts provide that proper behaviour within the family for centuries meant wives were to be kept at home and economically dependent on their husbands; they were owned by their husbands, and had to obey and respect them. In contrast, husbands had complete, unquestioned authority over their wives. These elements are still intact in some cultures, and are believed to be in society's best interest.[28]

---

[23] Ganley (2008), pp. 22–23 and 25.

[24] Herbert (1983), p. 2205; see also Metzger (1979).

[25] Fader (2020).

[26] Herbert (1983), p. 2205; see also Martin (1978).

[27] Herbert (1983), p. 2205; see also Davidson (1970).

[28] Herbert (1983), p. 2205.

2.4 Early Modern Domestic Violence in Europe

The history of domestic violence in Europe during the early modern period, between 1500 and 1800, suggests that the legal and social meaning of domestic violence in early modern societies was more a function of the position a person occupied within the household or community. Hence, a servant's violence toward the master was never acceptable, whatever the reason.[29] Men had the right to "chastise" their wives, servants, and apprentices. Churches and communities contributed by exercising pressure to bear such practices.[30] *Chastising one's wife* was considered a largely private affair. In the early modern period, the "Rules of Marriage" were established by the Church, which give absolute authority to a husband to discipline his wife. This was the way of life and law of the time.[31] Because male dominance was institutionalised through the medium of customs, laws, and practices, it had the appearance of being fair and normal. In the Bible, "God gave his male creation, Adam, the power to name all that he, Yahweh, created. That power, in addition, included the naming of his female helpmate, whom Adam called Eve."[32]

Any man who failed to maintain control over his wife, or other household members, would be undermined. If a wife or dependant was reputed to be drunken, quarrelsome, or violent, or suspected of adultery, then the violence employed by a husband was justified.[33] Murder of a wife by the husband for reasons such as talking back, scolding, and nagging, or for miscarrying children, was treated as a disciplinary action.[34] It wasn't about whether violence should be employed, but rather what levels and types of violence were necessary in order to assure household discipline.[35]

Under English common law, in Dublin at the time, a violent act by a woman against her husband or by a servant against a master was petty treason, whereas in Germany, the penalty for a woman who murdered her husband was decapitation. Civil and religious courts, as well as communities, tried to control the violent behaviour of husbands and wives toward each other.[36] Even the English law introduced to the American colonies allowed husbands to retain their right to physically abuse their wives.[37] The Mississippi State Supreme Court protected the husband's right to discipline his wife and held that family arguments were best left inside the walls of the home and were not proper matters for the court to intervene.[38]

---

[29] Hall (2016).

[30] Fee et al. (2002).

[31] Fader (2020).

[32] Fox (2002), p. 17.

[33] Hall (2016).

[34] Erez (2002).

[35] Hall (2016).

[36] Hall (2016).

[37] Erez (2002).

[38] Bradley v. State, 1 Miss. 156 (1824).

It stated that it would intervene only if excessive violence was inflicted.[39] The courts recognized the husband's right to use the necessary degree of force to compel the wife to "behave" and "know her place."[40] Whatever happened between wife and husband was regarded as private matters exclusively outside the ambit of the criminal justice system. The police and other justice officials followed the court.[41]

The Puritans, who were the English Protestants who fled Europe for America in search of religious freedom, established a legal system that was based on the social order of Medieval England. Though it didn't favor extreme violence, women and children were not acknowledged, and men possessed all the rights. Men were allowed to discipline their wives and children. Wives were at the mercy of their husbands and had no right to leave home or separate. The Puritans closely followed the biblical commands concerning proper husband and wife behaviour[42] The husband maintained superiority over his wife, children, and slaves for the next two centuries, until the Suffrage movement of 1848 and the Emancipation Proclamation in 1863, when attitudes toward women and minorities slowly began to change. Women came to be thought of as individuals, not merely as property.[43] A liberal pattern of gender equality began to develop considering women and men as separate but equal, though women were still most often considered subordinate and deprived of opportunities.[44]

In the late nineteenth century, lawmakers and judges were unsure whether a husband's physical cruelty toward his wife was a criminal act that could serve as a ground for divorce. In the twentieth century, major changes in the legal rights of married women in the US were brought about by the women's rights movement in the 1970s, which was instrumental in changing the prevailing attitude and approach toward domestic violence.[45] In the 1970s, remedial measures to reduce violence against women emerged; domestic violence even became a crime and a violation of law.[46] Laws and agencies were created in the US and in England extending support to helpless women. This change in attitude resulted in the further expansion of services. Social scientists, psychologists, women's rights activists, feminists, conciliation, mediation consultants, and other social service agencies provided support to victims in crisis.[47] The approach and attitude of the criminal justice system across countries has been inclined to protect women from battering incidents. This led to a

---

[39]State v. Black, 60 N.C. 262 (N.C. 1864) and State v. Oliver, 368 So. 2d 1331 (Fla. Dist. Ct. App. 1979).

[40]Joyner v. Joyner, 124 S.E. 2d 724 (1962).

[41]Erez and Belknap (1995); see also Erez (2002).

[42]Fader (2020).

[43]Fader (2020).

[44]Fox (2002), p. 26.

[45]Erez (2002).

[46]Erez (2002).

[47]Erez (2002).

reinvigoration of the civil rights movement and the UN Convention on the Elimination of All Forms of Discrimination Against Women (CEDAW) in 1979.

2.5 Men as Victims of Domestic Violence

Although it is commonly known that domestic violence originated in patriarchal society, where men are the perpetrators, there are also historical accounts indicating female violence against males from the nineteenth century.[48] For instance, the "chivari" customs in Central Europe ridiculed and publicly humiliated men who were beaten or abused by their wives. In the West of England during the sixteenth and seventeenth century there are recorded examples of the "Skimmington" procession, which publicly ridiculed men who had been beaten by their wives, parading them around on a horse or donkey. This was publicly approved by the senior figures in society since it was against natural law for a woman to be stronger than a man.[49] Generally speaking, if men were abused, they were defamed. This attitude did not change in the 1970s with the wave of feminism. Feminist lobbies advocated only for female victims of domestic abuse, which led to the mandatory arrest of men due to the pressure from the women's groups.[50] There was a great willingness to put men behind bars if they made any counter charges.[51]

2.6 Domestic Violence Against Gay Men

As a response to the women's rights movement, the men's rights movement emerged in the West subsequently. The movement focused on the discrimination and inequalities faced by men. The problem of domestic violence against men gained significant attention in the 1990s. The activists of the men's movement deployed sex role theory to argue that male gender role was similarly restrictive and damaging to men.[52] In the late 1970s, the sociologist Michael Messner wrote that "men's liberation had disappeared. The conservative and moderate wings of men's liberation became an anti-feminist men's rights movement, facilitated by the language of sex roles. The progressive wing of men's liberation abandoned sex role language and formed a pro-feminist movement premised on a language of gender relations and power.[53]

---

[48] Garratt (2012), p. 9.

[49] Garratt (2012), p. 10.

[50] Garratt (2012), pp. 10, 21.

[51] Garratt (2012), p. 22; see also George (2002).

[52] See "Men's Movement" by Flood (2007), pp. 418–422.

[53] Messner (1998).

According to Linda Kelly, most of the previously held feminist theories about domestic violence were based on the patriarchal view of male dominance. She states, "Violent behaviour is indiscriminate, or a product of either a physical or mental disorder, no patriarchal charge can be made [...] it logically follows that violence may be committed by women as well as men."[54] To account for the dearth of literature, Kelly contends, "Criticisms have ranged from personally attacking the researchers, to more academic efforts directed at attacking the work itself by denying the validity of the reports, to an outright defense of the violent behaviour of women or otherwise minimizing its significance [...] these policies are almost always led by the feminist debate." In other words, violence by women is not properly acknowledged, which has "debilitated the treatment of both domestic violence batterers and victims"[55]

Because domestic violence transcends gender and sexual orientation, stereotypes of domestic violence are invalid. Since battering is the result of "natural male aggression," it is present even among gay couples, who oftentimes imitate the heteronormative concept of marriage and family.[56] LGBT domestic violence therefore takes on many of the same forms as heterosexual domestic violence.[57] According to the WHO, "IPV [intimate partner violence] is related to any behaviour between a couple that involves acts of physical and sexual violence, emotional and psychological abuse, and controlling behaviour. According to numerous authors, the expression 'IPV' represents a form of violence that both men and women can enact, with no regard to age, marital status, or sexual orientations."[58] In other words, domestic violence is not about gender but more about control and power dynamics.[59]

Ideologies of masculinity and femininity regard homosexual men as less masculine than heterosexual men; similarly, lesbians are considered less harmful since women are perceived to be not physically dangerous.[60] In fact, many gays and lesbians have experienced additional victimization and homophobia after reporting the abuse to the police.[61] Because men are expected to defend themselves, gay men often ignore or underestimate violence in relationships and do not get the support they need.[62]

According to the National Violence Against Women Survey Report,[63] women living with female partners experienced less violence than women living with male partners. On the other hand, men living with male partners experienced more

---

[54] Kelly (2003).

[55] Kelly (2003).

[56] Herbert (1983), p. 2206.

[57] Ristock and Timbang (2005), p. 4.

[58] Rollè et al. (2018).

[59] Buttell and Cannon (2015).

[60] Rollè et al. (2018).

[61] Rollè et al. (2018).

[62] Ristock and Timbang (2005), p. 3.

[63] Tjaden and Thoennes (2000); see also Ristock and Timbang (2005), p. 6.

violence than men who lived with female partners. Around 15% of the men who have lived with a male intimate partner reported being raped, physically assaulted, or stalked by a male partner. The report concluded that "intimate partner violence is perpetrated primarily by men, whether against male or female intimates. Thus, strategies for preventing intimate partner violence should focus on risks posed by men."[64]

Service providers helping victims of domestic violence often use heteronormative language and lack awareness of same-sex relationships and same-sex violence, which leaves the impression that such services are for heterosexuals only. Also, LGBT persons are hesitant to ask for support because they are concerned about the maintenance of confidentiality.[65]

Most research on the prevalence of same-sex domestic violence has been conducted on a North American population; some have considered cases in China, Australia, Canada, South African, British, Brazil, Nigeria, Kenya, and India. The findings are similar across regions.[66] Over the past few decades, same-sex domestic violence has been researched in more depth by mental health professionals and psychologists. Historically, violence between intimate partners was only studied from a heterosexual perspective, which excluded same-sex relationships. Research on LGBT domestic violence initially surfaced in 1978 and expanded in the late 1980s.[67] Violence in the LGBT community was not discussed publicly for various reasons, after all, drawing attention to the existence of domestic violence in the LGBT community could lead to stigmatising the community at large or could give rise to negative reactions to feminism.

One of the earliest works addressing domestic violence among gay men is *Men Who Beat the Men Who Love Them: Battered Gay Men and Domestic Violence*. This book highlights the incidence of domestic violence among gay men in America, which is nearly double than that in heterosexual relationships. The book includes personal narratives, criminal code categories, and analyses criminal, mental health, medical, political, and interpersonal issues. It contends that battering is not gender-specific, and insists on criminalization of domestic violence. A wide-ranging governmental and private plan of action is proposed, including lists of necessary laws and policies, as well as outlines of awareness, necessary education, and training to understand the problem.[68]

Due to a data shortage, policymakers, law enforcement bodies, the LGBT community, and psychoanalysts fail to obtain a clear impression of this problem, which directly affects policies, services allotted to the LGBT community, and other public health matters, such as unprotected sex and related health hazards.[69]

---

[64]Ristock and Timbang (2005), p. 7.

[65]Ristock and Timbang (2005), p. 11.

[66]Rollè et al. (2018), p. 2.

[67]Stiles-Shields and Carroll (2014), pp. 2 and 7.

[68]Island and Letellier (1991).

[69]Stiles-Shields and Carroll (2014), p. 10.

2.7 A New Dialogue on Domestic Violence

Since the late 1970s, scholars have tried to explain violence against women by relating it to factors that are social, psychological, cultural, behavioral, personal, racial, ethnic, financial, biological, neurological, or environmental.[70] However, none of these factors can precisely explain why men commit violence against women. What is the reason?[71] No single reason explains or justifies men's criminal behavior.

Different theories have been applied to understand domestic violence.[72] Such theories pertain to gender inequality within the patriarchal social order. Many have been developed only to know why some men resort to violence. In doing so, scholars have ignored the gender-neutral aspect of violence and have only provided a one-sided explanation of the problem. Undoubtedly, women have been victimized by men for over 2000 years. Men have regarded women as the "other"[73] or as "separate." But domestic violence against women cannot be linked particularly to any one factor; we need to look at this problem from a broader perspective. Instead of asking why men violate laws or commit crimes against women, we need to ask why humans violate laws or commit crimes. What could be the reasons for humans to practice abusive or violent behavior?

2.8 Sri Aurobindo on Violence

While criticising Gandhi's *ahimsa* (benevolent principle of non-violence), Sri Aurobindo stated on July 23, 1923:

> I believe Gandhi does not know what happens to the man's nature when he takes to Satyagraha or non-violence. He thinks that men get purified by it. But when men suffer, or subject themselves to voluntary suffering, what happens is that their vital being gets strengthened. These movements affect the vital being only and not any other part. Now when you cannot oppose the force that oppresses, you say that you will suffer. That suffering is vital, and it gives strength. When the man who has thus suffered gets power, he becomes a worse oppressor.[74]

---

[70] Jackson (2008), p. 224.

[71] Carlson (2012), pp. 89–91.

[72] Javier and Herron (2018). See Patriarchy Theory, Feminist Theory, Family System Theory, Socio-Psychological Theories, Frustration Aggression Theory, Perversion Theory, Structural Theory, Psycho Social Theory of Learned Helplessness, Survivor Theory, Exchange Theory, Traumatic Bonding Theory, Power Theory, Cycle Theory of Violence, Stress Theory, Socio-Cultural Theory, System Tension and Feedback System Theory, Resource Theory, Social Learning Theory, Conflict Theory, Psychopathological Theory, Psychological Theory, Physiological Theory, and Social Bond Theory.

[73] Beauvoir (1949).

[74] Sri Aurobindo (2019).

Hence, he says later, "there is a need to transform the spirit of violence." Sri Aurobindo further states:

> But in this practice of Ahimsa / non-violence is not transformed. When you insist on such a one-sided principle, what happens is that can't, hypocrisy and dishonesty get in and there is no purification at all. Purification can come by the transformation of the impulse of violence. In that respect the old system in India was much better: the man who had the fighting spirit became the Kshatriya and then the fighting spirit was raised above the ordinary vital influence. The attempt was to spiritualize it. It succeeded in doing what passive resistance cannot and will not achieve. The Kshatriya was the man who would not allow any oppression, who would fight it out and he was the man who would not oppress anybody. That was the ideal.[75]

Sri Aurobindo's view on war and violence in the context of nationalism can be applied to abuse and violence in interpersonal relationships. Human evolution is a struggle and a collective journey of humanity. Just as there are cosmic forces[76] that assist, support, and deter the collective evolution of mankind, so are there individual forces that help or hinder individual evolution. Change is often resisted. When a new order or harmony replaces the old one, old forces try to disrupt. Even the forces that exist to advance evolution to the next level tend to cripple, dismantle, or refuse the change. This contradiction can lead to a crisis in relationships. The crisis might affect private life, for instance, in the form of domestic violence, and public life in the form of war or terror. The phenomenon is the same, but the impact differs since it is the reflection and notion of human consciousness on individual and collective levels, respectively. The challenge is to overcome these forces; the question becomes, how do we overcome these positive and negative forces? Sri Aurobindo writes in the following passage:

> For this Spirit, this Divine is only in outward from the Destroyer, Time who undoes all these finite forms: but in himself he is the Infinite, the Master of the cosmic Godheads, in whom the world and all its action are securely seated. He is the original and ever originating Creator, one greater than that figure of creative Power called Brahma which he shows to us in the form of things as one aspect of his trinity, creation chequered by a balance of preservation and destruction. The real divine creation is eternal; it is the Infinite manifest sempiternal in finite things, the Spirit who conceals and reveals himself for ever in his innumerable infinity of souls and in the wonder of their actions and in the beauty of their forms.[77]

It is commonly understood that everything has a metaphysical origin; destruction, too, has a metaphysical origin. If we relate this principle to interpersonal relationships, it would simply mean that when something went wrong *one could blame* it on god. But the difference is that, as per the metaphysics of consciousness, destruction is the destruction of the past,[78] the destruction of darkness, ignorance, obstruction, and negativity. Power is metaphysical. It originates with a specific purpose, but

---

[75] Sri Aurobindo (2019).

[76] The term "cosmic forces" has no standard definition. It tends to be a poetical stand-in for any "very powerful and unknown" forces, i.e., "we don't know."

[77] Sri Aurobindo (1922).

[78] Shanta (2015).

when power enters human consciousness, it becomes an object of human ego which creates one kind of disorder in the world. For instance, religion has power structures and originated to uplift humanity. But for the *human ego,* everything connected with *religion* is a means to further its own ends.[79] Human ego exploits or uses religion and power for its own expansion to satisfy greed and desire. This is what happens at the human level. Domestic violence reflects the human ego.[80] In other words, domestic violence is the ego of the past. Hostility, violence, darkness, ignorance, confusion, and misunderstanding have been a part of human life for centuries now. Our past is full of slaughter, murder, and war. Not even saints or children of god were spared. Rulers made arbitrary decisions and massacred to expand territories;[81] slavery was less about destruction and more a way of life.

Humans are conscious of their past errors; they feel disgusted with them. This is how human consciousness initially responds: it observes the extreme forms of violence from the outside and develops a feeling of disgust on the inside, which leads to change.[82] If we look at history, we see that negative forces have existed throughout. Hitler was one of the worst, because his regime propagated the horror of the Holocaust. Yet Stalin was also bad, and his regime killed far more people. The difference between the two regimes was quality versus quantity.[83]

We can draw parallels here. It's just a matter of degree but the origin is the same. Negativities will be manifested until they are resolved in human consciousness. In fact, this is the real challenge. As we work on the inside, the result will manifest on the outside.[84] For instance, when a husband restrains or controls his wife so that she does not act against his will, what does this indicate? Is there any difference between extremism like IS and this? Is there any difference between Nazism and IS? Again, it's just a matter of degree but the origin is the same. When we work toward destroying IS from the outside, we are also destroying this tendency of terror in human nature on the inside. It reflects upon our attitude that we do not want this tendency to expand. Exactly this is the situation at the interpersonal level among couples or intimate partners. Nowadays we discuss and debate issues pertaining to domestic violence, women rights, child rights, and elder rights, which we never did in the past. These questions were of no relevance in the past when violence was a way of life.

The evolution of humanity is fascinating.[85] It has started rejecting darkness, falsehood, and terror. We still have violence in relationships and in the world, but we also see large masses of people opposing it. Today, curtailing violence—whether private or public—is the responsibility of everyone. The idea of jus cogens means

---

[79] Thornton (2001).

[80] Baumeister et al. (1996).

[81] Puri (2020).

[82] Marchetti (2018).

[83] Snyder (2011).

[84] Marchetti (2018).

[85] Stringer (2011).

that we cannot allow genocide or crimes against humanity to happen. Domestic violence is an international public health issue that affects millions of individuals annually.[86] Hence, states have a duty under international law to prevent domestic violence and punish domestic violence offenders irrespective of gender.

2.9 Conclusion

This chapter has examined the definition of domestic violence in past and present contexts. It has elaborated the ancient, medieval, and modern legal history of domestic violence, which has led to the emergence of the women's and men's rights movements. Since the 1970s, scholars have focused on violence against women, thus failing to realize that violence transcends gender. From a philosophical perspective, the chapter has provided reasons for human violent behaviour: an aftereffect of the past and an international public health issue of the present.

References

Baumeister RF, Smart L, Boden JM (1996) Relation of threatened egotism to violence and aggression: the dark side of high self-esteem. Psychol Rev 103(1):5–33. https://doi.org/10.1037/0033-295x.103.1.5

Beauvoir S (1949) The second sex. Retrieved March 8, 2020 from https://www.marxists.org/reference/subject/ethics/de-beauvoir/2nd-sex/introduction.htm

Black's Law Dictionary (1999) West Group, St. Paul, Minnesota

Brown C (2008) Gender-role implications on same-sex intimate partner abuse. J Fam Violence 23:457–462. https://doi.org/10.1007/s10896-008-9172-9

Buttell F, Cannon C (2015) Illusion of inconclusion: the failure of the gender paradigm to account for intimate partner violence in LGBT relationships. Partner Abuse 6(1):65–77. https://doi.org/10.1891/1946-6560.6.1.65

Carlson BE (2012) Review of the book Sourcebook on Violence Against Women by Renzetti CM, Edleson JL, & Bergen RK. J Women Aging 24(1):89–91. https://doi.org/10.1080/08952841.2012.638880

Davidson T (1970) Conjugal crime: understanding and changing the wife beating pattern. Hawthorn Books, New York

Douglas H (1991) Assessing violent couples. Fam Soc: J Contemp Soc Serv 72(9):525–535. https://doi.org/10.1177/104438949107200902

Encyclopedia of Crime and Justice (1983) Macmillan Reference USA, New York

Erez E (2002) Domestic violence and the criminal justice system: an overview. Online J Issues Nurs 7(1):4. Retrieved March 8, 2020 from https://pubmed.ncbi.nlm.nih.gov/12044215/

Erez E, Belknap J (1995) Policing domestic violence. In: Bailey G (ed) Encyclopedia of police science. Garland Publishing, New York

---

[86] Stiles-Shields and Carroll (2014), p. 1.

Fader S (2020) A history of domestic violence: how much have things changed? Better Help. Retrieved March 10, 2020 from https://www.betterhelp.com/advice/domestic-violence/a-history-of-domestic-violence-how-much-have-things-changed/

Fee E, Brown TM, Lazarus J, Theerman P (2002) Domestic violence—medieval and modern. Am J Public Health 92(12):1908–1908. https://doi.org/10.2105/AJPH.92.12.1908

Flood M (2007) Men's movement. In: Flood M, Gardiner JK, Pease B, Pringle K (eds) International encyclopedia of men and masculinities. Routledge, London and New York, pp 418–422

Fox VC (2002) Historical perspectives on violence against women. J Int Women's Stud 4(1):15–34. Retrieved March 10, 2020 from https://vc.bridgew.edu/jiws/vol4/iss1/2/

Ganley AL (2008) Understanding domestic violence. Retrieved March 10, 2020 from https://www.familyjusticecenter.org/resources/understanding-domestic-violence-chapter-1/

Garratt Z (2012) Domestic violence against men – is it a forgotten crime? (Published Thesis). Birmingham City University, England. Retrieved March 10, 2020 from https://www.mankind.org.uk/wp-content/uploads/2015/05/ZOE-GARRATT-DISSERTATION.pdf

George MJ (2002) Skimmington revisited. J Men's Stud 10(2):111–127. https://doi.org/10.3149/jms.1002.111

Hall D (2016) Domestic violence has a history: early modern family violence. Australian Women's History Network. Retrieved March 10, 2020 from http://www.auswhn.org.au/blog/domestic-violence-history/

Herbert CP (1983) Wife battering. Can Fam Physician Médecin de famille canadien 29:2204–2208

Island D, Letellier P (1991) Men who beat the men who love them: battered gay men and domestic violence. Harrington Park Press, New York. https://www.researchgate.net/publication/247426723_Men_Who_Beat_the_Men_Who_Love_Them_Battered_Gay_Men_and_Domestic_Violence. Accessed 8 Mar 2020

Jackson NA (2008) Encyclopedia of domestic violence. Routledge, New York and London

Javier RA, Herron WG (2018) Understanding domestic violence: theories, challenges, and remedies. Rowman & Littlefield, London

Kaur G (2004) Domestic violence or violence against women: law and practice. Delhi Law Rev 26

Kelly L (2003) Disabusing the definition of domestic abuse: how women batter men and the role of the feminist state. Florida State University Law Review. Retrieved March 10, 2020 from https://time.com/wp-content/uploads/2014/12/kelly.pdf

Kury H, Smartt U (2006) Domestic violence: recent developments in German and English legislation and law enforcement. Eur J Crime Crim Law Crim Just 14(4):382–407. https://doi.org/10.1163/157181706780132850

Marchetti G (2018) Consciousness: a unique way of processing information. Cogn Process 19:435–464. https://doi.org/10.1007/s10339-018-0855-8

Martin JP (1978) Violence and the family. John Wiley and Sons, New York

Messner M (1998) The limits of "the male sex role": an analysis of the men's liberation and men's rights movements' discourse. Gend Soc 12(3):255–276. https://doi.org/10.1177/0891243298012003002

Metzger M (1979) A social history of battered women. Distributed at Consultation for Feminist Studies Training Program Coordinators, Sponsored by Secretary of State Women's Program, Ottowa, Canada

National Policing Improvement Agency's Guidance on Investigating Domestic Abuse (2008) Special Operations centre, Bedfordshire, England. Retrieved March 10, 2020 from http://library.college.police.uk/docs/npia/Domestic_Abuse_2008.pdf

Oxford Dictionary & Thesaurus, South Asian Edition (2005) Oxford University Press, Oxford

Puri S (2020) The great imperial hangover: how empires have shaped the world. Atlantic Books, London

Ristock J, Timbang N (2005) Relationship violence in Lesbian/Gay/Bisexual/Transgender/Queer [LGBTQ] communities: moving beyond a gender-based framework. Violence Against Women Online Resources. Retrieved March 10, 2020 from https://vawnet.org/material/relationship-violence-lesbiangaybisexualtransgenderqueer-lgbtq-communities-moving-beyond

Rollè L, Giardina G, Caldarera AM, Gerino E, Brustia P (2018) When intimate partner violence meets same sex couples: a review of same sex intimate partner violence. Front Psychol 9. https://doi.org/10.3389/fpsyg.2018.01506

Shanta BN (2015) Life and consciousness – the Vedantic view. Commun Integr Biol 8(5). https://doi.org/10.1080/19420889.2015.1085138

Snyder T (2011) Hitler vs. Stalin: who was worse? The New York Review. Retrieved March 10, 2020 from https://www.nybooks.com/daily/2011/01/27/hitler-vs-stalin-who-was-worse/

Sri Aurobindo (1922) Essays on the Gita. Retrieved March 10, 2020 from https://sriaurobindostudies.wordpress.com/2014/04/09/the-hidden-benevolence-of-the-divine-powers-of-destruction/

Sri Aurobindo (2019) Sri Aurobindo on Gandhi. eSamskriti. Retrieved March 10, 2020 from https://www.esamskriti.com/e/History/Great-Indian-Leaders/SRI-AUROBINDO-on-GANDHI-1.aspx

Stiles-Shields C, Carroll RA (2014) Same-sex domestic violence: prevalence, unique aspects, and clinical implications. J Sex Marital Ther 41(6). https://doi.org/10.1080/0092623X.2014.958792

Stringer C (2011) Human evolution: the long, winding road to modern man. The Guardian. Retrieved March 10, 2020 from https://www.theguardian.com/science/2011/jun/19/human-evolution-africa-ancestors-stringer

Thornton SP (2001) Freud, Sigmund. The Internet Encyclopedia of Philosophy. University of Limerick, Ireland. Retrieved March 10, 2020 from https://iep.utm.edu/freud/?fbclid=IwAR0UDjvuW7WXSI2pgVsL-SYhgOp2TfH4yMY1fHrPe_0FyyWrsiYq0ncgns4

Tjaden P, Thoennes N (2000) Extent, nature and consequences of intimate partner violence. Findings from the National Violence Against Women Survey. National Institute of Justice, Washington, D.C. Retrieved March 10, 2020 from https://www.ojp.gov/pdffiles1/nij/181867.pdf

Webster's New Collegiate Dictionary (1981) G & C Merriam Company, Springfield, Mass

Chapter 3
International Law and Domestic Violence

3.1 Understanding Domestic Violence

A growing challenge to international organizations, national governments, domestic violence agencies, and the LGBT communities is to integrate the problem of same-sex domestic violence into international deliberation. The rate of same-sex domestic violence victims is at least equal to the 25% of the heterosexual women who experience domestic violence during their lifetimes. Internalised homophobia while being raised in a heteronormative society could contribute to the increased risk of domestic violence among same-sex couples.[1]

Same-sex violence includes acts of physical, psychological, emotional, and sexual abuse that occur between two intimate partners of the same sex or gender. The consequences affect the victim's physical and mental health, family relationships, social networks, occupational functioning, and financial well-being.[2] Domestic violence inflicted by men against women has been taken very seriously by global activists, scholars, and policy makers, who have acknowledged that domestic violence violates the fundamental human rights of women. The United Nations has even introduced an international legal framework with binding and non-binding guidelines to prevent violence against women, a step which helped change public perception toward domestic violence against women across countries.[3] Nearly 89 states enacted legislations criminalising domestic violence and providing support services to the victims.[4]

---

[1] Seaman (2014).

[2] Murray and Mobley (2009), p. 361.

[3] McQuigg (2015).

[4] See the U.N. Secretary-General's study on violence against women: https://www.un.org/womenwatch/daw/vaw/violenceagainstwomenstudydoc.pdf (accessed on March 14, 2020).

Y. Naik, *Domestic Violence Against Male Same-Sex Partners in the EU with Special Reference to Refugee and Migrant Gay Men in Germany*, https://doi.org/10.1007/978-3-030-86807-9_3

The General Assembly of the United Nations requested the Secretary-General to establish a coordinated database on the extent, nature, and consequences of all forms of violence against women, and on the impact and effectiveness of policies and programs for eliminating such violence. The database was developed and launched in 2009 and was called the "UN Secretary-General's database on violence against women." In 2016, it was updated, redesigned, and relaunched as the "Global Database on Violence against Women."[5]

The causes and effects of domestic violence in same-sex and opposite-sex relationships are similar. LGBT survivors also experience the same agony leading to violation of basic human rights, especially their life, dignity, and bodily integrity, which is why there is an urgent need to incorporate same-sex domestic violence into the international discourse on LGBT human rights. This can be done by adapting or relying on existing remedies on domestic violence against women,[6] which means the similarities and differences of domestic violence in hetero- and homosexual relationships must be fully understood.

3.2 International Legal Framework on Violence Against Women

International law treats domestic violence as discrimination against women and as a violation of women's human rights. In 1996, the UN Special Rapporteur on Violence against women (VAW) stated, "The argument that domestic violence should be understood and treated as a form of torture and, when less severe, ill treatment, is one that deserves consideration."[7] In 2008, both the UN Committee Against Torture (CAT) and the UN Special Rapporteur on Torture and Other Cruel, Inhuman or Degrading treatment or punishment recognized that domestic violence could constitute torture.[8]

The General Assembly resolution on the Elimination of Domestic Violence against Women was the first Convention to recognize that domestic violence can take many different forms, including physical, psychological, and sexual violence, as well as economic deprivation and isolation. It was adopted by the General

---

[5]See the Global Database on Violence against Women: https://evaw-global-database.unwomen. org/en/about (accessed on March 14, 2020).

[6]Serra (2013).

[7]See the Report of the Special Rapporteur on violence against women, its causes and consequences, E/CN.4/1996/53, February 5, 1996: http://hrlibrary.umn.edu/commission/thematic52/53-wom.htm (accessed on March 15, 2020).

[8]See the General Comment No. 2, CAT/C/GC/2, January 24, 2008: https://www.refworld.org/docid/47ac78ce2.html (accessed on March 15, 2020) and the Report of the UN Special Rapporteur on torture and other cruel, inhuman or degrading treatment or punishment, Manfred Nowak, A/HRC/7/3, January 15, 2008: https://www.refworld.org/docid/47c2c5452.html (accessed on March 15, 2020).

Assembly in 1979 and entered into force in 1981.[9] The Convention is also described as the International Bill of Rights for Women ratified by 189 states.[10] The Convention aims to monitor the situation of women, promote women's rights, and bring to light the areas—especially political, economic, social, cultural, and civil—in which women are denied equality with men.[11]

The Convention provided certain guidelines to the state parties. Article 10 of the Convention provides that women shall have the same conditions for career and vocational education as men. They shall also have access to continuing education, including sports activities and physical education.[12] It also provided that the state parties shall confer on women the right to work and the right to choose a profession; equal pay as men; and the right to social security in cases of sickness, disability, or retirement. Also, it aims to eliminate discrimination against women in the field of health care.[13] The Convention provides for the upliftment of women in economic and social life. The state parties shall also not discriminate against women from rural areas and shall give them equal opportunity to participate in the development planning at all levels.[14] Women should be conferred equality with men before the law[15] and state parties shall eliminate discrimination against women in all matters relating to marriage and family relations.[16] According to Recommendation 19, which addresses domestic violence as a form of discrimination against women:

> Family violence is one of the most insidious forms of violence against women. It is prevalent in all societies. Within family relationships women of all ages are subjected to violence of all kinds, including battering, rape, other forms of sexual assault, mental and other forms of violence, which are perpetuated by traditional attitudes. Lack of economic independence forces many women to stay in violent relationships. The abrogation of their family responsibilities by men can be a form of violence, and coercion. These forms of violence put women's health at risk and impair their ability to participate in family life and public life on a basis of equality.[17]

---

[9] See the Convention on the Elimination of All Forms of Discrimination Against Women, December 18, 1979: https://www.ohchr.org/en/professionalinterest/pages/cedaw.aspx (accessed on March 15, 2020).

[10] See United Nations, *Treaty Series,* vol. 1249, p. 13: https://treaties.un.org/Pages/ViewDetails.aspx?src=TREATY&mtdsg_no=IV-8&chapter=4&lang=en (accessed on March 15, 2020).

[11] See the Convention on the Elimination of All Forms of Discrimination Against Women (CEDAW), December 18, 1979: https://www.ohchr.org/en/professionalinterest/pages/cedaw.aspx (accessed on March 15, 2020).

[12] Naik (2013), p. 115.

[13] Art. 12 CEDAW.

[14] Art. 13 CEDAW.

[15] Art. 15 CEDAW.

[16] Art. 16 CEDAW.

[17] See the Committee on the Elimination of Discrimination against Women, General Recommendation 19, Violence against women (Eleventh session, 1992), U.N. Doc. A/47/38 at 1 (1993): http://hrlibrary.umn.edu/gencomm/generl19.htm (accessed on March 15, 2020).

3.3   Gender-based Violence

Further, Recommendation 19 includes gender-based violence as a form of discrimination covered by the CEDAW:

> The definition of discrimination includes gender-based violence, that is, violence that is directed against a woman because she is a woman or that affects women disproportionately. It includes acts that inflict physical, mental or sexual harm or suffering, threats of such acts, coercion and other deprivations of liberty. Gender-based violence may breach specific provisions of the Convention, regardless of whether those provisions expressly mention violence.[18]

To prohibit gender-based violence, CEDAW recommends:

(a) State parties should take appropriate and effective measures to overcome all forms of gender-based violence, whether by public or private act;
(b) State parties should ensure that laws against family violence and abuse, rape, sexual assault and other gender-based violence give adequate protection to all women and respect their integrity and dignity. Appropriate protective and support services should be provided for victims. Gender-sensitive training of judicial and law enforcement officers and other public officials is essential for the effective implementation of the Convention;
(c) State parties should encourage the compilation of statistics and research on the extent, causes and effects of violence, and on the effectiveness of measures to prevent and deal with violence;
(d) Effective measures should be taken to ensure that the media respect and promote respect for women;
(e) State parties in their reports should identify the nature and extent of attitudes, customs and practices that perpetuate violence against women and the kinds of violence that result. They should report on the measures that they have undertaken to overcome violence and the effect of those measures;
(f) Effective measures should be taken to overcome these attitudes and practices. States should introduce education and public information programmes to help eliminate prejudices that hinder women's equality;
(g) Specific preventive and punitive measures are necessary to overcome trafficking and sexual exploitation;
(h) State parties in their reports should describe the extent of all these problems and the measures, including penal provisions, preventive and rehabilitation measures that have been taken to protect women engaged in prostitution or subject to trafficking and other forms of sexual exploitation. The effectiveness of these measures should also be described;
(i) Effective complaints procedures and remedies, including compensation, should be provided;
(j) State parties should include in their reports information on sexual harassment, and on measures to protect women from sexual harassment and other forms of violence of coercion in the workplace;

---

[18] See the General Comment 6, Committee on the Elimination of Discrimination against Women, General Recommendation 19, Violence against women (Eleventh session, 1992), U.N. Doc. A/47/38 at 1 (1993), reprinted in Compilation of General Comments and General Recommendations Adopted by Human Rights Treaty Bodies, U.N. Doc. HRI/GEN/1/Rev.6 at 243 (2003): http://hrlibrary.umn.edu/gencomm/generl19.htm (accessed on March 15, 2020).

(k) State parties should establish or support services for victims of family violence, rape, sexual assault and other forms of gender-based violence, including refuges, specially trained health workers, rehabilitation and counselling.[19]

3.4 Implementing International Legal Obligations

For the implementation of the provisions of the Convention, a Committee on Elimination of Discrimination Against Women has been established consisting of expert members of high moral standing. State parties are expected to report to the Committee on a periodical basis.[20] The Convention, however, did not provide for an individual complaint system. On October 7, 1999, the General Assembly adopted the Optional Protocol to the Convention on the Elimination of All Forms of Discrimination Against Women (CEDAW), which enables victims of sex discrimination, sexual exploitation, and other abuses to approach the Committee.[21] The Optional Protocol creates two procedures to monitor compliance with CEDAW. First, it establishes a communication procedure for individual women, or groups of women, to submit claims of violations after exhausting domestic remedies.[22] Second, the Optional Protocol creates an inquiry procedure which enables the Committee to investigate situations of "grave or systematic violations" of women's rights.[23] The decisions for such communications and inquiries are published on the UN Women website.[24] Both procedures can only be used in cases where the state is a party to the Convention and the Optional Protocol.

Other conventions exist to protect women. For instance, Convention on Political Rights of Women; Convention on consent of marriage, minimum age of marriage and registration of marriages; Convention on nationality of married women; and Convention on recovery abroad of maintenance.[25] Thus, by creating an effective legal framework of international law on violence against women, the problem of domestic violence has gained immense significance as a fundamental human rights concern. Due to this endeavour, several countries have criminalised domestic

---

[19] General Recommendation No. 19 (llth session, 1992) 24, made by the Committee on the Elimination of Discrimination against Women: https://www.un.org/womenwatch/daw/cedaw/recommendations/recomm.htm#recom19 (accessed on March 16, 2020).

[20] Naik (2013), p. 116.

[21] See Optional Protocol to CEDAW, https://www.un.org/womenwatch/daw/cedaw/protocol/text.htm (accessed on March 15, 2020).

[22] Art. 2, 4, Optional Protocol to CEDAW, https://www.un.org/womenwatch/daw/cedaw/protocol/text.htm (accessed on March 15, 2020).

[23] Art. 8, Optional Protocol to CEDAW, https://www.un.org/womenwatch/daw/cedaw/protocol/text.htm (accessed on March 15, 2020).

[24] "Decisions/Views," CEDAW: https://www.un.org/womenwatch/daw/cedaw/protocol/dec-views.htm (accessed on March 15, 2020).

[25] Naik (2013), p. 116.

violence through national legislations leading to an international crusade on this human rights issue.

3.5   The Charter and the Universal Declaration of Human Rights (UDHR)

Apart from these specific Conventions for the protection of women, there are other international instruments safeguarding women's rights. A fundamental principle of the United Nations Charter adopted in 1945 is the "equal rights of men and women," and protecting and promoting women's human rights is the responsibility of all states.[26] The Universal Declaration of Human Rights (UDHR) does not spell out any rights which apply to women, but it does emphasize that rights conferred under the Declaration apply to both men and women equally. It states that all human beings are born free and equal in dignity and rights.[27] That everyone is entitled to all the rights and freedoms set forth in the Declaration, without distinction of any kind, such as race, color, sex, or language.[28] Men and women of full age, without limitation, have the right to marry, to found a family, and divorce.[29] "Women" are only mentioned in Article 16. The Declaration also confers women an entitlement to special care and assistance for "motherhood."[30] Further, the right to life, liberty, and security of person,[31] and the right not to be subjected to torture or to cruel, inhuman or degrading treatment or punishment[32] are equally conferred upon both men and women. The right to vote in public,[33] and the right to work and equal pay,[34] are applicable to both men and women. Using words like "everyone" and "no one," the Declaration is gender neutral. It forbids discrimination based on sex as opposed to the earlier drafts, which stated that "all men are born free and equal." Instead, it says that all human beings are so born and entitled to the rights and freedoms set forth in the Declaration.[35]

---

[26] See Women's Human Rights and Gender Equality: https://www.ohchr.org/EN/Issues/Women/WRGS/Pages/WRGSIndex.aspx (accessed on March 16, 2020).

[27] Article 1 UDHR.

[28] Article 2 UDHR.

[29] Article 16 UDHR.

[30] Article 25 UDHR.

[31] Article 3 UDHR.

[32] Article 5 UDHR.

[33] Article 21 UDHR.

[34] Article 23 UDHR.

[35] Morsink (1991), p. 256.

3.6   International Covenant on Civil and Political Rights (ICCPR) and the International Covenant on Economic, Social and Cultural Rights (ICESCR)

Though the UDHR is of prime significance, it is not a treaty and therefore not binding, making it is a weak instrument of protection. A more precise and detailed formulation of the convention had to be drafted to bind state parties, which led to the adoption of two international covenants, which were only one in the original draft: the International Covenant on Civil and Political Rights (ICCPR) and the International Covenant on Economic, Social and Cultural Rights (ICESCR). Article 3 of these Covenants provides for equality between men and women in the enjoyment of all rights.[36] However, these Covenants are legally binding only when state parties sign/ratify them either with or without reservations.[37]

The ICCPR provides for political and civil rights identified in the Universal Declaration. It includes the right to life (Art.6), the right to freedom and security (Art. 9), and the respect of privacy (Art. 17). It prohibits torture and cruel, inhuman, or degrading treatments (Art. 7). It recognises freedom of thought, conscience and religion (Art. 18), freedom of movement (Art. 12), and freedom of association, including the right to form trade unions (Art. 22). It also guarantees the cultural rights of ethnic minorities (Art. 27).[38] Regarding women, it makes the principle of equality before the law and the principle of non-discrimination binding (Arts. 2–3). It also provides for equality between men and women at marriage and at its dissolution (Art 6), protects the right to participate in public life without discrimination (Art. 25), and prohibits the use of the death penalty on pregnant women (Art. 23).[39]

The Human Rights Committee implements human rights through a reporting procedure in which a report is submitted to the Secretary-General of the United Nations. The inter-state communication system allows complaints concerning violations of human rights. Under the 1996 Optional Protocol to the ICCPR, if a state party fails to fulfil its affirmative obligations, individual citizens are entitled to file complaints against the state parties violating civil and political rights.[40] Further,

---

[36] See the ICCPR: https://www.ohchr.org/en/professionalinterest/pages/ccpr.aspx (accessed on March 16, 2020) and the ICESCR: https://www.ohchr.org/en/professionalinterest/pages/ccpr.aspx (accessed on March 16, 2020).

[37] See the Vienna Convention on the Law of Treaties 1969, Art. 19: https://www.refworld.org/docid/3ae6b3a10.html (accessed on March 16, 2020).

[38] Gender and International Human Rights Law, Legal Assistance Centre, 2005, p. 30, http://www.lac.org.na/ (accessed March 16, 2020).

[39] Gender and International Human Rights Law, Legal Assistance Centre, 2005, p. 30, http://www.lac.org.na/ (accessed on March 16, 2020).

[40] See the Optional Protocol to the International Covenant on Civil and Political Rights, December 16, 1996, Art. 1: https://www.ohchr.org/en/professionalinterest/pages/opccpr1.aspx (accessed on March 16, 2020).

conciliation allows parties to settle the dispute amicably.[41] The ICESCR, on the other hand, requires state parties to promote the well-being of their citizens (Art. 4). It includes the right to work and professional training (Art. 6), the right to form and join trade unions (Art. 8), the right to social security (Art. 9), the right to health (Art. 12), and the right to education (Art. 13).[42] Regarding women, the Covenant once again emphasizes equality and non-discrimination (Arts. 2–3) and includes the principle of equal pay for equal work (Art. 7). It provides for the protection of motherhood (Arts. 10, 12), and calls for paid maternity leave or leave with adequate social security benefits (Art. 10).[43]

Although the ICESCR has set the principles which the state parties are required to achieve in future, its implementation measures are weaker than those provided in the ICCPR.[44] To implement the Covenant, the UN's Economic and Social Council established the Committee on Economic, Social and Cultural Rights (CESCR) in 1985. It consists of eighteen independent experts who are nominated and elected by state parties to the Covenant, who serve in their personal capacities. It monitors compliance with the Covenant by examining periodic reports submitted by state parties.[45] As a legal remedy, victims of domestic violence can invoke the ICCPR and other international treaties focused on women's rights, such as CEDAW, rather than seek recourse to the ICESCR.

Additionally, the United Nations has hosted several conferences focusing on the themes of women development, peace, equality,[46] state responsibility for violence against women,[47] and the role of women:[48] The World Conference on Women, 1985, in Nairobi; the World Conference on Human Rights, 1993, in Vienna; and the Fourth World Conference on Women, 1995, in Beijing. Other regional human rights instruments such as the European Convention for the protection of Human Rights and Fundamental Freedoms (ECHR), the American Convention on Human Rights (ACHR) and the African Charter on Human and People's Rights (African Charter) also provide protection to women from violence. Not all the provisions enlisted in these instruments relate to women's issues. State parties can sign or ratify these instruments either with or without reservations.

---

[41] Naik (2013), pp. 109–110.

[42] Gender and International Human Rights Law, Legal Assistance Centre, 2005, p. 32: http://www.lac.org.na/ (accessed on March 16, 2020).

[43] Gender and International Human Rights Law, Legal Assistance Centre, 2005, p. 32: http://www.lac.org.na/ (accessed on March 16, 2020).

[44] Naik (2013), p. 109.

[45] Gender and International Human Rights Law, Legal Assistance Centre, 2005, p. 32: http://www.lac.org.na/ (accessed March 16, 2020).

[46] See the UN Conferences on Women and Gender Equality: https://www.un.org/en/conferences/women (accessed on March 17, 2020).

[47] World Conference on Human Rights, Vienna, 1993: https://www.ohchr.org/en/aboutus/pages/viennawc.aspx (accessed on March 17, 2020).

[48] Beijing and its Follow up: https://www.un.org/womenwatch/daw/beijing/ (accessed on March 17, 2020).

3.7 The European Convention for the Protection of Human Rights and Fundamental Freedoms (ECHR)

The ECHR is a prominent regional achievement. It has established a European Commission and a European Court of Human Rights to deal with both state and individual complaints. The Commission and the Court are the most effective existing enforcement bodies despite their geographic limitations.[49] The European Commission proposed the EU sign the Istanbul Convention. The ECHR considers gender-based violence a form of discrimination against women. In *Eremia v the Republic of Moldova*,[50] the Court held that the first applicant was a victim of domestic violence at the hands of her husband, a police officer. Under the Council of Europe (CoE) Law, the Convention on preventing and combating violence against women and domestic violence (Istanbul Convention) condemns all forms of discrimination against women.[51]

In the context of migration, the CoE favors respect for fundamental rights and human dignity, as well as solidarity and shared responsibility. By following the adoption of Resolution A/HRC/35/17 on the Protection of the human rights of migrants, the CoE contributed a document to further the UN Compendium of principles, good practices and policies on safe, orderly and regular migration in line with international human rights law.[52] In 2015, the Secretary General of the CoE issued a guidance document to the 47 member states on the treatment of migrants and asylum seekers, including with regard to their reception and temporary living conditions, to ensure respect for their human rights.[53]

3.8 The American Convention on Human Rights (ACHR)

The ACHR may be invoked to protect the rights of abused women. The ACHR recognises the right to life and right to human treatment. Article 5 states, "Women, together with men, are equally entitled to these rights." The Convention imposes upon state parties an obligation to respect and ensure the rights and freedoms under the Convention, for "all persons without any discrimination on the grounds of of

---

[49] Kapoor (2011), p. 862.

[50] Application no. 3564/11: https://hudoc.echr.coe.int/eng#{%22itemid%22:[%22001-119968%22] (accessed on March 21, 2020).

[51] Handbook on European Non-Discrimination Law (2018), pp. 84, 86.

[52] See UN Compendium of principles, good practices and policies on safe, orderly and regular migration in line with international human rights law Contribution from the Council of Europe, 24th July 2017, www.ohchr.org (accessed on April 10, 2020).

[53] See UN Compendium of principles, good practices and policies on safe, orderly and regular migration in line with international human rights law Contribution from the Council of Europe, 24th July 2017, www.ohchr.org (accessed on April 10, 2020).

race, colour, sex, language, religion, political or other opinion, national or social origin, economic status, birth, or any other social conditions." Further, the ACHR affirms that "all persons are equal before the law and have equal protection of the law."[54]

3.9 Inter-American Convention on the Prevention, Punishment and Eradication of Violence Against Women

This was the first human rights treaty to highlight gender-based violence and to include special provisions that prohibit violence in the home. State parties are recommended to address causes of gender-based violence with special measures, such as introducing educational programs to counter gender stereotypes or providing social services for victims of violence. The convention helped shape the national laws in the entire region, especially concerning domestic violence.[55]

3.10 Inter-American Commission on Human Rights (IACHR) and the Inter-American Court of Human Rights (IACtHR)

The provisions under the Inter-American Convention on Violence against Women are interpreted and enforced by the IACHR and the IACtHR. The IACHR can receive and analyse communications alleging violations of human rights from state parties. The IACHR can even receive individual complaints or complaints from groups of persons or non-governmental entities concerning the violation of human rights.[56]

The IACHR can issue non-binding recommendations and refer the petitions to the IACtHR. The Commission plays an advisory role on violence against women. The IACtHR can issue binding decisions with respect to individual petitions by state parties. The IACtHR's decisions are final and not subject to appeal.[57] Thus, domestic violence victims can approach both regional authorities (the Commission and the Court) in order to safeguard their rights and hold the state parties liable for violations, if any.

---

[54] Agarwal (2007), pp. 453–454.
[55] Agarwal (2007), p. 454.
[56] Kapoor (2011), p. 882.
[57] Kapoor (2011), p. 884.

3.11   African Charter on Human and Peoples' Rights (African Charter)

The African Charter entered into force on October 21, 1986. It may be used by victims of domestic violence. The Charter imposes a general duty upon its state parties to "recognise the rights, duties and freedoms enshrined in the Charter and to adopt legislative or other measures to give effect to them."[58]

3.12   Protocol to the African Charter on Human and Peoples' Rights (ACHPR) on the Rights of Women in Africa (Protocol to African Charter)

The ACHPR is a more relevant document for domestic violence victims within the African region. This instrument was initiated by a working group in January 1998. A Special Rapporteur on the Rights of Women in Africa was also appointed in order to investigate the continued development of the Protocol. The Special Rapporteur recommends measures aimed at eliminating gender-based violence against women in Africa.[59]

3.13   The African Commission on Human and Peoples Rights (African Commission)

The African Commission was established in order to protect the rights delineated in the African Charter. The Commission protects and promotes human rights and interprets the provisions in this context. The Commission also oversees inter-state complaints and other communications, which include individual petitions.[60] Hence, its international legal instruments and obligations have helped and enabled state parties to take appropriate measures in order to reduce instances of violence against women.

---

[58] Agarwal (2007), pp. 456–457.

[59] See the Protocol to the African Charter on Human and People's Rights on the Rights of Women in Africa: https://www.ohchr.org/EN/Issues/RuleOfLaw/CompilationDemocracy/Pages/ProtocolCharter.aspx (accessed on March 17, 2020).

[60] Kapoor (2011), p. 892.

3.14 International Human Rights Law and LGBT Rights

In international discussions of LGBT human rights, these international instruments are often not mentioned in terms of same-sex domestic violence. Domestic violence against women is more acknowledged than same-sex domestic violence. The emerging dialogue on the LGBT International Human Rights law can help fill the gap between the international law on domestic violence against women and the international law on same-sex domestic violence. LGBT human rights have mainly centered on the resolutions of the UN General Assembly and the UN Human Rights Council (UNHRC).[61] Out of concern for the violation of human rights relating to sexual orientation and gender identity, the European Union supported the December 2008 UN General Assembly statement on human rights, sexual orientation, and gender identity (i.e., it is supported by sixty-eight countries from five continents).[62] In 2011, the UNHRC adopted a resolution on human rights, sexual orientation, and gender identity, which documented discriminatory laws against individuals based on their sexual orientation and gender identity; it was unanimously supported by the European Union.[63] Replying to the United Nations Human Rights Council's request, the Office of the United Nations High Commissioner for Human Rights (OHCHR) released its report on discriminatory laws and violation of LGBT Human Rights based on sexual orientation and gender identity.[64] In the following, the recent findings of the United Nations human rights bodies, regional organizations, non-governmental organizations, and information submitted by governments are discussed. Developments include:

1. Since 2011, 14 States have adopted or strengthened anti-discrimination and hate crime laws, extending protection on grounds of sexual orientation and/or gender identity and, in two cases, also introducing legal protections for intersex persons. Three States have abolished criminal sanctions for homosexuality; 12 have introduced marriage or civil unions for same-sex couples nationally; and 10 have introduced reforms that, to varying degrees, make it easier for transgender persons to obtain legal recognition of their gender identity.
2. In dozens of countries, police, judges, prison guards, medical staff and teachers are receiving gender and sexuality sensitivity training, anti-bullying programmes have

---

[61] Naik (2017).

[62] See the Guidelines to promote and protect the enjoyment of all human rights by lesbian, gay, bisexual, transgender and intersex (LGBTI) persons, Foreign Affairs Council meeting, Luxembourg, June 24, 2013: http://www.consilium.europa.eu/uedocs/cms_data/docs/pressdata/en/foraff/137584.pdf (accessed on March 18, 2020).

[63] See the UN Resolution on LGBT Human Rights: http://arc-international.net/wp-content/uploads/2011/09/HRC-Res-17-19.pdf (accessed on March 18, 2020). See also Discrimination on Grounds of Sexual Orientation and Gender Identity in Europe, *Council of Europe,* Strasbourg, June 2011, p. 52: https://rm.coe.int/discrimination-on-grounds-of-sexual-orientation-and-gender-identity-in/16809079e2 (accessed on March 18, 2020).

[64] See the U.N. High Comm'r for Human Rights, Discriminatory Laws and Practices and Acts of Violence Against Individuals Based on Their Sexual Orientation and Gender Identity: https://www.refworld.org/docid/5571577c4.html (accessed on March 18, 2020).

been launched in schools, and shelters have been built to house homeless lesbian, gay, bisexual and transgender (LGBT) youth. Popular television programmes have integrated LGBT characters in a positive way and celebrities have helped to raise awareness by "coming out" as LGBT persons themselves or speaking out in support of members of the LGBT community. In all regions, LGBT and intersex human rights defenders are more vocal and visible – in several cases successfully challenging in the courts attempts by authorities to restrict their legitimate activities.

3. While these advances are welcome, they are overshadowed by continuing, serious and widespread human rights violations perpetrated, too often with impunity, against individuals based on their sexual orientation and gender identity. Since 2011, hundreds of people have been killed and thousands more injured in brutal, violent attacks – some of which are chronicled below. Other documented violations include torture, arbitrary detention, denial of rights to assembly and expression, and discrimination in health care, education, employment and housing. These and related abuses warrant a concerted response from Governments, legislatures, regional organizations, national human rights institutions and civil society, as well as from United Nations bodies – the Human Rights Council included.

4. Concerns regarding the extent and gravity of violence and discrimination against LGBT and intersex persons have been raised repeatedly by United Nations human rights treaty bodies and special procedures. In recent years, the Office of the High Commissioner (OHCHR) has published a range of guidance and public information materials – including factsheets, booklets and short videos – and has sought to engage States in a constructive dialogue on ways to better protect the rights of LGBT and intersex persons.[65]

Oftentimes incidents of LGBT domestic violence and discrimination go unreported due to the stigma and fear of discriminatory treatment from the police or judges, which means there is a lack of proper statistics on LGBT domestic violence. International organs give more significance to violence against women, and international and national laws and respective authorities overlook the seriousness of this problem.

Despite suppression, significant progress has been made in the international discourse on LGBT human rights over the last two decades. Countries are committed to standing up to discrimination against LGBT people around the world. Judicial activism is also evolving on LGBT issues. We are witnessing recommendations from the public-spirited members of the community to governments and other influential leaders on how to improve laws and protect people's rights regardless of their sexual orientation or gender identity.[66] In some countries, awareness, acceptance, and tolerance are comparatively higher than in others who still refuse to repeal laws criminalizing homosexuality. Although hate crimes against LGBT persons have increased in all parts of the world, most jurisdictions at least claim they are working toward reducing instances of discrimination and violence.

---

[65] See the U.N. High Comm'r for Human Rights, Discriminatory Laws and Practices and Acts of Violence Against Individuals Based on Their Sexual Orientation and Gender Identity: https://www. refworld.org/docid/5571577c4.html (accessed on March 18, 2020).

[66] Amnesty International, LGBTI Rights: https://www.amnesty.org/en/what-we-do/discrimination/lgbt-rights/ (accessed on March 18, 2020).

Undoubtedly, progress is being made, but more work must be done. Awareness about the decriminalization of sexuality must be increased. The existing international discourse on LGBT domestic violence fails to address the depth of the problem and its adverse effects on the victims of LGBT domestic violence.[67] It is indispensable that victims of LGBT domestic violence are entitled to equality before law and equal protection of law irrespective of their sexual orientation or gender identity.[68] Every individual is equal in the eyes of the law and shall enjoy the same rights, privileges, and protections. Hence, states should confer upon them the right to seek recourse to both civil and criminal remedies. In the words of Natalie E. *Serra:*

> States that wish to provide equal protection and consistent enforcement of LGBT-inclusive domestic violence statutes should implement comprehensive training programs on how law enforcement officials can best serve LGBT communities and the unique needs of LGBT survivors. Failing to do so would make LGBT survivors more vulnerable to escalated violence by their partners, who could perpetrate abuse with impunity. Furthermore, when LGBT survivors expect homophobic responses from law enforcement, they are unlikely to report the abuse they experience, contributing to the lack of statistics on same-sex domestic violence and hampering the ability of states to adequately respond to the problem.[69]

Major international human rights instruments, including the United Nations Charter, the UDHR, the ICCPR, and the ICESCR have cherished the principle of non-discrimination and equality before the law. The International human rights law principle of equality before the law and non-discrimination based on sexual orientation and gender identity should be conferred upon the victims of LGBT domestic violence in the same way as it is afforded to heterosexual domestic violence victims. This will help recognize the principle that rights are equally conferred on all individuals.[70]

The Constitution of these conventions and treaties empower the authorities under the treaties to emphasize and uplift the principles of non-discrimination and equality before law. For instance, the Human Rights Committee (HRC) under the ICCPR stated, "Non-discrimination, together with equality before the law and equal protection of the law without any discrimination, constitute a basic and general principle relating to the protection of human rights."[71] And "Article 2, paragraph 1, of the International Covenant on Civil and Political Rights obligates each state party to respect and ensure to all persons within its territory and subject to its jurisdiction the rights recognized in the Covenant without distinction of any kind, such as race, color, sex, language, religion, political or other opinion, national or social origin, property, birth or other status." Article 26 not only entitles "all persons to equality before the law as well as equal protection of the law but also prohibits any

---

[67] Serra (2013), pp. 18–20.
[68] CCPR General Comment No. 18: Non-discrimination: https://www.refworld.org/pdfid/453883fa8.pdf (accessed on March 19, 2020).
[69] Serra (2013), p. 24.
[70] Human Rights and Domestic Violence (2010), pp. 72–73.
[71] CCPR General Comment No. 18: Non-discrimination: https://www.refworld.org/docid/453883fa8.html (accessed on March 20, 2020).

discrimination under the law and guarantees to all persons equal and effective protection against discrimination on any ground such as race, color, sex, language, religion, political or other opinion, national or social origin, property, birth or other status."[72] Article 3 obligates each state party "to ensure the equal right of men and women to the enjoyment of the rights set forth in the Covenant." While Article 14, paragraph 1, provides that "all persons shall be equal before the courts and tribunals, and paragraph 3 of the same article provides that, in the determination of any criminal charge against him, everyone shall be entitled, in full equality." Similarly, Article 25 provides for the "equal participation in public life of all citizens, without any of the distinctions mentioned in article 2."[73] State parties have the responsibility to confer equal rights upon all individuals without discrimination. They are also responsible for eliminating discrimination by public authorities, the community, or by private persons or bodies.[74]

International human rights instruments do not explicitly mention sexual orientation or gender identity as prohibited grounds of discrimination. However, it is accepted that "international instruments were not meant to be exhaustive in their enumeration of prohibited grounds for differential treatment."[75] On the other hand, international authorities responsible for interpreting these instruments have interpreted the prohibition of discrimination based on "sex" or "other status" to be prohibited as discrimination based on sexual orientation or gender identity. CESCR stated, "States should ensure that a person's sexual orientation is not a barrier to realizing Covenant rights, for example, in accessing survivor's pension rights." It further acknowledged, "persons who are transgender, transsexual or intersex often face serious human rights violations, such as harassment in schools or in the workplace."[76]

Growing evidence indicates that a significant number of LGBT people across countries are victims of violence, discrimination, harassment, or assault due to their sexual orientation and gender identity.[77] And there exist discriminatory national laws and practices in many countries which criminalize sexual orientation and gender identity. Hence, this issue is a matter of concern for many judicial and

---

[72] CCPR General Comment No. 18: Non-discrimination: https://www.refworld.org/docid/453883fa8.html (accessed on March 20, 2020).

[73] CCPR General Comment No. 18: Non-discrimination: https://www.refworld.org/docid/453883fa8.html (accessed on March 20, 2020).

[74] CCPR General Comment No. 18: Non-discrimination: https://www.refworld.org/docid/453883fa8.html (accessed on March 20, 2020).

[75] Human Rights and Domestic Violence (2010), p. 76.

[76] General Comment No. 20, Non-discrimination in economic, social and cultural rights (art. 2, para. 2, of the International Covenant on Economic, Social and Cultural Rights), p. 10: https://digitallibrary.un.org/record/659980?ln=en (accessed on March 20, 2020).

[77] See Discrimination on grounds of sexual orientation and gender identity in Europe, Council of Europe, November 2014, p. 51: https://rm.coe.int/discrimination-on-grounds-of-sexual-orientation-and-gender-identity-in/16807b76e8 (accessed on March 18, 2020).

legal systems around the world.[78] The international community has been reluctant to discuss issues pertaining to the violation of LGBT Human rights. In 1992, through a landmark decision, the HRC in *Toonen v Australia*[79] held that laws criminalizing consensual same-sex relations between adults are in violation of international human rights law. The Court acknowledged that sexual orientation was included in the anti-discrimination provisions as a protected status under the ICCPR. The following international law articles were invoked in this case: Article 2, paragraph 1 of the ICCPR (i.e., each state party to the present Covenant undertakes to respect and to ensure to all individuals within its territory and subject to its jurisdiction the rights recognized in the present Covenant, without distinction of any kind, such as race, colour, sex, language, religion, political or other opinion, national or social origin, property, birth or other status); Article 17 of the ICCPR (right to privacy); and Article 26 of the ICCPR (right to non-discrimination).

The Committee held that interference with consensual sexual activity was an interference with privacy under Article 17. The law could not be justified on public health grounds, because criminalization of same-sex consensual conduct could not be shown to be a reasonable or proportional means of preventing HIV/AIDS. The Committee noted that an appropriate remedy would be repeal of the law and gave Australia 90 days to report on the granted remedy. The Committee upheld Article 26 (right to equality before the law) to prohibit discrimination based on sexual orientation.[80]

In *Young v Australia,* a complaint regarding the Australian Government's refusal to extend welfare benefits to a gay man's partner, the HRC again confirmed that discrimination based on sexual orientation violates Article 26 of the ICCPR.[81] In this case, the Committee did not rely on the "sex" language in Article 26, but rather established "sexual orientation" as an independent protected classification under Article 26.[82] In *X v Colombia*, the HRC affirmed that "prohibition against discrimination under Article 26 [of the ICCPR] comprises discrimination based on sexual orientation."[83]

---

[78] Sexual Orientation, Gender Identity and International Human Rights Law, Practitioners Guide No. 4, International Commission of Jurists, Switzerland, 2009, p. 1: https://www.refworld.org/pdfid/4a783aed2.pdf (accessed on March 18, 2020).

[79] Communication No. 488/1992: http://hrlibrary.umn.edu/undocs/html/vws488.htm (accessed on March 18, 2020).

[80] Toonen v Australia, CCPR/C/50/D/488/1992: https://www.globalhealthrights.org/health-topics/health-care-and-health-services/toonen-v-australia/ (accessed on March 18, 2020).

[81] UN Human Rights Comm., Communication No. 488/1992 (Toonen v Australia): https://www.equalrightstrust.org/ertdocumentbank/Microsoft%20Word%20-%20Mr.%20Edward%20Young%20v.%20Austr.pdf (accessed on March 20, 2020).

[82] UN Human Rights Comm., Communication No. 488/1992 (Toonen v Australia): https://www.equalrightstrust.org/ertdocumentbank/Microsoft%20Word%20-%20Mr.%20Edward%20Young%20v.%20Austr.pdf (accessed on March 20, 2020).

[83] UN Human Rights Comm., Communication No. 1361/2005 (X v Colombia): http://www.worldcourts.com/hrc/eng/decisions/2007.03.30_X_v_Colombia.htm (accessed on March 20, 2020). See also Human Rights & Domestic Violence: An Advocacy Manual (2010), p. 77.

3.15   EU Non-discrimination Law

Protection against discrimination in Europe can be found within both the EU and Council of Europe law. The Court of Justice of the European Union (CJEU) interprets EU law in the light of the ECHR and the European Social Charter (ESC).[84] The EU Charter of Fundamental Rights (CFR) recognises rights enlisted in the ECHR. Individuals can complain to the EU if there is a violation of rights but such a complaint can be made before the national courts before approaching the European Court of Human Rights (ECtHR). The ECtHR will therefore not be competent to examine complaints of discrimination unless they fall within the ambit of one of the rights protected by the ECHR.[85]

The ESC expressly prohibits discrimination. Its wording is analogous to that of Article 14 of the ECHR. It provides protection from discrimination on the grounds of race, color, sex, language, religion, political or other opinion, national extraction or social origin, health association with a national minority, birth, or "other status."[86] The EU anti-discrimination law was initially limited to a provision prohibiting discrimination based on sex in employment, but its interpretation has been gradually expanded. Article 20 of the CFR states that everyone is equal before the law. Article 21 prohibits any discrimination on grounds such as sex, race, colour, ethnic or social origin, genetic features, language, religion or belief, political or any other opinion, membership of a national minority, property, birth, disability, age, or sexual orientation. Article 23 provides for gender equality.[87]

Under the ECHR, Article 13 confirms the right of access to justice, and Article 6 provides for the right to a fair trial.[88] Under EU law, access to justice is set out in Article 47 of the CFR. Article 20 of the Charter states that everybody is equal before the law, and Article 21 prohibits discrimination.[89] Further, the right for respect for private and family life is guaranteed under Article 8 of the ECHR and under Article 7 of the CFR.[90]

---

[84] Kuijer (2018).

[85] See European Convention on Human Rights: https://www.echr.coe.int/Pages/home.aspx?p=basictexts&c= (accessed on March 20, 2020).

[86] See European Convention on Human Rights: https://www.echr.coe.int/Pages/home.aspx?p=basictexts&c= (accessed on March 20, 2020).

[87] See European Union Charter of Fundamental Rights: https://ec.europa.eu/info/aid-development-cooperation-fundamental-rights/your-rights-eu/eu-charter-fundamental-rights_en (accessed on March 20, 2020).

[88] See European Convention on Human Rights: https://www.echr.coe.int/Pages/home.aspx?p=basictexts&c= (accessed on March 20, 2020).

[89] See European Union Charter of Fundamental Rights: https://ec.europa.eu/info/aid-development-cooperation-fundamental-rights/your-rights-eu/eu-charter-fundamental-rights_en (accessed on March 20, 2020).

[90] See European Convention on Human Rights: https://www.echr.coe.int/Pages/home.aspx?p=basictexts&c= (accessed on March 20, 2020), and European Union Charter of Fundamental

Over the years, the ECtHR has developed its general interpretation of Article 8 of the ECHR concerning private and family life as follows:

> the notion of "private life" within the meaning of Article 8 of the Convention is a broad concept which encompasses, inter alia, the right to establish and develop relationships with other human beings [...] the right to "personal development" [...] or the right to self-determination as such. It encompasses elements such as names [...] gender identification, sexual orientation and sexual life, which fall within the personal sphere protected by Article 8 [...] and the right to respect for both the decisions to have and not to have a child.[91]

The ECtHR applied this general principle while deciding cases of same-sex couples. For instance, in *Gas and Dubois v France*,[92] a biological mother's homosexual civil partner was refused simple adoption of her partner's child. Under French law, a simple adoption resulted in all the rights associated with parental responsibility being removed from the child's father or mother in favour of the adoptive parent, except where an individual adopted the child of his or her spouse. The ECtHR held that the situation of the applicants was not comparable to that of married couples because under French law, marriage conferred a special status on those who entered into it and the ECHR did not go so far as to compel states to provide for same-sex marriage. The ECtHR noted that a heterosexual couple in a civil partnership would also have had their application refused under the relevant provisions and as such, while the applicants were in a comparable legal situation, there was no difference in treatment based on their sexual orientation and consequently, no violation of Article 14 in conjunction with Article 8 of the ECHR.[93]

Under the ECHR, Article 14 does not explicitly list "sexual orientation" as a protected ground. However, the ECtHR has stated that sexual orientation is included among the "other" grounds protected by Article 14.[94] While interpreting the prohibition of discrimination on the grounds of sexual orientation, the ECtHR and CJEU affirm that cases relating to sexual orientation discrimination involve individuals receiving less favorable treatment because they are gay, lesbian or bisexual, but the grounds also prohibit discrimination on the basis of being heterosexual.[95] The Court's jurisprudence will be discussed in the next chapter.

Rights: https://ec.europa.eu/info/aid-development-cooperation-fundamental-rights/your-rights-eu/eu-charter-fundamental-rights_en (accessed on March 20, 2020).

[91] Handbook on European Non-Discrimination Law (2018), p. 141.

[92] Application no. 25951/07: https://hudoc.echr.coe.int/eng?i=001-109572 (accessed on March 21, 2020).

[93] Handbook on European Non-Discrimination Law (2018), p. 142.

[94] Handbook on European Non-Discrimination Law (2018), p. 178.

[95] Handbook on European Non-Discrimination Law (2018), p. 176.

3.16   Human Rights Defenders

Apart from the judiciary, human rights activists have persistently campaigned for the protection of LGBT rights and protested discrimination and violence.[96] They have been frequent targets, leading to persecution and human rights violations. This is especially the case in countries where homosexuality is criminalized.[97]

The following EU Guidelines on human rights defenders *can serve as an* appropriate starting point for guidance across countries:

1. Encouraging third countries to adopt a culture of general respect towards and recognition of the work carried out by human rights defenders, including those of human rights of LGBT people.
2. Prioritising its work in countries where there is a poor record of respect towards human rights defenders in general and specifically defenders of human rights of LGBT people, in particular where legislative changes and the imposition of criminal sanctions have had a negative impact on the work carried out by human rights defenders in relation to the human rights of LGBT people.
3. Reacting to apparent violations of the rights of human rights defenders in third countries, highlighting the EU position in relation to this issue and carrying out its work in the framework of the EU Guidelines on human rights defenders.[98]

3.17   The Yogyakarta Principles

In 2006, an acclaimed group of international human rights experts met in Yogyakarta, Indonesia, to layout a set of international principles relating to sexual orientation and gender identity. The result was the Yogyakarta Principles: a universal guide to human rights which guarantee binding international legal standards to be complied by all states. Further, Yogyakarta Principles plus 10 were adopted on November 10, 2017 as a supplement to the Yogyakarta Principles.[99] According to these principles, gay rights are considered both human rights and civil rights. The rights include but are not limited to the following: allowing men who have sex with men to donate blood; recognition of same-sex relationships such as marriage, partnership and union; allowing adoption; recognition of parenting by gay couples, anti-bullying laws and student non-discrimination laws to protect gay children and or students; immigration equality laws; anti-discrimination laws for employment and housing; hate crime laws providing enhanced criminal penalties for prejudice-motivated violence against gay people; equal age of consent laws; equal access to

---

[96]Tackling Discrimination against Lesbian, Gay, Bi, Trans, & Intersex People (2017).

[97]Promoting the Enjoyment of all Human Rights by Lesbian, Gay, Bisexual and Transgender People (2010), p. 12.

[98]Promoting the Enjoyment of all Human Rights by Lesbian, Gay, Bisexual and Transgender People (2010), p. 12.

[99]An Activist's Guide to The Yogyakarta Principles (2010).

assisted reproductive technology and legal recognition and assignment of preferred gender and laws related to sexual orientation and military service.[100]

The state is obliged to protect everyone from discrimination based on sexual orientation or gender identity and extend equality before law and the equal protection of the law without any discrimination on other grounds including gender, race, age, religion, disability, health and economic status. In this direction, the states shall:

1. embody the principles of equality and non-discrimination based on sexual orientation and gender identity in their national constitutions or other appropriate legislation, if not yet incorporated therein, including by means of amendment and interpretation, and ensure the effective realisation of these principles;
2. repeal criminal and other legal provisions that prohibit or are, in effect, employed to prohibit consensual sexual activity among people of the same sex who are over the age of consent, and ensure that an equal age of consent applies to both same-sex and different sexual activity;
3. adopt appropriate legislative and other measures to prohibit and eliminate discrimination in the public and private spheres based on sexual orientation and gender identity;
4. take appropriate measures to secure adequate advancement of persons of diverse sexual orientations and gender identities as may be necessary to ensure such groups or individuals equal enjoyment or exercise of human rights. such measures shall not be deemed to be discriminatory;
5. in all their responses to discrimination based on sexual orientation or gender identity, take account of the manner in which such discrimination may intersect with other forms of discrimination;
6. take all appropriate action, including programmes of education and training, with a view to achieving the elimination of prejudicial or discriminatory attitudes or behaviours which are related to the idea of the inferiority or the superiority of any sexual orientation or gender identity or gender expression.[101]

The state is also responsible for protecting the right to security of the person against violence or bodily harm, whether inflicted by government officials or by any individual or group. In doing so, states shall:

1. take all necessary policing and other measures to prevent and provide protection from all forms of violence and harassment related to sexual orientation and gender identity; take all necessary legislative measures to impose appropriate criminal penalties for violence, threats of violence, incitement to violence and related harassment, based on the sexual orientation or gender identity of any person or group of persons, in all spheres of life, including the family;
2. take all necessary legislative, administrative and other measures to ensure that the sexual orientation or gender identity of the victim may not be advanced to justify, excuse or mitigate such violence;
3. ensure that perpetration of such violence is vigorously investigated, and that, where appropriate evidence is found, those responsible are prosecuted, tried and duly punished, and that victims are provided with appropriate remedies and redress, including compensation;

---

[100] An Activist's Guide to The Yogyakarta Principles (2010). See also Naik (2017). For human rights defenders, see also Gross (2008).

[101] An Activist's Guide to The Yogyakarta Principles (2010), pp. 10–11.

4. undertake campaigns of awareness-raising, directed to the general public as well as to actual and potential perpetrators of violence, in order to combat the prejudices that underlie violence related to sexual orientation and gender identity.
5. take all appropriate action, including programmes of education and training, with a view to achieving the elimination of prejudicial or discriminatory attitudes or behaviours which are related to the idea of the inferiority or the superiority of any sexual orientation or gender identity or gender expression.[102]

The Yogyakarta Principles can be used as a guide by judges, court personnel, prosecutors, and lawyers concerning LGBT international human rights matters. They have been widely cited in different international publications pertaining to discourse on LGBT human rights.[103]

3.18   Conclusion

The chapter has extensively discussed the gaps between international law on domestic violence against women and the existing discourse on international law on same-sex domestic violence. Domestic violence against women is more recognized than same-sex domestic violence. The chapter has emphasized equality before the law and non-discrimination as two crucial principles for accessing legal remedies against same-sex domestic violence. International human rights instruments and authorities responsible for interpreting these instruments interpret the prohibition of discrimination based on "sex" or "other status" as discrimination based on sexual orientation or gender identity. The judicial interpretation and role of human rights defenders has been summarized. To fill these gaps, the chapter has recommended guidelines based on the Yogyakarta Principles.

References

Agarwal HO (2007) International law and human rights. Central Law Publications, India
An Activist's Guide to The Yogyakarta Principles (2010). Retrieved March 27, 2017 from www.yogyakartaprinciples.org
Gross AM (2008) Sex, love, and marriage: questioning gender and sexuality rights in international law. Leiden J Int Law 21(1):235–253. https://doi.org/10.1017/S0922156507004839
Handbook on European Non-Discrimination Law (2018) European Union Agency for Fundamental Rights and Council of Europe. Retrieved March 21, 2020 from https://fra.europa.eu/sites/default/files/fra_uploads/fra-2018-handbook-non-discrimination-law-2018_en.pdf
Human Rights & Domestic Violence: An Advocacy Manual (2010) Columbia Law School, Human Rights Clinic, & Sexuality & Gender Clinic. Retrieved March 20, 2020 from https://www.law.

---

[102] An Activist's Guide to The Yogyakarta Principles (2010), p. 13.
[103] Serra (2013).

columbia.edu/sites/default/files/microsites/human-rights-institute/files/dv%20advocacy%
  20manual.pdf
Kapoor SK (2011) International law and human rights. Central Law Publications, India
Kuijer M (2018) The challenging relationship between the European Convention on Human Rights
  and the EU legal order: consequences of a delayed accession. Int J Hum Rights 24(7):998–1010.
  https://doi.org/10.1080/13642987.2018.1535433
McQuigg RJA (2015) Domestic violence as a human rights issue: Rumor v. Italy. Eur J Int Law 26
  (4):1009–1025. https://doi.org/10.1093/ejil/chv057
Morsink J (1991) Women's Rights in the Universal Declaration. Hum Rights Q 13(2):229–256.
  https://doi.org/10.2307/762661
Murray CE, Mobley AK (2009) Same-sex intimate partner violence: a methodological review. J
  Homosex 56(3):361–386. https://doi.org/10.1080/00918360902728848
Naik Y (2013) Textbook on international law and human rights. Southern Book House
Naik Y (2017) Homosexuality in the Jurisprudence of Supreme Court of India. Springer Publishers,
  Germany
Promoting the Enjoyment of all Human Rights by Lesbian, Gay, Bisexual and Transgender People
  (2010). European Union. https://doi.org/10.2860/62206
Seaman AM (2014) Domestic violence common among same-sex partners: review. Reuters.
  Retrieved March 14, 2020 from https://www.reuters.com/article/us-domestic-violence-gay/
  domestic-violence-common-among-same-sex-partners-review-idUSKCN0HJ25X20140924?
  irpc=932
Serra EN (2013) Queering international human rights: LGBT access to domestic violence remedies.
  Am Univ J Gend Soc Pol Law 21(3):583–607. Retrieved March 14, 2020 from https://
  digitalcommons.wcl.american.edu/jgspl/vol21/iss3/3/
Tackling Discrimination against Lesbian, Gay, Bi, Trans, & Intersex People (2017) United Nations
  Human Rights, Office of the High Commissioner. Retrieved March 18, 2020 from https://www.
  unfe.org/wp-content/uploads/2017/09/UN-Standards-of-Conduct.pdf

Chapter 4
Judicial Activism and LGBT Rights

The norms to tackle domestic violence have evolved globally through the medium of law and jurisprudence. International, national, and regional law, as well as court judgments, serve as legal principles and precedents on the subject, respectively. Courts are efficiently dealing with domestic violence cases using improved methods and courses of actions. Specialized courts are designed to protect the interests of citizens, to secure the victims' safety, and to enhance defendant accountability. Since the 1980s, courts have emerged as problem solvers, leading to greater justice system accountability.

But this isn't enough to ensure social justice. Inaccessible justice can marginalize minorities.[1] There are often issues falling beyond the ambit of law and justice; they are dormant and fail to reach the court. In this context, LGBT issues pertaining to sexual orientation, gender identity, family rights, and domestic violence have challenged courts across countries to resolve cases without the backing of law and precedents. Since the scope of this study is limited to the European Union, this chapter will provide an overview of the formation, composition, jurisdiction, and the activism of the Court of Justice of the European Union (CJEU) and the European Court of Human Rights (ECtHR) on LGBT family rights.

---

[1] Monjurul Kabir (2014).

4.1   The Court of Justice of the European Union

The CJEU was established in 1952. The General Court was created in 1988, and the Civil Service Tribunal was created in 2004, which ceased to operate on September 1, 2016 after its jurisdiction was transferred to the General Court.[2] The CJEU is a multilingual institution. Each Member State has its own language and specific legal system.[3] In 2004, to relieve the burden of the CJEU and improve legal protection in the EU, the Council of the European Union attached a specialized court for civil service cases to the General court.[4] In 2015, however, the Union Legislature decided to gradually increase the number of judges at the General Court to 56 and to transfer to it the jurisdiction of the Civil Service Tribunal. The Tribunal was dissolved on September 1, 2016.[5]

4.2   Functions

In matters of Union Law, the CJEU acts as the highest judicial authority. Its main task is to ensure the interpretation and application of the Treaties in accordance with the law. This involves monitoring the application of Union law, both about the conduct of the EU institutions when implementing treaty provisions and about the fulfilment of obligations under Union law by the Member; interpreting Union law; developing Union law;[6] enforcing the law; annulling EU legal acts; ensuring the EU takes action; and sanctioning EU institutions.[7]

4.3   Composition

The CJEU is divided into two courts: The European Court of Justice (ECJ), which deals with requests for preliminary rulings from national courts, certain actions for annulment and appeals, and the General Court, which rules on actions for annulment that can be brought by individuals, companies, and, in some cases, EU

---

[2] See Court of Justice of the European Union: https://curia.europa.eu/jcms/jcms/Jo2_6999/en/ (accessed on April 8, 2020).

[3] See CJEU: https://curia.europa.eu/jcms/jcms/Jo2_6999/en/ (accessed on April 8, 2020).

[4] See Article 257 TFEU.

[5] Borchardt (2017), p. 80.

[6] Borchardt (2017), p. 80.

[7] See https://europa.eu/european-union/about-eu/institutions-bodies/court-justice_en (accessed on April 8, 2020).

governments in case of infringement of their rights.[8] Each judge and advocate general are appointed for a renewable six year term, jointly by national governments.[9]

4.4   Jurisdiction

Prof. Klaus-Dieter Borchardt has precisely explained the ECJ's scope and function:

> In carrying out these functions, the Court's work involves both legal advice and adjudication. Legal advice is provided in the form of binding opinions on agreements which the EU wishes to conclude with non-member states or international organisations. Its function as a body for the administration of justice is much more important. However, in exercising that function, it operates in matters that in the Member States would be assigned to different types of court, depending on their national systems. It acts as a constitutional court when disputes between Union institutions are before it or legislative instruments are up for review for legality; as an administrative court when reviewing the administrative acts of the Commission or of national authorities applying union legislation; as a labour court or industrial tribunal when dealing with freedom of movement, social security and equal opportunities; as a fiscal court when dealing with matters concerning the validity and interpretation of directives in the fields of taxation and customs law; and as a civil court when hearing claims for damages or interpreting the provisions on the enforcement of judgements in civil and commercial matters.[10]

Thus, the ECJ hears matters from a national court especially when a national court refers question on the interpretation of EU law to the ECJ. It interprets the legal provisions and sends the matter back to the national court for a final decision. Nevertheless, the national court is free to decide issues concerning their own nation's laws. Additionally, private individuals can also ask the ECJ to annul an EU act that directly concerns them.

The ECJ and the ECtHR are not related to each other. However, there are concerns about consistency in case law between the two courts. The ECJ refers to the judgments of the ECtHR and treats the ECHR as a part of the EU's legal system.

4.5   The European Court of Human Rights

The European Commission on Human Rights dissolved with effect from November 1, 1998. With effect from November 1, 1998, the only institution for the implementation of the provisions of the ECHR is the ECtHR. Article 19 of the ECHR sets up a

---

[8] See https://europa.eu/european-union/about-eu/institutions-bodies/court-justice_en (accessed on April 8, 2020).

[9] Borchardt (2017), p. 80.

[10] Borchardt (2017), p. 81.

European Court of Human Rights, which is to function on a permanent basis. The original Convention required at least eight State Parties to accept the jurisdiction of the Court. This requirement was fulfilled in September 1958; the Court was set up in January 1959, but only the state accepting its jurisdiction could bring a case before the Court.[11]

4.6   Composition of the Court

The ECtHR is composed of judges equal to that of the High Contracting States.[12] Currently, there are 47 judges from 47 Member States. There are no restrictions on the number of judges of the same nationality. Judges[13] are elected by the Parliamentary Assembly of the Council of Europe for a term of six years.[14] The judges shall be of high moral character and must possess the qualifications required for the appointment of high judicial office. Judges act in their individual capacity and are not represented by any State.[15] The term of office expires when they reach the age of seventy.[16] No judge may be dismissed from office unless other judges decide by a majority of two-thirds that he or she has ceased to fulfil the required conditions.[17]

4.7   Jurisdiction of the European Court of Human Rights

The jurisdiction of the Court extends to all matters concerning interpretation and application of the Convention and the Protocols thereto.[18] The Court has the following three types of jurisdictions:

1) **Inter-State cases**: The State Parties may refer to the Court any alleged breach of the provisions of the Convention and the Protocols thereto by other State Parties.[19]
2) **Individual applications**: The Court is empowered to receive individual applications for the violations of human rights. It receives applications from any person, non-governmental organisation, or group of individuals claiming to be the victim

---

[11] Kapoor (2018), pp. 886–867.
[12] Article 20 of the European Convention.
[13] Agarwal (2007), p. 451.
[14] Article 23.
[15] Article 21.
[16] Article 23.
[17] Article 24.
[18] Article 33, 34, and 47.
[19] Kapoor (2018), p. 869.

of a violation by one of the High Contracting Parties of the rights set forth in the Convention. Question of admissibility of cases brought by the individuals are decided by three judges of the Court.[20] The Court deals with the matter after all domestic remedies have been exhausted. The matter should be brought before it within a period of six months from the date on which the final decision was taken.[21] The Court does not deal with any individual application which is substantially the same as a matter that has already been examined by the Court or has already been submitted to another procedure of international investigation or settlement and contains no relevant new information.[22]

3) **Advisory opinions**: The Court, at the request of the Committee of Ministers, gives advisory opinions on legal questions concerning the interpretation of the Convention and protocols thereto.[23] Decisions of the Committee of Ministers to request an advisory opinion of the Court requires a majority role of the representatives entitled to sit on the Committee.[24] The Court gives reasons for its advisory opinion. If the advisory opinions do not represent, in whole or in part, the unanimous opinion of the Judges, any Judge shall be entitled to deliver a separate opinion.[25]

The Court has ruled matters pertaining to treatment of individuals,[26] refugees,[27] military actions,[28] freedom of speech,[29] religion,[30] interstate cases,[31] etc. It has tried to balance the aim of the ECHR, i.e., the effective protection of fundamental rights and the need to regard national traditional ethics and sensitivities. In doing so, it had to protect individuals against fundamental rights violations and to clarify on the general scope and meaning of the Convention.[32]

---

[20] Article 34.

[21] Article 35(1).

[22] Agarwal (2007), p. 451.

[23] Article 47, para 1.

[24] Article 47, para 3.

[25] Article 49.

[26] *Ireland v United Kingdom* (5310/71).

[27] *Cyprus v Turkey* (25781/94).

[28] *A and others v UK* (3455/05).

[29] *Appleby v UK* (44306/98).

[30] *Refah Partisi (the Welfare Party) and Others v Turkey* (41340/98, 41342/98, 41343/98).

[31] *Ireland v the United Kingdom* (5310/71, 5451/72), *Denmark v Turkey* (34382/97).

[32] Gerards and Senden (2009).

4.8   Judicial Activism of the ECtHR and ECJ on LGBT Rights

Activism of the ECtHR and ECJ means that judgments are made without the basis of law and treaties. EC law is at an early stage, so the treaties or laws do not cover every aspect, and are sometimes silent. And this is when the ECtHR and ECJ become activists. In doing so, both Courts go beyond the normal decision-making procedure in forming law and policy by their decisions. In this perspective, the cases of LGBT discrimination based on sexual orientation, gender identity, and family life serve as a litmus test for activism.

Many cases have reached the ECJ and the ECtHR that claim equal rights for homosexuals at par with heterosexual ones. In *Norris v Ireland*,[33] the claim that the criminalisation of homosexual acts between consenting adult men were in violation of Article 8 of the ECHR was upheld. As an effect of this judgment, homosexuality was decriminalised in Ireland in 1993.

The support extended by the ECtHR and ECJ toward the development of homosexual rights led to the granting of tenancy rights. In *Schalk & Kopf v Austria*,[34] the ECtHR denied same-sex couples in cohabitating relationships the right to marry. In doing so, it held that de facto partnership falls within the notion of "family life." At this stage, the ECtHR and the ECJ were both reluctant to accept the equal rights argument in favor of same-sex marriage.

It is interesting to note the stand of the ECJ and the ECtHR on the right to parenthood. The majority of national legislations from the EU member states are challenged by same-sex couples on discrimination grounds of Article 8 (right to family life) and Article 14 (the enjoyment of the rights and freedoms without discrimination on any ground such as sex, race, color, language, religion, political or other opinion, national or social origin, association with a national minority, property, birth or other status) of the ECHR.

In *Niemietz v Germany*,[35] the ECtHR openly refused to define private life. But in its later decision, the Court held that the right to respect for private life definitely comprises the right to establish and develop relationships with other human beings.[36] In *Bensaid v United Kingdom*,[37] the Court held that "gender identification, name and sexual orientation and sexual life" are protected by Article 8 of the ECHR.

In *Mata Estevez v Spain*,[38] the Court accepted same-sex relationships only to be protected by the right to respect for private life, and not the right to a family life.

---

[33] Application no. 6/1987/129/180, 26 October 1988.

[34] Application no. 30141/04, 24 June 2010.

[35] Application no. 13710/88, 16 December 1992, (1993) 16 EHRR 97, para 29.

[36] *Botta v Italy* (21439/93).

[37] Application no. 44599/98, 6 February 2001, (2001) 33 EHRR 205, para 59.

[38] Application no. 56501/00, 10 May 2001.

However, after two years, in *Karner v Austria*,[39] there was a turning point where the Court granted same-sex couples the right to succeed to a tenancy after the death of a partner as it exists for different-sex couples. Further, in *P.S. and J.S. v Austria*,[40] the Court reiterated the notion of "family life" to same-sex couples by extending health and accident insurance cover to the surviving companion. The ECtHR considered this to be a breach of Article 8 read with Article 14. It recognised that same-sex partners had the right to benefit from a companion's health insurance. However, conferring such rights in the absence of any European law on this point would depend on the national legislation of the member state.

Apart from the ECtHR, the ECJ has also protected same-sex couples rights. In *Tadao Maruko v Versorgungsanstalt der Deutschen Bühnen*,[41] it "ruled that the surviving registered life partner of a member of an occupational pension scheme was entitled to receive survivor benefits on the member's death." In *Jürgen Römer v Freie und Hansestadt Hamburg*,[42] the Court held that the existence of direct discrimination presupposes the existence of comparable situations. The ECJ is in favor of equating same-sex and different sex rights.

In *K.B. v NHS*,[43] a female employee wished to nominate R., a female-to-male transsexual, to access her survivor's pension rights, but could not because at the time UK law did not recognise sex change, which meant K.B. and R were unable to marry. Hence, K.B. was unable to nominate R. to receive her pension after death. The Court held that while there was no discrimination in the law restricting the right to the survivor's pensions to married spouses, UK law de facto prevented R. from qualifying by denying her the right to marry, which amounted to a violation of Article 157.[44] However, the ECJ left it to the national court to determine whether K.B. could rely on Article 157 to gain recognition of her right to nominate R. as beneficiary.[45] Although the ECtHR and the ECJ have shown tolerance and acceptance toward the civil rights of same-sex couples, there has been an absence of consensus on same-sex marriage and the right to choose parenthood.

---

[39] Application no. 40016/98, 24 July 2003.

[40] Application no 18984/02, 22 July 2010.

[41] ECJ, C-267/06, *Tadao Maruko v Versorgungsanstalt der deutschen Bühnen*, 1 April, 2008, (ECLI:EU:C:2008:179), https://uk.practicallaw.thomsonreuters.com/6-381-1777?__ lrTS=20190616044107766&transitionType=Default&contextData=(sc.Default)& firstPage=true&bhcp=1 (accessed on March 29, 2020).

[42] ECJ, C-147/08, *Jürgen Römer v Freie und Hansestadt Hamburg*, 10 May, 2011, (ECLI:EU: C:2011:286).

[43] ECJ, C-117/01, *KB v NHS Pensions agency and secretary of State for Health*, 7 January, 2004, (ECLI:EU:C:2004:7).

[44] Article 157 TFEU provides that: "Each Member State shall ensure that the principle of equal pay for male and female workers for equal work or work of equal value is applied." https://eur-lex. europa.eu/legal-content/EN/TXT/?uri=celex%3A12012E%2FTXT (accessed on March 29, 2020).

[45] Chalmers et al. (2010), p. 549.

4.9 The Right to Parenthood

The ECtHR is also careful when it comes to parenthood. First, it considers that there is no right to a child guaranteed by the Convention. Second, it is bound by the legislation of member states, which meets different requirements and cannot be easily unified. This is why the Court affirmed in *Gas and Dubois v France* that France did not violate the ECHR when it refused to allow donor insemination for homosexual couples.[46] Indeed, French legislation maintained that donor insemination was available to heterosexual couples "for therapeutic purposes only, with a view in particular to remedying clinically diagnosed infertility or preventing the transmission of a particularly serious disease." Prima facie, there is no right to a child conferred by the Convention and the laws in member states differ on this issue. Some disagree or deny conferring parental rights to same-sex couples. The ECtHR is aware of these positions on parental rights, which is reflected in its judgments.

For instance, in *Charron and Merle-Montet v France*[47] the ECtHR unanimously declared the application inadmissible. The application concerned a female married couple who had applied for medically assisted reproduction by means of artificial insemination. The application was rejected by Toulouse Hospital on the grounds that "the Bioethics Law currently in force in France did not authorise such medical provision for same-sex couples." Ms. Charron and Ms. Merle-Montet complained about the rejection of their application, relying on Article 8 (right to respect for private and family life) and Article 14 (prohibition of discrimination). Noting the importance of the subsidiarity principle, the Court considered that because Ms. Charron and Ms. Merle-Montet had not appealed to the administrative courts to set aside Toulouse Hospital's decision for abuse of authority, they had failed to exhaust domestic remedies.[48] The Court's diligence is clearly noticeable in this case. The Court was apprehensive of the legal and political situation; perhaps it did not wish to overrule.

However, in *E.B. v France* case,[49] "the Court acknowledged that there was no right under domestic law or the Convention to found a family or to adopt, nor was there such a right enshrined in any of the other relevant international instruments, such as the Convention on the Rights of the Child or the Hague Convention of 29 May 1993 on the Protection of Children and Co-operation in Respect of International Adoption. But, once a country had established a right and allowed for adoptive proceedings, it could not discriminate against potential parents. In this case, the French government had made it possible for single individuals to adopt, and hence could not refuse authorisation on the grounds that the child would not have a paternal

---

[46]ECtHR, *Gas and Dubois v France* (25951/07), 15 March 2012.

[47]ECtHR, *Charron and Merle-Montet v France* (22612/15), 16 January 2018.

[48]See: https://hudoc.echr.coe.int/app/conversion/pdf/?library=ECHR&id=003-5999215-7685226&filename=Decision%20Charron%20and%20Merle-Montet%20v.%20France%20-%20same-sex%20couple (accessed on March 30, 2020).

[49]ECtHR, *E.B. v France* (43546/02), 22 January 2008.

figure given the nature of E.B.'s same-sex relationship."[50] In *Gas and Dubois*,[51] the issue arose before the Court whether the legal provisions prohibiting a person in a same-sex relationship to adopt their partner's child violate the right to non-discrimination under the European Convention. While dismissing this application the Court held "there had been no violation of Article 14 in conjunction with Article 8, as the law did not provide for second-parent adoption in relation to opposite-sex couples, as well as same-sex couples. The difference in treatment was, therefore based on marital status, rather than sexual orientation. Furthermore, as established by previous jurisprudence of the Court, the European Convention does not provide a right to be able to marry same-sex couples."[52] Further, in *Fretté v France*,[53] a homosexual man complained that the decision dismissing his request for authorisation to adopt a child amounted to arbitrary interference with his private and family life. The Court held that there had been no violation of Article 14 (prohibition of discrimination) in conjunction with Article 8 (right to respect for private life) of the Convention. It found that the national authorities had been legitimately and reasonably entitled to consider that the right to be able to adopt, on which the applicant had relied, was limited by the interests of children eligible for adoption, notwithstanding the applicant's legitimate aspirations and without calling his personal choices into question. The Court further held that there had been a violation of Article 6 (right to a fair hearing) of the Convention, the applicant having been denied a fair hearing of his case in adversarial proceedings.[54]

In yet another case, *X and Others v Austria*,[55] after an Austrian court refused to grant one of the partners the right to adopt the son of the other partner without severing the mother's legal ties with the child (second parent adoption), a complaint was filed by two women who lived in a stable homosexual relationship. The Court held that there had been a violation of Article 14 (prohibition of discrimination) taken in conjunction with Article 8 (right to respect for private and family life) of the Convention on account of the difference in treatment of the applicants in comparison with unmarried different-sex couples in which one partner wished to adopt the other partner's child. It further held that there had been no violation of Article 14 taken in conjunction with Article 8 when the applicants' situation was compared with that of a married couple in which one spouse wished to adopt the other spouse's child. The Court found that the difference in treatment between the applicants and an unmarried heterosexual couple in which one partner sought to adopt the other partner's child had been based on the first and third applicants' sexual orientation. No convincing

---

[50] https://archive.crin.org/en/library/legal-database/eb-v-france.html (accessed March 30, 2020).

[51] ECtHR, *Gas and Dubois v France* (25951/07), 15 March 2012.

[52] https://archive.crin.org/en/library/legal-database/gas-and-dubois-v-france.html (accessed March 30, 2020).

[53] Application no. 36515/97.

[54] Factsheet, Sexual Orientation Issues, Council of Europe: https://www.echr.coe.int/Documents/FS_Sexual_orientation_ENG.pdf (accessed on April 6, 2020).

[55] Application no. 19010/07.

reasons had been advanced to show that such difference in treatment was necessary for the protection of the family or for the protection of the interests of the child. At the same time, the Court underlined that the Convention did not oblige States to extend the right to second parent adoption to unmarried couples. Furthermore, the case was to be distinguished from the case Gas and Dubois v. France (see above), in which the Court had found that there was no difference of treatment based on sexual orientation between an unmarried different-sex couple and a same-sex couple as, under French law, second parent adoption was not open to any unmarried couple, be they homosexual or heterosexual.

In all of these cases, the ECtHR has acknowledged that same-sex couples have the same civil rights as different sex couples. Member states must provide equal protection of those rights. The Court indirectly hinted that the member states have the power to decide who has the freedom to exercise parental rights.

Concerning the legal recognition of same-sex couples or same-sex marriage, the ECtHR is of the opinion that there is no right to marry for same-sex couples but that they do have the right to form a civil union. The Court relies on Article 12 of the ECHR, "Men and women of marriageable age have the right to marry and to found a family, according to the national laws governing the exercise of this right." Its approach is heteronormative. In *Rees v The United Kingdom*,[56] the Court stated that "the right to marry guaranteed by Article 12 refers to the traditional marriage between persons of opposite biological sex." In the Court's opinion, marriage is conditioned by the existence of a family, and there is no family without children. Therefore, there should be no marriage between people who cannot have children biologically. Thus, the Court links marriage to procreation, which is contrary to our modern societies and to the protection of individual freedoms. Since the Court found a close link between procreation and marriage, it firstly refused to grant transsexual couples the right to marry just as much as same-sex couples.[57] However, in *Christine Goodwin v UK*[58] the ECtHR appears to have accepted transgender families: "The Court held that Article 12 refers to the right of a man and a woman to marry and nonetheless found that such gender categories cannot be determined by biological criteria."[59] As a response to this judgment, the UK government came out with the Gender Recognition Act 2004. Under this Act, transgender people can legally have their gender recognized.[60]

Further, in *Cossey*[61] and *Sheffield and Horsham*,[62] the ECtHR held that marriage as protected under Article 12 was the union of two persons of the opposite biological

---

[56] *Rees v U.K.* (1987) 9 EHRR 56.
[57] Naik (2017).
[58] 11 July 2002, 32 EHRR 18.
[59] 11 July 2002, 32 EHRR 100.
[60] Hodson (2007).
[61] *Cossey v U.K.* (1991) 13 EHRR 622.
[62] *Sheffield and Horsham v U.K.* (1999) 27 EHRR 163.

sex. In *Botta v Italy*,[63] the ECtHR held that the right to respect private life includes the right to establish and develop relationships with other human beings. In *Bensaid v UK*,[64] the Court held that gender identification, name, sexual orientation, and sexual life are protected by Article 8 of the ECHR as part of "private life." In addition, the Court in the case of *Mata Estevez v Spain*[65] held, "With regard to private life, the Court acknowledges that the applicant's emotional and sexual relationship related to his private life within the meaning of Article 8(1) of the Convention."[66]

In *Burden v United Kingdom*,[67] two unmarried sisters who had lived together for more than thirty years in a house that they inherited from their parents claimed that when one of them dies, the other would be forced to sell the house to pay inheritance tax, while spouses or civil partners had exemption from charge. The ECtHR held that a relationship between siblings or other people in cohabitation is (legally) different from that between married couples and homosexual civil partners. The Court gave importance to the existence of a public undertaking, carrying with it a body of rights and obligations of a contractual nature. The Court further held that there was no similarity between married and civil partnership, on the one hand, and different-sex or same-sex couples who choose to live together but do not become husband and wife or civil partners, on the other hand. In doing so, the Court did not make any distinction in the sex of the persons in the marriage or civil union. Through this verdict the Court recognised the right for same-sex couples to enter a civil union.[68] While disagreeing that same-sex couples have family life, the ECtHR stated:

> The Grand Chamber commences by remarking that the relationship between siblings is qualitatively of a different nature to that between married couples and homosexual civil partners under the United Kingdom's Civil Partnership Act. The very essence of the connection between siblings is consanguinity, whereas one of the defining characteristics of a marriage or Civil Partnership Act union is that it is forbidden to close family members [. . .] The fact that the applicants have chosen to live together all their adult lives, as do many married and Civil Partnership Act couples, does not alter this essential difference between the two types of relationship.[69]

The Court further differentiated formalised family relationships and de facto ones:

> Moreover, the Grand Chamber notes that it has already held that marriage confers a special status on those who enter into it. The exercise of the right to marry is protected by Article 12 of the Convention and gives rise to social, personal and legal consequences. Since the coming into force of the Civil Partnership Act in the United Kingdom, a homosexual couple now also has the choice to enter into a legal relationship designed by Parliament to

---

[63] Application no. 21439/93, 24 February 1998, (1998) 26 EHRR 241, para 32.

[64] Application no. 44599/98, 6 February 2001, (2001) 33 EHRR 205, para 59.

[65] Application no. 56501/00, 10 May 2001.

[66] Application no. 56501/00, 10 May 2001.

[67] *Burden v The United Kingdom*, ECHR (2008), no. 1337/05, para 62, 65.

[68] *Burden v The United Kingdom*, para 62, 65.

[69] *Burden v The United Kingdom*, para 62.

correspond as far as possible to marriage. As with marriage, the Grand Chamber considers that the legal consequences of civil partnership under the 2004 Act, which couples expressly and deliberately decide to incur, set these types of relationship apart from other forms of co-habitation. Rather than the length or the supportive nature of the relationship, what is determinative is the existence of a public undertaking, carrying with it a body of rights and obligations of a contractual nature. Just as there can be no analogy between married and Civil Partnership Act couples, on one hand, and heterosexual or homosexual couples who choose to live together but not to become husband and wife or civil partners, on the other hand (. . .), the absence of such a legally binding agreement between the applicants renders their relationship of co-habitation, despite its long duration, fundamentally different to that of a married or civil partnership couple.[70]

However, by differentiating formalised and de facto relationships, the Court equated marriage and civil partnership. Later, it stated in *Courten v United Kingdom*, "The Court would note that while the Grand Chamber equated civil partnerships between homosexual couples with marriage this was on the basis that in both situations the parties had undertaken public and binding obligations towards each other."

In *Valliantanos and others v Greece*,[71] the Court held that homosexual couples committed to a stable relationship fell within the ambit of Article 8 of the Convention, on the right to family life. The ECtHR noted that the cohabitation agreements that were available to everyone, not just homosexuals, did not offer real protection to gay couples. It also recognized the trend among member states of the Council of Europe to provide for some form of legal recognition of same-sex couples.[72] Still the right for same-sex couples to enter a civil union was partial. In *Oliari and Others v Italy*,[73] the ECtHR further noted that Italian law did not provide any legal alternatives to same-sex couples although they were involved in committed relationships with no protection. The Court therefore held that Italy in the absence of its permitting marriage for same-sex couples had a positive obligation to provide other options, such as civil unions or registered partnerships. The Court observed that Article 12 does not impose a requirement on a state to recognize a right to marry for same-sex couples. Therefore, it did not find a violation of Article 12, and hence reiterated that Article 14 on discrimination has no standing alone; it complements the other substantive provisions of the Convention. The ECtHR concluded that Italy had violated Article 8 of the Convention.[74]

A similar argument to *Schalk & Kopf v Austria* was given by Judge Schermers in favour of equal marriage rights in *W. v UK*.[75] He opined that the fundamental human right underlying Article 12 ECHR should also be granted to same-sex couples, that

---

[70] *Burden v The United Kingdom*, para 63–65.

[71] Applications nos. 29381/09 and 32684/09.

[72] *Valliantanos and others v Greece*: https://www.loc.gov/law/foreign-news/article/european-court-of-human-rights-decision-on-gay-marriage-in-italy/ (accessed on March 31, 2020).

[73] Applications nos. 18766/11 and 36030/11 (July 21, 2015), HUDOC.

[74] See *Oliari and Others v Italy*: https://www.loc.gov/law/foreign-news/article/european-court-of-human-rights-decision-on-gay-marriage-in-italy/ (accessed on March 31, 2020).

[75] *W. v The United Kingdom*, ECHR (1989), no. 11095/84.

the right to marry and to found a family is of paramount importance for the individual and denial of this right would mean condemnation to solitude and loneliness.[76] This view resembles that of Judges Rozakis, Spielmann, and Jebens in *Schalk and Kopf v Austria*[77] concerning Article 14 ECHR and the vigorous justifications needed.[78] However, in *Hämäläinen v Finland*,[79] the ECtHR held that a Finnish rule requiring married applicants to convert their relationship to a registered partnership prior to obtaining recognition, was compatible with the right to private and family life under Article 8 ECHR.

Some others cases in Austria about registered partnerships, *Hörmann and Moser v Austria*[80] and *Dietz and Suttasom v Austria*,[81] were concluded before the District Administrative Authorities, while civil marriage was contracted before the Office for Matters of Personal Status. The applicants, two same-sex couple who had been living in a long-term relationship for several years, complained that they were discriminated on grounds of their sexual orientation. The Court claimed, "following legislative changes, as of 1 April 2017, the applicants would have the possibility to conclude a registered partnership before the Office for Matters of Personal Status. It therefore considered that the matter had been resolved within the meaning of Article 37 (striking out applications) of the Convention and decided to strike the applications out of its list of cases."[82]

Regarding the registration of marriage contracted abroad, in *Orlandi v Italy*,[83] the ECtHR condemned Italy for failing to legally protect same-sex couples who married abroad. The Court reaffirmed that the Council of Europe member states have an obligation to safeguard the family life of same-sex couples under Article 8 (right to respect for private and family life) and failing to recognise marriage contracted abroad (before the law on civil unions came into force in 2016) would be a violation of Article 8.[84]

With respect to family reunification rights of EU citizens who exercise EU free movement rights, the Court of Justice of the European Union (CJEU) on June 5, 2018 delivered its judgment in the case of *Relu Adrian Coman and others v Inspectoratul General Pentru Imigrari and Ministerul Afacerilor Interne;*[85] Coman, a Romanian citizen, legally married Mr. Hamilton, a United States national, while he

---

[76] Shahid (2017).

[77] Application no. 30141/04, 24 June 2010.

[78] Shahid (2017).

[79] Hämäläinen v Finland [2015] 1 FCR 379, [88]-[89].

[80] Application no. 31176/13.

[81] Application no. 31185/13.

[82] Factsheet, Sexual Orientation Issue, Council of Europe: https://www.echr.coe.int/Documents/FS_Sexual_orientation_ENG.pdf (accessed on April 6, 2020).

[83] Applications nos. 26431/12, 26742/12, 44057/12, and 60088/12.

[84] See https://www.ilga-europe.org/resources/news/latest-news/ecthr-orlandi-italy (accessed on April 1, 2020).

[85] ECJ, Case C-673/16.

resided in Brussels. The Court held that under EU law the same-sex spouse of an EU citizen can move and reside with the latter in the territory of another EU member state, just as opposite-sex spouses of EU citizens. The Court recognized that same-sex marriages must be treated in the same way as opposite-sex marriages for a specific legal purpose.[86] This judgment was in contrast to what the Court had previously decided in *D and Sweden v Council,*[87] where the Court found that "marriage means a union between persons of the opposite sex." With a liberal perspective, the Court in *Taddeucci and McCall v Italy*[88] held that the refusal to grant a residence permit on family grounds to an unmarried same-sex couple consisted in unjustified discrimination based on sexual orientation. The Court's restraint was visible in a recent case. In *Chapin and Charpentier v France,*[89] a French same-sex couple wanting to marry challenged the decision of the public prosecutor before the ECtHR. The public prosecutor had rejected their marriage application on the ground that only persons of different sex were able to marry. Even in this recent case the Court resorted to the heteronormative definition of marriage. However, it did acknowledge that the institution of marriage had undergone major social changes since the adoption of the ECHR. The Court reiterated that there was no European consensus on same-sex marriage.

This brings us to the pertinent question, Why do the Courts show a liberal attitude towards same-sex couples when it comes to conferring or protecting their civil rights, with the exception of same-sex marriage? The role of religion and religious leaders in influencing the masses indirectly imbibes within its fold "the judiciary." In this respect, the probability of judges considering the mood in countries like Poland cannot be negated. It certainly impacts sensitive issues and judicial decisions. There is oftentimes only one logic, namely, that "marriage is between man and woman." Undoubtedly, the ECtHR and the ECJ have helped same-sex couples acquire civil rights and legal protection. However, except for a few dissenting opinions of judges in favour of gay marriage rights, the ECtHR and the ECJ are more inclined to the heteronormative view of marriage. In most of these cases, the central argument was that "marriage has deep-rooted social and cultural connotations which may differ largely from one society to another. The Court reiterates that it must not rush to substitute its own judgment in place of that of the national authorities, who are best placed to assess and respond to the needs of society."[90]

---

[86] See http://centaur.reading.ac.uk/86389/ (accessed on April 1, 2020).

[87] Judgment of the Court of 31 May 2001 *D and Kingdom of Sweden v Council of the European Union.* Joined Cases C-122/99 P and C-125/99 P.

[88] ECtHR, *Taddeuci and McCall v Italy,* no. 51362/09, 30 June 2016.

[89] ECHR (2016), no. 40183/07.

[90] *Schalk & Kopf v Austria,* Application no. 30141/04, 24 June 2010, para 43; Scherpe (2013).

4.10 European Court of Justice

The ECJ is the main dispute settlement body of the European Union. It is weaker than domestic courts in member states. However, with its limited competence it is more powerful than other international tribunals like the International Court of Justice (ICJ).[91] A fundamental judgment of the ECJ concerning principles is found in the *Costa v ENEL* judgment: it shows that the European Economic Community (EEC) Treaty has created its own legal system, which has become an integral part of the legal systems of member states, and that community law takes precedence over national law.[92] In *Costa v ENEL*,[93] the ECJ held that when there is a conflict between international and national law, the latter prevails. Although the former assumes superiority over the latter, most states do not accord supremacy to international rules of law.

Even the member state liability for violations of EU law was proclaimed by the ECJ in *Francovich*.[94] In this case, the ECJ held that member states are liable in instances where they have failed to implement a directive which did not have direct effect because of the imprecise nature of the directive's wording. The ruling also allowed for "national private law remedies or their equivalent to be made available for breaches of Community law."[95] In the *Foto–Frost v Hauptzollamt Lübeck-Ost*[96] judgment, national courts were declared incompetent to decide on the validity of EU rules and had to approach the ECJ to declare rules void or invalid.

The ECJ helps to transmute the national law of member states to the benefit of European law. In the protection of human rights, the ECJ acts more like a supreme court than a dispute settlement court. The ECJ is neither an interpreter of treaty rules nor an agent of member states; rather, it is a defender of citizens' rights.[97] By extending protection to LGBT persons and by conferring rights upon them, the ECJ has gained the position of a norm reinforcer. For granting these rights, it went a step ahead of member states' governments.

The ECJ extended its competency to review the adopted EU legal act;[98] the rules of EU law relating to Member States' police and judicial cooperation in criminal

---

[91] Waele and Vleuten (2010), pp. 639–640 (accessed on April 3, 2020).

[92] (1964) Case 6/64, https://www.cvce.eu/content/publication/1999/1/1/cb4154a0-23c6-4eb5-8b7e-7518e8a2a995/publishable_en.pdf (accessed on April 3, 2020).

[93] (1964) Case 6/64.

[94] Francovich and Bonifaci v Republic of Italy (C-6, 9/90) [1991] I-5357.

[95] See https://www.lawteacher.net/cases/francovich-v-italy.php (accessed on April 3, 2020), Hanft (1991), p. 1273.

[96] Case 314/85 (22 October 1987).

[97] Waele and Vleuten (2010), pp. 640–641.

[98] Case 294/83, *Parti Ecologiste 'Les Verts' v Parliament*, 1986 E.C.R. 1365, Case C–70/88, *Parliament v Council* (Chernobyl), 1990 E.C.R. I–204. See Waele and Vleuten (2010).

matters;[99] and the CFSP rules regarding a common foreign and security policy of the member states.[100] It interpreted free movement of goods by removing the quantitative restrictions.[101] A similar approach was taken by the ECJ while deciding on the freedom to provide services and freedom of establishment.[102] The ECJ is known for its liberal approach in granting rights of free movement and social security benefits to member state nationals, irrespective of where they reside in the EU.[103] It believes in granting equal residence rights and social welfare benefits to EU citizens.[104] In the absence of specific rules regarding merger control in the Treaties, the ECJ warranted the creation of a judge-made law.[105]

The public opinion and political will of the member states differs on LGBT rights. In some states, the acceptance level is less than in others. This does influence LGBT rights in member states. Although the ECJ does not review their national legislations, it has delivered landmark judgments on gender identity and sexual orientation. It has acted as an interpreter of rules and has actively engaged in judicial activism. Even with respect to the protection of civil rights of LGBT persons, the ECJ has engaged in excessive activism. This is self-evident when analysing the series of ECJ judgments on LGBT rights.

In *Grant v South–West Trains Ltd*,[106] the ECJ held that a company's ban on the provision of travel perks to same-sex partners of employees did not violate European sex discrimination law. The ECJ reasoned that concession would have been refused to a male employee cohabitating with a male partner. The rule was not discriminatory as it applied in the same way to female and male workers. About the question whether discrimination based on sexual orientation should be considered sexual discrimination, the ECJ ruled that discrimination based on sexual orientation was not

---

[99] Case C–355/04 P, *Segi and Others v Council*, 2007 E.C.R. I–1657, Case C–303/05, *Advocaten voor de Wereld v Leden van de Ministerraad*, 2007 E.C.R. I–3633. See Waele and Vleuten (2010).

[100] Case C–91/05, *Comm'n v Council* (ECOWAS), 2008 E.C.R. I–3651. See Waele and Vleuten (2010).

[101] Case 8/74, *Procureur du Roi v Dassonville*, 1974 E.C.R.837, Case 120/78, *Rewe–Zentral AG v Bundesmonopolverwaltung für Branntwein*, 1979 E.C.R. 649. See Waele and Vleuten (2010).

[102] Case 2/74, *Reyners v Belg.*, 1974 E.C.R. 631, Case C–76/90, *Säger v Dennemayer & Co.*, 1991 E.C.R. I–4221, Case C–55/94, *Gebhard v Consiglio dell'Ordine degli Avvocati e Procuratori di Milano*, 1995 E.C.R. I–4165, Case C–212/97, *Centros Ltd v Erhvervs– og Selskabsstyrelsen*, 1999 ECR I–1459. See Waele and Vleuten (2010).

[103] Case 53/81, *Levin v Staatssecretaris van Justitie*, 1982 E.C.R. 1035; Case 139/95, *Kempf v Staatssecretaris van Justitie*, 1986 E.C.R. 1741; Case 196/87, *Steymann v Staatssecretaris van Justitie*, 1988 E.C.R. 6159; Case C–456/02, *Trojani v CPAS*, 2004 E.C.R. 1–7573. See Waele and Vleuten (2010).

[104] Case C–85/96, *Martínez Sala v Freistaat Bayern*, 1998 E.C.R. I–2691; Case C–184/99, *Grzelczyk v. Centre Public d'aide Sociale d'Ottignies–Louvain–la–Neuve*, Case C–184/99, 2001 E.C.R. 1–6193; Case C–413/99, *Baumbast v Sec'y of State for the Home Dep't.*, 2002 E.C.R. 1–7091. See Waele and Vleuten (2010).

[105] Case 6/72, *Europemballage Corporation v Comm'n of the European Comtys.*, 1973 E.C.R. 215. See Waele and Vleuten (2010).

[106] (C-249/96) [1998] IRLR 206, ECJ.

prohibited. This verdict was critiqued harshly by Paul L. Spackman, who asserted that the ECJ was "conservative" and largely ineffective, since its work is flawed by an "unwillingness to protect gays and lesbians in areas other than private consensual sex."[107]

In *Grant*, the ECJ observed that the member states lacked consensus on same-sex relationships and treated such relationships differently. However, it provided scope for future legislation on this issue by referring the newly included provision (with the Treaty of Amsterdam).[108] This paved the way for future EU legislations dealing with LGBT discrimination.

In *D. & Kingdom of Sweden. v Council*,[109] for the claim "household allowance" the ECJ refused to allow a registered partnership to be treated as equivalent to marriage. It therefore endorsed its hold to rule on the legal status of relationships despite objectional arguments from the side of the member states.

A ruling that has been hailed as a great leap toward equality is *Maruko v Versorgungsanstalt der Deutschen Bühnen*.[110] Mr. Maruko entered into a registered civil partnership (under German law) in 2001; following the death of his partner in 2005, Mr. Maruko applied for a widower's pension. The VddB[111] refused the pension on the ground that there was no provision for such survivor's benefits to be paid to registered civil partners. Applying the Directive 200/78/EC of 27 November 2000,[112] the ECJ upheld the right not be discriminated on the grounds of sexual orientation, and ruled that the refusal to grant such a pension because the partners had not married amounts to indirect discrimination based on sexual orientation, against the directive. Even though the partners had entered a same-sex union, the effect is the same as marriage. The ECJ further asserted that it is for the national court to determine whether the legal situation of spouses is like that of persons in a registered civil partnership.[113] Rational analysis of this decision can be better described in the words of Henri de Waele and Anna van der Vleuten:

> The ECJ ruled that the Member States are competent regarding marital issues, but that they have to exercise this competence within the boundaries of EU law—especially within the boundaries of the non–discrimination provisions—including those relating to sexual orientation. Admittedly, the ECJ did restrict the scope of its ruling by labelling Maruko as a case of direct discrimination, whereas it in fact constituted a case of indirect discrimination (the

---

[107] Spackman (1997), p. 1078.

[108] Article 13 EC Treaty and https://www.europarl.europa.eu/topics/treaty/pdf/amst-en.pdf (accessed on April 5, 2020) now TFEU, art. 19 (1). https://eur-lex.europa.eu/legal-content/EN/TXT/HTML/?uri=CELEX:12012M/TXT (accessed on April 5, 2020).

[109] 2001 E.C.R. I–4319.

[110] *Tadao Maruko v Versorgungsanstalt der deutschen Bühnen*, 1998 E.C.R. I–1757.

[111] Versorgungsanstalt der deutschen Bühnen (VddB).

[112] The directive establishes a general framework for equal treatment in employment and occupation.

[113] *Maruko v Versorgungsanstalt der Deutschen Bühnen* [2008] IRLR 250, ECJ https://www.sackers.com/pension/tadao-maruko-v-versorgungsanstalt-der-deutschen-buhnen-european-court-of-justice-1-april-2008/ (accessed on April 5, 2020).

unequal treatment was based on the in–itself neutral distinction between marriage and partnership). However, the ECJ magisterially put unequal treatment of a registered partnership on par with unequal treatment based on sexual orientation. It was able to do so because in Germany only same–sex couples are allowed to enter into a registered partnership.

The Court has also made bold decisions to protect transgender rights. In *P v S and Cornwall County Council*,[114] after rejecting the arguments of the respondent and applying the Equal Treatment Directive, the ECJ observed:

> The Directive is the expression of the principle of equality, which is one of the fundamental principles of Community law. In view of its purpose and the fundamental nature of the rights which it seeks to safeguard, the scope of the Directive also applies to discrimination based essentially, if not exclusively, on the sex of the person concerned. Where such discrimination arises, as in the present case, from the gender reassignment of the person concerned, he or she is treated unfavourably by comparison with persons of the sex to which he or she was deemed to belong before undergoing gender reassignment. To tolerate such discrimination would be tantamount, as regards such a person, to a failure to respect the dignity and freedom to which he or she is entitled, and which the Court has a duty to safeguard. Therefore, dismissal of a transsexual for a reason related to a gender reassignment must be regarded as contrary to Article 5(1) of the Directive.[115]

In *K.B. v Nat'l Health Servs. Pensions Agency*,[116] a transsexual female-to-male partner was not allowed to claim survivor's pension on the ground that the couple was not married and that the husband was registered as a woman even after undergoing gender reassignment surgery. UK Law did not allow sex change. The ECJ noted the earlier ruling of the ECtHR, namely, that UK Law was incompatible with the ECHR's right to marry,[117] and left it to the national court to determine whether or not to apply Article 157 to gain recognition of her right to nominate her husband as beneficiary.[118]

After two years, in *Richards v Secretary of State for Work and Pensions*,[119] the ECJ accepted the claim of a male-to-female transsexual who had been denied the right to the more favourable retirement age afforded to women in the U.K. for pension purposes. It further opined that this was an explicit case of discrimination of a male-to-female transsexual person. The Court relied on the *K.B. case* reasoning, "National legislation which precludes a transsexual, the absence of recognition of his new gender, from fulfilling a requirement which must be met in order to be entitled to a right protected by Community law must be regarded as being, in principle, incompatible with the requirements of Community law."[120]

---

[114] Case C-13/94, [1996] IRLR 347.

[115] See https://www.equalrightstrust.org/ertdocumentbank/Microsoft%20Word%20-%20P%20v%20S.pdf (accessed on April 5, 2020).

[116] 2004 E.C.R. I–541.

[117] *Christine Goodwin v UK.*

[118] Chalmers et al. (2010), p. 549.

[119] Case C–423/04, *Richards v Sec'y of State for Work & Pensions*, 2006 E.C.R. I–3585.

[120] Arsanjani et al. (2010), pp. 502–503.

On the continuing struggles of LGBT asylum seekers who do not wish to be sent back to the closet, in 2013 the Court held that "the competent authorities cannot reasonably expect, in order to avoid the risk of persecution, the applicant for asylum to conceal his homosexuality in his country of origin or to exercise reserve in the expression of his sexual orientation."[121] In another landmark case, *F. v Bevandorlasi es Allampolgarsagi Hivatal*,[122] the ECJ declared the illegality of the use of psychological reports based on projective personality tests in determining the sexual orientation of asylum seekers. It further ruled, "EU law does not prohibit authorities or courts from ordering the production of an expert report to help assess the facts and circumstances relative to an asylum seeker's claim, but only if the production of the report is consistent with human right law and the report is not relied upon solely or conclusively."[123]

Although the ECJ is not a constitutional court, it has become an active promoter of the fundamental human rights of LGBT people. In comparison, an examination of the factsheet on "Sexual Orientation Issues" illuminates the similar attitude of the European Court of Human Rights, especially how it has changed from a moderate role to an active one leading to social justice. Over the years, the Court has strived to achieve the goals and objectives of the ECHR.

It is not only in family matters, but the Court has extended protection to LGBT people in cases involving allegations of ill-treatment by the police or by private individuals. In *M.C. and C.A. v Romania*,[124] the applicants had participated in the annual gay march in Bucharest. On their way home in the metro, they were attacked by a group of six young men and a woman. The attackers punched and kicked them and shouted homophobic abuse at them. The applicants complained that the investigation into the attack against them had been inadequate. They alleged that the authorities had not considered the fact that the offences against them had been motivated by hatred against homosexuals. The Court held that there had been a violation of Article 3 (prohibition of inhuman or degrading treatment) read together with Article 14 (prohibition of discrimination) of the Convention, finding that the investigations into the applicants' allegations of ill-treatment had been ineffective as they had lasted too long, had been marred by serious shortcomings, and had failed to take into account possible discriminatory motives.[125]

In *Sabalić v Croatia*,[126] "The applicant, who was attacked in a bar by a man to whom she had disclosed her homosexual orientation, complained in particular of the

---

[121] *Minister voor Immigratie en Asiel v X and Y and Z v Minister voor Immigratie en Asiel*, C-199/12 to 201/12, para. 75–76.

[122] Case C-473/16.

[123] Zheng (2018).

[124] Application no. 12060/12, 12 April 2016.

[125] Factsheet, Sexual Orientation Issue, Council of Europe: https://www.echr.coe.int/Documents/FS_Sexual_orientation_ENG.pdf (accessed on April 6, 2020).

[126] Application no. 50231/13, 7 January 2014, see also the similar application pending in *Beus v Croatia* (no. 16943/17).

lack of an appropriate procedural response on the part of the local authorities to an act of violence by a private party motivated by her sexual orientation. She further complained that she did not have an effective domestic remedy concerning her complaints and that she was discriminated based on her sexual orientation. The Court gave notice of the application to the Croatian Government and put questions to the parties under Articles 3 (prohibition of inhuman or degrading treatment), 8 (right to respect for private life), 13 (right to an effective remedy), and 14 (prohibition of discrimination) of the Convention."[127]

The Court took a step forward in protecting rights of homosexual detainees. In *Stasi v. France*,[128] "the applicant complained that he had been the victim of ill-treatment by other inmates during his imprisonment, in particular because of his homosexuality, and he alleged that the authorities had not taken the necessary measures to ensure his protection. The Court held that there had been no violation of Article 3 (prohibition of inhuman or degrading treatment) of the Convention. It found that, in the circumstances of the case, and considering the facts that had been brought to their attention, the authorities had taken all the measures that could reasonably be expected of them to protect the applicant from physical harm."[129]

The Court has ruled in favour of homosexual refugees who would otherwise be at risk if returned to their country of origin. In *A.S.B. v the Netherlands*,[130] "the applicant complained that if expelled to Jamaica he would face a real and personal risk of treatment in violation of Article 3 (prohibition of inhuman or degrading treatment) of the Convention due to his homosexuality. The Court decided to strike the application out of its list of cases in accordance with Article 37 (striking out applications) of the Convention. It noted that the applicant had been granted asylum in the Netherlands and found that, consequently, there was no longer any risk of his expulsion to Jamaica."

In *A.E. v Finland*,[131] "there was the alleged risk of treatment in breach of Article 3 (prohibition of torture and inhuman or degrading treatment) of the Convention faced by a homosexual man in the event of his being returned to Iran. The Court struck the application out of its list of cases, in accordance with Article 37 (striking out applications) of the Convention, noting in particular that the applicant had been granted a continuous residence permit in Finland valid for a period of one year with a possibility of renewal and that he was thus no longer subject to an expulsion order.

---

[127] Factsheet, Sexual Orientation Issue, Council of Europe: https://www.echr.coe.int/Documents/FS_Sexual_orientation_ENG.pdf (accessed on April 6, 2020).

[128] Application no. 25001/07.

[129] Factsheet, Sexual Orientation Issue, Council of Europe: https://www.echr.coe.int/Documents/FS_Sexual_orientation_ENG.pdf (accessed on April 6, 2020).

[130] Application no. 4854/12, 10 July 2012.

[131] Application no. 30953/11, 22 September 2015.

The Court therefore considered that the matter giving rise to the complaints in the case had been resolved."[132]

4.11 Conclusion

This chapter has analysed the activism of the ECJ and the ECtHR on LGBT family rights. The EC Treaty regulates the jurisdiction of the European Court of Justice. With respect to the protection and promotion of LGBT rights, the Courts have developed a more elaborate concept to reduce discrimination with the help of the EU legislature. This has indirectly influenced the member states to adopt effective directives. In addition, the case laws have offered LGBT people in certain cases better protection than the Convention. On the other hand, fundamental rights and collective action to that effect have been more enhanced by the ECtHR than the ECJ. As a result, the two distinct legal orders are intertwined, which aren't easy to demarcate.[133] Although the Courts have adopted divergent approaches on certain issues, both strive to achieve similar objectives, which reflects their constructive and cooperative relationship in the protection of fundamental rights.

References

Agarwal HO (2007) International law and human rights, 1st edn. Central Law Publications, India
Arsanjani MH, Cogan J, Sloane R (2010) Looking to the future: essays on international law in honor of W. Michael Reisman. Brill Publishers, Leiden
Borchardt KD (2017) The ABC of EU Law. European Union. Retrieved March 18, 2020 from https://op.europa.eu/en/publication-detail/-/publication/5d4f8cde-de25-11e7-a506-01aa75ed71a1
Chalmers D, Davies G, Monti G (2010) European Union law: cases and materials. Cambridge University Press, Cambridge, England
de Vries SA (2013) Editorial EU and ECHR: conflict or harmony? Utrecht Law Rev 9(1):78–79. https://doi.org/10.18352/ulr.214
Gerards J, Senden H (2009) The structure of fundamental rights and the European Court of Human Rights. Int J Constit Law 7(4):619–653. https://doi.org/10.1093/icon/mop028
Hanft JE (1991) Francovich and Bonifaci v Italy: EEC Member State liability for failure to implement community directives. Fordham Int Law J 15(4):1273
Hodson L (2007) Different families same rights? Lesbian, Gay, Bisexual and Transgender Families under International Human Rights Law. ILGA-Europe. Retrieved March 30, 2020 from http://www.ilga-europe.org/sites/default/files/Attachments/different_families_same_rights_hr_law_2007.pdf
Kapoor SK (2018) International law and human rights. Central Law Publications, India

---

[132] Factsheet, Sexual Orientation Issue, Council of Europe: https://www.echr.coe.int/Documents/FS_Sexual_orientation_ENG.pdf (accessed on April 6, 2020).

[133] de Vries (2013).

Monjurul Kabir AH (2014) Societies can't be inclusive without equal access to justice. The Guardian. Retrieved April 11, 2020 from https://www.theguardian.com/global-development-professionals-network/2014/feb/20/justice-women-social-inclusion-development

Naik Y (2017) Homosexuality in the Jurisprudence of Supreme Court of India. Springer Publishers, Germany

Scherpe JM (2013) The legal recognition of same-sex couples in Europe and the role of the European Court of Human Rights. Equal Rights Rev 10:83–96. Retrieved April 2, 2020 from https://www.equalrightstrust.org/ertdocumentbank/ERR10_sp1.pdf

Shahid M (2017) The right to same-sex marriage: assessing the European Court of Human Rights' consensus-based analysis in recent judgments concerning equal marriage rights. Erasmus Law Rev 10(3). https://ssrn.com/abstract=3104533

Spackman PL (1997) Grant v. South-West Trains: equality for same-sex partners in the European Community. Am Univ Int Law Rev 12(6):1063–1120

Waele HD, Vleuten A (2010) Judicial activism in the European Court of Justice - the case of LGBT rights. Mich State J Int Law. Retrieved April 3, 2020 from https://www.researchgate.net/publication/254883449_Judicial_Activism_in_the_European_Court_of_Justice_-_The_Case_of_LGBT_Rights

Zheng J (2018) European Court of Justice bans homosexuality tests for asylum seekers. EJIL: Talk. Retrieved May 1, 2020 from https://www.ejiltalk.org/european-court-of-justice-bans-homosexuality-tests-for-asylum-seekers/

Chapter 5
Judicial Responses to Domestic Violence in the EU Member States

The Court of Justice of the European Union (CJEU) and the European Court of Human Rights (ECtHR) have made many sweeping and landmark decisions on LGBT family rights. Concerning the legalisation of same-sex marriage, both courts have adopted a heteronormative approach. Case laws are important for understanding judicial perception, as well as the offence of domestic violence. Since 2007, the ECtHR has delivered important judgments in cases involving domestic violence,[1] but these cases deal with issues of violence only against women, their family members and relatives, not same-sex domestic violence. In the absence of court judgments and European regional law on same-sex domestic violence, the European Courts judgments about opposite sex domestic violence must be reviewed and analysed. This chapter will analyse these judgments and assess the socio-legal situation of domestic violence in Germany at the national level. By examining the rules and principles applied by the Courts, the chapter provides a comprehensive legal analysis of state accountability for domestic violence.

5.1 Legal Protection Against Domestic Violence in the EU Member States

In most cases of domestic/intimate partner violence, the victims are women. Although the EU has several legislations and practical instruments in place for the rights and protection of women and children, same-sex domestic violence issues are mostly unconsidered. EU member states lack legislation and proper statistics on same-sex domestic violence. Twenty jurisdictions have legal protection for married/registered same-sex partners, and eighteen have rules protecting same-sex

---

[1] McQuigg (2015), p. 1009.

cohabiting partners, except Bulgaria and Greece. The legal situation is doubtful in Slovenia, Czech Republic,[2] Poland, and Romania. In 1995, Finland, Portugal, and Norway provided legal protection against domestic violence to same-sex cohabitants, and subsequently Austria (1997), Belgium (1998), and Sweden (1998). France joined in 1999, and later extended protection even to former or ex-partners (including cohabitants) in 2006. Finland (2004) and Portugal (2007) also extended protection to former or ex-partners.[3]

Rights and laws against violence were established in almost all cantons of Switzerland; these apply to cases of domestic violence and stalking by ex-partners, and they differ among the cantons. Civil Code 28b provides protection against violence, threats, and stalking. Code 28b can be applied independently in a penal prosecution. A restraining order can be issued by the police, and the accused can be prosecuted for Disobedience Against an Official Order under Penal Code 292. The punishment is a money fine, but the victim should provide enough evidence and bear the financial costs.[4]

The Netherlands have been providing protection since 2009. Italy doesn't explicitly include same-sex cohabitants for protection but prohibits different treatment of same-sex and opposite-sex cohabitants. These legal developments are the result of more jurisdictions recognising either marriage or registered partnership for same-sex partners during this period. Hungary extended legal protection against domestic violence to same-sex former cohabiting partners in 2014. Some NGOs in Spain believe that lawmakers should draft a specific law for same-sex couples, whereas others have proposed regulating the protection of these victims through a modification of the 2004 Organic Act against Gender Violence.[5] Denmark intends to make specific provisions in the Danish Criminal Code.[6]

To address LGBT issues, the Luxembourg Ministry for Equal Opportunity has consulted NGOs to draft a law based on the provisions of the Istanbul Convention.[7] As Per Article 140 of the Croatian Criminal Code, intrusive behavior committed against a current or former spouse, a common-law spouse or same-sex partner, a person with whom the perpetrator was in an intimate relationship, or a child, shall be punished by imprisonment of up to three years.[8] Article 215 punishes domestic violence and punishes a family member who by violence, abuse, or exceptionally

---

[2] See Herd (2019).

[3] Damonze (2017), pp. 74, 79–85.

[4] See "Stalking and Swiss Law": http://www.stalkingriskprofile.com/docs/Stalking%20and% 20Swiss%20Law.pdf (accessed on May 11, 2020).

[5] Carratalá (2016).

[6] *Report/Perspective and Action Plan* (2018).

[7] See *Luxembourg: Overview on the situation of lesbian, bisexual and queer women and recommendations to end violence, discrimination and invisibility* (2018), p. 4.

[8] See European Institute for Gender Equality: https://eige.europa.eu/gender-based-violence/ regulatory-and-legal-framework/legal-definitions-in-the-eu/croatia-intimate-partner-violence (accessed on May 2, 2020).

insolent conduct puts another family member into a humiliating position with imprisonment for six months to five years.[9]

In recent years, preventing domestic violence was a priority for the Estonian criminal justice system. LGBT people are not considered a separate group, so they do not receive any special treatment, but protection is extended without discrimination.[10] The last jurisdictions to provide protection to registered same-sex partners were Malta (2014), Greece (2015), and Italy (2016). Nevertheless, opposite-sex married couples, registered partners, and cohabiting partners receive more protection than same-sex partners against domestic violence.[11] The legal situation in Germany will be elaborated later.

5.2 Domestic Violence: Public or Private Matter?

Unlike in past decades, domestic violence is now considered a public crime; states are accountable to address domestic violence as a human rights violation. This development is mainly due to the efforts of international human rights instruments, court decisions, and vibrant social activism.[12] In particular, the ECtHR has emphasized legislative measures to protect and prevent domestic violence against women. Significantly, the ECtHR has refused to consider domestic violence as a private matter requiring private prosecution; rather, it made it obligatory for the authorities to regard Article 8 of the European Convention on Human Rights (ECHR) as a public crime. In *Bevacqua and S. v Bulgaria*,[13] Bevacqua, along with her minor son, left Bulgaria for Italy after her divorce. She applied for an interim custody order, stating that her husband had battered her. Over the course of one year, Bevacqua was unable to obtain the order, and continued to be harassed and assaulted by her ex-husband. Despite repeated assaults, the police did nothing to assist Bevacqua, and upon complaining of their inaction, Bevacqua was told that her issue was a "private matter". The Court held that Article 8 was violated based on the Bulgarian authorities' failure to protect Bevacqua and punish her husband for the assaults. The Court also found that the categorization by the Ministry of the Interior of the issue as a "private matter" was incompatible with the state's obligation to protect the applicant's family life. It is especially noteworthy that the Court chose to interpret Article 8 not as requiring the State to stay out of private and family matters, but

---

[9] See European Institute for Gender Equality: https://eige.europa.eu/gender-based-violence/regulatory-and-legal-framework/legal-definitions-in-the-eu/croatia-intimate-partner-violence (accessed on May 2, 2020).

[10] *Developing Directive-Compatible Practices for the Identification, Assessment and Referral of Victims* (2017).

[11] Damonze (2017), pp. 86–87.

[12] Hasselbacher (2010).

[13] Application no. 71127/01, (2008).

rather as requiring the State to intervene where women face situations of violence in the private sphere.[14]

It is noteworthy that *Bevacqua* was the first case in which the Court recognized domestic violence and harassment as a violation of Article 8 of the Convention, the right to respect for private and family life. Reiterating the same principle in *Opuz v Turkey,* the Court held, "[T]he issue of domestic violence, which can take various forms ranging from physical to psychological violence or verbal abuse … is a general problem which concerns all member States and which does not always surface since it often takes place within personal relationships or closed circuits and it is not only women who are affected. The [European] Court [of Human Rights] acknowledges that men may also be the victims of domestic violence and, indeed, that children, too, are often casualties of the phenomenon, whether directly or indirectly."[15]

The Court further held that there was a violation of the prohibition of discrimination in Article 14 ECHR.[16] It found that domestic violence in Turkey was gender-based, and that the Turkish State authorities failed to prevent such violence, even if they themselves had no intent to discriminate. The Court also acknowledged the fact that violence is gender neutral and both men and women can be victims of domestic violence.[17]

Apparent in these judgments is that the Court's language demonstrates its gender-neutral approach toward domestic violence: violence transcends sexual identity and orientation. Hence, a breach of state responsibility to prevent domestic violence means the state failed to act effectively, and silence implies condoning violence.

In *A v Croatia,*[18] where the victim experienced verbal and physical violence by her ex-husband who suffered from mental illness, the Court affirmed that violence experienced by the victim relates to the "right to private life" because it had intervened with the victims physical, moral, and psychological integrity, which falls within the ambit of private life. Referring Article 8 ECHR,[19] the Court further ruled that states have a positive obligation to take legal steps and protect private individuals from violence. Where instances of violence have been repeatedly brought to the notice of state authorities, it cannot overlook its responsibility. In

---

[14] See https://library.law.utoronto.ca/whrrdocument/bevacqua-and-s-v-bulgaria (accessed on April 14, 2020).

[15] *Opuz v Turkey*, Application no. 33401/02, § 132.

[16] Article 14 provides that the enjoyment of the rights and freedoms set forth in this Convention shall be secured without discrimination on any ground such as sex, race, colour, language, religion, political or other opinion, national or social origin, association with a national minority, property, birth or other status.

[17] Opuz v. Turkey, Application no. 33401/02.

[18] Application no. 55164/08, 14 October 2010.

[19] Article 8 provides a right to respect for one's "private and family life, his home and his correspondence," subject to certain restrictions that are "in accordance with law" and "necessary in a democratic society."

Hajduova v Slovakia,[20] the applicant's abusive ex-husband was ordered to receive psychiatric treatment at a hospital. When he was prematurely released after one week, the government did not try to enforce its order and the ex-husband began threatening the applicant and her attorney. The Court concluded that the government's failure to enforce the order and return the ex-husband to the hospital violated the Convention and that the government had a duty to prevent the applicant's psychological harm (caused by the ex-husband's threats). The Court found that the government of Slovakia failed to fulfil its obligations arising from the European Convention on Human Rights.

According to the Court, domestic authorities are obligated to take reasonable preventative measures when they know about or have reason to believe that there is an imminent threat or risk to an individual. Lack of action would amount to a breach of the state's positive obligations under Article 8 of the Convention to secure respect for the individual's private life. In a previous case,[21] the Court held that failure to protect women against domestic violence could be a violation of Article 8 (right to respect for private and family life) and Article 3 ECHR.

In *Kalucza v Hungary*,[22] the Court refused to apply Article 8 ECHR and dismissed the applicant's complaints about the violent behaviour shown by her former husband. It ruled that domestic violence is non-discriminatory; if both parties are involved in assaults, the purpose of providing adequate protection to victims would be seriously undermined.[23]

In *E.M. v Romania*,[24] the applicant E.M. was a Romanian national who was born in 1973 and lived in Bucharest. She alleged that the investigation into her criminal complaint of domestic violence committed in the presence of her daughter, aged one and a half, had not been effective. The Romanian courts had dismissed the applicant's complaints on the ground that her allegations had not been proven. Relying in substance on Article 3 ECHR,[25] the applicant was ensured effective protection by the Court.

In *D.P. v Lithuania*,[26] the Government of Lithuania acknowledged a procedural violation in a case of domestic violence. The implementation of the criminal-law mechanisms was defective, which led to a violation of the state's positive obligations under Article 3 of the Convention. Hence, the Court decided to strike the application out of its list of cases.

The Court has opposed cases where a legal framework exists but is not properly applied or is inconsistent with international standards. For instance, In *Bălşan v*

---

[20] Application no. 2660/03, 30 November 2010.

[21] *E.S. and others v Slovakia*, Application no. 8227/04, 15 September 2009.

[22] Application no. 57693/10, 24 April 2012.

[23] Application no. 57693/10, 24 April 2012, para 66 and 68.

[24] Application no. 43994/05, 30 October 2012.

[25] Article 3 (prohibition of torture and inhuman or degrading treatment).

[26] Application no. 27920/08, 22 October 2013.

Romania,[27] The applicant alleged that the authorities had failed to protect her from repeated domestic violence and to hold her husband accountable, despite her several complaints. The Court noted that the authorities were aware of the abuse but had failed to apply the relevant legal provisions in this case. Such an approach was inconsistent with international standards on violence against women. The Court held that there had been a violation of Article 3 (prohibition of inhuman or degrading treatment) of the Convention since the authorities had failed to adequately protect the applicant against her husband's violence. The Court also observed that there was a violation of Article 14 (prohibition of discrimination) of the Convention read in conjunction with Article 3, as it was a case of discrimination and gender-based violence.[28]

In *S.Z. v Bulgaria,*[29] the Court again acknowledged a structural problem of lack of effective investigation. In this case, the applicant complained of the ineffectiveness of the criminal proceedings for the false imprisonment, assault, rape, and trafficking in human beings perpetrated against her. The Court held that there had been a violation of Article 3 of the Convention on account of the shortcomings in the investigation, along with excessive delays in the criminal proceedings, and a lack of investigation into certain aspects of the offences. The Court also observed that it had already, in over 45 judgments against Bulgaria, found that the authorities had failed to comply with their obligation to carry out an effective investigation and considered that these recurrent shortcomings disclosed the existence of a systemic problem. It considered that it was incumbent on Bulgaria, in cooperation with the Committee of Ministers, to decide which general measures were required in practical terms to prevent other similar violations of the Convention in the future.

The Court has refused to accept the notion that repeated acts of domestic violence are of trivial nature. In *Valiulienė v Lithuania,*[30] a woman suffered from spousal abuse over a long period of time, there was delay in the criminal investigation, and the pre-trial investigations were discontinued. The Court ruled that by failing to protect the applicant and her children from domestic violence, Lithuanian law enforcement authorities violated Article 3 ECHR (prohibition of torture, inhuman and degrading treatment and punishment).

The Court has explicitly ruled against state authorities condoning sex discrimination i.e., discrimination against women. In *Eremia v The Republic of Moldova,*[31]

---

[27] Application no. 49645/09, 23 May 2017.

[28] See the presentation by Mykolas Černiauskas, "Gender Equality and Non-Discrimination from the Perspective of the European Court on Human Rights": http://secretariadegenero.pjud.cl/images/documentos/Eurosocial_PJUD/SeminarioII/Presentacion%20TEDH%20Cerniauskas.pdf (accessed on April 16, 2020).

[29] Application no. 29263/12, 3 March 2015.

[30] Application no. 33234/07, 26 March 2013.

[31] Application no. 3564/11, 28 August 2013.

Mudric v The Republic of Moldova,[32] *B. v The Republic of Moldova,*[33] and *T.M. and C.M. v The Republic of Moldova,*[34] the Court ruled that there was a violation of Article 3 (prohibition of torture, namely ill-treatment in the present cases). There were also violations of Article 8 (the right to respect for private and family life) in the *Eremia* and *Mudric* cases; and violations of Article 14 (prohibition of discrimination) in conjunction with Article 3 (ill-treatment) in *Eremia, Mudric,* and *T.M. and C.M.* Hence, the Court directed the state to provide financial compensation to the victims.[35]

In all of the above cases, the Court has relied on Article 3 (protection from inhuman or degrading treatment or punishment), Article 8 (right to private and family life), and Article 14 (protection from discrimination). According to the Court, the state is a recognised subject of international law and is responsible for protecting victims from domestic violence. The state responsibility to fulfil international duties is, therefore, a legal responsibility, for a state cannot abolish or create international law in the same way that it can abolish or create domestic law.[36] International responsibility now also involves the consideration of the position of international organisations and individuals.[37] Thus, the rules of international law regarding state responsibility concern the circumstances in which and the principles whereby the state becomes accountable for the injury or damage caused.[38]

Applying these principles, Article 3 can be utilised to address a wide range of ill-treatments including domestic violence among same-sex couples or intimate partners. The article can be applied to all circumstances or incidents involving state responsibility to protect against acts or ill-treatments of inhuman or degrading nature. The duty of the state is to exercise due diligence, and, where injurious acts have nevertheless been committed, to procure reparation for the wrongful act, by punishing the offenders and compelling them to pay compensation, if necessary.[39] However, since the Convention entered into force in 1953, this article has rarely been invoked to address discrimination based on sexual orientation.[40] The limited use of Article 3 is because sexual minorities are not interested in using this provision. The article has been used in asylum cases.[41] In most cases, Article 8 in conjunction with Article 14 has been invoked by sexual minorities to address discrimination against

---

[32] Application no. 74839/10, 16 July 2013.

[33] Application no. 61382/09, 16 October 2013.

[34] Application no. 26608/11, 28 January 2014.

[35] Irina Crivet, "ECtHR or CEDAW: Spoilt for Choice in Moldova?": https://strasbourgobservers. com/2018/12/07/ecthr-or-cedaw-spoilt-for-choice-in-moldova/ (accessed on April 17, 2020).

[36] Oppenheim (1955), p. 337.

[37] Kapoor (2011), p. 136.

[38] Starke (1989), p. 293.

[39] Kapoor (2011), p. 140.

[40] It was invoked in this regard in 2012. Johnson and Falcetta (2018), p. 2.

[41] ECHR (2004) *F. v United Kingdom*, 17341/03; ECHR (2004) *I.I.N. v the Netherlands*, 2035/04.

same-sex couples. Complainants often do not understand what constitutes inhuman or degrading treatment. Hence, less complaints are filed invoking this provision.[42]

Besides, the Convention should be interpreted in the background of changing social circumstances. For instance, acts or situations which were classified as inhuman or degrading treatment in the past could be classified differently in future. The majority of applications received by the Court invoking Article 3 are from asylum seekers. However, the Court has refused to apply this article even to complaints by same-sex asylum seekers, contending that they would suffer ill-treatment if deported to their country of origin, leading to violation of Article 3.[43]

Furthermore, the article has also never been invoked in cases of lack of access to or legal recognition of same-sex marriage and/discrimination against same-sex couples. This is because the Court has interpreted marriage under Article 12[44] as a heterosexual union. Putting it in the words of Johnson and Falcetta:

> the Courts refusal to compare unmarried same-sex couples and married different-sex couples for the purposes of considering complaints about discrimination based on sexual orientation under Article 14 of the Convention105 has produced a two track approach: on the one hand, the Court continues to develop its jurisprudence on numerous aspects of sexual orientation discrimination in respect of private and family life (under Article 8) whilst, on the other hand, it maintains the inflexible view that same-sex couples have no recourse to being excluded from the rights and benefits attached to marriage (under Article 12).[45]

The Court has otherwise acknowledged that same-sex couples have an equal right to enter a stable, committed relationship and are entitled to legal recognition and protection of their relationship.[46] Hence, the Court should include domestic violence among same-sex couples and intimate partners as a form of degrading treatment within the meaning of Article 3, and a form of discrimination within the meaning of Article 14 in conjunction with Article 3. In addition, the Court can also apply Article 8. Exclusion of domestic violence among same-sex couples from the ambit of Article 3 would amount to a form of degrading and discriminatory treatment under Article 3 and 14, respectively.

Also, the fact that none of the existing Conventions or legislations cover instances of same-sex domestic violence does not prevent the Court from invoking Articles 3, 8, and 14. The Court has otherwise decided cases which fell outside the scope of the Convention or which were not recognised by the Convention. For instance, in *Slyusarev v Russia*,[47] the Court held that depriving a prisoner of his reading glasses

---

[42] Johnson and Falcetta (2018), p. 10.

[43] See *Protecting Persons with Diverse Sexual Orientations and Gender Identities: A Global Report on UNHCRs Efforts to Protect Lesbian, Gay, Bisexual, Transgender, and Intersex Asylum-Seekers and Refugees* (2015).

[44] Article 12 provides, "Men and women of marriageable age have the right to marry and to found a family, according to the national laws governing the exercise of this right."

[45] Johnson and Falcetta (2018), pp. 32–33.

[46] See *Schalk and Kopf v Austria*, Application no. 30141/04, 24 June 2010; *Burden v United Kingdom*, Application no. 13378/05, 29 April 2008.

[47] *Slyusarev v Russia*, Application no. 60333/00 (ECtHR, 20 April 2010), paras 43–44.

amounted to degrading treatment contrary to Article 3. Similarly, in *Strelets v Russia*,[48] the fact that the Convention does not recognise the right of access to food or the right to sleep did not prevent the Court from deciding that depriving a prisoner of food and sleep between court hearings amounted to inhuman and degrading treatment.[49] Hence the Court should harmonise the provisions of the Convention especially when deciding contemporary cases. In fact, the founders had designed the Convention with these principles in mind.

The Court has also decided cases of domestic violence in the light of Article 2 ECHR.

According to Article 2: 1. Everyone's right to life shall be protected by law. No one shall be deprived of his life intentionally save in the execution of a sentence of a court following his conviction of a crime for which this penalty is provided by law. 2. Deprivation of life shall not be regarded as inflicted in contravention of this Article when it results from the use of force which is no more than absolutely necessary: (a) in defence of any person from unlawful violence; (b) in order to effect a lawful arrest or to prevent the escape of a person lawfully detained; (c) in action lawfully taken for the purpose of quelling a riot or insurrection.

Under Article 2, the state has an obligation to safeguard and protect the rights of individuals from violence. The right to life also includes the security of persons from third party criminal acts. The landmark decision in *Toonen v Australia*,[50] in which the UN Human Rights Committee held that all people—including lesbian, gay, bisexual, transgender and intersex (LGBTI) persons—are entitled to enjoy the protections provided for by international human rights law, including respect for right to life, security of person and privacy, the right to be free from torture and arbitrary arrest and detention, the right to be free from discrimination and the right to freedom of expression, association and peaceful assembly.[51] States have an obligation to exercise due diligence to prevent, punish, and redress deprivations of life and to investigate and prosecute all acts of violence.[52] States should prevent violence and discrimination on the ground of sexual orientation and gender identity. States are also obliged to protect the right to life, liberty, and security of persons irrespective of sexual orientation or gender identity.[53] The Court applied these general principles to the following domestic violence cases.

---

[48] *Strelets v Russia*, Application no. 28018/05 (ECtHR, 06 November 2012), para 47.

[49] Johnson and Falcetta (2018), p. 37.

[50] See Communication no. 488/1992, also *Young v. Australia*, Communication no. 941/2000 (CCPR/C/78/D/941/2000), para 10.4.

[51] See *Discriminatory laws and practices and acts of violence against individuals based on their sexual orientation and gender identity* (2011), p. 4. See also Naik (2017).

[52] *Discriminatory laws and practices and acts of violence against individuals based on their sexual orientation and gender identity* (2011), pp. 4–5.

[53] *Discriminatory laws and practices and acts of violence against individuals based on their sexual orientation and gender identity* (2011), p. 5.

In *Branko Tomasic and Others v Croatia*,[54] the Court found that there was violation of the right to life (Article 2) in this case on the basis that death threats were not taken seriously, despite being made to officials during psychiatric treatment in prison. The applicants, relatives of the mother and child victims, claimed that the state failed to exercise due diligence to protect the victim from her husband, who was released from prison. The husband was serving a jail sentence, along with compulsory psychiatric treatment, for threatening to kill his wife and their baby with a bomb. Shortly after his release, the husband shot and killed his wife and baby. The Court held that state officials, in this case, should have required the husband to undergo a psychiatric assessment before his release and should have searched his vehicle and home after the death threats were reported. A failure to undertake all these actions amounted to a violation of the state's positive obligations to uphold the right to life.[55]

Further, in *Kontrova v Slovakia*,[56] the Court went a step further and applied Article 13 in conjunction with Article 2. In this case, the complainant filed a criminal complaint against her husband, accusing him of assaulting her and beating her with an electric cable. Days later, she returned to the police station with her husband to modify the complaint such that her husband's alleged actions were treated as a minor offence, which called for no further action. The following month, the police were called by the complainant and a relative to report that the husband had a gun and was threatening to kill himself and the children. A few days later, he acted on these threats and killed the children. Although the domestic courts found that the tragedy was a direct consequence of the police's failure to act, the complainant was unsuccessful in seeking compensation. Considering these facts, the Court held that there had been a violation of Article 2, the right to life, given the failure of the domestic authorities to protect the lives of the applicant's children. The Court found that the police had failed in their obligations by not accepting the criminal complaint, launching an investigation, and commencing criminal proceedings. The Court also condemned the state's failure to act pursuant to the emergency calls placed shortly before the murders. Finally, the Court held that the state had also violated Article 13, the right to an effective remedy, stating that the complainant should have been able to apply for compensation where she had suffered harm as a result of police failures.[57]

Moreover, in *Opuz v Turkey*,[58] the Court established that a state's failure to protect women from violence can violate the right to non-discrimination, enshrined in Article 14. Turkey's failure to set up a system to protect domestic violence victims

---

[54] Application no. 46598/06, (2009).

[55] See https://library.law.utoronto.ca/whrrdocument/branko-tomasic-and-others-v-croatia (accessed on April 18, 2020).

[56] Application no. 7510/04, (2007).

[57] See https://library.law.utoronto.ca/whrrdocument/kontrova-v-slovakia (accessed on April 18, 2020).

[58] Application no. 34401/02, 50 Eur. H.R. Rep. 28, (2009).

and punish offenders was also found to violate the rights to life (Article 2) and freedom from degrading or inhuman treatment (Article 3). In this case, the complainant alleged that state authorities had failed to protect her and her mother from domestic violence at the hands of her husband, which led to the infliction of life-threatening injuries on the complainant and to the death of her mother. Several complaints had been filed over the course of seven years, with no action by the authorities. It was only after the complainant's mother was murdered that her husband was arrested, though he was released pending his appeal, and continued to threaten the complainant.[59]

In the case of *Durmaz v Turkey*,[60] the husband stated to the prosecutor that his wife had committed suicide by overdosing on her medications. The prosecutor never conducted an investigation into the allegations brought by the mother of the deceased, who claimed that her daughter's husband had beaten her twice before, ending in hospitalisations; afterwards, he apologized to his wife and persuaded her to change her mind by promising that he wouldn't be violent toward her again. The applicant alleged that the real problem in the present case was the national authorities' continuing tolerance toward domestic violence, which has been a severe problem in Turkey. The Court held that there had been a violation of Article 2 (right to life) of the Convention in its procedural aspect on account of the Turkish authorities' failure to carry out an effective investigation into the death of the applicant's daughter. The Court considered that the prosecutor's failure was a part of a judicial passivity to allegations of domestic violence referring to the Court's findings in the *Opuz v Turkey* case.

In *Civek v Turkey*,[61] the applicants' mother was murdered by their father. The applicants complained that the Turkish authorities had failed in their obligation to protect their mother's life. The Court held that there had been a violation of Article 2 (right to life) of the Convention. It found, in particular, that even though the Turkish authorities had been informed of the genuine and serious threat to the applicants' mother's life and despite her continued complaints of threats and harassment, they had failed to take the measures reasonably available to them in order to prevent her from being murdered by her husband.

In *Talpis v Italy*,[62] this case concerned the conjugal violence suffered by the applicant, which resulted in the murder of her son and her own attempted murder. The Court held that there had been a violation of Article 2 (right to life) of the Convention on account of the murder of the applicant's son and her own attempted murder. It found, in particular, that by failing to take prompt action on the complaint lodged by the applicant, the Italian authorities had deprived that complaint of any effect, creating a situation of impunity conducive to the recurrence of the acts of

---

[59] See https://library.law.utoronto.ca/whrrdocument/opuz-v-turkey (accessed April 19, 2020).

[60] Application no. 3621/07, 13 November 2014. See *Prosecution of Domestic Violence Against Women – A Public or Private Matter* (2019), pp. 11–12. See *Factsheet – Domestic violence* (2020).

[61] Application no. 55354/11 23 February 2016.

[62] *Talpis v Italy*, Application no. 41237/14, 2 March 2017.

violence, which had then led to the attempted murder of the applicant and the death of her son. The authorities had therefore failed in their obligation to protect the lives of the persons concerned. The Court also held that there had been a violation of Article 3 (prohibition of inhuman or degrading treatment) of the Convention on account of the failure of the authorities in their obligation to protect the applicant against acts of domestic violence.

In this respect, it noted in particular that the applicant had lived with her children in a climate of violence serious enough to qualify as ill-treatment, and that the manner in which the authorities had conducted the criminal proceedings pointed to judicial passivity, which was incompatible with Article 3. Lastly, the Court held that there had been a violation of Article 14 (prohibition of discrimination) of the Convention in conjunction with Articles 2 and 3, finding that the applicant had been the victim of discrimination as a woman on account of the inaction of the authorities, which had underestimated the violence in question and thus essentially endorsed it.[63]

In *N. v Sweden*,[64] the Court decided on the alleged risk of being subjected to domestic violence in case of deportation: The applicant, an Afghan national, arrived in Sweden with her husband in 2004. Their requests for asylum were refused several times. In 2005 the applicant separated from her husband. In 2008 her request for a divorce was refused by the Swedish courts as they had no authority to dissolve the marriage. Her husband informed the court that he opposed a divorce. In the meantime, the applicant unsuccessfully requested the Swedish Migration Board to re-evaluate her case and stop her deportation, claiming that she risked the death penalty in Afghanistan as she had committed adultery by starting a relationship with a Swedish man and that her family had rejected her. The Court held that the applicant's deportation from Sweden to Afghanistan would constitute a violation of Article 3 (prohibition of inhuman or degrading treatment or punishment) of the Convention finding that, in the special circumstances of the present case, there were substantial grounds for believing that if deported to Afghanistan, she would face various cumulative risks of reprisals from her husband, his family, her own family and from the Afghan society which fell under Article 3. The Court noted that the fact that the applicant wanted to divorce her husband and did not want to live with him any longer, might result in serious life-threatening repercussions. Lastly, to approach the police or a court, a woman had to overcome the public opprobrium affecting women who left their houses without a male guardian.[65]

In a right to a fair trial (Article 6 of the Convention) case *D.M.D. v Romania*,[66] the proceedings were brought by the applicant against his father for domestic abuse. The proceedings in question had lasted over eight years and ended in the father's conviction of physically and mentally abusing his child. The applicant complained

---

[63] See *Factsheet – Domestic violence* (2020).

[64] Application no. 23505/09, 20 July 2010.

[65] *Factsheet – Domestic violence* (2020).

[66] Application No. 23022/13, 3 October 2017.

that those proceedings had been ineffective and that he had not been awarded damages. In particular, the domestic courts had found at last instance that they did not have to examine the issue of compensation as neither he nor the prosecutor had made such a request before the lower courts. The Court held that there had been a violation of Article 3 (prohibition of inhuman or degrading treatment) of the Convention because the investigation into the allegations of abuse had lasted too long and had been marred by other serious shortcomings. The Court also held that that there had been a violation of Article 6 § 1 (right to a fair trial) of the Convention because the domestic courts had not examined the merits of the applicant's complaint about the failure to award him compensation, despite it being clearly worded in domestic law that they were under an obligation to rule on the matter of compensation in a case concerning a minor, even without a formal request from the victim.[67]

In *O.C.I. and Others v Romania,*[68] the first applicant, a Romanian national, decided not to go back to her husband in Italy with their two children. Before the Court, the first applicant and her children complained about the order to return the children to Italy. They alleged in particular that the Romanian courts had failed to take into account the grave risk of mistreatment they faced at the hands of their father, which was one of the exceptions under the Hague Convention of 25 October 1980 on the Civil Aspects of International Child Abduction to the principle that children should be returned to their habitual place of residence. The Court held that there had been a violation of Article 8 (right to respect for private and family life) of the Convention, finding that the Romanian courts had failed to give enough consideration to the grave risk of the applicant children being subjected to domestic violence when ordering their return to their father in Italy, which was one of the exceptions to the principle under international law that children should be returned to their habitual place of residence. The Court noted in particular that, even if there was mutual trust between Romania and Italy's child-protection authorities under EU law, that did not mean that Romania had been obliged to send the children back to an environment where they were at risk, leaving it up to Italy to deal with any abuse if reoccurred.

5.3 Confidentiality of Correspondence and Cyberbullying

In *Buturugă v Romania,*[69] where Buturuga argued that her rights in terms of the European Convention on Human Rights (European Convention) had been violated, particularly article 3—prohibition of torture and inhuman or degrading treatment—and article 8—right to respect for private and family life and correspondence; the

---

[67] *Factsheet – Domestic violence* (2020).
[68] Application no. 49450/17, 21 May 2019 (Committee judgment).
[69] Application no. 56867/15, 11 February 2020.

Court, noted that the domestic authorities had not addressed the facts from a domestic violence angle. Rather, their decisions had been based on the criminal code provisions penalising violence between private individuals, and not on those laying down harsher penalties for domestic violence. The Court was of the view that the findings of the domestic authorities were questionable, as they had failed to identify the individual responsible for the injuries. With regard to the investigation into the breach of confidentiality of Buturuga's correspondence, the Court pointed out in particular that cyberbullying was currently a recognised aspect of violence against women and girls, and could take on a variety of forms, including breaches of privacy, intrusions into the victim's computer and the capture, sharing and manipulation of data and images, including private data. The Court further accepted Buturuga's argument that acts such as illicitly monitoring, accessing or saving one's partner's correspondence could be considered by the domestic authorities when investigating cases of domestic violence. The Court therefore held that Romania had failed in its positive obligations under articles 3 and 8 of the European Convention and ordered the state to pay €10 000 to Buturuga.[70]

In the case of *M.G. v Turkey*,[71] the ECtHR held that there had been: a violation of Article 3 (prohibition of torture and inhuman or degrading treatment) of the European Convention on Human Rights, and a violation of Article 14 (prohibition of discrimination), taken in conjunction with Article 3. The case concerned the domestic violence experienced by M.G. during her marriage, the threats made against her following her divorce and the subsequent proceedings. The Court found that the authorities had taken a passive attitude, in that the criminal proceedings had been opened more than five years and six months after M.G. had lodged a complaint against her husband and that the proceedings were apparently still pending. The Court also held that after the divorce was pronounced (on 24 September 2007) and until the entry into force of a new Law (no. 6284) on 20 March 2012, the legislative framework in place did not guarantee that M.G., a divorcée, could benefit from protection measures, and noted that for many years after applying to the national courts, she had been forced to live in fear of her ex-husband's conduct.[72]

In *Halime Kılıç v Turkey*,[73] the applicant's daughter was killed by her husband despite having lodged four complaints and obtained three protection orders and injunctions. The Court held there had been a violation of Article 2 (right to life) and a violation of Article 14 (prohibition of discrimination) taken together with Article 2 of the Convention. It found that the domestic proceedings had failed to meet the requirements of Article 2 of the Convention by providing protection for the

---

[70] See https://altadvisory.africa/2020/02/12/european-court-recognises-cyberbullying-as-an-aspect-of-violence-against-women-and-girls/ (accessed on April 19, 2020).

[71] Application no. 646/10, 22 July 2016.

[72] See *The authorities' passivity with regard to a woman's experience of domestic violence was in breach of the Convention* (2016).

[73] Application no. 63034/11, 28 June 2016.

applicant's daughter. By failing to punish the failure by the latter's husband to comply with the orders issued against him, the national authorities had deprived the orders of any effectiveness, thus creating a context of impunity enabling him to repeatedly assault his wife without being called to account. The Court also found it unacceptable that the applicant's daughter had been left without resources or protection when faced with her husband's violent behaviour and that in turning a blind eye to the repeated acts of violence and death threats against the victim, the authorities had created a climate that was conducive to domestic violence on women.[74]

In *J.D. and A v the United Kingdom*,[75] the Court reasoned that there was discrimination in the reduction of housing benefits to two single mothers following a change in the national housing regulations:

> The Court held that there had been a violation of Article 14 (prohibition of discrimination) of the Convention in conjunction with Article 1 (protection of property) of Protocol No. 1 in respect of the second applicant. It noted that the regulation's aim to encourage people to move conflicted with the Sanctuary Scheme's goal of allowing victims of gender-based violence to stay in their homes. The impact of treating the second applicant in the same way as others subject to the new housing benefit rules was therefore disproportionate as it did not correspond to the legitimate aim of the measure. Moreover, the UK Government had not provided any weighty reasons to justify prioritising the aim of the scheme over that of enabling victims of domestic violence to remain in their homes.[76]

5.4 The Court of Justice (CJEU)

The CJEU's approach is similar to that of the ECtHR. In its judgments on two landmark cases, *Magette Gueye and Valentin Salmeron Sanchez*,[77] the CJEU held that the objective of law enforcement authorities is not only to protect the interests of victims but also to consider the larger interests of society:

> The Court further ruled that the mandatory imposition of an injunction to stay away for a minimum period, provided for as an ancillary penalty by the criminal law of a member State, on persons who commit crimes of violence within the family, even when the victims of those crimes oppose the application of such a penalty, is admissible. The Court also acknowledged that member States are permitted to exclude recourse to mediation in all criminal proceedings relating particular category of offences committed within the family.[78]

As a negotiation to all the case laws of the Courts on domestic violence against women, the Council of Europe adopted the Convention on Preventing and Combating Violence against Women and Domestic Violence in May 2011, which came into

---

[74] *Factsheet – Domestic violence* (2020).

[75] Applications nos. 32949/17 and 34614/17, 24 October 2019.

[76] *Factsheet – Domestic violence* (2020).

[77] Applications C483/09 and C-1/10.

[78] See *Prosecution of Domestic Violence Against Women – A Public or Private Matter* (2019), p. 13.

force in August 2014. The Convention proclaims that parties shall take the necessary legislative and other measures to exercise due diligence to prevent, investigate, punish, and provide reparation for acts of violence covered by the scope of the Convention that are perpetrated by non-state actors;[79] that parties shall ensure that investigations into or prosecution of certain offences shall not be wholly dependent upon a report or complaint filed by a victim and that the proceedings may continue even if the victim withdraws her or his statement or complaint.[80] However, as per the Convention provision, "any State or the EU may declare that it reserves the right not to apply or to apply only in specific cases or conditions the provisions laid down in Article 55, paragraph 1 regarding minor offences of physical violence."[81]

In all of the abovementioned cases, state authorities deliberately failed to fulfil their obligations to protect victims from violence. Either they failed to conduct proper investigations or to enforce the decisions of national courts. In some cases, they failed to compensate the victims. The Courts are objective in their approach to protect the right to private and family life, which includes a person's physical and psychological integrity and the right to a violence-free home environment (Article 8). This is true also with respect to the right to life (Article 2), prohibition of torture and inhuman or degrading treatment (Article 3), and prohibition of discrimination (Article 14). The state cannot deny its positive obligation to safeguard the rights and interests of citizens. The Courts, being gender neutral, believe that no person should be discriminated in the exercise of his or her right to enjoy private life and family; that no person should be subjected to torture, inhuman, or degrading treatment and discrimination. Especially the ECtHR affirmed the elements of due diligence, prevention, investigation, and prosecution of such violence. Furthermore, the Courts have explicitly condemned domestic violence, as well as the impassivity of state authorities toward such violence. National authorities are accountable to citizens whenever there is a likelihood of imminent threat or danger to life. Proper investigations and criminal proceedings should be initiated by state authorities. The misuse of power or negligence on the part of authorities need to be checked. Judicial remedies like free legal aid should be made accessible to the victims of violence without any discrimination.[82] In the absence of law, all these above judicial propositions can even be applied to cases of domestic violence among same-sex couples or intimate partners. In addition to state responsibility, the European Courts should encourage the political, administrative and judicial bodies of the member states to reform laws to include same-sex (unmarried) partners or their children.[83]

---

[79] Article 5, "State obligations and due diligence."

[80] Article 55, para 1.

[81] Article 78. See *Prosecution of Domestic Violence Against Women – A Public or Private Matter* (2019), p. 4.

[82] *Equal access to justice in the case-law on violence against women before* Greater Protection in Cases *the European Court of Human Rights* (2015), pp. 35–36.

[83] Waaldijk (2018), p. 17.

5.5 Germany's Commitment

Germany supports the EU instruments, international agreements, and policy frameworks aimed at achieving gender equality and empowering women. It is committed to the aims of CEDAW and the Istanbul Convention on violence against women and domestic violence. By signing both these Conventions, Germany pledged to implement tangible measures to guarantee legal and social equality between the sexes.[84]

5.6 German Law

Marriage and family are key structures in Germany. Both are protected by the state as a fundamental human right under Art. 6(1) GG (*Grundgesetz*—the German Constitution).[85] Several provisions of the family law were re-codified by the Act on Equal Rights of Men and Women in the Field of Civil Law (*Gleichberechtigungsgesetz*) of June 18, 1957.[86] In recent years, the landmark decisions of the Federal Constitutional Court (*Bundesverfassungsgericht*) have led to the legal reform of family law. According to the Federal Constitutional Court, non-marital cohabitation enjoys protection only under the general freedom of the action clause (*allgemeine Handlungsfreiheit*) of Article 2 (1) GG. This is relating to the legislative protection of tenants' rights.[87] This also applies to unregistered homosexual relationships. Fundamentally, the German Constitution considers marriage a legal relationship between a man and a woman.

The Registered Life Partnerships Act of February 16, 2001 allowed two persons of the same sex to register their partnership and is like marriage. Previously, from 2001 until 2017, same-sex couples could register their union under the Registered Life Partnerships Act (*Eingetragene Lebenspartnerschaft*).[88] This Act granted limited benefits to same-sex couples, which have been gradually extended by the Federal Constitutional Court (*Bundesverfassungsgericht*). For instance, in the beginning, partners did not have general adoption rights and only some custody rights. Marriage was not legally recognised. Since October 1, 2017, same-sex marriage has been recognised in Germany.[89]

---

[84] See Germany's commitment to women's rights: https://www.auswaertiges-amt.de/en/aussenpolitik/themen/menschenrechte/-/229112 (accessed on April 29, 2020).

[85] The Basic Law (Grundgesetz—GG) of 1949 established equality between men and women (Article 3 II GG).

[86] Reimann and Zekoll (2005), pp. 251–252.

[87] Reimann and Zekoll (2005), pp. 251–252.

[88] See Gesetz über die Eingetragene Lebenspartnerschaft (Lebenspartnerschaftsgesetz—LPartG): https://www.gesetze-im-internet.de/lpartg/BJNR026610001.html (accessed on April 23, 2020).

[89] See Gesetz zur Einführung des Rechts auf Eheschließung für Personen gleichen Geschlechts: https://www.bgbl.de/xaver/bgbl/start.xav?startbk=Bundesanzeiger_BGBl&

5.7 German Legal Framework on Domestic Violence

Until two decade ago, there was no specific legal framework on domestic violence. Today there is the Preventive Powers of Police (State Police Law), Federal Protection against Stalking and Violence Act (*Gewaltschutzgesetz* of 2001), and the Criminal Code. In the past, only the Police, civil courts (I and II), and child protection agencies were responsible for taking cognizance of the offence; there was no protection officer or comparable institution.[90]

Under the State Police Act, Police can intervene in case of mental or physical danger of life, limb, or liberty. The act can be registered as a criminal offence. Under such circumstances, any police officer has the right to act and remove the accused person from a shared household by issuing a prohibitive order against his or her return for up to 14 days without an extension. Physical force can be deployed by police officer to remove a person. If necessary, such an order can be extended or other protections orders may be issued.[91] Protection by Civil Court (I) is possible only if the aggrieved person applies for it. There must be a deliberate violation of one's mental or physical health, body, or liberty. A court order will be issued within the duration of the interim police order if an application is filed within that short time period. Such court orders substitute a police order.[92] A protection order issued by Civil Court (II) may cover, inter alia, (a) temporary removal from and interdiction of return to shared household and interdiction to return (6 months or longer, depending on ownership, rental contract, etc.); (b) interdiction of contact is possible outside the household and at specified places like school or the workplace; the perpetrator is not allowed to contact or meet with the victim, etc.; (c) interdiction of communication is also possible by technical means. A breach of protection order constitutes an offence punishable with imprisonment up to one year, or a fine.[93]

A brief overview of German legislative changes is found in the article of Helmut Kury and Ursula Smartt:[94] The First Right to Marriage Reform Act of June 14, 1976 (*Ehereformgesetz*) gave the married woman equal rights to her husband. In 1976, the Victim Compensation Act came into force (*Opferentschädigungsgesetz* of May 11, 1976). This Act was specifically aimed at the protection of the private life of victims involved in criminal proceedings (especially from the media). Victims who suffered damage to their health are compensated by the state. On April 1, 1987 the Victim Compensation Act was amended by the Victims of Criminal Acts 1987 (*Opferschutzgesetz* "for the improvement and support of victims in criminal proceedings"). The 1987 Act grants the victim increased protection from personal

---

jumpTo=bgbl117s2787.pdf#__bgbl__%2F%2F*%5B%40attr_id%3D%27bgbl117s2787.pdf%27%5D__1587545125456 (accessed on April 22, 2020).

[90] Arzt (2014).

[91] Arzt (2014).

[92] Arzt (2014).

[93] Arzt (2014).

[94] Kury and Smartt (2006), pp. 395–397.

questions during trial proceedings. In addition, "in camera" proceedings were allowed. The German Criminal Code (*Strafgesetzbuch*) was amended in 1997 by means of the 33rd Amendment Act (*Strafrechtsänderungsgesetz*). The Criminal Code now includes that offences such as "sexual assault causing a person to engage in sexual activity without consent (*sexuellen Nötigung*) and rape (*Vergewaltigung*) are now possible offences within marriage."

On December 1, 1998, the Victim Protection Act 1998 came into force (*Zeugenschutzgesetz*); it extended the statutory protection of victims, vulnerable persons, and witnesses under the age of 16 in criminal proceedings. The statutory provision of the parental right to inflict corporal punishment on children (*Züchtigungsrecht der Eltern gegen Kinder*) was abolished and substituted by an amendment to the Child Support Act of November 7, 2000. The father's right to punish his children by beating had existed since 1896 (§1631 BGB); likewise, the right to "chastise" his wife existed until 1928. The general right to "chastise" one's children continues to exist in customary law of most Germanic states.

On January 1, 2002, the Protection from Violence Act 2000 came into force (*Gewaltschutzgesetz*). This civil legislation acts as a "protection for victims of violence, persecution, and other unreasonable acts (such as stalking) and for the easement of legislation regarding the allocation of the domestic and marital home during divorce proceedings." The Act provides for an exclusion order to remove or ban one (married) partner from the marital home in cases of domestic violence. This Act protects married couples only when the violence takes place in the "marital home." Fights, incidents, or acts that take place outside the "marital home" are not covered. On September 1, 2004, the improvement of the Rights of Victims Act (in criminal proceedings) came into force (*Opferrechtsreformgesetz* of June 24, 2004, announced in BGBl I 2004 No. 31 of 30.6.2004). Under this Act victims of crime have a statutory right to legal aid and the assistance of an advocate, a confidant/e, or victim support person at every stage of criminal proceedings.[95]

In addition, the Act on Civil Law Protection against Violent Acts and Stalking also provides for sanctions under criminal law: section 4 of the Act provides for imprisonment of up to one year or a fine for violations of protective orders issued by the Court.[96] This Act was subsequently amended by the Federal Stalking Act (40. StRÄndG) of 22 March 2007, which entered into force on 31 March 2007 and made the act of stalking a punishable offence (Section 238 of Germany's Criminal Code) and the Family Procedure Reform Act (*Gesetz zur Reform des Verfahrens in Familiensachen und in den Angelegenheiten der freiwilligen Gerichtsbarkeit*, or FGG-RG), which entered into force on September 1, 2009.[97] The Act applies to the

---

[95] Kury and Smartt (2006), pp. 395–397.

[96] Gesetz zum zivilrechtlichen Schutz vor Gewalttaten und Nachstellungen (Gewaltschutzgesetz—GewSchG) 1: https://evaw-global-database.unwomen.org/en/countries/europe/germany/2002/act-on-civil-law-protection-against-violence%2D%2D2002- (accessed on April 22, 2020).

[97] Gesetz zum zivilrechtlichen Schutz vor Gewalttaten und Nachstellungen (Gewaltschutzgesetz—GewSchG) 1: https://evaw-global-database.unwomen.org/en/countries/europe/germany/2002/act-on-civil-law-protection-against-violence%2D%2D2002- (accessed on April 22, 2020).

right to use the marital home that is located in Germany as well as pertaining to prohibitions as to trespass, approaching and contact.[98] Furthermore, when a foreigner is affected by violence, the following provisions would apply:

> If a foreign wife or a foreign husband is affected by violence and wishes to separate from the violent person, this may affect his/her right of residence. As a rule, a foreign spouse who has come to join a spouse already living in Germany only acquires an independent right of residence in Germany if marital cohabitation has lawfully existed in the federal territory for at least three years (Section 31 (1) first sentence no. 1 of the Residence Act (Aufenthaltsgesetz)). If a separation before the expiry of this period should take place, it may be possible to enable the spouse to continue his or her residence in Germany in order to avoid hardship (Section 31 (2) of the Residence Act). Hardship shall be deemed to apply, for example, if the continuation of cohabitation is unreasonable because the foreigner or his/her children are suffering violence at the hands of the spouse. Separation from the violent spouse in combination with protection orders or the allocation of the home under the Act on Protection against Violence within the first three years in Germany therefore cannot lead to a loss of the right of residence. The family court's decision should in any case be submitted to the Aliens Authority (Ausländerbehörde), since it constitutes important grounds for a decision in favour of presuming that a hardship case exists pursuant to Section 31 (2) of the Residence Act. However, one restriction should be noted. The victim is only granted an independent right of residence if the extension of the residence permit of the violent spouse from whom the victim's right of residence derives was not ruled out, i.e. the violent spouse himself/herself had the prospect of permanent settlement. This prospect does not exist when an extension of the residence permit has been ruled out pursuant to Section 8 (2) of the Residence Act or when the purpose of the stay was temporary (e.g. a working visit limited to a period of four years as a speciality cook). In such cases— even in a hardship case—the victim has no individual right of residence independent of the legal residence status of the violent person as the foreigner who brought about family reunion. If the statutory requirements are fulfilled, however, the right of residence may be possible for a victim under Chapter 2 Section 5 of the Residence Act (residence on humanitarian grounds).[99]

Furthermore, as mentioned, the Council of Europe Convention on Preventing and Combating Violence against Women and Domestic Violence (Istanbul Convention) entered into force in Germany on February 1, 2018. As an impact of this new legal development, a "no means no" rule has been implemented. As per this rule, a sexual act is a crime if it takes place against the consent and will of the victim. The elements of "threat of violence" and "resistance" are no longer a prerequisite. Considering the provisions enlisted in the Istanbul Convention, it is now the responsibility of all levels of government—the Federal Government, the Länder (States), and local authorities—to ensure its implementation and to protect women against violence.[100] It is significant to note that same-sex domestic violence issues have been kept at bay

---

[98] Article 17a of the Introductory Act to the German Civil Code (Einführungsgesetz zum Bürgerlichen Gesetzbuch [EGBGB]).

[99] See *Greater Protection in Cases of Domestic Violence, Information on the Act on Protection Against Violence* (n.d.), p. 23.

[100] See *Report of the Federal Republic of Germany. Twenty-fifth Anniversary of the Fourth World Conference on Women and Adoption of the Beijing Declaration and Platform for Action (1995)* (2019), p. 4.

and were not a part of this Convention. The task of updating the Convention interpretation is simpler than extending the rules of the Convention to new fields of human rights.[101]

5.8 Reporting Domestic Violence Cases

The under-reporting of female victims of domestic violence is around 90%. More than 80% of abused women do not wish to press charges against their abuser.[102] An equal number of men (3.2%) and women (3.0%) reported that they had been victims of domestic violence; but women still form the majority (58.3%) compared with men (41.7%).[103] Lifestyles and behaviours have changed; there is an increasing number of victims of domestic violence on online forums. As mentioned, "stalking" is a rather new phenomenon in Germany—it did not exist in Germanic vocabulary before. It now figures in the new Protection from Violence Act (*Gewaltschutzgesetz* 2000).[104] Concerning "partnership abuse," a new German federal study reveals violence against and amongst males, including victims of domestic violence. Of the 266 males surveyed, 23% stated that they had experienced some form of physical or sexual abuse within their (past or current) relationships. The vast majority were abused outside the domestic or familial environment. The researchers noted that conducting this type of sensitive research was fraught with methodological difficulties, because of the social taboos such as homosexuality in Germany which has only been decriminalized recently.[105]

5.9 Police Attitude Toward Domestic Violence

Domestic violence is underreported in Germany since it is considered an internal family matter. It is highly likely that the offender will get off scot-free. This distrust in the criminal justice system by victims discourages them from reporting the offence.

Some decades ago, German police would send a complaining woman victim back home, advising her to compromise with her husband, amicably.[106] Since the 1980s, there has been a change in attitude among the German police. They began to try and

---

[101] Viljanen (2008), p. 263.

[102] Kury and Smartt (2006), p. 389.

[103] Lamnek and Luedtke (2005), p. 53.

[104] Kury and Smartt (2006), p. 390.

[105] See *Gewalt gegen Männer in Deutschland* (2004), p. 12. See also Kury and Smartt (2006), p. 394.

[106] Kury and Smartt (2006), p. 384.

settle the dispute between the couples through mediation, though many believed that approaching them would only worsen the problem. Even today, the same situation prevails in most cases. However, in contrast to the past, there is a new legislative measure that prevents domestic violence: the *Platzverweis*, a court or police order which places an injunction of an exclusion, displacement, or ban on the perpetrator. This order is valid for a short time. The order forms part of the Protection from Violence Act 2000 and came into force in 2005.[107] It is noteworthy that each of the 16 federal German states (*Länder*) has its own police laws. However, The German Criminal Penal Code (*Strafgesetzbuch*), a codified law, is still the most important legislation to get police protection in domestic violence cases.

5.10   Positive Judicial Findings

The German Judiciary has played a pivotal role in the empowerment of women. Courts are inclined to promote victim safety and increase batterer accountability by enforcing existing laws promptly and consistently. The Courts have not only extended equal protection to German women but also women asylum seekers.

In the *Verwaltungsgericht Stuttgart,* Urteil vom 23.01.2006—A 11 K 13008/ 04—Based on a complaint filed by an Iranian asylum seeker, the Stuttgart Administrative Court obliged the Federal Office for Migration and Refugees to determine that the applicant should not be deported to her husband. In other words, the Court justified a ban on forced deportation to escape from marital violence. The applicant traveled to Germany in February 2004. She had graduated from high school at the age of eighteen. She was only allowed to study four years later. Her parents are very religious. She was married in July 2003 by her parents against her will to her father's 50-year-old friend. After her marriage, she was prohibited from continuing her studies. The whole marriage was a pain for her. Her husband beat, tortured and raped her. She was hospitalized for two weeks because of a stomach tear and bleeding caused by the beatings. At the beginning of autumn 2003, she filed for divorce, but the judge rejected it because her arguments were not grounds for divorce.[108]

The 11th Chamber of the Administrative Court stated:

According to Section 60 (1) of the Residence Act, which now applies, persecution can also exist if the threat to life, physical integrity or freedom is linked solely to gender. A persecution of so-called non-state actors, who could also be private individuals if the state is unable or unwilling to offer protection against the persecution, is also relevant. The applicant met these requirements. She had given credibility to the fact that she was married to her father's boyfriend against her will and was regularly raped and brutally abused by her

---

[107] Kury and Smartt (2006), p. 398.

[108] See "Keine Abschiebung bei Zwangsheiratung": https://www.kostenlose-urteile.de/VG-Stuttgart_A-11-K-1300804_Keine-Abschiebung-bei-Zwangsverheiratung.news2299.htm (accessed on April 29, 2020).

husband during this marriage. The applicant had neither had the opportunity to divorce her husband, nor had she been able to count on the Iranian State to provide protection in view of the constant massive marital violence. According to the information available, women in Iran would still be treated as second-class people with regard to family law, civil law and criminal law. So, the husband has the right to divorce without having to justify the application for divorce; a woman, on the other hand, can only request that the court annul the marriage if the husband is mentally ill or impotent. If a woman wants a divorce, the police or a court will send her back to her husband. Women also had no way to take legal action against a violent husband. According to the Federal Foreign Office, they could not trust marital or domestic violence that effective state protection would be granted. The maltreatment committed by men against their women would be tolerated by the Iranian government. For the applicant there is also no possibility of regional evasion within Iran. If she were forced to move outside of her marital or family environment in Iran, she would run the risk of being raped, murdered or victims of traffickers. When the applicant returned to Iran, she was not sufficiently certain that she would not be persecuted again. Rather, she is threatened by the husband and a new persecution based on her gender.[109]

In *VG Karlsruhe,* Beschluss vom 16.08.2007—6 K 2446/07, Approving short-term eviction by Police in the event of domestic violence the 6th Chamber of the Administrative Court in Karlsruhe decided in an urgent procedure that "in the event of domestic violence, in order to protect the victim, the police may only briefly refer the victim to an apartment until the victim can apply for measures under the Violence Protection Act at the local court - the family court. As the administrative court stated, the violence protection law provides, at the victim's request, for a temporary ban on entry and a stay within a certain radius of the injured person's home. However, these measures should only be ordered by the competent district court - the family court. An expulsion order from the police authority is in principle permitted to prevent criminal offenses, in order to prevent (further) bodily harm or coercion of the victim in domestic conflicts. The police eviction is only a flanking, short-term measure to enable a first crisis intervention in cases of domestic violence and to assist victims before or until family legal protection can be reached. On the other hand, the local police authority does not have the power to take preliminary measures, as it were, in anticipation of any judicial regulations under the Violence Protection Act, which are reserved exclusively for the competent local court - family court - within the scope of the application of the Violence Protection Act."[110]

In *Bayerisches Landessozialgericht,* Urteil vom 06.04.2016—L 11 AS 355/15— A pertinent issue on who will ultimately have to bear the costs if woman and her children flee domestic violence to a women's shelter? The Bavarian State Social Court held that the local authority of origin must bear the costs for admission to a women's shelter. In this case, an aid recipient in H. became a victim of domestic violence and fled with her three underage children with the help of the police on April 15, 2013. After spending one week with relatives in different cities, she was

---

[109] See "Keine Abschiebung bei Zwangsheiratung": https://www.kostenlose-urteile.de/VG-Stuttgart_A-11-K-1300804_Keine-Abschiebung-bei-Zwangsverheiratung.news2299.htm (accessed on April 29, 2020).

[110] https://www.juraforum.de/urteile/begriffe/haeusliche-gewalt (accessed on April 29, 2020).

admitted to a women's shelter on May 1, 2013 in S. The JobCenter in S. granted the usage fees for the women's shelter as part of the unemployment benefit II payment, but reclaimed these costs from the job center from H. The job center refused to reimburse because the beneficiary had not least had her habitual residence in H. The Bavarian State Social Court, like the Nuremberg Social Court previously, ruled that the job center of the municipality of origin should bear the cost of admission to the women's shelter. The escape of a person affected by domestic violence does not preclude them from returning to the violent partner. The short stopovers with relatives would not have created a new habitual residence for the beneficiary. The legislature had also considered that the escape from domestic violence does not necessarily end seamlessly in a women's shelter but could previously lead to several stations that could possibly justify an actual stay. It is about the financial protection of the location.[111]

In *VG-LUENEBURG* – Aktenzeichen: 3 B 47/03 the Court observed:

According to § 1 of the Violence Protection Act, the court (family court) can regulate, at the request of an injured person, among other things, that the perpetrator does not enter the apartment of the injured person and is not within a certain radius of the apartment. According to this, it is regularly the responsibility of the injured person - such as the wife - to seek protection against acts of violence by another person - such as the husband. However, the applicability of the Violence Protection Act, which emphasizes the independent design of violent conjugal and other relationships, does not mean that a police order is not permitted in order to prevent the continuation of domestic violence. Rather, a removal order according to § 17 NGefAG is a necessary addition to the Violence Protection Act. Since the measures according to the Violence Protection Act can only be ordered by the family court, the initiation of the judicial process by the person concerned and the process itself must necessarily take a certain amount of time the police - as the 'first point of contact' for the victim of violence seeking help - have the opportunity to protect the injured person in the necessary manner until this judicial decision. As a rule, only a relocation within the meaning of section 17 (1) sentence 2 NGefAG can be considered, because this is the only way to counter the threat to the victim's health without the victim having to leave the apartment themselves, what should be avoided according to the purpose of the Violence Protection Act.[112]

Against this background, in cases in which a person has deliberately injured the body, health, or freedom of another person and thus fulfilled the requirements of Section 1 of the Protection Against Violence Act, it is "temporary" and usually still satisfies the principle of proportionality Measure within the meaning of section 17 (1) sentence 2 NGefAG to see a one-week removal order, in which the time until the decision of the family court is to be "bridged" and which therefore loses its validity as soon as the family court has made this decision. The dismissal is therefore an accompanying measure, without which the Violence Protection Act would not run empty. The removal order provides victims of violent marital and other relationships with better protection in advance of the family court decision. The removal order is a measure of the current crisis, a first emergency aid. It can also be assumed that a removal order under police law is not a sanction for past injustice. Rather, police law in

---

[111] See "Bayerisches LSG zur Kosten-tragungs-pflicht bei Unterbringung im Frauenhaus": https://www.kostenlose-urteile.de/Bayerisches-LSG_L-11-AS-35515_Bayerisches-LSG-zur-Kostentragungspflicht-bei-Unterbringung-im-Frauenhaus.news22789.htm (accessed on April 29, 2020).
[112] https://openjur.de/u/315194.html (accessed on April 29, 2020).

general and the removal order are intended to counter an impending danger, i.e., ward off a danger that is likely to threaten in the near future. The dismissal is therefore future-oriented and not past-oriented.[113]

It is clear that both the European Courts and the German Courts have played vital roles in the protection and promotion of human rights, but they have not always spearheaded new social developments. The Courts have at times adopted a conservative approach. They do not function in isolation but give due respect to the international instruments. However, when Courts face new challenges in the field of human rights, it is crucial to understand and examine issues or concerns beyond the ambit of law. The Courts need to become accustomed to this and adopt new methods and mechanisms to tackle new problems. This can make the Courts more vibrant to routinely review substantively important aspects of new human rights. In the context of the ECtHR, Jukka Viljanen states:

> It is obvious that the Court is not starting the discourse on a human rights problem, and it is not the final stage of the development of any human rights law in that question. The Court is not adapted to take a widespread role in the network of human rights instruments; its mission is to pass the torch to another actor and let the dialogue to continue; and maybe to return to the discourse in a later stage of the development process.[114]

5.11 From Persecution to Acceptance: LGBT Rights in Germany

Likewise, the legal history and evolution of LGBT rights in Germany from persecution to acceptance reveals the nature of legal and judicial evolution.

In 1957 the Federal Constitutional Court ruled on constitutional complaints brought by two men who had been found guilty of violating Article 175 of the German Criminal Code which prohibited homosexual relations between men. Arguments such as protection of the free development of one's personality and equal rights for men and women were rejected. According to the court there was no violation of the special equality. In fact, biological difference between the sexes was seen to be so decisive that hetero and homosexual couples could not be compared at all.[115]

Article 175 Criminal Code was abolished in 1969. On February 16, 2001 the Act of the Termination of the Discrimination of Same-Sex Couples entered into force. The Civil Partnerships Act introduced the legal status of homosexual partners (men or women) as of August 1, 2001. Rejecting the contention that registered same-sex couples threatened marriage and the special status of the traditional family in the German constitution, the Federal Constitutional Court ruled that the new German gay partnership law was fully constitutional. As per the court opinion, gay

---

[113] https://openjur.de/u/315194.html (accessed on April 29, 2020).

[114] Viljanen (2008), p. 263.

[115] Streinz (2013), p. 107.

partnerships are not "marriage with the wrong etiquette" but a completely different union between same-sex couples. "Marriage is neither damaged nor otherwise impaired by the partnership legislation," said the Court in its seventy-page ruling.[116] Based on this development, in 2010 the Federal Constitutional Court declared the unequal treatment of marriage and registered civil partnership in the Gift and Inheritance Act to be unconstitutional.[117] In 2013 followed the decision that the exclusion of registered civil partnerships from income splitting for spouses was unconstitutional.[118]

In 2017 Germany legalized same-sex marriage through a parliamentary vote. Federal Constitutional Court judges have repeatedly emphasized in their previous decisions that social change is considered in the interpretation of the Basic Law.[119] Later, the Federal Constitutional Court ordered tax equality for homosexual couples.[120] The Court also ruled in favour of same-sex adoption. It held that a member of a civil partnership should be permitted to adopt the partner's adopted child or stepchild; before this ruling, prospective parents in a civil union could only adopt a partner's biological child. The presiding judge claimed that "marriage and the family shall enjoy the protection of the state, in marriage as in a civil partnership, the act of adoption provides the child in the same manner with material advantages in terms of support, care and inheritance law."[121] As per the Court reasoning, while a lack of access to marriage per se did not comprise a violation of civil liberties, a same-sex couple's lack of legal options to protect their relationships might, in certain instances, and amount to violations of the Basic law's equal treatment clause (Article 3).[122] Thus, the Federal Constitutional Court assumed the role of an activist in balancing law and social interests. Although the development of homosexuality has ranged from punishment to equal treatment, many LGBT people still experience hostility and discrimination in Germany. The anti-discrimination law known as the General Equal Treatment Act (*Allgemeines Gleichbehandlungsgesetz*) protects individuals against discriminations they may face because of their skin color, country of origin, sex, religion, disability, age or sexual orientation/sexual identity. According to the law, complaints against sexual orientation or sexual identity, can be filed at the Anti-discrimination Agency.[123] Also, people persecuted in their home country due to their sexual orientation or sexual identity are eligible for asylum in Germany if there is an imminent threat to their life or fear of imprisonment or inhuman treatment due to their sexual orientation/identity. The persecution, however, must be quite

---

[116] See "New German gay partnership law is fully constitutional, court decides" (2002).

[117] Streinz (2013), pp. 108–109.

[118] Streinz (2013), p. 108.

[119] "Same-sex marriage in Germany: An issue for the court?" (2017).

[120] "German court orders gay tax equality" (2013).

[121] "German Court Strengthens Gay Adoption Rights" (2019).

[122] Davidson-Schmich (2017).

[123] See "LGBTQIA Which rights do I have in Germany?" https://handbookgermany.de/en/rights-laws/lgbtiq.html (accessed April 29, 2020).

severe, i.e., insults and the like are not considered to be sufficient ground for asylum.[124] The Frankfurt Administrative Court—while granting refugee status to an applicant who was deemed at risk of persecution due to his homosexuality—ruled that sexual orientation does not only constitute an unchangeable characteristic, but is so fundamental to the identity of a person that he/she should not be forced to denounce it.[125]

5.12   Conclusion

Relying on landmark judgments, the chapter clarified the public and private dichotomy on domestic violence. With the help of provisions of the ECHR, the chapter affirmed state obligations to protect women from domestic violence. Further, it elaborated domestic violence law in the jurisprudence of the European and German Courts. Although the issue of domestic violence has gained attention at international level in recent years, especially from international bodies like the United Nations, such bodies have still not addressed LGBT domestic violence to any great extent. Against this backdrop, the chapter assessed the legal history and evolution of LGBT rights in Germany.

In some countries, gay men face legal and social challenges that are not experienced by non-LGBT people, which is why they seek refuge in Germany. They arrive from different regions including Africa, the Middle East, and Asia. There are no statistics about the numbers of people requesting asylum based on sexual orientation and gender identity. The authorities do not keep records or statistical information on sexual orientation and gender identity. Many gay men seeking asylum prefer to settle in cities and do not wish to disclose their sexual orientation and gender identity to the authorities for various reasons. There is less private space and interpreters lack basic knowledge on this issue.[126] During the asylum process, many have complained about harassment by the officials and security staff. They are not allowed to study or work until the application process is complete, which can take months. Many undergo a phase of frustration and depression. Many are successful in providing letter from a psychologist on SOGI.[127]

Especially gay refugees in Germany face challenges because they have to live with other asylum seekers at a refugee shelter. They suffer from verbal, physical, and sexual abuse at the shelters and some have been forced to move out. Harassment,

---

[124] See "LGBTQIA Which rights do I have in Germany?" https://handbookgermany.de/en/rights-laws/lgbtiq.html (accessed April 29, 2020).

[125] Germany - Administrative Court Frankfurt / Oder, 11 November 2010, VG 4 K 772/10.A: https://www.asylumlawdatabase.eu/en/case-law/germany-administrative-court-frankfurt-oder-11-november-2010-vg-4-k-77210a (accessed April 29, 2020).

[126] Rajanayagam and Awadalla (2016).

[127] Rajanayagam and Awadalla (2016).

aggression, and discrimination are the norm at such shelters. Finding private spaces in this type of accommodation is difficult. In addition, they experience racist stereotypes and culture clashes. Though many have escaped conservative Muslim countries where homosexuality is illegal, they are still being victimized.[128]

Research findings reveal that due to the stigma attached to homosexuality, LGBT people in Germany are more than twice as likely to have been diagnosed with psychological distress or depressive disorder when compared to heterosexual people. There is a need to help improve LGBT inclusivity and visibility. This is possible by collecting information on sexual orientation in a broader range of surveys, for instance, on the LGBT labour force or information on gender identity to legally prohibit anti-LGBT discrimination in employment and social life.[129]

In the case of crime, reports at times blame refugees, yet the police records describe the accused as non-refugee men. This adds to further discrimination. Most cases go unreported. European privacy laws need to be amended. The Lesbian and Gay Federation based in Germany reported 106 cases of violence against homosexual and transgender refugees in the Berlin region, dating from August through the end of January 2016. Most of the cases took place in refugee shelters, and 13 included sexual abuse.[130]

According to Joerg Steinert, head of the federation in Berlin-Brandenburg, "refugees are reluctant to approach police for fear of jeopardizing their asylum applications, opting instead for pleading gay rights groups for assistance all over the country. In 2015, the federation relocated 50 individuals to private homes because the refugee centers were considered too dangerous."[131]

References

Arzt C (2014) Domestic violence and the legal system in Germany. Lecture at Symbolises Law School, Pune. Retrieved April 22, 2020 from https://www.hwr-berlin.de/fileadmin/portal/Dokumente/Prof-Seiten/Arzt/Domestic_Violence_Germany_21-1-14.pdf

Carratalá A (2016) Press coverage of same-sex domestic violence cases in Spain. Revista Latina de Comunicacion Social 71(71):40–65. https://doi.org/10.4185/RLCS-2016-1083en

Damonze D (2017) Statutory protection against domestic violence in Europe – a comparative case study. LawsAndFamilies Database. Retrieved May 1, 2020 from https://www.academia.edu/34020817/Statutory_protection_against_domestic_violence_in_Europe_a_comparative_case_study_of_question_2.7_in_the_LawsAndFamilies_Database

Davidson-Schmich LK (2017) LGBT politics in Germany: unification as a catalyst for change. German Polit 26(4):534–555. https://doi.org/10.1080/09644008.2017.1370705

---

[128] "The war isn't over for gay refugees as they face abuse in shelters in the EU" (2016).

[129] "Society at a Glance 2019: A Spotlight on LGBT People: How does Germany Compare?" (2019).

[130] "The war isn't over for gay refugees as they face abuse in shelters in the EU" (2016).

[131] "The war isn't over for gay refugees as they face abuse in shelters in the EU" (2016).

Developing Directive-Compatible Practices for the Identification, Assessment and Referral of Victims (2017) National Report Estonia, Institute of Baltic Studies. Retrieved May 2, 2020 from https://www.ibs.ee/wp-content/uploads/VICT-report-ESTONIA-3.pdf

Discriminatory laws and practices and acts of violence against individuals based on their sexual orientation and gender identity (2011) Annual report of the United Nations High Commissioner for Human Rights and reports of the Office of the High Commissioner and the Secretary-General. Retrieved May 2, 2020 from https://digitallibrary.un.org/record/719193?ln=en

Equal access to justice in the case-law on violence against women before the European Court of Human Rights (2015) Council of Europe. Retrieved April 20, 2020 from https://edoc.coe.int/en/gender-equality/6690-equal-access-to-justice-in-the-case-law-on-violence-against-women-before-the-european-court-of-human-rights.html

Factsheet – Domestic violence (2020) European Court of Human Rights. Retrieved April 29, 2020 from https://www.echr.coe.int/Documents/FS_Domestic_violence_ENG.pdf

German court orders gay tax equality (2013) Deutsche Welle. Retrieved April 29, 2020 from https://www.dw.com/en/german-court-orders-gay-tax-equality/a-16868143

German Court Strengthens Gay Adoption Rights (2019) Spiegel International. Retrieved April 29, 2020 from https://www.spiegel.de/international/germany/german-court-strengthens-gay-and-lesbian-adoption-rights-a-884278.html

Gewalt gegen Männer in Deutschland: Personale Gewaltwiderfahrnisse von Männern in Deutschland (2004) Bundesministerium für Familie, Senioren, Frauen und Jugend. Retrieved May 2, 2020 from https://www.bmfsfj.de/resource/blob/84590/a3184b9f324b6ccc05bdfc83ac03951e/studie-gewalt-maenner-langfassung-data.pdf

Greater Protection in Cases of Domestic Violence, Information on the Act on Protection Against Violence (n.d.) Federal Ministry for Family Affairs, Senior Citizens, Women and Youth. Retrieved April 22, 2020 from https://www.bmfsfj.de/blob/121760/b227b8b02448a576045c444efe81b792/mehr-schutz-bei-haeuslicher-gewalt-englisch-data.pdf

Hasselbacher L (2010) State obligations regarding domestic violence: the European Court of Human Rights, due diligence, and international legal minimums of protection. J Hum Rights 8(2). Retrieved April 20, 2020 from https://scholarlycommons.law.northwestern.edu/njihr/vol8/iss2/3/

Herd N (2019) The Istanbul Convention & the Czech Republic: barriers to ratification. Young Feminist Europe. Retrieved May 2, 2020 from https://www.youngfeminist.eu/2019/01/the-istanbul-convention-the-czech-republic-barriers-to-ratification/

Johnson PJ, Falcetta S (2018) Sexual orientation discrimination and Article 3 of the European Convention on Human Rights: developing the protection of sexual minorities. Eur Law Rev 43 (2):167–185

Kapoor SK (2011) International law and human rights. Central Law Publications, India

Kury H, Smartt U (2006) Domestic violence: recent developments in German and English legislation and law enforcement. Eur J Crime Crim Law Crim Justice 14(4):382–407. https://doi.org/10.1163/157181706780132850

Lamnek S, Luedtke J (2005) Gewalt in der Partnerschaft: Wer ist Täter, wer ist Opfer? In: Kury H, Obergfell-Fuchs J (Hrsg.) Gewalt in der Familie. Für und Wider den Platzverweis (Freiburg 2005), pp 37–69

Luxembourg: Overview on the situation of lesbian, bisexual and queer women and recommendations to end violence, discrimination and invisibility (2018) Rosa Lëtzebuerg-CIGALE Luxembourg. Retrieved May 2, 2020 from https://tbinternet.ohchr.org/Treaties/CEDAW/Shared%20Documents/LUX/INT_CEDAW_NGO_LUX_29967_E.pdf

McQuigg RJA (2015) Domestic violence as a human rights issue: Rumor v. Italy. Eur J Int Law 26 (4):1009–1025. https://doi.org/10.1093/ejil/chv057

Naik Y (2017) Homosexuality in the jurisprudence of Supreme Court of India. Springer Publishers, Germany

New German gay partnership law is fully constitutional, court decides (2002) The Irish Times. Retrieved April 29, 2020 from https://www.irishtimes.com/news/new-german-gay-partnership-law-is-fully-constitutional-court-decides-1.1088928

Oppenheim L (1955) International law. Longmans, Green & Co, London

Prosecution of Domestic Violence Against Women – A Public or Private Matter (2019) European Judicial Training Network. Retrieved April 19, 2020 from http://www.ejtn.eu/PageFiles/17913/TH-2019-01%20TEAM%20BULGARIA.pdf

Protecting Persons with Diverse Sexual Orientations and Gender Identities: A Global Report on UNHCRs Efforts to Protect Lesbian, Gay, Bisexual, Transgender, and Intersex Asylum-Seekers and Refugees (2015) United Nations High Commissioner for Refugees. Retrieved April 17, 2020 from https://www.refworld.org/pdfid/566140454.pdf

Rajanayagam I, Awadalla A (2016) LGBT*I*Q Refugees in Germany. Lernen aus der Geschichte. Retrieved April 27, 2020 from http://lernen-aus-der-geschichte.de/International/content/12840

Reimann M, Zekoll J (2005) Introduction to German law. CH Beck, München

Report of the Federal Republic of Germany. Twenty-fifth Anniversary of the Fourth World Conference on Women and Adoption of the Beijing Declaration and Platform for Action (1995) (2019) Retrieved April 24, 2020 from https://www.unece.org/fileadmin/DAM/Gender/Beijing_20/Germany.pdf

Report/Perspective and Action Plan (2018) Issued to the Danish Parliament by the Minister for Equal Opportunities. Retrieved May 2, 2020 from http://um.dk

Same-sex marriage in Germany: An issue for the court? (2017) Deutsche Welle. Retrieved April 29, 2020 from https://www.dw.com/en/same-sex-marriage-in-germany-an-issue-for-the-court/a-39527311

Society at a Glance 2019: A Spotlight on LGBT People: How does Germany Compare? (2019) The Organisation for Economic Co-operation and Development. Retrieved April 29, 2020 from https://www.oecd.org/germany/sag2019-germany.pdf

Starke JG (1989) Introduction to international law. Butterworths, Singapore

Streinz R (2013) The role of the German Federal Constitutional Court Law and Politics. Ritsumeikan Law Review 31. Retrieved April 29, 2020 from http://www.ritsumei.ac.jp/acd/cg/law/lex/rlr31/09streinz.pdf

The authorities' passivity with regard to a woman's experience of domestic violence was in breach of the Convention (2016) European Court of Human Rights 101 22.03.2016. Retrieved April 29, 2020 from https://rm.coe.int/168062cf75

The war isn't over for gay refugees as they face abuse in shelters in the EU (2016) Albawaba News. Retrieved April 29, 2020 from https://www.albawaba.com/news/war-isn%E2%80%99t-over-gay-refugees-they-face-abuse-shelters-eu-808596

Viljanen J (2008) The role of the European Court of Human Rights as a developer of international human rights law. Cuadernos constitucionales de la Cátedra Fadrique Furió Ceriol 62–63. Retrieved April 29, 2020 from https://www.corteidh.or.cr/tablas/r26759.pdf

Waaldijk K (2018) Extending rights, responsibilities and status to same-sex families: trends across Europe. Ministry of Foreign Affairs of Denmark. Retrieved May 2, 2020 from https://rm.coe.int/extending-rights-responsibilities-and-status-to-same-sex-families-tran/168078f261

Chapter 6
Domestic Violence Among German, Refugee, and Migrant Gay Men in Germany

In this chapter, the problem of sexual racism is considered in light of the increase of queer refugees and migrants in Germany. Through direct interviews with queer refugees, victims of domestic violence, and members of the German gay community, the queer refugee experience of living in Germany is captured. I found that queer refugees living in very close quarters with other refugees had to endure the same homophobic attitudes of their home country *as well as* the rejection of the German gay community. A major aspect of this picture, beyond the interviews, is the overt discrimination against refugee and migrant gay men by German gay men on gay chat websites, which is significant because these could be seen as the "hub" connecting the gay community. Beyond discrimination, this chapter examines the situation of sexual exploitation among queer refugees and Germans, which is surprisingly practiced by both. Finally, the work and knowledge of various European NGOs are taken into account, as well as implications of this research for practice, policy, and future research.

6.1 Sexual Racism

Much has been written about the sexual racism of White gay men toward Asian and Black men. Asian men are stereotyped by White gay men as feminized or desexualized and Black men as hypersexualized.[1] Also commonly reported are Asian men who discriminate or ignore races such as Arabs, Latinos, Blacks, and vice-versa, or how all of these races approve of White gay men. In the gay community, whiteness has always been the acceptable norm and non-whiteness

---

[1] Nguyen (2004), pp. 223–228; Gross and Woods (1999), pp. 235–253.

the exception,[2] reflecting racist power hierarchies.[3] According to the Britain-based Fact Site survey report, "more than two-thirds of the men from the Black, Asian and other minority ethnic backgrounds had personally experienced racism on the gay scene."[4]

White gay men have defended their actions by calling them "preferences" or "choices."[5] In the present day, racial preference has become a very common criteria on gay dating sites, as White gay men expect non-White gay men to disclose their ethnicity and origin.[6] Although most gay dating sites provide a voluntary option to mention user ethnicity, the demand to disclose ethnicity persists.

Sexual racism or racial preference is especially problematic in Germany, which currently also faces a migrant crisis. While the German gay community appears to be tolerant and liberal toward refugees and migrants, their acceptance is only superficial. Whereas British and American White gay men make offensive, racial comments to non-White men,[7] German gay men silently distance themselves from non-White gay men. In other words, they give the cold shoulder to non-White gay men or exploit them to satisfy their erotic desires. Through my research I have found that even some white German LGBT spaces specifically exclude LGBT gay refugees and migrants. These refugees have also been banned from entering mainstream LGBT spaces at times because their appearance is too masculine; they do not appear homosexual, e.g., a masculine gay refugee man is not allowed into a gay club, all of which manifests the doubt or distrust within the gay community itself.

6.2 Gay Refugees and Migrants in Germany

Many people from non-European countries have made it to Germany through the Balkan and Mediterranean route; among them are gay men. German Asylum law is very clear.[8] It provides that the refugees are entitled to asylum if they can demonstrate that they have been persecuted in their home country due to their sexual orientation and that they are in danger of being physically hurt, killed, imprisoned, or prosecuted or being exposed to humiliating or inhumane treatment or punishment. Acts of persecution include discrimination in education, health care, or employment. However, one cannot deny the probable misuse of the law.

---

[2]Nguyen (2004), pp. 223–228; Gross and Woods (1999), pp. 235–253.

[3]Callander et al. (2012).

[4]Haggas (2017).

[5]Paul et al. (2010).

[6]Paul et al. (2010).

[7]Paul et al. (2010). See also Flores (2017) and Allen (2020).

[8]See the Asylum Act: https://www.gesetze-im-internet.de/englisch_asylvfg/ (accessed on November 19, 2017).

The gay men who arrive in Germany quickly realize that they are facing the same people they feared in their home country, who have brought along with them the same conservative views about homosexuality. This means that the lives of gay refugees are not much different in Germany.[9] If they are visibly queer (feminine and gay), they are still verbally abused while walking down the street, especially by straight refugee men. One gay refugee complained to me that another person, someone he had never met, insulted him in his mother tongue in the middle of the street for being gay.

Many are still living in the closet and do not see any chance of coming out. They suppress their sexuality while living in refugee shelters. Many feel ashamed and are afraid of being attacked if they disclose their orientation. Their survival strategy, which is to hide their sexual orientation, rarely changes even after entering Germany. For instance, there have been reports about an attack on a Syrian gay couple seeking asylum in Germany;[10] there have also been reports about refugees suffering physical assault and threats from other refugees because of their sexuality. It is noteworthy that the most severe violence is most often perpetuated by non-Germans.

Many cases of violence occur in the LGBT refugee camps with other refugees. The risk of violence increases if the camp is located in rural areas or small cities, but this applies to all countries. While some cases are reported to the police, the outcome is always uncertain. Even if there is evidence of violence, refugees living in camps most often first report the violence to those who work there, and these people are usually not trained to take immediate action. They fail to report the case to the police at all, or even to their higher ups. If refugees are able to report the violence directly to the police, they often experience discrimination because they are either not believed or are considered perpetrators, e.g., black men are quite often seen as culprits. Also, for many victims, the psychological act of reporting violence is like coming out. Gay refugees are vulnerable, and refugee camps are breeding grounds for violence.

Furthermore, most refugees have a tough time convincing immigration authorities of their sexual orientation. Straight-acting gay men are often mistaken as heterosexual by the authorities. And some heterosexual men claim to be gay to take advantage of the legal situation. Interpreters, who usually accompany refugees before the immigration authorities, frequently have homo or transphobic attitudes;[11] and others have pressured men to falsely state homosexuality as a ground for claiming asylum. An interlocutor who works as an interpreter narrated his experience to me in the following words, "I was asked to change the facts or manipulate them [. . .] they begged, they pleaded with me to help them unlawfully, and I feared to do that. I finally refused."[12] Most newly arrived refugees presume that the corruption existing in their home country exists in Germany, which means they will have to bribe the authorities to avoid deportation. All these instances certainly

---

[9]Dammers (2016).

[10]"Gay asylum seekers beaten close to death in Germany" (2017).

[11]Rajanayagam and Awadalla (2016).

[12]Conversation, August 18, 2017.

present a challenge to the European Court of Justice, which ruled that sexuality tests for asylum seekers were banned.[13]

6.3   Overt Discrimination on Gay Chat Websites

Apart from the structural and institutional hardships faced by refugee gay men after arriving in Germany,[14] it is also significant to note how German gay men treat refugee and migrant men. Most face discrimination, sexual abuse, and harassment within the gay community itself.[15] Discrimination is invisible to the mainstream public but is a well-known fact among gay men. German gay men are divided in their approach toward the refugees and migrants. Some like them, others don't. In both cases, though, abuse is a common factor. Similar to Britain and the United States, the most common place for refugee and migrant men to experience sexual abuse and racism in Germany is on gay chat websites. German gay men usually defend themselves by claiming that they have been fooled or cheated in the past by the refugees or migrants either for money or for the purpose of obtaining a visa or passport. Some profile texts of German men on gay chat websites speak to this general attitude.

> **Profile text 1**: "I will not respond to any Messages from Asia, Africa and South America!"

> **Profile text 2**: "Guys from Africa, Asia, and East Europe etc. - no chance"

> **Profile text 3**: "bitte KEINE Neger, Flüchtlinge, Mohamedaner & Co - ich kann Euch einfach nicht mehr sehen [...] Geht zu den doofen Gutmenschen die Euch beklatschen - nicht zu mir!!!!!! Jeder Mensch hat eine Heimat - also geht wieder dorthin zurück.........
> Verschont mich mit Euren Moralsprüchen wie intollerant ich sei - das ist MEINE Meinung - und die darf doch frei geäußert werden????? " "(And please NO Negroes, refugees, Mohammedans & Co - I just cannot see you anymore. Go to the stupid good people who applaud you - not to me!!!!!! Everyone has a home - so go back there......... Spoil me with your moral quotes about how intolerant I am - that is MY opinion - and which may be freely expressed?????)

> **Profile text 4**: "No money boys and no gays from Russian and Africa etc."

> **Profile text 5**: "By the way – just interested in American or European guys! Not interested in guys living in Africa or Asia, pretending to be in Europe – sorry pals."

> **Profile text 6**: "African guys please note, that I am not interested at all to help anybody coming to Germany. You have to use the assistant of the Embassy or Consulate"

---

[13] See Judgment of the Court (Grand Chamber): http://curia.europa.eu/juris/document/document.jsf?text=&docid=160244&pageIndex=0&doclang=en&mode=req&dir=&occ=first&part=1&cid=143957 (18, November 2017).
[14] Rajanayagam and Awadalla (2016).
[15] Rajanayagam and Awadalla (2016).

Profile text 7: "Hello, I am a local guy who finds Arabic refugees hot! If you are straight, have blue b_lls from the long journey without sex? I'm a passive bottom who likes to give you a b__wjob, you can f__k me". "Refugee für nete Mann und heise Stunden?"

Profile text 8: "You know this Syrian called XXXXXX? Take care... I lost some thousand Euros to this refugee... Be warned and contact me, before you make the same mistake... (Kontaktiert mich, bevor ihr auf diesen Asylbewerber reinfallt").

Profile text 9: "Was ich nicht suche, ...keine Flüchtlinge, Einwanderer oder Mikranten ....Ich habe nichts gegen sie, bin selber bei der LINKE und akzeptiere sie auch hier .... aber leider nicht für Beziehung .....da nehme ich eher meines gleichen die aus Deutschland abstammen" (What I am not looking for, ... no refugees or migrants. . . . I am leftist and accept you . . . . but unfortunately not for relationship. . . . . .I would prefer to be with a German descent".)

The above narratives are only the tip of the iceberg.

6.4 Queer Refugee Activism

Many initiatives have been undertaken by gay rights activists to help refugees seeking asylum. Unfortunately, there has been less effort to eradicate discrimination, sexual abuse, and harassment within the community. Iris Rajanayagam and Ahmed Awadalla describe a typical act of discrimination, "There are initiatives, which are outright exploiting the name of queer refugees. A recent incident took place where a queer club organised a fundraising party for the benefit of queer refugees, but failed to organise any support for the refugees to enter the party, which led to a lesbian refugee to be turned out at the door."[16]

Queer refugees living in rural areas or camps have special needs, since they are highly vulnerable to attack there. To decrease the risk of violence, gay rights activists have opened shelters for gay refugees in cities like Berlin and Cologne.[17] Criticizing this queer refugee campaign, one LGBT activist expressed his opinion to me in the following words, "Even the opening of queer refugee cafés, refugee gay groups, and shelters for gay refugees involves ulterior motives to gain publicity, money, and sex." He added, "In fact, by providing separate shelters for gay refugees, the activists have tried to segregate them from the mainstream population. When migrants or refugees arrive in Germany, they have to obey the law of the host country. Under all circumstances they have to accept the culture and lifestyle in Germany. However, by opening separate shelters for refugee gay men, the activists have conveyed the wrong message. Is it justified to give preferential or privileged treatment to gay refugees (who have less fear of persecution) in comparison to the war victims?"[18]

---

[16]Rajanayagam and Awadalla (2016).

[17]See "Berlin opens Germany's first major gay refugee centre" (2016) and Rogers (2016).

[18]Conversation, November 11, 2017.

Activists have also alleged that immigration authorities are asking embarrassing questions to the refugee gay men;[19] that the decision-makers are not trained in LGBT issues; and that gays are being victimized.[20] However, one of the LGBT volunteers I interviewed had a totally different view, "The sole purpose of all these allegations is to expedite and influence the asylum process mainly with ulterior motives. The gravity of the hardships of gay refugees in Germany has been unnecessarily blown out of proportion by the activists."

6.5 Sexual Abuse Among Gay Men

Though the German gay community is divided concerning the queer refugee movement, gay asylum seekers still desperately seek life security in Germany. This desperation leads to submission to any and every demand. Most contacts happen discretely through the medium of gay chat websites. German men might offer them help, but in most cases their ulterior motive is to sexually exploit them. But the sexual exploitation goes both ways. Some refugee and migrant men agree to the exploitation; they are offered money for sex, or might agree to serve as private escorts, massagers, or travel companions, or do household chores like cooking, cleaning, and working in the garden.[21]

Further, some small entrepreneurs make them work in their warehouses even without work permits.[22] Some older men[23] desire to have young refugees and migrants in their home mostly for erotic fun. Some are also helped in finding rental accommodations.[24] Asians, Arabs, and African gay men tend to be victims of sexual exploitation since they are presumed to be submissive, hairy/manly, and have long penises, respectively. Most German men prefer hairy men and men with long c—ks.[25] A few German men who claim to be "international" use this as an opportunity to learn about different cultures. Some German men agree to act as guardians to young refugees,[26] and others are driven by the hope of a serious relationship leading to marriage. However, in most cases, the relationship breaks up. German men prefer men of their own ethnicity and origin for long-term relationships.

---

[19]Lowe (2017).

[20]Hauswedell (2017).

[21]Information obtained on the basis of interviews with refugee and migrant gay men, October 21, 2017.

[22]Information obtained on the basis of interviews with refugee and migrant gay men, October 4, 2017.

[23]White men, 45 years of age or older.

[24]Information obtained on the basis of interviews with refugee and migrant gay men, November 13, 2017.

[25]Information obtained from profiles on gay chat websites, November 15, 2017.

[26]Interview, September 28, 2017.

It is true that poverty makes gay men more vulnerable to sexual abuse.[27] Misusing or exploiting the economic status of refugee gay men is not uncommon.[28] They are given gifts or second-hand items like clothes, watches, and shoes. In all these instances, the relationship revolves around mostly money and sex.[29] An interlocutor narrated his experience to me in the following words: "My daddy provides me little money every time when I need it. There is always a 20 euro note hidden in my apartment, either in a flower pot or under the pillow, I only have to search for it or call up and ask for the place where it is hidden, it's like a treasure hunt."[30]

In opposition to the above accounts, there are also instances in which refugee and migrant men have exploited, assaulted, or sexually abused German men. This is confirmed in the account by the following interlocutor, "Migrant men are known for seeking benefits. I sensed that the guy only wanted visa benefits and entry in Germany. I avoided him. Later that guy found another older guy and through him he came to Germany. After a few months or years, he was not happy and started looking for younger guys, cheated on his partner and later separated." Another interlocutor discussed the issue in more depth; he claimed that many refugee or migrant gay men profess to wanting a serious relationship: "Often refugee or migrant men exploit German men by giving the impression that a prospective partnership or marriage is possible. They use you and then throw you away, or have sex in the name of a relationship. At times, there are reports of theft (money or gold) in the dating scene. One must be careful."

But the problem of theft is a minor one in comparison to the sexual abuse of German gay men by refugee or migrant men. One interlocutor told me, "I was blackmailed and asked to elope in another country by a guy who was in love with me. He was heterosexually married. I refused to elope. One day he entered my room and assaulted me with a knife, leaving me in blood pool. Finally my neighbors admitted me to the hospital. Currently my petition is before the Court and the guy is in jail. I still live in fear and am undergoing the psychotherapy recommended to me. I fear going to Muenster [Germany] since the incident took place in Muenster and the guy's family resides there."[31] Another reported his experience of sexual abuse and the subsequent court decision regarding his case, "I invited a refugee to my apartment whom I had known for around 6 months, my intention was to have a conversation but not sex. I am handicapped and can't do things on my own. I have heart problem and diabetes. The guy knew my health situation. Nevertheless, he started forcing me to have sex. I refused, he pulled my pants and started forceful

---

[27] Greenall (2008).

[28] See "Abuse in Same-Sex and LGBTIQ Relationships": http://www.humanservices.alberta.ca/documents/NCN1375-abuse-in-same-sex-LGBTQ-relationships-booklets.pdf.

[29] Information obtained on the basis of interviews with refugee and migrant gay men, October 21, 2017.

[30] Conversation, October 21, 2017.

[31] Conversation, September 26, 2017.

penetration. I shouted and screamed until the neighbours arrived, the guy just ran away in no time. My petition was before the local court but nothing happened, he could bring more witnesses (other refugees) and finally the Court order said that I was guilty for inviting him into my apartment. I was doubted by the authorities but not him. In fact they told me that the guy has already left Germany for his home country. I knew that it was a lie, but I had no option other than to suffer and keep my mouth shut."[32]

Men who have been sexually assaulted are much less likely than women to report their abuse or to seek medical care.[33] Studies on LGBT sexual abuse in Germany have been conducted mostly in the context of lesbian women.[34] There are many studies on the experiences and health care of women exposed to intimate partner violence,[35] but less pertaining to sexual abuse among consenting gay men. Many studies claim that there is a higher percentage of violence in gay relationships as opposed to heterosexual ones, but these studies are employing a very small sample group. According to them, percentages of violence in homosexual relationships range between 15 to 50%.[36]

The act of dominating, forcing, or pressuring unwanted sex acts leads to emotional or physical harm; the partner's performance is ridiculed or criticized.[37] While this is not an experience unique to refugees or migrants, it is more common among interracial gay couples or intimate partners.[38] Some consider sex as the only way to be cared for, and this attitude also amounts to sexual abuse. In addition, some young refugees and migrants are forced to use drugs or alcohol to enable unwanted sex practices especially for high or long duration sex performance.[39] Non-disclosure of STDs or HIV-positive status, removing condom before or during sex (stealthing), forcing partner not to use condoms, or commenting or touching body parts when the partner doesn't want them to be touched are quite common.[40] An interlocutor told me about his experience, "I dated a guy from Cologne for at least 4-5 times and he never told me that he was HIV positive. We had sex during this time but he told me about his HIV status nearly after 6 months since according to him it was not detectable and so he didn't feel the need to tell that. It was indeed shocking. I was

---

[32] Conversation, October 7, 2017.

[33] Tewksbury (2007), p. 31.

[34] Ohms and Müller (2001), Curtis (1999), Brückner (2002) and Schrötte and Ansorge (2008).

[35] Larsen et al. (2014).

[36] Losehand (2012).

[37] See "Abuse in Same-Sex and LGBTIQ Relationships": http://www.humanservices.alberta.ca/documents/NCN1375-abuse-in-same-sex-LGBTQ-relationships-booklets.pdf.

[38] See "Abuse in Same-Sex and LGBTIQ Relationships": http://www.humanservices.alberta.ca/documents/NCN1375-abuse-in-same-sex-LGBTQ-relationships-booklets.pdf and "LGBTQ Violence in Communities of Color": https://wocninc.org/wp-content/uploads/2018/11/LGBTQFAQ.pdf (accessed on November 23, 2019).

[39] Deimel et al. (2016).

[40] Information obtained on the basis of interviews with refugee and migrant gay men, dated October 21, 2017.

lucky not to get the virus." Another interlocutor explained to me about how many German gay men don't always feel they have an obligation to disclose their HIV status to foreigners as they do to other German men; he asserted, "In German eyes, foreigners are either dangerous criminals or imbeciles, or, at best, cute and sexy, ready to be exploited. But this is to be expected. Even in private matters like whether a person has HIV or AIDS, a German feels responsible for disclosing such a fact to a German but might not to a foreigner. Very often young people are used by elderly men suffering from HIV/AIDS, etc. They don't disclose this fact to the young foreigners but keep it secret and do get involved in intense sex because the feeling of being in bed with a young person is quite satisfying to them. Some even indulge in intense sex without disclosing the fact about their ill health."[41]

Another factor contributing to sexual abuse and relationship dysfunction among refugee and migrant gay men in Germany is the wide age differences. Because many contacts are developed through the medium of gay chat forums, there tends to be a wide age difference. Younger gay men (in their twenties or early thirties) who want to escape their home countries would rather enter a relationship with an elderly gay man than suffer in their home country. Since it is typical of elderly gay men in Europe to seek out younger gay men as erotic or travel partners, relationships are formed quickly. But when younger men arrive in Europe, they find that the differences due to various reasons like age gap or physical and mental non-compatibility become prominent. This is why many younger refugees and migrants seek better contacts and end their partnerships or marriage after acquiring permanent residency. A Hungarian gay man spoke to me about his foreign partner separating from him after he spent a good deal of money, time, and energy to bring him to Europe. He stated, "I travelled to India to find my love. I invested my time, money to bring him to Hungary. We got married but within a few months he found another man. He begged to me for his residency, I had to continue our marriage for three years until he could acquire permanent residency. It was a mental trauma with quarrels and misunderstandings every day."[42]

6.6 Implications, Policy, and Research

Research findings reveal that most abuse experienced in homosexual relationships is similar to that in heterosexual relationships. "Power dynamics, the cyclical nature of abuse and the escalation of abuse over time are similar to what happens in heterosexual couples."[43] The only difference being that it is less talked about and is

---

[41] Conversation with interlocutor, August 28, 2018, 10:00–11:00 A.M.

[42] Conversation with interlocutor, April 9, 2019, 20:42–21:15 PM.

[43] Dickens (2014). See also Luglio (2015).

invisible.[44,45] Despite the similarities, people usually assume that men can't be victims of sexual abuse and that men are supposed to be stronger and aggressive.[46] There is also the myth that most gay men are promiscuous and have high sex drives.[47] Even the awareness of sexual abuse of adult men is a recent development in the medical, health care, psychological, and sociological literature. Most of the early literature focussed on male children rather than adults.[48] The National Crime Victimization Survey by the United States Bureau of Justice Statistics found that 11% of all sexual assault victims are male.[49] England and Wales reported that male rape comprises 7.5% of all rape reported to criminal authorities.[50] However, not much has been reported about sexual abuse among gay men in intimate relationships or in the dating scene. The lack of awareness of sexual abuse and assault among gay men has been described by Lara Stemple: "Despite the grave and widespread nature of sexual violence against men and boys, the current international human rights framework is inadequate for addressing this problem [. . .] The international instruments that contain the most comprehensive and meaningful definitions of sexual violence exclude men on their face, reflecting and embedding the assumption that sexual violence is a phenomenon relevant only to women and girls."

Unlike opposite-gendered relationships, these problems go unreported; gay men view these problems as private affairs and do not feel they will receive a supportive response.[51] Also, most gay men never realize the seriousness of the abuse. Several reports reveal that sexual abuse victims (both men and children) are less likely to report their victimisation than female victims due to the social biases against them.[52] There is stigma, fear, and shame that their sexuality might be questioned.[53] These reasons especially discourage refugees and migrants from complaining about the abuse. Non-white gay men may be unwilling to report their abuse because of preconceived notions or racial stereotypes, for instance, the notion that the non-white partner in an interracial relationship is more likely to be the abuser. If

---

[44] Walby and Allen (2004).

[45] Michelini (2016).

[46] See "LGBTQ Violence in Communities of Color": https://wocninc.org/wp-content/uploads/2018/11/LGBTQFAQ.pdf (accessed on November 23, 2019).

[47] Stemple (2009).

[48] Tewksbury (2007), pp. 22–23.

[49] Stemple (2009). Callie Marie Rennison, U.S. Dep't of Justice, Publ'n No. NCJ 182734, National Crime Victimization Survey: Criminal Victimization 1999, at 6 (2000) (calculating a figure of 11% from the cited rates of three female rape victims per 1000 persons and 0.4 male rape victims per 1000 persons).

[50] Stemple (2009). Simmons et al. (2002): Crime in England and Wales 2001/2002, at app. 1, tbl.3.04 (2002) (using the 2001/2002 figures of 9008 reported rapes of females and 735 reported rapes of males to calculate that 7.5% of the total 9743 reported rapes had male victims).

[51] Donovan et al. (2006).

[52] Stemple (2009).

[53] Tewksbury (2007), pp. 22–35. See also Calderwood (1987), Hodge and Cantor (1998), Kaufman et al. (1980), McLean et al. (2005), Anderson (1982) and Scarce (1997).

both persons are non-white, the victim may fear harsh treatment of both partners by the police and criminal justice system. Due to the misconceptions of instability revolving around gay relationships, the public does not realize the gravity of the problem. Very few services exist for gay men who are being abused by other gay men. In order to overcome the stress and tension, many resort to alcohol, drugs, medications,[54] and unsafe sex practices leading to STDs.[55]

Even the public agencies lack education and awareness on the subject and hence are not able to respond effectively.[56] Hence, awareness raising campaigns and education, and the training of public agencies could be the first step toward reducing instances of sexual abuse.[57] There is very limited research in this field. Hence, future research in this area can effectively help address the issues and concerns of gay men.

6.7   NGO Reports on Domestic Violence

It should be noted that some NGOs have recorded some relevant data and good practices. NGOs collaborate to educate gay men in safe sex practices and their right to be free from abuse and violence. They help to create awareness and are a place where victims can report abuse and receive counseling. They also attempt to identify gaps in existing laws and policies relating to domestic violence.[58]

According to the data retrieved from the NGO RosaLinde, Leipzig, an organization devoted to understanding and ending any discrimination related to sexual orientation,[59] traumatic cases of domestic violence have been reported, but few have received adequate support. There are many cases of domestic violence in which family members target another member of the family because of their sexual orientation, for example, a homosexual child, sibling, uncle, aunt, or cousin. There are also cases of physical violence where parents have locked their homosexual child up for weeks. Queer refugees find themselves in a vulnerable position, similar to that of the homosexual child. The power imbalance, which arises for many reasons like lacking language skills, quickly leads to verbal, physical, and mental abuse. In intimate relationships, financial dependency is well-known as the most significant issue leading to a power imbalance which in turn leads to violence. Queer refugees or migrants are pressured to stay in the relationship out of necessity.

According to Rosa Strippe, a German NGO that counsels LGBT persons and their families, only 36 counselling sessions were conducted dealing with discrimination and violence in 2018. And according to data from HAZ Schwulenberatung, a similar

---

[54] Tewksbury (2007), pp. 25 and 29.

[55] Tewksbury (2007), p. 28.

[56] Donovan et al. (2001).

[57] Donovan et al. (2006).

[58] Watson (2014), pp. 3 and 50.

[59] Conversation with interlocutor RosaLinde, Leipzig, December 5, 2018, 14: 00–16:00 PM.

NGO in Switzerland offering counselling to people who question their sexual orientation or gender identity, "In Switzerland, physical, sexual violence has been reported mostly under the influence of alcohol and illegal substance such as cocaine or crystal meth. Refugee gay men often have a hard time in Switzerland, they find little connection in the scene. In mixed couples, the dependency ratio becomes a burden because the foreign partner cannot find work and does not have his own circle of friends. This significantly burdens the relationship, sometimes it comes to physical violence or drastic jealousy scenes. In most cases there is verbal abuse or insults and physical abuse. Both Swiss and non-Swiss are perpetrators and /or victims. Physical violence involves face slapping, blows on the face, kicking, scratching, biting, throwing objects or spitting on the partner. Mental abuse involves insults, threats, and refusal to have sex. Concerning sexual abuse, many refugee gay men narrate bad experiences in their country of origin. Also, of rape under the influence of some substance. Some gay refugees see themselves as sex objects for Swiss men. According to them, Swiss men only want to have sex with them, but otherwise do not wish to socialize with them. Unfortunately, insults are part of everyday gay life in Switzerland. Bad words like gay pig are common in schoolyards. Being gay and foreign is often a double stigma. There is no better protection against discrimination in the law. In this regard, there are too few offers for queer migrants."[60]

In Portugal, the Director of the NGO Associação Ilga told me, "There are many prejudices regarding same sex domestic violence irrespective of gays or lesbians. We work with police forces and we train them and there is this misconception that there is no power relation because both parties are of the same sex [. . .] Just two or three years back we established the first emergency shelter for male victims of domestic violence in the South of Portugal. These shelters are not for gay men in specific but all men. Male victims of domestic violence have approached us and we cooperate with other services to direct the cases to other service providers. Physical and psychological violence is usually reported. Most couples are local couples whereas some are interracial couples. Some victims have fled their home country because of an abusive relationship. Since homosexuality is illegal in those countries, nobody knew that the victims were in a relationship and they were not able to talk about it with anyone, so they decided to leave and seek asylum in Europe. In Portugal, there is no specific law penalizing domestic violence, but this offence is part of the criminal code, i.e., Section 151 of the criminal code. The law is gender neutral and applicable not only for formally married couples but also informal couples or those who are dating. It also applies to all nationalities, so foreigners in Portugal are entitled to seek protection. Awareness is needed on LGBT issues and EU directives. The judges, for instance, would apply the criminal code but not EU directives, like judgments of the ECHR or ECJ, etc. Even hate crimes are classified as physical offences. The Attorney General would not classify a case as a hate crime but as an assault. There are cases of domestic violence even among refugees, but this is not an

---

[60]Information received via email from HAZ Schwulenberatung, Zurich, July 1, 2019.

issue. Initially, they faced microaggressions due to cultural differences but those were amicably settled."

In Eastern European countries, NGOs are not as experienced working on LGBT domestic violence issues. They provide free legal assistance to asylum seekers, refugees, and stateless persons. Most NGOs have not come across cases of domestic violence among gay men, and refugee/migrant gay men have not approached them with such cases."[61]

6.8 Conclusion

Many gay men do not realize that they are victims of domestic violence; it can even be in the form of microaggressions, subtle behaviors or insults on a day-to-day basis. For instance, some try to make their partner feel small or dumb and apologize later just for the sake of it.[62] The mental health status of gay men who are victims of domestic violence can range from high emotional imbalances to controlled approaches wherein victims would prefer to conceal the trauma they might have suffered. Some prefer to hide their physical or mental victimization.[63]

Poverty, financial dependence, inequality, and economic crises further serve to bind the victim to the abuser, which leads to accepting the physical, mental, and sexual abuse.[64] In relationships where one partner earns considerably more money, some are forced to be in open relationships or even engage in sex with other men, e.g., a threesome.[65]

Apart from the financial inequality often occurring in relationships between German gay men and refugee or migrant gay men, there is the added problem of intercultural disputes, which is one of the top reasons for separation or divorce.[66] Some foreign gay men experience abuse due to language barriers and related issues. An interlocutor stated, "I am weak in studies, I needed time, but my ex-partner used to force me and insult me in front of his friends for not learning German language. I was new to Germany; this culture was new to me and I needed time. His friends made it worst for us, they fuelled up this issue and this led to constant quarrels between us. Due to such pressure and infidelity as well I decided to end our marriage."[67]

Survivors of same sex domestic abuse often experience post separation abuse after the relationship has ended. For a notable number of gay men living in abusive

---

[61] Information received via email from Hungarian Helsinki Committee, June 6, 2019.

[62] Tahseen (2019).

[63] Tewksbury (2007), p. 31.

[64] Conner (2014), pp. 396–397.

[65] Conversation with interlocutor, March 16, 2019, 10:30–11:02 AM.

[66] Marcen and Morales (2017).

[67] Conversation with interlocutor, March 23, 2019, 16:42–17:05 PM.

relationships, the abuse only intensifies after the separation. Such abuse could involve contacting the ex-partner on the telephone, sending text messages and emails, or even visiting his workplace, home, family, and friends. At times, it involves harassing the ex-partner with court cases or making financial demands.[68] An interlocutor stated, "My South Asian partner used to doubt me all the time, control my phone calls and act like a spy. When we separated, he couldn't accept the separation and used to constantly harass me, blame me on WhatsApp using abusive words. One day he even insulted my new boyfriend. It was my birthday party and he suddenly showed up and became very wild, even went to attack my boyfriend. But my other friends tried to control the situation. He filed for alimony, I had to pay him nearly eighty thousand euros and still his rattling doesn't stop."

Academic research of domestic violence among gay men is limited. For an analysis, there is no proper available data because cases are either underreported or gender is not specified. At the EU level, effective steps have been taken to collect data on intimate partner violence against women but no such steps have been taken to collect data on intimate partner violence against LGBT persons. Institutions such as the police and justice sectors are the most important and cost-effective sources of data collection across the EU. However, several challenges impair efforts to collect data within the member states.[69]

Concerning intimate partner violence against women, the European Institute for Gender Equality (EIGE) has developed country-specific recommendations to guide the improvement of administrative data collection on intimate partner violence at the national level. To reinforce these efforts at the European level, policy and technical recommendations for Eurostat on the specifics of data collection on gender-based violence have been proposed.[70] However, no such efforts are made considering the interests of LGBT persons. There is no available data on the scale of intimate partner violence among same-sex partners in the member states. Support mechanisms to deal with issues pertaining to domestic violence do exist in Germany and throughout Europe, but are not broad enough. Generally speaking, there is a lack of awareness and social support; it should not be forgotten that most gay men lack even the support of their family. At times, laws are better than the society.

References

Allen S (2020) 'No Blacks' is not a sexual preference. It's racism. The Daily Beast. Retrieved November 18, 2020 from https://www.thedailybeast.com/no-blacks-is-not-a-sexual-preference-its-racism

---

[68] Donovan et al. (2006).

[69] Police and justice sector data on intimate partner violence against women in the European Union, June 19, 2019: https://eige.europa.eu/publications/police-and-justice-sector-data-intimate-partner-violence-against-women-european-union (accessed May 31, 2020).

[70] See *Understanding intimate partner violence in the EU: The role of data* (2019).

Anderson CL (1982) Males as sexual assault victims: multiple levels of trauma. J Homosex 7 (2–3):145–162. https://doi.org/10.1300/J082v07n02_15

Berlin opens Germany's first major gay refugee centre (2016) The Local. Retrieved November 19, 2017 from http://www.newnownext.com/serbia-refugee-camp-germany-attack/07/2017/

Brückner M (2002) Gewalt im Geschlechterverhältnis – Möglichkeiten und Grenzen eines geschlechtertheoretischen Ansatzes zur Analyse häuslicher Gewalt. In: Göttert M, Walser K (eds) Gender und soziale Praxis. Helmer, Königsstein im Taunus

Calderwood D (1987) The male rape victim. Med Aspects Hum Sex 21(5):53–55

Callander D, Holt M, Newman C (2012) Just a preference: racialised language in the sex-seeking profiles of gay and bisexual me. Cult Health Sex 14(9):1049–1063. https://doi.org/10.1080/13691058.2012.714799

Conner DH (2014) Financial freedom: women, money, and domestic abuse. William Mary J Women Law 20. Retrieved November 18, 2020 from http://works.bepress.com/dana_harrington_conner/9/

Curtis F (1999) Gestalt-Paartherapie mit lesbischen Paaren: Anwendung von Theorie und Praxis auf die lesbische Erfahrung. In: Wheeler G, Beckmann S (eds) Gestalttherapie mit Paaren. Peter Hammer Verlag, Cologne

Dammers T (2016) This is what it's like to be a gay refugee in Germany. Vice. Retrieved November 20, 2017 from https://www.vice.com/en_us/article/yvxjgg/gay-refugees-germany-876

Deimel D, Stöver H, Hößelbarth S, Dichtl A, Graf N, Gebhardt V (2016) Drug use and health behaviour among German men who have sex with men: results of a qualitative, multi-centre study. Harm Reduct J 13(36). https://doi.org/10.1186/s12954-016-0125-y

Dickens SE (2014) Community assessment of same-sex survivors of intimate partner violence (IPV) in Humboldt County. Humboldt State University. Retrieved June 6, 2020 from https://www.semanticscholar.org/paper/Community-assessment-of-same-sex-survivors-of-(IPV)-Dickens/786629ee57a3a0d4392c4b53dfac52921bdacba4

Donovan C, Heaphy B, Weeks J (2001) Same sex intimacies: families of choice and other life experiments. Routledge, London and New York

Donovan C, Hester M, Holmes J, McCarry M (2006) Comparing domestic abuse in same sex and heterosexual relationships. University of Sunderland and University of Bristol. Retrieved November 27, 2017 from http://www.equation.org.uk/wp-content/uploads/2012/12/Comparing-Domestic-Abuse-in-Same-Sex-and-Heterosexual-relationships.pdf

Flores AR (2017) Yes, there's racism in the LGBT community. But there's more outside it. The Washington Post. Retrieved November 18, 2017 from https://www.washingtonpost.com/news/monkey-cage/wp/2017/07/07/yes-there-is-racism-in-the-lgbtq-community-but-not-as-much-as-outside-it/?utm_term=.3bfd583845dd

Gay asylum seekers beaten close to death in Germany (2017) Sogica. Retrieved November 27, 2017 from https://www.sogica.org/en/life_stories/gay-asylum-seekers-beaten-close-to-death-in-germany/

Greenall M (2008) Sex work and economics – a rapid annotated bibliography. Paulo Longo Research Initiative. Retrieved November 18, 2017 from http://www.plri.org/resource/sex-work-and-economics-%E2%80%93-rapid-annotated-bibliography

Gross LP, Woods JD (1999) The Columbia reader on lesbians and gay men in media, society, and politics. Between men—between women. Columbia University Press, New York

Haggas S (2017) Racism and the gay scene. GMFA. Retrieved June 24, 2021 from https://www.gmfa.org.uk/fs148-racism-and-the-gay-scene

Hauswedell C (2017) Hostile environment for homosexual refugees. DW. Retrieved November 18, 2017 from https://www.dw.com/en/hostile-environment-for-homosexual-refugees/a-39673732

Hodge S, Cantor D (1998) Victims and perpetrators of male sexual assault. J Interpers Violence 13 (2). https://doi.org/10.1177/088626098013002004

Kaufman A, Divasto P, Jackson R, Voorhees D, Christy J (1980) Male rape victims: noninstitutionalized assault. Am J Psychiatry 137(2):221–223. https://doi.org/10.1176/ajp. 137.2.221

Larsen M, Krohn J, Püschel K, Seifert D (2014) Experiences of health and health care among women exposed to intimate partner violence: qualitative findings from Germany. Health Care Women Int 35(4):359–379. https://doi.org/10.1080/07399332.2012.738264

Losehand J (2012) Gewalt Zwischen Homosexuellen Männern. Zentrum QWIEN. Retrieved November 18, 2017 from http://www.qwien.at/QWIEN_Gewalt_2012.pdf

Lowe J (2017) Refugees in Europe: German authorities question gay refugees on their sex lives. Newsweek. Retrieved November 19, 2017 from http://www.newsweek.com/germany-eu-refugees-crisis-gay-aylum-seekers-635334

Luglio (2015) Domestic violence in same-sex couples and the connection with the social and internalised homophobia. Bleeding Love Blog. Retrieved June 6, 2020 from https://www. bleedinglove.eu/the-domestic-violence-in-same-sex-couples-and-the-connection-with-social-and-internalized-homophobia/

Marcen M, Morales M (2017) Remain single or live together: does culture matter? MPRA. Retrieved May 31, 2020 from https://mpra.ub.uni-muenchen.de/77623/1/MPRA_paper_ 77623.pdf

McLean IA, Balding V, White C (2005) Further aspects of male-on-male rape and sexual assault in greater Manchester. Med Sci Law 45(3). https://doi.org/10.1258/rsmmsl.45.3.225

Michelini A (2016) Asexual perspective: when violence is as invisible as orientation. National LGBT Rights Organization. Retrieved November 18, 2020 from https://www.lgl.lt/en/? p=11900

Nguyen HT (2004) The resurrection of Brandon Lee: the making of a gay Asian American Porn Star. In: Williams L (ed) Porn studies. Duke University Press, Durham, North Carolina

Ohms C, Müller K (eds) (2001) Gut aufgehoben? Zur psychosozialen Versorgung lesbischer Frauen mit Gewalt- und/oder Diskriminierungserfahrungen im europäischen Vergleich. Frankfurt, Berlin

Paul JP, Ayala G, Choi K (2010) Internet sex ads for MSM and partner selection criteria: the potency of race/ethnicity online. J Sex Res 47(6):528–538. https://doi.org/10.1080/ 00224490903244575

Rajanayagam I, Awadalla A (2016) LGBT*I*Q Refugees in Germany. Lernen aus der Geschichte. Retrieved April 27, 2020 from http://lernen-aus-der-geschichte.de/International/content/12840

Rogers J (2016) Germany opens special migrant centre for gay refugees in Cologne. Express. Retrieved November 18, 2020 from https://www.express.co.uk/news/world/747730/Germany-Cologne-gay-refugees-migrant-centre

Scarce M (1997) Male on male rape: the hidden toll of stigma and shame. Insight Books/Plenum Press, New York

Schrötte M, Ansorge N (2008) Gewalt gegen Frauen in Paarbeziehungen: Eine sekundäranalytische Auswertung zur Differenzierung von Schweregraden, Mustern, Risikofaktoren und Unterstuetzung nach erlebter Gewalt. Bundesministerium für Familie, Senioren, Frauen und Jugend, Berlin

Simmons J et al (2002) Crime in England and Wales 2001/2002. Home Office Statistical Bulletin

Stemple L (2009) Male rape and human rights. Hast Law J 60:605–647

Tahseen I (2019) Are microaggressions driving a wedge in your relationship? Entertainment Times of India. Retrieved May 30, 2020 from https://timesofindia.indiatimes.com/life-style/are-microaggressions-driving-a-wedge-in-your-relationship/articleshow/72198271.cms

Tewksbury R (2007) Effects of sexual assault on men: physical, mental and sexual consequences. Int J Men's Health 6(1):22–35. https://doi.org/10.3149/jmh.0601.22

Understanding intimate partner violence in the EU: The role of data (2019) European Institute for Gender Equality. Retrieved May 31, 2020 from https://eige.europa.eu/publications/understanding-intimate-partner-violence-eu-role-data

Walby S, Allen J (2004) Domestic violence, sexual assault and stalking: findings from the British Crime Survey. Home Office Research Study 276. Retrieved November 27, 2017 from http://citeseerx.ist.psu.edu/viewdoc/download?doi=10.1.1.477.2558&rep=rep1&type=pdf

Watson C (2014) Preventing and responding to sexual and domestic violence against men: a guidance note for security sector institutions. DCAF, Geneva

Chapter 7
Epilogue: Domestic Violence and Happiness

Some social scientists claim that couples who fight often really do love each other: it is a sign of a mature relationship, care, strong connection, passion, etc. Others claim that fights or quarrels can contribute to several chronic health problems.[1] Both claims have much to do with happiness. Good relationships are the key to health and happiness. Being happy is a goal to achieve and to hold onto—a chain of decisions in everyday life. But how to be happy in a relationship and how to build a healthy relationship? There could be many answers. If two individuals love each other and want to live together, they should do so, and vice versa. It makes no sense to live together when the love has ceased to exist. They should be free to decide for themselves. Many crimes would be prevented if people were free in this respect. They would not have to conceal, pretend, or even commit violence or crimes to be separated. And if they truly love each other, they will continue to live together naturally without being forced to do so by law.[2]

In the Indian tradition, there is psychic love,[3] as, for instance, Sita has (Sita, in Hinduism is the consort of the god Rama)[4] when she keeps loving Rama (Rama, one of the most widely worshipped Hindu deities)[5] despite injustice being done to her. It is also often found in Bollywood films when the hero and heroine are prevented from loving each other by their family members; they keep loving each other in the face of adversity and eventually experience a happy end. Often, we find that the parents in such films change their minds in the end, overcoming their dark impulses or antiquated convictions out of love for their children. Underlying this is the ideal of

---

[1] Astbury et al. (2000) and Lawrence et al. (2019).

[2] Sri Aurobindo (1968), p. 236.

[3] Sri Aurobindo (1990).

[4] A central character in the great Hindu epic *Ramayana* ("Rama's Journey").

[5] His story is told briefly in the *Mahabharata* ("Great Epic of the Bharata Dynasty") and at great length in the *Ramayana* ("Rama's Journey").

© The Author(s), under exclusive license to Springer Nature Switzerland AG 2022   121
Y. Naik, *Domestic Violence Against Male Same-Sex Partners in the EU with Special Reference to Refugee and Migrant Gay Men in Germany*,
https://doi.org/10.1007/978-3-030-86807-9_7

psychic love or soul connection, which is a special characteristic of certain Indian movies.

Soul connection is deeper than the mood-driven vital love, more lasting, it keeps couples together even through severe crisis. The greater the soul development, the greater the capacity of overcoming vital clashes between partners. But it should be equally practiced by both partners, not only the meek partner. "The psychic love is pure and full of self-giving without egoistic demand," but it is human and can err and suffer.[6] Also, "When there is no demand or desire, only love and self-giving, that is the psychic love."[7] The German edition *Das seelische Wesen*[8] is a highly recommended reading, a subject of great interest and provides useful knowledge in all stages of life concerning love between friends and partners. It is closely related to Christian love, which has elements of forgiveness. In the ideal case, even the most violent emotional eruptions cannot kill the flame of soul connection, as the latter has the invincible stability of the Atman[9] behind it. However, it does not rule out divorce, which may take place despite the best intentions if living together is no longer constructive. If there is soul connection, for the benefit of children, for instance, partners will make harmonious arrangements and abstain from legal battles. I have several friends who practiced this successfully over a long period of time, for the sake of their children.

The causes of conflict are mostly on the vital level, due to jealousy, conflictive interests, and convictions. These conflicts may be overcome if there is a strong mutual attraction, but if the latter ceases, the clash becomes more likely—if not neutralized by soul connection. From the integral viewpoint, all this has a lot to do with education. If males learn that it is normal to beat women, for instance, they will mistreat all genders. Therefore, it is important to impart right values onto both sexes from the beginning.[10] This is similar to Aristoteles ethics, who believed that happiness comes from how we live our lives and not in pursuits of material wealth, power, or honor. It is more about lives lived and actions taken in pursuit of happiness.[11]

Furthermore, counselling can be a solution if the respective partner has a calm, neutral mind and is able to instill harmony into the relationship and overcome the force of violent aversion and distaste.[12] Ideally, a counselor will awaken the soul connection in the clients. This could also happen if both partners approach a person with psychic powers and sincerely seek their help and advice, but professional counsellors will probably rather try to appeal to reason and strengthen it. In any case, "soul connection" sounds very convincing. Until the late twentieth century, the work of relationship counselling was informally done by close friends, family

---

[6] Sri Aurobindo (1969), p. 13.

[7] Sri Aurobindo (1969), p. 14.

[8] Sri Aurobindo (1996).

[9] Ātman is a Sanskrit word that means inner self, spirit, or soul in Hindu philosophy.

[10] Prince-Gibson and Schwartz (1998).

[11] Moore (2020).

[12] Safta (2010). See also "Counselling Guidelines on Domestic Violence" (2001).

members, or local religious leaders. Even today, in many less advanced cultures, the institution of the family and the village or group elders do the work of relationship counselling.[13] Just as it was in the past, the purpose of counselling has been to help clients find happiness.

However, in modern times, rapid social development has been made possible due to the feminist movement, women's rights movement, and activism related to gender equality, identity, sexual orientation etc.[14] All of these social developments are ultimately triggered by the pursuit of happiness: adherents seek a system that ensures good chances and opportunities for as many people as possible. Protection from domestic violence is yet another addition to that development.

In addition, there is the phenomenon of the media in modern times. Media activism promoted important issues. As for philosophers and thinkers, they are the real actors presenting ideas that shape the future of a country. In ancient Greece and Rome, too, pamphlets and books were written transporting their ideas, but new ideals as those of the French revolution were always promoted by the Press.[15] It is the invention of printing which powerfully promoted many social movements. As already stated, the movement of gender equality has been promoted by media. For instance, until 1977, women required the permission of their husbands to open a bank account. Gradually, this was reformed due to public pressure supported by media.[16] Today, social media has intensified this movement.[17] For instance, social media has helped transgender people organize themselves and voiced their interests; the concrete result is that there is now a new option on legal records beyond male/ female, there is a third gender.[18] However, the media in some countries did not support such issues due to lack of government support. There was a report about this development in the radio: in the past, there were many people with all kinds of gender queer ideas, but they were too dispersed all over the country and world. Single persons or mini groups had no power. Today, people can assemble in larger groups due to the influence of social media and can work together to build up sufficient power to transport their ideas to the political arena. In the pursuit of happiness, they fight for what they aspire to have.

It is well-known that gender differences are not merely a social construct but biological and evolutionary.[19] For instance, no male with a sound mind would ever consider wearing mini-skirts or high-heeled shoes. The latter are very uncomfortable and unhealthy and yet tens of millions of women all over the world wear them every day, mostly voluntarily because they enjoy elegance and feel happy wearing them. And even if a male wears mini-skirts or high-heeled shoes because he wants to, he is

[13] Nichols and Schwartz (1998).

[14] Manzanera-Ruiz and Lizarraga (2015).

[15] Reichardt (2012).

[16] Cancian and Ross (1981).

[17] Kidd and McIntosh (2016).

[18] Graham (2019).

[19] McIntyre and Edwards (2009).

wearing those shoes because they make him feel happy. Certainly, there are also factors such as education and social conditioning, but these are not the only factors. One-sided theories denying basic gender differences and roles are absurd. To say that gender differences are a social construct is also a social construction. It is quite common, for instance, for the male partner to take the lead while dancing (also in ice skating performances, etc.), but it is wrong to consider the female partners as inferior for allowing this to happen. They both play different yet necessary roles, and if the performance is perfect, equal credit should be given to both.

Even sexual orientation and gay, lesbian, and bisexual identities are created by humans to describe their world of happiness. These categories are transitory and are likely to change throughout the course of human evolution.[20] Humans have internalized freedom for fundamental rights and the media gave impetus to the new claims as a pursuit of happiness. The same rule applies to other aspects of life, too.

Today's new development allows people to use social media to bypass any such blockage, powerfully pushing the matter until politicians are forced to submit to public demand.[21] Thus, in Northern Africa some time ago, a democracy movement was pushed out by several autocratic countries, against the will of their governments and the press controlled by them.[22] It had little success, because the people of those countries were not yet ready for the change. Also, major changes such as the liberation of slaves in America only became possible when the liberal philosophy behind it got the support of journalists spreading those ideas in the masses.[23] Even currently what we see in the U.S. and across countries is a terrible battle with both sides trying to sway people with the help of various media.

Concerning domestic violence, currently there are mixed responses on the gender issue of the prevalence of domestic violence. Some studies support that both men and women are equally likely to perpetrate violence; whereas other argue that men are far more likely to be perpetrators in a violent intimate relationship.[24] After years of debate, domestic violence is now perceived as a human problem rather than a gender problem.[25] In this sense, it has more to do with the happiness of humans than the happiness of genders. People who are happy attract others who are happy and build stronger relationships.[26]

Understanding the various pursuits of happiness can include many interpretations such as the ownership of property, life, liberty, freedom, or family life, which lead to the enjoyment of life to the fullest. Carli N. Conklin states,[27]

---

[20] Hammack (2005).

[21] Calderaro (2018).

[22] Maddy-Weitzman (2011).

[23] Drescher (2011).

[24] Chan (2011).

[25] Hamel and Nicholls (2007).

[26] Staley (2017).

[27] Conklin (2015), p. 261.

if the phrase "pursuit of happiness" seems empty, or too general, to us today, it is not because we, as a people, have lost the desire to pursue that which makes us happy, but because the most common contemporary understanding of the word "happy" aligns today with what the eighteenth-century philosophers would have called a "fleeting and temporal" happiness versus a "real and substantial" happiness. The first is a happiness rooted in disposition, circumstance, and temperament; it is a temporary feeling of psychological pleasure. The second is happiness as eudaimonia[28]—well-being or human flourishing. It includes a sense of psychological pleasure or "feeling good" but does so in a "real" or "substantial" sense. It is "real" in that it is genuine and true. It is substantial in that it pertains to the substance or essence of what it means to be fully human.[29]

And Layard states:

In the United States people are no happier, although living standards have more than doubled. There has been no increase in the number of "very happy" people, nor any substantial fall in those who are "not very happy". [...] The story is similar in Britain, where happiness has been static since 1975 and [...] is no higher than in the 1950s. This has happened despite massive increases in real income at every point of income distribution. A similar story holds in Japan.[30]

Similarly, individuals may suffer in an unhappy marriage or relationship despite having an abundance of material wealth and possessions. Improving relationship quality or boosting general happiness can provide immense benefits, including better health and longevity.[31] The goal of research on domestic violence, considering this perspective, is not to explore the ultimate, ideal human relationship truths but to make sense of the specific lived experiences influencing individual lives, cultures, and societies, which are always in flux.

References

Astbury J, Atkinson J, Duke J, Easteal P, Kurrle S, Tait P, Turner J (2000) The impact of domestic violence on individuals. Med J Aust 173(8):427–431. Retrieved May 31, 2020 from https://www.mja.com.au/journal/2000/173/8/impact-domestic-violence-individuals

Bayertz K, Gutmann T (2012) Happiness and law. Ratio Juris 25(2):236–246. https://doi.org/10.1111/j.1467-9337.2012.00511.x

Calderaro A (2018) Social media and politics. In: Outhwaite W, Turner S (eds) The Sage handbook of political sociology. Sage Publications LTD. https://doi.org/10.4135/9781526416513.n46

Cancian FM, Ross BL (1981) Mass media and the women's movement: 1900–1977. J Appl Behav Sci 17(1). https://doi.org/10.1177/002188638101700102

Chan KL (2011) Gender differences in self-reports of intimate partner violence: a review. Aggress Violent Behav 16(2):167–175. https://doi.org/10.1016/j.avb.2011.02.008

---

[28]Eudaimonia means achieving the best conditions possible for a human being, not only in happiness, but also virtue, morality, and a meaningful life.

[29]Conklin (2015), p. 261.

[30]Bayertz and Gutmann (2012).

[31]Lawrence et al. (2019).

Conklin C (2015) The origins of the pursuit of happiness. Wash Univ Jurisprud Rev 7(2):195–262. Retrieved June 30, 2021 from https://openscholarship.wustl.edu/cgi/viewcontent.cgi?article=1123&context=law_jurisprudence

Counselling Guidelines on Domestic Violence (2001) Canadian Public Health Association. Retrieved June 2, 2020 from http://www.endvawnow.org/uploads/browser/files/Counselling%20Guidelines%20on%20DV%20-%20Southern%20Africa%20-%20SAT%20and%20CIDA.pdf

Drescher S (2011) A history of slavery and antislavery. Eur Rev 19(01):131–148. https://doi.org/10.1017/S1062798710000396

Graham D (2019) Germans can now choose "third gender" option on legal records. Euronews. Retrieved June 30, 2021 from https://www.euronews.com/2019/01/01/germans-can-now-choose-third-gender-option-on-legal-records

Hamel J, Nicholls TL (2007) Domestic violence: a gender-inclusive conception. Family Interventions in Domestic Violence. Retrieved June 30, 2021 from https://www.researchgate.net/publication/252861765_Domestic_Violence_A_Gender-Inclusive_Conception

Hammack PL (2005) The life course development of human sexual orientation: an integrative paradigm. Hum Dev 48:267–290. https://doi.org/10.1159/000086872

Kidd D, McIntosh K (2016) Social media and social movements. Sociol Compass 10(9):785–794. https://doi.org/10.1111/soc4.12399

Lawrence E, Rogers R, Zajacova A, Wadsworth T (2019) Marital happiness, marital status, health, and longevity. J Happiness Stud 20(1):1–23. https://doi.org/10.1007/s10902-018-0009-9

Maddy-Weitzman B (2011) North Africa's Democratic Prospects. Foreign Policy Research Institute E-Notes. Retrieved June 2, 2020 from https://www.researchgate.net/publication/288761371_North_Africa%27s_Democratic_Prospects

Manzanera-Ruiz R, Lizarraga C (2015) Women's social movements and social development: opportunities for social work in Tanzania. Int Soc Work 60(1). https://doi.org/10.1177/0020872815574132

McIntyre M, Edwards C (2009) The early development of gender differences. Annu Rev Anthropol 38(1). https://doi.org/10.1146/annurev-anthro-091908-164338

Moore C (2020) What is Eudaimonia? Aristole and Eudaimonic Well-Being. Positive Psychology. Retrieved June 2, 2020 from https://positivepsychology.com/eudaimonia/

Nichols MP, Schwartz RC (1998) Family therapy: concepts and methods. Allyn & Bacon, Boston

Prince-Gibson E, Schwartz SH (1998) Value priorities and gender. Soc Psychol Q 61(1):49–67. https://doi.org/10.2307/2787057

Reichardt R (2012) The French Revolution as a European Media Event. EGO European History Online. Retrieved June 2, 2020 from http://ieg-ego.eu/en/threads/european-media/european-media-events/rolf-reichardt-the-french-revolution-as-a-european-media-event

Safta CG, Stan E, Iurea C, Suditu M (2010) Counseling and assistance for women victims of domestic violence in Romania - case study. Procedia - Soc Behav Sci 5:2034–2041. https://doi.org/10.1016/j.sbspro.2010.07.409

Sri Aurobindo (1968) Words of the Mother I. Sri Aurobindo Society

Sri Aurobindo (1969) Letters on Yoga II. Sri Aurobindo Society

Sri Aurobindo (1990) Psychic being: soul: its nature, mission and evolution. Sri Aurobindo Society

Sri Aurobindo (1996) Das seelische Wesen: Die Seele: Ihre Natur, Aufgabe und Evolution. Sri Aurobindo Society

Staley O (2017) What is the evolutionary purpose of happiness? Quartz. Retrieved June 2, 2020 from https://qz.com/930860/what-is-the-purpose-of-happiness/

Table of Cases

A.E. v Finland
A.S.B. v the Netherlands
A v Croatia
Bălşan v Romania
Bensaid v UK
Bevacqua and S. v Bulgaria
Botta v Italy
Bradley v State
Branko Tomasic and Others v Croatia
Burden v United Kingdom
Buturugă v Romania
B. v The Republic of Moldova
Chapin and Charpentier v France
Charron and Merle-Montet v France
Christine Goodwin v UK
Civek v Turkey
Cossey v UK
Costa v ENEL
Courten v United Kingdom
D and Sweden v Council
Dietz and Suttasom v Austria
D.M.D. v Romania
D.P. v Lithuania
Durmaz v Turkey
E.B. v France
E.M. v Romania
Eremia v the Republic of Moldova
Foto–Frost v Hauptzollamt Lübeck-Ost
Francovich v Italy

© The Author(s), under exclusive license to Springer Nature Switzerland AG 2022
Y. Naik, *Domestic Violence Against Male Same-Sex Partners in the EU with Special Reference to Refugee and Migrant Gay Men in Germany*,
https://doi.org/10.1007/978-3-030-86807-9

Fretté v France
F. v Bevandorlasi es Allampolgarsagi Hivatal
F. v United Kingdom
Gas and Dubois v France
Grant v South–West Trains Ltd
Hajduova v Slovakia
Halime Kılıç v Turkey
Hämäläinen v Finland
Hörmann and Moser v Austria
J.D. and A v the United Kingdom
Jürgen Römer v Freie und Hansestadt Hamburg
Kalucza v Hungary
Karner v Austria
K.B. v NHS
Kontrova v Slovakia
Magette Gueye and Valentin Salmeron Sanchez
Maruko v Versorgungsanstalt der Deutschen Bühnen
Mata Estevez v Spain
M.G. v Turkey
Mudric v The Republic of Moldova
Niemietz v Germany
Norris v Ireland
N. v Sweden
O.C.I. and Others v Romania
Oliari and Others v Italy
Opuz v Turkey
Orlandi v Italy
P v S and Cornwall County Council
P.S. and J.S. v Austria
Rees v The United Kingdom
Relu Adrian Coman and others v Inspectoratul General Pentru Imigrari and Ministerul Afacerilor Interne
Richards v Secretary of State for Work and Pensions
Sabalić v Croatia
Schalk & Kopf v Austria
Sheffield and Horsham v UK
Slyusarev v Russia
Stasi v. France
State v. Black
State v. Oliver
Strelets v Russia
S.Z. v Bulgaria
Tadao Maruko v Versorgungsanstalt der Deutschen Bühnen
Taddeucci and McCall v Italy
Talpis v Italy

T.M. and C.M. v The Republic of Moldova
Toonen v Australia
Valiulienė v Lithuania
Valliantanos and others v Greece
W. v UK
X and Others v Austria
X v Colombia
Young v Australia

CPSIA information can be obtained
at www.ICGtesting.com
Printed in the USA
LVHW081338021122
732111LV00009B/218

Dem Andenken meiner Mutter
Heilani Ayoub (1956–2017)

Vorwort

Auch im 21. Jahrhundert gestaltet sich die Buchproduktion immer noch höchst kollektiv. Die vorliegende Arbeit wurde im Februar 2014 unter dem Titel »Schrift- und Schreibmystik. Christina von Hane« von der Universität Oxford als Dissertationsschrift angenommen. Sie wurde für den Druck überarbeitet. Ohne die beständige, ehrliche und freundliche Hilfe von Freunden, Fachkollegen und vielen anderen Beteiligten dürfte dieses Buch so nicht vorliegen.

Mein aufrichtiger Dank gilt allen voran Almut Suerbaum, die mir als Dissertationsbetreuerin und auch weit darüber hinaus in der Revisionsphase kritisch und inspirierend zur Seite stand. Ein ganz besonderer Dank gebührt Nigel Palmer, der die Arbeit als Zwischenprüfer kommentierte, die Edition der Christina von Hane-Vita mit Adleraugen gegen die Handschrift überprüfte und auf zahlreiche E-Mails bis zur Drucklegung enthusiastisch antwortete.

Den Dissertationsprüferinnen Annette Volfing und Elizabeth Andersen möchte ich für das offene und freundliche Gespräch während der Dissertationsverteidigung danken. Mehrere Kollegen haben unterschiedliche Bearbeitungsstufen der Arbeit gelesen und kommentiert, so Ben Morgan, Freimut Löser, Burkhard Hasebrink, Susanne Köbele und Ursula Peters. Ihnen allen sei recht herzlich gedankt für wichtige Verbesserungsvorschläge. Monika Studer verbrachte einen sonnigen elsässischen Tag damit, mir bei der Bestimmung unzählbarer Lagen zu helfen, und Ruth Wiederkehr kommentierte einzelne Editionsteile. Auch bei ihnen möchte ich mich aufrichtig bedanken.

Das Dissertationsprojekt wurde im Rahmen der Marie-Curie-Maßnahmen der Europäischen Kommission mit einem großzügigen Stipendium und vielen Austauschmöglichkeiten, die das europäische Netzwerk *Mobility of Ideas and Transmission of Texts* eröffnete, gefördert. Ich danke allen Teilnehmern aus Oxford, Lecce, Freiburg i. Br., Antwerpen und Leiden, insbesondere Loris Sturlese, Dagmar Gottschall, Alessandra Beccarisi und Ubaldo Villani-Lubelli für die anregenden Gespräche während meines Forschungsaufenthaltes an der Università del Salento, Lecce. Auch die jährlich stattfindenden Graduiertentreffen der altgermanistischen Seminare und Institute der Universitäten Freiburg i. Br., Fribourg, Genf und Oxford haben die Arbeit sachlich und methodisch vorangebracht.

Ich danke den Herausgebern der Hermaea Stephan Müller und Christine Lubkoll für die Aufnahme in ihre Buchreihe. Jakob Klingner und Maria Zucker bin ich dankbar für die freundliche Verlagsbetreuung. Moritz Ahrens danke ich für die große Hilfe bei der sprachlichen Glättung und dem Setzen des Manuskripts. Meinen hilfswissenschaftlichen Assistentinnen Sina Hoche und Doris Sperber sei ebenfalls gedankt.

https://doi.org/10.1515/9783110536324-001

Außerdem möchte ich mich bei der Studienstiftung des deutschen Volkes für die langjährige Unterstützung und die ideelle Promotionsförderung bedanken. Ich danke auch der Harvard University, insbesondere dem Office of the Dean of the Arts & Humanities für die finanzielle Unterstützung der Druckkosten, dem Somerville College, Oxford, der Bibliothèque nationale et universitaire Strasbourg sowie der Faculty of Medieval and Modern Languages, Oxford.

Schließlich sei meinem Ehemann David William Hughes besonders gedankt.

Dumbarton Oaks, Washington D.C., im April 2017   Racha Kirakosian

Inhalt

Vorbemerkung

Teil A: **Untersuchung**

1	**Forschungsüberblick und methodische Grundlagen** —— **3**	
1.1	Christina von Hane – Kurzer Forschungsabriss —— **4**	
1.2	Untersuchungsbereiche und Forschungszusammenhänge —— **9**	
1.3	Methodische Vorüberlegungen —— **21**	

2	**Der Text(-körper): mystisch, hagiographisch** —— **37**	
2.1	Mystik und Hagiographie —— **39**	
2.1.1	Mystische Texte —— **40**	
2.1.2	Hagiographische Texte —— **45**	
2.1.3	Mystische Vita —— **51**	
2.2	Autorisierungsstrategien des hagiographischen Erzählens —— **71**	
2.2.1	Intertextualität —— **72**	
2.2.2	Konstitution von Heilsgewissheit —— **86**	
2.2.3	Narrativierung theologischer Modelle —— **93**	

3	**Ich-Konstitutionen und Perspektivenvielfalt** —— **99**	
3.1	Der implizite Hagiograph —— **99**	
3.1.1	Der nahestehende Ordensbruder —— **100**	
3.1.2	Der schreibende Vermittler —— **102**	
3.1.3	Der wertende Exeget —— **106**	
3.2	Der implizite Leser —— **116**	
3.2.1	Das lesende Du —— **119**	
3.2.2	Exkurs: Cod. Vat. lat. 4763 —— **127**	
3.2.3	Das betende und liturgisch gebundene Du —— **137**	
3.3	Die Mystikerin —— **145**	
3.3.1	Die stumme/schweigende Begnadete —— **146**	
3.3.2	Die Prophetin und Visionärin —— **151**	
3.3.3	Ein unabhängig reflektierendes Ich —— **163**	
3.4	Zusammenfassung —— **166**	

4	**Die mystische Braut: allegorisch, typologisch** —— **169**	
4.1	Allegorisch: die Seele —— **170**	
4.1.1	Die auserwählte Gottesbraut Christina —— **170**	
4.1.2	Die Vielfachbesetzung der mystischen Braut —— **187**	

4.2   Typologisch: Maria —— **195**
4.2.1   Maria memoranda —— **196**
4.2.2   Mater compassionis, mater misericordiae, mater Christi —— **205**
4.2.3   Maria als Vorbild für Königin und Braut —— **211**

5   Die Inszenierung dynamischer Textualität und die Evidenz materieller Buchschriftlichkeit —— 221
5.1   Schriftlichkeit und Vision —— **222**
5.2   Das Fließen der göttlichen Offenbarung —— **229**
5.3   Die Rede vom Buch als performativer Selbstbezug —— **242**

6   Schlussbemerkung —— 251

Teil B: Beschreibung der Handschrift und Editionen

1   Straßburg, Bibliothèque nationale et universitaire, Ms. 324 —— 259
1.1   Kodikologische und paläographische Beschreibung —— **259**
1.2   Inhalt der Handschrift —— **264**
1.3   Schreibsprache des deutschen Teils —— **268**
1.4   Beobachtungen zur Schreibertätigkeit —— **273**

2   Editionsprinzipien —— 277
2.1   Allgemeine Editionsprinzipien —— **277**
2.2   Vorbemerkungen zur Edition der Maria Magdalena-Bekehrungslegende —— **281**

3   Editionen —— 283
3.1   Vita der Christina von Hane —— **283**
3.2   Maria Magdalena-Bekehrungslegende —— **347**

Abbildungen —— 351
Abkürzungen —— 356
Bibliographie —— 357
     Textausgaben —— **357**
     Handschriften —— **360**
     Forschungsliteratur —— **361**
Register —— 393
     Namen-, Orts-, Sach- und Werkverzeichnis —— **393**
     Stellenverzeichnis der Christina von Hane-Vita —— **396**

Vorbemerkung

Christina von Hane ist eine bisher selten beachtete Mystikerin. Ihre Vita ist sonderbar: Scheint sie zunächst in weiten Teilen konventionell, erweisen sich einzelne Passagen als ungewöhnlich. Bereits Kurt Ruh stellte fest: »Die Christina von Hane-Vita bietet für den Leser, der nur noch Analogien zu bekannten Typen erwartet, Überraschungen, das heißt einmalige Besonderheiten.«* Und doch wurde die Christina von Hane-Vita in der Forschung weitgehend vernachlässigt. Mit der vorliegenden Arbeit wird erstmalig eine umfassendere Studie geliefert, die zu weiteren Untersuchungen anregen soll. Während der Beschäftigung mit der Vita und ihrer handschriftlichen Erscheinungsform erwies sich der Zusammenhang zwischen der Performativität des mystischen Textes und der materiellen Schriftpräsenz des Buches als gewinnbringend. Mit dieser Annäherungsweise soll ein Beitrag zu aktuellen Debatten in der mediävistischen Forschung geleistet werden. Die im ersten Teil dieses Buches vorgestellten Untersuchungen, die die Christina von Hane-Vita in ihrer handschriftlichen Präsenz berücksichtigen, legten es nahe, ebenfalls die mit ihr im Verbund tradierte Maria Magdalena-Bekehrungslegende zu edieren. Die kritische Edition beider Texte soll als Grundlage für weitere Forschungen dienen.

---

* Kurt Ruh: Geschichte der abendländischen Mystik. Bd. 2: Frauenmystik und Franziskanische Mystik der Frühneuzeit. München 1993, S. 121.

https://doi.org/10.1515/9783110536324-003

Teil A: **Untersuchung**

1 Forschungsüberblick und methodische Grundlagen

Dass eine Prämonstratenserin im Mittelpunkt einer mystischen Vita des Mittelalters steht, erscheint zunächst ungewöhnlich. Es sind insbesondere die Beginen und die Nonnen der Dominikaner- und Franziskanerorden, die für ihre Beteiligung an mystischen Diskursen ihrer Zeit bekannt sind. Dennoch ist das Feld der mystischen Spiritualität nicht erst mit Christina von Hane von den Prämonstratensern betreten worden, so gilt der Prämonstratensermönch Hermann Josef von Steinfeld († 7.4.1241/1252?) als der Dichter des ältesten bekannten Herz Jesu-Hymnus.[1] Als prominenter Vertreter einer Marienmystik, die von der von Bernhard von Clairvaux vorgezeichneten brautmystischen Liebessprache inspiriert ist,[2] war er u.a. als Seelsorger in Frauenklöstern des Eifelgebietes tätig, also geographisch unweit von der Region, aus der die Christina von Hane-Vita stammt;[3] und Hermann Josef kannte die Mystikerinnen seiner Zeit. In seiner Vita wird die ebenfalls bei Caesarius von Heisterbach für ihre besondere Frömmigkeit aufgeführte Hover Zisterzienserin Elisabeth genannt,[4] zudem soll er die Offenbarungen Elisabeths von Schönau gekannt haben.[5] Da die Mystik Hermann Josefs von Steinfeld deutliche Parallelen mit der Vita Christinas von Hane aufweist – bei beiden treten der Fokus auf die Einzelseele, die Betonung auf das Spiel mit dem Jesuskind und der Höhepunkt der mystischen Hochzeit stark hervor –, liegt es nahe, dass die Christina von Hane-Vita mit Hermann Josef von Steinfeld ein ordensinternes

---

1 Vgl. Friedrich Ohly: Du bist mein, ich bin dein. Du in mir, ich in dir. Ich du, du ich. In: Kritische Bewahrung. Beiträge zur deutschen Philologie. Festschrift für Werner Schröder zum 60. Geburtstag. Hrsg. von Ernst-Joachim Schmidt. Berlin 1974, S. 371–415, hier S. 376, und Karl Koch/Eduard Hegel: Die Vita des Prämonstratensers Hermann Joseph von Steinfeld. Ein Beitrag zur Hagiographie und zur Frömmigkeitsgeschichte des Hochmittelalters (Colonia sacra 3). Köln 1958, S. 85. Siehe auch Franz Josef Worstbrock: Hermann Josef von Steinfeld. In: ²VL 3 (1981), Sp. 1062–1066, hier Sp. 1065.
2 Vgl. Miri Rubin: Mother of God. A History of the Virgin Mary. London 2010, S. 266 f.
3 Vgl. Augustinus Kurt Huber: Hermann Joseph von Steinfeld. In: Neue Deutsche Biographie. Hrsg. von von der Historischen Kommission bei der Bayerischen Akademie der Wissenschaften. 25 Bde. Berlin 1953–2013, Bd. 8 (1969), S. 651 f., insbes. S. 651, und Ulrich G. Leinsle: Zur rechtlichen Ordnung prämonstratensischer Seelsorge im Mittelalter. In: Rottenburger Jahrbuch für Kirchengeschichte 22 (2003), S. 31–46, insbes. S. 34.
4 Siehe dazu Ingrid Ehlers-Kisseler: Heiligenverehrung bei den Prämonstratensern: Die Seligen und Heiligen des Prämonstratenserordens im deutschen Sprachraum. In: Rottenburger Jahrbuch für Kirchengeschichte 22 (2003), S. 65–94, insbes. S. 77.
5 Vgl. Hermann Josef Kugler: Hermann Josef von Steinfeld (um 1160–1241) im Kontext christlicher Mystik. St. Ottilien 1992, S. 58 f. und S. 101–103; siehe auch Koch/Hegel (1958), S. 101–105.

https://doi.org/10.1515/9783110536324-004

Vorbild hatte. Ihre Mystik bleibt dennoch singulär, wie in den folgenden Untersuchungen dargelegt werden soll.

1.1 Christina von Hane – Kurzer Forschungsabriss

Obwohl der 1120 von Norbert von Xanten gegründete Orden während des Mittelalters besonders attraktiv für Frauen gewesen sein soll,[6] wurde bisher keine ausführliche und ordensunabhängige Studie unternommen, um die Mystik der einzigen mittelalterlichen Prämonstratenser-Visionärin genauer zu untersuchen.[7] Die in der Straßburger Handschrift Bibliothèque nationale et universitaire, Ms. 324 unikal überlieferte Vita ist die älteste uns bekannte Quelle für das Leben der Prämonstratenserin Christina von Hane.

Die aus dem 16. Jahrhundert stammende Abschrift wurde 1958 zufällig von Franz Paul Mittermaier in der Straßburger Staats- und Universitätsbibliothek entdeckt und von ihm im *Archiv für Mittelrheinische Kirchengeschichte* herausgegeben. Erst seit Mittermaiers Beschäftigung mit der Handschrift ist bekannt, dass die traditionelle Zuweisung Christinas an das Stift Retters bei Königstein im Taunus eine frühneuzeitliche Erfindung gewesen sein muss.[8] Mittermaier und Krings rekonstruieren aus verstreuten Hinweisen in der Vita eine Biogra-

---

6 Vgl. Caroline Walker Bynum: Holy Feast and Holy Fast. The Religious Significance of Food to Medieval Women. Berkeley/Los Angeles/London 1987, S. 16.

7 Zur älteren Forschung gehört zunächst ein im Zusammenhang eines größer angelegten Werkes des Ilbenstädter Priors Johannes Haas verschollener Text über die Heiligen des Prämonstratenserordens, vgl. Kurt Köster: Leben und Gesichte der Christina von Retters (1269 bis 1291). In: Archiv für Mittelrheinische Kirchengeschichte 8 (1956), S. 241–269, insbes. S. 241; zu Johannes Haas und seinem Werk siehe Léon Goovaerts: Haas (Jean). In: Écrivains, artistes et savants de l'ordre de Prémontré. Dictionnaire bio-bibliographique. Hrsg. von Léon Goovaerts. 4 Bde. Brüssel 1899–1920. Bd. 1 (1899), S. 342. Außerdem wurde Christina von Hane unter dem Namen Christina von Retters in verschiedene enzyklopädische Hand- und Wörterbücher zum Mittelalter oder zu Heiligen allgemein aufgenommen, dazu Kurt Köster: Christina von Hane (Hagen), gen. Retters. In: ²VL 1 (1978), Sp. 1225–1228, insbes. Sp. 1127 f. Sie wird in einer Monographie über das Kloster Retters nur kurz erwähnt: Wilhelm Fink: Kloster (Hofgut) Retters v. d. Höh. Königstein 1931, S. 5. Im Kontext einer Abhandlung über die hochmittelalterliche Spiritualität des Prämonstratenserordens beschäftigte sich ausführlicher mit Christina von Hane François Petit: La spiritualité des Prémontrés aux XXᵉ et XIIIᵉ siècles (Études de thélogie de d'histoire de la spiritualité 10). Paris 1947, S. 119–124. Eine eigenständige und ordensunabhängige Untersuchung verfasste erst Köster (1956), der alle bis dato bekannten Texte auflistet. All diese Veröffentlichungen fallen hinter den Stand der Wiederentdeckung von Straßburg, Bibliothèque nationale et universitaire, Ms. 324 zurück.

8 Vgl. Teil B, Kap. 1.1.

phie Christinas von Hane, nach der sie auch aus historischer Sicht viel eher dem Stift von Hane bei Bolanden angehörte. Da über die Vita hinaus keine weiteren Quellen überliefert sind, die Christina einem bestimmten Kloster zuordnen ließen oder die sie gar nur erwähnen, wird als Hauptgrund für die Klosterzugehörigkeit der Bericht einer Armutsperiode des Klosters Hane angeführt, die in der Vita erwähnt wird und die sich für Christinas Lebenszeit in den Stiftsurkunden bezeugen lasse.[9] Diese Armutsperiode wird vor allem dadurch belegt, dass seit 1265 die Anzahl der Mitglieder des Konvents konstant unter 50 gehalten werden sollte.[10] Angesichts der für Hane überlieferten Schenkungsurkunden aus dem 13. Jahrhundert scheint die in der Vita erwähnte Armut des Klosters allerdings nicht den alleinigen Anlass zur Regulierung gegeben zu haben. Ein am Ende des 13. Jahrhunderts durch das Generalkapitel erlassenes Verbot der Aufnahme neuer weiblicher Mitglieder betraf den gesamten weiblichen Zweig des Ordens.[11] Wahrscheinlich wird die Kombination aus der wirtschaftlichen Situation der weiblichen Stifte und dem andauernden Zuwachs der Mitglieder zu diesem Aufnahmeverbot beigetragen haben. In Hane sank die Mitgliederzahl in den Jahren nach 1265 kontinuierlich und betrug um 1289 etwa 30 Nonnen.[12]

Die Familienzugehörigkeit Christinas von Hane zum Grafengeschlecht von Nassau lasse sich laut Mittermaier durch die Verbindungen zum Hause Bolanden erklären, die das Kloster Hane 1129 gestiftet hatten.[13] Zusätzlich dazu wird in den Visionen Christinas von der militärischen Funktion eines leiblichen Bruders berichtet, die vom Grafen Adolf von Nassau (1250–1298) bekleidet wurde: *Yn dem selben lyecht sache sie, daz zo Koillen eyn groiße stryt sulde geschen vnd daz vil lude da erslagen sulten werden. [...] Sie sache auch, das jre lyeplicher broder furte*

---

9 Vgl.: *Jn dem anderen jaire dar na da sie vß der scholen wart genommen, da worden die jonffrauwen durch yre armoit, vnd dyeße jonffrauwe myt jnne allen, gesant vß yrem cloister, ygliche zo yren altderen vnd frunten.* (CvH 9, 1–3) – Zu den Stiftsurkunden siehe Franz Paul Mittermaier: Wo lebte die selige Christina, in Retters oder in Hane? In: Archiv für Mittelrheinische Kirchengeschichte 12 (1960), S. 75–97, insbes. S. 79.

10 Vgl. Mittermaier (1960), S. 84–93.

11 Vgl. Manfred Heim: Prämonstratenserinnen. In: Mönchtum, Orden, Klöster. Von den Anfängen bis zur Gegenwart. Ein Lexikon. Hrsg. von Georg Schwaiger. 2. Aufl. München 1994, S. 366 f., insbes. S. 367.

12 Vgl. Bruno Krings: Die Frauenklöster in der Pfalz. In: Jahrbuch für westdeutsche Landesgeschichte 35 (2009), S. 113–202, insbes. S. 182.

13 Vgl. Mittermaier (1960), S. 92. Siehe auch Christine Kleinjung: Die Herren von Bolanden als Klostergründer. In: Alzeyer Geschichtsblätter 33 (2001), S. 17–33, insbes. S. 18 zur Stiftung durch Werner I. von Bolanden.

des byschoiffs banner (CvH 23, 19–24).[14] Mittermaier sieht in dieser Schilderung einen einschlägigen Grund dafür, Christina zur Schwester des hessischen Grafenkönigs zu erklären: »Es war freilich nicht die Stadt Köln, sondern der Erzbischof Siegfried von Köln«, dessen Bannerträger in der für ihn mit einer »vernichtenden Niederlage« endenden Schlacht bei Worringen am 5. Juni 1288 Graf Adolf von Nassau war.[15] Eine weitere in der Vita Christinas vorkommende Vision stützt Mittermaiers These: *Sye sach auch jn dem selben lyecht zo zweyne maillen, daz yrs broders kyntder zweyn, eyn knabe vnd eyn metgyn, bynne vyrtzen dagen sultden sterben ynwendich vnd sullen faren zo dem hemelrych.* (CvH 26, 9–11) Auch wenn der frühe Tod zweier Kinder des Grafen im Mittelalter gut bekannt war und dieses Detail allein daher nicht aussagekräftig genug ist,[16] führen weitere Parallelen zu historisch dokumentierbaren Ereignissen zur Annahme, dass Christina eine leibliche Schwester Adolfs von Nassau hätte gewesen sein können.[17] Dennoch kann die Vita nicht vorbehaltslos als authentischer Bericht verstanden werden, aus dem sich familiäre Verhältnisse ablesen ließen,[18] denn es ist nicht auszuschließen, dass nachträglich bewusst versucht wurde, Christina dem Grafengeschlecht von Nassau zu affiliieren. Historisch nachweisbar bleibt wenig.[19]

Mit einem gewissen biographischen Interesse geht auch Ralph Frenken vor, der das in der Vita beschriebene Leben Christinas von Hane aus psychologischer Sicht untersucht. Für ihn gehört die Prämonstratenserin zu einer Gruppe von Mystikerinnen und Mystikern, die als Kinder schwer misshandelt wurden und als

---

14 ›Die Vita der Christina von Hane‹, siehe unten im Handschriften- und Editionsteil B, Kap. 3.1. Im Folgenden abgekürzt als CvH. Die Stellennachweise geben Kapitel- und Zeilenzahlen an.

15 Mittermaier (1960), S. 86. Zum ersten sogenannten Grafenkönig von Nassau siehe Christine Reinle: Adolf von Nassau (1292–1298). In: Die deutschen Herrscher des Mittelalters. Historische Portraits von Heinrich I. bis Maximilian I. (919–1519). Hrsg. von Bernd Schneidmüller / Stefan Weinfurter. München 2003, S. 360–371.

16 Vgl. Mittermaier (1960), S. 88 f., Anm. 82.

17 Zu diesem Ergebnis kommt schließlich Mittermaier (1960), S. 88. Vorsichtiger formulierte Köster (1956), S. 247, dass Christina »mit einiger Wahrscheinlichkeit« dem Geschlecht der Grafen von Nassau entstamme. Mit Christinas Vision über einen Schwager weiß Mittermaier (1960), S. 88, freilich nichts anzufangen: *An dem selben lyecht sache sy yn dem geist, daz eyn rytter yrer geswygen broder erslagen haytte yn eyner stait, die da heiße Lansteyn.* (CvH 26, 1 f.) Mittermaiers Beobachtungen ist hinzuzufügen, dass in der Vita drei leibliche Schwestern Christinas erwähnt werden, vgl. CvH 23, 31–34.

18 Norbert Backmund: Die mittelalterlichen Geschichtsschreiber des Prämonstratenserordens (Bibliotheca Analectorum Praemonstratensium 10). Averbode 1972, S. 91, urteilt: »Für die Geschichtsschreibung ist die Vita nicht gerade ergiebig.«

19 Krings (2009), S. 192–196, 201 f., stellt die biographischen Hinweise der Vita Christinas und die daraus für Mittermaier resultierenden Ergebnisse als historisch erwiesen dar.

Folge der Traumata religiöse Phantasmen entwickelten.[20] Christina repräsentiere einen prototypischen Fall der psychoanalytischen Thesen, die Frenken vordergründig aus einer gestörten Sexualität herleitet; die Nonne weise »zudem die härtesten und folgenreichsten Dissoziationen« auf.[21] Solche Ansätze, die historische Realität mit historisierender Dokumentation verwechseln, tendieren dazu, die Erfahrungen der Mystiker, insbesondere der weiblichen, zu pathologisieren,[22] obwohl seit Peters' Studie ›Religiöse Erfahrung als literarisches Faktum‹ die Konstruiertheit mystischer Texte wiederholt in den Vordergrund gerückt wird.[23] Auch Williams-Krapp warnt davor, »anhand der uns überlieferten Werke medizinische Anamnesen auszustellen«, womit er sich gegen »die Forderung Peter Dinzelbachers [wendet], die Aussagen der Texte als autobiographisch zu werten«.[24] Gerade weil die von anderen Texten beeinflussten Viten oft die einzigen Lebenszeugnisse darstellen, kann es nicht darum gehen, die Psychologie der darin beschriebenen Figuren zu analysieren.[25] Die Vita selbst, nicht ihre Heilige, soll daher im Mittelpunkt der folgenden Untersuchung stehen.

Textgeschichtlich nahm Köster vor der Wiederentdeckung der Straßburger Handschrift an, dass die Überlieferung einer aus dem 17. Jahrhundert stammenden flämischen Version der Vita Christinas von Hane auf zwei Strängen basiere, von denen der ältere auf einen ursprünglich lateinischen Text zurückführe.[26] Zwar ist

---

20 Vgl. Ralph Frenken: Kindheit und Mystik im Mittelalter (Beihefte zur Mediävistik 2). Frankfurt a. M. 2002, S. 11–25.

21 Frenken (2002), S. 141.

22 Das beobachtet Amy Hollywood: Sensible Ecstasy. Mysticism, Sexual Difference and the Demands of History. Chicago 2002, S. 4. Siehe auch Rebecca L. R. Garber: Feminine Figurae. Representations of Gender in Religious Texts by Medieval German Women Writers. 1100–1375 (Studies in Medieval History and Culture 10). New York/London 2003, S. 126, für den Fall Margareta Ebners.

23 Ursula Peters: Religiöse Erfahrung als literarisches Faktum. Zur Vorgeschichte und Genese frauenmystischer Texte des 13. und 14. Jahrhunderts. Tübingen 1988.

24 Werner Williams-Krapp: ›Wir lesent daz vil sölichen sachen swerlich betrogen werdent‹. Zur monastischen Rezeption von mystischer Literatur im 14. und 15. Jahrhundert. In: Nonnen, Kanonissen und Mystikerinnen. Religiöse Frauengemeinschaften in Süddeutschland. Beiträge zur interdisziplinären Tagung vom 21. bis 23. September 2005 in Frauenchiemsee. Hrsg. von Eva Schlotheuber/Helmut Flachenecker/Ingrid Gardill (Veröffentlichungen des Max-Planck-Instituts für Geschichte 235, Studien zur Germania Sacra 31). Göttingen 2008, S. 263–278, hier S. 265f.

25 Susanne Bürkle: Literatur im Kloster. Historische Funktion und rhetorische Legitimation frauenmystischer Texte des 14. Jahrhunderts (Bibliotheca Germanica 38). Tübingen/Basel 1999, S. 38, weist ausdrücklich darauf hin, dass Thesen über vermeintliche »psycho-soziale Mechanismen und Auswirkungen, die das interne klösterliche Leben mit sich bringe« und die zur Ausbildung einer spezifischen Spiritualität führten, soziale Netzwerke, organisatorische Kompetenzen der Nonnen sowie klösterliche Strukturen mehr oder weniger ausblenden.

26 Vgl. Köster (1956), S. 245.

nach wie vor nicht auszuschließen, dass noch zu Lebzeiten Christinas ein ›Liber revelationum‹ womöglich unter ihrer Mitwirkung entstanden ist,[27] doch lässt das wiederentdeckte deutschsprachige Manuskript keinen Zweifel daran, dass es die von Köster auf der Grundlage der flämischen Übertragung angenommenen zwei Überlieferungszweige nicht gegeben hat, sondern dass allein der deutsche Text die Grundlage für die spätere flämische sowie für eine aus dem 18. Jahrhundert stammende lateinische Übersetzung darstellt.[28]

Auch nach der Mittermaierschen Edition, die in zwei Teilen 1965 und 1966 erschienen ist, blieb eine intensive Beschäftigung mit dem ältesten uns überlieferten Text über Christina von Hane aus.[29] Dass Christinas Fall bisher kaum Interesse erweckte, mag zum einen am Sprachstand des moselfränkischen

---

27 Vgl. Köster (1956), S. 242; Mittermaier (1960), S. 90; Ruh (1993), S. 125.
28 Vgl. Franz Paul Mittermaier: Lebensbeschreibung der sel. Christina, gen. von Retters. In: Archiv für Mittelrheinische Kirchengeschichte 17 (1965), S. 209–251, insbes. S. 218 und S. 220 f. Der flämische Text ist bei Joannes Ludolphus van Craywinckel: ›Het leven vande salighe maghet Christina‹. In: Legende der levens ende gedenck-weerdige daden van [...] persoonen [...] inde witte ordre vanden H. Norbertus het tweede deel. Hrsg. von Joannes Ludolphus van Craywinckel. 2 Bde. Mechelen 1664/Antwerpen 1665, Bd. 2, S. 730–759, gedruckt, der lateinische Text bei Caspar Lauer: ›Vita beatae Christinae‹. In: Spiritus literarius Norbertinus a scabiosis Casimiri Oudini calumniis vindicatur seu sylloge viros ex ordine Praemonstratensi. Hrsg. von Georg Lienhardt. Augsburg 1771, S. 597–602. Zum Vergleich der deutschen Vorlage mit der flämischen Überarbeitung siehe Racha Kirakosian: Rhetorics of Sanctity. Christina of Hane in the Early Modern Period – with a Comparison to a Mary Magdalene Legend. In: Oxford German Studies 43 (2014[b]), S. 380–399, insbes. S. 383–389.
29 Die früheste wissenschaftliche Beschäftigung mit Christinas Fall setzt ordensintern mit der Arbeit Backmunds (1972), S. 112, ein. Aus historischer Sicht nähert sich Krings (2009), S. 188–202, der Vita Christinas von Hane. Erst in neuester Zeit gibt es vereinzelte Studien im Rahmen komparatistischer Arbeiten zu frauenmystischen Texten, so etwa Bardo Weiss: Ekstase und Liebe. Die Unio mystica bei den deutschen Mystikerinnen des 12. und 13. Jahrhunderts. Paderborn 2000; am Rande auch Marzena Górecka: Das Bild Mariens in der Deutschen Mystik (Deutsche Literatur von den Anfängen bis 1700 29). Bern/New York 1999; neuerdings auch Annette Volfing: Verdoppelung und Verdrängung. Simultane Diskurse in der mystischen Literatur. In: Stimme und Performanz in der mittelalterlichen Literatur. Hrsg. von Nine Miedema/Angela Schrott/Monika Unzeitig (Historische Dialogforschung 4). Berlin 2017(a), und Caroline Emmelius: Das visionäre Ich. Ich-Stimmen in der Viten- und Offenbarungsliteratur zwischen Selbstthematisierung und Heterologie. In: Von sich selbst erzählen. Historische Dimensionen des Ich-Erzählens. Tagung Irsee 2013. Hrsg. von Sonja Glauch/Katharina Philipowski. Heidelberg 2017. Hauptsächlich zu Christina von Hane siehe Racha Kirakosian: Which is the Greatest? Knowledge, Love or Enjoyment of God? The Mystic Christina of Hane in Comparison to Meister Eckhart. In: Mystical Theology 23/1 (2014[a]), S. 20–33; dies. (2014b); dies.: Penitential Punishment and Purgatory. Christina of Hane and the Drama of Purification through Pain. In: Punishment and Penitential Practices in Medieval German Writing. Hrsg. von Sarah Bowden/Annette Volfing. London 2017(a); dies.: L'expérience transcendante dans l'espace immanent et le rôle du language performatif dans la biographie mystique de Chris-

Textes liegen, zum anderen am Stoff selbst, der sich einer einfachen Herangehensweise entzieht. Jedenfalls erweckten der Inhalt und die Erzählstruktur der
Vita für Kurt Ruh den Anschein von Distanz: »Über allem liegt eine Patina der
Unverbindlichkeit.«[30] Dennoch birgt die Vita, wie Ruh zugesteht, »Überraschungen, das heißt einmalige Besonderheiten«.[31] Die vorliegende Arbeit macht sich
zur Aufgabe, diese Besonderheiten unter Einbezug aktueller Forschungsdebat-
ten so in den Blick zu nehmen, dass Ruhs Forderung nach einer Textanalyse der
Christina von Hane-Vita endlich eingelöst wird.[32]

1.2 Untersuchungsbereiche und Forschungszusammenhänge

Die aktuelle Forschung zu den einzelnen Untersuchungsbereichen wird in den
entsprechenden Kapiteln ausführlich behandelt. An dieser Stelle soll zunächst
dargestellt werden, in welche größeren Forschungszusammenhänge die vorliegende Untersuchung zu stellen ist, um in einer anschließenden methodologischen Auseinandersetzung die theoretischen Implikationen gesondert aufzu-
zeigen. Zentral für die folgenden Untersuchungsbereiche ist das Paradigma der
Performativität. Die ursprünglich sprachpragmatische Diskussion um Performanz und Performativität hat längst auch die Geistes- und Kulturwissenschaften
erreicht,[33] wobei der performative Charakter mittelalterlicher Texte besonders
hervorgehoben wird. So konstatiert z. B. Suydam: »there is a fundamental oral,
interpretive, and performance orientation to all medieval texts«.[34] Allerdings wird
der Begriff des Performativen in solchen Kontexten oft inadäquat und auf eine
Vielzahl von Phänomenen angewendet.[35] Performative Qualitäten decken bei der

---

tina de Hane. In: Le Moyen Âge 123 (2017[b]), und dies.: Musical Heaven and Heavenly Music. At
the Crossroads of Liturgical Music and Mystical Texts. In: Viator 48 (2017[c]).
30 Ruh (1993), S. 124. Um welche Art von Unverbindlichkeit es sich dabei handeln soll, bleibt
ungewiss.
31 Ruh (1993), S. 121. Weiterhin heißt es bei Ruh (1993), S. 123: »Oft glaubt man nicht richtig
gelesen zu haben.«
32 Vgl. Ruh (1993), S. 122, Anm. 13.
33 Eine Übersicht der Anwendungsgebiete bietet Mary A. Suydam: Background. An Introduction to Performance Studies. In: Performance and Transformation. New Approaches to Late Medieval Spirituality. Hrsg. von Mary A. Suydam / Joanna E. Ziegler. Basingstoke 1999(b), S. 1–25.
34 Mary A. Suydam: Beguine Textuality, Sacred Performances. In: Performance and Transformation. New Approaches to Late Medieval Spirituality. Hrsg. von Mary A. Suydam / Joanna E. Ziegler.
Basingstoke 1999(a), S. 169–210, hier S. 179.
35 Vgl. David Gorman: Use and Abuse of Apeech-Act in Criticism. In: Poetics Today 20 (1999),
S. 93–119, und Jonathan Culler: Philosophy and Literature. The Fortunes of the Performative. In:
Poetics Today 21 (2000), S. 503–519.

Beschäftigung mit historischen Texten eine verdächtig große Bedeutungsvielfalt ab; sie beziehen sich z.b. auf Aufführungs- oder Nachahmungssituationen und interaktive Dimensionen des Lesens sowie des Erinnerns.[36] Trotz eines gemeinsamen Vokabulars sind die verschiedenen interpretativen Bereiche nicht immer methodologisch einheitlich. Der Ruf nach einer »multi-disziplinären Diskussion« eines umfassenden Verständnisses performativer Funktionsmechanismen besteht seit Längerem.[37] Auch die methodologischen Vorüberlegungen der vorliegenden Untersuchungen können natürlich keine umfassende Lösung des Problems bieten, doch trotz aller Kritik bilden Performativitätstheorien eine wichtige Grundlage für die Analyse der Christina von Hane-Vita. Mit der Einbindung von Körper- und Ritualstudien sollen die sprachpragmatischen Bedeutungsdimensionen des Textes auf das Materielle der Textüberlieferung ausgeweitet werden.

Zugleich bedarf die Bezeichnung des Textes als ›Vita‹ der begrifflichen Klärung, da ›Vita‹ nicht ohne weiteres als Gattung zu verstehen ist.[38] Im Umgang mit der Christina von Hane-Vita ist es angesichts der zunehmend zurückhaltenden Forschungseinstellung gegenüber starken Gattungsdefinitionen ratsam, von ›Texttypen‹ zu sprechen, da diese Definition flexibler im Umgang mit hybriden und multifunktionellen Formen erscheint. ›Texttyp‹ ist nicht als Synonym oder Oberbegriff zu ›Textsorte‹ oder ›Gattung‹ zu verstehen, wie Heinemann vorschlägt.[39] Stattdessen reflektiert die »terminologische Offenheit« des Begriffs, »dass der Prozess literarischer Entwicklung gerade nicht über eine stringente Gat-

---

36 Christine Stridde: Verbalpräsenz und göttlicher Sprechakt. Zur Pragmatik spiritueller Kommunikation ›zwischen‹ St. Trudperter Hohelied und Mechthilds von Magdeburg Das Fliessende Licht der Gottheit. Stuttgart 2009, S. 15–26 und S. 30–42, liefert eine ausführliche Übersicht pragmatischer Methoden in der Literaturwissenschaft.

37 Manuele Gragnolati/Almut Suerbaum: Medieval Culture ›betwixt and between‹. An Introduction. In: Aspects of the Performative in Medieval Culture. Hrsg. von Manuele Gragnolati/Almut Suerbaum (Trends in Medieval Philology 18). Berlin/New York 2010, S. 1–12, hier S. 12. Cornelia Herberichs/Christian Kiening: Einleitung. In: Literarische Performativität. Lektüren vormoderner Texte. Hrsg. von Cornelia Herberichs/Christian Kiening (Medienwandel – Medienwechsel – Medienwissen 3). Zürich 2008, S. 9–21, hier S. 10, sprechen vom »Reiz der gegenwärtigen Situation«, eine Schnittmenge der aus verschiedenen wissenschaftsgeschichtlichen Diskursen stammenden Ansätze sichtbar zu machen, und greifen dabei auf die Forderung Uwe Wirths: Der Performanzbegriff im Spannungsfeld von Illokution, Iteration und Indexikalität. In: Performanz. Zwischen Sprachphilosophie und Kulturwissenschaften. Hrsg. von Uwe Wirth. Frankfurt a.M. 2002, S. 9–60, zurück.

38 Siehe die ausführliche Diskussion dazu in Kap. 2.1.

39 Vgl. Wolfgang Heinemann: Textsorten. Zur Diskussion um Basisklassen des Kommunizierens. Rückschau und Ausblick. In: Textsorten. Reflexionen und Analysen. Hrsg. von Kirsten Adamzik (Textsorten 1). Tübingen 2000, S. 9–29, insbes. S. 16 f.

tungsentwicklung, sondern über die Kommunikation erfolgreicher Textmuster aus verschiedenen Gattungstraditionen stattfindet«, wie Kern feststellt.[40] Anders als ein fester Gattungsbegriff ermöglicht das Konzept des Texttyps daher ein dynamisches Verständnis von Text. Für die Untersuchung der Christina von Hane-Vita ist ein dynamischer Textbegriff geeignet, da aufgezeigt werden soll, wie das materielle Textzeugnis mit seiner performativen Textgenese zusammenhängt.

Für eine erste gattungstypologische Kontextualisierung der Vita wird die Frage nach dem Texttyp vor dem Hintergrund von Definitionsdebatten in der Mystik- wie Hagiographieforschung gestellt.[41] Viten und andere Texttypen wie Offenbarungen und Visionen von Mystikern werden u. a. von Theologen, Historikern und Literaturwissenschaftlern analysiert, wobei es selten Berührungspunkte zwischen den fachinternen Diskussionen gibt.[42] Die divergierenden Herangehensweisen an mystische Texte setzen oft bei gattungsterminologischen Kategorisierungen an und kommen dementsprechend zu unterschiedlichen Ergebnissen,[43] die sich nur zum Teil ergänzen, zuweilen jedoch widersprechen, wie das Beispiel der Forschung zu Hildegard von Bingen illustriert.[44] Seit den 1990er Jahren wird in interdisziplinären Arbeiten zunehmend auf die Multifunktionalität mystischer Texte hingewiesen, die zugleich erfordert, dass Sprachlichkeit, Spiritualität und Klösterlichkeit als Komplex wahrgenommen und untersucht werden.[45] Dabei

---

[40] Manfred Kern: ›Lyrische Verwilderung‹. Texttypen und Ästhetik in der Liebeslyrik des 15. Jahrhunderts. In: Texttyp und Textproduktion in der Literatur des deutschen Mittelalters. Hrsg. von Elizabeth Andersen / Manfred Eikelmann / Anne Simon (Trends in Medieval Philology 7). Berlin / New York 2005, S. 371–393, hier S. 374 f.

[41] Béatrice W. Acklin Zimmermann: Gott im Denken berühren. Die theologischen Implikationen der Nonnenviten (Dokimion 14). Fribourg 1993, S. 12–14, präsentiert die gattungstechnische Debatte für Nonnenviten.

[42] Siehe bereits Siegfried Ringler: Die Rezeption mittelalterlicher Frauenmystik als wissenschaftliches Problem, dargestellt am Werk der Christine Ebner. In Frauenmystik im Mittelalter. Hrsg. von Peter Dinzelbacher / Dieter R. Bauer Ostfildern 1985, S. 178–200, insbes. S. 183 und S. 192–196.

[43] Zu verschiedenen theoretischen Ansätzen in der Mystikforschung siehe Louise Nelstrop: Christian Mysticism. An Introduction to Contemporary Theoretical Approaches. Farnham / Burlington 2009, S. 1–20.

[44] Vgl. Frank J. Tobin: German Mystical Literature to 1350. In: A Companion to Middle High German Literature to the 14th century. Hrsg. von Francis G. Gentry. Leiden / Boston / Köln 2002, S. 345–377, insbes. S. 358.

[45] Ein solcher Ansatz wird in dem Band Jeffrey F. Hamburger / Susan Marti (Hrsg.): Crown and Veil. Female Monasticism from the Fifth to the Fifteenth Century. New York / Chichester 2008, verfolgt. In den letzten Jahrzehnten haben sich neue Dimensionen der Auseinandersetzung mit mystischen Texten aufgetan: Barbara Newman: Liminalities. Literate Women in the Long Twelfth Century. In: European Transformation. The Long Twelfth Century. Hrsg. von Thomas F.

meint ›Sprachlichkeit‹ hier nicht das philosophische Problem der Versprachlichung, sondern spielt auf den Status der Volkssprache an. In diesem Sinne eröffnet der von McGinn geprägte Terminus »vernacular theology« eine fünfte Kategorie neben einer scholastischen, einer monastischen, einer pastoralen und einer mystischen Theologie.[46] Auch wenn eine scharfe kategoriale Trennung zwischen diesen Bereichen letztlich nicht möglich ist, erlaubt der Begriff der volkssprachigen Theologie einen bestimmten Spielraum im Umgang mit mystischen Texten. McGinns Terminus wurde in der Forschung positiv aufgegriffen, scheint er doch wesentlich neutraler als der Begriff der »Erlebnismystik«,[47] der die Phänomenologie der mystischen Erfahrung aus biologistischer Sicht hervorhebt.[48] Wenn er hier verwendet wird, dann soll damit allerdings nicht suggeriert werden, dass diese volkssprachige Theologie im Gegensatz zu einer scholastisch-lateinischen Theologie stünde[49] – im Gegenteil: In volkssprachigen Texten ist die Grenze zur Latinität durchlässig.[50] Geschlechterspezifische Textunterschiede lassen sich

---

X. Noble/John Van Engen. Notre Dame 2012, S. 354–402, insbes. S. 354, spricht von einer feministischen Historiographie der vergangenen 30 Jahre, die die Aufarbeitung weiblicher Autorschaft im Mittelalter ermöglichte. Margot Fassler: Composer and Dramatist. Melodious Singing and the Freshness of Remorse. In: Voice of the Living Light. Hildegard of Bingen and her World. Hrsg. von Barbara Newman. Berkeley 1998, S. 149–175, insbes. S. 157–159, weist auf das pädagogische Programm des ›Scivias‹ der Hildegard von Bingen hin, das über eine dogmatische Theologie hinausgehe.

46 Vgl. Bernard McGinn: Meister Eckhart and the Beguines in the Context of Vernacular Theology. In: Meister Eckhart and the Beguine Mystics. Hadewijch of Brabant, Mechthild of Magdeburg, and Margerite Porete. Hrsg. von Bernard McGinn. New York 1994(a), S. 1–14, und ders.: The Flowering of Mysticism. Men and Women in the New Mysticism, 1200–1350. New York 1998, insbes. S. 19–24. Siehe auch Barbara Newman: God and the Goddesses. Vision, Poetry, and Belief in the Middle Ages. Philadelphia 2003, S. 295 f. – Daneben gibt es den Begriff der ›volkssprachigen Mystik‹: Marleen Cré: Vernacular Mysticism in the Charterhouse. A Study of London, British Library, MS Additional 37790 (The Medieval Translator 9). Turnhout 2006, behandelt darunter Texte von Heinrich Seuse, Juliana von Norwich, Birgitta von Schweden und Margareta Porete.

47 Vgl. Peter Dinzelbacher: Vision und Visionsliteratur im Mittelalter. Stuttgart 1981, S. 65–77.

48 Vgl. Frank J. Tobin: Mechthild von Magdeburg. A Medieval Mystic in Modern Eyes. Columbia, SC 1995, S. 115–132. Ähnlich problematisch verhält es sich mit dem Begriff der ›praktischen Mystik‹, siehe dazu Siegfried Ringler: Viten- und Offenbarungsliteratur in Frauenklöstern des Mittelalters. Quellen und Studien (MTU 72). Zürich/München 1980, S. 11. Siehe auch Bürkle (1999), S. 3 f.

49 Dass eine Einteilung nicht scharf getroffen werden kann, zeigt der Fall Hildegards von Bingen, die für Newman (2012), S. 356, eine Schwellenfigur zwischen verschiedenen Traditionen darstellt: »a liminal figure between the monastic humanism of the past and the prophetic mysticism of the future«. Siehe auch ebd., S. 366 f.

50 Vgl. Stephen Mossman: Marquard von Lindau and the Challenges of Religious Life in Late Medieval Germany. Oxford 2010, S. 25 f.; Susanne Köbele: ›Primo aspectu monstruosa‹. Schrift-

ebenfalls schwer greifen, wie bereits die Schriften Meister Eckharts oder Johannes Taulers zeigen, in denen trotz einer Nähe zu Formen von Nonnenspiritualität männliche Sprechinstanzen dominieren.[51] Auch eine Figur wie Hildegard von Bingen sprengt dieses binäre System und lässt sich nicht in die fünf McGinnschen Arten religiöser Schriftlichkeit einordnen.[52] All diese Benennungsversuche zeigen das Bemühen, Texten speziell aus dem weiblich-monastischen Milieu theologische Relevanz zuzusprechen, obwohl oder womöglich gerade weil diese seit jeher so umstritten ist. Erste Ansätze, die betroffenen Texte endlich auch auf ihren spekulativen, d.h. theologisch-theoretischen Inhalt hin zu lesen, wurden einzeln vorgeführt.[53] Insbesondere Mechthild von Magdeburg, Margareta Porete und Hadewijch werden neben einer auf die *unio* zwischen Seele und Gott ausgerichteten Mystik scholastisch-theologische Komponenten eingeräumt.[54]

---

auslegung bei Meister Eckhart. In: ZfdA 122 (1993[a]), S. 62–81; Almut Suerbaum: Sprachliche Interferenz bei Begriffen des Lassens. ›Lux Divinitatis‹ und das ›Fließende Licht der Gottheit‹. In: Semantik der Gelassenheit. Generierung, Etablierung, Transformation. Hrsg. von Burkhard Hasebrink/Susanne Bernhardt/Imke Früh (Historische Semantik 17). Göttingen 2012(b), S. 33–47, speziell zu Mechthilds von Magdeburg ›Fließendem Licht der Gottheit‹; Balázs J. Nemes: Von der Schrift zum Buch – vom Ich zum Autor. Zur Text- und Autorkonstitution in Überlieferung und Rezeption des ›Fließenden Lichts der Gottheit‹ Mechthilds von Magdeburg (Bibliotheca Germanica 55). Tübingen/Basel 2010.

51 Einer geschlechterspezifischen Einteilung verweigert sich insbesondere Heinrich Seuse, der für die brautmystische Vereinigung eine weibliche Rolle annimmt, siehe dazu Bynum (1987), S. 102 f. Siehe auch Barbara Newman: Some Medieval Theologians and the Sophia Tradition. In: Downside Review 108 (1990), S. 111–130, insbes. S. 122; Jeffrey F. Hamburger: The Visual and the Visionary. Art and Female Spirituality in Late Medieval Germany. New York 1998, S. 243; Barbara Newman: Henry Suso and the Medieval Devotion to Christ the Goddess. In: Spiritus. A Journal of Christian Spirituality 2 (2002), S. 1–14; Carolyn Diskant Muir: Bride or Bridegroom? Masculine Identity in Mystic Marriages. In: Holiness and Masculinity in the Middle Ages. Hrsg. von P. H. Cullum/Katherine J. Lewis (Religion & Culture in the Middle Ages). Cardiff 2004, S. 58–78; speziell zu Friedrich Sunder siehe Annette Volfing: ›Daughter Zion‹ in Medieval German Literature. Abingdon 2017(b).

52 Zur komplexen Frage der weiblichen Autorschaft siehe die Bände Laurie J. Churchill/Phyllis R. Brown/Jane E. Jeffrey (Hrsg.): Women Writing Latin. From Roman Antiquity to Early Modern Europe. 3 Bde. New York/London 2002.

53 Vgl. Hollywood (2002), S. 7.

54 Außerdem werden auch Hildegard von Bingen, Getrud von Helfta, und Elsbeth Stagel auf theoligische Fragen hin untersucht, vgl. den Band Béatrice W. Acklin Zimmermann (Hrsg.): Denkmodelle von Frauen im Mittelalter (Dokimion 15). Fribourg 1994. In der Literaturwissenschaft weitgehend unbeachtet blieb bezüglich einer solchen Herangehensweise die Arbeit von Zimmermann (1993).

Als besonders heikel erweist sich also immer wieder das Feld der sogenannten ›Frauenmystik‹.[55] Ruh versteht unter frauenmystischen Texten solche, die
höchstwahrscheinlich »für Frauen geschrieben oder von Frauen durch Diktat
oder Bericht [...] vermittelt worden sind«.[56] Somit dürfte die Christina von Hane-
Vita als frauenmystischer Text gelten.[57] Doch eine geschlechterspezifische Trennung bezüglich der Genese und Zielgruppe der traditionell zur Frauenmystik
gezählten Texte ist nicht unkompliziert, wie Nemes jüngst an der Überlieferungslage des ›Fließenden Lichts der Gottheit‹ zeigen konnte.[58] Anstatt auf die
Annahme zurückzugreifen, dass Frauen eine andere Art von Theologie betreiben
als Männer,[59] schlägt Newman vor, das Augenmerk darauf zu richten, wie die
Theologie eigentlich praktiziert wurde. Eine »imaginative theology« stelle daher
Fragen nach theologischen Methoden und nach der Epistemologie der Texte.[60]
Der praktische Wert mystischer Texte wird auf diese Weise zu Gunsten eines kreativen Umgangs mit ihnen hervorgehoben. Dieser Ansatz unterscheidet sich trotz
seines phänomenologischen Interesses grundsätzlich vom Konzept der Erlebnismystik, da es weniger um die berichteten Erlebnisse als um den performativen
Charakter der Texte geht.

---

55 Mittlerweile wird selbst der Begriff ›Frauenmystik‹ nur noch mit Bedacht und allenfalls in
Anführungszeichen verwendet, wie ein Beitragstitel von Williams-Krapp verdeutlicht, wobei
der Begriff selbst in seinem Aufsatz unerwähnt bleibt: ›Frauenmystik‹ in Nürnberg. Zu einem
bisher unbekannten Werk des Kartäusers Erhart Groß. In: Grundlagen. Forschungen, Editionen
und Materialien zur deutschen Literatur und Sprache des Mittelalters und der Frühen Neuzeit.
Hrsg. von Rudolf Bentzinger/Ulrich-Dieter Oppitz/Jürgen Wolf. Stuttgart 2013, S. 181–195. Borries
(2008), S. 454, lehnt ihn zumindest zur Beschreibung von spätmittelalterlichen Schwesternspie-
geln entschieden ab. Eine kurze Diskussion zum Begriff der Frauenmystik findet sich bei Ekkehard Borries: Schwesternspiegel im 15. Jahrhundert. Gattungskonstitution – Editionen – Untersuchungen. Berlin/New York 2008, S. 451–454.
56 Ruh (1993), S. 17.
57 Monologe aus der Sicht der Mystikerin am Vitenende könnten so als Rückstände einer frühen
Aufzeichnung gelesen werden. Auf die literarische Konstruiertheit solcher Unmittelbarkeit sti-
lisierenden Passagen in mystischen Texten weisen Nemes (2010), S. 23 f., und für Dorothea von
Montau Franziska Küenzlen: Sprechen und Sprecher in ›Das Leben der Heiligen Dorothea des
Johannes Marienwerder‹. In: Oxford German Studies 39, 2 (2010), S. 160–180, insbes. S. 163, hin.
58 Vgl. Nemes (2010), S. 17–27.
59 So noch bei Peter Dinzelbacher: Europäische Frauenmystik des Mittelalters. Ein Überblick.
In: Frauenmystik im Mittelalter. Hrsg. von Peter Dinzelbacher/Dieter R. Bauer. Ostfildern 1985,
S. 11–23, insbes. S. 15.
60 Vgl. Newman (2003), S. 297: »Discussions of vernacularity call attention to the problem of
›who‹ could write theology and who could read it. [...] Imaginitive theology, on the other hand,
focuses on ›how‹ theology might be performed; it draws attention to theological method and
epistemology.«

Wie aus den Diskussionen um Texttypen und volkssprachige Theologie bereits deutlich geworden ist, geht es bei geschlechterspezifischen Diskursen immer wieder auch um Fragen der Autorschaft. In diesem Kontext wurde insbesondere auf die Zusammenarbeit zwischen Mystikerinnen/Visionärinnen und ihren größtenteils männlichen geistlichen Betreuern hingewiesen.[61] So konstatiert Emmelius unter Rückgriff auf Peters, dass der Verschriftlichungsprozess der oft vorsprachlichen Erfahrung vielschichtig abgelaufen und zumeist von einer mündlichen Mitteilung ausgegangen sei.[62] Die schriftlich fixierte Offenbarung sei aber als Kriterium einer »authentische[n] Gotteserfahrung« wichtig, so Grubmüller mit Blick auf Mechthild von Magdeburg, da nur sie die »Teilhabe an der Autorität des klerikalen Mediums Schrift« ermöglichen könne.[63] Hier spiele laut Newman das Motiv des göttlichen Schreibauftrags eine entscheidende Rolle.[64] Dass Autorisierungsstrategien zu einer femininen Schreibweise oder Rede innerhalb der »von Männern geprägten Texttraditionen« gehören, diskutiert Schnell aus rhetorischer Sicht.[65] Festzuhalten bleibt allerdings, dass Autorisierungsstrategien weniger an das Geschlecht als an den jeweiligen Legitimationsbedarf eines

---

61 Vgl. den Band Catherine M. Mooney (Hrsg.): Gendered Voices. Medieval Saints and their Interpreters. Philadelphia 1999. Susanne Bürkle: Weibliche Spiritualität und imaginierte Weiblichkeit. Deutungsmuster und -perspektiven frauenmystischer Literatur im Blick auf die Thesen Caroline W. Bynums. In: ZfdPh 113 (1994), S. 116–143, insbes. S. 138, spricht daher von »Gemeinschaftsprojekten eines wie auch immer zusammengesetzten Autorenkollektivs«. Siehe auch Annette Volfing: ›Du bist selben eyn himmel‹. Textualization and Transformation in the Life of Dorothea von Montau. In: Oxford German Studies 39 (2010), S. 147–159, insbes. S. 147 f., zu Dorothea von Montau.
62 Vgl. Caroline Emmelius: Verborgene Wahrheiten offenbaren. Verschriftlichungsprozesse in frauenmystischen Texten zwischen Subversion und Autorisierung. In: Offen und Verborgen. Vorstellungen und Praktiken des Öffentlichen im Privaten in Mittelalter und Früher Neuzeit. Hrsg. von Caroline Emmelius u.a. Göttingen 2004, S. 47–65, insbes. S. 48 f. Je nach Entstehungssituation gebe es verschiedene Bearbeitungsschritte in der Textgenese, vgl. Caroline Emmelius: Begnadung und Zweifel. Zur Interaktion von Innen- und Außenraum in den ›Offenbarungen‹ der Adelheid Langmann. In: Innenräume in der Literatur des deutschen Mittelalters. XIX. Anglo-German Colloquium Oxford 2005. Hrsg. von Burkhard Hasebrink u.a. Tübingen 2008, S. 309–325, insbes. S. 310, unter Rückgriff auf Peters (1988), S. 108 f.
63 Klaus Grubmüller: Sprechen und Schreiben. Das Beispiel Mechthild von Magedeburg. In: Festschrift Walter Haug und Burkhart Wachinger. Hrsg. von Johannes Janota. 2 Bde. Tübingen 1992, Bd. 1, S. 335–349, hier S. 338.
64 Vgl. Newman (2003), S. 302.
65 Vgl. Rüdiger Schnell: Gender und Rhetorik in Mittelalter und früher Neuzeit. Zur Kommunikation der Geschlechter. In: Rhetorik 29 (2010), S. 1–18, insbes. S. 18. Siehe auch ebd., S. 7: »Autorinnen neigen dazu oder sehen sich gezwungen, sehr viel expliziter ihren Status als Autor zu legitimieren.«

Textes gebunden sind[66] und dass das Authentizitätsproblem, welches mit dem Bericht einer Vision oder einer mystischen Erfahrung einhergeht, mit Autorisierungsfragen zusammenhängt, denen sich nicht nur Autorinnen im Mittelalter stellen mussten.

Daher empfiehlt es sich, obwohl im vorliegenden Fall eine eigenhändige Niederschrift Christinas von Hane nicht auszuschließen ist, bei der Beschäftigung mit ihrer Vita weniger von einem Autor als von Autorisierungsstrategien auszugehen. In vielen mystischen Texten hat man es ungeachtet etwaiger Geschlechterzuordnungen mit »der zentralen Paradoxie« der »Versprachlichung des grundsätzlich die Sprache übersteigenden Augenblicks der ›unio‹« zu tun.[67] Das Unsagbarkeitsproblem in mystischen Schriften ist Teil einer von Dyonisius Areopagita geprägten apophatischen Theologie und wurde bisher vor allem in seiner scholastischen Ausprägung behandelt.[68] Zwar wies Hildegard Keller auf verschiedene Funktionen der *ineffabilia* in brautmystischen Texten hin,[69] doch steht es noch aus zu zeigen, warum sich Elemente der negativen Theologie nicht immer auf einen Unsagbarkeits-Topos reduzieren lassen.[70] In der Christina von Hane-Vita vermitteln Autorisierungsstrategien hagiographischen Erzählens eine Heilsgewissheit, die eine Diskrepanz zwischen der unbeweisbaren und unsagbaren mystischen Erfahrung und ihrer Verschriftlichung zu überbrücken versuchen. Im

---

66 Zum Forschungsstand von Autorisierungsstrategien in mystischen Texten siehe Almut Suerbaum: Die Paradoxie mystischer Lehre im ›St. Trudperter Hohenlied‹ und im ›Fließenden Licht der Gottheit‹. In: Dichtung und Didaxe. Lehrhaftes Sprechen in der deutschen Literatur des Mittelalters. Hrsg. von Henrike Lähnemann/Sandra Linden. Berlin/New York 2009, S. 27–40, insbes. S. 29. Außerdem sei mit Klaus Grubmüller: Erzählen und Überliefern. ›Mouvance‹ als poetologische Kategorie in der Märendichtung. In: PBB 125 (2003), S. 469–493, insbes. S. 470, daran erinnert, dass das Verhältnis von »Aufführung und Festigkeit mittelalterlicher Texte« noch nicht ausreichend geklärt wurde, um lebensweltliche Rückschlüsse zuzulassen. Diese Vorsicht ist auch bei Autorintentionen und Textentstehungsszenarien geboten.

67 Suerbaum (2009), S. 28. Siehe auch Emmelius (2004), S. 48 f.

68 Vgl. Pierre Hadot: Apophatisme et théologie négative. In: Hadot, Exercices spirituels et philosophie antique. Paris 1981, S. 185–193; Michael A. Sells: Mystical Languages of Unsaying. Chicago/London 1994, insbes. S. 34–62 und S. 146–205, zur apophatischen Mystik u.a. bei Johannes Eriugena, Meister Eckhart und Margareta Porete.

69 Vgl. Hildegard Elisabeth Keller: My Secret is Mine. Studies on Religion and Eros in the German Middle Ages (Studies in Spirituality Supplements 4). Leuven 2000(b), S. 105 f. und S. 172–175.

70 Aus rhetorischer Sicht handelt es sich um eine Hyperbel, wie Christina Lechtermann: Funktionen des Unsagbarkeitstopos bei der Darstellung von Schmerz. In: Schmerz in der Literatur des Mittelalters und der Frühen Neuzeit. Hrsg. von Hans-Jochen Schiewer/Stefan Seeber/Markus Stock (Transatlantische Studien zu Mittelalter und Früher Neuzeit – Transatlantic Studies on Medieval and Early Modern Literature and Culture 4). Göttingen 2010, S. 85–104, an der Kommunikation von Schmerz illustriert.

Rahmen dieser Untersuchung sollen daher Textualisierungsstrategien, wie z.B. die Narrativierung theologischer Modelle, im Vordergrund stehen.[71]

Zu den konzeptuellen Entwürfen von Schreibvorgängen gehören auch die verschiedenen in der Vita angelegten Ich-Konstruktionen und -perspektiven.[72] Die narratologische Untersuchung möchte diesen nachgehen und dabei das Einbinden eines impliziten Lesers in den Erzählakt besonders hervorheben: Wie wirkt sich die Anrede an einen impliziten Leser zur Artikulation von Heilsgewissheit auf das Spannungsverhältnis zwischen dem individuellen Leben der Mystikerin und ihrer klösterlichen Lebensgemeinschaft aus? Die Ansicht, dass die mitunter auch an körperlichen Zeichen geäußerte Sonderstellung einer Nonne dem Gemeinschaftsgedanken eines Konvents entgegenstand, erscheint historisch sinnvoll.[73] Emmelius hat nachgewiesen, dass schriftliche Zeugnisse von Visionen und »Erfahrungen« zum einen Erklärungen lieferten, um die »herausgehobene Einzelne« in ihr soziales Umfeld zu integrieren; zum anderen ermöglichten sie, »ihren spirituellen ›Nutzen‹ für die klösterliche Gemeinschaft herauszustellen«.[74]

---

71 Zum Prozess der Textualisierung in mystischen Texten siehe Volfing (2010), S. 148.

72 Zum textinternen Schreibthema als Bedingung einer Schriftmystik siehe Freimut Löser: ›Schriftmystik‹. Schreibprozesse in Texten der deutschen Mystik. In: Finden – Gestalten – Vermitteln. Schreibprozesse und ihre Brechungen in der mittelalterlichen Überlieferung. Freiburger Colloquium 2010. Hrsg. von Eckart Conrad Lutz (Wolfram-Studien 22). Berlin 2012, S. 155–201, insbes. S. 159 f.

73 Vgl. Hildegard Elisabeth Keller: ›înlougen‹. Blicke in symbolische Räume an Beispielen aus der mystischen Literatur des 12. bis 14. Jahrhunderts. In: Symbolik von Ort und Raum. Hrsg. von Paul Michel (Schriften zur Symbolforschung 11). Bern 1997. S. 353–376, insbes. S. 355. Die Absonderung einer einzelnen Nonne und der folgende Rückzug aus der Gemeinschaft geschehen nicht immer freiwillig, wie Hildegard Elisabeth Keller: Absonderungen. Mystische Texte als literarische Inszenierung von Geheimnis. In: Deutsche Mystik im abendländischen Zusammenhang. Neu erschlossene Texte, neue methodische Ansätze, neue theoretische Konzepte. Kolloquium Kloster Fischingen 1998. Hrsg. von Walter Haug / Wolfram Schneider-Lastin Tübingen 2000(a), S. 195–221, insbes. S. 202–205, darlegt. Dabei ist historisch nicht zu entscheiden, ob es zwischen den Prophezeiungen und dem sozialen Phänomen der Ausgrenzung einen kausalen Zusammenhang gibt, vgl. Bürkle (1999), S. 94. Lässt man sich bei der Konstruktion von Individuum (»self«) und Gemeinschaft (»community«) auf eine affektive Räumlichkeit (»affective space«) ein, dann hat man es laut Newman (2012), S. 355, bei weiblichen Autoren des monastischen Mittelalters mit Schwellenfiguren zu tun, die sich auf einem emotionalen Grenzgebiet bewegen (»emotional boundary zone«).

74 Caroline Emmelius: Begnadung und Zweifel. Zur Interaktion von Innen- und Außenraum in den ›Offenbarungen‹ der Adelheid Langmann. In: Innenräume in der Literatur des deutschen Mittelalters. XIX. Anglo-German Colloquium Oxford 2005. Hrsg. von Burkhard Hasebrink u.a. Tübingen 2008, S. 309–325, hier S. 313; siehe auch ebd., S. 323: »Die Offenbarungstexte [...] arbeiten [...] einer Hagiographisierung des Lebens der begnadeten Frau zu, die integrative Funktionen für den Konvent übernehmen kann.«

Mystische Berichte können auf diese Weise als didaktische »Einladung zum Nachvollzug« verstanden werden, wie auch Suerbaum konstatiert.[75]

Dieser Nachvollzug im Leseprozess muss für einen klösterlichen Gebrauchskontext vor dem Hintergrund des auf Lateinisch exerzierten liturgischen Alltags gesehen werden. Es ist dabei von einer Wechselwirkung auszugehen, denn die Liturgie hat sicherlich auch mystische Texte beeinflusst. Heinzer untersucht die Interdependenz von Liturgie und Vision und sieht die Rolle der Überlieferung von Visionstexten im Zusammenhang mit der »Frage der Brechung des sprachlich nicht adäquat formulierbaren Visions-*Erlebnisses* in der Aufzeichnung als Visions-*Text*«.[76] Inwieweit sich liturgische Praktiken auf mystische Texte niederschlugen, wurde bisher noch nicht hinreichend geklärt.[77] Der liturgische Aspekt spielt in dieser Arbeit eine maßgebliche Rolle, nicht zuletzt weil ein möglicherweise aus Hane stammendes Gebetbuch zum Vergleich mit dem Vitentext herangezogen werden kann.[78]

In der Christina von Hane-Vita lässt sich das Spannungsverhältnis zwischen der einzelnen Mystikerin und einem implizit angesprochenen Kollektiv auch auf der Ebene der Allegorie nachweisen. Obwohl die Allegorie der Braut Christi

---

75 Suerbaum (2009), S. 33.

76 Felix Heinzer: Imaginierte Passion – Vision im Spannungsfeld zwischen liturgischer Matrix und religiöser Erfahrung bei Elisabeth von Schönau. In: Nova de veteribus. Mittel- und neulateinische Studien für Paul Gerhard Schmidt. Hrsg. von Andreas Bihrer. München/Leipzig 2004, S. 463–475, hier S. 470 f. (Hervorhebungen im Original).

77 Suerbaum (2009), S. 40, beobachtet im Rahmen einer Untersuchung zur Hoheliedrezeption bei Mechthild von Magdeburg: »Für mittelalterliche geistliche Texte [...] wäre erst noch im Detail zu klären, wie stark solche Phänomene des ›Hymnischen‹ von liturgischen Mustern geprägt sind, denn liturgische Anklänge verleihen gerade in einem volkssprachlichen Text natürlich Dignität, binden damit das in ihnen Artikulierte aber auch zurück an Formen der Liturgie als Gemeinschaftsvollzug [...]« Siehe auch Susanne Köbele: Bilder der unbegriffenen Wahrheit. Zur Struktur mystischer Rede im Spannungsfeld von Latein und Volkssprache (Bibliotheca Germanica 30). Tübingen/Basel 1993(b), S. 86. Zur Liturgie bei Heinrich Seuse siehe Bernhardt (2012), S. 131 f.

78 Siehe Kirakosian (2017c) für den musikalischen Charakter der Visionen in ihrer liturgischen Einbettung. Einen ähnlichen Ansatz verfolgen Anna Harrison: ›I Am Wholly Your Own‹. Liturgical Piety and Community among the Nuns of Helfta. In: Church History. Studies in Christianity and Culture 78 (2009), S. 549–583, und Claire Taylor Jones: ›Hostia jubilationis‹. Psalm Citation, Eucharistic Prayer, and Mystical Union in Gertrude of Helfta's ›Exercitia spiritualia‹. In: Speculum 89 (2014), S. 1005–1039, für Gertrud von Helfta und zum Teil für Mechthild von Magdeburg. Die Verbindung zwischen Liturgie und mystischer Erfahrung im ›Legatus divinae pietatis‹ wird auch von Helga Unger: Interaktion von Gott und Mensch im ›Legatus divinae pietatis‹ (Buch II) Gertruds der Großen von Helfta. Liturgie – mystische Erfahrung – Seelsorge. In: Literatur und Liturgie. Historische Fallstudien. Hrsg. von Cornelia Herberichs/Norbert Kössinger/Stephanie Seidl (Lingua Historica Germanica 10). Berlin/Boston 2015, S. 133–165, behandelt.

sowohl für die einzelne Seele als auch für ein Kollektiv stehen kann, wird insbesondere in der amerikanischen Forschung oft weniger das Allegorische als das Körperliche der Braut betont und zwar erneut anhand von geschlechterabhängigen Attributen. Der Körper, so Hollywood, nehme eine besondere Rolle ein, wenn es um die göttlichen Erfahrungen begnadeter Frauen gehe.[79] Bereits Bynum hatte beobachtet, dass Frauen eher als Männer dazu neigten, »religiöse Erfahrungen« mit dem Körper zu erleben und diese anschließend mit dementsprechenden körperlichen Metaphern wiederzugeben.[80] Allerdings konstatiert Elliott: »Yet this experience of embodiment had the effect of rendering the female body a special medium for communication with the incarnate Christ, ushering in forms of religious expression grounded in physicality.«[81] Zwar ist das Thema der Verkörperung im Christentum auf Grund der Inkarnationsvorstellung eines Gottes in Jesus Christus zentral, doch deswegen muss in einer Textanalyse nicht unbedingt der menschliche Körper im Mittelpunkt stehen. Hier soll dagegen ein anderer Schwerpunkt der Brautallegorie gewählt werden: das Verhältnis zwischen der Brautallegorie und einer in der Vita angelegten mariologischen Typologie. Auf diese Weise wird das Marienbild der Vita im Vergleich zu anderen Texten analysiert.

Während der weiblich spezifizierte Körper der Mystikerin nicht Gegenstand dieser Untersuchungen sein kann, wird der Medienträger, das Buch, als Schriftkörper ins Zentrum gerückt. Hintergrund für diese Interessensverschiebung ist, dass selbst eine körperbetonte Religiosität von vornherein an die Niederschrift der vermeintlich göttlichen Erfahrung gekoppelt ist, dass also mystische und hagiographische Texte die Spannung zwischen einer spirituellen Wahrheit und ihrer materiellen Beweisführung widerspiegeln.[82] Die besonders in den Thesen Bynums und Gumbrechts dominierende Forschungsdebatte um (sakrale) Materialität und Präsenz wird so auf den eigentlichen Schriftträger der mystischen Vita

---

79 Vgl. Hollywood (2002), S. 8.

80 Vgl. Caroline Walker Bynum: Fragmentation and Redemption. Essays on Gender and the Human Body in Medieval Religion. New York 1991, S. 194.

81 Dyan Elliott: Flesh and Spirit. The Female Body. In: Medieval Holy Women in the Christian Tradition, c. 1100 – c. 1500. Hrsg. von Alastair J. Minnis / Rosalynn Voaden (Brepols Essays in European Culture 1). Turnhout 2010, S. 13–46, hier S. 21. Für John Wayland Coakley: Women, Men and Spiritual Power. Female Saints and their Male Collaborators. New York 2006, und ders.: Women's Textual Authority and the Collaboration of Clerics. In: Medieval Holy Women in the Christian Tradition, c. 1100 – c. 1500. Hrsg. von Alastair J. Minnis / Rosalynn Voaden (Brepols Essays in European Culture 1). Turnhout 2010, S. 83–104, gehen mit der körperlichen Sonderstellung Machtfragen einher, die das Verhältnis der Frau zum männlich dominierten Sakralsystem betreffen.

82 Zu dieser Spannung siehe Gail Ashton: The Generation of Identity in Late Medieval Hagiography. Speaking the Saint (Routledge Research in Medieval Studies 1). London / New York 2000, S. 137.

ausgeweitet.[83] Das hat zur Folge, dass die Handschrift als Schnittstelle zwischen Körper und Schriftlichkeit in den Vordergrund rückt.[84] Lentes hat für Evangelien-bücher des Mittelalters gezeigt, wie die Materialität des Buches einen sakralen Status durch die liturgische Einbettung erhält.[85] Kiening erörtert die Signifikanz der Buchschriftlichkeit für die Wirksamkeit der mystischen Rede und betont die Zuschreibung einer Heilswirkung der »Materie, in der so etwas wie eine Realprä-senz des Göttlichen anwesend ist«.[86] Mystische Texte ließen die Materialität des Buches zur »Bedingung für ein Wirksamwerden« erscheinen.[87] Wenn schriftonto-logische Erscheinungen in der Materialität des Buches als Verkörperung der an sich paradoxen mystischen Mitteilung verstanden werden, dann geht es auch immer um das Reaktualisierungspotenzial des zum Ausdruck Gebrachten.[88] So zeigen Hasebrink und Strohschneider, dass Texte mit sakralem Anspruch »die beständige kultische Erneuerung und Aktualisierung des Heilsgeschehens« ver-langen, »sodass kulturelle Praxis wie textuelle Form konstitutiv von einer Ver-gegenwärtigung des (transzendent) Fernen und (temporal) Vergangenen geprägt sind«.[89] Für die Beschäftigung mit der mystischen Vita Christinas von Hane bedeu-

---

83 Vgl. Caroline Walker Bynum: Christian Materiality. An Essay on Religion in Late Medieval Europe. New York 2011; Hans Ulrich Gumbrecht: Production of Presence. What Meaning Cannot Convey. Princeton 2004, und ders.: Präsenz. mit einem Nachwort von Jürgen Klein. Frankfurt a. M. 2012.

84 Anders geht Christian Kiening: Zwischen Körper und Schrift. Texte vor dem Zeitalter der Lite-ratur. Frankfurt a. M. 2003, damit um, wenn er das Performative »zwischen Körper und Schrift« verankert und dabei die Materialität der Überlieferung nicht thematisiert.

85 Vgl. Thomas Lentes: Textus Evangelii. Materialität und Inszenierung des textus in der Li-turgie. In: ›Textus‹ im Mittelalter. Komponenten und Situationen des Wortgebrauchs im schrift-semantischen Feld. Hrsg. von Ludolf Kuchenbuch / Uta Kleine (Veröffentlichungen des Max Planck Instituts für Geschichte 216). Göttingen 2006, S. 133–148.

86 Christian Kiening: Mystische Bücher (Mediävistische Perspektiven 2). Zürich 2011 (nochmals erschienen in: Codex im Diskurs. Hrsg. von Thomas Haye / Johannes Heimrath. Wiesbaden 2014, S. 59–86), S. 8.

87 Kiening (2011), S. 46.

88 Kiening (2011), S. 13, unterscheidet drei Funktionen der Schrift: eine materiell-auratische Funktion, »bei der das pure Dasein der Schriftzüge zählt«, eine performative, »bei der mit Worten gehandelt wird«, und eine operationale, »bei der die Schrift das Programm eines Handlungsvoll-zuges in sich trägt«. Zur operationalen Dimension von Schrift siehe auch Sybille Krämer: Ope-rationsraum Schrift. Über einen Perspektivenwechsel in der Betrachtung der Schrift. In: Schrift. Kulturtechnik zwischen Auge, Hand und Maschine. Hrsg. von Gernot Grube / Werner Kogge / Sy-bille Krämer. München 2005, S. 23–57.

89 Burkhard Hasebrink / Peter Strohschneider: Religiöse Schriftkultur und säkulare Textwissen-schaft. Germanistische Mediävistik in postsäkularem Kontext. In: Poetica 46 (2014), S. 277–292, hier S. 282.

tet dies, dass man von einer Textdynamik ausgehen muss, die die Mechanismen der Heiligkeitskonzeption über die Darstellung der begnadeten Person hinaus transzendiert und auf die Rezeption des Textes ausweitet.[90] Diesem dynamischen Textverständnis liegt zudem das von Löser ausgearbeitete Konzept der Schriftmystik zugrunde, wonach der mystische Text auf keiner Stufe als vollendet angesehen werden kann, sondern sich stets im Prozess seiner Entstehung befindet.[91] An der mystischen Vita Christinas von Hane lässt sich zeigen, wie eine prozesshafte Textualität durch performative und selbstreferenzielle Strategien die Paradoxie der Heiligkeitsdarstellung des Unverfügbaren aus sich selbst heraus freisetzt.

1.3 Methodische Vorüberlegungen

Ein zwischen Bericht und Vergegenwärtigung der mystischen *unio* changierender Vitentext bedarf einer Analysemethode, die skripturale Eigenschaften sowie soziale und ästhetische »Modalitäten mündlicher Kommunikation« berücksichtigt.[92] Hilfreich sind daher bestimmte in der Narratologie entwickelte Konzepte, deren Begrifflichkeit im Folgenden kurz vorgestellt werden soll. Zudem soll der Begriff der Performativität, auf den die einzelnen Untersuchungsbereiche immer wieder zurückgreifen, forschungsgeschichtlich kontextualisiert werden.

Der bereits eingeführte Begriff der Verschriftlichung weist auf ein Spannungsfeld zwischen Mündlichkeit und Schriftlichkeit hin, das in der Textlinguistik mit der medialen Unterscheidung zwischen phonischer und graphischer Mitteilung einhergeht. Diese sei nach Söll nicht automatisch mit der Unterscheidung zwischen gesprochener und geschriebener Äußerung analog zu setzen.[93] Das Modell nach Koch/Oesterreicher verdeutlicht hinsichtlich der medialen Beziehung, dass

---

90 Niklaus Largier: Rhetorik des Begehrens. Die ›Unterscheidung der Geister‹ als Paradigma mittelalterlicher Subjektivität. In: Inszenierungen von Subjektivität in der Literatur des Mittelalters. Hrsg. von Martin Baisch u.a. Königstein im Taunus 2005, S. 249–270, hier S. 261, spricht von einer »Verkörperung des Textes [...], die immer neu die Dynamik von Begehren und Genuss mit all den damit verbundenen Möglichkeiten subjektiver Wahrnehmung exploriert.«
91 Vgl. Löser (2012), der sich auf die Arbeit von Alois Maria Haas: Sermo mysticus. Studien zu Theologie und Sprache der deutschen Mystik (Dokimon 4). Fribourg 1979, insbes. S. 255–295, stützt.
92 Peter Strohschneider: Textualität der mittelalterlichen Literatur. Eine Problemskizze am Beispiel des ›Wartburgkrieges‹. In: Mittelalter. Neue Wege durch einen alten Kontinent. Hrsg. von Jan-Dirk Müller/Horst Wenzel. Stuttgart/Leipzig 1999, S. 19–41, hier S. 24.
93 Vgl. Ludwig Söll: Gesprochenes und geschriebenes Französisch (Grundlagen der Romanistik 6). Berlin 1985, S. 17–25.

es sich bei Verschriftlichung immer auch um eine konzeptionelle Verschiebung handelt,[94] die letztlich zum Ausdruck im graphischen Medium neigt.[95] Wenn man dieses textlinguistische Schema auf die mystische Vita anwendet, so hat man es mit einem Verschriftlichungssprozess zu tun, weil davon auszugehen ist, dass eine schreibende Instanz den mystischen Text strukturierte, ordnete, vereinheitlichte: »Schrift ist von vornherein ein systematisierendes Element«, konstatiert Grubmüller.[96] Über eine allgemeine Regelhaftigkeit von verschrifteter Sprache hinaus postuliert Haas für mystische Texte auch eine konzeptionelle Verschiebung: »Mystik begegnet uns als Sprache in Texten. Die Einheitserfahrung, die in diesen Texten sichtbar wird, ist je eine sprachlich schon interpretierte, strukturierte und auch analysierte.«[97] In diesem Sinne müssen Formen der graphisch-gesprochenen Rede im Text als redaktionell abgefasst angesehen werden, sodass eine konzeptionelle Verschriftlichung anzusetzen ist: Die mystische Mitteilung gibt vor, eine ursprünglich mündliche gewesen zu sein, die anschließend verschriftet wurde, stilistisch ist sie aber so bearbeitet, dass man deutlich von einer Verschriftlichung ausgehen kann.[98] Damit tritt der mystische Vitentext in die Nähe eines »literarischen Faktums« (Peters).

---

94 Vgl. Wulf Oesterreicher: ›Verschriftung‹ und ›Verschriftlichung‹ im Kontext medialer und konzeptioneller Schriftlichkeit. In: Schriftlichkeit im frühen Mittelalter. Hrsg. von Ursula Schaefer (ScriptOralia 53). Tübingen 1993, S. 267–292, und Peter Koch / Wulf Oesterreicher: Mündlichkeit und Schriftlichkeit von Texten. In: Textlinguistik. 15 Einführungen. Hrsg. von Nina Janich. Tübingen 2008, S. 199–215, insbes. S. 200; siehe auch Johannes Schwitalla: Gesprochenes Deutsch. Eine Einführung. 2. überarb. Aufl. (Grundlagen der Germanistik 33). Berlin 2003, und Söll (1985).
95 Vgl. Peter Koch / Wulf Oesterreicher: Gesprochene Sprache in der Romania. Französisch, Italienisch, Spanisch (Romanistische Arbeitshefte 31). Tübingen 1990, S. 12.
96 Klaus Grubmüller: Werkstatt-Typ, Gattungsregeln und die Konventionalität der Schrift. Eine Skizze. In: Texttyp und Textproduktion in der deutschen Literatur des Mittelalters. Hrsg. von Elizabeth A. Andersen / Manfred Eikelmann / Anne Simon (Trends in Medieval Philology 7). Berlin / New York 2005, S. 31–40, hier S. 32.
97 Alois Maria Haas: Die Verständlichkeit mystischer Erfahrung. In: Deutsche Mystik im abendländischen Zusammenhang. Neu erschlossene Texte, neue methodische Ansätze, neue theoretische Konzepte. Kolloquium Kloster Fischingen 1998. Hrsg. von Walter Haug / Wolfram Schneider-Lastin. Tübingen 2000, S. 9–29, hier S. 15. Im Gegensatz dazu werden bestimmte östliche Formen der Mystik als praktische Traditionen verstanden, vgl. Jerome Kroll / Bernard Bachrach: The Mystic Mind. The Psychology of Medieval Mystics and Ascetics. New York / London 2005, S. 2.
98 Eckart Conrad Lutz: Schreibprozesse? Zur Einleitung. In: Finden – Gestalten – Vermitteln. Schreibprozesse und ihre Brechungen in der mittelalterlichen Überlieferung. Freiburger Colloquium 2010. Hrsg. von Eckart Conrad Lutz (Wolfram-Studien 22). Berlin 2012, S. 9–22, hier S. 12, unterscheidet »[d]ie Herstellung (oder die Entstehung) eines Textes (›dictare‹)« von der »Herstellung (oder [der] Entstehung) einer Aufzeichnung (›graphein‹)«.

Dass der Vitentext trotz seines verschriftlichten Charakters einer ständigen Dynamik unterliegt, zeigen Textualisierungsstrategien einer medialen Prozesshaftigkeit.[99] Anstelle der Aufrechterhaltung eines Autor-Werk-Paradigmas gilt es daher, den Erzählakt als kontinuierliche Vermittlung hervorzuheben.[100] Die Bedingung einer prozesshaften Textualität beginnt damit, dass in der diegetischen Welt mündliche Kommunikation als Vermittlungsglied zwischen der göttlichen Rede und dem schriftlich Kommunizierten fungiert.[101] Die auf diese Weise unterschiedlich konstituierten Stimmwechsel zeugen von einer Vielschichtigkeit der Kommunikationsebenen, wie sie etwa von Küenzlen für die Vita Dorotheas von Montau systematisiert wurden.[102] In der Christina von Hane-Vita kommt eine komplexe Ich-Pluralität hinzu, die keine stilistische Einheit bildet, sodass, anders als in der Vita der Dorothea von Montau, keine stilistisch einheitliche Stimme konstruiert wird.[103] In der Vita der Christina von Hane impliziert das jeweilige Sprecher-Ich, anders als in Küenzlens Modell, nicht automatisch eine Form der direkten Rede. Für die Sprecher-Instanz der schriftlich-fixierten Kommunikationssituation bietet sich an den entsprechenden Stellen stattdessen die Bezeichnung ›Schreiber-Ich‹ an. Diese Entscheidung erfolgt im Zusammenhang mit der Verschriftlichungskonzeption nach Oesterreicher, wobei das Schreiber-Ich nicht mit dem realen Schreiber der Handschrift zu verwechseln ist, sondern auf der diegetischen Ebene als narrative Instanz zu verstehen ist. So bleibt die Perspektive des Schreiber-Ichs auch dann konstant, wenn zwischen erzählenden, sprechenden, lobenden oder auslegenden Stimmen gewechselt wird.

Um dieses Phänomen genauer zu beschreiben, sollen hier Begriffe aus der modernen Romantheorie, die insbesondere auf Genette zurückgehen, herangezogen werden, trotz der Gefahr, sie »aus der Sphäre zu reißen, in der sie entstanden

---

99 Hasebrink/Strohschneider (2014), S. 289, sprechen sich ausdrücklich für die »Umstellung von ›Literatur‹ auf ›Text‹« als konsequente Erweiterung von Peters' Ansatz aus, »um die Funktion von religiöser Rede mit Überlieferungsqualität für die Medialisierung von Heil und damit für Praktiken religiöser Vervollkommnung herauszuarbeiten«.

100 Zum Erzählakt als »Überliefertheit« siehe Peter Strohschneider: Höfische Textgeschichten. Über Selbstentwürfe vormoderner Literatur (Germanisch-Romanische Monatsschrift 55). Heidelberg 2014, S. 25–27 und S. 31.

101 Vgl. Volker Mertens: Sprechen mit Gott – Sprechen über Gott. Predigt und Legendendichtung im frühen 13. Jahrhundert (Rudolf von Ems, ›Barlaam und Josaphat‹). In: Sprechen mit Gott. Redeszenen in mittelalterlicher Bibeldichtung und Legende. Hrsg. von Nine Miedema/Angela Schrott/Monika Unzeitig (Historische Dialogforschung 2). Berlin 2012, S. 269–283, hier S. 269: »Erst das Sprechen mit Gott verleiht die Autorität, über Gott zu sprechen.«

102 Vgl. Küenzlen (2010), S. 160–167.

103 Küenzlen (2010), S. 163, weist darauf hin, dass mit »Dorotheas Stimme« stets »deren literarische Inszenierung« gemeint ist.

und entwickelt worden sind«.[104] Ein Beispiel für die Anwendung eines modernen
Begriffs auf Texte des Mittelalters ist mit dem Konzept des Autors gegeben. In
der kritischen Auseinandersetzung zeigt sich, dass mittelalterliche Schreibszenarien von einem Autorverständnis im modernen Sinne zu differenzieren sind.[105]
Dies gilt vor allem dann, wenn ein Dichtername als impliziter Autor fungiert, da
sich die dichtende Instanz allein textintern eines Autornamens bedient. Auch
moderne Vorstellungen von Urheberschaft lassen sich angesichts durchaus diachron vorkommender kollektiver Schreibszenarien selten auf mittelalterliche
Texte anwenden.[106] Während in modernen, von einem Autor verantworteten
Texten die Imagination dieses Autors als reale Instanz vorausgesetzt wird,[107]
lässt sich dies also für viele mittelalterliche Texte nicht ohne Weiteres durchfüh-
ren.[108] Für die Beschäftigung mit der Christina von Hane-Vita spielt – ob es ihn
nun wirklich gegeben hat oder nicht – ein historisch identifizierbarer Autor keine
Rolle, denn es gibt weder in der Vita selbst Anhaltspunkte für seine Signifikanz,
noch existieren andere historische Bezeugungen eines Hagiographen. Trotzdem
verweist der implizite Hagiograph der Vita immer wieder auf den Akt des Schreibens. Auch wenn es Bumke für verfehlt erachtet, mit dem Terminus des impliziten Autors zu arbeiten, da dieser oft nicht vom fiktiven Erzähler zu unterscheiden

---

104 Auf die allgemeine Gefahr, Begriffe aus ihrem ursprünglichen Kontext herauszureißen und
in neuen Kontexten anzuwenden, wies bereits Sigmund Freud hin, vgl. Das Unbehagen der Kultur. Stuttgart 2010 (Originalausgabe Wien 1930), S. 99.
105 Zur Differenzierung zwischen mittelalterlichem und modernem Erzählen siehe Nine Miedema: Zur historischen Narratologie am Beispiel der Dialoganalyse. In: Historische Narratologie.
Mediävistische Perspektiven. Hrsg. von Harald Haferland/Matthias Meyer (Trends in Medieval
Philology 19). New York 2010, S. 35–67, insbes. S. 35–37.
106 Jeder noch so individuell wirkende Text ist nach Rachel Fulton: From Judgement to Passion.
Devotion to Christ and the Virgin Mary. 800–1200. New York 2002, S. 162 f., einer oder mehreren
Traditionen verhaftet. Es liegt daher nahe, »die Sprecherrolle vom Autor zu trennen«, wie auch
Sonja Glauch: Ich-Erzähler ohne Stimme. Zur Andersartigkeit mittelalterlichen Erzählens zwischen Narratologie und Mediengeschichte. In: Historische Narratologie. Mediävistische Perspektiven. Hrsg. von Harald Haferland/Matthias Meyer (Trends in Medieval Philology 19). New York
2010, S. 149–185, insbes. S. 162, erörtert.
107 Vgl. Matias Martinez/Michael Scheffel: Einführung in die Erzähltheorie. 6. Aufl. München
2005, S. 95.
108 Schon Jürgen H. Petersen: Kategorien des Erzählens. In: Poetica 9 (1977), S. 167–195, insbes.
S. 169, betonte, dass der Ich-Erzähler der modernen Literatur nicht vergleichbar mit dem Erzähler der mittelalterlichen Literatur sei. Zur Diskussion des Autor-Werk-Konzepts in der mediävistischen Forschung siehe Elizabeth A. Andersen/Manfred Eikelmann/Anne Simon: Einleitung. In:
Texttyp und Textproduktion in der deutschen Literatur des Mittelalters. Hrsg. von Elizabeth A.
Andersen/Manfred Eikelmann/Anne Simon (Trends in Medieval Philology 7). Berlin/New York
2005, S. XI–XXV, insbes. S. XII f.

sei,[109] ist seine Verwendung für unsere Untersuchung dennoch vielversprechend, sofern es sich um eine diskursive Art von Autorschaft handelt, die ein realhistorisches Verfassertum nicht automatisch miteinschließt.

Trotz theoretischer Differenzen sind also einige wenige technische Termini aus der Romantheorie auch für unsere Analyse unerlässlich.[110] Die Frage, »ob es angemessen sei, das terminologische System der Narratologie« auf den Bereich der Mediävistik anzuwenden, beantwortet Miedema positiv, sofern erstens die untersuchten Texte »(Teil-)Phänomene« aufweisen, auf die die Terminologie angewendet werden könne; zweitens sollten auf der Seite der »mittelalterlichen Produzenten« zumindest Ansätze eines Bewusstseins für die narratologisch untersuchten Phänomene festgestellt werden können.[111] Beides trifft auf die Vita der Christina von Hane zu: Es gibt Anzeichen einer reflektierten Verwendung von Figurenrede, z.B. Gedanken- oder Bewusstseinsbericht und Gedankenrede. Das Innenleben der Mystikerin wird in verschiedenen Modi der erzählten Rede dargestellt; zudem sind Ansätze zur Perspektivierung und Fokalisierung vorhanden.[112] Es ist daher durchaus hilfreich, auf das von Genette geprägte Fachvokabular zurückzugreifen. Von der direkten Rede, die als solche markiert wird, unterscheidet er den »discours direct libre«: »sans signes démarcatifs, c'est l'état ›autonome‹ du ›discours immédiat‹«.[113] Solche Momente der »freien direkten Rede« häufen sich am Schluss der Christina von Hane-Vita. Für die Stimmenfiguration, die mit der Frage »Qui parle?« ermittelt werden könne, ist nach Genette zu beachten, dass auch die Erzählerstimme immer wie die Stimme einer Person stilisiert sei: »la voix du narrateur est bien toujours donnée comme celle d'une personne«.[114] Während die Erzählebenen als extra- und intradiegetisch unterschieden werden,

---

109 Vgl. Joachim Bumke: Autor und Werk. Beobachtungen und Überlegungen zur höfischen Epik. In: ZfdPh 116, Sonderheft (1997), S. 87–114, insbes. S. 106.
110 Monika Fludernik: The Diachronization of Narratology. In: Narrative 11 (2003), S. 331–348, und dies.: Einführung in die Erzähltheorie. Darmstadt 2006, S. 124–133, fordert für die Mediävstik eine historische Narratologie.
111 Miedema (2010), S. 36. Siehe auch Alastair Matthews: The Kaiserchronik. A Medieval Narrative. Oxford 2012, und Gert Hübner: Erzählformen im höfischen Roman. Studien zur Fokalisierung im ›Eneas‹, im ›Iwein‹ und im ›Tristan‹ (Bibliotheca Germanica 44). Tübingen 2003.
112 Ein Interesse für die »narrative Erschließung des Innenraums« (Jan-Dirk Müller: Höfische Kompromisse. Acht Kapitel zur höfischen Epik. Tübingen 2007, S. 339) ist in mittelalterlichen Texten durchaus nachweisbar, siehe dazu auch Hübner (2003) und Miedema (2010), S. 44.
113 Gérard Genette: Nouveau discours du récit. Paris 1983, S. 38.
114 Genette (1983), S. 43. Anders als dies bei Genette (1983), S. 48–52, konstatiert wird, ist in unserem Fall die Erzählstimme nicht immer extern fokalisiert. Vgl. Hübner (2003), S. 34–39, zur Diskussion der narratologischen Begriffe ›Stimme‹ und ›Fokalisierung‹ und ihrer Resonanz in der Literaturwissenschaft.

muss für das mittelalterliche Erzählen außerdem eine Differenzierung zwischen einer *histoire-* und einer *discours*-Ebene angesetzt werden, die zur veränderten Fokalisierung führen kann und den Ich-Bericht einer Figur auch außerhalb des Erzählrahmens ermöglicht.[115]

Auch Metapher und Allegorie bedürfen einer explizit textanalytischen Annäherungsweise, da spirituelle Phänomene in mystischen Texten oft in figurativer Sprache wiedergegeben werden.[116] Heinzer hat die »Bedingungen und Mechanismen« mittelalterlicher Visionen untersucht und fordert für die bildliche Rede in mystischen Texten, sie »aus der problematischen Engführung einer auf das Theologische und Religionspsychologische fokussierten Diskussion« herauszuführen, um sie stattdessen »als mediales Repräsentationssystem zu begreifen«.[117] Schneider, der im Rahmen seiner Auseinandersetzung mit der Mystagogie der Spätantike die Performativität der Allegorie untersucht, fasst Allegorie und Metapher als »indirektes Sprechen« auf.[118] Zum Verhältnis von Metapher und Allegorie weist er außerdem darauf hin, dass weder die Metapher schlichtweg als verkürzte Allegorie zu verstehen sei, noch die Allegorie nur als erweiterte oder systematische Metapher gelten könne.[119] In der vorliegenden Untersuchung wird im Anschluss an Köbeles Untersuchung der Metapherkonstellationen in Frauenlobs Dichtung die »analogisierende Veranschaulichung« eines metaphorischen Prozesses als »Zusammenspiel gegenläufiger Tendenzen« begriffen.[120] Allegorie und Metapher bleiben zwar schwer zu trennen, doch kann festgehalten werden, dass eine

---

115 Eine Zusammenfassung der theoretischen Auseinandersetzung findet sich bei Markus Stock: Figur. Zu einem Kernproblem historischer Narratologie. In: Historische Narratologie. Mediävistische Perspektiven. Hrsg. von Harald Haferland/Matthias Meyer (Trends in Medieval Philology 19). Berlin/New York 2010, S. 187–203, insbes. S. 189–196. Das Konzept eines ›Figuren-Ich-Erzählers‹ außerhalb des ›Dichter-Ich-Rahmens‹ formuliert Glauch (2010), S. 154.

116 Vgl. Jörg Seelhorst: Autoreferentialität und Transformation. Zur Funktion mystischen Sprechens bei Mechthild von Magdeburg, Meister Eckhart und Heinrich Seuse (Bibliotheca Germanica 46). Tübingen/Basel 2003, S. 62–67, zur Funktion der Metapher in der Mystik; vgl. Christoph Leuchter: Dichten im Uneigentlichen. Zur Metaphorik und Poetik Heinrichs von Morungen. Frankfurt a. M. 2003, S. 33–41, zur Differenzierung von Metapher, Gleichnis und Allegorie. Siehe auch Wolfgang Christian Schneider: Durch Sinnbilder zur Schau. Performative Momente in Allegorie, Typos-Bezug und Mystagogie des spätantiken Christentums. In: Performativität und Praxis. Hrsg. von Jens Kertscher/Dieter Mersch. München 2003, S. 175–194.

117 Heinzer (2004), S. 475.

118 Schneider (2003), S. 183.

119 Schneider (2003), S. 181, Anm. 21, sieht die Metapher als begrenzte Aussage und die Allegorie als weitgreifenden Aussagenzusammenhang mit zumeist diskursiver Entwicklung.

120 Susanne Köbele: Umbesetzungen. Zur Liebessprache in Liedern Frauenlobs. In: Geistliches in weltlicher und Weltliches in geistlicher Literatur des Mittelalters. Hrsg. von Christoph Huber/Burghart Wachinger/Hans-Joachim Ziegeler. Tübingen 2000, S. 213–235, hier S. 214.

Allegorie von dynamisch gearteten metaphorischen Prozessen lebt.[121] In Anlehnung an Michel, der das Problem von historischen Texten darin sieht, dass »uns unser Gefühl im Stich« lässt, wenn es um die besondere Wirkung der Metapher geht,[122] resümiert Leuchter: »Man wird letztlich nicht entscheiden können, was ein mittelalterliches Publikum als metaphorisch empfand und was nicht.«[123] Gleichzeitig aber sei eine Beschäftigung mit der Metapherntheorie während des Mittelalters breit dokumentiert, wie die auf Augustinus zurückgehende Unterscheidung von *res* und *signa* illustriere, die eine Rückübersetzung der Metapher prinzipiell möglich mache.[124] Aus der Sicht der modernen Linguistik nach Searle birgt allerdings der Versuch, für metaphorische Sätze wörtliche Paraphrasierungen zu finden, das Problem, dass immer Sinn verloren geht und dass für das Verstehen der Metapher die Wahrheitsbedingungen der Äußerung reproduziert werden müssen.[125] Daher folgt aus Searles Essay, dass es keine bessere Beschreibung für das Gemeinte als die Metapher selbst gibt. In diesem Sinne ist eine Rückübersetzung von vornherein zum Scheitern verurteilt, da es keinen primären Zustand geben kann, auf die eine alternative Beschreibung zurückgreifen könnte. Die Wahrheitsbedingungen einer Metapher weisen also über den schriftlichen Text hinaus und vermögen auf eine performative Weise »den Rahmen des herrschenden kulturellen Repräsentationssystems auf[zu]weichen«: Es handelt sich um »Metaphorizität als Form der Transgression«, wie Neumann und Warning betonen.[126] Daher ist auch der Nachvollzug einer figurativen Rede niemals eine passive Handlung,[127] denn in der Rezeption einer Metapher werden ihre Wahr-

---

121 Vgl. Erika Fischer-Lichte: Ästhetische Erfahrung. Das Semiotische und das Performative. Tübingen 2001, S. 121–127, die im Anschluss an Walter Benjamins Ausführungen Allegorie als Verfahren einer ästhetischen Bedeutungskonstitution erörtert.

122 Paul Michel: Alieniloquium. Elemente einer Grammatik der Bildrede (Zürcher germanistische Studien 3). Bern 1987, S. 163.

123 Leuchter (2003), S. 19.

124 Vgl. Leuchter (2003), S. 17–32.

125 Vgl. John Rogers Searle: Expression and Meaning. Studies in the Theory of Speech Acts. Cambridge 1979, S. 76, 103 f., 114–116.

126 Gerhard Neumann / Rainer Warning: Einleitung. In: Transgressionen, Literatur als Ethnographie. Hrsg. von Gerhard Neumann / Rainer Warning (Rombach Wissenschaften Litterae 98). Freiburg i. Br. 2003, S. 7–16, hier S. 7.

127 Schneider (2003), S. 184 f., beschreibt diesen Vorgang als ein Mithandeln im Vollzug des Verstehens. Bereits Wolfgang Iser: Der implizite Leser. Kommunikationsformen des Romans von Bunyan bis Beckett. München 1972, S. 38, betont ein entsprechendes »Interaktionsschema«.

heitsbedingungen reaktualisiert.[128] Es findet so eine »kommunikative Aneignung von Wirklichkeit« statt.[129]

Am Anfang dieser Kommunikation steht der Vitentext in seiner materiellen Verkörperung. Zwischen der Wahrnehmung der materiellen Erscheinung des Vitentextes und dem Vollzug des Verstehens befindet sich somit ein dynamischer Text, der sowohl den produktiven Prozess des Schreibens als auch das Vergegenwärtigungspotenzial des Nachvollzugs in sich trägt. Für die mystische Vita ließe sich pointierter formulieren: Ein Heiligkeit beanspruchendes Schreiben, das autoreferentiell im Text angelegt ist und sich als Teil der göttlichen Offenbarung ausweist, verfolgt gleichzeitig das Ziel einer heilbringenden Wirkung im Vollzug des Textes.[130] Diese einem Werkverständnis gegenläufige dynamische Textvorstellung setzt somit eine performative, also auf den Vollzug ausgerichtete Sprachlichkeit voraus.

Der Begriff des Performativen bedarf allerdings der Klärung, da Begriffe wie Performance, Performanz und Performativität je nach Disziplin unterschiedlich besetzt sind.[131] Der Begriff ›Performanz‹ wird häufig synonym für ›Performativität‹ gebraucht,[132] bezieht sich aber in der Linguistik traditionellerweise auf das Sprechen bzw. auf Gesprochenes, also *parole* im Saussureschen Sinne. Dieser sprachpragmatische Ansatz findet in der Literaturwissenschaft wohl deswegen großen Anklang, weil Austin Sprache mit einer »aktiven, kreativen Funktion« ausstattete und seinem Konzept von Performativität die nötige »linguistische und philosophische Rechtfertigung« gab.[133] Auf die Probleme und Unstimmigkeiten beim literaturtheoretischen Umgang mit dem Austinschen Modell hat Gorman ausführlich hingewiesen.[134] Austin führte das Adjektiv engl. ›performa-

128 Zum entsprechenden Phänomen der Medialität vgl. Niklaus Largier: Die Kunst des Begehrens. Dekadenz, Sinnlichkeit und Askese. München 2007, und Köbele (1993b).

129 So K. Ludwig Pfeiffer: Struktur- und Funktionsprobleme der Allegorie. In: Von der Materialität der Kommunikation zur Medienanthropologie. Aufsätze zur Methodologie der Literatur- und Kulturwissenschaften 1977–2009. Hrsg. von Ingo Berensmeyer / Nicola Glaubitz (Reihe Siegen 161). Heidelberg 2009, S. 159–187, hier S. 161, im Kontext seiner These, die Allegorie sei nicht nur als eine »literarische Struktur« zu verstehen.

130 Siehe auch Annette Volfing: Medieval Literacy and Textuality in Middle High German. Reading and Writing in Albrecht's Jüngerer Titurel. New York 2007, S. 8 f.

131 Wirth (2002) bietet eine grundlegende Einführung in das Thema.

132 Vgl. Joachim Scharloth: Performanz als Modus des Sprechens und Interaktionsmodalität. Linguistische Fundierung eines kulturwissenschaftlichen Konzepts. In: Oberfläche und Performanz. Untersuchungen zur Sprache als dynamischer Gestalt. Hrsg. von Angelika Linke / Helmuth Feilke (Germanistische Linguistik 283). Tübingen 2009, S. 233–254, insbes. S. 233.

133 Vgl. Culler (2000), S. 506.

134 Vgl. Gorman (1999).

tive‹ ein, das er selbst auf das Verb ›(to) perform‹ zurückführt, welches wiederum mit *action* im Zusammenhang gebraucht wird. Sprechakte sind demnach gleich »performing an action«.[135] Aus dem Neologismus ›performative‹ hat man das Substantiv ›performativity‹ abgeleitet, das seine Entsprechung im deutschen Terminus ›Performativität‹ findet. Während das Wort ›performance‹ im Alltagsgebrauch und außerhalb einer sprachtheoretischen Begriffsbildung existiert, hat dies im Deutschen zu den drei nebeneinander stehenden Neubildungen ›Performance‹, ›Performanz‹ und ›Performativität‹ geführt, die nicht immer klar voneinander getrennt werden.

Wenn ›Performance‹ als Entlehnung aus dem Englischen im Deutschen gebraucht wird, dann wird der Begriff, wie Belliger und Krieger beobachten, fast synonym zu dem der Ritualisierung im Sinne Turners (»soziales Drama«) und Goffmans verwendet. Geertz, Tambiah, Schechner und andere verstünden »kulturelle Performance« so als Darstellung und zugleich Reproduktion kultureller Sinn- und Handlungsmuster.[136] Eine Theatervorstellung oder andere aus dem Raum sich abhebende Aufführungen werden so in ihrer einmaligen Darbietung als Performance verstanden.[137] Für Schechner liegt überdies dann eine Performance vor, »when historical and social context, convention, usage, and tradition say it is«.[138] Auch Fischer-Lichte gebraucht den Begriff auf diese Weise, was innerhalb der Theater-Studien konventionell erscheint.[139] Mit den Gender Studies hat der Performance-Ansatz den Verkörperungsaspekt des Performativen gemeinsam.[140] Performativität ist also je unterschiedlich konnotiert und kann auf alles angewendet werden, das sich in einer kulturellen Praxis als handelnd herausstellt, d.h. im Unterschied zu Performanz kann sich Performativität auf mehr als allein gesprochene Sprechakte beziehen. Daher können schriftlich fixierte wie nonverbale Manifestationen, z.B. Objekte, als performativ bezeichnet werden,

---

135 John Langshaw Austin: How to Do Things with Words. 2. Aufl. Oxford 1975, S. 6.
136 Andréa Belliger/David Krieger: Einführung. In: Ritualtheorien. Ein einführendes Handbuch. Hrsg. von Andréa Belliger/David Krieger. 5. Aufl. Wiesbaden 2013, S. 7–35, S. 9 f.
137 Vgl. die Synonyme für ›Performance‹ im Duden-Online, URL: http://www.duden.de/suchen/ dudenonline/Performance [10.08.2017].
138 Richard Schechner: Performance Studies. An Introduction. 2. Aufl. New York/London 2006, S. 38.
139 Vgl. Erika Fischer-Lichte: Grenzgänge und Tauschhandel. Auf dem Wege zu einer performativen Kultur. In: Performanz. Zwischen Sprachphilosophie und Kulturwissenschaften. Hrsg. von Uwe Wirth. Frankfurt a. M. 2002, S. 277–300, insbes. S. 294–300, und dies.: Ästhetik des Performativen. Frankfurt a. M. 2004.
140 Vgl. Judith Butler: Gender Trouble. Feminism and the Subversion of Identity. New York/London 1990, und dies.: Bodies That Matter. On the Discursive Limits of Sex. New York/London 1993.

ohne dass damit Performanz im Austinschen Sinne, d.h. einer phonetisch vernehmbaren Sprachmanifestation, gemeint wäre.[141]

Performanz-Begriffe in Linguistik und Sprechakttheorie sind nur eine von mehreren theoretischen Orientierungen, die »nicht nur gesonderte Genealogien auf[weisen], sondern sich auch teilweise [widersprechen]«, wie Kertscher und Mersch anmerken.[142] Ein Beispiel dafür ist der Streit um das von Chomsky geprägte Begriffspaar Kompetenz/Performanz, der zu einer gesonderten Diskussion innerhalb der generativen Grammatik geführt hat, wo performanzbasierte Ansätze dominieren.[143] Die Performanzforschung innerhalb der Linguistik – erweitert durch Erkenntnisse aus der Neurolinguistik – bleibt nach wie vor einem System verhaftet, in dem Sprache isoliert behandelt wird.[144]

In der Literaturwissenschaft, so betont Stridde, sei »die Pragmatik nicht autonom gegenüber Semantik und Syntax«.[145] Semiotische Zugänge sind in der Performativitätsdebatte insofern wichtig, als sie den Fragen um Repräsentation und um Identifizierung von Zeichen als Repräsentation kritisch gegenüberstehen. Der von Austin inspirierte Ansatz bedeutet ja gerade, dass eine sprachliche Äußerung nicht nur die Welt repräsentiere, sondern sie zugleich konstituiere und daher also hervorbringe.[146] Derart funktioniert auch das mittelalterliche Prinzip der *similitudo*, das die Ähnlichkeit zwischen der metaphorischen Bezeichnung und dem Bezeichneten erst durch deren Verbindung schafft.[147] Diese Verbindung gründet aber in letzter Instanz im sozialen Charakter von Zeichengebräuchen, da es eines

---

141 Vgl. Schechner (2006), S. 30.

142 Jens Kertscher/Dieter Mersch: Einleitung der Herausgeber. In: Performativität und Praxis. Hrsg. von Jens Kertscher/Dieter Mersch. München 2003, S. 7–15, hier S. 8.

143 Vgl. Beatrice Primus: Performanz und Grammatik. In: Oberfläche und Performanz. Untersuchungen zur Sprache als dynamischer Gestalt. Hrsg. von Angelika Linke/Helmuth Feilke (Germanistische Linguistik 283). Tübingen 2009, S. 99–116, insbes. S. 100.

144 Vgl. Jörg Bücker: Sprachhandeln und Sprachwissen. Grammatische Konstruktionen im Spannungsfeld von Interaktion und Kognition (Sprache und Wissen 11). Berlin/Boston 2012, für den Versuch eines semiotisch, gesprächsanalytisch, sprachgebrauchstheoretisch und kognitionslinguistisch begründeten Zugangs zur Analyse und Modellierung verfestigter grammatischer Muster am Beispiel nicht-finiter Prädikationskonstruktionen. Siehe auch Douglas Robinson: Introducing Performative Pragmatics. New York 2006, für eine Studieneinführung in die Performativitätstheorien innerhalb der linguistischen Pragmatik.

145 Stridde (2009), S. 21. Für einen Forschungsüberblick über sprechakt-theoretisch-pragmatische Ansätze in literatur- und kulturwissenschaftlichen Bereichen vgl. ebd., S. 15–26 und S. 30–42.

146 Austin (1975), S. 6: »In these examples it seems clear that to utter the sentence [...] is not to ›describe‹ my doing [...] or to state that I am doing it: it is to do it.«

147 Vgl. Leuchter (2003), S. 28 f.

interaktiven Gebrauchs von Sprache bedarf, um Bedeutung zu konstituieren, so wie auch Searle den sozialen Kontext für das Verstehen einer Metapher betont.

Dass das Problem der von Austin und Searle geprägten Performativitätstheorie die »Abstraktion von der raum-zeitlichen Situierung des Sprechens [bleibt], die impliziert, dass Medienfragen erst gar nicht aufkommen«,[148] ist strittig, denn nach Austin finden Sprechakte in einem sozialen Rahmen statt.[149] Wenn Performanz als Sprachmanifestation verstanden wird, dann ist mit der Fixierung von Worten im Medium Text die Möglichkeit des Wiederholens geschaffen.[150] Diese Art von Performanz erlaubt es, den performativen Charakter von Sprache zu untersuchen. Culler beschreibt das Problem wie folgt: »[...] how should one conceive of the relation between what language does and what it says?«[151] In der konkreten Anwendung eines solchen Zugangs beschreibt Suydam die Mystik aus dem Umfeld der Beginen als »a set of fixed notations to guide past and future sacred performances. That is, the written text is a guide (and, itself a performance) that enables the performed text.«[152] Dabei ist zu beachten, dass schriftliche Sprechakte nicht tatsächlich geäußert worden sein müssen; sie können hingegen durchaus eine mündliche Situation simulieren. Der Kontext eines schriftlichen Sprechakts wie etwa die Ankündigung einer direkten Rede in einem narrativen Umfeld muss ebenso beachtet werden, wenn man textualisierte Formen der Performativität untersuchen will. Ob z.B. die sprechhandelnde Stimme zu ihrem Sprechakt autorisiert ist,[153] kann im narrativen Kontext erheblich von der übergeschalteten Stimme abhängen, die die Rede als solche kennzeichnet. Insbesondere für Textzeugnisse muss also der iterative Charakter des Zeichengebrauchs beachtet werden, der nach Butler Voraussetzung für die Autorisierung des Sprechmodus ist.[154] Auch Derrida hat in der Auseinandersetzung mit Austin und Searle auf die Iterabilität sprachlicher Zeichen, d.h. auf ihre Wiederholbarkeit, als Basis für

---

148 Sybille Krämer: Einleitung. In: Performativität und Medialität. Hrsg. von Sybille Krämer. München 2004, S. 13–31, hier S. 15.

149 Siehe dazu Culler (2000), S. 508.

150 Diese Relation könnte mit Michel Foucault: L'Archéologie du savoir. Paris 1969, S. 134, als »wiederholbare Materialität« (»matérialité répétable«) beschrieben werden. Auf Grund der Wiederholbarkeit ist ein statisches Verständnis vom Text zu hinterfragen.

151 Culler (2000), S. 518.

152 Suydam (1999a), S. 194.

153 Dass die Stimme, die einen Sprechakt vollziehen will, dazu autorisiert sein muss, wird von Austin (1975), S. 15, als eine Grundvoraussetzung für eine gelungene Sprechhandlung gesehen: »[...] the particular persons and circumstances in a given case must be appropriate for the invocation of the particular procedure invoked.«

154 Vgl. Butler (1993), S. 225 f. und S. 235. Siehe auch Culler (2000), S. 514.

das Regelhafte am Sprachgebrauch hingewiesen.[155] Diese Wiederholbarkeit der Zeichen impliziere Alterität und die Erzeugung von Differenz.[156] Performativität beschreibe demnach die Wiederholung von Zeichenausdrücken in zeit- und raumversetzten neuen Kontexten, was zugleich eine Veränderung der Zeichenbedeutung bewirke.[157]

Ob die zwei Theoriestränge innerhalb des Themas der Performativität, nämlich »(I) ›Handlungstheorien‹, woran vor allem sprachphilosophische Modelle anschließen, sowie (II) das Konzept von ›Wiederholung und Differenz‹, wie es auf den Poststrukturalismus und die Dekonstruktion zurückgeht«, stets klar voneinander zu trennen sind, ist fraglich.[158] Psychoanalytische Untersuchungen in der Literaturwissenschaft demonstrieren, wie die handlungsorientierte Sprechakttheorie mit postmodernen Theorien zu vereinen ist.[159] Performanz-Theorien in Anthropologie und Ethnographie, das Performanz-Konzept des französischen Poststrukturalismus bzw. der Dekonstruktion, sowie die Performativität im Sinne des Ereignisses überschneiden sich durchaus mit der Sprechakttheorie, wie interdisziplinäre Ansätze verdeutlichen, die verschiedene sprachwissenschaftliche Theorien mit den Kulturwissenschaften zu verbinden suchen.[160] Dennoch heißt es zuweilen, dass der *performative turn* der Kulturwissenschaften trotz seiner sprachtheoretischen Verankerung ohne linguistische Beteiligung

---

155 Vgl. Simon Morgan Wortham: The Derrida Dictionary. London / New York 2010, S. 78, zu Derridas Iterabilitätskonzept. Zur Debatte zwischen Derrida und Searle gemeinsam mit dem abgedruckten und zum Teil ins Englische übersetzten Schlagabtausch siehe Jacques Derrida: Limited Inc. Hrsg. von Gerald Graff. London 1998.

156 Vgl. Krämer (2004), S. 16 f., in Auseinandersetzung mit Butlers »Kreativität des Zitats«.

157 Auch in der traditionellen Rhetorik wird Abweichung im Sprachgebrauch als Performanz verstanden, siehe dazu Jürgen Fohrmann: Vorbemerkung. In: Rhetorik, Figuration und Performanz. DFG-Symposion 2002. Hrsg. von Jürgen Fohrmann (Germanistische Symposien, Berichtsbände 25). Stuttgart / Weimar 2004, S. VII–X, insbes. S. VII.

158 Vgl. Kertscher / Mersch (2003), S. 7.

159 Vgl. Shoshana Felman: The Literary Speech Act. Don Juan with J. L. Austin, or Seduction in Two Languages. Hrsg. von Catherine Porter. Ithaca 1983, und Elisabeth Strowick: Sprechende Körper – Poetik der Ansteckung. Performativa in Literatur und Rhetorik. München 2009. Siehe auch Stefan Seeber: Freud und die Mediävistik. Witztheoretische Überlegungen anhand von Wolframs ›Parzival‹. In: Oxford German Studies 41 (2012), S. 129–147, für die Verbindung von Performanz und Psychoanalyse. Für einen allgemeinen Überblick siehe Jutta Eming: Mediävistik und Psychoanalyse. In: Codierungen von Emotionen im Mittelalter / Emotions and Sensibilities in the Middle Ages. Hrsg. von Stephen Jaeger / Ingrid Kasten (Trends in Medieval Philology 1). Berlin / New York 2003, S. 31–44.

160 Vgl. den Band Christoph Wulf / Michael Göhlich / Jörg Zirfas (Hrsg.): Grundlagen des Performativen. Eine Einführung in die Zusammenhänge von Sprache, Macht und Handeln. Weinheim / München 2001. Siehe auch Kertscher / Mersch (2003), S. 8.

stattfand.[161] Dabei zeigen insbesondere die Arbeiten Fischer-Lichtes eine Ausein-andersetzung mit linguistischen Phänomenen, an einer Stelle in Anlehnung an Ingarden auch ausdrücklich mit »textuellen Systemen«.[162]

Im theaterwissenschaftlichen Bereich, wo Performativität mit Verkörpe-rungstheorien in Verbindung gebracht wird, spielen semiotische Beziehungen seit jeher eine wichtige Rolle. Als der Begriff der Verkörperung gegen Ende des 18. Jahrhunderts in der deutschen Theatertheorie aufkam, wollte man damit ausdrücken, dass »[d]er Schauspieler seinen phänomenalen sinnlichen Körper so weit in einen semiotischen transformieren [sollte], daß dieser instand gesetzt würde, für die sprachlich erzeugten Bedeutungen des Textes als Zeichenträger, als materielles Zeichen zu dienen.«[163] Fischer-Lichte zeigt, wie diese Vorstel-lung einer Zwei-Welten-Theorie verpflichtet ist, nach der sich der Schauspieler zunächst »entkörperlichen« muss, um den entsprechend gewünschten Sinn ver-körpern zu können.[164] In dieser bis weit ins 20. Jahrhundert gültigen Vorstellung steht der phänomenale Körper im Dienste eines semiologischen Bedeutungssys-tems. Mit einem seit den 1970ern zusehends verstärkten Blick auf den phäno-menalen Körper in den Kulturwissenschaften hat sich der Begriff der Verkörperung gewandelt, was sicherlich auch mit der Einführung des Begriffs ›embodiment‹ durch Csordas zusammenhängt.[165] Fischer-Lichte resümiert, dass es Aufgabe des Begriffs der Verkörperung sei, dem »Körper eine vergleichbar paradigmatische Position zuzugestehen wie dem Text, anstatt ihn unter dem Textparadigma zu subsumieren.«[166] Der phänomenale Körper wird als »Bedingung der Möglichkeit jeglicher kultureller Produktion« gesehen.[167]

---

161 Vgl. Helmut Feilke/Angelika Linke: Oberfläche und Performanz – Zur Einleitung. In: Ober-fläche und Performanz. Untersuchungen zur Sprache als dynamischer Gestalt. Hrsg. von Helmut Feilke/Angelika Linke (Germanistische Linguistik 283). Tübingen 2009, S. 3–17, insbes. S. 9.
162 Fischer-Lichte (2001), S. 194, beschreibt, wie jeder literarische Dialog aus Haupt- (auch Re-detext) und Nebentext (wer spricht, Haltung etc.) besteht, d.h. er »besteht also aus zwei unter-schiedlichen textuellen Systemen«. Zu Haupt- und Nebentext siehe auch Roman Ingarden: Das Literarische Kunstwerk. Mit einem Anhang von den Funktionen der Sprache im Theaterschau-spiel. 2. verb. u. erw. Aufl. Tübingen 1960, S. 403–425.
163 Fischer-Lichte (2001), S. 302; vgl. ebd., S. 301–309.
164 Fischer-Lichte (2001), S. 303.
165 Vgl. den Band Thomas J. Csordas (Hrsg.): Embodiment and Experience. The Existential Ground of Culture and Self (Cambridge Studies in Medical Anthropology 2). Cambridge 2001 (Nachdruck der Originalausgabe Cambridge 1994).
166 Fischer-Lichte (2001), S. 309.
167 Fischer-Lichte (2001), S. 309. Die Bestimmung des Körpers als Metapher mit der Präsup-position der Metapher als performative Größe, wie von Markus Hallensleben: Performance of Metaphor: The Body as Text – Text Implantation in Body Images. In: Performance and Performa-tivity in German Cultural Studies. Hrsg. von Carolin Duttlinger/Lucia Ruprecht/Andrew Webber

Die Frage »nach dem Argument der Körperlichkeit im Feld des Literarischen und nach der Körperbewegung und deren Bedeutung für die Texte« beeinträchtigt auch den Text-Begriff allgemein, wie Neumann und Warning feststellen.[168] Auch Wenzel und Lechtermann konstatieren, für die »Teilhabe am Text« sei dessen Verkörperung ein notwendiger Schritt.[169] Das Konzept der Verkörperung führt zum Verständnis von Performance als einer in Raum und Zeit bestimmbaren Darbietung zurück. Dass Performativität und Textualität im Bereich des (Schau-) Spiels eng miteinander verflochten sind, wie das etwa im historischen Kontext am geistlichen Spiel zu sehen ist, steht außer Frage.[170] Wie bereits das Lesen von Theaterstücken als performativer Akt verstanden werden kann,[171] so kann auch der Vollzug eines jeden Textes als ein Ereignis betrachtet werden. Wenn ein Ereignis immer eine spezifische Prozesshaftigkeit in sich trägt,[172] dann bedeutet dies für den textuellen Bereich, dass die Unterscheidungen zwischen Produktions-, Werk- und Rezeptionsästhetik nicht mehr ausreichen. Für Fischer-Lichte, die das Theater als Modell heranzieht, »müssten [a]n ihre Stelle die Begriffe »›Inszenierung‹, ›Wahrnehmung‹ bzw. ›ästhetische Erfahrung‹ und ›Ereignis‹« treten.[173]

Diese beiden Kategorisierungsmöglichkeiten, Produktion und Rezeption auf der einen Seite und Inszenierung und Wahrnehmung auf der anderen, müssen sich aber nicht gegenseitig ausschließen. So sprechen Herberichs und Kiening zwar von Produktion und Rezeption vormoderner Texte, betonen aber den dynamischen Charakter von Schrift im Mittelalter, »deren Herstellung wie Wahrnehmung prozessual erfolgten: im Nach- und Mitvollzug der Zeichen, unter

---

(German Linguistic and Cultural Studies 14). Oxford 2003, S. 241–255, insbes. S. 242, betrieben, fällt hinter der Debatte des phänomenalen Körpers zurück.

168 Neumann/Warning (2003), S. 8. Siehe auch Strowick (2009), S. 13, zur »Relevanz der Konzeption der Performativität des geschlechtlichen Körpers für die Literaturwissenschaften, den Akt des Lesens«.

169 Horst Wenzel/Christina Lechtermann: Repräsentation und Kinästhetik. Teilhabe am Text oder die Verlebendigung der Worte. In: Paragrana 10 (2001), S. 191–213, hier S. 197.

170 Vgl. den Band Ingrid Kasten/Erika Fischer-Lichte (Hrsg.): Transformationen des Religiösen. Performativität und Textualität im geistlichen Spiel. Berlin 2007.

171 Vgl. Boris Vejdovsky: The Act of Reading as Performance. In: Performance. Hrsg. von Peter Halter (SPELL 11). Tübingen 1999, S. 55–61. Siehe auch Erika Fischer-Lichte: Die verwandelnde Kraft der Aufführung. In: Die Aufführung. Diskurs – Macht – Analyse. Hrsg. von Erika Fischer-Lichte. München 2012, S. 11–23, insbes. S. 18, mit dem Beispiel der Dichterlesungen.

172 Vgl. Erika Fischer-Lichte: Performativität und Ereignis. In: Performativität und Ereignis. Hrsg. von Erika Fischer-Lichte (Theatralität 4). Tübingen 2003(a), S. 11–37, insbes. S. 12 und S. 31. Siehe auch Fischer-Lichte (2012), S. 18.

173 Erika Fischer-Lichte: Theater als Modell für eine Ästhetik des Performativen. In: Performativität und Praxis. Hrsg. von Jens Kertscher/Dieter Mersch. München 2003(b), S. 97–111, hier S. 110.

Beteiligung des Körpers, mit dem Ziel einer Eröffnung spiritueller Welten.«[174] Der Vollzug des Verstehens als Mithandeln wird insbesondere in liturgischen Handlungen deutlich,[175] für die der Kontext entscheidend ist. Die sogenannte linguistische Anthropologie versucht darum, über eine sprachpragmatische Herangehensweise auch historische und kulturelle Aspekte einzubeziehen. So stellt Hall in Abgrenzung zu Austin und Derrida fest: »for linguistic anthropologists, context must be identified, since speech acts are realized only through the cultural conventions that govern their use.«[176]

Bei der Suche nach performativen Strategien in historischen Texten können kontextbedingte Aspekte nicht unberücksichtigt bleiben. Sprachpragmatische Ansätze sind in der mediävistischen Spiritualitätsforschung vielfach diskutiert worden.[177] Trotz Hollywoods Zweifel am Erfolg der auf den »flüchtigen« Gegenstand angewendeten zeitgenössischen Theorien[178] konnte an einzelnen Fallstudien erfolgreich demonstriert werden, wie diese Herangehensweisen weiterführende Resultate erbringen.[179] Auch Aspekte der Materialität der Textzeugnisse

---

174 Herberichs/Kiening (2008), S. 16. Christine Stridde: Heinrich Wittenwiler: ›Der Ring‹ (um 1410). In: Literarische Performativität. Lektüren vormoderner Texte. Hrsg. von Cornelia Herberichs/Christian Kiening (Medienwandel – Medienwechsel – Medienwissen 3). Zürich 2008, S. 299–315, hier S. 311, spricht im Rahmen einer rezeptionsästhetischen Lektüre des Wittenwilers ›Ring‹ vom »Entscheidungsvermögen des Lesers«.
175 Vgl. Schneider (2003), S. 191.
176 Kira Hall: Performativity. In: Journal of Linguistic Anthropology 9 (2000), S. 184–187, hier S. 185. Die Forderung nach der historischen Kontextualisierung neben der grammatisch-logischen Bestimmung von sprachlichen Äußerungen formulierte bereits Michel Foucault in seiner Archäologie des Wissens. Letzteres muss vor dem Hintergrund von Foucaults Diskursanalyse erklärt werden, für den eine Gruppe von Äußerungen einen Diskurs formt und ein Diskurs wiederum »ne forme pas une unité rhétorique ou formelle, indéfiniment répétable«, was nach sich zieht, dass eine Äußerung nicht isoliert betrachten werden soll, sondern als »fragment d'histoire« (Foucault [1969], S. 153).
177 Vgl. den Überblick bei Stridde (2009), S. 15–26 und S. 30–42, und außerdem den Band Mary A. Suydam/Joanna E. Ziegler (Hrsg.): Performance and Transformation. New Approaches to Late Medieval Spirituality. Basingstoke 1999.
178 Vgl. Amy Hollywood: Rezension zu Mary A. Suydam/Joanna E. Ziegler: Performance and Transformation. New Approaches to Late Medieval Spirituality (1999). In: Hypatia 16 (2001), S. 106–108, hier S. 108: »Contemporary performance theory struggles with the ephemeral nature of its object.«
179 Catherine Müller: How to Do Things with Mystical Language. Marguerite d'Oingt's Performative Writing. In: Performance and Transformation. New Approaches to Late Medieval Spirituality. Hrsg. von Mary A. Suydam/Joanna E. Ziegler. Basingstoke 1999, S. 27–45, zeigt, wie die Performativität der mystischen Sprache Marguerites d'Oingt zur poetischen Strategie avanciert. Nicola Zotz: Otfrid von Weißenburg. ›Evangelienbuch‹ (863/71). In: Literarische Performativität. Lektüren vormoderner Texte. Hrsg. von Cornelia Herberichs/Christian Kiening (Medienwandel

werden beachtet, wenn z.B. beschrieben wird, dass sich Schrift in »ihrer Eigendynamik« präsentiere.[180] Zusätzlich dazu heben Herberichs und Kiening den Aspekt der »Wiederholbarkeit eines Aktes, der auf paradoxerweise den Eindruck von Einmaligkeit erzeugen und zugleich mit Dauer versehen kann«, hervor:[181]

> Selbst Gebetbücher und sprachpragmatische Texte, die in herausragendem Maße auf unmittelbare Wirkung angelegt scheinen, bringen in ihrer situationsabstrahierenden Schriftlichkeit zugleich Mittelbarkeiten hervor, nämlich Bedingungen für eine nicht gegenwärtige, sondern künftige Wirksamkeit.[182]

Mit dieser Formulierung verweisen Herberichs und Kiening auf das dynamisch-kreative Potenzial von schriftlich fixierter Sprache. Da performative und mimetische Verfahren immer aktive Vorgänge miteinschließen,[183] kann der Text unter Berücksichtigung seiner materiellen Erscheinung sowie seiner historischen Wahrnehmung auch in seinem Reaktualisierungspotenzial untersucht werden. Performativität wird demzufolge für die Untersuchung der Christina von Hane-Vita vorrangig als eine textuelle Strategie verstanden, d.h. auch die Darstellung von Vortragssituationen (fingierte Mündlichkeit) oder die Verkörperung von allegorischen Rollen (mystische Braut in Vielfachbesetzung) werden unter dem Aspekt einer textbasierten Performanz behandelt.[184]

– Medienwechsel – Medienwissen 3). Zürich 2008, S. 44–61, untersucht die Performativität des Evangelienbuches und sieht dabei »[d]as mediale Zeugnis des Textes und die Parallelführung, Verdichtung und Verschränkung von Transzendenz und Immanenz« als Verweis darauf (hier S. 58).

180 Christa M. Haesli: Sprachpragmatische Texte des Clm 536 (11./12. Jahrhundert). In: Literarische Performativität. Lektüren vormoderner Texte. Hrsg. von Cornelia Herberichs/Christian Kiening (Medienwandel – Medienwechsel – Medienwissen 3). Zürich 2008, S. 62–81, hier S. 77. Siehe auch Aleksandra Prica: Frau Ava. ›Johannes‹ und ›Leben Jesu‹ (um 1120). In: Literarische Performativität. Lektüren vormoderner Texte. Hrsg. von Cornelia Herberichs/Christian Kiening (Medienwandel – Medienwechsel – Medienwissen 3). Zürich 2008, S. 82–99, und Lentes (2006).

181 Herberichs/Kiening (2008), S. 10, ausführlich nochmals ebd., S. 13 f.

182 Herberichs/Kiening (2008), S. 17.

183 So Rüdiger Campe in Anlehnung an Wolfgang Iser, vgl. Martin Zenck: Erzeugen und Nachvollziehen von Sinn. Rationale, Performative und Mimetische Verstehensbegriffe in den Kulturwissenschaften. Eine Einleitung zu den drei Sektionen. In: Erzeugen und Nachvollziehen von Sinn. Rationale, Performative und Mimetische Verstehensbegriffe in den Kulturwissenschaften. Hrsg. von Martin Zenck/Markus Jüngling. München 2011, S. 13–26, insbes. S. 25.

184 Vgl. Suydam (1999a), S. 181 zum »staged text« und S. 179 zur »textual performance« bei Birgitta von Schweden.

2 Der Text(-körper): mystisch, hagiographisch

Die literarhistorische Verortung der Christina von Hane-Vita muss auch nach Texteinflüssen und Texttypen fragen. Ruh sah die Vita Christinas von Hane als das »Lebensbild« einer »visionären oder im Gnadenleben stehenden Frau« aus der Zeit, in der sich die »religiöse Frauenbewegung« auf ihrem Höhepunkt befand (13. Jahrhundert).[1] Wenn Ruh die Vita als typischen Ausdruck ihrer Entstehungszeit versteht, so steht das allerdings in einer gewissen Spannung zur handschriftlichen Überlieferung. Wie, wann und warum die Christina von Hane-Vita ab- und umgeschrieben wurde, kann nicht mit Sicherheit bestimmt werden. In der Forschung lässt sich seit Ruh eine Akzentverschiebung beobachten, in der immer seltener vom Werk und seiner entsprechenden Gattungszuweisung die Rede ist.[2] Parallelen einer solchen Akzentverschiebung bietet die Beschäftigung mit Mechthilds von Magdeburg ›Fließendem Licht der Gottheit‹, da man sich hier insbesondere seit der Arbeit Poors von einem werkorientierten Konzept fortbewegt.[3] Andere Ansätze akzeptieren im Falle Mechthilds das Konzept eines »ordentlichen Buches«, obwohl sich Kohärenz und Integrität zu verflüchtigen scheinen.[4] Wenn Ruh die Entstehungsumstände für die Christina von Hane-Vita anvisiert, so setzt er – wie Neumann für Mechthild von Magdeburg – voraus, dass sich diskrete Phasen und Intentionen der Textbearbeiter ausmachen lassen.[5]

---

1 Ruh (1993), S. 17.

2 Strohschneider (2014), S. 25–27, thematisiert die »Vorgaben klassizistischer Autor-Werk-Paradigmen« (S. 25) und weist mit einem ausführlichen Forschungsüberblick auf das »Problemfeld vormoderner Textualität« (S. 26) hin.

3 Vgl. Sara S. Poor: Mechthild of Magdeburg and Her Book. Gender and the Making of Textual Authority. Philadelphia 2004.

4 Vgl. Nigel F. Palmer: Kapitel und Buch. Zu den Gliederungsprinzipien mittelalterlicher Bücher. In: Frühmittelalterliche Studien 23 (1989), S. 43–88, insbes. S. 77 f. – Das Verständnis einer Einheit des Buches wird letztlich von der Überlieferungssituation bestätigt, siehe dazu Nemes (2010). Elizabeth A. Andersen: The Voices of Mechthild of Magdeburg. Bern 2000, S. 104–110, betont zudem das Selbstverständnis des ›Fließenden Lichts‹ als Buch.

5 Vgl. Hans Neumann: Beiträge zur Textgeschichte des ›Fließenden Licht der Gottheit‹ und zur Lebensgeschichte Mechthilds von Magdeburg. In: Altdeutsche und altniederländische Mystik. Hrsg. von Kurt Ruh (Wege der Forschung 23). Darmstadt 1964, S. 175–239, insbes. S. 216; siehe auch Hans-Georg Kemper: Allegorische Allegorese. Zur Bildlichkeit und Struktur mystischer Literatur. In: Formen und Funktionen der Allegorie. Symposium Wolfenbüttel 1978. Hrsg. von Walter Haug (Germanistische Symposien, Berichtsbände 3). Stuttgart 1979, S. 90–125, insbes. S. 96, und Andersen (2000), S. 98 f. Vgl. Ruh (1993), S. 125, zu Christina von Hane. Noch Ralf-Henning Steinmetz: Bearbeitungstypen in der Literatur des Mittelalters. Vorschläge für eine Klärung der Begriffe. In: Texttyp und Textproduktion in der deutschen Literatur des Mittelalters. Hrsg. von Elizabeth A. Andersen/Manfred Eikelmann/Anne Simon (Trends in Medieval Philology 7). Ber-

https://doi.org/10.1515/9783110536324-005

Schreibintentionen werden auf diese Weise oft an die Gattung der entsprechend entstehenden Texte gekoppelt. Bennewitz' Position ist hingegen, dass »die Gattungsfrage für die gesamte Literaturproduktion des Mittelalters keine [...] vorrangige Frage darstellt«. Dass »die Grenzen zwischen den einzelnen Genres immer wieder überschritten werden«,[6] schließt nicht aus, dass man sich im Mittelalter gewisser Texttypen bewusst war.[7] Für Grubmüller hingegen kann erst dann von Gattung die Rede sein, wenn eine »reflexionsgeleitete Typenbildung stattgefunden hat«, d. h. wenn der jeweilige Texttyp auf schriftlich fixierte Vorbilder zurückgeht.[8] Doch finden sich diverse Texttypen »häufig ganz verschieden zusammengefügt«, sodass die klare Gattungszuordnung eines Textes kaum möglich ist, wie auch Herbers beobachtet.[9]

Sollte also die Christina von Hane-Vita dominanten Oberkategorien wie ›Gnadenleben‹ oder ›Offenbarungsliteratur‹ eindeutig zugeordnet werden können? Obwohl vorweggenommen werden darf, dass eine stringente Gattungszuweisung für die Christina von Hane-Vita nicht definitiv vorgenommen werden kann, erscheint die Untersuchung nach Texttraditionen aufschlussreich, sofern sie Texteinflüsse sowie Texttypen umfasst. Die Auseinandersetzung mit den Merkmalen mystischer Texte sowie des hagiographischen Texttyps Vita kristallisiert zentrale Probleme heraus, die sich nicht allein auf Texttraditionen beschränken, sondern auch theologische Merkmalszuweisungen betreffen. Das Verhältnis von

lin/New York 2005, S. 41–61, insbes. S. 42 und S. 47, geht von der Intentionalität eines Textbearbeiters als ausschlaggebendes Argument gattungstypologischer Zuweisungen aus.

6 Ingrid Bennewitz: Jungfrau, Mutter, Königin. Vereinnahmung und Ausgrenzung von Weiblichkeit in mittelalterlichen Marienliedern. In: Lektüren der Differenz. Hrsg. von Ingrid Bennewitz. Berlin 2002, S. 55–74, hier S. 59.

7 Zu diesem Ergebnis kommt Hedwig Röckelein: Das Gewebe der Schriften. Historiographische Aspekte der karolingerzeitlichen Hagiographie Sachsens. In: Hagiographie im Kontext. Wirkungsweisen und Möglichkeiten historischer Auswertung. Hrsg. von Dieter R. Bauer/Klaus Herbers (Beiträge zur Hagiographie 1). Stuttgart 2000, S. 1–25, insbes. S. 4, in ihrer Studie zu Viten des Frühen Mittelalters.

8 Grubmüller (2005), S. 37. Zugleich räumt er ein (S. 32): »Literatur ist im allgemeinen nicht von vornherein eine in sich strukturierte, gar nach ›Gattung‹ geordnete Erscheinung, schon gar nicht die volkssprachige Literatur des Mittelalters, der eine formulierte Poetik ebenso fehlt wie eine kohärente organisatorische Basis und die [...] eng in Gebrauchssituationen eingebunden ist, die sich in der Regel der Systematisierung entziehen.«

9 Klaus Herbers: Hagiographie im Kontext. Konzeption und Zielvorstellung. In: Hagiographie im Kontext. Wirkungsweisen und Möglichkeiten historischer Auswertung. Hrsg. von Dieter R. Bauer/Klaus Herbers (Beiträge zur Hagiographie 1). Stuttgart 2000, S. IX–XXVIII, hier S. XVI. Siehe auch den ausführlichen kultur- und literarhistorischen Überblick zur »Viten- und Offenbarungsliteratur« bei Bürkle (1999), S. 9–56, insbes. S. 44, zur Komplexität gattungstypologischer Fragen.

Immanenz und Transzendenz wird sowohl für die Definition mystischer Texte als auch für die Funktionsmechanismen hagiographischen Erzählens herangezogen. Doch klären zu wollen, wie Mystik und Hagiographie zueinander stehen, wäre nicht zuletzt deswegen anmaßend, weil Texteinflüsse und -typen immer nur am Einzelfall bestimmt werden können. Stattdessen werden im Folgenden die definitorischen Diskurse einschließlich der Paradigmen von Innen und Außen, von Spiritualität und Körperlichkeit hinterfragt, um dynamische Konfigurationen zwischen Mystik und Hagiographie zu untersuchen. Zugleich werden Texttraditionen unter Berücksichtigung historischer und historiographischer Vorstellungen von Hagiographie betont. Daher sind auch Prozesse des Umschreibens, Abschreibens und Einschreibens (in bestimmte Diskurse) zu diskutieren.

2.1 Mystik und Hagiographie

Grundsätzlich operiert religiöses Sprechen, ob mystisch oder nicht, mit außersprachlichen Prinzipien. Köbele betont die »paradoxe Bedingung« religiösen Sprechens, die darin bestehe, »daß es nach einer Sprache sucht, die das Göttliche zugänglich machen will, indem sie zugleich an dessen Nichtdarstellbarkeit festhält«.[10] Laut Strohschneider gehören diese Grenzen der Kommunikabilität am »Übergangsbereich von Transzendenz und Immanenz« zur christlichen Heilsgeschichte.[11] Er konstatiert, dabei werde narrativen Diskursen »selbst unmittelbar wirklichkeitsverändernde Kraft zugetraut«.[12] Diese Feststellung ist für die folgenden Untersuchungen grundlegend, in denen narrative Diskurse und die bereits mehrfach betonte »Überliefertheit« in der Auseinandersetzung mit dem Text(-körper) im Spannungsfeld von Mystik und Hagiographie als konstitutiv für den Text an sich zu sehen sind.[13] Dass die Kopplung von Mystik und Hagiographie für Texte aus dem weiblichen monastischen Bereich von Relevanz ist, zeigt Bürkle mit ihrer Arbeit zu dominikanischen Schwesternbüchern. In der mystischen Ausrichtung der entsprechenden Texte verschränkten sich Klosterhistoriographie und -hagiographie, sodass die Genese der Texte von dem Ort

---

10 Susanne Köbele: Frauenlobs Lieder. Parameter einer literarhistorischen Standortbestimmung. Tübingen/Basel 2003, S. 236.
11 Strohschneider (2014), S. 29.
12 Strohschneider (2014), S. 30.
13 Strohschneider (2014), S. 26 f., zur »Überliefertheit« als Textbedingung. Siehe auch Franz Josef Worstbrock: Wiedererzählen und Übersetzen. In: Mittelalter und Frühe Neuzeit. Übergänge, Umbrüche und Neuansätze. Hrsg. von Walter Haug (Fortuna vitrea 16). Tübingen 1999, S. 128–142, insbes. S. 128.

ihrer Produktion und Rezeption nicht wegzudenken sei.[14] Auch wenn die Christina von Hane-Vita, anders als die spätmittelalterlichen Schwesternbücher, die Vollkommenheit einer einzigen Nonne präsentiert und nicht singuläre Qualitäten verschiedener Individuen,[15] sind in beiden jene Textstrategien erkennbar, die die im christlichen Mittelalter etablierten theologischen Konzepte, darunter auch das paradoxe Sprechen vom Unsagbaren, im hagiographischen Modus für einen kollektiven Umgang rezipieren und wiedergeben.[16] Bevor die Besonderheit der auf diese Weise entstehenden mystischen Vita vorgestellt wird, bietet es sich daher an, zunächst die einzelnen Bereiche Mystik und Hagiographie gesondert zu behandeln.

2.1.1 Mystische Texte

Nach einer kurzen Darstellung der allgemeinen Definitionsproblematik angesichts der Überlieferungslage mystischer Texte seien im folgenden einige wenige Forschungsstränge hervorzuheben, die den Status der Volkssprache, die *unio*-Zentrierung und die vermeintliche Kategorie der ›Frauenmystik‹ betreffen.

Tobin macht auf den anachronistischen Gebrauch des Begriffs ›Mystik‹ aufmerksam, da weder dieser noch die Bezeichnung ›Mystiker‹ in mittelalterlichen Texten verwendet würden. Dementsprechend werde das, was im Mittelalter nicht als separate Kategorie religiöser Schriften gegolten habe, heute allgemein unter mystischer Literatur subsumiert.[17] Williams-Krapp dagegen beobachtet, dass

---

14 Vgl. Bürkle (1999), S. 1–17 und S. 318.

15 Vgl. Garber (2003), S. 105 f. und S. 161, zum Vorbildcharakter der Nonnen. Siehe auch Johanna Thali: Beten – Schreiben – Lesen. Literarisches Leben und Marienspiritualität im Kloster Engelthal (Bibliotheca Germanica 42). Tübingen 2003, S. 218–221; Williams-Krapp (2008), S. 275 f.; Bernard McGinn: The Harvest of Mysticism in Medieval Germany (1300–1500) (The Presence of God 4). New York 2005, S. 2.

16 Vgl. Berndt Hamm: ›Gott berühren‹. Mystische Erfahrung im ausgehenden Mittelalter. Zugleich ein Beitrag zur Klärung des Mystikbegriffs. In: Religiosität im späten Mittelalter. Spannungspole, Neuaufbrüche, Normierungen. Hrsg. von Reinhold Friedrich/Wolfgang Simon (Spätmittelalter, Humanismus, Reformation 54). Tübingen 2011, S. 449–472, insbes. S. 458, zur spätmittelalterlichen Rezeption der Mystik.

17 Vgl. Tobin (2002), S. 345. Für eine Forschungsgeschichte über mystische Literatur siehe ebd., S. 346–350. Von dieser literarischen Bestimmung mystischer Texte ist zu unterscheiden, dass seit Dionysius Areopagita (um 500) Mystik als eine eigene theologische Disziplin verstanden wird, vgl. Kurt Flasch: Das philosophische Denken im Mittelalter. Von Augustin zu Machiavelli. 2. rev. u. erw. Aufl. Stuttgart 2011, S. 86–90, und ebd., S. 122–125 speziell zum mittelalterlichen Verständnis der Mystik als theologische Disziplin.

mystische Texte in überlieferungsgeschichtlichen Kontexten gebündelt sind und schließt daraus, dass diese Texte sehr wohl als eigene Kategorie verstanden werden können.[18] Wenn Tobin auf einen (fehlenden) metadiskursiven Umstand verweist, d.h. darauf, dass es im Mittelalter keine Diskussion über Mystik als Kategorie gegeben habe, dann stellt sich die Frage, ob eine fehlende Terminologie zwangsläufig auch auf eine fehlende Differenzierung hindeutet. Tobin und Williams-Krapp wenden für ihre Definitionen jeweils verschiedene Methoden an. Dass beide Ergebnisse berechtigt nebeneinander existieren, weist zugleich auf die Diskrepanz zwischen theoretischem Diskurs und textlicher Überlieferungslage hin. Im heutigen Forschungskontext spiegelt sich eine ähnliche Diskrepanz in dem Versuch wider, ein mystisches Korpus inhaltlich zu umreißen,[19] und wird insbesondere dann immanent, wenn es um die deutschsprachige Mystik geht.

Im Zusammenhang der internationalen Mediävistik ist es auffällig, dass in der Germanistik die deutschsprachige Mystik als eine besondere Ausformung wahrgenommen wird.[20] Für Haas gehört all das zum »Schriftkorpus der Deutschen Mystik«, bei dem es sich um eine *theologia spiritualis* oder *mystica* handelt, die trotz der verschiedenen »literarischen Gebrauchstypen« von einem Prozess des Transzendierens ausgeht.[21] Dennoch bleibt es kontrovers, inwiefern es sich bei der deutschsprachigen Mystik tatsächlich um einen Sonderweg handelt.[22] Haas' Definition lässt unbeachtet, dass auf lateinische Texte dieselben von ihm genannten Kriterien zutreffen können. Zum »Korpus des mystischen Schrifttums« würden laut Ruh indessen auch all diejenigen Texte gezählt werden, die ein Transzendieren nicht zum unmittelbaren Gegenstand haben, sondern Vorstufen beschreiben wie etwa die der Meditation, der *compassio* oder des Gebets.[23] Auch Williams-Krapp spricht sich für ein »erweiterte[s] Verständnis von ›Mystik‹ bzw. ›mystischer Literatur‹ aus, das die Berichte jeglicher Art über die Erfahrung mit dem Übernatürlichen umspannt (»Visionen, Auditionen, ›unio‹-Erfahrungen,

---

18 Vgl. Williams-Krapp (2008), S. 269.
19 Vgl. Bernard McGinn: The Growth of Mysticism. Gregory the Great Through the Twelfth Century (The Presence of God 2). New York 1994(b), und ders. (1998).
20 Vgl. McGinn (2005).
21 Alois Maria Haas: Geistliches Mittelalter (Dokimon 8). Fribourg 1984(a), S. 262 f.
22 Vgl. McGinn (1994a), S. 9: »Vernacular theology differed from both its monastic and scholastic cousins not only in audience, but also in how it organized and presented its teaching. [...] The characteristic genres of vernacular theology are less easy to describe.«
23 Kurt Ruh: Geschichte der abendländischen Mystik. Bd. 1: Die Grundlegung durch die Kirchenväter und die Mönchstheologie des 12. Jahrhunderts. München 1990, S. 15.

Exempla, Prophetien usw.«).[24] Doch bereits an den Randgebieten dieses Defi-nitionsbereichs kommt es zu Streitfragen: Die Unterscheidung von Vision und Ekstase z. B. zieht nach sich, dass »zahlreiche Werke – vor allem aus dem Bereich der Frauenmystik – ausgegliedert werden [müssten]«, so Williams-Krapp.[25] Diese Exklusion beträfe prominente Figuren wie Hildegard von Bingen, wie Tobin auf den Punkt bringt: »Though some would deny her the name ›mystic‹, maintain-ing that she made no contributions to the mystical tradition, others find in her broadly diverse writings some traces of mysticism.«[26] So dürfe man auch Hilde-gard von Bingen auf Grund des rein Visionären ohne jede Ekstase nicht »aus einer Geschichte der deutschen Mystik« ausgrenzen.[27] Hildegards Beispiel verdeut-licht, dass Korpora mystischen Schrifttums, ob spezifisch deutsch oder nicht, letztlich Prozessen der Kanonbildung unterliegen.[28]

Während die philosophiegeschichtliche Auseinandersetzung im Anschluss an Dionysius Areopagita »das Nachdenken über den befangenen, weil in Gegen-sätzen verbleibenden Charakter unseres Redens vom Einen« betont,[29] wird mystische Rede in der mediävistischen Germanistik spezifischer in ihrem wider-sprüchlichen Verhältnis von transzendentem Anspruch und semiotischer Kom-munikation untersucht: »die Anwesenheit des Transzendenten in der Immanenz birgt selbst eine Paradoxie in sich, insofern sich die Unbegreiflichkeit des Tran-szendenten zeichenhaft vermittelt.«[30] Bei aller Problematik, den Inhalt mysti-scher Texte zu definieren, spricht sich Hasebrink für ein enges Verständnis aus, wenn er die Vereinigung von Gott und Seele als thematische Mitte der Mystik

---

24 Williams-Krapp (2008), S. 268. Auch mystagogische Abhandlungen seien hinzuzuzählen, vgl. Werner Williams-Krapp: Mystikdiskurse und mystische Literatur im 15. Jahrhundert. In: Neuere Aspekte germanistischer Spätmittelalterforschung. Hrsg. von Freimut Löser u.a. (Ima-gines Medii Aevi 29). Wiesbaden 2012, S. 261–285, insbes. S. 261; siehe auch Ruh (1990), S. 14 f.

25 Williams-Krapp (2008), S. 264.

26 Tobin (2002), S. 358.

27 Williams-Krapp (2012), S. 261. Ausführlicher setzt sich Weiss (2000), S. 5–11, mit Hildegards Fall auseinander, der sich einer mystischen Definition entziehe, weil sie explizit Abstand von Elementen wie dem *raptus* oder der Ekstase nehme.

28 Vgl. Ruh (1990), S. 14 zur Kanonbildung.

29 Flasch (2011), S. 89.

30 Burkhard Hasebrink: ›Ich kann nicht ruhen, ich brenne‹. Überlegungen zur Ästhetik der Klage im ›Fließenden Licht der Gottheit‹. In: Das fremde Schöne. Dimensionen des Ästhetischen in der Literatur des Mittelalters. Hrsg. von Manuel Braun / Christopher Young (Trends in Medieval Philology 12). New York 2007, S. 91–107, hier S. 94. Siehe auch Walter Haug: Gotteserfahrungen im abendländischen Mittelalter. In: Positivierung von Negativität. Letzte kleine Schriften. Hrsg. von Ulrich Barton. Tübingen 2008(a), S. 225–250, hier S. 228, der die »Zwiespältigkeit der Kommuni-kationsverweigerung« behandelt.

bestimmt.[31] McGinn sieht den ›Sonderweg der Deutschen Mystik‹ weniger in der *unio*-Ausrichtung als in der »originellen Literaturproduktion«, die den Einbruch der Transzendenz in die Immanenz thematisiere.[32] Dass »häufig die literarische oder intellektuelle Qualität eines Werkes« zum Kriterium einer Zuweisung erhoben wird,[33] demonstriert auch die Debatte zwischen Dinzelbacher, der sich für eine »Erlebnismystik« ausspricht, und Ringler, der von gattungsimmanenten Gesetzen für mystische Texte ausgeht.[34] Köbele stellt dagegen die Opposition »erlebt/bewusst konstruiert« als verfehlt dar, indem sie überzeugend auf die von Augustinus geprägte Doppelstruktur religiösen Sprechens verweist, wonach sich die Aussage über ein persönliches Ereignis mit einem hohen literarisch-konzeptionellen Anspruch verträgt.[35]

Aus der vorgestellten Diskussion wird deutlich, dass das zu definierende thematische Zentrum von mystischen Texten jeweils an die textliche, z.T. auch als literarisch umschriebene Erscheinungsform gebunden ist, ob das nun die Sprache oder den Gebrauchstyp betrifft. Auf die »kategoriale Unschärfe eines zwiespältigen Basisbegriffs ›Literatur‹« weisen neuerdings Hasebrink und Strohschneider ausführlich hin.[36] Mit der entsprechenden Begriffsentwicklung in Säkularisierungskontexten wurde in der Altgermanistik ein erweiterter Literaturbegriff eingeführt, der Religiöses »allein unter der Bedingung seiner Aufspaltung in Ästhetisches auf der einen und Funktionales auf der anderen Seite« zulassen konnte.[37] Die Konsequenzen der entsprechenden Aufspaltung lassen sich insbesondere an der Diskussion um sogenannte ›frauenmystische‹ Texte sehen, wo sowohl produktions- als auch rezeptionsästhetische Kriterien für eine vornehm-

---

31 Burkhard Hasebrink: ›ein einic ein‹. Zur Darstellbarkeit der Liebeseinheit in mittelhochdeutscher Literatur. In: PBB 124 (2002), S. 442–465, insbes S. 443; siehe auch Köbele (1993b), S. 30 f.
32 Vgl. McGinn (2005), S. 2.
33 Williams-Krapp (2008), S. 264.
34 Vgl. Peter Dinzelbacher: Rezension zu Siegfried Ringler: Viten- und Offenbarungsliteratur in Frauenklöstern des Mittelalters. Quellen und Studien (1980). In: Anzeiger für deutsches Altertum und deutsche Literatur 93 (1982), S. 63–71, und ders.: Zur Interpretation erlebnismystischer Texte des Mittelalters. In: ZfdA 117 (1988), S. 1–23, insbes. S. 1–4; Ringler (1980).
35 Köbele (1993b), S. 22 und S. 198. In diesem Sinne ist auch für Hadot (1981), S. 192, der apophatische Diskurs nur dank der Differenzierung zwischen der Erfahrung selbst (»l'extase mystique«) und dem Sprechen (»les méthodes théologiques«) über diese Erfahrung möglich, sodass eine »apophatische Praxis« (»pratique apophatique«) die Aussage über einen unsagbaren Gott nicht ausschließe.
36 Hasebrink/Strohschneider (2014), S. 287.
37 Hasebrink/Strohschneider (2014), S. 288. Hasebrink und Strohschneider sprechen sich für eine »mediävistische Textwissenschaft« als eine »historische Textwissenschaft« im »postsäkularen Kontext« aus (ebd., S. 287 f.).

lich geschlechterspezifische Definition herangezogen werden.[38] Die Bezeichnung ›Frauenmystik‹ suggeriere die »Andersartigkeit weiblicher Frömmigkeit und weiblichen Schreibens«, so Thali.[39] Peters favorisiert eine literarästhetische Kategorisierung, indem sie von einem Sammelbegriff der Frauenmystik ausgeht, der poetisch anspruchsvolle Texte über religiöse Erfahrung, Viten- und Offenbarungstexte sowie lateinische Vitencorpora über *mulieres religiosae* umfasst.[40] An anderer Stelle jedoch demonstriert Peters am Beispiel der Beginenmystik, wie problematisch es ist, innerhalb des so definierten Korpus von ›Gattungen‹ zu sprechen. So sei es angesichts der Offenheit volkssprachiger Spiritualität unzulässig, die Beginenmystik als abgrenzbaren Sonderbereich aufzufassen.[41]

Gerade bei brautmystischen Inhalten handelt es sich selten um homogene Texttypen, da es »wegen der höchst unterschiedlichen Materialbasis« zu verschiedenen Konkretisierungsmöglichkeiten kommt.[42] Allein das Beispiel des ›Fließenden Lichts der Gottheit‹ Mechthilds von Magdeburg illustriert die Schwierigkeit, sein »Profil [...] gattungsmäßig zu charakterisieren«.[43] Was lange als eine Art Autobiographie galt,[44] entzieht sich einer eindeutigen Gattungszuweisung, auch wenn durchaus Elemente starker Kategorien vorhanden sind wie etwa die

---

38 Dies ist so bezeichnend, weil es den Gegenbegriff einer ›Männermystik‹ nicht gibt und stattdessen allenfalls von ›Brautmystik‹ gesprochen wird. Einen Forschungsüberblick zur Frauenmystik bietet Thali (2003), S. 48–54.

39 Thali (2003), S. 50.

40 Ursula Peters: Mittelalterliche Literatur am Hof und im Kloster. Ergebnisse und Perspektiven eines historisch-anthropologischen Verständnisses. In: Mittelalterliche Literatur und Kunst im Spannungsfeld von Hof und Kloster. Ergebnisse der Berliner Tagung, 9.–11. Oktober 1997. Hrsg. von Nigel F. Palmer/Hans-Jochen Schiewer. Tübingen 1999, S. 167–192, insbes. S. 184.

41 Peters (1988), S. 97–100. McGinn (1994a), S. 9, kommt für Gattungszuweisungen im Bereich der volkssprachigen Mystik letztlich auf dasselbe Ergebnis.

42 Ursula Peters: Das ›Leben‹ der Christine Ebner. Textanalyse und kulturhistorischer Kommentar. In: Abendländische Mystik im Mittelalter. Symposium Kloster Engelberg 1984. Hrsg. von Kurt Ruh (Germanistische Symposien, Berichtsbände 7). Stuttgart 1986, S. 402–422, hier S. 418; siehe auch dies. (1988), S. 39. – Aber auch in einem einzigen Text können sich verschiedene Formen verzahnen, vgl. Andersen (2000), S. 96, zu Mechthilds von Magdeburg ›Fließendem Licht‹: »As an integral literary work, the ›Fließendes Licht der Gottheit‹ does indeed elude categorisation in terms of a single genre, containing as it does a miscellany of visions, auditions, dialogue, monologues, prayers, hymns, love poetry, letters, allegories, parables and narratives.«

43 Elizabeth A. Andersen: ›Das Licht der Gottheit‹ und der Psalter. Dialogische Beziehungen. In: Dialoge. Sprachliche Kommunikation in und zwischen Texten im deutschen Mittelalter. Hamburger Colloquium 1999. Hrsg. von Nikolaus Henkel/Martin H. Jones/Nigel F. Palmer. Tübingen 2003, S. 225–238, hier S. 228.

44 Vgl. Nemes (2010), S. 25.

der Vita.[45] Die Forschungsdebatte über Frauenmystik als eigene Kategorie zeigt, dass eine Sonderkategorie von Mystik selten von der hagiographischen Tradition abgekoppelt werden kann. Mystische Texte, die sich mit dem Leben einer Frau beschäftigen, orientieren sich an hagiographischen Mustern, die, wie Peters beobachtet, den oft männlichen Bearbeitern zum Bau eines biographischen Gerüsts dienten.[46]

2.1.2 Hagiographische Texte

Was aber zeichnet einen hagiographischen Text abgesehen von seinem biographischen Gerüst eigentlich aus? Um dieser Frage nachzugehen, seien hier die Zusammenhänge zwischen Heiligenverehrung, Schreibintentionen und Textbearbeitungen sowie ordenspolitischem Interesse kurz vorgestellt.

»Die hagiographische Literatur hat eine Reihe von unterschiedlichen Textsorten hervorgebracht«, deren Gestaltung sich nach der Heiligenverehrung richte, so Ruhrberg.[47] Diese Bestimmung schlösse konsequenterweise all jene mystischen Texte aus dem Korpus hagiographischer Texte aus, die das Leben einer Nonne in den Mittelpunkt stellen, ohne dabei einen Kult initiieren oder approbieren zu wollen. Das Prinzip der Heiligenverehrung ist vor allem in lateinischen Kontexten wichtig, wo Passio, Gesta, Translatio, Miracula, Elevatio und andere Texttypen zu dem für die Kanonisierung erforderlichen hagiographischen Dossier gehören.[48] Für Vollmann ist die Vielzahl der mittellateinischen Viten ein Zeichen dafür, die

---

45 So bereits Alois Maria Haas: Mechthild von Magdeburg – Dichtung und Mystik. In: Amsterdamer Beiträge zur älteren Germanistik 2 (1972), S. 105–156, insbes. S. 111, und erneut Andersen (2000), S. 95, die die autobiographische Lesart als Anachronismus bezeichnet.
46 Zugleich gebe der Bearbeiter-Aspekt Anlass, von einer »gattungsspezifisch unterschiedlichen Ausrichtung« der entsprechend hagiographisch gefärbten Texte auszugehen, vgl. Peters (1988), S. 39: »Zwischen dem Bild, das die Viten von den literarischen Interessen und Aktivitäten der ›mulieres religiosae‹ zeichnen, und den Texten einer Hadewijch oder einer Mechthild klafft [...] – schon aufgrund der gattungsspezifisch unterschiedlichen Ausrichtung der Texte – eine Lücke, die sich nicht ohne weiteres schließen lässt.«
47 Christine Ruhrberg: Der literarische Körper der Heiligen. Leben und Viten der Christina von Stommeln (1242–1312) (Bibliotheca Germanica 35). Tübingen/Basel 1995, S. 156.
48 Vgl. Herbers (2000), S. XVI, und Monique Goullet/Martin Heinzelmann: Avant-propos. In: La réécriture hagiographique dans l'occident médiéval. Transformations formelles et idéologiques. Hrsg. von Monique Goullet/Martin Heinzelmann (Beihefte der Francia 58). Ostfildern 2003, S. 7–15, insbes. S. 7.

Vita als eine ursprünglich lateinischsprachige Gattung zu verstehen.[49] Demnach orientieren sich die klare Kennzeichen einer Vita tragenden volkssprachigen Texte an den lateinischen Vorgängern.[50] So versteht Nemes die volkssprachig entworfenen Lebensbilder Juttas von Sangerhausen als Viten, wofür er typische Merkmale auflistet; darunter die Herkunft aus einem Adelsgeschlecht, den Dienst an Kranken, Wundertaten und andere Gnadenauszeichnungen.[51] Diese thematischen Kriterien, so plausibel sie auf den ersten Blick erscheinen mögen, sind allerdings weiter auszudifferenzieren: Die noble Abstammung ist weniger eine hagiographische Voraussetzung als ein Zeugnis sozialer Verhältnisse, da adlige Klosterangehörige auf Grund ihrer Erziehung und ihres Prestigepotenzials viel eher zu prominenten Figuren heranwuchsen. Der Spitaldienst ist nur eine denkbare Form der Heiligkeit, die insbesondere nach der Zeit Elisabeths von Thüringen verbreitet ist. Nemes' Zugang scheint weniger an den theologisch-historischen Bedingungen interessiert als an der Ausgestaltung der Texte, die sich an bestimmten Mustern orientieren. Diesbezüglich mag es nicht verwundern, dass Viten auf bestimmte Traditionen zurückgreifen. Wiederkehrende Topoi und Themenkomplexe sind aber stets eingebettet in historische Kontexte.

Dazu gehören die *causae scribendi*, die auf den intendierten Gebrauchskontext hagiographischer Texte hinweisen.[52] Der mittelalterliche Begriff der Vita stammt zwar aus dem Kanonisierungsprozess, doch lassen bestimmte Gebrauchssituationen auch andere Funktionen des Heiligenlebens zu. Dass hagiographische Texte z. B. in liturgischen Kontexten gebraucht wurden, wird von Historikern konzeptionell vorausgesetzt, wie Dolbeau ausführt: »Au Moyen Âge, la production hagiographiques était conçue, en général, pour une lecture faite à haute voix

---

49 Vgl. Benedikt Konrad Vollmann: Vita. In: Lexikon des Mittelalters. 9 Bde. und Registerband. München 1980–1999. Bd. 8 (1997), Sp. 1751–1752, insbes. Sp. 1751. – Anders betont Ruhrberg (1995), S. 163, dass es sich auf Grund der Volkssprachigkeit bei mystischen Texten um »Gnadenviten« handle, ohne ein stichhaltiges Argument für diese Unterscheidung zu liefern.
50 So versteht Andersen (2000), S. 33, etwa, dass »the vision and the hagiographical ›life‹ emerge as two of the most characteristic genres subsumed under the heading of vernacular theology.«
51 Vgl. Balázs J. Nemes: Jutta von Sangerhausen (13. Jahrhundert). Eine ›neue Heilige‹ im Gefolge der Heiligen Elisabeth von Thüringen? In: Zeitschrift für Thüringische Geschichte 63 (2009), S. 39–73, insbes. S. 49 f. Freilich handelt es sich hierbei um Texte von nach 1500.
52 Zur hagiographischen Darstellungsabsicht siehe Gerd Althoff: ›Causa scribendi‹ und Darstellungsabsicht. Die Lebensbeschreibung der Königin Mathilde und andere Beispiele. In: Litterae medii aevi. Festschrift für Johanne Autenrieth zum 65. Geburtstag. Hrsg. von Michael Borgolte/ Herrad Spilling. Sigmaringen 1988, S. 117–133. Der Plural *causae* sei laut Herbers (2000), S. XVII, Anm. 37, zu bevorzugen.

et de durée limitée, le temps d'un repas ou des leçons liturgiques de matines.«[53] In vielen Fällen kann nur ein rezeptionsästhetischer Ansatz helfen, den Gebrauch eines Textes zu eruieren. Auch mit der Integration in liturgische Abläufe bewahren die hagiographischen Textstücke ihre narrative Natur.[54]

Zusätzlich zu den Entstehungsgründen sei zudem die Weitertradierung von Heiligenleben hervorzuheben.[55] So plädiert Monique Goullets für einen methodischen Ansatz der *réécriture*, der zur Zusammenarbeit zwischen Literaturwissenschaftlern und Historikern aufruft.[56] Da für die Christina von Hane-Vita eine konkrete Umschreibung nicht nachgewiesen werden kann, scheint es angemessener von Retextualisierung zu sprechen.[57] Christinas deutsche Vita könnte in diesem Sinne als ein lokal-bezogenes Unternehmen verstanden werden, das sehr

---

53 François Dolbeau: Transformations des prologues hagiographiques, dues aux réécritures. In: L'hagiographie mérovingienne à travers des réécritures. Hrsg. von Monique Goullet/Martin Heinzelmann/Christiane Veyrard-Cosme (Beihefte der Francia 71). Ostfildern 2010, S. 103–124, hier S. 103. Siehe auch Williams-Krapp (2012), S. 263: »Hagiographie für die tägliche Tischlesung.«
54 Vgl. Herbers (2000), S. XII.
55 Im Kontext der karolingischen Renaissance betont Friederike Sauerwein: Religiöse Identität oder ›Heiliger Schein‹? Weibliche Lebensgestaltung und hagiographische Überlieferung am Beispiel der hl. Lioba. In: Hagiographie im Kontext. Wirkungsweisen und Möglichkeiten historischer Auswertung. Hrsg. von Dieter R. Bauer/Klaus Herbers (Beiträge zur Hagiographie 1). Stuttgart 2000, S. 46–57, hier S. 50, »das Bemühen [des Hagiographen] um bessere Versionen älterer, stilistisch unbeholfener Texte«.
56 Bei der methodischen Herangehensweise der sogenannten *réécriture* werden neue Versionen eines Textes (Hypertext) mit einem vorangehenden Text (Hypotext) verglichen, um anschließend die Veränderungen nach quantitativen, strukturellen oder linguistischen Gesichtspunkten zu bestimmen, vgl. Monique Goullet: Vers une typologie des réécritures hagiographiques, à partir de quelques exemples du Nord-Est de la France. Avec une édition synoptiquedes deux Vies de saint Èvre de Toul. In: La réécriture hagiographique dans l'occident médiéval. Transformations formelles et idéologiques. Hrsg. von Monique Goullet/Martin Heinzelmann. (Beihefte der Francia 58). Ostfildern 2003. S. 109–144, insbes. S. 110. So attraktiv ein solcher analytischer Ansatz auch erscheinen mag, durch den signifikante Bedeutungsverschiebungen eruiert werden sollen, so schwierig gestaltet sich seine Umsetzung bei einer Überlieferungssituation, wie sie im Christina von Hane-Fall vorliegt. Das Prinzip der *réécriture* erklärt allenfalls, dass es sich bei dem uns überlieferten Text um eine Version handelt, die aus einem gewissen Anlass entstanden ist und deswegen vorheriges Material umschrieb.
57 ›Retextualisierung‹ bietet sich auch deswegen an, weil das Konzept der *réécriture* im Kontext literarischer Adaptationen anders verwendet wird, vgl. Michael Stolz: Medieval Canonicity and Rewriting. A Case Study of the Signune-Figure in Wolfram's ›Parzival‹. In: Textual Scholarship and the Canon. Hrsg. von Hans Walter Gabler/Peter Robinson/Paulius V. Subačius (Variants 7). Amsterdam/New York 2008, S. 75–94, insbes. S. 77. Siehe auch Strohschneider (1999), S. 28, zum »Status des Textes [...] in der Relationalität von Textversionen«.

wahrscheinlich auf existierende ältere Vorlagen zurückgriff und solche für eine ordensinterne Rezeption neu auflegte.[58]

Eine Nähe zur Observanzbewegung lässt sich zwar nicht ausschließen, zumal wir es mit einem relativ späten Textzeugnis zu tun haben, aber verglichen mit den spätmittelalterlichen Schwesternbüchern der Dominikaner- und Franziskanerorden ist die Vita kaum reguliert bzw. politisiert: Reform wird weder explizit angesprochen noch dem Rezipienten nahegelegt.[59] Im Kontext der *devotio moderna* bewegten sich Viten in einem Spannungsfeld zwischen dem Interesse für mystische Lebensweisen und dem steigenden Argwohn gegenüber jeder Form von radikaler Spiritualität,[60] wobei diese zweite Welle der weiblichen Spiritualität eine erhöhte Tendenz an Visionen aufwies.[61] Für das Kloster Hane bei Bolanden ist historisch nachweisbar, dass es an der monastischen Reformbewegung des 12. Jahrhunderts teilnahm.[62] An der Reformbewegung des 15. Jahrhunderts war der Prämonstratenserorden mit dem speziellen Anliegen, die Klausur durchzusetzen, allgemein beteiligt.[63] Ruh sieht in der Vita Christinas von Hane ein Indiz dafür, wie verbreitet die *cura monialium* in eigenen Frauenklöstern als Aufgabe

---

[58] Ein solcher lokal-personaler Bezug tritt ab der karolingischen Zeit in der Vitenproduktion auf, welche im Spätmittelalter insgesamt stark zurückgeht. Kritisch zu bewerten ist Vollmanns (1997), Sp. 1751, Aussage, wonach die Viten heiliger Witwen, Nonnen, Seherinnen und Mystikerinnen zwischen dem 12. und 15. Jahrhundert unter dem Einfluss »germanischen Denkens« gestünden hätten. Nach einer Blüte weiblicher Hagiographie in der Merowingerzeit bedeutete dies eine erneute Welle des Interesses an Frauenfrömmigkeit, die zwischen 750–1150 abgeebbt sei.

[59] Zur Observanzfrömmigkeit siehe Werner Williams-Krapp: Frauenmystik und Ordensreform im 15. Jahrhundert. In: Literarische Interessenbildung im Mittelalter. DFG-Symposion 1991. Hrsg. von Joachim Heinzle (Germanistische Symposien, Berichtsbände 14). Stuttgart/Weimar 1993, S. 301–313, insbes. S. 303. Siehe auch Hamm (2011), S. 449–453, zur Normierung in Texten der *devotio moderna*.

[60] Zur steigenden Skepsis gegenüber dem Übernatürlichen insbesondere bei Frauen siehe Williams-Krapp (2012), S. 263–267. Siehe auch Amy Hollywood: The Soul as Virgin Wife. Mechthild of Magdeburg, Marguerite Porete, and Meister Eckhart, Notre Dame (Studies in Spirituality and Theology 1). London 1995, S. 38: »Concerned particularly with keeping control over women's religious life through enclosure and supervision, these acts culminate in an increasing ›specularization‹ of their spirituality.«

[61] Vgl. Wybren Scheepsma: Check and Double-check. An Unknown Vision Cycle by a Religious Woman from the Low Countries. In: The Voice of Silence. Women's Literacy in a Men's Church. Hrsg. von Thérèse de Hemptinne/María Eugenia Góngora (Medieval Church Studies 9). Turnhout 2004, S. 207–221, insbes. S. 208.

[62] Vgl. Kleinjung (2001), S. 32.

[63] Vgl. Bruno Krings: Die Prämonstratenser und ihr weiblicher Zweig. In: Studien zum Prämonstratenserorden. Hrsg. von Irene Crusius/Lemut Flachenecker (Studien zur Germania Sacra 25). Göttingen 2003, S. 75–105, insbes. S. 101.

des Dominikanerordens wahrgenommen wurde, wobei er von der Lebenszeit der Prämonstratensernonne, d.h. vom späten 13. Jahrhundert, ausgeht.[64] Ganz allgemein kann unter der Annahme, dass der spätmittelalterliche Text in einer geistlichen Gemeinschaft entstanden und rezipiert worden ist, in der bevorzugt »mystische Bedürfnisse, Erfahrungen, Reflexionen und Anleitungen« Teil eines reformbewussten Lebens waren,[65] die Vita als Teil einer »mystischen Kultur« nach der Definition Thom Mertens' verstanden werden.[66] In dem mystischen Klima des Spätmittelalters »[finden jetzt] [a]uch kultmäßig eher unbedeutende Heilige im Gegensatz zum Zeitalter der Verslegende in breitem Umfang Berücksichtigung«, auch wenn dies die Heiligen anderer Orden weitaus weniger betrifft als die der Franziskaner und Dominikaner.[67]

Dass nicht jede Vita die Approbation des Heiligen als eine *causa scribendi* hatte, zeigen insbesondere die mittelalterlichen Viten der Prämonstratenser. Der Orden strebte in der Regel keine Kanonisation seiner Mitglieder an, obwohl »einige Prämonstratenser wie Heilige verehrt wurden«.[68] Da der Kanonisationsprozess ohnehin erst spät reguliert wurde, wäre es zudem anachronistisch, die mittelalterlichen Lebens- und Wunderberichte daran zu messen. Die Zusammenstellungen der Erzählungen waren »wohl meist für die unmittelbare Nachbarschaft« bestimmt.[69]

Möchte man einen Schritt weiter gehen, so könnte Christinas Vita als der Versuch angesehen werden, nicht allein ihre Sonderstellung in ihrem Konvent hervorzuheben, sondern auch die Rolle des Konvents zu unterstreichen und zwar im Sinne einer Klosterhistoriographie, wie sie etwa dem dominikanischen Ordenschronisten Johannes Meyer um die Mitte des 15. Jahrhunderts bei der Rezeption der populären Schwesternbücher vorschwebte. Ihm ging es nicht »nur um eine Revitalisierung der Gattung, sondern zugleich um deren Domestizie-

---

64 Vgl. Ruh (1993), S. 121.

65 Vgl. Hamm (2011), S. 451.

66 Vgl. Hamm (2011), S. 451, und Thom Mertens: Mystieke cultuur en literatuur in de Late Middeleeuwen. In: Grote lijnen. Syntheses over Middelnederlandse letterkunde Rijksuniversiteit Te Leiden. Hrsg. von Frits van Oostrom (Nederlandse literatuur en cultuur in de middeleeuwen 11). Amsterdam 1995, S. 117–135.

67 Werner Williams-Krapp: Deutschsprachige Hagiographie von ca. 1350 bis ca. 1550. In: Hagiographies. Histoire internationale de la littérature hagiographique, latine et vernaculaire, en Occident, des origines á 1550. Hrsg. von Guy Philippart (Corpus Christianorum Hagiographies 1). Turnhout 1994, S. 267–288, hier S. 269.

68 Kisseler (2003), S. 71.

69 Kisseler (2003), S. 71.

rung«, d.h. die Texte sollten nicht unreflektiert rezipiert werden.[70] Ein derartiger Eingriff lässt sich an der Christina von Hane-Vita nicht nachweisen. Ein ordensstrategisches Vorgehen ist in ihrem Fall erst für die zweite Hälfte des 17. Jahrhunderts nachweisbar, als sogar die Information ihrer Konventszugehörigkeit manipuliert wurde, womöglich weil ihre Promotion einem noch existierenden Kloster angesichts sinkender Mitgliederzahlen zu Gute kommen sollte.[71] Mit der Übertragung ihrer moselfränkischen Vita ins Flämische liegt hingegen eine hagiographische *réécriture* vor. Dadurch, dass zwischen der spätmittelalterlichen Textabschrift und ihrer frühneuzeitlichen Adaptation ein gewisser zeitlicher Abstand herrscht, muss diese flämische Rezeption in ihren respektiven historischen Kontext gesetzt werden. Im nachtridentinischen Europa hatte sich der mystische Trend dahin verschoben, approbierten Mystikerinnen der Gegenreformation eine prophetisch-politische Dimension zuzusprechen – ein Charakteristikum, das die Vita der Christina von Hane kaum vorweisen kann. Nur eine einzige prophetische Vision hat ihre Vita anzubieten, welche daher in der frühneuzeitlichen Bearbeitung umso stärker betont wird.[72] Andererseits tritt durch die starke Kürzung der Vita im Zuge der Übertragung ins Flämische die mystische Vereinigung Christinas mit ihrem Bräutigam in den Hintergrund. In der flämischen Ausgabe wird die mystische Vereinigung nicht mehr als Geschehen narrativ wiedergegeben, sondern durch die »wahrscheinliche Angleichung« von Braut und Bräutigam lediglich als Möglichkeit in Aussicht gestellt: *Het is nochtans waerschijnelijck dat sy ghelijck wierdt aenhaeren Bruydegom* (Craywinckel, ›Het leven vande salighe maghet Christina‹ XV, 747).[73] Offenbar eignete sich das brautmystische Material nicht für die entsprechende Heiligenkonzeption, die sonst in dem klosterhistoriographischen Kompendium Craywinckels vorzufinden ist.

Während sich die Forschungsdiskussionen zu mystischen Texten immer wieder um traditionelle Formen und theologisch relevante Inhalte drehen, scheint die Frage nach der Gattung für hagiographische Texte nur zweitrangig. Jedoch können in beiden Diskussionsbereichen Spannungsverhältnisse zwischen Innen und Außen, Körperlichkeit und Spiritualität, Geheimnis und Evidenz festgestellt werden. Anstatt diese Spannungen aufzulösen, etwa indem Kategorisierungen vorgenommen werden, sollen genau diese Spannungen als Bestandteile einer mystischen Vita unterstrichen werden.

---

70 Williams-Krapp (2012), S. 267. Siehe auch ders. (1993), S. 312.

71 Dazu ausführlich Kirakosian (2014b). Siehe auch Backmund (1972), S. 90; Mittermaier (1960), S. 96; Krings (2009), S. 188–192.

72 Vgl. Kirakosian (2014b), S. 387.

73 Die Stellennachweise geben Kapitel- und Seitenzahlen an.

2.1.3 Mystische Vita

In der Vita der Christina von Hane ist von Beginn an ersichtlich, dass ein brautmystischer Lebensweg entworfen wird, bei dem die Beziehung der Seele zu Gott im Vordergrund steht.[74] Williams-Krapp formuliert, dass »[v]or allem hagiographische Modelle mit ihrem charakteristischen Wahrheitsverständnis bestens geeignet [erschienen], die Biographien von ›mystischen‹ Begnadeten zu gestalten«.[75] Dass mystische Texte oft auch als hagiographische Texte verstanden wurden, ist keine neue Einsicht, doch wurde bisher der terminologische Gebrauch kaum hinterfragt. Ringler und in Anlehnung an ihn Ruhrberg und andere arbeiten mit dem Terminus »Gnadenvita« oder »Gnaden-Leben«, welcher die Innen- und Seelenwelt als Ort der Handlung und daher die »persönlichen Gnadenerfahrungen« betont.[76] Für Ringler sind die Ebenen der Textentstehung oder auch die »Bearbeitungsschritte« von der *unio* zur Vita als Gattungsindikatoren zu bewerten.[77] Mit dem Begriff der Gnadenvita ordnet er die entsprechenden mystischen Texte der Hagiographie zu. Offen bleibt, wie diese Zuteilung gerechtfertigt wird und in welchem Verhältnis die mystischen Texte zum traditionellen Vitencorpus stehen.[78]

Peters konstatiert, dass traditionelle Viten »als programmatische Entwürfe neuer Ausdrucksformen weiblicher Religiosität für eine literaturhistorische Analyse und Einordnung [...] von herausragender Bedeutung« seien.[79] Emmelius meint, die Vita erzähltheoretisch vom Offenbarungstext absetzen zu können: »Die retrospektiv konzipierte Vita hat Anfang, Mitte und Ende. Sie ist eine ›Erzählung‹, deren Zielsetzung – hier: das Evidentwerden von Heiligkeit – von vornherein feststeht.«[80] Diese Feststellung trifft aber auch auf andere hagiographische Formen wie die der Legende zu. Selbst in der Legende kann es ein Spiel mit der

---

74 Vgl.: *Eyne jonffrauwe na Christum yrem bruytgam ist sye genant Christina, die got, vnsere herre, yme selber vßerwilt hait zo eyner bruyt.* (CvH 1, 6 f.)

75 Williams-Krapp (2008), S. 266.

76 Ringler (1985), S. 188. Siehe auch Ruhrberg (1995), S. 163; Emmelius (2008), S. 311; Thali (2003).

77 Vgl. Ringler (1985), S. 187–191. So erneut Emmelius (2008), S. 310 f.

78 Für einen differenzierteren Umgang mit Ringlers Typus des Gnaden-Lebens spricht sich bereits Bürkle (1999), S. 294, aus.

79 Peters (1988), S. 38.

80 Emmelius (2008), S. 311. Überdies operiert Emmelius in Anlehnung an Ringler (1980), S. 339 f., mit dem Begriff des Gnaden-Lebens, der streng genommen hinter Peters zurückfällt. Peters (1986), S. 418, warnte davor, sich auf eine zwischen 1300 und 1360 entstandene »Gattung« der Gnaden-Leben zu fixieren, die »die verschiedensten Texte aus ihren engen literarischen Relationen zu anderen literarischen Formen reißen [würde]«.

Retrospektive geben (z. B. unerwartete Konversion), während in vielen mystischen Viten Heilsgewissheit nicht unbedingt von vornherein besteht. Texte, die das Visionäre (z. B. Offenbarungstexte) oder das Wunderhafte (z. B. Legenden) zum Zentrum haben, weisen durchaus die narrative Triade von Anfang, Mitte und Ende auf und können zudem ebenfalls aus retrospektiver Sicht erzählt werden.[81] In Visionstexten handelt es sich daher oft um eine inszenierte Gegenwart, die letztlich einem retrospektiven Rahmen verhaftet bleibt. Hagiographisches Erzählen – das betrifft also nicht allein die Vita –, mit Strohschneider gesprochen, »verhält sich stets retrospektiv«.[82]

Historische und textwissenschaftliche Zugänge zur Hagiographie erweisen sich als hilfreich bei der Beschäftigung mit mystischen Viten.[83] Dabei scheint der Begriff der »hagiographischen Mystik« zunächst dienlich,[84] doch hat man es oft mit mehr als einer einfachen »hagiographische[n] Stilisierung« zu tun, die als »notwendiger Legitimationsrahmen« dient.[85] Die Formen eines inneren und äußeren Heiligenlebens, wie sie von Ringler charakterisiert werden, schließen sich in der mystischen Vita nicht gegenseitig aus: »So ist die Heiligkeit in der Heiligenlegende wesentlich gerade dadurch charakterisiert, daß sie offenkundig ist; im ›Gnaden-Leben‹ dagegen ist sie wesentlich eine verborgene und ›heimliche‹ (im mhd. Wortsinn).«[86] Die Beschäftigung mit der Christina von Hane-Vita zeigt indes, dass beide Formen von Heiligkeitsausweis miteinander verbunden sind.

Die Darstellung einer Unmittelbarkeit der *unio mystica* ist immer narrativ gebunden, denn die Sprache der Mystik versucht »retrospektiv zu fassen, was der liebenden Seele geschehen ist, denn in der Unio selbst kann sie nicht sprechen«.[87] Epische Elemente verschaffen der mystischen Vita gleichzeitig Anspruch auf »die Zeitlosigkeit ewiger Transzendenz«.[88] Der Einbezug hagiographischer Strategien ist aber von der Bedingung der Heiligsprechung zu trennen. So sollte es nicht

---

81 Vgl. Susanne Köbele: Die Illusion der ›einfachen Form‹. Über das ästhetische und religiöse Risiko der Legende. In: PBB 134 (2012), S. 365–404, insbes. S. 377.

82 Strohschneider (2014), S. 170–190, hier S. 178.

83 Vgl. Ruhrberg (1995), S. 159–167, zur Verschränkung von Mystik und Hagiographie.

84 Vgl. die Apostrophierung »hagiographisch-frauenmystischer Literatur« bei Peters (1988), S. 189.

85 Köbele (1993b), S. 26.

86 Ringler (1980), S. 339 f.

87 Walter Haug: Gotteserfahrung und Du-Begegnung. Korrespondenzen in der Geschichte der Mystik und der Liebeslyrik. In: Geistliches in weltlicher und Weltliches in geistlicher Literatur des Mittelalters. Hrsg. von Christoph Huber / Burghart Wachinger / Hans-Joachim Ziegeler. Tübingen 2000, S. 195–212, hier S. 203.

88 Vgl. Strohschneider (2014), S. 178: »Bibelepik und Legende erzählen, was sie als unerzählbar konstituieren. Sie setzen die Zeitlichkeit vergangener Immanenz (als *Geschichte* des Heiligen)

verwundern, dass kaum eine deutsche Mystikerin in ein allgemeines Legendar aufgenommen wurde, und nur eine einzige je selig gesprochen wurde, und dies erst 600 Jahre nach ihrem Tod.[89] Die Viten deutscher Mystikerinnen wurden stattdessen in gesonderten oder in mystischen Sammelhandschriften tradiert.[90] Warum mystische Viten nicht im Verbund mit erfolgreichen, im Sinne von kirchlich approbierten Heiligengeschichten überliefert werden, mag an dem Fehlen posthumer Wunder und damit an der Abwesenheit eines entsprechenden Heiligenkults liegen. Dennoch darf der didaktische Gemeinschaftsbezug mystischer Viten nicht unterschätzt werden, da es in ihnen selten allein um »persönliche Gnadenerfahrungen« (Siegfried Ringler) geht. In mystischen Viten sind Bemühungen um Externalität und fast schon sinnlicher Greifbarkeit zu beobachten, und zwar insbesondere dann, wenn man vom Text als Instrument der Heilsvergewisserung ausgeht. Die Behandlung von Wundern als externalisierte Zeichen von Heiligkeit, von der Materialität der Überlieferung und vom Beichtvater als Hagiographen zeigen, dass in mystischen Viten des 13. bis 15. Jahrhunderts eine »innerliche Heiligkeit«[91] mit externalisierten Formen von Heilsgewissheit kombiniert wird, auch wenn sie nicht im Kontext konkreter Heiligsprechungsverfahren stehen.

Externalisierte Zeichen von Heiligkeit

Wunder sind »in deutschen Mystikerinnenviten kaum anzutreffen«, wie Williams-Krapp vermerkt.[92] Die andauernde göttliche Präsenz am Grabe der Heiligen, am prominentesten in Form von Wunderereignissen, ist nur ein Beispiel für die Grundlegung eines Kultes. Wie auch bei anderen Mystikern gibt es keine

---

und die Zeitlosigkeit ewiger Transzendenz (als Geschichte des *Heiligen*) in eins.« (Hervorhebungen im Original)

89 Die Seligsprechung Dorotheas von Montau erging im Jahre 1976. Hildegard von Bingen wurde im Jahre 2012 zur Kirchenlehrerin erhoben. Eine verkürzte Version des deutschsprachigen ›botten der götlichen miltekeit‹, der auf den ›Legatus divinae pietatis‹ mit Gertrud von Helfta im Mittelpunkt zurückgeht, wird im 15. Jahrhundert in süddeutsche Legendare aufgenommen. Zur Entstehung der sogenannten Trutta-Legende im Nürnberger Raum siehe Werner Williams-Krapp: Die deutschen und niederländischen Legendare des Mittelalters. Studien zu ihrer Überlieferungs-, Text- und Wirkungsgeschichte (Texte und Textgeschichte 20). Tübingen 1986, S. 259, Anm. 15 und S. 301. Dahingegen verortet Klaus Grubmüller: Gertrud von Helfta. In: ²VL 3 (1981), Sp. 7–10, insbes. Sp. 9, die Entstehung der Trutta-Legende im Wiener Raum. Wahrscheinlicher ist aber die Entstehung in Nürnberg.

90 Vgl. Williams-Krapp (2008), S. 269 f.

91 Ruhrberg (1995), S. 163.

92 Williams-Krapp (2008), S. 276.

entsprechenden Quellen über einen posthumen Christina von Hane-Kult. Doch auch in der Vita, die sich auf Christinas Lebenszeit beschränkt, scheinen für die Nachwelt approbierbare Wunder keine große Rolle zu spielen. Zu fragen ist also, ob das Vorhandensein oder Fehlen von Wunderberichten als Differenzkriterium zwischen Hagiographie und mystischer Vita taugt. Hollywood etwa betrachtet eine öffentliche, externe Sichtbarkeit der Heiligkeit als zentrales gattungstechnisches Merkmal hagiographischer Texte. In mystischen Texten dagegen gehe es zwar ursprünglich um eine internalisierte Heiligkeit, doch um Ansprüche auf Heiligmäßigkeit erheben zu können, würden Hagiographen die Geschichten insbesondere weiblicher Personen mit äußeren Körperaspekten versehen, damit das Innere und Unsagbare nachvollziehbar würde.[93] Es sei dies daher eine explizit hagiographische Vorgehensweise. Ungeklärt bleibt dabei, inwiefern sich am Körper der Heiligenfigur auftretende wundersame Phänomene, wie etwa Stigmata, von anderen Zeichen, z.B. von der Heiligenfigur bewirkte Wunder, unterscheiden. Hollywood erklärt die Darstellungsverschiebung eines inneren Mystischen zu einem äußeren Körperlichen aus historischer Sicht:

> While there is evidence that women hagiographers submit to genre expectations in the thirteenth century, bodily asceticism and paramystical phenomena do not begin to emerge in women's mystical writings until the fourteenth century, when, coincidentally, persecution of beguines and other religious women in northern Europe was given new impetus by the decrees of the Council of Venice. [...] Before this period, women's mystical treatises found their primary form of legitimation in the depiction of visionary experience and the erotic language of the Song of Songs, both of which lend themselves to, without enacting, the movement toward externalization and somatization [...].[94]

Hollywoods Beobachtung körperbetonter Aspekte weiblicher Religiosität kann auf weit vor das 14. Jahrhundert zurückreichende Texttraditionen somatischer Heiligkeit ausgeweitet werden.[95] Das politische Gewicht in der Entwicklung hagiographischer Tendenzen ist sicherlich, wie Hollywood ganz richtig betont, besonders im ausgehenden Mittelalter nicht zu unterschätzen. Das illustriert

---

93 Vgl. Hollywood (1995), S. 35–37.
94 Hollywood (1995), S. 38.
95 Vgl. Stephen J. Davis: Crossed Texts, Crossed Sex. Intertextuality and Gender in Early Christian Legends of Holy Women Disguised as Men. In: Journal of Early Christian Studies 10 (2002), S. 1–36, für das Körper- und Geschlechterbewusstsein bei frühchristlichen weiblichen Heiligen. Siehe auch Walter Haug: Die Wahrheit der Fiktion. Studien zur weltlichen und geistlichen Literatur des Mittelalters und der frühen Neuzeit. Tübingen 2003, S. 492, in seiner differenzierten Positionierung der *unio* als »metaphorische Körperlichkeit« wie bei Mechthild von Magdeburg und der *unio* »über die Dialektik von Wort und Körper« wie bei Elsbeth von Oye.

die u.a. von Jean Gerson im Kontext des Kanonisationsprozesses Birgittas von Schweden geforderte Unterscheidung der Geister.[96] Körperbetontheit und externalisierte Zeichen von Heiligkeit gehen einer ansteigenden Skepsis gegenüber jeglichen Formen weiblicher Spiritualität voraus. So befasst sich Ruhrberg mit einer somatischen Mystik am Beispiel Christinas von Stommeln, deren Vita noch zu Lebzeiten im 13. Jahrhundert verfasst wurde.[97] Auch die Lebensbeschreibungen anderer Mystikerinnen, darunter Angela von Foligno, Mechthild von Magdeburg, Mechthild von Hackeborn, Gertrud von Helfta und Agnes Blannbekin, weisen Tendenzen somatischer Erscheinungen auf, die nur bedingt als Reaktionen auf theologische und scholastische Debatten zu interpretieren sind.[98]

---

96 Vgl. Anna Fredrikkson Adman: An Heretical Saint? The Birgittine Case and Heymericus de Campo at the Council of Basel. In: University, Council, City. Intellectual Culture on the Rhine, 1300–1550. Acts of the XIIth International Colloquium of the Société Internationale pour l'Étude de la Philosophie Médiévale. Freiburg im Breisgau, 27–29 October 2004. Hrsg. von Laurent Cesalli/Nadja Germann/ Maarten J. F. M. Hoenen (Rencontres de philosophie médiévale 13). Turnhout 2007, S. 277–289.

97 Vgl. Ruhrberg (1995), S. 11 f.

98 Vgl. die folgenden Textstellen: Mechthild von Magdeburg: ›Das fließende Licht der Gottheit‹. Nach der Einsiedler Handschrift in kritischem Vergleich mit der gesamten Überlieferung. Hrsg. von Hans Neumann (MTU 100–101). 2 Bde. München 1990–1993, Bd. 1 (1990): Text, besorgt von Gisela Vollmann-Profe, I 5; I 7 (Die Stellennachweise geben Buch- und Kapitelzahlen an; gegebenenfalls werden auch die Zeilenzahlen referiert.); Mechthild von Hackeborn: ›Liber specialis gratiae‹. In: Revelationes Gertrudinæ ac Mechtildianæ II. Sanctæ Mechthildis virginis ordinis sancti Benedicti Liber specialis gratiæ, accedit sororis Mechthildis ejusdem ordinis Lux divinitatis. Opus ad codicum fidem nunc primum integre editum Solesmensium O. S. B. monachorum cura et opera. Paris 1877, S. 1–421, hier II 26, 168–171 (Die Stellennachweise geben Buch-, Kapitel- und Seitenzahlen an.); Gertrud von Helfta: ›Legatus divinae pietatis‹ III. In: Gertrude d'Helfta. Œuvres spirituelles III. Hrsg. von Pierre Doyère (Sources chrétiennes. Série des textes monastiques d'Occident 27). Paris 1968, 32, 2, 168 (Die Stellennachweise geben Kapitel-, Paragraph- und Seitenzahlen an.); von Agnes Blannbekin heißt es, dass sie nach der Ekstase körperlich geschwächt sei, vgl. ›Leben und Offenbarungen der Wiener Begine Agnes Blannbekin‹. Hrsg. von Peter Dinzelbacher/Renate Vogeler (Göppinger Arbeiten zur Germanistik 419). Göppingen 1994, 106, 7–10. (Die Stellennachweise geben Kapitelzahlen an; gegebenenfalls werden auch die Zeilenzahlen referiert.) Siehe auch die körperliche Andacht und das Fasten in Angela von Foligno: ›Memoriale‹. In: Il libro della Beata Angela da Foligno. Edizione critica. Hrsg. von Ludger Thier/Abele Calufetti (Spicilegium Bonaventurianum 25). Grottaferrata 1985, S. 125–401, insbes. I, 248–255 (Die Stellennachweise geben Kapitel- und Zeilenzahlen an.), und die körperliche Schwachheit bei einer ausgeprägten Visionstätigkeit in Angela von Foligno: ›Instructiones‹. In: Il libro della Beata Angela da Foligno. Edizione critica. Hrsg. von Ludger Thier/Abele Calufetti (Spicilegium Bonaventurianum 25). Grottaferrata 1985, S. 403–737, insbes. 21, 597 f. (Die Stellennachweise geben Instructionummern und Seitenzahlen an.)

Gerade die asketische Lebensweise, die von Hollywood explizit als spätmittelalterliche Zutat eingeschränkt wird, findet ihre Personifizierung in den
frühchristlichen Heiligen, den Einsiedlern und Wüstenvätern, deren hagiographische Berichte weiterhin tradiert und rezipiert wurden. In der Christina von
Hane-Vita nimmt Askese ihren Platz im Kontext des Lasterkatalogs ein: So hat
die Episode, in der Christina sich zur Bekämpfung sexuellen Verlangens auf glü-
hende Kohlen setzt, eine frühe Motivparallele in der merowingischen Heiligenfigur Radegunds.[99] Ein heilig-asketisches Leben ist stets körperbetont, gerade
weil es den Körper zu verneinen sucht.[100] Bereits die ersten Heiligen der frühen
Kirche übten radikales Fasten, und Nahrungsverweigerung ist auch im Hochmittelalter weiterhin ein umstrittenes Thema, wie kritische Äußerungen Hildegards
von Bingen nahelegen. Diese sprach sich im Gegensatz zu ihrer Lehrmeisterin
Jutta von Sponheim für eine mäßige, auf die Gesundheit Rücksicht nehmende
Enthaltsamkeit (*rationabilis abstinentia*) aus.[101] Christinas von Hane mit dem
Verzicht auf Nahrungsaufnahme einhergehender Kampf gegen die Völlerei führt
zum Bewusstseinsverlust: *Sie versmaet sich selber also gar, daz si vnder willen
van rechter cranckeit yn amacht fiel vber der taiffelen.* (CvH 14, 10 f.)[102] Dass die
Auswirkungen einer extremen Lebenspraxis eine zentrale Bedeutung für die
Spiritualität von Frauen einnahmen, hat bereits Bynum ausführlich gezeigt.[103]
Wunder- und Askesemotive sind daher weniger auf kirchenpolitisch bedingte
Faktoren zurückzuführen. Sie sind wiederkehrende Topoi eines nach wie vor
aktiven Repertoires hagiographischen Schreibens, das sich im Falle einer mys-

---

99 Vgl. Kirakosian (2017a).

100 Zur sexuellen Entsagung, Askese und Körperlichkeit im frühen Christentum siehe Peter
Brown: Body and Society. Men, Women, and Sexual Renunciation in Early Christianity. New York
2008 (Originalausgabe New York 1988).

101 Zum moderaten asketischen Leben nach Hildegard von Bingen siehe Franz Josef Felten:
›Noui esse uolunt... deserentes bene contritam uiam...‹. Hildegard von Bingen und Reformbewegungen im religiösen Leben ihrer Zeit. In: Im Angesicht Gottes sucht der Mensch sich selbst.
Hildegard von Bingen (1098–1179). Hrsg. von Rainer Berndt. Berlin 2001, S. 27–86, insbes. S. 58 f.
und S. 72 f.

102 Vgl. dazu Margareta Ebner: *und lag als ich tod wär, daz ich niht auzze noch trank* (›Offenbarungen der Margaretha Ebner‹. In: Margaretha Ebner und Heinrich von Nördlingen. Ein Beitrag zur Geschichte der deutschen Mystik. Hrsg. von Philipp Strauch. Amsterdam 1966, S. 1–166
[Nachdruck der Orignalausgabe Freiburg i. Br./Tübingen 1882], hier 3, 16 [Die Stellennachweise
geben Seiten- und Zeilenzahlen an.]). Siehe auch Christinas Kampf gegen *invidia* und *avaritia*,
vgl. CvH 10.

103 Vgl. Bynum (1987).

tischen Vita nicht von der Internalisierung der Begegnung mit dem Göttlichen trennen lässt.[104]

Wie eingangs dargelegt, lassen sich individuelle Texte selten kategorischen Modellen zuweisen. In der Christina von Hane-Vita scheinen approbierbare oder posthume Wunder völlig zu fehlen. Trotzdem weist Christinas als spirituell vorbildlich gezeichnetes Leben Momente auf, in denen ›wundersame Gnadenauszeichnungen‹ nachweisbar erscheinen. Dazu gehören neben der Augenzeugenschaft bei körperlichen Extremzuständen die sich im Nachhinein bewahrheitende prophetische Rede sowie die visionäre Identifizierung von Klosterreliquien.[105] Allerdings ist zu beobachten, dass der Text den Begriff *wunder/wonder* anders verwendet, als dies der heutige Sprachgebrauch annehmen lässt: Meistens wird *wonder* als superlativer Zustand göttlicher Qualitäten oder als relativ bedeutungsarme Hyperbel gebraucht.[106] An anderer Stelle wird *wonder* bedeutungsträchtiger, weil potenziell offener gebraucht; so etwa, wenn ein Wunderbericht angekündigt wird: *dan der heilge geist yn yre wyrcket durch nakomen wonder wunderliche dynge* (CvH 15, 5 f.). Weniger abstrakt, aber umso greifbarer werden diese Wunderwerke, wenn Christinas Seele als die Freude Gottes und der Seelen im Fegefeuer umschrieben wird: *Jre gesmacke hait got erfrauwet yn dem hemel vnd auch die engel vnd alle heilgen, die sunder yn der erden vnd die lyeben selen yn dem fegefůr, alstu noch hoiren wyrst groißen wonder her nache.* (CvH 30, 16–18) Die mehrfache Erlösung der Seelen durch Christina wird von der Erzählerstimme als etwas Erstaunliches angekündigt und als Wundersames interpretiert. Aus der

---

104 Vgl. Ruhrberg (1995), S. 159: »Ab dem 12. und verstärkt im 13. Jahrhundert erscheinen in der Hagiographie auch die mystischen Tendenzen und Phänomene, die ganz allgemein die Spiritualität der Zeit prägten.«

105 Vgl. CvH 32, 31–36. Auch in Margareta Ebners Fall fungieren die Mitschwestern als Zeuginnen für Todesqualen, vgl. ›Offenbarungen der Margaretha Ebner‹ 4, 3–5.

106 So z.B. in CvH 56, 12 und CvH 38, 2. Allein schon Christinas Existenz ist in diesem Sinne ein ›Wunder‹ der Gnade und der göttlichen Liebe: *Dan wairhaifftenclichen, wer dyße bůche vberleßet vnd gedencket daz wonder der genaden vnd der gotlicher lyebden, die got an dyeßer reyner jonffrauwen, syner vßerwilter bruyt Christinen, gedayn hait, der mache woil sprechen, das der selich sy geboren, den got dar zo vß erwilte hait, daz er der selicher creatuer denen sultde.* (CvH 39, 14–18) Auch die guten Werke, die Christina im Kampf gegen den Hass als Todsünde durch den Heiligen Geist wirkt, sind weniger als Wunder denn als erstaunliche Taten beschrieben, vgl.: *Dyeße vndogent des haißes, dar vß sprynget der nyt. Dem wiederstontde sie gar kreifftlichen vnd gar wyßelichen, dan der heilge geist yn yre wyrcket durch nakomen wonder wunderliche dynge.* (CvH 15, 2–6) Hier ist *wunderlîche* im Sinne von ›erstaunlich‹ verwendet, vgl. Matthias Lexer: Mittelhochdeutsches Handwörterbuch. Zugleich als Supplement und alphabetischer Index zum Mittelhochdeutschen Wörterbuche von Benecke-Müller-Zarncke. Nachdruck der Ausgabe Leipzig 1872–1878 mit einer Einleitung von Kurt Gärtner. 3 Bde. Stuttgart 1992, Bd. 3, Sp. 991.

Untersuchung der Fürbitten für die Fegefeuerseelen in Mechthilds von Magdeburg ›Fließendes Licht der Gottheit‹ schlussfolgert Suerbaum, dass der Mystikerin die »Gewissheit der Wirkmächtigkeit, die sonst nur Heiligen nach ihrem Tode
zukommt«, zufalle.[107] Die Bestätigung eines Wunders, das die Lossprechung
der Seelen aus dem Fegefeuer betrifft, ist aber ins Jenseits entrückt.[108] Eine Ausnahme dazu bildet in der Christina von Hane-Vita die Fürbitte für einen nicht
näher beschriebenen Ordensbruder namens Jacob, dessen Buße im Fegefeuer als
Folge ihres Gebets beendet wird, wie Christina in einer Vision von göttlicher Seite
bestätigt wird.[109] Zwar scheinen posthume Wunder nicht zentral, da weniger das
Nachleben als die Lebenszeit der Mystikerin im Mittelpunkt steht. Die wiederholte Bestärkung von wundersamen Geschehnissen und Zuständen zeigt jedoch,
dass ein Bemühen um externalisierte Zeichen von Heiligkeit besteht. Solche
Bestärkungen sind Teil einer Autorisierungsstrategie für eine an sich unverfüg-
bare Heiligkeit. Die lateinische Lebensbeschreibung eines Heiligen oder seit dem
ersten Jahrtausend eines zur Kanonisierung empfohlenen heiligmäßigen Menschen verfolge laut Vollmann die theologische Intention der Glaubensversiche-
rung und des Nachweises für die göttliche Präsenz auf Erden.[110] Dies ist auch
in mystischen Heiligenviten aus dem volkssprachigen Bereich wesentlich, weil
auf diese Weise das als unsagbar Dargestellte in berichtbare Zeichen verkörpert
wird. Ein transzendenter Anspruch wird so in die Präsenz körperlicher Imma-

---

107 Almut Suerbaum: Dialogische Identitätskonzeption bei Mechthild von Magdeburg. In: Dialoge. Sprachliche Kommunikation in und zwischen Texten im deutschen Mittelalter. Hamburger
Colloquium 1999. Hrsg. von Nikolaus Henkel/Martin H. Jones/Nigel F. Palmer Tübingen 2003,
S. 239–255, hier S. 252.
108 Obwohl die erfolgreichen Bemühungen Christinas um die Fegefeuerseelen nicht als Wunder gezählt werden können, scheint sich Christinas Heiligmäßigkeit darin ganz besonders zu
äußern, vgl.: *vnd das du den anderen schenckest van dyeßem borne yn dyeßer wyße* (CvH 84, 4 f.).
Siehe auch Maria E. Müller: Die heilige Margarete, der Teufel und André Jolles. In: Sprechen mit
Gott. Redeszenen in mittelalterlicher Bibeldichtung und Legende. Hrsg. von Nine Miedema/An-
gela Schrott/Monika Unzeitig (Historische Dialogforschung 2). Berlin 2012, S. 127–144, hier
S. 135, zu Margarete-Legenden: »Den Fürbittgebeten der Figur kommt Vorbildfunktion zu für die
kultische Verehrung der Heiligen [...].« – In der Prominenz des Fegefeuerfürbittmotivs steht
Christina von Hane Adelheid Langmann nah, vgl. ›Die Offenbarungen der Adelheid Langmann‹.
Klosterfrau zu Engelthal. Hrsg. von Philipp Strauch (Quellen und Forschungen zur Sprach- und
Kulturgeschichte der Germanischen Völker 26). Straßburg 1878, 5, 4 f.; 8, 20 f.; 12, 23–25; 17, 11 f.;
25, 22–28; 29, 19; 35, 2 f.; 39, 24. (Die Stellennachweise geben Seiten- und Zeilenzahlen an.)
109 Vgl.: *Sie hait gehoirt syn soiße stymme sprechenden yn yrem geist myt dyeßen wortten: [...]
Dru dusent selen myt broder Jacobs sele erloißen ich yn dyeßer nacht vß dem fegefuer vmb dyne
lyebde. Die selben sullent noch cccl jaire yn dem fegefuer syn gewest. Die lyebde hait sy dar vß
erloist.* (CvH 57, 3–10)
110 Vgl. Vollmann (1997), Sp. 1751.

nenz übersetzt. Vergewisserungsversuche von Heiligkeit setzen also weniger bei Sprache als bei deren Materialisierung an. Diese kommt als Immanenz in verschriftlichter Form vor. Daher wird hier die Materialität der Textlichkeit als ein fundamentales Element der mystischen Vita angesehen.

Materialität der Textlichkeit

Mit dem Aufkommen der Material Philology in den 1990ern ist der Ruf nach der Erfassung der ›materiellen Verkörperung der Texte‹ immer lauter geworden.[111] Die Materialität der Schrift weist auf die körperbetonten »Interaktionssysteme« vormoderner Texte hin, die im Gegensatz zur »körperabstrakten Kommunikation« der Neuzeit eine »hohe[ ] Partizipativität der Teilnehmer« bedingte und dabei auch »Sprechsituationen« privilegierte, wie Strohschneider hervorhebt.[112] Schrift in der Vormoderne funktioniere »immer auch als Medium von Nahkommunikation und Teilhabe«.[113] Diese nach Strohschneider »wichtige medienanthropologische Einsicht der jüngeren Mediävistik«[114] zeigt sich am Beispiel des mittelalterlichen Gebrauchs des Psalters, wo der Kontakt mit Schriftlichkeit »eine besondere Eigenständigkeit bewahrt«, wie Stolz erörert.[115] Bawden, die sich mit den »Praktiken der Gestaltung und Wahrnehmung von medial-materiellen Zwischenräumen im Mittelalter« beschäftigt,[116] konstatiert im Hinblick auf den Umgang mit Büchern, dass die Bildkünstler »[d]ie Gebrauchsdimension des Buches, das Umblättern [...] genutzt« hätten, um ihre theologische Botschaft zu unterstreichen.[117] Medial-materielle Strategien sind an der Schnittstelle zwischen Handschrift und Text anzusiedeln. So werden in der Christina von Hane-Vita Sin-

---

[111] Die Diskussion wurde grundlegend angefacht von einer Sonderausgabe der Zeitschrift *Speculum* im Jahre 1990. Siehe die Arbeiten von Stephen G. Nichols: Philology in a manuscript culture. In: Speculum 75 (1990), S. 1–10; ders.: Philology and Its Discontents. In: The Future of the Middle Ages. Medieval Literature in the 1990s. Hrsg. von William D. Paden. Gainesville 1994, S. 113–141; ders. Why material philology? Some Thoughts. In: Philologie als Textwissenschaft. Alte und neue Horizonte. Hrsg. von Helmut Tervooren/Horst Wenzel (ZfdPh 116, Sonderheft). Berlin 1997, S. 10–30.
[112] Strohschneider (2014), S. 23.
[113] Strohschneider (2014), S. 111.
[114] Strohschneider (2014), S. 111.
[115] Michael Stolz: Artes-liberales-Zyklen. Formationen des Wissens im Mittelalter (Bibliotheca Germanica 47). Tübingen/Basel 2004, S. 515 f.
[116] Tina Bawden: In Bewegung versetzte Betrachter: Überlegungen zur raumöffnenden Dimension klappbarer Bildmedien im Mittelalter. In: Bewegen im Zwischenraum. Hrsg. von Uwe Wirth (Wege der Kulturforschung 3). Berlin 2012, S. 297–319, hier S. 298.
[117] Bawden (2012), S. 303, mit dem Beispiel einer Bildsequenz der Gnadenerweise Christi und Marias.

neserfahrungen und Verkörperlichungsaspekte trotz der wiederholten Betonung des Unsagbaren herausgehoben, während auf einer grundsätzlich phänomenalen Ebene das direkt Taktile der Buchschriftlichkeit zur heiligmäßigen Materialität erhoben wird. Der Text ist in seiner Überliefertheit dadurch auch immer Textkörper.

Die Untersuchung der handschriftlichen Besonderheiten der Vitaüberlieferung lässt Strategien einer Materialität erkennen, bei der Rubrizierungen und Unterstreichungen über eine strukturierende Funktion hinaus bedeutungstragende Faktoren zukommen. Der Beginn des deutschen Handschriftenteils (Bl. 212^r–283^v) ist durchgängig rubriziert und fällt durch Unterstreichungen und Initialen auf. Initialen erfüllen dort eine grammatisch-strukturelle Funktion, wo der Sinnzusammenhang zu Missdeutungen führen könnte, wie etwa beim Übergang von direkter Rede zum Erzählbericht.[118] Tatsächlich unterbrechen die roten Initialen (Lombarden) einen, dem Kontext nach zu urteilen, zusammenhängenden Textausschnitt so, dass einzelne Blöcke entstehen. Drei Funktionsgruppen dieser auf diese Weise entstehenden Abschnitte lassen sich bestimmen: Die Initialen führen entweder einen narrativen Abschnitt, eine liturgische Kalenderinformation oder eine direkte Rede ein. Gerade im letzten Fall wird die strukturelle Funktion der Initialen deutlich. Bei einer wenig ausdifferenzierten Interpunktion, die keine Anführungsstriche zur Markierung einer direkten Rede kennt, machen die rot und größer gezeichneten Buchstaben den Anfang oder das Ende einer solchen deutlich:

aber eyns sprach er zo myr **O** mȳ vßerwilte sele ...

(Straßburg, BNU, Ms. 324, Bl. 305^v)

Uff sent maria magdalenē dage sprach er aber eyns zo yrer selen **O** Du heilge sele mȳ erfrauwe dich ...

(Straßburg, BNU, Ms. 324, Bl. 328^v)

Indem die satzgrammatischen Strukturen markiert werden, liefert der Schreiber (oder Rubrikator) logische Hilfen.[119] Die dabei entstehenden Blöcke belaufen

---

118 Zum Problem der Interpunktion in mittelalterlichen Handschriften siehe Malcolm Beckwith Parkes: Medieval Punctuation and the Modern Editor. In: Filologia classica e filologia romanza. Esperienze ecdotiche a confronto. Atti del Convegno. Roma, 25–27 maggio 1995. Hrsg. von Anna Ferrari (Incontri di studio 2). Spoleto 1998, S. 337–349.
119 Vgl. Malcolm Beckwith Parkes: Punctuation and the Medieval History of Texts. In: La Filologia testuale e le scienze umane. Atti del convengo internazionale. Roma, 19–22 aprile 1993. Hrsg. von Accademia Nazionale dei Lincei (Atti dei Convegi 111). Rom 1994, S. 265–277, hier S. 265:

sich insbesondere zu Beginn und erneut in der Mitte des Textes auf relativ kleine Einheiten, sodass über den instruktiven Charakter dieser Passagen spekuliert werden kann, d.h. darüber, inwiefern deren Lektüre nicht auch gleichzeitig auf einen Prozess des Memorierens hinausläuft.[120]

Eine vergleichbare strukturelle Funktion tragen rot verzierte Großbuchstaben in der Bekehrungslegende der Maria Magdalena aus demselben Kodex, wo sie das Ende einer wörtlichen Rede hervorheben:

> **D**a antwert maria vnd sprach mỹ vßerkorē sust' [...] laiße vns nŭ froeliche syñe myt eỹ ander wer weyße wie lange **D**es anderē dags zoge ...
>
> (Straßburg, BNU, Ms. 324, Bl. 352ʳ)

Dass die Rubrizierung eine strukturierende Funktion innehat und das gezielte Lesen und Aufschlagen von bestimmten Stellen erleichtern soll, wird zwar deutlich, doch ist schwer festzustellen, inwiefern sie bereits einer womöglich älteren Vorlage entstammt. Zudem muss man mit kollektiven Entstehungsszenarien rechnen,[121] die ein gleichzeitiges Lesen, Abschreiben und Abwägen mit Mitarbeitern in der Schreibstube denkbar machen, auch wenn der relativ kleine Konvent Hane, sofern man die Entstehung der Handschrift dort lokalisieren möchte, wohl kaum über eine entsprechend ausgebaute Schreibstube verfügte. In der Straßburger Handschrift lässt sich beobachten, dass im Vitentext an vielen Stellen auf graphische Lücken wie etwa Leerzeilen verzichtet wurde und stattdessen Initialen als Marker fungieren. Palmer erklärt dieses Phänomen allgemein: »Die mittelalterlichen Handschriften ersetzen die Paragraphenzeichen durch Initialen, und eine solche Einteilung in Initialenabschnitte war mit Sicherheit bei den meisten mittelalterlichen Werken schon vom Autor vorgesehen.«[122] Abgesehen

---

»Scribes and correctors were also readers, and, when they applied punctuation or deployed details of layout, they were concerned primarily to elucidate the meaning of a text as they understood it. Grammatical or rhetorical structures were indicated only in so far as it was necessary to clarify a particular passage where confusion was likely to arise, or to support a particular interpretation.«

120 Zu diesem Phänomen allgemein siehe Rachel Fulton: From Judgement to Passion. Devotion to Christ and the Virgin Mary. 800–1200. New York 2002, S. 174, und Mary Jean Carruthers: The Craft of Thoughts. Meditation, Rhetoric, and the Making of Images, 400–1200 (Cambridge Studies in Medieval Literature 34). Cambridge 1998, S. 101–105.

121 Suydam (1999a), S. 176–180, macht auf den öffentlichen Charakter der Kopiertätigkeit aufmerksam.

122 Palmer (1989), S. 48. Allerdings sind im Kontext dieser Untersuchung die Begriffe ›Werk‹ und ›Autor‹ problematisch, was auch allgemein an den Bedingungen einer Handschriftenkultur liegen mag, weil der ›Autor‹ hinter mittelalterlichen Schreibprozessen kaum fassbar ist, wie Lutz

von Autorintentionen, die den Entstehungsprozess betonen, ist die Wirkung der handschriftlichen Erscheinung eines Textes für den Gebrauchsvollzug nicht zu unterschätzen.[123]

Die Gebrauchsfunktion der Initialen ist wohl am stärksten gekennzeichnet, wenn mit ihnen ein deiktischer Satz eingeleitet wird, der den Bogen aus dem Text zu einem impliziten Leser schlägt:

> Hie myrcke die groiße ere vnd wirdicheit wie sie got erhabn̄ hait yn yrer selē vor allē hemelschn̄ heyre als er sprache zo yre yn dem hogetzijt der heilger marien nagdalenē ...
>
> (Straßburg, BNU, Ms. 324, Bl. 312ʳ)

Diesem Textausschnit folgt eine erneut mit rubrizierter Initiale eingeleitete direkte Rede auf der nächsten Handschriftenseite. Das Beispiel verdeutlicht, wie sich der didaktische Charakter des Textinhalts im Manuskript widerspiegelt, indem der hier zitierte Absatz auf Grund seiner Abgrenzung mit rubrizierten Initialen isoliert erscheint.

Die Nennung liturgischer Kalendertage hat eine ähnlich pragmatische Funktion. Der entsprechende Festtag wird speziell rubriziert und markiert einen jeweils neuen thematischen Abschnitt. Die Rubrizierungen, die unter anderem Kalendertage markieren, funktionieren im Kontext einer monastischen Lektüre (z.B. Tischlektüre) ähnlich wie Interpunktionszeichen, die in der Christina von Hane-Vita wie in der Maria Magdalena-Bekehrungslegende sehr rar sind und nur am Satzende, d.h. vor einer Initiale, vorkommen. Die Interpunktion unterstreicht dabei vorhandene rhetorische Strukturen und schafft zugleich logische Verbindungen zwischen verschiedenen Elementen. Auf diese Weise markiert sie die Inflektion der Stimme und bereitet so eine Vortragssituation vor, weswegen die Interpunktion eines Textes, sowohl was dessen Wahrnehmung als auch dessen

---

(2012), S. 14, anmahnt. Siehe auch Suydam (1999a), S. 179: »I believe that there is an important performance dimension associated with this phenomenon of mediated textuality. Authors expected audiences and copyists to interact with their texts.« Auf Grund der Überlieferungslage der Christina von Hane-Vita lässt sich Palmers allgemeine Frage danach, »welcher Platz dem Schriftsteller oder dem Schreiber zwischen Unabhängigkeit und Traditionsverbundenheit zuzumessen ist« (Palmer [1989], S. 44), hier wohl nicht klären.

123 Patricia Zimmerman Beckman: The Power of Books and the Practice of Mysticism in the Fourteenth Century. Heinrich of Nördlingen and Margaret Ebner on Mechthild's ›Flowing of the Godhead‹. In: Church History. Studies in Christianity and Culture 76 (2007), S. 61–83, insbes. S. 65 f., argumentiert, dass die handschriftliche Materialität eines Buches die Lesart des Textes beeinflusst.

Inszenierung angeht, erhellend sein kann. Parkes erläutert: »In the Middle Ages the capacity of punctuation to record semantic significance implicit in a text can be seen in the ways in which scribes and correctors drew upon experience from their wider reading in order to punctuate biblical texts.«[124] Das Satzzeichen kann so als »mediale Pause« gesehen werden,[125] wie auch in liturgischen Texten *punctus* und *comma* nicht nur rhetorische Strukturen markieren, sondern dem Zelebranten anzeigen, wo im Gebet pausiert werden soll.[126]

Die strukturelle Funktion von Gliederungseinheiten unterlag »im volkssprachlichen Schrifttum [einer eigenständigen Entwicklung], die u.a. auf das besondere Verhältnis zur Mündlichkeit, auf die zweisprachige Literatursituation und auf den Übersetzungscharakter vieler volkssprachlicher Texte zurückzuführen« ist.[127] Rubrizierte Buchstaben sind das in der Christina von Hane-Vita am häufigsten verwendete Gliederungsmittel; wie auch Initialen stehen sie in der Tradition mittelalterlicher Buchkultur. Ab dem 12. Jahrhundert trat mit der Überlieferung der deutschen Kaiserchronik »ein neuer Typ hervor, bei dem die Initialenabschnitte durch Großinitialen und Rubriken in größere Erzähleinheiten gruppiert werden, die den Regierungsperioden der einzelnen Kaiser entsprechen.«[128] Initialen in der Zeilenmitte dienen in ihrer Funktion als Gliederungseinheiten in einer Vorlesesituation dazu, den Sinnzusammenhang schneller zu erfassen. Ihr Vorhandensein im Straßburger Manuskript weist darauf hin, dass der Schreiber bzw. Rubrikator die Grundlage für eine Aufführungs-, d.h. hier eine Vorlesesituation herstellte.[129] Diese Annahme wird durch die Funktionsgruppen der Initialen in der Christina von Hane-Vita gestützt, wo der pragmatische Charakter auf einen performativen Gebrauch verweist.[130]

---

124 Malcolm Beckwith Parkes: Pause and Effect. An Introduction to the History of Punctuation in the West. Aldershot 1992, S. 72.
125 Parkes (1992), S. 73.
126 Vgl. Parkes (1992), S. 77.
127 Palmer (1989), S. 44.
128 Palmer (1989), S. 62.
129 Vgl. Nigel F. Palmer: Manuscripts for Reading. The Material Evidence for the Use of Manuscripts Containing Middle High German Narrative Verse. In: Orality and Literacy in the Middle Ages. Essays on a Conjunction and its Consequences in Honour of D. H. Green. Hrsg. von Mark Chinca/Christopher Young (Utrecht Studies in Medieval Literacy 12). Turnhout 2005, S. 67–102, hier S. 81: »[...] the scribes knew that they were preparing the ground for the performative act of reading out loud.«
130 Der pragmatische Charakter tritt insbesondere bei Akklamationen wie »O« oder »O we« hervor. Andere deutsche Handschriften des 15. Jahrhunderts weisen einen ähnlichen Gebrauch von Initialen und Mittelinitialen auf, wo diese als visuelle Indikatoren eines performativen Ge-

Neben Initialen fungieren auch Unterstreichungen und andere graphische Hervorhebungen als materiale Marker von Textlichkeit. Eine strukturierende Funktion tragen die Unterstreichungen auf den Bl. 261^v–262^v, wo sie die Auflistung von sieben Lehrstücken hervorheben. Der Rubrikator unterstrich im Christina von Hane-Teil größtenteils Schlüsselbegriffe, zu denen nahezu ausnahmslos die flektierten Formen der Wörter *kyntgen/kint, hertze, herre, sele, geist* und *jonffrauwe*, zudem die Eigennamen *Emaus, Jesus Christus, Ewangelium, (Sanctus) Gregorius* und *Christina* gehören. Die graphische Hervorhebung betrifft auch das Evangelium als Autoritätsträger und den Prophetenstatus (*propheta*). Unterstreichungen fungieren im Vortrag als visuelle Gedächtnisstütze; sie dienen aber auch der schnellen Erfassung von Schlüsselbegriffen. Man stelle sich vor, die Handschrift durchzublättern und nur die unterstrichenen Elemente wahrzunehmen; als Beispiel sei hier die Doppelseite 282^v–283^r herangezogen (siehe Abb. 1): vßerwilte – vßerwilter – Jch gebñ – hemelsche spyße – vßer|wilte – gebloymtes hertze – selen – dryne dagen – here – spegel – hemel – erde – spegel – sele– hogezijt – heren vffartze dage sprach – here – lyecht – lyecht – ende ‖ sele – pynstzdage – sprach – here – Jch – lyecht – Jch byn – lyechtz – Jch – soiße styme̅ – spyße – Jch byn – guden – soißicheit – hemel – lyebste sele – got – gode – hogezijt – lychams dage – Jch byn – wort – hertze̅ – hertze̅. Die auf diese Weise hervorgehobenen Begriffe dürften ein meditatives Lesen fördern. Die Materialität der Schrift lädt so zur interaktiven Teilhabe ein.

Die Hervorhebung des Christus-Namens erfolgt nicht allein durch eine Unterstreichung, sondern auch unter Verwendung der Abbreviatur des Christusmonogramms. Auch der Name ›Christina‹ leitet sich bis auf die erste Nennung im Titel immer aus der für Christus gebrauchten Abbreviatur ab, indem an das Monogramm die weibliche Namensendung *-ina* angehängt wird.[131] Davon ausgeschlossen ist die Schreibung von zwei gleichnamigen Reliquienspendern (*Cristine virgo, Cristine virgo*).[132] Mit der Verwendung des Christusmonograms für den Namen der Mystikerin wird graphisch nicht nur untertützt, was der Text vermitteln will, nämlich die Identifizierung der mystischen Braut mit ihrem Bräutigam, sondern das Christus vorbehaltene graphische Zeichen verleiht der visuellen Erscheinung des Christina-Namens einen quasi-sakralen Status. Die Materialität des Textkörpers trägt auf diese Weise heiligmäßigen Charakter. Der Textkörper kann so als externalisiertes Zeichen von Heiligkeit verstanden werden.

---

brauchs verwendet werden, vgl. die Rubrizierungen für »*O we*« in Bertholds ›Zeitglöcklein‹ in St. Gallen, Stiftsbibliothek, cod. 1142, S. 37.

131 Vgl. Straßburg, BNU, Ms. 324, Bl. 212^r, siehe Abb. 2.

132 Vgl. CvH 32 (Bl. 267^v).

Beichtvater als Hagiograph

Meist wird die Verschriftlichung mystischer Viten in den Texten selbst einem Beichtvater zugeschrieben. In der Forschung wurde deshalb auch immer wieder nach der Produktion der Texte gefragt. Hinweise auf Schreibintentionen oder den Gebrauch der Texte werden dabei gleichermaßen betont. Weibliche Religiosität, so die verbreitete Überzeugung, gehe mit einem männlichen Verfasser der entsprechenden Texte einher.[133] Im Anschluss an die Beobachtung, dass die Viten »spätmittelalterlicher heiliger Frauen« meistens von Männern geschrieben worden seien, bestimmt Coakley: »This hagiographical literature is indeed for the most part a clerical literature.«[134] Hier wird eine wie auch immer geartete klerikale Autorschaft als Indiz männlicher Urheberschaft verstanden. Auch bei Garber wird deutlich, dass eine geschlechterspezifische Trennung vorgenommen wird, wonach hagiographische Literatur als klerikal und lateinisch geprägt angesehen und damit als »male-authored« verstanden wird.[135]

Eine scharfe Trennlinie zu einer vermeintlich volkssprachig-weiblichen Tradition lässt sich jedoch nicht ziehen, wie etwa die Viten der Franziskaner- und Dominikanerorden zeigen, die nicht nur ordensinterne, sondern große ordensunabhängige Heilige betreffen und von einer reichen volkssprachigen Tradition zeugen.[136] Auch das Prinzip einer männlichen Verfasserschaft trifft nur bedingt zu. Die oft komplexe Überlieferung der Texte aus weiblich-religiösen Bereichen schließt Schreibeinflüsse durch die betreffenden Frauen nicht aus:[137] Hildegard von Bingen etwa betrachtete sich selbstsicher als Autorin,[138] Elisabeth von Schönau beteiligte sich maßgeblich am gemeinsamen Schreibprojekt mit ihrem Bruder Ekbert, Margareta Ebner stand im regen Austausch mit Heinrich von

---

133 Vgl. Coakley (2010), S. 90 f.

134 Coakley (2010), S. 84. Der Begriff »clerical literature« wird dabei unzulänglich damit erklärt, dass die Viten von Klerikern verfasst worden seien und neben der Heiligenfigur in gewissem Sinne auch vom jeweiligen Kleriker handelten.

135 Vgl. Garber (2003), S. 117–120; siehe auch Coakley (2010), S. 91.

136 Vgl. Williams-Krapp (1994), S. 278.

137 Elizabeth Alvilda Petroff: Body and Soul. Essays on Medieval Women and Mysticism. New York/Oxford 1994, S. 139–160, untersucht anhand überlieferter Dialoge den Einfluss der Frauen auf ihre Beichtväter und ignoriert dabei die Möglichkeit der literarischen Konstruktion. Bürkle (1999), S. 23 f., hingegen weist darauf hin, dass die aus den Viten gewonnenen Indizien für die Textproduktion das Verhältnis einer »enge[n] literarische[n] Zusammenarbeit zwischen Beichtvater und Schwester« rekonstruierten.

138 Siehe dazu im Speziellen Christel Meier: Prophetentum als literarische Existenz. Hildegard von Bingen (1098–1179). Ein Porträt. In: Deutsche Literatur von Frauen. Hrsg. von Gisela Brinker-Gabler. 2 Bde. München 1988, Bd. 1: Vom Mittelalter bis zum Ende des 18. Jahrhunderts, S. 76–87, insbes. S. 76–78.

Nördlingen,[139] und Katherina von Siena porträtierte sich als ausdrucksfähige Mittlerin in weltlichen Dingen.[140] Dennoch, so betont Mooney, neigten männliche Hagiographen dazu, die heiligen Frauen so weit zu »mystifizieren«, dass diese völlig außerhalb der Welt erschienen.[141] Den starken Einfluss der »größtenteils gelehrte[n] Beichtväter [...], die mit strengem Auge auf die dogmatische Korrektheit des Berichteten achteten und in zum Teil erheblichem Umfang mit hagiographischen Konventionen arbeiteten«, betont auch Williams-Krapp, der sodann schlussfolgert, »dass die Echtheit des Erlebens keine Kategorie hagiographischer Literatur war.«[142] Den Konstruktionscharakter der Texte betonend, sprechen sich demnach Mooney wie Williams-Krapp für eine Gattungszuweisung der Texte aus, die bereits bei der Produktion bewusst ergangen sein soll.

Ein produktionsästhetischer Vorgang ist nicht an jedem Text auf gleiche Weise nachvollziehbar: In den Texten zu Christine Ebner z.B. treten die Bemühungen eines anonym bleibenden Vertrauten der Mystikerin besonders hervor, wenn es darum geht, Material zu kompilieren und zu verarbeiten. Der Lebensbericht der Dominikanernonne des 14. Jahrhunderts präsentiert sich als ein komplexer Mischtext, der sich aus verschiedenen Texttypen wie Gebeten, Liedern und Visionsberichten speist und »nur unvollständig die Spuren seiner allmählichen Entstehung verdeckt.«[143] In der Vita Christinas von Stommeln flicht der Hagiograph Petrus von Dacien Elemente ein, die das selbstbewusste Schreiben

---

139 Johannes Janota: Freundschaft auf Erden und im Himmel. Die Mystikerin Margareta Ebner und der Gottesfreund Heinrich von Nördlingen. In: Impulse und Resonanzen. Tübinger mediävistische Beiträge zum 80. Geburtstag von Walter Haug. Hrsg. von Gisela Vollmann-Profe u.a. Tübingen 2007, S. 275–300, hier S. 276, spricht zum zuletzt genannten Paar von einem »erotisch eingefärbte[n] Gedankenaustauch«. Siehe auch Urban Federer: Mystische Erfahrung im literarischen Dialog. Die Briefe Heinrichs von Nördlingen an Margaretha Ebner (Scrinium Friburgense 25). Berlin/New York 2011, insbes. S. 220–294; siehe dazu die Buchbesprechung von Balázs J. Nemes: Rezension zu Urban Federer: Mystische Erfahrung im literarischen Dialog. Die Briefe Heinrichs von Nördlingen an Margaretha Ebner (2011). In: ZfdPh 132 (2013), S. 454–469.
140 Vgl. Catherine M. Mooney: Voice, Gender, and the Portrayal of Sanctity. In: Gendered Voices. Medieval Saints and Their Interpreters. Hrsg. von Catherine M. Mooney. Philadelphia 1999(a), S. 1–15, insbes. S. 10.
141 Vgl. Mooney (1999a), S. 11.
142 Williams-Krapp (2008), S. 266. Vgl. dahingegen jetzt Köbele (2012), S. 367, zur Legende: »Doch außerhalb gattungshybrider Grenzfälle versteht der idealtypische Legendenerzähler sich unmissverständlich als demütig-schlichter Chronist der Wahrheit.«
143 Peters (1988), S. 158. Siehe auch Peters (1986), S. 414–416, und Susanne Bürkle: Die ›Gnadenvita‹ Christine Ebners. Episodenstruktur – Text-Ich und Autorschaft. In: Deutsche Mystik im abendländischen Zusammenhang. Neu erschlossene Texte, neue methodische Ansätze, neue theoretische Konzepte. Kolloquium Kloster Fischingen 1998. Hrsg. von Walter Haug/Wolfram Schneider-Lastin. Tübingen 2000, S. 483–513.

hervorheben.[144] Ein weiteres Gegenbeispiel zu einem geregelten Produktionsablauf bietet Angela von Foligno, deren Seelsorger und Hagiograph immer wieder die eigene Unzulänglichkeit und Unfähigkeit betont, das Mitgeteilte adäquat wiederzugeben;[145] ein Topos, der als Strategie zur Teilhabe am mystischen Diskurs gelesen werden könnte, aber in erster Linie den Schreibprozess in seiner Bemühung um Authentizität thematisiert.

Hagiographische Konventionen sind in mystischen Viten zweifelsohne vorzufinden. Dennoch wurde der Beichtvater-Topos in seiner epistemologischen Abstraktion als wesentliches Gattungsmerkmal derjenigen mystischen Texte bestimmt, in denen der Erzählrahmen von der Stimme eines männlich spezifizierten Kollaborateurs dominiert wird.[146] Doch gerade der Beichtvater-Komplex verdeutlicht, dass es in vielen Fällen keine scharfe Trennlinie zwischen mystischen und hagiographischen Texttypen gibt, weil der Beichtvater zum einen als realer Verfasser, zum anderen als impliziter Autor verstanden werden kann.[147] Verzahnungen von textimmanenten mit gattungstypologischen Elementen führen zu Schemata, denen sich Einzelfälle wie die Christina von Hane-Vita entziehen. Trotzdem ist Backmund überzeugt, einen Autor für diese Vita festmachen zu können. Die Nennung eines nahestehenden Ordensbruders wird als das eindeutige Indiz für einen historisch bestimmbaren Hagiographen herangezogen:

> Aus dem Text geht klar hervor, dass der Verfasser Christina persönlich gekannt hatte, er sagt des öfteren: »... wie sie mir selbst gesagt hat«. Er war auch sicher Kleriker. Zweimal sagt er: »... nun komme ich zur Materie zurück«, was ein echt theologischer, ja scholastischer Ausdruck ist. Die meisterhafte Schilderung der mystischen Zustände und die gelegentlichen Zitate können nur von einem Geistlichen stammen. Dazu kommt, dass eine Nonne diese geistigen Erlebnisse, und ganz sicher die schweren Bußübungen, die zum Teil recht delikat sind, bestimmt niemand anders als ihrem Beichtvater anvertraut hat. Wir dürfen

144 Vgl. Ruhrberg (1995), S. 209–213.
145 Vgl. Paul Lachance: Introduction. In: Angela of Foligno. Complete Works. Hrsg. von Paul Lachance. Mahwa 1993, S. 15–119, insbes. S. 49; siehe auch Emmelius (2004), S. 54–59. – Insbesondere Angelas Beispiel zeigt, dass sich die von Berndt Hamm: Wollen und Nicht-Können als Thema der spätmittelalterlichen Bußseelsorge. In: Spätmittelalterliche Frömmigkeit zwischen Ideal und Praxis. Hrsg. von Berndt Hamm/Thomas Lentes (Spätmittelalter und Reformation, Neue Reihe 15). Tübingen 2001, S. 111–146, hier S. 112, festgestellte »spätmittelalterliche Auseinandersetzung mit der geistlichen Insuffizienz im Kontext eines weit verbreiteten Strebens nach religiöser Vollkommenheit und Leistungsfähigkeit auf dem Wege zum Heil« nicht auf die Mystikerin beschränkt, sondern auf den mitteilenden Seelsorger ausweitet, dessen Schreibakt dadurch gewissermaßen Anteil an der Heilsgewissheit nimmt.
146 Vgl. Coakley (2010), S. 89.
147 Vgl. Bürkle (1999), S. 27, zur typenspezifischen Ausgestaltung der Figur des Beichtvaters in Anlehnung an Peters (1988).

also den Beichtvater der Nonne von Hane um 1200–1300 als Autor vermuten, und das kann nur ein Chorherr des nahen Klosters Rothenkirchen gewesen sein, dessen Leitung Hane unterstand.[148]

Krings schließt sich diesen Beobachtungen zunächst an und schlussfolgert: »Der Autor der Vita war ein Mann, der seinen Namen nicht nennt. [...] Demnach kann es sich nur um den Beichtvater Christinas handeln«.[149] Backmund nennt weiterhin einen konkreten Propst (Godebert), der als Autor in Frage komme.[150] Auch Krings äußert sich zur historischen Identifizierung des Beichtvaters: »Als Propst von Hane ist am 9. April 1287 ein Rothenkirchener Kanoniker namens Gotsmann bezeugt, der am 13. Dezember 1293 als Abt von Rothenkirchen erwähnt wird. Er dürfte der Verfasser der Vita sein.«[151]

Wie Backmund und Krings für die Christina von Hane-Vita, nimmt auch Coakley allgemein an, dass die Hagiographen von Mystikerinnen wegen der »höchst privaten Mitteilungen« zugleich die Beichtväter gewesen sein mussten.[152] Hinter dieser Auffassung steht die Vermutung, dass weibliche Heiligkeitsdarstellung einer männlichen Vermittlung bedurfte.[153] Festzuhalten bleibt allerdings die wahrscheinliche, indes nicht nachweisbare Annahme, dass ein Christina »sehr nahe stehender Geistlicher ihres Ordens« ihre Lebensgeschichte »wohl ziemlich unmittelbar nach den Ereignissen niederschrieb«.[154] Als Vergleichspunkt bietet sich die Vita Christine Ebners an, deren Verfasser ebenfalls anonym bleibt.[155] Der implizite Autor des Textes lässt sich indes nicht mit einem realhistorischen Verfasser gleichsetzen. Versteht man den Autor hingegen als »textliches Konstrukt«, wie das Nemes im Kontext der Überlieferung des ›Fließenden Lichts‹ vorschlägt, wird auch der Umgang mit dem Beichtvater-Topos differenzierter, da der Beichtvater nicht mit einem männlichen Autor identifiziert werden muss.[156]

---

148 Backmund (1972), S. 90 f.
149 Krings (2009), S. 199 f.
150 Vgl. Backmund (1972), S. 91, Anm. 187.
151 Krings (2009), S. 200. Krings' Argumente stützen sich allein auf die textinternen Mitteilungen Christinas an das Schreiber-Ich. Krings' (ebd.) Annahme einer Krankensalbung durch den Probst lässt sich in der Christina-Vita nicht nachweisen.
152 Vgl. John Wayland Coakley: The Representation of Sanctity in Late Medieval Hagiography. Evidence from Lives of Saints of the Dominican Order. Cambridge, MA 1980 (Diss. Harvard), S. 249–263.
153 Vgl. Coakley (1980), S. 261.
154 Mittermaier (1960), S. 90.
155 Siehe dazu Peters (1988), S. 159, und ausführlich Bürkle (2000).
156 Nemes (2010), S. 17.

Warum geschlechterspezifische Merkmale einer Autorinstanz nach wie vor zentral erscheinen, erörtert Poor am Beispiel Mechthilds von Magdeburg:

> It is no mere coincidence that the shift in theological interest from the ›auctoritas‹ or divine truth of a scriptural text to its human ›auctor‹ in the thirteenth century coincides with the publication of texts written by semireligious or lay women as well as men who find themselves in the role of a scriptural author – that is, those who are recording messages from and conversations with God.[157]

Auf Grund des Zusammenspiels zwischen den Konzepten einer göttlich inspirierten *auctoritas* und einer menschlichen Ausführung (*auctor*) würden bestimmte Texttypen mit geschlechterspezifischen Autorkonstruktionen in Verbindung gebracht.[158] Dennoch ist, wie Hollywood betont, die Autorinstanz eines Textes nicht unbedingt an einen spezifisch männlichen Autor oder eine spezifisch weibliche Autorin gebunden. Gerade für mystische Texte seien solche Kategorisierungen problematisch, da männliche und weibliche Autorkonstruktionen unabhängig von den tatsächlich gegebenen Entstehungsbedingungen der Texte behandelt werden müssten.[159] Nemes verfolgt im Gegensatz dazu einen weitgehend genderfreien Ansatz, wenn er die Text- und Autorkonstitution in der Überlieferung und Rezeption von Mechthilds ›Fließendem Licht‹ untersucht: Das Ergebnis illustriert, warum »die Rückkoppelung editorischer Entscheidungen an eine Autorpersönlichkeit« heikel erscheint.[160] Moderne Interpreten müssten daran scheitern, herauszufiltern, was echt, d.h. was vom Autor stammt, und was unecht ist, d.h. was nachträglich im Zuge der Überlieferung hinzugekommen ist.[161]

Bei dem in der Christina von Hane-Vita gezeichneten Autorbild wird vor allem Wert darauf gelegt, dass er die Nonne selbst gekannt und begleitet habe: *Jch, broder der dyße schryben, was auch da geynwirdich. Vnd ich gedacht an die jemerliche erbiebonge des lyeblichen Jhesus, daz er leyt an dem crutze, da van das*

---

157 Poor (2004), S. 4.

158 Vgl. dazu Caroline Walker Bynum: Jesus as Mother. Studies in the Spirituality of the High Middle Ages (Publications of the Center for Medieval and Renaissance Studies 16). Berkeley 1982, S. 135–146, die von der »Feminisierung religiöser Sprache« spricht (»feminization of religious language«, S. 135).

159 Vgl. Hollywood (1995), S. 16 f. und S. 23–25. So auch bereits Ursula Peters: Hofkleriker – Stadtschreiber – Mystikerin. Zum literarischen Status dreier Autorentypen. In: Autorentypen. Hrsg. von Walter Haug/Burghart Wachinger (Fortuna Vitrae 6). Tübingen 1991, S. 29–49, und erneut Bürkle (1999). Für die Zusammenfassung dieser Diskussion siehe Nemes (2010), S. 17–27.

160 Nemes (2010), S. 51.

161 Nemes (2010), S. 48 f. Gerade hinsichtlich Mechthilds von Magdeburg ›Fließendes Licht‹ wurden kühne Annahmen über Autoren und Autorinnen gewagt, vgl. ebd., S. 21–23.

ertrich erbiebet (CvH 57, 45–48). Der Augenzeugenbericht funktioniert als eine Form von externalisierter Heiligkeit, da die Körperlichkeit des Geschehens auch gleichzeitig eine mentale ›(Be-)Greifbarkeit‹ einschließt, die der Hagiograph im Kommentarmodus christologisch aufwertet. Coakley zufolge, wäre diese Form von Vertrautheit zwischen Mystikerin und geistlichem Begleiter die Basis für die Entstehung des Textes durch den männlichen Autor. Doch wie Bürkle zu Coakley kritisch anmerkt, ist das eine allzu »schematisierte Perzeption von Heiligkeit«.[162] In Bürkles Gegenkonzept existiert das Autorbild einer »schreibenden Mystikerin«, die sich des Beichtvater/Hagiograph-Topos als Autorin hätte bedienen können.[163] Auch Watson erkennt Erwähnungen eines nahe stehenden Ordensbruders vordergründig als literarstrategisches Autorisierungsmittel an.[164] Weiterführend konstatiert Suerbaum, dass Rückschlüsse von literarischen Sprecher-Inszenierungen auf »konkrete Lebensumstände« problematisch und daher zu vermeiden seien.[165]

So verschieden die Forschungsansätze sind, im Großen und Ganzen nimmt man Abschied von einer »single-author mentality«,[166] wie sie etwa für Heinrich von Nördlingen als Hagiograph Mechthilds von Magdeburg lange praktiziert wurde.[167] Doch was für Mechthild von Hackeborn, Gertrud von Helfta, Margarete Ebner, Heinrich Seuse und Mechthild von Magdeburg mit Hilfe der Überlieferungslage differenziert dargestellt werden kann,[168] entzieht sich in Christinas Fall der Beurteilung, und nicht zuletzt deswegen, weil nur ein Textzeuge der Vita überliefert ist.[169] Jedenfalls trägt die Autorkonstituierung in der Christina von Hane-Vita eine diskursive Funktion. So ließe sich auch über eine hagiographische Autorschaft im Anschluss an Foucault sagen, dass die Zuschreibung eines Autors

---

162 Bürkle (1999), S. 198.

163 Bürkle (1999), S. 294–306.

164 Vgl. Nicholas Watson: Richard Rolle and the Invention of Authority. Cambridge 1991, S. I.

165 Suerbaum (2003), S. 250. Siehe auch Bürkle (1994), S. 139 f.

166 Poor (2004), S. 10.

167 Siehe dazu Nemes (2010), S. 27.

168 Vgl. Nemes (2010), S. 358–360.

169 Wenn die überlieferungsgeschichtliche Autorkonstituierung wenig Aufschluss über geschlechterspezifische Schreibstrategien gibt, bleiben allein textinhärente Merkmale heranzuziehen. Zu diesen Zwecken müsste Christina als realhistorische Figur verstanden werden, die sich dem Text gemäß mündlich mitgeteilt haben soll, worauf eine textlich-schriftliche Überlieferung folgte, bei der womöglich mehrere Autoren bzw. Bearbeiter direkt und indirekt beteiligt waren. Einen solchen rekonstruierten Weg schlägt Poor trotz der reichen Überlieferungslage für Mechthild von Magdeburg ein, vgl. Poor (2004), S. 15 und S. 201. Es ist allerdings darauf hinzuweisen, dass man sich mit einer realhistorischen Prämisse auf ein interpretatorisches Terrain begibt, wo Rückschlüsse auf die Autorschaft tautologischen Charakter tragen.

einen bestimmten Diskursmodus erfüllt, der nicht allein aus Formeln der Autorisierung besteht, sondern eine Art von Diskurs markiert, welcher das Behauptete als bewiesen darlegt.[170] In diesem Licht kann auch die Funktion der Autorschaft in der Christina von Hane-Vita verstanden werden:[171] Sofern wir von Diskursen im Foucaultschen Sinne ausgehen, verliert die Bedeutung eines echten Beichtvaters/Hagiographen ohnehin an Relevanz. Nachdem die historische Bedeutung eines Beichtvaters oder Bearbeiters für unseren Text ausscheidet, fragt sich, wodurch sich Autorisierungsstrategien des hagiographischen Erzählens in der mystischen Vita eigentlich auszeichnen.

2.2 Autorisierungsstrategien des hagiographischen Erzählens

Mystische Viten schreiben sich in etablierte hagiographische Diskurse ein, und zwar – das wird an der eigentlichen Definition von Mystik ersichtlich – weil sie das Paradox vom Sprechen über das Unsagbare in die Darstellbarkeit von Heiligkeit zu überführen versuchen. Strohschneider formuliert dazu:

> Im hagiographischen Erzählen ragt nicht Transzendenz substanziell in die Immanenz herein, sondern dieses weist umgekehrt über die Grenzen der Immanenz hinaus auf ein ganz Anderes, auf die radikale Negation aller Immanenz: auf die von allen Unterscheidungen unterschiedene Sphäre des Nichtunterschiedenen. In scharfer kategorialer Differenz zu dieser von ihr bezeichneten Transzendenz ist die hagiographische Narration selbst (in literaturwissenschaftlicher Perspektive) stets etwas Immanentes.[172]

Von der eigentlichen Materialität der Textlichkeit ist also die davon abstrahierte transzendente Bedeutung zu trennen. Im Anschluss an Strohschneider kann auch die Narration selbst als immanente Manifestation verstanden werden. Diese narrative Immanenz kann nur auf einer textuellen Ebene etabliert werden. Es seien daher die diskursiven Strategien des Textes zu erörtern, d.h. die Kontextualisierungen innerhalb bestimmter Schreibtraditionen. Diese Herangehens-

---

170 Vgl. Michel Foucault: Qu'est-ce qu'un auteur? In: Dits et écrits. 1954–1988. Hrsg. von Daniel Defert/François Ewald. 2 Bde. Paris 1994. 2. Aufl. des unveränderten Nachdrucks. Malesherbes 2008, Bd. 1: 1954–1975, S. 817–849, insbes. S. 828: »›Hippocrate a dit‹, ›Pline raconte‹ n'étaient pas au juste les formules d'une argument d'autorité; c'étaient les indices dont étaient marqués des discours destinés à être reçus comme prouvés.«
171 Ähnlich argumentiert Suerbaum (2003), S. 253, für den Prolog von Mechthilds ›Fließendem Licht‹, der den Schreibprozess thematisiert: »Es geht nicht darum, inwieweit diese Angaben historisch real sind, sondern allein um den literarischen Gestus, den sie verfolgen.«
172 Strohschneider (2014), S. 177.

weise nimmt Abstand von den Beobachtungen, die Ruh sowie Backmund an der Christina von Hane-Vita anstellen. Ruh unterscheidet stilistisch drei ›Blöcke‹ von Textarten: Der erste Teil weise am ehesten eine hagiographische Bearbeitung auf und sei daher als Tugend- und Gnadenleben zu charakterisieren.[173] Backmund hingegen sieht in dem gesamten Text ein »außergewöhnliches Bußleben«;[174] eine Zuschreibung, die allerdings nur einen frühen Teil von Christinas Lebensgang betrifft. Allmählich, d.h. ab Kapitel 41 in der vorliegenden Edition, trete, so Ruh, der brautmystische Charakter stärker hervor, wobei sich Visionen, Auditionen und andere Gottesbegegnungen an kirchlichen Festtagen orientieren. Zum Schluss, d.h. ab Kapitel 96, dominiere die Ich-Rede Christinas, die theologische Fragen des Spätmittelalters erörtere. »Mit Bestimmtheit stammt diese Partie nicht vom Autor, der für den brautmystischen Teil verantwortlich ist«, urteilt Ruh.[175] Es liege also ein »dreigeteiltes Werk unterschiedlicher Herkunft vor, das sich als eine Einheit ausgibt«.[176] Diesen Aussagen liegen gattungsinhärente Bestimmungen zu Grunde, die den komplexen Text mit einer Hypothese über die Vorlagen erklären wollen. Weder die Handschrift noch der Text geben uns Anhaltspunkte für eine solche Dreiteilung. Was sich so als Ganzes präsentiert, läuft einer teleologischen Herangehensweise, die vom Endprodukt einer bearbeiteten Vita ausgeht, entgegen. Sicherlich weist die Vita aus rhetorischer Sicht Stilbrüche auf; eine geglättete Vita liegt nicht vor. Stattdessen gehen verschiedene Textarten ineinander über, wobei die Übergänge fließend und, anders als bisher behauptet, nicht blockartig voneinander zu trennen sind. Das dabei entstehende Spiel thematisiert Erzählprozesse als textuelle Strategien. Im Folgenden werden drei dieser textuellen Strategien untersucht: Intertextualität, die narrative Konstitution von Heilsgewissheit sowie die Narrativierung theologischer Modelle.

2.2.1 Intertextualität

Intertextualität betrifft die Nähe eines Textes zu einem anderen Text, die sich in stofflichen und strukturellen Motiven niederschlagen kann.[177] Ein engeres Begriffsverständnis der Intertextualität geht von markierten Bezügen zwischen

---

173 Vgl. Ruh (1993), S. 122.
174 Backmund (1972), S. 89.
175 Ruh (1993), S. 124.
176 Ruh (1993), S. 125.
177 Vgl. Andersen (2000), S. 147 f.

einem Text und weiteren Texten oder Textgruppen aus.[178] Kraß diskutiert die Anwendbarkeit von Genettes Begriff der Intertextualität auf die Mediävistik.[179] Seine Untersuchung verschiedener Übertragungen der Mariensequenz ›Ave praeclara maris stella‹ zeigt, dass das Konzept der historischen Intertextualität zwar hilfreich ist, aber »im Falle der kollektiven Übersetzungen« nicht völlig zutrifft.[180] Stattdessen schlägt er den wiederum von Genette eingeführten Begriff der Architextualität vor, wonach Texte der gleichen Gattung aus vergleichbaren Milieus zusammengehören. Sicherlich sind diese Kategorien hilfreich, um eine Systematik der Textzusammenhänge zu erstellen. Eine genaue Bestimmung der Textverhältnisse ist aber nicht immer möglich, zumal inhaltliche wie sprachliche Verwandtschaften zwischen den Texten verschiedene Ursachen haben können. Weniger auf die Ursachen als auf die Wirkung konzentriert sich der folgende Ansatz, der die Funktion von Intertextualität als Legitimationsstrategie, hier des hagiographischen Erzählens, behandelt. Bezüge zur Bibel- und Legendenepik, zu alttestamentlichen Büchern und zu stofflichen Motiven aus dem religiösen Schriftbereich allgemein stellen auch immer einen Bezug zur eigenen Schriftlichkeit her. In diesem Sinne sind neben direkten Zitaten auch Annäherungen oder eine nicht weiter spezifizierbare Nähe als intertextuelle Bezüge zu behandeln.

Andersen stellt für die Aufzeichnungen Mechthilds von Magdeburg fest, dass diese mit der Nennung von alttestamentlichen Figuren in ein »dialogisches Verhältnis zur Heiligen Schrift« träten.[181] Auch in der Christina von Hane-Vita sind alttestamentliche Figuren zentral; so greift der Beginn der Vita auf Esther zurück. Über die Parallelführung Esthers mit der Prämonstratensernonne Christina stellt die Vita über die Bibel hinaus auch Bezüge zu theologischen Texten des Mittelalters sowie zum volkssprachigen Esther-Stoff des Spätmittelalters her.[182] Die typologische Interpretation Esthers klingt bereits in der Patristik an, wo Jungfrauen und Witwen des Alten Testaments (Esther, Judith, Susanna) mit Maria

178 Vgl. Manfred Pfister: Konzepte der Intertextualität. In: Intertextualität. Formen, Funktionen, anglistische Fallstudien. Hrsg. von Manfred Pfister/Ulrich Broich. Tübingen 1985, S. 1–30, insbes. S. 25.
179 Vgl. Andreas Kraß: ›Ich gruess dich gerne‹. Aspekte historischer Intertextualität am Beispiel von gereimten deutschen Übersetzungen der Mariensequenz ›Ave praeclara maris stella‹ in Mittelalter und Früher Neuzeit. In: Grundlagen: Forschungen, Editionen und Materialien zur deutschen Literatur und Sprache des Mittelalters und der Frühen Neuzeit. Hrsg. von Rudolf Bentzinger/Ulrich-Dieter Oppitz/Jürgen Wolf (ZfdA, Beiheft 18). Stuttgart 2013, S. 301–314, insbes. S. 301–303.
180 Kraß (2013), S. 314.
181 Andersen (2003), S. 225.
182 Zur typologischen Dimension siehe Kap. 4.2.

verknüpft werden.[183] Esther präfiguriert Maria außerdem auch für Richard von St. Victor.[184] Diese Tradition wird in der volkssprachigen Auseinandersetzung weitergeführt und ausgeweitet. In Heinrichs von Mügeln ›Tum‹ ist Esther eine figurative Station in der heilsgeschichtlichen Ordnung.[185] In den ›St. Georgener Predigten‹ wird Esther allegorisch gedeutet. Auf der Stufe des *sensus spiritualis* steht sie für die Seele des Gläubigen, während Assuerus Gott symbolisiert:[186] *Bi deme kúnige Assvero ist bezachinot ѷnsir herre Ihesus Cristus, vnde bi der kúniginne Hester ist bezaichinot dú sele.* (›St. Georgener Predigten‹ 2, 66–68)[187] Ähnlich sieht es Tauler, für den Assuerus Gott oder den Heiligen Geist, Esther die Seele des gläubigen irdischen Menschen versinnbildlicht.[188] In der Christina von Hane-Vita heißt es über die Prämonstratensernonne:

> *Sie ist woil die ander Hester, die dem gewaren Assůero vnder anderen jonffrauwen getzogen vnd gehalten wart yn dem hußße, daz da hieße der jonffrauwen huße, das sye yme getzirt myt gantzer doegenden vnd myt heilger hoger lyebden yme zo gelacht wůrde, dan man leßet also, daz frauwe Hester was die aller suberlichste vnd die aller lyeblichste vnd gar angeneme.* (CvH 1, 10–15)

Die Qualifikation Christinas als *die ander Hester* ist dabei ein Typologiesignal, weil das *ander* ein analoges Verhältnis schafft.

In den ›St. Georgener Predigten‹ wird ähnlich wie in Christinas Vita die Ausschmückung der Seele mit Esthers Erwählung und ihrer Vorbereitung auf den Ehevollzug analog gesetzt:

---

183 Vgl. Ambrosius: ›De viduis‹. In: PL 16 (1845), Sp. 233A–262D, insbes. Kap. 4, Sp. 241A–242C.

184 Vgl. Richard von St. Victor: In Cantica Canticorum explicatio. In: PL 196 (1855), Sp. 405A–523B, insbes. Kap. 42, Sp. 522C.

185 Vgl. Heinrich von Mügeln: ›Der Tum‹. In: Die kleineren Dichtungen Heinrichs von Mügeln. Erste Abteilung. Die Spruchsammlung des Göttinger Cod. Philos. 21. Hrsg. von Karl Stackmann. 3 Teilbde. (DTM 50–52). Berlin 1959, Bd. 2, S. 147–219, hier 169, 9. (Die Stellennachweise geben Strophen- und Verszahlen an.)

186 Vgl. Manfred Caliebe: Hester. Eine poetische Paraphrase des Buches Esther aus dem Ordensland Preussen. Edition und Kommentar (Quellen und Studien zur Geschichte des Deutschen Ordens 21). Marburg 1985, S. 301 f. und S. 268–270, für das im Mittelalter gängige exegetische Typologieverfahren, Esther und Assuerus als Typus und Maria und Christus als Antitypus zu verstehen.

187 ›Die St. Georgener Predigten‹. Hrsg. von Regina D. Schiewer und Kurt Otto Seidel (DTM 90). Berlin 2010. (Die Stellennachweise geben Predigtnummern und Zeilenzahlen an.)

188 Vgl. ›Die Predigten Taulers‹. Aus der Engelberger und der Freiburger Handschrift sowie aus Schmidts Abschriften der ehemaligen Straßburger Handschriften. Hrsg. von Ferdinand Vetter (DTM 11). Berlin 1910, insbes. die Predigten 27, 38 und 53. (Die Stellennachweise geben Predigtnummern an; gegebenenfalls werden auch die Seitenzahlen referiert.)

Bi der kúnegin Hester ist bezaichint ain iechliche seligú sela. ›Hester‹ daz sprichit ›ain virborgene vrouwe, dú wol geziert ist‹. Daz ist dú sele, dú ist nu uirborgin. Dú sol wol gezierte sin vnd geclaidit mit edelen tuginden, swenne der himilsche kúnic nah ir sende, daz sie mit eron ze houe uar vúr den grozin got uon himilriche und vúr alliz ingesinde. (›St. Georgener Predigten‹ 5, 231–235)

In der Christina von Hane-Vita wird zusätzlich zur mystischen Vereinigung zwischen Seele und Gott auch der Erlösungsaspekt der Esther-Geschichte hervorgehoben: *Er entboitde auch freden alle synem lantde vnd er gaiff synen vnderthanen groiße konenckclichen gaben, dar er bruytlaufft myt yr macht. Dyß ist alles geistlich an dyeßer jonffrauwen ernuwet.* (CvH 1, 19–22) Der kollektive Nutzen Esthers wird hier auf die Mystikerin übertragen und auf den Dienst Christinas an die Seelen im Fegefeuer vorausweisend eschatologisch verklärt.[189] In der spätmittelalterlichen ›Hester‹-Prosa wird die Funktion Esthers als Erlöserin dem typologischen Verständnis nach als eine marianische Qualität verstanden.[190] Der Epilog der ›Hester‹ der Deutschordensdichtung schlägt ebenfalls die Brücke zu Maria und mündet in ein Fürbittengebet:

ich enmac noch enwil
nicht hie von geschriben vil
sunder daz alleine,
daz wir die gar reine,
uz alles herzen truwe
an mardocheo, mit ruwe
unse hester anschrien,
ich meine di lieben marien,
daz sie den kunic assuerum,
den edelen iesum christum,
vor uns getruwelichen bite
daz uns sine helfe wone mite. (›Hester‹, V. 1945–1954)[191]

Unter den hier vorgeführten Ester-Figuren scheint die Christina von Hane-Vita der Deutschordensdichtung besonders nahe zu stehen. Die Krönung der ›Königin‹

---

189 Diese endzeitliche Auslegung des Buches Esther ist auch bei Berthold von Regensburg zu finden, vgl. Berthold von Regensburg: Vollständige Ausgabe seiner Predigten mit Ammerkungen von Franz Pfeiffer. Mit einem Vorwort von Kurt Ruh. 2 Bde. Berlin 1965 (Neudruck der Originalausgabe Wien 1862/1880), Bd. 1, Predigt 24, S. 378, Z. 8 – S. 379, Z. 20.
190 Vgl. Kurt Ruh: Hester. In: ²VL 3 (1981), Sp. 1201–1203, insbes. Sp. 1202.
191 ›Hester‹. In: Caliebe (1985), S. 11–123.

wird in beiden Texten betont, in der Handschrift der Christina von Hane-Vita ist das Wort ›kroyne‹ zusätzlich unterstrichen:

> *die kunicliche crone*
> *satzete er ir uf vil schone*
> *die jene hete vor getragen.* (›Hester‹, V. 405–407)

> *Dar vmbe da sie zo dem konynck yn wart gefort, da gefielle sie yme gar woille yn synen augen, vnd er hait sie lyeffe, als da steth geschreben, vor allen anderen frauwen, vnd erkreget vor sym angesiecht genade vnd barmhertzicheit vor allen yren gespiellen, also daz er yr alleyn die kroyne vff saitzet.* (CvH 1, 15–19)

Insbesondere die in beiden Texten ähnlich formulierte und wiederholt ergehende Aufforderung nach der Willensbekundung Esthers/Christinas durch Assuerus/Christus ist auffällig:

> *beger an mir swes du wilt* (›Hester‹, V. 1243)

> *vrowe lieb, nu gere an mir*
> *swaz du wilt, daz gebe ich dir,*
> *ez sie ouch wenic oder vil.* (›Hester‹, V. 1273–1275)

> *hester, nu bite swes du wilt,*
> *wand mich kein dir nicht bevilt*
> *ob ez joch halb min riche sie* (›Hester‹, V. 1529–1531)

> *sage an, vrowe gut,*
> *welch not betrubet dinen mut?*
> *wiltu icht han an mir?* (›Hester‹, V. 1643–1655)

> *O du aller lyeblichste sele myn, heyße van myr, was du wilt. Du vßerwilte sele myn, die ich myr vßerwylt hayn, heyße van myr, was du wylt.* (CvH 23, 4–6)

> *O du aller lyeblichste sele myn, was wyltu me?* [...] *O du aller selichste sele myn, was wyltu nu me?* (CvH 56, 3–7)

> *O du aller sanfftmodichste sele myn, wes begerstu me?* [...] *O du aller myldichste sele myn, was wyltu me?* [...] *O aller kůste sele myn, wes begerstu me?* (CvH 57, 4–8)

> *Sele myn, was wiltu nu me?* (CvH 69, 4 f.)

> *Eya lyebe sele myn, was wyltu me?* (CvH 87, 6 f.)

> *O seliche sele myn, was wylttu me?* (CvH 89, 7)

> *O lyebe sele myn, was wyltu me?* (CvH 93, 4 f.)

> *Heische van myr, was du wilt.* (CvH 97, 24)

Die Parallelen sind nicht so eng, dass eine Kenntnis der Deutschordensdichtung vorausgesetzt werden muss; ganz auszuschließen ist eine Beeinflussung indes nicht. Darauf deutet auch der Überlieferungskontext: Eine Handschrift der ›Hester‹-Deutschordensdichtung überliefert die einzige mitteldeutsche Reisefassung des ›Brandan‹,[192] und da anzunehmen ist, dass das Fischinsel-Motiv aus dem ›Brandan‹-Stoff in die Christina von Hane-Vita Eingang fand, liegt es nicht ganz fern, die überlieferungstechnische Nähe an dieser Stelle textgeschichtlich aufzuwerten. Die entsprechende Passage in der Vita lautet:

> [...] *da du wyrste vynden eytzelichen wort, da groiße befyndunge der genaden vnd soißicheit myt wonderlicher ynwendiger beschauwonge, die also vnsprechlichen vnuerstendich synt vnser groppicheit zo begryffen, als eynem wayllen eynen dutzen zo verstayn.* (CvH 39, 23–26)

Die Unmöglichkeit, Gott zu begreifen, wird damit verglichen, einen Wal merklich anzustoßen. In Brandans Reise realisiert der Wal nichts von dem, was auf seinem Rücken geschieht.[193] Das sogenannte Fischinsel-Motiv war allerdings im Hoch- und Spätmittelalter weit verbreitet.[194] Schließlich war das Fischinsel-Motiv aus anderer Quelle wie z. B. aus Konrads von Megenberg ›Das Buch der Natur‹ bekannt gewesen.[195] Ob bei dem Vergleich zwischen Wal und Menschenverstand tatsächlich Brandans Reise verarbeitet wird, muss daher offen bleiben, doch legt die gemeinsame Überlieferung mit der Hesterdichtung dies nahe.

Intertextuelle Bezüge zur Bibel sind in der Christina von Hane-Vita dahingegen greifbarer. Alt- und neutestamentliche Referenzen fungieren insbesondere im Kontext der Darstellung des Kampfes gegen die sieben Todsünden als etablierte Autoritätsquellen. An moral-theologisch aufgeladenen Stellen wird eine vermeintlich patristische oder biblische Quelle angegeben, um so das Behauptete zu stützen: *Also schrybet sanctus Gregorius: ›So der mensche me na dem hemel wyrbet, so yme der vyant ye behentlicher zo gehet vnd ye me stercklichen myt yme strydet.‹* (CvH 9, 9–11) Der Bezug zu Gregor dem Großen steht am Anfang des Abschnitts, der Christinas Abkehr von allen weltlichen Dingen illustriert. Die feindlichen, nächtlichen Heimsuchungen des Teufels (*heißichster fyant*) werden

---

192 Es handelt sich um Berlin, Staatsbibliothek Preußischer Kulturbesitz, Ms. germ. oct. 56.
193 Vgl. ›Brandan‹. Die mitteldeutsche ›Reise‹-Fassung. Hrsg. von Reinhard Hahn/Christoph Fasbender (Jenaer germanistische Forschungen NF 14). Heidelberg 2002, hier V. 165–225.
194 Vgl. Reinhard Hahn/Christoph Fasbender (Hrsg.): ›Brandan‹. Die mitteldeutsche ›Reise‹-Fassung (Jenaer germanistische Forschungen NF 14). Heidelberg 2002, S. 99 f.
195 Vgl. Konrad von Megenberg: ›Das Buch der Natur‹. Hrsg. von Robert Luff/Georg Steer (Texte und Textgeschichte 54). 4 Bde. Tübingen 2003, Bd. 2: Kritischer Text nach den Handschriften, Buch III. D. 7, S. 274, Z. 12–19.

mit Christinas Streben nach himmlischen Dingen erklärt. Ob damit der im Spätmittelalter zunehmend an Bedeutung gewinnende Diskurs um die sogenannte »Unterscheidung der Geister« angesprochen ist,[196] bleibt dabei unwesentlich. Auch wenn der Teufel als Feindbild skizziert wird, geht es in Christinas Fall nicht um die Authentizität einer Vision und daher auch nicht im strengeren Sinn um die Unterscheidung der Geister.[197] Christinas sieben Jahre lang andauernder Kampf gegen die Todsünden wird viel mehr im Sinne einer tiefgründigen *purificatio* als Vorstufe der Seelenveredelung skizziert. Der erfolgreiche Widerstand steht im Verbund mit der Entwicklung innerer Tugenden. Die Überwindung einer jeden Kardinalsünde fördert zugleich die entsprechende Kardinaltugend, z.B.: *Also vberwant sie die hoiffart myt rechter oitmodicheit.* (CvH 13, 19 f.). Dieser Vorgang der *purificatio*, dem eine Phase der kontemplativen Übung Christinas folgt,[198] steht im Kontext monastisch-asketischer Modelle.[199] Der implizite Hagiograph weiß jedoch zu unterstreichen, dass keines der Heiligenvorbilder Christinas Strenge überstieg:

> *Jch eyn hayn noch nyt geleßen van keynem der menschen, der also swerlichen vnd auch also manchfeldenclichen hebe gestreden wieder die anfechtonge vnd auch also enxtlichen vnd gentzelichen vberwonden. Myr leßen woil van etzelichen heilgen, die gar stercklichen myt etzelichen vndogenden stretden vnd sie auch gar vollenkommenclichen vberwonden.* (CvH 9, 17–21)

Der indirekte Bezug zu Heiligengeschichten überhöht somit Christinas Askese, indem ihr Beispiel als überragend dargestellt wird.

---

196 Williams-Krapp (2012), S. 264 f. Rosalynn Voaden: God's Words, Women's Voices. The Discernment of Spirits in the Writing of Late-Medieval Women Visionaries. Woodbridge/Rochester 1999, S. 45, bringt den Diskurs um die Unterscheidung der Geister mit dem apophatischen Diskurs zusammen: »it [the discourse] establishes a language in which the ineffable can be articulated – and in which those articulations are examined, and either endorsed or condemned«.
197 Vgl. ähnlich Niklaus Largier: Rhetorik des Begehrens. Die ›Unterscheidung der Geister‹ als Paradigma mittelalterlicher Subjektivität. In: Inszenierungen von Subjektivität in der Literatur des Mittelalters. Hrsg. von Martin Baisch u.a. Königstein im Taunus 2005, S. 249–270, insbes. S. 250 und S. 261–266.
198 Vgl. CvH 16.
199 Siehe Susanne Köbele: Bonaventura. ›Itinerarium mentis in Deum‹ (1259). In: Literarische Performativität. Lektüren vormoderner Texte. Hrsg. von Cornelia Herberichs/Christian Kiening (Medienwandel – Medienwechsel – Medienwissen 3). Zürich 2008, S. 157–178, insbes. S. 157–160, zum Modell Bonaventuras. – Angela von Foligno durchlebt eine graduelle Entwicklung, die sich durch sieben Schritte auszeichnet, vgl. Elizabeth Alvilda Petroff: Medieval Women's Visionary Literature. New York/Oxford 1986, S. 10. Siehe auch Kirakosian (2017a) für einen Vergleich von Christinas Kampf gegen die Todsünden mit Radegunds Vita.

Für Christina von Hane geht diese Seelenläuterung mit der Kontemplation der Passion Christi einher.[200] Diese *imitatio Christi* schließt das eigene Leiden mit ein, wie es auch etwa in extremer Ausrichtung im Leidenskonzept Elsbeths von Oye vorzufinden ist.[201] Zur *imitatio Christi* kann auch die Versuchung durch den Teufel gezählt werden.[202] Christinas eigene Heimsuchung wird so zum Zeichen der Gotteserwählung verkehrt.[203] Der Erfolg ihres Widerstands wird als Teil eines Heilsplans skizziert: ›*Aber die got van herzen lyebt haynt, den wyrt alle dynge van gode zo dem aller besten gekeret*‹, *als sanctus Paulus spricht* (CvH 10, 55 f.).[204] Der Verweis auf den Paulusbrief an die Römer unterstreicht die Erwählung Christinas, da ihr die Zuversicht Gottes von vornherein – das schließt ihren Kampf gegen die Versuchung mit ein – zugesprochen wird. Weitere ›Anfechtungen‹ werden in diesem Sinne umgedeutet: *da wultde sie vnser lyeber here baßer versuchen vnd er verhenget aber vber sie dieselbe bekarunge des fleiß gar sere swerlichen.* (CvH 10, 59 f.)[205] Auch Christinas Versuchung im Bereich der *luxuria*, hier insbesondere der sexuellen Lust, gibt sich als Teil eines heilsgeschichtlichen Plans:

---

200 Vgl. CvH 16, 1–4. Siehe auch ähnliche Verbindungen in ›Die Offenbarungen der Adelheid Langmann‹ 1, 10 f. Siehe auch die ersten 19 Schritte Angelas von Foligno, (siehe dazu Lachance [1993], S. 18), vgl. insbes. Angela von Foligno: ›Memoriale‹ I, 212 f.: *Et tunc reclusi me in passione Christi; et data est mihi spes quod ibi poteram liberari.*

201 Zu Elsbeth von Oye siehe Burkhard Hasebrink: Elsbeth von Oye. Offenbarungen (um 1340). In: Literarische Performativität. Lektüren vormoderner Texte. Hrsg. von Cornelia Herberichs/ Christian Kiening (Medienwandel – Medienwechsel – Medienwissen 3). Zürich 2008, S. 259–279, und Gregor Wünsche: Imitatio Ioannis oder Elsbeths Apokalypse. Die ›Offenbarungen‹ Elsbeths im Kontext der dominikanischen Johannesfrömmigkeit im 14. Jahrhundert. In: Schmerz in der Literatur des Mittelalters und der Frühen Neuzeit. Hrsg. von Hans-Jochen Schiewer/Stefan Seeber/Markus Stock (Transatlantische Studien zu Mittelalter und früher Neuzeit 4). Göttingen 2010, S. 167–190. Die Edition der Vita Elsbeths von Oye ist in Vorbereitung durch Wolfram Schneider-Lastin, siehe dazu Monika Gsell: Das fließende Blut der Offenbarungen Elsbeths von Oye. In: Deutsche Mystik im abendländischen Zusammenhang. Neu erschlossene Texte, neue methodische Ansätze, neue theoretische Konzepte. Hrsg. von Walter Haug/Wolfram Schneider-Lastin. Tübingen 2000, S. 455–482.

202 Vgl. die in der Bibel geschilderten Versuchungen Christi durch den Teufel in der Wüste: Mt 4,1–11; Mc 1,12 f.; Lc 4,1–13. – Gefolgt wird hier und in allen weiteren Bibelverweisen der fünften Auflage der Vulgata-Ausgabe: Robert Weber/Roger Gryson (Hrsg.): Biblia Sacra Vulgata. 5. Aufl. Stuttgart 2007.

203 Eine andere Lesart würde in den Darstellungen eines Feindes die Nähe zum Grundton des Psalmisten sehen, wie das Andersen (2003), S. 232–234, für Mechthilds von Magdeburg ›Fließendes Licht‹ darlegt.

204 Vgl. Rm 8,28: *scimus autem quoniam diligentibus Deum omnia cooperantur in bonum his qui secundum propositum vocati sunt sancti.*

205 Bezüglich der Themen Anfechtung und Krisenerfahrung im ›Fließenden Licht der Gottheit‹ resümiert Suerbaum (2003), S. 251: »Auch in der Versuchung durch den Teufel manifestiert sich so letztlich Gottes Güte, die die Seele durch Leiden auf den Weg zu Gott zurücklenkt.«

Dyße swere lange anfechtonge verhenget vnser lyeber here vber sie nyt an sachen, want er woilt sie versuchen vnd beweren als den heilgen Tobiam, zo dem der engel sprache: ›So du gode woil befellest, so was noit, daz dich anfechtonge vnd vngemache beweret.‹ Auch ist geschreben yn dem boiche der wyßheit: ›Der here hait geprobert syne vßerwilten als daz golt yn dem oben des fürs.‹ (CvH 10, 8–13)

Hier wird ausdrücklich erläutert, dass es keinen eigentlichen Grund für Christinas Versuchung gibt (*nyt an sachen*), sondern dass diese stattdessen als Auszeichnung zu verstehen sei. Christinas Bewährung wird exegetisch untermauert, wobei der Vergleich zum Buch Tobias auf zwei Ebenen funktioniert. Sarah, Tobias' zukünftige Schwiegertochter, wird von einem ihr Sexualleben beeinflussenden bösen Geist befreit. Zuvor mussten alle sieben Bräutigame in ihrer jeweiligen Hochzeitsnacht sterben.[206] Die Verbindung zu Christinas Widerstand gegen sexuelle Lust macht deutlich, dass es bei diesem Vergleich um den gemeinsamen Nenner einer unschuldigen Jungfrau geht, die von einer äußeren, dämonischen Kraft beeinflusst wird und die nur vom richtigen, d.h. göttlich vorbestimmten Bräutigam von ihrem Fluch befreit werden kann.[207] Zum anderen wird das harte Schicksal des als gottesfürchtig dargestellten Tobias bereits im Bibeltext als Bewährungsprobe dargelegt: *hanc autem temptationem ideo permisit Dominus evenire illi ut posteris daretur exemplum patientiae eius sicut et sancti Iob* (Tb 2,12). Der Bezug zur alttestamentlichen Figur Tobias in der Leidensdarstellung ist nicht außergewöhnlich. In den ›St. Georgener Predigten‹ wird auf diese Weise erklärt, warum Gott dem ihn liebenden Menschen Leid aufbürdet:

Wan liset daz in manege wis in der scrift, den menschin, den got minnot, daz er deme arbaite git. [...] Do kan der engil unde troste in vnde sprach: ›[...] Ez můs sin unde sol sin, daz du arbaite habest, wan got der minnet dich.‹ Owe, sæliger mensche, daz sol dir ain trost sin in der nöte, daz du gedenchest, daz dich got minnet, so er dir arbaite git. (›St. Georgener Predigten‹ 26, 170–176)

Wie bei Tobias ist auch Christinas Versuchung keine Strafe sondern eine Belohnung und eine Auszeichnung, die den didaktischen Nutzen mit sich bringt, ein Vorbild zu sein.[208]

---

206 Vgl. Tb 3,8.

207 Diese Interpretation legt auch der Vergleich mit der Maria Magdalena-Bekehrungslegende nahe, siehe unten Kap. 2.2.2.

208 Siehe auch die folgende Textstelle: *Auch so wil ich eyn deyl hie schryben, wie wyßlich myt starcker vbonge sie wieder stontde vnd alle vndogent vberwant vnd sie alle vnder sich tratte, daz dyße eyn spegel vnd eyn forme sy aller der, die yn dyeßem leben stryden wullent wieder die anfechtonge der vndogent.* (CvH 9, 13–16)

Die sieben Jahre asketischer Übung im Kampf gegen die Todsünden werden für den impliziten Leser des Textes zusammengefasst und resümiert:

> *Nyt eyn verwonder dich, daz eyn also zarte jonffrauwe also swerlichen versucht wart durch bekarunge vnd die also rytterlichen vberwonden hait als dyeße jonffrauwe, dan sie ist geproifft als daz golt yn dem füer.* (CvH 15, 14–17)

In einer imperativischen Negation soll der Leser in seinem Verständnis gelenkt werden. Zusätzlich dazu wird ein biblischer Kontext eröffnet, der Christinas Besonderheit betont und ihren Leidensweg nur als Bestätigung dessen darlegt.[209] Die beiden Schlagwörter *golt* und *füer* sind im Manuskript unterstrichen, sodass bereits ein überfliegendes Lesen einen biblischen Referenzrahmen hervorzurufen vermag.[210] Auch an anderer Stelle soll der Vergleich mit dem im Feuer geprüften Gold die Härte von Christinas Kampf, der Krankheit und Versuchung miteinschließt, vor Augen führen. Die Heilsgewissheit dieser Umstände wird zum einen durch den Trost, den sie anschließend erfährt, bestätigt, zum anderen durch das Opfer, das sie der ganzen Welt zuliebe leide.[211] Gerade letzteres stellt die Verbindung zur *imitatio Christi* her, womit die Modellhaftigkeit des einzelnen Lebens

---

209 Vgl. 1. Pt 1,7 (im Feuer bewährtes Gold); Mal 3,3 (Gold und Silber unter Prüfung); Ps 66,10 (Silber, das geläutert wird). Verstärkend wird das Bild des geprüften Goldes im Feuerofen, das im Textverlauf erneut auftritt, hervorgerufen. Es geht auf die Geschichte der Jünglinge im Feuerofen aus dem alttestamentlichen Buch Daniel zurück und kann als Redewendung u.a. in den Sprüchen wiedergefunden werden, vgl. Dan 3. Geprüftes Edelmetall im Ofen kommt sonst auch in Prv 17,3 (Gold und Silber im Ofen geprüft als Vergleich für die Prüfung des menschlichen Herzens) und Is 48,10 (Silber im Ofen) vor.

210 Die Kindheit und Jugend Christinas werden weiterführend veranschaulicht: *Jre kyntliche tzijt hait sie gedroncken die mylche der troistlicher vnd lustlicher beschauwonge yn der kyntheit vnsers heren Jhesu Cristi. Aber yn der bloender jogent ist sie gespyste worden myt eym grauffen broyt, daz sie wurde gesterckt vnd bereyt zo groißeren dyngen vnd vollenkommener wege.* (CvH 15, 17–20) – Die Analogisierung von flüssiger Nahrung (Milch) in der Kindheit und fester Nahrung (Brot) in der Jugend trägt eucharistische Züge. Die Muttermilch-Metaphorik, d.h. die Liebe, mit der man zu Gott aufgezogen wird, begegnet so auch im ›St. Trudperter Hohenlied‹, vgl. ›Das St. Trudperter Hohelied‹. Eine Lehre der liebenden Gotteserkenntnis. Hrsg. von Friedrich Ohly (Bibliothek des Mittelalters 2, Bibliothek deutscher Klassiker 155). Frankfurt a.M. 1998, hier 139, 24–26. (Die Stellennachweise geben Vers- und Zeilenzahlen an.)

211 Vgl.: *Vnd also hait sie gelieden vnsprechelichen krenckten yrs lybes vnd yres hertzen. Also als daz golt wyrt geproffet yn dem füer, also ist sie gantze durch luter worden jnwendich vnd vßewendich durch yre groiße lyebde vnd gedult, die sy leytde vor alle die gantze werelt.* (CvH 65, 27–30) Vgl. dazu die Anrede Christi an Adelheid Langmann: *ich gib dir offt ze leiden dor üm, daz ich sein [vater] gerüemen müg in dem himel.* (›Die Offenbarungen der Adelheid Langmann‹ 11, 10 f.)

thematisiert wird.[212] So ist auch die Bewährung des Goldes im Feuer ein weiteres Bild für den Christina auszeichnenden ›Seelenadel‹.[213]

Die Versicherung, dass es sich insbesondere bei den körperlichen Leiden um eine Station auf dem Weg zu Gott handelt,[214] wird auch in anderen mystischen Texten des Spätmittelalters mit biblischen Bezügen unterstrichen.[215] Ein Vergleich zur deutschen Version von Gertruds ›Legatus divinae pietatis‹ veranschaulicht, dass bei Christina wie bei Gertrud eine Mystik des Herzens im Vordergrund steht: Gott möchte dabei im Herzen jenes Menschen wohnen, welchen er zuvor durch Leid geläutert hat.[216] Auch bei Getrud wird dieser Prozess mit einem Verweis auf den biblischen Text erläutert. So heißt es im deutschen ›botten der götlichen miltekeit‹:

> *Von got, der sin wurtschaft haben wil mit den kinden der mônschen, wart ir eines moles ingesprochen, das es dig geschehe, wen got kein redelich ursach hat, das er mit reht gewonen mûge by dem mônchen, so sendet er im liden und trûpsal, darumb das er mit dester besserem reht by im blibe. Wenn die geschrift der worheit sprichet also: Der herre ist den nohe, die ein betrûbtes hertze haben und die versmeht sint. Er sprichet ôch: In der betrûpsal wil ich by in sin.* (Gertrud von Helfta, ›ein botte der götlichen miltekeit‹ 43, 2–8)[217]

---

212 Vgl. die Analogisierung von Adelheid Langmanns Leiden mit der Passion Christi (›Die Offenbarungen der Adelheid Langmann‹ 61, 5–11). Für Margaretha Ebner siehe auch Garber (2003), S. 110 f.

213 Bereits im Kindesalter zeichnet sich der Seelenadel ab, vgl.: *dan die jonge zarte sele van yrem adel wart erkant* (CvH 2, 4 f.).

214 Siehe auch Leiden als Manifestation der Heiligkeit bei Dorothea von Montau, vgl. Johannes Marienwerder: ›Das Leben der heiligen Dorothea von Montau‹. Hrsg. von Max Töppen. In: Scriptores rerum Prussicarum. Die Geschichtsquellen der preußischen Vorzeit bis zum Untergange der Ordenherrschaft. Hrsg. von Theodor Hirsch/Max Töppen/Ernst Strehlke. Bd. 2. Leipzig 1863 (Nachdruck Frankfurt a. M. 1963), S. 197–350, hier II 25, 266; I 5, 205; II 16, 250. (Die Stellennachweise geben Buch-, Kapitel- und Seitenzahlen an.)

215 Im ›Fließenden Licht‹ Mechthilds von Magdeburg wird diese Verbindung mit einem elaborierten Gleichnis zwischen der Seele und der Passion Christi dargestellt, vgl. Mechthild von Magdeburg, ›Das fließende Licht der Gottheit‹ III 10. Siehe auch das Leiden zur Ehre Gottes bei Heinrich Seuse: ›Büchlein der ewigen Weisheit‹. In: Heinrich Seuse. Deutsche Schriften Hrsg. von Karl Bihlmeyer. Stuttgart 1907 (unver. Nachdruck Frankfurt a. M. 1961), S. 196–325, insbes. 13, 248–254. (Die Stellennachweise geben Kapitel- und Seitenzahlen an.)

216 Ruh (1993), S. 122, schließt nicht aus, dass Christinas»Vitenschreiber Kenntnis des ›Liber specialis gratiae‹ und des ›Legatus divinae pietatis‹ hatte.«

217 Gertrud von Helfta: ›ein botte der götlichen miltekeit‹. Hrsg. von Otmar Wieland (Studien und Mitteilungen zur Geschichte des Benediktiner-Ordens und seiner Zweige. Ergänzungsband 22). Ottobeuren 1973. (Die Stellennachweise geben Kapitelzahlen an; gegebenenfalls werden auch die Zeilenzahlen referiert.)

Das himmlische Wirtschafthalten, von dem hier die Rede ist, steht in Verbindung mit dem Wohnen Gottes im Menschen;[218] ein gängiges Bild für das geistliche Leben, wie es auch in den ›St. Georgener Predigten‹ im Verbund mit Esthers Hochzeitsfest vorkommt, wo das *gotliche gezelt* als Bild für die ›Vermählung‹ zwischen Gott und Seele verwendet wird.[219] Wie bei Gertrud von Helfta wird in der Christina von Hane-Vita der Leidensprozess mit dem Einzug Christi ins Herz des Menschen belohnt:

> *Da wart yre hertze geliche der luterer sonnen, yn der daz lyebliche kyntgyn da vor betzeichenclichen vor yr yn der sonnen yn dem chore gespellet haitte, als der propheta yn dem selter spricht: ›Vnser lyeber here hait syn huyße, daz ist syne wannunge, gesaitzet yn die sonne.‹*
> (CvH 4, 25–29)

Das Psalmzitat ist dabei in den Kontext des Erzählerkommentars eingebettet, indem ein Attributsatz daran angeknüpft wird: Was »der Prophet« im Psalm singt (*in sole posuit tabernaculum suum*, Ps 18,6), wird hier spezifiziert und so ausgelegt, dass der Bezug zu Christinas Geschichte ersichtlich wird. Denn schon im Kindesalter sieht Christina das Jesuskind in der Sonne spielen, *als abe iß yme eyn beytgen wultde machen vß der sonnen. Also gaiffe er yr zo verstayn, daz er alleyn wille rogen yn dem hertzen, daz da luter ist als die sonne.* (CvH 3, 6–8)[220] Das wiederholte Motiv, Gott wolle wohnen/ruhen in dem Herzen, das heller als die Sonne leuchte, fällt dabei besonders auf. Es verweist nicht nur textintern darauf, dass Christinas Herz bereits der Sonne gleiche; der Bezug zum Psalmisten als Autoritätsquelle untermauert außerdem die Interpretation des Vergleichs Sonne–Herz und gibt so der Aussage über Christinas reines Herz die maßgebliche Fundierung.

Bibelzitate werden auch in die direkte Rede Christinas transponiert:

> *da sprach sie: ›Got eyn laiste die nummerme, die yn ynne hoiffent.‹ Van den der prophete spricht: ›Die begertde der armen hait der here gehoirt, syne augen sehent zo den armen. Der mylde troister aller bedruppter hertzen, die zo yme haitte gesufftzet, er hait an gesehen synne arme dyrne, sy zo troisten jn yrem noitde.‹* (CvH 10, 87–91)

---

218 Vgl. Nigel F. Palmer: Herzeliebe, weltlich und geistlich. Zur Metaphorik vom ›Einwohnen im Herzen‹ bei Wolfram von Eschenbach, Juliana von Cornillon, Hugo von Langenstein und Gertrud von Helfta. In: Innenräume in der Literatur des deutschen Mittelalters. XIX. Anglo-German Colloquium Oxford 2005. Hrsg. von Burkhard Hasebrink u. a. Tübingen 2008, S. 197–224, insbes. S. 204–208. Ältere Arbeiten zum Motiv des Wohnens im Herzen sind bei Keller (2000a), S. 214, Anm. 86 angegeben.
219 ›St. Georgener Predigten‹ 5, 132–257.
220 Vgl. die Jesuskind-Vision Adelheid Langmanns, ›Die Offenbarungen der Adelheid Langmann‹ 18, 21 f. – 19, 10.

Zwar lässt sich der Beginn der Rede klar mit einem Psalmvers identifizieren (*et confident in te qui noverunt nomen tuum quoniam non dereliquisti quaerentes te Domine*, Ps 9,11), doch was im Anschluss als die vermeintlichen Worte des Propheten folgt, erinnert wegen der Erwähnung der darauffolgenden *armen dyrne* eher an das Magnifikat,[221] auch wenn dieses selbst zum Teil erneut auf Psalmen zurückgeht.[222] Vor allem aber wird Christina selbst zum Sprachrohr der biblischen Worte.[223] Was dieses Sprecher-Ich über Gott ausdrückt, soll auf es selbst zurückfallen: Christina autorisiert ihre eigenen Erfahrungen mit den entsprechenden biblischen Worten.

Der chronologische mit dem Kirchenjahr verflochtene Erzählstrang stellt immer wieder Bezüge zu den als historisch dargestellten Ereignissen im Evangelium her, wie z.B. in der folgenden Passage:

> *Jn dem selben jaire da daz hogetzijt quam der gebort vnsers heren, als daz lyebe kyntgyn Jhesus geboren wart, dyße seliche jonffrauwe haitte alle yre begerde vnd gedancken vnd alle betrachtonge an vnderlaiß by dem lyeben kyntgyn, vnd van der kyntheit Jhesu wart yre begerde gemeret vnd me entzŭndet van dem geynwerdichen hogetzijt der gebort des gotlichen jonfferlichen kyngyns, wie sie sich bereytden moicht entgeyn daz lyebe kyntgyn, daz iß geistlich yn jre hertze vnd sele sich wultde veruerdichen geboren zo werden, vff daz sie sich des lyeben kyngyns nach yrs hertzen begerde woille gebruchen mocht.* (CvH 5, 2–9)

Historisches Ereignis, liturgische Feier und innere Anbetung des Kindes durch Christina fallen zusammen.[224] Die Sonderstellung Christinas wird an anderer Stelle durch ihr Gebet an Pfingsten mit den Jüngern in der Apostelgeschichte verglichen:

---

221 Vgl. Lc 1,46–55.

222 Vgl. Ps 103,13 und 17; Ps 34,11; Ps 107,9.

223 Zu diesen Formen göttlichen Sprechens siehe Andersen (2003), Suerbaum (2003) und Annette Volfing: Dialog und Brautmystik bei Mechthild von Magdeburg. In: Dialoge. Sprachliche Kommunikation in und zwischen Texten im deutschen Mittelalter. Hamburger Colloquium 1999. Hrsg. von Nikolaus Henkel/Martin H. Jones/Nigel F. Palmer. Tübingen 2003, S. 257–266.

224 Historisch, d.h. mit anderen dokumentierten Erwähnungen, kann Christinas Lebenszeit ohnehin nicht abgeglichen werden. Mittermaiers Bemühung, seiner Edition Jahreszahlen beizufügen, wo sie nicht explizit genannt waren, musste angesichts der sich häufig wiederholenden Festtage ohne Jahresangabe in eine uneindeutige Zuordnung münden, vgl. ›Lebensbeschreibung der sel. Christina, gen. von Retters‹. Hrsg. von Franz Paul Mittermaier: In: Archiv für Mittelrheinische Kirchengeschichte 17 (1965), S. 226–251, und Archiv für Mittelrheinische Kirchengeschichte 18 (1966), S. 203–238. Die wenigen Jahresangaben im Text sind als Strategie hagiographischen Schreibens zu verstehen, das zum Ziel hat, das Leben der begnadeten Person in einen zeitlich nachvollziehbaren und dadurch heilsgeschichtlich linearen Rahmen zu setzen.

An dem pynxste abent zo nacht saße sie an yrem stoille byß zo metten tzijt wachende jn groißer burnender begerden, das yr got woilt senden daz lyecht vnd das füre des heilgen geistes, da van daz yre sele erlucht moichte werden yn erkentenyß vnd entzonte yn lyebden, als die heilgen apostelen worden entfencket. (CvH 21, 1–5)

Dem entsprechenden Festtag zugeordnet, verweist die Feuer-Metaphorik auf das Pfingstgeschehen. Ein weiterer Bezug zur Apostelgeschichte rückt Christina in den Status eines biblischen Jüngers Christi:

Da wart jre hertze freuden voille. Aber da sie myt froelicher begerden na yme gryffen woiltde, daz sie daz aller lyeplichste kyntgen vmbfangen, gehelßet vnd gekůßet hette vnd zertlichen an yre hertze gedrucket hette, da fant sie yne nyt, dan er was verswonden van yre, als er auch in Emaůs vor den jongeren verswant, als daz ewangelium spricht. (CvH 3, 13–17)

Die Parallele zu den Jüngern von Emmaus impliziert, dass Christina das Jesuskind leiblich, d. h. mit sinnlichen Augen, gesehen hat.[225] Für das hagiographische Schreiben erscheint hier erneut die Quelle der Autorisierung wichtig. Biblische Verse werden nicht nur als Anspielungen, sondern als Brücken zu einem außerzeitlichen Geschehen genutzt. In einer Vision wird so betont, dass die Taube der Taufe Christi am Jordan dieselbe sei, die nun auf Christinas Haupt fliege: *Dyß ist die dube: der heilge geist, der jn der gestailt eyner duben, als man yme ewangelio leßet, daz eyn dube floge vff vnseren heren, als er getaufft wart van sent Johannes. Dyße dube floge nu vff dyße jonffrauwe, synne brůyt* (CvH 7, 30–33).[226] Mit der Rückbindung an das biblische Geschehen soll kein Zweifel an der Heiligkeit Christinas gelassen werden, obgleich die Taube im Neuen Testament nur als Vergleich zum Heiligen Geist gebraucht wird (*et testimonium perhibuit Iohannes dicens quia vidi Spiritum descendentem quasi columbam de caelo et mansit super eum*, Io 1,32.). Christinas Leben wird dadurch in eine zeitlose Sphäre versetzt, in der ihre Heiligkeit Teil eines großen, universellen Heilsgeschehens ist.

Das hagiographische Schreiben operiert mit traditionellen Instrumenten der Bibelexegese wie der allegorischen Parallelisierung.[227] Oftmals handelt es sich, wie an den oben zitierten Stellen zu sehen ist, um kurze Anspielungen, aber diese reichen aus, um eine bestimmte Gedankenwelt hervorzurufen. Im monastischen Referenzrahmen, in dem Bibeltexte und patristische Schriften zur alltäglichen Literatur gehören, handelt es sich daher um eine argumentative Strategie, die

---

225 Vgl. Lc 24,13–35. Siehe auch bei Adelheid Langmann das Verschwinden Christi im Moment der Erkenntnis, ›Die Offenbarungen der Adelheid Langmann‹ 19, 10.
226 Zu dieser und anderen Visionen der Christina von Hane-Vita siehe jetzt Kirakosian (2017b).
227 Vgl. Röckelein (2000), S. 3.

ihre Autorisierung erst in der Textrezeption gänzlich entfaltete. In den angeführten Beispielen tritt die illokutionäre Dimension eines Sprechakts deutlich hervor: Indem die Aussagen als direkte Reden oder wörtliche Zitate der entsprechenden Autoritäten dargestellt werden, wird ihnen ein Wahrheitscharakter beigemessen, der seine Gültigkeit außerhalb des Textes zu beziehen vorgibt, sodass der nötige Rückhalt bei etablierten Quellen eingeholt wird. Ob es sich dabei um ›echte‹ Zitate handelt, die in anderen Schriftzeugnissen belegt sind, ist nicht immer nachweisbar, scheint aber für die jeweilige Heiligkeitsdarstellung nicht von Belang. Es geht nämlich weniger um die Authentizität des Zitatinhalts als um die Autorisierung des Erzählten in einem als approbiert dargestellten Referenzrahmen.

2.2.2 Konstitution von Heilsgewissheit

Erwählung, Einsicht in die eigene Sündenhaftigkeit, Läuterung, der Tugendkatalog und die starke Dominanz des Bittgebets sind Themen dieser und anderer Viten.[228] Die *narratio* der Christina von Hane-Vita weist ebenfalls eine hagiographische Struktur auf, mit Anfang (Initiation des heiligen Lebens durch Klostereintritt)[229] und Mitte (Leidensweg und Wundertätigkeit in Visionen und Fürbittenpraxis); der Text endet hier, sodass nicht sicher auszumachen ist, ob er mit Tod und Nachleben geendet hätte. Mit dem Versuch, ein rundes Leben darzustellen, wird eine historisch-biographische Dimension beansprucht.[230] Auch

---

228 Vgl. Suerbaum (2003), S. 253, und Ringler (1980), S. 10. Siehe auch Gisela Vollmann-Profe: Mechthild in der Provinz. ›Das fließende Licht der Gottheit‹ und ›Das Leben der heiligen Dorothea‹. In: Impulse und Resonanzen. Tübinger mediävistische Beiträge zum 80. Geburtstag von Walter Haug. Hrsg. von Gisela Vollmann-Profe u. a. Tübingen 2007, S. 265–274, insbes. S. 268 f., speziell zu Dorothea von Montau.
229 Christina wird auf Anraten Gottes ins Kloster gebracht, vgl. CvH 1, 7–9. Vergleichbar ist der ausdrückliche Gotteswille, Adelheid Langmann an ein Kloster zu übergeben: *ja ez ist mein wille. ich will si haben swo si ist, da si ein ist mit mir* [...] *da si niman ist* (›Die Offenbarungen der Adelheid Langmann‹ 2, 5–8). – Vgl. Eva Schlotheuber: Klostereintritt und Übergangsriten. Die Bedeutung der Jungfräulichkeit für das Selbstverständnis der Nonnen der alten Orden. In: Frauen – Kloster – Kunst. Neue Forschungen zur Kulturgeschichte des Mittelalters. Beiträge zum internationalen Kolloquium vom 13. bis 16. Mai 2005 anlässlich der Ausstellung ›Krone und Schleier‹. Hrsg. von Jeffrey F. Hamburger / Carola Jäggi. Turnhout 2007, S. 43–55, zur Symbolik und Praxis des Klostereintritts einer Nonne im Mittelalter und ihrer anschließenden Erziehung zum Tugendleben.
230 Vgl. Balázs J. Nemes / Almut Märker: ›Hunc tercium conscripsi cum maximo labore occultandi‹. Schwester N von Helfta und ihre ›Sonderausgabe‹ des ›Legatus divinae pietatis‹ Gertruds von Helfta in der Leipziger Handschrift Ms 827. In: PBB 137 (2015), S. 248–296, insbes. S. 293, Anm. 125, zum hagiographischen Versuch historisch-biographischer Konkretisierung.

das entspricht dem hagiographischen Erzählen, wie bereits die ersten deutschen Prosa-Viten im Bereich der Klosterhistoriographie zeigen.[231] So ist in unserem Fall selbst die historisierende Angabe für Christinas Geburt im ersten Textabschnitt – das Jahr 1275 in römischen Ziffern und erneut ausgeschrieben – als Gestus zu verstehen, der den Authentizitätsgrad des Erzählten steigern soll.[232] Rhetorische Autorisierungsstrategien nehmen einen großen Stellenwert ein, weil ein Wahrheitsanspruch erhoben wird, bei dem allerdings allein die Wirkkraft der Sprache den Tatbestand schafft: Hagiographie will verfügen und nachweisen, Heiligkeit handelt aber vom Unverfügbaren. Bevor die Textlektüre der Vita fortgesetzt wird, soll an dieser Stelle eine kurze Forschungsposition, die das legendarische Erzählen thematisiert, skizziert werden.

Obwohl oder gerade weil es in der Hagiographie im engeren Sinne um die sprachliche Beweisführung von Heiligkeit geht, bleibt allein die Rhetorik, um dieses epistemologische Ungleichgewicht zu balancieren. Das »Gelingen der Erzählung«, so Köbele, sei die einzige Möglichkeit, das Vakuum zu füllen, wo Evidenzen für die Heiligkeit grundsätzlich fehlten.[233] Was Strohschneider für das legendarische Erzählen als konstitutiv bestimmt – dass es »durch ein unaufhebbares Geltungsdefizit« gekennzeichnet sei –, gilt auch allgemein für hagiographisches Erzählen:

> Die narrative Rede über Heiligkeit selbst verfügt keineswegs immer schon über höchste Geltung. Im Gegenteil: Sie ist ja stets ein Immanenz-Moment, ein Teil von ›Welt‹, und das bedeutet, dass schon insofern der Erzählakt hier immer von seinem Erzählgegenstand her devaluiert wird.[234]

---

231 Vgl. Konrad Kunze: Deutschsprachige Hagiographie von den Anfängen bis 1350. In: Hagiographies. Histoire internationale de la littérature hagiographique, latine et vernaculaire, en Occident, des origines á 1550. Bd. 2. Hrsg. von Guy Philippart (Corpus Christianorum Hagiographies 2). Turnhout 1996, S. 211–238, insbes. S. 225. – Siehe auch Michael Angold: The Fourth Crusade. Event and Context. Harlow 2003, S. 12, zur allgemeinen Annahme, dass im Kontext der hochmittelalterlichen Geschichtsschreibung Verse der Unterhaltung dienten, während Prosa von der Wahrheit handelte.
232 Zum Spannungsfeld zwischen Historiographie und Hagiographie siehe Röckelein (2000), S. 2–7, und die Beiträge im Band Richard Corradini/Max Diesenberger/Meta Niederkorn-Bruck (Hrsg.): Zwischen Niederschrift und Wiederschrift. Hagiographie und Historiographie im Spannungsfeld von Kompendienüberlieferung und Editionstechnik (Forschungen zur Geschichte des Mittelalters 18). Wien 2010.
233 Für die Legende erörtert dies Köbele (2012), S. 396 f.
234 Peter Strohschneider: Textheilung. Geltungsstrategien legendarischen Erzählens im Mittelalter am Beispiel von Konrads von Würzburg ›Alexius‹. In: Über die Stabilisierung und Legitimierung institutioneller Ordnungen. Hrsg. von Gert Melville/Hans Vorländer. Köln/Weimar/Wien 2002, S. 109–147, hier S. 116 f.

Zu fragen wird also sein, ob die Christina von Hane-Vita einen solchen insbesondere religiösen Texten anzuhaften scheinenden Legitimierungsbedarf aufweist, und wenn ja, wie sie ihn kompensiert.[235]

Ein Vergleich mit der im Kodex Straßburg, BNU, Ms. 324 mitüberlieferten fragmentarischen Bekehrungslegende der Maria Magdalena schärft den Blick auf eine hagiographische Rhetorik in der Christina von Hane-Vita. Beide Abschriften sind wahrscheinlich gemeinsam entstanden. Dass in der selben Handschrift zwei so unterschiedliche Texte von gleicher Hand und in unmittelbarer Abfolge überliefert werden, erscheint angesichts der Diversität der hagiographischen Texttypen im Spätmittelalter plausibel; so kann im Zuge der Reformbewegungen eine anwachsende Popularität der Legenden und eine damit einhergehende Intensivierung der Heiligenverehrung beobachtet werden.[236] Ringler plädiert für ein gattungsbewusstes Tradieren der Legendenform:

> Das konsequente Schreiben in legendarischen Stilformen darf auch im Bereich der Nonnenliteratur nicht länger als das Ungenügen einer wenig gebildeten, wundersüchtigen Verfasserin gelten, sondern muss als formbewusster Gebrauch einer ausgeprägten literarischen Aussageweise ernst genommen werden.[237]

Legendentraditionen gehen bei allem Formbewusstsein dynamisch mit ihrem Stoff um. Das demonstriert die Figurenkonstruktion Maria Magdalenas im Mittelalter. Drei verschiedene biblische Personen schmolzen hier zu einer Figur zusammen: die von Dämonen besessene und schließlich bekehrte Maria von Magdala, die den Kreuzestod Christi miterlebt,[238] Marthas und Lazarus' Schwester Maria von Bethanien[239] und eine namenlose Sünderin, die Christi Füße mit ihren Tränen befeuchtet und mit ihren langen Haaren trocknet.[240] Zudem steuerten apokryphe

---

235 Zum Legitimierungsbedarf siehe Beate Kellner: Wort Gottes – Stimme des Menschen. Textstatus und Profile von Autorschaft in Otfrids von Weißenburg ›Evangelienbuch‹. In: Geltung der Literatur. Formen ihrer Autorisierung und Legitimierung im Mittelalter. Hrsg. von Beate Kellner/Peter Strohschneider/Franziska Wenzel (Philologische Studien und Quellen 190). Berlin 2005, S. 139–162, insbes. S. 141.
236 Vgl. Williams-Krapp (1993) und ders. (1994), S. 269.
237 Ringler (1980), S. 11. Zur gattungstheoretischen Forschungsdiskussion der Legende siehe Strohschneider (2014) S. 177, Anm. 112.
238 Vgl. die folgenden Bibelstellen: als Jüngerin Lc 8,1–3, am Kreuz und bei der Grablegung Mt 27,55–61; Mc 15,40–47; Lc 23,49–56; Io 19,25, am Auferstehungsgrab Mt 28,1–8; Mc 16,1–8; Lc 24,1–10; Io 20,1–13, als Zeugin und Verkünderin der Auferstehung Mt 28,9 f.; Mc 16,9–11; Io 20,14–18.
239 Vgl. die folgenden Bibelstellen: als Schwester von Martha und Lazarus Lc 10,38–42; Io 11,1–45; Salbung Christi durch Maria von Bethanien Mt 26,6–13; Mc 14,3–9; Io 12,1–8.
240 Vgl. Lc 7,36–50.

Legenden wie die der Maria von Ägypten Elemente bei.[241] Die mit der Christina von Hane-Vita überlieferte Magdalenenlegende ist Teil einer Legendenrezeption im deutschsprachigen Raum, die »unbedingt die niederländische Produktion« miteinbezieht.[242] Die Handschrift des mittelniederländischen Magdalenenlegendentexts nach *G* (Den Haag, Koninklijke Bibliotheek, cod. 133 F 17) tradiert u.a. auch Jan Ruusbroecs ›Van den gheesteliken Tabernakele‹.[243] In der Den Haager Handschrift wie im volkssprachigen Teil von *S* (Straßburg, BNU, Ms. 324) ist also das Nebeneinander einer Legende mit einem oder mehreren spirituellen oder mystischen Texten zu beobachten.

Während die Überlieferung in *S* die Christina von Hane-Vita und die Maria Magdalena-Bekehrungslegende miteinander verbindet, scheinen sie sich als Texttypen dennoch zu unterscheiden: In der Christina von Hane-Vita liegt ein finales Erzählen mit linearer Heilsgewissheit vor. Die Andersartigkeit der Protagonistin im Vergleich zu ihrem Umfeld wird bereits im Kindesalter etabliert.[244] Der Weg zur Veredelung der Seele entspricht einer kalkulierten Heiligkeit, während in der *conversio*-Legende das unerwartete Ereignis die plötzliche Läuterung bringt. Köbele macht einen derartigen Unterschied in der Heilsdarstellung rhetorisch fest. Die Legende sei ein besonderer Texttyp der Hagiographie, deren »Hauptfunktion [...] die narrative Stabilisierung von Heilsgewissheit« darstelle.[245] Das Besondere an diesem Texttyp bestehe darin, dass die »Heils-Selbstverständlichkeit« nicht linear wiedergegeben werde, wie das finale Erzählen zunächst glauben lasse.[246] Dem Protagonisten dürfe die Selbstevidenz der eigenen Heiligkeit nicht ersichtlich sein, was sich auf die narrative Struktur der Erzählung auswirke.[247] Zu

---

241 Vgl. Katherine Ludwig Jansen: The Making of the Magdalen. Preaching and Popular Devotion in the Later Middle Ages. Princeton/Chichester 2000, zum Bild Maria Magdalenas im Mittelalter.

242 Williams-Krapp (1994), S. 267.

243 Zu *G* und zur gesamten Parallelüberlieferung der Maria Magdalena-Bekehrungslegende siehe unten im Teil B, Kap. 1.2 und 2.2.

244 Vgl. CvH 1–2. – Die besondere Stellung Adelheid Langmanns wird ebenfalls im Kindesalter ersichtlich: *der heilig geist mit ir gewont hot von kind uf* (›Die Offenbarungen der Adelheid Langmann‹ 1, 3 f.); *daz kint füeget nit wann in ein closter* (›Die Offenbarungen der Adelheid Langmann‹ 1, 13 f.); siehe dazu Emmelius (2008), S. 317.

245 Köbele (2012), S. 366. Siehe auch André Jolles: Einfache Formen. Legende, Sage, Mythe, Rätsel, Spruch, Kasus, Memorabile, Märchen, Witz (Konzepte der Sprach-und Literaturwissenschaft 15). 5. Aufl. Tübingen 1974 (Originalausgabe Tübingen 1930), S. 33.

246 Köbele (2012), S. 399.

247 Vgl. Susanne Köbele: ›heilicheit durchbrechen‹. Grenzfälle von Heiligkeit in der mittelalterlichen Mystik. In: Sakralität zwischen Antike und Neuzeit. Hrsg. von Berndt Hamm/Klaus Herbers/Heidrun Stein-Kecks (Beiträge zur Hagiographie 6). Stuttgart 2007, S. 147–169.

einem ähnlichen Schluss kommt auch Strohschneider, der anhand zweier Legenden aus dem Passional zeigt, dass die Heiligwerdung ein am Heiligen vollzogenes
Ereignis ist, das vom selben auch erst mitvollzogen werden muss.[248] Das heißt,
dass das Muster der *conversio*-Geschehnisse dem Heiligen nicht von vornherein bekannt ist. Strohschneider kommt es dabei weniger »auf die traditionsbil-
dende Kraft eines Konversionsmodells« als auf die an eine Lektüre gebundenen
»Erzähl-Kräfte« an.[249] Der Unterschied zwischen Heiligenvita und Legende liege
also im thematischen Wendepunkt, der sich auf die Erzählstrategien auswirke.
So bedarf es in der Legende auch keiner Autorisierungsstrategie, weil es zum
Texttyp gehört, so »tun zu müssen«, als sei das Wunder evident.[250] Rhetorische
Beweisführungen würden dieses Prinzip in Frage stellen, während sie in der Vita
die Heiligkeit erst konstituieren.

Denkbar ist auch, dass in der Christina von Hane-Vita eine »ambivalente
Rhetorik-Einstellung«,[251] bei der die Heiligkeit der Protagonistin verdeckt bleiben
kann, zu kurz greift, weil sie weder eine bekannte Figur noch eine approbierte
Heilige betrifft. Zugleich kann nicht von einer ausnahmslos innerlichen Heiligkeit gesprochen werden, denn trotz des mystischen Lebensweges muss Christinas
Heiligkeit evident werden, d.h. externalisiert werden, und zwar nicht nur auf die-
getischer Ebene. Auch in rhetorischer Hinsicht dienen der einführende Textabschnitt in seiner Bildhaftigkeit (z.B. *roiße vnder anderen blomen* [CvH 1, 10]), die
verschiedenen direkten und indirekten Bibelallusionen sowie die patristischen
Zitate als Strategien einer formalen Darstellung ihres Heiligenstatus.

Dennoch gibt es strukturelle und thematische Gemeinsamkeiten zwischen
den beiden Texttypen Vita und Legende. Mit Ecker gesprochen weisen beide
eine dogmatische (theologisch-ideologische) Dimension mit einer appellativen
(»pragmatisch rezeptiven«) Struktur auf, die den Leser über die Unterhaltung
hinaus zu einer kritischen Reflexion mit dem eigenen Leben führen möchte und
die daher Anspruch auf eine praktische Relevanz des Berichteten erhebt.[252] Vor
allem die christlich-areopagitische Moral der *purificatio* (z.T. mit vorauslaufen-
der *conversio*) wird in beiden Texten angesprochen:[253] Christina überwindet die

---

248 Vgl. Strohschneider (2014), S. 203.
249 Strohschneider (2014), S. 212.
250 Köbele (2012), S. 395.
251 Köbele (2012), S. 401.
252 Vgl. Hans-Peter Ecker: Die Legende. Kulturanthropologische Annäherung an eine literarische Gattung (Germanistische Abhandlungen 76). Stuttgart/Weimar 1993, S. 11–91 und S. 116–235.
253 Zum Prinzip einer läuterbaren Seele siehe Alois Maria Haas: Die deutsche Mystik im Spannungsbereich von Theologie und Spiritualität. In: Literatur und Laienbildung im Spätmittelalter
und in der Reformationszeit. Symposion Wolfenbüttel 1981. Hrsg. von Ludger Grenzmann/Karl

sieben Hauptsünden; Maria Magdalena kehrt sich von ihrem sündigen Leben ab.[254] Beide Lebenswege dienen als exemplarische Vorbilder und tragen so eine didaktische Funktion.[255]

Wie viele Legenden entwirft die Vita ein Modell vorbildlichen Lebens. Schon in der patristischen Theologie entwickelte sich eine Tradition der Maria / Martha-Exegese, die Auswirkungen auf spirituelle Vorstellungen von Frauenfrömmigkeit im Mittelalter hatte. Der ab dem ausgehenden 13. Jahrhundert zunehmende Kult um die bethanischen Schwestern diente im Kloster als Modell für die Kombination von *vita activa* und *vita contemplativa*.[256] Die Bedeutung der mit Martha symbolisierten *vita activa* kann insbesondere an der Spitaltätigkeit der Prämonstratenserinnen und späterhin der Beginen gesehen werden.[257] Die Kombination eines aktiven/äußerlich wirkenden Lebens und eines kontemplativen/innerlich wirkenden Lebens ist durchaus vorhanden in der Christina von Hane-Vita, wo ein aktives Leben das kontemplative begleitet.[258] Heilsgewissheit spielt in der

---

Stackmann (Germanistische Symposien, Berichtsbände 5). Stuttgart 1984(b), S. 604–639, insbes. S. 622.

254 Außerdem weisen beide Texte stoffgeschichtliche Parallelen zu Gregor dem Großen auf: insbesondere die Hiobexegese kann zum Hintergrundverständnis der Christina von Hane-Vita dienen; Gregors Magdalenahomilien stellen die exegetische Voraussetzung für die Legenden um die Figur Maria Magdalenas dar, siehe dazu Madeleine Boxler: ›ich bin ein predigerin und appostlorin‹. Die deutschen Maria Magdalena-Legenden des Mittelalters (1300–1550). Untersuchungen und Texte. (Deutsche Literatur von den Anfängen bis 1700 22). Bern 1996, S. 42–45.

255 Eine weitere Gemeinsamkeit sind die Konzepte aus der höfischen Welt, vgl.: *O sele myn, jch hayn dich getzogen yn ryttersschafft* (CvH 18, 29 f.); *Lazarus namme eyn groiße deylle yn der stait van Jerusalem vnd er ubet sich yn ritterschaifft, want er was eyn rytter* (›Maria Magdalena-Bekehrungslegende‹ Z. 8–10, siehe unten im Handschriften- und Editionsteil B, Kap. 3.2). Neben dem Reue-Motiv ist außerdem Maria Magdalena als Modell der *pietas* hervorzuheben, zu deren *imitatio* (in der Liebe zu Christus) u.a. Bonaventura anhielt, siehe dazu Frank O. Büttner: Imitatio pietatis. Motive der christlichen Ikonographie als Modelle zur Verähnlichung. Berlin 1983, S. 136–142. Zur Behandlung des Maria Magdalena-Materials in Straßburg, BNU, Ms. 324 im Vergleich mit der Christina von Hane-Vita siehe Kirakosian (2014b).

256 Zur Auseinandersetzung der Erzählung von Martha und Maria als weibliche Modelle bei Meister Eckhart siehe Seelhorst (2003), S. 25 f., und McGinn (2005), S. 189–193.

257 Vgl. Martina Wehrli-Johns: Maria und Martha in der religiösen Frauenbewegung. In: Abendländische Mystik im Mittelalter. Symposium Kloster Engelberg 1984. Hrsg. von Kurt Ruh (Germanistische Symposien, Berichtsbände 7). Stuttgart 1986, S. 354–367, insbes. S. 356.

258 Eine *vita activa* äußert sich ansatzweise in Christinas Küchen- und Krankendienst: *Vnd sy wart sich also sere vben yn rechter oitmodicheit, also das sie dick den meyden vnd auch den jonfferen die schoißel vß yren henden namme vnd jn vor woißche. Vff daz sie sich moicht vollenkommenclichen oitmodigen, so vnderwarffe sie sich, den siechen zo dyenen vnd sonderlichen jn den wercken, die aller oitmodichste vnd versmelichste vnd aller vnfledichste waren.* (CvH 13, 13–18) – Von einer *vita mixta*, wie von Haas (1984b), S. 605, vorgestellt, kann aber nicht die Rede sein, weil sich

Legende wie in der Vita, wenn auch auf verschiedene Weise konstituiert, eine besondere Rolle, da stets der Einzelfall (die Heilige) als Beispiel für die Heilsgeschichte (das Heilige) fungiert.

Die vorangehenden Überlegungen haben nachgewiesen, wie stark der Christina von Hane-Text von einem »vitenähnlichen Grundriss«[259] geprägt ist. Ringlers Verständnis von volkssprachiger »Nonnenliteratur« als »Viten- und Offenbarungsliteratur« trifft zunächst auf die Christina von Hane-Vita zu: Ein spätmittelalterlicher Text berichtet vom Leben einer Nonne des 13. Jahrhunderts und findet wahrscheinlich im Zuge der Reformbewegung seine Rezeption.[260] Der mystische Lebensweg Christinas von Hane wird mit Referenzen angereichert, die auf ein hagiographisches Erklärungsbedürfnis hinweisen. Ein spannungsgeladenes Verhältnis zwischen mystischem Inhalt und hagiographischer Ausformung besteht bereits mit der von einem Heiligen erwarteten Wundertätigkeit, die in Kontrast zum nach innen gewandten mystischen Leben zu stehen scheint. In der Christina von Hane-Vita werden Wege gesucht, Wundersames, d.h. göttliche Zeichen, an der begnadeten Person zu externalisieren. So weist der Text legendenähnliche Strukturen auf, weil die Heiligkeit der Protagonistin immer wieder präsentiert und exemplifiziert werden muss, auch wenn sie von Anfang an für die Heiligkeit prädestiniert ist. Ringlers folgende Hypothese verbindet die legendarische Form mit dem Zweck der Nonnenviten, die zur Erbauung dienen sollten:

> Die Belehrung, welche in den Nonnenviten gegeben werden soll, ist eine Lehre von der praktischen Mystik, vermittelt in denjenigen Formen, die dem mittelalterlichen Menschen die vertrautesten sind: in den Formen der Legende.[261]

Gerade die didaktische Funktion spielt in der Christina von Hane-Vita eine entscheidende Rolle. Der Überlieferungsverbund mit der Maria Magdalena-Bekehrungslegende unterstreicht eine zu ähnlichen Zwecken dienende Rezeption. Gleichzeitig ist es der Vergleich zwischen diesen beiden Texten des Straßburger Kodex, der einen wesentlichen Unterschied in der Heiligenkonstitution der betreffenden Hauptpersonen kennzeichnet, auch wenn ihnen gemeinsam ist,

---

Christinas aktiver Dienst auf die Zeit vor dem ausnahmslos spirituellen Leben bezieht und so die Vorbereitung darauf darstellt. Daher stehen sich *vita activa* und *vita contemplativa* auch nicht im Wege; auch Friedrich-Wilhelm Wentzlaff-Eggebert: Deutsche Mystik zwischen Mittelalter und Neuzeit. Einheit und Wandlung ihrer Erscheinungsform. Berlin 1969, S. 17, betont, dass beide Lebenskonzepte nicht unbedingt ein »Gegensatzpaar« ergäben.
259 Ringler (1980), S. 10.
260 Ringler (1980), S. 3.
261 Ringler (1980), S. 14.

was Köbele folgendermaßen auf den Punkt bringt: »Dass Legenden von der Evidenz des Heiligen erzählen, kann nicht darüber hinwegtäuschen, dass die das auch und gerade deswegen tun, weil Evidenzen fehlen.«[262] In der Legende wird die Illusion einer einfachen Form aufrechterhalten, da die heilige Person sich ihres eigenen Status nicht bewusst ist, sodass die Exemplifizierung der Heiligkeit in der Legende notgedrungen nach außen gerichtet sein muss, wo sich der Protagonist in einer Reihe von Erlebnissen bewährt.[263] In der mystischen Vita, die die begnadete Person von Beginn an als solche kennzeichnet, lässt sich analog von der Illusion einer Kohärenz sprechen, welche als autorisierungsstrategisches Mittel für eine nicht verfügbare Heiligmäßigkeit fungiert.[264]

2.2.3 Narrativierung theologischer Modelle

Ruhs Beobachtungen zur Vita der Christina von Hane bringen die Textkomposition mit dem theologischen Inhalt in Verbindung. So werden der wechselnde »Charakter des Textes« und die inkonsistenten Aussagen als Elemente uneinheitlichen Erzählens angeführt: »verschiedene Vorstellungen folgen einander, vermischen sich, sind nicht selten unvereinbar. Jegliche theologische Kontrolle fehlt.«[265] Bei »aller Verschiedenheit der drei Textblöcke« gebe es dennoch »durchgehende Elemente«.[266] Was sich bei Ruh wie eine Kritik an der Textkohärenz lesen lässt, wird zuweilen als rhetorisches Stilelement verstanden: Der Authentizitätsgrad der an Autorisierung mangelnden Erzählung steige durch einen Stil der »Unmittelbarkeit«.[267] Als unbearbeitet erscheinende Elemente entsprächen der »inneren« Seite der Textentstehung, die »die gedankliche Verarbeitung von (Liebes)Erfahrung, die meditative Reflexion oder geistliche Begnadung, die dem

---

262 Köbele (2012), S. 396.

263 Vgl. Köbele (2012), S. 395.

264 Ähnlich verhält es sich in der lateinischen Vita der Margareta Contracta, wo der Hagiograph insbesondere im Epilog Redewendungen und Bibelzitate zum Einsatz bringt, um am Wahrheitsgehalt der Mitteilung keine Zweifel zu lassen, vgl. Johannes von Magdeburg: ›Die Vita der Margareta contracta‹. einer Magdeburger Rekluse des 13. Jahrhunderts. Hrsg. von Paul Gerhard Schmidt (Studien zur katholischen Bistums- und Klostergeschichte 36). Leipzig 1992, insbes. Kap. 70, S. 101.

265 Ruh (1993), S. 124.

266 Ruh (1993), S. 125.

267 Vgl. Peter Dronke: Women Writers of the Middle Ages. A Critical Study of Texts from Perpetua (203) to Marguerite Porete (1310). Cambridge 1984, S. x, der von »immediacy« spricht. Für eine kritische Diskussion dieser Herangehensweise siehe Poor (2004), S. 193–199. Nemes (2010), S. 151, sieht in dem Phänomen die »Unmittelbarkeit des Schreib- und Entstehungsprozesses«.

poetischen Schaffensprozess vorausgeht«, beschreibe. Daher zählt Peters solche Elemente zu einer Vorstufe der Verschriftlichung.[268] Was die Christina von Hane-Vita angeht, verschränkt Ruh beide Aspekte, den des unmittelbaren Erzählens und den der Volkssprachigkeit:

> Nun könnte es sein, dass deren [Christinas Vita] Quelle eine lateinische Fassung gewesen und verlorengegangen ist. Eine solche Annahme ist indes weniger naheliegend, als es scheint, und dies, weil der deutsche Text alles andere als eine Einheit darstellt.[269]

Einer Literarizität des Lateinischen wird hier eine strukturelle Kohärenz zugeordnet, die die Christina von Hane-Vita nicht vorweise.[270] Hasebrink kommentiert: »Eine lateinische Quelle dachte Ruh sich offenbar hier als Garant der Einheit eines Textes, während er der Volkssprache eine größere Heterogenität zumisst.«[271] Zudem wird eine vermeintlich spezifisch affektive Spiritualität der Nonnenviten von scholastisch geprägten Diskursen kontrastiert.[272] Für Ruh ist es undenkbar, dass eine Nonne aus dem 13. Jahrhundert so gelehrt sein konnte, an der Entstehung der theologisch-spekulativen relevanten Textteile teilzunehmen:

> Da ist die Frage nach dem Primat von Erkenntnis oder Liebe [...], da sind Fragen nach inner-trinitarischen Vorgängen, nach dem Mysterium der hypostatischen Union: alles spekulative Aussagen, die weit über den geistigen Horizont Christinas hinausgehen.[273]

---

268 Vgl. Ursula Peters: Werkauftrag und Buchübergabe. Textentstehungsgeschichten in Autor-bildern volkssprachiger Handschriften des 12. bis 15. Jahrhunderts. In: Autorbilder. Zur Media-lität literarischer Kommunikation in Mittelalter und Früher Neuzeit. Hrsg. von Gerald Kapfham-mer/Wolf-Dietrich Löhr/Barbara Nitsche (Tholos Kunsthistorische Studien 2). Münster 2007, S. 25–62, insbes. S. 29.
269 Ruh (1993), S. 121.
270 Ruh (1993), S. 125, nimmt für den ersten Teil eine lateinische Vorlage an, weil dieser seiner Auffassung nach kohärent sei. Allgemein zu geschlechterspezifischen Interpretationen in Texten siehe Joan Cadden: Meanings of Sex Difference in the Middle Ages. Medicine, Science, and Cul-ture (Cambridge History of Medicine). Cambridge 1993, S. 180 f., und Jessica A. Boon: Trinitarian Love Mysticism. Ruusbroec, Hadewijch, and the Gendered Experience of the Divine. In: Church History. Studies in Christianity and Culture 72 (2003), S. 484–503, insbes. S. 485 f.
271 Burkhard Hasebrink: Koreferat zum Referat ›Saintly Writing and Writing Saints‹ von Racha Kirakosian. Public Final Meeting Marie Curie Network MITT, Freiburg 11.04.2013 (unveröffent-licht), S. 1.
272 Ausführlich zu dieser Unterscheidung siehe Bürkle (1999), S. 40.
273 Ruh (1993), S. 124.

Ähnlich urteilt Backmund, wenn er sicher von einem männlich-klerikalen Hagiographen ausgeht,[274] während sich Krings der gesamten Problematik entzieht.[275]

Dabei lässt sich aus historischer Sicht das Gegensatzpaar lateinisch/männlich und volkssprachig/weiblich als konstruiert verstehen.[276] So zeigt Suerbaum in einer diskursiven Analyse der lateinischen und deutschen Mechthild von Magdeburg-Texte, dass die Artikulation gelehrt-theologischer Reflexionen nicht ausschließlich an die eine oder andere Sprache gebunden ist.[277] Ruh selbst findet die sonst vordergründig im Lateinischen ausgehandelten theologischen Positionen in der Christina von Hane-Vita überraschend.[278] Hasebrink erläutert:

> Ruh trifft mit seiner Kenntnis und seinem Spürsinn genau jene Spannung, die literaturwissenschaftlich an der Vita Christinas interessiert: die Spannung zwischen dem spezifischen literarischen Profil des Textes und dem Facettenreichtum seiner einzelnen Bestandteile. Einheit und Vielheit, Zentrierung und Dezentrierung, Autorschaft und Kompilation, Narration und Diskurs scheinen sich wechselseitig zu bedingen, abzulösen und zu überlagern.[279]

Die Beschäftigung mit der von Hasebrink zuletzt genannten Wechselseitigkeit zwischen Narration und Diskurs hilft auch die Frage nach der Einheit des Textes zu beleuchten. Handelt es sich wirklich um disparate Blöcke oder wie hängen Narration und Diskurs zusammen?

Ein von Ruh explizit genanntes Beispiel illustriert, wie ein theologischer Themenkomplex in die Vitenerzählung eingebunden wird:[280] In der scholastischen

---

274 Vgl. Backmund (1972), S. 90 f.

275 Vgl. Krings (2009), S. 200, Anm. 477: »Die Frage, wieweit theologische Spekulation des Autors in seine Erläuterungen mit eingeflossen ist – man denke an die genannten Traktate am Schluss der Vita –, ist in diesem Zusammenhang nicht zu beantworten.«

276 Vgl. Sara S. Poor: Mechthild von Magdeburg, Gender, and the ›Unlearned Tongue‹. In: Journal of Medieval and Early Modern Studies 31 (2001), S. 213–250, insbes. S. 213–221.

277 Vgl. Suerbaum (2012b). Siehe auch Johanna Thali: ›andaht‹ und ›betrachtung‹. Zur Semantik zweier Leitvokabeln der spätmittelalterlichen Frömmigkeitskultur. In: Semantik der Gelassenheit. Generierung, Etablierung, Transformation. Hrsg. von Burkhard Hasebrink/Susanne Bernhardt/Imke Früh (Historische Semantik 17). Göttingen 2012, S. 226–267.

278 Vgl. Ruh (1993), S. 121. Es kann nur spekuliert werden, ob womöglich häretisches Material entfernt wurde. Schließlich standen im Spätmittelalter andere viel prominentere Figuren wie etwa Birgitta von Schweden (1303–1373) unter Häresieverdacht, siehe dazu Barbara Newman: What Did it Mean to Say ›I saw‹? The Clash Between Theory and Practice in Medieval Visionary Culture. In: Speculum 80 (2005), S. 1–43, insbes. S. 41, und Adman (2007), S. 279 und S. 288.

279 Hasebrink (unveröffentlicht), S. 1 f.

280 Weitere Diskurse in der Christina von Hane-Vita betreffen die Themen Zeit und Zeitlosigkeit, monastisches Tugendstreben, Trinität, Vernunft und der Mensch als Abbild Gottes (*imago Dei*).

Form einer *disputatio* wird die Frage nach dem Primat von Erkenntnis, Liebe oder *gebruchen* für das ewige Leben eingeführt:

> *Da hoirt myn sele, daz die meyster stryedent vnder eyn ander, an wylchen dyngen lyge daz ewige leben. Die eyne sprachen: »An bekentenyß.« Die anderen sprachen: »An der lyebden.« Die drytten sprachen: »An gebruchen.« Got vffenbait aber myner selen, daz man nyt eyn mache lyebe gehaben, man bekenne yn dan. Van wem ich nyt eyn weyße, der ist verre van myr, daz eyn kayn ich nyt lyeffe gehayn. So ich got ye baße bekennen, so myn sele ye stercklicher jn lyeffe hayt. Got ist endeloiße, dar vmb moiße daz bekentenyß endeloiß syn, daz got bekennen sal, vnd yn dem bekentenyß got lyeffe hayn vnd yn der lyebden gotze gebruchen. Also wyste got myn sele, das eyns sonder das ander nyt gesynne eyn mache, want bekennen vnd lyeffe haben vnd got gebruchen ist myner selen gezeuget eyn ewiche leben yn gode. Dan synt alle dynge vollenkomen yn gode, wanne iß wyrckeit an hydernyß.* (CvH 98, 6–18)

Mit der Gegenüberstellung der verschiedenen scholastischen Parteien erinnert diese Passage an eine ähnliche Auseinandersetzung bei Meister Eckhart:

> *Die besten meister sprechent, daz der kerne der sælicheit lige an bekantnisse. Ein grôzer pfaffe kam niuwelîche ze Parîs, der was dâ wider und ruofte und donte gar sêre. Dô sprach ein ander meister wol bezzer dan alle, die von Parîs bezzer hielten: ›meister, ir ruofet und donet vaste; enwære ez niht gotes wort in dem heiligen êwangeliô, sô ruoftet ir und dontet ir gar sêre‹. Bekantnisse rüeret blôz, daz ez bekennet. Unser herre sprichet: ›daz ist daz êwige leben, daz man dich aleine bekenne einen wâren got.‹ Volbringunge der sælicheit liget an beiden: an bekantnisse und an minne.* (DW III, 70, 188)[281]

Weitere Bezüge zu einer von Eckhart geprägten mystischen Theologie zeigen, dass sich die Christina von Hane-Vita durchaus an scholastischen Diskursen beteiligt und dabei individuelle Positionen bezieht.[282] Im Wechselverhältnis von *intellectio* und *volitio* (oder auch *dilectio*, eine klare Distinktion ist hier nicht möglich) wird der Aspekt der *fruitio* eingeführt. In der Christina-Vita nimmt *gebruchen* einen anderen Platz ein als bei Eckhart und unterscheidet sich gerade durch seine scholastische Einbindung außerdem von Hadewijchs und Mechthilds von Magdeburg Konzepten.[283] Es wird in die Debatte um Erkenntnis und Liebe eingebettet und als gleichwertig zu diesen für die *unio* zwischen Gott und Seele betrachtet. Zusätzlich

---

281 Meister Eckhart: Die deutschen und lateinischen Werke. Hrsg. i. A. der Deutschen-Forschungsgemeinschaft. Die Deutsche Werke [DW]. Bd. 1–3. Hrsg. und übers. von Josef Quint. Stuttgart 1958–1976 (unveränd. Nachdrucke 1986–1999), hier DW III (1976). (Die Stellennachweise geben Band- und Predigtnummern sowie Seitenzahlen an.)
282 Vgl. Kirakosian (2014a) für eine ausführliche Untersuchung der zitierten Stellen.
283 Zu Hadewijch und Mechthild von Magdeburg siehe McGinn (2005), S. 185. Siehe jetzt auch die komparatistische Untersuchung von Andrea Zech: Spielarten des Gottes-Genusses. Semanti-

zu der scholastischen Ausführung, die den Stellenwert von *gebruchen* diskutiert, ist der »Genuss« der Gottesvereinigung sinnlich konnotiert. Über die Vereinigung heißt es: *Da bekennet sy [die sele] got vnd smacket got yn gotlicher naturen* (CvH 100, 66 f.). Das Wort *gebruchen* wird im Kontext der Gottesvereinigung im Bild des ›Zerfließens‹ und ›Einmündens‹ der Seelen in Gott verwendet:

> *Da zofloißen sie yn got myt eym vnsprechelichen gebruchen der soißer gotheit vnd lyeblicher menscheit. Dyese selen worden myt luterer lyebden jn got gebreyt, also daz alle yre vernoifft erfoilt worden myt freuden. Das geschet, wanne got syne gotliches lyecht yn sie gußet, daz dan die selen van vnsprechlicher vbersoißicheit vnd vbersoißer woillust vberfließent.* (CvH 56, 24–28)

Weiterhin wird ausgeführt: *Got ist soiße vnd mylde, als er wylle, vnd smacket er, wanne die sele yn lyebe hait* (CvH 97, 9 f.). Die kausale Verknüpfung zwischen Liebe und ›Gott schmecken‹ weist trotz aller in der *disputatio* erörterten Gleichwertigkeit zwischen *lyebden* und *gebruchen* auf eine konsekutive Bewegung oder Transformation hin, wonach *gebruchen* auf Liebe folgt. Das Schmecken Gottes äußert sich für Christina von Hane konkret im Empfang der Eucharistie.[284] Vor dem Hintergrund der Transsubstantiationslehre könnte die Eucharistie als eine liturgisch induzierte Verkörperung der *unio* angesehen werden, die den Menschen transformieren soll. Wenn Christina selbst zum Geschmack für Gott und die himmlische Heerschar wird, dann wird dieser Transformationsprozess, ein theologisches Modell, narrativ verarbeitet:

> *Jre gesmacke hait got erfrauwet yn dem hemel vnd auch die engel vnd alle heilgen, die sunder yn der erden vnd die lyeben selen yn dem fegefûr* (CvH 30, 16–18).

Andersherum ließe sich das am Vitenende scholastisch erörterte Primat von Liebe und Erkenntnis als nachträgliche theologische Begründung für die Bezie-

---

ken des Genießens in der europäischen Frauenmystik des 13. Jahrhunderts (Historische Semantik 25). Göttingen 2015.

284 Vgl.: *Dar nach da der pryester die buße vß detde, da foillet sie den aller soisten gesmacke vnd geroiche, van yre hertze vnd yre lyffe vnd alle jre gelyeder gestercket vnd erquicket worden, die van starcker begerden verkrencket waren* (CvH 31, 9–12); *Da was jre vnser here also soiße yn yrem montde als honyck, vnd die soißicheit floiße yn yre hertze vnd yn yre sele* (CvH 22, 6 f.). – Die Verbindung von *fruitio* und Eucharistie findet sich auch bei Eckhart, siehe dazu Burkhard Hasebrink: ›mitewürker gotes‹. Zur Performativität der Umdeutung in den deutschen Schriften Meister Eckharts. In: Literarische und religiöse Kommunikation in Mittelalter und Früher Neuzeit. DFG-Symposium 2006. Hrsg. von Peter Strohschneider. Berlin / New York 2009(b), S. 62–88, insbes. S. 85.

hung zwischen Christina und Gott verstehen. Von göttlich figurierter Seite wird ihr wiederholt zugesichert:

> ›[...] *Du leyffest yn dem gesmacke myner gotlicher soißicheit, da ersterckestu dich yn die jnwendigen soißicheit myner gotheit.‹* (CvH 68, 7–9)

> ›*O du aller lobelichste sele myn, erfrauwe dich, wanttu scheppest jn dem abgruntde myns hertzes den vbersoißen gesmacken vnd die heillicheit myner gotlicher lyebden, die dich doyt vergeyßen aller vergencklicher dynge. Wan du flugest vber dich myt eynem luteren hertzen jn myn luter gotheit, da wyrt dyn edel sele erlucht gotlichen, vnd sie wyrt geleret myt gotlicher soißicheit, myt vberster vollenkomenheit.‹* (CvH 82, 18–23)

Doch die ineinander verflochtenen Ebenen von Diskurs und Narration sind nicht unbedingt hierarchisch aufzulösen. Auch ein klares Abwechseln dieser Ebenen ist nicht immer gegeben. Theologisch relevante Diskurse finden sich zwar konzentriert in scholastischer Redeweise am Ende des Textes, aber sie kommen vereinzelt bereits vorher im Text vor und zwar nicht als disparate Versatzstücke sondern als in den narrativen Kontext integrierte Ausführungen. Dabei werden dieselben Begriffe benutzt, sodass auch sprachlich bestimmte Motive wiederholt auftreten. Bezüglich der eingangs erläuterten Aussage, wonach volkssprachige Texte durch Inkohärenz oder, um es mit Hasebrink positiver auszudrücken, »Heterogenität« gekennzeichnet sind, lässt sich konstatieren, dass in der Christina von Hane-Vita abstrakte Probleme, die in Form einer *quaestio*, *lectio* oder *summa* behandelt werden, dem Charakter einer volkssprachigen Mystik nicht widersprechen. Die Vita bedient sich verschiedener aus der monastisch geprägten Theologie stammenden Formen und Themen und das jenseits geschlechterspezifischer Orientierungen, welche ohnehin zum Teil eher moderne Vorbehalte denn mittelalterliche Tatbestände widerspiegeln.[285] Die Narration des Heiligenlebens vollzieht auf diese Weise, worum es in den jeweiligen theologischen Gesichtspunkten geht.[286]

---

285 Ähnlich argumentiert Andersen (2000), S. 33, für das ›Fließende Licht der Gottheit‹ Mechthilds.
286 Auf die performative Kraft narrativer Diskurse, denen »selbst unmittelbar wirklichkeitsverändernde Kraft zugetraut« wird, weist Strohschneider (2014), S. 30, hin. Siehe auch Strowick (2009), S. 11, zum »Akt des Erzählens«.

3 Ich-Konstitutionen und Perspektivenvielfalt

Da die Vita der Christina von Hane durch eine Überlagerung wechselnder Stimmen gekennzeichnet ist, ist es angebracht, die Sprecherrollen zu untersuchen. Das folgende Kapitel hat zum Ziel, diese verschiedenen Sprecher in ihren Ich-Konstitutionen vorzustellen, wobei dem Wechsel von der dritten zur ersten Person im letzten Drittel des Textes besondere Bedeutung zukommt. Anschließend wird die Signifikanz dieser Perspektivenvielfalt für die Erzeugung von Präsenz innerhalb des Textes diskutiert. Während die Stimme des mystischen Bräutigams auf Grund der Komplexität theologischer Fragestellungen hier nicht gesondert vorzustellen ist,[1] stehen die Stimmen des impliziten Hagiographen und der Mystikerin im Vordergrund. Auf diese Weise werden Erzähler und Gegenstand der Erzählung gegenübergestellt. Dazwischen lässt sich der implizite Adressat des Textes als Teilnehmer im Erzählakt schalten, sodass der Text im Rekurs auf die Ausführungen de Certeaus als ein dynamischer Zwischenraum verstanden wird, in dem Schreibvorgang und Vollzug aufeinandertreffen.[2]

3.1 Der implizite Hagiograph

Im Kontext des hagiographischen Schreibens ist die Perspektive des Erzählers bereits erwähnt worden, der verschiedene Rollen einnimmt, wobei sich freilich fragen lässt, ob es sich dann jeweils noch um dieselbe Stimme handelt. Weil jedoch kein Stimmenwechsel, d.h. keine neue Ich-Figuration, erkennbar ist, handelt es sich um funktionale Rollen, deren sich der implizite Autor bedient. Von einer fiktiv-chronologischen Folge der Vermittlung ausgehend werden diese Rollen und deren Konstitutionen der Reihe nach vorgestellt, angefangen bei dem Christina nahestehenden Ordensbruder, über den schreibenden Berichterstatter bis hin zum Exegeten. Allerdings sind die Erzählerfunktionen im Kontext selbst selten zu trennen, wie an einigen Stellen gezeigt werden kann.

---

1 Die Rolle des göttlich figurierten mystischen Gegenübers wird an einer Stelle direkt adressiert: *Honger vnd dorst vnd gebrechen wullŭstu myt vns vnd durch vns lyden* (CvH 16, 7 f.). Mehr zur göttlich figurierten Stimme in Kap. 5.2.
2 Vgl. Michel de Certeau: L'expérience religieuse. Connaissance vécue dans l'église. In: Le voyage mystique. Michel de Certeau. Hrsg. von Luce Giard. Paris 1988, S. 27–51. Siehe auch Uwe Wirth: Zwischenräumliche Bewegungspraktiken. In: Bewegen im Zwischenraum. Hrsg. von Uwe Wirth (Wege der Kulturforschung 3). Berlin 2012, S. 7–34, insbes. S. 23 f.

https://doi.org/10.1515/9783110536324-006

3.1.1 Der nahestehende Ordensbruder

Erst im Verlauf des Textes wird ersichtlich, dass die erzählende Instanz eine intradiegetische Perspektive einnimmt und sich damit als eine Figur aus dem nahen Lebensumfeld Christinas darstellt, selbst wenn an keiner Stelle eine Figurenrede aus ihrer Sicht stattfindet.[3] Das Erzähler-Ich beschreibt sich an einer Stelle als gegenwärtiger, d.h. miterlebender *broder* (CvH 57, 45). Die intradiegetische Fokalisierung dient der Augenzeugenschaft und verstärkt daher die autorisierte Rede (*auctoritas*) insbesondere während extremer körperlicher Zustände Christinas.[4] Zugleich wird die verbale Kommunikation zwischen Mystikerin und Bruder an einer Stelle explizit gemacht: *Vnd sie sprache zo myr: ›Vff die tzijt [...].‹* (CvH 31, 15 f.) Eine Augenzeugenschaft und die direkte Adressierung durch Christina werden außerdem derart kombiniert, dass die Worte der Mystikerin zur Verifikation des ohnehin visuell Wahrgenommenen dienen: *Aber daz ich selber sache, sagen sie myr dyß wort vnd sprach: › Jn dießem vngemache [...].‹* (CvH 80, 16 f.)

Die Funktion einer beglaubigenden Instanz ist dort am prominentesten, wo der Ich-Bericht Christinas (der allerdings direkte Gottesrede einschließen kann) und die Erzählerstimme unvermittelt nebeneinanderstehen, sodass der Erzähler die in der ersten Person gefasste persönliche Erfahrung bestätigt:

> ›Da was ich yn der soißer begerunge myns aller soisten bruytgams vnd er sprache zo myr: »Kynt myns, lege dyne lyden kreifflichen yn mych. Du salt noch hude erbieben an allen dynen geliederen, als myn menscheit erbiebt an dem heilgen crutze vmb die menscheliche nature, vnd daz sal dyr geschegen vmb die selbe tzijt.«« Vnd daz geschache also. Van sexten byß zo nonen leyt sy vnsprecheliche erbiebonge vnd brechonge aller yrer gelieder vnd krachonge des hertzen van groißer lyebden gelicher wyße eyns sweren sterbens yn aller wyß, als da vor geschreben ist. (CvH 63, 47–54)

Was von göttlicher Seite im futurischen Modus vorausgesagt wird (*vnd daz sal dyr geschegen vmb die selbe tzijt*)[5] bestätigt das Sprecher-Ich des impliziten Hagiographen aus einer vergangenen Perspektive der eigenen Erfahrungswelt (*vnd*

---

3 Zur Differenzierung zwischen Erzähler- und Figurenrede siehe Miedema (2010), S. 37–44.
4 Vgl.: *Jch, der dyße schryben, sache dyß selber myt mynen augen, das sie soilche pyne leyte* (CvH 80, 7 f.).
5 Das umschriebene Futur erwächst aus Bezeichnungen für Nuancierungen der Modalität und der inchoativen Aktionsart. Die Modalität, die hier durch *salen* (sollen) mit Infinitiv ausgedrückt wird, setzt den Verbalvorgang in Beziehung zum Willen des Sprechenden und verleiht ihm zugleich den Charakter des Zukünftigen, siehe dazu Hermann Paul u.a. (Hrsg.): Mittelhochdeutsche Grammatik. 24. Aufl. überarb. von Peter Wiehl/Siegfried Grosse. Tübingen 1998, S. 295 f., § 314–§ 315b.

daz geschache also).[6] Die unmittelbare Wiederholung der Satzkonstruktion ist in den Berichtmodus transferiert und aus der direkten Adressierung herausgehoben, was der an Christina gerichteten Weissagung eine Gültigkeit verleiht, deren Bewahrheitung nur der miterlebende Berichterstatter attestieren kann. Mit den folgenden detaillierten Beobachtungen von Christinas Leiden verschafft sich der Augenzeugenbericht einmal mehr eine autoritative Position, die im Selbstbezug zur Schrift die Bedeutung des Geschriebenen als Nachweisbares hervorhebt (*als da vor geschreben ist*). Das erzählende Ich konstituiert sich als ein erlebendes Ich, womit der *auctoritas*-Wert des Erzählten gesteigert wird.[7] Wie Bürkle gezeigt hat, ist dieses für »die Legendenprologe typische Verfahren der Wahrheitsbeteuerung« konstitutiv für ein in der »neuen Hagiographie« des 13. Jahrhunderts entworfenes Heiligkeitskonzept.[8] In diesem Sinne ist die Intimität zwischen Beichtvater-Hagiograph und Heiliger als eine textinterne Figurenkonstellation zu verstehen.

Die Rolle des nahestehenden Bruders hängt also mit einem Schreibprozess zusammen. Doch die unpersönliche Perspektive auf das Geschriebene verweist dabei nicht auf einen historischen Beichtvater »am Rande eines Verschriftlichungsprojekts« der religiösen Erfahrung,[9] wie das etwa für die Vitentexte im

---

6 Vgl. damit die im Erzählbericht nachträglich unterstützte göttliche Rede bei Adelheid Langmann: ›dor umb daz ir hin bliben seit‹ (›Die Offenbarungen der Adelheid Langmann‹ 74, 9); *als unser geminter herre Jesus Crist gesprochen do het* (›Die Offenbarungen der Adelheid Langmann‹ 74, 13 f.).
7 Die Fokalisierung auf Christina (d.h. ihr Innenleben wird aus der Perspektive des nahestehenden Bruders erzählt) kann als Wahrheitsbedingung der Erfahrung verstanden werden. In der *evidentia*-Lehre der römischen Rhetorik »kann der Redner die Wahrscheinlichkeit seiner Erzählung befördern, indem er für den Anschein von Evidenz insbesondere dort sorgt, wo ein Mangel an Evidenz herrscht,« fasst Gert Hübner: ›evidentia‹. Erzählformen und ihre Funktion. In: Historische Narratologie. Mediävistische Perspektiven. Hrsg. von Harald Haferland / Matthias Meyer (Trends in Medieval Philology 19). New York 2010, S. 119–147, hier S. 123, zusammen, der als konkrete Mittel neben der Figurenrede auch die deskriptive Detaillierung und die affektische Emphatisierung nennt: »Indem der Redner ihre [der handelnden Personen] Innenwelt, vor Augen ›führt‹ und ›durchschaubar macht‹, stärkt er die Glaubwürdigkeit seiner Erzählung von ihrem Handeln«, ebd., S. 124.
8 Bürkle (1999), S. 200 f.
9 Zur erzähltypologischen Abgrenzung zwischen Subjekt der Rede und dem Sprecher vgl. Hans-Joachim Ziegeler: Erzählen im Spätmittelalter. Mären im Kontext von Minnereden, Bispeln und Romanen (MTU 87). München 1985, S. 66. Siehe auch Glauch (2010), S. 157: »In den Fällen, in denen das Ich im Zentrum der Erzählung im Grunde verschwindet, weil es dort nur eine Beobachterposition einnimmt, macht es sich vorwiegend an den Rändern des Textes bemerkbar, die Ich-Rede wird zu einem Rahmen [...].«

brabantisch-lüttichen Raum der Fall ist. Für diese konnte Peters feststellen, dass Beichtväter

> zwar als glaubwürdige Augenzeugen und Chronisten des spirituellen Wegs der religiös bewegten Frauen [gelten], sie [...] jedoch in den Lebensberichten keineswegs einen herausragenden Part als Initiatoren bei der literarischen Fixierung der spirituellen Erlebnisse dieser Frauen [haben].[10]

Im Gegensatz dazu lässt sich die Perspektive des Beichtvaters in der Christina-Vita nur schwer auf ein historisches Szenario der Vermittlung beschränken, da keine genaueren Umstände der Verschriftlichung bekannt sind. Wie bereits mehrfach deutlich geworden ist, ist ein historischer Ansatz für die Vita kaum möglich. Jedoch deckt die Sprecheruntersuchung Narrationstechniken auf, die wiederum auf den Schreib- und Interpretationsakt eines impliziten Autors hinweisen, der auf diese Weise an einem Schreibprozess im Dienste eines von Christina auf den impliziten Leser auszuweitenden Heilsplans teilnimmt.

3.1.2 Der schreibende Vermittler

Die Formel *Nu komen ich wieder an die materie* verdeutlicht einen Vermittlungsakt, der in seinem Vollzug eine autoreferentielle Erzählsituation hervorruft (CvH 2, 1).[11] Der performative Selbstbezug wird erhöht, indem die Formel an

---

10 Peters (1988), S. 116.

11 Die *materie* ist hier mit der *diegesis* zu vergleichen, die Hagiographen seit der Antike selbstreferentiell nutzen, vgl. Claudia Rapp: Storytelling as Spiritual Communication in Early Greek Hagiography. The Use of Diegesis. In: Journal of Early Christian Studies 6 (1998), S. 431–448, insbes. S. 432. Sie ist also weniger die *materi* eines mündlich stilisierten Gelehrtendiskurses (siehe dazu Caroline Emmelius: Gesellige Ordnung. Literarische Konzeptionen von geselliger Kommunikation in Mittelalter und Früher Neuzeit [Frühe Neuzeit 139]. Tübingen 2009 [Diss. Göttingen 2005], S. 332–383), wie das etwa im Prosaroman ›Florio und Bianceffora‹ der Fall ist (siehe auch Silke Schünemann: Florio und Bianceffora (1499). Studien zu einer literarischen Übersetzung [Frühe Neuzeit 106]. Tübingen 2005 [Diss. Göttingen 2003], S. 146–148 und S. 204–209), sondern eher *historia*, ähnlich gebraucht in mittelalterlichen Prosaerzählungen, namentlich in Chronik und Heldenepik (vgl. Ludger Lieb/Stephan Müller: Situationen literarischen Erzählens, Systematische Skizzen am Beispiel von ›Kaiserchronik‹ und Konrad Flecks ›Flore und Blanscheflur‹. In: Erzähltechnik und Erzählstrategien in der deutschen Literatur des Mittelalters. Hrsg. von Wolfgang Haubrichs/Eckart Conrad Lutz/Klaus Ridder [Wolfram-Studien 18]. Berlin 2004, S. 33–57, insbes. S. 41, und Jürgen Wolf: Narrative Historisierungsstrategien in Heldenepos und Chronik – vorgestellt am Beispiel von ›Kaiserchronik‹ und ›Klage‹. In: Erzähltechnik und Erzählstrategien in der deutschen Literatur des Mittelalters. Hrsg. von Wolfgang Haubrichs/Eckart

anderer Stelle leicht verändert wiederholt wird. Die Erzählinstanz hebt so die erneute (*wieder vmb*) Erzählbewegung hervor: *Nv komen ich wieder vmb vff die materie.* (CvH 6, 1) In der französischen Prosa-Lancelot-Forschung wurde das Prinzip der verschiedenen Erzählstränge (*entrelacement*) in seiner narrativen Funktion hervorgehoben.[12] Auf diese Weise werden, so Pauphilet, unabhängige narrative »Fäden« (»fils diversement colorés«) zusammengeführt.[13] Im Christina-Text verbinden sich zwei Ebenen mit dem direkten Mittel des *entrelacement*: der chronologische Fortgang der Erzählung mit der allgemeinen Bedeutung des Heiligenlebens. Die zweite Ebene beschreibt einen didaktischen Modus, der im textdiegetischen Bezug an den genannten Stellen einen gesteuerten Erzählfluss konstruiert und durch Verben der akustischen Wahrnehmung einen impliziten Adressaten evoziert, so z. B. in Verweisen auf den Fortgang des Textes: *alstu her na fyndest geschreben* (CvH 3, 10).[14]

Der implizite Autor nimmt die Rolle eines aktiv schreibenden Bruders an, dessen Tätigkeit eine gegenwärtige ist, d. h. die Vermittlung der göttlichen Erfahrung spielt sich zeitlich während des Schreibprozesses ab: *Jch, der dyße schryben* (CvH 80, 7 f.). Neben Rück- und Vorverweisen finden sich auch andere Formulierungen, die einen Selbstbezug zur Schrift herstellen: *manchfeldenclichen me, dan hie geschreben ist* (CvH 10, 17); *die nyt hie geschreben eyn synt* (CvH 29, 2). Mit diesen Formulierungen soll der eigentliche Aussagewert des zu übermittelnden Inhalts bekräftigt und überhöht werden. Das *hie* Geschriebene ist zugleich beides: eine Auswahl besonderer Ereignisse und die Bestätigung von Christinas Erwählung. Bezeichnenderweise sind in beinahe allen Fällen die mit dem Mitteilungsprozess zusammenhängenden Schlüsselwörter in der Handschrift unterstrichen

---

Conrad Lutz / Klaus Ridder [Wolfram-Studien 18]. Berlin 2004, S. 323–346, insbes. S. 333); siehe auch Karina Kellermann: ›Exemplum‹ und ›historia‹. Zu poetologischen Traditionen in Hartmanns ›Iwein‹. In: Germanisch-Romanische Monatsschrift 42 (1992), S. 1–27, insbes. S. 5, und Walter Haug: Literaturtheorie im deutschen Mittelalter. Von den Anfängen bis zum Ende des 13. Jahrhunderts, 2. überarb. und erw. Aufl. Darmstadt 1992(a), S. 125–128.

12 Vgl. Ferdinand Lot: Étude sur le Lancelot en prose. Paris 1918, S. 27. Siehe auch Eugène Vinaver: A la recherche d'une poétique médiévale. Paris 1970, S. 131–138.

13 Vgl. Albert Pauphilet: Études sur la Queste del Saint Graal attribuées à Gautier Map. Paris 1921, S. 162. Siehe auch Almut Suerbaum: Entrelacement? Narrative Technique in Heinrich von dem Türlîn's ›Diu Crône‹. In: Oxford German Studies 34 (2005), S. 5–18, insbes. S. 8, die von »tapestry« und »fabric of the narrative« spricht.

14 Vgl. weitere textdiegetische Verweise: *alstu her nach dicke wyrdest fynden geschreben* (CvH 4, 32); *als her na geschreben stet* (CvH 57, 54); *alstu herna fyndest geschreben* (CvH 5, 31). Auch Rückverweise erfolgen: *als auch da vor geschreben steyt* (CvH 63, 15); *als da vor geschreben ist* (CvH 63, 54); *iß auch da vor geschreben ist* (CvH 65, 9); zum Teil in auralen Wendungen: *als da vor gesprochen ist* (CvH 6, 18).

(*schryben, swigen, geschreben*), sodass der Schreibakt in der materiellen Schriftlichkeit nochmals graphisch betont wird und damit mehr als nur semantisch auf sich selbst rückverweist.

Indem sich der Schreibakt als unmögliche Aufgabe präsentiert, schließt er sich dem apophatischen Diskurs der mystischen Theologie an.[15] Das Paradox einer verschriftlichten Mystik besteht darin, vom nicht Vermittelbaren zu handeln.[16] Hasebrink vermerkt dazu, dass »[...] die Anwesenheit des Transzendenten in der Immanenz, selbst eine Paradoxie in sich [birgt], insofern sich die Unbegreiflichkeit des Transzendenten zeichenhaft vermittelt«.[17] In der Christina von Hane-Vita formuliert das Erzähler-Ich *expressis verbis* die Inadäquatheit der sprachlichen Vermittlung göttlicher Inhalte: *Ich meynen, daz keynne zonge moge vß gelegen die soißicheit, den troiste vnd woillust, die die edel sele da haitte.* (CvH 6, 22–24) Die Unzulänglichkeit des sprachlichen Ausdrucks wird qualitativ bestimmt, was in verschiedenen Formeln wiederholt wird, in denen erneut der basale Schreibakt eines impliziten Autors zum Vorschein tritt:

> *Nach den vj wochen als dyeße seliche jonffrauwe eynzucket was yn eyn gotliches lyecht, da sie vil gesehen vnd gehoirt hait, die nyt hie geschreben eyn synt [...].* (CvH 29, 1 f.)

und an anderer Stelle

> *Jhesus, yre eyniges lyebe, spyltte myt yrer selen eyn also lyeblich soiße mynnen spielle, daz keynne zonge dar van gesagen eyn kayn ader auch keyn hant geschryben eyn kayn.* (CvH 34, 6–8)

Kombiniert wird die Unsagbarkeit der göttlichen Begegnung mit ihrer quantitativ ebenfalls eingeschränkten Beschreibung, doch wird im textdiegetischen Verweis

---

15 Zum apophatischen Diskurs als negative Theologie innerhalb der Mystik siehe Sells (1994), S. 6–10.

16 Vgl. Bruce Millem: The Unspoken Word. Negative Theology in Meister Eckhart's German Sermons. Washington D.C. 2002, S. 179, der das Scheitern einer Versprachlichung göttlicher Unverfügbarkeit (»the mystery of God's revelation«) als wesentlich für das Konzept der negativen Theologie und des apophatischen Diskurses ansieht (»essential to the project of negative theology and apophatic discourse«). Eine andere und schlüssige Position nimmt de Certeau (1988), S. 34, ein, der den apophatischen Diskurs damit erklärt, dass die mystische Erfahrung selbst immer unvollkommen bleibe: »La présence à Dieu ne reste pas dans le silence d'une pure lumière ou d'une pure nuit. Elle n'est pas une communion dans un instant de plénitude et de transparence. Elle reste toujours imparfaite et éphémère au moment même où elle se réalise. C'est pourquoi elle se dit.«

17 Hasebrink (2007), S. 94.

auf einen folgenden Teil vertröstet, der sich an den Festtagen der Heiligen orientiert:

> *O, was lyeblichen gesprechs, das got gewonlichen hait gehait, wyrstu dicke hoiren her na, da du wyrste vynden eytzelichen wort, da groiße befyndunge der genaden vnd soißicheit myt wonderlicher ynwendiger beschauwonge, die also vnsprechlichen vnuerstendich synt vnser groppicheit zo begryffen, als eynem wayllen eynen dutzen zo verstayn. Doch synt her geschreben der soißer sprechonge eyn deylle yn die hogetzijden [...].* (CvH 39, 22–27)

Die Auswahl der geschilderten Momente wird explizit in die narrative Ordnung der liturgischen Festtage eingereiht. Der Selbstbezug einer Schriftmystik vollzieht sich in der Verbindung von göttlicher Erfahrung und wörtlicher Vermittlung im kirchlich gebundenen Rahmen – und das Schreiber-Ich macht auf diese verschachtelte Kommunikation aufmerksam.[18] Die apophatische Aussage gewinnt daher an konkretem Boden, indem sie in ein liturgisch vollzogenes Sprachfeld, hier den kirchlichen Kalender, gesetzt wird.

Zu diskutieren ist, ob sich der implizite Autor einen eigenen Willen zuschreibt oder im futurischen Modus spricht, wenn seine Stimme mehrfach betont: *Doch wil ich eyn teylle her na schryben* (CvH 7, 39).[19] In jedem Fall ist damit ein prozesshaftes, nicht abgeschlossenes Schreiben evoziert, das die Grundlage für jedwedes Wissen über Christina bildet und über die Vermittlung ihres begnadeten Lebens verfügt. Die Möglichkeit eines bewussten Vorenthaltens steigert diesen Verfügungsbereich eines schreibenden Ichs: *Ich wille aůch nyt swigen der groißer genaden [...].* (CvH 8, 1) Gleichzeitig scheint das Schreiber-Ich eine Ausnahmestellung innerhalb des apophatischen Diskurses zu beziehen:

> *Die ruwe was vol soißicheit vnd also lyeblichen, das jre sele sach da so groiße freude vnd so groiße verborgenheit der wunderlicher gotheit, da van vnmoglichen were eynigen menschen zo reden.* (CvH 78, 27–29)

Wer eigentlich zum Reden von der göttlichen Erfahrung befähigt ist, bleibt in dieser Aussage unklar; so könnte die Ausnahmeposition jeden betreffen, der die *unio* erlebt. Eine alternative Deutung verortet den impliziten Autor unter die Schar dieser Erwählten. Die Erwählung liegt dann nicht in dem mystischen Heiligenleben selbst, sondern darin, Zeugnis über ein solches Leben zu geben. Zum

---

18 Ausführlich zur Schrift- bzw. Schreibmystik siehe Kap. 5.
19 Vgl. auch die folgenden Textstellen: *Auch so wil ich eyn deyl hie schryben, wie* (CvH 9, 13); *als ich eyn teylle her na schryben wylle* (CvH 9, 26 f.). – Zur voluntativen Bedeutung mit futurischer Färbung von *wollen* mit Infinitiv siehe unten Anm. 76.

Teil grenzt ein impliziter Schreibauftrag an einen Schreibzwang, der auch immer mit der Selektion des Materials einhergeht:

> *Ist eyn deyle schemelichen zo schryben, so iß doch ist eyn zeychen groißer lyebden, die sie haitte, wie sie yren vyant moichte vberwynnen vnd wie sye den schaitze yrrer kußheit behylde vnbefleckte. Dar vmb eyn mache ichs nyt vnderwegen gelaißen, ich eyn schrybe dan eyn deylle dar van.* (CvH 10, 36–40)

In einer ausschweifenden Begründung für die folgende Verschriftlichung von Christinas Selbstverstümmelung figuriert sich das schreibende Ich als moralisch-wertende Instanz mit persönlichem Einfluss, was die Vermittlung besonderer Einzelheiten angeht. Diese Art des Schreibens ist zwar von einem Phänomen der geheimen Niederschrift, wie von Nemes und Märker am Beispiel der jüngst entdeckten Sonderausgabe des ›Legatus divinae pietatis‹ beschrieben, zu unterscheiden, weil es dem impliziten Hagiographen der Christina-Vita nicht vordergründig um eine Buchentstehungsgeschichte geht.[20] Dennoch gibt es auch in der Christina-Vita ein Spiel mit dem Geheimen in seiner Spannung zum Kollektivbezug, welches das Schreiber-Ich zu beherrschen und zu bestimmen vorgibt, wenn es sich eine Entscheidungskraft über das Mitgeteilte zuschreibt. Dieses Phänomen ist vielleicht eher als Konsequenz prophetischen Sprechens zu verstehen; Köbele erläutert für die Prophetenrolle, dass dieser sich »zur Aufdeckung von Verborgenem und Künftigem berufen« fühle. Diesen prophetischen Aspekt beansprucht auch der implizite Hagiograph der Christina von Hane-Vita. Auch eine »aktive Deutungsmacht und exklusive Autorschaft«, wie sie sonst dem Propheten zukommen, sind Attribute seiner Rollenfiguration als Sprachrohr der Mystikerin. Aus einer solchen »Spannung von Offenbarungsevidenz und Auslegungsbedürftigkeit«, wie Köbele an der Frage prophetischer Autorschaft allgemeinhin formuliert, resultiert so dann die exegetisch-hermeneutische Dimension des Vitentextes.[21]

3.1.3 Der wertende Exeget

Schreibprozesse werden in der Vita zum einen an autoreferentiellen Aussagen des schreibenden Ichs deutlich, zum anderen an der heilsgeschichtlichen Funk-

---

20 Nemes/Märker (2015), S. 288. Siehe auch Bürkle (1999), S. 243 f.

21 Susanne Köbele: Verheißung als Erfüllung. Zur Transformation prophetischer Autorschaft um 1300. In: Prophetie und Autorschaft. Charisma, Heilversprechen und Gefährdung. Hrsg. von Christel Meier/Martina Wagner-Egelhaaf. Berlin 2014, S. 169–196, hier S. 169.

tion der Verschriftlichung von religiöser Erfahrung, sodass der Vermittlungsakt auch jenseits der diegetischen Welt Anspruch auf einen kollektiven Nutzen
erhebt.[22] Das Sprecher-Ich nimmt eine apostolische Rolle ein. Der prophetische
Charakter der Vermittlung geht mit dem entsprechenden Lektüremodus und mit
einer Einladung zum Nachvollzug einher, der sich letztlich auf Christinas Aus-
nahmezustand bezieht und auf die Heiligung des Lesers abzielt.

Der implizite Hagiograph präsentiert sich als ein pflichtbewusster Erzähler, wenn er von der erfolgreichen Bewahrung von Christinas Jungfräulichkeit
berichtet. Christinas rigorose Maßnahmen zur Bekämpfung sexueller Versuchungen nuanciert der implizite Hagiograph, indem er die Tat selbst zwar kritisiert,
die Intention dahinter jedoch in einer abaelardschen Denkweise anerkennt: *Jch
loben viel me die sach vnd die meynunge, yn der sie iß dede, dan ich die daytde
loben. Dan iß was eyn vnuernoifftige kaistigonge.* (CvH 10, 53–55) Die hier inter-
pretierende Stimme des Schreiber-Ichs nimmt eine Seelsorger-Funktion an, was
für einen spirituellen Text aus dem monastischen Milieu nicht ungewöhnlich
ist;[23] doch ist nicht Christina die Empfängerin der Seelsorge, da auf der erzählten
Ebene Christina nie Adressatin der wertenden Worte ist, sodass von einem Austausch zwischen einem nahestehenden Bruder und der Mystikerin nicht die Rede
sein kann. Alle wertenden und kommentierenden Aussagen sind im Präsens
formuliert und bewegen sich auf der zeitlich-fiktiven Ebene eines Schreibprozesses.[24] Mit der kausalen Konjunktion *dar vmb* argumentiert der implizite Hagiograph, warum trotz des *schemelichen* Tatbestands die Bewahrung von Christinas
Jungfräulichkeit von Interesse ist (vgl. CvH 10, 36).[25] Mit dem *zeychen* ist daher
ein interpretierendes Verfahren der Erzählstrategie angesprochen. Die Rolle des

---

22 Vgl. Volfing (2007), S. 9, zum ›Jüngeren Titurel‹. – Die Lehre und Lehrhaftigkeit des Textes
äußern sich diskursiv bzw. im Prozess der sprachlichen Vermittlung, wie das Suerbaum (2009),
S. 35–38, für das ›St. Trudperter Hohelied‹ erläutert.
23 Vgl. Haas (1984b), S. 604. Zur Verbindung von Nonnenseelsorge und Textproduktion siehe
Bürkle (1999), S. 67–71; zum Seelsorger als Hagiograph in lateinischen Vitentexten siehe ebd.,
S. 193–233.
24 Es handelt sich trotzdem nicht um eine »Frömmigkeitstheologie, die aus den Erfahrungen
der Seelsorge hervorwächst und für die Seelsorge bestimmt ist, die in Reflexion und Anleitung
ausschließlich der rechten, heilsamen Lebensgestaltung der Christen dienen will und dabei besonders der Frage nachgeht, wie Menschen in ihrer geistlichen Schwäche, ihrer Verhärtung oder
Verängstigung, Ansporn und Trost, Stärkung und Schutz gegeben werden kann«, Hamm (2001),
S. 111. Seelsorgerische Empfehlung im engeren Sinne, wie sie z.B. bei Marquard von Lindau zu
finden ist (dazu Mossman [2010], S. 29–32 und S. 174), bietet die Vita der Christina von Hane
hingegen nicht.
25 Vgl. argumentative Strategien der Erzählinstanz zur Steigerung der Aufnahmebereitschaft
beim Publikum im Leben Dorotheas von Montau, siehe dazu Küenzlen (2010), S. 164–169.

impliziten Hagiographen als Exegeten göttlicher Zeichen gilt es daher im Folgenden zu untersuchen.

Die Funktionen einer beobachtenden Instanz auf der einen Seite und einer kommentierenden auf der anderen spielen sich auf zwei virtuell voneinander getrennten Ebenen ab, obwohl es sich immer um dieselbe Perspektive einer Sprecherrolle handelt. Daher kann der Erzähler, der sich ja zugleich als impliziter Hagiograph konstituiert, nicht allein von Christinas körperlichem Extremzustand Zeugnis geben, sondern überdies den Vergleich zur Passion Christi herstellen und auf diese Weise das Motiv der *imitatio Christi* in den Text einflechten:

> *Jre augen stunden vffen. Noch nye keyns adems eyn wart man gewar, daz ich selber versucht vnd befant. Vnd alle, die by yre waren, die sprachen, daz sy nye grußelicher doit gesehen hetten, als sie leyt zo eym yecklichen mail. Jch, broder der dyße schryben, was auch da geynwirdich. Vnd ich gedacht an die jemerliche erbiebonge des lyeblichen Jhesus, daz er leyt an dem crutze, da van das ertrich erbiebet [...].* (CvH 57, 42–48)

Die Erfahrungen Christinas ins richtige Licht rückend stilisiert sich das wertende Ich eines schreibenden, miterlebenden Bruders mit diesem Vergleich überdies als Kenner einer spezifischen spirituellen Lebensweise in der Nachfolge Christi, womit seine Apostel-Rolle mit Sendungsauftrag hergestellt ist.[26] Mit der Passionsmystik hängt eine Erlösungstheologie zusammen, die im nachempfindenden Vollzug des Leidens Christi die Heilsgewissheit »je neu aktuell im Zusammenhang individuellen und kirchlichen Lebens« umsetzt.[27] Die Ausrichtung der mystischen Erfahrung auf »die Frage des Heils, die Ich und Gesellschaft in all ihren Dimensionen betrifft«,[28] wird mit der pastoralen Rolle des impliziten Hagiographen hergestellt. Dabei wird ersichtlich, dass nicht die Mystikerin selbst die Verbindung zwischen spiritueller Erfahrung und theologischer Bedeutung konstituiert, wie dies Haas in seinen größtenteils auf männliche Figuren wie Seuse, Tauler und Eckhart gerichteten Ausführungen voraussetzt, sondern dass ein hagiographischer Erzähler diese heilsgeschichtliche Funktion übernimmt.[29]

In der Christina von Hane-Vita wird die spezifisch semiotische Bedingung eines erkenntnis- und glaubenstheoretischen Apostolats im thomistischen Sinne, in dem »das ›enuntiabile‹ des Glaubens je neu durchsichtig werden [muss] auf

---

26 Vgl. ähnlich die Sprecherperspektive Mechthilds im ›Fließenden Licht‹, siehe dazu Suerbaum (2003), S. 245. Siehe auch Nigel F. Palmer: Das Buch als Bedeutungsträger bei Mechthild von Magdeburg. In: Bildhafte Rede in Mittelalter und früher Neuzeit. Probleme ihrer Legitimation und ihrer Funktion. Hrsg. von Wolfgang Harms. Tübingen 1992, S. 217–235, insbes. S. 229.
27 Haas (1984b), S. 629.
28 Haas (1984b), S. 612.
29 Vgl. Haas (1984b), S. 605.

die ›res‹, die eine Lebenswirklichkeit ist«,[30] wortwörtlich umgesetzt, indem das Schreiber-Ich den mystischen Bericht auf seinen zeichenhaften Charakter hinweisend immer wieder von seiner persönlichen unzugänglichen Natur auf eine allgemeine lebensweltliche Botschaft herunterbricht. Dieses Übersetzungsverfahren wird insbesondere an dem Gebrauch des Zeichenbegriffs deutlich: *zeichen/ zeychen, bezeychenunge, betzeychen/bezeichen* und *betzeienclichen* finden sich vor allem an solchen Stellen, an denen göttliche Manifestationen mittels bildhafter Rede zusätzlich sinnstiftend erläutert werden.[31] So wird z.B. der Flug einer Christina in einer Vision erscheinenden Taube als Nachahmungsaufforderung gedeutet: *Die dube floge vber yre, als abe sie der heilge geist da myt betzeichent, daz sie vber sich na yme flegen sultde.* (CvH 7, 35 f.) Die Visualität des Taubenflugs illustriert auf diese Weise den an sich unsagbaren mystischen *raptus*, von dem es im Anschluss heißt: *Wie hoch vnd wie ferre sie dar nach vber sich myt hoger beschauongen geflogen was, daz eyn kan keyn hertze vß gesprechen, iß eyn were dan myt yrer selen yn got geflogen.* (CvH 7, 37–39)[32] Göttliche Zeichen bedürfen der Auslegung des impliziten Hagiographen, der die Sichtbarkeit phänomenaler Zustände mit transzendenter Bedeutung ausstattet. Lebensweltliche Erscheinungen werden so zu Offenbarungen, wie das folgende Beispiel vor Augen führt:

Das yre hertze also ynwendich verseret were van smertzen vnd van mytlyden der pynen vnd des doitze yrs aller lyebsten heren, das vffenbairt vnser here vßwendich vnd betzeychent iß myt eynem vffenbairen zeichen. Vff eyn tzijt, da sie yre heubt van rechter cranckeit yn yre lyncke hant hait geneyget, da fiel yr eyn troppen bloitze van yrem hertzen vß dem lyncken augen vff den fynger, an den man den ryncke yn doit. Man dreyt den ryncke dar vmb an dem fynger, want van dem hertzen gechet eyn ader in den vynger. Also woilt vnser here betzeychen, daz iß eyne mynnetroppe were vnd were van deme hertze gefalle vß dem augen, das da entge dem hertze steyt, vnd vff den fynger, yn dem die ader vß dem hertzen gechet. Auch wart der smertzen yrs hertzen noch me gevffenbart. (CvH 17, 12–22)

Der implizite Hagiograph schickt hier die Begründung bzw. Interpretation dem eigentlichen Phänomen voraus, sodass der Übersetzungsakt in Umkehrung dargestellt wird: Am Anfang steht das Nacherleben der Passion, erst anschließend folgt dessen Offenbarung in einem äußerlichen (*vffenbairen*) Zeichen.[33]

---

30 Haas (1984b), S. 615.

31 Vgl. die folgenden Textstellen: CvH 5, 25 f.; CvH 22, 16–18; CvH 36, 16 f.; CvH 37, 10–14.

32 Zum Taubenflug als performative Strategie siehe Kirakosian (2017b).

33 Der auf den Ringfinger fallende Blutstropfen ist zudem als Auszeichnung der Braut Christi zu lesen (siehe auch den Ringaustausch zwischen Gott und Seele in CvH 81, 14 f.). So ist der Ring im ›Legatus‹ Gertruds von Helfta ein Zeichen für die brautmystische Erwählung, vgl.: *sicut annulus signum est desponsationis, sic adversitas tam corporalis quam spiritualis verissimum signum est*

Der implizite Hagiograph hebt auf diese Weise für den impliziten Leser hervor, dass den bildhaften Darstellungen höhere Bedeutungen zukommen – in der gegebenen Passage wird so der Blutstropfen als Passionsnachempfinden gedeutet. Dass Bilder entsprechender Übersetzungen bedürfen, hat daher weniger mit Christinas Unverständnis zu tun, als damit, dass ihre Erkenntnis in Visionen nachdrücklich ausgeführt und erklärt werden muss und zwar von einer Stimme, die die persönliche Erfahrung autoritativ untermauert: von der interpretierenden Stimme eines exegetisch ausgebildeten Bruders.[34] Dieser macht es sich zur Aufgabe, den Offenbarungsakt auf verschiedenen Sinnebenen zu reproduzieren. Das zeichenhafte Interpretieren ist Teil einer Prophetenrolle, die hier die *auctoritas* des impliziten Autors schafft und den gewünschten Lektüremodus des Textes ausweist.[35]

Diese didaktische Lektüre ist eingebettet in die monastische Kultur der *memoria*. Bei der Vermittlung von komplexen Texten halfen Metaphern, Allegorien, Paradoxien, Ironie und andere Tropen das Gelesene oder Gehörte zu memorieren, doch war die Entschlüsselung bestimmter Bilder zum Gelingen dieses Prozesses essentiell, wie Fulton präzisiert: »It was the process of unlocking these images« that would fix them in the mind and incite the meditant to love.«[36] Mit Blick auf die meditative Rezeption der Heiligen Schrift, weist Carruthers auf die Funktion illustrierender und dadurch erklärender Ornamentationen in Texten hin, die den Leser im Prozess des Nachvollziehens leiten sollen.[37] Die Kommentare und Ausführungen in der Christina-Vita können so als exegetische Hilfen verstanden werden, die die Voraussetzungen für die Rezeption im Sinne einer *lectio divina* schaffen. In der Vita werden mehrfach mit den Kommentaren implizite Rückverweise über Kapitelgrenzen hinweg hergestellt, sodass verschiedene

---

electionis divinae et quasi desponsatio animae cum Deo (Gertrud von Helfta, ›Legatus divinae pietatis‹ III, 2, 1, 18).

34 Anders verhält es sich bei Langmann, wo die Christus-Figur die allegorische Baumvision mit lateinischen Versatzstücken auslegt, vgl. ›Die Offenbarungen der Adelheid Langmann‹ 49, 28–50, 5. Siehe auch den Bericht Langmanns: *ich verstunt des nit wol. do kom under herre und legt ez also auz* (›Die Offenbarungen der Adelheid Langmann‹ 95, 18 f.).

35 Vgl. Christian Seebald: Hermeneutischer Dialog. Rudolfs von Ems ›Barlaan und Josaphat‹ und die Lehre der ›bezeichnunge‹. In: Sprechen mit Gott. Redeszenen in mittelalterlicher Bibeldichtung und Legende. Hrsg. von Nine Miedema / Angela Schrott / Monika Unzeitig (Historische Dialogforschung 2). Berlin 2012, S. 285–303, insbes. S. 299, zu *bezeichen* als Markierung eines »hermeneutisch-exegetische[n] Verfahren[s]«.

36 Fulton (2002), S. 263.

37 Vgl. Carruthers (1998), S. 116 f.

Aspekte sinn- und bildhaft miteinander verbunden werden, wie das folgende Beispiel illustriert:

> *want als sie myr selber gesaitte hait, daz sie xij funffzich Pater noster gebet hette, myt veniem, myt beden, myt begeronge sich also verarbet vnd vermoit hait, daz yre naturliche craifft gebrache, daz sie wieder gebeden noch begeren mocht.* (CvH 5, 18–21)

Christinas hier beschriebene Betpraxis wird mit einer darauffolgenden Vision rückgekoppelt:

> *Da sache sie aber daz zarte aller suberlichstes kyntgen stayn vor dem elter yn eyner wegen vnd iß was gedecket myt eym dechelach van roißen vnd vff eynem yecklichen blaytde der roißen stontde geschreben Pater noster vnd iß hait eyn crantze vff sym heubt van xij gar schonen roißen vnd got gaiffe yre so verstayn, daz iß waren die czwolff funfftzich Pater noster, die sie dem kynde Jhesu gesprochen haitte.* (CvH 6, 5–10)

Christinas Vision eines ›Pater noster‹-Kranzes aus Rosen erinnert an die visuelle meditative Praxis des Mittelalters, bei der Diagramme, Zeichnungen, und Glasmalereien das Gebet schematisierend begleiteten und unterstützten.[38] Zugleich ist eine kreative Gebetspraxis denkbar, wie das beim sogenannten handwerklichen Gebet der Fall ist.[39] Inwiefern die in der Vita geschilderte Vision Ausdruck oder Folge solcher Praktiken war, lässt sich nur schwer bestimmen. In jedem Fall wird zum einen Christinas Gebet damit veranschaulicht und zum anderen wird die Vision mit Sinn aufgeladen. Die deiktische Rückbindung innerhalb des Erzählvorgangs wird im Manuskript mit dem wiederholten Unterstreichen der Schlüsselwörter (Ziffern und das ›Pater noster‹) graphisch unterstützt. Das ausdrückliche Entschlüsseln bestimmter Komplexe verleiht dem Text einen sakralen

---

38 Vgl. Mary Jean Carruthers: The Book of Memory: A Study of Memory in Medieval Culture (Cambridge Studies in Medieval Literature 70). Cambridge 1990, S. 248–257 zu Diagrammen und meditativen Praktiken; siehe auch Kathryn Vulic: Prayer and Vernacular Writing in Late-Medieval England (unveröffentlichte Diss. University of California 2004), insbes. Kap. 2: Beyond words. The Paternoster diagram and meditative prayer, S. 105–185. Siehe auch Anna Gottschall: The Lord's Prayer in Circles and Squares. An Identification of some Analogues of the Vernon Manuscript's Pater Noster Table. In: Marginalia 7 (2008), URL: http://merg.soc.srcf.net/journal/08confession/circles.php [10.08.2017].
39 Vgl. Hamburger (1998), S. 78. Zum Rosenkranzgebet speziell siehe Hanneke van Asperen: Praying, Threading, and Adorning. Sewn-in Prints in a Rosary Prayer Book (London, British Library, ADD. MS 14042). In: Weaving, Veiling, and Dressing. Textiles and Their Metaphors in the Late Middle Ages. Hrsg. von Kathryn M. Rudy/Barbara Baert (Medieval Church Studies 12), Turnhout 2007, S. 82–100, insbes. S. 105: »Prayer is not represented metaphorically, but tangibly.«

Status, da dieses Verfahren sonst in der Regel angewendet wird, wenn der Exeget die Bibel auslegt. In der Vita wird zudem betont, dass die exegetische Auflösung von göttlicher Seite geschieht (*got gaiffe yre so verstayn*). Der Erzähler erscheint dagegen auf der Textoberfläche lediglich als Vermittler. Wie Suerbaum hinsichtlich des didaktischen Aussagewertes des ›St. Trudperter Hohenlieds‹ feststellt, wird auch in der Christina von Hane-Vita »Lehre [...] auf zwei Ebenen realisiert«.[40] Einerseits ist das tugendhafte Leben Christinas sprachlich nacherzählbar, andererseits bedarf es der Auslegung symbolischer Momente. In unserem Fall ist zusätzlich zur »Notwendigkeit einer Metaphernphrase«, wie sie von Egerding für den mystischen Mitteilungsprozess ausgeführt wird,[41] außerdem die narratologische Perspektivierung zu betonen, weil die Rolle des kommentierenden Schreiber-Ichs (die Stimme des nahestehenden Bruders) die Autorisierung des Interpretierten beeinflusst.[42]

Zur prophetischen Funktion des Schreiber-Ichs gehört außerdem die Aufgabe, Christinas Heiligenleben auf eine Weise mitzuteilen, die den Stoff für den impliziten Leser aufbereitet. Mit Hilfe eines Gelehrtentopos wird die Ausnahmestellung Christinas unter den Heiligen begründet:

> *Jch eyn hayn noch nyt geleßen van keynem der menschen, der also swerlichen vnd auch also manchfeldenclichen hebe gestretden wieder die anfechtonge vnd auch also enxtlichen vnd gentzelichen vberwonden. Myr leßen woil van etzelichen heilgen, die gar stercklichen myt etzelichen vndogenden stretden vnd sie auch gar vollenkommenclichen vberwonden. [...] Aber dyeße heilge jonffrauwe Christina hait nyt gestretden myt etzelichen als myt tzweyn ader dryn. Sie eyn hait auch nyt gestreden eyn jaire ader zweyn, dan sie streyde vij gantzer jaire wieder die sieben heubt sunden, myt yglicher eyne gantze jaire [...].* (CvH 9, 17–26)

Der Christinas Besonderheit demonstrierende argumentative Aufbau ist rhetorisch so gestaltet, dass sich zunächst das Schreiber-Ich als belesen in den Heiligenleben darstellt, um erst anschließend denselben Horizont in einem kollektiven *myr* vorauszusetzen, zu dem es sich als zugehörig zählt. Im letzten Schritt wird der Vergleich mit Christina angestellt.[43] Die Stimme des interpretierenden Vermittlers konstituiert sich als Teil einer Gemeinschaft, in der das Lesen von

---

40 Suerbaum (2009), S. 37.

41 Michael Egerding: Die Metaphorik der spätmittelalterlichen Mystik. Bd. 1: Systematische Untersuchung. Paderborn u. a. 1997(a), S. 35 f.

42 Mit Egerdings (1997a), S. 36, Terminologie ausgedrückt, werden dadurch die »Bedeutungskomponenten« beim »Bildempfänger« verändert.

43 Zum ›St. Trudperter Hohelied‹ stellt Suerbaum (2009), S. 36, fest: »Charakteristisch ist vielmehr die häufige Verwendung des kollektiven ›Wir‹, mit dem sich das Sprecher-Ich in die Gemeinschaft der christlichen Leser einbezieht.«

Heiligenleben üblich zu sein scheint, sodass der Gebrauchskontext der Vita impliziert wird. Wie im ›Fließendem Licht‹ Mechthilds von Magdeburg geht es dabei weniger um »Gelehrsamkeit« denn um »Erfahrungswissen«.[44] Dieses erlaubt, das Vorwissen des impliziten Lesers argumentativ zu nutzen, so z.B. wenn eine rhetorische Frage auf die Unnötigkeit weiterer Ausführungen anspielt: *Kortzelichen, wanne sie allergernst hette geßen vnd auch woil gedorfft hette, so hoirt sie vff vnd saiße dan vngeßen. Was sal ich vil sagen?* (CvH 14, 8–10). Durch das Adverb *kortzelichen* verweist der implizite Hagiograph auf sein resümierendes Erzählverfahren.[45] Auf diese Weise färbt der Heilsnutzen der Mystikerin auf den Erzähler ab, dessen Aufgabe die Aufbereitung der persönlichen Erfahrung für ein größeres Publikum ist.

So wird auf den gemeinschaftlichen Nutzen von Christinas Leben mehrfach hingewiesen, wobei es erneut exegetischer Betrachtungen bedarf (*vß legen*), damit ihr Beispiel letztlich auch lehrreich wirken kann: *Aber zo eyner lerunge den anderen, daß eyn eynfeldiche mensche baße verstene konne, so wille ich eyn deylle vß legen, als ich van yre selber gehoirt hayn* (CvH 8, 3–5).[46] Die in der Handschrift unterstrichenen Wörter weisen auf die Kernaussage dieser Textstelle hin: *anderen – mensche.* Auch aus göttlicher Sprecherperspektive wird hervorgehoben, dass sie als Vorbild für andere steht,[47] sodass der Text, wie das ›Fließende Licht‹, als »Schnittpunkt der persönlichen Geschichte […] mit der allumfassenden Heilsgeschichte der christlichen Offenbarung« erscheint.[48] Christinas Bedeutung für das Gemeinschaftsheil steht dabei nach wie vor mit einem als unzulänglich dargestellten Schreibakt in Verbindung:

> *Wie hoch vnd wie ferre sie dar nach vber sich myt hoger beschauongen geflogen was, daz eyn kan keyn hertze vß gesprechen, iß eyn were dan myt yrer selen yn got geflogen. Doch wil ich eyn teylle her na schryben, als abe ich eynen troppen neme vß dem mere.* (CvH 7, 37–40)

Hier wird die Möglichkeit eines abstrakt gesetzten Erzählens vom Bericht des impliziten Hagiographen abgelöst. Folglich wird das personifizierte Erzählen,

---

44 Suerbaum (2009), S. 30; siehe auch ebd.: »Lehre setzt Autorität aufgrund von Gelehrsamkeit und damit Bildung voraus, ist gebunden an die Sphäre der Schriftlichkeit.«

45 Ähnlich bei Adelheid Langmann, wo es um die Schlussfolgerung des Abts von Kaisheim, Ulrich III. Niblung, in einem Brief geht, vgl. *kürtzlichen* (›Die Offenbarungen der Adelheid Langmann‹ 93, 28).

46 Vgl. ebenso: *Auch verhencket vnser here zo dem anderen mail dyeße groiße anfechtonge vber sie, dar vmb daz yre strytde eyn lere were allen den die bekarunge vnd anfechtonge lydent.* (CvH 10, 13–15)

47 Vgl. CvH 78.

48 Andersen (2003), S. 229.

hier als Schreibprozess dargestellt, als unvollständig klassifiziert, indem der bildhafte Vergleich mit dem Tropfen aus dem Meer die Vita als minimalen Ausschnitt aus Christinas Leben portraitiert. Hyperbolisch wird auch ein *ieglich troph des meres* im Kontext des Gotteslobs in Heinrichs von Mügeln ›Tum‹ verwendet.[49] Zugleich ist damit eine Metapher gewählt, die auf die unendliche Natur der Gottheit hinweisen will, wie an anderer Stelle in der Christina von Hane-Vita deutlich wird: *Da sprach er aber zo yre: ›O du gar zarte sele myn, ich wylle dich senden yn die dyeffte des mers, daz ist yn daz abgront der lyebden der heilgen dryueldickeit [...].‹* (CvH 78, 13–15) Bei Rudolf von Biberach ist in Anlehnung an Damascenus' *De fide orthodoxa* die Weite des Meers ein Bild für Gott: *got ist, als ein vngendot vnd vngezilot mer der substancie* (Rudolf von Biberach: ›Die siben strassen zu got‹ 134, 15 f.).[50] Den wohl griffigsten Vergleich für das in der Vita verwendete Bild des Tropfens aus dem Meer bietet aber ein Ausschnitt aus Meister Eckharts deutschen Predigten:

> *Nû merket, wie sich got vereinet mit den dingen. Er vereinet sich mit den dingen und beheltet sich doch ein an im selben, und alliu dinc an im ein. Hie von sprichet Kristus: ir sult gewandelt werden in mich und ich niht in iuch. Daz kumet von sîner unwandelhafticheit und von sîner unmæzlicheit und von der dinge kleinheit. Dâ von sprichet ein wîssage, daz alliu dinc sint als kleine wider gote als ein tropfe wider dem wilden mer. Der einen tropfen würfe in daz mer, sô verwandelte sich der tropfe in daz mer und niht daz mer in den tropfen.* (DW III, 80, 386 f.)

Eckhart weist das Bild des Tropfens aus dem Meer als Jesus Sirach-Zitat aus: *numerus dierum hominum multum centum anni quasi guttae aquae a mare* (Eccl 18,8). Bei Eckhart wird der bildhafte Ausdruck aufgeladen mit der Vorstellung der *unio* als das Einmünden in die göttliche Natur. Zunächst ist aber mit dem Tropfen, wie in der alttestamentlichen Quelle, die *kleinheit* der Dinge bezeichnet. In der Vita wie in der Eckhart-Predigt wird das *mer* für die *unwandelhafticheit* und *unmæzlicheit* Gottes im Kontext der *unio* gebraucht. Wenn der Erzähler der Vita einen Tropfen aus dem Meer nimmt, dann ist dieser Tropfen in qualitativer Hinsicht genauso beschaffen wie das Meer. Der der Vita zugrundeliegende theologische Gedanke der Wandlung ist bei Eckhart hingegen ausgeführt. Dass etwa ein Tropfen Weihwasser ein ganzes mit ordinärem Wasser gefülltes Becken verän-

---

49 Vgl.: *Wer aller künste zins, / schatz wisheit, richtum alles sinns / verrunet in mins herzen flins, / versigelt mit der witze wachs, / und wer ein ieglich troph / des meres an der wolken schoph / gezünet, dines lobes zoph / volflechte nicht irs sinnes flachs* (›Der Tum‹ 179, 1–8).
50 Rudolf von Biberach: ›Die siben strassen zu got‹. Die hochalemannische Übertragung nach der Handschrift Einsiedeln 278. Hrsg. von Margot Schmidt (Spicilegium Bonaventurianum 6). Quaracchi-Florentiae 1969. (Die Stellennachweise geben Seiten- und Zeilenzahlen an.)

dern kann, entspricht dieser Vorstellung von der Einheit Gottes mit den Dingen. Daher ist auch der Erzählakt des impliziten Hagiographen in gewisser Hinsicht vollkommen. Wie ein Tropfen zur Heiligung des Wassers ausreicht, so reicht auch seine unvollständige Erzählung aus.

Trotz einer Einheitsvorstellung verweist also das Bild des Tropfens aus dem Meer quantitativ gesehen auf eine lückenhafte Erzählung. Dabei nimmt der implizite Hagiograph der Christina-Vita eine aktive Rolle bei der noch so inadäquaten Vermittlung der *unio*-Erfahrung Christinas ein, denn er ist es, der die Teilhabe daran mit seinem Schreibakt erst ermöglicht. Im Anschluss an die oben zitierte Stelle, die den Taubenflug im Schlafsaal beschreibt, heißt es:

> *Die dube, die yre da gesant, wart auch alles zo mail alles vmb vnd vmb daz slaiffhuße der jonffrauwen. Da myt verstene ich daz zo bezeychen, daz van der sendonge des heilgen geistes die gantze versamenunge geheilget sulte werden durch yren verdynst.* (CvH 7, 40–43)

Der implizite Hagiograph macht auf die Heiligung der Klosterangehörigen aufmerksam, doch gleichzeitig ist eine andere Heiligung angesprochen: die des impliziten Lesers des Textes. Der vorausgehende Bezug zum Schreibprozess macht ja bereits auf die sich erst im Vollzug auswirkende Heiligung aufmerksam. Mit Löser ließe sich daher von einer Schriftmystik sprechen, die sich stets in einem ontologischen Prozess befindet.[51]

In der Vita ist also die Verbindung zwischen Rezeption und Intention rhetorisch inszeniert. Damit verfolgt die Erwähnung des Schreibakts deutlich mehr als die Funktion einer Berichterstattung mit dem Ziel einer akkuraten Erzählung: Hier geht es vielmehr um Heiligung, die einen Prozess des Interpretierens miteinschließt (*da myt verstene ich daz zo bezeychen*). Haas' Postulat einer mittelalterlichen Mystik, die auch immer eine interpretierte ist,[52] kann dort festgemacht werden, wo der implizite Autor auf seine exegetische Tätigkeit hinweist. Diese Art von Selbstinszenierung, d.h. »das eigene prophetische Sprechen als diskursive Rede unter der paradoxen Bedingung der Nichtdiskursivierbarkeit des Erkannten auszuweisen« gehört zugleich, so Köbele, zur Autorrolle des christlichen Propheten.[53] Auf diese Weise erklärt sich der implizite Hagiograph der Christina von Hane-Vita zum unabdingbaren Glied der Heilsverheißung. Erzählung und Heilsgeschichte werden von ihm zusammengeführt. Das Urteil und die Wertung eines Augenzeugen sind daher nicht nur auf einer hagiographischen Autorisie-

---

51 Vgl. Löser (2012).
52 Vgl. Haas (2000), insbes. S. 15.
53 Köbele (2014), S. 175.

rungsebene von Bedeutung.[54] Die Stimme eines exegetisch versierten Hagiographen führt über die Erzählebene hinaus und richtet sich dabei nicht wie so oft im Beichtvater-Topos angenommen realhistorisch an die Mystikerin, sondern mit textpragmatischem Anspruch an den impliziten Leser.

3.2 Der implizite Leser

Die Christina von Hane-Vita richtet sich intradiegetisch an historische Adressaten, die dem Kontext nach Angehörige oder Vertraute des Klosters Hane hätten sein müssen. Das ist an den für das Kloster relevanten, z.T. prophetischen Aussagen ersichtlich, wie etwa an den Details der vornehmlich dort aufbewahrten Reliquien der elftausend Jungfrauen:

> Vnd die eylff dusent, wylcher heubtder yn vnserem gotz huße synt, yn sonderheit erkant sy sie myt yrem namen vnd geslecht, det sie an schryben, als noch yn den rollen yn dem cloister fonden wyrt, vnd synt dyeße: Ceomate virgo, Petrisse virgo, Elyzabet virgo, Benedicta virgo, Juliana virgo, Anne virgo, Cunigondis virgo, Gertrudis virgo, Cristine virgo, Cristine virgo, Elyzabet filie cesaris. (CvH 32, 31–36)

Auch klostertopographische Angaben in Visionserscheinungen wie ein Kruzifix im Schlafsaal, ein Kreuzgang auf dem Weg zum Kapitelsaal oder eine Nikolauskapelle lassen auf das Vorwissen spezifischer Lokalitäten zurückschließen.[55] Einmal wird ein historisch nicht weiter identifizierbarer Ordensbruder namens Jacob erwähnt, für dessen Seelenheil Christina betet, wobei die Namensnennung die Verbindung zu einem direkten Adressatenkreis herstellt.[56] Doch sind diese konkreten Benennungen zu vage, als dass sich daraus Rückschlüsse auf realhistorische Umstände ziehen ließen.[57] Stattdessen sollen im Folgenden die ein bestimmtes Bild des Lesers erzeugenden narrativen Strategien ermittelt werden.

---

54 Köbele (2014), S. 170, hebt in diesem Sinne die zwei zentralen Aspekte von Autorschaft auf der einen Seite und Zeugenschaft und Urheberschaft auf der anderen hervor.
55 Vgl. die folgenden Textstellen: *Svnderlichen so stont eyne crucifix vff dem dormiter ader slaiffhuyße* (CvH 7, 7); *durch den crutzganck yn das cappittel huße* (CvH 20, 8); *da hieß sie sich furen yn sent Nycolais cappel* (CvH 17, 2); *Sie was vff eyn tzijt jn sent Nyclais capelle* (CvH 28, 3); *da wart sie gefort yn sent Nyclaes capelle* (CvH 36, 2).
56 Vgl. CvH 57, 8–13.
57 Der historische Ansatz von Krings (2009), S. 201, z.B. rekurriert auf die Braut-Allegorie: »Für welche Leser aber schreibt er [der Verfasser]? Für solche, die wie Christina, den Weisungen des Evangeliums gemäß leben, das heißt, Christus nachfolgen. Das sind in erster Linie die Frauen von Hane, die Bräute Christi sein wollen und einen Ring tragen, der sie daran erinnern soll.«

Die zuvor getroffene Dissoziation zwischen einem realhistorischen Autor und einem impliziten Autor als Rollenkonstitution des Erzählers bedingt gleichermaßen die Konstituierung eines impliziten Lesers im Kontrast zu realhistorischen Adressaten. So geht man in der Forschung zum höfischen Roman von einem fiktiven Rezipientenkreis aus, der im Text selbst angelegt ist.[58] In der rezeptionsästhetischen Analyse moderner Romane nach Iser spricht man zudem von einem »Beteiligungsangebot, das dem Leser gemacht werden muß«:

> Die Beteiligung des Lesers könnte sich gar nicht entfalten, wenn ihm alles vorgesetzt würde. Und das bedeutet doch, daß sich der formulierte Text über Andeutungen und Suggestionen in das von ihm Nicht-Gesagte, aber dennoch Gemeinte abschattet. Denn erst hier kommt die Einbildungskraft des Lesers zu ihrem Recht; der geschriebene Text stattet sie mit Anweisungen aus, sich das vorzustellen, was er selbst verschweigt.[59]

Das Leerstellen-Modell Isers geht von einer kreativen und imaginativen Beteiligung des Lesers aus. In der neueren Forschung werden der »Akt des Lesens« wie auch der »Akt des Erzählens« als Performativa verstanden.[60] Bereits Hasebrink wies auf die Performativität mittelalterlicher Predigttexte hin, bei denen die appellativ-inzitative Rede die Identifizierung des Lesers als Adressaten des Heilsereignisses ermögliche.[61] Der Leseprozess als solcher ist bei vormodernen Texten weiterhin nach sozialen Praktiken zu differenzieren, weil es sich hier um »zeremonielle, rituelle oder doch ritualnahe Vollzugsformen« des Lesens handelt.[62] Insbesondere Viten sind Texte, die vorgelesen wurden. Dieser mündliche Vollzugsmodus spiegelt sich in den Texten entsprechend wider.

Die »fingierte Mündlichkeit« eines Textes kann dabei als »bewusste Schreibstrategie« verstanden werden,[63] deren wichtigste Funktion es nach Goetsch sei, die »Illusion einer Sprache der Nähe« herzustellen.[64] Das Paradigma der fiktiven Oralität, das auf Burrows Arbeit basiert und u.a. von Coleman und Green

---

58 Vgl. Eberhard Nellmann: Wolframs Erzähltechnik. Untersuchungen zur Funktion des Erzählers. Wiesbaden 1973, S. 26.

59 Iser (1972), S. 59.

60 Strowick (2009), S. 11–13.

61 Vgl. Burkhard Hasebrink: Formen inzitativer Rede bei Meister Eckhart. Untersuchungen zur literarischen Konzeption der deutschen Predigt (Texte und Textgeschichte 32). Tübingen 1992(b), S. 40–43.

62 Strohschneider (2014), S. 265. Siehe auch Largier (2007), S. 37.

63 Paul Goetsch: Fingierte Mündlichkeit in der Erzählkunst entwickelter Schriftkulturen. In: Poetica 17 (1985), S. 202–218, hier S. 202.

64 Goetsch (1985), S. 217.

weiter entwickelt wurde,[65] trennt die Inszenierung eines Textes von seiner realen Rezeption, ohne dass dabei die akustische Wahrnehmung vernachlässigt würde. Zumthor hingegen operiert mit dem Begriff der »vocalité«, weil er die Opposition Mündlichkeit/Schriftlichkeit für zu vereinfachend hält und die Kommunikation im Mittelalter als eine komplexe unterstreichen will.[66] In ihrer Kritik an dem auf die Stimme abzielenden Konzept der Vokalität betonen Chinca und Young, dass das mediale Zusammenspiel dabei in den Hintergrund gerate.[67] Unter Berücksichtigung medialer Fragen führt Coleman dagegen das Konzept der öffentlichen Vortragssituation im Mittelalter, der sogenannten »aurality« ein: »the reading of a written text aloud to one or more people«.[68] Inwiefern eine öffentliche von einer privaten Lesesituation getrennt werden kann, bleibt dabei zu hinterfragen.[69] Zumindest aber ist mit »Auralität« die im Mittelalter vorherrschende Rezeption des Vorlesens hervorgehoben.[70] Die »aurale« Dimension eines Textes verweist also auf die in der Schriftlichkeit festzumachenden Inszenierungsoptionen des Hörens wie Lesens. Sie wird daher von Green als eine Zwischenstufe der Rezep-

---

65 Vgl. John Anthony Burrow: Ricardian Poetry. Chaucer, Gower, Langland and the Gawain Poet. 2. Aufl. London 1992.

66 Vgl. Paul Zumthor: La Poésie et la voix dans la littérature médiévale. Paris 1987. Siehe auch in dessen Nachfolge Ursula Schaefer: Vokalität. Altenglische Dichtung zwischen Mündlichkeit und Schriftlichkeit (ScriptOralia 39). Tübingen 1992, und Jan-Dirk Müller: Spielregeln für den Untergang. Die Welt des Nibelungenliedes. Tübingen 1998.

67 Vgl. Mark Chinca/Christopher Young: Orality and Literacy in the Middle Ages. A Conjunction and its Consequences. In: Orality and literacy in the Middle Ages. Essays on a conjunction and its consequences in honour of D. H. Green. Hrsg. von Mark Chinca/Christopher Young (Utrecht Studies in Medieval Literacy 12). Turnhout 2005, S. 1–15, insbes. S. 5, und Dennis Howard Green: Terminologische Überlegungen zum Hören und Lesen im Mittelalter. In: Eine Epoche im Umbruch. Volksprachliche Literalität 1200–1300. Cambridger Symposium 2001. Hrsg. von Christa Bertelsmeyer-Kierst/Christopher Young. Tübingen 2003, S. 1–22, insbes. S. 12 f.

68 Joyce Coleman: Interactive Parchment. The Theory and Practice of Medieval English Aurality. In: The Yearbook of English Studies 25 (1995), S. 63–79, hier S. 64. Siehe auch dies.: Public Reading and the Reading Public in Late Medieval England and France, 2. Aufl. (Cambridge Studies in Medieval Literature 26). Cambridge 2005, S. 55 und S. 109 f.

69 Dennis Howard Green: Medieval Listening and Reading. The Primary Reception of German Literature 800–1300. Cambridge 1994, S. 169–202, sucht nach einer Balance zwischen diesen Polen, bietet aber letztlich in seiner Kritik zu Coleman und Manfred Günther Scholz: Zur Hörerfiktion in der Literatur des Spätmittelalters und der frühen Neuzeit. In: Literatur und Leser. Theorien und Modelle zur Rezeption literarischer Werke. Hrsg. von Gunter Grimm. Stuttgart 1975, S. 135–147, kein alternatives Modell an; siehe auch Dennis Howard Green: Fictive Orality. A Restriction on the Use of the Concept. In: Blütezeit. Festschrift für L. Peter Johnson zum 70. Geburtstag. Hrsg. von Mark Chinca/Joachim Heinzle/Christopher Young. Tübingen 2000, S. 161–174.

70 Vgl. Coleman (2005), S. 27–32.

tion (»intermediate mode of reception«), insbesondere für volkssprachige deutsche Texte ab 1200, betont.[71]

Im Folgenden ist dennoch der Begriff der Inszenierung dem der Rezeption vorzuziehen, weil die in der Christina von Hane-Vita angelegten Momente fingierter Mündlichkeit sowohl kollektive wie auch individuelle Inszenierungsszenarien verschiedener medialer Beschaffenheit visuell wie akustisch hervorrufen.[72] Zusätzlich dazu ist im Anschluss an Largiers Ausführungen zur »Vergegenwärtigung des Vergangenen mit praktischen Mitteln« im Mittelalter der implizite Leser auf zwei Ebenen zu untersuchen:[73] die Konfiguration eines lesenden Du in der Vergegenwärtigung der Schrift, z.B. im Schriftgebrauch als Gedächtnisübung, und die Rollenzuweisung eines betenden und liturgisch gebundenen Du in einem virtuellen Wahrnehmungsraum, d.h. hier in der angewendeten Sinneserfahrung. Den Beobachtungen zur Gebetspraxis mit Hinblick auf die Rolle des impliziten Lesers der Vita läuft der Vergleich mit einem wahrscheinlich aus Hane stammenden deutsch-lateinischen Gebetbuch voraus.

3.2.1 Das lesende Du

Der mittelhochdeutsche Anwendungsbereich von *lesen* lässt nahezu alle Erkenntnisformen zu – von ›zu sich nehmen‹, ›aufnehmen‹, ›sammeln‹, ›sich erinnern‹, bis hin zum modernen Verständnis von ›lesen‹. Dennoch wird in der Vita der Christina von Hane deutlich, dass es sich speziell um das Hören oder Sehen von Worten handelt. Wenn es also um Lesen geht, dann ist damit vordergründig die Wahrnehmung von Sprache gemeint. In der Christina-Vita machen zwei Aussagen deutlich, wie das materielle Schriftkorpus mit dem Leseakt in Verbindung steht: *als du woil machest myrcken, abe du dyße buchelgyn myt flyße dyns hertzen wylt vber leßen* (CvH 6, 15 f.) und *wer dyße buche vberleßet vnd gedencket* [...] (CvH 39, 14 f.). Ein lesendes Du ist also auch ein sehendes Du, das in dem »begegnungsstiftenden Blick« nicht nur, wie Heinzer ausführt, die Visionen der Mystikerin imaginiert, sondern zu allererst den Zugang zu einer »Schaufrömmigkeit« des Buches hat.[74] In beiden aus der Vita zitierten Textstellen wird die Lektüre deik-

---

71 Vgl. Green (1994), S. 169–230 und S. 299 f.

72 Vgl. die Parallelität von lesen und hören in den folgenden Textbeispielen: *als daz ewangelium spricht* (CvH 38, 32); *als ym ewangelio wyrt geleißen* (CvH 15, 7).

73 Largier (2007), S. 37–42 gründet seine Beobachtungen auf die im Mittelalter herrschende Vorstellung über den Leser, »der immer als ein in einen zeitlichen Prozess eingebundener Praktiker vorgestellt werden muss« (hier S. 37).

74 Heinzer (2004), S. 472.

tisch gebunden (*dyße buchelgyn/bůche*), was die Vergegenwärtigung von Schrift und ihre Autoreferentialität hervorhebt. In Rück- und Vorverweisen wird der mediale Vollzug erst durch ein Du ermöglicht, indem das implizite Schreiber-Ich dieses Du in der direkten Anrede konfiguriert: [...] *alstu her na fyndest geschreben* (CvH 3, 10).[75] Ein lineares Verhältnis gemäß des Textverlaufs (*her na*) wird zur materiellen Schriftlichkeit (*geschreben*) in Bezug gesetzt, wobei diese Verbindung nur durch ein Du zustande kommt (*asltu*), das den Text wahrnimmt (*fyndest*). Das verknüpfte Vergleichspartikel (*als* in *alstu*) lädt den impliziten Leser dazu ein, das schriftliche Material zu erkunden und kann als Autorisierungsmarker verstanden werden, weil das Gesagte als durch die Lesermanipulation überprüfbar dargestellt wird. Dies wird ganz besonders an einer retrospektiven Darstellung des Leseprozesses deutlich:

> *Siche an, wie gar jemerlichen die pyne vnd daz sterben was, vnd auch war vmb iß got vber sie verhenget. Daz fyndestu geschreben yn dem jaire vor dyeßem an aller heilgen dage. Da lyestu van eyner semlicher erschuttunge, erbiebonge vnd ersterbonge.* (CvH 80, 13–16)

Der implizite Leser wird aufgefordert, eine dreifache Leistung zu erbringen, die (Ein-)Sehen, Aufschlagen und Lesen einschließt und letztlich das nicht Nachvollziehbare materiell zugänglich macht. Die vorausweisenden und daher wohl zum Textbeginn gehäuft auftretenden Formulierungen (*her na*) dienen dem Anschein einer abgeschlossenen Heiligengeschichte, auf die im *buchelgen* punktuell zurückgegriffen werden kann:

> *Das was eyn zeychen, daz got vnßer here dar na waschen wolte yn yrem hertzen, das er sie van syner kyntheit zo hoger lyebden zehen woillte, als du woil machest myrcken, abe du dyße buchelgyn myt flyße dyns hertzen wylt vber leßen, wie sie got van eymme zo dem anderen myt syner gotlicher wyßheit vff gezogen haitte.* (CvH 6, 13–18)

Ein Erkenntnisgewinn als Folge des Leseaktes ist konditional und futuristisch bestimmt (*abe du* [...] *wylt*).[76] Der von Christina erfahrene Gnadenerweis weitet sich auf ein Du aus, wie die Axialität von *yrem hertzen* und *dyns hertzen* ver-

---

75 Siehe oben Anm. 14. Siehe auch den konkreten Rückverweis innerhalb der kalendrischen Textstruktur: *Siche an, wie gar jemerlichen die pyne vnd daz sterben was, vnd auch war vmb iß got vber sie verhenget. Daz fyndestu geschreben yn dem jaire vor dyeßem an aller heilgen dage.* (CvH 80, 13–16)

76 Nach Paul (1998), S. 297, § 315, hat »›will‹ mit dem Infinitiv [...] überwiegend voluntative Bedeutung; es kann aber auch eine stark futuristische Bedeutungskomponente aufweisen, und beides kann unmittelbar nebeneinander stehen«. Im Kontext des gesamten Satzes, der mit einem anderen Modalverb eingeläutet (*machest*) und mit einer konditionalen Konjunktion (*abe*) fortge-

deutlicht. Ist dieses Du aber ein persönliches Du, das sich direkt an den Leser richtet, oder handelt es sich um den unpersönlichen Gebrauch des Pronomens? An nur wenigen Stellen wird die zweite Person zugunsten einer spezifizierten Leserschaft aufgegeben, z.B. *Hie mache eyn vollenkomen hertze myrcken, wie* [...] (CvH 5, 11). An nur einer Stelle jedoch ist die direkte Anrede ganz sicher unpersönlich gebraucht. Bei der Aufzählung von zunächst unpersönlichen Lehrsätzen wechselt das Subjekt im letzten Lehrsatz in die persönliche Anrede: *Das irste ist, daz der mensche* [...] *Das siebente, dastu vmb nyemans lyebe ader leyt laißes vnderwegen, was du myt gode haist zo schaiffen.* (CvH 29, 6–17) Dieses Du ist somit eine personifiziert erscheinende Fortführung der allgemein an den Menschen gerichteten Grundsätze. Grundsätzlich aber ist das Du des Textes als ein Gegenüber konstituiert, das das »Büchlein« in den Händen hält.

Um also die Seelenentwicklung Christinas zu verstehen, muss das Lesen mit *flyße dyns hertzen* geschehen. Im Textverlauf wird auf das Gelesene wie auf das noch zu Lesende verwiesen. Der Akt des Lesens, oder das Leseereignis, verhält sich auf diese Weise parallel zum Erzählvorgang. Das Schreiber-Ich resümiert:

> *O flyßicher leißer, nu haistu gehoret, wie die seliche jonffrauwe Christina yre kyntliche jaire hait gestanden yn der schoillen. Nyt alleyn hait sie geleret die bustabe, sonder auch nach dem geistlichen leben. Iß ist yetzont genoch gesait van der kyntheit, was da ist geschet yn yrer jogent.* (CvH 8, 31–34)

Die im Manuskript unterstrichene Adressierung des eifrigen Lesers (*flyßicher leißer*) wird durch die vorauslaufende Akklamation zusätzlich hervorgehoben, bevor sie den impliziten Leser in eine neue zeitliche Dimension überführt. Wurde das Du bisher auf Zukünftiges hingewiesen, wird hier zum ersten Mal seine Präsenz auf die zeitliche Linie des Erzählten ausgedehnt. Der implizite Hagiograph strukturiert die Narration im Rückblick und kehrt mit dem Mittel des *entrelacement* zum Erzählfluss zurück (*genoch gesait van*), wobei er das Gesagte als Bezugsgröße wählt. Dazu passt das Gehört-Haben des impliziten Adressaten (*nu haistu gehoret, wie*), sodass die fingierte Mündlichkeit die Identität eines lesenden Du vergegenwärtigt. Mit der Strategie des suggestiven Rückverweises auf einen vorausgehenden Abschnitt wird der Leser im Vergegenwärtigungsprozess als bewusst erfahrend dargestellt und in den Prozess des Erzählens aktiv eingebunden. Das wird besonders deutlich, wenn das Schreiber-Ich an einer Stelle nach dem Eindruck des Lesers fragt: *Wie meynnestu, daz yr jonfferliches hertze yn*

---

führt wird, liegt ein konjunktivischer Modus im abhängigen Satz vor (Konjunktiv Praesentis), der durchaus eine futuristische Nuance trägt, vgl. ebd., S. 409, § 446.

gedancken dick floiße yn groißer vocht des gotlichen tzorns? (CvH 10, 17–19) Es ist dies aber eine rhetorische Frage, wie der mit Bibelzitaten angereicherte Kontext dieser Formulierung deutlich macht. Es geht um Vorwissen, um Bibelkenntnis und um Leseerfahrung, die der implizite Hagiograph voraussetzt und die er mit seinem Leser zu teilen scheint.

Abgesehen von unpersönlichen Formulierungen (*man leßet also* [CvH 1, 14])[77] gibt es also auch ein lesendes Wir, zu dem sich der implizite Hagiograph zählt.[78] Die gemeinsame Referenzwelt etabliert sich mit personalen (*myr*) und possessiven Pronomen (*vnser*) und basiert explizit – anders konstituiert sich das aus Christinas Sicht geäußerte *myr*[79] – auf der Kenntnis geistlicher und hagiographischer Texte (des Neuen Testaments sowie der Heiligenleben).[80] Die Vita verweist indirekt auf die gemeinsame Bibellektüre bzw. liturgische Lesung im Klosteralltag, geht es doch hier wahrscheinlich um ein Vorlesen, wie auch die Zuhörerschaft implizierende Passivkonstruktion *wyrt geleißen* nahelegt.[81] Ähnlich verhält es sich mit der unpersönlichen Formel *als man yme ewangelio leßet* (CvH 7, 31), die auf eine liturgische und paraliturgische Lesepraxis hinweist. Autorisierung läuft demnach über die von einem Kollektiv geteilten Konventionen der Lesepraktiken und Leseinhalte. Die Figur Christinas fungiert im sprachlichen Vollzug des Textes als verbindende Instanz zwischen einem biblischen Gott und einer klösterlichen Glaubenspraxis. Es ist die »Schriftlektüre«, die das Leservorwissen mit

---

77 Siehe auch die folgeden Textbeispiele: *als ym ewangelio wyrt geleißen* (CvH 15, 7); *als man yme ewangelio leßet* (CvH 7, 31).

78 Dem steht an zwei Stellen ein pluraler Adressat gegenüber: *Nu salt ir hoiren* (CvH 9, 3); *sult yr hoiren* (CvH 9, 13). Vor dem Hintergrund des Colemanschen Modells liegt hier die Spur einer kollektiven Vortragssituation vor.

79 Wenn Christina im pluralen Modus spricht, dann geht es um die Gemeinschaft der Christen jenseits einer Leserfiguration, vgl. die folgenden Textstellen: *also werden myr alle d age gedaufft yn dem dauffe, als der engel sprach zo der jonffrauwen Maria* (CvH 99, 18 f.); *Da hvbe sie an van freuden vnd sprache: ›Myr sullen lyebe haben, myr sullen loben, myr sullen sehen!‹* (CvH 23, 30 f.) Kongruent dazu richtet sich die vom göttlichen Sprecher-Ich ausgehende plurale Anrede an ein Seelenkollektiv, vgl.: ›*Heillich, heillich syt yr yn myner gotheit, vollenkomen yn myner ewiger lyebden.‹* (CvH 32, 40 f.); *›Komet, yr gebenediten myns vader, vnd besytzet daz ryche, daz vch ist bereyt van anbegynne der werelt.‹* (CvH 57, 20 f.); *Jch setzen mych vor vch zo eynigen ewigen verbande, daz yr mych ewenclichen sullent loben. Vnd yr sullent erkennen mynne wonderliche wonder […]* (CvH 58, 11–13). Die pluralen Adressierungen schließen auf Grund der direkten Anrede stets den impliziten Leser ein.

80 Vgl.: *Des hayn myr woil eyn exempel van vnserem herren Jhesu Cristo* (CvH 39, 7 f.); *als myr dick leßen van yme* (CvH 39, 11). Siehe auch: *Myr leßen woil van etzelichen heilgen* (CvH 9, 19 f.); *als wyr van etzelichen leßen* (CvH 10, 45 f.). – Hier sei nur am Rande auf die Autoreferentialität des Lesens von Heiligenleben innerhalb des Vitentextes hingewiesen.

81 Vgl.: *als daz ewangelium spricht* (CvH 38, 32); *als ym ewangelio wyrt geleißen* (CvH 15, 7).

dem Vergegenwärtigen des vorliegenden Textes in Einklang bringt.[82] Erst vor dem Hintergrund dieses kollektiven Wissens kann Christina als Ausnahmefall in der Gemeinschaft eingeordnet werden, sodass der implizite Hagiograph auf ein Du angewiesen ist: Diese Rollenzuweisung schafft die Grundlage für ein gelenktes Leseverständnis von Christinas Vita.

Das Ziel des Leseereignisses wird mit dem Sendauftrag des impliziten Hagiographen spezifiziert:

> *Aber zo eyner lerunge den anderen, daß eyn eynfeldiche mensche baße verstene konne, so wille ich eyn deylle vß legen, als ich van yre selber gehoirt hayn.* (CvH 8, 3–5)

Der Interpretationsvorgang des wertenden Schreiber-Ichs dient dem Seelenheil der anderen, d. h. all derer, die von Christina erfahren. Der didaktische Anspruch (*lerunge*) setzt dabei ein Du voraus, das auf die Vermittlung samt seiner Auslegung angewiesen ist. Das Motiv des einfältigen und unwürdigen Menschen, wie z. B. im ›Fließenden Licht‹ die Sprecherin charakterisiert wird,[83] wird hier auf den impliziten Leser ausgeweitet. Dass Christina anderen als Vorbild dienen soll, ist eine erneute Bekräftigung ihres Heiligenstatus. Ihr Platz in der Heilsgeschichte wird auch von der göttlichen Sprecherrolle bestätigt: *vnd dastu dar zo myt dyner geduldicheit ynne [den anderen] gude exempel gebest vnd myt dynen wortten vnd wercken gude lere* (CvH 84, 8 f.). Indem nicht nur auf die Werke sondern auch auf die Worte Christinas hingedeutet wird, geht dem Nachvollzug von Christinas beispielhaftem Charakter eine verbale Kommunikation voraus. Das Schreiber-Ich weist an anderer Stelle darauf hin, dass das beispielhafte Verhalten Christi durch ein wiederholtes Lesen bekannt sei (*als myr dick leßen van yme*), und zieht anschließend die Parallele zum Verhalten Christinas, wie es im vorliegenden Buch zu lesen sei.[84] Der Platz von Christinas Leben innerhalb der gemeinsamen Referenzwelt wird so erst durch den Lesevollzug eines Du konstituiert.

Der textpragmatische Anspruch führt über den Lesevollzug hinaus, indem ein an den Imperativen gut erkennbarer didaktischer Charakter den impliziten Leser lenken will.[85] Deiktische Verweise (*hie myrcke …*) haben im Leseprozess die

---

82 Vgl. Largier (2007), S. 36, zur Schriftlektüre und Deixis als Vergegenwärtigung.

83 Vgl. Palmer (1992), S. 227.

84 Vgl. CvH 39, 10–12.

85 Vgl. die folgenden Textstellen: *Gedencke hie yn, wie* (CvH 12, 31); *Nyt eyn verwonder dich, daz* (CvH 15, 14); *Myrcke, das* (CvH 30, 10); *Hie myrcke van* (CvH 57, 11 f.); *Hie myrck an, wie* (CvH 62, 1); *Gedencke, wie* (CvH 64, 11); *Hie myrcke die groiße ere vnd wirdicheit, wie* (CvH 74, 1). – An einigen Stellen ist die intradiegetische Figur Christina die Adressatin des Imperativs, vgl.: *O seliche jonffrauwe Christina, gedencke* (CvH 15, 20 f.); *Erwyrffe genade der andacht* (CvH 17, 35). An einer

Funktion eines Lesezeichens, das den Textverlauf strukturiert und als Interpretationshilfe dient. Die Mündlichkeit des Lesevollzugs wird mit dem imperativischen *hoire* hervorgehoben (im Manuskript zusätzlich unterstrichen): *Jn purificacione beate Marie virginis wie yre sele myt gode vereyniget hait gestanden, hoire, wie er sprache zo yre.* (CvH 41, 1 f.) In diesem Modus wird *hoire* nur ein weiteres Mal verwendet und zwar, wenn das göttliche Sprecher-Ich Christina zum Hören auffordert: *O myn sele, hoire myn stymme vnd behalt myn wort.* (CvH 59, 9) Was Christina textintern von Gott mitgeteilt wird, gilt hier durch die Aufforderung des Hörens auch für den Leser des Textes.[86] Die intradiegetische Appellstruktur des göttlichen Sprecher-Ichs ist mit dem Anspruch des Erzählers und impliziten Hagiographen an einen impliziten Leser vereinbar. Auch er hält seinen »fleißigen Leser« (vgl. CvH 8, 31) zur Befolgung seiner von Christinas vorbildhaftem Charakter zeugenden Worte an. Deshalb kann die zitierte Ansprache des göttlichen Sprecher-Ichs als eine offene, auf den Leser ausgeweitete Adressierung verstanden werden.

Dass Christinas Beispiel dem »fleißigen Leser« gilt, wird anschließend mit genau dieser Attribuierung für Christinas Kampf gegen die Todsünden weiterhin verstärkt: *Nu salt ir hoiren, wie gar flyßelichen sie dar range, daz yre hertze worde getzeret myt allen dogenden.* (CvH 9, 3 f.) Auf Grund der Identifizierungsmöglichkeit durch die gemeinsame Qualität des fleißigen oder eifrigen Bemühens überlappt sich die Perspektivierung Christinas mit der des impliziten Lesers. Die

---

Stelle richtet sich Christina mit einem Imperativ an einen impliziten Adressaten: *Als nu dyeße heilge jonffer also lache entzucket yn dem geist, da sprach sie dyeße wort: ›Die lyebde, die wyrt entfencket van dem fuer, sy wyrt erluchtet van dem lyecht. Gedencke van dem wyne, der hoger, soißer, luterer gotheit, der dyner sele ist zo gefueget.‹* (CvH 24, 1–4) Davon zu trennen ist ein reflektives Du, mit dem sich Christina im inneren Monolog selbst anspricht: *Auch vnderwillen wanne sie alleyn saiße by der bache vnd sache daz waißer hynne flyeßen, so gedacht sie: ›Also ist alle dynge hynne gefloißen, die du vnnützelich haist zo bracht, vnd koment nummerme erwyeder.‹* (CvH 8, 24–27). Das Motiv der verronnenen Zeit kann als »eine Art Zubehör der Hauptsünde ›acedia‹, der religiös-sittlichen Trägheit« angesehen werden, so Alois Maria Haas: Fülle der Zeit. Ein Durchblick durch die Mystik. In: Mystik – Überlieferung – Naturkunde. Gegenstände und Methoden mediävistischer Forschungspraxis. Tagung in Eichstätt am 15. und 17. April 1999, anlässlich der Begründung der ›Forschungsstelle für Geistliche Literatur des Mittelalters‹ an der Katholischen Universität Eichstätt. Hrsg. von Robert Luff/Rudolf Kilian Weigand (Germanistische Texte und Studien 70). Hildesheim/Zürich/New York 2002, S. 179–195, hier S. 179. Beichtformulare aus dem 9. und 10 Jahrhundert erwähnen Zeitverschwendung als Sünde. Vgl. auch die Bußthematik bei Tauler, siehe dazu Haas (1984b), S. 625: »Zur ›weselichen ker‹ gehört die Bereuung der Sünden«.
86 Eine direkte Aufforderung, verbunden mit einem intentionalen Schreibzweck, findet sich bei Adelheid Langmann: *ir sült auch wizzen, all di di daz hörent oder lesent, daz hie mit gemeint sint alle di, di mit den kreutzen gingen, sie sint geistlich oder werltlich.* (›Die Offenbarungen der Adelheid Langmann‹ 73, 1–3)

Rollenfiguration eines impliziten Lesers ist im Text vielfach angelegt (z.B. textpragmatisch als betende Figur, s.u.), d.h. zusätzlich zum Konzept der fingierten Mündlichkeit wird eine Leserrolle auch jenseits des medialen Nachvollzugs
konfiguriert. Das lesende Du nimmt an einer heilsbringenden Kommunikations-
kette teil, die bei Gott und Christina beginnt und über das Textzeugnis vermittelt
wird:[87]

> *Dan wairhaifftenclichen, wer dyße bůche vberleßet vnd gedencket daz wonder der genaden*
> *vnd der gotlicher lyebden, die got an dyeßer reyner jonffrauwen, syner vßerwilter bruyt Chris-*
> *tinen, gedayn hait, der mache woil sprechen, das der selich sy geboren, den got dar zo vß*
> *erwilte hait, daz er der selicher creatur̄en denen sultde. Also sprache vnser here yn yrer selen*
> *van dyeßen dryn jonffrauwen: ›Dyeße dry jonffrauwen synt selich vnd sy dragent reyne hertzen*
> *yn mynem namen.‹ Dyße was eyn anfancke mannyches fruntlichen zosprechens, daz got yn*
> *yrer selen dick gar sere fruntlichen hait gereyt van dyeßen dryn jonfferen. O, was lyeblichen*
> *gesprechs, das got gewonlichen hait gehait, wyrstu dicke hoiren her na, da du wyrste vynden*
> *eytzelichen wort, da groiße befyndunge der genaden vnd soißicheit myt wonderlicher ynwendi-*
> *ger beschauwonge, die also vnsprechlichen vnuerstendich synt vnser groppicheit zo begryffen,*
> *als eynem wayllen eynen dutzen zo verstayn. Doch synt her geschreben der soißer sprechonge*
> *eyn deylle yn die hogetzijden, dar durch die gotliche lyebhauenden hertzen got lobent sullent*
> *vmb genade vnd wirdicheit, die da verstanden wyrt manchfeldenclichen.* (CvH 39, 14–29)

Ausgehend von der sprachlichen Mitteilung des göttlich figurierten Sprecher-Ichs
an Christina nimmt auch der Leser das *gesprech* und das *zo sprechen* auditiv war
(*wyrstu dicke hoiren*), was sicherlich mit der fingierten Mündlichkeit der direkt
wiedergegebenen Rede zusammenhängt, aber auch metaphorisch als generelle
Wahrnehmung gedeutet werden kann.[88] Dass es nicht nur um artikulierte Sprache
geht, unterstützt die möglicherweise von dem Brandanschen Fischinsel-Motiv
inspirierte Metapher des Wals, der keinen Sinn aus einem Stoß (*dutzen*) ableiten
kann. Angesprochen ist damit auch ein rationalitätskritischer Ansatz, wie er in

---

87 Ähnlich verhält es sich mit dem Prolog in der ›Lux divinitatis‹ Mechthilds von Madgeburg,
vgl.: *Sic etiam omnes qui hunc librum scripturi vel lecturi sunt, si tamen pia intentione intenderint,*
incrementum consolationis et gratiæ spiritus, sicut in ipso promissum est a Domino, consequen-
tur. (Mechthild von Magdeburg: ›Lux divinitatis‹. In: Revelationes Gertrudinæ ac Mechtildianæ
II. Sanctæ Mechtildis virginis ordinis sancti Benedicti Liber specialis gratiæ, accedit sororis
Mechtildis ejusdem ordinis Lux divinitatis. Opus ad codicum fidem nunc primum integre editum Solesmensium O.S.B. monachorum cura et opera. Paris 1877, S. 435–710, hier S. 436) Siehe
dazu Palmer (1992), S. 226. Die Aufforderung zum Lesen steht in der prophetischen Tradition der
Johannesoffenbarung, vgl.: *beatus qui legit et qui audiunt verba prophetiae et servant ea quae in*
ea scripta sunt tempus enim prope est (Apc 1,3).
88 Vgl. Green (2000).

der Bernhardinischen Mystik anzutreffen ist.[89] Demnach sind die Gnadenerwei-
sungen Gottes auf eine unaussprechliche Weise unzugänglich (*vnsprechlichen
vnuerstendich*). Erneut wird die Vorstellung schlichter und unkundiger Adressaten aufgerufen, zu denen sich das Schreiber-Ich gesellt (*vnser groppicheit*),
sodass sich die Ambivalenz der Rationalität auch auf den Rezipienten erstreckt.[90]
Dennoch wird eine Lösung zum Verständnis der göttlichen Wahrheit angeboten.
Diese wird auf die Wirkung des Textvollzugs umgeleitet, denn trotz des apophatischen Diskurses wird immer wieder auf die Präsenz der Schrift (*dyße buche,
eytzelichen wort, her geschreben*) hingewiesen, die es auf eine bestimmte Weise
wahrzunehmen gelte, damit das Göttliche nachvollzogen werden könne. Dabei
findet der pragmatische Vollzug des in den liturgischen Kalender eingebetteten
Textes im Lesen und Gedenken statt und mündet in ein Sprechen desjenigen, der
das göttliche Wunder verstanden hat, um nunmehr die Erwählung Christinas zu
bezeugen und zu bekunden (*der mache woil sprechen*).[91] Sicherlich muss dieses
Sprechen erneut metaphorisch verstanden werden, doch das ändert nichts daran,
dass die Rollenzuweisung des impliziten Lesers mit dem Akt des Lesens/Hörens
und des Erzählens/Sprechens zusammenhängt und sich auf einen Kommuni-
kationskontext außerhalb der vorliegenden Schriftlichkeit ausdehnt. Lesen und
Hören bedingen einander und sind in den Prozess des Erzählens derart einge-
flochten, dass sie zum Sprechen des Adressaten überführen wollen.

---

89 Siehe dazu Annette Volfing: ›der sin was âne sinne‹. Zum Verhältnis von Rationalität und
Allegorie in philosophischen und mystischen Texten. In: Relation und Inszenierung von Ratio-
nalität in der mittelalterlichen Literatur. Blaubeurer Kolloquium 2006. Hrsg. von Klaus Ridder
(Wolfram-Studien 20). Berlin 2008, S. 329–350, insbes. S. 350. Siehe auch Otto Langer: Affekt und
Ratio. Rationalitätskritische Aspekte in der Mystik Bernhards von Clairvaux. In: Zisterziensische
Spiritualität. Theologische Grundlagen, funktionale Voraussetzungen und bildhafte Ausprä-
gungen im Mittelalter. 1. Himmelroder Kolloquium. Hrsg. von Clemens S. Kasper (Studien und
Mitteilungen zur Geschichte des Benediktinerordens und seiner Zweige. Ergänzungsband 34).
St. Ottilien 1994, S. 33–52.
90 Vgl. den Kommentar der Christus-Figur nach einer Allegorese in den Offenbarungen Langmanns: *wi aber dem sei: daz kan kein sin uf ertrich bedenken noch betrahten. in den ewigen freuden wert ir ez sehen, di mein derwelten. hie sult ir ez einfelticlichen glauben und niht vil do noch
trahten* (›Die Offenbarungen der Adelheid Langmann‹ 50, 6–9).
91 Die Formel des Gedenkens verweist auf den Zustand des »beredten Schweigens«, der in der
monastischen Kultur eine meditative Praxis darstellt, vgl. Mireille Schnyder: Topographie des
Schweigens. Untersuchungen zum deutschen höfischen Roman um 1200 (Historische Semantik 3). Göttingen 2003, S. 135 f. So kann das Zusammenspiel aus mündlichem und schriftlichem
Gebetsraum eine innere Sprachlichkeit des Lesers evozieren. – Nach Paul (1998), S. 264, § 276,
bezeichnet das Modalverb *mugen, mügen* (hier *machen*) »von Haus aus fast immer das physische
Vermögen ›können, imstande sein‹ und behält diese Funktion bis ins Frühnhd. hinein.«

Das Erzählen avanciert also zum kollektiven Unternehmen, das die Opposition von mündlichem Vollzug und geschriebenem Text überwindet.[92] Die inhärente Appellstruktur einer fingierten Mündlichkeit kann in ihrer dramatischen Inszenierung als Faktor der in der Augustinischen Tradition tief verwurzelten Empathie verstanden werden.[93] Das Hören und Gedenken der Worte der Vita konstituiert sich somit als eine aktive Beteiligung am christlichen Heilsplan. »In the Middle Ages, it was not adequate only to hear the message of salvation«, schreibt Vrudny und erklärt auf Carruthers zurückgreifend: »the work of memory was seen as intricately related to salvation.«[94] Der implizite Leser der Vita wird eingeladen, sich mit Christina zu identifizieren und ihre Erwählung aktiv nachzuvollziehen.[95] Der Identifikationsfaktor geht über die Lektüre hinaus und erstreckt sich auf meditative Übungen wie Gebete, dabei die potenzielle Erwählung des impliziten Lesers provozierend.[96]

3.2.2 Exkurs: Cod. Vat. lat. 4763

Im Vergleich mit wahrscheinlich aus Hane stammenden und heute in der Vatikanischen Bibliothek aufbewahrten deutsch-lateinischen Gebeten lassen sich Strukturmerkmale in der Vita festmachen, die »die Vielfalt von Themenbereichen und literarischen Diskurstypen« aufdecken.[97] Ringler hatte betont, dass die Rezeption religiöser Texte, ob volkssprachig oder lateinisch, die Viten von Mystikerinnen beeinflusst habe.[98] Einige aus dem Hochmittelalter überlieferte Gebete geben den einzigen Anhaltspunkt für eine entsprechende Rezeption im monastischen Umfeld Christinas von Hane.[99] Die Beschäftigung mit dem prag-

---

92 Vgl. Volfing (2007), S. 7.
93 Vgl. Fulton (2002), S. 3.
94 Kimberly Vrudny: Friars, Scribes, and Corpses. A Marian Confraternal Reading of ›The Mirror of Human Salvation‹ (›Speculum humanae salvationis‹) (Mediaevalia Groningana New Series 12). Paris / Leuven 2010, S. 111 f.
95 Zum ›Fließenden Licht‹ Mechthilds von Magdeburg formuliert Suerbaum (2009), S. 33: »Differenziert wird hier also zwischen Lehre als Vermittlung lernbarer Inhalte, die normativen Charakter haben, und der Prozesshaftigkeit von Lehre, die sich im Nachvollzug äußert und perfektioniert.«
96 Ein in der Christina von Hane-Vita formuliertes Gebet richtet sich direkt an Christina, vgl. CvH 15, 20–24.
97 Peters (1991), S. 44, zu Mechtild von Magdeburg im Kontext literarischer Rezeption.
98 Vgl. Ringler (1980), S. 11.
99 Dem sei eine kürzlich wiederentdeckte Meister Eckhart-Handschrift aus dem Prämonstratenserkloster Altenberg hinzuzufügen, die das Interesse der Prämonstratensernonnen an der

matischen Gehalt dieser Gebete lohnt allein schon deshalb, weil damit die Vita auch im historischen Kontext hinsichtlich ihrer didaktischen Funktion sowie ihres performativen Gebrauchs untersucht werden kann.[100] Es ist also von einem Netz intertextueller Beziehungen auszugehen, ohne dass direkte Rezeptionsstufen nachweisbar wären.

Aus welchem Jahrhundert Rom, Bibliotheca Vaticana, Cod. Vat. lat. 4763, in dem die erwähnten Gebete zu finden sind, genau stammt, ist noch nicht ausreichend geklärt.[101] Wie der spezifische Heiligenkalender nahelegt, stammt der Kodex aus der Mainzer Diözese,[102] zu der im Mittelalter auch Hane gehörte.[103] Wilhelm klassifiziert den Hauptteil der Handschrift als Brevier,[104] während

---

von Eckhart geprägten rheinischen Mystik weiterhin nahelegt, dazu Balázs J. Nemes/Markus Vinzent: Neue Texte aus dem Kreis der Kölner Eckhartisten? Eine wiederentdeckte Handschrift auf der Wartburg bei Eisenach mit Übersetzungen aus Meister Eckharts Bibelkommentaren und ihre Bedeutung für die Eckhart-Philologie (in Vorbereitung); siehe auch Balázs J. Nemes: Meister Eckhart auf der Wartburg. Fundbericht anlässlich der Wiederentdeckung einer frühen Eckhart-Handschrift aus dem Prämonstratenserinnenstift Altenberg im Bestand der Wartburg-Stiftung. In: Wartburg-Jahrbuch 15 (2017), S. 176–202.

100 Zur frühen Entwicklung des Klosters Hane siehe Kleinjung (2001) und Norbert Backmund: Monasticon Praemonstratense. id est historia circariarum et canoniarum candidi et canonici Ordinis Praemonstratensis, 2. Aufl. Berlin/New York 1983 (Originalausgabe Straubing 1949). Allgemein zum weiblichen Zweig des Prämonstratenserordens siehe Heim (1994); Bynum (1987), S. 16; Krings (2003), S. 79–83; Felten (2001), S. 28 f. und S. 48; Newman (2012), S. 379–381; zur frühen Observanzbewegung bei den Prämonstratensern siehe Stefan Weinfurter: Reformkanoniker und Reichsepiskopat im Hochmittelalter. In: Historisches Jahrbuch 97/98 (1978), S. 158–193, insbes. S. 163, und Caroline Walker Bynum: ›Docere verbum et exemplo‹. An aspect of Twelfth-Century Spirituality (Harvard Theological Studies 31). Missoula 1979, S. 195–197.

101 Friedrich Wilhelm: Denkmäler deutscher Prosa des 11. und 12. Jahrhunderts. Abteilung A: Text; Abteilung B: Kommentar (Münchener Texte 8). München 1914/1916 (Nachdruck in einem Band [Germanistische Bücherei 3]. München 1960), S. 156 f., schließt nicht aus, dass die Gebete und mit ihnen das lateinische Stundenbuch auf das 12. Jahrhundert zurückgehen, wenn auch der Mainzer Kalender (Bl. 1–7), der dem eigentlichen Hauptteil vorausgeht und der die Nekrologien insbesondere der Familien von Randecke und von Boland verzeichnet, aus dem 14. Jahrhundert stammt. Siehe dazu Eberhard König/Gabriele Bartz: Das Stundenbuch. Perlen der Buchkunst. Die Gattung in Handschriften der Vaticana. Stuttgart/Zürich 1998, S. 34: »Wie viele spätere Stundenbücher diente auch dieses Exemplar für persönliche Eintragungen unter anderem der im pfälzischen Raum ansässigen Familie Bolanden.«

102 Vgl. Hanns Swarzenski: Die lateinischen illuminierten Handschriften des XIII. Jahrhunderts. In den Ländern am Rhein, Main und Donau. Berlin 1936, S. 25.

103 Die heutige dort stehende protestantische Kirche befindet sich nunmehr in der Diözese Speyer, vgl. Backmund (1983), S. 96.

104 Vgl. Wilhelm (1960), S. 157, in Anlehnung an Carl Greith: Spicilegium Vaticanum. Beiträge zur nähern Kenntniss der Vatikanischen Bibliothek für deutsche Poesie des Mittelalters. Frauenfeld 1838, S. 69, der es als »Breviarium pro monialibus« bezeichnet.

König und Bartz von einem Stundenbuch ausgehen »mit geradezu klassischem Aufbau aus Kalender, Marien-Offizium, Bußpsalmen und Litanei, Toten-Offizium und daran angeschlossenen Gebeten in Latein und Deutsch sowie einem Kurzpsalter am Schluss«.[105] Ob eine klare Trennung zwischen einem Brevier und einem Stunden- oder Gebetbuch tatsächlich nur selten möglich ist, wie jüngst Wolf behauptet hat, sei in Frage gestellt und kann nur am Einzelfall diskutiert werden.[106] Hamburger weist ausführlich auf die Definitionsprobleme für Stunden- und Gebetbücher aus dem deutschsprachigen Gebiet hin und thematisiert dabei speziell Fragen des Kontextes.[107] Während Gugumus den Inhalt von Cod. Vat. lat. 4763 als Chor- und Privatgebet ausweist, schränkt Krings den Gebrauch auf einen ausschließlich privaten Kontext ein.[108] Krings schließt aus der fehlenden Erwähnung der relevanten Familien als Gönner des Klosters sowie dem nicht-prämonstratensischen Kalender darauf, dass das Gebetbuch weder im Kloster Hane entstanden ist, noch dort gebraucht wurde.[109] Das vorliegende Gebetbuch enthält in der Tat keine Chorgebete und weist deshalb in seiner Struktur zunächst auf einen laikalen Gebrauch. Auch die deutschen Gebetsanweisungen verweisen auf eine, wie Palmer präzisiert, »semi-literate devotee who needed the instructions to be in German«.[110] Trotzdem ist Krings entgegenzuhalten, dass ein privates Gebetbuch auch innerhalb der Klostermauern gebraucht werden konnte; einige Nonnen besaßen eigene Bücher, die sie z. T. beim Klostereintritt mitbrachten. Auch wenn weder der Ursprung noch der Gebrauch sicher in Hane lokalisiert werden kann, rücken die folgende Bildbeschreibung und die Sprach-

---

105 König/Bartz (1998), S. 34. Siehe auch Greith (1838), S. 69 f.

106 Vgl. Jürgen Wolf: Psalter und Gebetbuch am Hof. Bindeglieder zwischen klerikal-literater und laikal-mündlicher Welt. In: Orality and Literacy in the Middle Ages. Essays on a Conjunction and its Consequences in Honour of D. H. Green. Hrsg. von Mark Chinca/Christopher Young (Utrecht Studies in Medieval Literacy 12). Turnhout 2005, S. 139–179, insbes. S. 140; Wolf bezeichnet Cod. Vat. lat. 4763 als »(Nonnen-)Gebetbuch« (ebd., S. 177, Nr. 72).

107 Vgl. Jeffrey F. Hamburger: Another Perspective. The Book of Hours in Germany. In: Books of Hours Reconsidered. Hrsg. von Sandra Hindman/James Marrow. Turnhout 2013, S. 97–152, Anm. auf S. 505–510, insbes. S. 95 f.

108 Vgl. Johannes Emil Gugumus: Die Handschrift Vatican. latin. 4763 der Vatikanischen Bibliothek. In: Blätter für Pfälzische Kirchengeschichte und religiöse Volkskunde 26 (1959), S. 133–145, insbes. S. 135.

109 Vgl. Krings (2009), S. 186.

110 Nigel F. Palmer: Manuscripts of the Earliest Middle High German Prayers, ca. 1150–1250. In: Vernacular Manuscript Culture. Hrsg. von Erik Kwakkel (Studies in Medieval and Renaissance Book Culture). Leiden 2017.

standanalyse des deutschen Gebetsanteils den Kodex Vat. lat. 4763 in die Nähe der rhein- und moselfränkischen prämonstratensischen Klosterlandschaft.[111]

In dem Mainzer Heiligenkalender des Stundenbuches befindet sich ein auf Goldgrund gezeichnetes ganzseitiges Bild (Bl. 6ᵛ), auf das der Beginn der Marien-Matutin folgt. Palmer hebt den historischen Wert dieser Darstellung hervor: »The miniature harmonizes with the high-grade script: this is one of the most professionally and carefully executed high-status manuscripts with German vernacular texts to have been preserved from the first half of the thirteenth century.«[112] Die Miniatur mit zwei Registern stellt die thronende Muttergottes in der Tradition der *sedes sapientiae* mit dem Jesuskind auf dem Schoß und der Hostie in der Hand dar.[113] Die Architektur des vom Kreuz überhöhten Baldachins identifiziert Maria als *Ecclesia*, wie Hamburger beobachtet.[114] Zur Linken Marias steht die Heilige Katharina, zur Rechten die Heilige Margaretha, die beide nur dank eines gotischen Schriftzugs identifizierbar sind; beide sind mit Palmzweigen, dem Insignium des Martyriums, abgebildet. Auf der unteren Hälfte der stark byzantisierenden – und damit noch in der Tradition romanischer Malerei stehenden – Darstellung sind von links nach rechts die Heilige Elisabeth, der Heilige Petrus mit seinen Insignien Schlüssel und Buch, und der Heilige Nikolaus mit den Zeichen des Bischofs (Krummstab, Mitra, gesalbte runde Male auf den Händen) dargestellt. Da die Heilige Elisabeth bereits 1231 gestorben war und vier Jahre später kanonisiert wurde, wird der Kalender nicht vor diesem Zeitpunkt angefertigt worden sein,[115] sodass seine Entstehung durchaus in die vermutete Lebenszeit Christinas von Hane fallen könnte. Die Kombination von Petrus, Elisabeth und Nikolaus würde die Zuweisung dieses Buches samt seiner deutschen Gebete nach Hane plausibel machen, dessen Stiftskirche Petrus geweiht war.[116] Auch das Übergewicht der weiblichen Figuren, darunter die beiden Schutzpatroninnen der Jungfräulichkeit Katharina und Margaretha, sprechen für einen weiblichen

---

111 Zudem verweisen die im Cod. Vat. lat. 4763 genannten Familien (Bolanden, Wildgrafen, Randecke) auf den Entstehungsort und Gebrauchskontext in Hane, siehe auch Nigel F. Palmer: The German Prayers in their Literary and Historical Context. In: The Prayer Book of Ursula Begerin. Hrsg. von Jeffrey F. Hamburger/Nigel Palmer. 2 Bde. Dietikon 2015, Bd. 1: Art-historical and literary introduction; with a conservation report by Ulrike Bürger, S. 377–488, insbes. S. 411.
112 Palmer (2017).
113 Abb. zuerst bei Swarzenski (1936), Tafel 2, Abb. 12; in Farbe bei König/Bartz (1998), S. 35, wo es trotz des Auftretens auf Bl. 6ᵛ (der Mainzer Kalender beginnt früher) »als Eröffnung des Buches« angesehen wird. Siehe auch Hamburger (2013), S. 103 mit einer kurzen Bildbeschreibung.
114 Vgl. Hamburger (2013), S. 103.
115 Vgl. König/Bartz (1998), S. 34.
116 Vgl. Wilhelm (1960), S. 157.

Kontext. Außerdem wird hier die in der Mainzer Diözese rasch verehrte Heilige Elisabeth neben solcherart prominenten Figuren positioniert, dass die Frauen nicht allein quantitativ in der Überzahl stehen, sondern auch im Prestigegehalt erhaben erscheinen.[117] Schließlich befand sich, den Angaben in der Christina von Hane-Vita folgend, eine Nikolauskapelle im Kloster Hane.[118] Auch Palmer hält die Herkunft der Handschrift aus Hane für möglich.[119]

Die in Cod. Vat. lat. 4763 enthaltenen lateinischen Gebete mit deutschen ausführlicheren Gebetstexten auf den Bl. 107ʳ bis 128ᵛ wurden von Schneider auf die erste Hälfte des 13. Jahrhunderts datiert.[120] Der sprachliche Befund rückt das Stundenbuch in die geographische Nähe des Klosters Hane bei Bolanden:[121] Der allgemeine *n*-Antritt an die 1. Pers. Präs. und die Lenisierung von mhd. <t> in der Wortmitte und im Anlaut zu <d> sind Kennzeichen des Mittelfränkischen.[122] Es ist allerdings problematisch, den Sprachstand der deutschen Gebetsteile mit

---

117 Die Elisabethenverehrung im Prämonstratenserorden und in der Gegend um Hane erklärt sich allein schon aus der Tatsache, dass ihre Tochter Gertrud dem Rommersdorfer Prämonstratenser-Frauenkloster Altenberg an der Lahn als langjährige Meisterin vorstand; zu Gertrud von Altenberg siehe Krings (2003), S. 104. Der im Heiligenkalender von Cod. Vat. lat. 4763 am 17. März gedachten Gerdrudis ist aber nicht die Tochter Elisabeths, sondern die u.a. im Maingebiet verehrte karolingische Gertrud von Nivelles. Gertrud von Altenberg wurde erst nach ihrem Tod 1297, d.h. nach der Entstehung des Kodex, kultisch verehrt (ihr Heiligentag ist der 13. August).

118 An drei Stellen ist von einer Nikolauskapelle in naher Reichweite oder innerhalb des Klosters die Rede: *da hieß sie sich furen yn sent Nycolais cappel* (CvH 17, 2); *Sie was vff eyn tzijt jn sent Nyclais capelle* (CvH 28, 3); *da wart sie gefort yn sent Nyclaes capelle* (CvH 36, 2). Dabei ist jedes Mal die örtliche Angabe, die Nikolauskapelle, im Manuskript vom Rubrikator unterstrichen. Nur einmal erscheint der Heilige Nikolaus im Kalenderblatt der Vita, erwähnt im Zusammenhang einer mystischen Audition (vgl. CvH 60). Mittermaier (1960), S. 85, indes konnte keine weiteren Quellen für eine Nikolauskapelle in Hane finden. Kleinjung (2001), S. 29, erwähnt für Hane die Erwerbung einer Kapelle im Jahr 1160, führt aber keine weiteren Quellen an (ebd., Anm. 61 ist fehlerhaft). In Frage gestellt sei, ob es ein Verhältnis zum Prämonstratenserkloster Hagenau im Elsass gibt, welches dem Heiligen Nikolaus geweiht war (zu diesem Kloster siehe Backmund [1983], S. 99), und mit der lateinischen Bezeichnung für ›Hane‹, nämlich *Hagen* verwechselt werden könnte. Diese These würde den Entstehungsort der Vita nach Hagenau verlagern, was allerdings mit dem Sprachstand und der Erwähnung südhessischer Gebiete unvereinbar ist.

119 Vgl. Palmer (2015), S. 411.

120 Vgl. Karin Schneider: Gotische Schriften in deutscher Sprache I. Vom späten 12. Jahrhundert bis um 1300, Text- und Tafelband. Wiesbaden 1987, S. 112 und S. 161.

121 Wilhelm (1960), S. 158 entscheidet sich allgemein für einen rheinfränkischen Sprachstand.

122 Das betrifft in den ›Vatikanischen Gebeten‹. In: Denkmäler deutscher Prosa des 11. und 12. Jahrhunderts. Abteilung A: Text; Abteilung B: Kommentar. Hrsg. von Friedrich Wilhelm (Münchener Texte 8). München 1914/1916 (Nachdruck in einem Band [Germanistische Bücherei 3]. München 1960), S. 69–73: *sprechen ich* (69, 7; 70, 22; 70, 40); *gruozen/gruzen* (69, 12; 70, 27); *loben* (69, 12); *biden* (70, 45; 71, 63); *bevelhen* (70, 50; 70, 53; 71, 58); *flihen* (71, 57); *minnen* (69, 13). Nie-

dem Mittelhochdeutschen zu vergleichen, weil ein älterer Sprachstand vorliegt, was an den betonten Endungen und der Hebung von *o* zu <u> deutlich wird.[123] Die Sprache wirkt nur z.T. archaisierend, weil verschobene mit unverschobenen Formen variieren.[124] Trotz seines jüngeren Sprachstandes steht der rheinfränkische Text dem moselfränkischen Dialekt sehr nahe, was aus geographischer Sicht nicht verwundert. Das bedeutet freilich, dass auch jedes andere Kloster in der Gegend als Entstehungsort in Frage käme.

Die inhaltlichen Parallelen zwischen den Gebeten und der Vita betreffen die Gebetsschwerpunkte und deren praktische Anweisungen. Inhaltliche Gemeinsamkeiten sieht auch Gugumus:

> Im visionären Werk Christinas treten besonders die Passion Christi, die Marienmystik und Heiligenverehrung sowie das Armseelenmotiv auf. Es sind die gleichen Elemente der Frömmigkeit, die auch in unserer Handschrift [Cod. Vat. lat. 4763] wenigstens kurz wiederkehren.[125]

Der Fürbittencharakter in den Gebeten richtet sich nicht nur auf die *memoria* Marias (*sancte dei genitricis et urginis marie memoriam agimus*, ›Vatikanische Gebete‹ 70, 37 f.),[126] sondern auch auf die persönlichen Verwandten der jeweiligen Betenden und darüber hinaus auf die Seelen aller Gläubigen: *so beuelhen ich dir mine sela. unde mines uader sela. unde miner muder sela. unde alle geloubigen selen* (›Vatikanische Gebete‹ 70, 53 f.).[127] Im weiten Sinne kann Christinas

---

derdeutsche Formen: *bidden* (70, 31); *bluode* (70, 49); *vader* (70, 53); *muder* (70, 54); *dot* (71, 6; 72, 125); *dreffen* (71, 62); *drost* (71, 67). (Die Stellennachweise geben Seiten- und Verszahlen an.)

123 ›Vatikanische Gebete‹: *herro* (69, 8; 71, 52); *frowa* (69, 10; 69, 13; 70, 25; 70, 43; 70, 45; 70, 50); *era* (69, 11; 70, 26; 70, 44; 71, 64); *kundda* (70, 27); *sela* (70, 51; 70, 53; 70, 54; 71, 59; 71, 68); *sinemo* (70, 49); *driwa* (70, 52); *gnada* (70, 51; 71, 58); *minna* (71, 63); *helfa* (71, 57; 71, 68); *sundiga* (71, 57). Hebung in: *sun* (70, 38; 71, 63; 71, 67); *froweda* (72, 129); *sacha* (72, 130).

124 ›Vatikanische Gebete‹: *dene* (71, 77) mit *dineme* (71, 65); *mine* (70, 53) mit *heiligen* (70, 42); in einem Wort *driuveldickeide* (70, 42).

125 Vgl. Gugumus (1959), S. 136. Allerdings kann man nicht von einer Interdependenz ausgehen, weil diese Themen viel zu allgemein sind, als dass sie einen direkten Zusammenhang zwischen der Christina-Vita und dem Stundenbuch zuließen.

126 Fulton (2002), S. 218, zufolge tritt die Marienanbetung nach der Jahrtausendwende immer häufiger auf, da nach dem Ausbleiben der Wiederkehr Christi ihr Gnadenerweis nunmehr mit der Erlösung in Verbindung gebracht werde.

127 Die *memoria* der Angehörigen ist ein rekurrierendes Motiv in Klostergebeten. Man kann bei Fürbitten auch allgemein von einem Gemeinschaftsbezug ausgehen, vgl. Ruth Wiederkehr: Das Hermetschwiler Gebetbuch. Studien zu deutschsprachiger Gebetbuchliteratur der Nord- und Zentralschweiz im Spätmittelalter (Kulturtopographie des alemannischen Raums 5). Berlin/Boston 2013, S. 148 f.

starke Neigung zur Fürbitte für ihre leiblichen Verwandten und für weitere Seelen im Fegefeuer mit dieser Tradition in Verbindung gebracht werden.[128] Außerdem erscheint die Präsenz der Jungfrau Maria in beiden Texten für die private Andacht wichtig.[129] Nur das vierte vatikanische Gebet führt im lateinischen Titel Maria, obwohl sich die vorangehenden drei Gebete ebenso an sie richten. Doch im Gegensatz zu den ersten, lateinisch beginnenden Gebeten ist der Haupttext des vierten von Anfang an auf Deutsch verfasst. Der deutsche Teil der ersten drei Gebete rekurriert zunächst auf den lateinischen Vers: *Diz heilige uers. unde diz heilige lob sprechen ich dir herro zelobe unde zeren diner heiligen gotheide* (›Vatikanische Gebete‹ 69, 7 f.).[130] Die lateinischen Teile in den ersten Gebeten sind im Plural formuliert (*credimius* (!), *adiuuemur, sentiamus*, etc.), während die volkssprachigen Ausführungen von einer singulären Stimme zu sprechen sind. Der lateinische Teil des Gebets erscheint daher als Gemeinschaftspraxis im sakralen Vollzug.[131] Deswegen ist die These eines privaten Gebetbuches einer Nonne (einzelne Gebete innerhalb einer klösterlichen Gemeinschaft) zu bevorzugen. Das Zusammenspiel von formgebendem Rahmen und individuellem Gebet findet sich auch in der Lebensgeschichte Christinas, wo die einzelne Nonne auf das Angelusläuten reagiert: *Auch vff eyn tzijt als man Aue Maria zo abent luytde, da ylet sy sych also sere zo der erden, daz sie eyn knee also swerlichen verwont hait.* (CvH 27, 6 f.) Das Hinknien Christinas wird in einem anschließenden Traum, in welchem ihr Maria erscheint, thematisiert, wobei die Körperlichkeit des Gebets und deren Wirkung zum Mittelpunkt der Traumvision werden: *sy ist yre erscheynen yn dem slaiffe vnd sy droge yn yren zarten henden eyn boiße myt koistlicher salben vnd sie hait yre dyenerßen gesont gemacht vnd sye hait yre befollen, daz sy vortter sennfftlichen sulde nyeder kneen.* (CvH 27, 9–12) Eine verkörperlichte Art des Gebets wird in den praktisch ausgerichteten Vatikanischen Gebeten ebenfalls in den Vordergrund gerückt: *unde sprich der heiligen gotheide [...] uffe dinen knin stende* (›Vatikanische Gebete‹, 71, 135).[132]

---

128 Vgl.: *Auch so ist iß zo verstayn, daz sie den heren haitte gebeden vor dyeße lyepliche gesusteren, als sie auch dick haitte gebeden vor ville der lebendiger vnd der doden, der da ist geweste sonder zaille* (CvH 23, 31–34).

129 Damit bewegen sich beide Texte innerhalb einer im Hochmittelalter ansetzenden Marienverehrung mit Maria als Fürsprecherin der Menschen; siehe Rubin (2010), S. 221–224 zum Niederschlag dieser Entwicklung in Stundenbüchern.

130 Siehe auch ›Vatikanische Gebete‹ 70, 22 f; 70, 40 f.

131 Wiederkehr (2013), S. 144 f., weist auf das Verhältnis von Deutsch und Latein in spätmittelalterlichen Gebetstexten hin und untersucht die darin beschriebenen paraliturgischen Abläufe.

132 Thali (2012), S. 257, zeigt für Seuse, dass sich die Gebetspraxis des Hinkniens auch in Gedanken abspielen kann. Diese »Imaginationstechnik« schließt eine Körperlichkeit des Gebets ein.

Doch sind nicht allein die Körperhaltung und die Worte des Betenden von Bedeutung: Auch der göttlich figurierte Kommunikationspartner ist im Gebet verkörpert und nimmt daran teil. Das Gebet ist immer als eine zweiseitige Bewegung gedacht. Verkörperung kann in diesem Sinne als »Schwellenphase zwischen diesseitiger und jenseitiger Welt« verstanden werden. In Anlehnung an das Konzept der Übergangsriten nach Gennep erläutert Wirth:

> In besonderer Weise stellt sich die Frage nach den magisch-religiösen Bewegungsformen im Zwischenraum, wenn sie sich nicht erst auf dem Weg ins Jenseits vollziehen, sondern noch auf der Erde ausgeführt werden: von Handlungsträgern, deren Körperstatus sich im Übergang befindet.[133]

Wirths Beschreibung von rituellen Bewegungsabläufen lässt sich auch auf die Christina von Hane-Vita mit ihrem Anspruch auf Kommunikation mit dem Göttlichen anwenden. So wird sowohl in der Christina-Vita als auch in den deutsch-lateinischen Gebeten eine Gebetspraxis beschrieben, die sich an real-sakralen Gegenständen orientiert, d.h. an Objekten, die das Göttliche verkörpern wollen. Am prominentesten ist das Kreuz: *Stant uor daz cruce unde sich iz ane. unde sprich diz gebet mit inneclicheme hercen. DOMINe [...], Pater nosteR. Nu dene dine henne unde sprich zu dem heiligen cruce* (›Vatikanische Gebete‹ 71, 72–77).[134] Auch Christina breitet ihre Arme in Andacht vor dem Kreuz aus und imitiert dabei gewissermaßen den gekreuzigten Christus.[135] Die Gewohnheit Christinas, sich zum Gebet vor das Kreuz im Schlafsaal hinzuknien und mitunter mit ausgestreckten Armen hinzulegen, erinnert in seinem Ablauf an die Vatikanischen deutsch-lateinischen Gebete, weil von einer Bewegung innerhalb des Gebets, das ebenfalls als innig und herzenstief beschrieben wird,[136] die Rede ist:

---

133 Wirth (2012), S. 14.

134 Zu einer ähnlichen Gebetspraxis vorm Kreuz in einem Psalter um 1200 siehe Ursmar Engelmann: Ein Gebet an den Gekreuzigten aus dem Anfang des XIII. Jahrhunderts. Eine Novene aus der ersten Hälfte des frühen 13. Jahrhunderts. In: Scriptorium 10 (1956), S. 103–105, und Ulrich Kuder: Mittelalterlicher Bildgebrauch: Überlegungen zum ersten Blatt eines Psalters aus der Zeit um 1200. In: Die Schönheit des Sichtbaren und Hörbaren. Festschrift für Norbert Knopp zum 65. Geburtstag. Hrsg. von Matthias Bunge. Wolznach 2001, S. 61–85.

135 In der Tradition der an Christus gerichteten Gebete waren solche private Formen von Frömmigkeit seit dem 11. Jahrhundert üblich, vgl. Fulton (2002), S. 150.

136 Vgl. ›Vatikanische Gebete‹ 71, 94; 72, 101. Die christliche Tradition von Tertullian über Augustinus zu Bernhard von Clairvaux betont, dass Gebete vom Herzen gesprochen werden sollen, vgl. dazu Veerle Fraeters: Gender and Genre. The Design of Hadewich's ›book of visions‹. In: The Voice of Silence. Women's Literacy in a Men's Church. Hrsg. von Thérèse de Hemptinne / María

Want sie vor daz gynge, als sie myr selber gesait hait, so was yr nummer also woil, sie fielle nyeder vff jre knee vor daz crucifix vnd dancket vnserem heren des jemerlichen doitz, den er durch daz menschen willen leyt am crutze. Vnd auch dick, wanne sie dar vor hyn gynge, so gedacht sie myt groißer andacht: ›Ach, hie stet myn lyebhaber vnd bettet myn vnd er hait syne armen vff gethayn entgeyn myr zo spreyt, daz er mych myt synen armen vmbfange vnd mych zo yme zehe.‹ Myt dyeßen gedancken spreyt sy yre armen van yre vnd sprache myt groißer beger-den vnd andacht yrs hertzen: ›Gegrußet systu, heilges crutze, du byst eyn eyniger zoversicht vnsers heils.‹ Also fiel sie dan nyeder myt den vßgestrechten armen vff die erde vnd lache vor dem crutze eyn tzijt lanck yn yrer gestreckster venien [...]. (CvH 7, 7–18)

Dabei ist nicht zu unterschätzen, dass in der Straßburger Handschrift die Wörter *armen, knee, crutze* und *veniem* (Dat. Pl. *venien*) in der entsprechenden Passage vom Rubrikator unterstrichen sind: Die Indikatoren einer verkörperten Kommunikation mit dem Göttlichen werden also in der Handschrift auch graphisch hervorgehoben. Die aus Miniaturen und anderen in Gebetbüchern auffindbaren Bildern erschlossene soziale Praxis des Gebets, wie sie von Hamburger untersucht wird,[137] ist also hier um eine weitere graphische Sinnebene zu erweitern, nämlich die der Visualität der Schrift.

Der Formelcharakter der vatikanischen Gebete ist selbstverständlich texttypisch bedingt, zumal einige Gebetsteile Messformularen entnommen sind, die einen konventionellen liturgisch orientierten Ablauf vorgeben.[138] Doch auch die Formelhaftigkeit des in der Vita begegnenden religiösen Lebens ist hervorzuheben. Das wiederkehrende Kalenderblatt, ein praktischer Tugendkatalog, der Kampf gegen die Todsünden und die verschiedentlich aufgelisteten göttlichen Gaben weisen allesamt Strukturen auf, die den sprachlichen Vollzug des Textes mittels einer gelebten spirituellen Praxis nahelegen wollen. Der Vollzug im Lesen wird in beiden Texttypen thematisiert, womit der Bezug zu einer performativen Nachahmung gegeben ist.[139] Selbst die Christina zugeschriebenen Gebetsabläufe, die mit dem ›Pater noster‹ oder dem ›Ave Maria‹ und zusätzlich mit dem phy-

---

Eugenia Góngora (Medieval Church Studies 9). Turnhout 2004, S. 57–81, insbes. S. 65. Siehe auch Thali (2012), S. 258–261, zur Notwendigkeit der Liebe und Öffnung des Herzens.
137 Vgl. Hamburger (2013), S. 103.
138 Auch Wiederkehr (2013), S. 128–132, unterscheidet zwischen Gebetsinhalten und Gebetsabläufen, zu denen die Körperhaltung zählt.
139 Vgl. die folgenden Textstellen: *Unde lis danne uespera uon den doden. Placebo. Dilexi. unde die anderen di dar zu horent. Diz gebet salt du noun dage lesen* (›Vatikanische Gebete‹ 72, 125–127); *abe du dyße buchelgyn myt flyße dyns hertzen wylt vber leßen* (CvH 6, 16); *wer dyße büche vberleßet* (CvH 39, 14 f.).

sischen Hinknien präzisiert werden,[140] können als formelhaft gelesen werden, sodass die praktisch-didaktischen Bezüge auf unterschiedlichen Ebenen gegeben sind, wie das auch für die Vatikanischen Gebete der Fall ist.[141] Auch in Cod. Vat. lat. 4763 wird wird das Lesen in bestimmten Passagen graphisch gelenkt.[142] Das Gebet konstituiert sich zudem nicht allein durch sprachliche Kommunikation, sondern erfordert den Einsatz des gesamten Körpers. Materiell verkörpert sind auch sakrale Objekte, auf die sich das Gebet räumlich und gedanklich richtet. Direkte Leseaufforderungen und sich wiederholende sprachliche Strukturen laden in beiden Texten zum Vollzug von Sprache und darüberhinaus zur Nachahmung der vorgestellten Praktiken ein.[143] Diese Faktoren unterstreichen den kollektiv pragmatischen Wert der mystischen Vita, obwohl sich der Inhalt höchst privater Erfahrungen zunächst einem kollektiven Nutzen zu entziehen scheint.[144] Auch ein hagiographisch orientierter und deskriptiv erscheinender mystischer Text weist daher performative Strukturen auf, die der ursprünglichen Austin-

---

140 So z. B.: *want als sie myr selber gesaitte hait, daz sie xij funffzich Pater noster gebet hette, myt veniem, myt beden, myt begeronge sich also verarbet vnd vermoit hait* (CvH 5, 18–20). – Unterstrichen sind in der Handschrift erneut die körperbetonten Schlagwörter und das Gebet selbst (*funffzich Pater noster, veniem, verarbet, vermoit*).

141 Sylvia Huot: Polytextual Reading. The Meditative Reading of Real and Metaphorical Books. In: Orality and Literacy in the Middle Ages. Essays on a Conjunction and its Consequences in Honour of D. H. Green. Hrsg. von Mark Chinca / Christopher Young (Utrecht Studies in Medieval Literacy 12). Turnhout 2005, S. 203–222, hier S. 204 f., spricht von einem »polytextuellen Lesen«, in dem die Gebete im Zuge eines meditativen Lesens modellhaft sind.

142 In den Gebeten markieren Punkte relativ kleine Satzeinheiten und farbige Majuskeln Gebetsansätze wie beim ›Pater noster‹, vgl. Wilhelm (1960), S. 158.

143 Ein weiterführender Vergleich zu anderen zeitnahen volkssprachigen Gebetbüchern wäre vonnöten, um zum einen die sprachlichen Eigenschaften klarzustellen, und zum anderen die aufgestellten Thesen über die Schwerpunkte in den religiösen Praktiken zu erhärten. Es bietet sich aus Gründen der regionalen Nähe ein Zisterzienserinnengebetbuch aus der Diözese Trier an, das um 1300 begonnen wurde, im Stift St. Thomas an der Kyll entstanden ist und bis 1316 dort weitergeführt wurde, vgl. dazu Wolfgang Jungandreas: Ein moselfränkisches Zisterzienserinnengebetbuch im Trierer Raum um 1300. In: Archiv für mittelrheinische Kirchengeschichte 9 (1957), S. 195–213, insbes. S. 196. In dem Zisterzienserinnengebetbuch werden im moselfränkischen Dialekt die Gebetstitel des ›Pater noster‹ und ›Ave Maria‹ angeführt, siehe dazu Andreas Heinz: Die Zisterzienser und die Anfänge des Rosenkranzes. Das bisher unveröffentlichte älteste Zeugnis für den Leben-Jesu-Rosenkranz in einem Zisterzienserinnengebetbuch aus St. Thomas a. d. Kyll (um 1300). In: Analecta Cisterciensia 33 (1977), S. 262–309, insbes. S. 266–271.

144 Vgl. Suerbaum (2003), S. 253, für die ›Lux divinitatis‹ Mechthilds von Magdeburg: »Einerseits ist das Leben der Heiligen Beweis spezieller Gnade, andererseits aber dient es anderen als Beispiel zur Nachahmung, sowohl im heiligmäßigen Leben als auch im Hinblick auf das Lob Gottes.«

schen Sprechakttheorie entsprechend ganze rituelle Handlungen betreffen.[145] Sprechhandlungen, dazu zählen Gebete, produzieren oder konstruieren erst im Verbund mit einer zeremoniellen Prozedur eine soziale Praxis. Für die Vita der Christina von Hane heißt dies, dass ein Vollzug des Textes im Kontext eines gewissen sozialen Rahmens sakramentale Gebetshandlungen einschließt.

3.2.3 Das betende und liturgisch gebundene Du

Innerhalb des mystischen Heiligenlebens entfalten Gebetsanweisungen und direkt wiedergegebene Gebete einen performativen Charakter, der sich auf den Leser als Sprechhandelnden auswirkt.[146] Da die Christina von Hane-Vita durch ihren exegetischen Charakter zur Rezeptionsform einer *lectio divina* einlädt, ist die Transformation eines Lesers mitinbegriffen, der die Worte nicht einfach nur wahrnimmt, sondern diese »auskostet«, wie Fulton anschaulich formuliert:

> Reading was to be done slowly, with frequent pauses, and charged with emotion [...]; words were not so much to be spoken as chewed; texts were to be savoured on the tongue, to be assimilated into the mind much as food was assimilated into the body. Reading in this way was expected not simply to instruct but, rather, to transform the reader; it was the basis for creating the spiritual self, much as eating created the physical.[147]

Zusätzlich zur Performativität des Gebets und dessen *memoria*-Funktion steht nun daher der implizite Leser in seiner Beziehung zur Gebetsthematik im Vordergrund. Largier führt in Anlehnung an Tkacz aus, dass eine Praxis der *memoria* auch immer eine »sakramentale Mimesis« einschließe, die das Nachempfinden im Leseprozess ermögliche.[148] So wie es in der Geschichte des christlichen Gebets

---

145 Anders als spätere (streng linguistische) Lesarten geht Austin (1975), S. 17–20 und S. 33–36, explizit auf die sozialen und rituellen Umstände von Sprechhandlungen ein.

146 Vgl. Christian Kiening: Gebete und Benediktionen von Muri (um 1150/1180). In: Literarische Performativität. Lektüren vormoderner Texte. Hrsg. von Christian Kiening/Cornelia Herberichs (Medienwandel – Medienwechsel – Medienwissen 3). Zürich 2008, S. 101–118, hier S. 102, zur Flexibilität des Subjekts des Gebets, das »sowohl das Selbst wie ein Anderer sein« kann.

147 Fulton (2002), S. 156. Siehe auch ebd., S. 173, über die *lectio divina* nach Cassian. In diesem Sinne stehen sich Gebet und Meditation sehr nahe, vgl. ebd., S. 156.

148 Niklaus Largier: Medieval Mysticism. In: The Oxford Handbook of Religion and Emotion. Hrsg. von John Corrigan. Oxford 2008, S. 364–379, hier S. 366. Catherine Brown Tkacz: Singing Women's Words as Sacramental Mimesis. In: Recherches de théologie ancienne et médiévale 70 (2003), S. 275–328, hier S. 275, beschreibt liturgische Akte als »sacramental mimesis«: »liturgical imitation that was described and experienced by Christians as bringing them into likeness with Christ and the Saints«.

»zwei einander ergänzende und beeinflussende Richtungen« gibt, so soll auch hier zum einen das »emotionale Augustinische Prinzip der Zwiesprache mit Gott« und zum anderen das »ordnende benediktinische Prinzip, das den Tag in die liturgischen Gebetszeiten einteilt«, behandelt werden.[149]

In der Religionswissenschaft wird das Gebet als »Kulturen und Zeiten durchziehendes Grundelement eines sich in der Sprache vollziehenden Austauschs des Menschen mit Gott« verstanden.[150] Neben einer an der Vielzahl formal-einheitlicher Typen des Lob- und Bittgebets, z.B. in den Psalmen, ersichtlichen objektiven Dimension tritt eine subjektive Dimension hinzu, die »eine Haltung, eine Einstellung, eine Absicht zum Ausdruck [bringt], an deren Angemessenheit wiederum die Wirksamkeit geknüpft werden kann«.[151] In der Christina von Hane-Vita drückt sich das persönliche Gebet Christinas in den meisten Fällen als Andacht aus, in deren Zentrum das Leiden Christi steht.[152] Obwohl diese Gebetspraxis an meditative Übungen erinnert,[153] handelt es sich oft um Zwiegespräche, in denen z.T. Christinas Worte direkt ausformuliert werden. So bilden sie in dieser Form

---

[149] Gerard Achten: Das christliche Gebet im Mittelalter. Andachts- und Stundenbücher in Handschrift und Frühdruck. 2. verb. Aufl. (Staatsbibliothek Preußischer Kulturbesitz. Ausstellungskataloge 3). Berlin 1987, S. 7. Hrabanus Maurus' ›Unterweisung für Geistliche‹ (819), bis ins 12. Jahrhundert oft abgeschrieben, bringt die beiden Prinzipien zusammen, indem das Gebet als innerlicher geographisch ungebundener Vorgang verstanden wird, der sich an kanonische Gebetszeiten orientiert, vgl. Kiening (2008), S. 103. Ein Beispiel aus der Christina-Vita führt diese Verknüpfung vor, wenn Christina einer persönlichen bis zur Erschöpfung reichenden Gebetspraxis am Weihnachtsabend nachgeht, vgl. CvH 5.
[150] Vgl. Kiening (2008), S. 101, in Anlehnung an Friedrich Heiler: Das Gebet. Eine religionsgeschichtliche und religionspsychologische Untersuchung. 5. Aufl. mit Nachträgen. München 1923. Siehe auch Maryvonne Hagby/Dagmar Hüpper: Die Gebete als dialogische Reden. Die ›Königstochter von Frankreich‹ (1400) und die ›Belle Hélène de Constantinople‹ (14. Jahrhundert). In: Sprechen mit Gott. Redeszenen in mittelalterlicher Bibeldichtung und Legende. Hrsg. von Nine Miedema/Angela Schrott/Monika Unzeitig (Historische Dialogforschung 2). Berlin 2012, S. 191–216, insbes. S. 191 f.
[151] Kiening (2008), S. 102.
[152] Prototypisch für diese Art der Andacht sind die rheinischen ›Vita Christi‹-Texte aus dem 14. Jahrhundert (für eine Zusammenfassung im englischsprachigen Bereich siehe Michelle Karnes: Imagination, Meditation, and Cognition in the Middle Ages. Chicago 2011, S. 11–13). Sie gehen auf die ›Vita Christi‹ des Italieners Michael de Massa († 1337) zurück, vgl. Tobias A. Kemper: Die Kreuzigung Christi. Motivgeschichtliche Studien zu lateinischen und deutschen Passionstraktaten des Spätmittelalters (MTU 131). Tübingen 2006, S. 116–133. Sarah McNamer: Affective Meditation and the Invention of Medieval Compassion. Phildadelphia 2010, S. 95, plädiert für eine geschlechterspezifische Rezeption der ›Vita Christi‹-Textgruppe, die bereits beim frühsten Vorläufer, den ›Meditationes vitae Christi‹ (um 1300, nicht nach 1320/1330), ansetze und den affektiven Modus einer weiblichen Leserschaft repräsentiere.
[153] Gebetsausführungen werden auch als *vbonge* bezeichnet (z.B. CvH 65, 42).

ein Gebet, das im Vollzug dem Leser eine Stimme verleiht, die sich an Gott rich-tet.[154] Die Vergegenwärtigung des Textes bringt mit der multiplen Besetzungs-möglichkeit dieser Sprecherrolle mit, was Largier die »Animation der Sinne« oder die »Spontaneität des Erlebens« nennt.[155] Dem phänomenologisch orientierten Zugang zur Schriftlektüre liegen textinhärente Strategien zu Grunde, die den impliziten Leser in das Funktionieren des Textes einbinden.

Im kollektiven »Wir« integriert der Erzähler den impliziten Leser in verschie-dene spontane Gebete, die z. T. vom Beten selbst handeln:

> *Dar vmbe, o vnser seliche moder, bede vor vns alle, dan dyne stymme ist soiße yn den oren des heren, vff daz myr selenclichen mogen komen vß den sorgen dyeßer tzijt zo dem hemelschen paradijß.* (CvH 15, 24–27)

Auch aus Christinas Perspektive wird ein spontaner Ausruf im kollektiven Modus geäußert, der den impliziten Leser im performativen Sprachgebrauch einbezieht: *Da hvbe sie an van freuden vnd sprache: ›Myr sullen lyebe haben, myr sullen loben, myr sullen sehen!‹* (CvH 23, 30 f.)[156] Der Gesprächspartner Gott antwortet auf das Gebet in Visionen und Auditionen. Die göttliche Rede wird im Text stets direkt wiedergegeben, sodass das darin angesprochene Du, das zwar intradiegetisch an Christina gerichtet ist, auch immer den Leser mitanspricht.[157] Auf Christinas Gebet aus der Ich-Perspektive wird geantwortet:

> *Jn dem selben lyecht sprach sie zo vnserem lyeben heren: ›O myn zartes lyeffe, als ich dich hie vor mails hayn gebeden vor die lebendigen vnd doitden, so beden ich dich, dastu myr nyt eyn wullest weygeren myn bede.‹ Da sprache vnser lyeber here zo yre: ›O du myn aller lyebste, ich hayn dich sicher gemacht des ewigen lebens myt eyner stedicher sicherheit.‹* (CvH 24, 4–8)

---

154 Vgl.: ›*O getruwer here vnd vader myn, bystu alleyn der, den ich myt alle mynen sachen meyn-nen vnd an dem ich allen mynen troist vnd zoversicht hayn gelacht?*‹ (CvH 10, 81–83) Auch wenn die Entstehung und Rezeption der Vita in einem weiblichen Umfeld anzusetzen ist, bleibt die Sprecherposition der darin formulierten Gebete geschlechtlich unspezifisch, sodass auf der Vollzugsebene keine eindeutig weibliche Identität figuriert wird. Ein Beispiel für eine weiblich figurierte Gebetsstimme bietet das Begerin-Gebetbuch, vgl. Jeffrey F. Hamburger / Nigel Palmer (Hrsg.): The Prayer Book of Ursula Begerin. 2 Bde. Dietikon 2015.
155 Largier (2007), S. 37. Siehe auch ders. (2005), S. 261.
156 Ein ähnliches Gebet, allerdings im singulären Modus und weit ausführlicher findet sich in den Offenbarungen Langmanns, vgl. ›Die Offenbarungen der Adelheid Langmann‹ 80, 20–91, 28.
157 Das Du ist an einer Stelle durch die Formelhaftigkeit des Segenausspruches offen gehalten: ›*Mensche ganck hyn ane focht vnd syt froelich. Der heilge geist ist yn dyr vnd vber dyr vnd myt dyr*‹ (CvH 7, 28 f.).

Innerhalb der Dialoghaftigkeit wird Christinas Gebet als wirksam dargestellt, sodass ihr Gebetshandeln einen gelungenen performativen Sprechakt vollführt.[158] Als erfolgreiches Modell führt Christina dem Leser ein vorbildliches Verhältnis zu Gott vor. Ihre subjektive Position wird weiterhin als allgemeingültig dargestellt, wenn in der göttlichen Rede spezifiziert wird, wie sie zu beten hat:

> ›*Wanne du beden wylt, so gancke yn dyne kamer vnd bede an dynen vader yn dem verborgen, als die dore besloißen ist, vnd dyne vader erhoirt vnd er sal dyr wieder loyne geben.*‹ (CvH 10, 102–104)

Die Aufforderung zum stillen Gebet mit Gott ist ein Bibelzitat (Mt 6,6).[159] Es bewirkt durch die direkte Ansprache an ein Du, dass der geäußerte Ratschlag auch dem impliziten Leser gilt.[160] Im selben Kontext wird impliziert, dass ein Übersetzungsakt aus der ursprünglich lateinischen Gottesrede in die Sprache der schriftlichen Textmitteilung stattgefunden hat: *wie woil sie nyt gelert eyn was, so verstonde sy doch daz latyne woil yn der selen* (CvH 10, 100 f.). Die Adressierung an den als ungelehrt figurierten (*eynfeldiche*) Leser ist dadurch gesichert. Wie Kiening an einem mischsprachigen alemannischen Gebetbuch des späten 12. Jahrhunderts zeigt, zielt auch hier die Subjektivierung im Gebet »nicht auf ein singuläres Individuum«.[161] Die für Christina gezogene Lehre am Abschnittsende richtet sich genauso an den impliziten Leser: *Da wart sie gelert yn yrem verstentenyß, yn allen sachen zo flegen zo dem gebede, alleyn myt gode zo reden vnd zo myden alle vnnutze reden.* (CvH 10, 104–106)[162]

---

158 Die Bestätigung des Fürbittengebets für die Erlösung der Seelen aus dem Fegefeuer erfolgt vordergründig aus göttlich figurierter Perspektive, vgl. CvH 51; CvH 56, 4–7; CvH 57, 8–16; CvH 58, 8 f.; CvH 63, 25 f.; CvH 70; 78, 32–39; CvH 83, 8–11; CvH 91, 11–15; CvH 95, 2–24. – Anders verhält es sich bei Adelheid Langmann, wo zwar ebenfalls Fegefeuerseelen durch das physische Leiden der Nonne befreit werden, doch wo kein entsprechendes Gebet zuvor präzisiert wird, vgl. ›Die Offenbarungen der Adelheid Langmann‹ 5, 4 f.; dahingegen mit Gebet ebd., 7, 15–18.
159 Zu einer ausführlicheren Passage bei Cassian und zum stummen Gespräch mit Gott allgemein siehe Schnyder (2003), S. 152–154.
160 Vgl. die direkte Anweisung der Christus-Figur über die zu sprechenden Worte bei der Andacht: *Vmbfancke mych fruntlichen myt hertzelicher lyebden vnd betzwynge mych myt dynen armen sprechenden:* »*Die lyebde ist also starcke als der doit.*« (CvH 42, 3–5) Siehe auch die Gebetsanweisung inklusive Selbstgeißelung Christi bei Langmann, vgl. ›Die Offenbarungen der Adelheid Langmann‹ 37, 13–23.
161 Kiening (2008), S. 105. – Wiederkehr (2013), S. 115 f., zeigt, dass es sich dabei, nicht wie noch von Kiening angenommen, um ein Gebetbuch aus Muri handelt.
162 Ähnlich verhält es sich mit Christinas Gebet an die Jungfrau Maria, das im Nachhinein ebenfalls mit einer direkten Anweisung beantwortet wird, vgl. CvH 27. Siehe auch ein Gebet, in dem sie sich nach einem gottgetreuen Leben erkundigt, vgl. CvH 96. – Wiederkehr (2013), S. 147,

Das Gebet in seiner liturgischen Ausrichtung wird als klosteralltägliche Praxis behandelt. Einzelne Stundengebete dienen dem impliziten Leser als Orientierung, weil sie mit ihrer formalen Vorgabe auf ein allgemeingültiges System und auf eine kollektive Gebetspraxis verweisen.[163] Eingebettet in bestimmte Gebetszeiten, erscheint Christinas Praxis so auch jenseits des Textes nachvollziehbar. Ein direkter Ausruf vor dem sechsten Responsorium lädt zu einer »konstruktiven Phantasie der Lektüre« ein.[164] Der *jubilatio*-Gesang wird dem Leser gewissermaßen in den Mund gelegt: *O frolicher jubile!* (CvH 6, 19 f.) Erst im darauffolgenden Satz wird der Freudengesang auf Christina bezogen: *Ach, wie froelich yre hertze vnd sele da syngen moicht!* (CvH 6, 20)

Das liturgisch gebundene Du betrifft auch ein sich erinnerndes Du, denn ein Großteil der christologischen Liturgie verschreibt sich der *memoria*. Carruthers betont, dass der monastische Umgang mit Schriftlichem stets einen meditativen Prozess des Erinnerns bedeutet.[165] Diesbezüglich ist eine Passage der Vita besonders auffällig: *O du vßerwilte bruyt Christi [...] o soiße jonffrauwe Christina!* (CvH 17, 31–36) Die direkte Anrede erweckt den Anschein eines Gebetsanrufs an Christina. Gleichzeitig ist mit dem Du der implizite Leser angesprochen. Dessen Identifikation mit der Mystikerin ist möglich,[166] weil das Gebet der Mystikerin selbst eine Praxis der *memoria passionis* ist, in der sie sich im Grunde mit der Maria-Figur am Fuße des Kreuzes vergleicht, wenn sie die eigene Schwachheit beklagt und Gottes Trost verlangt.[167] Die Ebenbildlichkeit Christinas mit ihrem marianischen Vorbild wird also auf ein liturgisch gebundenes Du im Vollzug der *memoria* übertragen. Während Largier für solche Beschreibungen die emotionalen Effekte in den Vordergrund rückt, ist der Text selbst mit seinem performativen Potenzial zu

---

kommt in ihrer Untersuchung ebenfalls zu dem Ergebnis, dass sich Gebetstexte an den Leser richten.

163 Vgl. das kollektiv gesprochene Totengebet in CvH 8, 21, die Sequenz und den Hymnus CvH 27, 3–6, den Messgesang CvH 76, 1 sowie Christinas Gebetsandacht an Ostern CvH 83, 1 f.

164 Vgl. Largier (2007), S. 39.

165 Vgl. Carruthers (1998).

166 Wie Brautmystik und liturgisches Sprechen zusammenhängen, zeigt Köbele (1993b), S. 86, die konstatiert, dass mit der Hohelied-Rezeption bei Mechthild von Magdeburg »eine enge Affinität zum liturgischen Sprechen, zum Hymnus« erreicht werde.

167 Die Tendenz zur marianisch inspirierten Gebetspraxis ist allgemein seit dem 11. Jahrhundert zu beobachten, vgl. Fulton (2002), S. 150. Vgl. in unserem Text die entscheidende Passage: *O seliche jonffrauwe Christina, gedencke [...] Dar vmbe, o vnser seliche moder, bede vor vns alle [...].* (CvH 15, 20–25) Siehe ähnlich den Trost Gottes bei Angela von Foligno, ›Instructiones‹ 31, 660.

untersuchen, d. h. ohne dabei zwangsläufig lebensweltliche Umstände zu rekonstruieren.[168]

Die Gebete, die sich wie bei Gertrud von Helfta und Mechthild von Hackeborn an eine klösterliche Gemeinschaft richten,[169] evozieren in der Christina von Hane-Vita einen sinnlichen Vollzug, der sich im liturgischen Raum abspielt.[170] Die liturgische Dramatisierung ist wie im ›Fließenden Licht‹ Mechthilds auch bei Christina auf »Wiederaufführung« angelegt.[171] Christina, die sonst an wenigen Stellen in dem ersten Teil ihrer Vita aktiv zu Wort kommt, präzisiert eine Gebetshandlung, die vom dramatischen Element einer impliziten Regieanweisung begleitet wird: ›*Ach, hie stet myn lyebhaber vnd bettet myn vnd er hait syne armen vff gethayn entgeyn myr zo spreyt, daz er mych myt synen armen vmbfange vnd mych zo yme zehe.*‹ (CvH 7, 11–13)[172] Das Kreuz kann sich der implizite Leser mit dieser Beschreibung plastisch vorstellen. Das »dramatische Potenzial der Liturgie«[173] tritt aber am deutlichsten zur Zeit des Hochgebets hervor, d. h. während der eucharistischen Feier. Insbesondere im Rahmen der eucharistischen Visionen entfalten sich Christinas Erlebnisse wie ein dramatisches Stück auf der Bühne. Die Liturgie bietet sich als räumliche Folie der *unio*-Erfahrung an; mit Köbele gesprochen: Es findet eine »liturgische Mediatisierung der ›unio‹« statt.[174] Während der Messe werden Altar– und Chorraum so zum Ort einer virtuellen Zeremonie, die sich trotz ihres visionären Charakters im konkreten raumzeitlichen Kontext abspielt. In Analogie zum lebensweltlichen Geschehen vor dem Altar sieht Christina Christus mit Engeln eine Messe in der Luft zelebrieren.[175] Akribisch genau wird der spi-

---

168 Vgl. Largier (2007), S. 38: »Nicht Memoria, nicht fromm erinnerndes Gedenken ist das Ziel, sondern eine Entfaltung der sinnlichen und affektiven Erfahrungsmöglichkeiten als neue, künstlich induzierte Bewusstseinszustände.«

169 Vgl. Suerbaum (2003), S. 251 f.

170 Ob sich dadurch ein bestimmtes Wahrnehmungsmuster produziert (vgl. Largier [2005], S. 261), bedürfte der weiteren Klärung.

171 Burkhard Hasebrink: Spiegel und Spiegelung im ›Fließenden Licht der Gottheit‹. In: Deutsche Mystik im abendländischen Zusammenhang. Neu erschlossene Texte, neue methodische Ansätze, neue theoretische Konzepte. Kolloquium Kloster Fischingen 1998. Hrsg. von Walter Haug/Wolfram Schneider-Lastin. Tübingen 2000, S. 157–174, hier S. 172.

172 Auch Angela von Foligno erwähnt liturgisch inspirierte Gesten, vgl. Joy A. Schroeder: The Feast of the Purification in the Liturgical Mysticism of Angela of Foligno. In: Mystics Quarterly 32 (2006), S. 35–67, insbes. S. 36.

173 Vgl. Fulton (2002), S. 266: »dramatic potential of the liturgy«.

174 Köbele (1993b), S. 112. Siehe jetzt auch Kirakosian (2017c).

175 Ähnlich nimmt Elsbeth Achler von Reute an einer alternativen Messzeremonie teil, die von Christus und Engeln parallel gefeiert wird. Ihr Fall ist mit einem Hostienwunder verbunden, vgl. Karl Bihlmeyer (Hrsg.): Die schwäbische Mystikerin Elsbeth Achler von Reute († 1420) und die

rituelle Messablauf beschrieben,[176] der mit dem direkt wiedergegebenen Verstitel *Te deum laudamus* (CvH 33, 3 f.) initiiert wird und den liturgischen erneut direkt zitierten Worten *Jte missa est* (CvH 33, 23) endet.[177] Das Besondere an diesen Sprechakten ist, dass sie parallel zur in ihrem Verlauf nur angedeuteten realen Messe auf die Vorstellungswelt des impliziten Lesers setzen. Das wird besonders dann ersichtlich, wenn die virtuelle Erweiterung eines liturgischen Akts gefordert wird, wie etwa bei der Nennung des ambrosianischen Lobgesangs: *sie hoirt die engelschen schairen yn der luyffte gar soißelichen syngen ›Te deum laudamus‹ gantze vß* (CvH 33, 3 f.); oder wie nach dem Entlassungsruf mit anschließendem Segen: *Da er ›Jte missa est‹ saitde vnd den senne gaiff* (CvH 33, 23 f.). Die fragmentarischen Ausrufe werden von der Imagination des Lesers ergänzt.

Auch an anderen liturgischen Stellen findet sich diese den Leser zum unabkömmlichen Glied des Textvollzug erhebende Strategie.[178] Der implizite Leser hat dabei die mit textpragmatischen Markern versehenen Leerstellen zu füllen. Christinas Vision schließt die im realen Raum Anwesenden ein:

> *Dar na gynge der conuent zo vnd vnser here bereychte sie. Da sach sie, daz vnser herre by etzelichen verleyffe vnd by etzelichen nyt. Da er ›Jte missa est‹ saitde vnd den senne gaiff, da wart jre gevffenbairt, alle die des wirdiche waren. Daz waren die, den die wyße crentze worden vffgesaitzet vff yre heubtder.* (CvH 33, 22–25)

So wie der feierliche Vorgang der spirituellen Kommunion sich trotz ihrer Unkenntnis auch auf Christinas Mitschwestern ausweitet,[179] so soll der implizite Leser durch sein quasiliturgisches Engagement ebenfalls zur Schar der Kommu-

---

Überlieferung ihrer Vita. In: Festgabe Philipp Strauch zum 80. Geburtstage am 23. September 1932 dargebracht von Fachkollegen und Schülern. Hrsg. von Georg Baesecke/Ferdinand Joseph Schneider (Hermaea 31). Halle 1932, S. 96–109, hier Abschnitt 11, S. 105 f.; siehe auch Angela von Foligno, ›Memoriale‹ VII, 226–241. Siehe Zimmermann (1993), S. 90–105, zur spirituellen Vision.

176 Damit wird die Auratisierung des Messvorgangs (vgl. Kiening [2008], S. 103) im Lesevollzug evoziert.

177 Sprechhandlungen sind essentiell und Regieanweisungen sichern die richtige Anrufung, was beim daher auch *oratio periculosa* genannten Hochgebet des Abendmahls bedeutend ist, »weil bei ihrem Vollzug die Gefahr bestand, Fehler zu machen und damit die eigentliche Wirkung zu verfehlen«, Arnold Angenendt: Liturgik und Historik. Gab es eine organische Liturgie-Entwicklung? (Quaestiones disputatae 189). Freiburg/Basel/Wien 2001, S. 121 f.

178 Vgl. die folgenden partiell angegebenen Lieder: ›Gloria in excelsis‹ *gantze vß* (CvH 20, 24); ›Te sanctum dominum in excelsis‹ *gantze vß myt dem Gloria patri* (CvH 31, 9); ›Ego sum panis viuus‹ etc. (CvH 22, 25); ›Der here ist vff gestanden van dem grabe‹ *vnd ander ville gar schoner wort* (CvH 20, 13 f.).

179 Vgl. die Krönung derjenigen, die ihrer würdig sind sowie die Krone der Jungfrauen bei Agnes von Blannbekin (›Leben und Offenbarungen der Agnes Blannbekin‹ 12); siehe auch die

nizierenden gehören. Mehr noch, er vernimmt die Stimme des sich an Christina richtenden Lammes, das die Aufnahme Christi im Abendmahl bestätigt:

> ›O du aller lyeblichste, erfrauwe dich, erfrauwe dich. Du haist yn dyr den hemelschen heillant dyner selen, der da ist eyne konynck aller konynck, got, godes sone, der myt syner genaden dynen honger vß gedunne kan vnd dyner dorste myt syner soißichet verleßen.‹ (CvH 33, 33–36)

Mit Christinas Eucharistievision ist vollzogen, was mittelalterliche Theologen theoretisch diskutierten, nämlich dass die Liturgie an sich, insbesondere in Verbindung mit der Rezeption des dialogischen Hohenlieds, ein »dramatisches Drehbuch« mit entsprechenden Sprechpartien darstellt, mit Zeiten der Stille und mit bestimmten Gesten.[180] Für Honorius Augustodunensis z.B. macht das Konzept der Liturgie als Drama möglich, dass himmlische Stimmen gehört werden können.[181] Die Vita der Christina von Hane wendet Textstrategien an, die direkt vernommene Reden Christi oder Marias ebenfalls an der Leser gerichtet erscheinen lässt. Dramatische Inszenierungen setzen dabei auf verschiedenen Ebenen an: Diegetisch finden sich Dialoge zwischen Christina und göttlicher Stimme sowie ganze Handlungsabläufe wie z.B. die visionäre Messe. Textpragmatisch wird in verschiedenen Appellstrukturen die Inszenierung der Vita selbst vorbereitet. Der Wirkungszusammenhang von irdischem Wort und transzendenter Bedeutung wird mit Sprechhandlungen erweitert, die in ihren multiplen Figurationsmöglichkeiten auch immer den impliziten Leser ansprechen.

Im Kontext der liturgischen Feier sind Akte der Verkündigung wie Prophetie, eucharistische Kommunikationsformeln und Gebetstexte an Sprachereignisse als Wortgeschehen gebunden.[182] Im Lesevollzug sind die Gebete in die *narratio* der Vita eingebettet, die ihrerseits dem liturgischen Kalenderblatt folgt und dialogische Partien aufweist, sodass sich ein dichtes Gewebe ergibt, das die multiple Adressierung der direkten Rede bei Gebeten und Gebetsanweisungen ermöglicht. Die *narratio* folgt einer Wiederholungsstruktur, die zwar chronologisch geordnet ist, auf Grund der sich wiederholenden Jahresfeiern jedoch auch analogische Beziehungen zulässt. Für den medialen Vollzug des Textes erlaubt diese Beziehung eine situative, körperliche und durchaus mündliche Umsetzung. Mit Kiening kann daher festgehalten werden, dass die Schriftlichkeit, die einer

---

crone der warheit im ›Fließenden Licht der Gottheit‹ (Mechthild von Magdeburg, ›Das fließende Licht der Gottheit‹ I 46, 52–54).

180 Fulton (2002), S. 267, spricht von einem » dramtic – or, rather ›tragic‹ – script«.

181 Vgl. Fulton (2002), S. 268.

182 Zum Gebet als Sprechakt siehe Karl-Heinrich Bieritz: Liturgik. Berlin/New York 2004, S. 252–270.

Gebetspraxis vorauszulaufen scheint, performative Möglichkeitsbedingungen reflektiert.[183] In diesem Sinne ist einmal mehr die Bedeutung der in sich performativen Schriftlichkeit hervorzuheben, die sich als »Ergebnis eines heilsorientierten Schreib- und Arbeitsprozesses« präsentiert.[184]

3.3 Die Mystikerin

Die Stimme Christinas artikuliert sich erst allmählich im Erzählverlauf und nur in direkter Rede des übergeschalteten Erzählers, wo sie ihre Visionen größtenteils in monologischen Erzählberichten mitteilt.[185] Vermehrt tritt gegen Ende der Vita Christinas Stimme unabhängig von jedweder metadiegetischen Ebene auf, sodass die zuvor als Monologe erscheinenden Gespräche mit der göttlich figurierten Stimme (Auditionen) nun unmittelbarer als Dialoge wiedergegeben werden, wobei die Zwiegespräche mit Gott zum Ende hin aus Christinas Perspektive erfolgen, d.h. Christina wird zum direkten Sprachrohr Gottes.[186] Auch wenn bei diesen Perspektivenwechseln die Fragmentierung des Sprecher-Ichs nicht so fortgeschritten ist wie etwa bei Mechthild von Magdeburg,[187] können aus narrativer Sicht unterschiedliche Ich-Figurationen für Christinas Stimme festgestellt werden. Christina nimmt – ähnlich wie der implizite Autor – verschiedene Rollen ein, die sich im Erzählverlauf graduell entwickeln und zum Teil überlappen.[188] Zunächst ist die Figur Christinas die stumme Begnadete, deren Stimme kaum hörbar ist; nur in indirekter Rede wird wiedergegeben, was sie gesagt haben soll. Die Abwesenheit ihrer Stimme bestärkt auf diese Weise die Rolle eines intradiegetisch als eine Art Beichtvater figurierten impliziten Hagiographen.[189] Nach der Darstellung der Seelenveredelung entfaltet Christina eine mitteilende Stimme, die

---

183 Vgl. Kiening (2008), S. 115.
184 Kiening (2008), S. 104.
185 Zur entsprechenden Rahmentechnik siehe die Graphik bei Glauch (2010), S. 155.
186 Vgl. Andersen (2003) zu dieser Art des prophetischen Sprechens.
187 Vgl. Volfing (2003), S. 257.
188 Die Rollenvielfalt ist nicht so reich angelegt wie etwa im ›Fließenden Licht‹ Mechthilds von Magdeburg, vgl. Andersen (2000), S. 96: »As the narrator, Mechthild casts herself in the role of visionary, prophet, teacher, critic, lover, counsellor and mediator, adopting the appropriate registers of speech.«
189 Ein feministischer Standpunkt würde hier womöglich von einem geschlechterspezifischen Sprechverhalten ausgehen, bei dem Männer stärker an der Sprecherrolle interessiert sind als Frauen, vgl. Marijke Schnyder: Geschlechtsspezifisches Gesprächsverhalten. Höraktivitäten und Unterbrechungen in Radiogesprächsrunden (Sprach- und Literaturwissenschaft 36). Pfaffenweiler 1997 (Diss. Fribourg 1994), S. 170–173.

sich auf den intradiegetischen Zirkel zu beschränken scheint, weil sie immer vom Haupterzähler eingeleitet diegetisch wohl an diesen oder an ihre Mitschwestern adressiert ist. Erst gegen Ende des Vitentextes dominiert der Ich-Bericht, wenn Christinas Rolle als theologisch versierte Mystikerin am stärksten hervortritt.

3.3.1 Die stumme/schweigende Begnadete

Die Stimmlosigkeit Christinas spielt sich auf mehreren Ebenen ab, die erzähltechnisch, diegetisch und theologisch relevant sind. Christinas Leben wird dem hagiographischen Ton gemäß generell im Erzählbericht wiedergegeben. Zu Beginn wird die Prämonstratensernonne an nur wenigen Stellen mit aus der Bibel stammenden Ausrufen zitiert.[190] Besonders auffällig ist dabei der die *imitatio Christi* hervorhebende Ausruf Christinas beim Empfinden großer Schmerzen, der an die Worte Christi im Garten Gethsemane anlehnt: *Ist iß dyn wille, so erloiße mych van dießen bantden des lyffs vnd der selen.* (CvH 10, 84 f.)[191] Bibelzitate werden Christina nicht immer direkt in den Mund gelegt. Auch in narrativen Passagen nehmen die entsprechenden Zitate Bezug auf Christinas Erlebnisse:

> *O, wie woil mocht sie sprechen, als die bruyt spricht yn canticis:* ›*Verkondiget mym vßerwilten lyeben, daz ich van lyebden krancke byn geworden.*‹ *O du vßerwilte bruyt Christi, wer hait dyne hertze verwont myt der straillen der lyebden anders dan der aller schonester van formen vor allen kynderen der menschen, des schoiße also scharppe synt?* (CvH 17, 29–33)

Solche Erzählerkommentare lenken die Leserrezeption, indem sie Christina zur Braut des Hohenlieds stilisieren (*adiuro vos filiae Hierusalem si inveneritis dilectum meum ut nuntietis ei quia amore langueo*, Ct 5,8).

Der Erzähler gibt auch die göttlich figurierte Stimme direkt wieder, obwohl er darauf insistiert, dass allein Christina diese vernommen habe. Der Umstand, dass die an Christina adressierten Auditionen vom Erzähler wiedergegeben werden,

---

190 Vgl. die starke Parallele zwischen der Vita und dem Lukasevangelium: ›*Was nyt myn hertze burnen yn myr van Jhesu, wylchen ich hayn gesehen, wylchen ich lyeffe hayn?*‹ (CvH 3, 18 f.); vgl.: *et dixerunt ad invicem nonne cor nostrum ardens erat in nobis dum loqueretur in via et aperiret nobis scripturas* (Lc 24,32).

191 Vgl.: *dicens Pater si vis transfer calicem istum a me verumtamen non mea voluntas sed tua fiat* (Lc 22,42). Siehe auch das folgende Beispiel und seine Nähe zu Bibelversen: *da sprach sie:* ›*Got eyn laiste die nummerme, die yn ynne hoiffent*‹. *Van den der prophete spricht:* ›*Die begertde der armen hait der here gehoirt, syne augen sehent zo den armen.* [...]‹ (CvH 10, 87–89); vgl.: *et sperent in te qui noverunt nomen tuum quoniam non dereliquisti quaerentes te Domine* (Ps 9,11); *quia respexit humilitatem ancillae suae* (Lc 1,48).

ohne dass eine Zwischenvermittlung markiert werden müsste, ist insofern auffällig, als die Perspektive Christinas dadurch in den Hintergrund gerät, auch wenn sie stets unausgesprochen vorausgesetzt wird.[192] Begegnungen mit dem Göttlichen und ihre Wirkung auf Christina werden also aktiv von der Erzählinstanz vorgestellt. Nur zu Beginn der Vita wird die Kommunikation zwischen einem impliziten Autor und der Mystikerin thematisiert.[193] Der dominierende Erzählbericht eines Hagiographen und die Passivität der Begnadeten am Sprechanteil verstärken den Eindruck einer ›entrückten‹ Figur Christinas, die sich der direkten Mitteilung entzieht und deren Innenleben allein durch eine schreibende dritte Instanz vermittelt werden kann.[194] Allenfalls in der indirekten Rede wird der Austausch zwischen Christina und einer göttlichen Instanz thematisiert:

> *Da bait sie vnseren lyeben heren myt groißer begerden, daz er yn yre sele myt syner genaden*
> *wultde flyeßen.* (CvH 8, 11 f.)

> *Da so hobe sie an zo schreye myt groißem jamer vnd claget gode myt heyßen threnen, daz sie*
> *yn nyt alle yre dage myt allem flyße gesucht haitte.* (CvH 8, 27–29)

Christina ist nicht nur auf narratologischer Ebene gesehen stumm, sondern entzieht sich auch als Figur in der erzählten Welt dem sprachlichen Ausdruck: Ihre Mühen gegen die Todsünde des Hasses münden in einen anatomischen Sprachentzug. Sie beißt sich so lange auf die Zunge, bis ihr das Blut aus Mund und Nase schießt:

> *Vnder willen beyß sie yn die zonge, daz das bloit dar vß gynge. Daz dede sie, wanne sy yn*
> *tzorne keyn wort yn vngedult eyn wult antwerden. Dar vmb geschage vff eyn mail, das sie*
> *van eyner frauwen yn dem cloister swerlichen myt vngedult wart angefecht, wie woille daz*
> *sie yr doch nye keyn wort myt nye keynme vngeduldichen wort antwerden eyn woille, vnd sie*
> *drucket iß alles yn sich, also daz iß yr also na vnd swerlichen yn gynge yn das hertze, byß daz*
> *yr das bloitte zo monde vnd naßen vß gynge.* (CvH 12, 23–29)

---

192 Vgl.: *Yn dyeßen roißen spielte daz hemelsche kyntgen entgene der jonffrauwen zo betzeychen yre na komen leben, als abe iß spreche: ›Myr eyn genochet nyt [...]‹* (CvH 5, 25–27). Die konditionelle Rede im Konjunktiv impliziert, dass diese Rede nicht eigentlich geäußert wird und dass es sich stattdessen um eine virtuelle Stimme handelt. Dadurch wird das Deutungspotenzial eines impliziten Hagiographen markiert. – Zur Perspektive und Fokalisierung bei Figurenkonstitutionen siehe Stock (2010), S. 191.
193 Über Christinas *raptus* (hier: *zoge*) weiß das Schreiber-Ich seine direkte Informationsquelle anzugeben: *als sie myr selber sagete* (CvH 10, 98).
194 Anders ist es z.B. bei Margareta Ebner, die im Ich-Bericht ihre Erfahrungen wiedergibt.

Die Verstümmelung der Zunge spiegelt auf diese Weise die Prävention von »Zungensünden« wider, einem christlichen Konzept, das sich u. a. in der Volkspredigt bei Berthold von Regensburg finden lässt.[195] Die Assoziation des klösterlichen Schweigens (Schweigegelübde) mit der Zungenkastration ist Teil einer sich durch das Mittelalter ziehenden Debatte, die sich auf biblische Quellen stützt und in lateinischen wie volkssprachigen Texten geführt wird, bei Augustinus beginnt, und über Bernhard von Clairvaux und Gregor den Großen bis hin zum ›St. Trudperter Hohenlied‹ reicht.[196] Eine Vertiefung und Gegenüberstellung der Bernhardinischen Konzepte *circumcisio* und *abscissio linguae* kann bei der Einordnung von Christinas Handeln weiterhelfen.[197] Wörtlich betrachtet beschreibt die *abscissio linguae* das totale Herausschneiden der Zunge (Kastration), während die *circumcisio* – ähnlich wie die Beschneidung der männlichen Vorhaut – ein partielles Abtrennen meint. Metaphorisch verstanden kann daher der erste Begriff auf den völligen Verlust der Sprachfähigkeit bezogen werden. Die *circumcisio* kann als das Vermeiden schlechten Sprechens angesehen werden. Die letztere Vorstellung, d. h. die *circumcisio linguae,* trifft auf Christina zu, die sich auf die Zunge

---

195 Vgl. Uwe Ruberg: Beredtes Schweigen. In lehrhafter und erzählender deutscher Literatur des Mittelalters (Münstersche Mittelalter-Schriften 32). München 1978, S. 73–76, hier S. 75. – Es handelt sich bei Christina nicht um das Verstummen durch physische Verletzung, wie Schnyder (2003), S. 119–131, für den höfischen Roman diskutiert, sondern um eine intendierte Sprechunfähigkeit.

196 Vgl. Ruberg (1978), S. 78–87. Weitere Beispiele u. a. aus der ›Crône‹ Heinrichs von dem Türlin, aus Neidharts ›Winterliedern‹, aus dem ›Winsbecke‹ und aus Hugos von Trimberg ›Renner‹ zeugen von einem weitläufigen Diskurs der zweckorientierten Manipulation der Zunge in volkssprachigen Texten, vgl. ebd. Zum Schweigen in der didaktischen, monastischen und homiletischen Literatur siehe Volker Roloff: Reden und Schweigen. Zur Tradition und Gestaltung eines mittelalterlichen Themas in der französischen Literatur (Münchener Romanistische Arbeiten 34). München 1973. Für einen Forschungsüberblick zum Schweigen in der Frühen Neuzeit, mit einem kurzen Abriss der mediävistischen Forschung und des linguistischen und sprachtheoretischen Bereichs, siehe Claudia Benthien: Barockes Schweigen. Rhetorik und Performativität des Sprachlosen im 17. Jahrhundert. Paderborn 2006, S. 24–29. Doch bleibt Benthien in ihrer Abhandlung der theoretischen Implikationen eines performativ verstandenen Begriffs vom Schweigen sehr allgemein, vgl. ebd., S. 18–23. Weitere Schwächen der Arbeit bespricht Ralf Bogner: Rezension zu Claudia Benthien: Barockes Schweigen. Rhetorik und Performativität des Sprachlosen im 17. Jahrhundert (2006). In: Arbitrium 26 (2008), S. 67–71, ausführlich.

197 Vgl. die Predigt ›De triplici custodia, manus, linguae et cordis‹, insbes.: *Alioquin si sola inesset vita, nec circumcisio quidem ei; si sola mors, etiam abscissio deberetur.* (Bernhard von Clairvaux: Sermones de diversi. In: PL 183 [1854], Sp. 537A–748C, hier 583A–587B [586B]). – Ruberg (1978), S. 78, bleibt in seiner Auseinandersetzung mit Bernhards von Clairvaux Unterscheidung unspezifisch.

beißt, um sich vor sündigem Sprechen zu ›hüten‹.[198] Vor diesem Hintergrund entspricht das selbstauferlegte Schweigen Christinas einer qualitativen Kategorie des Nicht-Redens, das eine sprachlose Sprechhandlung darstellt:[199] Schweigen als Kommunikation.[200] Der Sprachverlust gibt sich so als Teil eines selbstauferlegten Zuchtprogramms im Kampf gegen die Kardinalsünden mit dem Ziel des Seelenheils. Es scheint dabei um mehr als ein optimales Gesprächsverhalten mit den Mitmenschen zu gehen, wie das etwa die *artes dicendi* vorschreiben (so z. B. beim ›Welschen Gast‹ Thomasins von Zerklaere),[201] denn Schweigen ist in der abendländischen und in der vorchristlichen Tradition eine Kardinaltugend mit heilsgeschichtlicher Relevanz.[202] Doch auch »Ermahnungen im geistlichen Bereich assoziieren sich mit Regeln des Hofes«, wo Schweigeregeln von einer höfischen *zuht* diktiert werden.[203] So wie in der höfischen Welt kein lauter Zorn geäußert werden soll,[204] so unterdrückt auch Christina ihre Worte, um gegen die Todsünde des Zorns anzutreten. Bestätigt wird die Tugendhaftigkeit dieses Verhaltens, wenn das Schweigen, ähnlich wie bei Adelheid Langmann, als göttliches Gebot ausgegeben wird.[205] Ein besonderer Fall des Schweigens und der Zungenmanipulation präsentiert Adelheid Langmann, die zur Abwehr einer teuflischen Heimsuchung ein Kreuz mit ihrer Zunge formt (vgl. ›Die Offenbarungen der Adelheid Langmann‹ 76, 3f.). Wie der Kontext auch hier nahelegt, handelt

---

198 Mhd. *huote* kommt in der Christina von Hane-Vita zwar in einem anderem Kontext vor, wird jedoch ebenfalls im Zuge des Kampfes gegen die Hauptsünden erwähnt, vgl.: *Eyns mails da quam eyn man. Den hoirt sy reden myt eyner frauwen van fleißelichen vnd werenclichen sachen. So sie myt loiste zo hoirt vnd vergaiß yrer huytde, vnd sie gaiffe orsache zo der bekarunge, da quam der bekarer [...].* (CvH 10, 70–72)
199 Vgl. Ruberg (1978), S. 11.
200 Vgl. Alois Hahn: Rede- und Schweigeverbote. In: Kölner Zeitschrift für Soziologie und Sozialpsychologie 43 (1991), S. 86–105.
201 Siehe dazu Nine Miedema: Gesprächsnormen. Höfische Kommunikation in didaktischen und erzählenden Texten des Hochmittelalters. In: Text und Normativität. XX. Anglo-German Colloquium. Hrsg. von Elke Brüggen u. a. Boston 2012, S. 251–278.
202 Vgl. Ruberg (1978), S. 19–26, insbes. S. 24 f.; für einen ausführlichen Überblick zum Schweigen in der christlichen Theologie siehe Diarmaid MacCulloch: Silence. A Christian History. New York 2013.
203 Schnyder (2003), S. 156.
204 Vgl. Schnyder (2003), S. 167.
205 Vgl. die folgenden Textstellen: *alleyn myt gode zo reden vnd zo myden alle vnnutze reden* (CvH 10, 105 f.); *du solt dich hüetten vor unnützer rede* (›Die Offenbarungen der Adelheid Langmann‹ 20, 26). Das Gebot vom unnützigen Sprechen entspricht der höfischen Gesprächskultur, die sich im 12. und 13. Jahrhundert entwickelt, wonach (junge) Frauen das Sprechen meiden sollen, wie das etwa im ›Welschen Gast‹ Thomasins von Zerklaere durchdekliniert wird, siehe dazu Miedema (2012), S. 255–257.

es sich nicht etwa um das monastische Schweigen der *contemplatio*.[206] Die auf alttestamtliche Texte zurückgehende Funktionsbestimmung des Schweigens als Präventions- und Disziplinarmaßnahme wurde zusätzlich von Augustinischen Vorstellungen geprägt.[207] Christinas erzwungenes Schweigen bedeutet daher weniger die gewaltsame Unterwerfung des Körpers als vielmehr dessen Ausnutzen für ein tugendhaftes Leben.

Es bleibt zu fragen, inwiefern das Schweigen Christinas als eine textuelle Strategie verstanden werden kann, die die Unsagbarkeit der mystischen Erfahrung auf eine performative Weise demonstriert. Könnte mit diesem Ansatz erklärt werden, warum die Redeanteile der göttlich figurierten Stimme bis auf den Schlussteil der Christina-Vita stark überwiegen? Christinas Schweigen wird im Kontext des Klosteralltags als ein »beredtes Schweigen« dargestellt.[208] Denn in ihrer Andacht ist sie sprechunfähig:

> *So dyße heilge jonffrauwe vnder wyllen was myt den anderen jonffrauwen vff dem kyrchoff, so fylle yre dyßen gedancken yn ire hertze, daz sie der doden gebet nyt eyn mocht gesprechen myt den anderen.* (CvH 8, 19–22)

Ganz in Gedanken versunken, kann Christina das Totengebet nicht mit den anderen Klosterangehörigen sprechen.[209] Allerdings werden ihre Schilderungen während der Gottesschau in weiten Strecken aus zweiter Hand, d.h. vom Erzähler wiedergegeben, während die göttliche Rede immer direkt wiedergegeben wird, sodass sich Zwiegespräche zwischen Gott und Christina fast als Monologe präsentieren und nur virtuell dialogisch zu denken sind.[210] Dass Christina in diesen Dialogen abgesehen vom Ende des Vitentextes einen schweigsamen Part einnimmt, könnte mit einer bestimmten textstrategischen Darstellung der

---

206 Zum monastischen Schweigen siehe Schnyder (2003), S. 136 f.
207 Die entsprechenden Bibelverse sind Ps 34,13 und Iob 27,4. Vgl. die bei Ruberg (1978), S. 241–248, aufgelisteten mittelalterlichen Texte zum Nutzen des Schweigens.
208 Zum kontemplativen Schweigen siehe Schnyder (2003), S. 135–140.
209 Dass Christina nicht mitsingt, unterstreicht gleichzeitig ihren Sonderstatus. Eine ähnliche Spannung zwischen individueller Begnadung und kollektivem Alltag findet sich im ›botten der göttlichen miltekeit‹: *Zůhant wart sú innewendig mit got also gar vereinet, das sú vergas, das sú sich uswendig mit ir gederde zů dem convent nit glichet. Do wart sú gemanet von einer anderen. Zůhant do det sú also die anderen. Do bat sú got, das er sú behůten wolte, das sollich sunder wise an ir nit me gemerket wurde. Des gewert sú der herre, also das sú fúrbas mit got also ser niemer vereinet wart, sú rihtet sich dennoch uswendig noch dem convent.* (Gertrud von Helfta, ›ein botte der götlichen miltekeit‹ 77, 35–41)
210 Zum Halbdialog siehe unten Kap. 4.1.2.

mystischen Ekstase zusammenhängen.[211] Der vielfach diskutierte apophatische Diskurs würde auf diese Weise zum Reflex eines Verstummens in der kontemplativen Schau werden. Dicke fragt in diesem Sinne für Mechthilds ›Fließendes Licht‹: »Wo brechen die Dialoge unvermittelt ab und verstummen, wie sie es müssten, sollten sie zur Unio hinführen und sie zum Ereignis haben?«[212] Eine abrupt einsetzende Stille, ein bewusstes Schweigen im Moment der Reaktualisierung der Vereinigung als performative Kehrtwende der Vermittlung kennt die Vita der Christina von Hane hingegen nicht.[213] Textstrategien, die zugleich auf eine Theologie des Schweigens deuten könnten, lassen sich in der Vita also nicht finden. Dennoch bleibt in den folgenden Ausführungen zu diskutieren, wie sich Christinas Stimmenfiguration mit einer spezifisch visionären und mystischen Rollenidentität vereinen lässt.

3.3.2 Die Prophetin und Visionärin

Ob Christinas Visionsberichte inhaltlich differenziert werden können, dürfte sich anhand der intertextuellen Verweise klären lassen, so wie etwa Andersen für Mechthilds ›Fließendes Licht‹ beobachtet, dass Referenzen auf das Hohelied die mystische Stimme und solche auf den Psalter die prophetische Stimme markieren.[214] Zwar lässt sich auch für Christina bestimmen, dass Verweise aufs Hohelied im Zusammenhang mit der Rolle der mystischen Braut erfolgen und Psalterzitationen die Rolle einer autoritativen Stimme betreffen, doch gibt es so wenige Belegstellen, dass sich keine klare Unterscheidung treffen ließe. Stattdessen ist die Perspektivierung der Visionsberichte in der Vita zu betonen, weil sich – anders als etwa bei Mechthild von Magdeburg – die Stimme der Visionärin narratologisch erst allmählich entwickelt und sich erst zum Schluss selbstständig,

---

211 Vgl. Roloff (1973), S. 55.

212 Gerd Dicke: Aus der Seele gesprochen. Zur Semantik und Pragmatik des Gottesdialogs im »Fließenden Licht der Gottheit« Mechthilds von Magdeburg. In: Dialoge. Sprachliche Kommunikation in und zwischen Texten im deutschen Mittelalter. Hamburger Colloquium 1999. Hrsg. von Nikolaus Henkel/Martin H. Jones/Nigel F. Palmer. Tübingen 2003, S. 267–278, hier S. 272. Aus theologischer Sicht nähert sich Seelhorst (2003), S. 22–24, dem Problem des Sprechens angesichts der *unio*-Erfahrung.

213 Als Paradebeispiel dient die Augustinische Stille im Visionsbericht von Ostia, vgl. Schnyder (2003), S. 59 f.

214 Vgl. Andersen (2000), S. 148.

d.h. im Ich-Bericht und ohne vorherige *inquit*-Formel, äußert.[215] Hier soll daher die Stimme der sprechenden Visionärin Christina auf zwei Ebenen diskutiert werden: Zunächst werden die intradiegetischen Mitteilungen der Mystikerin an ihr Umfeld, d.h. an den Kreis ihrer Mitschwestern, vorgestellt, mit der Frage, ob und wie sich Christina als Prophetin etabliert. Im zweiten Schritt wird die Perspektivierung der Visionen vorgestellt. Auf der Textoberfläche ergibt sich so ein nuanciertes Bild der Sprecherverteilung, die eine geschlechterspezifische Diskussion nach sich zieht. Zum Schluss wird die Frage nach Diskursen und Schreibprozessen des Visionären aufgeworfen.

Das Wort ›Prophet‹ oder ›prophetisch‹ wird im Zusammenhang mit Christina im Text zwar nicht erwähnt, doch gehören einige ihrer Offenbarungen in den Bereich des prophetischen Sprechens, weil es darin um privilegiertes Wissen außerhalb des normalmenschlich Zugänglichen handelt, welches in der persönlichen Begegnung zwischen Gott und der Prophetin kommuniziert wird.[216] In einer direkten Anrede Gottes werden Christina nämlich drei Gaben zuteil, zu denen die *vber fludige maiße* gehört, die von der Stimme des Kommentators gedeutet wird: *Die vberfloedige maiße was, daz sie alles sache vnd das sie das alles zo dem besten kert.* (CvH 35, 9 f.) Christinas göttliche Gabe der Prophetie ist demnach mit einer Berufung zur Besserung des Allgemeinwohls verbunden,[217] wie das auch für Birgitta von Schweden gilt, wenn Gott der Mystikerin mitteilt, dass er ihr alle Geheimnisse zeigen will.[218] Außerdem werden Christina die sieben Gaben des Heiligen Geistes zuteil (*Du byst versiegelt myt den sieben gaben des heilgen geistes*

---

215 Zu den wechselnden Sprecherpositionen im ›Fließenden Licht‹ siehe Andersen (2003), S. 237; siehe auch Suerbaum (2003), S. 255. Anders als das für die Christina von Hane-Vita der Fall ist, weist das ›Fließende Licht‹ aber eine »zentrale narrative Stimme« auf, so Volfing (2003), S. 257. Siehe auch Andersen (2000), S. 17: »Mechthild's ›book‹ is an integral literary work«.

216 Vgl. Hildegard von Bingen als Prophetin, siehe dazu Barbara Newman: Hildegard and Her Hagiographers. The Remaking of Female Sainthood. In: Gendered Voices Medieval Saints and their Interpreters. Hrsg. von Catherine M. Mooney. Philadelphia 1999, S. 16–34, und Kathryn Kerby-Fulton: Prophet and Reformer. Smoke in the Vineyard. In: Voice of the Living Light. Hildegard of Bingen and Her World. Hrsg. von Barbara Newman. Berkeley 1998, S. 70–90.

217 Vgl. den Zweck der göttlichen Gaben: *also daz der crystenheit nutze vnd hulffe dar van queme, gode zo lobe, vnd zo beßerunge manyches menschen* (CvH 57, 60 f.).

218 So etwa in den Offenbarungen Birgittas von Schweden, vgl. Sancta Birgitta: ›Revelaciones‹ I. Hrsg. von Carl-Gustaf Undhagen (Samlingar utgivna av Svenska fornskrift-sällskapet. Ser. 2, Latinska skrifter 7). Uppsala 1978, 2, 3, 245. (Die Stellennachweise geben Kapitel-, Vers- und Seitenzahlen an.) – Zu Birgittas von Schweden Modell einer prophetischen Berufung siehe Claire L. Sahlin: Birgitta of Sweden and the Voice of Prophecy. Woodbridge 2001, S. 5.

yn der heilger dryfeldicheit. [CvH 72, 5 f.]),[219] zu denen der biblisch christlichen Tradition nach die Prophetie gehört.[220]

Von Gott offenbartes Wissen kann sich laut Gregor dem Großen auf die Vergangenheit oder die Zukunft, aber auch auf die Gegenwart richten, d.h. zum Bereich des Prophetischen gehören trotz einiger gegenteiliger Stimmen des Mittelalters nicht nur Weissagungen.[221] Christinas Prophezeiungen betreffen allesamt Geschehnisse in der Gegenwart, sodass der Vermittlungsakt der prophetischen Rede in erster Linie an die anwesenden Schwestern gerichtet ist: *Dyße sach sie alles yn dem geist vnd sayt iß den, die by yre waren* (CvH 23, 26), heißt es über Christinas Einsicht in die trügerischen Ereignisse am »römischen Hof« (päpstliche Kurie)[222] und über weitere Vorgänge, die zum Teil ihren leiblichen Bruder oder klosterinterne Vorgänge – wie z.B. das Verstecken von Honig und Feigen einiger Schwestern – betreffen.[223] In diesem Sinne ist die Rolle der Prophetin als göttlich inspirierte Moralwächterin hervorzuheben.[224]

Die Funktion der Augenzeugenschaft wird in anderen prophetischen Visionen von den Mitschwestern bedient: *Dyße saget sie allen den jonfferen, die by yre waren vnd dar van wysten.* (CvH 25, 13 f.)[225] Das Mitwissen ist fundamental für die

---

219 Bei Tauler geschieht die Aufnahme des Heiligen Geistes im Menschen mit der siebenfaltigen »Selbstauslegung« der Gaben (vgl. ›Die Predigten Taulers‹ 23), »damit der Mensch in der Tiefe der Gottheit versinken darf« (Haas [1984b], S. 624). Siehe auch die sieben Gaben des Heiligen Geistes im ›St. Trudperter Hohenlied‹ 43, 17; 145, 28–147, 25, und als Stufenleiter zur Vervollkommnung der Seele ebd., 44, 4.

220 Vgl. 1 Sm 10,11 und 1 Rg 12,8–10. – Zu diskutieren bleibt, wie sich in der Christina-Vita die Gabe der Weisheit zur Prophetie verhält, siehe dazu CvH 38 über zehn Weisheitssätze und CvH 92 zur obersten Weisheit; vgl. dazu alttestamentlich 1 Rg 3,5–28.

221 Zu Gregors Untergliederung der Prophetie im ›Fließenden Licht‹ Mechthilds von Magdeburg siehe Palmer (1992), S. 220. Gregors Ansichten waren weit verbreitet, wie die Rezeption von Thomas von Aquin unter Beweis stellt, vgl. Sahlin (2001), S. 36 f.

222 Mechthild von Magdeburg äußert vergleichbare Kirchenkritik, vgl. Górecka (1999), S. 442 f. Christinas Kirchenkritik bleibt zwar vage, doch in ihrem Vorkommen unterstützt sie die Rolle der Prophetin, wie sie etwa bei Hildegard von Bingen ausgeprägter zu finden ist, vgl. Jeroen Deploige: Priests, Prophets, and Magicians. Max Weber and Pierre Bourdieu ›vs‹ Hildergard of Bingen. In: The Voice of Silence. Women's Literacy in a Men's Church. Hrsg. von Thérèse de Hemptinne/María Eugenia Góngora (Medieval Church Studies 9). Turnhout 2004, S. 3–22, insbes. S. 11 f.

223 Vgl.: *Dar vmb so sy vnder willen begert honych ader fygen, so sache sy yn dem geist, wo iß die jonfferen yn yren kysten ader anders wo haitten.* (CvH 23, 17 f.) Siehe auch CvH 23 und CvH 26 zu familienbezogenen Prophezeiungen.

224 Vgl. Sahlin (2001), S. 11 f.

225 Siehe auch die folgende Textstelle: *Dyße saget sie auch den jonfferen na yrer gewanheit, die by yre waren.* (CvH 26, 11 f.)

Verifizierung der prophetischen Rede, wie sich retrospektiv herausstellt,[226] und wird besonders dann evident, wenn sich das Prophezeite in weiter Ferne zuträgt, weil sich Christinas Informationsvorsprung erst mit der Divergenz von Wissen und geographischer Lage etabliert:

> *An dem selben lyecht sache sy yn dem geist, daz eyn rytter yrer geswygen broder erslagen haytte yn eyner stait, die da heiße Lansteyn. Vnd sy sach auch, das er an der selen ewenclichen verloren was. Dar vmb schreye sy gar jemerlichen. Vnd sy saytde iß den jonffrauwen, die by yre waren, myt groißem bedroppenyß, daz die sele verloren sultde werden. Vnd sy nante yn auch den rytter vnd auch die stait, da iß geschet was. Dyße verwonderten sich die jonffrauwen gar sere, daz iß also ferre yn eym anderen lantde was. Dar vmb frageten sy dar na vnd erforen, daz iß vff dem selben dage dort geschette was, als sy gesehen vnd gehoirt haitte vnd auch gesaget haitte.* (CvH 26, 1–9)

Die intradiegetische Autorisierung der Prophezeiung wird in den Nachforschungen der Schwestern eingeholt, indem diese den von Christina bereits mitgeteilten Tod ihres Verwandten bestätigen.[227] Zudem kann Christinas aktive Vermittlungsarbeit zur Loslösung der Seelen im Fegefeuer zu den Funktionen der prophetischen Gabe gezählt werden, wie das Deploige etwa für die Zisterzienserin Aleidis van Schaarbeek (gest. 1250) bestimmt.[228] Suerbaum argumentiert, dass eine solche Fürsprecher-Rolle eine göttlich offenbarte Form von Autorität voraussetze.[229] Momente persönlicher Offenbarung verstärken die Rolle Christinas als authentische Vermittlerin zwischen Mensch und Divinität.[230]

Dabei liegt insofern ein passiv dargestellter Mitteilungsprozess vor, als die Kommunikation von Christinas Seite aus unbewusst erfolgt, da sie in Offenbarungsmomenten z.T. als im entrückten Zustand beschrieben wird, z.B.: *Aber da sie wieder zo yre selber qůam, da eyn wyste sie nyt eyn wort dar van* (CvH 24, 13 f.). Diese Art von Bewusstlosigkeit bedeutet zwar, der äußerlichen Sinne beraubt zu sein, wie mehrfach nahegelegt wird:

---

226 Vgl. die folgenden Textstellen: *Die selben erforen dar na, daz iß alles geschet was vff den dage vnd vff die stonde, wie sy yn gesayt haitte.* (CvH 23, 26–28); *Dyße geschache auch balde dar na.* (CvH 25, 10)

227 Auch Birgitta von Schweden wird der Tod ihres Sohns Karl in einer Vision offenbart, vgl. Sancta Birgitta: ›Revelaciones‹ VII. Hrsg. von Birger Bergh (Samlingar utgivna av Svenska fornskrift-sällskapet. Ser. 2, Latinska skrifter 7). Uppsala 1967, 13, 1–7, 152 f.

228 Vgl. Deploige (2004), S. 20.

229 Vgl. Suerbaum (2003), S. 249.

230 In der Spannung zwischen Verlangen und Erfüllung artikuliert die Stimme der Mystikerin eine innige Beziehung zwischen Seele und Gott, wobei ein Austausch über vereinbarte, zum Teil erfüllte Absprachen stattfindet, vgl.: ›O du myn aller lyebste, ich hayn dich sicher gemacht des ewigen lebens myt eyner stediocher sicherheit.‹ (CvH 24, 7 f.)

wie woil daz yre vßerliche synne slyeffen (CvH 24, 10)

Da wart yr sele sonder alle hyndernyß ruwen yn den armen yrs bruytgams vnd alle yre vßerlichen synne slyeffen. (CvH 78, 25–27)

Daz lyecht jn der entzückonge wertte seße wochen. Vnd van der kraifft des ynnerlichen lyechtes was sie die vj wochen beraubet yrs vßerlichen gehoirs. (CvH 23, 9–11)

Zugleich wird aber deutlich, dass sie auch während dieser passiven Bewusstseinszustände spricht und singt:

Aber sy sancke myt der stymmen, daz alle die hoirtten, die by yre wairen, die iß yr her na saytten. (CvH 24, 11–13)

Yn den iiij wochen lache sie, daz sie noch nye nust eyn wyste vßerlich, was da geschage. Aber was sie ynwendich sach jn dem geist, daz saget sie dick vßewendich myt dem montde, das sy iß nyt eyn wyste selber. (CvH 18, 17–20)

dan alles, das sie yn den seße wochen sache, da eyn wyste sy nyt eyne wort vmb. Dan was sie ynwendich jn dem geist sach, da rette der lypliche mont van vßwendich, daz sy iß nyt eyn wyste. (CvH 26, 12–15)

Dass es sich in diesen Momenten um ekstatische Zustände handelt, macht die Nähe zur Augustinischen Definition deutlich, wonach während der Ekstase (*ecstasis*) alle Körperfunktionen lahmgelegt sind, damit die *visio spiritualis* einsetzen kann.[231] Eine klare Trennung zwischen »ekstatisch-mystischer« und »autoritativ prophetischer« Stimme, wie sie Andersen etwa für Mechthild von Magdeburg trifft,[232] kann indes nicht vorgenommen werden, da prophetische Visionen in der Christina von Hane-Vita grundsätzlich im entrückten Zustand der begnadeten Nonne stattfinden und mystische Erfahrungen von der kommentierenden Hagiographenstimme mit einem autoritativen Heilsnutzen versehen werden.

Auf narratologischer Ebene ist die autorisierte Form der prophetischen Rede zu betonen, da der Bericht aus männlicher Perspektive zugleich die Überprüfung eines schreibenden und daher reflektierenden nahestehenden Ordensbruders miteinschließt. So wird die sich auf einen einzigen zusammenhängenden Teil des Textes konzentrierende Rolle der Prophetin aus der Perspektive des Erzählers

---

231 Vgl. Augustinus: De Genesi ad litteram XII. In: PL 34 (1845), Sp. 245–486, insbes. Kap. 12, Sp. 463 f. Siehe auch Kirakosian (2017b).
232 Vgl. Andersen (2000), S. 148.

etabliert. Dieser unterstreicht Christinas göttliche Gabe effektvoll, die Prophezeiungen an ihren realen zum Teil gesellschaftlich relevanten Folgen messend.[233]

Innerhalb der prophetisch gestalteten Berichte erfolgen nur wenige Worte in der Rede Christinas. Es sind die göttlichen Zusprüche und allenfalls affektive Interjektionen Christinas, die aus ihrer Perspektive direkt wiedergegeben werden.[234] Eine solchermaßen gewichtete Stimmenverteilung, die einen geschlechterspezifischen Charakter von prophetischen Visionen im Mittelalter anzusprechen scheint, wird in der Forschung kontrovers diskutiert. Zunächst sei klarzustellen, dass die Passivität Christinas in der Stimmenverteilung keine allgemeine männliche Machttendenz mittelalterlicher Prophezeiungen widerspiegelt, aus der, so Sahlin, Frauen viel leichter ausgeschlossen werden konnten.[235] Ein weiteres Argument hinterfragt die Autorität weiblicher Propheten: Unter dem Vorzeichen, dass sich Hildegard von Bingen selbst als ungelehrt und schwach beschreibt, hält es Powell für paradox, dass dieselbe eine prophetische Identität annehme.[236] Dahingegen betont Meier, dass das Prophetenamt als göttlicher Auftrag sehr wohl mit der Figur der schwachen und kranken Frau vereinbar sei.[237] Vor diesem Hintergrund ist hervorzuheben, dass Christinas eigener gebrechlicher Körperzustand und ihre visionäre Begabung sie von Kindheit an für eine Prophetenrolle vorbestimmt erscheinen lassen. Außerdem missachtet ein absolut gefasstes geschlechterspezifisches Verständnis von prophetischer Rede, dass das Bild der Prophetin bereits biblisch etabliert ist und besonders in frühchristlichen und legendenepischen Traditionen fortbesteht.[238] Damit ist eine Umdeutung von Schwäche gegeben: Sie ist nicht Hindernis, sondern Prädestinierung.

Eine weitere Problematik betrifft den teilweise beigemessenen gesellschaftspolitischen Wert von Visionstexten von und über Frauen. »It is but very rarely that the mysticism of these thirteenth-century women, which we mainly know

---

233 Über einen von Christina aufgedeckten Mord heißt es: *Also quam iß van yre vß, daz er sie ermort haitte, vnd dar vmb so moist er das lant rümen.* (CvH 25, 16 f.)

234 *Da hvbe sie an van freuden vnd sprache: ›Myr sullen lyebe haben, myr sullen loben, myr sullen sehen!‹* (CvH 23, 30 f.) Siehe auch: *Da sie dyße sache yn dem geist, da ryeffe sy vnd schreye vnd sprache: ›O we, geschruwe sy vber den morder!‹* (CvH 25, 3–5)

235 Vgl. Sahlin (2001), S. 7 f.

236 Vgl. Morgan Powell: ›Vox ex negativo‹. Hildegard of Bingen, Rupert of Deutz and Authorial Identity in the Twelfth Century. In: Unverwechselbarkeit. Persönliche Identität und Identifikation in der vormodernen Gesellschaft. Hrsg. von Peter von Moos (Norm und Struktur 23). Wien 2004, S. 267–295, insbes. S. 268.

237 Vgl. Meier (1988), S. 78, zu Hildegard von Bingen. Siehe auch Poor (2001), S. 232, und Petroff (1986), S. 26, zu Mechthild von Magdeburg.

238 Vgl. Tobin (1995), S. 11 f. Siehe auch den Band Beverly Mayne Kienzle/Pamela J. Walker (Hrsg.): Women Preachers and Prophets through Two Millennia of Christianity. Berkeley 1998.

from hagiographical texts, was meant to function as a type of social or religious criticism or that it served in a political context«, urteilt Deploige, der mit dieser Aussage Figuren wie Hildegard von Bingen und Mechthild von Magdeburg marginalisiert.[239] Zudem liegt der literarische Wert einer prophetischen Stimme zunächst auf einer rein textlichen Ebene vor und sollte daher von einer realhistorischen Wirksamkeit getrennt werden.[240]

Ob die Etablierung einer gültigen Prophetenrolle mit den Autorisierungsmechanismen weiblichen Sprechens zusammenhängt, bleibt in unserem Fall eine offene Frage, die dadurch kompliziert wird, dass sich in der Christina von Hane-Vita die Verteilung der Sprecherpositionen mit dem Charakter der Visionen verschiebt. Während die Visionen mit prophetischem Gehalt aus hagiographischer Sicht berichtet werden und in dieser männlichen Stimmenkonfiguration an die Visionsberichte Elisabeths von Schönau erinnern,[241] erfolgen die Himmels- und Eucharistievisionen zunehmend aus der Perspektive Christinas.[242] Damit ist das Thema einer genuin weiblichen Spiritualität angerissen. Da sich in der niederländischen und rheinischen mystischen Tradition ab dem 13. Jahrhundert Visionen immer mehr von Prophezeiungen abkoppeln, geht die Forschung im Anschluss an Bynum vielmehr von einer personalisierten und weiblichen Spiritualität als von einer prophetischen Berufung aus.[243] So behauptet Fraeters: »Thirteenth-century religious visionary literature is gender-specific«.[244] Deutlich mehr visionäre Textzeugnisse seien von Frauen als von Männern überliefert, was Fraeters mit den theoretischen Konzepten über Körperlichkeit und ekstatische Erfahrungen erklärt.[245] Gegen eine solche Unterscheidung muss eingewendet werden, dass in der Theorie wie in den Visionstexten selbst Ekstase und Vision nicht immer zusammenfallen, sodass Fraeters, die in diesem Punkt beide spirituellen Formen zusammenwirkt, irrigerweise Hildegard ekstatische Erfahrungen zuschreibt.[246]

---

239 Deploige (2004), S. 19.

240 Vgl. Meier (1988), S. 82 f.

241 Siehe dazu Palmer (1992), S. 224.

242 Ob nicht prophetische Visionen zugleich private Offenbarungen sind, wie das etwa Fraeters (2004), S. 57, für Elisabeth von Schönau bestimmt oder Andersen (2000), S. 21–23, allgemein diskutiert, bleibt allerdings fraglich, da auch solche Visionen einen didaktischen und daher auch kollektiven, d.h. eben nicht ausschließlich privaten Charakter haben.

243 Vgl. Bynum (1991), S. 53–78 und S. 318–329; siehe auch Dinzelbacher (1981); Newman (2012), S. 354 und S. 385.

244 Fraeters (2004), S. 57.

245 Vgl. Fraeters (2004), S. 58.

246 Vgl. Fraeters (2004), S. 59. Siehe dahingegen Andersen (2000), 25: »However, unlike Mechthild and other visionaries of the thirteenth century, she [Hildegard of Bingen] does not receive these visions in ecstatic rapture.« Siehe auch Weiss (2000), S. 6. Anders als Fraeters nimmt

Als Paradigma innerhalb der weiblichen Visionstexte wird aber auch die Art der Vermittlung betont.[247] Wenige weibliche Autorinnen gäben ihre Visionsberichte in der ersten Person wieder, bestimmt Fraeters diesbezüglich, Mechthild von Magdeburg, Hildegard von Bingen und Gertrud von Helfta als Gegenbeispiele aufzählend.[248] Männliche Kleriker berichteten dementsprechend nur in der dritten Person und in Latein von Nonnenvisionen.[249] In unserem Fall stellen sich solche Kategorisierungen als problematisch heraus: Zwar wird in der Vita der Christina von Hane die begnadete Nonne an keiner Stelle als schreibende Figur stilisiert[250] und auch ein Teil ihrer Visionen wird, wie oben dargelegt, indirekt von der männlich figurierten Stimme des nahestehenden Ordensbruders wiedergegeben. Trotzdem sind die direkt wiedergegebenen Visionsberichte Christinas aus ihrer eigenen Perspektive formuliert. Eine historische Trennung zwischen schreibendem Kleriker und begnadeter Nonne gestaltet sich daher schwierig, da selbst in den Erzählberichten des impliziten Hagiographen die unvermittelte Rede Christinas hineingewirkt ist. Weil auch Teile ein und derselben Vision aus verschiedenen Perspektiven wiedergegeben werden,[251] empfiehlt es sich, die Rollenkonfigurationen innerhalb des Textes hervorzuheben, anstatt bei starken geschlechterspezifischen, sich an den gesamten Text *en bloc* richtenden Kategorien anzusetzen.[252]

Visionen werden im fortgeschrittenen Verlauf des Textes aus Christinas Perspektive geschildert, was in verschiedenen Stufen der unmittelbaren Rede aufeinander aufbaut und argumentativ vorbereitet wird, sodass von einer Stimmenentwicklung gesprochen werden kann. Wird zunächst Christinas direkte Rede als solche vom übergeschalteten Schreiber-Ich, vom Erzähler, eingeleitet,[253] erfolgen

---

Powell (2004), S. 267, an, dass sich eine einst geschlechtergeteilte Visionspraxis historisch entwickelt und zu Gunsten der weiblichen Visionärinnen verschoben habe.

247 Vgl. Ruh (1993), S. 68: »Was jetzt mit Hildegard und Elisabeth und allen späteren Visionärinnen einsetzt, ist die visionäre und auditive Vermittlung der ›Inhalte‹ der Schauung.«

248 Vgl. Fraeters (2004), S. 59.

249 Vgl. Fraeters (2004), 61. Siehe auch Coakley (2010), S. 85, und Petroff (1986), S. 29.

250 Vgl. als Gegenbeipsiel die in Mechthild »fließende Schrift« (Mechthild von Magdeburg, ›Das fließende Licht der Gottheit‹ VI 43, 2–5), siehe dazu Andersen (2000), S. 53.

251 Vgl. CvH 21 und CvH 31.

252 Eine derartige Stimmenalternanz findet sich an wenigen Stellen bei Birgitta von Schweden (vgl. Sahlin [2001], S. 63) und öfter bei Angela von Foligno (vgl. Angela von Foligno, ›Memoriale‹ III, 246–250), wo allerdings der Mitteilungs- und Verschriftlichungsprozess zwischen Bruder A. und der Mystikerin immer wieder *expressis verbis* unterstrichen wird (vgl. Angela von Foligno, ›Memoriale‹ II, 97–173; V, 193–197; V, 219–221; VII, 258 f.; IX, 495–532).

253 Vgl.: *Da sprach dyeße seliche jonffrauwe: ›Da ich was yn dyeßem lyeblichen lyecht, da sache ich [...].‹* (CvH 56, 10 f.)

allmählich unabhängige Berichte, d. h. ihre Stimme wird nicht mehr angekündigt. In solchen Visionsberichten erscheint die Visionärin als unmittelbares Sprachrohr Gottes, dessen Stimme auf diese Weise direkt wiedergegeben wird.[254] Auch innerhalb eines Sinn- sowie in der Handschrift durch Initialen gekennzeichneten Abschnittes können die Stimmen des berichtenden Bruders und der Visionärin abrupt wechseln.[255] Die letztliche Eigenständigkeit in der Vermittlung der Visionsberichte aus Christinas Perspektive wird narrativ mit langen Monologen vorbereitet, die den Haupterzähler völlig verdrängen.[256] Ein letztes Mal meldet sich das Erzähler-Ich des hagiographischen Berichtes mit der Ankündigung einer Visionsdarstellung; doch autorisiert sich im Anschluss daran Christinas Stimme selbst zur Verkündigung der göttlichen Botschaft: *got bewyst myr alle dynge yn dem hemel vnd yn der erden. Vnd er bewyste myr* [...]. (CvH 97, 4 f.)[257] Es bedarf keiner Approbation einer dritten Vermittlerperson mehr, um das Nichtnachvollziehbare als gültig darzustellen; stattdessen reicht der autorisierte Ich-Bericht der Visionärin, in dem der Akt des Sehens betont wird.[258] Wie Newman betont, ist Letzterer eine Grundvoraussetzung zur autorisierten Rede über göttliche Visionen.[259] Dass Christinas Augen weit aufgerissen sind, ohne ihre Umgebung wahrzunehmen, unterscheidet die Vision vom Traum.[260] Das Sehen geht mit dem Sprechen einher: Christina kann sich autorisiert über theologische Fragen äußern, weil ihr von Gott selbst offenbart wird, wie es sich damit verhält.[261]

---

254 Vgl.: ›*Da ich vnsprechlichen troistonge haitte myt gode. Vnd dar na aber eyns sprach er zo myr:* »*O myn vßerwilte sele* [...].«‹ (CvH 65, 11–13)

255 Vgl.: *In der selber nacht begerte sie zo hoiren die crystemyße vnd yre hertze was vol burnender begerden vnd furyger lyebden.* ›*Da wart myr der hemel vff gedayn* [...].‹ (CvH 62, 2 f.)

256 Vgl. den längeren Monolog in CvH 80.

257 Siehe auch: *Dyß alles erwult got myt syner crefftiger lyebden, also daz iß myr luterlichen bewyste wart.* (CvH 97, 26 f.)

258 Vgl.: *Vnd ich sache, wie got ist vber alle* (CvH 97, 6 f.). Zum »Anspruch auf eine mit Autorität ausgestattete Ich-Rolle« im ›Fließenden Licht‹ siehe Suerbaum (2003), S. 240 f.

259 Vgl. Newman (2005), S. 4.

260 Vgl.: *Jre augen stunden vffen.* [...] *vnd yre sele was yn eym hemelschen lyecht. Vnd sy was vereyniget myt gode yn lyebden vnd freuden selencklichen* (CvH 57, 42–54). Besonders ausgeprägt ist das Motiv des Wachseins in den Offenbarungen der Birgitta von Schweden, vgl. Sancta Birgitta: ›Revelaciones‹ IV. Hrsg. von Hans Aili (Samlingar utgivna av Svenska fornskrift-sällskapet. Ser. 2, Latinska skrifter 7). Göteborg 1992, 139, 1, 388; 46, 10, 161; 142, 1, 395 (*vigilanti/vigilans* oder *non dormiens*); siehe außerdem ›Revelaciones‹ VII 4, 1, 118; 13, 8, 153; 27, 1, 196. Zum Argwohn gegenüber Traumvisionen Birgittas siehe Sahlin (2001), S. 62–65.

261 Vgl. insbes. die folgenden Textstellen: *Da myn sele daz gesache, da entphynge sie ynnerlichen also snelle yn dem augenblycke der zijt, da got mensche wart, daz ich sprechen, das die vereynionge vnd alles daz werck, dasta geschet ist, das dat gescheet sy sonder zijt.* (CvH 100, 35–38); *Da hoirt ich vnd sache daz ewige wort, daz iß fleysche wart* (CvH 100, 48 f.).

Trotz der Dominanz der hagiographischen Perspektive findet man in Monologen, direkten und unabhängigen Reden Christinas jenen volkssprachigen Ich-Bericht, der so bezeichnend für schreibende Mystikerinnen wie etwa für Hadewijch ist, selbst wenn der Schreibprozess darin nicht explizit betont wird. Er ist aber in verschiedenen Textualisierungsstrategien impliziert, zu denen sowohl die Adaptation des apophatischen Diskurses wie des liturgischen Kalenders gehört. Ähnlich wie der Erzähler vorgibt, das ihm von der Gottesschau (*betrahtonge*) Berichtete nicht adäquat wiedergeben zu können, so räumt auch Christina in einer direkten Rede – d. h. in der ersten Person – ein, keinen vollständigen Visionsbericht liefern zu können: ›*Da was myn geist yn dem lyecht dry dage vnd drye nacht. Got gaiffe myr zo beschauwen vnd zo erkennen vil vnd vil yn dem hemel vnd yn der erden, des ich nyt alles eyn kayn gesaget.*‹ (CvH 22, 29–32) An einer Stelle wird ein imperfektes Erinnerungsvermögen als Grund für den inadäquaten Bericht angegeben: *An dem hertzen stonde geschreben* ›*O sapiencia Jhesus Christi*‹ *vnd noch me, das yr vß dem gedechtenyß was gegangen.* (CvH 21, 30–32) Was sich aber als Insuffizienz der Mitteilung ausgibt, hebt den apophatischen Charakter der Vision hervor. Eine solche Äußerung insbesondere aus der Sicht Christinas kann als Autorisierung der göttlichen Begegnung angesehen werden, weil damit die »ambivalente Funktion der Vermittlung von Unmittelbarkeit« vorgeführt wird, wie sie etwa Köbele für die »grundsätzliche Unabschließbarkeit religiöser Symbolisierungsprozesse« spezifiziert.[262] Da aber eine apophatische Aussage von der Mystikerin selbst getroffen wird, liegt ein Akt des Erinnerns vor. Diese Retrospektive unterscheidet sich von den zuvor genannten prophetischen Visionen, bei denen es sich um den hagiographischen Bericht einer unbewussten Mitteilung Christinas handelt. Die »Spannung zwischen Rede und Schrift« gehört zur Prophetie.[263] Mit dem zurückblickenden Vergegenwärtigen Christinas wird so ein Schreibprozess jenseits jeglichen realhistorischen Verfassertums thematisiert. Die subtile Einschreibung der Mystikerin in Verschriftlichungsdiskurse ist zudem auch an der Übernahme der liturgischen Kalendertage festzumachen. Im Ich-Bericht führt das Sprecher-Ich Christinas dieses vom impliziten Hagiographen vorgegebene Ordnungsprinzip fort. Mit dieser Struktur- und Erzählweise erinnert die Vita an den ›Legatus divinae pietatis‹, wo ebenfalls ein Perspektivenwechsel der Sprecher von kirchlichen Festtagen umrahmt wird. Die Ausrichtung am kirchlichen Kalender bietet dort eine wiederkehrende extern existierende Struktur, wo keine interne Gliederung erkennbar ist. Der ›Legatus‹ allerdings kennt die strukturelle Einteilung in Bücher. Während auch das ›Fließende Licht‹ eine Einteilung

---

262 Köbele (2014), S. 171.
263 Köbele (2014), S. 172.

in Bücher und Kapitel aufweist, die eine scholastisch-gelehrte Orientierung der Schreibertätigkeit nahelegt,[264] fehlt der Christina-Vita eine eindeutige systematische Einteilung.[265] Doch bleibt selbst Mechthild ein spezieller Fall, denn »[i]m Unterschied zu den meisten mittelhochdeutschen Verstexten wird [ihre] Prosa durch einen nahezu vollständigen Gliederungsapparat der traditionellen Art begleitet«, wie Palmer erläutert.[266] Beim liturgischen Kalendertag der Christa von Hane-Vita handelt es sich hingegen um eine Gliederungsformel, die einen integralen Bestandteil des Textes bildet und in der Straßburger Handschrift teilweise unabhängig von den roten Überschriften erfolgt.[267] Wenn die unvermittelte Rede der Visionärin am Absatzbeginn einsetzt, dann wird zum Teil der Festtag angegeben, was die allgemeine strukturelle Ordnung stützt, an wenigen Stellen aber eine wiederholte Angabe bedeutet.[268] Wenn die Vision aus Christinas Perspektive liturgisch eingeordnet, d.h. realweltlich systematisiert wird, dann bekommt ihr Bericht eine neue Qualität, da der Mitteilungsprozess nicht einfach unbewusst und entrückt dargestellt wird. Er verfolgt stattdessen eine den Schreibprozess thematisierende Textstrategie und das obwohl es sich rein formell nicht um eine schreibende Mystikerin handelt.

Liturgie und Vision sind in der Vita auf zweierlei Weise verbunden: An einigen Stellen sind liturgische Vorgänge Auslöser einer Vision,[269] an anderen gibt das liturgische Fest das Thema der Vision vor.[270] Thematische Wiederklänge

---

264 Vgl. Palmer (1989), S. 57 und S. 43: »Die mittelalterlichen volkssprachlichen Handschriften und Texte, die eine solche mehrfach gestufte Gliederung aufweisen, übernehmen Strukturen aus dem Bereich des lateinischen Schrifttums, die ihrerseits in einem Traditionszusammenhang mit den griechischen und arabischen Handschriften des Mittelalters stehen, oder sie wandeln diese Strukturen ab.« Die Anlehnung an die lateinische Tradition der Bücher kann bis zur Nachahmung einer lateinischen Vorlage führen, wie z.B. das mitteldeutsche ›Leben der hl. Elisabeth‹ demonstriert, vgl. ebd., S. 67.

265 Trotzdem wird in der vorliegenden Edition (Teil B, Kap. 3.1) eine Einteilung in Kapitel vorgenommen; zur Begründung siehe Teil B, Kap. 2.1.

266 Palmer (1989), S. 77. Doch auch die Interpunktion als die kleinste Gliederungseinheit in der Christina-Vita verweist in diesem Sinne auf eine gelehrte Tradition; zur Interpunktion siehe Parkes (1992), S. 80 f.

267 So wie das auch der Fall für Konrads von Megenberg ›Buch der Natur‹ ist, vgl. Palmer (1989), S. 80 f.

268 Vgl. CvH 63; wiederholt auch im übergeschalteten Erzählbericht in CvH 35.

269 Vgl. Christinas Marienvision nach dem liturgischen Gesang ›Ave praeclara‹ in CvH 27, siehe dazu unten Kap. 4.2.

270 Vgl. das Grab- und Auferstehungsthema mit Christus im weißen Kleid an Ostern (CvH 20); das Feuer des Heiligen Geistes an Pfingsten (CvH 21), jedoch den an Johannes den Evangelisten angelehnten Adlerflug am selben Pfingsttag (ebd.). »The flight of the eagle becomes a journey into heaven«, stellt Annette Volfing: John the Evangelist in Medieval German Writing. Imitating

des jeweiligen Festtages in der Vision sind auch bei Gertrud von Helfta und Elisabeth von Schönau festzustellen, die sich mit einer derartigen Organisation von anderen Visionärinnen, insbesondere von Hildegard von Bingen unterscheiden.[271] Heinzer kontrastiert die Verzahnung von Liturgie und Vision, wie sie bei Hildegard vorkommt, mit der bei Elisabeth von Schönau. Während Visionen bei Hildegard zur Musik führten, sei die Liturgie in ihrer musikalischen Einheit von Harmonie und Wort Auslöser der Visionen bei Elisabeth von Schönau.[272] Die Vita der Christina von Hane kennt beide Arten der musikalischen Liturgie–Vision-Beziehung.[273] Hier ist Musik nicht nur Auslöser, sondern auch Produkt der Vision.[274] In jedem Fall bietet die musikalische Seite der Vision zugleich eine pragmatische Schnittstelle zwischen Text und implizitem Leser; Heinzer spricht von einer »memoriale[n] Präsenz und emotionale[n] Kraft«.[275] Zugleich sind nicht alle Visionen Christinas von Hane inhaltlich vom kirchlichen Kalender oder von einem spezifischen Gebet bestimmt. Insbesondere Auditionen sind in der Christina-Vita nicht auf die angegebenen liturgischen Festtage abgestimmt.[276] Generell ist die Vita wiederum mit Mechthilds ›Fließendem Licht‹ vergleichbar, wo die Verbindung zwischen Liturgie und Vision nicht ausschlaggebend zu sein scheint,[277] da sich die göttliche Begegnung viel mehr auf die Psalmen und auf das Hohe-

---

the Inimitable. Oxford 2001, S. 45 f., für dieses Motiv fest; für weitere Darstellungen des Evangelisten als Adler in der Literatur siehe ebd., S. 94 und S. 136; siehe auch Jeffrey F. Hamburger: St John the Divine. The Deified Evangelist in Medieval Art and Theology. Berkeley/London 2002, S. 47. Bei Hadewijch und Mechthild von Magdeburg wird der Adler ebenfalls Johannes zugeordnet, vgl. ebd., S. 75 und S. 92 f. Anders als in diesen Beispielen jedoch handelt es sich in Christinas Vision um Christus als Adler.

271 Vgl. Fraeters (2004), S. 66, und Jeffrey F. Hamburger: The Rothschild Canticles. Art and Mysticism in Flanders and the Rhineland Circa 1300. New Haven/London 1990, S. 26. Jean-Claude Schmitt: L'exception corporelle. À propos de l'assomption de Marie. In: The Mind's Eye. Art and Theological Argument in the Middle Ages. Hrsg. von Jeffrey F. Hamburger/Anne-Marie Bouché. Princeton 2006, S. 151–185, hier S. 152 f., unterscheidet kritisch zwischen Elisabeth von Schönau und Hildegard von Bingen: »Elisabeth se distingue des autres visionnaires contemporains (au premier rang desquels Hildegarde de Bingen), par l'organisation liturgique de ses extases, dont le récit suit, année après année, l'ordre des fêtes religieuses.« – Weiterhin sind bezüglich der engen Verbindung von Vision und Liturgie Adelheid Langmann und Margareta Ebner zu nennen.
272 Vgl. Heinzer (2004), S. 474.
273 Sieh dazu ausführlich Kirakosian (2017c).
274 Vgl. insbes. CvH 22, 24 und CvH 32.
275 Heinzer (2004), S. 474.
276 Ein liturgischer Anhaltspunkt äußert sich in der Eucharistievision während der Kommunion, vgl. CvH 31. Zur Bedeutung der eucharistischen Frömmigkeit vgl. Bynum (1991), S. 119–150.
277 Vgl. Walter Haug: Grundformen religiöser Erfahrung als epochale Positionen. Vom frühmittelalterlichen Analogiemodell zum hoch- und spätmittelalterlichen Differenzmodell. In: Re-

lied stützt und von einem brautmystischen Verlangen nach der Vereinigung von Gott und Seele ausgeht. Christinas Fall stellt also eine Art Mittelweg dar, weil die innerlich spirituelle Beziehung zu Gott jenseits der äußerlich liturgischen Welt in den Mittelpunkt gerückt und dabei narrativ von einem strukturell kirchlichen Rahmen zusammengehalten wird, der an einigen Stellen die Visionswelt der Mystikerin zu reflektieren scheint. Obwohl damit ein wesentlicher Unterschied zu Hadewijch gegeben ist, deren Visionen ganz losgelöst vom jeweiligen Kalenderblatt ergehen, bleibt die Funktion der liturgischen Erwähnung ähnlich wie bei der flämischen Mystikerin, wo sie weniger einer Autorisierungsstrategie gleichkommt, sondern sich im Bewusstsein über den literarischen Prozess entfaltet.[278]

3.3.3 Ein unabhängig reflektierendes Ich

Spekulationen und eine aktiv formulierte Teilnahme an theologischen Diskursen konzentrieren sich auf den letzten Teil des Textes, der aus narrativer Sicht durch die unmittelbare Rede, den Ich-Bericht Christinas hervorsticht. Die z.T. erlebte Rede hingegen könnte mit der Fokalisierung der Figurenrede als Beschreibung des Innenlebens erklärt werden, sodass sich von einer Reflektorfigur sprechen ließe, die insbesondere in Heiligenlegenden des 13. Jahrhunderts ebenfalls nur in kleineren Textsegmenten vorzufinden ist.[279] Das zöge nach sich, dass sich Christinas Gedankenwelt und ihre nach außen gerichtete Kommunikation weiterhin im übergeschalteten Erzählrahmen abspielten. Doch ist neben fehlenden *inquit*-Formeln, der Stil dieses neuen, letzten Abschnitts zu betonen, von dem Ruh annahm, dass er von einem anderen Redaktor stamme.[280] Doch jenseits einer theologischen Herangehensweise verändert sich der Text auch sprachlich, weswegen Abstand von der Annahme einer Reflektorfigur genommen werden muss, die eine für die Christina-Vita nicht verfügbare konsistente Literarizität voraus-

---

ligiöse Erfahrung. Historische Modelle in christlicher Tradition. Hrsg. von Walter Haug / Dietmar Mieth. München 1992(b), S. 75–108, insbes. S. 94–100.
278 Vgl. Fraeters (2004), S. 67 f., über Hadewijch
279 Siehe Miedema (2010), S. 45, in Anlehnung an Hübner (2003), S. 398, für das fokalisierte Erzählen im höfischen Roman des 12. Jahrhunderts. Siehe auch Monika Fludernik: The Fictions of Language and the Languages of Fiction. London / New York 1993, S. 93–99, und Martin Schuhmann: Reden und Erzählen. Figurenrede in Wolframs ›Parzival‹ und ›Titurel‹ (Frankfurter Beiträge zur Germanistik 49). Heidelberg 2008, S. 36–38. Zur Reflektortechnik in der Narratologie siehe Hübner (2003), S. 46–55.
280 Vgl. Ruh (1993), S. 124.

setzt.[281] Der stilistische Umschwung äußert sich zunächst auf der terminologischen Ebene mit einem Zuwachs an scholastischen Redewendungen, wie die Formulierungen *die meyster stryedent vnder eyn ander* (CvH 98, 7) oder *[d]ie meyster sprechent* (CvH 100, 53) zeigen, die sowohl eine Anlehnung an theologische Diskurse markieren wie auch die Exklusion daraus, weil Christinas Sprecher-Ich Stellung bezieht und sich dementsprechend anders verortet.[282] Längere zu Beginn als solche vom Erzähler-Ich eingeführte Monologe Christinas lassen dichte Visionsbilder unkommentiert stehen. Diese Art des Visionsberichts unterscheidet sich deutlich von der Stimme des auslegenden impliziten Hagiographen.[283] An einer Stelle ist eine Spaltung von Christinas Sprecher-Ich und Seele zu beobachten, die noch im selben Abschnitt aufgehoben wird, indem der *lyebhaber zo myr* spricht, anstatt wie zuvor *zo myner selen*:

> *›Vff die tzijt, als ich mynen aller lyebstes lyeffe entphynge, da zofloiße van soißer sicheit myn sele, vnd sie wart versencket yn eynen abgront der woillüstiger lyebden. Vnd da sprache der lyebhaber zo myner selen: »Du byst myn vßerwilte bruytde, myn dube, myn konynckynnen. Jch wil dich edel machen myt myner wyßheit.« Da wart myn sele getzogen gotlichen yn eyn groiße wytte konncklich huße woil aller freuden vnd wunnen. [...] Da sprache der lyebhauer zo myr: »O sele myn, sehest lyecht yn lyecht? Jch befelen dyr die lebendigen myt den doden. Ich wil dyr myn wonden vff doyn.« Dar nach neygete sich die verwentte sele myn vff yren lyebhauer. Myt dem wart sy vereyniget yn eym soiße roge, yn eynem lyeblichen slaiffe.‹* (CvH 31, 16–33)

Obwohl das Sprecher-Ich hier selbstreflexiv die göttliche Rede an ein erlebendes Ich richtet, folgt in der direkt wiedergegebenen Rede der eigentliche Adressat, die *sele myn*. Auf diese Weise ist, was grammatisch inkonsistent erscheint, semantisch wiederhergestellt.[284] Mittermaier hatte sich in seiner Edition an einigen kritischen Stellen für eine Setzung von Redezeichen zu Gunsten der Sprechanteile des Erzählers entschieden:[285]

---

281 Zu bedenken wäre, ob es sich wie beim höfischen Roman um eine *discours*-Ebene handelt, die sich von der *histoire*-Ebene durch die veränderte Fokalisierung auszeichnet, vgl. dazu Stock (2010), S. 190 f. und S. 201.

282 Zur scholastischen Redeweise in der Vita siehe Kirakosian (2014a).

283 In diesem Sinne ist die erlebte Rede als »Möglichkeit des mündlichen Sprachgebrauchs« hervorzuheben, dazu Hübner (2003), S. 50 f.

284 Vgl. ähnlich: *Da was myn sele [...] vnd sie sach [...]*. (CvH 97, 48 f.)

285 Mittermaiers Setzung von Redezeichen ist an einer Stelle verwirrend: *Die drytten sprachyn: ›An gebruchen.‹ Got vffenbait aber myner selen, ›daz man nyt eyn mache lyebe gehabyn, man bekenne yn dan; van wem ich nyt eyn weyße, der ist verre van myr; daz eyn kayn ich nyt lyeffe gehayn‹. So ich got ye baße bekennen [...]*, ›Lebensbeschreibung der sel. Christina, gen. von Retters‹ (1966), 235. (Die Stellennachweise geben das Jahr der Teilveröffentlichung und Seitenzahlen an.)

»Vff der heiliger dry konynck dage da was myn sele [...]. Da sprach vnser here: ›Wullent [...] Jch hayn sye gesaitzet van dem dode vnd gebyn yn daz ewige leben na dyeßem lebyn.‹«
Jn dem oister dage dede got vff syner bruytde eyn groiße lyechte. Vnd yn dem lyechte sache sie, wie alle geiste sich erewyrdichsten vnd ernuweten sich yn dem gotlichyn lyecht. Vnd alle jre hertzen worden gespyste vnd entfenget myt gotlichem lyecht vnd troiste. »Vnd got bewyst myr alle dynge [...].« (›Lebensbeschreibung der sel. Christina, gen. von Retters‹ [1966], 233)

und erneut

»[...] Da was myn sele yn groißer genaden, vnd got bewyst myr syne groiße wonder, wie er syne genade gußet yn die guden vnd yn die boißen.« Vnd sie sach, wie er syn gebenedistes [!] bloyt goiße yn die, die sich vor den sunden hoytdent. »Da sprache myn sele: ›Here, was wyltu doyn myt dyeßen?‹ [...]« (›Lebensbeschreibung der sel. Christina, gen. von Retters‹ [1966], 235)[286]

Die auf diese Passage folgende konsistente Spaltung von Sprecher-Ich und *sele/ bruytde* spricht jedoch für den durchgehenden Ich-Bericht der Christina-Figur. Ihre Stimme unterscheidet sich schon dadurch von der des kommentierenden Schreiber-Ichs, dass kein Modus des Deutens vorliegt, sondern alle Angaben indikativisch dargestellt werden. Im Kontrast zum Erzählerkommentar (z.B. *Da myt verstene ich daz zo bezeychen* [CvH 7, 41]) formuliert Christinas Sprecher-Ich theologisch umstrittene Thesen mit logischen Konsekutivpartikeln wie *also* und *dar vmb*, die den rhetorischen Argumentationsaufbau eines Gedankens unterstreichen.[287]

Christina bezieht sich für ihre spekulative Position auf eine unantastbare Quelle: Neben der nachdrücklichen Betonung der Vision (*da gaiffe myr got eyn groiße vnd eyn wonderliche lyechte zo sehen* [CvH 100, 1 f.]) werden die Prädikate *vffenbairen* und *wysen* mit Gott als Subjekt verwendet, sodass grammatikalisch Gott als Handlungsträger hervortritt.[288] Kombiniert mit performativen Verben der assertiven/repräsentativen Klasse, die die eigentliche Proposition zum Ausdruck bringen, wird so die Autorisierung des Gesagten auf grammatikalischer, theologischer und textpragmatischer Ebene verstärkt. Zu untersuchen bleibt, ob die Entwicklung einer eigenständigen Stimme Christinas auch thematisch mit ihrer Seelenentwicklung in Verbindung gebracht und womöglich parallelisiert werden kann. Der theoretische Hintergrund des verloschenen Eigenwillens, der im Text indirekt thematisiert wird, könnte auf diese Weise die Grundlage für das

---

286 Vgl. im Kontrast dazu CvH 96 zu CvH 97 in der hier vorgelegten Edition.
287 Vgl. *also* und *dar vmb* als Konsekutivpartikel in CvH 94, 21; CvH 95, 36; CvH 98, 13; CvH 99,7 f.
288 Die entsprechenden Teilphrasen lauten: *Got vffenbait aber myner selen* (CvH 98, 9 f.); *Alsos wyste got myn sele* (CvH 98, 15).

Verständnis von Christinas Perspektivenwechsel bilden: Mit Volfing ließe sich fragen, ob als Voraussetzung für diesen Wechsel der »Prozess der Assimilation zwischen dem Sprecher-Ich und seiner vorbildlichen Rolle« nunmehr vollzogen sei.[289] Tatsächlich findet die neue reflexive Perspektivierung erst statt, nachdem Christina nach einer erfolgreich dargestellten Seelenveredelung als gottgleich beschrieben wird.[290] Da es in ihrer Rückschau um einen Vergegenwärtigungsakt geht, der nur außerhalb der *unio* stattfinden kann, liegt ohnehin eine Dissoziation zwischen Sprecher-Ich und Seele vor, denn »Sprechen heißt immer schon: getrennt sein«.[291] Die Spannung zwischen dem unabhängigen Sprecher-Ich und der in der Einheit mit Gott verstummten Seele liegt darin, dass die eine Stimme ein Ich voraussetzt, während die andere in Gott aufgelöst kein Ich mehr darstellt.[292] Die figurative Spaltung spiegelt erzähltechnisch die Unvereinbarkeit einer mystischen Sprecherposition wieder.

3.4 Zusammenfassung

Die narratologische Beschäftigung mit der Christina von Hane-Vita zeigt, wie das Erzählen als ein kollektives Projekt funktioniert, das auf die textpragmatische Interaktion mit dem Leser angewiesen ist. Das Du der Erzählebene ist ein lesendes Du, welches auf Grund seines vorausgesetzten Referenzwissens die Besonderheit von Christinas Leben etablieren kann. Darüber hinaus beteiligt sich der implizite Leser mit Hilfe des wiederkehrenden Kalenders und der verstreuten Gebetstexte an dem liturgischen und memorialen Nachvollzug. Das im Text angelegte Reaktualisierungspotenzial ist also ein medial inszeniertes: Hören, Sehen und Beten sind performative Akte. Das den Erzählrahmen konstituierende Ich stilisiert sich als ein erlebendes Ich im Umfeld Christinas, was seine Schreib- und Interpretiertätigkeit autorisiert. Ein solcher Identitätsentwurf ist, wie Meier erläutert, auf ein exemplarisches Ich zentriert, das für seine eigenständige Interpretation einer plausiblen Legitimation bedarf: »Autor-Identitäten werden [...] mit dem

---

289 Volfing (2003), S. 265.

290 In der Anrede der Gottesfigur an Christina heißt es: *Du byst myr gemacht geliche.* (CvH 95, 50 f.)

291 Walter Haug: Das Gespräch mit dem unvergleichlichen Partner. Der mystische Dialog bei Mechthild von Magdeburg als Paradigma für eine personale Gesprächsstruktur. In: Das Gespräch. Hrsg. von Karlheinz Stierle/Rainer Warning (Poetik und Hermeneutik 11). München 1984, S. 251–279, hier S. 277.

292 In der Vereinigung ist die Seele *bloiße yrs selbes* (CvH 100, 70).

Anspruch auf Autorität angeboten [...].«[293] Im Spannungsbereich zwischen einem männlich autorisierten Erzählen und der diegetischen Mitteilung der weiblichen Mystikerin erscheint der prophetische Gehalt von Christinas Visionen innerhalb der erzählten Welt sinnstiftend. Dabei verweist der hagiographische Ton der prophetischen Visionen weniger auf eine geschlechterspezifische Visionskultur oder eine weibliche Theologie; vielmehr geht es um textuelle Strategien, die den Schreibprozess thematisieren. In der paradoxen Nacherzählung der mystischen Unmittelbarkeit inszeniert sich das Schreiben als heilsvergewissernder Akt. Der implizite Hagiograph nimmt auf diese Weise teil am Anspruch der auf die Visionärin zukommenden prophetischen Gabe. Die Stimme des impliziten Autors wird allmählich von einem selbstständigen Sprecher-Ich der Mystikerin abgelöst, bis die diegetische Mitteilung an eine dritte Person hinfällig wird. Die auf diese Weise inszenierte Unmittelbarkeit bleibt aber mit denselben ambivalenten, dem Sprechen über das Unsagbare charakteristischen Sinnentzügen behaftet. Trotz einer klaren und starken Sprecherposition zum Textende hin, liegt eine fragmentierte Ich-Figuration Christinas vor. Inwiefern diese mit einer allegorisch ausgerichteten Rolle der mystischen Braut zusammenhängt, steht im Fokus des folgenden Untersuchungsteils.

---

[293] Christel Meier: Autorschaft im 12. Jahrhundert. Persönliche Identität und Rollenkonstrukt. In: Unverwechselbarkeit. Persönliche Identität und Identifikation in der vormodernen Gesellschaft. Hrsg. von Peter von Moos (Norm und Struktur 23). Köln/Weimar/Wien 2004. S. 207–266, hier S. 263.

4 Die mystische Braut: allegorisch, typologisch

Christina von Hane wird in ihrer Vita mit der *sponsa Christi* identifiziert, deren allegorischer Gehalt auf dem Hohenlied und dessen Rezeption fußt. Haug zeichnet die Geschichte der christlichen Hoheliedauslegung folgendermaßen nach:

> Für das Frühmittelalter galt, daß die Braut auf die Kirche und der Bräutigam auf Christus gedeutet wurden. Im 12. Jahrhundert kam es nun zu einer folgenreichen Interpretationswende, indem an die Stelle der Kirche die Seele des einzelnen Gläubigen trat. Damit war ein neues Denk- und Vorstellungsmuster für die Gottesbegegnung geschaffen.[1]

Die Vita der Christina von Hane steht in der Tradition jener hochmittelalterlichen Hoheliedinterpretationen, die eine Vielfachbesetzung der *sponsa* von ekklesiologischen über mariologische bis hin zu psychologischen Identitäten erlauben.[2] Volfing argumentiert, dass eine solche multiple Rollenzuweisung an sich »bereits eine teilweise Erklärung für die unvollzogene Individuation des Sprecher-Ichs« von Mechthild im ›Fließenden Licht‹ biete.[3] In der Christina von Hane-Vita scheint die *sponsa*-Allegorie vornehmlich für die eine auserwählte Gottesbraut Christina zu stehen, doch sind auch weitere Rollenbesetzungen der *sponsa* impliziert, sodass auch hier nach der pluralen Identität der Brautfiguration gefragt werden muss. Im Anschluss an die allegorische Untersuchung der Gottesbraut stellt sich die Frage nach der typlogischen Deutung der mystischen Braut, denn in der christlichen Theologie wird Maria, die neutestamentliche Mutter Christi, in der Braut des Hohenlieds präfiguriert. Typologische Beziehungen schaffen auf Grund analoger Bezüge eine Dynamik von Identität und Differenz.[4] In diesem

---

1 Haug (2000), S. 200.

2 Vgl. Largier (2008), S. 365. Die traditionellen Interpretationen für die Braut des Hohenlieds sind die Kirche, die Jungfrau Maria und die einzelne Seele, vgl. Newman (2012), S. 388.

3 Volfing (2003), S. 258.

4 Zur Typologie vgl. Friedrich Ohly: Halbbiblische und außerbiblische Typologie. In: Simboli e simbologia nell'alto medioevo. Settimane di studio del centro italiano di studi sull'alto medioevo XXIII. 3–9 aprile 1975. Hrsg. von Centro italiano di studi sull'alto medioevo. 2 Bde. Spoleto 1976, Bd. 2, S. 429–472, und Schneider (2003), S. 180–182. Das typologische Verfahren stammt aus dem theologischen Bereich, wo es die Vergegenwärtigung des Alten Testaments in neuen Bezügen beschreibt, siehe dazu Paul Michel: Übergangsformen zwischen Typologie und anderen Gestalten des Textbezugs. In: Bildhafte Rede im Mittelalter und früher Neuzeit. Probleme ihrer Legitimation und ihrer Funktion. Hrsg. von Wolfgang Harms/Klaus Speckenbach. Tübingen 1992, S. 43–72, insbes. S. 44 f.; siehe ebd., S. 54 f., zum Neuen Testament. Kritisch zur Differenzierung zwischen Typologie und Allegorie äußert sich David A. Wells: Allegorie als Interpretationsmittel mittelalterlicher Texte. Möglichkeiten und Grenzen. In: Bildhafte Rede im Mittelalter und früher

https://doi.org/10.1515/9783110536324-007

Sinne avanciert auch Christina letztlich über die Brautrolle hinaus, indem ihre Figur marianische Eigenschaften annimmt. In dieser Untersuchung bietet es sich daher an, die Interpretationsebenen zu differenzieren: Christina kann erst im zweiten Schritt mit Maria in Bezug gesetzt werden. Voraussetzung dafür ist die Identifikation ihrer Seele mit der mystischen Braut. Folglich soll zunächst die mystische Braut des Vitentextes in ihrer allegorischen Beschaffenheit untersucht werden. In einer ausführlichen Auseinandersetzung mit dem mittelalterlichen Symbolbegriff erinnert Stolz aber daran, dass

> in Patristik und Mittelalter anders als in der neuzeitlichen Ästhetik kein Unterschied zwischen den Begriffen der Symbolik und der Allegorik gemacht wird, sodass dort die ›symbolicae formae‹ weitestgehend mit dem allegorischen Prinzip des ›aliud dicitur‹, ›aliud demonstratur‹ konvergieren.[5]

Vor diesem theoretischen Hintergrund soll die Allegorie der Gottesbraut in ihrer Symbolik, d.h. hier also in ihrem auf ein Anderes verweisenden Charakter untersucht werden.

4.1 Allegorisch: die Seele

4.1.1 Die auserwählte Gottesbraut Christina

Dass Christina als auserwählte Braut Gottes gedeutet wird, bleibt zunächst eine Zuweisung der hagiographischen Erzähler-Stimme im Erzählbericht; gleich zu Beginn der Vita wird sicher gestellt, welchen spirituellen Status die Prämonstratensernonne hat: *Christina, die got, vnsere herre, yme selber vßerwilt hait zo eyner bruyt* (CvH 1, 7). Indirekt spielen Bibelallusionen auf dieselbe Identifikation mit der Braut des Hohenlieds an, z.B. *als geschreben ist in canticis canticorum* (CvH 30, 8 f.); *O, wie woil mocht sie sprechen, als die bruyt spricht yn canticis* (CvH 17, 29 f.). Auch aus eigener Perspektive nimmt Christina die Rolle der an dem Hohenlied orientierten geliebten Braut an, indem sich ihre Ausrufe mit den entsprechenden Bibelversen decken:

Neuzeit. Probleme ihrer Legitimation und ihrer Funktion. Hrsg. von Wolfgang Harms/Klaus Speckenbach. Tübingen 1992, S. 1–23, insbes. S. 7–9.

5 Stolz (2004), S. 107.

Da sprache yre sele yn vnsprechlicher lyebden: ›O yr dochter van Jerusalem, verkondiget mym lyeben, want ich van leybden krancke byn worden.‹ (CvH 52, 8–10)

adiuro vos filiae Hierusalem si inveneritis dilectum meum ut nuntietis ei quia amore langueo (Ct 5,8)

und

Da sprach sie zo yrem vßerwilten: ›Myn aller lyebster, kome her abe yn dynen garten.‹ (CvH 53, 6 f.)

surge aquilo et veni auster perfla hortum meum et fluant aromata illius (Ct 4,16).

Kongruent dazu wird Christus wiederholt als ihr *bruytgam* und *lyebhaber* bezeichnet. Die bereits mit diesen Rollenzuweisungen etablierte Liebesbeziehung bringt erotische Konnotationen mit sich, die der Bernhardinisch geprägten Hoheliedauslegung inhärent sind.[6] In der Christina von Hane-Vita werden insbesondere erotisch gefärbte Anspielungen vom impliziten Hagiographen als zu dechiffrierende Zeichen verstanden. In den exegetischen Diskursen der Vita werden so die erotischen Komponenten der brautmystischen Allegorie symbolisch ausgewertet.

Die Erotik der Vereinigung

Erotisch aufgeladene Metaphern und das Vokabular einer Sprache der Liebenden sind Charakteristika der Brautmystik.[7] Oft wird in diesem Zusammenhang die Sexualität von Mystikerinnen betont: Bynum geht von genuin weiblichen sexuellen Erfahrungen aus, die sich in einem religiösen Diskurs entladen.[8] Mazzoni geht in ihrem realhistorischen Ansatz weiter, wenn sie aus den erotischen Visionen der Angela von Foligno schlussfolgert, dass sie von einer Vertrautheit mit dem männlichen Körper zeugten, die nur eine einst verheiratete Frau wie Angela zu beschreiben wüsste.[9] Obwohl Coakley am Beispiel John Donnes zeigt, dass

---

6 Vgl. grundlegend zur erotisierenden Brautmystik McGinn (1994b), S. 158–224; siehe auch E. Ann Matter: The Voice of my Beloved. The Song of Songs in Western Medieval Christianity. Philadelphia 1990.
7 Diese Sprache der Liebenden bezieht sich nicht allein auf Mystikerinnen, wie Julie B. Miller: Eroticized Violence in Medieval Women's Mystical Literature. A Call for a Feminist Critique. In: Journal of Feminist Studies in Religion 15 (1999), S. 25–49, insbes. S. 25, behauptet.
8 Vgl. Bynum (1991), S. 190, und dies. (1987), S. 248: »sexual feelings were [...] not so much translated into another medium as simply set free.«
9 Siehe Cristina Mazzoni: Angela of Foligno. In: Medieval Holy Women in the Christian Tradition, c. 1100 – c. 1500. Hrsg. von Alastair J. Minnis/Rosalynn Voaden (Brepols Essays in European Culture 1). Turnhout 2010, S. 581–600, hier S. 591: »This vision is regularly evoked for its beauty

auch männliche Mystiker sich erotisch aufgeladener Sprache bedienen, bleibt ihr Ansatz ebenfalls an eine realphysische Sexualität orientiert; sexuelles Verlangen und das Verlangen nach Gott seien ineinander verwoben.[10] Jantzen ruft sogar zu einem wörtlichen Verständnis sexueller Schilderungen in jenen Texten auf, die von weiblicher Mystik handeln. Diese »explizite Sexualität« sei der grundlegende Unterschied zum intellektualisiert-erotischen Diskurs männlicher Mystiker.[11] Solche Ansätze sind problematisch, weil sie die diskursive Natur der jenseits von realer physischer Sexualität angesiedelten Liebessymbolik verkennen.[12] Das jüdisch-christliche Hohelied als ein Liebesgedicht, das verschiedene Interpretationen, darunter nicht-sexuelle, zulässt,[13] ist nur eine von vielen Manifestationen einer Philosophie der Liebe, die eine körperliche Sexualität transzendiert. Das prominenteste Beispiel für eine solche Philosophie bleibt wohl das Eros-Konzept Diotimas in der Rede des Sokrates in Platons ›Symposion‹: Sexuelles Verlangen ist hier nur ein Initiator und allenfalls Wegbegleiter der Erkenntnis, die höchste Form von Liebe ist aber völlig losgelöst von jeglichem sexuellen Verlangen. Selbst wenn die westeuropäische Welt des Mittelalters keinen direkten Zugang zum ›Symposion‹ hatte, so ist doch die Vorstellung der Liebe als des Schönen in Bezug auf die Gottheit mit Plotins Rezeption von Platon erstmals allegorisch

---

and its positive representation of the body, for its realism and for the confirmation that a married woman who knows what the body of a man feels like will have an experience of Christ's presence different from a virgin.«

10 Siehe Sarah Coakley: ›Batter my heart…?‹ On Sexuality, Spirituality, and the Christian Doctrine of the Trinity. In: Graven Images 2 (1995), S. 74–83, hier S. 76: »[…] ›messy entanglement‹ of sexual desire and desire for God«. Die Wahl des Adjektivs »messy« scheint auf Grund der – ob gewollten, das sei in Frage gestellt –Doppelbedeutung von chaotisch und verschmutzt unglücklich. Die These des sexuellen Verlangens nach Gott vertritt Sarah Coakley erneut in: Powers and Submissions. Spirituality, Philosophy and Gender. Oxford 2002, S. 54 f., und dies.: God, Sexuality and the Self. An Essay ›on the Trinity‹. Cambridge 2013.

11 Grace M. Jantzen: Power, Gender and Christian Mysticism (Cambridge Studies in Ideology and Religion 8). Cambridge 1995, S. 133: »The sexuality is explicit, and there is no warning that it should not be taken literally.«

12 Bernard McGinn: The Language of Inner Experience in Christian Mysticism. In: Spiritus. A Journal of Christian Spirituality 1 (2001[b]), S. 156–171, setzt sich mit der diskursiven Natur mystischer Texte auseinander, wenn er die Tradition einer »Sprache der Innerlichkeit« untersucht und dabei die linguistischen Aspekte der insbesondere von Origines und Gregor von Nyssa beeinflussten Hoheliedrezeption des Mittelalters betont.

13 Vgl. Kallirroe Linardou: The Couch of Solomon, a Monk, a Byzantine Lady and the Song of Songs. In: The Church and Mary. Papers Read at the 2002 Summer Meeting and the 2002 Winter Meeting of the Ecclesiastical History Society. Hrsg. von Robert Norman Swanson. Suffolk / New York 2004, S. 73–85.

gedeutet und so indirekt weitertradiert worden,[14] und schließlich im Augustinischen, z.T. auf Plotin basierenden Neuplatonismus ins Christliche gewendet.
Die Versöhnung von christlicher Liebesidee (neutestamentliche Agape) mit dem
platonischen Eros-Konzept geht zudem auf Abhandlungen und Briefe des Dionysius Areopagita zurück. Das neuplatonische Liebesprinzip wurde nun in eins
gesetzt mit dem christlichen Schöpfergott, was sowohl das Ausströmen Gottes
zu seinen Geschöpfen wie das Zurückfließen der gottsuchenden Schöpfung einschließt. Wie Haug erläutert, wurde im Neuplatonismus »der erotische Aufstieg
des Einzelnen in eine kosmische Ontologie« eingebaut.[15] Das Aufstiegsprinzip
dieses Liebeskonzepts führt also über das Irdisch-Sinnliche hinaus und will das
Irdisch-Körperliche hinter sich lassen. Daher könne auch, so Haug, die mittelalterliche Liebesmystik als ein Versuch begriffen werden, die Dichotomie von Geist
und Leib zu überwinden.[16]

Trotz einer im Platonismus verwurzelten Tradition der Einheit von Liebe und
Erkenntnis scheint Volfing eine Opposition zwischen Vernunft und affektiver
Liebe festmachen zu können, die sich in mystischen Texten des Mittelalters auch
auf die allegorische Ebene auswirke:

> Wenn man als gegeben ansieht, dass der (buchstäblich verstandene) Sexualtrieb traditi-
> onell als sinnlich, affektiv und unvereinbar mit einem höheren Streben nach Vernunft
> angesehen wird, scheint die Frage legitim, ob möglicherweise diese Spannung auch auf die
> allegorische Ebene übertragen wird.[17]

Doch eine Spannung zwischen Sexualtrieb und Streben nach Vernunft muss
nicht immer »gegeben« sein, weil in vielen Texten der sinnliche Akt die Gotteserfahrung nicht verhindert, im Gegenteil diese zu begleiten und sogar zu befördern
scheint. So wird bei Mechthild von Magdeburg die erotische »Anschauung im
Detail immer wieder allegoretisch gebrochen«;[18] Haug konstatiert:

> Es verwischen sich die Grenzen zwischen Allegorese, Metaphorik und anschaulicher Unmit-
> telbarkeit; und wenn dann die liebende Vereinigung geschildert wird, fällt überhaupt alles

---

14 Zur allegorischen Deutung von Diotimas Eros-Konzept bei Plotin siehe Teresa Chevrolet:
L'Eros De Diotime comme mythe intertextuel. Lectures néo-platoniciennes d'un passage du
Banquet. In: Bibliothèque d'Humanisme et Renaissance 51 (1989), S. 311–330, insbes. S. 313–317.
15 Haug (2000), S. 197.
16 Vgl. Haug (2000), S. 200.
17 Volfing (2008), S. 333.
18 Haug (2000), S. 201.

Deuten aus. Natürlich weiß man, daß hier von der Seele und von Gott die Rede ist, aber die Schilderung der Unio vertraut sich ungebrochen dem sinnlichen Akt an.[19]

In diesem Sinne ist der Körper Medium der Gotteserfahrung, sodass keine klare Grenze zwischen Geistigem und Leiblichem gezogen werden kann.[20]

In der Vita der Christina von Hane spiegelt sich genau diese Dichotomie, die dennoch keine Opposition darstellt, wider. Christus wendet sich an die Nonne und versichert ihr: *O zarte sele myn, ich geben dyr starcken glauben vnd waire zoversicht, heilge wyßheit vnd geistliche begerde.* (CvH 76, 40 f.) Ein »geistliches Begehren« ergründet das christliche Kernverständnis der Hoheliedrezeption.[21] So finden sich in der Christina-Vita trotz der mehrfach angesprochenen mystischen Vereinigung vergleichsmäßig wenige erotische Anspielungen darauf.[22] Die Vita ist darin etwa mit den Offenbarungen Birgittas von Schweden vergleichbar, wo nur gelegentlich der eheliche Verkehr im brautmystischen Sinne zwischen Seele und Gott erwähnt wird.[23] Es liegt keine intensive erotisierende Liebesbeziehung

---

19 Haug (2000), S. 202 f.
20 Vgl. Haug (2000), S. 203.
21 Vgl. Linardou (2004), S. 83. Siehe auch Largier (2008), S. 364–366.
22 Abgesehen von der brautmystischen Vereinigung, die im übrigen selten als Ehevollzug etikettiert (vgl. *lusteliche wyrtschafft* [CvH 37, 4]) und an nur einer Stelle als *mynnen spielle* (CvH 34, 7) bezeichnet wird, könnte eine kindliche Vision Christinas als ›spirituelle Defloration‹ gedeutet werden, wenn Christina das Jesuskind eng an ihren Körper schmiegt als Zeichen des spirituellen Begehrens: *Da nu daz kyntgen also eyn wille vor yre myt der sonnen gespelte, da macht iß sich vff vnd gynge vor yr vnd drat alles vor sich, byß daz iß zo yr quam, vnd da sloiffe iß yr vnder daz jonfferliche mentelgen.* (CvH 3, 10–13) Andererseits könnte dies auch ein Bild für die *imitatio* einer Schutzmantelmadonna sein, siehe dazu Górecka (1999), S. 93. Siehe auch Christa Belting-Ihm: ›Sub matris tutela‹. Unterschungen zur Vorgeschichte der Schutzmantelmadonna. Heidelberg 1976 zur Genese des Schutzmantelmadonna-Motivs; siehe James France: Cistercians under Our Lady's Mantle. In: Cistercian Quarterly 37 (2002), S. 393–414, über den Zugang der Zisterzienser zum Motiv; siehe Rosemary Drage Hale: Rocking the Cradle. Margaretha Ebner Be(holds) the Divine. In: Performance and Transformation. New Approaches to Late Medieval Spirituality. Hrsg. von Mary A. Suydam/Joanna E. Ziegler. Basingstoke 1999, S. 211–239, insbes. S. 224, für Beispiele aus Adelhausen und Weiler; siehe David Kinsley: The Goddesses' Mirror. Visions of the Divine from East to West. Albany 1989, S. 231–233, zum Mutteraspekt. Der bunte und aus besonderem, »himmlischen« Stoff angefertigte Schutzmantel bei Agnes Blannbekin ist eine Gabe Gottes an Maria, die darunter ›unendlich‹ vielen Seelen Schutz und Gnade erweist (vgl. ›Leben und Offenbarungen der Agnes Blannbekin‹ 183, 9–28). Das Motiv kommt auch bei Adelheid Langmann vor (vgl. ›Die Offenbarungen der Adelheid Langmann‹ 51, 13–15), siehe dazu Thali (2003), S. 187.
23 Vgl. BvS I 1, 12, 244.

wie etwa bei Dorothea von Montau vor.[24] Anders als bei Mechthild von Magdeburg und Gertrud von Helfta wird auch kein himmlisches Ehebett als Ort der
Vereinigung erwähnt.[25] Auch Ruh resümiert: »So sehr das Ganze brautmystisch
orientiert ist, erotische Geistigkeit gewinnt – wie bei Mechthild von Hackeborn –
keinen Raum.«[26]

Dennoch bleibt auch die Christina von Hane-Vita von einer mit der entsprechenden Bildlichkeit einhergehenden Liebesbeziehung zwischen der Seele und
Christus dominiert. Verben des Küssens und des Umarmens zeichnen diese
innige Liebesbeziehung aus, wie das auch bei Mechthild von Magdeburg, Margareta Ebner, Gertrud von Helfta, Heinrich von Nördlingen, Seuse, Tauler, und,
wenn jener über die Paulinische Entrückung spricht, Meister Eckhart der Fall ist.[27]

---

24 Siehe dazu Almut Suerbaum: ›O wie gar wundirbar ist dis wibes sterke!‹ Discourses of Sex,
Gender, and Desire in Johannes Marienwerder's Life of Dorothea von Montau. In: Oxford German
Studies 39 (2010), S. 181–197, insbes. S. 196 f. Siehe auch Annette Volfing: Ever-growing Desire.
Spiritual Pregnancy in Hadewijch and in Middle High German Mystics. In: Desire and Dante and
the Middle Ages. Hrsg. von Manuele Gragnolati et al. London 2012, S. 45–57, insbes. S. 49, und
Volfing (2010), S. 155.
25 Vgl. Mechthild von Magdeburg, ›Das fließende Licht der Gottheit‹ VI 1, 108; III 10, 45; II 23, 40.
Siehe Seelhorst (2003), S. 86–95, zur Erotik Mechthilds von Magdeburg; siehe auch Joelle Mellon:
The Virgin Mary in the Perception of Women. Mother, Protector and Queen. Since the Middle
Ages. Jefferson 2008, S. 120 für Gertrud von Helfta.
26 Ruh (1993), S. 124.
27 Die entsprechenden Stellen in der Christina-Vita lauten: *Da vmbfynge der here sy myt synen
gotlichen armen yre sele vnd er geboitde yre auch, myt yren lyplichen armen yn zo vmbfange, vnd
er druckt sy an syne hertze.* (CvH 21, 16–18); [...] *vmbfynge der lyeblicher got yre sele gar sere fruntlichen myt synem vmbfengen myt beytden armen* (CvH 37, 26 f.). Vgl. mit dem ›Fließenden Licht‹:
halsen und kússen und unbegriflliche got umbevahen (Mechthild von Magdeburg, ›Das fließende
Licht der Gottheit‹ VII 1, 95 f); mit Margareta Ebner: *ich [got] wil dich frölich enphahen und min-
neklich umvahen in daz ainige aine, daz ich bin* (›Offenbarungen der Margaretha Ebner‹ 69, 26 f.);
mit dem ›Legatus‹: *Dominus utrisque brachiis blande ipsam circumplectens, et fortiter sibi astrin-
gens* (Gertrud von Helfta, ›Legatus divinae pietatis‹ III, 21, 1, 112); mit Heinrich von Nördlingen:
ie enger das minenbet ist ie neher der umbfang get ie susser smecket das wessenlich mundküssen
(›Briefe Heinrichs von Nördlingen‹. Margaretha Ebner und Heinrich von Nördlingen. Ein Beitrag
zur Geschichte der deutschen Mystik. Hrsg. von Philipp Strauch. Amsterdam 1966, S. 169–270
[Nachdruck der Orignalausgabe Freiburg i. Br. / Tübingen 1882], Brief XLVI, S. 252, Z. 53 f.); mit
Seuse: *Ach, minú lieben kint, sendent unser ellenden hertzen in den minneklichen umbvang, bis
daz die sele hin nach kome!* (Heinrich Seuse: ›Das grosse Briefbuch‹. In: Heinrich Seuse. Deutsche Schriften Hrsg. von Karl Bihlmeyer. Stuttgart 1907 [unver. Nachdruck Frankfurt a. M. 1961],
S. 405–495, hier IX. Brief, S. 433); mit Tauler: *in einem unsprechlichen umbevange* (›Die Predigten
Taulers‹ 39, 156); mit Meister Eckhart: *in einem lieplïchen umbevange* (DW III, 86, 486 f.). Das Bild
des Küssens und Umarmes des mystischen Brautpaares basiert auf dem Text des Hohenlieds:
leva eius sub capite meo et dextera illius amplexabitur me (Ct 2,6).

Bereits in einer Vision im Kindesalter geht ein starkes Begehren von Christina aus, das in dem Kuss zwischen den Liebenden münden will:[28]

> *Da sie daz lyebe kyntgyn gesache, da begert sie, daz iß zo yr quemme. Zo hant gynge vnd gynge iß byß also lange daz iß by sie quam, vnd iß stonde yn dem stoille vor sie vnd iß woiße also groiße vor yre, daz iß wart eyn schoner jongelyn also groiße, daz syn heubt reicht an yren mont.* (CvH 6, 10–13)

Freilich liegt erotisches Potenzial in der Entwicklung des Jesuskinds zum sexualfähigen Jüngling, der sich Christina körperlich annähert. Doch weiß die Erzählerstimme die orthodoxe Deutung der Vision bereitzustellen und die spirituelle Allegorese zu liefern: *Das was eyn zeychen, daz got vnßer here dar na waschen wolte yn yrem hertzen, das er sie van syner kyntheit zo hoger lyebden zehen woiltte* (CvH 6, 13–15). Während Christina ein schöner Jüngling erscheint, wird Christus von Adelheid Langmann in einer vergleichbaren Vision beschrieben als *ein alter herre und was sein antlutzze also wunnenclichen schön* (›Die Offenbarungen der Adelheid Langmann‹ 8, 9 f.).[29] In anderen Visionen Langmanns bleibt die Gestalt Christi die eines achtzehnjährigen Jünglings, während in der Christina von Hane-Vita das Alter der Christuserscheinung nicht näher beschrieben wird.[30] Auch im ›botten der götlichen miltekeit‹ steht eine ähnliche Vision eines Jünglings für die Liebesbeziehung zwischen Gertruds Seele und Christus.[31] Der Vergleich zu anderen Fällen macht an dieser Stelle deutlich, dass eine sexual-erotische

---

28 Siehe Górecka (1999), S. 339 und S. 347, zum Kuss als Bild des Einheitsereignisses. Als Grundlage aus dem Hohenlied vgl. den Bibelvers *osculetur me osculo oris sui quia meliora sunt ubera tua vino* (Ct 1,2).
29 Garber (2003), S. 128–130, meint am Adelheid Langmann-Text den Einfluss weltlicher Liebeslyrik zu erkennen. Keller (2000b), S. 30, und Anne Clark Bartlett: Male Authors, Female Readers. Representation and Subjectivity in Middle English Devotional Literature. Ithaca 1997, S. 72 f., untersuchen die Visionen Langmanns, die Christus als männlichen, großherzigen und attraktiven Jüngling porträtieren. Zum brautmystischen Bild Gottes als Mann siehe auch Bardo Weiss: Die deutschen Mystikerinnen und ihr Gottesbild. Das Gottesbild der deutschen Mystikerinnen auf dem Hintergrund der Mönchstheologie. 3 Bde. Paderborn 2004, Bd. 3, S. 2190 f.
30 Vgl.: [...] *do kom unser herre in eins junglings weise in ahzehen jaren für si und fuert sein mueter an der hant* [...] (›Die Offenbarungen der Adelheid Langmann‹ 29, 30); und über eine Traumvision heißt es: *Aines nahtes traumt ir, wi unser herre im kor stunt als ein junglink um ahzehen jor* (›Die Offenbarungen der Adelheid Langmann‹ 67, 3 f.).
31 Vgl.: *Do sach ich einen zarten schönen júngeling wol by xvj joren.* (Gertrud von Helfta, ›ein botte der götlichen miltekeit‹ 7, 5 f.)

Deutung der Zusammenkunft Christinas mit Christus als Frau und Mann an klare Grenzen stößt.[32]

Der Klang der Vereinigung

Dennoch gibt es eine Sinnlichkeit der Vereinigung, durchaus in ihrer körperbetonten Natur, wie das in der Vita der Christina von Hane besonders an der Verbindung von Klang, auch Tanz, und mystischer Vereinigung gezeigt werden kann. Christinas wie Marias Stimme werden als *soiße yn den oren des heren/mynen oren* bezeichnet (CvH 15, 25 f.; CvH 62, 8). Diese Eigenschaft deckt sich mit der Stimme der Christusfigur, die von sich behauptet: *Jch byn eyn soiße stymme. Jch byn eyn spyße.* (CvH 47, 2).[33] In Mechthilds von Magdeburg ›Fließendem Licht der Gottheit‹ wird die intrinsische Verbindung vom Klang der Stimme und der Liebesbezeugung expliziert:

> So sprichet er: »Eya du liebú tube, din stimme ist ein seitenspil minen oren, dinú wort sint wurtzen minem munde, dine gerunge sint die miltekeit miner gabe.« (Mechthild von Magdeburg, ›Das fließende Licht der Gottheit‹ I 2, 25–27)

> So sprichet der jungeling: ›Ich hôre ein stimme, die lutet ein teil von minnen. Ich han si gefriet manigen tag, das mir die stimm nie geschach. Nu bin ich beweget, ich mûs ir engegen! Sú ist die jene, die kumber und minne miteinander treit.‹ (Mechthild von Magdeburg, ›Das fließende Licht der Gottheit‹ I 44, 10–13)

Das *Nu*, der Augenblick des gegenseitigen Erkennens, baut auf das Hören der von Liebe zeugenden Stimme auf. Ein Rufen und Gerufen-Werden führt in die Präsenz dieses *Nu*. Zudem begleitet Wohlklang die Gottesbegegnung: *der fúrste wil úch gegen komen in dem tôwe und in dem schônen vogelgesange* (Mechthild von Magdeburg, ›Das fließende Licht der Gottheit‹ I 44, 16 f.). Abgesehen vom kosmischen Lobgesang der Engel, in den die Schar der menschlichen Seelen einstimmt (vgl. CvH 97, 40 f.), spielt Klang auch in der Christina von Hane-Vita in Momenten der Gottesbegegnung eine besondere Rolle. In einer Vision, die in ihrer Bildhaftigkeit

---

32 Die Tradition der Hoheliedrezeption schließt stets eine erotische Deutung ein, innerhalb derer der *locus amoenus* und die Dialektik der Liebesfreude durch Selbstaufopferung zu betonen sind, vgl. dazu Erik Gray: Come be my Love. The Song of Songs, ›Paradise Lost‹, and the Tradition of the Invitation Poem. In: PMLA 128 (2013), S. 370–385, insbes. S. 370–375. Die Vita verfolgt dennoch kaum ein Programm des erotischen Begehrens, wie es Largier (2005), S. 251 f., in einer Rhetorik der Hoheliedauslegung beobachtet.
33 Wiederholt wird die Stimme der Christusfigur als süß beschrieben, vgl. CvH 57, 3; CvH 57, 21; CvH 53, 7.

an mittelalterliche Darstellungen von Christus als Baum anlehnt,[34] sieht und hört Christina Christus als Vogel inmitten einer Vogelschar singen:

> [...] *er sancke myt eyner soißer stymme den anderen fogellen vor dyße wort: ›Ego sum panis viuus‹ etc. Da songen yme alle die anderen fogel nach myt soißem thone: ›Tu es panis viuus in quo omnes viuimus in eternum‹.* (CvH 22, 24–26)

Auf die Antiphon *Ego sum panis* erfolgt aber eine gespiegelte Antwort, zudem eine melodische, wie die Bezeichnung *thone* nahelegt. Die Umkehrung in die direkte Anrede (*Tu es panis*) stellt einen kreativen Umgang mit der Liturgie dar, der spezifisch für die Vita der Christina von Hane zu sein scheint, denn kein mittelalterliches Gesangbuch verzeichnet ein entsprechendes Responsorium. Das offizielle Responsorium *Si quis manducaverit ex hoc pane, vivet in æternum* wird hier in die direkte Anrede gewendet. *Ego sum panis* ist die Antiphon zum Benedictus der Laudes an Fronleichnam. In der Vita wird das Morgengebet in dem Chor der Vögel verbildlicht. Der Kontext des Hochfests der leiblichen Gegenwart Christi im Sakrament der Eucharistie unterstreicht die in der Vita angelegte Verbindung von Klang und Gottesvereinigung.

Die Bilder einer Liebessprache vermischen sich mit der Resonanz des Gesangs. Zu dem Widerklang tritt aber auch ein Neuklang hinzu. Das wird an zwei weiteren Textpassagen deutlich, die ganze Liedzeilen wiedergeben:

> *Vnder des als yre sele yn der soißer begerunge myt yrem hertzen lyeben was, da sancke die vberschone jonffrauwe vnd moder Maria myt soißer vnd frolicher stymmen eyn lyebliches lyetgyn zo dryn stonden na eyn ander, vnd daz kyntgyn Jhesus sange myt yre also: ›O myn aller lyebste fruntdynnen, ich hayn dyr gegeben die sicherheit vnd daz ewige leben.‹ Dyß gesicht vnd auch der sanck was alles yn dem geist vnd nyt yn den vßewendigen synnen.* (CvH 34, 9–14)

> *Da sancke myn lyebhaber myner selen myt froelicher stymmen dyeßen sancke: »Myn fruntdynnen, kere dich her zo myr, daz myr dich ansehen. Dyne stymme ist soiße yn mynen oren, vnd dyne angesicht ist suberlich.«* (CvH 62, 6–8)

Zwar wird an einer Stelle betont, dass der Gesang nicht mit den äußeren Sinnen zu vernehmen sei, doch schlägt die Beschreibung *soißer vnd frolicher stymmen eyn lyebliches lyetgyn* gemeinsam mit der darauffolgenden Textwiedergabe eine

---

34 Die Baumvision der Christina-Vita erinnert an eine Illumination der sogenannten *Rotschild Canticles* (New Haven, Beinecke Library, MS 404, Bl. 5ʳ), vgl. Hamburger (1990), S. 39 f., Abb. 4. Von der Christina-Vita unterschieden sind allerdings die Funktionszuordnungen der Vögel und die Erscheinung Christi: In der Christina-Vita ist Christus ein Vogel, in den *Rotschild Canticles* erscheint er als der Gekreuzigte.

klanginduzierte und sich daher performativ entfaltende Unmittelbarkeit der Gottesbegegnung vor. Dem »ästhetische[n] Potential« einer »klanginduzierte[n] Liebesrhetorik« sei daher ein performatives Potential hinzuzufügen.[35] Köbele, die den Zusammenhang von Sinn und Klang im Minnesang diskutiert, weist auf den »Hiat zwischen Stimme und Schrift« hin:[36]

> Wenn Liebe nicht nur Gegenstand der Lyrik ist, sondern, als Sinnlichkeit zum Klang drängend, Gegenstand und Medium zugleich, dann bleibt Unmittelbarkeit notgedrungen immer eine medial inszenierte, unter anderem klanginduzierte.[37]

Das Lied als Produkt der Gottesbegegnung ist in der Christina von Hane-Vita nicht allein auf der erzählten Ebene thematisiert. Mit der Angabe der Typen Lobgesang und Reigen an zwei weiteren Stellen sowie der dazugehörigen Liedtexte ist eine lyrische Unmittelbarkeit geschaffen, die den impliziten Leser zur klanglichen Inszenierung einlädt.

> *Vnd yre vßerwilter bruytgam vnd syne moder songen jre myt eyner soißer stymmen dyeßen lyeblichen loiffe: ›Sicheit des ewigen lebens geben ich dyr vnd vollenhyrtunge byß an das ende.‹* (CvH 63, 57–59)

> *Das gotliche lamp sange vor myt vbersoißem thone vnd die jonffrauwen sangen alles na myt froelichen stymmen vnd hertzelichen freuden, alles na yme vnd er myt ynne sonder eynnige wandelonge. Eya woil eyn kauffen! Eya woil eyn dantze! Eya woil eyn sancke! Eya woil eyn lyeblich spielle! Dyße was der reyne, den er vor songe: ›Heillich, heillich syt yr yn myner gotheit, vollenkomen yn myner ewiger lyebden.‹* (CvH 32, 36–41)

Der sonst kollektive Charakter der Melodien wird in der Vita mit der gegebenen Stimmenfiguration des Bräutigams und seiner Mutter göttlich überhöht, wenn Christus und Maria spezifizierte Lieder singen. Der genannte Reigen (*reyne*) fügt dieser Gottesteilhabe an einer außerliturgischen Klangwelt die Dimension des Tanzes hinzu. Der Rundtanz wird hier als Lied ausgezeichnet, das dem Kontext nach das göttliche Lamm, also erneut Christus, der Schar der elftausend Jungfrauen vorsingt. Doch ist der Reigen in der Vita sowohl Gesang als auch Tanz. Das Bild des mit einer Schar von Jungfrauen tanzenden Christus wird von dem Rhythmus der Sprache getragen. Am Ende der vierfachen Wiederholung des *Eya*, der Interjektion als Kreismotiv, überrascht die abschließende nunmehr verdoppelte

---

35 Susanne Köbele: Rhetorik und Erotik – Minnesang als ›süßer Klang‹. In: Poetica 45 (2013), S. 299–332, hier S. 330.
36 Köbele (2013), S. 303.
37 Köbele (2013), S. 324.

Kadenz *lyeblich spielle*. Dabei muss offen bleiben, ob nicht doch die anschließenden Worte der direkten Rede der Christusfigur den Reigen darstellen sollen (*Heillich, heillich ...*). Doch bis auf die Wiederholung von *heillich* weist hier rhythmisch gesehen nicht besonders viel auf einen Reigen hin. Die unvermittelten von *Eya* eingeläuteten Ausrufe hingegen sind nicht nur lyrisch raffinierter, sondern auch unmittelbarer, weil sie von der Erzählstimme, so scheint es, affektiv ausgerufen werden. Auf diese Weise wirkt die Gottesbegegnung, die Gegenstand des Berichts ist, fast schon sinnlich greifbar. Einen Tanz, den Gott die Seele lehrt, kennt zwar auch das ›Fließende Licht der Gottheit‹, doch bleibt dieser eine abstrahierte Bewegung der einzelnen Seele,[38] während sich der Tanz in der Christina-Vita als eine kollektive Praxis präsentiert. Andere Aspekte der Christina von Hane-Vita heben zugleich die besondere Liebesbeziehung zwischen Christinas Seele und ihrem Bräutigam Christus hervor.[39] In der allegorischen Beschaffenheit der brautmystischen Metaphern wird Christinas Seele mit der Geliebten des Hohenlieds identifiziert.

Die Bilder der Vereinigung

Anhand von zwei besonders prominenten Bildern, Palmbaum und Kuss, lässt sich das in der Christina von Hane-Vita dominierende brautmystische Verhältnis diskutieren. Der Vergleich mit anderen mystischen Texten hilft dabei, die Mystik der Vita zu kontrastieren und profilieren. Anschließend wird nach der Bewegung der sich punktuell erfüllenden Liebe gefragt, nach Zusammenkunft und Trennung.

Während einer in der Vita früh geschilderten Entrückung spricht Christina von der Liebesentfachung und mahnt den impliziten Leser, der Gottheit in der eigenen Seele zu gedenken:

> *Als nu dyeße heilge jonffer also lache entzucket yn dem geist, da sprach sie dyeße wort: ›Die lyebde, die wyrt entfencket van dem fuer, sy wyrt erluchtet van dem lyecht. Gedencke van dem wyne, der hoger, soißer, luterer gotheit, der dyner sele ist zo gefueget.‹* (CvH 24, 1–4)

---

38 Vgl. Mechthild von Magdeburg, ›Das fließende Licht der Gottheit‹ I 44, 33 f. Die Dreierfolge von Liebe (*minne*), Erkenntnis (*bekantnisse*) und Genießen (*gebruchunge*) in dieser Passage des ›Fließenden Lichts‹ erinnert an die theologisch spekulative Diskussion in der Christina von Hane-Vita (CvH 98), siehe dazu Kirakosian (2014a).
39 Die Verbindung von Musik und Mystik in der Christina von Hane-Vita konnte hier nur am Rande umrissen werden, siehe dazu ausführlicher Kirakosian (2017c).

Das brautmystische Wachsen, d.h. die Aszendenz oder auch der Seelenaufstieg, spiegelt sich besonders gut in der Palmbaumallegorie: ein Bild aus dem Hohenlied, das in verschiedenen Illuminationen aufgegriffen wird, Gegenstand eines anonym überlieferten Traktats ist und auch in unserem Text mehrmals ausgemalt wird.[40] In direkter Anspielung auf die biblische Quelle sieht die erleuchtete Christina einen Baum in ihrer Seele wachsen, der mit einem Palmbaum verglichen wird.[41] Der intertextuelle Verweis und die gleichzeitige Erklärung der Vision folgen:

> Wan dyeßem baůme vnd van syner bezeychenunge hait yr der here gegeben zo verstayn yn dem lyecht, als geschreben ist in canticis canticorum: ›Jch sal vff stigen yn den palmen baume vnd ich sal vmbfangen syn frucht.‹ (CvH 30, 7–9)

Dass es sich bei diesem Bild um den im Hohenlied angelegten Topos des Wachsens der Liebe handelt,[42] machen weitere Ausführungen zur Beschaffenheit des Baums deutlich, von denen eine aus der Erzählerperspektive kommentiert wird:

> Der was vben gar breyt vnd groiß vnd vnden smaille vnd cleyn. [...] Myrcke, das der palmen baume ist vnden smaille vnd stincht vnd vben breyt van laube vnd edel van fruchten. Also ist yre leben hie yn dyeßer tzijt cleyn gewest durch eyn oitmodiges erkentenyße yrs selbs vnd sy ist vol stiche gewest van bytterheit der bedroppenyß jn abezeonge, yn spyßen vnd dranck, yn krenckten, yn harten cleyderen vnd leger, alstu da vor haist gehoirt. Aber vffen is sy sere breyt gewest yn gotlicher lyebden entgene yre vyant vnd fruntde, edel van soißen fruchten der dogent. (CvH 30, 6–16)

Daran anschließend wird in der direkten Rede der Gottesfigur das brautmystische Bild unter Rückgriff auf die Formulierung des Erzählberichts als Wachsen der Liebe ausgelegt: ›[...] Jch hayn dich ryche gemacht myt der gedult vnd ich hayn dich verbreytde yn der lyebden vnd ich hayn dich erhaben van dem nyedersten byß zo dem vbersten.‹ (CvH 30, 20–22) Die Charakterisierung des Baums als unten schmal und oben weit entspricht der vom 13. bis 16. Jahrhundert weit verwendeten und ursprünglich wohl aus dem Altfranzösischen stammenden Allegorie der

---

40 Siehe z.B. die Illumination in den *Rotschild Canticles*, dazu Hamburger (1990), S. 35, Abb. 4. Vgl. Wolfgang Fleischer: Untersuchungen zur Palmbaumallegorie im Mittelalter (Münchener Germanistische Beiträge 20). München 1976, S. 277–287, zum ›Palmbaumtraktat‹.
41 Vgl.: *Yn dem lyecht sach sie geistlichen eyn baume vß yrer selen waißen als eynen palmen baume.* (CvH 30, 5 f.) Siehe auch die Baumallegorie im ›Legatus‹ (vgl. Gertrud von Helfta, ›Legatus divinae pietatis‹ III, 18, 6, 84–86).
42 Vgl. dazu Gray (2013), S. 371.

palma contemplationis.[43] Mit ihr wird allgemein die tugendhafte Seele gemeint, die sich in der mittelhochdeutschen Rezeption der Allegorie auch explizit als Braut Gottes identifizieren lässt, wie das im ›St. Trudperter Hohenlied‹ der Fall ist: *der PALMBOUM der ist bî der erde smal unde / rûch. er ist wasse unde ist obenân breit unde / vil schoene. alsô sint die gotes briute.* (›Das St. Trudperter Hohelied‹ 119, 12–14) Die geschlechterspezifische Baumart hingegen, wie sie im biblischen Hohenlied anzutreffen ist, wird in der Christina-Vita überwunden, denn Christinas Liebe/Seele wächst wie ein Palmbaum (Frau), der Früchte trägt (Mann).[44] Der im Hohelied dem männlichen Dialogpartner zugeordnete Baum wird im Erzählerkommentar der Vita mit der menschlichen Seele bzw. mit dem Leben der Mystikerin identifiziert, obwohl die anfängliche Visionsbeschreibung und die göttliche Bestätigung offen lassen, ob es sich beim Baum nicht auch um den mystischen Bräutigam handeln könnte. Christina als Braut und ihr Bräutigam sind daher nicht zu unterscheiden. Was sich im ›St. Trudperter Hohenlied‹ allegorisch lesen lässt, wird in der Christina von Hane-Vita explizit betont: eine zweistufige Entwicklung, die sich auf das diesseitige Leben einerseits und auf ein jenseitiges Leben andererseits zu richten scheint. Auf Erden (*bî der erde/yre leben hie yn dyeßer tzijt*) mag das nicht ersichtlich sein, aber in der Vereinigung, die topographisch *obenân/vffen* angesiedelt ist, gleicht die *gotes briut/seliche jonffrauwe* ihrem Bräutigam. Daher bezieht sich im ›St. Trudperter Hohenlied‹ wie in der Christina-Vita die positiv umschriebene Palmkrone (*breit unde uil schône/sere breyt* [...] *Edel van soißen fruchten*) weniger auf ein Leben nach dem Tod als auf die Teilhabe am Göttlichen durch das kontemplative, tugendhafte Leben auf Erden. Dieses Aufsteigen der Seele, die Aszendenz, mündet in die *elevatio*,[45] ein

---

43 Siehe dazu Fleischer (1976); siehe auch Hamburger (1990), S. 35–42. Eine dreifache Auslegung der Palmbaumallegorie ist möglich: die Palme als Kreuz Christi, als Bußmetapher, als Metapher für die göttliche Begegnung, vgl. Hamburger (1990), S. 36. Zu Gott als Baum in mystischen Texten siehe Weiss (2004), Bd. 3, S. 2166–2170.

44 Vgl.: *statura tua adsimilata est palmae et ubera tua botris / dixi ascendam in palmam adprehendam fructus eius et erunt ubera tua sicut botri vineae et odor oris tui sicut malorum / guttur tuum sicut vinum optimum dignum dilecto meo ad potandum labiisque et dentibus illius ruminandum* (Ct 7,7–9). Bezüglich des Apfelbaums vgl.: *malus* [...] *et fructus eius dulcis gutturi meo* (Ct 2,3) und *arbore malo* (Ct 8,5). – Zu diskutieren bleibt, ob die Früchte (Weintrauben) auch dem Palmbaum angehören. Dann würde keine genderspezifsche Aufteilung vorliegen. In einer Vision Langmanns ist zwar nicht explizit von einem Palmbaum die Rede, aber von einem Früchte bringenden Baum, der für das Wachsen der Tugenden steht, wie ihr von göttlicher Seite versichert wird, vgl. ›Die Offenbarungen der Adelheid Langmann‹ 5, 16–22.

45 Die Aszendenz wird in den *Rotschild Canticles* mit den verschiedenen aufwärts reichenden Zweigen und Vögeln illustriert, siehe dazu Hamburger (1990), S. 38: »The elevation of the soul is represented by the swallow who feeds only in the air. [...] The seventh and final branch of the

Konzept, das je nach literarischer Ausformung und philosophischem Kontext unterschiedlich bezeichnet wird.[46]

Die Erhebung wird im Bild des Seelenflugs festgehalten und steht in der Christina-Vita im Zusammenhang mit dem brautmystischen Kuss, der vom Heiligen Geist ausgeht und in seinem bildlichen Pendant der Taube erscheint.[47] Die enge Beziehung zwischen Gott und der Seele wird in Anlehnung an das Hohelied u.a. auch bei Gertrud von Helfta und Mechthild von Magdeburg im Bild des Kusses veranschaulicht.[48] Eine »noch intensivere Form der Beziehung« meint Egerding in der Wendung Mechthilds *Ich bin in dir und du bist in mir* (Mechthild von Magdeburg, ›Das fließende Licht der Gottheit‹ III 5, 12 f.) lesen zu können, die eine Hoheliedrezeption mit volkssprachig geprägten Liedversen, hier dem sogenannten Tegernseer Liebesgruß, assoziiert.[49] Ähnliche Passagen, die sich wie

---

›Palma contemplationis‹ is designated ›defectio‹ or ›gansiv suzichait‹. Both these terms signify a state of spiritual rapture or ecstasy.«

46 Siehe dazu Volfing (2008), S. 329.

47 Vgl. die Vision in CvH 7; siehe dazu ausführlich Kirakosian (2017b). Die Nähe der Vision zu Illuminationen, in denen Taubenflügel das menschliche Gesicht berühren (vgl. Hamburger [1990], S. 71, Abb. 129), betont den piktorialen Wert der brautmystischen Vision. Gregor der Große benutzt ebenfalls die Flugmetapher im mystischen Sinne, wobei ihn die »Flügel der Kontemplation« in die Höhe erheben: *Aut rara valde aut nulla hoc in sublimibus penna contemplationis levat* (Gregor der Große: Registrum Epistolarum. Hrsg. von Paul Ewald/Ludwig M. Hartmann [MGH Epp. 1–2]. 2 Bd.e. Berlin 1891/1899, Bd. 2 [1899], Buch IX, Nr. 227, S. 219, Z. 22 f.). Auch Johannes Eriugena geht in seinem Johannes-Kommentar auf den Flug der Gottesschau ein, siehe dazu Ruh (1990), S. 184. Siehe auch Weiss (2004), Bd. 3, S. 2177–2180. Letztlich geht das Bild des Fluges auf neuplatonische Beschreibungen der Gottesschau zurück, wie etwa die der Augustinischen Vision zu Ostia, vgl. Sancti Augustini Confessionum libri XIII. Hrsg. von Lucas Verheijen (CCSL 27). Turnhout 1981, Buch IX, Kap. x, S. 147 f.

48 Vgl. Gertrud von Helfta: ›Legatus divinae pietatis‹ IV. In: Gertrude d'Helfta. Œuvres spirituelles IV. Hrsg. von Jean-Marie Clément (Sources chrétiennes. Série des textes monastiques d'Occident 48). Paris 1978, 14, 6, 160 (Die Stellennachweise geben Kapitel-, Paragraph- und Seitenzahlen an.); Mechthild von Magdeburg, ›Das fließende Licht der Gottheit‹ II 23, 38; III 10, 5 f.; VI 1, 211; VII 1, 78.

49 Vgl. Michael Egerding: Die Metaphorik der spätmittelalterlichen Mystik. Bd. 2: Bildspender – Bildempfänger – Kontexte. Dokumentation und Interpretation. Paderborn u.a. 1997(b), S. 149. Ähnliche Formulierungen finden sich bei Adelheid Langmann: *dein hertz is mein, ich wil in deim hertzen sein* (›Die Offenbarungen der Adelheid Langmann‹ 46, 24); *dein sel ist mein, dein leip ist mein* (›Die Offenbarungen der Adelheid Langmann‹ 46, 30); *du pist mein und ich pin dein. wir sein vereint und süllen vereinet ewiclichen sein* (›Die Offenbarungen der Adelheid Langmann‹ 47, 9–11). Basis der brautmystischen Interpretation derartiger Wendungen ist erneut das Hohelied: *Dilectus meus mihi, et ego illi* (Ct 2,16). Ohly (1974) stellt den allgemeinhin als zum frühen Minnesang gezählten Tegernseer Liebesgruß in den weitläufigen Kontext der mittelhochdeutschen Literatur und widmet dabei der Hoheliedrezeption einen großen Raum. Siehe auch Helmut Ter-

lyrische Versatzstücke lesen lassen, mag Christinas Brautmystik einem ordensinternen Vorbild entnommen haben:[50]

> Die vom Hohenlied inspirierte und bis ins Wort bestimmte Lyrik der affektiven Prämonstratenser- und Zisterziensermystik bernhardischer Prägung mit dem Verlangen der Seele nach Vereinigung mit dem Bräutigam Christus steht der deutschen Strophe näher als irgend sonst bisher Bekanntes.[51]

Ohly denkt u.a. an den Prämonstratenser Hermann Josef von Steinfeld, der wohl das älteste Herz-Jesu-Lied dichtete und in seinem Jesus-Jubilus ganz der Liebessprache des Hohenlieds verhaftet ist.[52] Bei Hermann Josef tritt die spirituelle Vereinigung von Gott und Seele deutlich hervor,[53] so wie auch Christina eine Einheit mit ihrem Bräutigam bildet: *O du zarte sele myn, du byst myn vnd ich byn dyne, ich ewenclichen by dyr wille syn.* (CvH 49, 7 f.)[54] Einen designierten Ort dieser Vereinigung im Sinne eines *locus amoenus* thematisiert die Vita hingegen nicht direkt;[55] eine Bewegung der Liebe wie im Hohenlied wird nur impliziert, fehlt aber nicht völlig, wie etwa Ruh annimmt.[56] Der kaum explizit als solcher bezeichnete Aufstieg der Seele und das Verlangen nach dem noch in einer Vision wahrgenommenen verschwundenen Christus lassen Ansätze des brautmystischen Dilemmas von Zusammenkunft und Trennung erkennen.[57]

---

vooren: Minnesang, Maria und das Hohe Lied. Bemerkungen zu einem vernachlässigten Thema. In: Vom Mittelalter zur Neuzeit. Festschrift für Horst Brunner. Hrsg. von Dorothea Klein. Wiesbaden 2000, S. 15–47, hier S. 20, der die intertextuellen Parallelen zwischen Minnesang und Hoheliedexegese als »funktionale Zitate« deutet.

50 An einer Stelle wird der Liebesgruß um die deutsche Übertragung der Formel *in saecula saeculorum* (Phil 4,20) erweitert: *Jch byn yn dyr vnd du salt syn yn myr yn ewicheit der ewicheit.* (CvH 73, 10 f.)

51 Ohly (1974), S. 376.

52 Siehe dazu jetzt Racha Kirakosian: Das göttliche Herz im ›Fließenden Licht der Gottheit‹ Mechthilds von Magdeburg. Eine motivgeschichtliche Verortung. In: Euphorion 112 (2017 [d]).

53 Vgl.: *Sit in te et tu in eo, / Ut quiescat sic cum Deo / fiatque unus spiritus.* (Str. 9, zit. nach Ohly [1974], S. 377)

54 Hier wird der rhythmisierte Reim aufrecht erhalten, indem ›dyne‹ zu ›dyn‹ synkopiert wird.

55 In der Vita werden die Bilder des Weinkellers und des Gartens genannt; zum metaphorischen Gebrauch des *locus amoenus* in mystischen Texten siehe Volfing (2008), S. 346.

56 Vgl. Ruh (1993), S. 124: »Auch vom Hohenlied, häufig zitiert, geht kein Sehnen und Verlangen, kein Suchen und Finden aus.« Ruhs (ebd.) Aussage darüber, dass »[d]ie Seele [...] bereits am Ziel« sei, ist entgegenzuhalten, dass Christinas allmähliches Fortschreiten im Tugendleben und ihr allegorisches Hinaufziehen zum Liebhaber durchaus Entwicklungen darstellen.

57 Vgl. die folgenden Textstellen aus verschiedenen Sprecherpositionen (Christina, göttliche Stimme, Erzählerstimme): *Dar na an dem sondage da wart myn sele van groißer lyebden vff getzo-*

Die Grammatik der Vereinigung

Zusammenkunft und Trennung, Einheit und Abbruch sind auch auf der Organisationsebene des Vitentextes zu finden, wo sich in einer an das Hohelied angelehnten Reihung von Gottesbegegnungen eine »lockere, unsystematische Streuung der szenisch gebundenen oder metaphorischen Liebesgebärden« als »Wechsel von Liebessituationen« gibt, wie es Ohly für das ›St. Trudperter Hohelied‹ formuliert. Bei aller Unterschiedlichkeit der beiden Texte kann dasselbe für die Vita Christinas behauptet werden, wo der Perspektivenwechsel von Erzählbericht, göttlicher Rede und Ich-Bericht zu einer Art Liebesbewegung führen.[58]

Die Liebesbewegung ist auf der allegorischen Ebene eine gegenseitige, denn auch der Bräutigam sehnt sich an einer Stelle nach seiner Braut Christina.[59] Das Begehren Christinas wird oft in der Antizipation auf die eucharistische, d.h. mit der Kommunion einhergehende, Vereinigung artikuliert.[60] Daher ist die Eucharistie als liturgischer Raum der Vereinigung sowohl raumzeitlich als auch spirituell möglich, was sich mit der Erfüllung der Palmbaumallegorie auf Erden deckt. Die Trennung, der Liebesverlust nach der Vereinigung wird in der Brautmystik als eine körperliche Erfahrung verstanden, bei dem ein konkreter physischer Schmerz die Distanz zwischen Gottheit und Mensch markiert.[61] Andersherum ließe sich argumentieren, dass die Vita die mystische Vereinigung nicht einfach nur als eine punktuell und zeitlich auf Erden klar begrenzte und von einer Tren-

---

gen vor got. (CvH 64, 22 f.); *Jch komen schieer vnd holen dich.* (CvH 22, 10); *Da wart van stonden an die groiße freude zo soißem truren gewant vnd yr groiße begert wart da van gemeret* (CvH 3, 19–21).
58 Friedrich Ohly: Gebärden der Liebe zwischen Gott und Mensch im St. Trudperter Hohelied. In: Literaturwissenschaftliches Jahrbuch 34 (1993), S. 9–31, hier S. 10.
59 Vgl.: *Jn dem hogetzijt des heilgen Nycolay hait der lyebliche got, der soiße troiste aller bedroiffter hertzen, mit begerden vnd verlangen als eyn bruytgam zo syner aller lyebster bruyt gesprochen zo der selen* (CvH 60, 1–3).
60 Vgl.: *Des selben dags vnder der myßen begert sie gar des heilgen sacramentz yrs gemynten bruytgams.* (CvH 20, 17–19); *da begert sie auch yre lyeben heren zo entphangen myt groißer genaden. Da der pryster das heilge sacrament bracht getragen [...]* (CvH 22, 1–3); *da die seliche jonffrauwe daz heilge sacrament sultde entphangen, da brantte yre sele yn groißer lyebden* (CvH 32, 1 f.); *Da nu der pryster die boiße vff dede vnd sie nach jrem vßerwilten gyrlichen begerdte [...]* (CvH 32, 8 f.); *da hait sie entphangen daz wirdige heilge sacrament myt groißer lyebden vnd begerden* (CvH 35, 3 f.); *da sie vnseren heren myt groißer begerden entphangen haitte [...]* (CvH 78, 1 f.). Bei Hadewijch stehen Begehren und Erfüllung ebenfalls immer im Verbund, siehe dazu Almut Suerbaum: Between Unio and Alienation. Expressions of Desire in the Strophic Poems of Hadewijch. In: Desire and Dante and the Middle Ages. Hrsg. von Manuele Gragnolati u.a. London 2012(a), S. 152–163, insbes. S. 157. Siehe auch Monika Studer: Im Schatten der Gottesbraut. Engel in Mechthilds ›Fliessendem Licht der Gottheit‹. In: Euphorion 103 (2009), S. 225–251, insbes. S. 233, zur Eucharistie-Frömmigkeit bei Mechthild von Magdeburg.
61 Vgl. Haug (2000), S. 202.

nung gefolgten Einheit darstellen will. Der Vitentext siedelt die Inszenierung der mystischen Vereinigung jenseits jeglicher Zeitlichkeit an, sodass sie in zweifacher Hinsicht als Überwindung und Überbrückung, als Transzendenzerfahrung funktioniert; auf der erzählten Ebene zwischen Gottheit und menschlicher Seele, wo die Vereinigung das Diesseits wie das Jenseits einschließt:

> *Da sy also yn dyeßer beschauonge was vnd da myt yn gotlicher gebruchen myt vberflußicher soißicheit yn dießem paillas, vmbfynge der lyeblicher got yre sele gar sere fruntlichen myt synem vmbfengen myt beytden armen, myt eym yngoiße syner meynnunge, das er syne vßerwylten hie yn dyeßem leben vmbfencket myt synem lyncken armen myt soißer genaden vnd na dyeßem leben myt dem rechten armen der ewiger freuden.* (CvH 37, 24–29)

und zugleich auf einer textpragmatischen Ebene, wo das Reaktualisierungspotenzial des Textes die mystische Vereinigung als eine sich ständig im Werden begriffene performative Größe ermöglicht.[62]

Die Vereinigung vollzieht sich auch auf grammatisch-syntaktischer Ebene: Wenn es sich bei den oben diskutierten Stimmenbesetzungsmöglichkeiten sowohl um Christinas als auch um die göttliche Stimme handelt, dann hat man es mit der performativen »Einheit zweier Sprecher« zu tun.[63] Die Einheit der Sprechenden wird auch inhaltlich thematisiert, wenn Christina und Christus aus einem Munde zu singen scheinen:

> *Da sie daz seste responsorium syngen sult, da sach sie daz zarte kyntgyn vff dem boiche sitzen vnd myt yre syngen, daz iß yre vnd sy yme jn synem mont sancke.* (CvH 6, 20–22)

Diese stimmliche Verschachtelung demonstriert die Vereinigung als eine klanginduzierte Inszenierung. Eine Verschachtelung der Personen ist im Text auch direkt thematisiert:

> *›[...] Jch hayn dyr gegeben die clairheit, die myr myn vader hait geben, daz myr vereyniget syn. Myn vader ist yn myr vnd ich yn yme vnd du byst yn vns. Alles das ich hayn, das ist dyne, vnd was du haist, daz ist myn.‹* (CvH 71, 4–7)

Die »Konstruktion dieser Liebeseinheit« spiegelt sich in einer »Grammatik der Liebessprache wider«, wie das Hasebrink am Beispiel von Mechthilds ›Fließen-

---

62 S. u. Kap. 5.
63 Dicke (2003), S. 270. Vgl. ebd., S. 271, Anm. 20, mit Kritik an Haug (1984), S. 258, bezüglich Mechthilds von Magdeburg Gott-Seele-Dialoge und dem »rekapitulierenden« Versuch, eine vergangene *unio*-Erfahrung wiederabzurufen.

dem Licht‹ demonstriert.⁶⁴ Mechthilds ›Fließendes Licht‹ lässt sich in diesem Sinne mit der Vita der Christina von Hane vergleichen, da dort die Braut ebenfalls mit ihrem Geliebten eins wird und dies »sprachlich in der Form einer chiastischen Gegenüberstellung realisiert [wird]«.⁶⁵ Doch wie in der oben zitierten Passage gehen auch andere Stellen über einen »umgekehrten Parallelismus« hinaus,⁶⁶ und zwar wenn die Verschachtelung einer Einheit immer den Vater mitdenkt: ›[...] Jch byn yn mym vader vnd du byst yn myr vnd ich yn dyr.‹ (CvH 67, 4) Der Schluss des ersten kausallogischen Prämissenpaares innerhalb der Beziehungskette wäre, dass Christina im Vater ist, da sie in Christus und dieser im Vater ist. Stattdessen erfolgt hier die chiastische Liebesverklammerung von Braut und Bräutigam, die also in Gott vereint sind. Durch diese Dreierbeziehung bzw. diese Einheit in einem Dritten wird die Symmetrie der brautmystischen Verbindung nicht aufgehoben,⁶⁷ sondern in den Vater überführt.

4.1.2 Die Vielfachbesetzung der mystischen Braut

Es liegt in der Natur der Allegorie, dass die Rolle der mystischen Braut generell mehrfach besetzt werden kann. So betont Iser einer Hegelschen Ästhetik gemäß, dass ein allegorisches Wesen niemals ein Subjekt sei.⁶⁸ Dennoch sei ein »Interaktionsschema« vorhanden: »Wird der Leser [...] zu den Bedingungen des Autors tätig, dann ergibt sich die Chance, daß er die ihm zugedachte Rolle annimmt. Um eine solche Tätigkeit zu steuern, sind bestimmte Strategien notwendig.«⁶⁹ Eine solche »Leserregie« koppelt den rezeptionsästhetischen Ansatz deutlich an einen produktionsästhetischen.⁷⁰ Für die brautmystische Allegorie sind jedoch weniger die produktionsästhetischen Intentionen eines Autors ausschlaggebend als der traditionelle Interpretationsraum, den die Hoheliedrezeption in der monasti-

---

64 Hasebrink (2002), S. 444.
65 Hasebrink (2002), S. 446. Vgl. die in der Christina-Vita vorkommenden chiastischen Phrasen: *Du byst myn vßerwelte brůyt vnd ich byn dyne lyebhaber* (CvH 43, 4) und *du byst myn vßerwilte vnd ich byn dyn vßerwilter* (CvH 45, 2). Siehe auch die Willensvereinigung, die nach demselben chiastischen Prinzip formuliert wird: *Want myn wylle dyne wylle ist vnd dyn wylle myn wille ist.* (CvH 92, 15 f.)
66 Hasebrink (2002), S. 446.
67 Vgl. Hasebrink (2002), S. 445.
68 Iser (1972), S. 37. Nach Walter F. Otto (ohne Angabe), sei die Allegorie »in Wahrheit keine Personifikation, sondern eine Entpersonifizierung«, vgl. ebd.
69 Iser (1972), S. 67.
70 Iser (1972), S. 71.

schen Schriftlektüre öffnet. Sicherlich spielen Leserregie und Textstrategien auch im folgenden Untersuchungsteil eine besondere Rolle, doch geht es dabei weniger um eine bewusste Steuerung als um die Wirkkraft und Referenzwelt der Allegorie im Lektürekontext.

Die gesamte Christenheit als mystische Braut

Wie Volfing am Beispiel Mechthilds von Magdeburg vorführt, kann die Braut nicht nur für die einzelne Seele oder für Maria stehen, sondern auch die gesamte Christenheit bezeichnen.[71] Diese Option lässt sich an der Vita der Christina von Hane sowohl auf allegorischer wie auf grammatisch-narratologischer Ebene zeigen. Theologisch gesehen stehen sich bei der traditionellen Hoheliedauslegung die Konzepte der Braut-Kirche und der individuellen Braut nicht im Wege.[72] In der Christina von Hane-Vita führt ein auf alle auserwählten Seelen ausgedehntes Bild der brautmystischen Vereinigung in den allegorischen Weinkeller Gottes,[73] wo der sinnliche Genuss der göttlichen Vereinigung ›ausgekostet‹ wird: *Da wyrt eyn ygliche sele van lyebden droncken* (CvH 56, 30 f.).[74] Christinas Anspielung auf die entsprechenden alttestamentlichen Verse bezieht sich überdies explizit auf die Vereinigung Gottes mit allen Seelen: *Da wart got vnd die seliche selen vereyniget myt eynem willen ewanclichen.* (CvH 56, 21 f.)[75] Das Konzept der nüchternen Liebestrunkenheit wird in der patristischen Exegese von Ct 5,1 ([...] *cum aromatibus meis comedi favum cum melle meo bibi vinum meum cum lacte meo comedite amici bibite et inebriamini carissimi*) als die »Entwerdung in der Gotteserfahrung« gedeutet.[76] Während in der Christina-Vita das Weinkeller-Motiv auf eine Mehrzahl von Seelen angewendet wird, ist im ›Fließenden Licht der Gottheit‹ die einzelne Seele *wantrunken in der minne* und *übertrunken* (Mechthild von Magdeburg, ›Das

---

71 Vgl. Volfing (2003), S. 261.
72 Vgl. Volfing (2008), S. 346.
73 Siehe dazu Ruh 1990, S. 262.
74 Siehe ähnlich bei Adelheid Langmann: *und mich trenkest und mich trunken machst mit dem kipperwein deiner süezzen gotheit* (›Die Offenbarungen der Adelheid Langmann‹ 89, 3 f.). Siehe auch Volfing (2012), S. 264, zum auf dem Hohenlied (Ct 2,4) basierenden Motiv bei Mechthild von Magdeburg. Volfing (2001), S. 34 f., sieht die mystische Trunkenheit im Zusammenhang mit der Hochzeit von Kana, wo der Wein nicht zur Berauschung führe. Siehe auch Volfing (2008), S. 337 f., und Weiss (2000), S. 207–218, zum Konzept der nüchternen Liebestrunkenheit.
75 Auch bei Mechthild von Magdeburg steht das Weintrinken für die Vereinigung, wie Seelhorst (2003), S. 89, deutet, dabei jedoch das Konzept der nüchternen Trunkenheit ignorierend und so von einem nicht weiter differenzierten »Rauschzustand« sprechend.
76 Margot Schmidt (Hrsg.): Rudolf von Biberach. ›Die siben strassen zu got‹. Die hochalemannische Übertragung nach der Handschrift Einsiedeln 278. Quaracchi, Florentiae 1969, S. 159*.

fließende Licht der Gottheit‹ III 3, 12 f.) oder *minnenvúrig trunken* (Mechthild von Magdeburg, ›Das fließende Licht der Gottheit‹ VII 33, 4).[77] Dementsprechend schlägt Langer vor, dass in der Bernhardinischen Brautmystik die Allegorie des Weinkellers mit dem Privatbereich der einzelnen Seele assoziiert werde.[78]

Die Spannung zwischen einer einzigen erwählten Braut Gottes und der Schar der Einzelseelen,[79] wird in der Christina-Vita in einer Mehrfachadressierung der betroffenen Seelen evident. Die zuvor aus dem Fegefeuer befreiten Seelen sieht Christina in einer Vision (*yn dyeßem lyeblichen lyecht*) in die *hemelsche herbyrge* einziehen:

> *Da was der hemelsche vader wyrtde, der sone trosches vnd der heilge geiste was schencker, der sie selber drencket myt dem cyperen wynne, van dem geschreben steyt yn dem mynnenbuche: »Jch sal drencken myn vßerwylten van dem wyne des drubens Cypri.«* (CvH 56, 13–17)

Wie bei Mechthild von Magdeburg ist die Herberge hier ein Bild der brautmystischen Vereinigung, bei dem die (Gast-)Wirtschaft für das *connubium* oder *commercium* steht.[80] Anders als bei Mechthild, wo die Mystikerin zur Wirtin (*hûsvrouwe*) avanciert, bleibt für Christina der Vater Hausherr.[81] In ihrer *commercium*-Allegorie sind andere Seelen betroffen, die dank Christinas Fürbitte in den ›Genuss‹ der göttlichen Vereinigung kommen.[82] Damit vollführt Christina eine *imitatio Mariae*, denn Maria ist traditionellerweise diejenige, die für die Seelen im Fege-

---

[77] In einer weiteren Belegstelle wird das Hohelied erwähnt: *in dem bûche Canticis, da dú brut so trunken kûne vunden ist* (Mechthild von Magdeburg, ›Das fließende Licht der Gottheit‹ III 20, 14 f.).

[78] Vgl. Langer (1994), S. 51 f. Siehe auch Urban Küsters: Der verschlossene Garten. Volkssprachliche Hohelied-Auslegung und monastische Lebensform im 12. Jahrhundert (Studia humaniora 2). Düsseldorf 1985, S. 275, zur traditionellen Hoheliedexegese, wo das Weinkellermotiv im Gegensatz zum auf das Gemeinschaftsleben anspielende Gartenmotiv mehr Zurückgezogenheit bedeute.

[79] Auf die Problematik zwischen dem Vater-Kind- und Braut-Bräutigam-Verhältnis in der Beziehung von Gott und der Gesamtheit der Menschen weist Volfing (2003), S. 259, hin.

[80] Vgl. Mechthild von Magdeburg, ›Das fließende Licht der Gottheit‹ III 9, 30 f. Siehe auch Mechthild von Magdeburg, ›Das fließende Licht der Gottheit‹ IV 5, 14 und V 24, 25. – In Lamprechts von Regensburg ›Tochter Syon‹ steht das *connubium* mit der Weinmetapher in Verbindung, vgl. Volfing (2008), S. 338.

[81] Die Rolle des Bräutigams wird mit dem Schafhüter identifiziert, sodass die Vorstellung einer Seelenschar mit dem Bild der Schafherde überlappt, vgl.: *vnd er sprache also: ›Jch byn eyn guter hyrt, der gut hyrt vnd soiße bruytgam byn ich. Jch hayn myn schaiffe gefort yn die hemelsche weydte […].‹* (CvH 57, 23 f.)

[82] Das Konzept *gebruchen* geht mit der Vereinigung einher, vgl.: *Da zofloißen sie yn got myt eym vnsprechelichen gebruchen der soißer gotheit vnd lyeblicher menscheit.* (CvH 56, 24 f.)

feuer zuständig ist.[83] Die Erwählung der als Bräute identifizierten Seelen wird in der Christina von Hane-Vita innerhalb einer Baum-Allegorie plural gefasst:

> *Da wart myn sele getzogen gotlichen yn eyn groiße wytte konncklich huße woil aller freuden vnd wunnen. Dar yn waren gesamet eyn versamenunge der vßerwilten, die da noch hie vff der erden lyeffeten. Der erkant ich vil, wie woil ich der noch nye kaynt gesehen eyn haitte. Mytten jn dem huße gynge vff eyn baume vnd woische byß zo dem hemel. Der waiße hailffe roißen vnd hailffe lylien, want van des baumes frucht worden gespyßet alle die vßerwilten vnd got myt yn. Des baumes stamme detde sich mytden vff vnd darvß scheynne eyn hemels lecht.* (CvH 31, 20–27)

Der sinnbildlich mit jungfräulichen Seelen (Lilien) und Märtyrern (Rosen) geschmückte Baum verweist auf die Johannesoffenbarung, wo der Baum des Lebens die himmlische Bevölkerung speist.[84] Hier handelt es sich also um eine Jenseitsvision, in der die endgültige Vereinigung des mystischen Brautpaares alle erwählten Seelen umfasst.[85]

Auf der Textoberfläche wird die Mehrfachadressierung der mystischen Braut grammatisch und narratologisch durch die direkte, stets einen Leser implizierende Du-Anrede und durch die Perspektivierung der Sprecherstimmen evident. Wenn die Formel *O du vßerwilte bruyt Christi* (CvH 17, 31) erfolgt, dann ist damit potenziell jeder Leser angesprochen, was auch durch die nachträgliche Präzisierung *o soiße jonffrauwe Christina* (CvH 17, 36) nicht aufgehoben wird.[86] Ähnlich sind auch alle intradiegetisch an Christina gerichteten Anreden der göttlichen Stimme zu verstehen, die aber in ihrer Halbdialogartigkeit im Grunde offen adressiert sind.[87] Das wird an einer Stelle besonders deutlich, wenn der zuvor als *du eirwirdige sele myn* (CvH 65, 19 f.) angesprochene Adressat *eyn konynckynnen yn*

---

83 Zu Maria als Beauftragte des Fegefeuers siehe Klaus Schreiner: Maria, Jungfrau, Mutter, Herrscherin. München 1994, S. 162; siehe auch Maria als *co-redemptrix* bei Büttner (1983), S. 89, und Kinsley (1989), S. 237–244. Zu Maria im Zusammenhang mit der heilsgeschichtlichen Schwangerschaft siehe Kinsley (1989), S. 226–231. Rubin (2010), S. 131, verbindet die Bußfrömmigkeit mit der Marienandacht: »Mary was attractive not only for her purity, but for the intimacy that linked her to the redemption by her son«; siehe auch ebd., S. 224: »Mary was imagined as an intercessor of great force who could determine the destiny of souls.« Thali (2003), S. 7, stellt eine Verbindung zwischen dem Aufkommen der Marienfrömmigkeit und der Geburt des Fegefeuers im 12. Jahrhundert her.

84 Vgl. Apc 2,7 und Apc 22,2.

85 Vgl. Petrus W. Tax: Die große Himmelsschau Mechthilds von Magdeburg. In: ZfdA 108 (1979), S. 112–137, insbes. S. 119, zu Mechthilds von Magdeburg »große[r] Himmelsschau«.

86 Vgl. Suerbaum (2009), S. 37, zur textexternen Adressierung im ›St. Trudperter Hohenlied‹.

87 Hier wird der Definition von ›Halbdialog‹ nach Bernd Bastert: ›den wol er lêren rehte tuon‹. Der ›Winsbecke‹ zwischen Didaxe und Diskussion. In: Text und Normativität. XX. Anglo-German

mynem ryche (CvH 65, 27) sein soll. Die Unbestimmtheit der Königin zieht nach sich, dass mehr als nur eine Königin denkbar ist. Eine Multiplizierung der mystischen Braut wird somit vorausgesetzt. Die multiplen Besetzungsmöglichkeiten gehen so weit, dass zum Schluss der Vita nicht mehr klar ist, von wem eigentlich die Rede ist, von potenziell jeder jungfräulichen Seele, von Christinas Seele oder gar von Maria.[88]

Begriffsbezeichnungen wie Besetzung, Adressierung und Identifikation, mit denen hier gearbeitet wird, verweisen in ihrem performativen Charakter auf das Verständnis der brautmystischen Allegorie als einer Bühnenrolle mit entsprechendem Inszenierungspotenzial. Diese theatrale Indienstnahme der Allegorie bedingt aber die Vorstellung eines Verwandlungsvorgangs, einer Verkörperung. Brandstetter lokalisiert die Wirkkraft von Verwandlung im Theaterbereich am »Theatervorhang« und geht dabei von einer Doppelung des Geschehens aus, von einer »Bühne des Theaters« und einer »Bühne der Imagination«.[89] In der medialen Gegebenheit der Christina von Hane-Vita ist der Text selbst als ein dramatisches Script zu verstehen, in dem die phänomenalen Prozesse einer vom impliziten Leser imaginierten Bühne vorbereitet werden. Die Allegorie der mystischen Braut ermöglicht dem impliziten Leser die Vorstellung einer Verkörperung. Mit dem dramatischen Mittel des Dialogs wird dieses Inszenierungspotenzial nicht nur skizziert, sondern vollführt.

Dialoghaftigkeit

Der Dialog wurde als »zentrale Sprachform mystischer Texte« beschrieben.[90] Vom Vorherrschen der Dialogform wie etwa in Mechthilds ›Fließendem Licht‹ oder in den Offenbarungen Elisabeths von Schönau kann für die Christina von

---

Colloquium. Hrsg. von Elke Brüggen u.a. Berlin/Boston 2012, S. 303–318, insbes. S. 307, gefolgt; demnach ist ein Halbdialog dann gegeben, wenn nur eine Sprechpartie präzisiert wird.

88 Der letzte Textabschnitt scheint anfänglich hauptsächlich von Maria zu handeln, kippt aber im letzten Satz in *Die sele, die got beschauwen* (CvH 100, 72) um, sodass das zuvor verwendete weibliche Personalpronomen revidiert bzw. als die menschliche Seele betreffend gedeutet werden kann.

89 Gabriele Brandstetter: Lever de Rideau – die Szene des Vorhangs. In: Szenen des Vorhangs. Schnittflächen der Künste. Hrsg. von Gabriele Brandstetter/Sibylle Peters (Rombach Scenae 9). Freiburg 2008, S. 19–44, hier S. 25.

90 Seelhorst (2003), S. 71. Bereits Haas (1984b), S. 628, spezifizierte, dass der Dialog zwischen Braut und Bräutigam ein Gesprächsmodell der »älteren Mystik« sei und zählte darunter die Viktoriner, Bonaventura und Mechthild von Magdeburg. Der dialogische Rahmen hängt sicherlich mit der Hoheliedrezeption zusammen, vgl. Gray (2013), S. 371. Siehe auch Largier (2008), S. 367, zur mystischen Dialoghaftigkeit.

Hane-Vita zwar nicht die Rede sein.[91] Dennoch lassen sich systematische Ähnlichkeiten feststellen, wenn es um das persönliche Wechselgespräch zwischen den Figuren Christina und Gott geht. Die Dialogpartner lassen sich zudem auf die impliziten Adressaten des Textes ausweiten.[92] In der folgenden Dialoganalyse handelt es sich daher um eine virtuelle Performanz, also nicht um eine »historische Pragmatik«, die eine reale Gesprächssituation nachzeichnen möchte.[93] Das Potenzial einer dramatischen Performativität haftet dem Vitentext trotz seiner grundlegend narrativen Natur an, da das geschriebene Wort im mittelalterlichen Gebrauchskontext zugleich ein ausgesprochenes Wort sein will.[94]

Die Dialoghaftigkeit ist in der Christina-Vita zum größten Teil impliziert, denn es handelt sich zumeist um Halbdialoge, in denen nur ein Sprecher zu Wort kommt und in denen kein reziprokes Gespräch stattfindet. Es ist die göttlich figurierte Stimme, die sich wiederholt an ein Du richtet. Die auf diese Weise konstituierten Auditionen geben eine entkörperte Stimme jenseits jeglichen Gesprächskontexts wieder.[95] Auf die Frage Christinas hin, was Gott sei, erhält sie die Antwort, dass er u. a. eine Stimme sei:

> ›O wunderlicher got, was bystu?‹ Da quamme yre eyn antwert vß dem gotlichen hertzen: ›Jch byn eyn burnendes fûer, eyne luchtes lyecht. Jch byn eyn stymme, eyne wille. [...]‹ (CvH 21, 36–38)

Unterstreichungen im Text begleiten diese Passage, doch nur eine Phrase ist durchgehend, d. h. ohne Unterbrechungen der Linie an Wortgrenzen, unterstrichen: *Jch byn eyn stymme*. Das darauffolgende Konzept (*wille*) ist dagegen graphisch nicht hervorgehoben. Hier weist einmal mehr die schriftliche Materialität des Textes auf die Kernaspekte hin. Das Verlauten der Stimmen, das schließt die der göttlichen Figur ein, kann aber erst durch den Vollzug des Lesers erfolgen, der mit seiner Inszenierung als virtueller Dialogpartner auch die Halbdialoge vervollständigt.

---

91 Siehe zu Mechthilds ›Fließendem Licht‹ Andersen (2003), S. 235, und dies. (2000), S. 18 und S. 27 f.
92 Vgl. Suerbaum (2003), S. 243, zu Mechthilds ›Fließendem Licht‹.
93 Zur historischen Pragmatik siehe Angela Schrott: Heiligenrede in altspanischen Texten. Dialogprofile und Techniken der Redeinszenierungen bei Gonzalo de Berceo. In: Sprechen mit Gott. Redeszenen in mittelrerlicher Bibeldichtung und Legende. Hrsg. von Nine Miedema / Angela Schrott / Monika Unzeitig (Historische Dialogforschung 2). Berlin 2012, S. 107–126, insbes. S. 107.
94 Vgl. Suydam (1999a), S. 181–184.
95 Von den direkt wiedergegebenen Sprechanteilen, die in Bezug auf Christina als Adressatin erfolgen, sind solche zu unterscheiden, die ohne *inquit*-Formel eingeführt, d. h. nicht explizit adressiert sind, so z. B. in CvH 45, CvH 70, CvH 81 und CvH 82.

Anders verhält es sich mit den expliziten Dialogen, in denen die dramatische Inszenierung ein »distanzloses Erleben« ermöglicht.[96] Ein ausgeprägtes Frage-und-Antwort-Spiel, wie es bei Mechthild von Magdeburg oder bei Elisabeth von Schönau vorkommt,[97] gibt es in der Christina-Vita nur in Ansätzen. Wenige im Text verstreut auftretende Zwiegespräche weisen eine komplexe Gesprächsstruktur auf.[98] Rhetorische, von der göttlichen Sprecherposition ausformulierte Fragen heben den vollkommenen Status der mit Gott vereinten Seele hervor, und Antworten erscheinen unnötig, da die Evidenz des besonderen Status der Seele auf Grund der direkten Adressierung bereits gegeben ist. Fast inflationär gebrauchte Formulierungen wie *aller lyebste sele, wes begerstu nu me?* oder *aller lyeblichste sele myn, was wyltu me?* begleiten die göttlich figurierten Sprechanteile. Diese Phrasen, in denen es um die Fürbitte oder die Befreiung der Seelen aus dem Fegefeuer geht, erlauben, wie das auch bei Mechthild von Magdeburg der Fall ist,[99] ohnehin wenig Variation. Im starken Kontrast zu diesen repetitiven Formulierungen steht eine rasche Folge von kurzen Fragen und Antworten, die ein dramatisches Rückschlagspiel evoziert. Christina sieht in einer Vision, *wie er [got] syne genade gußet yn die guden vnd yn die boißen*:

> Da sprache myn sele: »Here, was wyltu doyn myt dyeßen?« Da sprache vnser here: »Jch doyne myn hertze vff entgene sy, dan iß ist wontde van lyebden.« Da sprach myn sele: »Here, wie bystu myt den, die dych alleyn lyeffe haynt vnd alle dynge dyeßer werelt versmehent?« Da sprach vnser here: »Die wille ich setzen yn guder luytde hertzen vnd ich wille yre arbeit eym gemeynne mynen riche gutde machen.« Da sprach myn sele: »Here, wie wyltu doyn den, die sich jn allen dogenden vbent?« Da sprach vnser here: »Jch gyßen myn genade yn sie, daz sie bloent vor mym angesicht, als der meye doyt yn syner rechter zijt.« Da sprach ich: »Here, wie wyltu myt den doyn, die gerren dyn lyden erent?« Da sprach vnser here: »Jch wylle yn setzen eynen stoylle yn myne grondeloiße gotheit.« Da sprach ich: »Here, was wyltu doyn myt den sonderen?« Da sprach vnser here: »Myt den wille ich syn dache vnd nacht vnd alle tzijt, vnd ich eyn wille mych nummer van yn gescheytden, byß daz sie also dyeffe yn die sunden fallent, daz sie mych vnder yre fuße tredent. Dan wil ich mych ewenclichen van yn scheytden.« Vnd vnser here sprache: »Die myr volgent, die wille ich brengen, da ich byn.« Vnd ich sache, daz got goiße dyeße funffe sachen sonderlichen yn eynen menschen, vnd er wyrcket daz alles yn gotlicher vereynionge vnd myt soißer gebruchonge syner selen. (CvH 97, 50–67)

---

96 Dicke (2003), S. 274.
97 Siehe dazu Andersen (2000), S. 27; siehe auch Ernst Benz: Die Vision. Erfahrungsformen und Bilderwelt. Stuttgart 1969, S. 152.
98 Darunter zählen Passagen in CvH 21, CvH 24, CvH 53 (vgl. hier das Motiv des Herabkommens in den Garten aus Ct 4,16) und CvH 62.
99 Vgl. Suerbaum (2003), S. 252.

Das Tempo der Schilderungen in dieser Passage lässt erst dann nach, sobald die göttliche Antwort mehr als nur einen einfachen Satz darstellt und im Anschluss daran – als würde der Dialog fortgesetzt – eine erneute *inquit*-Formel erfolgt, die narratologisch überflüssig ist, da der Sprecher nicht wechselt (*Da sprach vnser here* [...] *Vnd vnser here sprache*). Der Ich-Bericht Christinas rundet das verlangsamte Zwiegespräch ab. Der gesamte Abschnitt ist in sich logisch aufgebaut, sodass die anfängliche Vision nach einer Reihe von Auskünften am Absatzende in ihrem Zusammenhang und in ihrer Auswirkung zusammengefasst wird. Die Spaltung der Ich-Perspektive Christinas von der Stimme der Seele scheint am Anfang der Passage einleuchtend, da es sich um die Kommunikation zwischen Gott und jenem Part des Menschen handelt, der zu dieser Art von Kommunikation fähig ist, also der Seele. Zum Schluss kehrt die Stimme zum Ausgangssubjekt zurück und die Distanz zwischen Körper und Seele wird eingeholt; die Sprecherpositionen fallen zusammen. Ein solches inkonsistentes Verhältnis zwischen den Sprecherpositionen und ihrer Perspektivierung stellt an und für sich nichts Außergewöhnliches dar und kommt vor allem in Mechthilds ›Fließendem Licht‹ vor.[100] Der Wechsel zwischen erster und dritter Person in der vorgestellten Passage der Christina-Vita weist auf ein reflexives Selbstverständnis der Mystikerin hin. Doch spielt sich die Absetzung des Ichs von der Seele nicht wie bei Mechthild in »Körper-Seelen-Dialogen« ab;[101] sie konstituiert sich stattdessen im Dialog mit Gott. Die Begegnung der Seele mit dem Göttlichen erscheint dadurch direkter und im Leseakt nachvollziehbar.[102] Auch dass sich der Leser die Halbdialoge als vollkommen vorzustellen hat, schafft im textpragmatischen Sinn ein Reaktualisierungspotenzial, das zur Vermittlung der göttlichen Erfahrung dient. Während Largier in solchen Vergegenwärtigungsstrategien »die Narrativität des Textes« aufgebrochen sieht, die »in eine Ebene unreduzierbarer Gegenwart« überführt,[103] betont Seelhorst, dass es sich dabei immer noch um »Textphänomen[e]« handelt.[104] Die Christina von Hane-Vita stellt wohl eher einen Mittelweg dar, denn selbst wenn man kein biographisch-reales Erlebnis außerhalb des Textes supponieren will, kann der

---

100 Vgl. Dicke (2003), S. 273.

101 Suerbaum (2003), S. 248.

102 Vgl. Corey Wronski-Mayersak: Dialogic Melting: Representing Mystical Union and Its Instability in Marguerite Porete's ›Mirror of Simple Souls‹. In: Viator 42 (2011), S. 157–182, insbes. S. 173 f. Siehe auch ebd. zum Dialog in Margareta Poretes ›Spiegel der einfachen Seelen‹ als Ausdruck der Vereinigung zwischen Gott und Seele.

103 Niklaus Largier: ›Anima mea liquefacta est‹. Der Dialog der Seele mit Gott bei Mechthild von Magdeburg und Heinrich Seuse. In: Internationale katholische Zeitschrift Communio 16 (1987), S. 227–237, hier S. 236.

104 Seelhorst (2003), S. 72.

Dialog auf Grund des unmittelbaren Wechselgesprächs als »höchste Form der Vergegenwärtigung« und als »Ort der stärksten Präsenz« der Vereinigung angesehen werden.[105] Eine solche Vergegenwärtigung tritt besonders stark in dem oben zitierten einzigen ausführlichen und expliziten Dialog der Christina-Vita hervor.

4.2 Typologisch: Maria

Traditionell gesehen liegt der Hoheliedexegese eine mariologische Ausrichtung zugrunde, sofern »Maria als ›typus ecclesiae‹ und die einzelne Seele als Glied der Kirche verstanden werden«, so Ruh.[106] Maria wird seit dem 12. Jahrhundert symbolisch mit der mystischen Braut aus dem Hohenlied assoziiert,[107] wobei entsprechend der Trinitätsmystik »hier im Bräutigam nicht der historische Christus, sondern der dreifaltige Gott oder einzelne Personen der Dreifaltigkeit gesehen [werden], allen voran der Heilige Geist.«[108] Vor diesem Hintergrund erstaunt es, wie vernachlässigt die mariologische Komponente in der deutschsprachigen brautmystischen Forschung vor der Studie Thalis gewesen ist.[109] Auf die Identifi-

---

105 Haug (1984), S. 271, für Mechthild von Magdeburg. Darauf, dass die Unmittelbarkeit von Mechthilds mystischen Erfahrungen in den wechselhaften Dialogen inszeniert ist, hat bereits Wolfgang Mohr: Darbietungsform der Mystik bei Mechthild von Magdeburg. In: Märchen, Mythos, Dichtung. Festschrift zum 90. Geburtstag Friedrich von der Leyens. Hrsg. von Hugo Kuhn/Kurt Schier. München 1963, S. 375–399, insbes. S. 384, hingewiesen.

106 Ruh (1990), S. 254. Neben dieser rein exegetischen Deutung darf das kirchenpolitische Interesse nicht außer Acht gelassen werden, das zu dieser Interpretation führte. Da man selbst im Neuen Testament wenig über Maria erfährt, waren die Kirchenväter bemüht, Vorandeutungen der Jungfrau Maria im Alten Testament zu finden; zu diesem Problem und zu den verschiedenen Lösungsansätzen der Patristen siehe George H. Tavard: The Genesis of Mariology. In: A Feminist Companion to Mariology. Hrsg. von Amy-Jill Levine. London/New York 2005, S. 106–120, insbes. S. 107–116. Nicht allein das Alte Testament, auch apokryphe Schriften und mythische Modelle wurden herangezogen, um ein christliches Marien- und damit Frauenbild zu entwerfen. Kulturgeschichtlich hatte diese Form der teleologischen Exegese große Auswirkungen, wie das Beispiel der Schwarzen Madonna illustriert, deren Kult theologisch mit dem Vers Ct 1,5 (*nigra sum sed formosa*) erklärt wird, vgl. Jaroslav Pelikan: Mary through the Centuries. Her Place in the History of Culture. New Haven/London 1996, S. 25 f.; siehe dazu auch Schreiner (1994), S. 239–242.

107 Vgl. Mellon (2008), S. 118.

108 Górecka (1999), S. 339.

109 Thali (2003), S. 12, konstatiert ein »weitgehende[s] Desinteresse« der Forschung gegenüber Marientexten. Anne Bezzel: Der gesegnete Leib. Die Schwangerschaft Mariens als Gegenstand der Devotion im Kontext einer somatischen Religiosität des ausgehenden Mittelalters. In: Frömmigkeit – Theologie – Frömmigkeitstheologie. Contributions to European Church History. Festschrift für Berndt Hamm zum 60. Geburtstag. Hrsg. von Gudrun Litz/Heidrun Munzert/Roland

kation der Mystikerin mit der schwangeren Maria hat kürzlich Volfing hingewiesen und dabei deutlich gemacht, dass das Motiv der spirituellen Schwangerschaft nicht nur als Allegorie innerhalb der religiösen Kultur des Mittelalters verstanden werden sollte, sondern als Teil eines größeren Kontextes, bei dem es um die Frage nach dem Transzendenten (»Unendlichen«) im Immanenten (»Endlichen«) geht.[110] Zwar kennt die Christina von Hane-Vita kein ausgeprägtes spirituelles Schwangerschaftsmotiv, wie es von anderen Mystikerinnen bekannt ist,[111] jedoch nimmt Maria einen besonderen Platz ein, der im Folgenden unter verschiedenen Gesichtspunkten untersucht wird. Inwiefern die Figur Marias in der Vita in einem typologischen Verhältnis zur mystischen Braut steht, bleibt trotz der traditionellen Besetzungsmöglichkeit der Brautrolle durch Maria kritisch zu hinterfragen.[112] Die mariologische Deutung der mystischen Braut kann aber nur in Beziehung mit der Christina-Figur untersucht werden, da sich beide Figuren in einem beinahe kompetitiven Spannungsverhältnis zueinander konstituieren. Der Vergleich mit anderen Texten, die von Maria und ihrer Bedeutung für religiöse Praktiken handeln, schärft den Blick für die Besonderheit der Christina von Hane-Vita.

4.2.1 Maria memoranda

Zunächst ist die liturgische Dimension einer institutionalisierten Marienfrömmigkeit für spirituelle Texte des Mittelalters zu betonen.[113] Die Erwähnung Marias

---

Liebenberg (Studies in the History of Christian Traditions 124). Leiden/Boston 2005, S. 105–118, insbes. S. 111–115, geht auf Marias Schwangerschaft und deren Widerhall bei Mystikerinnen ein, verwendet aber wenige Primärtexte.

110 Vgl. Volfing (2012), S. 48: »Spiritual pregnancy should therefore not be seen as an isolated motif within medieval religious writing, but as part of a wider engagement with the problem of how the finite might contain the infinite.« – Auf die spirituelle Schwangerschaft wurde auch in der Birgitta von Schweden-Forschung hingewiesen, siehe dazu Sahlin (2001), S. 78 f.

111 In der Christina von Hane-Vita wird die Schwangerschaft Marias in der traktatähnlichen Abhandlung zum Wort *fiat* thematisiert, vgl. CvH 100.

112 Die Christina-Vita schlägt dieses typologische Verfahren vor. Ein alternatives Vorgehen, wie z. B. gestützt auf die Charakterisierung der *imitatio Mariae* Newmans, würde die brautmystische Komponente vernachlässigen, vgl. Barbara Newman: Intimate Pietis. Holy Trinity and Holy Family in the Late Middle Ages. In: Religion and Literature 31 (1999[b]), S. 77–101, hier S. 86: »To mourn Christ's death with his tearful mother, to plead beside him as his prayerful sister, to be crowned in heaven as his humble daughter, constituted three dimensions of an ›imitatio Mariae‹ that promised deification through an intimate, multiform union with God.«

113 Vgl. Thali (2003), S. 104–115. Siehe auch Heinzer (2004) und ders.: Die ›heilige Königstochter‹ in der Liturgie. Zur Inszenierung Elisabeths im Festoffizium ›Laetare Germania‹. In: Elisabeth

innerhalb des kirchlichen Kalenders lässt sich in der Christina von Hane-Vita von der Erwähnung anderer Heiligen insofern unterscheiden, als nur Maria gegenüber die Verehrung Christinas explizit genannt wird:

> *Dyße heilge jonffrauwe hait auch gehait sonderliche andacht zo der konynclicher jonffrauwen Marien, der moder godes. Also hait die moder godes auch sonderliche neygonge zo yre vmb die lyebde yrs sons.* (CvH 27, 1–3)

Das Verhältnis zwischen Maria und Christina bezieht stets Christus mit ein. Mit der hier betonten Verehrung Marias durch Christina ist der Bezug zur Organisation der Vita nach den Heiligenfesttagen gegeben. Marias Figur ist zunächst auf dieser strukturellen Ebene fassbar: an den jeweiligen ihr gewidmeten Festtagen, die in der mittelalterlichen Kirche die Alltäglichkeit einer *memoria*-Praxis markieren. Die Untersuchung Marias als typologische Besetzung der mystischen Brautrolle schließt die *memoria* ein, denn gerade allegorische Bedeutungskonstitutionen, folgt man dem Verständnis Walter Benjamins, vollziehen sich »im Modus der Erinnerung«, wie Fischer-Lichte anmahnt.[114] Der Sinnbezug ist also an die Praxis des Erinnerns gebunden. In der Christina-Vita ruft die Nennung eines kirchlichen Festtages solche Erinnerungs- und Vergegenwärtigungsprozesse auf.[115] Wie präsent das Gedenken Marias in der Christina von Hane verankert ist, lässt sich daher anhand der liturgischen Kontextualisierung der fünf traditionellen Marienfeste zeigen: Lichtmess (auch Mariä Reinigung, 2. Februar), Verkündigung (25. März), Himmelfahrt (15. August), Geburt (8. September) und unbefleckte Empfängnis (8. Dezember).[116]

Insbesondere das auf Lc 2,22–24 basierende Fest Mariä Reinigung wird wegen einer betonten Körperlichkeitsthematik traditionellerweise mit einer weiblichen Spiritualität zusammengebracht; freilich unter der Prämisse, dass es sich bei weiblicher zugleich um eine somatische Spiritualität handelt.[117] Paradox ist allerdings, dass sich Maria, die Jesus ohne Schmerzen zur Welt gebracht haben soll, dem jüdischen Reinigungsritual nach der Geburt gestellt haben sollte, doch die

---

von Thüringen – eine europäische Heilige. Hrsg. von Dieter Blume/Matthias Werner. Petersberg 2007, S. 215–225, zu liturgischen Aspekten mittelalterlicher Spiritualität.

114 Fischer-Lichte (2001), S. 129.

115 Largier (2008), S. 366, betont eine mit Erinnerungsprozessen zusammenhängende Nachempfindungspraxis als Teil der mystischen Kontemplation von Bibel, Gebet und Liturgie.

116 Allein die Lichtmess und die Verkündigung gehen auf biblische Quellen zurück. Die restlichen Feiertage sind apokryph, vgl. Mellon (2008), S. 82.

117 Schroeder (2006), S. 39, hebt den Aspekt der mütterlichen Identifikation der Mystikerin mit Maria während der Lichtmess hervor.

kirchliche Tradition erkläre diesen Umstand damit, so Mellon, dass Maria aus Demut und Ehrfurcht vor dem Brauch gehandelt habe.[118] Was die Christina von Hane-Vita betrifft, lässt sich am Festtag der Lichtmesse keine besonders somatische Mystik ablesen.[119] Zu diesen Anlässen spricht stets der göttliche Bräutigam zur Seele Christinas, wobei an einer Stelle wenigstens die Erleuchtung der Seele betont wird:

> *Jn purificacione beate Marie virginis wie yre sele myt gode vereyniget hait gestanden, hoire, wie er sprache zo yre : ›O myn seliche fruntdynnen, jch byn die soiße lyebde, die yn dyner selen ist. Jch byn der, der sy erluchte. Jch byn yre ewyge lyecht, sie schauwet yn myr. Dar vmb saltu hayn freude vnd freude sonder ende.‹* (CvH 41, 1–4)

Kiening zufolge tritt das Licht-Motiv an Mariä Reinigung in Visionstexten deswegen auf, weil Licht als besonderes Medium des Göttlichen galt.[120] Eine systematische Assoziation mit dem Licht-Motiv an diesem Kalendertag kennt die Christina von Hane-Vita allerdings nicht. Alle weiteren Visionen und Auditionen an diesem Festtag ignorieren das Licht-Motiv, welches hingegen zu anderen Anlässen erwähnt wird.[121] Stattdessen werden an Mariä Lichtmess Christinas mit dem Lilienvergleich etablierte Jungfräulichkeit und ihre Integration in der Trinität hervorgehoben (vgl. CvH 94).[122] Die Charakterisierung als reine Jungfrau rückt Christina in die Nähe Marias. In Konrads von Würzburg Mariengedicht die ›Goldene Schmiede‹ wird Marias Jungfräulichkeit mit der Abwesenheit sexueller Körperlichkeit begründet:

> *din herze luterbære*
> *was darunder also kalt*
> *von kiuschekeite manecvalt*
> *unt von ir reinen wirde,*
> *daz alles fleisches girde*
> *und heizer brœdekeit gelust*

---

118 Vgl. Mellon (2008), S. 82.
119 Ganz anders verhält es sich mit Angela von Foligno, wenn die Nacktheit des Jesuskindes, das man ihr an Mariä Reinigung in die Arme legt, wiederholt betont wird, vgl. Angela von Foligno, ›Instructiones‹ 19, 586–588.
120 Vgl. Kiening (2008), S. 109.
121 So z. B. an Gründonnerstag, vgl. CvH 43. – Allenfalls die Anrede als *aller clairste sele myn* an Mariä Reinigung kann als Lichtmetapher verstanden werden (CvH 94, 4). Dafür spricht der textinterne Vergleich von Licht mit Klarheit: *als der dage erlucht wyrt van der sonnen, also ist alle der hemelsche hoiffe erfrauwet worden van der clairheit jrer entgeynwirdicheit* (CvH 67, 8–10).
122 Damit besetzt Christina zentrale marianische Eigenschaften. Siehe Newman (1999b), S. 78 und S. 85 f., zu Marias dynamischem Familienverhältnis innerhalb der Trinität.

verloschen was in diner brust
unz uf den grunt der sinne. (›Die Goldene Schmiede‹ V. 1774–1781)[123]

Im Rahmen von Christinas Kampf gegen die sieben Todsünden wird das Austreiben sexueller Lust besonders betont. Was in der ›Goldenen Schmiede‹ allegorisch bleibt – Maria musste sich nicht spirituell reinigen, denn *verloschen* verweist nicht auf einen Prozess sondern auf einen Zustand – wird in der Christina-Vita ganz konkret:

daz sie wulte myt dem lyplichen fure leißen daz geistlichen fûre yrs fleiße. Vnd dar na eyn gaiffe sie nyt alleyn den lyffe yn daz fuer, als wyr van etzelichen leßen, daz sie bloiße satzen vff gluenden kolen, vnd damyt dede sie vß daz fûre der bekarunge. (CvH 10, 44–47)

Maria liefert als die Verkörperung aller Tugenden, als die bereits Perfekte, das Vorbild für Christina. Keuschheit wird, wie Kesting betont, als eine der Haupttugenden Marias angesehen.[124] Weiterhin wird *humilitas*, insbesondere im Kontext der Hoheliedexegese hervorgehoben, wie z. B. bei Rupert von Deutz und Honorius Augustodunensis. Das ›Arnsteiner Mariengebet‹ (oder auch ›Arnsteiner Marienleich‹) nennt ebenfalls ausdrücklich die *otmuode*. Dieser mittelrheinische Marienpreis aus der Mitte des 12. Jahrhunderts bietet sich zum Vergleich mit der Vita Christinas von Hane hervorragend an, weil es sich dabei um einen »im Umkreis prämonstratensischer Marienfrömmigkeit entstandenen, wohl zum Gebrauch in einer (klösterlichen) Gebetsgemeinschaft bestimmten« Text einer »Verfasserin« handelt.[125] Im ›Arnsteiner Marienleich‹ werden die Vorstellung der *imitatio* sowie die moralischen Qualitäten Marias unterstrichen, zu denen auch die Demut zählt:

Des eines bin ich van dir gewis   daz, frowe, sus geret bis
durch die dine groze guode,   durch du dine otmuode
durch du dine suvercheit,   durch du dine groze mildecheit.
(›Arnsteiner Marienleich‹ 30, 1–3)[126]

---

123 Konrad von Würzburg: ›Die Goldene Schmiede‹. Hrsg. von Edward Schröder. Göttingen 1926.

124 Vgl. Peter Kesting: Maria-frouwe. Über den Einfluss der Marienverehrung auf den Minnesang bis Walther von der Vogelweide (Medium Aevum 5). München 1965, S. 27.

125 Konrad Kunze: ›Arnsteiner Mariengebet‹. In: ²VL 1 (1978), Sp. 498–500, hier Sp. 498.

126 ›Der Arnsteiner Marienleich‹. In: Die Religiösen Dichtungen des 11. und 12. Jahrhunderts. Hrsg. von Friedrich Maurer: Bd. 1. Tübingen 1964, S. 433–452. (Die Stellennachweise geben Strophen- und Zeilenzahlen an.) – Demut wird weiterhin im ›Arnsteiner Marienleich‹ 49, 2 thematisiert.

Marianische Attribute werden in der Christina von Hane-Vita der menschlichen, d.h. im Erzählkontext Christinas Seele zugeordnet. An Mariä Lichtmess werden Christinas Seele eine unerschöpfliche Tugendhaftigkeit, die Wohnung Gottes, die sich auf alle Seelen erstreckende Liebe, die Weisheit und die Willenserfüllung Gottes zugesprochen.[127] Zwar scheint sich die Erwähnung des Kalendertags hier nicht direkt auf den Visionsinhalt auszuwirken, da die Aussagen nicht mit dem eigentlichen Inhalt der Lichtmessfeier in Verbindung stehen.[128] Anders als bei den Mystikerinnen Mechthild von Magdeburg und Margareta Ebner wird nichts über die Umstände der Geburt Christi oder das folgende Reinigungsritual erwähnt.[129] Dennoch ist die identifizierende und typologische Funktion der *Maria memoranda* hervorzuheben, denn die Beschreibung Christinas steht ganz im Sinne einer *imitatio Mariae*.

Als Braut Christi orientiert sich Christina an Maria als ultimatem Vorbild, mehr noch: Sie wird ihr zunehmend gleichgestellt. An Mariä Verkündigung nämlich werden Christina die »sieben Freuden der seligen Jungfrau Maria« *gevffenbairt* (CvH 67, 1 f.), was aus der Sprecherposition der Mystikerin nachdrücklich betont wird, dabei auslassend, dass es sich um marianische Eigenschaften handelt: *Als ich was yn dießem lyecht, da verkontdiget got myr die sieben freuden* (CvH 67, 4 f.). Die Attribuierung auf Maria wird im weiteren Verlauf nicht noch einmal aufgegriffen. Selbst wenn die folgenden sieben Freuden unpersönlich formuliert sind, richten sie sich textintern an Christina, die dadurch als Mutter Gottes stilisiert wird:[130] 1. Sie steht über der Schar der Engel und Heiligen, 2. sie ist über alle Engelchöre erhaben,[131] 3. ihre Gegenwart ist himmlisches Licht, 4. sie ist eine Mutter des höchsten Königs, 5. ihr Wille ist vereinigt mit dem Willen der Trinität, 6. sie belohnt alle ihre Diener, 7. ihre Freude ist ewiglich (vgl. CvH 67).[132] Besonders in der offenen Formulierung *eyner moder des vbersten konyncks* wird deutlich, dass es sich hier nicht allein um die biblische Mutter Gottes handelt, sondern vielmehr um die Besetzung einer Rolle, sodass Maria in den Hintergrund rückt und allenfalls als Vergleichsfolie der zentralen Figur Christinas dient. Die

---

127 Vgl. CvH 64.

128 Im Gegensatz dazu steht die Liturgie bei Angela von Foligno im Vordergrund, siehe dazu Schroeder (2006), S. 45 f. Die Liturgie beeinflusst Visionen auch bei Margery Kempe und Birgitta von Schweden, siehe dazu ebd., S. 48.

129 Zu Mechthild von Magdeburg und Margareta Ebner siehe Bezzel (2005), S. 111.

130 Siehe auch die sieben Marianischen Tugenden in den ›St. Georgener Predigten‹ 20, 132–140.

131 Maria als Führerin der himmlischen Chöre steht in Anlehnung an die alttestamentliche Figur Miriams, vgl. Pelikan (1996), S. 28.

132 Die Bedeutsamkeit dieser Passage wird in der Handschrift mit vermehrten roten Verzierungen hervorgehoben, vgl. Straßburg, BNU, Ms. 324, Bl. 308ʳ–309ʳ.

Freuden selbst beschreiben ausnahmslos himmlische Freuden, womit Christinas Vita dem ›Liber specialis gratiae‹ Mechthilds von Hackeborn nahesteht, wo die sieben geläufigen irdischen, auf Marias Lebensgeschichte basierenden Freuden spirituell erhöht werden.[133] Während an anderer Stelle Christina an Mariä Verkündigung weitere Attribute Marias von der göttlich figurierten Stimme zugesprochen werden (vgl. CvH 75), weist der letzte Abschnitt der Vita ganz besonders auffällige theologische Standpunkte zur mariologischen Brautmystik auf (vgl. CvH 100).[134]

Am Festtag Mariä Himmelfahrt spricht die göttlich figurierte Stimme fast immer direkt, wobei die Audition an einer Stelle innerhalb der Vision Christinas stattfindet.[135] Im Kontext der Himmelfahrt erfährt Christina sieben Weisheiten, die sie in ihrem spirituellen Werdegang unterstützen.[136] Christina wird hier offenbar mit Maria als *sedes sapientiae* verglichen, auch wenn damit keineswegs die *artes liberales* gemeint sind, für die Maria im Mittelalter Patin stand.[137] Christinas Lehren (*stucke*) greifen hingegen auf den zweiten Teil des Buches der Weisheit zurück und stehen systematisch mit dem salomonischen (in der Exegese durchaus mariologischen) Thron in Verbindung (vgl. 1 Rg 10,8),[138] wie das etwa in der ›Goldenen Schmiede‹ explizit wird.[139] Als Tochter Gottes belehrt die Weisheit wie eine liebende Mutter (vgl. Sap 6,21–8,18), womit Anknüpfungspunkte zu

---

133 Vgl. Mechthild von Hackeborn, ›Liber specialis gratiae‹ I 41, 125. Einen Überblick über die textgeschichtliche Entwicklung der sieben Freuden bietet Elke Bayer: Sieben Freuden Marias. 1. Mittelhochdeutsche Literatur. In: Marienlexikon. Hrsg. von Remigius Bäumer / Leo Scheffczyk. 6 Bde. St. Ottilien 1988–1994, Bd. 6 (1994), S. 154 f. Siehe auch Thali (2003), S. 134 f., zu den sieben Freuden bei Friedrich Sunder.

134 Siehe unten Kap. 5.2 und Kap. 5.3.

135 Vgl. CvH 100 und CvH 52. Im Kontrast zu diesen Auditionen innerhalb des Visionsberichts steht eine Audition in direkter Rede innerhalb des Erzählberichts: *In dem hogezijtlichen dage assumpsionis Marie reyte er aber eyns myt yre vnd sprach also zo yrer selen dyeße wortte* […] (CvH 87, 1 f.).

136 Vgl. CvH 29. Kurt Köster: Christina von Hane (Hagen), gen. Retters. In: ²VL 1 (1978), Sp. 1225–1228, hier Sp. 1227, meint in diesen sieben Weisheiten die Ankündigung einer »besondere[n] Andacht für die hl. Weisheit« zu lesen, die später »Seuse in der Frauenmystik heimisch machen sollte«.

137 Siehe dazu Michael Stolz: Maria und die Artes liberales. Aspekte einer mittelalterlichen Zuordnung. In: Maria in der Welt. Marienverehrung im Kontext der Sozialgeschichte 10.–18. Jahrhundert. Hrsg. von Claudia Opitz u. a. (Clio Lucdenensis 2). Zürich 1993, S. 95–120.

138 Auch ikonographisch lässt sich eine Verbindung zwischen dem Festtag und dem Thronmotiv herstellen, da die Himmelfahrt im Laufe des Hochmittelalters immer stärker mit Marias Himmelskrönung repräsentiert wurde, siehe dazu Rubin (2010), S. 142. Zur brautmystischen Konnotation des Thrones siehe ebd., S. 266.

139 In der ›Goldenen Schmiede‹ ist Maria Salomons Thron, vgl. ›Die Goldene Schmiede‹ V. 1734–1785.

einer sich auf die Liturgie auswirkenden Mariologie gegeben sind.[140] Die Christina offenbarten Weisheiten lassen sich im Erzählbericht wie ein Tugendkatalog lesen, der im Zusammenhang mit der besonders reinen Seele Marias steht, da Maria dem mittelalterlichen Verständnis nach zu denjenigen gehört, die auf Grund ihrer Reinheit und ihrer besonderen Beziehung zu Christus mit ihrem irdischen Körper in den Himmel auffahren.[141] Der nicht verfallende Körper Marias stünde dann in allegorischer Beziehung zur geistlichen Askese, die Christina den Lebensweisheiten zufolge einhalten soll, um in eine *gotliche heymmelicheit* zu gelangen (CvH 29, 13 f.).

An nur einer von insgesamt drei Stellen, die das Fest der Mariä Geburt betreffen, wird das Thema der Geburt motivisch aufgegriffen:[142]

> *Jn dem hogezijt der geburte der jonffrauwen Maria sprache got der vader also zo yre: ›Du gebenedite sele myn, erfrauwe dich. Du haist yn dyr mynen eynigen gebornen sonne [...].‹* (CvH 88, 1–3)

In der zuletzt zitierten Passage wird die Teilhabe am Sohn thematisiert. Hier handelt sich nicht etwa um die Geburt Marias, sondern um das Weihnachtsgeschehen.[143] Neben der historisch-biblischen Gegebenheit der Menschwerdung (*eynigen, gebornen sonne*) wird aber auch auf die andauernde Gottesgeburt angespielt.[144] Jedenfalls zeigt sich, dass der liturgische Rahmen an der genannten Stelle nur auf der Textoberfläche das Thema der Geburt aufgreift.[145]

Das im modernen Kirchenjahr erste Marienfest der unbefleckten Empfängnis ist im Mittelalter eher christologisch angelegt.[146] Da sich der Kult dafür erst

---

140 Vgl. Josef Scharbert: Weisheitsbücher. In: Marienlexikon. Hrsg. von Remigius Bäumer/Leo Scheffczyk. 6 Bde. St. Ottilien 1988–1994, Bd. 6 (1994), S. 702 f., insbes. S. 703. Siehe auch Rubin (2010), S. 274: »[...] Mary herself was the embodiment of knowledge.«

141 Die Himmelfahrt wird dabei mit einem Einschlafen assoziiert (*dormitio*), vgl. Schmitt (2006).

142 An anderen Festtagserwähnung spielt die Geburt keine Rolle, vgl. CvH 30 und CvH 53.

143 Siehe Büttner (1983), S. 77–85, zur Geburt Christi innerhalb der Marienverehrung.

144 Es ist der letzte Abschnitt der Vita, der das Thema der Geburt im spirituellen Sinne aufgreift. Zur Gottesgeburt in der Seele siehe unten Kap. 5.2.

145 Die Erwähnung der Geburt Chrisi am Festtag der Mariengeburt dürfte aus historisch-exegetischer Sicht nicht überraschen, da auf Grund einer wiederholten unüblichen Geburt eine Analogie zwischen Marias Geburt und der ihres Sohnes besteht, die man als paradigmatische Beziehung bezeichnen kann. Zur historischen Debatte über Marias Erzeugung siehe Rubin (2010), S. 173–176.

146 Bis ins 18. Jahrhundert hinein verweigerten Päpste, das Fest der unbefleckten Empfängnis mariologisch zu verstehen, vgl. Mellon (2008), S. 85. Zum Verständnis der unbefleckten Empfängnis im Mittelalter, siehe auch Ann W. Astell: Chaucer's ›St. Anne Trinity‹. Devotion, Dynasty, Dogma, and Debate. In: Studies in Philology 94 (1997), S. 395–416.

nachmittelalterlich entwickelt, überrascht es nicht, dass dieses Fest wenig Raum in der Christina von Hane-Vita einnimmt.[147] Im Rahmen der einzigen Erwähnung handelt die Audition vom Emanationsgedanken und von der Gottesvereinigung.[148]Allerdings wird auch auf die Inthronisierung der Seele angespielt (*Du haist gegryffen yn mynen vbersten throne* [CvH 59, 3 f.]), welche als mariologische Komponente gedeutet werden könnte.

Neben den liturgischen Festtagen werden in der Vita zwei der zu bestimmten Zeiten gesungenen Lobgesänge auf Maria genannt.[149] Christina befindet sich im Gebet an Maria, als eine Mariensequenz eine Vision evoziert:

> *Also ist iß geschyt vff eyn tzijt, als yn dem conuent wart gesongen die sequencia Aue preclara vnd der den verße Audi nos, da sach sy die moder godes vff yren kneen beden vor den conuent.* (CvH 27, 3–6)

Sowohl die Sequenz ›Ave praeclara‹ als auch das ›Ave Maria‹ werden nicht ausschließlich an Marienfesttagen gesungen. Der siebte Vers des ›Ave praeclara‹ beginnt mit den hier erwähnten Worten *Audi nos*. An dieser Stelle sieht Christina Maria kniend für den Konvent beten, womit der fünfte Vers der Sequenz aufgegriffen wird: *Ora, virgo, nos illo pane caeli dignos effici* (Hermann von Reichenau, ›In assumptione B. Mariae‹).[150] Der Sequenztext und die Vision Christinas sind ineinander verflochten. Liturgie und Vision befinden sich in einem Wechselverhältnis, wie es Heinzer für Elisabeth von Schönau beobachtet, nämlich dass die Liturgie den Visionsinhalt beeinflusst.[151] Während diese Vision eine kniende, d.h. fürbittende Madonna darstellt, wirft sich Christina beim nächsterklingenden Mariengesang, ihr Vorbild imitierend, auf den Boden:

> *Auch vff eyn tzijt als man Aue Maria zo abent luytde, da ylet sy sych also sere zo der erden, daz sie eyn knee also swerlichen verwont hait. Dyße hait erkant die aller soiste jonffrauwe vnd aller myldicheste moder Maria, vnd sie hait getroiste yre aller getruweste dyenerynnen vnd sy ist yre erscheynen yn dem slaiffe vnd sy droge yn yren zarten henden eyn boiße myt koistlicher salben vnd sie hait yre dyenerßen gesont gemacht vnd sye hait yre befollen, daz sy vortter sennfftlichen sulde nyeder knen.* (CvH 27, 6–12)

---

147 In ihren Untersuchungen zur Marienspiritualität im Kloster Engelthal lässt Thali (2003), S. 108, dieses Kirchenfest dementsprechend gänzlich aus.

148 Vgl. CvH 59.

149 Siehe Rubin (2010), S. 191–196, zur gesungenen Marienverehrung in der Liturgie.

150 Hermann von Reichenau: ›In assumptione B. Mariae‹. In: Analecta hymnica Medii Aevi. Hrsg. von Clemens Blume / Guido M. Dreves. Leipzig 1886–1915. Bd. 50 (1907), Nr. 241, S. 313 f.

151 Vgl. Heinzer (2004), S. 474.

Das Läuten des ›Ave Maria‹ deutet auf eine Angelusglocke im Kloster Hane oder zumindest auf einen entsprechend erkennbaren Rhythmus des Glockenläutens hin.[152] Jedenfalls initiiert die Akustik der monastischen Lebenswelt das Gebet Christinas.[153] Dabei ist ihre Gebetshandlung von der zuvor beschriebenen Marienvision inspiriert. Christinas *imitatio Mariae* wird anschließend im Schlaf anerkannt, indem Maria als *mater misericordiae* die Wunden Christinas pflegt.[154] Damit ist eine bestimmte Rollenfiguration Marias gegeben, die liturgisch-pragmatisch definiert ist und dann hervortritt, wenn die *memoria* in lebensweltliche Folgen umschlägt. In diesem Beispiel ist es die Rolle der fürsorglichen Maria, die sich in Christinas Traum niederschlägt – genauer: die in dem vorlaufenden Gebet thematisierte Fürbitte für das Kloster unterstreicht diese besondere Funktion Marias, die in Marientexten der Zeit einen prominenten Platz einnimmt, wie das der ›Arnsteiner Marienleich‹ demonstriert:

> *Hilf dinen armen luden   die dich van allen landen*
> *widene ane ruofent   und des an dir gesuochent!* (›Arnsteiner Marienleich‹ 46, 1–2)

> *Ich bevelen dinen hulden   die mine sunderholden,*
> *die mir sint alse lief   alse min selves lif.*
> *daz du unsen heren   gewerdes des gewillen,*
> *daz er sie behuode naht unde dach   van aller slahten ubele daz in gewerren mach.*
> *daz er in geven wille   die sine lieven hulde*
> *unde ze lezzes uns gesamene   in deme ewigeme levene* (›Arnsteiner Marienleich‹ 48, 1–6)

Die *memoria Mariae* im klösterlichen Kontext ist, wie die Christina von Hane-Vita illustriert, neben der privaten Anbetung auch an den Festtagen präsent, die zu

---

152 Maria Crăciun: Ora pro nobis sancta Dei genitrix. Prayers and Gestures in Late Medieval Transylvania. In: Ritual, Images, and Daily Life: The Medieval Perspective. Hrsg. von Gerhard Jaritz. Wien 2012, S. 107–138, insbes. S. 109, beschreibt, wie das im 13. Jahrhundert von den Franziskanern eingeführte Angelusläuten rasch verbreitet und päpstlich bestätigt wurde.
153 John H. Arnold/Caroline Goodson: Resounding Community. The History and Meaning of Medieval Church Bells. In: Viator 43 (2012), S. 99–113, hier S. 121, unterstreichen den »aktivierenden Effekt« des Glockenläutens für das tägliche Leben im Mittelalter: »A key term here is ›roused‹ (›excitare‹): that the faithful be not just summoned, but roused to spiritual activity.« Siehe auch Richard Kieckhefer: ›Ihesus ist unser!‹ The Christ Child in the German Sister Books. In: The Christ Child in Medieval Culture: Alpha es et O! Hrsg. von Mary Dzon/Theresa M. Kenney. Toronto 2012, S. 380–399, insbes. S. 167, der von einer »liturgischen Vitalität« beim Hören des Glockenläutens spricht.
154 Zur im Schlaf erscheinenden Maria in Legendenerzählungen siehe Jean-Marie Sansterre: La Vierge Marie et ses images chez Gautier de Coinci et Césaire de Heisterbach. In: Viator 41 (2010), S. 147–178, insbes. S. 156 f.

den feierlichsten Ereignissen des Kirchenjahres gehören.[155] Das analoge Verhältnis zwischen Christina und Maria wird durch die sich wiederholenden Ereignisse im Laufe mehrerer Kirchenjahre konstituiert, sodass Christinas Leben in eine allgemeine Heilsgeschichte eingebettet erscheint. Mit dem Titel dieses Unterkapitels, einer Gerundivum-Konstruktion auf die Funktion der liturgischen Maria hin ausgerichtet, wird die Vollzugsnatur des Gedenkens formuliert.[156] So wie Christina in ihrer Marienandacht kann sich der Leser in die *memoria* Christinas vertiefen. Dass Maria selbst als betende Figur vorkommt, dient intradiegetisch Christina als Vorbild. Eine *memoria Mariae* ist hier fast schon autoreferentiell: Der mittelalterlichen Theologie nach ist Maria der erste Mensch, der die *memoria*-Praxis ausführt, und zwar in ihrer Funktion als *mater compassionis*.

4.2.2 Mater compassionis, mater misericordiae, mater Christi

Mittelalterliche Leidens- bzw. Nachempfindungskonzepte sind zentral für die Rolle Marias als barmherziger Mutter.[157] Bereits die Kirchenväter betonten Maria als *mediatrix* und wohl seit dem in karolingischer Zeit entstandenen Hymnus ›Ave maris stella‹ wird sie auch in der Liturgie um aktive Hilfe bei der Erlangung des Seelenheils gebeten. Bereits in der frühen lateinischen Hymnenpoesie nimmt sie eine »Mittlerrolle zwischen dem sündigen Menschen und dem streng als Richter auftretenden Gottessohn« ein.[158] Im ›Arnsteiner Minneleich‹ wird die Rolle als Mittlerin mit intertextuellen Verweisen auf die Hymnik etabliert:[159]

> *Maria godes druden,*   *Maria trost der armen,*
> *Maria stella maris,*   *zuofluht des sundæris,*
> *porze des himeles,*   *burne des paradises,*
> *dan uns du genade zu gefloz,*   *du uns ellenden entsloz*
> *daz unse rehte vaterlant,*   *nu gif uns, frowe, dine hant.* (›Arnsteiner Marienleich‹ 42, 1–5)

> *Maria gratia plena,*   *du bis vol aller gnaden* (›Arnsteiner Marienleich‹ 50, 3)

---

155 Vgl. Fulton (2002), S. 196.
156 Vgl. Gerhard Fink/Friedrich Maier/Karl Bayer (Hrsg.): System-Grammatik Latein. Bamberg/München 1997, S. 169, zur Verwendung des Gerundivums zur Bezeichnung eines Vorgangs.
157 So z. B. in Priester Wernhers ›Marienleben‹; vgl. Strohschneider 2014, S. 160–162, insbesondere zur heilsgeschichtlichen Typologie Marias und dem Funktionskonzept von Schmerz.
158 Caliebe (1985), S. 269, Anm. 19. Siehe auch Kesting (1965), S. 23.
159 Vgl. ›Arnsteiner Marienleich‹ 42–47.

Fulton argumentiert, dass die Mittlerrolle Marias als brautmystische Komponente verstanden werden kann, weil die Hoheliedexegese die Identifikation
mit Marias Leiden ermögliche.[160] Der im 11. und 12. Jahrhundert ansteigende
Marienkult hängt mit der neutestamentlichen *compassio* zusammen, die nicht
vom alle Erfahrungen übersteigenden Leiden Christi, sondern von einer nachvollziehbaren Art des Leidens im Erinnern handelt.[161] In diesem Sinne könnte
man verleitet sein, das Nachempfinden der Passion Christi bei Mystikerinnen als
eine doppelte *imitatio* zu verstehen, die auf das Mitgefühl Marias gründet, mit
welcher sich die Mystikerin sodann identifiziert. Sicherlich gibt es entsprechende
Hinweise bei Birgitta von Schweden und anderen Mystikerinnen, wo das Leiden
Christi auf diese zweistufige Weise nachempfunden wird; in der Christina von
Hane-Vita wird jedoch mehrfach betont, dass Christinas Leiden in ihrem Aufop-
ferungscharakter dem Christi gleich komme.[162] Es handelt sich also nicht nur um
ein innerliches, meditatives oder imaginatives Leiden, das sie verspürt, sondern
um reale körperliche Zustände, die auch äußerlich sichtbar werden.[163] Das ist ein
Indiz dafür, dass Christina das innerliche Leiden Marias überhöht.[164]

Die Dominanz der somatischen Spiritualität in der Christina von Hane-Vita
schlägt sich auch in einer starken Eucharistiefrömmigkeit nieder, wie sie etwa
im ›Legatus‹ Gertruds von Helfta zu finden ist.[165] Die Eucharistie-Frömmigkeit

---

160 Vgl. Fulton (2002), S. 197.

161 Vgl. Fulton (2002), S. 199–201.

162 Vgl.: *Also als daz golt wyrt geproffet yn dem füer, also ist sie gantze durch luter worden jnwendich vnd vßewendich durch yre groiße lyebde vnd gedult, die sy leytde vor alle die gantze werelt.*
(CvH 65, 28–30); *Dyne arbeit dragen ich myt dyr, dan du lydest vor alle die crystenheit myt myr*
(CvH 64, 17 f.). – Als Leidensmystikerin ähnelt Christina in ihrer Verbundenheit mit Christus Margareta Ebner, siehe dazu Janota (2007), S. 275 f. und S. 299.

163 Ein innerliches Nachempfinden geschieht in der Betrachtung des Leidens Christi, vgl.
CvH 16 und CvH 17. Siehe auch die äußerlich wahrnehmbaren Krankheitszustände in CvH 30; CvH
38; CvH 57; CvH 63; CvH 65. Damit steht Christina von Hane in der Tradition einer Verinnerlichung
der Passion, wie sie in patristischen Quellen vorgezeichnet wird, siehe dazu McGinn (2001b).

164 In den spätmittelalterlichen Marienklagen, Marienleben, Passionshymnen und -spielen
wird Marias innerer Schmerz analog gesetzt zu den äußeren Schmerzen Christi, vgl. Schreiner
(1994), S. 104 f.

165 Allerdings ist im ›Legatus‹ die Eucharistiefrömmigkeit stark mit der Inkarnation Christi im
Körper Marias verbunden, vgl. Gertrud von Helfta, ›Legatus divinae pietatis‹ IV 3, 4, 50–52; siehe
dazu Volfing (2012), S. 52; siehe auch Ella Johnson: To Taste (›Sapere‹) Wisdom (›Sapientia‹).
Eucharistic Devotion in the Writings of Gertrude of Helfta. In: Viator 44 (2013), S. 175–200. Die
Eucharistie lässt sich aber im Fall Christinas von Hane nicht wie etwa bei Hildegard von Bingen
mit Maria in Verbindung bringen, wo die Gebärmutter Voraussetzung der Fleischwerdung Christi
ist, vgl. dazu Sally Cunneen: In Search of Mary. The Woman and the Symbol. New York 1996,
S. 162–165. Auch Agnes von Blannbekin äußert sich in einer eucharistischen Vision über den

könnte darauf hinweisen, dass die Marienrolle weiterhin in den Hintergrund gerät. So führt Fulton für die monastische Welt aus, dass während Christus täglich in Form des Sakraments präsent sei und inkorporiert werden könne, es sich bei Maria hingegen um eine »virtuelle Präsenz« auf dem Altar handele.[166] Dass Maria aber gerade in ihrer Rolle als Erlöserin der Kranken und Schwachen sehr wohl mit dem Gedanken der Wandelkraft der Eucharistie assoziiert wurde, zeigt ein Auszug aus Konrads ›Goldener Schmiede‹:

> *die siechen und die weichen*
> *kan din genade spisen,*
> *du bist ein oblatisen*
> *des lebenden himelbrotes.* (›Die Goldene Schmiede‹ V. 494–497)

In der Christina von Hane-Vita bedeutet die Präsenz Marias auf dem Altar ungeachtet eucharistischer Anklänge den Zugang des Menschen zu einer von Gott autorisierten Fürsorge.[167] Affektive Züge der Marienverehrung treten im gesamteuropäischen Kontext erst ab dem 12. Jahrhundert in den Vordergrund.[168] Mechthild von Magdeburg spricht schon zu Beginn des ›Fließenden Lichts‹ von *sin minnenklichú muoter Maria* (Mechthild von Magdeburg, ›Das fließende Licht der Gottheit‹ I 2, 16); Maria nennt Adelheid Langmann *libez mein kint* und versichert ihr: *ich will dir tuon als ein getriwiu muter irm kind* (›Die Offenbarungen der Adelheid Langmann‹ 12, 9–13).[169] Auch andere Mystikerinnen wie Gertrud von Helfta und Margery Kempe heben den mütterlichen Aspekt Marias hervor, indem sie beschreiben, wie ihnen Maria das Jesuskind ans Herz legt.[170] Eine ähnliche Szene kennt auch die Vita der Christina von Hane:

Uterus Marias, in dem sie das sich abbildende männliche Kind sieht, vgl. ›Leben und Offenbarungen der Agnes Blannbekin‹ 54, 4–15. Zu Marias Schwangerschaft im Verbund mit einer Eucharistiefrömmigkeit siehe Alexandra Barratt: Context. Some Reflections on Wombs and Tombs and Inclusive Language. In: Anchorites, Wombs and Tombs. Intersections of Gender and Enclosure in the Middle Ages. Hrsg. von Liz Herbert McAvoy/Mari Hughes-Edwards. Cardiff 2005, S. 27–38, insbes. S. 31; siehe auch Rubin (2010), S. 262.

166 Fulton (2002), S. 245.

167 Vgl. *moderlichen* als Adverb für Marias aggressives Verhalten (CvH 28, 6). Außerdem wird im Erzählbericht die Liebe Marias zu Christina um Jesu Willen erläutert, vgl. CvH 28.

168 Vgl. Bezzel (2005), S. 110; Mellon (2008), S. 134.

169 Siehe auch Thali (2003), S. 286–193, zu Langmanns Marienfrömmigkeit.

170 Vgl. Mellon (2008), S. 140. Siehe auch Volfing (2012), S. 45 f. Newman (1999b), S. 88–92, stellt eine Verbindung zwischen dem mütterlichen Aspekt Marias und Margery Kempes sowie Birgittas von Schweden eigener Mutterschaft her. Zur Beziehung Birgittas mit der Jungfrau Maria siehe Claire L. Sahlin: His Heart was my Heart. Birgitta of Sweden's Devotion to the Heart of

Jn dem lyecht quam die hemelsche konynckynnen Maria myt yrem allersoisten kyntde Jhesus,
daz sie haitte vff jren moderlichen armen, vnd sie lacht jre daz lyebliche kyntgyn yn yre hertze.
(CvH 34, 4–6)

Die im Manuskript unterstrichenen Wörter *kyntde Jesus, moderlichen, kyntgen*
betonen den mütterlichen sowie den herrschaftlichen Aspekt Marias (*hemelsche konynckynnen Maria*). Ob es sich bei der Mutterrolle zugleich um eine *Maria
lactans* handelt, wie es die mittelalterliche Theologie vorsieht,[171] geht aus der
Christina-Vita nicht hervor. Viel eher handelt es sich um ein spirituelles ›Verpflan-
zen‹ des Jesuskindes, das Christina, wie der Text ja explizit macht, »ins Herz«
anstatt an die Brust gelegt wird.[172] Eine derartige ›innige‹ Beziehung zum Jesuskind gehört dennoch zur spirituellen Mutterschaft, die eine der primären Eigenschaften der allegorischen Gottesbraut darstellt.[173]

Die Konfiguration der vielfach besetztbaren Rolle der mystischen Braut zieht
aber eine Überschneidung zwischen Christina und Maria nach sich, welche in der
Vita an einer Stelle besonders evident wird, indem der Gesang des Jesuskinds in
der Ansprache an die Geliebte des Hohenlieds sowohl an die Mutter als auch an
Christina gerichtet erscheint:[174]

Jhesus, yre eyniges lyebe, spyltte myt yrer selen eyn also lyeblich soiße mynnen spielle, daz
keynne zonge dar van gesagen eyn kayn ader auch keyn hant geschryben eyn kayn. Vnder des

---

Mary. In: Heliga Birgitta – budskapet och förebilden. Hrsg. von Alf Härdelin/Mereth Lindgren.
Stockholm 1993, S. 213–227, und dies.: The Virgin Mary and Birgitta of Sweden's Prophetic Vocation. In: Maria i Sverige under Tusen År. Hrsg. von Sven-Erik Brodd/Alf Härdelin. Skellefteå
1996, S. 227–254.

171 Das Konzept der *Maria lactans* basiert auf der Seligpreisung von Marias Brüsten in Lc 11,27.
Zur stillenden Gottesmutter siehe Schreiner (1994), S. 192–196, und Rubin (2010), S. 211–216.
Siehe auch Adelheid Langmann als stillende Mutter (vgl. ›Die Offenbarungen der Adelheid Lang-
mann‹ 66, 28–67, 3).

172 In den Offenbarungen Langsmanns tritt die Integration des Kindes im Herzen klarer hervor:
und nam unser frau ir kindelein und legt irz in ir hertze. do tet sich ir hertze wider zu und unser
frau machet der swester ein creutz über ihr hertze und sprach: ›du solt ewiclichen in disem hertzen
bleiben.‹ (›Die Offenbarungen der Adelheid Langmann‹ 33, 23 f.)

173 Zur spirituellen Schwangerschaft bei Adelheid Langmann etwa erklärt Volfing (2012), S. 47:
»The fact that Mary later refers to her own historical pregnancy in terms of her having carried
Christ under her heart makes it clear that we are dealing with a form of spiritual pregnancy
here.« Zur spirituellen Schwangerschaft bei Birgitta von Schweden siehe Sahlin (2001), S. 52.

174 Górecka (1999), S. 418, geht auf diese Passage ein: »Die Metapher von [!] Minnespiel weist
darauf hin, dass hier ein Akt der Vereinigung der Mystikerin mit Gott gemeint ist.« Dieser Deutung ist nichts entgegenzusetzen, allerdings impliziert Górecka im nächsten Satz, dass dies eine
»marianische Vorstellung« sei (ebd.). Ansonsten beschäftigt sich Górecka nicht noch einmal mit
der Christina von Hane-Vita, sodass ihr Urteil isoliert und verallgemeinernd wirkt.

als yre sele yn der soißer begerunge myt yrem hertzen lyeben was, da sancke die vberschone jonffrauwe vnd moder Maria myt soißer vnd frolicher stymmen eyn lyebliches lyetgyn zo dryn stonden na eyn ander, vnd daz kyntgyn Jhesus sange myt yre also: ›O myn aller lyebste frunt-dynnen, ich hayn dyr gegeben die sicherheit vnd daz ewige leben.‹ (CvH 34, 6–13)

Inwiefern Maria im brautmystischen Sinne ein Vorbild für Christina darstellt, bleibt trotzdem schwer einzuschätzen, da sich Marias mütterliche Fürsorglich-keit auf die spezielle Weise manifestiert, Christina eine Ohrfeige zu verabreichen:

Auch hait sye entphangen vff eyn mail yre dysciplynen van der moder godes vmb vberyche penitencie, die sy yre swerlichen vff lacht, alstu hie vor gehoirt haist. Sie was vff eyn tzijt jn sent Nyclais capelle vnd sy beytde myt gantzer andacht yrs hertzen vor dem bylde vnser lyeber frauwen. Das bylde vff dem altare recket syne jonfferliche hant vß vnd gaiffe yre eynen backen slage vnd sie straiffet sie moderlichen vnd sprache zo yr: ›Laiße dyr genoichen myt dem gem-meynen.‹ Da hait sy sich selber erkant vnd sy ist vff gestanden vnd sy ist gefallen vor daz crutzcifixe zo den sijten des altares vnd sy baidte myt groißen ruwen yrs hertzen vmb genade vor dem sone vnd sy baidte auch vor den tzorne der moder vnd sy begert genaden van dem heren. (CvH 28, 1–10)

Das geschilderte Ereignis ist nicht mit einer Vision der inneren, d.h. spirituel-len Organe zu verwechseln, denn hier geht es um eine raumzeitliche Begeben-heit, bei dem das Altarbild, mit Marin gesprochen, die repräsentative Funktion übersteigt und die Macht des Bildspenders erlangt.[175] Unterstrichen wird die

---

175 Vgl. Louis Marin: Des pouvoirs de l'image. Gloses. Paris 1993, S. 236 zu »la pussicane d'origine« und ebd., S. 12, zu »l'énergie d'autoprésentation«. – Ausführlich zu dieser Passage und zur Visionsthematik in der Christina von Hane-Vita siehe Kirakosian (2017b). Zu Marienmirakeln und animierten Bildern und Skulpturen siehe auch Alexa Sand: Vindictive Virgins. Animate Ima-ges and Theories of Art in some Thirteenth-Century Miracle Stories. In: Word & Image. A Journal of Verbal/Visual Enquiry 26 (2010), S. 150–159; Bruno Boerner: Le rôle de l'image sculptée dans les couvents féminins allemands à la fin du Moyen Âge. In: Bibliothèque de l'École des chartes 162 (2006), S. 119–131; Jean-Marie Sansterre: ›Omnes qui coram hac imagine genua flexerint ...‹ La vénération d'images de saints et de la Vierge d'après les textes écrits en Angleterre du milieu du XIe aux premières décennies du XIIIe siècle. In: Cahiers de civilisation médiévale 49 (2006), S. 257–294; ders. (2010); Rubin (2010), S. 228–242; Katherine Allen Smith: Bodies of Unsurpassed Beauty. ›Living‹ Images of the Virgin in the High Middle Ages. In: Viator 37 (2006), S. 168–187. Zu Verkörperungen in Visionen siehe: Hamburger (1998); ders.: Speculations on Speculation. Vision and Perception in the Theory and Practice of Mystical Devotion. In: Deutsche Mystik im abendländischen Zusammenhang. Neu erschlossene Texte, neue methodische Ansätze, neue theoretische Konzepte. Kolloquium Kloster Fischingen 1998. Hrsg. von Walter Haug/Wolfram Schneider-Lastin. Tübingen 2000, S. 353–408; Newman (2005); Éric Palazzo: Visions and Litur-gical Experience in the Early Middle Ages. In: Looking Beyond. Visions, Dreams and Insights in Medieval Art and History. Hrsg. von Colum Hourihane (Occasional papers Princeton University. Department of Art and Archaeology. Index of Christian Art 11). Princeton 2010, S. 15–29; Jacque-

Verkörperung Marias durch die von Christina vernommene Stimme. Der imperativische Impetus ihrer Worte und die aggressive Gewalttat scheinen die Rolle einer Gnade erweisenden Mutter zu untergraben, zumal vom *tzorne der moder* die Rede ist.[176] Doch die *mater misericordiae* ist auch traditionell mit einem strengen Urteil vereinbar.[177] Schließlich passt auch die Aufforderung Marias, sich mit dem Einfachen abzufinden, zu einer vorbildlichen Demut:[178] Christina solle sich in Demut üben, denn in ihrer Bußpraxis habe sie übertrieben. Im Textabschnitt vor der Altarbild-Szene erfüllt Maria ihre tröstende Funktion, indem sie die Knie Christinas mit einer Salbe heilt (vgl. CvH 27, 10 f.).[179] Christina wird im Nachhinein dennoch getadelt – mit der Begründung: *Laiße dyr genoichen myt dem gemeynnen.* Die Zurechtweisung Marias öffnet Christina die Augen (*Da hait sy sich selber erkant*), sodass die Strafmaßnahme im Kontext pädagogisch wertvoll erscheint. Die Botschaft ist: Maria führt Christina auf den richtigen Weg. Ihr aggressives Verhalten wird so heilsgeschichtlich konnotiert. Diese Deutung führt somit zurück zu Marias heilsgeschichtlicher Funktion. In der ›Goldenen Schmiede‹ kann sie Sünden abwenden, die Seele retten (*von sünden uns bekere / schier unde in kurzen stunden, / strich an der sele wunden / des heiles erzenie*, ›Die Goldene Schmiede‹ V. 1880–1883) und wird selbst als heilende Salbe bezeichnet:[180]

der siechen sele wunden
verheilen kan din süezer list,
wan du dem sündesiechen bist
ein salbe und ein lactwarje; (›Die Goldene Schmiede‹ V. 806–809)

line Elaine Jung: The Tactile and the Visionary. Notes on the Place of Sculpture in the Medieval Religious Imagination. In: Looking Beyond. Visions, Dreams and Insights in Medieval Art and History. Hrsg. von Colum Hourihane (Occasional Papers Princeton University. Department of Art and Archaeology. Index of Christian Art 11). Princeton 2010, S. 203–240.

176 Christina wird weiterhin von ihrer Priorin bzw. Meisterin für ein verantwortungsloses Betverhalten gestraft, vgl. CvH 7.

177 Dass beide Rollen zusammenhängen, weiß Fulton (2002), S. 247, zu erklären:»The implication is not only that Mary should help the creatures who recognize her as their mistress but, more important, that if she does not, they will have very little hope of salvation.«

178 Vgl. Teresa Reed: Shadows of Mary. Reading the Virgin Mary in Medieval Texts. Cardiff 2003, S. 7, zu Maria als Mutter der Demut.

179 Für einen Überblick zu Maria als Heilerin siehe Kinsley (1989), S. 249–254.

180 Weitere Textbelege zur heilenden Funktion Marias in der ›Goldenen Schmiede‹ sind: *din trost den siechen heilet / der an der sele ist ungesunt, / davon dich manec wiser munt / gelichet edeln criutern. / din helfe kan lgeliutern / wol trüeben sin den siechen* (›Die Goldene Schmiede‹ 1328–1333); *din helfe uz tiefer sorgen bade / vil mangen hat erledeget* (›Die Goldene Schmiede‹ 152 f.).

Die Anrufung Marias um Gnade und Seelenheil im ›Arnsteiner Marienleich‹ unterstreicht die Wirkung ihrer Fürbitte bei Gott:

> *Hilf mir bit flize*   *daz ich du hellewize*
> *niemer ni relide,*   *dad ich ouch vermide*
> *hinne vord alle dinc*   *die wider godes hulden sint.* (›Arnsteiner Marienleich‹ 34, 1–3)

Voraussetzung dieser wirkmächtigen Kraft ist ein herrschaftliches Bild Marias.[181] Die Vorstellung von der *mater misericordiae* als tatkräftige Retterin hängt wohl damit zusammen, dass Christus dem mittelalterlichen Verständnis nach Maria keinen Wunsch abschlagen könne.[182] Diese Willenseinheit mit Christus kommt in der Christina von Hane-Vita auch der menschlichen Seele zu, wie im Laufe der Untersuchung gezeigt werden konnte.[183] Aus der Verbindung von Willenseinheit und Fürbittenfunktion wird deutlich, dass Christinas wichtigster Verdienst für die Fegefeuerseelen eine klar marianische Eigenschaft ist, mehr noch: die in Christina verkörperte mystische Braut erlangt denselben Maria vorbehaltenen Status der himmlischen Königin.

4.2.3 Maria als Vorbild für Königin und Braut

Maria, die typologische Gottesbraut des Hohenlieds, wird in zahlreichen Texten auch als himmlische Königin beschrieben.[184] In Notkers Sequenz ›In Assumptione sanctae Maria‹ ist sie die *regina caeli*; bereits Venantius Fortunatus verherrlicht

---

181 Anne L. Clark: The Priesthood of the Virgin Mary. Gender Trouble in the Twelfth Century. In: Journal of Feminist Studies in Religion 18 (2002), S. 5–24, insbes. S. 18–21, sowie Mellon (2008), S. 134 f., beschreiben, dass zur Zeit Elisabeths von Schönau (12. Jahrhundert) Marias Rolle als himmlische Königin besonders hervortrat, was sich auf die Maria-Figur der Visionen niedergeschlagen habe. Zum Marienverständnis Elisabeths von Schönau im Vergleich zu Hermann Josefs von Steinfeld Marienmystik, wo es eine mystische Vermählung zwischen der Seele und Maria gibt, schreiben Koch/Hegel (1958), S. 104: »Wie die Frömmigkeit Hildegards von Bingen im ganzen, so gehört die Frömmigkeit Eckberts und Elisabeths zum Teil noch einer früheren Stufe an. Wollte man diese als Stufe der Ehrfurcht bezeichnen, so könnte man die Frömmigkeit der Hermann Josef-Vita die Stufe der Inbrunst nennen.«
182 Vgl. Caliebe (1985), S. 272.
183 Insbesondere die Typologie zu Esther und die Einheit der Seele mit Christus als marianische Tugend unterstreichen diese Willensvereinigung.
184 Für einen Überblick dieser Zuschreibung siehe Kinsley (1989), S. 244–249.

sie als *gloriosa domina*.[185] In ihrer das Jesuskind tragenden Darstellung wird Maria in diesem Sinne als Thron Jesu, als *sedes sapientiae* verstanden.[186] In einer Himmelsvision Christinas von Hane sieht die Bestuhlung des königlichen Palasts einen besonderen Platz für die Himmelskönigin vor (vgl. CvH 37), so wie auch in der ›Goldenen Schmiede‹ Maria *mit im an den briutestuol [gesetzet]* ist (›Die Goldene Schmiede‹ V. 306 f.). Typlogisch gesehen werden neben der Geliebten des Hohenlieds auch andere alttestamentliche Figuren als Präfigurationen Marias verstanden. Der ›Arnsteiner Marienleich‹ macht auf diese typlogischen Bezüge aufmerksam und schließt in dem Gebet nach Demut eine Aufforderung zur *imitatio Mariae* ein:

> *Unde rouche mich gesterken   in allen guoden werken,*
> *daz ich bege minen lif   alse die heilige wif,*
> *die uns aller dugende   gegeven havent bilede:*
> *unser muoder Sara du otmudige,   Anna du geduldige,*
> *Hester du milde,   Judit du wizzige*
> *und andere die frowen   die in godes forhten*
> *hie sich so bedrageden   daz sie gode wole behageden.* (›Arnsteiner Marienleich‹ 35, 1–7)

> *Ouch na diner guode,   na diner otmuode*
> *muz ich gesceppen minen lif,   des hilf mir heiligez wif!*
> *an dine hant ich begeven   mich und allez daz min leven.*

> *dir bevelen ich alle mine leit,   daz du mir willes sin gereit,*
> *in swelechen minen noden   ich dich iemer ane geruofen.* (›Arnsteiner Marienleich‹ 36, 1–5)

Dass marianische Tugenden, wie hier etwa Demut, vom Menschen angenommen werden können, unterstreicht die didaktische Natur der Vorbildfunktion Marias. Zugleich steht außer Frage, dass nur Maria *an alles mittel bey got* ist, wie es im ›Marienleben‹ des Heinrich von St. Gallen heißt.[187] Stolz erklärt, dass der Theorie nach Maria über allen Künsten stehe, welche selbst letztlich unzulänglich blieben, um zu Gott zu gelangen.[188] Die Christina von Hane-Vita scheint die Unantastbarkeit des Marienstatus herauszufordern, indem Christinas Seele wie Maria

---

185 Die Anrede *O gloriosa domina* findet sich im Hymnus ›Quem terra pontus aethara‹, vgl. Venantius Fortunatus: Opera poetica. Hrsg. von Friedrich Löwe (MGH Auct. ant. 4, 1). Berlin 1881, Lied VIII, S. 385, Z. 21. Siehe auch den Marienpreis ›In laudem Sanctae Maria‹, ebd., Lied 1, S. 371–380.
186 Vgl. Reed (2003), S. 7. Auch bei Heinrich Seuse wird Maria bildhaft als *sedes sapientiae* dargestellt, vgl. Rubin (2010), S. 267.
187 Zitiert nach Stolz (2004), S. 255.
188 Vgl. Stolz (2004), S. 255.

den Vollkommenheitsgrad erreicht. So trifft die Bezeichnung der Königin vier Mal auf Maria, drei Mal auf Christina zu.[189] Christinas Aufnahme in die Engelchöre verweist auf die kosmische Bedeutung Marias, wie diese etwa in Konrads ›Goldener Schmiede‹ ausgeführt wird: *du hast in sinen koeren / enphangen wernde gnade* (›Die Goldene Schmiede‹ V. 222 f.). In der Christina-Vita wird in dem Kontext der Engelchöre auch der Aufstieg der Seele bis »vor die Trinität« erwähnt: *Da wart yre sele gefůrt durch die ix chore der engel vnd vor die heilge dryfeldicheit.* (CvH 63, 28 f.) Die *imitatio Mariae* wird bis zu einer *corporatio Mariae* getrieben (vgl. CvH 54).

Diese marianische Rollenfiguration Christinas von Hane wird bereits im ersten Textabschnitt der Vita vorgezeichnet, indem Christina mit der alttestamentlichen Figur Esther typologisch in Bezug gesetzt wird: *Sie ist woil die ander Hester* (CvH 1, 10 f.).[190] Was Esther in irdischen Kategorien erreichen kann, erfüllt Christina auf spiritueller Ebene: *Dyß ist alles geistlich an dyeßer jonffrauwen ernuwet.* (CvH 1, 21 f.) Damit ist der angestellte Vergleich weniger eine Erhöhung oder Steigerung (Antitypus) des alttestamentlichen Bezugsobjekts (Typus) als deren Reaktualisierung im spirituellen Kontext.[191] Auch wenn die Figur Esther zunächst gar nicht dem Leben einer mittelalterlichen Nonne zu entsprechen scheint, gelingt es der Christina-Vita, dort Analogien zu etablieren, wo es um die Königsbraut geht und wo die Rettung der Seelen aus dem Fegefeuer auf Christinas Fürbitten hin angesprochen wird, weil diese mit Esthers gelungener Rettung des jüdischen Volkes verglichen werden kann (vgl. Est 8). Insbesondere die hervorgehobene Stellung Esthers als Braut des Perserkönigs Xerxes wird umgedeutet: Ein dreifaches Lob preist die Gefälligkeit Christinas vor dem himmlischen König und weist eine Struktur nach dem Muster des Hochzeitsrituals aus Est 2,17 auf: Zuerst findet der König Gefallen an seiner Auserwählten, dann krönt er sie und schließlich teilt er zum Hochzeitsanlass Geschenke aus. In der Christina von Hane-Vita ist mit dem Hochzeitsfest die mystische Vereinigung angesprochen: *want er hait yn rechter vereynionge wyrtschaift myt yrer selen gemacht ewenclichen.* (vgl. CvH 1, 24 f.) Das

---

189 Die entsprechenden Textstellen für Christina als Königin sind: CvH 31, 19; CvH 65, 27; CvH 85, 9. Für Maria als Königin: CvH 27, 2; CvH 32, 26; CvH 34, 4; CvH 37, 11.

190 Die »halbbiblische Typologie« setzt das Alte zum Neuen in ein Spannungsverhältnis, »und zwar in gesteigerter Spiegelung«, so Ohly (1976), S. 432.

191 Vgl. Ohly (1976), S. 433: »Gegenstand der Typologie ist, wie der Typus und der Antitypus der Erhöhung zeigen, vornehmlich die Geschehensdeutung, insofern das alte und das neue Geschehen sich wechselseitig so erhellen, dass das Alte als Verkündigung des Neuen, das Neue als Erfüllung des Alten zu verstehen ist im Sinne des ›non veni solvere, sed adimplere‹.«

spezielle Bild der Krönung innerhalb des Esther-Vergleichs erscheint im Gesamt-kontext der Christina-Vita ebenfalls brautmystisch:[192]

> *Dar vmbe da sie zo dem konynck yn wart gefort, da gefielle sie yme gar woille yn synen augen, vnd er hait sie lyeffe, als da steth geschreben, vor allen anderen frauwen, vnd erkreget vor sym angesiecht genade vnd barmhertzicheit vor allen yren gespiellen, also daz er yr alleyn die kroyne vff saitzet.* (CvH 1, 15–19)

Die Motive *gespiellen* und *kroyne* tauchen im Textverlauf erneut auf. Christina verhält sich bereits im Kindesalter anders als ihre gleichaltrigen Mitschwestern (*gespellen*).[193] Mit diesem wiederkehrenden Motiv – zunächst auf Esther, dann auf Christina bezogen – wird Christinas Sonderstellung betont. Das Motiv der Krone erweitert die paradigmatischen Bezüge um Maria, die himmlische Königin, sodass sich eine dreigestufte Typologie zwischen Esther, Maria und Christina als den drei auserwählten Bräuten Gottes eröffnet.[194] In ihrer heilsgeschichtlichen Ausrichtung rechtfertigt sich Christinas Fall als ein weiterer »Bund zwischen Gott und seiner Schöpfung«.[195] Der »allegorische Synkretismus« des brautmystischen Modells bedeutet aber, dass sich diese Heilsgewissheit auf prinzipiell jede Seele übertragen lässt.[196]

Als himmlische Königin trägt Maria in der christlichen Tradition eine ihren Status repräsentierende Krone.[197] Die Krone wird der Seele in der Christina-Vita von der göttlichen Figur verliehen, sodass es nicht die Mystikerin selbst ist, die sich diese Zuschreibung anmaßt.[198] Als Visionsgegenstand tritt das Motiv der Krönung zweimal im Erzählbericht auf.[199] Ein Vergleich mit anderen mystischen Texten demonstriert die relative Sonderstellung der Christina von Hane-Vita, in der durchgehend Gott die Krone vergibt, anders als etwa bei Birgitta von Schwe-den, welcher in einer Kindheitsoffenbarung im Alter von sieben Jahren Maria

---

192 Das Krönungsmotiv ist im Hohenlied angelegt, vgl.: *Veni de Libano, sponsa veni de Libano, veni, coronaberis* (Ct 4,8).

193 Vgl. CvH 2.

194 Vergleichbare typologische Steigerungen weist Volfing (2012) in verschiedenen Beispielen der spirituellen Schwangerschaft bei Mystikerinnen nach.

195 Volfing (2003), S. 262, über Mechthild von Magdeburg.

196 Volfing (2003), S. 261.

197 Vgl. Reed (2003), S. 6 f., zum mariologischen Kronenmotiv.

198 Vgl.: *Du salt dyne jonffrauweliche crone dragen myt sonderlicher wirdicheit* (CvH 73, 7 f.); *Du haist [...] die crone dyner eren* (CvH 75, 2 f.); *Die heilge dryfeldicheit ist dyn crone* (CvH 97, 23 f.).

199 Vgl.: *Dar na quam der lyebhaber vnd kroynet sy myt iiij cronen [...]. [...] Vnd yre sele wart gecronet myt eyner cronen van zwolff steynen gelicher als zwolffe sternen.* (CvH 63, 34–56); *In der luterheit sach sie, daz got yre sele gecronet haitte myt eyner gulden cronen* (CvH 81, 6 f.).

die Krone aufsetzt.[200] Agnes von Blannbekin sieht in der Krone die Menschnatur Christi, d. h. der Sohn setzt die Krone auf das Haupt der Mutter.[201] Auf den typologischen Gehalt des Krönungsmotivs weist die Christina von Hane-Vita indirekt hin, wenn die zwölf Steine an der Krone Christinas mit zwölf Sternen verglichen werden, somit die Bildquelle aus Apc 12,1 evozierend: *Vnd yre sele wart gecronet myt eyner cronen van zwolff steynen gelicher als zwolffe sternen.* (vgl. CvH 63, 55 f.)[202] Die zwölf Sterne an der Krone sind traditionellerweise mit Maria assoziiert, wie verschiedene Mariendichtungen darlegen.

> *des liebte dich din alder friedel schone*
> *und gab durch minne brüte dir zu lone*
> *von sternen zwelf ein krone,*
> *uß der lücht aller tugende stein.* (›Der Tum‹ 131, 9–12)

In Heinrichs von Mügeln ›Tum‹ ist folgend jedem Edelstein eine allegoretische Strophe gewidmet. Im ›Marienleich‹ Frauenlobs wird der Glanz der zwölf Steine bereits im ersten Versikel benannt: *zwelf steine ich zu den stunden / kos in der krone veste* (Frauenlob, ›Marienleich‹ I, 7 f.).[203] In der ›Goldenen Schmiede‹ wird sinnbildlich der Strahlenglanz der Sterne betont:

> *got der hat dich gegestet*
> *mit einem liehten cranze:*
> *zwelf sternen mit ir glanze*
> *din houbet zieret schone,*
> *die siht man dir ze lone*
> *da brehen unde schinen.* (›Die Goldene Schmiede‹ V. 1834–1839)

---

200 Vgl. Sahlin (2001), S. 59. Auch Adelheid Langmann wird eine Krone von Christus aufgesetzt, vgl. ›Die Offenbarungen der Adelheid Langmann‹ 7, 14.

201 Vgl.: *Nam ipsa corana repraesentabat et significabat humanitatem Christi* (›Leben und Offenbarungen der Agnes Blannbekin‹ 183, 8–10).

202 Daneben steht die goldene Krone mit drei Edelsteinen für die Trinität, vgl. CvH 81, 6 f.; siehe auch an anderer Stelle: *Die heilge dryfeldicheit ist dyn crone* (CvH 97, 23 f.). Ein besonderes Zahlenspiel des Kronenmotivs findet sich auch bei Adelheid Langmann (vgl. ›Die Offenbarungen der Adelheid Langmann‹ 7, 14 f.) und Agnes Blannbekin (vgl. ›Leben und Offenbarungen der Agnes Blannbekin‹ 13, 80). Bernhard von Clairvaux deutet in seiner Marienhimmelfahrtspredigt die zwölf Sterne der Krone als die bei der Himmelfahrt anwesenden Aposteln, vgl. Stolz (2004), S. 493.

203 Frauenlob (Heinrich von Meissen): ›Marienleich‹. In: Leichs, Sangsprüche, Lieder. 1. Teil: Einleitungen, Texte. Auf Grund der Vorarbeiten von Helmuth Thomas. Hrsg. von Karl Stackmann / Karl Bertau. Göttingen 1981, S. 236–283. (Die Stellennachweise geben Versikel- und Verszahlen an.)

In ›Der meide kranz‹ werden die zwölf Künste als Sterne an Marias Krone chiffriert.[204] Die zwölfsteinige Krone in der Christina von Hane-Vita gilt aber zweifelsohne der menschlichen Seele. Christinas Seele wird dementsprechend als *eyn konynckynnen yn mynem ryche* bezeichnet (CvH 65, 27). Ganz ungewöhnlich ist das nicht, denn auch Mechthild von Magdeburg wird von Gott als *kúneginne* bezeichnet (Mechthild von Magdeburg, ›Das fließende Licht der Gottheit‹ II 25, 68). Dass es sich bei der Krönung der Seele aber prinzipiell um einen Teilaspekt der brautmystischen Allegorie handelt, tritt im ›botten der götlichen miltekeit‹ deutlich hervor, wenn die Seele im Anschluss an den Ringaustausch als Zeichen der *gemahelschaft* ebenfalls gekrönt wird: ›*Und hat mich gekrônet mit einer kronen also sin gemahel.*‹ (Gertrud von Helfta, ›ein botte der götlichen miltekeit‹ 49, 13 f.)[205]

Visionäre Krönungsszenarien sind an die Feier der Profess angelehnt, in der die Nonne ihre ordensgemäße Kopfbedeckung empfängt. Dass der Ordensschleier auch im spirituellen Sinne für die *corona sponsae* steht, illustriert ein Altarbild des Prämonstratenserstifts Altenberg: Der um 1330 entstandene Altar zeigt im rechten oberen Teil die Krönung Marias durch Christus, im rechten unteren Teil wird die Heilige Elisabeth von einer Prämonstratensernonne angebetet, wobei ein Engel die himmlische Krone über Elisabeths Kopf hält.[206] Die Kopfbedeckung einer Nonne war also Teil ihrer Identität als Braut Christi.[207] Die Profess ähnelte mit dem Besuch der Familie und den Geschenken zu diesem feierlichen Anlass einer Hochzeit. Dass diese lebensweltliche Realität in der Christina von Hane-Vita als Vorbild der himmlischen Krönung dient, macht vor allem die typologische Beziehung zur Figur Esthers deutlich, weil hier die Hochzeitsfeier samt Krönung ausgeführt wird (vgl. CvH 1).

Eine Krönung hat immer einen zeremoniellen Charakter. In der Regel wirkt sich das auf den Status des zu Krönenden aus. In der Christina von Hane-Vita bedeutet so die Krönung zugleich die Erhebung auf den himmlischen Thron. Das Bild der *sedes sapientiae*, von dem bereits die Rede war, stellt eine thronende

---

204 Vgl. Stolz (2004), S. 556.

205 In der lateinischen Vorlage, dem ›Legatus divinae pietatis‹, findet sich dementsprechend ebenfalls die Bezeichnung *sponsa*: *et tamquam sponsam decoravit me corona*. (Gertrud von Helfta, ›Legatus divinae pietatis‹ III, 2, 1, 20)

206 Abgedruckt und vorgestellt in Caroline Walker Bynum: Crowned with Many Crowns. Nuns and Their Status in Late-Medieval Wienhausen. In: The Catholic History Review 101 (2015), S. 18–40, hier S. 32.

207 In diesem Zusammenhang muss auch Christinas Kampf gegen Hochmut gesehen werden, wenn sie sich vor dem Chorgang ein Geschirrtuch um den Kopf wickelt, um so Demut zu demonstrieren (vgl. CvH 13). Das Motiv der Krone wird hier also subvertiert, wobei die marianische Tugend der Demut exemplifiziert wird.

Maria dar.[208] In der Vita ist es allerdings erneut Christinas Seele, die vom göttlich figurierten Sprecher als Thron Gottes angesprochen wird: *Jch hayn mynen throne jn dich gesaitzet vnd du byst der throne, yn dem ich wannen.* (CvH 74, 9 f.) Dabei verschieben sich die Bilder des göttlichen Throns und der Seele als Thron ineinander: *Du haist gegryffen yn mynen vbersten throne* (CvH 59, 3 f.) und *ich hayn dich erhoirt jn mynem hogen throne* (CvH 35, 12). Auch wenn dadurch die Analogie zu Gott, dem *konynck yn dem hemelschen throne* (CvH 64, 2 f.), verfestigt wird, ist die eigentliche Bezugsgröße nach wie vor eine brautmystisch konfigurierte Maria. Der Thron bleibt auch in der Vita mit der Rezeption des Hohenlieds verknüpft, wie der Anschluss an eine Passage, in der Christinas Seele als Thron aus Elfenbein beschrieben wird,[209] deutlich macht: *Dyne sele ist vol jn brunstiger begerden. Du byst myn frundynnen, myn dube, myn suster, myn bruytde.* (CvH 81, 21 f.)[210]

Zwar wird Maria in der Christina von Hane-Vita nicht explizit als Gottesbraut dargestellt, doch ihre Konfiguration als himmlische Königin rückt das Brautmystische dennoch ins Zentrum. In Mechthilds ›Fließendem Licht‹ hingegen wird Maria explizit als *brut der heiligen drivaltekeit* und *gotes brut* bezeichnet (Mechthild von Magdeburg, ›Das fließende Licht der Gottheit‹ I 22, 48 und 54). In der ›Goldenen Schmiede‹ sichert die Ringmetapher das Verständnis der Vermählung von Marias Seele mit Christus (vgl. ›Die Goldene Schmiede‹ V. 1892–1907). Das ›St. Trudperter Hohelied‹ hebt »die heilsgeschichtliche Bedeutung der Brautschaft Mariens hervor«.[211] In der Vita der Christina von Hane ist es vor allem der letzte Textabschnitt, der diese theologisch relevante Brautschaft vor dem Hintergrund der Empfängnis thematisiert. Das historisch biblische Ereignis der Empfängnis wird hier mit der Vereinigung der Seele mit der Trinität analog gesetzt, sodass Maria, die nun *vnser lyebe frauwe* heißt (CvH 100, 18), klar die mystische Braut darstellt. Im Anschluss an schöpfungstheologische Gedanken illustriert die Verkündigung die zeitlich entrückte Vereinigung (*sonder zijt*). Auch Meister Eckhart erwähnt die Schwangerschaft Marias im Kontext der Gottesgeburt.[212] Mit der Verbindung von trinitäts- und schöpfungstheologischen mit mariologischen Elementen rückt die Christina von Hane-Vita weiter in die Nähe der rheinländischen Mystik. Anders als einige Mystikerinnen ihrer Zeit kennt die Vita Christinas das

---

208 Vgl. Newman (1999b), S. 81 f.
209 Das Motiv des Elfenbeinthrones geht auf den Thron König Salomos zurück (vgl. 1 Rg 10,8; 2 Par 9,17), mit dem auch das Hohelied assoziiert wird. Außerdem liegt ein mariologisches Bild vor, vgl. Schreiner (1994), S. 160.
210 Diese Passage verarbeitet die folgenden Verse des Hohenlieds: Ct 1,15; Ct 2,14; Ct 6,4; Ct 7,1–7; insbes. Ct 4,8–10.
211 Górecka (1999), S. 340.
212 Vgl. McGinn (2005), S. 118–124 und S. 164–181.

Phänomen des Schwangergehens mit Christus nicht, das sich in der spätmittelalterlichen Devotion zur schwangeren Maria »in tatsächlichen somatischen Symptomen manifestierte«.[213] Der Schwerpunkt liegt dagegen auf der Jungfräulichkeit Marias als Gottesbraut.[214] Aus brautmystischer Sicht ist die *imitatio Mariae* seit der Vorstellung der Gottesgeburt in der Seele eine spirituelle Tugend[215] – und trotzdem geht es hier nicht darum, dass Christina ausdrücklich die Marienrolle annimmt, wie das Mellon verallgemeinernd für jede Nonne des Mittelalters darstellt.[216] Während z.B. der mystische Kuss als Ausdruck der Beziehung zu Gott im ›St. Trudperter Hohenlied‹ oder im ›Fließenden Licht‹ viel stärker mit einer *imitatio Mariae* in Verbindung steht,[217] bleibt in der Christina von Hane-Vita die Gottesgeburt in der menschlichen Seele an das Wort gebunden und mit der *conceptio Christi* verknüpft.

Die Auseinandersetzung mit der Rolle Marias in der Christina von Hane-Vita macht deutlich, dass Christina ähnlich wie Clara von Assisi und Angela von Foligno vor allen Dingen eine *imitatio Christi* anstrebt, sodass Maria allenfalls als Mutter und Königin im Hintergrund dargestellt wird.[218] Gleichzeitig ist die mariologische Deutung Teil der traditionellen Brautmystik und für die Vita durchaus relevant,[219] sofern die menschliche Seele Maria darin abzulö-

---

213 Bezzel (2005), S. 112. Hale (1999), S. 215, spricht auf Grund der Schwangerschaft bei Christina Ebner von »mother mysticism« und zählt dazu auch Margareta Ebner und Adelheid Langmann. Siehe auch Rubin (2010), S. 263–266.

214 Zur Bedeutung der Jungfräulichkeit Marias im Mittelalter siehe Fulton (2002), S. 248–250.

215 Vgl. Volfing (2012), S. 46.

216 Mellon (2008), S. 133, leitet aus der spätmittelalterlichen Vorstellung nach Jean Gerson ab, dass sich Nonnen auf Grund ihrer perfekten jungfräulichen Beziehung zu Gott natürlicherweise mit Maria identifizierten. Siehe auch Hale (1999), S. 217: »Mary was a primary exemplar for nuns«. Doch selbst wenn Schwangerschaft und Mutterschaft genuin weibliche Erfahrungsbereiche sind, ist die spirituelle Schwangerschaft nicht auf Mystikerinnen begrenzt, wie Volfing (2012), S. 47 f., zeigt.

217 Vgl. ›Das St. Trudperter Hohelied‹ 8, 5–9 und 8, 32–34; Mechthild von Magdeburg, ›Das fließende Licht der Gottheit‹ I 22, 27 f.

218 Siehe Catherine M. Mooney: Imitatio Christi or Imitatio Mariae? Clare of Assisi and her interpreters In: Gendered Voices. Medieval Saints and Their Interpreters. Hrsg. von Catherine M. Mooney. Philadelphia 1999b, S. 52–77, insbes. S. 53, zu Clara von Assisi. Lachance (1993), S. 99 f., geht hingegen wenig auf die Rolle Marias für Angela von Foligno ein.

219 Christinas spiritueller Weg zur Vervollkommnung führt sowohl über die *imitatio Christi* als auch über den Status der brautmystischen Geliebten. Garber (2003), S. 107, unterscheidet diese beiden Bereiche und teilt dem einen Margareta Ebner, dem anderen Adelheid Langmann zu, was eine allzu starre, wenn nicht irrige Kategorisierung ist, da auch Adelheid ansatzweise das Leiden Christi nachempfindet (vgl. ›Die Offenbarungen der Adelheid Langmann‹ 61, 5–11) und Margare-

sen scheint.[220] Zeitlich nah zur vermeintlichen Lebenszeit Christinas von Hane gewinnt im 13. Jahrhundert neben der herrschaftlichen Rolle Marias ihre Funktion als irdische Mutter an Bedeutung.[221] Die konfliktreiche Beziehung Christinas zu dieser mütterlichen Figur erinnert zum Teil an Gertruds von Helfta Visionen, in denen Maria ebenfalls verärgert auf das Verhalten der Nonne reagiert.[222] Von einer Marienmystik, wie z.B. bei Christinas Ordensbruder Hermann Josef von Steinfeld, kann indes nur in eingeschränkter Form die Rede sein.[223] Trotz alledem stehen Christina und Maria nicht in Konkurrenz zu einander, denn die »gesteigerte Wiederkehr« reiht sich in die göttliche Ordnung der Heilsgeschichte ein.[224] Maria ist bereits mit der Bibelexegese als Braut Gottes etabliert und die Christina-Vita baut auf dieses Verhältnis auf, sodass sich von einem Reaktualisierungspotenzial der Brautallegorie sprechen ließe.[225] Im ›St. Trudperter Hohenlied‹ z.B. wird die Titulatur der Braut Gottes von Maria auf prinzipiell jede (jungfräuliche) Seele übertragen.[226]

Volfing erklärt, dass der »Rollenaustausch« zwischen Seele, Kirche oder Maria konventionell sei, weil Christus stets Bräutigam bleibe.[227] Dieser grundlegenden Voraussetzung der Brautallegorie sei die narrative Dimension des Vitentextes samt seiner didaktischen Appellstruktur und seinen performativen Elementen des Mitteilungsprozesses hinzuzufügen. Die Rolle des Erzählers verhält

---

ta durchaus brautmystische Anklänge aufweist, was sich insbesondere in ihren *unio*-Berichten niederschlägt, siehe dazu Hale (1999), S. 215 und S. 226.

220 Hasebrink (2000), S. 160 f., diskutiert für Mechthild von Magdeburg die vielschichtige Rollenbesetzung der Braut und die Identifizierung mit dem jeweiligen Sprecher-Ich.

221 Im 14. Jahrhundert wurde der mütterliche Aspekt deutlich über den der Himmelskönigin gesetzt, wie etwa die Offenbarungen Birgittas von Schweden unterstreichen, vgl. Mellon (2008), S. 137. Zu Maria in der Rolle der *mulier fortis* als Antwort auf Spr 31, 10 (*mulierem fortem quis inveniet*) siehe Pelikan (1996), S. 27. Rubin (2010), S. 285, betont wiederum die wachsende Bedeutung Marias für herrschaftliche Repräsentationszwecke im 15. Jahrhundert.

222 Zu Gertruds Marienverständnis siehe Sharon Elkins: Gertrude the Great and the Virgin Mary. In: Church History. Studies in Christianity and Culture 66 (1997), S. 720–734, insbes. S. 723–731.

223 Siehe Rubin (2010), S. 266 f., zur Braut- und Marienmystik Hermann Josefs.

224 Ohly (1976), S. 435, über Typologieverhältnisse. Siehe auch Michel (1992), S. 55: »Typologisches Denken hat exegetische Kraft.«

225 Vgl. Walter Haug: Transzendenzerfahrung in Bildern des Abschieds. In: Positivierung von Negativität. Letzte kleine Schriften. Hrsg. von Ulrich Barton. Tübingen 2008, S. 354–370, insbes. S. 361 zum Reaktualisierungspotenzial. Siehe auch Ohly (1976), S. 434, für den die »prästabilisierte Konkordanz von Alt und Neu die providentielle Folgerichtigkeit des Zeitengangs zu einer dem Auge vergegenwärtigenden Evidenz« führt.

226 Vgl. Sg. *gotes brût* (›Das St. Trudperter Hohelied‹ 117, 33) und Pl. *gotes briute* (ebd., 119, 14,); siehe dazu Suerbaum (2009), S. 37 f.

227 Vgl. Volfing (2008), S. 346.

sich wie ein Dreh- und Angelpunkt, was der hagiographischen Schreibweise entspricht, wie Rapp präzisiert:

> The multifaceted connections that tie together the saint, the hagiographer and his work, and the audience are implicit in the topoi commonly encountered in the prefaces to hagiographical works. [...] [T]he hagiographer is a disciple of the saint and thus can claim for himself the status and authority of an eyewitness of the events he describes.[228]

Die allegorisch und typologisch konstituierte mystische Braut bietet einen textlich verarbeiteten Modus der Hoheliedrezeption. Hagiographische Elemente heben die Bedeutung der Schriftlichkeit für die Lehre aus der Vita Christinas hervor und lenken das Augenmerk auf ein wechselseitiges »Implikationsverhältnis von Mündlichkeit und Schriftlichkeit, von Sprecher(in), Schreiber(in) und Hörer(in)«,[229] das dem schriftlichen Wort Lebendigkeit verleiht. Zugleich funktioniert der Leseprozess gemäß einer Habitualisierung, die eine geistliche Vervollkommnung anstrebt.[230] Christina führt ein auf zweifache Weise wirksames Heiligenleben vor: zum einen auf eine darstellbare Weise (»Visualität der Heiligkeit«)[231] und zum anderen durch den Nachvollzug der Textualität als Nachbildung dieser Heiligkeit. Mit einem derartigen Reaktualisierungspotenzial ist weniger das Nacherleben von Christinas Erfahrung angesprochen als die textinhärente Disposition einer performativen Sprachlichkeit.

---

228 Rapp (1998), S. 432.
229 Kiening (2008), S. 106, in der Auseinandersetzung mit deutsch-lateinischen Gebeten.
230 Vgl. Hasebrink (2008) und ders.: Erecs Wunde. Zur Performativität der Freundschaft im höfischen Roman. In: Oxford German Studies 38 (2009[a]), S. 1–11, insbes. S. 8, Anm. 28.
231 Almut Schneider: ›er liez ze himel tougen erhellen sîner stimme dôn‹. Sprachklang als poetische Fundierung normativen Sprechens. In: Text und Normativität. XX. Anglo-German Colloquium. Hrsg. von Elke Brüggen u. a. Berlin/Boston 2012, S. 199–216, hier S. 209.

5 Die Inszenierung dynamischer Textualität und die Evidenz materieller Buchschriftlichkeit

Wenn der Schreibakt Teil der mystischen Mitteilung wird, wie verhalten sich dann Text und Schriftlichkeit zueinander? Äußern sich neben der Thematisierung von Schreibprozessen auch bestimmte Schriftkonzepte in der Vita der Christina von Hane? Zuletzt hat Freimut Löser auf die Schrift als elementare Bedingung der mittelalterlichen Mystik hingewiesen.[1] Angesichts der dynamischen Beschaffenheit von Text mag es allerdings, so soll hier entwickelt werden, angemessener sein, von ›Schreibmystik‹ zu sprechen. So steht die Selbstreferentialität der Schrift, welche die Mystik als sprachliche Mitteilung hervorhebt, im Vordergrund der folgenden abschließenden Untersuchungen. Dabei erscheint es wichtig, sich noch einmal vor Augen zu führen, dass »Vorgaben klassizistischer Autor-Werk-Paradigmen« zumindest aus medienanthropologischer Sicht in vormodernen Texten nicht greifen.[2] Im Rekurs auf Worstbrock plädiert Strohschneider für die »Überliefertheit« als das Konstitutive von vormoderner Textualität.[3] Überliefertheit ist nicht nur produktionstechnisch gesehen ein Komplex, der die Zusammen- und Folgearbeit durch ein Kollektiv beansprucht. In der Thematisierung des vermittelten, d.h. überlieferten religiösen Sprechakts ist die mystische Vita ein im Grenzbereich der Kommunikabilität angesiedelter Sprechakt, zu dessen Gelingen mehrere Teilnehmer nötig sind. Mit Köbele gesprochen liegt im religiösen Sprechakt »eine paradoxe Simultanthematisierung« vor, paradox deshalb, weil die unmögliche Aufgabe besteht, Transzendenz in Immanenz zu verkehren.[4] Dadurch befindet sich der Text gerade in seiner schriftlichen Beschaffenheit selbst aber am »Übergangsbereich von Transzendenz und Immanenz«.[5] Im Rahmen der christlichen Heilsgeschichte kommt deswegen der Schriftlichkeit eine besondere, nahezu reliquienhafte Funktion zu. Jede Schriftmystik nach der Definition Lösers ist der Prämisse verpflichtet, dass die transzendente Erfahrung in Worten ausgedrückt werden muss.[6] Dabei ist das Paradoxon des apophatischen Diskurses bisher größtenteils nur aus theologischer und philosophischer Sicht diskutiert worden,[7]

---

1 Vgl. Löser (2012), S. 159 f.
2 Strohschneider (2014), S. 25.
3 Strohschneider (2014), S. 26 f. Siehe auch Worstbrock (1999), S. 128.
4 Köbele (2003), S. 236.
5 Strohschneider (2014), S. 29.
6 Vgl. Löser (2012). »Theologie ist in Glaubensrede unverzichtbar«, formuliert auch Haas (1984b), S. 615.
7 Z. B. Sells (1994).

https://doi.org/10.1515/9783110536324-008

während es Literaturwissenschaftler meistens als Unsagbarkeits-Topos und so als ein rhetorisches Mittel klassifizieren.[8] Stattdessen soll im Folgenden ein Ansatz verfolgt werden, der textwissenschaftliche und poetologische Aspekte um die Dimension einer sprachpragmatischen Schriftlichkeit erweitert, um das Zusammenspiel von Textualität, Schrift und Schriftkörper zu untersuchen. Zunächst soll die Bedeutung von Schriftlichkeit in der Vita, zu denen hier vor allen Dingen die Visionsbeschreibungen zählen, vorgestellt werden. In der Vita der Christina von Hane wird die göttliche Mitteilung als eine sprachlich dynamische dargestellt, die im Zusammenhang mit der neuplatonischen Emanationslehre steht. In diesem Kontext bietet sich der Querblick zu Meister Eckhart besonders gut an. Ergänzende Verweise zu anderen Texten, insbesondere aus der Mariendichtung, beleuchten weiterhin die Signifikanz eines dynamischen Textverständnisses. Zugleich schafft die Bedeutung von Schrift einen Bezug zur Materialität, wie das etwa auch im ›Fließenden Licht der Gottheit‹ der Fall ist (vgl. Mechthild von Magdeburg, ›Das fließende Licht der Gottheit‹ II, 26). In ihrer sprachpragmatischen Untersuchung des Münchener Kodex Clm 536 betont Haesli den »Gedanken der Fleischwerdung des Wortes in Christus, der mit der Schriftwerdung des Fleisches korrespondiert.«[9] Die Schrift in der Handschrift präsentiere sich »in ihrer Eigendynamik« und verweise »auf die Vorstellung von ihrer göttlichen Herkunft und kosmologischen Einbindung«.[10] Auch wenn die »Exkarnation« – so der Begriff Haeslis für die Inkarnation im Buch – in der die Christina von Hane-Vita überliefernden Straßburger Handschrift nicht medial-materiell vorkommt,[11] sei dennoch auch hier die Phänomenologie der materiellen Buchschriftlichkeit in den Mittelpunkt der letzten Teiluntersuchung zu rücken.

5.1 Schriftlichkeit und Vision

Das alte Stereotyp der ungebildeten Nonnen gilt längst als überholt; stattdessen war, wie Schreiner für das 13. und 14. Jahrhundert bestimmt, »[d]ie Literarisierung religiöser Themen und Erfahrungen [...] gleichermaßen Frauen- und

---

8 Z.B. Lechtermann (2010).
9 Haesli (2008), S. 76. Siehe auch Horst Wenzel: Die Schrift und das Heilige. In: Die Verschriftlichung der Welt. Bild, Text und Zahl in der Kultur des Mittelalters und der Frühen Neuzeit. Hrsg. von Horst Wenzel/Wilfried Seipel/Gotthart Wunberg (Schriften des Kunsthistorischen Museums 5). Wien 2000, S. 15–57, insbes. S. 51.
10 Haesli (2008), S. 77.
11 Haesli (2008), S. 76, in Bezug auf die Illustration eines aufgeschlagenen Buches, vgl. München, Bayerische Staatsbibliothek, Clm 536, Bl. 84^r.

Männersache.«[12] Die Bildung und Literarizität der Beginen ist einigermaßen
erforscht;[13] im Prämonstratenserorden trafen Frauen, wenn es um Bildung ging,
wohl auf mehr Hürden.[14] Trotzdem waren diejenigen prämonstratensischen Frauenklöster, die keinem männlichen Konvent unterstellt waren, im liturgischen und
wirtschaftlichen Leben weitgehend selbstständig.[15] Dort waren die Nonnen den
Mönchen ihres Ordens so weit gleichgestellt, dass sie als Chorfrauen, *dominae*,
bezeichnet wurden: Sie sangen das Chorgebet, d. h. verrichteten den liturgischen
Dienst, konnten lesen und schreiben.[16] Dass Christina viel eher zu dieser liturgisch gebildeten Gruppe gezählt werden darf als zu den ungebildeten Laien-
schwestern, liegt für Krings auf der Hand; jedenfalls beherrscht sie der Vita nach
bereits als Kind das Chorgebet, besucht die Klosterschule und legt ihre Profess
ab. Gemäß den Ordensstatuten aus dem 13. Jahrhundert ist sie dadurch als klau-
surierte Nonne qualifizierbar.[17] Von Beginn der Vitenerzählung an wird Christinas Ausbildung thematisiert, wenn auch nur im Nebensatz:

> *Wanne sye sich abe gescheytden kontde van yren gespillen, die myt jre yn der scholen waren,*
> *so was sie gar gerne alleyn, daz sie yre sele myt heilgen gedancken gespyßen moicht.* (CvH 8,
> 5–7)

---

12 Zur Bildung von Frauen im Mittelalter siehe Schreiner (1994), S. 137–148, hier 144. Demnach
»verliefen die Konfliktlinien [...] nicht zwischen Männern und Frauen, sondern zwischen hart-
gesottenen Konservativen [...] und zwischen theologischen Neuerern, die, weil sie die Frau als
legitime Leserin der Heiligen Schrift anerkannten, mit Leidenschaft taten, was an der Zeit war.«
13 Hier war der Austausch von Manuskripten üblich, wobei viele Beginen niedrigen Standes
keinen Zugang zur Bildung hatten, vgl. Walter Simons: ›Staining the Speech of Things Divine‹.
The Use of Literacy in Medieval Beguine Communities. In: The Voice of Silence. Women's Literacy in a Men's Church. Hrsg. von Thérèse de Hemptinne/María Eugenia Góngora (Medieval
Church Studies 9). Turnhout 2004, S. 85–110, insbes. S. 110. Kritischer über die literarische Tätigkeit von Beginen äußert sich Geert Warnar: ›Ex levitate mulierum‹. Masculine Mysticism and
Jan van Ruusbroec's Perception of Religious Women. In: The Voice of Silence. Women's Literacy
in a Men's Church. Hrsg. von Thérèse de Hemptinne/María Eugenia Góngora (Medieval Church
Studies 9). Turnhout 2004, S. 193–206, insbes. S. 197.
14 Vgl. Bynum (1987), S. 15 f.
15 Das trifft streng genommen nicht auf das Kloster Hane zu, das unter der Aufsicht Rothenkir-
chens stand, vgl. Kleinjung (2001), S. 32.
16 Vgl. Krings (2003), S. 102 und S. 104.
17 Vgl. Krings (2003), S. 103 f. Kritisch zu Krings' Teiledition der prämonstratensischen Ordensstatuten (Bruno Krings [Hrsg.]: Die Statuten des Prämonstratenserordens von 1244/46 und ihre
Überarbeitung im Jahr 1279. In: Analecta Praemonstratensia 83 [2007], S. 5–127) äußert sich
Christian Lohmer: Rezension zu Bruno Krings: Die Statuten des Prämonstratenserordens von
1244/46 und ihre Überarbeitung im Jahr 1279 (2007). In: Deutsches Archiv für Erforschung des
Mittelalters 65 (2009), S. 214.

Eine Spannung zwischen dem Lehrinhalt in der Klosterschule und den inneren Gedanken, denen sich Christina zuwendet, zeichnet sich hier bereits ab und wird erneut im Kontext der klösterlichen Ausbildung konkret benannt:

> O flyßicher leißer, nu haistu gehoret, wie die seliche jonffrauwe Christina yre kyntliche jaire hait gestanden yn der schoillen. Nyt alleyn hait sie geleret die bustabe, sonder auch nach dem geistlichen leben. (CvH 8, 31–33)

Angesprochen ist damit ein kontroverses Verhältnis zwischen Gelehrsamkeit und Spiritualität, wobei letztere betont wird, indem auf Grund der syntaktischen Anordnung diese Qualifikation als eine zusätzliche, eine besondere hervorgehoben wird (Nyt allein ... sonder ...).[18] Auch wenn Christina zunächst als schriftkundig dargestellt wird, ist schwer zu beurteilen, ob sie damit auch eine gelehrte Nonne darstellt, da sie in keiner Erwähnung als schreibend porträtiert wird, wie das etwa bei Hildegard von Bingen der Fall ist.[19] Stattdessen wird Christina explizit als ungelehrt dargestellt: wie woil sie nyt gelert eyn was, so verstonde sy doch daz latyne woil yn der selen (CvH 10, 100 f.). Ähnlich formuliert Mechthild im ›Fließenden Licht‹ an ihren mystischen Bräutigam: Nu gebristet mir túsches, des latines kann ich nit (Mechthild von Magdeburg, ›Das fließende Licht der Gottheit‹ II 3, 48). Die Spannung zwischen gelehrtem Wissen und göttlicher Gnadenerkenntnis, die Palmer als wiederholtes Thema im ›Fließendem Licht‹ erkennt, wo zudem der Mangel an Lateinkenntnissen thematisiert wird, lässt sich also punktuell auch in der Christina-Vita nachweisen.[20] Sicherlich spielt bei der Ungelehrten-Darstellung der Topos der Demut eine besondere Rolle, wie gerade das Beispiel Hildegards von Bingen zeigt.[21] Zugleich gestaltet sich das Spannungsfeld zwischen Latein und Volkssprache in der Christina von Hane-Vita subtiler. Zum einen gibt es ein Nebeneinander von lateinischen und deutschen Gesangstiteln. So wird der ›Surrexit‹-Gesang im Text auf Deutsch zitiert (CvH 20, 13 f.),

---

18 Allgemein zum Spannungsbereich von Theologie und Spiritualität siehe Haas (1984b).

19 Vgl. Deploige (2004), S. 4 f. Zugleich beschreibt sich Hildegard als schwach und ungelehrt, vgl. Powell (2004), S. 268.

20 Vgl. Palmer (1992), S. 223 f. Siehe auch Köbele (1993b), S. 33–37, und Poor (2001), S. 217 f., Mechthild von Magdeburg, die sich selbst als ungebildete Frau identifiziert, muss »im laikalen Sinn alles andere als ungebildet« gewesen sein, erörtert Andersen (2003), S. 231. Zum allgemein Bildungsstand von Frauen des 13. Jahrhunderts vgl. Andersen (2000), S. 52–58. Zur Bildung unter den Dominikannerinnen siehe auch Marie-Luise Ehrenschwendtner: Die Bildung der Dominikanerinnen in Süddeutschland vom 13. bis 15. Jahrhundert (Contubernium 60; zugl. Diss. Tübingen 1999). Stuttgart 2004.

21 Vgl. Deploige (2004), S. 6: »Hildegard presented herself as a simple and uneducated woman, chosen by God to communicate his messages to mankind.«

während sonst wie gewöhnlich die lateinischen Titelanfänge angezeigt werden.[22] Andererseits erweisen sich lateinische Einsprengsel als Versatzstücke biblischer Referenzen, welche in ihrer intertextuellen Natur auch immer den Selbstbezug zur eigenen Textualität evozieren. An einer Stelle benutzt Christinas Sprecher-Ich den deutschen Begriff *mynnenbuch* (CvH 56, 16). Um auf das Hohelied zu verweisen, spricht der männlich figurierte Erzähler der Vita dahingegen von den *cantica canticorum* (CvH 30, 8 f.). Zugleich wird aus Christinas Perspektive ein lateinischer Begriff dem deutschen Kasus gemäß richtig bzw. gemischt dekliniert: *myt dem cyperen wynne / van dem wyne des drubens Cypri* (CvH 56, 15–17). Der aus Apc 22,13 stammende prägnante Satz des *ego sum alpha und omega* wird in einer Vision Christinas ins Deutsche übersetzt: *iß was vmb syn heubtgen geschreben also: ›Jch byn das anbegyn vnd daz ende.‹* (CvH 31, 14 f.) Eine klare Zuteilung von Latein und Volkssprache auf eine männliche respektive weibliche Stimme ist auf der Textoberfläche trotzdem nicht möglich.[23] Lateinsprachige liturgische und biblische Referenzen sind in die Vitenerzählung derart verflochten, dass es keine eindeutigen Zuweisungen nach Geschlecht oder Funktion gibt. Die Frage der intellektuellen versus affektiven Gotteserkenntnis, die immer auch mit Sprache zu tun hat, wird dagegen auf anderen Ebenen verhandelt; daher soll, wie es die zuletzt zitierten Textpassagen bereits andeuten, der Zusammenhang zwischen Schriftlichkeit und Vision genauer untersucht werden.

In den Visionen Christinas wird die Wahrnehmung geschriebener Visionsbotschaften mit einer spirituellen Gottesnähe verbunden. Schrift ist in der Form von Inschrift präsent:

Da sache sie aber daz zarte aller suberlichstes kyntgen stayn vor dem elter yn eyner wegen vnd iß was gedecket myt eym dechelach van roißen vnd vff eynem yecklichen blaytde der roißen stontde geschreben ›Pater noster‹. (CvH 6, 5–7)

An dem hertzen stonde geschreben ›O sapiencia Jhesu Christi‹ vnd noch me, das yr vß dem gedechtenyß was gegangen. (CvH 21, 30–32)

---

22 Vgl.: *Gloria in excelsis* (CvH 20, 24), *Te sanctum dominum in excelsis* [...] *Gloria patri* (CvH 31, 9), *Ego sum panis viuus* (CvH 22, 25) und die Mariengesänge *Aue preclara* (CvH 27, 4) und *Aue Maria* (CvH 27, 6).
23 Newman (2012), S. 354 f., betont für weibliche Schriftlichkeit, dass die Grenzen zwischen gebildet und ungebildet, Latein und Volkssprache überschritten werden. Zudem stellt Suerbaum (2012b), S. 34, fest, dass »eine scharfe Trennung zwischen einzelsprachig gebundenen Bedeutungen und übersprachlichen Diskursen nicht ohne Weiteres möglich ist«.

Ähnlich sieht Marguerite d'Oingt eine lateinische Inschrift in ihrer Vision.[24] Auch dieser volkssprachige (frankoprovenzalische) Text verwendet Latein nur in Verweisen auf Bibelstellen.[25] Im Beispiel der Christina von Hane-Vita visualisiert der Gebetstitel des ›Pater noster‹ die Gebetserfüllung Christinas. Die figurative Vision wird durch die darin vorkommende Schriftlichkeit erweitert. Liturgische Elemente der Eucharistie werden mit Hilfe der Visualität von Schrift in mystische Visionen hineingewoben, z.B. wenn Christina während der Messe die Litanei des ›Agnus Dei‹ in goldenen Buchstaben ausgeschrieben sieht:

> *Da nu der pryster die boiße vff dede, vnd sie nach jrem vßerwilten gyrlichen begertde, da sach sie vben yn der boißen eyn lamgyn slaiffen, vnd iß hait eyn crentzgyn vff synem heubt, daz was vmbschreven myt gulden bustaben ›Agnus dei qui tollit peccata mundi‹. ›Zo haynt entwacht das lemgyn vnd sprancke snel yn des prysters hant vnd strebete zo myr, als syne begert zo myr stontde.‹* (CvH 32, 8–13)

An dieser Stelle vermischt sich die raumzeitliche Dimension der Liturgie mit Christinas Vision vom Lamm Gottes, das sich ihr als Abendmahl mitteilt.[26] Die unvermittelte direkte Rede scheint gleichermaßen aus der Ebene des Berichts in einen dramatischen Modus zu wechseln. Das geschriebene ›Agnus Dei‹ ist in der Form eines physisch greifbaren Sakramentales denkbar; ein Wachstäfelchen mit einem Lammrelief, das i.d.R. in einer monstranzartigen Metallkapsel (hier *boiße*) aufgehoben wurde. Hier jedoch steht das ›Agnus Dei‹ auf dem Nimbus des Lamms. Der Schriftzug ist also Teil der visionären Erscheinung. In Christinas Visionen sind visuelle Schriftzüge ›vertextlicht‹: Sie erscheinen als Inschriften.[27] Dennoch kann man allein aus der Erwähnung der Schrift nicht darauf schließen, dass Christina Latein lesen konnte, da es sich um gängige Worte der Liturgie oder des Gebets handelt. Newman erläutert:

---

24 Vgl. ›Les Œuvres de Marguerite d'Oingt‹. Hrsg. von Antonin Duraffour/Pierre Gardette/Paulette Durdilly (Publications de l'Institut de Linguistique Romane de Lyon 21). Paris 1965, §145, S. 146.

25 Vgl. Müller (1999), S. 33

26 Zur brautmystischen Vereinigung in der zum Lamm gewandelten Hostie siehe Renana Bartal: Bridal Mysticism and Eucharistic Devotion. The Marriage of the Lamb in an Illustrated Apocalypse from Fourteenth-Century England. In: Viator 42 (2011), S. 227–246.

27 Ähnlich erklärt sich der Verweis auf das ›Pater noster‹ bei Margareta Ebner (vgl. ›Offenbarungen der Margaretha Ebner‹ 5, 26 und 8, 25) oder auch das Vorkommen des ›Amen‹ im ›Fließenden Licht der Gottheit‹ (vgl. Mechthild von Magdeburg, ›Das fließende Licht der Gottheit‹ I 44, 95 und II 26, 53). Siehe auch Adelheid Langmanns Verwendung liturgischer Phrasen und Worte in Visionen (z.B. ›Die Offenbarungen der Adelheid Langmann‹ 68, 21).

[...] women continued to perform the Divine Office in Latin throughout the Middle Ages, so they would have had at least a passive understanding, and even the least literate recluses and lay sisters could recite the ›Pater noster‹, the ›Ave Maria‹, and perhaps a few psalms.[28]

Versatzstücke täglicher Rezitationen finden also genauso Wiederhall in den Visionen, wie sich auch plastische und räumliche Elemente des Klosters darin spiegeln.

Eine nicht liturgisch geprägte Art von Schriftlichkeit liegt in solchen Visionen vor, in denen die Namen verstorbener Menschen Erwähnung finden. Während einer österlichen Vision sieht Christina Christus in den Kreuzgang des Konvents schreiten und sich vor einem Grab niederknien. Daraufhin vernimmt sie den Auferstehungsgesang (›Surrexit Dominus‹):

Vnd die engel furtten gar vil selen myt groißer freuden yn den hemel vnd sonderlichen die sele vff dem grabe, unser here vff gkneet haitte vnd eyn crutze dar vber gemacht hait. Des selben menschen sach sie synen namen geschreben myt gulden bůstaben. (CvH 20, 14–17)

In der Handschrift unterstrichen, macht die goldene Farbgebung (hier *bůstaben*) zusätzlich auf die Materialität des Schriftzugs aufmerksam. Selbst wenn der Name des verstorbenen Menschen unbekannt bleibt, stellt der Schriftzug eine Art Legitimationsstrategie dar, mit der die prinzipiell nicht nachvollziehbare göttliche Erfahrung überprüfbar erscheint. Strohschneider führt diesbezüglich aus, es gebe verschiedene Verfahren, um Schrift in einer göttlichen Offenbarung als sinnfällig auszuweisen: »Visionäre Erscheinungen und Engelsboten gehören dazu, die dem Propheten oder Apokalyptiker eine Schriftrolle, einen kleinen Codex zu essen geben«.[29] Dass es sich um eine textuelle Autorisierungsstrategie des an sich unzugänglich Heiligen handelt, zeigt insbesondere eine Vision Christinas von Hane, in der sie die Namen jener Märtyrerinnen erkennt, deren Reliquien im Kloster aufbewahrt sind (vgl. CvH 32, 31–36). Wie im Falle der Prophetie erhebt die Vision dadurch einen kontrollierbaren Wahrheitsanspruch auf Zustände in der realen Welt. An keiner Stelle wird behauptet, dass Christina den Schriftanteil ihrer Visionen auch tatsächlich liest.[30] Stattdessen geht es um ein allgemeines Wahrnehmen des Göttlichen, das sich über die Sprachlichkeit hinaus entfaltet, sodass die Christina-Vita in den größeren Zusammenhang eines »intensiv geführten philosophisch/theologischen Diskurses« im Mittelalter eingebettet werden

---

28 Newman (2012), S. 360.
29 Strohschneider (2014), S. 106.
30 Zu fragen ist, inwiefern es sich daher um ein metaphorisches Verständnis von Schrift handelt im Unterschied zu einem wörtlichen; zu dieser Unterscheidung siehe Volfing (2010), S. 152 f.

könnte, bei dem im Mittelpunkt die Frage danach stand, »wie Gott aber auf Erden überhaupt erfahrbar sein konnte«: Williams-Krapp führt aus, dass im volkssprachigen Schrifttum, wo »die große Mehrheit der ›mystisch‹ Begnadeten aus den Reihen der ›illiterati‹« stamme, der Anspruch herrsche, »über eine höhere spirituelle Legitimation und mithin in geistlichen Fragen unerschütterlichere ›auctoritas‹ zu verfügen als die Gelehrten.«[31] Ein solcher Anspruch ist zum Teil auch in der Christina von Hane-Vita spürbar.[32] Christinas Verständnis der göttlichen Erkenntnis wird dabei als wandelbar und prozesshaft dargestellt: *Da wart sie geleret yn yrem verstentenyß, yn allen sachen zo flegen zo dem gebede, alleyn myt gode zo reden vnd zo myden alle vnnutze reden.* (CvH 10, 104–106) Die Begriffsnuancen von *verstentenyß* werden an anderen Stellen ausgehandelt.[33] Dass die rationale Fakultät der Seele, die in der Christina-Vita mit dem ekstatischen Element verbunden wird, wie die Wendung *entzucket van yrem verstentenyß* (CvH 10, 97) zeigt, eine Gabe Gottes bleibt, weiß das Sprecher-Ich Christinas auszuführen:

> *Want die sele alleyn geschaiffen ist, got zo erkennen, so eyn mach sie doch van yre selber nyt vber sich selber komen, sie eyn werde dan gotlichen vff erhaben van dem, nach dem sie geschaiffen ist. Das ist die natuerliche wirdicheit der verstentlicher creaturen. Alleyn sie van yre selber gotliche dynge nyt eyn mache begryffen, so mache sye doch gotliche dynge entphangen, abe yr van gode gehoilffen wyrt.* (CvH 80, 51–56)

In den Offenbarungen Adelheid Langmanns heißt es ebenfalls, dass *ir ward aber ze versten geben* (›Die Offenbarungen der Adelheid Langmann‹ 69, 14). Die Gabe erscheint hier wichtig, denn so ist das intellektuelle Verstehen als Gnadenerweis ausgestellt. Von einer Gegenüberstellung einer affektiven versus scholastischen

---

31 Williams-Krapp (2008), S. 264.

32 So insbesondere in der Gegenüberstellung der Meinung der Meister (Scholastiker) mit der Erkenntnis Christinas (vgl. CvH 98), siehe dazu Kirakosian (2014a).

33 Vgl. die folgenden Textstellen: *da verlore sie van rechtem jamer vnd hertzen leyde alle yre verstentenyß fier wochen* (CvH 18, 16 f.); *Das erkante sie vnd alles, was man yn dem cloister reden was, daz hoirte sie, ader wo man iß reytde, daz hoirte sie ynwendich yn dem verstentenyß* (CvH 23, 14–16); *da was yre sele, daz ist das vberste verstentenyß der selen ader des ynnerlichen menschen, das was yn der vbersoißer begerunge* (CvH 57, 49 f.); *Dar na wart yr geist, yre vberst verstentenyß, vber sich getzogen yn die dryueldicheit* (CvH 78, 17 f.); *Yn dem lyecht vnd yn der lyebden wart myn hertze vnd myn verstentenyß vff erhaben zo beschauwen vnd zo bekennen gotliche dynge […]. Da myn sele yn dem lyecht der luterer verstentenyß erhaben wart vber menscheliche nature, da wart auch myn lyffe vff erhaben van der craifft godes zo sieben maillen […]* (CvH 80, 23–29); *Myt dyeßem gesicht quamme yr eyn starcke schrecken, daz sie wart entzucket van yrem verstentenyß* (CvH 10, 96 f.); *jn dem hyne zucke yrs verstentenyß* (CvH 80, 47); *Du haist entphangen jn myner gotheit eyn selichen yn fluß der soißer freuden, also bystu yn myr aller soiste. Hiemyt ist erlucht dyne verstentenyß* (CvH 95, 3–5).

Mystik, wie zuletzt von Maarten Hoenen verteidigt,[34] kann daher keine Rede sein.[35] Intellektuelle und spirituelle Visionen schließen sich in der Christina-Vita nicht gegenseitig aus. Stattdessen wird, wie das Volfing am Beispiel des ›Speculum Virginum‹ darlegt, das Klischee von weiblicher Irrationalität in Frage gestellt.[36] Dabei ist zu beachten, dass nicht allein die Verwendung rational-scholastischer Konzepte für die Beschreibung visionärer Entrückungen zu diesem Schluss führt, denn in der Christina-Vita findet die Auseinandersetzung mit der Frage nach Sprache und göttlicher Mitteilung auch auf der Diskursebene statt. Dieser Auseinandersetzung gilt das Augenmerk des nächsten Teilkapitels.

5.2 Das Fließen der göttlichen Offenbarung

Die Frage, wie sich Gott eigentlich mitteilt, wird explizit von Christinas Sprecher-Ich gestellt. Zwar wird vorhergehend konstatiert, dass Gott eine Stimme sei (vgl. CvH 21, 37), doch wird erst im letzten Abschnitt der Vita, die eine Auslegung der Verkündigungsszene darstellt, die göttliche Offenbarung explizit als ein (Aus-) Fließen dargelegt. Zudem führt die Schlusspassage aus, wie das Sprechen Gottes mit der Trinität zusammenhängt:

> *Da sache sie an dem vß floiße, daz ist die vffenbarunge, daz er sich selber vffenbairt, vnd syne vffenbairen, daz ist syne sprechen. Also sache die sele die ordenunge der engel, daz got myt yn spricht. Got eyn hait nyt zunge noch mont noch nuste. Wo myt sprycht er dan? Sye sprechent, myt den engelen ist, daz er sich eym yecklichen engel vffenbart, als er zo gode geordent ist. Gat vße floiße, daz ist eyn blenckender wylle vnder eym lyechte eyner reden, das der sone ewige ist van dem vader gefloißen myt der naturen vnd myt der personen, vnd der vader vnd der sone hugent jren geist yn der ewicheit.* (CvH 100, 8–15)

Die Formulierungen *ordenunge der engel* und *sich eym yecklichen engel vffenbart, als er zo gode geordent ist* verweisen auf eine von Dionysius Areopagita geprägte

---

34 Vgl. Maarten J. F. M. Hoenen: Translating Mystical Texts from the Vernacular into Latin. The Intentions and Strategies behind Laurentius Surius' edition of John Ruusbroec's Complete Works (Cologne 1552). In: Per perscrutationem philosophicam. Neue Perspektiven der mittelalterlichen Forschung. Loris Sturlese zum 60. Geburtstag gewidmet. Hrsg. von Alessandra Beccarisi/Ruedi Imbach/Pasquale Porro (Corpus philosophorum Teutonicorum Medii Aevi. Beihefte 4). Hamburg 2008, S. 348–374, insbes. S. 358 f.
35 So hängen in der Christina von Hane-Vita z. B. Vernunft und *fruitio* zusammen (vgl. CvH 56).
36 Vgl. Volfing (2008), S. 346.

mystische Theologie.[37] Thema ist also die auf den Areopagiten zurückgehende Vorstellung, dass Engel Gott besonders nahe seien. Wenn man die im Mittelalter weit verbreitete u.a. von Boethius beeinflusste kosmologische Vorstellung des Engelgesangs (*musica celestis*) voraussetzt,[38] dann stellt sich die Frage, ob die Vita eigentlich Gesang meint, wenn sie das »Sprechen Gottes in der Ordnung der Engel« thematisiert. Die göttlich figurierten Sprechpartien in der Christina-Vita haben in der Tat einen besonderen Sprachklang; Wort- und Phrasenwiederholungen, parataktische Satzanreihungen und Gleichklänge führen zu einer rhythmisierten Prosa. Laut vorgelesen erreicht so musikalische Sprache den Anschein einer klanginduzierten Liebesvereinigung zwischen Seele und göttlichem Bräutigam.[39] Dabei bedeutet die Trinität auch in der Christina von Hane-Vita, wie Haas für Meister Eckhart resümiert, »ein[en] Vorgang des göttlichen Sich-selbst-Aussprechens«.[40] Im Ausfließen, im Sprechen wird der Sohn geboren; die Vereinigung von Vater, Sohn und Heiligem Geist ist eine sich ewig wiederholende, die in der Christina-Vita entlang der Interpretation des Wortes *fiat* erklärt wird, das zum neutestamentlichen Ausruf der Bereitwilligkeit Marias zur Empfängnis gehört: *Dixit autem Maria: Ecce ancilla Domini; fiat mihi secundum verbum tuum et discessit ab illa angelus* (Lc 1,38). In der mittelalterlichen Rezeption der Verkündigungsszene spielt die verbale Kommunikation eine entscheidende Rolle für die Empfängnis.[41] In der Vita der Christina von Hane wird der Engelgruß als Bestätigung Marias in ihrer Disposition zur Gottesgebärerin beschrieben:

---

37 Zur Areopagitischen Engelsordnung siehe Rosemary A. Arthur: Pseudo-Dionysius as Polemicist. The Development and Purpose of the Angelic Hierarchy in Sixth Century Syria. Aldershot 2008.

38 Vgl. die drei Arten von Musik bei Boethius: *musica mundana, musica humana* und *musica instrumentis*, Boethius: ›De institutione musica‹. In: De institutione arithmetica libri duo. De institutione musica libri quinque. Accedit Geometria quae fertur Boetii. Hrsg. von Gottfried Friedlein. Leipzig 1867 (unveränd. Nachdruck Frankfurt a. M. 1966), S. 175–371, hier S. 187–189.

39 Carolyn Muessig: Prophecy and Song: Teaching and Preaching by Medieval Women. In: Women Preachers and Prophets through Two Millennia of Christianity. Hrsg. von Beverly Mayne Kienzle/Pamela J. Walker. Berkeley 1998, S. 146–158, insbes. S. 148, betont die Verbindung zwischen Musik und weiblicher Spiritualität: »[...] we see the significance and importance of song in allowing women a vehicle for expressing their spiritual learning«. Jakob von Vitry hielt den Gesang einer Jungfrau für die Manifestation der Vereinigung ihrer Seele mit dem brautmystischen Christus, vgl. ebd., S. 149.

40 Haas (1984b), S. 619.

41 Vgl. Horst Wenzel: Die Verkündigung an Maria. Zur Visualisierung des Wortes in der Szene oder: Schriftgeschichte im Bild. In: Maria in der Welt. Marienverehrung im Kontext der Sozialgeschichte 10.–18. Jahrhundert. Hrsg. von Claudia Opitz u.a. (Clio Lucdenensis 2). Zürich 1993, S. 23–52, insbes. S. 48. Auf der Basis der Verkündigungsszene wird das Hören des göttlichen Wortes als grundlegend in der Mystik beschrieben, vgl. Flasch (2011), S. 39 f.; siehe auch Burk-

Der engel sprach zo vnser lyeber frauwen: »Aue gracia plena dominus tecum.« Des irsten
wortze eyn achte sy nyt viel. Als er sprache, daz sie were vol genaden vnd daz got myt yre were
geistlichen steitlichen yn yrer selen, dan das got lyplichen van yre geboren soiltde werden [...].
(CvH 100, 38–41)

Die mariologische Lesart gestaltet sich historisch-biblisch einerseits und als zeitlose Vereinigung Marias mit Gott andererseits.[42] Der brautmystische Charakter
der Christina-Vita hebt die typologische Beziehung von Maria und menschlicher
Seele hervor und daher auch das Sich-Aussprechen Gottes im performativen
Sprechhandeln als Voraussetzung und gleichzeitige Folge der Vereinigung, die
daher sowohl in die Gottesgeburt mündet als auch dieselbe darstellt.[43] Schließlich geht die menschliche Seele die Vereinigung mit Gott ein: *Das drytte »fiat«,*
daz gesprochen ist, daz ist degelichs yn eyner ewicheit vnd yn der zijt zo der zarter
selen, die myt gode vereyniget ist. (CvH 100, 65 f.) Diese außerzeitliche Vereinigung
wird als Geburt dargestellt.

Eine derartige Gottesgeburt in der Seele findet sich auch in der Philosophie
Meister Eckharts. Der letzte Abschnitt der Christina-Vita weist ohnehin deutliche
Parallelen zu der deutschen Predigt Meister Eckharts zur Verkündigung nach
dem Lukasevangelium auf (Lc 1,26–28).[44] Die Begründung der Gottesgeburt in der
menschlichen Seele rekurriert sowohl bei Eckhart als auch in der Christina von

---

hard Hasebrink: Das Predigtverfahren Meister Eckharts. Beobachtungen zur thematischen und
pragmatischen Kohärenz der Predigt Q 12. In: Die deutsche Predigt im Mittelalter. Internationales Symposium am Fachbereich Germanistik der Freien Universität Berlin vom 3.–6. Oktober
1989. Hrsg. von Volker Mertens/Hans-Jochen Schiewer. Tübingen 1992, S. 150–168, insbes. S. 158.
In diesem Sinne wird die Andacht Marias, in der sie sich zum Zeitpunkt des Engelbesuchs be-
funden haben soll, traditionell als eine kontemplative Schriftlektüre hervorgehoben. Vgl. Klaus
Schreiner: Marienverehrung, Lesekultur, Schriftlichkeit. Bildungs- und frömmigkeitsgeschicht-
liche Studien zur Auslegung und Darstellung von Mariä Verkündigung. In: Frühmittelalterliche
Studien 24 (1990), S. 314–368, insbes. S. 318–331, zur mittelalterlichen Rezeption und Exegese der
Verkündigungsszene, wonach Maria eine kontemplierende, mit Gott die Vereinigung eingehende
Figur darstellt. Siehe auch Büttner (1983), S. 70–72, zur Verkündigung als Andachtspraxis.
42 Diese zwei Ebenen finden sich auch in Taulers Weihnachtspredigt zu den drei Geburten, vgl.
›Die Predigten Taulers‹ 1.
43 Vgl. Seelhorst (2003), S. 24–28, zur Diskussion der *unio* als Sprachprinzip.
44 Vgl. insbesondere: *Ûz der lûterkeit hât er mich êwiclîche geborn sînen einbornen sun in daz*
selbe bilde sîner êwigen vaterschaft, daz ich vater sî und geber den, von dem ich geborn bin. Ze
glîcher wîs, als ob einer stüende vor einem hôhen berge und ruofte: ›bistû dâ?‹ der gal und der hal
ruofte wider: ›bistû dâ?‹ Spræche er: ›kum her ûz!‹ der gal spræche ouch: ›kum her ûz!‹ Jâ, der in
dém liehte ein holz sæhe, daz würde ein engel und würde vernünftic, und niht aleine vernünftic, ez
würde ein lûter vernunft in der êrsten lûterkeit, diu dâ ist ein vülle aller lûterkeit. Alsô tuot got: er ge-
birt sînen einbornen sun in daz hœhste teil der sêle. In dem selben, daz er gebirt sînen eingebornen

Hane-Vita auf die vorauslaufende geistliche Geburt durch die Jungfrau Maria, wie sie bereits Augustinus entwickelt:[45]

> *Ich spriche: und hæte Marîâ niht von êrste got geistlîche geborn, er enwære nie lîplîche von ir geborn worden.* (DW I, 22, 375)

> *Aber were got nyt also lyeblichen vnd gruntlichen yn yrer selen gewest, er eyn were nye lyplichen van yre geboren worden.* (CvH 100, 44–46)

Auffällig erscheint hier der Gebrauch von *gruntlichen* in der Christina von Hane-Vita, weil er, anders als die Verwendung von *grunt* im Rest der Vita, dem Eckhartschen Konzept des Seelengrundes nahe zu stehen scheint. In jedem Fall wird sowohl in der Eckhart-Predigt als auch in der Christina von Hane-Vita das gesprochene Wort als Initiator jeglicher Gottesbewegung verstanden. *Were daz wort nyt gescheyt, alle syn gescheffze eyn were nuste gewest*, heißt es in der Vita (CvH 100, 25 f.), während Eckhart ausführt:

> *Dô got die sêle geschuof, dô geschuof er sie nâch sîner hœhsten volkomenheit, daz si solte sîn ein brût des eingebornen suns. Wan er diz wol bekante, sô wolte er ûzgân ûzer sîner heimlîcher triskamer der êwigen veterlicheit, in der er êwiclîche geslâfen hât, ungesprochen inneblîbende.* (DW I, 22, 387 f.)

Eckhart bleibt nicht bei dem Bild des sich-aussprechenden und dadurch stetig gebärenden Gottes stehen. Die Rückkehr Gottes mit der Seele in seine Schlafkammer führt zurück in den Zustand des ›Unausgeprochenen‹.[46] Zu fragen bleibt, ob die fragmentarisch erscheinende Christina von Hane-Vita letztlich auch zu diesem Umkehrschluss kommt, insofern der plötzliche Textabbruch als eine performative Strategie des Unausgesprochenen verstanden werden kann. Festzuhalten ist jedenfalls, dass sowohl in der Eckhart-Predigt wie auch in der Christina von Hane-Vita die Umkehrung in eine Außersprachlichkeit den höchsten Zustand der Seele bedeutet:[47]

---

sun in mich, sô gebir ich in wider in den vater. Daz enwas anders niht, dan daz got den engel gebar wider dem, daz er von der juncvrouwen geborn wart. (DW I [1958], 22, 382 f.)

45 Dass dieser Gedanke der spirituellen Schwangerschaft auch in anderen mystischen Texten behandelt wurde, zeigt die oben genannte Predigt Taulers, insbes. ›Die Predigten Taulers‹ 1, 11.

46 Vgl.: *Dâ er ûzgienc von dem allerhœhsten, dâ wolte er wider îngân mit sîner brût in dem allerlûtersten und wolte ir offenbâren die verborgene heimlicheit sîner verborgenen gotheit, dâ er ruowet mit im selber mit allen crêatûren* (DW I, 22, 388).

47 Zum weiteren Vergleich, insbesondere mit den letzten Sätzen der Christina von Hane-Vita, sei Eckharts Beschreibung des Seelengrunds (hier: *kraft in dem geiste*) herangezogen: *Ez ist von*

Einez ist in der sêle, in dem got blôz ist, und die meister sprechent, ez sî namelôs, und ez enhabe keinen eigenen namen. Ez ist und hât doch kein eigen wesen, wan ez ist noch diz noch daz noch hie noch dâ; wan ez ist, daz ez ist, in einem andern und jenez in disem; wan, daz ez ist, daz ist ez in jenem und jenez in disem; wan jenez vliuzet in diz und diz in jenez — (DW I, 24, 417 f.);

Das drytte »fiat«, daz gesprochen ist, daz ist degelichs yn eyner ewicheit vnd yn der zijt zo der zarter selen, die myt gode vereyniget ist. Da bekennet sy got vnd smacket got yn gotlicher naturen. Dan got sie vber schynnet als die sone den maynt. Da flußet got yn got. Da wyrt sie van genaden, das got ist van naturen, vnd wyrt gesencket yn den grondeloißen bornen der gotlicher naturen. Dan ist sie bloiße yrs selbes, als got ist aller namen. Also sterbet sie yn den wonderen der gotheit. Da flußet got yn gode, daz sie nyt begryffen kayne die gotliche nature. (CvH 100, 65–71)

In beiden Abschnitten wird das Bild des Fließens gebraucht, um die Beziehung zwischen Seele und Gott zu illustrieren. Das mystische Konzept der Emanation hängt mit der Geburt des Gottessohnes als Wortinkarnation zusammen. Hasebrink zeigt, wie Eckhart in seiner Exegese des Schriftwortes nach Lc 11,28 das göttliche Sprechen als Selbstmitteilung erschließt.[48] In der Christina von Hane-Vita wird das göttliche Wort mit der Geburt des Sohnes in der Bewegung des Fließens gefasst:

Gat vße floiße, daz ist eyn blenckender wylle vnder eym lyechte eyner reden, das der sone ewige ist van dem vader gefloißen myt der naturen vnd myt der personen, vnd der vader vnd der sone hugent jren geist yn der ewicheit. Da synt alle creaturen got yn gode vnder dem vßfloiße. (CvH 100, 12–16)

Die Eckhart-Predigt zur Verkündigung lässt sich hier erneut gegenüberstellen:[49]

Hier inne is ze verstânne, daz wir sîn ein einiger sun, den der vater êwiclîche geborn hât. Dô der vater gebar alle crêatûren, dô gebar er mich und ich vlôz ûz mit allen crêatûren und bleip doch inne in dem vater. (DW I, 22, 376)

Der »Ausfluss« wird vom Sprecher-Ich Christinas als Ursprung allen Lichts, als kreatürliche Quelle beschrieben:

---

allen namen vrî und von allen formen blôz, ledic und vrî zemâle, als got ledic und vrî ist in im selber. (DW I, 2, 40)

48 Vgl. Hasebrink (1992b), S. 215–218.

49 Siehe auch Eckharts Erklärung der (Un-)Ähnlichkeit von Grashalmen: *Ein meister sprach: daz alle grasspier sô unglîch sint, daz kumet von der übervlüzzicheit gotes güete, die er stürzet übervlüzziclîche in alle crêatûren, daz sîn hêrschaft deste mê geoffenbâret werde. Dô sprach ich: ez ist wunderlîcher, wie alle grasspier sô glîch sint [...].* (DW I, 22, 384 f.)

> *Vnd ich sache yn dem lyecht, das er ist eyn oirsproncke alles lyechtes vnd eyn borne alles*
> *lebens vnd eyne vß floiße alles wesens. Vnd alle das gůt, daz alle creaturen entphangen*
> *mogent, das eyn ist nůste entgene dem, daz got, der lebendige borne, ist yn yme selber.* (CvH
> 99, 2–5)

Dieses kreatürliche Verständnis eines überfließenden Gottes findet auch in anderen Texten im Emanationsbild des Brunnens seinen Niederschlag. Wie Köbele jüngst für den ›Marienleich‹ Frauenlobs gezeigt hat, ist »Marias heilsgeschichtliche Funktion sehr eng mit dem Schöpfergott verbunden«, wobei das »weltschöpferische Prinzip« als ein zeitloser Verlauf, also als eine *creatio continua*, vorzustellen sei.[50] In der ›Goldenen Schmiede‹ dagegen wird der Schöpfungsakt durch das Gotteswort hervorgebracht.[51] Hier wird die Erlösung der Seele durch Maria mit der Taufmetaphorik als Wiedergeburt illustriert. Wie der Adler, der seine Kinder fallen lässt:

> *also versuochest du si gar*
> *diu din tugent widerbar*
> *in des toufes brunnen.*
> *do si den tot gewunnen,*
> *do gebære du si wider.* (›Die Goldene Schmiede‹ V. 1069–1073)

In der ›Goldenen Schmiede‹ ist das Fließmotiv stets marianisch konnotiert (vgl. ›Die Goldene Schmiede‹ V. 525–575, 651–671, 936–955). Im ›Tum‹ ist das Motiv des fließenden Sprechens auf die Marienpreis-Dichtung selbst ausgeweitet.[52] Zugleich ist Maria ein Jungbrunnen:

> *Du brunn und heiles mar,*
> *in dem des himels adelar*
> *sich jungt und sin gefider gar* (›Der Tum‹ 129, 1–4).

In der ›Goldenen Schmiede‹ ist Maria hingegen der *kiusche brunne* (›Die Goldene Schmiede‹ V. 1350), in Frauenlobs ›Marienleich‹ ein *zuckersüzer brunne* (Frauenlob, ›Marienleich‹ XII, 1), im ›Arnsteiner Marienleich‹ ein *burne des paradises* (›Arnsteiner Marienleich‹ 42, 3). In der Exegese von Ct 5,12 und Ps 41,2–3 steht der *fons* nach Pseudo-Dionysius, Bernhard, Thomas Gallus und Robert Grosse-

---

50 Köbele (2014), S. 192.

51 Vgl.: *sin wort und sines mundes ruof / mag elliu dinc gewürken* (›Die Goldene Schmiede‹ V. 1694 f.).

52 Vgl.: *Meit, aller güt inguß, / hab ich ich nicht blünder sprüch influß / geleitet sam her Tullius / in dines hoen lobes tich* (›Der Tum‹ 175, 1–4).

teste für den Urquell des lebendigen Wassers.[53] In der ›Goldenen Schmiede‹ ist es
Maria, die das lebendige Wasser liefert.[54] In Rudolfs von Biberach ›siben strassen
zu got‹ figuriert wiederum, wie das auch in der Christina von Hane-Vita der Fall
ist, zweifelsohne Gott den Brunnen.[55] Diese Beispiele zeigen, dass das Brunnen-
motiv mit dem Fließen des göttlichen Aussprechens assoziiert wird, und zwar
unabhängig davon, ob Maria als Empfängerin oder als Geberin des lebendigen
Wassers dargestellt wird. In der Christina von Hane-Vita wird deutlich dargelegt,
dass die Emanation mit dem Sprechen einhergeht. Hier führt das Sprechen Gottes
zur Gottesgeburt in der Seele, die sodann in das *enunciare* des Wortes mündet,
wie das etwa Laird für die Mystik Gregors von Nyssa diskutiert. Wenn auch Lairds
tautologischer Neologismus »logophatic« unglücklich zusammengesetzt scheint,
macht er die Auswirkung der unsagbaren *unio*-Erfahrung in ihrem Mitteilungs-
drang deutlich.[56] Auf einen solchen Mitteilungscharakter weist auch Hasebrink
hin. Den für die Predigten Eckharts von Hasebrink ausgearbeiteten worttheologi-
schen Kategorien nach ist in der Christina-Vita ganz besonders die »Dialogizität
von göttlichem Sprechen und Hören« evident.[57] Die Vereinigung ist also auch im
Dialog umgesetzt und nicht nur narrativ dargestellt.[58]

---

53 Vgl. Schmidt (1969), S. 140*. Das Motiv des lebendigen Wassers im Neuen Testament findet
sich in der Geschichte der Samariterin am Brunnen, vgl. Io 4,1–30.

54 Vgl.: *lesch uns den eweclichen durst / mit diner tugent frühtec, / daz wir niht wazzersühtec /
beliben an der sele dort* (›Die Goldene Schmiede‹ V. 1336–1339).

55 Vgl.: *Min sel hat geturst zů gotte, der ein brunne des lebendes ist* (Rudolf von Biberach: ›Die
siben strassen zu got‹ 112, 14 f.); *Der vatter, der ein brvnne der sůzikeit ist* (ebd., 17, 17); *Iesus [...] ist
ein brv̇nlichv̇ genv̇cht der inflv̇ssen gŏtlicher sůzzikeit* (ebd., 182, 19 f.).

56 Vgl. Martin S. Laird: Gregory of Nyssa and the Grasp of Faith. Union, Knowledge, and Divine
Presence (Oxford early Christian studies). Oxford 2004, S. 155: »The union is apophatic, but the
effect is logophatic; for the Word fills the mouth of the bride ›with words of eternal life.‹« Dass
die *unio*-erfahrung zum mystischen Sprechen führt, stand auch vor der Begriffsfindung Lairds
außer Frage, vgl. Seelhorst (2003), S. 23. Für Angela von Foligno entseht im Anschluss an das
Hören des Gotteswortes ein Mitteilungsbedürfnis, vgl: *Iterum adhuc Deus venit in animam, et
loquitur ei verba dulcissima in quibus multum delectatur, et sentit eum, in quo sentimento valde
delectatur* (Angela von Foligno, ›Memoriale‹ VII, 288 f.); *Sed hic certificatur anima quod Deus est
intus in ea, quia sentit eum aliter quam consuevit, quia sentit eum cum tanto duplicato sentimento
et cum tanto amore et igne divino, quo aufertur ei omnis timor animae et corporis. Et loquitur ea,
quae nunquam audivit ab aliquo mortali, et intelligit ea cum maximo lumine, et est ei poena tacere
illa* (Angela von Foligno, ›Memoriale‹ VII, 294–298).

57 Hasebrink (1992b), S. 57.

58 Daher ist in den Momenten der Vereinigung die Stimme Gottes in einer Dialoginszenierung
›vernehmbar‹ und zwar sowohl diegetisch als auch auf der Textoberfläche; siehe auch Volfing
(2008), S. 333.

Auf metaphorischer Ebene ist die fließende Gottesmitteilung in der Christina-Vita in dem Bild des Siegels greifbar.[59] Solche Schriftmetaphern finden sich auch in anderen Texten. So weist Löser nach, wie bei Mechthild von Magdeburg das Fließen eine Metapher für Schrift ist und daher auch als Akt des Mitteilens gesehen werden kann.[60] In der Vita der Christina von Hane verbinden sich die Komplexe Sprache und Fließen vor dem Hintergrund der Ebenbildlichkeit der menschlichen Seele mit Gott. In einer Ansprache der göttlichen Stimme wird Christina als »lebendiges Buch« angesprochen: *Du byst eyn lebendiges buche, gezeyget myt der heilger dryfeldicheit. Du byst versiegelt myt den sieben gaben des heilgen geistes yn der heilger dryfeldicheit.* (CvH 72, 4–6) In Gertruds von Helfta ›Legatus‹ ist die Vorstellung des siebenfach versiegelten Buches auf die Handschrift selbst ausgeweitet, wobei die sieben Siegel explizit als Metapher für die Gaben des Heiligen Geistes ausgewiesen werden.[61] In der Christina-Vita greift das aus der Johannesoffenbarung gespeiste Bild des siebenfach versiegelten Buches auf eine Episode zurück,[62] in der sich Christina Gott als *yngesegel* aufs Herz einprägen soll: *O myn aller lyebste bruyt, lege mych als eyne yngesegel vff dyne hertze.* (CvH 42, 2 f.)[63] Das *yngesegel* wird seit dem 12. Jahrhundert als ein Verweis auf die theologische Bedeutung der analogen Beziehung zwischen Gottheit und Mensch-

---

59 Die Honig-Metapher illustriert ebenfalls den fließenden Charakter von Sprache, vgl.: *vnd da hait der lyebelicher got aber eynße gesprochen zo yrer selen also myt honynchfluyßichen wortten* [...] (CvH 94, 2 f.). Das Bild des Honigs hängt üblicherweise mit der Exegese von Ct 4,11 zusammen, siehe dazu Friedrich Ohly: Süße Nägel der Passion. Ein Beitrag zur theologischen Semantik. In: Collectanea philologica. Festschrift für Helmut Gipper zum 65. Geburtstag. Hrsg. von Günter Heintz/Peter Schmitte. 2 Bde. (Saecula spiritualia 14–15). Baden-Baden 1985, Bd. 2, S. 403–613, insbes. S. 481–498. In den Offenbarungen Langmanns ist die Rezeption des Hoheliedverses evident: *dein munt ist süezzer denn ie lein hongseim. hong und milch ist unter deiner zungen* (›Die Offenbarungen der Adelheid Langmann‹ 22, 18 f.); siehe auch ›Die Offenbarungen der Adelheid Langmann‹ 26, 13 f. Zur Geschmacksqualifikation Gottes und der trinitarischen Personen als süß siehe Ohly (1985), S. 436–445.
60 Vgl. Löser (2012), S. 160–169. Dass sich im ›Fließenden Licht‹ Gott durch sein Wort offenbart, stellt bereits Andersen (2003), S. 232, fest.
61 Vgl.: ›[...] *Das bůch wil ich decken mit minem heiligen leben; [...] und wil es versygelen mit miner götlichen krafft, mit den sůben goben des heiligen geistes reht also mit sůben ingesygelen [...].*‹ (Gertrud von Helfta, ›ein botte der götlichen miltekeit‹ 3, 26–29)
62 Die sieben Gaben des Heiligen Geistes in der Passage der Christina-Vita spielen auf die sieben Siegel aus der Johannesoffenbarung an, vgl. Apc 5,5. Weitere biblische Siegelreferenzen speisen das Bild des versiegelten Buches, vgl. Io 6,27; 2 Cor 1,21 f.; Eph 1,13 f.; Eph 4,30; Apc 7,3.
63 Die gesamte Formulierung ist dem Hohenlied entnommen, vgl.: *pone me ut signaculum super cor tuum* (Ct 8,6).

heit verwendet.[64] Während das Wort *yngesegel* im Deutschen ursprünglich aus der Urkundensprache stammt, hat es hier die Bedeutung des Abbilds: Christina soll sich Gott buchstäblich in ihr Herz einprägen.[65] Die Nuance des Abbildens für lat. *signaculum* oder *sigillum* findet sich schon in der frühmittelalterlichen Scholastik, wo der Stempel des (göttlichen) Siegels einerseits das Eigentumsverhältnis anzeigt (die menschliche Seele gehört Gott) und andererseits die *similitudo* zwischen Matrix und bearbeitetem Material verdeutlicht (die menschliche Seele ist zwar nicht Gott, aber dessen Abbild).[66] Entsprechend wird in der Mönchstheologie die Vereinigung mit Gott als Schmelzvorgang der Braut beschrieben (Ct 5,6), in die sich Gott wie ein Siegel eindrücken kann;[67] Bernhard von Clairvaux und Richard von St. Viktor betonen das Weich- und Flüssigwerden der Seele und im ›St. Trudperter Hohenlied‹ wird die Seele von der Hitze des Heiligen Geistes geschmolzen.[68] Wie Christina von Hane verwenden auch die Mystikerinnen von Helfta die Vorstellung des Schmelzens der Seele zur Darstellung der *unio*-Erfah-

---

64 Vgl. Fulton (2002), S. 256, über die Zeit des Honorius Augustodunensis: »The dualistic nature of the seal came into its own, however, in contemporary attempts to explain the mysteries of the faith, particularly the mysteries of the Godhead and the relationship between that Godhead and humanity.« Der Gedanke der Einprägung geht auf Augustinus' Lehre vom *caracter sacramentalis* zurück, die auf Rm 4,11 basiert; vgl. Daniel Weidner: Ein Beispielfall nach der Reformation. Sakrament, Rhetorik und Repräsentation bei Théodore de Bèze. In: Sakramentale Repräsentation. Substanz, Zeichen und Präsenz in der Frühen Neuzeit. Hrsg. von Stefanie Ertz / Heike Schlie. München 2012, S. 29–48, insbes. S. 37 f.

65 Vgl. »ingesigel« in Lexer (1872), Sp. 1433. Schmidt (1969), S. 105* f., führt aus, dass für Rudolf von Biberach das Siegel »ein reines Wort der Kanzleisprache als Prägestempel oder Abdruck« sei, das »sinnbildlich das Gezeichnetsein von Gott nach dem Maße seiner Wahl« bedeute, »um die Seele dem göttlichen Willen gleichförmig zu machen, ganz nach Gott zu bilden, zur Identität zu führen«. Das Verhältnis von Abbild und Abdruck ist ausgeführt von Christinas Sprecher-Ich: *Vnd syne bylde ist yn mym hertzen gedrucket* [...] (CvH 62, 10 f.).

66 Vgl. Fulton (2002), S. 254–256.

67 Vgl. den Matthäuskommentar bei Rupert von Deutz: *et in me demissa totam compleuit animae meae substantiam, eo modo mihi impressa, quem uerbis exprimere nullatenus possum, multo citius atque profundius, quam cera, quamuis mollisima, sigillum fortiter impressum admittere possit. Protinus somno qui uix obrepserat excussus sum, et uigilans sensi dulce pondus, uigilans delectatus sum, et quid dicam? Anima mea liquefacta est* (Rupert von Deutz: ›De gloria et honore filii hominis super Mattheum‹. Hrsg. von Rhaban Haacke [CCM 29]. Tournai 1979, Buch XII, S. 383, Z. 785-791); siehe dazu Weiss (2000), S. 524–526 und S. 535 f. Zu Ruperts von Deutz mariologischer Hoheliedauslegung siehe Rubin (2010), S. 159 f. Auch bei Langmann kommt die Siegel-Wachs-Metapher vor: *daz si dauht, si klebot in im als ain wahs in ainem insigel* (›Die Offenbarungen der Adelheid Langmann‹ 67, 30 f.).

68 Vgl. Weiss (2000), S. 524–526, und Fulton (2002), S. 257.

rung.[69] So spricht die Prämonstratenserin, ähnlich wie Gertrud von Helfta, ihre Seele sei weich geworden:[70]

› [...] *Da sprach myn sele zo yme myt groißer freuden:* »*Myn sele ist weche geworden, als myn lyeffe myr hait gereyt.* « *Vnd syne bylde ist yn mym hertzen gedrucket myt eyniger furiger lyebden, die nummerme verleißen eyn mache.* ‹ (CvH 6, 9–11)

Die göttliche Stimme bestätigt diesen veränderten Seelenzustand als Schmelz-vorgang in der Vereinigung: *Du byst altzo mail myt myr vereyniget vnd van myner gotlicher lyebden zosmoiltzen vnd gentzelichen yn mych zoflußen* (CvH 89, 3–5).[71]

---

69 Die folgenden Textstellen betreffen den Schmelzvorgang: [...] *das des moenschen herze be-ginnet ze brennende und sin sele ze smelzende und sin ovgen ze vliessende* (Mechthild von Mag-deburg, ›Das fließende Licht der Gottheit‹ VI 13, 8 f.), vgl. die fließenden Augen in der Vita der Christina von Hane: *also daz yre hertze vnd yre augen myt eyn ander worden fließen van eym soißen ynbrunstigen schryen* (CvH 4, 13 f.). Im ›Liber‹ heißt es: *Anima mea liquefacta est?* (Mecht-hild von Hackeborn, ›Liber specialis gratiae‹ VI 8, 387); *Sicque anima tota Christo incorporata et amore divino liquefacta, tamquam cera a facie ignis, totaque absorpta in Deo, sicut cera sigillo impressa, similitudinem illius praetendit* (ebd., I 1, 9); [...] *qui pro beneplacito suo et secundum quod animae expedire novit, eam sua dulcedine allicit, et amore suo liquescere facit* (ebd., III 9, 208); vgl. das Schmelzen durch die Süße Gottes bei Christina: *du versmiltzest van der gotlicher soißecheit yn myr* (CvH 70, 6). Siehe auch: *Anima vero tota in dilectum eliquabatur, ita ut quasi unus spiritus cum eo facta sibimet videretur.* (Mechthild von Hackeborn, ›Liber specialis gratiae‹ I 23, 83); *Unde et ardens amor cordis ipsius erga me continue liquefacit intima mea erga se in tantum quod sicut adeps in igne liquescit, sic dulcedo divini Cordis mei a calore cordis ipsius resoluta jugi-ter distillat in animam ejus.* (Gertrud von Helfta: ›Legatus divinae pietatis‹ I. In: Gertrude d'Helfta. Œuvres spirituelles II. Hrsg. von Pierre Doyère [Sources chrétiennes. Série des textes monas-tiques d'Occident 25]. Paris 1968, 3, 6, 140 [Die Stellennachweise geben Kapitel-, Paragraph- und Seitenzahlen an]); vgl. in verkehrter Weise das Schmelzen der Seele von der göttlichen Hitze bei Christina: *Du haist entfangen yn myr das fuer der gotlicher hytzsten. Dyner lyebden bewegonge spannet sich yn mych vnd du versmiltzest van der gotlicher soißecheit yn myr* (CvH 70, 4–6). – Siehe auch das Zerfließen der Seele bei Langmann (vgl. ›Die Offenbarungen der Adelheid Langmann‹ 65, 26 f.) und im ›St. Trudperter Hohenlied‹ (vgl. ›Das St. Trudperter Hoheliied‹ 1, 10 f.; 13, 13).

70 Vgl. mit dem Schmelzen des Herzens und der Seele in Gertruds von Helfta: ›Legatus divinae pietatis‹ V. In: Gertrude d'Helfta. Œuvres spirituelles V. Hrsg. von Jean-Marie Clément/Bernard de Vregille (Sources chrétiennes 331). Paris 1986, 27, 7, 218, und ›Legatus divinae pietatis‹ II. In: Gertrude d'Helfta. Œuvres spirituelles II, 23, 8, 338. (Die Stellennachweise geben Kapitel-, Para-graph- und Seitenzahlen an.) – Honorius Augustodunensis beschreibt in seinem exegetischen Werk ›Sigillum‹ die menschliche Seele als Wachs, in das sich der göttliche Siegel eindrückt, vgl. Fulton (2002), S. 257. Es handelt sich bei Honorius um eine mariologisches Lesart, vgl. Rubin (2010), S. 159.

71 Christinas Sprecher-Ich beschreibt die Liebesvereinigung mit Bildern des Feuers: *Vnd wanne yre got smacket, so drynget sie vff yn got myt starckem ernste vnd myt furiger lyebden vnd myt groißem lobe.* (CvH 97, 17 f.) Die mit Feuer angefachte Liebesekstase findet sich auch bei Maria von Oignies, Ivette von Huy, Ida von Nijvel, Beatrijz von Nazareth, Hadewijch, Mechthild von

Ein Blick auf die Mariendichtung zeigt, dass die Siegelmetapher im Zusammenhang mit dem Zerschmelzen der Seele mariologisch gedeutet werden kann. In Frauenlobs ›Marienleich‹ ist Maria in der Lage, alle Siegel (Apc 5,1) zu öffnen (vgl. Frauenlob, ›Marienleich‹ XIII, 33–38).[72] In Heinrichs von Mügeln ›Tum‹ rückt Maria an die Position Gottes, wenn sie über die Prägefähigkeit des Siegels verfügt: *o reine meit, in unsers herzen tigel / drück unde smelz der tugende ingesigel* (›Der Tum‹ 130, 9 f.).[73] Die Logik des Mariengedichts erlaubt diese Machtverschiebung vom Schöpfergott zur Schöpferin, weil Maria als die perfekte Gottesbraut jegliche Seele präfiguriert.[74] In der Christina von Hane-Vita mündet die mit den sieben Gaben des Heiligen Geistes ausgestattete Seele Christinas in die Dreieinigkeit Gottes und wird so mit der Gottheit vereint.[75] Über eine Analogie mit Christus, den das Neue Testament als das lebendige Wasser bezeichnet, wird sie von der göttlich figurierten Stimme angesprochen erhöht: *Du byst eyn was aller dogent, myt dem ich werden gedrencket* (CvH 70, 7 f.).[76] Das Schmelzen und Flüssigwerden ist die Voraussetzung, um in Gott zu fließen und anschließend selbst überzufließen.[77] Geschmolzen und als flüssiges Wasser gleicht Christinas Seele ihrem göttlichen Bräutigam, der in Anlehnung an das Hohelied (Ct 4,15) als *der lebendige*

Madgeburg, Ida von Gorsleeuw, Margarita von Ypern, Ida von Löwen, Mechthild von Hackeborn und Agnes Blannbekin, vgl. Weiss (2000), S. 519–524.

72 Siehe dazu Köbele (2014), S. 191 f.

73 Das Bild des Einprägens trägt die Konnotation der Fruchtbarkeit, des ›Vorgebärens‹ (aus lat. *prae* + *gnasci*).

74 Vgl.: *Got brach naturen rigel / und goß des himels ingesigel, / gebrechte in der meide tigel / nach unser münze sin gestalt* (›Der Tum‹ 183, 1–4). Siehe auch in den Sprüchen Heinrichs von Mügeln: […] *was hilfet dann sin ingesigel, / das er uß sines herzen milde riffte / und goß es in der meide tigel, / bi dem er himel, mer und erde stifte?* (Heinrich von Mügeln, Str. 32, V. 7–10). In: Karl Stackmann (Hrsg.): Die kleineren Dichtungen Heinrichs von Mügeln. Erste Abteilung. Die Spruchsammlung des Göttinger Cod. Philos. 21. 3 Teilbde (DTM 50–52). Berlin 1959, Bd. 1, S. 47. Auch in der ›Goldenen Schmiede‹ ist Maria das perfekte Abbild Gottes: *du bist ein warez ingesigel, / darin nach menschlicher art / diu gotheit gedrücket wart / und an sich nam ir zeichen* (›Die Goldene Schmiede‹ V. 490–493).

75 Der Vermittlungsakt der Vereinigung liegt als reversibler Prozess (aus dem dreieinigen Gott herausgeflossen) im ›Fließenden Licht‹ Mechthilds von Magdeburg vor, vgl. Palmer (1992), S. 231.

76 Siehe auch CvH 80, 46–48. Vgl. die entsprechenden Bezeichnungen in der Bibel: *aquam vivam* (Io 4,10 f.). Siehe auch: *qui credit in me sicut dixit scriptura flumina de ventre eius fluent aquae vivae* (Io 7,38). Im typologischen Verfahren wird eine brautmystische Verbindung zum Hohenlied hergestellt, vgl.: *fons hortorum puteus aquarum viventium* (Ct 4,15).

77 In der mystischen Vereinigung wird die Seele Christinas der überfließenden Natur Gottes gleich, wie die Christus-Figur Christina versichert: *Du flußest myt vberfludicher lyebden. Jch byn yn dyr vnd du salt syn yn myr yn ewicheit der ewicheit.* (CvH 73, 10 f.) Siehe auch Meister Eckhart zum Schmelzen der Seele: *Ein heilige sprichet: ich enpfinde etwenne solcher süezicheit in mir, daz ich mîn selbes und aller crêatûren vergizze und zemâle wil zervliezen in dich.* (DW III, 79, 369 f.)

borne (CvH 99, 5) beschrieben wird, sodass das Weichwerden der Seele und das Fließen Gottes in analoger Beziehung zueinander stehen, so wie es die Tradition der Bernhardinischen Brautmystik für die Vergöttlichung der Seele vorsieht.[78]

In einem letzten Schritt verbindet das Christina-Ich im Moment der Vereinigung beide Bilder, das des Fließens und das des Siegels:[79]

> *Da van versmyltzet myn sele vber alle vnd sie wyrt weche van yrer gewonlicher harticheit vnd entphenget van dem fuer des heilgen geistes vnd flußet als eyn smeltzenden waiße yn daz gotliche bylde, daz sie gesehen haitte jn dem hyne zucke yrs verstentenyß, vnd entphenget an sich die forme der gelichenyß des yn druckes. Her zo eyn mach der mensche nyt komen van yme selber myt keynem synem fliße [...].* (CvH 80, 44–49)

Während die Seele wassergleich ins *gotliche bylde* fließt, empfängt sie einen stempelartigen Abdruck (*yn druck*); die menschliche Seele wird zum Abbild Gottes.[80] Das Schmelzen der Seele wird auf diese Weise Voraussetzung für den Siegelaufdruck. Ungewöhnlich ist hierbei, wie der Vergleich mit anderen Texten erweist, die Wassermetaphorik für die Gottesgleichheit. Im ›Fließenden Licht‹ *komen zwo reine nature zesamene: Das heisse für der gotheit und das vliessende wahs der minnenden selen* (Mechthild von Magdeburg, ›Das fließende Licht der Gottheit‹ III 24, 9–11).[81] Wenn die Seele schmilzt, dann wird sie als dynamisches Wesen dargestellt, wie auch das göttliche Wort als eine kontinuierliche Offenbarung dar-

---

78 Siehe Hamm (2011), S. 455 f., zur Vergöttlichung der Seele in der Bernhardinischen Brautmystik.

79 Die homographische und homophone Nähe des Wortes *fliße* zu *fließen* hat in der Christina-Vita keine Auswirkungen auf eine etwaige Mehrdeutigkeit der entsprechenden Konzepte.

80 Daneben gibt es auch das Konzept des Ebenbildes; der Spiegel ist in der Christina von Hane-Vita Ausdruck der Gleichheit von menschlicher Seele und Gott: *Dyne angesicht ist yn dem vnbefleckten spegel myner gotheit gar lyeblichen* (CvH 81, 19 f.); *Du wannest yn dem spegel der gotheit* (CvH 91, 7 f.). Adelheid Langmann formuliert die Ebenbildlichkeit direkter: *spigil deiner gothait* (›Die Offenbarungen der Adelheid Langmann‹ 89, 13). In der Christina-Vita wird die Spiegelmetapher an einer Stelle explizit mit dem Fließen in Verbindung gebracht: *Also wart yn dyeßem gotlichen spegel daz ewige wort fleße* (CvH 100, 56 f.); siehe auch: *vnd sie werdent gesencket yn den gotlichen spegel* (CvH 56, 32 f.). Siehe auch Mechthild von Magdeburg, ›Das fließende Licht der Gottheit‹ I 5, 4; die Verwendung der Spiegelmetapher für die »interpersonale Zweiheit von Geliebter und Geliebtem« wurde für Mechthilds ›Fließendes Licht‹ ausführlich von Hasebrink (2000), S. 161, vorgestellt. Siehe Thomas Cramer: Das Subjekt und sein Widerschein. Beobachtungen zum Wandel der Spiegelmetapher in Antike und Mittelalter. In: Inszenierungen von Subjektivität in der Literatur des Mittelalters. Hrsg. von Martin Baisch u.a. Königstein im Taunus 2005, S. 213–229, hier S. 220, zum Spiegel im Augustinischen Sinne als »Metapher der Erkenntnis nach dem Prinzip der unähnlichen Ähnlichkeit«.

81 Allerdings lässt auch Mechthild Gott über die Seele sagen, dass diese ein Bach sei, vgl. Mechthild von Magdeburg, ›Das fließende Licht der Gottheit‹ I 19, 3.

gelegt wird. Das göttliche Sprecher-Ich der Christina-Vita charakterisiert sich als *das lebendige wort* (CvH 48, 1 f.), das in Christinas Herzen wohne. Die Offenbarung Gottes erfolgt durch das Schöpferwort und ist ein sprechendes Fließen aus dem *born der heilgen dryueldicheit* (vgl. CvH 84, 3).[82] Diese Offenbarung wird wie im lateinischen Prolog des ›Lux divinitatis‹ Mechthilds von Magdeburg durch die Trinität initiiert.[83] Auch im deutschsprachigen ›Fließenden Licht‹ ergeht der göttliche Gruß aus dem Brunnen der fließenden Dreifaltigkeit.[84] Eine Verbindung der beiden Aspekte ›Wort‹ und ›Brunnen‹ findet sich ebenfalls bei Margareta Ebner.[85] Das Bild des Schmelzens für die Vereinigung und das Fließen des Wassers treffen sich im Emanationsgedanken,[86] der in der *fiat*-Abhandlung Christinas von Hane die Geburt des Sohnes in der menschlichen Seele einschließt. Wenn Christina in ihrem Abbild Gott gleicht und sich mit der Dreifaltigkeit vereint, dann hat das zur Folge, dass auch sie zur Heilsbringerin wird:

> *Du wyrckest die wercke der barmhertzicheit, dar vmb ist dyr vffgesloißen der abgront des borns der heilger dryueldicheit, also daz du mochest scheppen also viel, alstu jn dich begryffen machst, vnd das du den anderen schenckest van dyeßem borne yn dyeßer wyße, also dastu, myn fruntdynnen, yn mogest myt dynem lyden erwerben erkentenyß yrer sunden vnd*

---

[82] Vgl. Stolz (2004), S. 508, zur Menschwerdung Christi als Wortschöpfung in den ›Artes‹-Auslegungen. Siehe auch Stolz (2004) S. 221, Anm. 15, zum mariologischen Aspekt der Inkarnation Christi.

[83] Vgl. Palmer (1992), S. 220 f.

[84] Vgl. Mechthild von Magdeburg, ›Das fließende Licht der Gottheit‹ I 2, 1 f. Zum Motiv des Fließens in Verbindung mit der Trinität siehe Patricia Zimmerman Beckman: Swimming in the Trinity. Mechthild of Magdeburg's Mystical Play. In: Spiritus. A Journal for Christian Spirituality 4 (2004), S. 60–77.

[85] Z. B. wenn Christus als ewiges Wort aus dem *ursprung des lebenden brunnen* fließt (›Offenbarungen der Margaretha Ebner‹ 166, 1 f.).

[86] Mit dem Aspekt des Fließens hängt auch das passionsmystische Bild der fließenden Adern Christi zusammen, vgl.: *Ich sache dry aderen vberfludenclichen fließen van gode* (CvH 63, 24); *Der kelche was also groiße, als recht aber grondeloiße were, vnd das heilge bloytde floiße durch verborgen aderen* (CvH 33, 20 f.). Die fließenden Adern Christi kommen auch in anderen mystischen Texten vor: *Owe, dú milt ader, dú nie erseig an erbermde, dú ist an mit armen ersigen!* (Heinrich Seuse: ›Leben‹. In: Heinrich Seuse. Deutsche Schriften Hrsg. von Karl Bihlmeyer. Stuttgart 1907 [unver. Nachdruck Frankfurt a. M. 1961], S. 7–195, hier Kap. 38, S. 127); *Do sach ich flússen einen cristallenen bach us der lincken syten des herren* (Gertrud von Helfta, ›ein botte der götlichen miltekeit‹ 8, 2 f.). Das Bild kann sich auch auf Maria beziehen: *du bist ein fliezend ader* (›Die Goldene Schmiede‹ V. 524). Neben dem Emanations- und Passionsgedanken ist an einer Stelle in der Christina-Vita eine anatomische Ader des menschlichen Körpers gemeint, die allerdings sogleich allegorisch überhöht wird: *Also woilt vnser here betzeychen, daz iß eyne mynnetroppe were vnd were van deme hertze gefalle vß dem augen, das da entge dem hertze steyt, vnd vff den fynger, yn dem die ader vß dem hertzen gechet.* (CvH 17, 18–21)

dastu dar na, myn dube, ynne mogest myt dyner lyebden genade erwerben vnd dastu dar zo myt dyner geduldicheit ynne gude exempel gebest vnd myt dynen wortten vnd wercken gude lere. (CvH 84, 2–9)

Der zitierte Abschnitt hebt Christinas heilsgeschichtliche Funktion besonders hervor. Neben einer intradiegetischen Lesart dieser Worte – als solche an Christinas Mitschwestern gerichtet – ist damit aber auch ein Bezug zur Textualität der Vita selbst gegeben. Wenn Christina vom göttlichen Sprecher-Ich als *eyn lebendiges buche* (CvH 72, 4) bezeichnet wird, dann vollzieht sie damit die Transformation der Menschwerdung Gottes, die Inkarnation vom Abstrakten zum Konkreten.[87] Ihre Ebenbildlichkeit mit dem christologischen Buch der Apokalypse überhöht zugleich die schriftmaterielle Präsenz des mystischen Textes.[88] Auf diese Weise wird trotz der mystischen Rede das Sprechen Gottes in der physischen Präsenz des Buches als manifest dargestellt.

5.3 Die Rede vom Buch als performativer Selbstbezug

Christus ist ein lebendiges Buch gewest

Das lebendige Buch des Lebens uns zu lesen,
Ist Christus auf der Welt mit Red und That gewesen. (›Cherubinischer Wandersmann‹ V 176)[89]

In der Vorstellung von Christus als ein sich selbst lesendes Buch, das daher Subjekt und zugleich Nutzer oder Vollstrecker seiner selbst ist, beschreibt Silesius mittels eines hermetischen Umkehrschlusses den performativen Selbstbezug von Buchschriftlichkeit. Die Rede vom Buch ist in mystischen Texten im Grunde unabdingbar. Doch ist es weniger ein Defizit an Legitimation innerhalb der apophatischen Tradition, der zu diesem Diskurs führt, als ein durch die Verbindung

---

87 Andreas Kablitz: Inkarnation, Überlegungen zur Konstitution eines Kulturmusters (›Novum Testamentum‹ – Dante. ›Vita nova, Commedia‹). In: Transgressionen, Literatur als Ethnographie. Hrsg. von Gerhard Neumann/Rainer Warning (Rombach Wissenschaften Litterae 98). Freiburg i. Br. 2003, S. 39–79, hier S. 61, spricht von der Menschwerdung Gottes als die »Verwandlung des Mediums der Schöpfung zu ihrem Subjekt«.
88 Bei Seuse wird die Ebenbildlichkeit in der Siegelmetaphorik als Buchschriftlichkeit ausgelegt, siehe dazu Kiening (2011), S. 59–61.
89 Angelus Silesius: ›Cherubinischer Wandersmann‹. In: Sämtliche poetische Werke. Hrsg. von Hans Ludwig Held. 3 Bde. 3. erw. Aufl. München 1949–1952, Bd. 3 (1949). (Die Stellennachweise geben Buchzahlen und Reimnummern an.)

vom Inkarnations- mit dem Emanationsgedanken entstehender Sinnüberschuss, der sich in der materiellen Buchschriftlichkeit entlädt.[90] Welche Rolle spielt Buchschriftlichkeit in der Vita der Christina von Hane? Wie wird der Anspruch auf eine mystische Botschaft materiell präsentiert? Hier soll abschließend geklärt werden, wie sich Mitteilungsprozesse in Buchmetaphern niederschlagen und dabei eine typologische Dimension der Bildbeziehung konstituieren.

Bereits bei der Rollenfiguration als stumme Begnadete ist die Parallelisierung Christinas zur Bibel auffällig, da ihr Worte in den Mund gelegt oder allegorische Beziehungen zwischen der Bibel und der auserwählten Braut Christina hergestellt werden. Die Stimme Christinas wiederholt die als heilig erachteten Worte der Bibel und autorisiert auf diese Weise den Vitentext. Der Vitentext erhebt mit seiner Motivik des fließenden Wortes einen in Anlehnung an die Johannesoffenbarung heilbringenden Anspruch auf den Schriftvollzug: Lesen oder Hören der Worte bringt Gnade und Heiligung (vgl. CvH 84; CvH 39).[91] Strohschneider diskutiert im Kontext einer schriftbezogenen mantischen Praxis im ›Simplicissimus‹ den reliquienähnlichen Status des Schriftträgers und beschreibt Selbstentwürfe von Erzählungen,

> in denen sich anstelle der diskursiven Seite der ›narratio‹ vielmehr die phänomenale Materialität des Trägers jener Schrift in den Vordergrund schiebt, in welcher die Erzählrede gespeichert ist. Weil dabei von der ›histoire‹ der jeweiligen Hagiographie keineswegs abgesehen werden kann, weil im Gegenteil das Erzählte mit diesen Schriftträgern subtile Beziehungen unterhält, kommt diesen Schriftträgern ein reliquiärer oder doch reliquienanaloger Status zu.[92]

Mit Strohschneider ausgedrückt, befasst sich die narrative Seite der Christina-Vita mit der göttlichen Mitteilung an die Prämonstratensernonne. Dem liegt der theologische Gedanke eines fließenden, d.h. sich aussprechenden Gottes zu Grunde. Auf der hagiographischen Ebene richtet sich die *histoire* an den impliziten Leser. Die *narratio* wird zum einen als Produkt von Mitteilungs- und Schreibprozessen

---

90 Auch texttraditionelle Begründungen der Buchmetapher sind zu beachten, vgl. Alois Maria Haas: Sinn und Tragweite von Heinrich Seuses Passionsmystik. In: Die Passion Christi in Literatur und Kunst des Spätmittelalters. Hrsg. von Walter Haug/Burghart Wachinger. Tübingen 1993, S. 94–112, hier S. 97, Anm. 10: »Seuses Anwendung der Buchmetapher auf Christus dürfte bonaventurischen Hintergrund haben.«

91 Vgl.: *Beatus qui legit et qui audiunt verba prophetiae et servant ea quae in ea scripta sunt tempus enim prope est.* (Apc 1,3) – Zur Rolle des Evangelisten als fließende Weisheit siehe Volfing (2010), S. 156.

92 Strohschneider (2014), S. 131.

dargestellt,[93] zum anderen wird die evidente Schriftlichkeit als ein lebendiges Buch inszeniert. Die Mystikerin verkörpert das theologisch-abstrakte Ausfließen des göttlichen Sprechens und ist selbst vertreten im physisch greifbaren Objekt des *buchelgyn* (CvH 6, 16), das der Leser in seinen Händen hält. Die Schreibmystik äußert sich im lebendigen Buch, das in seiner Christusanalogie erhöht wird und das gleichzeitig heruntergebrochen wird auf seine materielle Erscheinung.[94] Eine in der Schrift verkörperte Mystik ist als Inkarnation des göttlichen Sprechens im Buch immanent, sodass das Paradoxe der verschrifteten Mystik in dieser Umkehrung das Transzendente materiell reproduziert.[95] Obwohl in der Christina-Vita die Beziehung zwischen Schriftlichkeit und Heiligkeit nicht so ausdrücklich an die Buchproduktion gekoppelt ist, wie das z.B. in Gertruds ›Legatus‹ der Fall ist,[96] wird die Präsenz des Buches als verkörperte Gottesoffenbarung dennoch immanent und zwar ganz besonders im typologischen Bezug zu Maria.

Die mariologische Buchmetaphorik etabliert sich schon im Frühchristentum und bleibt mit verschiedenen Metaphern des Buchwesens bis ins Spätmittelalter wirkmächtig.[97] Der typologische Bezug zu Maria basiert auf Jesajas Schreiben auf

---

93 Vgl. Palmer (1992), S. 226, zu Mechthilds von Magdeburg Buch, das »aus Gott geflossen« sei. Im Unterschied dazu betont Peter von Moos: Was galt im lateinischen Mittelalter als das Literarische an der Literatur? Eine theologisch-rhetorische Antwort des 12. Jahrhunderts. In: Literarische Interessenbildung im Mittelalter. DFG-Symposion 1991. Hrsg. von Joachim Heinzle (Germanistische Symposien, Berichtsbände 14). Stuttgart/Weimar 1993, S. 431–451, hier S. 433, einen »schriftstellerischen Prozess«. Die entsprechende Schlüsselstelle lautet: *Dise Schrift, die in disem bůche stat, die ist gevlossen us von der lebenden gotheit in swester Mehtilden herze und ist also getrůwelich hie gesetzet, alse sie us von irme herzen gegeben ist von gotte und geschriben mit iren henden. Deo gratias.* (Mechthild von Magdeburg, ›Das fließende Licht der Gottheit‹ IV 63, 2–5)
94 Ein derartig duales Verständnis des Buches vertritt Isaac von Stella, vgl. Lentes (2006), S. 133 f.
95 Ähnlich argumentiert Kiening (2011), S. 35–66, zur Buchschriftlichkeit bei Mechthild von Magdeburg, Gertrud von Helfta und Heinrich Seuse.
96 Vgl. Gertrud von Helfta, ›ein botte der götlichen miltekeit‹ 78, 2–77, zur Verbindung zwischen Buchproduktion und der Passion Christi. Siehe auch Bruno Quast: ›drücken und schreiben‹. Passionsmystische Frömmigkeit in den Offenbarungen der Margarethe Ebner. In: Gewalt im Mittelalter. Realitäten – Imaginationen. Hrsg. von Manuel Braun/Cornelia Herberichs. München 2005, S. 293–306, hier S. 294, zum Status der Ding- und Schriftzeichen in ihrer passionsmystisch gefärbten religiösen »Erfahrung« bei Margareta Ebner.
97 Vgl. Schreiner (1994), S. 157 f., und ders.: ›wie Maria geleicht einem puch‹. Beiträge zur Buchmetaphorik des hohen und späten Mittelalters. In: Archiv für Geschichte des Buchwesens 11 (1971), S. 1437–1464, insbes. S. 1437–1445. Siehe auch Mary McDevitt: ›The Ink of Our Mortality‹. The Late-Medieval Image of the Writing Christ Child. In: The Christ Child in Medieval Culture: Alpha es et O! Hrsg. von Mary Dzon/Theresa M. Kenney. Toronto 2012, S. 224–253, insbes. S. 239–

die Tafel,[98] womit »er die übernatürliche Empfängnis des Gottessohns im Schoß der Jungfrau vorausverkündet«.[99] Bei Petrus von Celle (1115–1183) wird in einem akribischen Vergleich zur Buchentstehung die Menschwerdung des Gottessohnes als Beschriftung von Marias jungfräulichem Schoß verstanden.[100] Auf gleiche Weise ist in der Schreibmystik Christinas von Hane die spirituelle Gottesgeburt als im realphysischen Buch verkörpert anzusehen. Wie Schreiner darlegt, fand »[d]ie in lateinischer Sprache entfaltete Buchmetaphorik [...] im Laufe des 13. Jahrhunderts Eingang in die volkssprachliche Literatur«, wovon auch mystische Texte betroffen gewesen seien.[101] Im 15. Jahrhundert sei die Buchanalogie so weit nuanciert, dass Maria als geschriebener Text verstanden werde, wofür der Dominikanerbischof Antonius von Florenz (1389–1459) einstehe: Jedwede Bestimmungen des »gedachten, gesprochenen und geschriebenen Wortes würden – allegorisch betrachtet – auch von Maria gelten«, wobei das gedachte Wort dem vom Vater gezeugten und von Maria geborenen Wort entspreche, das gesprochene Wort dem vom Propheten vorausverkündeten Wort Gottes und das *verbum inchartatum seu scriptum* für das im Schoß der Jungfrau Fleisch annehmende Wort stehe.[102] Dieser Aufteilung folgend bedeutet eine geschriebene von der Vereinigung der Seele mit Gott handelnden Brautmystik auch immer eine Inkarnation Christi.[103]

Wie bereits die Vielfachbesetzung der brautmystischen Rolle gezeigt hat, darf man nicht bei der Maria-Mystikerin-Analogie stehenbleiben, da die Vereinigung auf die menschliche Seele allgemein abzielt. Was im Text als didaktisches Programm ausgedrückt wird, hängt mit der apophatischen Natur des mystischen Diskurses zusammen, weil trotz der Unbegreifbarkeit Gottes der Schriftvollzug der Heiligung dienen will. Der implizite Leser avanciert in seiner Rezeption der Schreibmystik genauso zum Buch wie es die modellhafte Maria und im typologischen Bezug Christina tun.[104] Mit der Reaktualisierung des Textes in Bezug zur

---

242. Die folgenden Bibelstellen liegen der entsprechenden Buchmetaphorik zugrunde: Is 29,11 und Apc 5,1.

98 Vgl.: *et dixit Dominus ad me sume tibi librum grandem et scribe in eo stilo hominis Velociter spolia detrahe Cito praedare* (Is 8,1).

99 Schreiner (1994), S. 158.

100 Vgl. Schreiner (1994), S. 159 f. Newman (1999b), S. 91, sieht das marianische Verständnis des Petrus von Celle eng mit der Trinität verknüpft.

101 Vgl. Schreiner (1994), S. 163–167, hier S. 163. Siehe auch Schreiner (1971), S. 1453–1464.

102 Vgl. Schreiner (1994), S. 169.

103 In diesem Sinne entspricht die Buch-Typologie der engen Definition Ohlys (im Diskussionsbericht bei Michel [1992], S. 72), wonach das typologische Prinzip der Steigerung Christus als Sinnmitte bewahre.

104 Die Verkehrung der Unsagbarkeit Gottes und die Verkörperung der Schrift durch den Leser ist wohl am prägnantesten bei Silesius, vgl. *Was Gott ist, weiß man nicht* (›Cherubinischer

kirchlichen Referenzwelt fügt das liturgisch-gebundene Du eine weitere medial
induzierte Ebene der von akustischen Gesängen und Litaneien geprägten Wahrnehmung hinzu. Die synästhetische Wiederholung von Christinas mystischen
Erfahrungen, die sich im semi-liturgischen Raum abspielen – selbst im virtuellen
Lesevollzug – führt zu einer »typologischen Mehrschichtigkeit«, wie sie von Ohly
beschrieben wird: »Das Gegenwärtige wird – selbst ein Antityp – zur Präfigura-
tion des Kommenden.«[105] Dieses Kommende wird in der Christina von Hane-Vita
in Himmelsvisionen als das verheißene Gottesreich dargestellt. Damit steht der
Text inmitten eines typologischen Dreierschritts, der das Mittelalter als »die echte
hohe Zeit der Mitte (›media aetas‹), die mit Christus anhob«, sieht und auf das
Jenseits zielt.[106] Christinas Seele ist in diesem Sinne die Nachfolgerin einer brautmystischen Maria aber auch eines heilbringenden Christus. Die Manifestation der
Schreibmystik im Buch macht sie zur Schablone jeder Seele, die ihr Potenzial,
zum lebendigen Buch Gottes zu werden, im Textvollzug entfaltet. Die typologische
Beziehung zwischen Maria und Christina weitet sich also über die allegorische
Mehrfachbesetzung der mystischen Braut auch auf den Schriftkörper als Buch
aus: Die Verkörperungsmöglichkeit äußert sich im physisch greifbaren Material.
Damit sind Körperlichkeits- und Materialitätsaspekte als Bedeutungsträger ange-
sprochen, wie sie vor allem von Bynum und Gumbrecht diskutiert werden.[107]
Während Bynum von sakral-repräsentativem Material ausgeht und Gumbrecht
weitgehend theoretisch bleibt, zeigt die Untersuchung der Christina von Hane-
Vita, dass die Materialität des Buches mit dem theologischen Diskurs über die
göttliche Mitteilung verknüpft ist. Der Emanationsgedanke äußert sich in deik-
tischen Wendungen und in einer Appellstruktur an ein lesendes Du als textliche
Sprachmanifestation und somit als immanente Verlängerung des transzendenten
Gotteswortes, das dank der Buchschriftlichkeit nunmehr wiederholbaren Reak-
tualisierungsprozessen zur Verfügung steht.[108] Es geht bei dieser Verkörperung
der sprachlichen Mitteilung um eine textuelle sowie materielle Reinszenierung
mit einem Anspruch auf Sakralität.[109] Zuletzt hat Strohschneider auf die taktile

---

Wandersmann‹ IV 21: *Der unbekannte Gott*) und *So geh und werde selbst die Schrift und auch das
Wesen* (›Cherubinischer Wandersmann‹ VI 263: *Die Welt ist ein Sandkorn*).

105 Ohly (1976), S. 446 f. Folgend erklärt Ohly, wie die Liturgie als überzeitliches Element die
Brücke über die drei Zeiten schlägt.

106 Ohly (1976), S. 447.

107 Vgl. Bynum (2011) und Gumbrecht (2004).

108 Dass Mechthilds mystischer Text als Wort Gottes empfunden wurde, beweisen Randvermer-
ke in der Einsiedler Handschrift des ›Fließenden Lichts der Gottheit‹, vgl. Palmer (1992), S. 234.

109 Ob damit eine »Technik der Verlebendigung« wie bei Hoheliedlektüren gegeben ist, bleibt
zu hinterfragen, vgl. Largier (2005), S. 261, der Bezug nimmt auf Elaine Scarry: On Vivacity. The

Bedeutung des Schriftkörpers in Priester Wernhers ›Marienleben‹ hingewiesen: Die Buchmaterialität in Verbindung mit der »Gegenwärtigsetzung« von Heiligem in der Schrift führe zum Status einer »Schrift-Reliquie«.[110] In der textuellen Kultur der mittelalterlichen Mystik ist das Schreiben immer ein prozesshafter Vorgang, der sich wie Gott im Emanationsgedanken als Akt des Fließens äußert: Die Mitteilung der mystischen Erfahrung im Buch spiegelt Gottes Sprechen wider.[111] Die Identifikationskette von Gott, der sich im Menschensohn verkörpert, weitet sich so auf das im Buch verkörperte Gotteswort aus, welches wiederum als Teil einer mittelalterlichen Praxis der *memoria* nachvollzogen werden kann. Der implizite Leser, der von Christinas Leiden in der Nachfolge Christi liest,[112] findet in Maria als Bindeglied ein Modell für seinen eigenen Nachvollzug, weil sie der Tradition nach die erste Person ist, die das Leiden Christi am Kreuz meditativ nachempfindet (*mater compassionis*).[113] Auch bei Heinrich Seuse, Mechthild von Magdeburg und Dorothea von Montau steht das *buoch* mit dem *gekruzigten lip* in Verbindung.[114] Egerding erläutert bezüglich Seuse:

Difference between Daydreaming and Imagining-Under-Authorial-Instruction. In: Representations 52 (1995), S. 1–26.

110 Vgl. Strohschneider (2014), S. 166–168.

111 Vgl. Friedrich Ohly: Eine Lehre der liebenden Gotteserkenntnis. Zum Titel des St. Trudperter Hohelieds. In: ZfdA 121 (1992), S. 399–404, insbes. S. 400–403, zur Verwendung des mystischen Buches als Spiegel.

112 Vgl. Haas (1979), S. 281, der mit dem Konzept der Schriftmystik die Nachfolge Christi beschreibt.

113 Vgl. Maria als »exemplary ›pietas‹ to inspire imitation, as well as empathy and devotion«, Newman (1999b), S. 81. Siehe auch Amy Neff: The Pain of ›Compassio‹. Mary's Labor at the Foot of the Cross. In: Art Bulletin 80 (1998), S. 254–273, und Rubin (2010), S. 243–249.

114 Vgl.: *Daz ist der anevang in der schůle der wisheit, den man liset an dem ufgetanen zertenneten bůch mines gekrúzgeten libes.* (Seuse, ›Büchlein der ewigen Weisheit‹ 3, 209) Im ›Fließenden Licht‹ steht das Buch z. T. für den gekreuzigten Christus, vgl. Mechthild von Magdeburg, ›Das fließende Licht der Gottheit‹ II 26, siehe dazu Palmer (1992), S. 231; siehe auch: *Daz buoch is drivaltig und bezeichnet alleine mich* (Mechthild von Magdeburg, ›Das fließende Licht der Gottheit‹ II 26, 10 f.), siehe dazu Wenzel (1993), S. 43, und Palmer (1992), S. 231. Siehe auch die Verbindung von Passionsmystik und Buchschriftlichkeit bei Dorothea von Montau: *In sulchir wyse, mit so grosin wundin, smertzen und castyunge druckte sy in ire sele eyn stete gedechtnis der heiligen wunden und narwen Crist des herren, in den sy als in eynem buche laz di libe und das lyden Cristi unsers herren* (›Das Leben der heiligen Dorothea von Montau‹ I 17, 213). Bei Adelheid Langmann gestaltet sich der Zusammenhang zwischen Schrift, Trinität und dem Leiden Christi subtiler, indem Analogien zwischen den fünf Buchstaben des Jesu-Namens und den fünf Wunden Christi einerseits und zwischen der Mystikerin und der Dreifaltigkeit andererseits hergestellt werden, vgl. ›Die Offenbarungen der Adelheid Langmann‹ 16, 15–26.

> Die Buchmetapher erscheint zur Erfassung der lehrhaften Bedeutung, die im gekreuzigten Leib Jesu enthalten ist; dem Lesen ähnlich gewinnt man aus der Beschäftigung damit die Erkenntnis, dass die Vernichtung aller Begierden und aller Lust erforderlich ist, wenn man sich Jesus angleichen will im Leiden.[115]

Die Aufforderung zur Nachfolge Christi im Leiden fasst Bernhardt unter dem Begriff der impliziten Pragmatik zusammen.[116] An Egerdings Beobachtung ist hingegen der didaktische Anspruch der Buchmetapher hervorzuheben. Mit der Aufforderung nach Partizipation an ein Du wird das Paradox des Unsagbaren zudem in die physische Präsenz der Schrift, in das Buch überführt, denn mit Gumbrecht gesprochen weist das Buch mit seinen »effects of presence« auf einen Umgang mit Schrift hin, der sich im Verkörperungsakt transzendenter Vorgänge äußert.[117] Die Lesetätigkeit der Heiligen Schrift war ausgehend von der Rezeption der Verkündigungsszene seit dem 13. Jahrhundert ein Element der *imitatio Mariae*;[118] auch die Christina von Hane-Vita präsentiert sich als Offenbarung Gottes, wonach Christinas Leben und dessen Mitteilung (*dyne wortte vnd wercke*) aus der Quelle der Dreifaltigkeit entspringen und Vorbildcharakter aufweisen (vgl. CvH 84). In der brautmystischen Ansprache erfüllt Christina die Rolle der Mutter Gottes und des Erlösers zugleich. Die *unio* mit der Trinität bewirkt den Zusammenfall ihrer Identität mit Braut und Bräutigam, Mutter und Sohn, Gott und Seele.[119] Ihre Seele wird konsequenterweise selber unaussprechlich.[120] Damit schließt sich der Kreis eines performativen Selbstbezugs, der die eigene Buchschriftlichkeit vergöttlicht.

---

115 Egerding (1997b), S. 158.

116 Vgl. Susanne Bernhardt: Die implizite Pragmatik der Gelassenheit in der ›Vita‹ Heinrich Seuses. In: Semantik der Gelassenheit. Generierung, Etablierung, Transformation. Hrsg. von Susanne Bernhardt/Burkhard Hasebrink/Imke Früh (Historische Semantik 17). Göttingen 2012, S. 115–142, insbes. S. 116–119.

117 Gumbrecht (2004), S. 18.

118 Vgl. Schreiner (1990), S. 339.

119 Vgl.: *Du byst gebyldet nach der heilger dryueldicheit vnd ich, dyne bruytgam, byn gecleydet myt dem cleytde dyner menscheit* (CvH 91, 3–5); *Ich hayn dich yn der heilger dryueldicheit geliche gemacht eyner wyßer lylien vnder mynen jonffrauwen* (CvH 94, 5 f.).

120 Wenn die Seele Gott gleich geworden ist, dann wird auch sie zum Gegenstand der negativen Theologie, mit anderen Worten: Wie Gott unnennbar ist, erreicht auch die Seele diesen Status, vgl.: *Got der âne namen ist – er enhât enkeinen namen –, ist unsprechelich, und diu sêle in irm grunde ist sie ouch unsprechelich, als er unsprechelich ist* (DW I, 17, 284). Siehe auch DW III, 77, 337 f. und DW III, 80, 380; zu Eckharts Gottes- und Seelennamenlosigkeit siehe Sells (1994), S. 16. Dementsprechend wird auch Christinas Seele gegen Ende der Vita wiederholt als unaussprechlich bezeichnet, dreimal in Folge spricht das göttliche Sprecher-Ich sie auf diese Weise direkt an (vgl. CvH 95), insbes.: *Du byst eyn vnsprechlich weßen yn der wunderlicher dryueldicheit, daz allen heilgen eyn loiffe ist vnd allen crysten selen troiste, vnd iß ist allen hertzen vnbekante.* (CvH

Die Verkettung vom Buch als fließende Mitteilung mit dem Fließen als die in Gott mündende Seele ist der logische Höhepunkt der Vita, geht man denn von der Vorstellung des göttlichen Ausflusses und einer philosophischen Ausrichtung auf die Inkarnation im Wort aus. Die allerletzten Worte der Vita würden somit die Gottesvereinigung im Lesevollzug vollführen:[121]

> ›[...] *Also sterbet sie yn den wonderen der gotheit. Da flußet got yn gode, daz sie nyt begryffen kayne die gotliche nature. Die sele, die got beschauwen, die sal doit syn aller befleckonge der sunden.‹ etc.* (CvH 100, 70–72)

Die hier vorgeführte Argumentation macht daher denkbar, dass die nur in der Straßburger Handschrift überlieferte mystische Vita vielleicht gar kein Fragment ist, denn sie endet ja mit dem der Gottesschau vorauslaufenden Sterben der Seele Christinas.[122] Das Ende der Vita könnte auf diese Weise als eine raffiniert performative Erhöhung des die Seele überführenden Einigungsprinzips gelesen werden, das im finalen *etc.* eine unaufhörliche Kontinuität des Mitteilens einschließt.

95, 10–12) Nicht allein aus der Sicht der Philosophie Meister Eckharts hat die Seele damit den höchsten Stand erreicht (siehe dazu Bernard McGinn: The Mystical Thought of Meister Eckhart. The Man from Whom God Hid Nothing. New York 2001[a], S. 45–47); die Vita der Christina von Hane präzisiert ebenso: *Dyeße vereynigonge myt gode ist der selen hochste vollenkommheit yn dyeßem leben.* (CvH 80, 58 f.)

121 Siehe bereits die Statusbeschreibung Christinas durch die Gottesstimme: *Du byst dyr doit vnd lebest ewenclichen yn myr* [...]. (CvH 61, 11 f.) Dieser Seelenannihilierung geht ein Aufruf zur ›Gelassenheit‹ voraus: *Du salt got durch got laißen, das ist myn hogester wille vnd dyne hogester loyne* [...]. (CvH 59, 9 f.) Vgl. dazu den Gedanken der Seelenannihilierung bei Eckhart: *Der mensche, der alsô stât in gotes minne, der sol sîn selbes tôt sîn und allen geschaffenen dingen, daz er sîn selbes als wênic ahtende sî als eines über tûsent mîle. Der mensche blîbet in der glîcheit und blîbet in der einicheit und blîbet gar glîch; in in envellet kein unglîcheit. Dirre mensche muoz sich selben gelâzen hân und alle dise werlt. Wære ein mensche, des alliu disiu werlt wære, und er sie lieze als blôz durch got, als er sie enpfienc, dem wölte unser herre wider geben alle dise werlt und ouch daz êwige leben.* (DW I, 12, 201 f.)

122 Die Gottesschau ist auch für Eckhart der erhabenste Zustand der Seele, vgl.: *Wenne aber diu gnâde wirt volbrâht ûf daz hœhste, sô enist ez niht gnâde; ez ist ein götlich lieht, dar inne man got sihet.* [...] *Die wîle wir menschen sîn und die wîle iht menschlîches an uns lebet und in einem zuogange sîn, sô engesehen wir got niht; wir müezen ûferhaben werden und gesast in eine lûter ruowe und alsô got sehen.* (DW III, 70, 196) – An dieser Stelle wäre zu erwägen, ob die Fragmentartigkeit der Christina von Hane-Vita die Perfektion der Seele nach dem Tod unterstreicht bzw. textuell umsetzt, sodass das Verschriftlichte immer als unvollendet dargestellt wird. Für die Fälle Margareta Ebners und Adelheid Langmanns wird ein ähnlich performativer Gedanke ansatzweise von Garber (2003), S. 105, skizziert. Siehe auch Mark S. Burrows: Raiding the Inarticulate. Mysticism, Poetics and the Unlanguageable. In: Spiritus. A Journal of Christian Spirituality 4 (2004), S. 173–194, insbes. S. 187, zur Fragmentartigkeit des sprachlichen Ausdrucks als mystische Ästhetik.

6 Schlussbemerkung

Gewiss scheint die Vita der Christina von Hane im Vergleich mit traditionellen Viten auf eine uneinheitliche Weise zusammengestellt worden zu sein. Vor allem die Erzählstruktur ist vielschichtig: Sie beginnt im hagiographischen Ton und weist mehrere Stimmwechsel auf. In ihrer Orientierung an einer hagiographischen Modellhaftigkeit sowie in ihrem spekulativen Anteil weist die Vita Ähnlichkeiten mit der Mystik von Helfta auf, während der besonders von der starken Präsenz des liturgischen Kalenders geprägte strukturelle Charakter an Texte wie die Offenbarungen der Adelheid Langmann, Margareta Ebner und Agnes Blannbekin erinnert. Zweifelsohne geben brautmystische Elemente Zeugnis von Christinas von Hane vermeintlicher Lebenszeit. Neben Visionen und Auditionen finden sich aber auch theoretische, beinahe scholastische Elemente, die v.a. Diskurse des 14. Jahrhunderts reflektieren. Vielleicht weisen diese Aspekte auf die Kopier- und Kollationstätigkeit eines Schreibers hin, der es mit mehreren Vorlagen zu tun hatte.[1] In der relativ späten Abschrift könnte aber auch ein Textzeugnis vorliegen, das näher an einer ersten Niederschrift angesiedelt ist als zunächst vermutet.[2] Doch die Frage nach der Originalität oder der »Einheit« des Textes muss unbeantwortet bleiben.[3] Sie ist indes weniger wichtig als oft angenommen, da sie einem Werk- und Autorbegriff verpflichtet ist, der der Christina von Hane-Vita nicht angemessen ist. Stattdessen hat diese Untersuchung auf die innertextlichen Reflektionen über die eigene Schriftlichkeit der Vita hingewiesen. Insbesondere aus narratologischer Sicht zeigt die in der Vita angesetzte Stimmenvielfalt, dass ein Gnadenprinzip von der Mystikerin auf den impliziten Leser erweitert werden soll. Das mystische Leben konstituiert sich so im Vergegenwärtigungsprozess jedes Mal neu und kann sich von der Mystikerin, die nur noch eine virtuelle Besetzung der Brautrolle ist, loslösen. Die Liebesbeziehung ist daher eine szenisch dargestellte, die zwischen narrativem Bericht, Dialog und traktatähnlicher Abhandlung changiert. Begleitet von liturgischen und akustischen Referenzen wird im Vollzug des Textes die Vereinigung als eine klanginduzierte *unio* konstituiert. Das Postulat der literarischen Konstruktion reicht daher nicht aus, um die textuelle Prozesshaftigkeit, die der Christina-Vita inhärent ist, zu erklären. Dieser Text stellt kein sich als Einheit ausgebendes monolithisches Werk dar. Prozesse des Abschrei-

---

1 So schlussfolgert Ruh (1993), S. 125.
2 Vgl. Peters (1988), S. 109. Emmelius (2008), S. 311, weist darauf hin, dass frühe Niederschriften mystischer Offenbarungen oft strukturell uneinheitlich waren und auch »inhaltliche Diskrepanzen« aufwiesen.
3 Vgl. Ruh (1993), S. 121.

https://doi.org/10.1515/9783110536324-009

bens, Umschreibens und Einschreibens heben eine komplexe und vielschichtige Textualität hervor. Die Vita bedient sich aus lateinischen und volkssprachigen Traditionen stammenden Diskursen und entwickelt einen individuellen Umgang mit der Vermittlung spiritueller Inhalte. Eine derartige spirituelle Praxis führt vor, was abstrakt debattiert wird, und trägt darüber hinaus performative Züge.[4] Peters' Feststellung über das Schreiben, das »in den Prozess der Begnadung einbezogen ist«, ist in dieser Hinsicht zu erweitern, denn es bleibt nicht beim »Movens der Rekapitulation spiritueller Erfahrungen und zugleich verstärkende[n] Medium der Begnadung«, sondern führt darüber hinaus in eine Interaktion mit dem in die Textgestaltung integrierten Leser.[5] Die Besonderheit des mystischen Lebens besteht darin, dass es über die hagiographische Darstellung hinaus eine gelebte Praxis voraussetzt, die sich im Lesen des Textes vollzieht. Damit sind der didaktische Bezug und diejenigen Strukturmerkmale gemeint, die eine Lesesituation vorzubereiten scheinen. Der Text will somit eine Lesesituation animieren; denn Schriftlichkeit im Mittelalter kann nicht adäquat beschrieben werden, ohne die Mündlichkeit mitzudenken, in der jene immer eingebettet war und zwar sei es im Prozess der Verschriftlichung oder im Leseprozess, der das Aussprechen des Wortes implizieren konnte.[6] Auch auf der materiellen Ebene weisen die graphischen Besonderheiten der Handschrift auf den pragmatischen Charakter des Textes hin, indem z. B. gewisse Wörter unterstrichen sind, die die Aufmerksamkeit auf sich ziehen und so zu einer besonderen Beachtung einladen.[7] Der Vergleich

---

4 Vgl. Beckman (2007), S. 67, über Mechthilds von Magdeburg ›Fließendes Licht‹: »a sacramental object that can produce holiness through its performance and rhetoric.«

5 Peters (1988), S. 146, über Margareta Ebner und deren literarische Zusammenarbeit mit Heinrich von Nördlingen. Texte bedeuteten Inspiration für das spirituelle Leben einer mittelalterlichen Nonne, die als Schreiberin in ihrer Tätigkeit eine spirituelle Übung sah, ähnlich wie auch das Lesen als Übung verstanden wurde, vgl. Thérèse de Hemptinne: Reading, Writing and Devotional Practices. Lay and Religious Women and the Written Word in the Low Countries (1350–1550). In: The Voice of Silence. Women's Literacy in a Men's Church. Hrsg. von Thérèse de Hemptinne/María Eugenia Góngora (Medieval Church Studies 9). Turnhout 2004, S. 111–126, insbes. S. 126.

6 Vgl. Palmer (2005), S. 86: »continuos tradition of linguistic formulae such as requests for attention, ›Amen‹ and ›Tu autem‹ that marked out the performative aspect of the literary text [...].« Siehe auch Green (1994), S. 15–17 und S. 30–35, sowie Chinca/Young (2005), S. 4: »[...] the written word was spoken and heard as well as seen, it was also the case that the spoken word was implicated in the ›literate‹ domains of writing and visual apperception.« Das Sehen der Wörter kann physisch gemeint sein, aber auch als imaginäre Vision dessen, was wiedergegeben wird (»seeing with the mind's eye«, ebd.). Siehe auch Green (2003), S. 7–11.

7 Vgl. Palmer (2005), S. 91, der die graphischen Hervorhebungen in einem handschriftlichen Text nicht nur als Markierungen für Aufführungssituationen versteht, sondern auch als Anregung, sich in einer privaten Lektüre mit dem Text auseinanderzusetzen.

mit den möglicherweise aus dem Lebenskontext Christinas stammenden latei-
nisch-deutschen Gebeten zeichnet den mystischen Text in seinem performativen
Vollzug aus. Die in der grundsätzlich narrativen Christina von Hane-Vita angelegten performativen Aspekte auf der materiellen, sprachlichen und didaktischen
Ebene verweisen immer wieder auf den Schreibvorgang,[8] der sich als ein zu weiteren Formen des Erlebens hinführenden Gnadenakt ausgibt.[9] Die sich am Kirchenjahr orientierenden Textualisierungsstrategien machen die Schreibmystik
innerhalb einer liturgischen Rezeption erfahrbar, weil dadurch der Nachvollzug
des Textes durch ritualisierte spirituelle Handlungen vorgegeben ist. Diese Art
von Reinszenierung verleiht ähnlich einer »Rhetorik des Begehrens« dem Leben
der Mystikerin eine Zeitlosigkeit, welche sich auf der einen Seite in paradigmati-
scher Beziehung zum Bibelgeschehen abspielt, und auf der anderen mit der Iterabilität des Textes im Lesevollzug begründet wird.[10] Die Figur Christinas funktioniert typologisch als Braut und Wort Gottes, die eine Mehrfachbesetzung dieser
Rollen ermöglicht.[11] Dabei spielt weniger die menschliche Verkörperung der Braut
als der Buchkörper eine besondere Rolle. Das Buch wird dank des Nachvollzugs
eines Lesers zum Beweis des Unnachweisbaren und reiht sich mit dem didaktischen Anspruch des Textes in die Folge der christlichen Heilsgeschichte ein. Das
illustriert die Typologie der Buchmetapher, die in ihrer Schriftnatur das Wort
Gottes mit dem Konzept der Emanation zusammenführt. Der Metapherngebrauch
entfaltet nur in einer performativen Anwendung seine Wirkungskraft, sodass der
Vollzug der Christina-Vita das Buch zum gesprochenen und fließenden Wort
transformiert.[12] Mittels dieser performativen Elemente positioniert sich die mystische Vita so zwischen Inszenierung und Evidenz. Eine Spannung zwischen der
Verfügbarkeit und dem gleichzeitigen Entzug von Heiligkeit ist in der Vita insbesondere dort lokalisierbar, wo verschiedene Autorisierungsdiskurse nebeneinander laufen, biblische Assoziationen evozierend, sich auf Kirchenväter berufend,
einen männlichen Hagiographen stilisierend und Augenzeugenschaft für nach-

---

8 Vgl. Suerbaum (2009), S. 31, zur Verbindung von Mystik und Didaxe im handschriftlichen
Bezug. Zur entsprechenden Kontroverse im ›Fließenden Licht der Gottheit‹ siehe Palmer (1992).
9 Vgl. Suerbaum (2009), S. 28. Siehe auch Suydam (1999a), S. 186: »devotional books were
believed to have transformative power.«
10 Vgl. Largier (2005), S. 258–261. Es sei zudem angemerkt, dass auch mittelalterliche Gelehrte
jeden religiösen Text – das schließt auch die Bibel ein – als Gegenstand der Rhetorik ansahen,
eine göttliche Beredsamkeit voraussetzend und dabei den literarischen Status von heiligen Texten anerkennend, siehe dazu Moos (1993), S. 437 und S. 450.
11 In diesem Zusammenhang bedeutet das Lesen eine Praxis individueller Formierung (»pratique d'invduation «), vgl. Marielle Macé: Façons de lire, manières d'être. Mayenne 2011, S. 18.
12 Vgl. Suydam (1999a), S. 179, ähnlich für Birgitta von Schweden.

weisbare Prophezeiungen anführend, möglicherweise aus demselben Legitimationsbedarf heraus auf den apophatischen Diskurs zurückgreifend.[13] Eine strikte Verschriftlichungstheorie des Vitentextes, wie sie Ringler für Offenbarungstexte bestimmt, ist für die Christina von Hane-Vita dagegen nicht auszumachen.[14] Stattdessen ist der dynamische Charakter des Schriftlichen und Verschriftlichten hervorzuheben, wie ihn Löser für prominentere Mystiker diskutiert.[15] Die vorliegende Untersuchung hat gezeigt, wie sich Schrift- und Schreibmystik und Hagiographie in der Vorstellung von der Verkörperung des Göttlichen treffen, d. h. von der prinzipiellen Möglichkeit des Immanentwerdens des Transzendenten.[16] Es geht dabei nicht um den Körper der Mystikerin, so wie eine Theologie der Weiblichkeit dies womöglich sehen mag.[17] Stattdessen ist der Schriftkörper als externalisierte Präsenz der Heiligkeit in den Vordergrund zu rücken,[18] da das Buch im Prozess des sprachlichen Vollzugs als fließendes Wort Gottes seine Heiligung beansprucht und damit als »heilige Materialität« gelten will.[19] Es handelt sich mit der Textualität zugleich um eine »iterable Materialität« (Foucault), die als christologisch fundiertes *verbum incarnatum* auf das Gespräch Gottes mit dem Menschen

---

13 Es handelt sich daher um eine mögliche (im Gegensatz zu einer bestimmten) »sprachliche Realisierung [...] der uneinholbaren Transzendenz Gottes«, die für Seelhorst (2003), S. 50, die Grundannahme jeder negativen Theologie bildet.

14 Vgl. Ringler (1985), S. 190: »In der sprachlichen Formulierung zeigt sich ein Streben nach Vereinheitlichung und Glättung; [...]. Inhaltlich, sprachlich und strukturell sind Legendarisierungsprozesse zu beobachten.«

15 Vgl. Löser (2012).

16 Vgl. Sells (1994), S. 43–45, zu Gottes Anwesenheit in der Welt (Theophanie) als Problem des mystischen Schrifttums.

17 Siehe dazu Newman (2012), S. 385.

18 Joachim Bumke: Höfischer Körper – Höfische Kultur. In: Modernes Mittelalter. Neue Bilder einer populären Epoche. Hrsg. von Joachim Heinzle. Frankfurt a. M. 1994, S. 67–102, insbes. S. 97 f., und Hans Ulrich Gumbrecht: Beginn von ›Literatur‹ / Abschied vom Körper? In: Der Ursprung von Literatur. Medien, Rollen, Kommunikationsformen zwischen 1450 und 1550. Hrsg. von Gisela Smolka-Koerdt/Peter-Michael Spangenberg/Dagmar Tillmann-Bartylla. München 1988, S. 15–50, betonen den ›Körperlichkeitsaspekt‹, der jedem sprachlichen Vollzug zugrunde liege, und schlagen das Begriffspaar ›Körperlichkeit und Schriftlichkeit‹ vor. Doch auch diese Unterscheidung wird der Sprachlichkeit im Mittelalter nicht gerecht, wie Chinca/Young (2005), S. 6, betonen: »Common to both the traditional terms and these newcomers is their isolation of what one might call the instrumental aspect of communication: the materials deployed, the organs of the body that are brought into play, and the senses involved in the production and reception of discourse.«

19 In Anlehnung an den Begriff »holy matter«, Bynum (2011), S. 25.

aufbaut,[20] und die im Nachvollzug das »Beteiligtsein des Menschen an der heils-mächtigen Wirksamkeit des trinitarischen Lebens in Gott« inszeniert.[21] Mystische Vitentexte lassen sich, das haben die vorgestellten Teiluntersuchungen nachge-wiesen, nicht auf ihre somatischen, brautmystischen oder historiographisch rele-vanten Anteile (z.B. für das Verhältnis zwischen männlicher und weiblicher Autorschaft) reduzieren; sie müssen in ihrer Vielschichtigkeit wahrgenommen werden. Dabei ist die Phänomenologie der Quelle hervorzuheben: das materielle Erscheinen als heiliges Buch, als Manifestation des göttlichen Wortes. Die mysti-sche Vita der Christina von Hane ist nur ein Beispiel für eine Schrift- und Schreib-mystik, in der sich Elemente materieller Präsenz, sprachlichen Ausdrucks und brautmystischer Verkörperung verzahnen. Das Zusammenspiel von der Evidenz eines Heiligschreibens und der Inszenierung eines heiligen Schreibens steht aber im größeren Kontext einer Vergegenwärtigungspraxis im und durch das Buch.

---

20 Vgl. Udo Kern: Wir sind ein Gespräch. Existential-ontologische theologische Überlegungen. In: Unerwartete Theologie. Festschrift für Bernd Hildebrandt. Hrsg. von Tilman Beyrich (Theolo-gie. Forschung und Wissenschaft 17). Münster 2005, S. 135–154, insbes. S. 140.
21 So Haas (1984b), S. 623, für Meister Eckhart und Tauler.

Teil B: **Beschreibung der Handschrift und Editionen**

1 Straßburg, Bibliothèque nationale et universitaire, Ms. 324

Als Mittermaier in den Jahren 1965 und 1966 die moselfränkische Vita der Prämonstratensernonne Christina von Hane nach der Handschrift Straßburg, Bibliothèque nationale et universitaire, Ms. 324 herausgab, steckte die Forschung zur weiblichen Beteiligung an einer deutschsprachigen Mystik noch in Kinderschuhen. Ruh sprach sich 1993 in seinem Grundlagenwerk zur abendländischen Mystik für eine kritische Edition der nur in einem einzigen Überlieferungsträger vorkommenden Vita Christinas von Hane aus.[1] Dass im Verbund dieser nun vorgelegten Edition auch eine mitüberlieferte Legende von der Bekehrung Maria Magdalenas herausgegeben wird, erklärt sich aus dem Forschungsinteresse, die Texte in ihrem gemeinsamen Entstehungs- und Gebrauchskontext nachzuvollziehen. Wie die Christina von Hane-Vita im Straßburger Kodex zufällig wiedergefunden wurde, nachdem sie Köster noch 1956 für verschollen hielt,[2] dokumentiert Mittermaier.[3] Dort sind auch sämtliche frühneuzeitliche Zusätze zu der Handschrift, in der die Vita enthalten ist, detailliert dargelegt. Die dazugehörende Geschichte, die sich dem frühneuzeitlichen Gebrauch der Handschrift widmet, ist hinreichend erforscht.[4] Die im 17. Jahrhundert auf die leeren Seiten der Handschrift nachgetragenen Texte und Notizen sowie die im Vitenteil vorgenommenen Randbemerkungen aus den Folgejahrhunderten sind ebenfalls bei Mittermaier nachzulesen und werden daher in dieser Handschriftenbeschreibung und in der Edition nicht weiter berücksichtigt.[5]

1.1 Kodikologische und paläographische Beschreibung

Der moderne Rückentitel von Straßburg, BNU, Ms. 324 präzisiert den Inhalt des Kodex als *Statuta sacri et canonici Ordinis Praemonstratensis sub Anno 1505.*[6] Auf

---

1 Vgl. Ruh (1993), S. 122, Anm. 13.
2 Vgl. Köster (1956).
3 Vgl. Mittermaier (1965), insbes. S. 209–210.
4 Siehe Mittermaier (1965), S. 218–223, und Kirakosian (2014b), S. 381–384.
5 Siehe Mittermaier (1965), S. 210–217.
6 Nachdem Ludwig Clemm: Das Totenbuch des Stifts Ilbenstadt. In: Archiv für hessische Geschichte und Altertumskunde. N.F. 19 (1936), S. 169–274, insbes. S. 193, Anm. 38, aus dem Kloster Ilbenstadt stammende Ordensregeln in der Sammelhandschrift vermutete, stellte Mittermaier (1965), S. 209, Anm. 7, fest, dass es sich dabei um eine Rezension derselben handelt.

https://doi.org/10.1515/9783110536324-010

welchen Bibliothekskatalog sich die ältere Signatur L Lat. 273 (Bl. 1ʳ und Band-
rücken von derselben Hand, die auch den Titel schrieb) bezieht, kann nicht mit
Sicherheit bestimmt werden. Jedenfalls befand sich der Band bis zu seiner Säku-
larisierung zu Beginn des 19. Jahrhunderts im Prämonstratenserstift Ilbenstadt.
Nach Straßburg wird die Handschrift noch vor 1918 gekommen sein, worauf der
Stempel der Kaiserlichen Universitäts- und Landesbibliothek schließen lässt.
Zum Verbleib des Bands in der Zwischenzeit lässt sich nichts Genaueres bestim-
men.[7]

Der Rückseite des Vorsatzblattes (Bl. Iᵛ) ist zu entnehmen, dass der Kodex 1662
auf Geheiß des Rommersdorfer Abts Petrus Diederich gebunden wurde. Dieselbe Hand aus der zweiten Hälfte des 17. Jahrhundert präzisierte, dass sämtliche Texte im Kloster Engelport gefunden wurden. Im Wesentlichen besteht der
Band aus zwei kodikologisch und inhaltlich unterscheidbaren Hauptteilen: einer
lateinischen Rezension der Statuten des Prämonstratenserordens aus dem Jahr
1505 im ersten Faszikel (Bl. 1ʳ–210ʳ) und im zweiten Faszikel aus der in deutscher
Sprache abgefassten Vita Christinas von Hane (Bl. 212ʳ–349ᵛ, CvH-Teil) sowie im
Anschluss daran einer unvollständigen ebenso deutschen Legendenerzählung
von der Bekehrung Maria Magdalenas (Bl. 350ʳ–355ᵛ, MM-Teil). Es gibt im übrigen
keinen Grund zur Annahme, dass die beiden Hauptteile auch vor dem Binden im
17. Jahrhundert zusammengehörten. Zwei aus der Feder des Prämonstratenserpri-
ors Pieters de Waghenare von S. Nicolas zu Veurne stammende Hymnen sind im
17. Jahrhundert auf den letzten Seiten des Bands nachgetragen worden (Bl. 356ʳ–
359ᵛ). Pieter de Waghenhares 23-strophiger lateinischer Hymnus auf Christina
von Hane (1661) geht der Korrespondenz Petrus Diederichs nach zu urteilen
auf eine heute verschollene Kopie der Vita zurück, die der Rommersdorfer Abt
nach seinem Fund in Engelport anfertigen und seinem flämischen Ordensbruder
zukommen ließ. In seinem Brief drückt er sich für die Kürzung der Vita aus.[8] Dabei
nennt er die Mystikerin immer Christina von Retters. Dass die Affiliation zu einem
anderen Prämonstratenserkloster erst bei einer nachträglichen Überarbeitung
eingeführt wurde, lässt sich auch an der Straßburger Handschrift sehen, wo in
die Worte *Hane* und *Bolant* mit dunklerer Tinte *Rithers* und *Koningstein* geschrieben wurden.[9] Diese jüngere Tinte ist mit der Zeit ausgeblichen, sodass heute die

---

7 Vgl. Mittermaier (1965), S. 223–225.

8 Vgl. Köster (1956), S. 242.

9 Mittermaier (1960), S. 76 und S. 96 f., macht dafür den Rommersdorfer Abt Petrus Diederich
verantwortlich, der das Kloster Retters mit der Promotion einer Hausheiligen aus der Säkularisie-
rung hätte zurück holen wollen. Christina trägt bis zur Wiederentdeckung der Straßburger Hand-

ursprünglichen geographischen Angaben wieder gut erkennbar sind (vgl. Straßburg, BNU, Ms. 324, Bl. 212ʳ, siehe Abb. 2). Schon im 18. Jahrhundert war man sich dieser Änderung wohl bewusst: Auf der verso-Seite des beim Binden hinzugefügten Bl. 211 schrieb eine Hand, die womöglich mit dem Ilbenstädter Prior Johannes Haas zu identifizieren ist,[10] den Titel der folgenden Lebensbeschreibung: *Vita Beatae Christinae Monasterij olim Hanensis – siue vt bibliotheca Praemonstr. In indice inscribit Ragenensis – Ordinis Praemonstratensis diocesis siue tractus Moguntini prope Bolant.* Dieselbe Hand ist für wenige Randnotizen im Vitenteil verantwortlich.[11] Caspar Lauer, der letzte Abt von Ilbenstadt, der vor der Erlangung der Abtswürde (30. Juni 1789) lange Zeit Stiftsbibliothekar war, griff später in den Titel auf Bl. 211ᵛ ein und korrigierte *Bolant* zu *Bolandium*. Er erweiterte außerdem die geographische Angabe mit *versus Cruciniacum in Palatinatu* (Bad Kreuznach in der Pfalz).

Datierung und Provenienz: Der lateinische Teil ist auf den 22. April 1505 datiert (Bl. 210ʳ), wobei dies das Datum des ursprünglichen Erlasses der reformierten Statuten des Prämonstratenserordens ist.[12] Daher ist die Entstehung mit Sicherheit nach dem 22. April 1505 anzusetzen. Die Provenienz des lateinischen Teils ist unbekannt. | Nach Ansicht von Krings ist der zweite Teil des Kodex (Bl. 212–355) »mit der Vita Christinas und der Legende von der Bekehrung Maria Magdalenas im 15. Jahrhundert abgeschrieben worden«.[13] Mittermaier verortet die Entstehung

---

schrift im 20. Jahrhundert immer den Beinamen »von Retters«, so etwa in einer lateinischen Übersetzung von Lauer (›Vita beatae Christinae‹) und einer relativ spät herausgegebenen französischen Vita (Ignace van Spilbeeck: Une fleur cachée. La bienheureuse Christine du Christ, religieuse du monastère de Rhetirs. Namur 1885). – Eine weitere Fälschung durch Petrus Diederich, die eine Seligsprechungsurkunde Gertruds von Altenberg betrifft, konnte Thomas Doepner: Das Prämonstratenserinnenkloster Altenberg im Hoch- und Spätmittelalter. Sozial- und Frömmigkeitsgeschichtliche Untersuchungen (Untersuchungen und Materialien zur Landesgeschichte 16). Marburg 1999, S. 72, Anm. 73, nachweisen.

10 Vgl. die Zuschreibung der Hände bei Mittermaier (1965), S. 216.

11 Nach einer späteren Angabe Caspar Lauers soll Johannes Haas aus der vorliegenden Vita für sein Sammelwerk über Heilige des Prämonstratenserordens geschöpft haben, vgl. Mittermaier (1965), S. 212, Anm. 17, und Köster (1956), S. 244 f. und S. 253, Anm. 3. Darüber, wie die Handschrift von Rommersdorf nach Ilbenstadt kam, können nur Spekulationen angestellt werden, vgl. Franz Paul Mittermaier: Das Verhältnis des Altenberger Priors Petrus Diederich (1643/55) zu den Prämonstratenserstiften Ober- und Nieder-Ilbenstadt in der Wetterau. In: Wetterauer Geschichtsblätter 7/8 (1959), S. 117–131, insbes. S. 124.

12 Vgl. Emile Valvekens: Le chapitre général de Prémontré et les nouveaux statuts de 1505. In: Analecta Praemonstratensia 14 (1938), S. 53–94, insbes. S. 83 f.

13 Krings (2009), S. 192.

um die Mitte des 15. Jahrhunderts im Kloster Hane, schlägt aber als Verantwortliche der Abschrift die Meisterin des Klosters Hane Margareta Cratz von Scharfenstein vor, die bis 1532 im Amt geblieben sein soll.[14] Krings hingegen schlägt vor, dass ein Kanoniker der Abtei Sayn die vorliegende Vita und die Legende im Kloster Rothenkirchen abschrieb.[15] Allerdings lässt sich der deutsche Teil der Handschrift auf das erste Viertel des 16. Jahrhunderts neudatieren; dafür sprechen die Wasserzeichen und die verwendete Bastardschrift,[16] die sich von der Bastarda des lateinischen Teils deutlich abhebt. Die Provenienz des deutschen Handschriftteils ist nicht gesichert. Ob das Manuskript in Hane selbst entstanden ist, muss daher offen bleiben, doch schließen die kodikologischen und paläographischen Befunde diese Annahme nicht aus.[17]

Papier: Papier unterschiedlicher Stärke in den beiden Hauptteilen der Handschrift. Blattgröße 137 × 97 mm. Blätter im Schnitt rot gefärbt. 360 Bl. Moderne Bleistiftfoliierung in der rechten oberen Ecke der recto-Seite. Ältere Paginierung zentriert oben auf Bl. 212ʳ–349ᵛ (S. 1–282). Bl. 211, 357–360 hinzugefügt beim Binden des Kodex. Herausgeschnittene Bl. zwischen Bl. 116–117, 161–162, 163–164, 172–173, 177–178 | 279–280. Die Zählung wurde erst nach diesen Veränderungen vorgenommen.

---

14 Vgl. Mittermaier (1965), S. 223. Die Liste der Meisterinnen und Äbtissinen von Hane bei Krings (2009), S. 187, weist an dieser Stelle eine Lücke auf.
15 Die Nonnen von Hane unterstanden stets den Chorherren von Rothenkirchen. Krings (2009), S. 192, zeichnet ein mögliches Überlieferungsszenario der in Straßburg, BNU, Ms. 324 überlieferten Christina-Vita und der Magdalenenlegende nach, das auf der Annahme der Abschrift im 15. Jahrhundert basiert: »Wir haben schon erfahren, dass Engelport bis in die sechziger Jahre des 16. Jahrhunderts der Abtei Sayn unterstand und außerdem, das der Sayner Abt Johann von Berka 1478 die Abtei Rothenkirchen reformierte und hierzu Sayner Kanoniker nach Rothenkirchen entsandte, von denen einer, Johann von Mayen, Abt von Rothenkirchen wurde und dieses Amt bis 1495 bekleidete. Einer der Sayner Kanoniker dürfte die Vita in Rothenkirchen abgeschrieben und die Handschrift nach Sayn geschickt haben. Von dort kam sie dann als Erbauungsschrift für die Schwestern nach Engelport.«
16 Zur Datierung siehe auch Kirakosian (2014b), S. 389–391.
17 Nachdem 1525 im Kontext der Bauernkriege das Kloster teilweise verwüstet wurde, wurde es schließlich 1564 oder 1566 aufgelöst, vgl. Krings (2009), S. 185, für das Jahr 1566; für das Jahr 1564 vgl. Backmund (1983), S. 97, und Paul Schotes: Reformbasilika Hane Bolanden. Bolanden 2009, S. 3. In der Zwischenzeit jedoch blieb das kommunitäre Leben bestehen, vgl. Backmund (1983), S. 97. In den 1540er Jahren blühte es unter der Meisterin Margarete von Engelsstadt kurz auf, vgl. Schotes (2009), S. 3.

Wasserzeichen: Im lateinischen Teil Reste nicht mehr identifizierbarer Wasserzeichen. | Im deutschen Teil nur noch Motivgruppen bestimmbar. Lagen 39, 40 (Bl. 309, 310, 320): PO-82651 (Braunschweig 1528),[18] PO-82652 (Trier 1531).[19] Lagen 41, 42 (Bl. 330, 331, 333, 340, 341, 343, 346, 353): Motivgruppe Piccard Krone IV 46 (Oberrhein 1526–1528),[20] Perlenanreihung auf der Kronenunterseite sowie Maße entsprechen hingegen der Papiermarke Basler Krone (1529–1532).[21] Obwohl eine präzise Identifikation der Wasserzeichen nicht möglich ist, weisen die Wasserzeichenreste auf die Entstehung des deutschen Handschriftenteils in der späteren ersten Hälfte des 16. Jahrhunderts hin.

Lagenstruktur: Lagenformel nicht gesichert. Im lateinischen Teil kann nicht immer mit Gewissheit bestimmt werden, welche Blätter genau fehlen, da der lateinische Text nicht untersucht wurde. Die im lateinischen Teil vermehrt vorkommenden Wortteile auf der rechten unteren Ecke der verso-Seite, die vom Buchbinder z.T. abgeschnitten worden sind, sind keine Reklamanten. 28 Lagen im lateinischen Teil: IV-1^7, IV^{15}, IV-1^{22}, IV^{30}, V^{40}, III^{46}, V^{56}, IV^{64}, III^{70}, VI-1^{81}, II^{85}, VII^{99}, IV^{107}, V-1^{116}, V-1^{125}, II^{129}, VIII^{145}, VI-1^{156}, III-1^{161}, II-1^{164}, IV-1^{172}, I^{174}, II-1+1^{178}, IV+1^{187}, 2 IV^{203}, I^{205}, I+2 I^{210}. Vorsatzblatt: I-1^{211}. | 12 Lagen im deutschen Teil: 4 VI^{259}, V^{269}, VI-1^{280}, VII^{294}, V^{304}, VII^{318}, V^{328}, IX^{346}, IV+1^{355}. Nachsatzblätter: I^{357}, II-1^{360}.

Schrift: 3 Schreiberhände: A (Bl. 1^r–124^v), B (Bl. 124^v–210^r) | C (Bl. 212^r–355^v: CvH-Teil, MM-Teil). Die Schreiber der lateinischen Statutenrezension bedienen sich beide einer schleifenlosen Bastarda mit einstöckigem a, bei welcher die Unterlängen von langem ſ und f unter die Grundzeile reichen, mit spitzen Brechungen bei den runden Teilen der Buchstaben, charakteristischen Verzierungen an den Oberlängen, besonders ausgeprägt bei l, die gut zu der Zeit um 1500 passen. | Im

---

18 Landesarchiv Baden-Württemberg: Wasserzeichen-Informationssystem, DE3285-PO-82651, URL: http://www.wasserzeichen-online.de/wzis/?ref=DE3285-PO-82651 [10.08.2017]. Die relevanten Wasserzeichen sind nicht bei Charles-Moïse Briquet: Les filigranes. Dictionnaire historique des marques du papier dès leur apparition vers 1282 jusqu'en 1600. Bd. 1: A-Ch, Bd. 2: Ci-K. Mansfield Centre 2007 (Originalausgabe Paris 1907), gelistet.
19 Landesarchiv Baden-Württemberg: Wasserzeichen-Informationssystem, DE4440-PO-82652, URL: http://www.wasserzeichen-online.de/wzis/?ref=DE4440-PO-82652 [10.08.2017].
20 Landesarchiv Baden-Württemberg: Wasserzeichen-Informationssystem, DE8100-HBVI52_999, URL: http://www.wasserzeichen-online.de/wzis/?ref=DE8100-HBVI52_999 [10.08.2017].
21 Landesarchiv Baden-Württemberg: Wasserzeichen-Informationssystem, DE4200-Ettenheimmünster44_999a, URL: http://www.wasserzeichen-online.de/?ref=DE4200-Ettenheimm%C3%BCnster44_999 [10.08.2017].

264 Straßburg, Bibliothèque nationale et universitaire, Ms. 324

Unterschied dazu handelt es sich bei der Schrift der Schreiberhand C um eine deutsche Bastarda mit einstöckigem a, mit Unterlängen bei f und f, Schleifen an den Buchstaben b, h, zumeist k und gelegentlich l. Diese Variationen bei k und besonders bei dem Buchstaben l lassen erkennen, dass es sich um eine unregelmäßige Variante einer deutschen Bastardschrift handelt, die eher auf das späte 15. und den Anfang des 16. Jahrhunderts hinweist. Als besonderes Charakteristikum kommt hinzu, dass die Schleifen immer schräg gestellt und mit dünner Feder ausgeführt sind. Weitere Merkmale sind die gebrochene Form des Buchstaben g mit rechtsschrägem Oberstrich sowie die tief nach links hinuntergezogene Unterlänge des y. Die Feststellung, dass es sich bei dem CvH-Teil und dem MM-Teil um eine einzige Schreiberhand handelt, beruht auf diesen paläographischen Beobachtungen.[22] Insgesamt macht die Schrift den Eindruck, dass der deutsche Teil zwischen 1490–1530 geschrieben worden ist, d.h. etwa zeitgleich mit dem lateinischen, am ehesten aber im späteren Abschnitt der genannten Zeitspanne.

Maße und Einband: Einspaltig. Schriftraum (schwankend): Bl. 1^r–210^r: 105 × 72 mm, 14–17 Zeilen. | Bl. 212^r–355^v: 110 × 75 mm, 16–22 Zeilen. Rote Initialen, Unterstreichungen und Strichelungen auf Bl. 212–355 (Ausnahmen s.u. Kap. 1.4 Beobachtungen zur Schreibertätigkeit). Einband des 17. Jh.: Pergament überzogene Holzdeckel. Außenmaß 140 × 100 mm.

Schreibsprache: Latein Bl. 1^r–210^r. | Moselfränkisch Bl. 212^r–355^v (CvH-Teil, MM-Teil). Anhand der Schreibsprache kann die Provenienz des deutschen Teils im moselfränkischen Dialektraum verortet werden (zur Schreibsprachenbestimmung s.u. Kap. 1.3).[23]

1.2 Inhalt der Handschrift

Adolf Becker: Die deutschen Handschriften der Kaiserlichen Universitäts- und Landesbibliothek zu Straßburg (Katalog der Kaiserlichen Universitäts- und Landesbibliothek in Straßburg 6). Straßburg 1914, S. 134.

---

22 Mittermaier (1965), S. 216, unterscheidet zwölf Hände, einschließlich acht Nachtragshände des 17.–18. Jahrhunderts (Randbemerkungen und Nachträge). Als Haupthände unterscheidet er A (Bl. 1^r–124^v) und B (Bl. 124^v *manuum*–210^r) für den lateinischen Teil und für den deutschen Teil H (Bl. 212^r–349^v, CvH-Teil) und Q (Bl. 350^r–355^v, MM-Teil). Er betrachtet die Schreiberhände H und Q als Hände »der gleichen Schule« und datiert sie auf die Mitte des 15. Jahrhunderts.
23 Kirakosian (2014b), S. 391, erörtert die historischen Bedingungen einer möglichen Abschrift in Hane.

Ernest Wickersheimer: Strasbourg (Catalogue Général des Manuscrits des Bibliothèques Publiques de France, Départements 47). Paris 1923, S. 138 f.

(Vorsatzblatt I): Hinzugefügtes Bl. beim Binden des Kodex

1. 1ʳ–210ʳ Lateinische Rezension der Prämonstratenserordensstatuten von 1505.
Iohannes permissione diuina abbas monasterij premonstratensis Laudunensis dijocesis ... Statuta hec per reverendissimos dominos meos ordinis premonstratensis abbates hoc anno superius dicto et die infra scripto recepta sunt capitulum generalem celebrantes. testor meo signeto manuali et apposito anno jam dicto et die xxijᵃ mensis aprilis

Lit. Lefèvre (1946);[24] Valvekens (1938); Valvekens (1939)[25]

(211:) Hinzugefügtes Bl. beim Binden des Kodex

2. 212ʳ–349ᵛ Vita der Christina von Hane
Dyß ist van der selicher Jonffrauwen Crystina genant die eyn cloister Jonffrauwe ist gewest zom hane gelegen by bolant yn mentzer strome ordens van premonstreye. Na der gebort vnsers heren Jhesu Cristi ... Also sterbet sie yn den wonderen der gotheit da flußet got yn gode daz sie nyt begryffen kayne die gotliche nature die sele die got beschauwen die sal doit syn aller befleckonge der sunden etc.

Ausg. Mittermaier (1965/1966)
Lit. Ruh (1993), Kirakosian (2014a), Kirakosian (2014b), Emmelius (2017), Kirakosian (2017a), Kirakosian (2017b), Kirakosian (2017c), Volfing (2017a)

---

24 Placide F. Lefèvre: les Statuts de Prémontré réformés sur les ordres de Grégoire IX et d'Innocent IV au XIIIe siècle Louvain 1946 (Bibliothèque de la Revue d'histoire ecclésiastique 23), S. 146–151.
25 Emile Valvekens: Textes relatifs à la réforme des status Prémontrés en 1505. In: Analecta Praemonstratensia 15 (1939), S. 25–41.

3. 350ʳ–355ᵛ Legende von der Bekehrung Maria Magdalenas (*S*) – Fragment
Die bekerunge der selicher marien magdalenen ist geschehet
als die lerer schrybent vff den irsten dag des mertze Maria
magdalena was geboren van eym edelen stame vnd eirlichem
geslecht ... Vnd also moiße ich dyne boiße gerucht allezijt horen
wo ich hyn komen Magdalena eyn konde sich nyt langer enthal-
den da sy martha sache schryen Da sprache sie myt schryenden
augen Ach lyebe suster iß ist

Parallelüberlieferung der Magdalenen-Legende:

B1: Berlin, Staatsbibliothek Preußischer Kulturbesitz,
Ms. germ. quart. 261, Bl. 186ʳ–190ᵛ
Datierung und Provenienz nach Degering (1926), S. 47:
16. Jh.; Kartause St. Barbara Köln[26]
Ripuarisch

B2: Berlin, Staatsbibliothek Preußischer Kulturbesitz,
Ms. germ. quart. 524, Bl. 159ʳ–163ʳ
Datierung nach Degering (1926), S. 92: 15. Jh.
Mittelniederdeutsch

D: Darmstadt, Universitäts- und Landesbibliothek, cod. 814,
Bl. 230ʳᵃ–233ʳᵇ
Datierung und Provenienz nach Staub/Sänger (1991), S. 63,
Nr. 35: um 1471; Augustinerinnenkloster St. Maria Magdalena
Köln[27]
Maria Magdalena-Legende auf Bl. 230–233: Nachtrag 16. Jh.
(1. Viertel)
Ripuarisch

G: Den Haag, Koninklijke Bibliotheek, cod. 133 F 17,
Bl. 162ʳᵃ–168ʳᵇ

---

[26] Hermann Degering: Kurzes Verzeichnis der germanischen Handschriften der Preußischen Staatsbibliothek II. Die Handschriften in Quartformat (Mitteilungen aus der Preußischen Staatsbibliothek VIII). Graz 1970 (Nachdruck der Originalausgabe Leipzig 1926).
[27] Kurt Hans Staub/Thomas Sänger: Deutsche und niederländische Handschriften. Mit Ausnahme der Gebetbuchhandschriften (Die Handschriften der Hessischen Landes- und Hochschulbibliothek Darmstadt 6). Wiesbaden 1991. Williams-Krapp (1986), S. 67, formuliert die Provenienz vorsichtiger.

Datierung nach de Vreese (1902), S. 465: 1479[28]
Provenienz nach van Eeghen (1941): Augustinerinnenkloster
St. Maria Magdalena (Bethanië) Amsterdam[29]
Mittelniederländisch
Ausg. Boxler (1996), S. 489–495; De Vooys (1905), S. 33–40[30]

K1: Köln, Historisches Archiv Best. 7008 (GB 8) 141, Bl. 187^r–199^r
Datierung nach Menne (1937), S. 526: 16. Jh.[31]
Ripuarisch

K2: Köln, Historisches Archiv 7020 (W* 8) 72, Bl. 21^r–46^r
Datierung nach Menne (1937), S. 174: 1550–1579
Ripuarisch

N: Nürnberg, Germanisches Nationalmuseum, Cod. 8826,
Bl. 13ra–17vb
Datierung und Provenienz nach Kurras (1974), S. 61: 1490–93;
Niederrhein[32]
Ripuarisch

Die von Williams-Krapp an verschiedenen Stellen für diese
Legendenversion aufgeführte Darmstädter Handschrift, Uni-
versitäts- und Landesbibliothek, cod. 2196 weist hingegen eine
andere Version der *conversio*-Legende auf.[33]

Lit. Kirakosian (2014b)

---

28 Willem de Vreese: De handschriften van Jan Ruusbroec's werken (Vlaamsche academie voor taal- & letterkunde. Uitgaven. VI. reeks. Bekroonde werken 24). Gent 1900.
29 Isabella Henriette van Eeghen: Vrouwenkloosters en Begijnhof in Amsterdam. Van de 14e tot het eind der 16e eeuw. Amsterdam 1941.
30 De Vooys, C. G. N.: De legende van sunte maria magdalena bekeringhe. In: Tijdschrift voor nederlandsche Taal- en Letterkunde 24 (1905), S. 16–44.
31 Karl Menne: Deutsche und niederländische Handschriften. Mitteilungen aus dem Stadtarchiv von Köln. Die Handschriften des Archivs. Heft 10, Abt. 1, Teil 2. Köln 1937.
32 Lotte Kurras: Die deutschen mittelalterlichen Handschriften, Erster Teil: Die literarischen und religiösen Handschriften. Anhang: Die Hardenbergschen Fragmente (Kataloge des Germanischen Nationalmuseums Nürnberg 1,1). Wiesbaden 1974.
33 Vgl. Williams-Krapp (1985), Sp. 1263, und ders. (1986), S. 438. Eine genaue Einordnung von Darmstadt, Universitäts- und Landesbibliothek, cod. 2196, Bl. 158ra–163va steht daher noch aus.

(4. 356ʳ–359ᵛ) Hinzugefügte Bl. beim Binden des Kodex
Abschriften aus Pieter de Waghenare: ›Vita beati Hermanni Josephi‹. 2. Aufl. Antwerpen 1661.
Hymnus auf Christina von Hane (356ʳ–358ʳ)
Hymnus auf Gertrud von Altenberg (358ʳ–359ᵛ)

Ausg. Christina-Hymnus: Mittermaier (1958), S. 355–358[34]

1.3 Schreibsprache des deutschen Teils

Verschiedene Beobachtungen bezüglich der Schreibsprache weisen auf einen Kopisten um 1520. Auf Grund des zwischen dem spätmittelhochdeutschen und frühneuhochdeutschen angesiedelten Sprachstandes der Christina von Hane-Vita muss offen gelassen werden, ob nicht womöglich mehrere benachbarte Dialekte über einen langen Zeitraum Einfluss auf den moselfränkischen Text ausübten.[35] Vergleichend werden für die folgende Untersuchung vordergründig der rheinfränkische bzw. mittelfränkische Dialekt und kontrastierend die Mainzer Schreibsprache herangezogen.[36]

Konsonantismus: Nach Jungandreas sind die Wahrung des <t> in *dat* und des <d> wie in *doit* und *vader* Kennzeichen des Mittelfränkischen.[37] Ein rheinfränkisches Merkmal ist das Nebeneinander von unverschobenem <t> und verscho-

---

34 Franz Paul Mittermaier: Ein bislang verschollener Hymnus auf die sel. Christina gen. von Retters. In: Archiv für mittelrheinische Kirchengeschichte 10 (1958), S. 353–355.
35 Der Text wurde bereits von Mittermaier (1965), S. 223, als moselfränkisch charakterisiert.
36 Die rheinfränkischen Merkmale sind aus Nigel F. Palmer: ›In kaffin in got‹. Zur Rezeption des ›Paradisus anime intelligentis‹ in der Oxforder Handschrift MS. Laud. Misc. 479. In: ›Paradisus anime intelligentis‹. Studien zu einer dominikanischen Predigtsammlung aus dem Umkreis Meister Eckharts. Hrsg. von Burkhard Hasebrink/Nigel F. Palmer/Hans-Jochen Schiewer. Tübingen 2009, S. 69–131, insbes. S. 102–104, entnommen. Der Mainzer Dialekt ist an Rudolf Schützeichel: Mundart, Urkundensprache und Schriftsprache. Studien zur Sprachgeschichte am Mittelrhein (Rheinisches Archiv 54). Bonn 1960, orientiert. Ein Vergleich der moselfränkischen Schreibsprache zu ripuarischen und niederfränkischen Sprachbelegen wäre weiterhin möglich. Zu diesen Dialektgrenzen siehe Theodor Frings: Mittelfränkisch-niederfränkische Studien. Bd 1: Das ripuarisch-niederfränkische Übergangsgebiet (Beiträge zur Geschichte der deutschen Sprache und Literatur 41). Halle 1917, und Roland Martin: Untersuchungen zur rhein-moselfränkischen Dialektgrenze (Deutsche Dialektgeographie 11a). Marburg 1992. Alle folgenden Wortbeispiele sind der Christina von Hane-Vita entnommen, sofern nicht anders vermerkt.
37 Vgl. Jungandreas (1957), S. 197.

benem <z> in *dat/daz*, aber sonst immer die verschobenen Schreibungen bei mhd. *z*.[38] Dieses Alternieren könnte aber auch diachron erklärt werden; z.B. ist für den Mainzer Sprachraum »ein relativ starkes Hervortreten der mundartlichen *dat*-Formen« im 15. Jahrhundert nachweisbar.[39] Ein Alternieren der nieder- und hochdeutschen Formen *dat/daz* ist laut Weimann in moselfränkischen Dialekten dagegen eher selten.[40] Das nur vereinzelte Vorkommen von *dat* an insgesamt vier Stellen in der Christina von Hane-Vita unterstützt diese Annahme. Wie im Rheinfränkischen üblich, kommen unverschobenes <p->, <-pp-> und <-rp> vor, z.B. *pyxntage*, *schepper* und *scharppe*.[41] Voralthochdeutsch *p* ist verschoben, z.B. *geschaffen*.[42] Es variieren durchgängig die Formen von *lyffe* und *lybe* sowie *loiffe* und *lobe*. Wie allgemein für das Westmittel- und Oberdeutsche üblich, steht im Anlaut für mhd. *t* immer <d->, so z.B. *dage* und *dogende*, aber *karfrytage* neben *oisterdage*.[43] Mit dem Mainzer Dialekt und mit dem Ripuarischen hat dieser Text den gelegentlichen Abfall von <ch> bei *nach* gemeinsam, so dass sowohl *na* wie *nach* auftreten. »Der insbesondere für das nördliche Rheinfränkische und westliche Hessische charakteristische Schwund von /r/ in der Gruppe /rht/«[44] ist auch in der Christina von Hane-Vita erwiesen (z.B. *vochtes*).[45] Im Anlaut erscheint <s> für *sch* in Worten wie *sicket* und *snelle(n)*.[46] *kauffen* für die Zusammenkunft zum Tanz und Gesang (mhd. *côvenanz*) führt einen doppelten stimmlosen Frikativ anstelle eines stimmhaften.[47] Dieser lautliche Wechsel ist im Text auch an

---

38 *dat* in CvH 21 (Bl. 251ᵛ), CvH 33 (Bl. 268ʳ), CvH 95 (Bl. 336ʳ), CvH 100 (Bl. 347ᵛ).

39 Schützeichel (1960), S. 46.

40 Vgl. Britta Weimann: Moselfränkisch. Der Konsonantismus anhand der frühesten Urkunden (Rheinisches Archiv 157). Wien/Köln/Weimar 2012, S. 144 f. Weimanns Beobachtungen beschränken sich auf den Konsonantismus in moselfränkischen Urkunden.

41 *pynxtage* in CvH 21 (Bl. 253ʳ); *schepper* in CvH 38 (Bl. 279ʳ), CvH 95 (Bl. 337ʳ), *scheppest* in CvH 82 (Bl. 325ᵛ), CvH 94 (Bl. 334ʳ), *scheppen* in CvH 84 (Bl. 326ᵛ), *oppert* in CvH 57 (Bl. 294ʳ), CvH 76 (Bl. 313ᵛ); *troppen* in CvH 7 (Bl. 225ʳ), CvH 17 (Bl. 244ᵛ, Bl. 245ᵛ), *mynnetroppe* in CvH 17 (Bl. 245ʳ), *kepper* in CvH 38 (Bl. 277ᵛ); *scharppe* in CvH 17 (Bl. 245ᵛ).

42 *geschaffener* in CvH 100 (Bl. 347ʳ⁻ᵛ); *geschaffen* in CvH 100 (Bl. 349ʳ).

43 *oisterdage* in CvH 20 (Bl. 248ᵛ), in einer Überschrift CvH 38 (Bl. 276ᵛ), CvH 97 (Bl. 342ᵛ); *karfrytage* in CvH 19 (Bl. 247ᵛ); *siechtagen* in CvH 20 (Bl. 248ᵛ); *pynxtage* in CvH 21 (Bl. 253ʳ), CvH 72 (Bl. 331ᵛ); *dornstage* CvH 63 (Bl. 301ᵛ), CvH 64 (303ᵛ); *crystage* in CvH 5 (219ᵛ), CvH 79 (Bl. 319ʳ).

44 Barbara Lenz-Kemper: Die hessischen Reimpredigten. 2 Bde. (DTM 89). Berlin 2008–2009. Bd. 1: Untersuchungen zu Überlieferung, Sprache und Herkunft (2008). Bd. 2: Texte (2009), hier Bd. 1 (2008), S. 159.

45 CvH 10 (Bl. 230ᵛ, 232ʳ), CvH 15 (Bl. 242ʳ), CvH 52 (Bl. 285ᵛ), CvH 82 (Bl. 324ᵛ).

46 *sicket* CvH 32 (Bl. 266ᵛ); *snellen* CvH 33 (Bl. 270ᵛ), *snelle* CvH 100 (Bl. 347ᵛ). Zur Graphemproblematik von vorahd. /s/ in hessischen Texten siehe Lenz-Kemper (2008), S. 104.

47 Aus dem Kontext (CvH 32) ergibt sich, dass *kauffen* womöglich eine seltene Ableitung von MHD *côvenanz* (oder *govenance*) darstellt, vgl.: *Die schaffen daz man schon begiesse / in der stu-*

anderer Stelle bezeugt: *myt eym grauffen broyt*.[48] Das *grawe brot* wäre wohl das schimmelige Brot und nicht, wie man leicht annehmen könnte, das Graubrot, d.h. das Brot ohne Weizenmehl, welches erst in der frühen Neuzeit aufkommt. Zwar wäre die Schreibung *grauffen* für *grauwen* lautlich schwer erklärbar, doch erwähnt Moser die intervokalische <-ff>-Schreibung für *naffe* (mhd. *nâwe*), die im Hessischen öfter im 15. und 16. Jahrhundert vorkomme, und erklärt diese mit der Entlehnung aus italienisch *nave*.[49]

Vokalismus: Im Vokalbereich ist die regelmäßige Schreibung <y> für mhd. *i* fast durchgängig, so. z.B. *sye* und *yre*. Weitere rheinfränkische Merkmale betreffen die Senkung von *u* zu <o>, z.B. in *son* und *wonder*, <a> für *o*, z.B. in *ader* und *wanen* (allgemein im südwestdeutschen Sprachbereich) sowie fast immer <i> als Vokalnachschlag in allen Kombinationen, z.B. *hait, saitzet, noit* und *rytterschaiffe*. Dieser Dehnungsvokal ist auch ein Charakteristikum der Mainzer (Urkunden-) Sprache und kann ebenso im Ripuarischen beobachtet werden.[50] Der intervokalische Schwund von *g* mit anschließender Senkung von *u* zu <o>, zumeist in Substantiven, bringt kontrahierte Erscheinungsformen mit sich (*grontfestionge, gebenedionge, verkondionge*), die zum Teil neben regelmäßigen Formen stehen (*vereynionge/vereynigun, eynionge/eynigunge, sayt/saget*). Besonders scheint außerdem der sporadische und unsystematische Vokalnachschlag <v> nach *u*, der zu parallelen Erscheinungen wie etwa *fůre/fure* und *baůme/baume* führt. Dialektale Lautprozesse sind in der Vokalverschiebung von mhd. *ei* zu <ai> erkennbar, z.B. in *kayn(t)* für mhd. *kein*.[51] An einigen Stellen findet sich <ie> für Mittelhochdeutsch ê (z.B. *zeirret, getzeirt, zeirheit*),[52] wie auch andere hessische Texte des 14. Jahrhunderts belegen.[53] Zugleich findet sich die alternative Schreibweise *zeyrcheit*,[54] *zeyrden*,[55] *gezeyrt*.[56]

---

ben uber al, / daz die iungen niht verdriesse. / da'z dem meier ist der schal, / da hôret man den govenanz. / Chůnzel, Heinzel, lat da schowen, / daz mit zůhten ge der tanz. (Neidhart-Lieder. Texte und Melodien sämtlicher Handschriften und Drucke, Hrsg. von Ulrich Müller u.a. 3 Bde. Berlin/New York 2007, Bd. 1, C 274 III, S. 502.)

48 CvH 15 (Bl. 242ʳ).

49 Vgl. Virgil Moser: Frühneuhochdeutsche Grammatik. Bd. 3: Lautlehre. Heidelberg 1951, S. 89, § 131, Anm. 19.

50 Vgl. Schützeichel (1960), S. 52.

51 Z.B. CvH 31 (Bl. 265ʳ) und CvH 80 (Bl. 319ᵛ).

52 *zeirret* (CvH 22 [Bl. 254ʳ]); *getzeirt* (CvH 5 [Bl. 220ᵛ]); *zeirheit* (CvH 95 [337ʳ]).

53 Vgl. Lenz-Kemper (2008), S. 68.

54 CvH 81 (Bl. 323ᵛ).

55 CvH 88 (Bl. 329ᵛ).

56 CvH 33 (Bl. 269ʳ).

Morphologie: Auf morphologischer Ebene weist der Text wie andere südhessische Quellen zahlreiche *ent*-Schreibungen für die 3. Pers. Pl. Präs. auf, z.B. *sullent*,[57] *sprechent*,[58] *werdent*.[59] »[D]er allgemeine *n*-Antritt an die 1. Pers. Praes.«, z.B. *Jch loben*,[60] gehört zu den allgemeinen Kennzeichen des Hessischen sowie Mittelfränkischen.[61] Der im Präteritum sowie an einer Stelle im Präsens der 3. Pers. Sg. vorkommende *n*-Antritt ist hingegen ungewöhnlich, z.B. *daz er yre hertze wultden bluwen machen*;[62] *Aber daz ich selber sache, sagen sie myr dyß wort vnd sprach*;[63] *dan so gynth zorǔcke die dogent*.[64] Das Nebeneinander von -*er* und -*en* bei Adjektivendungen ist hingegen typisch für das Moselfränkische.[65] Das schwache Verb *legen* wird an einigen Stellen im Präteritum stark flektiert, z.B. *wie der eyn kynt yn der wegen vor syner moder zo Nazareth lache*[66] und *an dem ich allen mynen troist vnd zo versicht hayn gelacht*.[67] Im Rheinfränkischen und Hessischen treten *lahte* und *gelaht* als schwache Präteritalformen von *legen* auf (aber nicht stark *lache* wie in der Christina von Hane-Vita).[68] Dass sich der Schreiber in einem Lautverschiebungsprozess befindet, wird an einer Stelle besonders deutlich, wenn er *byß* (3. Ps. Sg. Prät, mhd. *bîzen*, Ablautreihe I) mit einer interlinearen Ergänzung von <e> zur älteren Form *beyß* korrigiert.[69] Da *kyntheit* nur einmal maskulin erscheint (*van den kyntheit*)[70] zur sonst immer femininen Deklination, liegt an dieser Stelle weniger eine Kasusvarianz als ein Schreibfehler vor.[71] Das Substantiv *erkentenyß* hingegen ist sowohl als Neutrum (*daz lyecht*

---

57 CvH 23 (Bl. 256ᵛ).
58 CvH 56 (Bl. 289ᵛ).
59 CvH 56 (Bl. 289ᵛ).
60 CvH 10 (Bl. 232ᵛ).
61 Jungandreas (1957), S. 197. Siehe auch Lenz-Kemper (2008), S. 115. Der Wegfall von -*n* im Infinitiv an nur einer Stelle im Vitentext deutet wahrscheinlich auf einen Schreibfehler hin: *Da so hobe sie an zo schreye* (CvH 8 [Bl. 227ʳ]). Der *n*-Antritt an die 1. Pers. Prät. an einer Stelle scheint ebenfalls fehlerhaft: *Vnder den luchten sy* (CvH 1 [Bl. 2121ᵛ]).
62 CvH 8 (Bl. 226ᵛ).
63 CvH 80 (Bl. 320ʳ).
64 CvH 38 (Bl. 277ᵛ).
65 Vgl. Jungandreas (1957), S. 197.
66 CvH 2 (Bl. 214ᵛ).
67 CvH 10 (Bl. 234ʳ).
68 Vgl. Lenz-Kemper (2008), S. 166.
69 CvH 12 (Bl. 238ʳ).
70 CvH 8 (Bl. 227ᵛ).
71 CvH 2 (Bl. 214ᵛ), CvH 5 (Bl. 219ʳ), CvH 6 (Bl. 221ᵛ), CvH 7 (Bl. 222ᵛ), CvH 15 (Bl. 242ʳ).

des erkentenyß,[72] *durch eyn oitmodiges erkentenyße*[73]) wie als Femininum bezeugt (z.B. *myt steder lyebden vnd hoger erkentenyß*[74]).

Syntax: Einige Formulierungen des Schreibers scheinen zumindest dem heutigen Leser ungrammatisch, z.B. Passivkonstruktionen (*nyt myt der stymmen, daz man gehoirt mocht*[75]) und stark flektierte Adjektivendungen trotz definiter Artikel (*daz zarte aller suberlichstes kyntgen*[76]). Die Präposition *by* nimmt sowohl Akkusativ (z.B. *by die reynne jonffrauwen,*[77] *by sie*[78]) als auch Dativ an (z.B. *by yre waren*[79]). Abbreviaturen könnten daher an einigen Stellen mit Dativ oder Akkusativ aufgelöst werden, z.B. *by eȳ graiffe,*[80] *eyn* im Akkusativ oder *eym* im Dativ. Da in den ausgeschriebenen Fällen *by* + Dativ überwiegt, werden diese Abbreviaturen mit dem Dativ aufgelöst. Inkongruenz von Plural und Singular kommt an wenigen Stellen vor, z.B. *er gaiffe allen dyngen yren weßen;*[81] *Dan synt alle dynge vollenkomen yn gode, wanne iß wyrckeit an hyndernyß.*[82] Ganze Satzinversionen sind üblich, z.B. *du machtz frylichen als eyn adeler flyehen yn die vberste hoheit, vnd die luteren augen dyner selen festigen yn dem wieder glantze der ewiger gotlicher sonnen, vnd yn daz lyebliche angesicht der ewiger gotheit.*[83] Der Satz ist nur verständlich, sofern die letzte von *vnd* eingeleitete Phrase zum Satz mit *machtz flyehen* als Prädikat zugehörig gesehen wird, so dass der dazwischengeschobene Satz als Nebensetz derselben Ordnung erscheint. Die Konjunktion *vnd* besetzt eine Vielzahl an Bedeutungen, die modal, temporal, konsekutiv und selbst konditional übersetzt werden können.

Lexis: Das archaisch anmutende Wort *wyne* für den Liebhaber könnte ein Hinweis auf einen älteren Sprachstand sein.[84] Es wird durchgängig *van* für nhd. *von* benutzt, was diesen Text in die Nähe des Koblenzer Sprachraums rückt, geo-

---

72 CvH 8 (Bl. 225ᵛ).
73 CvH 30 (Bl. 263ʳ).
74 CvH 8 (Bl. 227ʳ).
75 CvH 24 (Bl. 257ᵛ).
76 CvH 6 (Bl. 221ʳ).
77 CvH 4 (Bl. 217ʳ).
78 CvH 6 (Bl. 221ᵛ).
79 CvH 6 (Bl. 222ʳ).
80 CvH 20 (Bl. 249ʳ).
81 CvH 98 (Bl. 343ᵛ).
82 CvH 98 (Bl. 344ʳ).
83 CvH 79 (Bl. 319ʳ).
84 CvH 24 (Bl. 257ʳ).

graphisch durchaus stimmig ist und auch für weite Teile des Moselgebiets gilt.[85] Wie bei den Formen *broder* und *lyeff* handelt es sich auch bei *van* um niederdeutsche Spracheinflüsse am Mittelrhein, die auch im Ripuarischen zu finden sind. Für Schützeichel zeugen solche Fälle von einer »Unsicherheit«, die letztlich eine »Übernahme südlicher Sprachgewohnheiten« begünstigte.[86] Obwohl *demoidcheit* mit *oitmodicheit* abwechselt, wobei die letztere niederdeutsche Form überwiegt,[87] handelt es sich nicht unbedingt um den Einfluss einer niederdeutschen Textrezeption: Das Moselfränkische ist eine Mischsprache, in der südlich-oberdeutsche Einflüsse häufiger und eher auffindbar sind als etwa im benachbarten Ripuarisch.[88] Die Vita führt zudem einige seltene Wörter auf, z.B. *anhebonge* für die mystische Entrückung,[89] *nunuste* für das Genitivadverbium mhd. *niuwenes*[90] und *vberentzicher* für einzigartig.[91]

1.4 Beobachtungen zur Schreibertätigkeit

Im Vitenteil der Handschrift fallen viele vom Schreiber (oder von der Schreiberin) vorgenommene Verbesserungen auf, die auf eine Abschrift hinweisen. Eine besondere Unregelmäßigkeit ergab sich durch ein nachträglich beschriebenes Blatt (Bl. 281): Trotz einer zu einem Viertel frei gebliebenen verso-Seite (Bl. 281[v]) sind die Zeilenzwischenräume und der Schriftsatz kleiner als auf den vorauslaufenden und nachfolgenden Blättern (siehe Abb. 3). Das Enden des Nachtrags mit der Abkürzung *etc.* deutet nicht notwendigerweise auf Unvollständigkeit hin, sondern könnte die Fehleinschätzung des Kopisten bestätigen. Das von Mittermaier als »flüchtigere Schrift« umschriebene Schriftbild auf diesem Blatt entspricht dem Vitenteil ab Bl. 328.[92] Die Linien und Kurven in der Schrift werden

---

85 Vgl. Schützeichel (1960), S. 70.

86 Schützeichel (1960), S. 58.

87 In der Christina von Hane-Vita kommt *oitmodicheit* an den folgenden Stellen vor: CvH 13 (Bl. 239[v]–240[r]), CvH 18 (Bl. 248[r]), CvH 30 (Bl. 263[v]), CvH 37 (Bl. 275[v]), CvH 65 (Bl. 306[r]), CvH 76 (Bl. 315[r]), CvH 81 (Bl. 324), CvH 95 (Bl. 336[r]). Dahingegen *demodicheit* nur zweimal: CvH 13 (Bl. 239[r]), CvH 76 (Bl. 316[r]).

88 Vgl. Britta Weiman: Überlegungen zur Entwicklung der Mündlichkeit und Schriftlichkeit in Luxemburg. In: Vielfalt der Sprachen, Varianz der Perspektiven. Zur Geschichte und Gegenwart der Luxemburger Mehrsprachigkeit. Hrsg. von Heinz Sieburg (Interkulturalität. Studien zu Sprache, Literautr und Gesellschaft 3). Bielefeld 2013, S. 251–262, insbes. S. 253.

89 CvH 8 (Bl. 225[v]).

90 CvH 15 (Bl. 242[r]).

91 CvH 23 (Bl. 256[r]).

92 Mittermaier (1965), S. 215.

flüssiger und generieren beinahe eine ununterbrochene Kontinuität, die nur oberflächlich einer kursiven Handschrift ähnelt.[93] Aus inhaltlicher Sicht ist beim Nachtrag des Blatts zunächst kein Bruch erkennbar. Die chronologische Abfolge des kirchlichen Kalenderjahrs ist hingegen durcheinandergebracht: Während vor Bl. 281 von einer Vision an Ostern berichtet wird, beziehen sich alle drei auf Bl. 281 genannten liturgischen Festtage auf die Zeit vor Ostern (Tag der Heiligen Agnes, Mariä Reinigung und Sonntag Invocavit).[94] Diese Unstimmigkeiten werden noch auf Bl. 282^r fortgeführt, wo Gründonnerstag (*abenteßen des heren*) erwähnt wird, bevor die Festtage auf die Zeit *nach oisteren* übergehen. Die Zeitspanne vom Tag der Heiligen Agnes bis zum Gründonnerstag füllt hingegen eine von Epiphanias bis zum Ostertag klaffende Lücke im Text ab Bl. 339^v.[95] Aus diesen Beobachtungen lässt sich ablesen, dass der Kopist um Vollständigkeit bemüht war und zumindest oberflächlich kohärente Übergänge herzustellen versuchte.

Unterstreichungen und rote Verzierungen einzelner Buchstaben kommen ausgeglichen und fast immer durchgängig auf einer Doppelseite vor. An wenigen Stellen fehlt die Lombarde, für die der Schreiber entsprechend Platz ließ. Ab Bl. 283^v hören Verzierungen und Unterstreichungen völlig auf mit der Ausnahme der Bl. 346^v und 348^r. Schon die Bl. 260^v, 263^v und 264^r, 265^v und 266^r, 267^v und 268^r sowie 269^r weisen keine Unterstreichungen auf. Die Lagenbeschaffenheit gibt keinen Aufschluss über diese Inkongruenz. Die letzten roten Überschriften finden sich auf Bl. 276^v (*Van dem Oisterdage*) und Bl. 334^v (*Annunciacio Marie*). Der Text von der Bekehrung Maria Magdalenas hingegen weist bis auf die rote Überschrift und die Lombarde zum Textbeginn (Bl. 350^r, siehe Abb. 4) gar keine Unterstreichungen oder roten Verzierungen auf.

Im Kontext von Bearbeitungstypen wie Neufassung, Adaption, Version und Werk lassen sich zwar Bearbeiter generell von »Urheber[n] von handschriftlich überlieferten Texten, die keinen Bearbeitungswillen erkennen lassen, sondern nur iterierende Varianten und versehentlich entstandene Fehler« als »bloße Schreiber« unterscheiden.[96] Doch auch ein Schreiber bzw. Kopist verfügte über gewisse Gestaltungsmöglichkeiten und griff nicht selten ganz bewusst in den Text ein, um

---

93 Dieses Phänomen wird von Malcolm Beckwith Parkes: Their Hands Before our Eyes. A Closer Look at Scribes. The Lyell Lectures Delivered in the University of Oxford 1999. Aldershot 2008, S. 73, als »hasty scribe« bezeichnet.
94 Vgl. CvH 39 f.
95 Vgl. CvH 96 f.
96 Steinmetz (2005), S. 53.

ihn zu verändern, zu interpretieren und zu gliedern.[97] Die häufigen Kopierfehler im deutschsprachigen Teil von Straßburg, BNU, Ms. 324 führen zu der Annahme, dass der Schreiber mit einer Vorlage arbeitete und wenig in den Text eingriff.[98] Dabei ist durchaus denkbar, dass er seinen eigenen zuvor zusammengestellten Text kopierte. Für die Annahme, dass die vorliegende Christina von Hane-Vita die Bearbeitung einer älteren Vorlage ist, spricht die Bezeichnung ›Meisterin‹ (*meysterschen*) für die Priorin des Klosters im Text,[99] denn ab 1495 bezeichneten sich die Meisterinnen vom Kloster Hane als Äbtissinnen.[100] Ob man dabei von Material ausgehen kann, das »ohne Zweifel schon bald nach ihrem [Christinas] Tode aufgeschrieben [wurde]«, wie Backmund vorschlägt, ist indes nicht nachweisbar.[101] Selbst wenn Bearbeitung »das Ergebnis wie den dazu führenden Vorgang« bedeuten kann,[102] gibt der deutsche Teil der Handschrift, von einer Hand mit mehreren Unterbrechungen geschrieben, wenig Aufschluss über die Bearbeitung oder den Entstehungsvorgang.[103]

---

97 Vgl. Parkes (2008), S. 55–145.

98 Auch wenn die Rolle des Schreibers für die Ausrichtung des Textes schwer zu bestimmen ist, zeigt sich an der Gestaltung der Handschrift, dass sein Einfluss nicht unterschätzt werden darf. Schließlich korrigierte sich der Schreiber trotz aller Nachlässigkeit an einigen Stellen. Es ist daher ebenfalls nicht auszuschließen, dass bereits seine Kopiervorlage Fehler aufwies.

99 CvH 7 (Bl. 223[v]).

100 Vgl. Krings (2009), S. 184.

101 Backmund (1972), S. 89.

102 Steinmetz (2005), S. 47.

103 Ruh (1993), S. 125, zieht die Möglichkeit in Erwägung, dass ein Teil des Textes aus dem Lateinischen übersetzt wurde, dass ein zweiter Teil in der erhaltenen Form eine Überarbeitung darstellt und dass ein dritter Teil »aus neuer Quelle« hinzugefügt wurde. Auf diese Vorschläge kann nicht eingegangen werden, weil es keine Möglichkeit gibt, die Vorgeschichte des in der Straßburger Handschrift unikal überlieferten Textes zu überprüfen.

2 Editionsprinzipien

2.1 Allgemeine Editionsprinzipien

Die hier vorgelegte Edition der Vita der Christina von Hane zielt auf einen Kompromiss zwischen einer diplomatischen Transkription der in moselfränkischer Schreibsprache abgefassten Handschrift *S* und einem gut les- und zitierbaren Text, der als Grundlage für weitere Forschungen dienen kann. Zu diesem Zweck erfolgt auch eine Unterteilung in Kapitel mit jeweils eigener Zeilenzählung. Die Kapitelzählung ist zu Beginn der entsprechenden Passage im Außensteg notiert, während sich die Zeilenzählung im Bundsteg befindet. Die Zählung der eigenständig nummerierten Kapitel ist hinzugefügt und richtet sich generell nach der episodenartigen Schilderung und der Nennung der Festtage des Kirchenjahres, sofern damit auch graphisch ein Abschnitt markiert ist, d.h. sofern eine Initiallombarde den entsprechenden Text einleitet.[1] An wenigen Stellen in der Handschrift geht die Erwähnung des Festtags oder einer Kardinalsünde in Form einer Überschrift der jeweiligen Initiale voraus. Zu Beginn der Vita sind es Episoden aus Christinas Kindheit und ihr siebenjähriger Kampf gegen die Kardinalsünden, die zusammenhängende Abschnitte bilden.[2]

Weil die Forschungsuntersuchungen dieses Bandes die Bedeutung der Buchschriftlichkeit für das Verständnis der Christina von Hane-Vita hervorheben, gibt die Edition bestimmte materielle Aspekte der Handschrift wie Lombarden und rubrizierte Titel wieder: rot geschriebene Schriftzüge und Lombarden werden **fett** gedruckt. Der Zeilenfall der Handschrift wird nicht nachgebildet und auch gelegentliche graphische Zeilenfüller in Form von Schleifen werden nicht wiederge-

---

1 Einige wenige Ausnahmen mussten gemacht werden: Kap. 26, 28 und 29 werden trotz Lombarden in der Zeilenmitte auf Grund separater Visions- bzw. Auditionsschilderungen als eigenständige Episoden aufgefasst. In Kap. 64 bis 69 und Kap. 95 stehen die Lombarden z.T. in der Zeilenmitte und markieren zumeist direkte Rede. Kap. 97 weist unter einem Festtag zwei mit Initiallombarden eingeleitete Abschnitte auf. In Kap. 52 kommen zwei Festtage vor.
2 Ab Bl. 281ʳ (Kap. 40) markiert fast durchgängig der kirchliche Kalender die verschiedenen Abschnitte. Diese liturgische Struktur wird im Vitentext angekündigt: *Doch synt her gescreben der soißer sprechonge eyn deylle yn die hogetzijden, dar durch die gotliche lyebhauenden hertzen got lobent sullent vmb genade vnd wirdicheit, die da verstanden wyrt manchfeldenclichen* (CvH 39 [Bl. 281ʳ]). Daher werden ab Kap. 40 einige wenige durch Lombarden initiierte Abschnitte, die keinen Festtag nennen, nicht als eigenständige Kapitel dargestellt. Zugleich bilden Kap. 40 bis 55 eine Reihe kürzerer Abschnitte, wobei in Kap. 43 und 44 der entsprechende Festtag im der Lombarde vorauslaufenden Fließtext erwähnt wird.

https://doi.org/10.1515/9783110536324-011

geben. Einzig in der Handschrift durch Initialen markierte Zeilenanfänge werden in der Edition reproduziert.

Grundsätzlich ist jeder nicht in der Handschrift vorkommende, das heißt editorisch hinzugefügte Text *kursiv* gedruckt. So stehen auch Angaben zur Foliierung in kursiven eckigen Klammern (*[...]*) und Bibelstellen in kursiven und runden Klammern (*(Mt 28,18)*). Näherungszitate werden durch *vgl.* eingeleitet. Die Bibel wird nach der fünften Auflage der Stuttgarter Vulgata-Ausgabe zitiert, auch bei der Psalmenzählung.

Alle Emendationen sind im Apparat vollständig aufgeführt. Konjekturen, die sich aus dem Kontext ergeben oder im Fall der Maria Magdalena-Bekehrungslegende aus anderen Handschriften übernommen sind, stehen in spitzen Klammern (<...>) und sind im Apparat vermerkt. Gleichermaßen sind übernommene Ergänzungen jüngerer Hände (*v. j. H.*) sowie Auslassungen gegenüber der Handschrift im kritischen Apparat immer gekennzeichnet. Dittographien werden dort getilgt, wo es sich nicht um rhetorische Wiederholungen handelt. Eine nicht genau zu bestimmende Anzahl unleserlicher Zeichen wird im Apparat mit dem Auslassungszeichen (...) indiziert. Wenn die Anzahl der unleserlichen Graphen festzumachen ist, wird pro nicht identifizierbarem Graph ein trianguläres Kolon gesetzt (:). Liegt ein nichtrekonstruierbarer Textverlust (wie z.B. auf Grund von Papierzerstörung auf den Bl. 223–224) vor, wird dies im Apparat zusätzlich vermerkt. Ergänzungen des Schreibers über der Zeile und marginale Korrekturen stehen in eckigen interlinearen Einfügungsklammern (ˈ ˈ), wobei nur marginale Korrekturen zusätzlich im Apparat als solche benannt sind (= *am Rande*). Ein Zeilenwechsel wird im Apparat mit einem vertikalen Strich (|), ein Blattwechsel mit zwei vertikalen Strichen (||) dargestellt.

Die Schreibsprache ist unnormalisiert. Daher werden alle Kasusvarianten beibehalten, sofern es sich nicht um eindeutige Schreibfehler handelt. Morphologisch-lexematische Varianten bleiben unverändert (wie z.B. *vereynigun* zu sonst immer kontrahiert *vereynionge*, der n-Schwund in *vernoifft* und *vnuernoifftige*, einmal *verlangen* gegenüber immer *verlangeren*, *ewanclichen* an zwei Stellen bei sonst immer *ewenclichen*), damit ein möglichst authentischer Eindruck vom Sprachstand des Textes vermittelt werden kann. Schreibfehler werden emendiert (z.B. zweimal *hoirfart*, einmal *honfart* bei sonst immer *hoiffart*), wobei inkorrekte lateinische Formen nur bei deutlichen Verschreibungen verbessert werden (z.B. *Dominaca* anstatt wie sonst *Dominica*, beibehalten dahingegen die Varianzen *assumpcionis/assumpsionis* und *purificacionis/purificacione*).

Bis auf wenige Ausnahmen bestand keine Notwendigkeit, von der Worttrennung in der Handschrift abzuweichen. Stets zusammengeschrieben werden: untrennbare Präfixe mit dem folgenden Verb (z.B. *zofloiße* anstatt wie in der Handschrift *zo floiße*, *vmbfangen* anstatt *vmb fangen*), Adverbien des Typs *zorŭcke* und *zosamen*, die in der Handschrift nur selten getrennt geschriebenen Adjektive *ynwendich* und *vßwendich* sowie das in der Handschrift an nur zwei Stellen auseinandergeschriebene Kompositum *lyebhaber*. Die an wenigen Stellen vorkommende Zusammenschreibung von *sprach* und *er* wird der besseren Lesbarkeit wegen stets getrennt geschrieben (ebenso *salt ir* anstatt *saltir*, beibehalten dahingegen kontrahiert *saltu*, *systu*, *hyßes*). Die in der Handschrift alternierenden Schreibweisen sind so wiedergegeben bei: trennbaren Präfixen (z.B. *vber fludige/vberfloedige*, *vber leßen/vberleßet*, *wieder stontde/wiederstonde*), Adverbien des Typs *da myt*, *dar vmbe* und *altzo mail* (auch an einer Stelle *war vmb*), der proklitischen Negation *eyn* (z.B. *eyn mache*), Adjektiven mit Präfixen (z.B. *ynbrunstig/jn brunstig*) und bei den in der Handschrift stark variierenden Wörtern *ynfluß* und *vßfloiß*.

Die Groß- und Kleinschreibung wird behutsam angepasst: Orts- und Eigennamen sowie Satzanfänge erscheinen groß, während die in der Handschrift gelegentlich groß geschriebenen Wörter wie *Ewenclichen* und *Jonffrauwe* ebenso wie Bücher der Bibel und kirchliche Festtage klein dargestellt werden. Hymnen, Gebete und lateinische Einsprengsel beginnen i.d.R. groß.

Zur Erleichterung der Lektüre wird eine moderne Interpunktion sparsam eingesetzt. Die Vita der Christina von Hane weist eine komplizierte Syntax mit verschachtelten Nebensätzen der zweiten und z.T. dritten Ordnung auf. Auf Grund mehrdeutiger Konjunktionen und Pronomina kann nicht immer eine eindeutige und konsequente Anwendung moderner Satzzeichen erfolgen. Die Edition versucht der spezifischen Syntax der Vita Rechnung zu tragen, indem eine dem heutigen Leserempfinden angemessene Interpunktion dann an der Grenze zweier Hauptsätze angewendet wird, wenn dies das Leseverständnis vereinfacht. Wegen der Tendenz des Textes zur Aneinanderreihung von Hauptsätzen kommt es regelmäßig zum Satzbeginn durch die Konjunktion *vnd*. Die in der Handschrift zur Unterstützung syntaktischer Einheiten verwendeten Großbuchstaben können der modernen Rechtschreibung gemäß klein wiedergegeben werden. Gelegentlich werden lange, verschachtelte Sätze in der Edition nicht verkürzt, weil sonst der Sinnzusammenhang verloren ginge. Nebensätze werden von darauffolgenden mit *vnd* eingeleiteten Hauptsätzen höherer Ordnung durch Komma getrennt. Außerdem werden einige parataktische Satzketten nur mit Komma unterbrochen, da ein Eingriff zur Anpassung an die moderne Syntax an diesen Stellen den entsprechenden Leseeffekt verzerren würde. Direkte Rede wird mit Doppelpunkt eingeleitet und steht in einfachen Anführungszeichen; direkte Rede zweiter Ordnung erscheint in doppelten Anführungszeichen. Auch bei der direkten Rede ergeben sich an einigen Stellen mehrdeutige Interpretationen. Die Edition bietet an solchen Stellen nur einen möglichen Vorschlag.[3]

Grapheme werden der Handschrift gemäß wiedergegeben. Für das Moselfränkische bedeutet dies die Beibehaltung von ij anstatt ähnlich y. Die Schreibungen i/j, i/y, u/v, u/ǔ, w/v, f/w sind beibehalten. Das gilt auch für die Lombarden und hat zur Konsequenz, dass *Uff* mit Initial-U geschrieben ist (anders als *vff* im Fließtext). Die Formen für *Ich/Jch* variieren hingegen je nach I- oder J-Lombarde. Die Unterscheidung zwischen Schaft-ſ und rundem s bleibt unberücksichtigt. Deutsches sz wird als ß wiedergegeben.

Gängige Abbreviaturen sind systematisch aufgelöst. Der Schreiber verwendet gelegentlich eine Schleife mit nach links gezogener Unterlänge am Wortende für unbetontes e. Die Abbreviatur *he'* wird in der Edition mit *here* aufgelöst, wobei in der Handschrift ausgeschrieben beide Formen *here* und *herre* auftreten. Ergänzungen bei radikalen Abkürzungen stehen in spitzen Klammern (<...>), so z.B. *s<elige>* oder *h<eilige>*. Die Handschrift kennt mehrere Abbreviaturen für die unbetonte Silbe *-en*: Neben der Abbreviatur <-ē> für *-en* am Wortende darf auch die Unterlänge von <ŋ> am Wortende mit <-en> aufgelöst werden, weil nicht abgekürzte Wortformen diese Endung nahelegen. Der Schreiber benutzt die Abbreviatur <ȳ> für *-yn* in unbetonten sowie betonten Endungen, wobei sich das Graphem für y durch einen schräg nach links gezogenen und verlängerten Unterstrich deutlich vom n in finaler Stellung unterscheidet. Die in der Handschrift willkürliche Alternierung zwischen den unbetonten Endungen <-yn> und <-en> wird in der Edition beibehalten.

Da *S* den einzigen Textzeugen für die Vita der Christina von Hane überliefert, wird im Apparat der entsprechenden Edition auf die Handschriftensigle verzichtet.

---

3 In CvH 99 (Bl. 345ʳ⁻ᵛ) z.B. wird zunächst aus der Perspektive Christinas berichtet, bevor ein Ich konfiguriert wird, das dem Sinnzusammenhang nach nur die göttliche Stimme darstellen kann: *Also wart vff dem dauffe gehoirt die stymme des vaders, vnd der sone bereitte daz waßer, vnd der heilge geist wart gesehen yn eym gelichenyßen eyner duben, vnd die gotliche craifft fluße durch die menscheit yn das waßer, dastu nyt moges sprechen, wie vyl gebresten du da habest, du habes ye myner genade entphangen.*

2.2 Vorbemerkungen zur Edition der Maria Magdalena-Bekehrungslegende

Es gelten die allgemeinen Editionsprinzipien der Christina von Hane-Vita. Ziel dieser Teiledition ist es, den im Verbund mit der Vita überlieferten Text der Maria Magdalena-Bekehrungslegende zugänglich zu machen. Damit der Überlieferungscharakter möglichst getreu wiedergegeben wird, wird auf die Edition einer Fortsetzung der Legende verzichtet. Die Parallelüberlieferung wird nur an lückenhaften Stellen beachtet, d.h. wenn der Schreiber von *S* ein zum Textverständnis erforderliches Wort ausließ, welches in den anderen Textzeugen zu finden ist. Der textkritische Apparat vermerkt also hauptsächlich Tilgungen und Ergänzungen gegenüber der Handschrift *S*.[4]

Die vorliegende Legende der Bekehrung Maria Magdalenas geht wahrscheinlich auf eine aus dem 14. Jahrhundert stammende und unter dem Namen Isidors von Sevilla überlieferte mittellateinische Legende aus dem niederländischen Sprachraum zurück.[5] Williams-Krapp ordnet die »mittelfränkische« Überlieferung der Maria Magdalena-Bekehrungslegende als eine von insgesamt drei deutschen Versionen ein, die auf mittelniederländische Übersetzungen des lateinischen Pseudo-Isidors zugeschriebenen Konversionsberichts zurückgehen. Die Entstehung der hier relevanten, vor allem im Kölner Raum verbreiteten »mittelfränkischen« Version falle dabei ins 15. Jahrhundert.[6] Auf Grund ihrer verschiedenen Überlieferungen, die das Mittelfränkische, Ripuarische, Niederdeutsche sowie Niederländische einschließen, bietet sich aber vielmehr die Bezeichnung als eine ›niederrheinische‹ Legendenversion an. Chronologisch lassen sich drei Stufen der Überlieferung dieser Magdalenen-Legende erkennen: die lateinischen Texte,[7]

---

4 Da sich die Textparallelen adäquater im digitalen Medium aufzeigen lassen, soll demnächst eine vollständige, auch die lateinischen Vorlagentexte näher in den Blick nehmende Edition von einem an der Harvard University basierten Forschungsprojekt geboten werden.

5 Die anonyme Erzählung der ›Conversio beatae Mariae Magdalenae‹ ist handschriftlich seit dem 14. Jahrhundert bekannt, Boxler (1996), S. 48 f. Zur Überlieferung von Pseudo-Isidor siehe ebd., S. 69.

6 Williams-Krapp (1985), Sp. 1263. Siehe auch den Nachtrag von Werner Williams-Krapp: Maria Magdalena. In: ²VL 11 (2004), Sp. 967–977, insbes. Sp. 968. Die Entstehung der niederrheinischen Legende kann nicht mit Sicherheit auf das 15. Jahrhundert datiert werden.

7 Insgesamt drei lateinische Texte der Maria Magdalena-Legende Pseudo-Isidors sind bekannt, wobei die Abhängigkeiten Hans Hansel: Die Maria-Magdalena-Legende. Eine Quellen-Untersuchung. Bottrop 1937 (Diss. Greifswald 1931), S. 119, zufolge einen deutlichen »Urtext« erkennen lassen: Brüssel, Bibliothèque royale de Belgique, ms. 7917, Bl. 145ʳ–146ʳ; Brüssel, Société des Bol-

die mittelniederländischen Texte[8] und die niederrheinischen Texte (dazu zählt die Legende in *S* samt die in der Handschriftenbeschreibung aufgeführte Parallelüberlieferung). Dabei ist ungeklärt, ob die niederrheinische nicht doch auf einer zeitlichen Ebene mit der niederländischen Überlieferung steht, da *G* (niederländisch) die niederrheinische Version überliefert und nicht früher angesiedelt werden dürfte als *B2* (niederdeutsch) und *D* (ripuarisch).[9] Die Kollation der niederrheinischen Legendenversion legt nahe, dass es sich in den verschiedenen Handschriften jeweils um gleichwertige Versionen handelt.[10]

---

landistes, ms. 347, Bl. 23–24; Kopenhagen, Kongelige Bibliotek, Cod. Gl. kgl. S. 205, Bl. 89–90. Die Editionen der lateinischen Texte sind bei Hansel (1937), S. 115–119, abgedruckt.

8 Im Kontext seiner Beschäftigung mit den mittelniederländischen Prosatexten der Bekehrungslegende konnte De Vooys (1905), S. 22–27, insgesamt vier voneinander unabhängige mittelniederländische Fassungen aus dem 15. Jahrhundert ausmachen: Den Haag, Koninklijke Bibliotheek, cod. 71 H 6, Bl. 235^r–239^r; Berlin, Staatsbibliothek Preußischer Kulturbesitz, Ms. germ. quart. 1122, Bl. 332^v–340^r; Den Haag, Koninklijke Bibliotheek, cod. 133 F 17, Bl. 162^r–168^r (hier: *G*); Groningen, Universiteitsbibliotheek, cod. 9 Mss. societas pro excolendo iure patrio, Bl. 173^v–176^r. Bereits das Verhältnis zwischen diesen mittelniederländischen Übertragungen konnte nicht hinreichend geklärt werden, vgl. De Vooys (1905), S. 25 f. Die Teileditionen der niederländischen Versionen befinden sich ebd., S. 28–44.

9 Die jeweilige Nähe der mittelniederländischen Texte zu den lateinischen Vorlagen des 14. Jahrhunderts stellt Hansel (1937), S. 121, vor. Demnach dürfe der Text von *G* als eine »besonders freie« Übertragung aus dem Lateinischen angesehen werden.

10 Ob eine erste Übertragung ins Niederdeutsche, ins Niederländische oder doch ins Ripuarische stattgefunden hat, kann daher letztlich nicht mit Sicherheit bestimmt werden. Zudem fanden innerhalb dieser niederrheinischen Überlieferung sicherlich Wechselwirkungen der verschiedenen Sprachen statt.

3 Editionen

3.1 Vita der Christina von Hane

**Dyß ist van der selicher jonffrauwen Crystina genant, die eyn cloister jon-
ffrauwe ist gewest zom Hane gelegen by Bolant yn Mentzer strome ordens
van Premonstreye.**

Na der gebort vnsers heren Jhesu Christi als man schreyffe mcclxxv dusend vnd   **Kap. 1**
5   zweye hondert vnd funff vnd sieb*entzich jaire, da woiße vff eyn schone lylie
vnder den dornen. Eyne jonffrauwe na Christum yrem bruytgam ist sye genant
Christina, die got, vnsere herre, yme selber vßerwilt hait zo eyner bruyt. Da sie
was umb yre seße jaire, van dem *[212ᵛ]* rayde godes yres bruytgams gaben sye yre
fruntde jn eyne cloister zo anderen guden jonffrauwen, die wyße cleytder drogen.
10   Vnder den luchten sy als eyn roiße vnder anderen blomen. Sie ist woil die ander
Hester, die dem gewaren Assůero vnder anderen jonffrauwen getzogen vnd gehalten wart yn dem hußße, daz ˹da˺ hieße der jonffrauwen hußße, *(vgl. Est 2,3)* das sye
yme getzirt myt gantzer doegenden vnd myt heilger hoger lyebden yme zo gelacht
[213ʳ] wůrde, dan man leßet also, daz frauwe Hester was die aller suberlichste
15   vnd die aller lyeblichste vnd gar angeneme. Dar vmbe da sie zo dem konynck yn
wart gefort, da gefielle sie yme gar woille yn synen augen, *(vgl. Est 2,9)* vnd er hait
sie lyeffe, als da steth geschreben, vor allen anderen frauwen, vnd erkreget vor
sym angesiecht genade vnd barmhertzicheit vor allen yren gespiellen, also daz er
yr alleyn die kroyne vff saitzet. *(vgl. Est 2,17)* Er entboitde auch *[213ᵛ]* freden alle
20   synem lantde vnd er gaiff synen vnderthanen groiße konenckclichen gaben, dar
er bruytlaufft myt yr macht. *(vgl. Est 2,18)* Dyß ist alles geistlich an dyeßer jonffrauwen ernuwet. Ach, wie ist sye vor den augen des ewigen konyncks also sere
woille gefellich! O, wie hait er sie also wirdenclichen gecroynnet vor vns allen! O,
wie dick hait er freden vnd genade alle dyeßem lantde durch sie gegeben, want
25   er hait yn rechter vereynionge wyrtschaift myt yrer selen gemacht ewenclichen.

Nu komen ich wieder an die materie.   **Kap. 2**
Da sie yn dem cloister was, byß *[214ʳ]* das sie x jaire alt was vnd dar na noch yn
der schullen na ordens gewanheit was vnd auch yn dem anderen jaire dar na, da
fließichet sie sich alle tzijt alleyn zo synne, dan die jonge zarte sele van yrem adel
5   wart erkant, daz yre bruytgam also bloitde was, daz er nyt myt yre koißen eyn
woiltde, dan da er yre daz cleynoit der gotlicher lyebden geben woiltde. Dar vmb

---

4 mcclxxv] MCClxv *radiert*   **5** siebentzich] s:eßentzich *radiert v. j. H.*   **12** daz ˹da˺] daz ˹die˺

https://doi.org/10.1515/9783110536324-012

verstailt sie sich, want sie eyn moicht van den anderen kyntderen, yren gespellen, nyt abegetzegen, vff daz sie yre kyntdes wyße mochte gelaißen, *[214ᵛ]* vff daz yre wyße hertze myt steter betrachtonge sich mocht bekommeren myt der kyntheit vnsers lyeben heren. Dyeße jonffrauwe betracht vnder willen, we schone vnd 10 eyn lyebliches kyntgen Jhesus were, wie lyeblichen er myt den anderen kyntderen spielt vnd wie der ryche got, der alle engel myt syner clairheit cleytdet, hait gelegen yn der cryppen eyn cleynes kyntgen, jn snoitde docher gewylckelt wart, der alle wyßheit yn yme besloißen hait, wie der eyn kynt yn der wegen vor syner moder zo Nazareth lache. Dyeße betrachtonge droge dyße jonffrau*[215ʳ]*we sonder 15 vnderlaiße yn yrem hertzen. Ach, wie dick sie daz kyntgyn jn rechter begerden an die armen jrer selen also lyeblichen vnd fruntlichen lacht! O, wie dicke sie iß myt yren trenen yn yrem hertzen andechtenclichen gebaith hait! O, wie dick sie yme myt andechtigem lobe jn yrer selen genante hait vnd swygenden gesongen hait, dan daz kyntgen ist gerne, da man yme zartet vnd zertlichen myt yme quintdelt 20 vnd lyeblichen myt yme spellen kanne.

Kap. 3 Iß geschage yn den selben tzijtden, da yrs hertzen betrachtonge *[215ᵛ]* also stetlichen was na dem lyeben kyntgyn Jhesus, da stontde sie yn dem chore by den anderen jonffrauwen vnd sie sache yn der sonnen, die zo eyner fynsteren yn scheynne yn den chore, das aller suberlichste kyntgyn, nach dem yre hertze konde getrachten. Das was Jhesus, daz aller lyeblichstes kyntgen der heilger jon- 5 ffrauwen Marien. Das kyntgen spielte myt der sonnen vor jre, als abe iß yme eyn beytgen wultde machen vß der sonnen. Also gaiffe er yr zo verstayn, daz er alleyn wille rogen yn dem hertzen, daz da luter ist als die sonne. Nach der tzijd kerte sie *[216ʳ]* alle yren flyße dar zo, wie sie yre hertze gelutert myt eyner vollenkomen lycht, alstu her na fyndest geschreben. Da nu daz kyntgen also eyn wille vor yre 10 myt der sonnen gespelte, da macht iß sich vff vnd gynge vor yr vnd drat alles vor sich, byß daz iß zo yr quam, vnd da sloiffe iß yr vnder daz jonfferliche mentelgen. Da wart jre hertze freuden voille. Aber da sie myt froelicher begerden na yme gryffen woiltde, daz sie daz aller lyeplichste kyntgen vmbfangen, gehelßet vnd gekußet hette vnd zertlichen an yre hertze ge*[216ᵛ]*drucket hette, da fant sie 15 yne nyt, dan er was verswonden van yre, als er auch in Emaũs vor den jongeren verswant, *(vgl. Lc 24,31)* als daz ewangelium spricht. O, we macht sie da woil myt lyeplichen vnd dyeffen sufftzen sprichen: ›Was nyt myn hertze burnen yn myr van Jhesu, *(Lc 24,32)* wylchen ich hayn gesehen, wylchen ich lyeffe hayn?‹ Da wart van stonden an die groiße freude zo soißem truren gewant vnd yr groiße 20 begert wart da van gemeret, also daz sie zo stont gar ynnenclichen schryen wart

---

3,1 da] da is   **3** sonnen] sonden   **7** sonnen] sonden   **10** kyntgen] kyntten *oder* kyngen *unsichere Lesung*   **11** vff vnd] vff vñ vnd   drat] drat vnd | trat

myt groißem jamer vnd verlangeren nach dem aller suberlich*[217ʳ]*sten kyntgyn Jhesus.

Jn den selben tzijtden zo eym anderen mail da begontde sie zo duncken, daz yr **Kap. 4** hertze nyt genoche luter eyn were, dem lyeplichen kyntgyn Jhesus dar jn geistlichen zo wannen, wie woil nach der wairheit yre sunden gar sere cleynen waren, want sie eyn reynne vnd luter jonffergen van seße jairen was, da sy yre altderen
5 yn daz cloister gedayn haynt by die reynne jonffrauwen, die dar yn waren. Doch weche sie jre sunden gar groiße yn yrem hertze, want der gerecht ist eyn schuldicher syns selbs. *(vgl. Ps 31,5)* Dar vmb gynge *[217ᵛ]* alle yre betrachtonge dar vff, wie sie yrem abt gentzelichen alle yre sunden bychten wultde, vff daz sie yre hertze altzo mail gelutert van allem gestüppe der sunden. Dyße betrachtonge
10 vnd dyße truricheit vmb yre sunden droge sie yn yrem hertzen stede. Eynes dags vnder eyner mysßen, da sie sich myt dyeßen gedancken yn yren stoille gelacht haitte, da begoiße sye vnser l<ieber> here myt genaden eyns vollenkomen ruwes, also daz yre hertze vnd yre augen myt eyn ander worden fließen van eym soißen ynbrunstigen schryen. Vnd da sie nu van dem schryen vff stontde, als sie vnseren
15 heren da *[218ʳ]* sache yn des prysters henden aber daz aller lyeblichstes kyngen, da wart abereyße yre synne erhaben vnd yr hertze yn vbermessicher freuden, vnd da wart yre hertze vnd sele eyntzundet van lyebden des zarten vnd suberlichen kyntzgyns, vnd sye wultde abereyße wartten dar na, are sy yres hertzen freude sehen sultde. Da was daz kyngyn van yren augen verswonden. Da wart
20 aber yre freude in eyn groiße betroppenyß gewandelt. Aber der getruwe got, der da alleyn eyn troister ist, die na yme trurent, der troiste sie so gar fruntlichen myt yme selber, den *[218ᵛ]* sie van gantzem hertzen begert. Vff eyne tzijt wart sie hoiren eyn stymme eyns geistlichen ynsprechs, als vnser here zo yrer selen sprach: ›Kynt myns, dyße gesicht sy dyr eyn waire vrkuntde, daz dyr alle dyne
25 sunden synt vergeben, die du noch ye gedayn haist.‹ Da wart yre hertze geliche der luterer sonnen, yn der daz lyebliche kyntgyn da vor betzei*ch*enclichen vor yr yn der sonnen yn dem chore gespellet haitte, als der propheta yn dem selter spricht: ›Vnser lyeber here hait syn huyße, daz ist syne wannunge, gesaitzet yn die sonne.‹ *(Ps 18,6)* Daz ist, daz er alleyn wille syn yn dem reynnen hertzen, daz
30 luter ist als die sonne. O, we hait er eyn also wonnencliche vnd stede *[219ʳ]* wannunge getzymmert vnd geplantzet yn die sonne des luteren hertzes dyeßer reyner jo*n*ffrauwen, alstu her nach dicke wyrdest fynden geschreben.

4,23 ynsprechs] yn sprechs   **26** betzeichenclichen] betzeien | clichñ   **32** jonffrauwen] joffrauwē

Kap. 5 **An dem hogetzijt natiuitatis domini**

Jn dem selben jaire da daz hogetzijt quam der gebort vnsers heren, als daz lyebe
kyntgyn Jhesus geboren wart, dyße seliche jonffrauwe haitte alle yre begerde vnd
gedancken vnd alle betrachtonge an vnderlaiß by dem lyeben kyntgyn, vnd van
der kyntheit Jhesu wart yre begerde gemeret vnd me entzůndet van dem geyn-   5
werdichen hogetzijt der gebort des gotlichen jonfferlichen kyngyns, wie sie sich
bereytden moicht entgeyn daz lyebe kyntgyn, daz iß geistlich yn *[219ᵛ]* jre hertze
vnd sele sich wultde veruerdichen geboren zo werden, vff daz sie sich des lyeben
kyngyns nach yrs hertzen begerde woille gebruchen mocht. So wachet sie die
gantze nacht an dem crystage vnd sie verleyffe alleyn vnd lyeße sich die nacht   10
yn dem chore besließen. Hie mache eyn vollenkomen hertze myrcken, wie groiße
lyebde vnd groiße begerde sy mocht hayn na dem lyeben kyntgen, daz sye die
lyebde also vberwant, da sy nach was eyn jonges jonffergyn vnd nochtan naturliche bloedicheit an jre verloire, daz sie sich nyt eyn focht, eyn fynster lange nacht
alleyn yn eym moister syn besloißen. Als Maria Magdalena fant by dem grabe   15
Jhesum yren heren, *(vgl. Io 20,11)* den sie lyebe haitte, also *[220ʳ]* fant dyeße
alleyn yn dem chore das lyebe kyntgyn Jhesum, daz sie lyebe haitte, vnd begert
yn van gantzem hertzen *zo* fynden, want als sie myr selber gesaitte hait, daz sie
xij funffzich Pater noster gebet hette, myt venien, myt beden, myt begeronge sich
also verarbet vnd vermoit hait, daz yre naturliche craifft gebrache, daz sie wieder 20
gebeden noch begeren mocht. Da lyeße sy sich nyeder an eyn rogen yres geistes.
Yn der roge sache *sie* yn eynem geistlichen gesicht daz aller lyeblichstes kyntgen
Jhesus vor yr vff dem stoille gayn spellen vnd waden yn den aller suberlichsten
roißen, die vff erden noch ye geworden. Iß waren keyn yrdeschen roißen, *[220ᵛ]*
sie waren hemelsche. Yn dyeßen roißen spielte daz hemelsche kyntgen entgene   25
der jonffrauwen zo betzeychen yre na komen leben, als abe iß spreche: ›Myr eyn
genochet nyt dan yn eym reynen hertzen, daz da sonder fflecken ist der sunden
vnd luter ist als die sone, want iß moiße auch reyne syn, sal ich dar yn wanne. Iß
moiße auch getzeirt syn myt hemelschen roißen, daz ist myt allen doegenden.‹
Zo hantze dar na flyßichet sie sich myt allem flyße vnd myt starcker vbonge nach   30
allen doegenden, alstu herna fyndest geschreben.

Kap. 6 **Nv** komen ich wieder vmb vff die materie. Van dyeßem gesicht *[221ʳ]* des lyeblichen kyntgynß wart yre hertze vnd yre sele vol freuden, soißicheit vnd troistes.
Da man die metten lůytte, da sancke sie myt den anderen jonfferen yn groißem
jubilo vnd myt groißen freuden yres hertzen, *so* da wart angehaben van der
gebort des kyntges. Da sache sie aber daz zarte aller suberlichstes kyntgen stayn   5

5,13 *nach* nochtan] nalru *gestrichen* **18** zo] so **21** *nach* noch] ge *gestrichen* **22** sache sie]
sache **6,4** so] zo

vor dem elter yn eyner wegen vnd iß was gedecket myt eym dechelach van roißen
vnd vff eynem yecklichen blaytde der roißen stontde geschreben ›Pater noster‹
vnd iß hait eyn crantze vff sym heubt van xij gar schonen roißen vnd got gaiffe
yre so verstayn, daz iß waren die czwolff funfftzich *[221ᵛ]* Pater noster, die sie

10 dem kynde Jhesu gesprochen haitte. Da sie daz lyebe kyntgyn gesache, da begert
sie, daz iß zo yr quemme. Zo hant gynge vnd gynge *iß* byß also lange, daz iß by
sie quam, vnd iß stonde yn dem stoille vor sie vnd iß woiße also groiße vor yre,
daz iß wart eyn schoner jongelyn also groiße, daz syn heubt reicht an yren mont.
Das was eyn zeychen, daz got vnßer here dar na waschen wolte yn yrem hertzen,

15 das er sie van syner kyntheit zo hoger lyebden zehen woillte, als du woil machest
myrcken, abe du dyße buchelgyn myt flyße dyns hertzen wylt vber leßen, wie sie
[222ʳ] got van eymme zo dem anderen myt syner gotlicher wyßheit vff gezogen
haitte. Da daz lyebe kyntgen vor yre vnd by yre wosche, als da vor gesprochen ist,
was sie da sancke ader laiße, daz sancke vnd laiße daz kyntgyn myt yr. O frolicher

20 jubile! Ach, wie froelich yre hertze vnd sele da syngen moicht! Da sie daz seste
responsorium syngen sult, da sach sie daz zarte kyntgyn vff dem boiche sitzen
vnd myt yre syngen, daz iß yre vnd sy yme jn synem mont sancke. Ich meynen,
daz keynne zonge moge vß gelegen die soißicheit, den troiste vnd woillust, die
die edel sele da *[222ᵛ]* haitte. Dan van rechter zarter verwenter woilluste wart yre

25 hertze vnd augen vber flyßen yn eym soißen lyeblich schryen. Vnd daz schryen,
daz werte die gantze metten durch.

Unser here vor quam dyße <se>lige jonffrauwe gar bytzijde myt dem sene vnd   **Kap. 7**
gebenedionge syner genaden. Dan van anbegynne daz sie yn daz cloister wart
gegeben, wie woil daz sie noch eyn kynt was van vj jairen, so gaiffe yre got doch
die genade vor den anderen, das sie yn yrer kyntheit gar andechtenclichen

5 eret myt neygen vnd myt venien vnd myt beden vnsers heren martel, wo die
gema*[223ʳ]*let ader gezeychent staynt.
Svnderlichen so stont eyne crucifix vff dem dormiter ader slaiffhuyße. Want sie
vor daz gynge, als sie myr selber gesait hait, so was yr nummer also woil, sie fielle
nyeder vff jre knee vor daz crucifix vnd dancket vnserem heren des jemerlichen

10 doitz, den er durch daz menschen willen leyt am crutze. Vnd auch dick, wanne
sie dar vor hyn gynge, so gedacht sie myt groißer andacht: ›Ach, hie stet myn
lyebhaber vnd bettet myn vnd er hait syne armen vff gethayn entgeyn myr zo
spreyt, daz er mych myt synen armen vmbfange vnd mych *[223ᵛ]* zo yme zehe.‹
Myt dyeßen gedancken spreyt sy yre armen van yre ⌐...⌐ vnd sprache myt groißer

15 begerden vnd andacht yrs hertzen: ›Gegrußet systu, heilges crutze, du byst eyn
eyniger zoversicht vnsers heils.‹ Also fiel sie dan nyeder myt den vßgestrechten

---

11 gynge iß] gynge   **7,1** <se>lige] | lige   **16** zoversicht] zo versicht

armen vff die erde vnd lache vor dem crutze eyn tzijt lanck yn yrer gestreckster venien, wie woil sye dicke van yrer meysterschen swerlichen gestraifft wart, vnderwillen hertlichen geslagen wart, daz sie zo lange was geweste by den crutze yn yrem gebede. Aber daz straiffen vnd die slege vnd alles daz yre zo quam zo 20 lyden, *[224ʳ]* daz was yre all soiße durch den, der also groiße pyne leyt durch sie an dem crutze, dar vmb daz sie nyt abe laißen eyn woilt, sunder sie woilte vollenhyrtten an der genaden godes, die yr got gegeben haitte. So geschache iß vff eyn mail, daz sie aber yn yrer andacht vor dem crutze stonde, da sache sie gar eyn schone wyße dube flegen vß dem mont des crucifyx. Die dube floge durch alle 25 den dormiter ader slaiffhuße vnd floge da zo yre vmb yre heubt, daz sie myt yren floegellen yre heubt vnd yren mont rort. Da sie die dube fangen woiltde, da hoirt sie eyn stymmen van der du*[224ᵛ]*ben, vnd sie sprache also: ›Mensche, ganck hyn ane focht vnd syt froelich. Der heilge geist ist yn dyr vnd vber dyr vnd myt dyr.‹ Vnd myt der stymmen verswant die dube. Dyß ist die dube: der heilge geist, der 30 jn der gestailt eyner duben, als man yme ewangelio leßet, daz eyn dube floge vff vnseren heren, als er getaufft wart van sent Johannes. *(vgl. Mt 3,16)* Dyße dube floge nu vff dyße jonffrauwe, synne brůyt, als daz er yre hertze vnd sele macht yme zo eyner wannunge vnd tempel des h<eiligen> geistes, starcke vnd stede yn groißem lyden, alstu her na hoiren wyrdest. Die dube floge vber yre, als abe sie 35 der heilge geist da myt *[225ʳ]* betzeichent, daz sie vber sich na yme flegen sultde. Wie hoch vnd wie ferre sie dar nach vber sich myt hoger beschauongen geflogen was, daz eyn kan keyn hertze vß gesprechen, iß eyn were dan myt yrer selen yn got geflogen. Doch wil <ich> eyn teylle her na schryben, als abe ich eynen troppen neme vß dem mere. Die dube, die yre da gesant, wart auch alles zo mail alles vmb 40 vnd vmb daz slaiffhuße der jonffrauwen. Da myt verstene ich daz zo bezeychen, daz van der sendonge des heilgen geistes die gantze versamenunge geheilget sultde werden durch yren verdynst.

Kap. 8 *[225ᵛ]* Jch wille aůch nyt swigen der groißer genaden, die yr got dede yn der tzijt yrer anhebonge. Das was daz lyecht des erkentenyß, das yre got gaiffe, also daz *sie* got yn allen creaturen konde fynden. Aber zo eyner lerunge den anderen, daß eyn eynfeldiche mensche baße verstene konne, so wille ich eyn deylle vß legen, als ich van yre selber gehoirt hayn. Wanne sye sich abe gescheytden kontde van 5 yren gespillen, die myt jre yn der scholen waren, so was sie gar gerne alleyn, daz sie yre sele myt heilgen gedancken gespyßen moicht. Dan wanne sie alleyn was, dan fant sie got yn den *[226ʳ]* creatǔren. Vnd wanne sie alleyn stonde by

---

18 sye] sye:: *nach* wart] V... **21** all] all:: **22** darvmb] Dar...vmb **25** *nach* schone] dube *gestrichen* **35** *nach* hoiren] wilt *gestrichen* **37** beschauongen] beschauongen sie **39** <ich>] iß **8,2** daz sie] dz

dem born vnd sache daz dryncke vaße vberfließen van dem waißer, so gedacht
10 sie, wie die vbersuße gotheit flußet yn syne engel vnd heilgen yn hemelryche
vnd her abe vff dyße ertrich. Da bait sie vnseren lyeben heren myt groißer begerden, daz er yn yre sele myt syner genaden wultde flyeßen. Was sie aber yn dem
gartten vnd sache daz ertrich getzeret myt blomen vnd myt graiße, so entphynge
sie groiße freude, als auch der heilge konynck Dauid gynge nye yn synen gartten,
15 er entphyn[226ᵛ]ge alle maille den heilgen geist. Also gedacht dyße heilge jonffrauwe, wie schone vnd wie wunnenclichen vnd lustlichen got yn yme selber
ist, der daz ertriche also zerlichen hait gecleyt mannychfalt. Dan so bait sie myt
groißer begerten vnseren lyeben heren, daz er yre hertze wultden bluwen machen
myt geistlichen bloemen der dogende. So dyße heilge jonffrauwe vnder wyllen
20 was myt den anderen jonffrauwen vff dem kyrchoff, so fylle yre dyßen gedancken yn ire hertze, daz sie der doden gebet nyt eyn mocht gesprechen myt den
anderen. Auch wanne sie die [227ʳ] baủme sache vff gerecht entgene dem hemel,
so fant sie aber got vnd bait yn, daz er yre hertze zo ym kerte vnd rychten wultde
myt steder lyebden vnd hoger erkentenyß. Auch vnderwillen wanne sie alleyn
25 saiße by der bache vnd sache daz waißer hynne flyeßen, so gedacht sie: ›Also
ist alle dynge hynne gefloißen, die du vnnützelich haist zo bracht, vnd koment
nummerme erwyeder.‹ Da so hobe sie an zo schreye myt groißem jamer vnd
claget gode myt heyßen threnen, daz sie yn nyt [227ᵛ] alle yre dage myt allem
flyße gesucht haitte. Nu kurtzelichen so fant sie got also yn allen dyngen, das alle
30 yre synnen, sehen vnd horen, got vß allen creaturen schepten vnd yn yre hertzen
goißen vnd yn jre sele braichten. O flyßicher leißer, nu haistu gehoret, wie die
seliche jonffrauwe Christina yre kyntliche jaire hait gestanden yn der schoillen.
Nyt alleyn hait sie geleret die bustabe, sonder auch nach dem geistlichen leben.
Iß ist yetzont genoch gesait van der kyntheit, was da ist geschet yn yrer jogent.

[228ʳ] Jn dem anderen jaire dar na da sie vß der scholen wart genommen, da **Kap. 9**
worden die jonffrauwen durch yre armoit, vnd dyeße jonffrauwe myt jnne allen,
gesant vß yrem cloister, ygliche zo yren altderen vnd frunten. Nu salt ir hoiren, wie
gar flyßelichen sie dar range, daz yre hertze worde getzeret myt allen dogenden.
5 Da sie erkant, daz got alleyn woiltde wannen vnder den bloeme des dogenhaiff-
tichen hertzen, da kerte sie alle yren flyße dar zo, das yre hertze bloeende werde
myt vollenkomen dogenden. Aber der aller heißichster fyant, dem alle dogent
wieder synt, der kerte allen synen flyße dar zo, daz er daz gehynderen moicht vnd
daz er sie [228ᵛ] myt vndogenden vberwonde. Also schrybet sanctus Gregorius:
10 ›So der mensche me na dem hemel wyrbet, so yme der vyant ye behentlicher zo
gehet vnd ye me stercklichen myt yme strydet.‹ Van dyeßem stryde, wie lange

27 schreye] schreye sie   34 der] den   9,6 da] Da he

vnd wie manchfeldenclichen sie der vyant myt allen vndogenden an fechte, sun-
derlichen myt den sieben doitsunden, sult yr hoiren. Auch so wil ich eyn deyl hie
schryben, wie wyßlich myt starcker vbonge sie wieder stontde vnd alle vndogent
vberwant vnd sie alle vnder sich tratte, daz dyße eyn spegel vnd eyn forme sy aller 15
der, die yn dyeßem leben stryden wullent wieder die anfechtonge der vndogent.
Jch eyn hayn noch nyt *[229 r]* geleßen van keynem der menschen, der also swerlichen vnd auch also manchfeldenclichen hebe gestretden wieder die anfechtonge
vnd auch also enxtlichen vnd gentzelichen vberwonden. Myr leßen woil van etzelichen heilgen, die gar stercklichen myt etzelichen vndogenden stretden vnd sie 20
auch gar vollenkommenclichen vberwonden. Also strydent noch vil guder lude
vff ertrich, yglicher myt etlicher anfechtonge, die myt godes hulffe vberwyntdent.
Aber dyeße heilge jonffrauwe Christina hait nyt gestretden myt etzelichen als
myt tzweyn ader dryn. Sie eyn hait auch nyt gestreden eyn jaire ader zweyn, dan
sie streydte vij *[229 v]* gantzer jaire wieder die sieben heubt sunden, myt yglicher 25
eyne gantze jaire, byß daz sie die alsammet vberwant vollenkomenclichen, als
ich eyn teylle her na schryben wylle.

Kap. 10 **D**a dyße heilge jonffrauwe was gesant zo yren fruntden, alstu vor gehoirt haist,
vnd voille eyn hailffe jare yn der werelt waz gewest vnd wieder vmb heymme
quam yn yre cloister, da warff yr der vyant vor myt boißen gedancken die werelt
vnd werntlichen sachen, die sie yn der werelt hatte gesehen vnd gehoirt. Vnd myt
den gedancken goiße er yre ynne also starcken anfechtonge vnd bekarunge des 5
fleiße, daz sy dick selber duchte, hette sy got nyt ey*[230 r]*gentlichen myt der hant
syner barmhertzicheit vnd genaden vffenthaillen, iß were vnmogelichen gewest,
das sie moicht die selbe erlieden hayn. Dyße swere lange anfechtonge verhenget
vnser lyeber here vber sie nyt an sachen, want er woilt sie versuchen vnd beweren
als den heilgen Tobiam, zo dem der engel sprache: ›So du gode woil befellest, so 10
was noit, daz dich anfechtonge vnd vngemache beweret.‹ *(vgl. Tb 2,12)* Auch ist
geschreben yn dem boiche der wyßheit: ›Der here hait geproberet syne vßerwilten als daz golt yn dem oben des fürs.‹ *(Sap 3,6)* Auch verhencket vnser here zo
dem anderen mail dyeße groiße anfechtonge vber sie, dar vmb daz yre strytde eyn
lere were allen den, *[230 v]* die bekarunge vnd anfechtonge lydent. Dyeße heilge 15
jonffrauwe haitte van yrer jogent an die genade godes zertlichen spelende yn
soißer befyndonge manchfeldenclichen me, dan hie geschreben ist. Wie meynnestu, daz yr jonfferliches hertze yn gedancken dick floiße yn groißer vocht des
gotlichen tzorns? O, was lyeblicher trene floißen van yren augen, dan dyße bekarunge wert eyn gantzes jaire, daz sie alles daz jaire also verre menscheliche craifft 20
gereichen moicht, alle tzijt ryngen vnd wieder stryden moiste wieder die vnkuß-
heit, daß sie yre hertzen vnd lybes reynicheit behalten moicht. Dar vmb dryeffe
sie van yre alle sunden vnd orsachen der sunden, daz ist alle stetde vnd lude vnd

alle sachen, *[231ʳ]* die yr moichten syn eyn orsache zo der bekarungen. Sye hyelte
25 sich yn groißer hirtickeit, daz sie da myt des fleiße woilluste an yre moicht verlie-
ßen, want sie dan dem vyant, der sie myt flyße anfecht, durch den dage also
stercklichen wieder stontde. So sye des nachtes slaiffen sultde gayn, so bracht er
yr yme slaiffe vor boiße dreume, boiße wullust vnd bekarunge. Aber daz sie yme
auch dar vmb festelichen wiederstonde vnd vberwant, want sie yn der nacht
30 erwachte, so stontde ⌜sie⌝ also swygenden vff van dem bette vnd gynge an eyn
heymeliche stait vnd zoge sich vß vnd name drye starcker dysciplynen myt eym
beyßem. Eyne dysciplyne name sie vor alle sunder. Die ander vor alle selen, *[231ᵛ]*
die yn dem fegefure synt. Die drytte vor alle gude lude, daz die got bestedigen
wultde an rechter kußheit. Dyße detde sie alle nacht eyn gantze jare, daz sie iß
35 wieder vmb froste ader vmb ander franckeit nyt eyn ließe. Aber dyß ist noch eyn
cleyn dyncke weder dem, daz noch hie vor ist. Ist eyn deyle schemelichen zo
schryben, so iß doch ist eyn zeychen groißer lyebden, die sie haitte, wie sie yren
vyant moichte vberwynnen vnd wie sye den schaitze yrrer kußheit behylde vnbe-
fleckte. Dar vmb eyn mache ichs nyt vnderwegen gelaißen, ich eyn schrybe dan
40 eyn deylle dar van. Da sie nu sache, daz sie daz fure yrs fleiße, das yre der heißi-
che *[232ʳ]* vyant dage vnd nacht yn yre entfengen woiltde, daz sie daz selbe nyt
eyn mocht geleißen myt starken slegen vnd groißer harttickeit yrs lybes vnd
lebens, da gedacht sie, so der lyp daz fuer me vocht vnd erschrycket dan alle
ander creaturen, daz sie wulte myt dem lyplichen fure leißen daz geistlichen fure
45 yrs fleiße. Vnd dar na eyn gaiffe sie nyt alleyn den lyffe yn daz fuer, als wyr van
etzelichen leßen, daz sie bloiße satzen vff gluenden kolen, vnd damyt dede sie vß
daz fure der bekarunge. Sie dede, was noch groißer was. Das eyn mensche synen
lyffe gyfft yn daz fure, daz ist eyn erschreckliche dynge der naturen. Aber daz was
noch erschrecklicher, das sie daz fuer dede yn yren lyffe. Das dede sie van ynwen-
50 dicher groißer *[232ᵛ]* begerden, daz sie die boißen geist vnd yre anfechtunge des
fleiße moicht vberwynnen. Zo eym anderen mail namme sie eyn burnende hoiltze
vnd stieße daz selbe also gluedich yn yren lyffe, also daz daz lypliche fure das
fure yrer bekarunge myt groißen smertzen verleyst. Jch loben viel me die sach vnd
die meynunge, yn der sie iß dede, dan ich die daytde loben. Dan iß was eyn
55 vnuernoifftige kaistigonge. ›Aber die got van herzen lyebt haynt, den wyrt alle
dynge van gode zo dem aller besten gekeret‹, *(Rm 8,28)* als sanctus Paulus spricht,
want die lyebde bedecket die vilheit der sunden. Aber wan der pynen des smert-
zes wart verleißen die bekarunge vnder willen *[233ʳ]* lange byß vff eyn ander
mail, da wultde sie vnser lyeber here baßer versuchen vnd er verhenget aber vber
60 sie dieselbe bekarunge des fleiß gar sere swerlichen. Da gedacht dyße jonffrauwe, wie der smertzen der pynen ernuwette mocht werden, also daz das fleiße

30 ⌜sie⌝] *am Rande* **43** alle] alle cre | ature͞

vergeiße der wulluste, die yme der duffel anwarffe myt der bekarunge. Dar vmb
dede sie aber gar eyn grußelich swere dynge. Das was, si nam kalcke vnd essich,
vnd macht dar vße eynen deiche vnd dede den aber yn yren lyffe, so sie aller
ferste kontde. Wer kayn gesaigen, was groißen smetzen sie leyt? Da myt verswal- 65
len der lyffe van den fußen an byß an den gurtel, das keynne waiße van yre
moicht komen. Daz wertte woil echt *[233ᵛ]* dage. Dar na gynge drye dage vnd dry
nachten bloit van yr yn der stait, da daz waißer her komen sult. Also vberwant sie
aber, also daz van dem smertzen die bekarunge verleischen wart an jre vff eyn
tzijt lange dar na. Eyns mails da quam eyn man. Den hoirt sy reden myt eyner 70
frauwen van fleißelichen vnd werenclichen sachen. So sie myt loiste zo hoirt vnd
vergaiß yrer huytde, vnd sie gaiffe orsache zo der bekarunge, da quam der bekarer
vnd fechte sie an aber myt der bekarunge des fleyße. Da macht sie aber myt kalcke
vnd harne, als sie vor haitte gedayn. Als sie nu noch gar sere crancke was van
dem irsten czweyn pynen beytde van dem fuer vnd van dem kalcke, da quam sie 75
van dyeßem drytten yn *[234ʳ]* also groiße cranckeit, daz yre alle yre lyffe also sere
swalle, als abe sie wasser suchtich were gewest, daz alle die, die sie sachen, die
verzwyfelten an yrem leben. Da na quam sie yn eyn groiße truricheit vnd focht,
das sie wieder godes wille also verre gegryffen haitte wieder die bescheytdenheit.
Vnd sie sprache myt schryenden augen vnd myt eym andechtigen hertzen also zo 80
vnserem lyeben heren: ›O getruwer here vnd vader myn, bystu alleyn der, den ich
myt alle mynen sachen meynnen vnd an dem ich allen mynen troist vnd zoversicht hayn gelacht? Nu so beden ich dich durch die lyebde, die dich vor mych bant
an daz crŭtz: Ist iß dyn wille, so erloiße mych van dießen bantden des *[234ᵛ]* lyffs
vnd der selen.‹ In der ander nacht dar na da sie lache yn groißen smertzen, also 85
das yre yetzont van groißem vngemacht vnd betruppenyß an naturlichen kreyfften gebresten wultde, da sprach sie: ›Got eyn laiste die nummerme, die yn ynne
hoiffent.‹ Van den der prophete spricht: ›Die begertde der armen hait der here
gehoirt, *(vgl. Ps 9,10)* syne augen sehent zo den armen. Der mylde troister aller
bedruppter hertzen, die zo yme haitte gesufftzet, er hait an gesehen synne arme 90
dyrne, *(vgl. Lc 1,48)* sy zo troisten jn yrem noitde.‹ Vff eyn tzijt erscheyn jre vnser
here Jhesus Christus. Den sache sie myt yren lyplichen augen vnd geistlichen
augen als eynen groißen vnd mechtigen heren myt funffe wunden. Die wairen
also wyte *[235ʳ]* als eyns mans spanne. Vnd vnser here sprache zo yre: ›Sieche
heryn jn myne wonden. Synt sy nyt wyte genunge, dastu dynen vngemache yn 95
myr verbergest? Hie vyndestu artzedie wieder alle anfechtonge.‹ Myt dyeßem
gesicht quamme yr eyn starcke schrecken, daz sie wart entzucket van yrem
verstentenyß. Jn dem zoge dede yre got die genade, daz sie na der tzijt, als sie myr
selber sagete, nummerme van keyner fleißelicher bekarunge berurt wart. Vnd da

---

82 zoversicht] zo versicht **86** kreyfften] keyfftē **92** here] hrʼ **95** heryn] her yn

100 sie got den heren myt alle yrem hertzen loifft, da sprach vnser lyeber here zo yrer
selen, wie woil sie nyt gelert eyn was, so verstonde sy doch daz latyne woil yn der
selen: ›Wanne du *[235 ᵛ]* beden wylt, so gancke yn dyne kamer vnd bede an dynen
vader yn dem verborgen, als die dore besloißen ist, vnd dyne vader erhoirt vnd er
sal dyr wieder loyne geben.‹ Da wart sie geleret yn yrem verstentenyß, yn allen
105 sachen zo flegen zo dem gebede, alleyn myt gode zo reden vnd zo myden alle
vnnutze reden.

Contra accidiam

In dem anderen jare darna daz was yn dem drytten jaire, da fecht sie an groiße
traicheit jrß lybes vnd swermodicheit vnd bedruppenyße yn allen guden dyngen.
Der wyederstayn sie dede myt der eygenschaifft dar zo gehoirret, das was hairtte
5 kastigonge des lychams vnd des fleische. Vnd sie vbet sich myt der hende
ar*[236 ʳ]*bet nach der tzijt. Da dyße heilge jonffrauwe sache, daz yre glieder vnd
yre lyffe also trache vnd wiederspennich was zo dem dynste godes, da gynge sie
alle morgens vnd saiße yn dem snee vnd berache yre beynne vnd yren lyffe byß
vber die hoiffen yn den snee. Vnd sie saiße da also lange, byß das jre lyffe durch-
10 kalt wart gelich dem snee. Dan name sie eyn starcke gerte vnd sloige yre lyffe vnd
die durchkalten beyn, byß daz yr das fleiße gantze fryße wart van den slegen. Dar
zo, was dem lybe wee dede, dar an vbet sie sich *[236 ᵛ]* stetlichen. Wie kalt die
nacht was, so die anderen jonffrauwen na der metten zo dem fuer saißen, so eyn
woiltde sie yrem lybe nyt also vil gemachs an doyn, als daz sie sich wermete. Das
15 dede sie alles. Das dem lybe zo gemache sultde geschen, auch van naturlicher
noitdurfit, das zoge sie yme abe. Myt soilicher hartticheit verdreyffe sie alle tra-
cheit van yr, also daz yre lyffe altzo mail gehoirsam wart dem geist.

Contra jram

Aber na dem jaire streytte sie eyn gantze jaire wieder den zorne vnd vngedult. So
alwege vngedult *[237 ʳ]* komet van zweyn dyngen, so namme sie fließelichen war
yrer bewegonge. Sie dede als eyn wyße kemperynnen yn dem geistelichen strytde,
5 want dem menschen, der da wilt geistlich werden, dem wertdent vor gehaltden,
daz er gerne hartte wortte, swere arbeit, gebrechen der noitdurfft moiße lyden.
Das ist das irste, da van vngedult komme: vnbewegonge des gemoitze. Zo dem
anderen mail komet vngedult dar van, das dem lybe wyrt benomen, was er gern
hette als sam*f*te wort, frun*tt*sacht van den luden, ere, troist, frede, eygen willen,
10 gemache vnd was dem *[237 ᵛ]* lyebe woil dede. Dar vmb daz sie auch die vngedult
vberwunde, als was der lyffe beger, das name sie yme. Aber was yme wieder was,
daz lacht sy yme vff. Vnd das der lyffe daz geduldenclichen entphynge, so lacht

12,4 *nach* dem] peistl *gestrichen*   **9** samfte] samste   frunttsacht] früffsacht

sie yme dick me vff, dan er gedrayn macht. Vnder willen lacht sie yre beth vol
neßelen, das alle jre lyffe eyn blaitter wart. So sie des morgens sultde gayn zo
der metten, so eyn kontde sie die schoe nyt an gedoyn vor den blaitteren. Vnd 15
sie moiste die metten barfuße stayn vff dem kalden esterich, das sie auch vnder
willen vff den steynen also erkalt, daz sie van *[238ᵗ]* rechter cranckeit hatte: da
van daz sie die nacht vngeslaiffen was verlyeben vnd auch dar zo, daz sie van
den steynen also erkalt was vnd daz sie myt starcker ander arbeit den lyffe haitte
gekastiget vnd vber laytden, daz sie van rechter cranckeit yn dem chore vil yn 20
amacht. Auch dede sie das myt vollenkomener macht was: Wieder allen tzorne
czwange sie yre gemoide, wie zornlichen man yre zo rechte, daz sie yme keyn
tzornich wort nummer gereth ader geantwert. Vnder willen beyß sie yn die zonge,
daz das bloit dar vß gynge. Daz dede sie, wanne sy yn tzorne keyn wort *[238ᵛ]* yn
vngedult eyn wult antwerden. Dar vmb geschage vff eyn mail, das sie van eyner 25
frauwen yn dem cloister swerlichen myt vngedult wart angefecht, wie woille daz
sie yr doch nye keyn wort myt nye keynme vngeduldichen wort antwertden eyn
woille, vnd sie drucket iß alles yn sich, also daz iß yr also na vnd swerlichen
yn gynge yn das hertze, byß daz yr das bloitte zo monde vnd naßen vß gynge.
Doche so bezwancke sie sich, daz sie der selber nye myt eynem vngeduldichen 30
wort woilt antwertden ader zoreden. Gedencke hie yn, wie stercklichen das sie
der vndůgent des tzornes wie*[239ᵗ]*derstonde.

Kap. 13 Contra superbiam

Die funffte doitsůnde, das ist hofart. Myt der selber streyt sie auch eyn gantze
jaire myt yn beytden geistlichen vnd werenclichen. Sie haitte aber also vberwonden alle hofart, also das sie nyt eyn mocht vollenbrengen myt den wercken, das
vollenbracht sie myt der begerden. Jren lyffe vnd yre heubt zirte sie als vil sy ver- 5
moicht nach der gewanheit. Der hoiffart wiederstont sie myt rechter demodicheit.
Vff eyn tzijt da ziert sie yre heubt durch hoiffart gar herlich. Aber vnder der ves-
peren sach sie hyn an das crucifix vnd *[239ᵛ]* sie gedacht, wie das lyebliche heubt
Jhesu Christi myt dornen gecroynet vnd durch stochen was. Vnd das selbe gynge
yre also sere yn yre hertze, das sie alle getzierde yrs heubts van yre warffe, vnd 10
sie namme eyne schoißel duche als eyn koiche mayt vnd bant daz selbe vmb yre
heubt vnd sie gynge da myt yn den chore vnder die lude. Also wart yn jre alle
hofart yn recht oitmodicheit gekert. Vnd sy wart sich also sere vben yn rechter oitmodicheit, also das sie dick den meytden vnd auch den jonfferen die schoißel vß
yren henden namme vnd jn vor woißche. Vff daz sie sich moicht vollenkomenc- 15
lichen oitmodi*[240ᵗ]*gen, so vnderwarffe sie sich, den siechen zo dyenen vnd

23 beyß] byˑeˑß 27 antwertden] antwert den **30** so] zo **13,6** hoiffart] hoirfart
7 hoiffart] hoirfart

sonderlichen jn den wercken, die aller oitmodichste vnd versmelichste vnd aller vnfledichste waren. Vnd daz dede sie dan also willich, froelich vnd begerlichen yn der meynnonge, als abe sy iß gode selber gedayn hette. Also vberwant sie die
20 hoiffart myt rechter oitmodicheit.

Contra gulam
Kap. 14

Myt der seister vndogent streyt sie auch eyn gantze jaire. Die heißet gula, daz ist vngenosamheit ader des fleiße begerde an eßen vnd dryncken vber die natůre noitdurfft. Dyeßer vndogent wiederstont sie myt aller starckster abstinencie,
5 *[240ᵛ]* also daz ⌐sie⌐ nyt alleyn yre abe brache myt esßyn vnd dryncken vber die noitdurfft, sie eyn gaiffe auch die recht noitdurfft dem lybe nyt hailffe. So sie ⌐l⌐vst haitte, daz sie gerne geßen hette vnd auch woil gedorfft hette, so saitze sie iß van yr vnd gaiffe iß eyner anderen. Kortzelichen, wanne sie allergernst hette geßen vnd auch woil gedorfft hette, so hoirt sie vff vnd saiße dan vngeßen. Was sal ich
10 vil sagen? Sie versmaet sich selber also gar, daz sie vnder willen van rechter cranckeit yn amacht fiel vber der taiffelen. Also vberwant sie an yr die maiße aller vngenosamheit des lybs.

Contra odium
Kap. 15

Auch eyns jaires fechte sie an *[241ʳ]* die siebende doit sunde. Daz ist haiß, der fecht dick an myt vngonst vnd rache entgeyn die sie betruppten. Dyeße vndogent des haißes, dar vß sprynget der nyt. Dem wiederstontde sie gar kreifftlichen vnd
5 gar wyßelichen, dan der heilge geist yn yre wyrcket durch nakomen wonder wunderliche dynge. Dar vmb na dem raytde vnsers heren Jhesu Christi, *(vgl. Mt 5,44)* als ym ewangelio wyrt geleißen, daz sie auch dyeßer vndogent gentzelichen wiederstonde, so tzwancke sie sich dar zo, wer sie aller meyste beswert vnd bedroifft vnd aller mynste genade zo yre haitten, daz sie den selben aller meyste denet vnd
10 yrs willen aller meyste *[241ᵛ]* wartte vnd den selben aller gůtlichste vnd das aller beste dede, daz sie vermoicht. Also vberwante sie dieße vndogent gar kreifftenclichen myt der dogent, die dar zo gehoret. Das ist die lyebde zo gode vmb sich selber vnd zo dem nesten vmb got. Wie groiße beyder lyebde ist gewest, wyrdestu herna vynden vnd vil hoiren werden. Nyt eyn verwonder dich, daz eyn also zarte
15 jonffrauwe also swerlichen versucht wart durch bekarunge vnd die also rytterlichen vberwonden hait als dyeße jonffrauwe, dan sie ist geproifft als daz golt yn dem fůer. Jre kyntliche tzijt hait sie gedroncken *[242ʳ]* die mylche der troistlicher vnd lustlicher beschauwonge yn der kyntheit vnsers heren Jhesu Christi. Aber yn der bloender jogent ist sie gespyste worden myt eym grauffen broyt, daz sie wurde

---

14,3 ader] aber   **15,1** Contra odium] *am Abschnittsende auf Bl. 242ᵛ vom Schreiber nachgetragen*

gestercket vnd bereyt zo groißeren dyngen vnd vollenkommener wege. O seliche 20
jonffrauwe Christina, gedencke der arbeit, myt der du haist gegangen durch den
bytteren wege dyße ellendes, vnd gedencke der genadenricher hulffe godes, der
dich hait vß gefurt vff die wege der gerechticheit, da du dich nunuste des boißes
eyn vochtes, sonder du rogest nů yn dem schey*[242ᵛ]*den dyns brůytgams. Dar
vmbe, o vnser seliche moder, bede vor vns alle, dan dyne stymme ist soiße yn den 25
oren des heren, vff daz myr selenclichen mogen komen vß den sorgen dyeßer tzijt
zo dem hemelschen paradijß.

Kap. 16 **D**a nu dieße aller heillichste jonffrauwe alle vndogentde vberwonden haitte vnd
got der here yme selber sy also bereyt hait, da zoge er sy van der vbonge zo den
hogeren dyngen, want woille drue jaire vbet sye sich stetlichen myt betrachtonge
na der pynen vnsers heren vnd synem doitde. Sie bedacht myt rechtem bekenn-
tenyß na der grondeloißer lyeb*[243ʳ]*den, die den lyeblichen godes sone dar zo 5
zwancke, der eyn konynck ist vber alle konynck vnd aller engel vnd eyn here aller
heren *(vgl. I Th 6,15; Apc 17,14)* des hemels vnd des ertrichs. Honger vnd dorst vnd
gebrechen wullůstu myt vns vnd durch vns lyden me dan xxxiij jaire. Sie lacht
sich vor die augen yrer selen myt anschauwen sonder vnderlaiße syne armoit, syn
smacheit, syne arbeit vnd syne betrubenyße vnd syne bytter martzel vnd synen 10
doit, den er also jemerlichen an dem crutze leytde. Dyeße betrachtonge was also
dieffe yn yrem hertzen, daz sie dick ny*[243ᵛ]*der sich viel yn amacht beytde van
bytterheit des mytlydens vnd van der soißicheit, die sie entphynge van rechter
erkentenyße der getruwer lyebden, die yn vor vns zwancke zo dem jemerlichen
doitde. Die groiße lyebe bracht yre jre hertze, aber yn der betrachtonge wart 15
yrem hertzen gegeben also groiße soißicheit, das sie vnder willen, wanne sy den
namen des zarten heren Jhesu hoirt nennen, der den doit also sere getruelichen
gelieden hait vor vns, so wart yre mont van dem namen vol soißicheit.

Kap. 17 In dem drytten ⌈jare⌉ yrer betrachtong yn dißer wyße nyt lange dar vor e sie sich
zo beth *[244ʳ]* lacht, da hieß sie sich furen yn sent Nycolais cappel, daz sie da yn
mysse hoirt, vnd iß was yn der vasten. Da sie nu yn der cappel verleiffe sytzen
alleyn vnd sie begonde na yrer gewanheit zo gedencken na den lyden vnsers
heren vnd sie hobe an van dem anbegyn syns vngemachs vnd lacht das alles yn 5
yre hertze myt bytterheit vnd da sie quam jn betrachtonge vff den berge Oliueti
vnd sie gedacht, wie der lyeblicher sone godes, der da ist eyn borne aller freuden,
der da van rechter betruppenyß vnd van fochten bludigen sweiße swytzet vor
synem dode, *(vgl. Lc 22,44)* da wart yr hertze also woil smertzen, daz sie nyt vor
sich moicht myt der betrachtonge. Dan sie ducht, als sie myr selber *[244ᵛ]* gesaget 10

16,12 *nach* dick] hi *gestrichen* nyder] hy ‖ der **17** heren] hrerē hait, hette sie iß vor sich betracht, daz yre hertze yn yrem lybe moiste zoberste syn van groißen smertzen. Das yre hertze also ynwendich verseret were van smertzen vnd van mytlyden der pynen vnd des doitze yrs aller lyebsten heren, das vffen-bairt vnser here vßwendich vnd betzeychent iß myt eynem vffenbairen zeichen.

15 Vff eyn tzijt, da sie yre heubt van rechter cranckeit yn yre lyncke hant hait geney-get, da fiel yr eyn troppen bloitze van yrem hertzen vß dem lyncken augen vff den fynger, an den man den ryncke yn doit. Man dreyt den ryncke dar vmb an dem fynger, want van dem hertzen gechet eyn ader in den vynger. Also woilt vnser [245ʳ] here betzeychen, daz iß eyne mynnetroppe were vnd were van deme hertze

20 gefalle vß dem augen, das da entge dem hertze steyt, vnd vff den fynger, yn dem die ader vß dem hertzen gechet. Auch wart der smertzen yrs hertzen noch me gev-ffenbart. Want sie yre susteren ⌜wieder⌝ zo dem beth sultde fůire vnd also gerynge sie yr den lyncken armen woiltde roren entgene dem verwoinden hertzen, da schoiße yre daz bloit van dem hertze zo dem montde hervß vnd naiße, das man

25 sie van groißer cranckeit nyt vorter eyn mocht gefuren, vnd sie verleyffe eyn wille yn dem crutzganck sietzen. Da fielen [245ᵛ] jre drye troppen bloitze van yrem hertzen vß dem lyncken augen vff den hertze fynger. Also wart sie myt arbeit zo leste gefuret zo dem bethe, da lache sie verlaißen van allen vßerlichen kreyfften, gar verlaißen. O, wie woil mocht sie sprechen, als die bruyt spricht yn canticis:

30 ›Verkondiget mym vßerwilten lyeben, daz ich van lyebden krancke byn gewor-den.‹ *(Ct 5,8)* O du vßerwilte bruyt Christi, wer hait dyne hertze verwont myt der straillen der lyebden anders dan der aller schonester van formen vor allen kyn-deren der menschen, des schoiße also scharppe synt? Durch eyn seliche betrach-tonge syner lyebden vnd bytteren lydens ist dyn hertze durchstochen myt der

35 heilsamer straillen [246ʳ] des mytlydens. Erwyrffe genade der andacht vns armen kyntderen jn der betrachtonge des lydens Christi, o soiße jonffrauwe Christina!

Dar nach als die lyebde was pynichen die seliche jonffrauwe Christina, ist sie **Kap. 18** gefort worden zo dem bette, vnd da verleyffe sie lygen als yn eyner rogen. O, wie wunderlichen ist got yn synen heilgen vnd der da wyrckt die <wonder> yn yne! Aber der die wonde geschoißen haitte, der wyste sy auch woil zo heillen. In der

5 rogen wart yre sele entzucket yn eyn claire lyecht, jn dem sach sie geistlichen myt den augen der selen eyn gar wonderliche suberliche roiße, die was [246ᵛ] also breyt als alle ertrich. Yn der roßen sach sie alle die gantze werelt vnd alle, die yn der werelt waren, vnd alle ordenunge vnd alle, die yn allen orden waren. Vnd sie gewanne gar eyn groiße betroppenyß vber alle, die yn doitsunden waren,

10 want sie sach sy alle beytde, die yn den orden waren vnd auch die vßewendich

---

18 dem] der   **24** hervß] her vß   **26** *nach* fielen] dryff *gestrichen*   **27** fynger] fynge
18,3 <wonder>] wōderlichñ

den orden waren. Aber die yn doit sunden waren, die kru̇chen vff der erden als vnsuber kreden. In dießem lyecht sach sie auch myt eyner foelunge ynwendich yn der selen alles, daz got noch ye geleyt vff der erden vor den menschen. Vnd da sie yn dem lyecht erkant, daz syn martel, syn bloit, syn bytter doit an also vil menschen *[247ʳ]* verloren sultde werden, vnd die sie sach yn doit sunden, vnd 15 daz sie krochen vff der erden als kretden, da verlore sie van rechtem jamer vnd hertzen leytde alle yre verstentenyß fier wochen. Yn den iiij wochen lache sie, daz sie noch nye nust eyn wyste vßerlich, was da geschage. Aber was sie ynwendich sach jn dem geist, daz saget sie dick vßewendich myt dem montde, das sy iß nyt eyn wyste selber. Die by yre waren, die hoirten iß. Jn dem selben betru̇ppenyß 20 vnd yn dem lyecht sprach vnser here zo yrer selen: ›Sele myn, du salt nyt jamer noch betruppenyß hayn *[247ᵛ]* vmb die, die mych versmeten haynt myt yren sunden. Du salt dich me erfrauwen, das myn vader hait van anbegyn vor sehen yn syner gotheit alle, die zo yme gehoirent.‹ Also lache sie die iiij wochen yn groißer crancheit, daz man yre alle nachtes wachen moiste. Vnd yn den iiij wochen gaiffe 25 yr vnser here groiße gaben. Vnd zo eyner yecklicher gaben wart die suchte des vßeren lybs gewandelt, also daz die jonfferen waynten, sie hette sich vmb gekeret van eyner suchten. Vnd sie wart dar na also sere crancke, daz sie alle verzwylfelten an yrer gesuntheit. Dieße wort sprache der here zo yrer selen: ›O sele myn, jch hayn dich getzogen *[248ʳ]* yn rytterschafft. Die engelße scharen synt die, die na 30 mynem willen farent vnd komment. O myn vßerwilte bruyt, du byst den engellen gelich myt dogenden. Du haist an dyr kußheit, gehorsamheit, furige lyebde, vnd ordenunge der oitmodicheit haistu an dyr, als die engel hay*n*t.‹

Kap. 19 Jn der selber vasten an dem karfrytage vor mytternacht byß an den mytdage lache sie aber yn der betrachtunge na der pynen vnd doit vnsers heren. Yn der betrachtonge wart sie aber entzucket, das sie yn dem geist wart sehen alle die pynen vnsers heren vnd alle die stede, da er die martel leyt. Dyße sach sie alles eygenclichen myt den augen der selen. Vnd *[248ᵛ]* yn der beschauwonge lache sie byß zo 5 der nonen. Da iß quam vmb die zijt, als vnser here verscheytde an dem cru̇tze vnd syne sele befaillen synem hemelschen vader, da sache dyeße heilge jonffrauwe eyn wyße dube, vnd die floge yr vff daz heubt. Vnd sie ducht, daz sich alle yre lyffe vff dede vnd daz die dube alle yre gelyeder durch gynge vnd erfoilt sie myt vnsprechlicher soißicheit, also daz yre smertzen wart gekeret yn soißicheit vnd 10 geistliche freude.

---

33 haynt] hayt

An dem oisterdage darna da man metten sancke, da lache sie yn eyner gotlicher **Kap. 20**
betrachtonge nach der vfferstentenyß vnsers heren vnd sy begert des an got, das
sie myt yme vfferstonde van yren siechtagen vnd van allen gebrechen *[249ʳ]* des
lybs vnd der selen. Da erscheyn jre vnser here yn eym wyßen cleyt vnd vmbfencke
5 sie gar fruntlichen vnd koiste sie gar lyeblichen vnd sprach zo yr: ›Jch byn das
leben dyner selen. Dyne heille hait dich vmbfangen.‹ Da er die wort zo yr sprach,
da gyng er van yr, vnd sie gynge yme na, aber sie eyn maicht yn nyt erfoilgen.
Also gynge er vor yr hynne durch den crutzganck yn das cappittel huße, byß daz
er quam by eym graiffe. Da erkant sie yn dem geist, wer yn dem graiffe lache
10 begraben. Vff den sargen des grabes knyete vnser here vnd er machet eyn crutze
vber daz graifft. Vnd vff dem grabe erfolgt si yn vnd sie wult yn hayn vmbfangen, da verswant er vor yren ‹augen›, *[249ᵛ]* vnd sie hoirte gerynge yn dem geist
eyn groiße schaire der engel gar soißelichen syngen yn der luyfft ›Der here ist vff
gestanden van dem grabe‹ vnd ander ville gar schoner wort. Vnd die engel furtten
15 gar vil selen myt groißer freuden yn den hemel vnd sonderlichen die sele vff dem
grabe, vnser here vff gekneet haitte vnd eyn crutze dar vber gemacht hait. Des
selben menschen sach sie synen namen geschreben myt gulden bůstaben. Des
selben dags vnder der myßen begert sie gar des heilgen sacramentz yrs gemynten
bruytgams. Da yr der prister nach der mysßen vnseren heren bracht, da duchte
20 sie, daz das sieche huße alles vol gotliches lyechtz *[250ʳ]* vnd gar soißen gerochs
were. Da sie vnseren heren myt groißer lyebden vnd yn vnsprechlicher lyebden
vnd begerden entphangen, da wart yre hertze erfoilt myt soißicheit, als abe alle
yre gelyeder vol soißicheit weren. Yn der woillust vnd soißicheit hoirt sie die engel
gar froelichen syngen yn der luyfft ›Gloria in excelsis‹ gantze vß. Jn dießem lyecht
25 der erzückunge gaiffe vnser here der selicher jonffrauwen Christine zo erkennen,
daz dyße was van syner gebort mcclxxxviij.

An dem pynxste abent zo nacht saße sie an yrem stoille byß zo metten tzijt **Kap. 21**
wachende jn groißer burnender begerden, das yr got woilt senden daz lyecht
[250ᵛ] vnd das fůre des heilgen geistes, da van daz yre sele erlucht moichte
werden yn erkentenyß vnd entzonte yn lyebden, als die heilgen apostelen worden
5 entfencket. Jn dyeße begerden zofloiße yre sele yn yrem lybe myt villen trenen
byß an mytternacht. Dar nach sach sie myt den augen yrer selen sweywen vber
yre eyne groißen wonnenclichen adeler. Syne augen branten als eyn fackel vnd
sie gaben eyn schone lyecht van ym vnd hynder yme, war er floge. Da erkant sie
gotlichen, daz der adeler was yre aller lyebster here. Vnd sie begert myt lyeblicher
10 begerden, daz er syne floegel zo yre kerte vnd sich gutlichen ergebe jn yre sele,
die yn syner lyebden begert nach yme. Da swancke *[251ʳ]* der aller lyebste syne

---

20,12 ‹augen›] *u. d. Z. v. j. H.* **21,9** here] here was **10** jn] jn yn

floegel zo jre eyn mail vnd aber eyn mail vnd also dick kerte er sich van yre. Da
wart alles ye me vnd me gemeret, die lyebde vnd die begert yn jre. Zo dem vertten
mail, da yr sele van wonderlicher begertden was jn der arbeit, da lyeße sich der
konynck der hemel her abe yn jre sele. Da wart sie myt wonderlicher freuden 15
erfoilt vnd myt gotlicher woillust begoißen. Da vmbfynge der here myt synen gotlichen armen yre sele vnd er geboitde yre auch, myt yren lyplichen armen yn zo
vmbfange, vnd er druckt sy an syne hertze. Aber als iß morgen wart, daz sy gayn
sult, yre lyebhaber zo entphangen, da ducht sie, daz sy gynge *[251ᵛ]* jn den wul-
lusten, vnd yre fůße eyn royrtden nyt der erden, dan die lyebde droge sie eyn 20
wege. Da sach sie, daz dat gotz huße was vol gotlicher genaden. Da entphynge sie
van dem pryster myt dem sacrament yren aller lyebsten heren vnd yre sele wart
erfoilt myt vngewonlycher freuden vnd genaden, also daz sie van soißer woillust
zofloiße als eyn honynchsem, vnd sie wart also mail gesencket yn eyn wunnenc-
liches lyecht. Da sach sie yn dem geist den hemel vffen vnd eyn groiße lyecht 25
dar jne. Van dem hemel lyeß sich her abe eyn lyecht, daz lucht vnd brant. Iß
was als alle ertrich. Vnd yn dem lyechte sach sie eyn *[252ʳ]* leuendich hertze. Das
dede sich selber vff vnd zo. Wanne iß sich vff dede, so goiße <iß> eyn wunderli-
ches lyecht vß yme. Van dem lyechte wart hemel vnd erde, vnd was dar yn was,
erlucht vnd myt vnsprechlicher freuden erfoilt. An dem hertzen stonde geschre- 30
ben ›O sapiencia Jhesu Christi‹ vnd noch me, das yr vß dem gedechtenyß was
gegangen. Da begert sie, das sich daz lyecht myt dem hertzen yn jre sele lyeße,
vnd das geschach also. Da vmbfynge sie daz lyecht vnd wart also hytzich van
der furiger lyebden, vnd van dem gotlichen lyecht wart sie also gantze erlucht.
Van der *groißer* soißicheit vnd van wunderlichem bekentenyß *[252ᵛ]* sprach sie: 35
›O wunderlicher got, was bystu?‹ Da quamme yre eyn antwert vß dem gotlichen
hertzen: ›Jch byn eyn burnendes fůer, eyne luchtes lyecht. Jch byn eyn stymme,
eyne wille. Jch byn eyn genongede vnd dyne vbersoißicheit vnd aller begerlicher
hertzen vnd aller heilger.‹ Hie van quam sie yn gotliche beschauwonge vnd van
der soißer beschauwonge quam sie van yre selber. Vnd sie wart also hytzich van 40
lyebden vnd fůrich ynwendich, also daz van der selen van hytzste auch der lyffe
vßwendich also groiße hytzste entphynge, das die waire furyge groiße hytzste myt
kaldem waißer nyt mochten werden erleßen, des sich die vil vnd lange versuch-
ten, die by yre waren. Vnd auch myt der dogent der lye*[253ʳ]*bden, die myt yre
also geweldenclichen ranck vnd yren lyeben an sich jn der selen czwanck, so 45
name die krefftige lyebde vberthant, das der lyffe ynwendich zoreyße, daz sy den
gebresten lyden moiste na godes willen vnd das auch gerne leyt. Das was yre eyn
selicher pynxtage.

---

16 here] here sy **20** royrtden] roytdē **25** geist] geist da sach sie **28** <iß>] ist **31** Jhesu
Christi] J̄hs x̄p̄us **35** groißer] goißer

In dem hogetzijt als man syngt van vnsers heren lycham, da begert sie auch yre **Kap. 22**
lyeben heren zo entphangen myt groißer genaden. Da der pryster das heilge
sacrament bracht getragen, da sach sy ynwendich durch die muren des huße, das
der pryster vnseren heren bracht als eyn claire lyecht. Jn dem lyecht ducht sie,
5 daz sie berycht wortden van den henden godes, *[253ᵛ]* wie woil sie auch berecht
wart van des prysters hende. Da was jre vnser here also soiße yn yrem montde *als*
honyck, vnd die soißicheit floiße yn yre hertze vnd yn yre sele. Da reytde yre lyebhaber myt yrer selen: ›Lyebe, habe mych lyeffe. Jch komen schyre vnd erfrauwen
dich. Lyebe, habe mych lyeffe. Ich komen schyeer vnd troisten dich. Lyebe, habe
10 mych lyeffe. Jch komen schieer vnd holen dich.‹ Dyeße soiße beschauwonge vnd
gebruchen der selen yn der tzijt ist vnselich gewest. Dyße geschage yre gewon-
lich also lange, byß daz yre vnser here yn eyn beßers vnd hogers verwandelt,
wanne sy vnseren heren entphynge, das er yn *[254ʳ]* yrem montde was also soiße,
vnd die soißicheit gyncke yn yre sele vnd hertze vnd durchfloiße alle yr gelieder.
15 Aber yn dyeßer irster beschauwonge sach sie geistlichen eynen baume waßen
vß yrem hertze. Des wortzel was grone, zo betzeychen, daz das hertze sal grone
syne jn gode myt dogenden vnd guden wercken vnd heilgen gedancken vnd myt
soißer begerden. Der stamme was luter vnd claire, daz bezeichet die luter clairheit vnsers hertzes. Der baume was woil getzeret vnd suberlich vnd vben woil
20 geblomet. Eyn yechliche blome haitte eyn sonderliche varbe. Daz betzechent, daz
got die sele myt mancherley dogenden cleytdet vnd zeirret yn dem hemelrich. Vff
eyner *[254ᵛ]* yeclicher blome saße eyn fogelgyn vnd vff der vberster blomen saße
eyn fogel groiße vnd suberlich vber sie alle als eyn adeler. Syne augen waren als
eyn claire lyecht vnd er sancke myt eyner soißer stymme den anderen fogellen
25 vor dyße wort: ›Ego sum panis viuus‹ etc. Da songen yme alle die anderen fogel
nach myt soißem thone: ›Tu es panis viuus in quo omnes viuimus in eternum‹. Da
dede sich der vberste fogel, vnser here Jhesus Christus, ⌐vff⌐ als eyn lyecht vnd
die cleynen fogelger alle vmb yn, vnd er besloiße ⌐sie⌐ alle yn ym. Da det sich der
hemel vff, vnd fort sie alle myt ym dar yn myt groißer freuden. ›Da was myn geist
30 yn dem lyecht dry dage vnd drye nacht. *[255ʳ]* Got gaiffe myr zo beschauwen vnd
zo erkennen vil vnd vil yn dem hemel vnd yn der erden, des ich nyt alles eyn kayn
gesagen.‹

Jn dem hogetzijt des selichen Johannes des deuffers was dyße heilge jonffrauwe **Kap. 23**
nach yrer gewanheit yn hytzicher andacht. Na yrer gewanheit sy was yn hytzicher
andacht vnd begerten. Vnd sie wart jn dem geist gezucket yn eyn groiße lyecht.
Vnd der lyeblicher bruytdegam spelet myt syner bruyt vnd er sprache zo yre: ›O
5 du aller lyeblichste sele myn, heyße van myr, was du wilt. Du vßerwilte sele myn,

---

22,6 montde als] montde   **13** yn] yn ‖ jn

die ich myr vßerwylt hayn, heyße van myr, was du wylt. Jch byn *[255ᵛ]* die gotliche lyebde vnd der sone des lebens hait dich gecleyt myt dem ewigen lyecht.
Du haist van myr daz ewige leben vnd alles gut. Die wyßheit ist dyn leben yn der
ewiger gotheit.‹ **D**az lyecht jn der entzŭckonge wertte seße wochen. Vnd van der
krafft des ynnerlichen lyechtes was sie die vj wochen beraubet yrs vßerlichen   10
gehoirs. Yn dem lyecht sach sie dicke, daz vff die tzijt zo Rome gesache mancherley falscheit vnd betregenyß vnd auch ander sachen, die yn dem houe geschagen.
Wer auch yn der tzijt quam vor sie, yn der hertzen sache sie, *[256ʳ]* was yn yrem
hertzen verborgen. Das erkante sie vnd alles, was man yn dem cloister reden was,
daz hoirte sie, ader wo man iß reytde, daz hoirte sie ynwendich yn dem versten-   15
tenyß. Jn der tzijt van vberentzicher soißicheit yrs hertzen eyn moicht sy nyt me
dan soiße spyße gessen. Dar vmb so sy vnder willen begert honych ader fygen, so
sache sy yn dem geist, wo iß die jonfferen yn yren kysten ader anders wo haitten.
Daz sache sie vnd hyßes yn dan. Yn dem selben lyecht sache sie, daz zo Koillen
eyn groiße stryt sultde geschen vnd daz vil lude da erslagen sultden werden.   20
Dyße sayt sy den, die by yre wa*[256ᵛ]*ren. Aber des dags vnd yn der stonden, da
der strytde geschache, da sache sie yn dem geist, daz eylffe dusent menschen
worden erslagen vnd daz yre selen alle sament sullent faren jn die helle. Sie sache
auch, das jre lyeplicher broder furte des byschoiffs banner vnd daz alle die, die
van symme geslecht waren, die sullen alle gefangen werden vnd yrer keyner wart   25
erslagen. Dyße sach sie alles yn dem geist vnd sayt iß den, die by yre waren. Die
selben erforen dar na, daz iß alles geschet was vff den dage vnd vff die stonde,
wie sy yn gesayt haitte. Yn den selben vj wochen saytde vnser here zo yr: ›Drye
susteren synt, die da sullent sterben, also das ye eyn sal erloiste *[257ʳ]* werden ⌐vß
dem fegefuer¬, ye daz die ander sterbe.‹ Da hvbe sie an van freuden vnd sprache: 30
›Myr sullen lyebe haben, myr sullen loben, myr sullen sehen!‹ Auch so ist iß zo
verstayn, daz sie den heren haitte gebeden vor dyeße lyepliche gesusteren, als
sie auch dick haitte gebeden vor ville der lebendiger vnd der doden, der da ist
geweste sonder zaille, alstu hoiren wyrst her na.

Kap. 24 **A**ls nu dyeße heilge jonffer also lache entzucket yn dem geist, da sprach sie dyeße
wort: ›Die lyebde, die wyrt entfencket van dem fuer, sy wyrt erluchtet van dem
lyecht. Gedencke van dem wyne, der hoger, soißer, luterer gotheit, der dyner sele
ist zo gefueget.‹ Jn dem selben lyecht sprach sie *[257ᵛ]* zo vnserem lyeben heren:
›O myn zartes lyeffe, als ich dich hie vor mails hayn gebeden vor die lebendigen   5
vnd doitden, *so* beden ich dich, dastu myr nyt eyn wullest weygeren myn bede.‹
Da sprache vnser lyeber here zo yre: ›O du myn aller lyebste, ich hayn dich sicher
gemacht des ewigen lebens myt eyner stedicher sicherheit.‹ In den selben tzijt-

9 Daz] *Lombarde steht in der Zeilenmitte.* **24,6** so] zo

den da sy also van yr selber was yn gotlicher beschauwonge, vnd sie was gantze
10 myt jme vereyniget, wie woil daz yre vßerliche synne slyeffen, da sancke yre der
vßerwilt eyn lyeplich lyette, nyt myt der stymmen, daz man gehoirt mocht. Aber
sy sancke myt der stymmen, daz alle die hoirtten, die by yre wairen, die iß yr her
na saytten. Aber *[258ʳ]* da sie wieder zo yre selber qŭam, da eyn wyste sie nyt eyn
wort dar van, dan sy kontde die wort vnd die wyße, die der here yrer selen geson-
15 gen haitte, daz ist dyße: ›Jhesus gedechtenyß is*t* soiße vnd des hertzen soiße
freude. Gegrußet systu, dornen crone, gebenediet sy die persone, dem du zosta-
chen haist daz konynckliches heubet. Du dorne crone, durch Christus gebeytde
gyffe myr daz ryche vnd daz keyßertum. O zijerde der crystenheit, du ersamer
dorne, eyn croyne des konyncks der eren, du artzedie der werelt, eyn soißicheit
20 yn vnseren enxsten vnd eyne balsame, behailt alle, die dich hude zo dage lobent,
vor boißen fellen.‹

[258ᵛ] Jn dem selben lyechte sache dyeße heilge jonffrauwe vber yr yn der luyffte **Kap. 25**
myt geistlichem gesicht, das eyn man syne eliche frauwe myt eyme seßel erslŭche,
vnd er stieße sy also lange zo der erden, byß daz er sy ermordet. Da sie dyße sache
yn dem geist, da ryeffe sy vnd schreye vnd sprache: ›O we, geschruwe sy vber den
5 morder!‹ Dyße hoirten die jonffrauwen, die by yre waren. Auch so sache sy, daz
die selbe frauwe nyt alleyn doit was an dem lybe, sonder sy was auch doit an der
selen, dan sy was jn dem willen gestorben, daz sy sich gerochen wultde hayn an
yrem man vnd wultde yn auch ermort hayn. Sie erkante auch yn dem geiste, daz
der man ewenclichen verloren *[259ʳ]* was vnd eyns boißen doitze sultde sterben.
10 Dyße geschache auch balde dar na. Nyt vber eyn lange tzijt wart er vmb ander
syne boißheit erdrencket yn dem Rynne. Aber vff die tzijt da er syn frauwe ermort,
da sache sy yn dem geist, daz er sy bracht doit gefŭrt zo yrem cloister, daz man
sie da begrobe. Dyße saget sie allen den jonfferen, die by yre waren vnd dar van
wysten. Da aber die frauwe vnd die anderen daz hoirten, da lyeffen sy hyn an die
15 fynster. Vnd sy sachen, daz eyner dort her van eym dorffe quam vnd bracht eyn
doit frauwe vnd bait sy, daz man sie dar begrobe. Also quam iß van yre vß, daz er
sie ermort haitte, vnd dar vmb so moist *[259ᵛ]* er das lant rŭmen.

An dem selben lyecht sache sy yn dem geist, daz eyn rytter yrer geswygen broder **Kap. 26**
erslagen haytte yn eyner stait, die da heiße Lansteyn. Vnd sy sach auch, das er an
der selen ewenclichen verloren was. Dar vmb schreye sy gar jemerlichen. Vnd sy
saytde iß den jonffrauwen, die by yre waren, myt groißem bedroppenyß, daz die
5 sele verloren sultde werden. Vnd sy nante yn auch den rytter vnd auch die stait,
da iß geschet was. Dyße verwonderten sich die jonffrauwen gar sere, daz iß also

---

15 ist] iß   **26,1** An] *Lombarde steht in der Zeilenmitte.*

ferre yn eym anderen lantde was. Dar vmb frageten sy dar na vnd erforen, daz iß vff dem selben dage dort geschette was, als sy gesehen vnd gehoirt haitte vnd auch *[260ʳ]* gesaget haitte. Sye sach auch jn dem selben lyecht zo zweyne maillen, daz yrs broders kyntder zweyn, eyn knabe vnd eyn metgyn, bynne vyrtzen dagen 10 sultden sterben ynwendich vnd sullen faren zo dem hemelrych. Dyße saget sie auch den jonfferen na yrer gewanheit, die by yre waren. Dan alles, das sie yn den seße wochen sache, da eyn wyste sy nyt eyne wort vmb. Dan was sie ynwendich jn dem geist sach, da rette der lypliche mont van vßwendich, daz sy iß nyt eyn wyste. Da sy den jonfferen van den zweyn kyntderen haitte gesait, da erforen sy 15 dar na, das die kynder alle beyde waren gestorben vff die selbe tzijt, als sy iß yn haitte gesayt.

Kap. 27 **D**yße heilge jonffrauwe hait auch gehait sonderliche an*[260ᵛ]*dacht zo der konynclicher jonffrauwen Marien, der moder godes. Also hait die moder godes auch sonderliche neygonge zo yre vmb die lyebde yrs sons. Also ist iß geschyt vff eyn tzijt, als yn dem conuent wart gesongen die sequencia Aue preclara vnd der den verße Audi nos, da sach sy die moder godes vff yren kneen beden vor 5 den conuent. Auch vff eyn tzijt als man Aue Maria zo abent luytde, da ylet sy sych also sere zo der erden, daz sie eyn knee also swerlichen verwont hait. Dyße hait erkant die aller soiste jonffrauwe vnd aller myldicheste moder Maria, vnd sie hait getroiste yre aller getruweste dyenerynnen vnd sy ist yre erscheynen yn dem slaiffe vnd sy droge yn yren zarten henden *[261ʳ]* eyn boiße myt koistlicher 10 salben vnd sie hait yre dyenerßen gesont gemacht vnd sye hait yre befollen, daz sy vortter senfftlichen sultde nyeder kneen.

Kap. 28 **A**uch hait sye entphangen vff eyn mail yre dysciplynen van der moder godes vmb vberyche penitencie, die sy yre swerlichen vff lacht, alstu hie vor gehoirt haist. Sie was vff eyn tzijt jn sent Nyclais capelle vnd sy beytde myt gantzer andacht yrs hertzen vor dem bylde vnser lyeber frauwen. Das bylde vff dem altare recket syne jonfferliche hant vß vnd gaiffe yre eynen backen slage vnd sie straiffet sie 5 moderlichen vnd sprache zo yr: ›Laiße dyr genoichen myt dem gemeynnen.‹ Da *[261ᵛ]* hait sy sich selber erkant vnd sy ist vff gestanden vnd sy ist gefallen vor daz crutzcifixe zo der sijten des altares vnd sy baitde myt groißen ruwen yrs hertzen vmb genade vor dem sone vnd sy baitde auch vor den tzorne der moder vnd sy begert genaden van dem heren. 10

28,1 Auch] *Lombarde steht in der Zeilenmitte.*   **6** Da] Da ‖ Da

Nach den vj wochen als dyeße seliche jonffrauwe eynzucket was yn eyn gotliches **Kap. 29**
lyecht, da sie vil gesehen vnd gehoirt hait, die nyt hie geschreben eyn synt, als
nu daz hogetzijt ist komen assumpcionis beate et gloriose virginis Marie, vnder
anderen genaden vnd sůßicheit so hait vnser here sy sonderlichen gewyst vnd
5 geliert sieben stŭcke, die da zo gehoirent allen den, die da got wullent lyeffe hayn
vnd woil befallen: Das irste ist, daz der mensche sich *[262ʳ]* sal abezegen van yrtz-
deschen dyngen, want wer daz hertze gyfft zo vergencklichen sachen, daz macht
das hertze van genaden ledich. Das ander ist, das der mensche die gedancken
syns hertzen altzijt sal vff rechten zo gode, da van wyrt daz hertze geistlichen.
10 Das drytte, daz der mensche sal sich keren vnd geben zo betrachtonge nach gode
myt andacht, daz erlucht die sele. Das iiij, das eyn mensche syns frŭndes nummerme eyn sal vergeißen, das ist rechte lyebden. Das v, das der mensche altzijt
syn hertze sal bereytden myt begerunge nach sym lyebhaber, das brenget gotliche
heymmelicheit. Das vj, das der mensche got alwege vor augen sal hayn, dastu
15 doest alles, daz yme lyeffe ist, vnd mydest, was yme leyt ist, vnd geduldenclichen
lydest, was er vber dich ver*[262ᵛ]*henget. Das siebente, dastu vmb nyemans lyebe
ader leyt laißes vnderwegen, was du myt gode haist zo schaiffen.

Jn dem hogtetzijt der selicher jonffrauwen Marien als sie geboren wart, da hait **Kap. 30**
dyeße seliche jonffrauwe vnseren heren entphangen myt groißer lyebden vnd
ynwendicher begerden. Da wart jre sele ynwendich vmbfangen myt eyme clairen
lyecht vnd yre hertze vnd alle yre gelyeder worden vbergoißen myt der vberster
5 soißicheit. Yn dem lyecht sach sie geistlichen eyn baume vß yrer selen waißen
als eynen palmen baume. Der was vben gar breyt vnd groiß vnd vnden smaille
vnd cleyn. Wan dyeßem baŭme vnd van syner bezeychenunge hait yr der here
gegeben zo ver*[263ʳ]*stayn yn dem lyecht, als geschreben ist in canticis canticorum: ›Jch sal vff stigen yn den palmen baume vnd ich sal vmbfangen syn frucht.‹
10 *(Ct 7,8)* Myrcke, das der palmen baume ist vnden smaille vnd stincht vnd vben
breyt van laube vnd edel van fruchten. Also ist yre leben hie yn dyeßer tzijt cleyn
gewest durch eyn oitmodiges erkentenyße yrs selbs vnd sy ist vol stiche gewest
van bytterheit der bedroppenyß jn abezeonge, yn spyßen vnd dranck, yn krenckten, yn harten cleyderen vnd leger, alstu da vor haist gehoirt. Aber vffen is sy
15 sere breyt gewest yn gotlicher lyebden entgene yre vyant vnd fruntde, edel van
soißen fruchten *[263ᵛ]* der dogent. Jre gesmacke hait got erfrauwet yn dem hemel
vnd auch die engel vnd alle heilgen, die sunder yn der erden vnd die lyeben selen
yn dem fegefŭr, alstu noch hoiren wyrst groißen wonder her nache. Da sprache
der here yn dem lyecht zo yrer selen: ›Ich hayn vff gerechte dyne leben myt aller
20 oitmodicheit. Jch hayn dich getziert myt aller reynicheit. Jch hayn dich ryche

---

29,1 Nach] *Lombarde steht in der Zeilenmitte.*   **30,8** canticorum] caticor'   **15** entgene] Entgne

gemacht myt der gedult vnd ich hayn dich verbreytde yn der lyebden vnd ich
hayn dich erhaben van dem nyedersten byß zo dem vbersten.‹

Kap. 31 **Vff sent Mychals dage**

Dyeße heilge jonffrauwe haitte also groiße burnende *[264ʳ]* lyebde nach yrem
aller lyebsten heren, den zo entphangen yn dem heilgen sacrament, vnd da yn
der pryster bracht, da erkant sy yn yre selber, daz der edel lycham godes alles
spellenden zo jre quam myt ylonge. Vnd yn dem gotlichen lyecht sach sie den 5
pryster zo yre komen myt vnserem lyeben heren, ye dan sy yn sege myt den
lyplichen augen. Vnd da sache sie, daz vier herlycher lyechtdreger da waren:
zweyn gyngen vor vnd zweyn hynden. Vnd sy songen myt hemelschen stymme
›Te sanctum dominum in excelsis‹ gantze vß myt dem Gloria patri. Dar nach da
der pryester die buße vß detde, da foillet sie den *[264ᵛ]* aller soisten gesmacke 10
vnd geroiche, da van yre hertze vnd yre lyffe vnd alle jre gelyeder gestercket vnd
erquicket worden, die van starcker begerden verkrencket waren. Da der pryster
jre den heilgen lycham boitde, da sach sie daz aller suberlichstes kyntgyn, daz
da was leuendich, wyße vnd roytde, vnd iß was gantze suberliche vnd iß was
vmb syn heubtgen geschreben also: ›Jch byn das anbegyn vnd daz ende.‹ Vnd 15
sie sprache zo myr: ›Vff die tzijt, als *ich* mynen aller lyebstes lyeffe entphynge, da
zofloiße van soißer sicheit myn sele, vnd sie wart versencket yn eynen abgront
der woillůstiger lyebden. Vnd da sprache der lyebhaber zo myner selen: »Du byst
myn vßerwilte bruytde, *[265ʳ]* myn dube, myn konynckynnen. Jch wil dich edel
machen myt myner wyßheit.« Da wart myn sele getzogen gotlichen yn eyn groiße 20
wytte konyncklich huße woil aller freuden vnd wunnen. Dar yn waren gesament
eyn versamenunge der vßerwilten, die da noch hie vff der erden lyeffeten. Der
erkant ich vil, wie woil ich der noch nye kaynt gesehen eyn haitte. Mytten jn dem
huße gynge vff eyn baume vnd woische byß zo dem hemel. Der waiße hailffe
roißen vnd hailffe lylien, want van des baumes frucht worden gespyßet alle die 25
vßerwilten vnd got myt yn. Des baumes stamme detde sich mytden vff vnd darvß
scheynne eyn hemels lecht. Yn dem lyecht sprache die stymme godes: *[265ᵛ]* »Jch
byn das lycht der werelt. *(Io 8,12)* Wairhefftich syt yre selich. Yre sytte alle myt
erben myns vaders. Jr bloet vor myr als die lylien.« Da sprache der lyebhauer zo
myr: »O sele myn, sehest lyecht yn lyecht? Jch befelen dyr die lebendigen myt den 30
doden. Ich wil dyr myn wonden vff doyn.« Dar nach neygete sich die verwentte
sele myn vff yren lyebhauer. Myt dem wart sy vereyniget yn eym soiße roge, yn
eynem lyeblichen slaiffe.‹

31,6 *nach* den] gotlichen *gestrichen* 13 daz aller] dz eÿ aller 15 anbegyn] anbeyn
16 als ich] als 17 van] van vā sicheit] *verkürzt für* sicherheit, *so auch in* Kap. 63 (Bl. 302ᵛ)
24 hailffe] haiffe

In dem hogetzijt der heilger eylffe dusent jonffrauwen da die seliche jonffrauwe   **Kap. 32**
daz heilge sacrament sultde entphangen, da brantte yre sele yn groißer lyebden.
Da der pryster das heilge sacra*[266ʳ]*ment bracht, da sache sie eyn furyges lycht,
vnd yn dem lyecht sach sie komen yren aller lyebsten heren. Vnd vor yme gynge eyn
5 groiße schaire der engel als die rytterschaiffe vor eynem konynck vnd sy songen
alle myt soißem schaille. Da wart daz sieche huße vol vbersoißen gerochs. Vff die
tzijt were yre hertze jn yrem lybe zobroiste, sultde sye <len>ger hayn eyn keren
des lyebhauers yrer selen. Da nu der pryster die boiße vff dede vnd sie na<ch>
jrem vßerwilten gyrlichen begertde, da sach sie vben yn der ⌐boißen¬ eyn lamgyn
10 slaiffen, vnd iß hait eyn crentzgyn vff synem heubt, daz was vmbschreben myt
gulden bustaben ›Agnus dei qui tollit *[266ᵛ]* peccata mundi‹. ›Zo haynt entwacht
das lemgyn vnd sprancke snel yn *des* prysters hant vnd strebete zo myr, als syne
begert zo myr stontde.‹ Da sie entphynge daz lyebliche lampe godes, da wart yre
sele vbersoißer freuden vol, vnd yr sele wart yn dem geist gefoirt yn eyn konynck-
15 lich pailas, das was also wytte als alle ertrich. Mytten dar yn stonde herlich der
throne godes. Gestuellet was das pailas alle vmb. Das gestulles was gewyrcket
van lylien. Vnd iß was alles vol gar soißen geroichs. Da sach sy yren aller lyebsten
heren als eyn lamp vnd er sprach yr zo: ›Jch byn daz geware lebendige lampe,
daz da schaiffet vnd sicket yn dyr alle dynge.‹ Des *[267ʳ]* vaders stymme sprache
20 auch zo yr: ›Myn lyeber sone sal myt dyr synne byß zo dem ende der werelt.‹ Dyß
lamp haitte vff synem rucke eyne fanne, die strechte sich yn drue ende. Eyn ende
vberzoge alle das pailas, daz ist die crystenheit, want er die behelt vnd beschir-
met myt syner lanckmodicher barmhertzicheit. Das ander deylle yn daz fegefüer,
da myt er die selen troisttet vnd yn yre pyne erlyechtet. Das drytte deylle vberzoge
25 den hemel, daz da betzeytget alle, die er behall*t*en wylt. Die erlucht er vnd erfult
sy myt syner gotlicher genaden. Aber die konynckynne, vnser frauwe, die entphenget den *[267ᵛ]* ynfloiße des gotlichen lyechtz vnd die woillust aller meyste
vnd zo aller irste, vnd dar na die anderen heilgen alle. Vnd dar na wart die fanne
verwandelt yn eynen spegel, dar yn sach *sy* vnser frauwe myt allen heilgen jonf-
30 frauwen. Die erkant sy myt yren namen vnd wie eyn ygliche was vor gode myt
loyne vnd wirdicheit. Vnd die eylff dusent, wylcher heubtder yn vnserem gotz
huße synt, yn sonderheit erkant sy sie myt yrem namen vnd geslecht, det sie an
schryben, als noch yn den rollen yn dem cloister fonden wyrt, vnd synt dyeße:
Ceomate virgo, Petrisse virgo, Elyzabet virgo, Benedicta virgo, Juliana virgo, Anne
35 virgo, Cunigondis virgo, Gertrudis virgo, Cristine virgo, Cristine virgo, Elyzabet
filie cesaris. Das got*[268ʳ]*liche lamp sange vor myt vbersoißem thone vnd die
jonffrauwen sangen alles na myt froelichen stymmen vnd hertzelichen freuden,

---

32,7 sye] sye vst   <len>ger] hurger   **8** na<ch>] nare   **9** ⌐boißen¬] boiß' *am Rande*   **12** des] das
25 behallten] behallē   **27** den] den ‖ den   **29** sach sy] sach   **37** hertzelichen] hertzēlichñ

alles na yme vnd er myt ynne sonder eynnige wandelonge. Eya woil eyn kauffen!
Eya woil eyn dantze! Eya woil eyn sancke! Eya woil eyn lyeblich spielle! Dyße was
der reyne, den er vor sange: ›Heillich, heillich syt yr yn myner gotheit, vollenko- 40
men yn myner ewiger lyebden.‹ Dar na sprach er zo yn: ›Jch byn der weche der
vollenkomenheit, der hoge vnd groiße lyebde dreyt. Jch byn die luter wairheit,
die vch van anbegyn vnd yn anbegyn *[268ᵛ]* ist bereyt.‹ Dar na lyeß sich jre sele
yn yrs lyebhabers schoiß jn eyn soiße rǔge vnd lyebliche vmbfangen.

Kap. 33 Jn dem hogetzijt aller heilgen begert dieße heilge jonffrauwe myt groißer begerden, mysße zo hoiren vff dyeßen dage. Da wart sie van groißer begerunge erweckt
vnd sie hoirt die engelschen schairen yn der luyffte gar soißelichen syngen ›Te
deum laudamus‹ gantze vß. Da van wart sie entzucket desta me. Vff dießem dage
hailffe man yr zo dem gotz huße. Vnd da sie begontden ne*che*n der kyrchen, da 5
sach sie, das dat monster vnd daz gantze ertrich vol hemel*[269ʳ]*schen geroichs
vnd lyechtz was. Da man zo chore an hobe die myße, da sach sie yn der luyfft
bereytde eynen herlichen altare, gezeyrt vben myt lylien vnd vor myt roißen, zo
beytden sytten myt vyolen. Da was vnser here pryster, sanctus Gabriel was dya-
conus, sanctus Mychael subdiaconus. Das misse gewant vnsers herren was als 10
eyn claire steyn durch sichtich, also daz man hyndern yme sach, was vor yme
geschage. Da hobe der here die mysße an myt eyner aller soister stymmen vnd
die hiemelsche chore sangen alle, myt vnsprechelicher freuden sangen sie *[269ᵛ]*
die misse vß. Aber da iß quam, daz er sulte vff heben daz heilge sacrament, da
erscheyn eyn furiges lyecht. Das verbreyt synen schynne den heilgen allen yn 15
dem hemel vnd yn der erden vnd der heilger crystenheit, vnd iß deyllet sich auch
yn daz fegefeur, den selen allen zo troiste vnd zo genaden. Da er deylte die hostie
yn dru deylle, da sache sie an dem deylle, das yn den kelche gelacht was, eyn
crutze vnd dar an den gecrutzigeten myt blodigen wonden. Das selbe sache sie
auch an den anderen zweyn deyllen. Der kel*che* was also groiße, als recht aber 20
grondeloiße were, vnd das heilge bloytde *[270ʳ]* floiße ⌐durch⌐ verborgen aderen.
Dar na gynge der conuent zo vnd vnser here bereychte sie. Da sach sie, daz vnser
herre by etzelichen verleyffe vnd by etzelichen nyt. Da er ›Jte missa est‹ saitde
vnd den senne gaiff, da wart jre gevffenbairt alle, die des wirdiche waren. Daz
waren die, den die wyße crentze worden vff gesaitz*et* vff yre heubtder. Vnder des 25
hait der pryster yn dem chore die mißße vß <gesangen>, byß daz die jonffrauwen zo vnserem heren gyngen vnd er sy berycht. Da sach sie vff dem altare daz
aller suberlichste lempgyn varen spelenden. Vff synem rucke was eyne *[270ᵛ]* royt
crutze. Vnd daz lempgyn dede eynen snellen sproncke zo yr vnd iß vore vmb sy

---

38 eyn kauffen] eȳ zo kauffñ **33,5** nechen] neckē **20** kelche] kelcke **25** gesaitzet] gesaitz
Vnder] Vñ der **26** vß <gesangen>] vß

30 gar froelichen. Da wan wart yre sele freuden vol. Da gaiffe yr der pryster yren lyebhaber, den entphynge sie myt groißer freuden vol vberfloißicher soißicheit. Da
vmb<fynge> daz waire lamp jre sele ynwendich myt syner genaden yn eyn lyebliche helsonge vnd sprache zo yre: ›O du aller lyeblichste, erfrauwe dich, erfrauwe
dich. Du haist yn dyr den hemelschen heillant dyner selen, ⸢der⸣ da ist eyne
35 konynck aller konynck, got, godes sone, der myt syner genaden dynen honger
vß gedunne kan vnd dyner dorste myt syner soißichet verleßen.‹ *[271ʳ]* Da wan
wart yre sele getzogen vnd versencket yn also groiße lyebde, daz yr yn eym augen
blycke wart vff gedayn hemel vnd erde vnd auch daz fegefúer. An den drynen
steden erkant sie ville lude vnd gar vil dynges. Vnd sie verleyffe also yn vnspre-
40 chelicher lyebden vnd gotlicher woilluste myt der selen dry dage vnd nacht, daz
sie van yr selber komen was vnd sy eyn gebruchet sich nyt der vßerlicher synne.

Dar na an dem heilgen crystdage da man schreyffe mcclxxxix jaire, da Christus **Kap. 34**
geboren wart, da was sie yn groißer andacht *[271ᵛ]* vnd freuden des hogetzij-
tes. Da vberfloiße yre lyffe myt genadenricher soißicheit vnd eyn hemels lyecht
erscheyne yn yre vnd vber yr. Jn dem lyecht quam die hemelsche konynckynnen
5 Maria myt yrem allersoisten kyntde Jhesus, daz sie haitte vff jren moderlichen
armen, vnd sie lacht jre daz lyebliche kyntgyn yn yre hertze. Jhesus, yre eyniges
lyebe, spyltte myt yrer selen eyn also lyeblich soiße mynnen spielle, daz keynne
zonge dar van gesagen eyn kayn ader auch keyn hant geschryben eyn kayn.
Vnder des als yre sele yn der soißer begerunge myt yrem hertzen *[272ʳ]* lyeben
10 was, da sancke die vberschone jonffrauwe vnd moder Maria myt soißer vnd frolicher stymmen eyn lyebliches lyetgyn zo dryn stonden na eyn ander, vnd daz
kyntgyn Jhesus sange myt yre also: ›O myn aller lyebste fruntdynnen, ich hayn
dyr gegeben die sicherheit vnd daz ewige leben.‹ Dyß gesicht vnd auch der sanck
was alles yn dem geist vnd nyt yn den vßewendigen synnen.

Vff der heilger dry k<onynck> **Kap. 35**
Uff der heilger dry konynck dage da man schreyff mcclxxxix dar na an dem
zwolfften dage, da hait sie entphangen daz wirdige heilge sacrament myt groißer
lyeb*[272ᵛ]*den vnd begerden. Da sprach yre lyeffe yn yre, nyt myt vßerlicher
5 stymmen, sonder yn der selen, also das jn syner begeronge was: ›Jch geben dyr
myn aller lyebster drye gaben: Jch verzijgen dyr alle dyn sunden. Jch zegen dich
zo myr. Jch bestedigen dich yn myr selber, als wer iß sach, dastu noch nye eyn
hettes gesundiget. Vnd vber dyß sal ich dyr geben eyn vber fludige maiße.‹ Die
vberfloedige maiße was, daz sie alles sache vnd das sie das alles zo dem besten

---

32 vmb<fynge>] vmb   **34** ⸢der⸣ da] Da ⸢der⸣   **34,1** mcclxxxix] mcclxxx:ix *unsichere Lesung*
35,1 k<onynck>] k'

kert. Vnd da sie also yn syner lyebden sich bekommeren was, da sprach *[273ʳ]* er 10
zo yr: ›Jch hayn dich lyeffe, o du seliche sele, van gantzem mynem hertzen vnd
ich hayn dich erhoirt jn mynem hogen throne.‹

Kap. 36 Jn dem hogetzijt purificacionis da die andechtige jonffrauwe sultde entphangen
yren aller lyebsten heren, da wart sie gefort yn sent Nyclaes capelle, vnd da beytde
sie yrs lyeben. Yre pyne was also groiße, daz yr sele van burnender begerden alles
langens verdroiß. Eyne lyecht quam jn yre sele, daz ynwendich vnd vßwendich
lucht und brant. Der pryster bracht van dem chore ge*[273ᵛ]*dragen den lyeblichen 5
lycham godes. Den sach sie brengen, dan daz lyecht luchtet yn yrer selen vnd
durch die mům̆re. Daz eyn was nyt wonder. Got, der ist eyn bornendes fům̆er. Dar
vmb so sach sie yn, eer dan er quam. Da yre daz heilge sacrament gegeben wart,
da zofloiße yre sele als honyche vor dem fure van soißer lyebden vnd lyeblicher
soißicheit, sich zo gebruchen gotlicher woillust. Das gotliche lyecht was by yr. Als 10
der jonffrauwen by na dryßich zo dem heilgen sacrament gyngen, da sach sie yn
dem gotlichen lyecht, nyt myt den vßerlichen augen, das der jonffrauwen nuwe
waren, die sie myt namen woil *[274ʳ]* kante, daz yre hertzen sich vff daden als die
roißen, die sich entsließent yn dem dauwe vnd entgene der sonnen yre bleytder
vßstreckent vnd gantze vff gaynt. Vnd sy sach, daz das aller lyeblichstes kyntgen 15
Jhesus sich saitzet lyeblichen yn die roißen, vnd die roißen sloißen sich zo. Die
roißen betzeichent die reyne lyebde der hertzen. Da van wart yr ⌐sele⌐ gemeret
van lyebden vnd freuden myt groißer soißicheit. Sie fraget dar na eyn vnder den
nuwen, wie iß yr da gegangen hette, als sie daz heilge sacrament entphangen
hette. Da antwert sie yre, daz sie also groiße genade vnd soiß*[274ᵛ]*icheit hette 20
gehaitte vnd troiste van der entphanonge des heilgen sacramentz, als sie yn lange
zijt noch <ye> hette gehait.

Kap. 37 Uff daz hogetzijt der verkondionge Marie die verwende sele eyn haitte nyt rům̆ege
dan alleyn yn yrem lyebhaber. Also zoge sie die lyebliche begeronge, als sie dick
haitte gedayn vnd entphangen den hogelopten heren. Der macht myt yrer selen da
eyn lusteliche wyrtschafft myt vberflußicher soißicheit syner entgeynwirticheit.
Da bewyste yre got eyn konynckcliches pails. Daz was groißer dan das gantze 5
ertrich vnd iß was *[275ʳ]* jnwendich grone als graiße. Das was woil schonheit, her-
licheit, vnd alle freude was da yn, vnd iß was gestullet vmbet vmb. Aber sonderlichen was bereyt eyn gar lustlicher, zyerlicher throne vmbzyrckelt, doch so waren
dar an dry stulle vnderscheytden. Eyner was van roißen, der ander van lylien, der
drytte van vyolen. Dyßer throne myt synen vnderscheytden stullen was eyner der 10
hemelscher konynckynnen aller neste vnd bezeichent dryerley lude, die gode die

---

36,22 <ye>] be *? unsichere Lesung*

aller neste synt, als iß yr vffenbairt was worden: Die roißen beduten die getruwe
gantze lyebhaber, die lylien die reyne luter hertzen, *[275ᵛ]* die violen betzeychen-
ten die geware oitmodicheit. Da sach sie, das ⌐der⌐ aller lyebster here geynwir-
15 dige was yn yrer selen myt freuden. Syne augen brantten yn synem heubt als
eyn fackel. Eyne roiße woische vß synem hertzen, die gynge vff vnd sy verbreyte
yre bleyder also wyt vnd rychlichen, daz alle syne lycham vberzogen wart myt
der roißen gelicher wyße als myt eym cleytde. Die roiße woische vff vorbas vnd
streckste sich wonderlichen vnd vberzoge geweldenclichen myt yren blederen das
20 paillas als eynem dache, das *[276ʳ]* da by bezeichent wart, das die getruwe lyebde
vß dem gotlichen hertzen gewaißen was vber alle achtonge vnd vber alle lyebde
der engel vnd der lude. Die lyebde zwancke yn dar zo, daz er mensche geworden
ist, vnd er leyt den doit vmb vnser erloißonge willen. Die lyebde vbergeyt vnd
vbertryfft alle lyebde. Da sy also yn dyeßer beschauonge was vnd da myt yn got-
25 licher gebruchen myt vberflußicher soißicheit yn dießem paillas, vmbfynge der
lyeblicher got yre sele gar sere fruntlichen myt synem vmbfengen myt beytden
armen, myt eym yngoiße syner meynnunge, das er syne vßer*[276ᵛ]*wylten hie yn
dyeßem leben vmbfencket myt synem lyncken armen myt soißer genaden vnd na
dyeßem leben myt dem rechten armen der ewiger freuden. Da sprache der here zo
30 jrer selen: ›Erffrauwe dich, sele myn. Du haist mych also sicherlichen entphangen
yn dich, als myn moder mych entphynge yn yren reynen jonfferlichen lycham. Jch
wannen vil lyeber yn dyr dan yn mynem hemel.‹ Dar na ergaiffe sich yr sele vnd
lyeß sich yn eyne soiße ruwe vnd lyebde yn got.

Van dem oisterdage
Jn dem osterlichen hogezijtde die sele der selicher jonffrauwen was *[277ʳ]* jn eyme
gotlichen lyecht, da sie vil wonder schauwet vnd vnsprechelichen groiße genade
befant. Jn dem selben lyecht bewyste yr got x stuck der gotlicher wyßheit: das
5 irste, daz der mensche mache erkennen, wanne got myt syner genaden zo der
selen kommet, vnd daz geschyt myt eyner froelicher vnd soißer bewegonge des
hertzen. Die ander wyßheit ist, daz der mensche erkennet, wanne daz sich got
van der selen scheytdet, dan zo zuget er yr abe die genaden des soißen troistes vnd laist jr da betruppenyß. Die drytte wyßheit lyget gantze an der burnen-
10 der lyebden vnd begerden zo gode. *[277ᵛ]* Die iiij wyscheit ist, daz der mensche
erkennet, wanne er abe nemet an eym dogentlichen leben. Daz geschyet, wanne
die andacht vnd die hytziche begerde begynnet trache vnd kalt zo werden, dan
so gynth zorǔcke die dogent. Das eyn ist aber nyt abe genomen, dastu yetzont
wenich bedes, vastes vnd wachest ader alsoliche dynge yn vßerlichyen vbonge
15 abe legest, die wille du yn dyr beheldes daz fǔer vnd daz lyechte der lyebden,

---

16 fackel] falckel

want da wyrt die vßerliche vbonge hyn gezogen, vnd die ist vnnutzelicher dan
<ynnerliche> vbonge als gult vnd kepper. Die v wyßheit, daz der mensche erken-
net alle sunden *[278ʳ]* vnd vndogent, also daz sich der keyn eyn verbergen yn yme
eyn mache van reyner consciencien, was boiße an der selen ist. Die vj wyßheit ist,
daz der mensche erkenne*t*, was gutde ist, daz ist gotliche genade vnd alle dogent,   20
vnd lyden myt gedult vngemache an dem lybe, an gebresten, an noitdurfft, an
versmechen vnd an sulchen sachen, die genade vnd loyne mogent brengen. Die
vij wyßheit, daz man sich kan wyßelichen abegescheytden van dem boißen. Dan
ist iß die allerbeste wyßcheit, daz man eyner yglicher anfechtunge entgegen
mache komen vnd sy vberwynde, der ist beytde geistlich vnd auch fleß*[278ᵛ]*lich.   25
Die viij wyßheit, daz man sich kayn wyßelichen vben an dogenden vnd an guden
wercken. Dar vmb gyfft got genade vnd geistliche gaben, das der mensche die
also wyßelichen an leget vnd sy brenge byß zo guder vbonge der dogent, als eyn
vader befelet synem sone vnder syne hende eyn pont ader me, daz er das wyßelichen anlege vnd da myt gewynne als eyn wyßer kaůffman. Leget er das woil   30
an, er gyfft yme me. Jst er aber versůmelich, er nymt iß ym das selbe vnd er gyfft
iß eym anderen, als daz ewangelium spricht. *(vgl. Mt 25,14–30; Lc 19,11–28)* Die
9 wyscheit, daz der mensche syne hertze recht kayn vff gerechten an allen
sachen, iß sy geyn got vnd entgeyn synen *[279ʳ]* eben crysten, entgene prelaten,
entgene vndertanen, geyn fruntde, geyn vyantde, geyn yme selber, also daz er   35
doch alles verlybe vff dem rechten wege. Die x wyßheit, daz der mensche got
lobet yn allen dyngen, jn allen creaturen als eynen wyßen schepper vnd behelder, vnd yn allem, daz er doit ader vff erden verhenget vff yn ader yn dem hemel
vnd jn dem aptgront. Der loiffe komet vß eym guden wyllen, der myt gode vereyniget ist. Der zarte edel bruytgam hait yme syn bruyt bereyt na sym woil befallen.   40
Dar vmb hait sie alwege gehait eynnen lyffe vol lydens vnd eyn sele vol *[279ᵛ]*
alles guden. Sie hait zo beth gelegen verwont an yrem lybe beytde jnwendich yrs
lybs vnd vßwendich jn groißen krenckten, alstu hoirest beytde van godes verhen-
ckenyß vnd auch van groißer abstinencien.

Kap. 39 Drye jonfferen plagen zo denen dyeßer bruyt Christi, des heren, myt groißem
flyße vnd myt groißer andacht. Vnd vmb die groiße truwe, die sy zo yre haitten,
dar vmb macht sie sy deylhaifftich der wyrschaifft. Wanne sie was yn dem troiste
vnd gebruchen yrs aller lyebsten herens, dan so baitde sie alwege vor sie. Dar vmb
dede yn vnser here groiße vnd sonderliche genade, als daz woil zo myrcken ist,   5
dan *[280ʳ]* man eyn kayn noch eyn mache nyemans lyebers gedeynen ader gut
gedoyn dan synen lyeben fruntden. Des hayn myr woil eyn exempel van vnserem

17 <ynnerliche>] vßerliche **20** erkennet] erkennē **24** daz] eȳ daz **39,4** herens] herēs
Korrektur des Schreibers aus herès

herren Jhesu Christo, da er sent Johannes syne moder woille befellen, daz er yr
pleger were. *(vgl. Io 19,26)* Dar vmb dede er yme sonderliche genade. Er ließe yn
10 vff synem hertzen rogen. Er was alwege myt sonderlicher lyebden zo yme geney-
get, als myr dick leßen van yme. *(vgl. Io 13,23)* Also geschach iß auch dyeßen
heilgen jonffrauwen. Dar vmb das sie dyeßer vßerwilter fruntdynnen godes also
getruwelichen deyntten, so dede vnser herre yn sonderliche ˹genade˺ zo heil vnd
selicheit zo lybe vnd zo der selen. Dan wair*[280ᵛ]*haifftenclichen, wer dyße bǔche
15 vberleßet vnd gedencket daz wonder der genaden vnd der gotlicher lyebden, die
got an dyeßer reyner jonffrauwen, syner vßerwilter bruyt Christinen, gedayn hait,
der mache woil sprechen, das der selich sy geboren, den got dar zo vß erwilte hait,
daz er der selicher creaturen denen sultde. Also sprache vnser here yn yrer selen
van dyeßen dryn jonffrauwen: ›Dyeße dry jonffrauwen synt selich vnd sy dragent
20 reyne hertzen yn mynem namen.‹ Dyße was eyn anfancke mannyches fruntlichen
zosprechens, daz got yn yrer selen dick gar sere fruntlichen hait gereyt *[281ʳ]* van
dyeßen dryn jonfferen. O, was lyeblichen gesprechs, das got gewonlichen hait
gehait, wyrstu dicke hoiren her na, da du wyrste vynden eytzelichen wort, da
groiße befyndunge der genaden vnd soißicheit myt wonderlicher ynwendiger
25 beschauwonge, die also vnsprechlichen vnuerstendich synt vnser groppicheit zo
begryffen, als eynem wayllen eynen dutzen zo verstayn. Doch synt her geschreben der soißer sprechonge eyn deylle yn die hogetzijden, dar durch die gotliche
lyebhauenden hertzen got lobent sullent vmb genade vnd wirdicheit, die da verstanden wyrt manchfeldenclichen.

Jn dem hogetzij Agnetis virginis da sprach der here zo yrer selen: ›O du aller   **Kap. 40**
lyebste sele myn, jch byn eyn lyecht dyns hertzes, du byst myn lyebde vnd jch byn
der, der yn dyr rogen. Du salt myn ewige bruyt verlyben yn ewicheit.‹

[281ᵛ] Jn purifi*ca*cione beate Marie virginis wie yre sele myt gode vereyniget hait   **Kap. 41**
gestanden, hoire, wie er sprache zo *yre*: ›O myn seliche fruntdynnen, jch byn die
soiße lyebde, die yn dyner selen ist. Jch byn der, der sy erluchte. Jch byn yre ewyge
lyecht, sie schauwet yn myr. Dar vmb saltu hayn freude vnd freude sonder ende.‹

Dominica Inuocauit sprache der here zo syner lyebhaberynnen: ›Jch byne dyne   **Kap. 42**
bruytgam. Jch byn dyr eyne lyecht der clairheit aller wyßheit. O myn aller lyebste
bruyt, lege mych als eyne yngesegel vff dyne hertze. Vmbfancke mych fruntlichen
myt hertzelicher lyebden vnd betzwynge mych myt dynen armen sprechenden:
5 »Die lyebde ist also starcke als der doit.«‹ etc.

---

17 *nach* das der] got *gestrichen* **41,1** purificacione] purificione **2** zo yre] zo **42,1** Dominica
Inuocavit] Dominaca | Inuocavit **5** *nach* etc.] Die lyebde ist also starcke als ‖ der doit

Kap. 43 *[282ʳ]* An dem abent eßen des heren sprach der here zo yre:
›Ich byn das ewiche lyecht. Jch byn die lebendige sone, die da durchlucht vnd
schynnet yn dyne hertze. Jch geben mych dyr vnd ich fuegen mych zo dyner sele.
Du byst myn vßerwelte brŭyt vnd ich byn dyne lyebhaber.‹

Kap. 44 Nach oisteren hoirt sie dyeße wort:
›Jch byn eyn vader des lyechtz, yn dem dyne sele ewenclichen erlucht wyrt. Got
ist yn dyner selen vnd dyne sele ist yn gode vnd sy verlybet alwege by yme.‹

Kap. 45 In dem hogetzijt des heilgen Johannes vor der latyneser porten:
[282ᵛ] ›**O** du byst myn vßerwilte vnd ich byn dyn vßerwilter. Jch geben dyr die
hemelsche spyße vnd ich geben mych dyr gantze. O myn vßerwilte, gyffe myr
dyn gebloymtes hertze, da yn wille ich roigen myt dyner selen.‹ Da nach na dryne
dagen sprach der here zo yre: ›Ich byn der lebendige spegel, der da erluchtet den   5
hemel vnd die erde vnd das mere vnd alles, das dar yn ist. Jn dem spegel wyrt
erlucht dyne sele.‹

Kap. 46 Jn dem hogezijt vnsers heren vffartze dage sprach vnser here zo yre: ›Jch byn eyn
lyecht, daz da erlucht alle lyecht, yn dem alle dynge lebent sonder ende, yn dem
dyn *[283ʳ]* sele verlyfft ewenclichen.‹

Kap. 47 An dem pynstzdage sprach der here zo yr: ›Jch byn eyn burnendes lyecht. Jch
byn eyn erluchter des lyechtz. Jch byn eyn soiße stymme. Jch byn eyn spyße. Jch
byn eyn geber alles guden, aller soißicheit, vnd ich erfoillen hemel vnd erde myt
myner groißheit. Erfrauwe dich, du myn aller lyebste sele. Du salt syn, da got ist,
vnd du salt vereyniget werden myt gode.‹   5

Kap. 48 Jn dem hogezijt vnser heren lychams dage sprach der here zo yr: ›Jch byn das
lebendige wort vnd ich wannen jn dynem hertzen vnd du byst eyn tempel myns
hertzen. O myn vßerwil*[283ᵛ]*te sele, erfrauwe dich. Jch hayn dich lyeffe. O myn
sele, erfrauwe dich. Du byst myn vßerwilte, du salt gayn zo dem hemel vnd dich
erfrauwen myt mynen vßerwilten.‹   5

Kap. 49 An dem hogezijt der gebort des selichen Johannes des deuffers da was sie yn
groißer beschauwonge vnd soißer begerden. Der lyebhaber sprach zo yre: ›Du
aller lyebste sele myn, heiße van myr, was du wylt. O du aller vßerwilte myn,
heyße van myr, waz du wylt. Jch byn die gotliche lyebde. Die sone des lebens, die
hait dich gecleyt myt dem ewige lyecht. Du haist van myr alles gut. Die wyßheit   5

45,3 vßerwilte] vßer | wilte *radiert aus* vßer | wilter

ist dyn leben yn der ewi*[284ʳ]*ger gotheit.‹ In dem selben lyechte sprach der here zo yrer selen: ›O du zarte sele myn, du byst myn vnd ich byn dyne, ich ewenclichen by dyr wille syn. Jch byn der schone got, der riche got, der starcke got, der ewige got, der wyße got.‹ Vnd da sprache der here zo yr: ›Nu so fuege dyße
10 alles zosamen yn dyner selen. So byn ich schone van richeit vnd ich byn die riche schonet, die starcke wyßheit vnd die wyße starckeit, die seliche ewicheit vnd die ewige selicheit.‹

Jn dem dage des heilgen Vdalrici hait der here gereyt zo syner lyebhauerynnen **Kap. 50**
sprechenden zo yr: *[284ᵛ]* ›O myn eynige sele, ich hayn dyr gegeben die sicherheit myt dem coße myns montze. Frauwe dich, myn eynige sele. Du haist yn dyr dynen vßerwilten heren Jhesum Christum. Du myn eynige durdel dube, ich sal hayn die
5 wyrtschafft myt dyner selen.‹

Jn dem hogezijt der selicher Marien Madalenen sprach der here zo yre: ›O eynige **Kap. 51**
sele myn, dyne leben ist gar lyeblich. Du byst myn gar geweldich. Dyne bede wille ich erhoiren vnd ich wille erfullen dynen willen. Die selen, vor die du mych bedest, die sullent balde erloiset werden.‹ Sie hait gebeden vor dusent selen vnd
5 Hertwiges *[285ʳ]* sele. Vor die selen heiße sy dru hundert mißen leßen. Der here sprach zo yrer selen: ›O du aller selichste sele, jch hayn dich entfangen zo myr. Ich wille dich auch lyebhaben yn ewicheit. Jch rogen yn dyr als yn mym woilluystigen ryche. Jch wille dich myr geliche machen, als werre iß myr mogelichen ist.‹

An dem hogezijt der vffnemonge der selicher jonffrauwen Marien was dyeße **Kap. 52**
seliche jonffrauwe na yre gewonlicher wyße yn soißer beschauwonge vnd begerden. Da hait sie yren aller soisten heren entphangen. Er sprach zo yre: ›O du aller soiste sele myn, erfrau*[285ᵛ]*we dich. Jch hayn dich lyeffe. Du salt mych vmbfan-
5 gen myt der heilger vocht vnd myt der heilger lyebden, das synt die armen dyner selen, myt den du mych lyeblichen salt vmbfangen. Vnd wanne du mych also vmbfangen haist, so halt mych vaste na alle dynem willen, dan ich wille dich vbergißen vnd sencken yn der engel soißicheit.‹ Da sprache yre sele yn vnsprechlicher lyebden: ›O yr dochter van Jerůsalem, verkondiget mym lyeben, want ich
10 van lyebden krancke byn worden.‹ *(Ct 5,8)* Er sprach auch zo yr yn dem hogezijt der entheubtdigonge sent *[286ʳ]* Johannes: ›Myn aller lyebste fruntde, die kastigen ich hie vff erden. Myn lyeben fruntde, die behoitden ich vor gelucke dyeßer werelt. Myn aller lyebste fruntde, die zegen ich myt myner vederlicher roytden.‹ etc.

An dem hogezijt der gebort der selicher jonffrauwen Marien sprach der here zo **Kap. 53**
yrer selen: ›O du aller lyebste sele myn, jch byn eyn bornender got. Jch byn eyn

geweldicher got. Jch byn eyn erluchtender got. Jch byn eyn erluchter der selen. Jch byn der, der dyn hertze wyt machet jn der lyebden des ewigen lebens. *[286ᵛ]* Jch machen myt mym troist fruchtber dyne sele. Mych geluste zo sehen dyne 5 angesicht.‹ Da sprach sie zo yrem vßerwilten: ›Myn aller lyebster, kome her abe yn dynen garten.‹ *(Ct 4,16)* Da sprach der here zo yr myt soißer stymmen: ›Jch byn eyne bloyme dyns hertzens vnd eyn ruge dyner selen.‹

Kap. 54 Jn dem hogezijt des heilgen Mychaelis sprache der herre zo yre: ›O du ewirdige sele, ich hayn dich lyeffe. Jch wille dich machen dogenhaiffich. Jch wille dich setzen yn myn gezyertes ryche vnd yn den chore der engel, der yrtzengel, cherubyn vnd seraphyn, die van burnender lyebden *[287ʳ]* entphynt synt yn myner lyebden. Myt den saltu myn aller lyebste syn ewenclichen sonder ende myt 5 freuden. Da saltu dryncken nuwen wyne van myr van der stedicher flyeßender soißicheit myner gotheit vnd gotlicher naturen. O myn fruntdynnen, jch byn dyns hertzen vnd selen freude vnd eyn spegel dyner augen.‹

Kap. 55 Jn dem hogezijt der eilffe dusent jonfferen sprache der herre zo jre: ›O du vßerwilte bruytde myn, erfrauwe dich, want dyn allersoister bruytgam hait dich lyeffe. Jch spelen yn dyr das lyebliche spele. Myne freude vnd myn woillust *[287ᵛ]* ist yn dyr. Dyn sele ist yn myr gotlichen vereyniget. Du, myn bruyt, erkennest mych yn der luterheit dyns hertzes vnd du rŭegest altzijt soißelichen yn myr.‹ 5

Kap. 56 In dem hogezijt aller heilgen hait der aller lyeblichste myt soißelichen reytden gesprochyn zo syner vßerwilter: ›O du aller lyebste sele, wes begerstu nu me? Du haist eyn voil burnde lyebhaber. Du lebest na mynem willen. O du aller lyeblichste sele myn, was wyltu me? Du haist eyn sele vol ⌈der⌉ gotheit. Die dusent selen, da du vor gebeden haist, vnd Hertwyges sele, die erloißen ich yn dießer 5 nacht van der pynen vß dem fegefŭer vmb dyne lyebde. Dyeße selen saltu *[288ʳ]* alle myt freuden sehen yn myr. O du aller selichste sele myn, was wyltu nu me? Du haist eynen lyffe altzo mail vol guder wercke dyn. Dyne lyebhaber lebet yn dyr van den dusent selen, die der ewige got durch dyne lyebde vff aller heilgen nacht ledich vnd loiße zo freuden nam.‹ Da sprach dyeße seliche jonffrauwe: ›Da 10 ich was yn dyeßem lyeblichen lyecht, da sache ich also groiße lyebde vnd wunderlichen wonder, wie sere lyeblichen vnd fruntlichen der lyebliche got dyeße vorgenante selen entphynge yn die hemelsche herbryge. Da was der hemelsche vader wyrtde, der sone trosches vnd der heilge gei*[288ᵛ]*ste was schencker, der sie selber drencket myt dem cyperen wynne, van dem geschreben steyt yn dem 15 mynnenbuche: »Jch sal dryncken myn vßerwylten van dem wyne des drubens

---

5 Mych] Mẙch **56,1** In] N *Initiale fehlt* **2** wes] we:s

Cypri.« *(vgl. Ct 8,2)* Da sprach vnßer here zo den selichen selen: »Kommet, yre
gebenediten myns vaders, yn daz ryche, das vch ist bereyt van anbegynne.«‹
(Mt 25,34) Dar na sache sie, wie got eyn ygliche sele saitzet nach yrer wirdicheit.

20 Da erkant sie, daz die selen worden gode vnd sie zoegen yn sich die gotliche
lyebde yn vnsprechlicher soißicheit. Da wart got vnd die seliche selen vereyniget
myt eynem willen ewanclichen. *[289ʳ]* Alzo hantze worden dyeße selen erfoilt myt
gotlicher soißicheit vnd sie worden gespyßet myt dem hemel broitde, also daz
sie alle yrs vngemachs vergaißen. Da zofloißen sie yn got myt eym vnsprecheli-

25 chen gebruchen der soißer gotheit vnd lyeblicher menscheit. Dyese selen worden
myt luterer lyebden jn got gebreyt, also daz alle yre vernoifft erfoilt worden myt
freuden. Das geschet, wanne got syne gotliches lyecht yn sie gußet, daz dan die
selen van vnsprechlicher vbersoißicheit vnd vbersoißer woillust vberfließent.
Dan *[289ᵛ]* so sprechent sie myt groißer freuden: ›Myr hayn vnser heyllant vnd

30 selicheit vmbfangen. Myr eyn sullent jn nu noch nummerme gelaißen.‹ Da wyrt
eyn ygliche sele van lyebden droncken vnd van allen heilgen freuden. So werdent
sie swymmen van groißer lyebden vnd sie werdent gesencket yn den gotlichen
spegel, da yn werdent sie schauwen nue wonder, nue freude sonder vnderlaiße,
vnd dan so werdent sie sprechen dyeße wort van groißem wonder, das sie yn got

35 beschauwent: ›O almechtiger here, daz hal*be* deyl eyn hoirten myr nyt, da myr
noch waren yn dem leben, daz myr nu befyn*[290ʳ]*den. O herre, selich synt alle,
die da wannent yn dynem husche. Yn ewicheit der ewicheit sullent sy dich loben.‹

In dem hogezijt aller heilgen da was die seliche jonffrauwe jn woillust des geistes **Kap. 57**
vereyniget myt yrem lyeben. Vnd yre gebet was zo yrem lyeben vor die leben-
dichen vnd die doden. Sie hait gehoirt syn soiße stymme sprechenden yn yrem
geist myt dyeßen wortten: ›O du aller sanfftmodichste sele myn, wes begerstu

5 me? Du haist eyn hertze vol heilger begerunge vnd ynbrunsticher begerunge der
groißer lyebden. *[290ᵛ]* O du aller myldichste sele myn, was wyltu me? Du byst
myn eynige sele, die da vol ist der eyniger gotheit vnd wonderlicher dryfeldicheit.
O aller kůste sele myn, wes begerstu me? Dru dusent selen myt broder Jacobs sele
erloißen ich yn dyeßer nacht vß dem fegefeur vmb dyne lyebde. Die selben sullent

10 noch cccl jaire yn dem fegefeur syn gewest. Die lyebde hait sy dar vß erloist. Du
salt sie myt freuden beschauwen yn wonderlichem lyecht der ewicheit.‹ Hie
myrcke van yren groißen krenckten. Sie haitte des nachtes myt groißem ernste got
[291ʳ] gebeden vor dru dusent selen vnd vor broder Jacobs sele. Des gewert sy der
lyebliche got myt freuden yn dem edelen lyecht der hemelscher beschauwonge,

15 want jn dem lyecht sach sie groiße wonder, als we die heilgen engel myt groißen
schairen quammen vnd hoilten dyeße selen vß dem fegefůer. Vnd myt groißem

---

35 halbe] halte **57,1** In] N *Initiale fehlt* **16** schairen] scha:rē

schalle vnd froelichem gesange brachten sie yre lyeben burger gefurt zo hobe vor
den hemelschen konynck. Vnd vnser lyeber here entphynge sie myt allen hemelschen heyrre gar sere lyeblichen vnd froelichen. Vnd er sprache myt sym soißen
montde: ›Komet, yr ge[291ᵛ]benediten myns vader, vnd besytzet daz ryche, daz vch 20
ist bereyt van anbegynne der werelt.‹ Dyße was eyn vber soiße stymme vol alles
troistes. Da sache sie, daz vnser herre saitzste eyn ygliche sele yn yre wirdicheit,
vnd er sprache also: ›Jch byn eyn guter hyrt, der gut hyrt vnd soiße bruytgam byn
ich. Jch hayn myn schaiffe gefort yn die hemelsche weydte, yn daz grone bluende
paradijß vnd yn die engelsche chore vnd yn daz vnsprecheliche lyecht myner 25
gotheit vnd yn die suberlicheit myner menscheit vnd zo der rechter lyebden myns
vaders vnd zo der gutden des [292ʳ] heilgen geistes vnd zo der ewiger rugen, da
sie vnbedeckte sullen sehen mych, got vnd menschen, jn myner vollenkommener
tzyerheit, da sie luterlichen sullent beschauwen daz ewige wortte. Da synt dusent
jaire als der dage, der gysteren ist vergangen.‹ Jn dyeßem lyecht sprach got zo yr: 30
›Du salt van lyebden durch mych me lyden, dan du vor ye gelyeden haist, vnd
daz doch geduldenclichen nach alle mynem willen.‹ Das geschache zo hantze.
Got lacht eyn wonderliche groiße krenckt vff sye, die sie angynge yn dem dage
vnd yn der nacht [292ᵛ] cehen stonde, vnderwyllen mynner, vnderwillen me. Vnd
daz lyden daz wert byß nach der completen, das der conuent slaiffen quam. Vnd 35
iß was eyn amacht vnd dar na eyne groiße erbieben aller yrer gelyeder myt eym
erschuderen aller yrer lybs, byße also lange daz alle yre gelyeder zobrachen vnd
erstorben. Dar na wart eyn hertze brechen. Vnd auch wart gehoirt vnderwillen die
groiße kreche, die van yrem hertzen quammen, das man iß hoirt jn aller wyße als
eyn lyebliche sterben vnd jemerliche doitlich verscheyden. So eyn vil yre dan das 40
heubt. Vnd alle yre gelye[293ʳ]der lagen vor doit eyn lange tzijt. Yre zeynne byße
sie hart zosamen. An alle yrem lybe sluck ader weget noch nye keynne ader. Jre
augen stunden vffen. Noch nye keyns adems eyn wart man gewar, daz ich selber
versucht vnd befant. Vnd alle, die by yre waren, die sprachen, daz sy nye grußeli-
cher doit gesehen hetten, als sie leyt zo eym yecklichen mail. Jch, broder der dyße 45
schryben, was auch da geynwirdich. Vnd ich gedacht an die jemerliche erbiebonge des lyeblichen Jhesus, daz er leyt an dem [293ᵛ] crutze, da van das ertrich
erbiebet, so iß aber lancke wart, ee sy wieder zo yre selber quemme. Aber die tzijt
als die crenckt noch wert, da was yre sele, daz ist das vberste verstentenyß der
selen ader des ynnerlichen menschen, das was yn der vbersoißer begerunge, als 50
sie myr selber hait gesait. Auch van der tzijt an wart yre vff gedayn der hemel byß
zo der metten tzijt. Da wart yre abe genomen die geynwyrdiche crenckt vnd yre
sele was yn eym hemelschen lyecht. Vnd sy was vereyniget myt gode yn lyebden
vnd freuden [294ʳ] selencklichen, als her na geschreben stet beytde als van der

37 yrer] yrer aller yrer 47 dem] den

55 krenteit vnd auch van der schonen gaben, die yre got gaiffe yn der krenckten.
Das doch noch vil me was, daz der edel got yren lyffe vnd yre sele gereyniget van
allen yren sunden, vnd er hait yme selber eyn woil befallende wannunge da yn
erkoren, so wolt er sy zegen na alle synem willen vnd woiltde sy machen yn der
lyebden, daz sye yme were eyne wieder bezaillunge syner marterlen vnd daz sie
60 da van oppert, also daz der crystenheit nutze vnd hul*ffe* dar van queme, gode
zo lobe, *[294ᵛ]* vnd zo beßerunge manches menschen. Dar vmb so gaiffe yr got
dyeße krancheit van lyebden, die er jre auch abe namme yn der zijt, als er yr auch
vor verkundiget haitte.

Jn dem dage der heilger Katherynnen sprach er zo yre: ›Erfrauwe dich, zarte **Kap. 58**
bruytde myn, du soiße blome myns hertzen. Jch erfrauwen mych yn alle dynen
gelyederen. Jch wyrcke yn dyner selen vnd yn allen dynen gelyederen der hoger
lyebden wercke myt der vereynionge dyns willens myt myner gotheit vnd myt der
5 *[295ʳ]* luterer erkentenyß mynner gotheit vnd ewicher wyßheit, da yn du nyt eyn
machs bedrogen werden. Du byst eyn hemelsche suylle der lebendigen vnd der
doden. Die lebendigen heillestu yn lyebden vor myr, als jch sy yn lyebden hayn
erloist myt mynem durberen bloytde an dem crutze myt myns vaders kraifft. Aber
die doden erloistu stetlichen vß dem fegefeur myt dynem lyden.‹ Dar na sprache
10 vnßer here dyeße wort: ›Myn wyßheit vnd clairheit synt yn myr besloißen myt
ewi*[295ᵛ]*ger freuden, fryheit vnd soißer ruwe vnd vol aller selicheit. Jch setzen
mych vor vch zo eynigen ewigen verbande, daz yr mych ewenclichen sullent
loben. Vnd yr sullent erkennen mynne wonderliche wonder, den ich wyrcken
durch myn heilgen sonder vffhoirunge. Jn myr synt alle dynge vollenbracht vnd
15 besloißen.‹

Jn dem hogezijt der entfanonge der selicher jonffrauwen Maria sprache der here **Kap. 59**
zo yre: ›O du vßerwillette bruytde myns hertzes, wes begerstu me? Du haist die
hoge gedoit*[296ʳ]*de lyebde. O myn sele, wes begerestu me? Du haist gegryffen yn
mynen vbersten throne, daz ist yn myn ere vnd hogen keyßerlichen ynflußen vnd
5 der soißer lyebden ynfloiße, die dyne sele durch floißen hait vnd sencket dich
stetlichen yn mynne gotheit, vnd die kraifft dyner lyebden flußet wieder vmb yn
mych. Das ist daz waißer der hoger lyebden vnd aller heilgen ynfluße, der zo allen
zijtden flußet sonder vff hoiren. In den bystu gesencket myt vbersoißer woillust.
O myn sele, hoire myn stymme vnd be*[296ᵛ]*halt myn wort. Du salt got durch got
10 laißen, das ist myn hogester wille vnd dyne hogester loyne vnd ist der groißer
lyebden recht.‹

---

60 hulffe] hul | ffpe   **59,3** gedoitde] *Bedeutung unklar*

Kap. 60 Jn dem hogetzijt des heilgen Nycolay hait der lyebliche got, der soiße troiste aller bedroiffter hertzen, mit begerden vnd verlangen als eyn bruytgam zo syner aller lyebster bruyt gesprochen zo der selen: ›O du aller heillichste sele myn, erfrauwe dich vnd erfrauwe dich. Dyn aller lyebster bruytdegam kommet zo dyr vnd er suchet heymlicheit by dyr vnd er gußet sich gentz*[297ʳ]*elichen yn dych myt 5 eym gotlichen jnfluße alles guden. Vnd ich vereynigen mych myt dyr myt selicher gantzheit, vff dastu myt myr werdest eyn geist. Myt vnsprechlicher freuden wyrstu gesencket yn das ewige wort.‹ Vnd daz ist eyn vereynionge des heilgen geistes.

Kap. 61 Jn dem hogetzijt der gebort Christi die gewaire sonne Christi vnd der schyne des vederlichen hertzens erlucht yre hertze, vnd got was bereyt, yme zo machen eyn waillustige wannunge yn yr, vnd er sprach also zo yrer selen: ›O du aller beste sele myn, erfrauwe dich vnd erfrauwe dich der groißen *[297ᵛ]* lyebden, want der behelder der werelt wannet yn dyr. Du byst myr die aller lyebste vnd die aller 5 lyeblichst wannunge myn, die ist jn dyr. Du byst die arche, yn der ich besloißen byn. Jch byn eyn lychter sterne yn dyr luchten, der nummerme vnder geyt. Jch byn eyn schynne des ewigen lyechtz, entgene dem alle lichter eyn dusternyß synt. Aber yn dem selben lyecht bystu erlucht. Jch byn eyn spegel der luterer clairheit, yn dem dyn sele erluchtet ist, vnd yn dem lyecht sehet sy myn groiße wonder 10 wercke. Du byst dyr doit vnd lebest ewenclichen yn myr myt froelicher vnd geistlicher *[298ʳ]* freuden vnd myt groißer jubilacio ewiger lyebden.‹

Kap. 62 Hie myrck an, wie sie yre hertze myt gantzer begerden keret zo gode.
In der selber nacht begerte sie zo hoiren die crystemyße vnd yre hertze was vol burnender begerden vnd furyger lyebden. ›Da wart myr der hemel vff gedayn vnd beytde hemel vnd erde was fließen van honych vnd mylche. Da wart myn sele van godes hant erfolt myt eym gotlichen ynfluße vnd myt allen geistelichen 5 freuden. Da sancke myn lyebhaber myner selen myt froelicher stymmen dyeßen sancke: »Myn fruntdynen, kere *[298ᵛ]* dich her zo myr, daz myr dich ansehen. Dyne stymme ist soiße yn mynen oren vnd dyne angesicht ist suberlich.« *(Ct 2,14)* Da sprach myn sele zo yme myt groißer freuden: »Myn sele ist weche geworden, *(Ct 5,6)* als myn lyeffe myr hait gereyt.« Vnd syne bylde ist yn mym hertzen gedru- 10 cket myt eyniger furiger lyebden, die nummer me verleißen eyn mache.‹

60,2 syner] syner se|len **61,1** gebort Christi] gebort xp̄s sonne Christi] sonne xp̄c
10 wonder] wor|der **62,2** In] N *Initiale fehlt* **11** lyebden] lyebe|dē

Van vnsprechlicher krenckten, die sie leyt jn dem dage der vnschuldiger kynder. **Kap. 63**
›Jn dem dage der vnschuldiger kynder wart myn hertze ynbrunstige vol aller starcker lyebden, als abe iß van lyebden *[299ʳ]* wultde zobrechen. Da sprach myn
lyebehauer yn myr: »Die lydonge dyner k*renck*ten, die du vor aller heilgen dage
5 gelyeden haist beytde ynwendich vnd vßwendich, an dynem hertzen van kreyff-
tiger lyebden vnd vßewendich van vnmacht, byß her, die sal van dießem dage
werden gemert an dyr ynwendich vnd vßwendich byß vber ix wochen also swerlichen, daz alle dyne gelyeder erbieben vnd erkrachen sullent. Vnd sie sullent
swerlichen lyden durch myner lyebden willen, dan du byß heren haist gelyeden,
10 vnd daz *[299ᵛ]* na alle mynem willen. Myt dyeßer kranckeit saltu myr geben eyn
wieder beloynunge myt eyner danckberer lyebden myns lydens, daz ich vor dich
vnd alle die werelt gelyeden hayn.«‹ Das geschache alles, als yr got verkondiget,
daz yr dyeße kranckeit zo komen sultde. Vber eyne kortze zijt da vielle sie an also
groiße kranckeit des hertzes vnd des lybes, das sich alle die verwondertden, die
15 sy sachen, als auch da vor geschreben steyt. Die gotliche lyebde nam vberthant
an yr myt also groißer *[300ʳ]* mans kraifft vnd myt also woillustiger soißicheit vnd
myt also groißer lyebden, das dyeße hertze die volheit der vnsprechlicher lyebden
nyt enthalden mocht vnd van der gotlicher vbersoißicheit des hertzen bewegonge
sich vßbreyt siechtlichen, also daz das hertze myt dem lybe vff woische hoge.
20 Vnd die noit, die das hertze leytde van der gotlicher hytzsten, die streckte sich
vß van dem hertzen yn die armen, das sie alle yre gelyeder also streckte van yr.
Vnd sie verlyeffe gerat vnd gantze verstreckte als eyn staiffe. Dyße wert byß zo
sent Agneten dage. ›Da sach *[300ᵛ]* ich myt eyner geistlicher beschauonge yn
dem gotlichen lyechte. Ich sache dry aderen vberfludenclichen fließen van gode.
25 Vnd got der here sprache zo myr: »Das ist daz bloitde, da myt du vil menschen
behalden machest hie vff ertrich, vnd du erloißes vil selen vßer dem fegefuer.«‹
Vnd alles hemelsche heyre erfrauwet sich desselben dags, da yr lycham was jn
der kranckeit vnd die sele yn der soißer lyebden sich zo bekommeren. Da wart
yre sele gefůrt durch die ix chore der engel vnd vor die heilge dryfeldicheit. Da
30 besloiße er sy yn syne gotliches hertze. Da be*[301ʳ]*schauwet yre sele sich selber,
wie sie was gecleyt myt eym roytden cleytde. Da sprache der lyebhauer zo yre: ›O
myn allerlyebste sele, ich hayn dich edel gemacht myt mym durberen bloitde vnd
ich hayn dich getzijert myt myner luterer gotheit vnd ich hayn dich gespyßet myt
des heilgen geistes soißicheit.‹ Dar na quam der lyebhaber vnd kroynet sy myt iiij
35 cronen: zo dem irsten myt der cronen der gerechticheit vnd myt der cronen gotlicher dogent vnd myt der cronen gotlicher wyßheit vnd myt der cronen gotlicher
lyebden. Sehent, *[301ᵛ]* wie woillenkomenclichen sy gezert ist gewest yn allen
dogenden vnd wie hytzich sy ist geweste entphenget yn der gotlicher lyebden.

4 krenckten] kenthtē

Dar vmb er yr hait geloifft zo geben die mytgeselschafft der ix chore der engel,
vff daz sie yn stediger hytzsten der lyebden alwege sultde verlyben ynne gebe- 40
nedienden myt den furygen engelen. Er hait yr auch geloifft dar zo den verdynst
aller heilgen, als *er* sprache zo yrer selen den dornstage na sent Agneten dage: ›O
du lyebhauende sele myn, erfrauwe dich. Du byst eyn claires lyecht vor mynen
augen. Jch wille dyr vff doyn na dyeßem leben die ix *[302ʳ]* chore der furiger
engel. Jch wille dyr geben aller merteler loyne vnd aller heilgen vnd aller engel 45
freude, vnd aller jonffrauwe wyrdicheit saltu yn dem chore der furiger seraphyn
besytzen.‹ ›Da was ich yn der soißer begerunge myns aller soisten bruytgams vnd
er sprache zo myr: »Kynt myns, lege dyne lyden kreifflichen yn mych. Du salt
noch hude erbieben an allen dynen geliederen, als myn menscheit erbiebet an
dem heilgen crutze vmb die menscheliche nature, vnd daz sal dyr geschegen vmb 50
die selbe tzijt.«‹ Vnd daz geschache also. Van sexten byß zo nonen leyt sy vnsprecheliche er*[302ᵛ]*biebonge vnd brechonge aller yrer gelieder vnd krachonge des
hertzen van groißer lyebden gelicher wyße eyns sweren sterbens yn aller wyß,
als da vor geschreben ist. Da wart jre sele gezucket yn den nunten chore vnd da
wart yre bewyst jre wirdicheit, die sie ewenclichen besytzen sultde. Vnd yre sele 55
wart gecronet myt eyner cronen van zwolff steynen gelicher als zwolffe sternen.
(vgl. Apc 12,1) Vnd yre vßerwilter bruytgam vnd syne moder songen jre myt eyner
soißer stymmen dyeßen lyeblichen loiffe: ›Sicheit des ewigen lebens geben ich
dyr vnd vollenhyrtunge byß an das ende.‹

Kap. 64 *[303ʳ]* Jn dem hogetzijt purificacione beate Marie sprach der here troistenden zo
yrer selen: ›O du aller myldeste sele myn, erfrauwe dich. Der konynck yn dem
hemelschen throne hait dich lyeffe vnd van allen dynen geliederen hait er freude
van dyr. Jch, dyne got, wyrcken yn dyner selen die edel wercke der hoger lyebden
myt nuwer freuden als yn dem hemel. Vnd ich eyn mach myn angesicht nyt van 5
dyr gekeren, dan ich hayn eyn wannunge fonden yn dyr na alle mynem willen.
Dyne lyebde ist yn dyr eyn orspruncke aller dogent. Du verbreytdest dyne *[303ᵛ]*
lyebde yn die gantze werelt den lebendigen vnd den doitden. Dar vmb saltu yr
aller loyne vnd wirdicheit entphangen. Du byst eyn duyffte myner wyßheit. Myn
wille ist an dyr gantze erwoilt.‹ Vff den dornstage na dem hogezijt lyecht mysse 10
da was die andechtige sele yn yrer betrachtonge. Gedencke, wie sie got troiste yn
yrem lyden, vnd er sprach also:
›Erfrauwe dich, myn dochter, das der vndoitlicher got doitlichen ist worden vmb
dich. Dyne pyne ist myr eyn freude. Dyne arbeit ist myr eyn ruwe. Dyne armoit
ist myr eyn rychtum. Dyne smaicheit ist myr eyn ere. Dyne doit ist myr *[304ʳ]* eyn 15
leben.‹ Dar na vff den frytdage sprach er aber eynß zo yre: ›O myn sele, erfrauwe

dich. Dyne arbeit dragen ich myt dyr, dan du lydest vor alle die crystenheit myt myr, want dyn dogenhaifftich leben wyrstu myt myr vereynigen hie vff dyeßem ertrich. Dar vmb saltu gar na by mych gesaitzet werde als myn bruyt yn daz hemel-
20 riche. Dyn lyebde erfoilt alle myn wunden, die ich leyt, vnd alle myn gelyeder beytde nacht vnd dage. Seße dusent dru hondert lxxij wonden die fließent vol myldicheit, soißicheit vnd lyebde vnd barmhertzicheit.‹ ›Dar na an dem sondage da wart myn sele *[304ᵛ]* van groißer lyebden vff getzogen vor got. Da was myn sele vereyniget myt gode yn eyner soißer gebrǔchonge. Da sancke der lyebhaber
25 myner selen dießen sancke: »**E**rffrauwe dich durch die ix chore der engel, dye synt yn dyr van myner geynwyrdicheit. Jch byn wairhefftich ane dyr vfferstan-den. Du haist erfoilt mynen willen myt allen dogenden heillenclichen. Du haist an dym bloytde vnd an dynem lybe vmb myner lyebden willen vor alle die werelt gelyeden, als ich auch jn groißer lyebden hayn gelyeden vor dich. Hemel vnd erde
30 erfrauwen sich van dynem lyden. Du wannest yn der grondeloißer dyefften der heilger *[305ʳ]* dryfeldicheit.«‹

Sie sehent, wie sie also groiße vnsprecheliche krenckten lyet vor den conuent vnd **Kap. 65** vor alle sunder, als er sprache zo yre yn dem dage des heilgen Valentini: ›**E**rfrauwe dich, du myn zarte daube. Du salt van lyebden lyden gar groiße pyne. Jch byn myt dyr vnd helffen dyr dragen alle dyne arbeit. Du salt vor dyeßen
5 conuent vnd vor alle sunder erbieben, als myn menscheit vor alle der werelt erbiebet an dem crutze. Du hast erfoilt die sieben flyeßende fluße myns bloitze, yn den du stetlichen wannest.‹ Syne bloyt ist darvmb sieben flußich, want iß verstrau*[305ᵛ]*wet hait die sieben heubt sunden. Das erbieben geschache zo hantze yn aller wyße, iß auch davor geschreben ist. Na dem hertzen brechen
10 da wart jre sele gesencket yn eyn gotliches lyecht vnd sie wart vereyniget jn got yn der heymlicher vber woillustiger lyebden. ›Da ich vnsprechlichen troistonge haitte myt gode. Vnd dar na aber eyns sprach er zo myr:
»**O** myn vßerwilte sele, du salt dyne arbeit froelichen lyden jn myr, want die gewailt myner gotheit vollenbrenget mynen willen an dyr. Als myn menscheit
15 erbiebet an dem crutze, also saltu erbieben van lyebden zo v stonden, also daz man auch eyn crachen sal hoiren van alle dynen *[306ʳ]* glyederen. O seliche sele myn, als ich van lyebden hayn gelyeden vor dich, also lydestu viel vnd groiße dynge geduldenclichen durch mych. Dar vmb so wille ich erhogen *dich* zo gar groißem loyne yn dem ewigen leben.« Aber eyns sprache der herre zo *myr*: »**O** du
20 eirwirdige sele myn, erfrauwe dich. Du, die da byst edel gemacht vnd getzijrt myt dem goltde myner groißer lyebden, du byst gecleyt myt dem wyßen helfenbey-

---

25 Erffrauwe] *Lombarde steht in der Zeilenmitte.* **65,1** Sie] *Lombarde steht in der Zeilenmitte.*
18 erhogen dich] erhogen **19** zo myr] zo O] *Lombarde steht in der Zeilenmitte.*

nnen *(vgl. Ct 5,14)* myner menscheit vnd myner reyner oitmodicheit. Du salt vmb myner lyebden willen drye stonden erbieben vnd erkrachen vor alle die werelt vnd vor alle selen yn dem fegefuer vnd vor alle sunder, als ich vor die werelt erbyebet hayn an dem stamme des crutze. *[306ᵛ]* Alle heilgen vnd alle engel vnd 25 alle geist erfrauwent sich vnd verwonderent sich van dynem lyden. Du salt syn eyn konynckynnen yn mynem ryche.«‹ Vnd also hait sie gelieden vnsprechelichen krenckten yrs lybes vnd yres hertzen. Also als daz golt wyrt geproffet yn dem fůer, *(vgl. Prv 17,3)* also ist sie gantze durch luter worden jnwendich vnd vßewendich durch yre groiße lyebde vnd gedult, die sy leytde vor alle die gantze werelt. 30 Aber alle yre krenckten vnd lyden synt gekeret worden yn eyn groiße soißicheit. Vnd dar na sprach er zo yre:

›O du luter lůchtende sele myn, myne suberliche durdeldube, du byst sonder flecken. Du salt *[307ʳ]* van myner lyebden zwoe stonden erbieben vnd erkrachen, als myn menscheit erbiebet an dem crutze. Du, myn lyebe bruytde, lyedeste vor 35 alle die werelt vnd vor alle selen, als ich auch van lyebden gelyeden hayn vor alle die werelt. Du, myn frundynen, byst eyn vberwynnerynnen, die myt myr vberwunden hait, als ich vberwonden hayn an dem crutze. Myns vaders willen wart an myr erfoilt vnd myn wille ist an dyr erfoilt. Die pyne dyns erbiebens sal noch hude eyn ende nemen an dyr. O myn sele, ich hayn dich hoge erhaben myt selen 40 vnd myt lybe yn eyne gotliches lyecht vnd yn die lyebde des heilgen geiste, das alle *[307ᵛ]* dyne wercke vnd vbonge sullent getzogen werden yn daz burnende fůer der gotlicher sonnen, daz nummer verleßen eyn sal yn dyner selen. Jch geben mych dyr na alle dynem willen.‹

Kap. 66 Dar na yn dem sondage Jnuocauit sprach er aber eyns zo yrer selen: ›Erfrauwe dich vnd habe mych lyeffe vnd lobe mych. O dochter van Syon, vßerwilte bruytde godes, was wyltu me? Hemel vnd erde synt erfoilt van der groißheit dyner lyebden vnd dyner wirdicheit. O sele myn, ich hayn dich erhaben vber die ix chore der engel. Du byst gotlichen gesencket yn die hemelsche wyrtschafft, yn 5 die soiß*[308ʳ]*icheit myner zarter gotheit.‹

Kap. 67 Van den vij freuden der selicher jonffrauwen Marien, wylche yr got hait gevffenbairt. Yn dem hogezijt der verkondige Marie hait der here aber eyns zo yr gereyt sprechende: ›O du alle vberste sele myn, erfrauwe dich. Myn hertze hait dich lyeffe. Jch byn yn mym vader vnd du byst yn myr vnd ich yn dyr.‹ ›Als ich was yn dießem lyecht, da verkontiget got myr die sieben freuden: Die irste ist, daz 5 die vollenkomenheit der eren yrs sons alleyn vbertryfft alle ere der engelen vnd aller heilgen. Die ij ist, daz sie vber alle chore der engel ist erha*[308ᵛ]*ben vnd sy

---

33 *vor* O] A *Lombarde* **38** hait] haist **67,3** O] *Lombarde steht in der Zeilenmitte.*

ist der heilger dryfeldicheit der aller neste. Die iij freude ist, als der dage erlucht
wyrt van der sonnen, also ist alle der hemelsche hoiffe erfrauwet worden van der
10 clairheit jrer entgeynwirdicheit. Die iiij freude ist, daz alle die burger des hemelschen hoiffs yre sonderliche ere vnd eirwirdicheit erbiedent als eyner moder des
vbersten konyncks. Die v freude ist, das der wille der heilger dryfeldicheit vereyniget ist myt yrem willen. Als was da befellet yren willen, das ist auch yn der vereynionge des willens der heilger dryfeldicheit. Die vj freude ist, das alle die, die
15 yre deynent, das den nach yrs hertzen *[309ʳ]* willen der loyne da wyrt gegeben.
Die vij freude ist, daz sy des alle zo mail sicher ist, daz die vollenkomenheit jrer
freuden nummer van yre genomen eyn salle werden ader gemyndert werden.‹

In dem sondage yn dem lyden vnßers heren hait er aber eyns myt yre gereyt myt   **Kap. 68**
eym fruntlichen vnd lyeblichen zoreytdunge der soißer wort. Vnd er sprach zo
yrer selen:
›**O** du aller starckste sele myn, erfrauwe dich, myn frundtynnen. Jch hayn dich
5 geclarificeret jn myner lyebden vnd yn myner lyebden saltu vmber vnd ewenclichen leben. Myt hoger lyebden der beschauonge hayn ich mych dyr ge*[309ᵛ]*geben.
Du haist eyn vollenkomen ‹...›. O du aller lyebste sele, wes begerstu me? Du ley-
ffest yn dem gesmacke myner gotlicher soißicheit, da ersterckestu dich yn die
jnwendigen ‹soißicheit› myner gotheit.‹
10 **D**ominica jn passione hait er aber eyns myt yre gereyt myt gutlichen wortten. Vnd
er sprache zo yrer selen:
›**O** du aller starckiste sele myn, erfrauwe dich myn, frundynnen myn. Jch hayn
dich yn myner lyebden geclarificeret. Jn myner lyebden saltu vmmer vnd evenc-
lichen leben.‹

In cena domini dixit jterum ad animam: ›**O** aller eirwirdichste sele myn, erfrauwe   **Kap. 69**
dich, frundynnen myn. Du haist den *[310ʳ]* rychen genaden ort besetzen eytzont,
der dich hie selich macht vnd yn myns vaders ryche ewanclichen. Du haist mych
luterlichen vnd soißelichen jn die vberste wailluste verborgen. Sele myn, was
5 wiltu nu me? Dyne lyebde, die burnet als seraphyn. Myne wille ist, das vrer wille
vmmer me vor sich gehe. Alle vre bedruppenyß sal eyne gut ende nemen.‹

---

15 deynent] deÿnet **68,1** In] *Lombarde steht in der Zeilenmitte.* **7** *nach* vollenkomen]
Der Satz bricht unvollständig ab. **9** ‹soißicheit› myner] myner *Konjektur aus ähnlich Kap. 71*
(Bl. 311ʳ) **10–14** Dominica *bis* leben] *leicht variierte Wiederholung der vorherigen Passage*
13 *nach* Jn myner] selen *gestrichen* **69,1** In] *Lombarde steht in der Zeilenmitte.*
O] *Lombarde steht in der Zeilenmitte.* **2** dich] dich myn

Kap. 70 Jn dem dage der wiedervfferstentenyß vnsers heren synt erloiste worden zwoilffe
dusent selen van yren verdynsten.

›O aller suberlichste sele myn, erfrauwe dich. Du byst eyn getzijert ryche, yn
dem ich froelichen ruwen vnd selenclichen wannen. Du haist *[310ᵛ]* entfangen
yn myr das fůer der gotlicher hytzsten. Dyner lyebden bewegonge spannet sich   5
yn mych vnd du versmiltzest van der gotlicher soißecheit yn myr. Du byst das
broit der gotlicher lyebden, myt dem ich gespyßet werden. Du byst eyn was aller
dogent, myt dem ich werden gedrencket. Du byst eyn arche der genaden, jn der
ich, got vnd mensche, wannen myt eynem claren lyecht vnd myt ewiger lyebden
als yn mynem hemel. Jch nemen yn dyßer nacht xii m selen vß dem fegefůer, die 10
haistu myt der arbeit dyns lydens vnd myt der biebonge dyner gelyeder erloist. Sie
solden zwey dusent jare vnd dru hundert jaire yn der pynen synne gewest. Durch
dyner lyebden *[311ʳ]* willen synt sy alle erloiste worden. Du salt myt yn allen loyne
entphangen vnd du salt sie myt freuden sehen jn dem spegel der heilger dryfeldicheit.‹   15

Kap. 71 Jn dem dage der vffstigonge des heren hait er gesprochen zo yr: ›Du aller edelste
sele myn, erfrauwe dich. Jch byn der weche, den du gehest yn die ynwendige
soißicheit myner gotheit. Da wyrstu geleret alle wairheit. Dar na bystu komen
myt luterheit vnd du segest an den willen myns vaders. Jch hayn dyr gegeben die
clairheit, die myr myn vader hait geben, daz myr vereyniget syn. Myn vader ist yn   5
myr vnd ich yn yme vnd du byst yn vns. Alles das ich hayn, das ist dyne, vnd was
du haist, daz ist myn.‹

Kap. 72 Vff den pynxstage sprach der here *[311ᵛ]* zo yrer sele:
›O du gar geweldige sele myn, erfrauwe dich, fruntdynnen myn. Ich behaltden
dich yn myner clairer gotheit. Dyne hertze ist eyn huße vol lyechtz vnd dyne sele
ist eyn tempel vol myner gotheit. Du byst eyn lebendiges buche, gezeyget myt der
heilger dryfeldicheit. Du byst versiegelt myt den sieben gaben des heilgen geistes   5
yn der heilger dryfeldicheit.‹

Kap. 73 Jn dem dage des selichen Johannes des deufferß sprach der here aber eyns zo
yrer selen:
›O du aller suberlichste sele myn, erfrauwe dich, frundynnen myn. Du byst myn
seliche wannunge, die ich myr hayn vßerwilt vnder mynen heilgen. Jch ruwen
stetlichen myt mynen *[312ʳ]* freuden yn dyr als yn mynem hemel, vnd des byn ich,   5
Jhesus Cristus, dyn lyeber bruytgam. Du byst eyn roiße vnder den merteler van
dynen lyden. Du salt dyne jonffraueweliche crone dragen myt sonderlicher wir-

---

70,10 dyßer] dußer   **71,2** weche] we:che   gehest] gehet

dicheit. O du aller lyebste sele myn, wes begerstu me? Du byst myt myr vereyniget
jn gotlicher lyebden yn dem abgront myner gotlicher lyebden vnd vnsprecheli-
10 cher gutdicheit. Du flußest myt vberfludicher lyebden. Jch byn yn dyr vnd du salt
syn yn myr yn ewicheit der ewicheit.‹

Hie myrcke die groiße ere vnd wirdicheit, wie sie got erhaben hait yn yrer selen **Kap. 74**
vor allen hemelschen heyre, als er sprache zo yre yn dem hogetzijt der heilger
Marien Magdalenen:
[312ᵛ] ›**O** du aller begerlichste sele myn, erfrauwe dich myt selen vnd myt lybe
5 ewenclichen yn myner gotlicher eren. Du haist yn dyner koistelicher selen den
wieder glantz des gotlichen schyntze. Der gotliche mynnen fluße der vberster
soißicheit ist also groißelichen yn dyr, das alle geist sich verwonderen van der
dyefften des vnsprechelichen gutz, daz da verborgelichen ist yn dyr. O seliche
sele myn, wes begerstu me? Jch hayn mynen throne jn dich gesaitzet vnd du byst
10 der throne, yn dem ich wannen. Dyne wille ist myt mynem willen vereynget.‹ O,
was groißer soißicheit vnd troistes hait sie da befonden jn der vereynigun, ⌐die⌐
da vnmogelichen synt den menschelichen zongen [313ʳ] vß zo sprechen, wylche
got yre hait gevffenbairt hie yn dieße leben.

Vnd er sprache zo yre also in assumpcione beate Marie virginis: **Kap. 75**
›**O** du aller myldeste sele myn, erffrauwe dich. Du haist der engel leben yn dyner
selen clairheit vnd zyerde dyner freuden vnd die crone dyner eren vnd den schaitze
des vbersten gůtz. Selicheit alles rychtums vnd aller eren vnd wallust wannet yn
5 dyr. O seliche sele, wes begerstu me? Du erkennest mych myt vollenkomenheit
vnd du schauwest yn den spegel der gotlicher wairheit. Jn dem grußestu mych
myt fruntlicher heymlicheit vnd ich grußen dich yn myner zarter soißicheit yn
dem clairrer dryfeldicheit. Yn der eren myner gotheit da bystu, eynige sele [313ᵛ]
myn, vol lyech*tz* myner soißicheit, vnd du byst hohe an der vollenkomenheit.‹

Uff sent Johannes dage als er entheubt wart, vnder des das man die misse sancke, **Kap. 76**
da was sie alleyn vff dem sieche huße. Vnd sy soiltde bynden yre v wonden, die
sye an yre haitte myt groißen smertzen. Da gedacht sie der funffe wonden yres
bruytgams, die er durch sie leyt an dem h<eiligen> crutze, vnd oppert da alle
5 yren smertzen der wonden yn syne wonden myt eynem groißen willen, also daz
sye alle yren vngemache willenclichen vnd froelichen vmb synen willen woiltde
lyden. Da wart sie also van gode getroiste, daz alle yre smertzen vnd bytterheit yn

---

74,7 soißicheit] soißicheit | soißicheit **10** myt] mȳt **75,1** in] N *Initiale fehlt* **3** *nach* den] sat
gestrichen **9** lyechtz] lyezhe *Korrektur des Schreibers aus* lyeche **76,1** er] er ent

eyn gotliche soißicheit wart verwandelt. *[314ʳ]* Want ʾgotʾ, der ware troister aller
bedrupter hertzen, der bracht yre selber synen heilgen fronen lycham vnd gaiffe
yr den myt syner eygener haynt yn yren mont vnd yn yre sele. Vnd er sprach also 10
zo syner lyeber bruytde:
›Erfrauwe dich, sele myn, wanttu haist mych wairheffenclichen yn dyr. Du byst
eyn van den, die myr myn vader hait gegeben. Jch wille dich leren den wege myns
lebens: Das ist smacket lyden myt gedult, armoit dragen wyßelich, eyn luter con-
scientze behalden yn groißer hoytde. Vnd du salt eyn hertze hayn vol burnender 15
lyebden, das ist myn wille, also was myn leben, dyße sal altzijt yn dynem hertzen
wannen.
[314ᵛ] **O** du hertze lyebe sele myn, weß begerstu me? Du haist mych eyntphan-
gen, als ich wart entphangen yn Jherusalem. Dyne beheder vnd dyn got, eyn
konynck, der da ist vber alle konynck, vnd dynen fursten, der eyn furste ist aller 20
fursten, der hait dich gar groißelichen geeret. Dyne weßen ist vort gegangen
van der groißer wirdicheit des aller vbersten. Dar vmb hayn ich dich gecleytde
myt dem roytden sament der gotlicher lyebden, van der du nummer doit sunde
gedoyn eyn machest. O sele myn, erkenne dyne schonheit vnd dyne wirdicheit.
Du byst gecleyt myt dem wyßen sammet gantzer kußheit des lybes vnd der selen. 25
Das ist das cleyt, daz myr woille gefellet an dyr vnd daz ich gar sere lyeffe hayn. O
du aller *[315ʳ]* schonste myn, erfrauwe dich. Du haist die soißicheit der vbersten
dogent, dar vmb so bystu gecleyt myt dem wairhaifftigen sament rechter oitmodicheit, die da wyrt erlucht yn allen gedancken vnd yn allen dynen wercken. Das
ist die dogent, die mych vß myns vaders schoiße vff daz ertriche bracht hait, want 30
oitmodicheit ist die doegent, vff der myn geist begert zo ruwen. O sele myn, want
du also dogenclichen gecleyt byst, so wille ich ewenclichen yn dyr rogen.‹ O was
groißer luste vnd freuden haitte got, yn yrer selen zo wannen, als er haitte gesprechen: ›Myn woilluste synt, zo syn myt den kynderen der menschen, doch wielle
me yn eyner woil getzertter selen, dʾieʾ da ist vmbsaitzet myt den hogesten dogen- 35
den.‹ Myt wylchen dyeße edel sele ist versichert gewest, als er sprache zo yr:
[315ᵛ] ›O du aller myldeste sele myn, erfrauwe dich. Jch hayn groißen troist yn dyr.
Des ewigen vaders wort ist vereyniget myt dyr, des du dich ewenclichen gebruchen
salt hie myt der genaden, vnd her nach saltu yn sehen van angesicht zo angesicht
yn dem hemelryche na alle dynem willen. O zarte sele myn, ich geben dyr star- 40
cken glauben vnd waire zoversicht, heilge wyßheit vnd geistliche begerde. O aller
lyebste sele myn, ich geben dyr gerechticheit vnd meßicheit, geistliche sterckste
vnd stedicheit alle die zijt dyns lebens. O lyebhauende sele myn, ich geben dyr
kuße ʾvnd luterʾ reynicheit geyn allen creaturen, also was du sichtz, hoirest ader
gedenckest, abe iß woil yn yme selber wieder die reynicheit were, das iß dyr doch 45

36 gewest] gewest | ist **41** zoversicht] zo versicht

nyt geschayt*[316ʳ]*den eyn mache noch die reynicheit dyner selen nyt beflecken
eyn mache. Want yn der reynicheit, da ich alle creature ynne hayn geschaiffen,
yn der saltu verlyben. O vßerwilte sele myn, jch geben dyr vollenkomen demodicheit, gantze getruwheit vnd waire gedult byß an das ende dyns lebens. O du
50 lyebe sele myn, du byst myt allen dogenden gecleyt.‹

In aller heilgen abent van groißem lyden yrer cranckeit da troiste sie vnser here gar   **Kap. 77**
zertlichen na syner getruwer gewanheit, also daz yre alle yre gelieder gestercket
vnd begoißen worden myt gotlicher genaden vnd myt sonderlicher soißicheit,
als vnser here zo yr gesprochen hait: ›Nyt eyn laiße dich verlangeren dyns vnge-
5 machs. Du haist mych yn *[316ᵛ]* dyr, als mych die engel vnd die heilgen haynt.‹
Vnd yr was da, als yre got vnd lyebehaber yn yre were. Da begert sie van gode vnd
sie hyeße jre begerunge van yme, als er yr loynen sultde vmb yren groißen smertzen, vnd sie hieße funffe M selen <van yme>.

Aber des morgens vff aller heilgen dage da sie vnseren heren myt groißer beger-   **Kap. 78**
den entphangen haitte vnd yre hertze vnd sele erfrauwet wart vnd erwoilt myt
soißicheit van lyebden, also daz sie duchte, were yre hertze eyn bercke gewest,
iß sult syn zobrosten van soißicheit, want van der soißicheit eyn kaynne keynne
5 menschen zunge gereden, yn der soißicheit vnd jn dem lyecht der vereynionge
sprach jre liebhauer zo yrer selen dyeße wort:
›**O** aller starckste sele *[317ʳ]* myn, erfrauwe dich. Dyn leben ist yn eyner verey-
nicheit myns lebens, mych gar hoge lyepe zo haben myt groißer vollenkomenheit. Du byst myn eynige sele. Du quelest van myner lyebden vnd dich durstet na
10 dem drancke myner lyebden. Dar vmb wille ich dich drencken myt der lyebden
aller creaturen vnd aller guder lude vff ertrich vnd aller heilgen vnd engelen yn
dem hemelriche. Der aller lyebde wille ich dyr geben, dastu mych myt aller yren
lyebde lyebhabest.‹ Hye myt genunget jrer selen nyt. Da sprach er aber zo yre: ›O
du gar zarte sele myn, ich wylle dich senden yn die dyeffte des mers, daz ist yn
15 daz abgront der lyebden der heilgen dryueldickeit. Da yn wil ich dich drencken yn
[317ᵛ] myner lyebden vnd yn mynem willen vnd gaben vnd genaden vnd yn dogenden vßwendich vnd ynwendich, als ich dich jn ewicheit vorsehen hayn.‹ Dar na
wart yr geist, yre vberst verstentenyß, vber sich getzogen yn die dryueldicheit vnd
yrer selen wart da vff gedayn eyn groiße lyecht. Vnd jn dem lyecht worden yre
20 bewyste vil verborgenner wonder wercke vnsers heren. ›Vnder anderen dyngen
sache ich, daz vor gode dem heren stonden alle vßerwylten, eyn yecklichen yn
synem loyne.‹ Da waz yre sele also myt gode vereyniget, daz yre was, als eyn

46 noch] nach   **77,5** dyr] yn dyr   **6** lyebehaber] lyebe haber   **8** *nach* selen] *Der Satz bricht
unvollständig ab.*

were nyemans me gewest dan got vnd sy alleyn yn dem hemelrich. Vnd van der
vnsprechlicher vereynionge jres geist myt gode sy dochte, daz sy got myt gode
were vnd was sy yn allen dyngen woille, daz got daz *[318ʳ]* auch wultde. Da wart yr 25
sele sonder alle hyndernyß ruwen yn den armen yrs bruytgams vnd alle yre vßerlichen synne slyeffen. Die ruwe was vol soißicheit vnd also lyeblichen, das jre sele
sach da so groiße freude vnd so groiße verborgenheit der wunderlicher gotheit,
da van vnmogelichen were eynigen menschen zo reden. Dar na yn der nacht des
selben dags da sprach vnser here zu yrer selen: ›O du vßerwilte sele myn, heiße 30
van myr, was du wylt. Myn hertze ist dyr vff gedayn. Jch byn van dyner lyebden
vberwonden. Jch eyn mach dyr nuste versagen. Funffe M selen erloißen ich yn
dyeßer nacht vß dem fegefuer durch dyne lyebde vnd geben ynne ewenclichen
myn vaders ryche. Sie soiltden noch v hondert jare yn der bußen des fegefůer
[318ᵛ] syn gewest.‹ Das verstonde sie also nyt, daz eyn eyckliche sele sultde v 35
hondert jaire yn dem fegefuer syn gewest, dan eyner jglicher selen was yre zyelle
vff gesaitzet nach yren sunden, vnd der zyelle der zaile was alle zosamen vc. ›Dan
du haist sye myt dyner lyebden erloiste, dar vmb salt du sonderlicher wirdicheit
myt jnne hayn vnd myt yn allen besytzen daz ewiche leben.

O du bloiende vnd aller suberlichste sele vnd aller heillichste sele vnd du vßer- 40
wilte dube myn, du salt erhaben werden byß zo dem ixten chore der engel. Wes
begerstu me? Die vberste lyebde yst yn dynem hertzen eyn grontfestionge aller
dogent. Dyne edel sele ist vor mynen augen eyn bant aller vollenkomenheit *[319ʳ]*
vnd selicheit. Du haist van genaden, daz ich hayn van naturen. Dyß alles saltu,
zarte sele, myt vns gemeyn hayn jn der vberster wairheit.‹ 45

Kap. 79 Vnd dar na vff dem heilgen crystage sprach er aber eyns zo yr:
›**O** du wonderliche sele myn, erfrauwe dich. Du haist eynen selichen yn ganck
yn myn luter gotheit yn dem hemelschen paradijß, da du sonder hyndernyß der
sunden myns vaders angesicht altzijt sehen salt. O erluchte sele myn, du machtz
frylichen als eyn adeler flyehen yn die vberste hoheit, vnd die luteren augen 5
dyner selen festigen yn dem wieder glantze der ewiger gotlicher sonnen, vnd yn
daz lyebliche angesicht der ewiger gotheit.‹

Kap. 80 In dem hogetzijt der h‹eilgen› dry ko*[319ᵛ]*nynck des abentz vnd auch des dags
da leyt sy so groiße vngemache vnd pyne an dem hertzen vnd an dem lybe, daz
alle yre glyeder erschutten vnd ersturben an yre, also daz keyn mensche nye also
grußelichen doitze erstarbe. Als jemerlichen sie ist erstorben an dem hertzen vnd
an dem lybe van aller heilgen dage an byß an den zwolfften dage alle nacht dry 5
stonden ane ander hant manych vngemache vnd groiße vnd stediges amechtiget

---

24 gode sy] gode vñ sy **80,2** vnd an] vñ dē an **5** van aller heilgen dage an] *gestrichen v. j. H.*

jres hertzes, daz an nye keynem menschen me gesehen was worden. Jch, der dyße
schryben, sache dyß selber myt mynen augen, das sie soilche pyne leytde, soilche
quale vnd soilche amacht, soilche erschutten yrer gelyeder, soilche ersterben vnd
10 solche wieder lebendige werden, van den keyn zunge gereden eyn kayn noch eyn
mache, want iß was altzo *[320ᵛ]* mail wieder den lauffe der naturen, want keyn
craifft der naturen eyn mocht daz gewyrcken an eym menschen. Aber got alleyn
myt synem gotlichen wonder woilt dyß wyrcken an yre vnd myt yre. Siche an, wie
gar jemerlichen die pyne vnd daz sterben was, vnd auch war vmb iß got vber sie
15 verhenget. Daz fyndestu geschreben yn dem jaire vor dyeßem an aller heilgen
dage. Da lyestu van eyner semlicher erschuttunge, erbiebonge vnd ersterbonge.
Aber daz ich selber sache, sagen sie myr dyß wort vnd sprach: ›Jn dießem vngemache wart myn sele durchgoißen vnd erlucht myt der gotlicher lyebden, vnd
myn geist swebet yn got. Vnd myr was, als ich yn yetzont gewyrdich hette vnd
20 als mynen lyebhaber zertlichen zo myner selen zwyngen vnd daz ich yn froelichen an sehe, myt eynem erluchten hertzen vnd selen zo yme floge *[320ᵛ]* vnd
sie yme yn drŭcket myt der genedicheit vnd myt der gedursticheit, myt der ich
yme gare getruwen, daz er mych gentzelichen lyeb hait. Yn dem lyecht vnd yn der
lyebden wart myn hertze vnd myn verstentenyß vff erhaben zo beschauwen vnd
25 zo bekennen gotliche dynge, vnd myn begerunge wart entzundet zo bekennen
vnd zo smacken, wie vber soiße myn lyebhaber ist. Jch haitte heymeliche freude
vnd wunder myt den fruntden godes, der alle vyant vberwynt. Da myn sele yn
dem lyecht der luterer verstentenyß erhaben wart vber menscheliche nature, da
wart auch myn lyffe vff erhaben van der craifft godes zo sieben maillen, daz der
30 conuent sache vnd alle, die by myr waren. Die gotliche lyebde vnd die hytziche
begerde, die zwey zyegent myn sele zosamen, daz sie also droncken wyrt van der
vber floißicher yn gyeßonge des *[321ᵛ]* heilgen geistes, da ich also sterckelichen
yn lygen. Als vnder willen erschynt er myr yn eym zucke als eyn blycke des gotlichen lyechtz. Vnd er zucket mynen geist vber sich, das ich yetzont begeren got
35 zo sehen als yn eyn spegel. Da gebryst menschelicher bescheytdenheit, wan ich
slaiffen yetzont soißelichen yn der beschauwunge godes vnd yn den armen myns
zarten bruytdegams. Vnd er bewyst myr viel, daz yn got verborgen ist, vnder des
an zo sehen, das myr nyemans daz benemen eyn mache, die freude vnd die luterheit der gotlicher genaden, der ich yetzont gesmacket hayn. Der gotliche schynne
40 vnd daz lyecht gußet sich yn mych vnd vermenget sich zo myr vnd machet van
zweyn, daz ist van myner selen vnd got, eyn geist, vnd myn sele wyrt got myt
gode vnd gantze vereyniget myt gode. Dyße verey*[321ᵛ]*nionge geschyt nyt dan
yn der aller groister hytzsten der lyebden vnd yn der aller soister begerunge yn
der lyebden. Da van versmyltzet myn sele vber alle vnd sie wyrt weche van yrer

---

9 soilche] soiche *(2×)*   **21** eynem] eȳne   **26** lyebhaber] lyeb ha|ber   **27** wunder] wŭde

gewonlicher harticheit vnd entphenget van dem fuer des heilgen geistes vnd 45
flußet als eyn smeltzenden waiße yn daz gotliche bylde, daz sie <gesehen> haitte
jn dem hyne zucke yrs verstentenyß, vnd entphenget an sich die forme der gelichenyß des yn druckes. Her zo eyn mach der mensche nyt komen van yme selber
myt keynem synem fliße, sonder alleyn der heilge geiste zuget den menschen
yn synem lyechte vnd yn syner lyebden da hynne, da alle menscheliche craifft 50
stylle swyget, ruwet, vnd wyrcket da alleyn die gotliche craifft. Want die sele
alleyn geschaiffen ist, got zo erkennen, so eyn mach sie doch van yre selber nyt
[322ʳ] vber sich selber komen, sie eyn werde dan gotlichen vff erhaben van dem,
nach dem sie geschaiffen ist. Das ist die natuerliche wirdicheit der verstentlicher
creaturen. Alleyn sie van yre selber gotliche dynge nyt eyn mache begryffen, so 55
mache sye doch gotliche dynge entphangen, abe yr van gode gehoilffen wyrt. Das
eyn vermache keyn ander creature, dan die na gode gebyldet ist, also ⌐so⌐ das der
hyntzoge yn got ist. Dyeße vereynigonge myt gode ist der selen hochste vollenkomenheit yn dyeßem leben.‹
Jn der vereynionge jrer selen myt gode sprach yre lyebhaber dyeße wort zo yrer 60
selen:
›Eya gotliche sele myn, erfrauwe dich van ewicheit zo ewicheit vnd syncke mynen
namen, den ich yn dich *[322ᵛ]* gegruntfft hayn. Du byst gebyldet na dem byltde
der heilger dryfeldicheit, getzeret myt mynem gelichenyß. Du byst myr vertruwe
yn eyn bruytde jn ewicheit myt rechtem glauben, so ich dich erloiste hayn myt 65
mynem koistelichen bloytde. O du seliche sele myn, du byst dar zo geordent,
dastu ewenclichen myt den heilgen engelen wannen salt. Vnd du machest aller
heilgen selicheit yn myr begryffen. Du byst eyn erbe myner ewiger gotheit vnd
eyn deylhaffionge der dryueldicher eynicheit. Was begerstu me? Dyne sele vnd
myn hemel, der yn dyr ist, *synt* myt den sterren vnd myt dem mayntde vnd myt 70
der sonnen getzeret. Die sterren, da myt die sele ist getzeret, daz synt die bloi-
tende dogent. Der maynt ist der luter crysten glauben myt rechtem zoversicht. Die
sonne ist die rechte furige lyebde entgene got vnd dynen eben*[323ʳ]*menschen.‹
Also hait got yre sele zo eynem hemel gemacht vnd er hait sy getzyeret myt allen
dogenden. Yn dießem selben lyecht sprach auch yre lyebehauer zo yrer selen: 75
›Sele myn, ich hayn dich gecroynt myt funffe groißen dogenden. Das ist gotliche
lyebde, wyßheit, gerechticheit, maißicheit vnd sterckte.‹ Also hait yre sele freude
vnd freude yn dem heilgen geist alle tzijt ewenclichen sonder ende.

---

46 <gesehen>] gehñ **54** natuerliche] natuerlicher **63** gegruntfft] *Bedeutung unklar*
70 synt myt] myt **72** zoversicht] zo | versicht

Uff sent Agneten dage da was yre sele vnd hertze yn vnsprechlicher freuden vnd **Kap. 81**
yn soißer genaden yrs lyebhauers, das yr was, als syne gewalt vnd syne soißicheit
yn jre sele fließen also genunchelichen, daz sie also groiße hytzste yn brunstiger
lyebden yn sich entphynge, daz sie dochte, daz yre sele gotlichen myt *[323ᵛ]* gode
5　got were. Vnd sie haitte also groiße clarheit, daz sie luterlichen jn got verbyldet
wart. In der luterheit sach sie, daz got yre sele gecronet haitte myt eyner gulden
cronen, die da hait dry groißer koistelicher steyne, also daz aller der hemelscher
hoiffe sonderliche freude vnd zeyrcheit hait van der schonheit der cronen. Der
irste steyn, der yn der cronen was, daz was die freude, die sie sonderlichen hait
10　van der gotheit vnd menscheit vnsers lyeben heren. Der ander steyn was die
freude, die sie van der moder godes haitte. Der drytte steyn was die freude, die
yre sele sonderlichen van allen heilgen vnd van allen engelen haitte. Zo dyeßer
cronen gaffe vnser lyeber ⌐here⌐ yrer selen eyn truwen ryncke zo eym zeychen
rechter lyebden vnd gantzer vereynionge, *[324ʳ]* die thuschen gode vnd yrer selen
15　yetzont ist vnd nummerme gescheytden eyn sal werden. Jn dießem lyechte vnd
yn dießer genaden was yre sele alle tzijt dache vnd nacht.
›O lyebliche sele myn, erfrauwe dich. Du byst myn throne, gemacht van hel-
ffenbeynnen, *(II Par 9,17)* vff dem ich alleyn ruwen wille. Myn fruntdynnen, was
wyltu me? Der heilge geist wyrcket yn dyr vier lyeblicher dynge: Dyne angesicht
20　ist yn dem vnbefleckten spegel myner gotheit gar lyeblichen. Dyne sieden synt
woil geordent. Dyne hertze ist vol gotlicher lyebden. Dyne sele ist vol jn brunstiger begerden. Du byst myn frundynnen, myn dube, myn suster, myn bruytde.
(vgl. Ct 4,9) Was begerstu nu me? Jch hayn dyn leben vff gerecht myt *[324ᵛ]* rechter
oitmodicheit vnd bestediget myt geduldicheit vnd vollenbracht myt der gewaner
25　lyebden. Dyne leben ist eyn bloytende roiße vor myner gotheit.‹

Uff sent Gregorius dage da was yre sele yn groißer soißicheit vnd sie wart **Kap. 82**
⌐v⌐ereyniget myt gode. Jn der vereynionge begert yre sele, das got sie wultde vff
rechten vff eyn dogenthaifftiges leben nach sym aller lyebsten willen. Da sprach
vnser lyeber here zo yrer selen: ›Habe mych lyeffe vnd fochte mych vnd vollen-
5　brenge yn allen dyngen mynen willen. Vnd wes du bedarfft an lyffelicher noitdurfft ader an geistlichem troiste, des eyn wille ich dyr nummer laißen gebresten.‹
Da was yre sele jn groißer soißicheit van metten *[325ʳ]* tzijt byß zo mytdage,
also daz sie duchte, daz die soißicheit der lyebden also groiße were, das yre sele
gantze myt gode vereynychet were vnd daz yre sele vnd got alleyn weren yn dem
10　hemelryche, vnd doichte auch daz, daz vff der erden nyemantz mee eyn were dan
sie vnd daz sye alleyn eyne wille myt gode were. Da duchte jre sele, daz sie were

---

81,4 myt] myt ‖ myt　**10** gotheit] *Korrektur des Schreibers aus* hotheit　**82,9** vereynychet]
vereynycheit

yn die gewalt vnd yn die wyßheit vnd yn die gude godes also dyeffe gesencket, das <sie> doyn vnd laißen machet na alle yrem willen, als sie got yn gode were. Van dyeßer soißicheit yrer selen wart yre menscheliche nature also verkrencket, als abe sie eytzont vergene wultde. Da gaiffe got yrer selen eyn bescheytdenheit, 15 daz sie yren lyebhauer her abe zoge yn siche myt groißer freuden vnd froelicher soißicheit.

[325ᵛ] ›O du aller lobelichste sele myn, erfrauwe dich, wanttu scheppest jn dem abgruntde myns hertzes den vbersoißen gesmacken vnd die heillicheit myner gotlicher lyebden, die dich doyt vergeyßen aller vergencklicher dynge. Wan du 20 flugest vber dich myt eynem luteren hertzen jn myn luter gotheit, da wyrt dyn edel sele erlucht gotlichen, vnd sie wyrt geleret myt gotlicher soißicheit, myt vberster vollenkomenheit.‹

Kap. 83 Jn dem dage des oisterlichen hogezijt was die andechtige junffrauwe aber yn yrem gebet vnd andacht vor die selen nach yrer gewonheit. Da hait der soiße here gesprochen zo yrer selen: ›O du erbere sele myn, wes begerstu me, wanttu byst alzo mail schone vnd luter vnd gantze *[326ʳ]* reyne. Dyne luterheit ist ⌐yn⌐ myr myt der clairheit dyns hertzes. Vnd myt der hoger vollenkomenheit der dogent der 5 beschauwonge bystu gantze versencket ⌐yn⌐ myner lyebden. Du beschauwest myt den augen dyner selen yn dem wunderlichen spegel der heilger dryueldicheit, yn dem aller lyebsten willen myns vaders. O seliche sele myn, wes begerstu me? Jn dyeßer nacht nemen ich zweyn dusent selen vß dem fegefuer. Sie sullent ffunffe hondert jaire yn dem fegefuer syn gewest, aber die craifft dyner lyebden hait sie 10 erloiste van allen yren pynen vnd hait sie erloiste van allen flecken yrer sunden. Du salt van yn allen sonderliche wirdicheit entphangen vnd sonderlichen den loyne vnd *[326ᵛ]* die ere vnd die danckberheit, die sie entgene eyn ander haynt. Das saltu, sele myn, alles entphangen yn dem spegel der gotlicher wirdicheit.‹

Kap. 84 Jn dem hogezijte ascensionis domini sprach er aber eyns zo yre: ›Du vnvberwynt-liche sele myn, wes begerstu me? Du wyrckest die wercke der barmhertzicheit, dar vmb ist dyr vffgesloißen der abgront des borns der heilger dryueldicheit, also daz du mochest scheppen also viel, alstu jn dich begryffen machst, vnd das du den anderen schenckest van dyeßem borne yn dyeßer wyße, also dastu, myn 5 fruntdynnen, yn mogest myt dynem lyden erwerben erkentenyß yrer sunden vnd dastu dar *[327ʳ]* na, myn dube, ynne mogest myt dyner lyebden genade erwerben vnd dastu dar zo myt dyner geduldicheit ynne gude exempel gebest vnd myt

---

12 gesencket] gesencket wer⏐re **13** <sie>] so **83,1** oisterlichen] oirsterlichñ **3** O] *Lombarde steht in der Zeilenmitte.*

dynen wortten vnd wercken gude lere. O sele myn, du byst, die ich myr hayn
10 vßerwilt nach mym hertzen. Dar vmb sal myn wille an dyr gantze erwoilt werden.‹

Uff dem heilgen pynxste dage da sie was yn groißer soißicheit vnd hytzicher   **Kap. 85**
lyebden, da hait got der here gesprochen zo yrer selen: ›**O** du myn heilge sele,
erfrauwe dich. Du byst eyn hogede der vollenkomenheit aller dogent. O du claire
lyebde vnd luter sele myn, wes begerstu me? Jch byn eyn fuer alle tzijt yn dynem
5 hertzen bornen, daz dich soißelich erluchte vnd dich senfftichen entphenget. O
myn *[327ᵛ]* zarte sele, wes begerstu me? Jch byn der borne der myldicheit, der
loiffe der engel, die ere der heilgen. Du byst gewandelt yn mych vnd ich gyßen
myn gotliche ynflusche jn dich.

O du selige konynckynnen, du sonderliche freude der engel vnd du sonderliche
10 zierheit der frauwen vnd aller heilgen, erfrauwe dich. Du haist vmbfangen die
ewige selicheit, yn der aller dyne wille wyrt erfoilt, vnd die da brenget froelichen
die genade dyner selen. Jch hayn dyne sele vmbfangen myt myner gotlicher eren
vnd ich hayn alle dyne synne getzogen yn die luterheit der ynwendiger soißicheit.
Da wyrt dyn hertze erluchte myt der vberster lyebden vnd wyßheit.
15 *[328ʳ]* **O** du soiße sele myn, erfrauwe dich. Jch byn wairhefftich yn dyr vnd ich
machen dich sicher, dastu nummerme salt gescheytden werden. Myne woillus-
tige wannunge ist yn dyr. O selige sele myn, wes begerstu me? Du suchest mych
myt soißem, froelichem, wyrdichem gesancke, vnd du vyndest mych altzijt
nach dyns hertzen begerden yn soißer lyebden vnd du entphengest mych yn der
20 gotlicher soißicheit myt vollem durste vnd du gebruchest dich mynner selenclichen myt der soißer genaden, der genaden der selicher selicheit, jn der alles
gut besloißen ist. O zarte sele myn, wes begerstu me? Ich geben mych dyr myt
begerden jn gantzer lyebden, dastu dich alle tzijt *[328ᵛ]* gebruchest der lyeblicher
gebrŭchonge myner gotlicher naturen, yn der besloißen ist das vberste gutde.‹

Uff sent Maria Magdalenen dage sprach er aber eyns zo yrer selen: **Kap. 86**
›**O** du heilge sele myn, erfrauwe dich. Dyn gantze leben ist eyn gotlich leben, dyn
begeren ist vollenkomen yn luterer lyebden. O sele, myn hertze ist dyr alle zo
mail geneyget. Wes begerstu me vorbas, want den schaitze der wirdicheit dyns
5 bruytgams haistu beseßen yn dem vbersten hemel der wyßheit der ynwendiger
luterheit. Mynne lyebde ist yn dyr eyn heil des fredens, eyn craifft des lybes, eyn
senffticheit des hertzes, eyne sicher fryheit des gemoides, eyn hoge erkentenyß
dyns selbes vnd myner gotheit, vnd ist eyn voiler durste aller soißicheit. Dyße
[329ʳ] haistu alles fonden, zarte sele mynne, jn der heilger heymmelicheit der

---

85,2 O] *Lombarde steht in der Zeilenmitte.*

wairer lyebden dyns eynigen lyebhabers, der dich also stercklichen byndet vnd 10
yn geistlicher freuden also wyßelichen leret.‹

Kap. 87 In dem hogezijtlichen dage assumpsionis Marie reyte er aber eyns myt yre vnd
sprach also zo yrer selen dyeße wortte:
›**O** du seliche sele myn, erfrauwe dich. Du haist daz ewige leben aller soißicheit
yn dyr. O zarte sele myn, wes begerstu me? Alle dyne wercke vnd leben ist eyn
gotliche wyrckonge, die got an dyr wircket. Dar vmb synt myn gotliche wercke 5
altzijt gut an dyr vnd vff gerecht vff daz aller beste. Eya lyebe sele myn, was wyltu
me? Ich leren dich vnd ich hayn dich lyeffe. Die ewige got*[329ʳ]*liche wyßheit,
die dyne hertze entfencket yn vollenkommener lyebden, vnd alle die engel vnd
die heilgen luchtent vnd bornent yn der clairheit myner gotheit, vnd burnet dyne
edel sele jn stediger lyebden vor mynem gotlichen angesicht.‹ 10

Kap. 88 Jn dem hogezijt der geburte der jonffrauwen Maria sprache got der vader also
zo yre: ›Du gebenedite sele myn, erfrauwe dich. Du haist yn dyr mynen eynigen
gebornen sonne, der da ist vol genaden vnd wairheit. *(vgl. Io 1,14)* Want myt der
genaden bystu erluchte vnd myt der wairheit wyßelichen geleret zo bekennen
mynen willen. O seliche dochter myn, wes begerstu me? Jch byn eyne zeyrden 5
dyner selen yn de*r* selichen myl<dicheit> myner vnsprechelicher lyebden. Du
byst *[330ʳ]* behoit myt sicherheit yn der soißer weytden, yn der wunnenclichen
ruwen der gebruchonge der burnender lyebden. Da yn saltu wannen ewenclichen
sonder ende.‹

Kap. 89 In dem hogezijt des ertz engels Mychaelis da was sie yn groißer andacht vnd yn
hytzicher lyebden. Da sprach er zo yrer selen:
›**O** du erwyrdige sele myn, du lyecht der crystenheit, erfrauwe dich. Du byst altzo
mail myt myr vereyniget vnd van myner gotlicher lyebden zosmoiltzen vnd gentzelichen yn mych zoflußen, also daz ich van dyner lyebden werden lyeffe gehait 5
vnd du van myner lyebden wyrst lyeffe gehait. Aber du haist lyeffe van genaden,
aber ich van naturen. O seliche sele myn, was wylttu me? Alles, daz ich *[330ᵛ]*
wyrcken yn dyr vnd dastu sichstes vnd hoires yn myr, daz eyn ist nyt anders dan
eyn wyrckonge der gotheit, die vßer myr flußet yn dich. Jch schencken dyr an
vnderlaiß den drancke der engel vnd der heilgen lyebde, vnd ich leben alle tzijt 10
myt nuwer genaden vnd wunder yn dyr.‹

Kap. 90 Uff der eylffe dusent jonfferen dage sprach er zo yrer selen: ›Du lyebe sele myn,
erfrauwe dich. Du byst gantze vereyniget myt dyeßer vollenkomener lyebden vnd

---

88,6 der] dē   myl<dicheit>] myl...   **89,6** haist] haist haist

myt dyner groißer lere. O zarte sele myn, wes begerstu me? Du byst altzijt erfoilt
myt gode, also das alle dyne wercke synt jn myr eyn luter gutte vnd eyn vorsich-
5 tige gotliche ordenunge, die du haist entphangen van mynem vader. *[331ʳ]* O sele
myn, wes begerstu me? Dyne lyebde weißet alle tzijt vber sich vnd gehet yn daz
hogest gut.‹

Jn dem hogezijt aller heilgen sprach er zo yrer selen also yn dießer wyße: ›O du Kap. 91
hogelobte sele, eyn waßende sel*ich*eit van der wyrckonge der heilger dryueldicheit, o du zarte sele myn, wes begerstu me? Du byst gebyldet nach der heilger dryueldicheit vnd ich, dyne bruytgam, byn gecleytdet myt dem cleytde dyner men-
5 scheit. Aber daz wyrt dyne aller meyste freude syn yn dem hemelryche, dastu
dich myner menscheit vnd myner gotheit ewenclichen gebruchen salt nach alle
dynem wyllen. O vßerwylte *[331ᵛ]* sele, was begerstǔ me? Du wannest yn dem
spegel der gotheit myt stediger vollen hyrtten der dogent, myt sicherheit der gotlicher lyebden, die dich hait ernuwet myt vnsprechelicher freuden vnd myt ewiger
10 soißicheit, die dich nacht vnd dage van mynner myldicheit durchflußet. O wonderliche sele, wes begerstu me? Dyn angesicht ist myr lyeblichen. Dyne lyebde
hait mych betzwungen, daz ich yn dyeßer nacht dru dusent selen erloißen van
der pynen des fegefuers durch die vnsprechelichen arbet, die dyne lyebde lydet.
Sie soiltden drue hondert vnd vyrtzich jaire yn dem fegefure syne gewest, want
15 daz dyn lyebe vnd dyne groiße lyden hait die schult vor sie betzailte. Dar vmb
saltu van *[332ʳ]* eyner iglicher selen sonderliche wyrdicheit yn dem hemel hayn.‹

Uff den irsten sondage yn dem aduente was er aber eynß reden myt *yr* vnd er Kap. 92
sprache zo yrer selen: ›O du aller myldeste brǔyt myn, erfrauwe dich. Jch byn yn
dyr daz leben dyner selen, daz wort vnd die wyßheit des vaders, der dich leret
gotliche alle wyßheit, alle dogent vnd alles gutte. Want ich byn alle tzijt yn dyr
5 myt vollenkomenner wyßheit vnd gude vnd myt soißer lere. Want ich byn die
vberste wyßheit der hogester gutden, die alle tzijt yn dyner selen bloet vnd yn
dynem hertzen wannet.
O du aller lyebste sele myn, erfrauwe dich. Du byst vffgegangen als die sonne yn
yrer *[332ᵛ]* crayfft zo heylle der crystenheit. Vnd daz myn freude yn dyr sy, so dryn-
10 gestu myt der hulffe myner gotheit yn die hogetde des lyechtes der heilger dryueldicheit. O wunderliche sele, wes begerstu me? Du leuffes yn der hoger lyebden
myner gotlicher wyßheit, daz ist yn der heilger woilluste, jn vollenkomenheit der
genaden, jn der groißheit der andacht des yn brunstigen willen, yn der furiger
lyebden vnd yn der sonnen der gotlicher clairheit vnd yn dem spegel der heilger
15 dryueldicheit, dar an du myr woille gefellest. Want myn wylle dyne wylle ist vnd

---

91,2 selicheit] selechte **92,1** myt yr] myt **7** *nach* wannet] *zwei Leerzeilen in der Handschrift*

dyn wylle myn wille ist. O aller lyebste sele myn, myt dießer wonderlicher hant-
fest sonderlicher lyebden bystu vor den anderen gotlichen vmbfangen.‹

Kap. 93 *[333ʳ]* Jn dem hogezijt der heilger dry konynck sprach er aber zo yrer selen also:
›O du aller lyebste sele myn, erfrauwe dich. Du haist yn dyner edeler selen den
hogen schatze der engel freude vnd der heilgen heillicheit, destu nyt beraubet
eyn machest werden. Du byst bestediget yn myner gotheit. O lyebe sele myn, was
wyltu me? Du flugest den hogen phat yn myn luter gotheit myt groißer fryheit.   5
Dar vmb wylle ich dich vnder myn engel vnd heilgen erheben, vnd ich wylle dich
setzen yn vnsprecheliche wyrdicheit.‹

Kap. 94 Aber dar na yn dem hogezijt purificacionis Marie was yre sele yn groißer
andacht vnd yn hytzicher lyebden, vnd da hait der lyebelicher got aber eynße
ge*[333ᵛ]*sprochen zo yrer selen also myt honynchfluyßichen wortten: ›O aller
clairste sele myn, erfrauwe dich. Du byst eyn blome myner heilgen yn myner
ewicheit. Du byst eyn soiße frucht myner heilgen. Ich hayn dich yn der heilger   5
dryueldicheit geliche gemacht eyner wyßer lylien vnder mynen jonffrauwen. O
sele myn, wes begerstu me? Du erkenste mych luterlichen yn allen dyngen. Du
haist mych stetlichen lyeffe vnd luterlichen, das ist, du haist mych lyeffe alleyn
vmb mynen willen. Du haist mych lyeffe ane maiße vnd du gebruchest dich
mynner na alle dynem willen. O myn bruytde, laiße dyr genogen. Du haist eynen   10
hemelschen lyffe vnd eyn engelsche sele. O myn aller zarte sele, wes begerstu
me? Ich hayn eyn wannunge yn dyr gemacht. *[334ʳ]* Du byst myr eyn woillustiger
gartten vnd mych geluste by dyr zo syn. Vnd du salt ewenclichen by myr wannen
yn der vberster freuden, da du salt sehen die zierheit aller heilgen vnd die hoge-
heit aller engel vnd die ere myner konynclicher maiestate, des vaders gewalt, des   15
sons wyßheit vnd des heilgen geistes gudicheit. Da saltu, zarte bloeme, luterlichen erkennen die heilge dryueldicheit. O du reyne sele myn, erfrauwe dich. Jch
hayn dich gesencket jn die duyffte myner gotheit, da du scheppest die rychtum
aller rychtum, die soißicheit aller soißicheit vnd die clairheit aller clairheit. O
selige sele myn, *[334ᵛ]* ich hayn dich groißelichen geedelt vnd stercklichen lyeffe   20
gehait, vnd dar zo hayn ich dich vßerwylt, also das myn wille vnd der dyne gotlichen werdent vereyniget.‹

Kap. 95 **Annunciacio Marie**
›O vnsprecheliche sele myn vnd groiße verborgen heymlichet myns gotlichen
hertzes, wes begerstu me? Jch, got vnd mensche, byn yn dyr myt der genaden. Du

---

16 dyn] *Korrektur des Schreibers aus* mÿ

haist entphangen jn myner gotheit eyn selichen yn fluß der soißer freuden, also
5 bystu yn myr aller soiste. Hie myt ist erlucht dyne verstentenyß.

O du heilge sele myn vnd groiße verborgen heymlicheit myns gotlichen hertzes,
wes begerstu me? Du byst eyn suylle des gotlichen tempels. Alle die gantze
werelt wyrt *[335ʳ]* geseliget vor mynnem vader van dynem lyden vnd van dyner
lyebden. Du lobest mych vnd du lebest myt den heilgen jn myner gotheit. Du byst
10 eyn tempel godes vol aller heillicheit. O lyebe sele, was wyltu me? Du byst eyn
vnsprechlich weßen yn der wunderlicher dryueldicheit, daz allen heilgen eyn
loiffe ist vnd allen crysten selen troiste, vnd iß ist allen hertzen vnbekante. O du
bloende fruchtber sele myn, wes begerstu me? Du byst eyn blome aller dogent. O
lyebliche sele myn, wes begerstu me? Ich vollenbrengen yn myner lyebden dyn
15 wyllen myt mynem hogen wercke. O sele myn, wes begerstu me? Du borrest myt
hogen erkentenyßen yn der gotheit myns vaders, yn dem du ver*[335ᵛ]*sichert byst
worden. Vnd alle dyn wylle ist vereyniget myt mynem willen. Dar vmb ist dyn
leben loblich yn der heilger dryueldicheit. O lobeliche sele, dyne hertze bloet.
Dastu durch mych van lyebden haist vergoißen, daz hayn ich entphangen yn myn
20 gotliches hertze. Myne gefangen wille ich dyr geben, want ich eyn mach dyr nuste
versayn. Jch nemen yn dyeßer nacht dusent selen vß dem fegefuer. Die haistu
erloist myt dynem bloitde vnd myt dyner groißer arbeit vnd myt dynem lyden. Sie
soiltden dru hundert *jaire* yn der pynen syne geweste. Dyne getruwe lyebde hait
sie alleyn erloiste. Dar vmb saltu sonderlichen loyne entphangen myt jn alle jn
25 dem spegel der heilger *[336ʳ]* dryfeldicheit.

O vnsprecheliche sele myn, wes begerstu me? Want ich hayn alle dyn meynunge
nach mym hertzen vnd nach alle mynem willen vffgerycht vnd geordeneret yn
allen dyngen myt vffenbairer wairheit. Durch der dogent willen alles, was du
wylt, daz dat auch myn wylle ist. O seliche sele, wes begerstu? Dyne hertze bloet
30 myt voiler genaden vnd dyne dogent bloitent myt heilgem wercke. Dyne sele
luchte*t* myt lobelicher lyebden yn myner lyeblicher gotheit, yn der du byst erfoilt
myt freuden vnd soißicheit yn der eynicheit der heilge dryfeldicheit.

Follenkomen sele myn, erfrauwe dich. Du haist die waire oitmodicheit, die keyns
lobs begert. Myn *[336ᵛ]* gotliche genade ist yn dyr verborgen vor allen menschen
35 hertzen. O du heilge sele, wes begerstu me? Du haist yn allen dogenden ynwendich eyn vollenkomen freude, also daz dyn hertze van wortten noch van wercken
noch van keynnem vnrecht nyt eyn mach bedruppt werden. Noch der freuden,
der du dich gebruchest yn myner gotheit, eyn mache nyt gemyndert werden. O
selige sele, erfrauwe dich. Du haist dynen lyffe yn mynem gotlichen dynste also
40 vberwonden, daz er dem geist gehoirsam ist nach mym wyllen.

---

23 hundert jaire] hundert **31** luchtet] luchte byst] bystʳuˀ, u *am Rande* **33** Follenkomen]
Fvlnkemē **40** *nach* wyllen] *eine Leerzeile in der Handschrift*

O du lyebe sele myn, erfrauwe dich. Du haist eyn soiße gedechtenyß dyns lyebhabers, der dich yn der hoheit syner wyßheit hait bestediget myt syner wonderlicher *[337ʳ]* zeirheit. O durtel dube myn, erfrauwe dich. Du haist die gewaire vnd
hoge genade van dynem schepper vnd van keynner creaturen nyt. Alle vergenck-
liche dynge haistu versmeet. O du lyebe sele myn, ich byn dyne lyebhaber. Dyne 45
edel sele mache nyemantz ervollen dan alleyn die heilge dryfeldicheit, dar na sy
gebyldet ist.

O wyrdige sele myn, erfrauwe dich. Du haist yn dich getzogen erkentenyß myner
gotheit myt burnender soißicheit, yn der du byst myt myr vereyniget yn wonderlicher heymlicheit vnd erkentenyßen myner verborgen ortel. Du byst myr gemacht 50
geliche. O selige luter sele, wes begerstu me? Du haist die *[337ᵛ]* fruchtber lyebde,
die nyemant gemynneren eyn kayn ader verleßen eyn mache. Dyne lyebde luchtet
durch die engelsche chore als die clairheit der sonnen yn myner gotheit. Da saltu
myt freuden ewenclichen wannen yn den hogen burnenden seraphyn.

O du koistliche sele myn, erfrauwe dich. Jch hayn dich yn ewycheit dar zo erwe- 55
llet, das myn groiße, ewige vnd vnsprecheliche gutde vnd genade wyrcke yn dyr
na der begerden myns hertzens. O seliche sele, wes begerstu me? Myn vader hait
dich lyeffe vnd hait dyr barmhertzicheit gegeben vber myn zo doyn. Vnd also
vylle, da me du vol byst myt barmhertzicheit, als vyel da wyrdiger haistu lyeffe
mynen vader vnd also vyel da me zwyn*[338ʳ]*get er dich, die barmhertzicheit zo 60
geben. Dar vmb geben ich dyr zo hulffe die frucht myns lebens yn der menscheit
vff ertrich, zo erloißen die sunden viellens folcks. O myn lyebe fruntdynnen, also
ist dyne leben gedayn zo dem fruchtbarren loyne myner menscheit, zo hulffe
zo komen dem menschelichen geslecht. Vnd van der beloynunge myner pynen
sullent sy vollenkomenclichen getroiste werden.‹   65

Kap. 96 ›Uff der heilger dry konynck dage da was myn sele yn groißer genaden vnd sache
yn eym wunnenclichen lyecht, wie got was yn synen vßerwelten kynderen eyn
burnender got vnd eyn krefftiger got vnd eyn lǔchtender got vnd eyn troistender
got vnd eyn fruchtber got. Vnd got myt syner burnender *[338ᵛ]* lyebden yn sy
goiße den floiße des ewigen lebens, daz yre aller hertzen entfencket worden van 5
lyebden na dem, daz iß vor gode wirdiche was, vnd erlucht sie myt eym gotlichen
lyecht, daz sie yren eygen gebresten worden erkennen vnd den wege der wairheit. Vnd er stercket sye myt syner genaden. So ynne eytzont wultde gebresten an
yren krefften geistlichen, so guße er syne gotliche genade vnd craifft yn sie, das
sie worden gestercket yn yme. Vnd er troiste sie myt sym gotlichen troiste. So er 10
vff sie lacht syne vederliche roytde vnd so yn yetzont wultde gebresten an men-

---

47 *nach* ist] *eine Leerzeile in der Handschrift* **54** *nach* seraphyn] *eine Leerzeile in der*
Handschrift **61** *nach* frucht] dyns *gestrichen* **62** fruntdynnen] frūtdy̆nē my̆

schelicher lydunge, so goiße er yn sie myt freuden die geloibde, daz er ynne das
hemelriche geloisset hait vnd <sich> ewenclichen selber. Vnd er macht myt syner
genaden fruchtber alle die do*[339ʳ]*gent yrer selen, das yn soiße vnd nuwe wart
15 alles yre leben yn got. Ich begert vff eyn tzijt zo beden vor eynen menschen, daz
myr got gebe zu bekennen, wie yre leben were. Da sprache vnser here: »Wullent
myn kynder sicher gut werden, so sullent sie vier sachen doynne, so doyn ich
yn vier dargene: das irste, daz sie yre fruntde laißent vmb mych, so geben ich yn
soiße gedancken. Das ander, daz sy yre vyant lyeffe habent vmb mych, so geben
20 ich ynne eyn burnende lyebde. Das drytte ist, daz sie lobe der menschen sullent
fliegen vmb mych, so geben ich jn groiße begerde zo myr. Das iiij, daz sie gedul-
dich syn yn yrer arbeit vmb mych, so geben ich yn groißen loyne vnd dogent
myt stedigem flyße, vnd ich geben mych selber yn zo lone *[339ᵛ]* ewenclichen.
Jch hayn sye gesaitzet van dem dode vnd geben yn daz ewige leben na dyeßem
25 leben.«

Jn dem oister dage dede got vff syner bruytde eyn groiße lyechte. Vnd yn dem   **Kap. 97**
lyechte sache sie, wie alle geiste sich erewyrdichten vnd ernuweten sich yn dem
gotlichen lyecht. Vnd alle jre hertzen worden gespyste vnd entfenget myt gotlichem lyecht vnd troiste. Vnd got bewyst myr alle dynge yn dem hemel vnd yn
5 der erden. Vnd er bewyste myr alle syne wercke nyt geliche, want er gaiffe eym
yechlichen na dem, daz er iß entphangen mocht. Vnd ich sache, wie got ist vber
alle, vnd er ist doch me yn den guden luden dan yn den anderen. Vnd wanne myn
sele got erkente als er ist, so ist sy als er ist, vermogenden vnd geweldich als er
ist. Got ist soiße vnd mylde, als er wylle, vnd smacket er, *[340ʳ]* wanne die sele
10 yn lyebe hait, vnd sie entphenget soißicheit van gode vnd hait yn lyeffe. Dar vmb
so hait sie got lyeffe vmb got. Wanne daz soiße mytweßen gotz yn der selen ist,
dan so ist der selen eyn vber smachafftiche soißicheit gotz yn gode. Das ist got
lyebhauen vmb got. Aber sich selber lyeffe haben vmb got ist vollenkomen. Also
hait die lyebhabende sele lyeffe got vmb got vnd sie hait eyn rechte lyebe, wanne
15 sie got lyeffe hait nyt vmb yrs eygen noitze vnd vmb daz sie gotz nyt entberen eyn
kayn, sonder sie hait yn lyeffe luterlichen durch jn selber vmb syne luter gutde.
Vnd wanne yre got smacket, so drynget sie vff yn got myt starckem ernste vnd
myt furiger lyebden vnd myt groißem lobe. Got ist der selen eyn verzertes fůer.
[340ᵛ] Der rauche des fůers ist ruwe eym yecklichen menschen an sym hertzen.
20 Vnser ruwe burnet yn dem hemel, daz ist got, wanne vns alle yrdeschen dynge
nyt me eyn synt dane esche vnd gestůpt. Da myn sele vff dyeßem heilgen oister
dage myt gode also vereyniget wart, da sprache myn leybhaber zo myner selen:

---

13 <sich>] sie   **97,2** erewyrdichten] erewyrdichstē   **9** smacket] smackeit   **11** mytweßen] myt
weßñ

»O du spegel aller guder sieden, du byst gesaitzet yn godes freden. Die heilge dryfeldicheit ist dyn crone. Heische van myr, was du wilt.« Da heiße myn sele zwo nuntzich vnd sieben hondert vnd nuntzich dusent sele vnd dru hondert sonder zo bekeren, vnd daz got alle gude lude wultde bestedigen. Dyß alles erwult got myt syner crefftiger lyebden, also daz iß myr luterlichen *[341ʳ]* bewyste wart. Jch sach, daz got die zaille der vor genanten selen van syner genaden vß dem fegefuer namme vnd fort sie yn syn hemelsche weytde vnd saitzet sie yn syne vollenkomen zyerheit, eyn yecklicher nach syner wyrdicheit. Da was yre freude aller yn got gefloißen. Vnd got haitte eyn yeckliche sele also lyeffe, daz er die heymlicheit, die er myt yn haitte vnd hayn wylle, myt eyner yecklicher yn sonderheit yn der ewicher freuden *haitte.* Die eyn weiße vnser lyebe frauwe nyt, noch keyn engel, noch keyn creature, want daz got also wylt syn myt eyner yecklicher selen, als eyn were nyemans me dan got vnd die sele alleyn. Also sprach vnser here zo dyeßen vor genanten selen: *[341ᵛ]* »Koment, myn vßerwilten lyeben kynder, zo der genaden, die vch bereyt ist van dem anbegynne der werelt, dar vmb daz jre hait gedayn mynen willen. Jch salle vch bewyßen myn konyncklichen herschaifft. Dar an endet sich alle vre vngemache.« Sie synt komen yn die hemelsche schonheit. Da bewyßet got jn syne gotheit. Sie syngent ym da den froelichen gesancke Alleluja myt hoger vnd soißer stymmen. Die engel syngent myt yn. Sye syngent alle gelich, yre geluyt gehet yn den hemel, sie sprechent alle: »Myr loben vnseren troiste*r*, dan myr wairen verloren, vnd durch yn syn myr worden erloist van der dusternyß der hellen. Vnser groiße vngemache hait eyn ende. *[342ʳ]* Dar vmb sagen myr dyr ere vnd loiffe, soißer vader vnd got, daz myr dich erkennen yn der duyfften dyner grondeloißer gotheit.« Dießer selicher oisterdage was myr eyne lyeblicher, soiße, froelicher dage.

Da was myn sele yn groißer genaden vnd got bewyst myr syne groiße wonder, wie er syne genade gußet yn die guden vnd yn die boißen, vnd sie sach, wie er syn gebenedites bloyt goiße yn die, die sich vor den sunden hoytdent. Da sprache myn sele: »Here, was wyltu doyn myt dyeßen?« Da sprache vnser here: »Jch doyne myn hertze vff entgene sy, dan iß ist wontde van lyebden.« Da *[342ᵛ]* sprach myn sele: »Here, wie bystu myt den, die dych alleyn lyeffe haynt vnd alle dynge dyeßer werelt versmehent?« Da sprach vnser here: »Die wille ich setzen yn guder luytde hertzen vnd ich wille yre arbeit eyn gemeynne mynen riche gutde machen.« Da sprach myn sele: »Here, wie wyltu doyn den, die sich jn allen dogenden vbent?« Da sprach vnser here: »Jch gyßen myn genade yn sie, daz sie bloent vor mym angesicht, als der meye doyt yn syner rechter zijt.« Da sprach ich: »Here, wie

---

24 *nach* zwo] ⌜xcij⌝ **25** *nach* hondert vnd] ⌜xc⌝ **33** freuden haitte] freudē **39** schonheit] schoheit **43** troister] troistē **47** *nach* dage] *eine Leerzeile in der Handschrift* **50** gebenedites] ge | benedistes

wyltu myt den doyn, die gerren dyn lyden erent?« Da sprach vnser here: »Ich
60 wylle yn setzen eynen stoylle yn myne grondeloiße gotheit.« Da sprach ich: »Here,
was wyltu doyn myt den sonderen?« Da sprach vnser here: *[343ʳ]* »Myt den wille
ich syn dache vnd nacht vnd alle tzijt, vnd ich eyn wille mych nummer van yn
gescheytden, byß daz sie also dyeffe yn die sunden fallent, daz sie mych vnder yre
fuße tredent. Dan wil ich mych ewenclichen van yn scheytden.« Vnd vnser here
65 sprache: »Die myr volgent, die wille ich brengen, da ich byn.« Vnd ich sache, daz
got goiße dyeße funffe sachen sonderlichen yn eynen menschen, vnd er wyrcket
daz alles yn gotlicher vereynionge vnd myt soißer gebruchonge syner selen.

Uff sent Johans dag des deuffers da was myn sele yn groißer freuden vnd wunnen **Kap. 98**
myt gode, *[343ᵛ]* vnd myn sele sache vnd hoirte viel wonders vnd bekentenys, wie
got ordineret, vnd er gaiffe allen dyngen yren weßen. Aber daz aller lustlichste
an allem dem, das got gyfft, das ist daz leben. Da sprache myn sele: »Here, was
5 ist daz leben?« Da sprache vnser here: »Das ist daz ewige leben, daz sie mych
erkennent vnd mynen eynigen geboren sone, den ich gesant hayn.« Da hoirt myn
sele, daz die meyster stryedent vnder eyn ander, an wylchen dyngen lyge daz
ewige leben. Die eyne sprachen: »An bekentenyß.« Die anderen sprachen: »An
der lyebden.« Die drytten sprachen: »An gebruchen.« Got vffenbairt aber myner
10 selen, daz man nyt eyn mache lyebe gehaben, man bekenne yn dan. Van wem ich
nyt eyn weyße, der ist verre van myr, daz eyn kayn ich nyt *[344ʳ]* lyeffe gehayn.
So ich got ye baße bekennen, so myn sele ye stercklicher jn lyeffe hayt. Got ist
endeloiße, dar vmb moiße daz bekentenyß endeloiß syn, daz got bekennen sal,
vnd yn dem bekentenyß got lyeffe hayn vnd yn der lyebden gotze gebruchen.
15 Also wyste got myn sele, das eyns sonder das ander nyt gesynne eyn mache,
want bekennen vnd lyeffe haben vnd got gebruchen ist myner selen gezeuget eyn
ewiche leben yn gode. Dan synt alle dynge vollenkomen yn gode, wanne iß wyrckeit an hyndernyß.

Uff vnsers heren lychams dage was myn sele yn eym stylle swebenden lyechte. **Kap. 99**
Vnd ich sache yn dem lyecht, das er ist eyn oirsproncke alles lyechtes vnd eyn
borne alles lebens vnd eyne vß floiße alles wesens. Vnd alle das gůt, daz alle
creaturen entphangen mogent, *[344ᵛ]* das eyn ist nŭste entgene dem, daz got,
5 der lebendige borne, ist yn yme selber. Vnd ich sache, daz eyn yechliche sele
gode naher ist, dan sye yre selber ist. Vnd wer got hie nyt erkennet, der eyn sal
sich synner nummer gebruchen na dyeßer zijt. Dar vmb sal eyn mensche gehen
van allen gebresten zo eynem vollenkomen weßen, also daz der mensche syner
jnwendicher andacht alle zijt genunch sy. Da sprach myn sele: »Here, ich doyn

99,9 jnwendicher] Jn wēdicher

alles, daz ich vermache. Wyltu aber me, dan ich vermache, so mache ich doch 10
numme gedoyn, als ich yn dyr vermache.« Dar na ruwet myn sele drye dage in
gode. Wanne die sele yn eyner gantzer gesaitzichet stet vff yre selber, so hait sie
roge. An dem drytten dage wart sie claire als die sonne, das ist, daz got wyrcket
alleyn yn *[345ʳ]* der selen vngehyndert. Also wyrcket er sich wairhefftiche yn
der selen vnd sie wart also claire als die wairheit. Vß yre eyn luchtet nyt dan die 15
wairheit. Jn dem lyechte sache myn sele vier dauffe. Der irste weste abe die erb-
sunde vnd der dauffe reyniget vßewendich vnd ynwendich. Vnd als got geboren
wart eyns van vnser lyeber frauwen, also werden myr alle dage gedaufft yn dem
dauffe, als der engel sprach zo der jonffrauwen Maria: »Der heilge geist sal vber
dich komen, zo reynige dyne bloytde vnd dyne fleische. Vnd die craifft des aller 20
vbersten sal dich vmbschedigen, das des vaders bylde wyeder yn dyr erschynne.
Vnd der sone sal berůren dich, also daz er sich wyeder yn dyr verbylde.« *(vgl.
Lc 1,35)* Also wart vff *[345ᵛ]* dem dauffe gehoirt die stymme des vaders vnd der
sone bereitte daz waßer vnd der heilge geist wart gesehen yn eym gelichenyßen
eyner duben *(vgl. Lc 3,22)* vnd die gotliche craifft fluße durch die menscheit yn 25
das waßer, dastu nyt moges sprechen, wie vyl gebresten du da habest, du habes
ye myner genade entphangen. Dyeßer dauffe geschyt eyns, aber die craifft des
dauffes vnd die bezeychenunge, die geschyt yn der selen nyt eyns mails yn dem
dage, sonder alle zijt des dags.

Kap. 100 Jn annunciacione beate Marie virginis da gaiffe myr got eyn groiße vnd eyn wonderliche lyechte zo sehen. Yn dießem lyechte sprache eyn stymme »fiat«. Daz ist
das edelste wort, daz noch ye gesprochen wart. Iß sprycht also vyl: Iß geschee
[346ʳ] eyne ynnycheit an vnderlaiß yn der dryer personen eynigunge yn gotlicher
naturen. Dyeße wort ist auch gesprochen worden yn der tzijt yn der eynionge got- 5
licher vnd menschelicher naturen yn eyner personen. Iß ist auch gesprochen yn
der eynicheit vnd yn der zijt der vereynigunge, da die sele myt gode vereyniget ist.
Da sache sie an dem vß floiße, daz ist die vffenbarunge, daz er sich selber vffenbairt, vnd syne vffenbairen, daz ist syne sprechen. Also sache die sele die ordenunge der engel, daz got myt yn spricht. Got eyn hait nyt zunge noch mont noch 10
nuste. Wo myt sprycht er dan? Sye sprechent, myt den engelen ist, daz er sich eym
yecklichen engel vffenbart, als *[346ᵛ]* er zo gode geordent ist. Gat vße floiße, daz
ist eyn blenckender wylle vnder eym lyechte eyner reden, das der sone ewige ist
van dem vader gefloißen myt der naturen vnd myt der personen, vnd der vader
vnd der sone hugent jren geist yn der ewicheit. Da synt alle creaturen got yn gode 15
vnder dem vß floiße. Da gyffet sich got myt vnderscheyt, daz irste den engelen,

---

17 vßewendich] vße | wēdich   ynwendich] yn wēdich   **21** das] vñ das   **100,1** annunciacione
beate Marie virginis] *gestrichen v. j. H.*   **11** Wo myt] Wo myt wo myt   **12** Gat] *Bedeutung unklar*

daz ander den menschen. Dyeße doyt alles got. Das ander »fiat«, daz da gesprochen wart yn der tzijt, daz geschage vnder de*n* worten, die vnser lyebe frauwe
sprache zo dem engel: »Fiad mihi secundum verbum tuum.« *(Lc 1,38)* Dyße wort
20 »fiat«, daz vnser lyebe frauwe sprachen sultde, begert die heilge dryueldicheit yn
der eynigunge. Die vereynionge ist des vaders, an dem *[347ʳ]* er iß versehen hait,
der sone, an dem iß gescheyt ist, der heilge geist, na dem daz er myt wyrcken
sultde. Vnd alle creaturen begerten des wortze, na dem daz iß ewenclichen vorsehen was yn gode, zo vorsehen an vnser lyeber frauwen zo des menschen selicheit
25 yn sonderlicher eren gotze vnd aller syner creaturen. Were daz wort nyt gescheyt,
alle syn geschefftze eyn were nuste gewest. Die tzijtliche vereynionge, die da
ewiche was yn gode, die sulte geschegen vber das wort, das vnser lyebe frauwe
sultde sprechen. Dar vmb begert iß sonderlichen alles menscheliche geslecht.
Doch beytde sie viel zo lange, ye sy iß sprechen wultde. Sie bekante woil, daz
30 iß was vber nature aller ge*[347ᵛ]*schaffener dynge. Jn dyeßem lyechte sache myn
sele, vnder dem wortte »fiat« entphynge vnßer lyeffe ffrauwe got lyplichen na der
menscheit. Vnd jn dem selben wort »fiat« an eyner gelicher zijt, da geschache die
vereynionge des lybes myt der sele, wie die vereyniunge myt yn beytden ist, vnd
sonderlichen die vereynnionge der gotlicher naturen vnd menschelicher naturen
35 an eyner personen. Da myn sele daz gesache, da entphynge sie ynnerlichen
also snelle yn dem augenblycke der zijt, da got mensche wart, daz ich sprechen,
das die vereynnionge vnd alles daz werck, dasta geschet ist, das dat gescheet
sy sonder zijt. Der engel sprach zo vnser lyeber frauwen: »Aue gracia p<lena>
d<ominus> t<ecum>.« *(Lc 1,28) [348ʳ]* Des irsten wortze eyn achte sy nyt viel. Als
40 er sprache, daz sie were vol genaden vnd daz got myt yre were geistlichen steitlichen yn yrer selen, dan das got lyplichen van yre geboren soiltde werden, das
alleyne die gotliche ordenunge vnd syn wyßheit yn menschelicher naturen <...>.
Damyt wart vollenbracht dyeße ordenunge. Were iß sache gewest, daz sye eer
were gestorben, dan vnser here were, sie were gefaren zo der vor hellen. Aber
45 were got nyt also lyeblichen vnd gruntlichen yn yrer selen gewest, er eyn were nye
<lyplichen> van yre geboren worden. Da hoirte ich, wie sie die engel vnd heilgen
lobten van yren dogenden, der sie also vil *[348ᵛ]* an yre haitte, want alle dogent
waren yn yre weselichen myt gode stede an vnderlaiße. Da hoirt ich vnd sache daz
ewige wort, daz iß fleysche wart, das da stetlichen van dem vader flußet als eyn
50 schynne. Vnd were eyn man also groiße, daz yme daz heubt an den hemel gynge
vnd die fuße yn den abgrunt vnd die armen also wyte vße recht als daz firma-
ment, der yn hylde vor eynem cleynen spegel, man sehe yn vber alle dar yn. Des
ist auch eyn gelichenyß yn der sonnen. Die meyster sprechent, das der mynste

---

18 den] dem   **42** *nach* naturen] *Der Satz bricht unvollständg ab.*   **44** *nach* here were]
ge:::telt   **46** <lyplichen>] lyeblichn̄

sterne vnder den gestanden sternen groißer ist dan alle daz ertrich. Dar vmb so ist
die sonne verre groißer dan die werelt. Der eynen cleynnen *[349ʳ]* spegel hyltde 55
entgene die sonne, noch wortde die sonnen gantze gesehen yn dem spegel. Also
wart yn dyeßem gotlichen spegel daz ewige wort fleße, vnd er nam die men*sche*-
liche nature an sich vnd nyt die persone, vnd van dem wercke des heilgen geistes
wart der lycham geschaffen yn dem aller lutersten vnd aller reynste gebloitde des
jonferlichen hertzes Marien, vnd das geschache alles yn eynem cleynen augen- 60
blycke der zijt, vnd keyns dyeßer werck eyn geschage vor noch na, want geliche
zo eynem mail wart got vnd mensche entphangen yn eyner personen. Da was der
sone godes gantze yn dem jonfferlichen lycham, da sie dyße wort sprache »fiat«.
Dyeße wort *[349ᵛ]* »fiat« ist eyn edel wort, yn dem alle vnser selicheit besloiße
ist. Das drytte »fiat«, daz gesprochen ist, daz ist degelichs yn eyner ewicheit vnd 65
yn der zijt zo der zarter selen, die myt gode vereyniget ist. Da bekennet sy got
vnd smacket got yn gotlicher naturen. Dan got sie vber schynnet als die sone den
maynt. Da flußet got yn got. Da wyrt sie van genaden, das got ist van naturen,
vnd wyrt gesencket yn den grondeloißen bornen der gotlicher naturen. Dan ist
sie bloiße yrs selbes, als got ist aller namen. Also sterbet sie yn den wonderen der 70
gotheit. Da flußet got yn gode, daz sie nyt begryffen kayne die gotliche nature.
Die sele, die got beschauwen, die sal doit syn aller befleckonge der sunden.‹ etc.

57 menscheliche] mēseliche

3.2 Maria Magdalena-Bekehrungslegende

Die bekeronge der selicher Marien Magdalenen ist geschehet, als die lerer schrybent, vff den irsten dags des mertze.

Maria Magdalena was geborren van eym edelen stame vnd eirlichem geslecht der stait van Jherusalem. Yre vader hieße Cierus vnd yre moderen Euckaria, vnd sy
5 haitten zwe dochter vnd eynen sone. Die eyne dochter hieße Martha vnd die ander Maria. Der sone hieße Lazarus vnd er was der, wylcher vnser here vff erwecket van dem dode, da er vyer dage doit jn dem grabe hait gelegen. Na dem dode yrer alderen deylten die kynder yr vederliches erbe. Lazarus namme eyn groiße deylle yn der stait van Jherusalem vnd er ubet sich yn rytterschaifft, want er was
10 eyn rytter. Martha gelobet, *[350ᵛ]* got zo dyenen yn reynicheit. Vnd sie <wart> eyne wyrttynnen vnd herbrycht die pylger, vnd sonderlichen vmb yrs hailgen lebens willen was sie wirdiche zo herbrygen vnseren lyeben heren Jhesum Christum vnd syne lyebe moder Maria vnd die heilgen apostelen. Vnd yre deyl was das stetgyn van Bethanyen gelegen by Jherusalem. Vnd was yre vber verlyehen van
15 yrer renten, das gaiffe sie den armen vmb got. Maria namme zo yrem deylle das sloiße geheißen Magdalum vnd da van wart yre der namen Magdalena gegeben. Alle yre gut vnd rentten bracht sie zo yn groißen sunden myt boißer geselschaifft. Vnd die boißen geist brachten sie zo falle durch yren boißen willen vnd manchueldige sunden: zo dem irsten mail yn hoifferdicheit, *[351ʳ]* want sie was also hou-
20 erdich van hertzen, das <yr> duchte, das nyemantz gelychen were yn suberlicheit yn edelheit vnd yn rychheit. Auch was sie also houerdich yn den wortten vnd wercken myt cleytderen vnd myt zyertheit yrs lychams. Sie was auch sere gyrich yn tzijtlichen dyngen: gut, ere vnd woilluste der werelt. Auch was sie vnkusche myt wortten vnd myt wercken, also daz sie yre gut geruchte vnd yren eygen namen
25 verlore, vnd auch also swerlichen, daz sie eyne vffenbair sunderschen wart geheißen, als vns saget der ewangelysta sanctus Lucas, want sie sundiget swerlichen myt yrem gesicht vnde myt *[351ᵛ]* handelonge der vngelicher personen. Aber yre lyebe suster Martha claget daz leben yrer suster der moder Christi myt schryenden augen vnd bayt sie, daz sye Christum wolde vor sie beden. Der lerer Ysiderus,
30 der dyeße leben beschreben haitte yn dem buche, das da ist geheißen das buche van dem dode der heilgen, sprache also, das dyeße susteren quamen zosamen zo Bethanien vnd Maria Magdalena gegynck sytzen vor eynen spegel vnd sie flichet yre schones haire vnd sie zieret yren lycham. Da sprache zo yre Martha, yre suster, myt clegelicher stymmen: ›Also zierestu dich na dem flesche vnd dyne schone
35 sele, die da geschaiffen ist na dem bylde godes, *[352ʳ]* befleckestu myt dynen

---

4 Euckaria] enttkaria *S*   **8** yr] yr | jre *S*   **10** <wart>] *fehlt in S, Konjektur nach N, B1, D*
20 yr] *fehlt in S, Konjektur nach B1*

groißen sunden. Jch beden dich, lyebe suster, gedencke, das dyn lycham hait
schult van der selen, vnd gedencke, das dyne schone lycham, den du zyerst myt
gultde vnd myt sylber, das der selbe saille werden eyn spyße der worme.‹ Da
antwert Maria vnd sprach: ›Myn vßerkoren suster, na dem das ich so suberlich
byn an dem lycham vnd yn rycheit dyeßer werelt, so beden ich dich, syst zofreden   40
vnd laiße mych myn gut verzeren myt freuden vnd myt den lyebhaueren dyeßer
‹werelt›. Vnd laiße vns nů froeliche synne myt eynander, wer weyße wie lange!‹
Des anderen dags zoge Maria zo huyße vnd Martha schreye aller bytterlichs, das
jre suster also wyllte was. Dar na vber *[352ᵛ]* zweyn mande haitten die jongeren
von Constantinopel yren hoiffe zo Jherusalem vnd waren da froelich. Vnd dar zo   45
wart auch geroiffen Maria Magdalena. Vnd sye quam auch dar myt groißer koist-
licheit vnd zyerheit yres lychams als eyn lyebhaues dyeßer werelt. Vnd sy spron-
gen vnd dantzten zweyn dage vnd zwe nachtten, also das sie nauwe die spyße
nemen moichten van groißer froelicheit vnd wyltdicheit. ‹Da› zo dyeßer zijt
vername yre suster, das vnser lyeber herre Jhesus Christus was yn den galylee-   50
schen lantde vnd er wultde zo yre komen yn Bethanyen. Da gynge Martha vnd
Marttylla, yre mayt, des morgens froe zo Jherusalem zo kauffen spyße vor den
heren. Vnd als Martha gynge vber *[353ʳ]* den markte, da quam van dem rayt huyß
myt pyffen vnd besunen Maria Magdalena varen yn dem reye myt groißer houer-
dicheit. Da sache Martilla, das Maria Magdalena geleyt wart yn groißer eren vnd   55
froelicheit. Da sprache sy zo yrer frauwen Martha: ›Sehet vmb uch!‹ Vnd als sie
yre suster ersache, da wart sie bytterlichen schryen, vnd sie wande yre hende
zosamen vnd sprache ynwendichs jn yrem hertzen: ›Ach got, myn here vnd myn
schepper, wee mych! Mych dunckket, das myn suster gedynt hait den boißen
geisten. Nochtant beden ich dich, dastu sie wullest ansehen myt dynen barmher-   60
tzichen augen. Vnd gyffe yre eynen anderen synne, also daz sie beßer yre leben.‹
Vnd also myt bedunge verleyffe Martha *[353ᵛ]* stayn vnd sy beytdet yrer suster
Maria. Vnd da Maria naer quame zo yrer suster, da sprach sie Martha zo vnd fragt
sie, wie iß werre, das sie also froe yn die stait wultde gayn. Martha, die heilge
jonffrauwe, myt groißer oitmodicheit antwert sy yrer suster vnd sprach, daz sie   65
dar vmb dar komen were zo keuffen die spyße yren gesten. Vff die zijt eyn haitten
die zwe susteren nyt vyl wort myt eyn ander vmb des volcks wyllen, das dar by
stontde. Aber Maria sprache myt eynem lachenden montde: ›Lyebe suster, keuffe
auch etwes vor mych. Jch wylle zo dyr komen vnd myt dyr essen.‹ Her van sprecht
der heilge lerer sanctus Augustinus, das Maria alle die dage yres lebens nye beßer   70
spyße aße dan vff die tzijt, want da *[354ʳ]* wart sie bekert van yrem sundigen
leben. Des anderen dags van groißer modicht wegen gynge Maria heymelichen

---

38 eyn] eȳ | eȳ *S*   **42** ‹werelt›] *fehlt in S, Konjektur nach N, B1, K1, D*   **49** ‹Da›] Ja *S*
53 markte] martte *S*   **55** sache] sacha *S*

vßer Jherusalem vnd quamme zo Martha yrer suster huße zo Bethanya, die sie
sere lyeblich entphynge myt groißer frolicheit vnd hyeße nyeder sytzen. Da
75 sprache Maria: ›Ach suster, das doyt myr sere noyt vnd bedarffe iß gar woil, das
ich ruwe, want ich hayn zweyn gantzer dage vnd zwe nacht gesprongen vnd
gedantzet. Vnd ich byn gantze froelich gewest myt den jongeren van Jherusalem.
Vnd ich eyn byn nye yn allen den dagen myns lebens vff eyn tzijt also froelich
gewest als da. Vnd ich hayn die gantze stait van Jherusalem froeliche gemacht.‹
80 Recht abe sy sprechen wultde: ›Nu eyn dantzen *[354ᵛ]* ich nummerme.‹ Dar vff
antwert Martha, die heilge jonffrauwe, yrer suster vnd sprache zo yr: ›Lyebe
suster, na dem daz jre also froelich syt gewest, haittet yr auch den konynck by
vch, der alle hertzen froelich macht, vnd der da aller suberlichst ist vber alle
konynck?‹ Da antwert yre Maria: ›Myt vns eyn waren keynne konynck. Wenne
85 meynestu, den keyßer Tyberius?‹ Martha sprach: ›Jch eyn meynne nyt Tyberi, der
da ist eyn konynck der menschen, sonder ich meynen den konynck aller konynck,
der da ist eyn rychter vber hemelrych vnd ertrich. Vnd der selbe ist eyn erloißer
der kynder van Israhel vnd er hait an yme alle die suberlicheit alle der gantzer
[355ʳ] werelt. Vnd syne vader ist got vnd syne moder ist eyne reyne jonffrauwe,
90 die geboren ist van konyncklichem stamme Davitz.‹ Da fraget Maria nach den
lyebhaberen der werelt vnd sprach also: ›Ach lyebe suster, sage myr, des beden
ich dich, wo ist dyeßer konynck? Jst er also suberlich, so wylle ich yn myt mynem
gelde vnd <goide> zo myr nemen zo mynem lyeben, vnd ich wylle synne frunt-
schaifft erkryegen.‹ Martha antwert yre vnd sprach: ›Aller lyebste suster, den
95 konynck, den ich meynen, daz ist myn lyeber here Jhesus Christus, der da ist eyn
meyster der selen.‹ Vnd myt den wortten wart Martha beweget myt schryen, dar
vmb das Maria dyße nyt eyn verstonde geistlich, <so>nder fleyßelich. Da Maria
sach, daz *[355ᵛ]* jre suster schreye, da fraget sie jre lyebe suster vnd sprache:
›Lyebe suster, war umb schryet yre alle zijt, als ich zo vch komen? Jst das myn
100 schult, so saget myr das selbe, so wille ich nyt me here komen.‹ Da sprache sie zo
yre: ›Ach lyebe suster, ich mach woille schryen, want ich hoiren alle tzijte, dastu
dyne geru̇cht, das da beßer ist dan gult vnd sylber, das haistu verloren. Vnd dyne
geselschaifft eyn ist nyt gut vnd du befleckest dyne schone sele myt dynen groißen
sunden. Vnd also moiße ich dyne boiße gerucht allezijt horen, wo ich hyn komen.‹
105 Magdalena eyn konde sich nyt langer enthalden, da sy Martha sache schryen. Da
sprache sie myt schryenden augen: ›Ach lyebe suster, iß ist <...>‹

78 yn allen] yn alle yn allē *S*   **82** haittet] haitte *S*   **86** eyn] eyne *? unsichere Lesung*
93 <goide>] *fehlt in S, Konjektur nach N, B1, K1*   **97** <so>nder] ...nder *S Textverlust durch*
Blattschaden   **106** nach ist] ... *S Textverlust durch Blattschaden, danach Textabbruch durch*
Blattverlust

Abbildungen

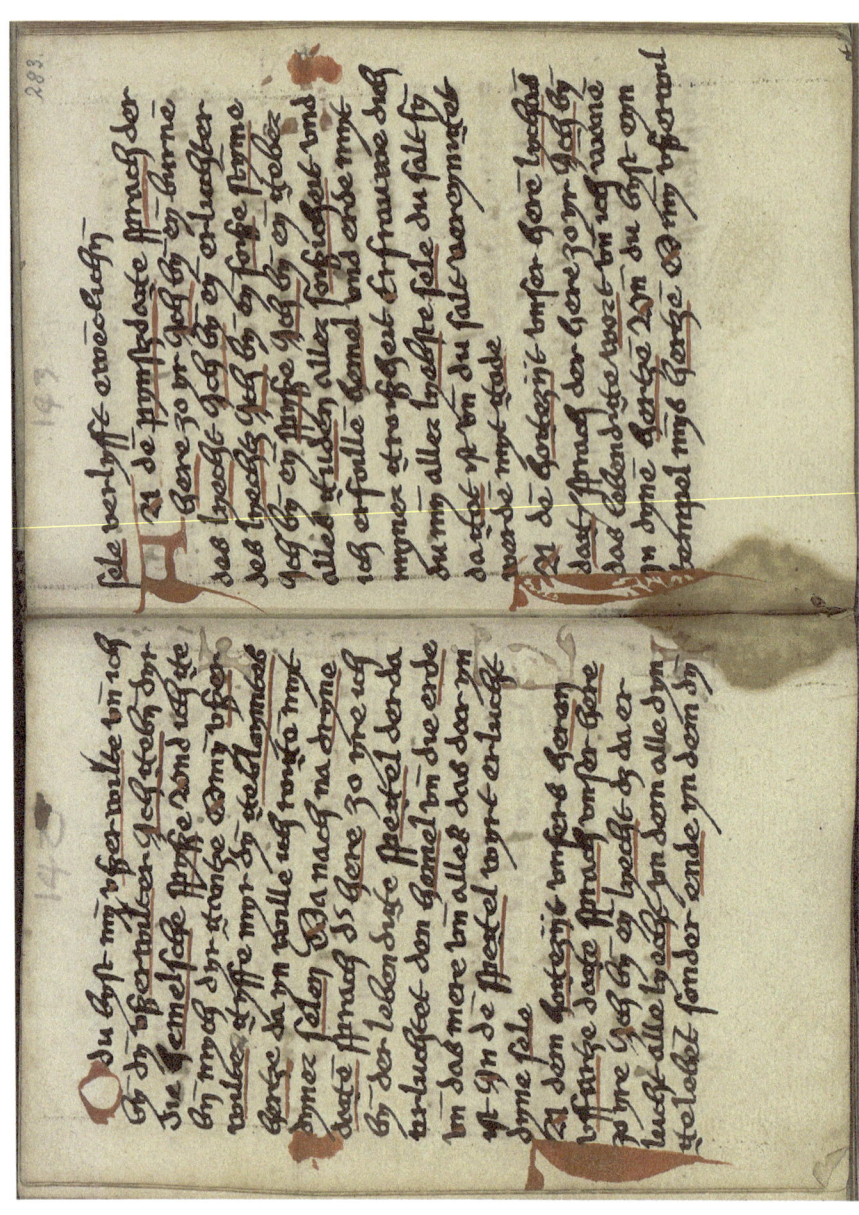

Abbildung 1: Straßburg, Bibliothèque nationale et universitaire, Ms. 324, Bl. 282ᵛ–283ʳ –
Reproduktion: Bibliothèque nationale et universitaire de Strasburg

https://doi.org/10.1515/9783110536324-013

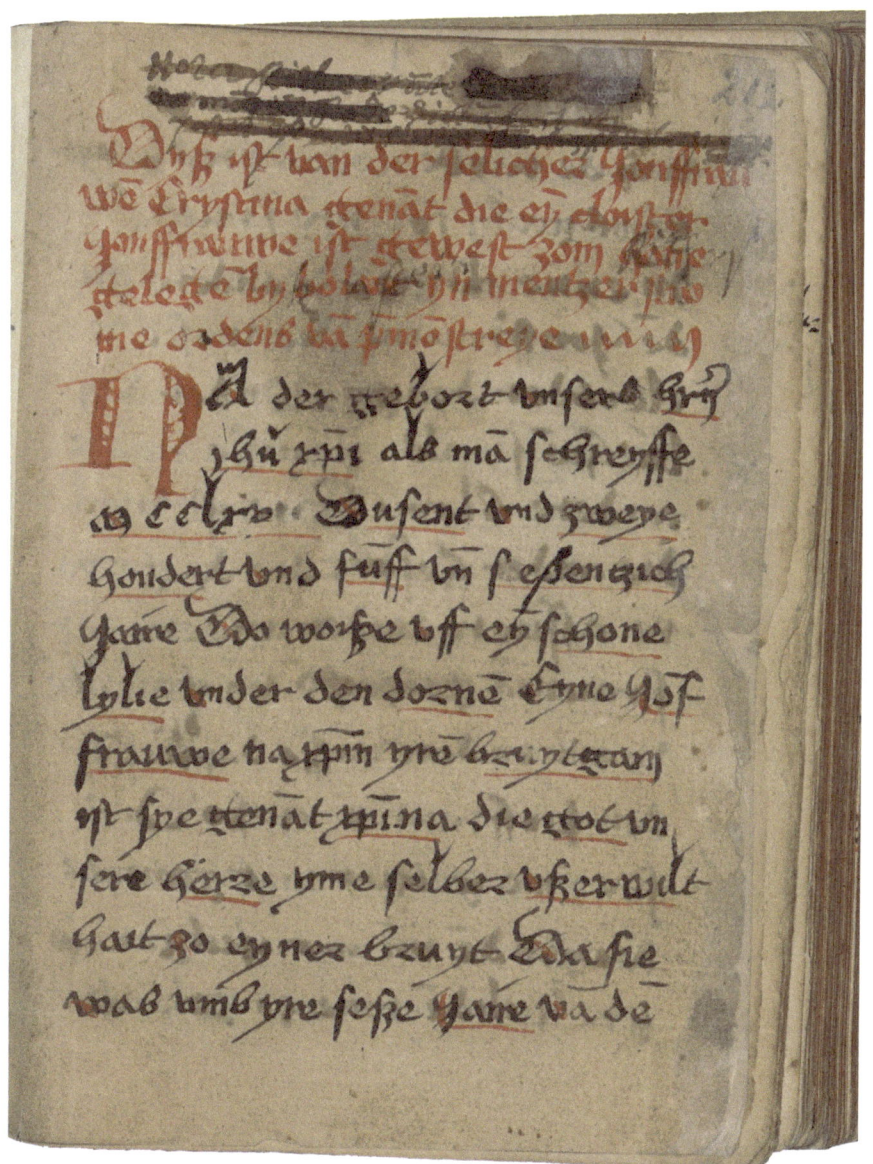

Abbildung 2: Straßburg, Bibliothèque nationale et universitaire, Ms. 324, Bl. 212ʳ – Reproduktion: Bibliothèque nationale et universitaire de Strasburg

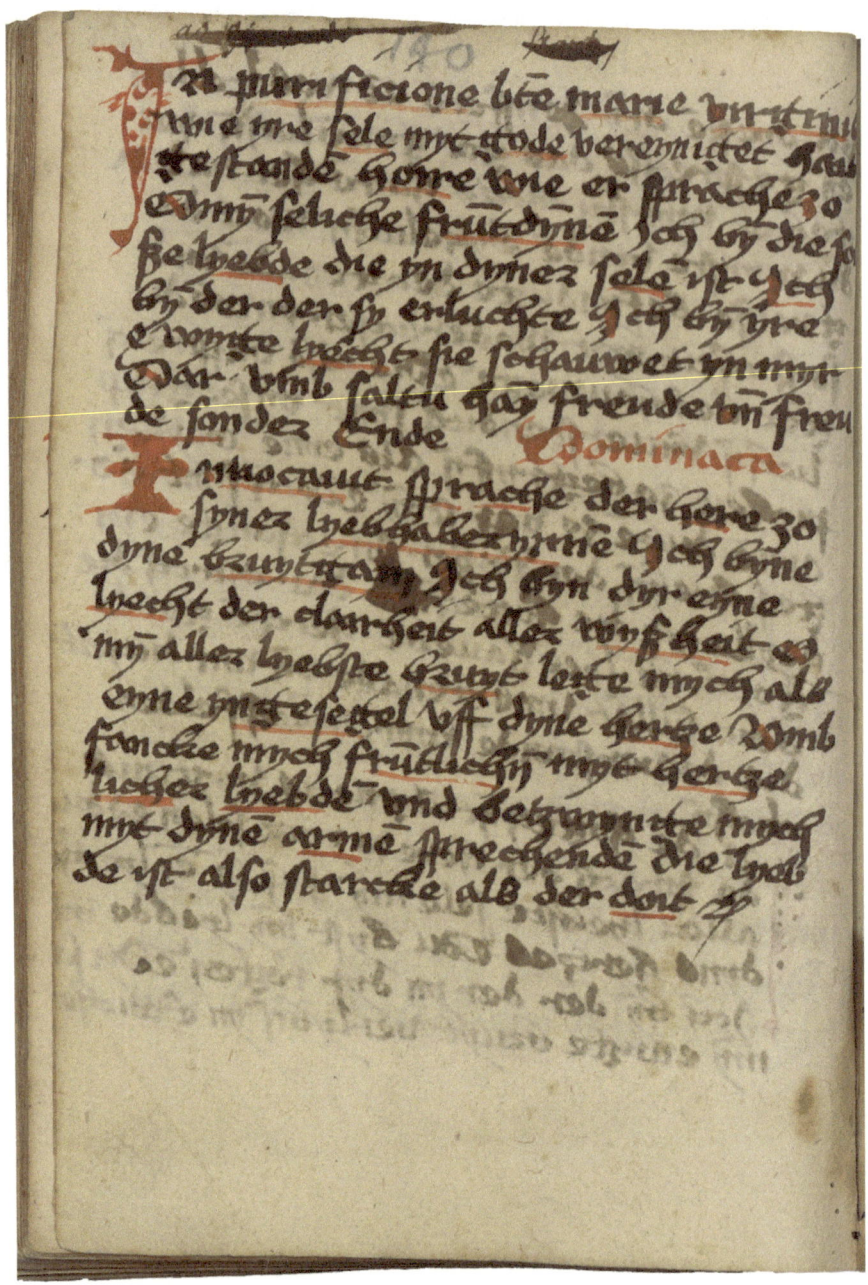

Abbildung 3: Straßburg, Bibliothèque nationale et universitaire, Ms. 324, Bl. 281ᵛ – Reproduktion: Bibliothèque nationale et universitaire de Strasburg

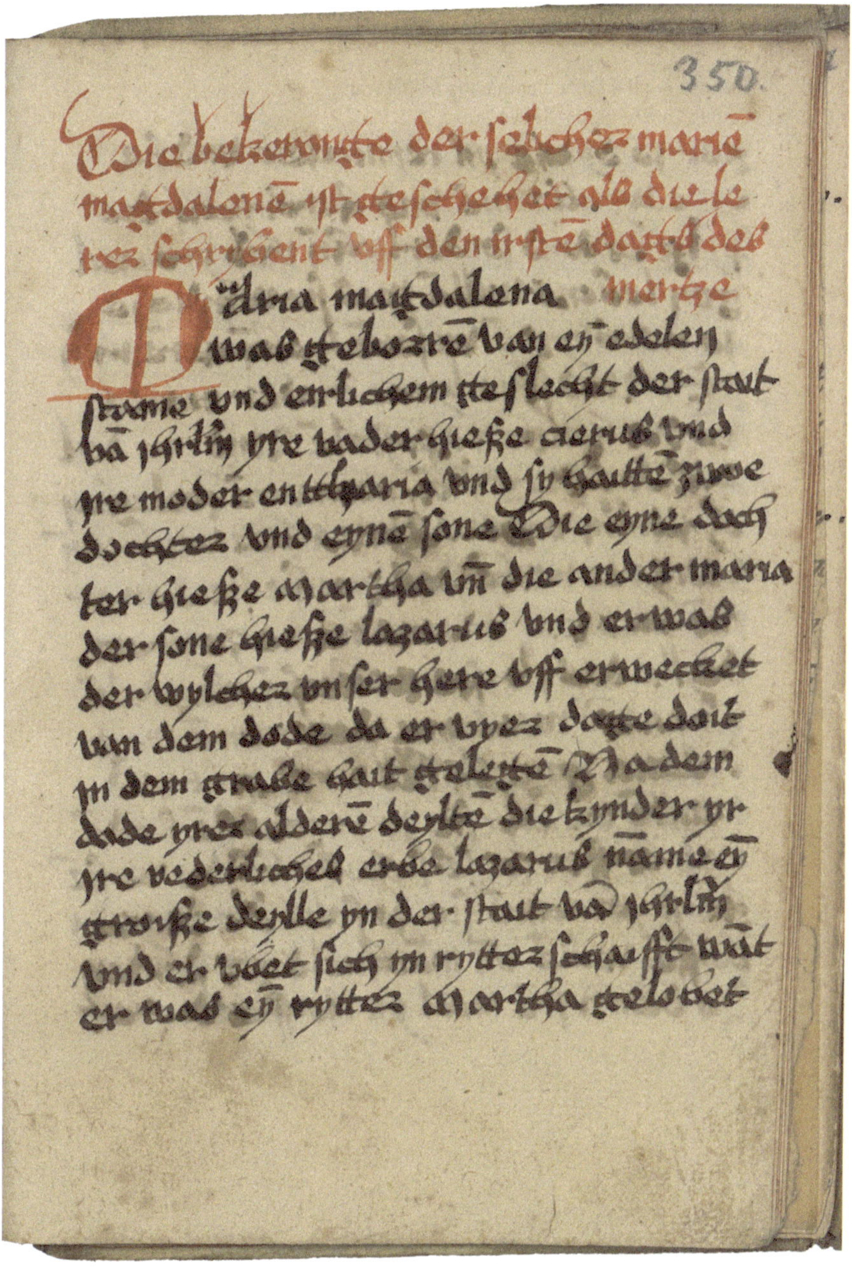

350.

Die bekerunge der selicher marie
magdalenē ist geschehen als die le
rer schribent uff den irstē dagtō des

Aria magdalena merge
was geborzē van eȳ edelen
stame vnd erlichem geslecht der stat
bā iherlm yre vader hieße cierus vnd
yre moder en tilgaria vnd sy hatte zwe
dochtez vnd eynē sone Die eyne doch
ter hieße martha vñ die ander maria
der sone hieße lazarus vnd er was
der wylchez vnser herre vff erwecket
von dem dode da er vyer dage doit
yn dem grabe hait geleytē Nadem
dode yres alderē deyltē die kynder yr
yre vederliches erbe lazarus name ē
groiße deylle yn der stat bā iherlm
vnd er voet sich yn ryttez schaufft wat
er was eȳ ryttez martha geloebet

Abbildung 4: Straßburg, Bibliothèque nationale et universitaire, Ms. 324, Bl. 350ʳ – Reproduktion: Bibliothèque nationale et universitaire de Strasburg

Abkürzungen

CCM	Corpus Christianorum. Continuatio Mediaevalis
CCSL	Corpus Christianorum Series Latina
CvH	›Die Vita der Christina von Hane‹
DTM	Deutsche Texte des Mittelalters
DW I/III	Meister Eckhart: Die deutschen und lateinischen Werke. Hrsg. i. A. der Deutschen-Forschungsgemeinschaft. Die Deutsche Werke Bd. 1/3. Hrsg. und übers. von Josef Quint. Stuttgart 1958/1976 (unveränd. Nachdrucke 1986/1999).
MGH	Monumenta Germaniae Historica
MTU	Münchener Texte und Untersuchungen zur deutschen Literatur des Mittelalters
PL	Patrologia cursus completus, omnium ss. patrum, doctorum scriptorumque ecclesiasticorum sive Latinorum, sive Graecorum. Series Latina (Vol. 1–221). Hrsg. von Jacques-Paul Migne. Paris 1844–1864.
PBB	Beiträge zur Geschichte der deutschen Sprache und Literatur
PMLA	Publications of the Modern Language Association of America
²VL	Die deutsche Literatur des Mittelalters. Verfasserlexikon. Begründet von Wolfgang Stammler, fortgeführt von Karl Langosch. 2., völlig neu bearb. Aufl. Hrsg. von Kurt Ruh / Burghart Wachinger u. a. 14 Bde. Berlin / New York 1978–2008.
ZfdA	Zeitschrift für deutsches Altertum und deutsche Literatur
ZfdPh	Zeitschrift für deutsche Philologie

https://doi.org/10.1515/9783110536324-014

Bibliographie

Textausgaben

Ambrosius: ›De viduis‹. In: PL 16 (1845), Sp. 233A–262D.

Angela von Foligno: ›Instructiones‹. In: Il libro della Beata Angela da Foligno. Edizione critica. Hrsg. von Ludger Thier / Abele Calufetti (Spicilegium Bonaventurianum 25). Grottaferrata 1985, S. 403–737.

Angela von Foligno: ›Memoriale‹. In: Il libro della Beata Angela da Foligno. Edizione critica. Hrsg. von Ludger Thier / Abele Calufetti (Spicilegium Bonaventurianum 25). Grottaferrata 1985, S. 125–401.

›Der Arnsteiner Marienleich‹. In: Die Religiösen Dichtungen des 11. und 12. Jahrhunderts. Hrsg. von Friedrich Maurer. 3 Bde. Tübingen 1964–1970, Bd. 1 (1964), S. 433–452.

Sancti Augustini Confessionum libri XIII. Hrsg. von Lucas Verheijen (CCSL 27). Turnhout 1981.

Augustinus: De Genesi ad litteram XII. In: PL 34 (1845), Sp. 245–486.

Bernhard von Clairvaux: Sermones de diversi. In: PL 183 (1854), Sp. 537A–748C.

Berthold von Regensburg: Vollständige Ausgabe seiner Predigten mit Ammerkungen von Franz Pfeiffer. Mit einem Vorwort von Kurt Ruh. 2 Bde. Berlin 1965 (Neudruck der Originalausgabe Wien 1862/1880).

Bihlmeyer, Karl (Hrsg.): Die schwäbische Mystikerin Elsbeth Achler von Reute († 1420) und die Überlieferung ihrer Vita. In: Festgabe Philipp Strauch zum 80. Geburtstage am 23. September 1932 dargebracht von Fachkollegen und Schülern. Hrsg. von Georg Baesecke / Ferdinand Joseph Schneider (Hermaea 31). Halle 1932, S. 96–109.

Sancta Birgitta: ›Revelaciones‹. Bd. 1, 4, 7. Hrsg. von Carl-Gustaf Undhagen / Hans Aili / Birger Bergh (Samlingar utgivna av Svenska fornskrift-sällskapet. Ser. 2, Latinska skrifter 7). Uppsala / Göteborg 1967–1992.

›Leben und Offenbarungen der Wiener Begine Agnes Blannbekin‹. Hrsg. von Peter Dinzelbacher / Renate Vogeler (Göppinger Arbeiten zur Germanistik 419). Göppingen 1994.

Boethius: ›De institutione musica‹. In: De institutione arithmetica libri duo. De institutione musica libri quinque. Accedit Geometria quae fertur Boetii. Hrsg. von Gottfried Friedlein. Leipzig 1867 (unveränd. Nachdruck Frankfurt a. M. 1966), S. 175–371.

›Brandan‹. Die mitteldeutsche ›Reise‹-Fassung. Hrsg. von Reinhard Hahn / Christoph Fasbender (Jenaer germanistische Forschungen NF 14). Heidelberg 2002.

›Lebensbeschreibung der sel. Christina, gen. von Retters‹. Hrsg. von Franz Paul Mittermaier: In: Archiv für Mittelrheinische Kirchengeschichte 17 (1965), S. 226–251 / Archiv für Mittelrheinische Kirchengeschichte 18 (1966), S. 203–238.

›Offenbarungen der Margaretha Ebner‹. In: Margaretha Ebner und Heinrich von Nördlingen. Ein Beitrag zur Geschichte der deutschen Mystik. Hrsg. von Philipp Strauch. Amsterdam 1966, S. 1–166 (Nachdruck der Orignalausgabe Freiburg i. Br. / Tübingen 1882).

Meister Eckhart: Die deutschen und lateinischen Werke. Hrsg. i. A. der Deutschen-Forschungsgemeinschaft. Die Deutschen Werke. Bd. 1. Hrsg. und übers. von Josef Quint. Stuttgart 1958 (unveränd. Nachdruck 1986).

Meister Eckhart: Die deutschen und lateinischen Werke. Hrsg. i. A. der Deutschen-Forschungsgemeinschaft. Die Deutschen Werke. Bd. 3. Hrsg. und übers. von Josef Quint. Stuttgart 1976 (unveränd. Nachdruck 1999).

https://doi.org/10.1515/9783110536324-015

Frauenlob (Heinrich von Meissen): ›Marienleich‹. In: Leichs, Sangsprüche, Lieder. 1. Teil: Einleitungen, Texte. Auf Grund der Vorarbeiten von Helmuth Thomas. Hrsg. von Karl Stackmann / Karl Bertau. Göttingen 1981, S. 236–283.

Venantius Fortunatus: Opera poetica. Hrsg. von Friedrich Löwe (MGH Auct. ant. 4, 1). Berlin 1881.

Gertrud von Helfta: ›ein botte der götlichen miltekeit‹. Hrsg. von Otmar Wieland (Studien und Mittelungen zur Geschichte des Benediktiner-Ordens und seiner Zweige. Ergänzungsband 22). Ottobeuren 1973.

Gertrud von Helfta: ›Legatus divinae pietatis‹. In: Gertrude d'Helfta. Œuvres spirituelles II–V. Hrsg. von Pierre Doyère / Jean-Marie Clément / Bernard de Vregille (Sources chrétiennes. Série des textes monastiques d'Occident 25, 27, 48). Paris 1968–1986.

Gregor der Große: Registrum Epistolarum. Hrsg. von Paul Ewald / Ludwig M. Hartmann (MGH Epp 1–2). 2 Bde. Berlin 1891/1899.

Heinrich von Mügeln: ›Der Tum‹. In: Die kleineren Dichtungen Heinrichs von Mügeln. Erste Abteilung. Die Spruchsammlung des Göttinger Cod. Philos. 21. Hrsg. von Karl Stackmann. 3 Teilbde. (DTM 50–52). Berlin 1959, Bd. 2, S. 147–219.

›Briefe Heinrichs von Nördlingen‹. Margaretha Ebner und Heinrich von Nördlingen. Ein Beitrag zur Geschichte der deutschen Mystik. Hrsg. von Philipp Strauch. Amsterdam 1966, S. 169–270 (Nachdruck der Orignalausgabe Freiburg i. Br. / Tübingen 1882).

Hermann von Reichenau: ›In assumptione B. Mariae‹. In: Analecta hymnica Medii Aevi. Hrsg. von Clemens Blume / Guido M. Dreves. Leipzig 1886–1915. Bd. 50 (1907), Nr. 241, S. 313 f.

›Hester‹. Eine poetische Paraphrase des Buches Esther aus dem Ordensland Preussen. Edition und Kommentar. Hrsg. von Manfred Caliebe (Quellen und Studien zur Geschichte des Deutschen Ordens 21). Marburg 1985, S. 11–123.

Joannes Ludolphus van Craywinckel: ›Het leven vande salighe maghet Christina‹. In: Legende der levens ende gedenck-weerdige daden van [...] persoonen [...] inde witte ordre vanden H. Norbertus het tweede deel. Hrsg. von Joannes Ludolphus van Craywinckel. 2 Bde. Mechelen 1664/Antwerpen 1665, Bd. 2, S. 730–759.

Johannes von Magdeburg: ›Die Vita der Margareta contracta‹. einer Magdeburger Rekluse des 13. Jahrhunderts. Hrsg. von Paul Gerhard Schmidt (Studien zur katholischen Bistums- und Klostergeschichte 36). Leipzig 1992.

Johannes Marienwerder: ›Das Leben der heiligen Dorothea von Montau‹. Hrsg. von Max Töppen. In: Scriptores rerum Prussicarum. Die Geschichtsquellen der preußischen Vorzeit bis zum Untergange der Ordensherrschaft. Hrsg. von Theodor Hirsch / Max Töppen / Ernst Strehlke. Bd. 2. Leipzig 1863 (Nachdruck Frankfurt a. M. 1963), S. 197–350.

Konrad von Megenberg: ›Das Buch der Natur‹. Hrsg. von Robert Luff / Georg Steer (Texte und Textgeschichte 54). 4 Bde. Tübingen 2003.

Konrad von Würzburg: ›Die Goldene Schmiede‹. Hrsg. von Edward Schröder. Göttingen 1926.

Krings, Bruno (Hrsg.): Die Statuten des Prämonstratenserordens von 1244/46 und ihre Überarbeitung im Jahr 1279. In: Analecta Praemonstratensia 83 (2007), S. 5–127.

›Die Offenbarungen der Adelheid Langmann‹. Klosterfrau zu Engelthal. Hrsg. von Philipp Strauch (Quellen und Forschungen zur Sprach- und Kulturgeschichte der Germanischen Völker 26). Straßburg 1878.

Caspar Lauer: ›Vita beatae Christinae‹. In: Spiritus literarius Norbertinus a scabiosis Casimiri Oudini calumniis vindicatur seu sylloge viros ex ordine Praemonstratensi. Hrsg. von Georg Lienhardt. Augsburg 1771, S. 597–602.

›Les Œuvres de Marguerite d'Oingt‹. Hrsg. von Antonin Duraffour / Pierre Gardette / Paulette
    Durdilly (Publications de l'Institut de Linguistique Romane de Lyon 21). Paris 1965.
›Conversio beatae Mariae Magdalenae‹. Hrsg. von Hans Hansel. In: Die Maria-Magdalena-
    Legende. Eine Quellen-Untersuchung. Bottrop 1937 (Diss. Greifswald 1931), S. 115–127.
›Van sunte maria magdalena bekeringhe‹. Hrsg. von C. G. N. de Vooys. In: De legende van sunte
    maria magdalena bekeringhe. Tijdschrift voor nederlandsche Taal- en Letterkunde 24
    (1905), S. 28–44.
Mechthild von Hackeborn: ›Liber specialis gratiae‹. In: Revelationes Gertrudinæ ac
    Mechtildianæ II. Sanctæ Mechthildis virginis ordinis sancti Benedicti Liber specialis
    gratiæ, accedit sororis Mechthildis ejusdem ordinis Lux divinitatis. Opus ad codicum
    fidem nunc primum integre editum Solesmensium O. S. B. monachorum cura et opera.
    Paris 1877 S. 1–421.
Mechthild von Magdeburg: ›Das fließende Licht der Gottheit‹. Nach der Einsiedler Handschrift
    in kritischem Vergleich mit der gesamten Überlieferung. Hrsg. von Hans Neumann (MTU
    100–101). 2 Bde. München 1990–1993, Bd. 1 (1990): Text, besorgt von Gisela Vollmann-
    Profe.
Mechthild von Magdeburg: ›Lux divinitatis‹. In: Revelationes Gertrudinæ ac Mechtildianæ II.
    Sanctæ Mechthildis virginis ordinis sancti Benedicti Liber specialis gratiæ, accedit sororis
    Mechthildis ejusdem ordinis Lux divinitatis. Opus ad codicum fidem nunc primum integre
    editum Solesmensium O. S. B. monachorum cura et opera. Paris 1877, S. 435–710.
Neidhart-Lieder. Texte und Melodien sämtlicher Handschriften und Drucke. Hrsg. von Ulrich
    Müller u. a. 3 Bde. Berlin / New York 2007.
Richard von St. Victor: In Cantica Canticorum explicatio. In: PL 196 (1855), Sp. 405A–523B.
Rudolf von Biberach: ›Die siben strassen zu got‹. Die hochalemannische Übertragung nach der
    Handschrift Einsiedeln 278. Hrsg. von Margot Schmidt (Spicilegium Bonaventurianum 6).
    Quaracchi-Florentiae 1969.
Rupert von Deutz: ›De gloria et honore filii hominis super Mattheum‹. Hrsg. von Rhaban Haacke
    (CCM 29). Tournai 1979.
Heinrich Seuse: ›Büchlein der ewigen Weisheit‹. In: Heinrich Seuse. Deutsche Schriften Hrsg.
    von Karl Bihlmeyer. Stuttgart 1907 (unver. Nachdruck Frankfurt a.M. 1961), S. 196–325.
Heinrich Seuse: ›Leben‹. In: Heinrich Seuse. Deutsche Schriften Hrsg. von Karl Bihlmeyer.
    Stuttgart 1907 (unver. Nachdruck Frankfurt a.M. 1961), S. 7–195.
Heinrich Seuse: ›Das grosse Briefbuch‹. In: Heinrich Seuse. Deutsche Schriften Hrsg. von Karl
    Bihlmeyer. Stuttgart 1907 (unver. Nachdruck Frankfurt a.M. 1961), S. 405–495.
Angelus Silesius: ›Cherubinischer Wandersmann‹. In: Sämtliche poetische Werke. Hrsg. von
    Hans Ludwig Held. 3 Bde. 3. erw. Aufl. München 1949–1952, Bd. 3 (1949).
Ignace van Spilbeeck: Une fleur cachée. La bienheureuse Christine du Christ, religieuse du
    monastère de Rhetirs. Namur 1885.
Stackmann, Karl (Hrsg.): Die kleineren Dichtungen Heinrichs von Mügeln. Erste Abteilung. Die
    Spruchsammlung des Göttinger Cod. Philos. 21. 3 Teilbde. (DTM 50–52). Berlin 1959.
›Die St. Georgener Predigten‹. Hrsg. von Regina D. Schiewer und Kurt Otto Seidel (DTM 90).
    Berlin 2010.
›Das St. Trudperter Hohelied‹. Eine Lehre der liebenden Gotteserkenntnis. Hrsg. von Friedrich
    Ohly (Bibliothek des Mittelalters 2, Bibliothek deutscher Klassiker 155). Frankfurt a.M.
    1998.

›Die Predigten Taulers‹. Aus der Engelberger und der Freiburger Handschrift sowie aus Schmidts Abschriften der ehemaligen Straßburger Handschriften. Hrsg. von Ferdinand Vetter (DTM 11). Berlin 1910.

›Vatikanische Gebete‹. In: Denkmäler deutscher Prosa des 11. und 12. Jahrhunderts. Abteilung A: Text; Abteilung B: Kommentar. Hrsg. von Friedrich Wilhelm (Münchener Texte 8). München 1914/1916 (Nachdruck in einem Band [Germanistische Bücherei 3]. München 1960), S. 69–73.

Pieter de Waghenare: ›Vita beati Hermanni Josephi‹. 2. Aufl. Antwerpen 1661.

Weber, Robert / Gryson, Roger (Hrsg.): Biblia Sacra Vulgata. 5. Aufl. Stuttgart 2007.

Handschriften

Berlin, Staatsbibliothek Preußischer Kulturbesitz, Ms. germ. oct. 56

Berlin, Staatsbibliothek Preußischer Kulturbesitz, Ms. germ. quart. 261

Berlin, Staatsbibliothek Preußischer Kulturbesitz, Ms. germ. quart. 524

Berlin, Staatsbibliothek Preußischer Kulturbesitz, Ms. germ. quart. 1122

Brüssel, Bibliothèque royale de Belgique, ms. 7917

Brüssel, Société des Bollandistes, ms. 347

Darmstadt, Universitäts- und Landesbibliothek, cod. 814

Darmstadt, Universitäts- und Landesbibliothek, cod. 2196

Den Haag, Koninklijke Bibliotheek, cod. 71 H 6

Den Haag, Koninklijke Bibliotheek, cod. 133 F 17

Groningen, Universiteitsbibliotheek, cod. 9 Mss. societas pro excolendo iure patrio

Köln, Historisches Archiv Best. 7008 (GB 8) 141

Köln, Historisches Archiv 7020 (W* 8) 72

Kopenhagen, Kongelige Bibliotek, Cod. Gl. kgl. S. 205

München, Bayerische Staatsbibliothek, Clm 536

New Haven, Beinecke Library, MS 404

Nürnberg, Germanisches Nationalmuseum, Cod. 8826

Rom, Bibliotheca Apostolica Vaticana, Cod. Vat. lat. 4763

St. Gallen, Stiftsbibliothek, cod. 1142

Straßburg, Bibliothèque nationale et universitaire, Ms. 324

Forschungsliteratur

Achten, Gerard: Das christliche Gebet im Mittelalter. Andachts- und Stundenbücher in
   Handschrift und Frühdruck. 2. verb. Aufl. (Staatsbibliothek Preußischer Kulturbesitz.
   Ausstellungskataloge 3). Berlin 1987.
Adman, Anna Fredriksson: An Heretical Saint? The Birgittine Case and Heymericus de Campo
   at the Council of Basel. In: University, Council, City. Intellectual Culture on the Rhine,
   1300–1550. Acts of the XIIth International Colloquium of the Société Internationale pour
   l'Étude de la Philosophie Médiévale. Freiburg im Breisgau, 27–29 October 2004. Hrsg.
   von Laurent Cesalli / Nadja Germann / Maarten J. F. M. Hoenen (Rencontres de philosophie
   médiévale 13). Turnhout 2007, S. 277–289.
Angold, Michael: The Fourth Crusade. Event and Context. Harlow 2003.
Althoff, Gerd: ›Causa scribendi‹ und Darstellungsabsicht. Die Lebensbeschreibung der Königin
   Mathilde und andere Beispiele. In: Litterae medii aevi. Festschrift für Johanne Autenrieth
   zum 65. Geburtstag. Hrsg. von Michael Borgolte / Herrad Spilling. Sigmaringen 1988,
   S. 117–133.
Andersen, Elizabeth A.: The Voices of Mechtild of Magdeburg. Bern 2000.
Andersen, Elizabeth A.: ›Das Licht der Gottheit‹ und der Psalter. Dialogische Beziehungen. In:
   Dialoge. Sprachliche Kommunikation in und zwischen Texten im deutschen Mittelalter.
   Hamburger Colloquium 1999. Hrsg. von Nikolaus Henkel / Martin H. Jones / Nigel F. Palmer.
   Tübingen 2003, S. 225–238.
Andersen, Elizabeth A. / Eikelmann, Manfred / Simon, Anne: Einleitung. In: Texttyp und
   Textproduktion in der deutschen Literatur des Mittelalters. Hrsg. von Elizabeth A.
   Andersen / Manfred Eikelmann / Anne Simon (Trends in Medieval Philology 7). Berlin / New
   York 2005, S. XI–XXV.
Angenendt, Arnold: Liturgik und Historik. Gab es eine organische Liturgie-Entwicklung?
   (Quaestiones disputatae 189). Freiburg / Basel / Wien 2001.
Arnold, John H. / Goodson, Caroline: Resounding Community. The History and Meaning of
   Medieval Church Bells. In: Viator 43 (2012), S. 99–113.
Arthur, Rosemary A.: Pseudo-Dionysius as Polemicist. The Development and Purpose of the
   Angelic Hierarchy in Sixth Century Syria. Aldershot 2008.
Ashton, Gail: The Generation of Identity in Late Medieval Hagiography. Speaking the Saint
   (Routledge Research in Medieval Studies 1). London / New York 2000.
Asperen, Hanneke van: Praying, Threading, and Adorning. Sewn-in Prints in a Rosary Prayer
   Book (London, British Library, ADD. MS 14042). In: Weaving, Veiling, and Dressing. Textiles
   and Their Metaphors in the Late Middle Ages. Hrsg. von Kathryn M. Rudy / Barbara Baert
   (Medieval Church Studies 12), Turnhout 2007, S. 82–100.
Astell, Ann W.: Chaucer's ›St. Anne Trinity‹. Devotion, Dynasty, Dogma, and Debate. In: Studies
   in Philology 94 (1997), S. 395–416.
Austin, John Langshaw: How to Do Things with Words. 2. Aufl. Oxford 1975.
Backmund, Norbert: Die mittelalterlichen Geschichtsschreiber des Prämonstratenserordens
   (Bibliotheca Analectorum Praemonstratensium 10). Averbode 1972.
Backmund, Norbert: Monasticon Praemonstratense. id est historia circariarum et canoniarum
   candidi et canonici Ordinis Praemonstratensis, 2. Aufl. Berlin / New York 1983 (Original-
   ausgabe Straubing 1949).

Barratt, Alexandra: Context. Some Reflections on Wombs and Tombs and Inclusive Language. In: Anchorites, Wombs and Tombs. Intersections of Gender and Enclosure in the Middle Ages. Hrsg. von Liz Herbert McAvoy / Mari Hughes-Edwards. Cardiff 2005, S. 27–38.

Bartal, Renana: Bridal Mysticism and Eucharistic Devotion. The Marriage of the Lamb in an Illustrated Apocalypse from Fourteenth-Century England. In: Viator 42 (2011), S. 227–246.

Bartlett, Anne Clark: Male Authors, Female Readers. Representation and Subjectivity in Middle English Devotional Literature. Ithaca 1997.

Bastert, Bernd: ›den wolt er lêren rehte tuon‹. Der ›Winsbecke‹ zwischen Didaxe und Diskussion. In: Text und Normativität. XX. Anglo-German Colloquium. Hrsg. von Elke Brüggen u.a. Berlin / Boston 2012, S. 303–318.

Bawden, Tina: In Bewegung versetzte Betrachter: Überlegungen zur raumöffnenden Dimension klappbarer Bildmedien im Mittelalter. In: Bewegen im Zwischenraum. Hrsg. von Uwe Wirth (Wege der Kulturforschung 3). Berlin 2012, S. 297–319.

Bayer, Elke: Sieben Freuden Marias. 1. Mittelhochdeutsche Literatur. In: Marienlexikon. Hrsg. von Remigius Bäumer / Leo Scheffczyk. 6 Bde. St. Ottilien 1988–1994, Bd. 6 (1994), S. 154 f.

Becker, Adolf: Die deutschen Handschriften der Kaiserlichen Universitäts- und Landesbibliothek zu Straßburg (Katalog der Kaiserlichen Universitäts- und Landesbibliothek in Straßburg 6). Straßburg 1914.

Beckman, Patricia Zimmerman: Swimming in the Trinity. Mechthild of Magdeburg's Mystical Play. In: Spiritus. A Journal for Christian Spirituality 4 (2004), S. 60–77.

Beckman, Patricia Zimmerman: The Power of Books and the Practice of Mysticism in the Fourteenth Century. Heinrich of Nördlingen and Margaret Ebner on Mechthild's ›Flowing of the Godhead‹. In: Church History. Studies in Christianity and Culture 76 (2007), S. 61–83.

Belliger, Andréa / Krieger, David: Einführung. In: Ritualtheorien. Ein einführendes Handbuch. Hrsg. von Andréa Belliger / David Krieger. 5. Aufl. Wiesbaden 2013, S. 7–35.

Belting-Ihm, Christa: ›Sub matris tutela‹. Unterschungen zur Vorgeschichte der Schutzmantelmadonna. Heidelberg 1976.

Bennewitz, Ingrid: Jungfrau, Mutter, Königin. Vereinnahmung und Ausgrenzung von Weiblichkeit in mittelalterlichen Marienliedern. In: Lektüren der Differenz. Hrsg. von Ingrid Bennewitz. Berlin 2002, S. 55–74.

Benthien, Claudia: Barockes Schweigen. Rhetorik und Performativität des Sprachlosen im 17. Jahrhundert. Paderborn 2006.

Benz, Ernst: Die Vision. Erfahrungsformen und Bilderwelt. Stuttgart 1969.

Bernhardt, Susanne: Die implizite Pragmatik der Gelassenheit in der ›Vita‹ Heinrich Seuses. In: Semantik der Gelassenheit. Generierung, Etablierung, Transformation. Hrsg. von Susanne Bernhardt / Burkhard Hasebrink / Imke Früh (Historische Semantik 17). Göttingen 2012, S. 115–142.

Bezzel, Anne: Der gesegnete Leib. Die Schwangerschaft Mariens als Gegenstand der Devotion im Kontext einer somatischen Religiosität des ausgehenden Mittelalters. In: Frömmigkeit – Theologie – Frömmigkeitstheologie. Contributions to European Church History. Festschrift für Berndt Hamm zum 60. Geburtstag. Hrsg. von Gudrun Litz / Heidrun Munzert / Roland Liebenberg (Studies in the History of Christian Traditions 124). Leiden / Boston 2005, S. 105–118.

Bieritz, Karl-Heinrich: Liturgik. Berlin / New York 2004.

Boerner, Bruno: Le rôle de l'image sculptée dans les couvents féminins allemands à la fin du Moyen Âge. In: Bibliothèque de l'École des chartes 162 (2006), S. 119–131.

Bogner, Ralf: Rezension zu Claudia Benthien: Barockes Schweigen. Rhetorik und Performa-
   tivität des Sprachlosen im 17. Jahrhundert (2006). In: Arbitrium 26 (2008), S. 67–71.
Boon, Jessica A.: Trinitarian Love Mysticism. Ruusbroec, Hadewijch, and the Gendered
   Experience of the Divine. In: Church History. Studies in Christianity and Culture 72 (2003),
   S. 484–503.
Borries, Ekkehard: Schwesternspiegel im 15. Jahrhundert. Gattungskonstitution – Editionen –
   Untersuchungen. Berlin / New York 2008.
Boxler, Madeleine: ›ich bin ein predigerin und appostlorin‹. Die deutschen Maria Magdalena–
   Legenden des Mittelalters (1300–1550). Untersuchungen und Texte. (Deutsche Literatur
   von den Anfängen bis 1700 22). Bern 1996.
Brandstetter, Gabriele: Lever de Rideau – die Szene des Vorhangs. In: Szenen des Vorhangs.
   Schnittflächen der Künste. Hrsg. von Gabriele Brandstetter / Sibylle Peters (Rombach
   Scenae 9). Freiburg 2008, S. 19–44.
Briquet, Charles-Moïse: Les filigranes. Dictionnaire historique des marques du papier dès
   leur apparition vers 1282 jusqu'en 1600. Bd. 1: A–Ch, Bd. 2: Ci–K. Mansfield Centre 2007
   (Originalausgabe Paris 1907).
Brown, Peter: Body and Society. Men, Women, and Sexual Renunciation in Early Christianity.
   New York 2008 (Originalausgabe New York 1988).
Bücker, Jörg: Sprachhandeln und Sprachwissen. Grammatische Konstruktionen im
   Spannungsfeld von Interaktion und Kognition (Sprache und Wissen 11). Berlin / Boston
   2012.
Bumke, Joachim: Höfischer Körper – Höfische Kultur. In: Modernes Mittelalter. Neue Bilder
   einer populären Epoche. Hrsg. von Joachim Heinzle. Frankfurt a. M. 1994, S. 67–102.
Bumke, Joachim: Autor und Werk. Beobachtungen und Überlegungen zur höfischen Epik. In:
   Philologie als Textwissenschaft. Alte und neue Horizonte. Hrsg. Helmut von Tervooren /
   Horst Wenzel (ZfdPh 116, Sonderheft). Berlin 1997, S. 87–114.
Bürkle, Susanne: Weibliche Spiritualität und imaginierte Weiblichkeit. Deutungsmuster und
   -perspektiven frauenmystischer Literatur im Blick auf die Thesen Caroline W. Bynums. In:
   ZfdPh 113 (1994), S. 116–143.
Bürkle, Susanne: Literatur im Kloster. Historische Funktion und rhetorische Legitimation
   frauenmystischer Texte des 14. Jahrhunderts (Bibliotheca Germanica 38). Tübingen / Basel
   1999.
Bürkle, Susanne: Die ›Gnadenvita‹ Christine Ebners. Episodenstruktur – Text-Ich und
   Autorschaft. In: Deutsche Mystik im abendländischen Zusammenhang. Neu erschlossene
   Texte, neue methodische Ansätze, neue theoretische Konzepte. Kolloquium Kloster
   Fischingen 1998. Hrsg. von Walter Haug / Wolfram Schneider-Lastin. Tübingen 2000,
   S. 483–513.
Burrow, John Anthony: Ricardian Poetry. Chaucer, Gower, Langland and the Gawain Poet. 2.
   Aufl. London 1992.
Burrows, Mark S.: Raiding the Inarticulate. Mysticism, Poetics and the Unlanguageable. In:
   Spiritus. A Journal of Christian Spirituality 4 (2004), S. 173–194.
Butler, Judith: Gender Trouble. Feminism and the Subversion of Identity. New York / London
   1990.
Butler, Judith: Bodies That Matter. On the Discursive Limits of Sex. New York / London 1993.
Büttner, Frank O.: Imitatio pietatis. Motive der christlichen Ikonographie als Modelle zur
   Verähnlichung. Berlin 1983.

Bynum, Caroline Walker: ›Docere verbum et exemplo‹. An aspect of Twelfth-Century Spirituality (Harvard Theological Studies 31). Missoula 1979.

Bynum, Caroline Walker: Jesus as Mother. Studies in the Spirituality of the High Middle Ages (Publications of the Center for Medieval and Renaissance Studies 16). Berkeley 1982.

Bynum, Caroline Walker: Holy Feast and Holy Fast. The Religious Significance of Food to Medieval Women. Berkeley/Los Angeles/London 1987.

Bynum, Caroline Walker: Fragmentation and Redemption. Essays on Gender and the Human Body in Medieval Religion. New York 1991.

Bynum, Caroline Walker: Christian Materiality. An Essay on Religion in Late Medieval Europe. New York 2011.

Bynum, Caroline Walker: Crowned with Many Crowns. Nuns and Their Status in Late-Medieval Wienhausen. In: The Catholic History Review 101 (2015), S. 18–40.

Cadden, Joan: Meanings of Sex Difference in the Middle Ages. Medicine, Science, and Culture (Cambridge History of Medicine). Cambridge 1993.

Caliebe, Manfred: Hester. Eine poetische Paraphrase des Buches Esther aus dem Ordensland Preussen. Edition und Kommentar (Quellen und Studien zur Geschichte des Deutschen Ordens 21). Marburg 1985.

Carruthers, Mary Jean: The Craft of Thoughts. Meditation, Rhetoric, and the Making of Images, 400–1200 (Cambridge Studies in Medieval Literature 34). Cambridge 1998.

Carruthers, Mary Jean: The Book of Memory: A Study of Memory in Medieval Culture (Cambridge Studies in Medieval Literature 70). Cambridge 1990.

Certeau, Michel de: L'expérience religieuse. Connaissance vécue dans l'église. In: Le voyage mystique. Michel de Certeau. Hrsg. von Luce Giard. Paris 1988, S. 27–51.

Chevrolet, Teresa: L'Eros De Diotime comme mythe intertextuel. Lectures néo-platoniciennes d'un passage du Banquet. In: Bibliothèque d'Humanisme et Renaissance 51 (1989), S. 311–330.

Chinca, Mark/Young, Christopher: Orality and Literacy in the Middle Ages. A Conjunction and its Consequences. In: Orality and literacy in the Middle Ages. Essays on a conjunction and its consequences in honour of D.H. Green. Hrsg. von Mark Chinca/Christopher Young (Utrecht Studies in Medieval Literacy 12). Turnhout 2005, S. 1–15.

Churchill, Laurie J./Brown, Phyllis R./Jeffrey, Jane E. (Hrsg.): Women Writing Latin. From Roman Antiquity to Early Modern Europe. 3 Bde. New York/London 2002.

Clark, Anne L.: The Priesthood of the Virgin Mary. Gender Trouble in the Twelfth Century. In: Journal of Feminist Studies in Religion 18 (2002), S. 5–24.

Clemm, Ludwig: Das Totenbuch des Stifts Ilbenstadt. In: Archiv für hessische Geschichte und Altertumskunde. N.F. 19 (1936), S. 169–274.

Coakley, John Wayland: The Representation of Sanctity in Late Medieval Hagiography. Evidence from Lives of Saints of the Dominican Order. Cambridge, MA 1980 (Diss. Harvard).

Coakley, John Wayland: Women, Men and Spiritual Power. Female Saints and their Male Collaborators. New York 2006.

Coakley, John Wayland: Women's Textual Authority and the Collaboration of Clerics. In: Medieval Holy Women in the Christian Tradition, c. 1100 – c. 1500. Hrsg. von Alastair J. Minnis/Rosalynn Voaden (Brepols Essays in European Culture 1). Turnhout 2010, S. 83–104.

Coakley, Sarah: ›Batter my heart…?‹ On Sexuality, Spirituality, and the Christian Doctrine of the Trinity. In: Graven Images 2 (1995), S. 74–83.

Coakley, Sarah: Powers and Submissions. Spirituality, Philosophy and Gender. Oxford 2002.

Coakley, Sarah: God, Sexuality and the Self. An Essay ›on the Trinity‹. Cambridge 2013.

Coleman, Joyce: Interactive Parchment. The Theory and Practice of Medieval English Aurality. In: The Yearbook of English Studies 25 (1995), S. 63–79.

Coleman, Joyce: Public Reading and the Reading Public in Late Medieval England and France, 2. Aufl. (Cambridge Studies in Medieval Literature 26). Cambridge 2005.

Corradini, Richard / Diesenberger, Max / Niederkorn-Bruck, Meta (Hrsg.): Zwischen Niederschrift und Wiederschrift. Hagiographie und Historiographie im Spannungsfeld von Kompendien-überlieferung und Editionstechnik (Forschungen zur Geschichte des Mittelalters 18). Wien 2010.

Crăciun, Maria: Ora pro nobis sancta Dei genitrix. Prayers and Gestures in Late Medieval Transylvania. In: Ritual, Images, and Daily Life. The Medieval Perspective. Hrsg. von Gerhard Jaritz. Wien 2012, S. 107–138.

Cramer, Thomas: Das Subjekt und sein Widerschein. Beobachtungen zum Wandel der Spiegel-metapher in Antike und Mittelalter. In: Inszenierungen von Subjektivität in der Literatur des Mittelalters. Hrsg. von Martin Baisch u. a. Königstein im Taunus 2005, S. 213–229.

Cré, Marleen: Vernacular Mysticism in the Charterhouse. A Study of London, British Library, MS Additional 37790 (The Medieval Translator 9). Turnhout 2006.

Csordas, Thomas J. (Hrsg.): Embodiment and Experience. The Existential Ground of Culture and Self (Cambridge Studies in Medical Anthropology 2). Cambridge 2001 (Nachdruck der Originalausgabe Cambridge 1994).

Cunneen, Sally: In Search of Mary. The Woman and the Symbol. New York 1996.

Culler, Jonathan: Philosophy and Literature. The Fortunes of the Performative. In: Poetics Today 21 (2000), S. 503–519.

Davis, Stephen J.: Crossed Texts, Crossed Sex. Intertextuality and Gender in Early Christian Legends of Holy Women Disguised as Men. In: Journal of Early Christian Studies 10 (2002), S. 1–36.

Degering, Hermann: Kurzes Verzeichnis der germanischen Handschriften der Preußischen Staatsbibliothek II. Die Handschriften in Quartformat (Mitteilungen aus der Preußischen Staatsbibliothek VIII). Graz 1970 (Nachdruck der Originalausgabe Leipzig 1926).

Deploige, Jeroen: Priests, Prophets, and Magicians. Max Weber and Pierre Bourdieu ›vs‹ Hildegard of Bingen. In: The Voice of Silence. Women's Literacy in a Men's Church. Hrsg. von Thérèse de Hemptinne / María Eugenia Góngora (Medieval Church Studies 9). Turnhout 2004, S. 3–22.

Derrida, Jacques: Limited Inc. Hrsg. von Gerald Graff. London 1998.

Dicke, Gerd: Aus der Seele gesprochen. Zur Semantik und Pragmatik des Gottesdialogs im »Fließenden Licht der Gottheit« Mechthilds von Magdeburg. In: Dialoge. Sprachliche Kommunikation in und zwischen Texten im deutschen Mittelalter. Hamburger Colloquium 1999. Hrsg. von Nikolaus Henkel / Martin H. Jones / Nigel F. Palmer. Tübingen 2003, S. 267–278.

Dinzelbacher, Peter: Vision und Visionsliteratur im Mittelalter. Stuttgart 1981.

Dinzelbacher, Peter: Rezension zu Siegfried Ringler: Viten- und Offenbarungsliteratur in Frauen-klöstern des Mittelalters. Quellen und Studien (1980). In: Anzeiger für deutsches Altertum und deutsche Literatur 93 (1982), S. 63–71.

Dinzelbacher, Peter: Europäische Frauenmystik des Mittelalters. Ein Überblick. In: Frauenmystik im Mittelalter. Hrsg. von Peter Dinzelbacher / Dieter R. Bauer. Ostfildern 1985, S. 11–23.

Dinzelbacher, Peter: Zur Interpretation erlebnismystischer Texte des Mittelalters. In: ZfdA 117 (1988), S. 1–23.

Doepner, Thomas: Das Prämonstratenserinnenkloster Altenberg im Hoch- und Spätmittelalter. Sozial- und Frömmigkeitsgeschichtliche Untersuchungen (Untersuchungen und Materialien zur Landesgeschichte 16). Marburg 1999.

Dolbeau, François: Transformations des prologues hagiographiques, dues aux réécritures. In: L'hagiographie mérovingienne à travers des réécritures. Hrsg. von Monique Goullet / Martin Heinzelmann / Christiane Veyrard-Cosme (Beihefte der Francia 71). Ostfildern 2010, S. 103–124.

Dronke, Peter: Women Writers of the Middle Ages. A Critical Study of Texts from Perpetua (203) to Marguerite Porete (1310). Cambridge 1984.

Ecker, Hans-Peter: Die Legende. Kulturanthropologische Annäherung an eine literarische Gattung (Germanistische Abhandlungen 76). Stuttgart / Weimar 1993.

Eeghen, Isabella Henriette van: Vrouwenkloosters en Begijnhof in Amsterdam. Van de 14e tot het eind der 16e eeuw. Amsterdam 1941.

Egerding, Michael: Die Metaphorik der spätmittelalterlichen Mystik. Bd. 1: Systematische Untersuchung. Paderborn u. a. 1997(a).

Egerding, Michael: Die Metaphorik der spätmittelalterlichen Mystik. Bd. 2: Bildspender – Bildempfänger – Kontexte. Dokumentation und Interpretation. Paderborn u. a. 1997(b).

Ehlers-Kisseler, Ingrid: Heiligenverehrung bei den Prämonstratensern: Die Seligen und Heiligen des Prämonstratenserordens im deutschen Sprachraum. In: Rottenburger Jahrbuch für Kirchengeschichte 22 (2003), S. 65–94.

Ehrenschwendtner, Marie-Luise: Die Bildung der Dominikanerinnen in Süddeutschland vom 13. bis 15. Jahrhundert (Contubernium 60). Stuttgart 2004 (Diss. Tübingen 1999).

Elkins, Sharon: Gertrude the Great and the Virgin Mary. In: Church History. Studies in Christianity and Culture 66 (1997), S. 720–734.

Elliott, Dyan: Flesh and Spirit. The Female Body. In: Medieval Holy Women in the Christian Tradition, c. 1100–c. 1500. Hrsg. von Alastair J. Minnis / Rosalynn Voaden (Brepols Essays in European Culture 1) Turnhout 2010, S. 13–46.

Eming, Jutta: Mediävisitik und Psychoanalyse. In: Codierungen von Emotionen im Mittelalter / Emotions and Sensibilities in the Middle Ages. Hrsg. von Stephen Jaeger / Ingrid Kasten (Trends in Medieval Philology 1). Berlin / New York 2003, S. 31–44.

Emmelius, Caroline: Verborgene Wahrheiten offenbaren. Verschriftlichungsprozesse in frauen-mystischen Texten zwischen Subversion und Autorisierung. In: Offen und Verborgen. Vorstellungen und Praktiken des Öffentlichen im Privaten in Mittelalter und Früher Neuzeit. Hrsg. von Caroline Emmelius u. a. Göttingen 2004, S. 47–65.

Emmelius, Caroline: Begnadung und Zweifel. Zur Interaktion von Innen- und Außenraum in den ›Offenbarungen‹ der Adelheid Langmann. In: Innenräume in der Literatur des deutschen Mittelalters. XIX. Anglo-German Colloquium Oxford 2005. Hrsg. von Burkhard Hasebrink u. a. Tübingen 2008, S. 309–325.

Emmelius, Caroline: Gesellige Ordnung. Literarische Konzeptionen von geselliger Kommunikation in Mittelalter und Früher Neuzeit (Frühe Neuzeit 139). Tübingen 2009 (Diss. Göttingen 2005).

Emmelius, Caroline: Das visionäre Ich. Ich-Stimmen in der Viten- und Offenbarungsliteratur zwischen Selbstthematisierung und Heterologie. In: Von sich selbst erzählen. Historische Dimensionen des Ich-Erzählens. Tagung Irsee 2013. Hrsg. von Sonja Glauch / Katharina Philipowski. Heidelberg 2017.

Engelmann, Ursmar: Ein Gebet an den Gekreuzigten aus dem Anfang des XIII. Jahrhunderts. Eine Novene aus der ersten Hälfte des frühen 13. Jahrhunderts. In: Scriptorium 10 (1956), S. 103–105.

Fassler, Margot: Composer and Dramatist. Melodious Singing and the Freshness of Remorse. In: Voice of the Living Light. Hildegard of Bingen and her World. Hrsg. von Barbara Newman. Berkeley 1998, S. 149–175.

Federer, Urban: Mystische Erfahrung im literarischen Dialog. Die Briefe Heinrichs von Nördlingen an Margaretha Ebner (Scrinium Friburgense 25). Berlin/New York 2011.

Feilke, Helmuth/Linke, Angelika: Oberfläche und Performanz – Zur Einleitung. In: Oberfläche und Performanz. Untersuchungen zur Sprache als dynamischer Gestalt. Hrsg. von Helmuth Feilke/Angelika Linke (Germanistische Linguistik 283). Tübingen 2009, S. 3–17.

Felten, Franz Josef: ›Noui esse uolunt… deserentes bene contritam uiam…‹. Hildegard von Bingen und Reformbewegungen im religiösen Leben ihrer Zeit. In: Im Angesicht Gottes sucht der Mensch sich selbst. Hildegard von Bingen (1098–1179). Hrsg. von Rainer Berndt. Berlin 2001, S. 27–86.

Felman, Shoshana: The Literary Speech Act. Don Juan with J.L. Austin, or Seduction in Two Languages. Hrsg. von Catherine Porter. Ithaca 1983.

Fink, Gerhard/Maier, Friedrich/Bayer, Karl (Hrsg.): System-Grammatik Latein. Bamberg/München 1997.

Fink, Wilhelm: Kloster (Hofgut) Retters v. d. Höh. Königstein 1931.

Fischer-Lichte, Erika: Ästhetische Erfahrung. Das Semiotische und das Performative. Tübingen 2001.

Fischer-Lichte, Erika: Grenzgänge und Tauschhandel. Auf dem Wege zu einer performativen Kultur. In: Performanz. Zwischen Sprachphilosophie und Kulturwissenschaften. Hrsg. von Uwe Wirth. Frankfurt a.M. 2002, S. 277–300.

Fischer-Lichte, Erika: Performativität und Ereignis. In: Performativität und Ereignis. Hrsg. von Erika Fischer-Lichte (Theatralität 4). Tübingen 2003(a), S. 11–37.

Fischer-Lichte, Erika: Theater als Modell für eine Ästhetik des Performativen. In: Performativität und Praxis. Hrsg. von Jens Kertscher/Dieter Mersch. München 2003(b), S. 97–111.

Fischer-Lichte, Erika: Ästhetik des Performativen. Frankfurt a.M. 2004.

Fischer-Lichte, Erika: Die verwandelnde Kraft der Aufführung. In: Die Aufführung. Diskurs – Macht – Analyse. Hrsg. von Erika Fischer-Lichte. München 2012, S. 11–23.

Flasch, Kurt: Das philosophische Denken im Mittelalter. Von Augustin zu Machiavelli. 2. rev. u. erw. Aufl. Stuttgart 2011.

Fleischer, Wolfgang: Untersuchungen zur Palmbaumallegorie im Mittelalter (Münchener Germanistische Beiträge 20). München 1976.

Fludernik, Monika: The Fictions of Language and the Languages of Fiction. London/New York 1993.

Fludernik, Monika: The Diachronization of Narratology. In: Narrative 11 (2003), S. 331–348.

Fludernik, Monika: Einführung in die Erzähltheorie. Darmstadt 2006.

Fohrmann, Jürgen: Vorbemerkung. In: Rhetorik, Figuration und Performanz. DFG-Symposion 2002. Hrsg. von Jürgen Fohrmann (Germanistische Symposien, Berichtsbände 25). Stuttgart/Weimar 2004, S. VII–X.

Foucault, Michel: L'Archéologie du savoir. Paris 1969.

Foucault, Michel: Qu'est-ce qu'un auteur? In: Dits et écrits. 1954–1988. Hrsg. von Daniel Defert/François Ewald. 2 Bde. Paris 1994. 2. Aufl. des unveränderten Nachdrucks. Malesherbes 2008, Bd. 1: 1954–1975, S. 817–849.

Fulton, Rachel: From Judgement to Passion. Devotion to Christ and the Virgin Mary. 800–1200. New York 2002.

Fraeters, Veerle: Gender and Genre. The Design of Hadewijch's ›book of visions‹. In: The Voice of Silence. Women's Literacy in a Men's Church. Hrsg. von Thérèse de Hemptinne / María Eugenia Góngora (Medieval Church Studies 9). Turnhout 2004, S. 57–81.

France, James: Cistercians under Our Lady's Mantle. In: Cistercian Quarterly 37 (2002), S. 393–414.

Frenken, Ralph: Kindheit und Mystik im Mittelalter (Beihefte zur Mediävistik 2). Frankfurt a.M. 2002.

Freud, Sigmund: Das Unbehagen der Kultur. Stuttgart 2010 (Originalausgabe Wien 1930).

Frings, Theodor: Mittelfränkisch-niederfränkische Studien. Bd 1: Das ripuarisch-niederfränkische Übergangsgebiet (Beiträge zur Geschichte der deutschen Sprache und Literatur 41). Halle 1917.

Garber, Rebecca L. R.: Feminine Figurae. Representations of Gender in Religious Texts by Medieval German Women Writers. 1100–1375 (Studies in Medieval History and Culture 10). New York / London 2003.

Genette, Gérard: Nouveau discours du récit. Paris 1983.

Glauch, Sonja: Ich-Erzähler ohne Stimme. Zur Andersartigkeit mittelalterlichen Erzählens zwischen Narratologie und Mediengeschichte. In: Historische Narratologie. Mediävistische Perspektiven. Hrsg. von Harald Haferland / Matthias Meyer (Trends in Medieval Philology 19). Berlin / New York 2010, S. 149–185.

Goetsch, Paul: Fingierte Mündlichkeit in der Erzählkunst entwickelter Schriftkulturen. In: Poetica 17 (1985), S. 202–218.

Goovaerts, Léon: Haas (Jean). In: Écrivains, artistes et savants de l'ordre de Prémontré. Dictionnaire bio-bibliographique. Hrsg. von Léon Goovaerts. 4 Bde. Brüssel 1899–1920. Bd. 1 (1899), S. 342.

Górecka, Marzena: Das Bild Mariens in der Deutschen Mystik (Deutsche Literatur von den Anfängen bis 1700 29). Bern / New York 1999.

Goullet, Monique: Vers une typologie des réécritures hagiographiques, à partir de quelques exemples du Nord-Est de la France. Avec une édition synoptiquedes deux Vies de saint Èvre de Toul. In: La réécriture hagiographique dans l'occident médiéval. Transformations formelles et idéologiques. Hrsg. von Monique Goullet / Martin Heinzelmann (Beihefte der Francia 58). Ostfildern 2003. S. 109–144.

Goullet, Monique / Heinzelmann, Martin: Avant-propos. In: La réécriture hagiographique dans l'occident médiéval. Transformations formelles et idéologiques. Hrsg. von Monique Goullet / Martin Heinzelmann (Beihefte der Francia 58). Ostfildern 2003, S. 7–15.

Gorman, David: Use and Abuse of Speech-Act in Criticism. In: Poetics Today 20 (1999), S. 93–119.

Gottschall, Anna: The Lord's Prayer in Circles and Squares. An Identification of some Analogues of the Vernon Manuscript's Pater Noster Table. In: Marginalia 7 (2008), online: http://merg.soc.srcf.net/journal/08confession/circles.php [10.08.2017].

Gragnolati, Manuele / Suerbaum, Almut: Medieval Culture ›betwixt and between‹. An Introduction. In: Aspects of the Performative in Medieval Culture. Hrsg. von Manuele Gragnolati / Almut Suerbaum (Trends in Medieval Philology 18). Berlin / New York 2010, S. 1–12.

Gray, Erik: Come be my Love. The Song of Songs, ›Paradise Lost‹, and the Tradition of the Invitation Poem. In: PMLA 128 (2013), S. 370–385.

Green, Dennis Howard: Medieval Listening and Reading. The Primary Reception of German Literature 800–1300. Cambridge 1994.

Green, Dennis Howard: Fictive Orality. A Restriction on the Use of the Concept. In: Blütezeit. Festschrift für L. Peter Johnson zum 70. Geburtstag. Hrsg. von Mark Chinca / Joachim Heinzle / Christopher Young. Tübingen 2000, S. 161–174.

Green, Dennis Howard: Terminologische Überlegungen zum Hören und Lesen im Mittelalter. In: Eine Epoche im Umbruch. Volksprachliche Literalität 1200–1300. Cambridger Symposium 2001. Hrsg. von Christa Bertelsmeier-Kierst / Christopher Young. Tübingen 2003, S. 1–22.

Greith, Carl: Spicilegium Vaticanum. Beiträge zur nähern Kenntniss der Vatikanischen Bibliothek für deutsche Poesie des Mittelalters. Frauenfeld 1838.

Grubmüller, Klaus: Gertrud von Helfta. In: ²VL 3 (1981), Sp. 7–10.

Grubmüller, Klaus: Sprechen und Schreiben. Das Beispiel Mechthild von Magdeburg. In: Festschrift Walter Haug und Burghart Wachinger. Hrsg. von Johannes Janota. 2 Bde. Tübingen 1992, Bd. 1, S. 335–349.

Grubmüller, Klaus: Erzählen und Überliefern. ›Mouvance‹ als poetologische Kategorie in der Märendichtung. In: PBB 125 (2003), S. 469–493.

Grubmüller, Klaus: Werkstatt-Typ, Gattungsregeln und die Konventionalität der Schrift. Eine Skizze. In: Texttyp und Textproduktion in der deutschen Literatur des Mittelalters. Hrsg. von Elizabeth A. Andersen / Manfred Eikelmann / Anne Simon (Trends in Medieval Philology 7). Berlin / New York 2005, S. 31–40.

Gsell, Monika: Das fließende Blut der Offenbarungen Elsbeths von Oye. In: Deutsche Mystik im abendländischen Zusammenhang. Neu erschlossene Texte, neue methodische Ansätze, neue theoretische Konzepte. Hrsg. von Walter Haug / Wolfram Schneider-Lastin. Tübingen 2000, S. 455–482.

Gugumus, Johannes Emil: Die Handschrift Vatican. latin. 4763 der Vatikanischen Bibliothek. In: Blätter für Pfälzische Kirchengeschichte und religiöse Volkskunde 26 (1959), S. 133–145.

Gumbrecht, Hans Ulrich: Beginn von ›Literatur‹ / Abschied vom Körper? In: Der Ursprung von Literatur. Medien, Rollen, Kommunikationsformen zwischen 1450 und 1550. Hrsg. von Gisela Smolka-Koerdt / Peter-Michael Spangenberg / Dagmar Tillmann-Bartylla. München 1988, S. 15–50.

Gumbrecht, Hans Ulrich: Production of Presence. What Meaning Cannot Convey. Princeton 2004.

Gumbrecht, Hans Ulrich: Präsenz, mit einem Nachwort von Jürgen Klein. Frankfurt a.M. 2012.

Haas, Alois Maria: Mechthild von Magdeburg – Dichtung und Mystik. In: Amsterdamer Beiträge zur älteren Germanistik 2 (1972), S. 105–156.

Haas, Alois Maria: Sermo mysticus. Studien zu Theologie und Sprache der deutschen Mystik (Dokimon 4). Fribourg 1979.

Haas, Alois Maria: Geistliches Mittelalter (Dokimon 8). Fribourg 1984(a).

Haas, Alois Maria: Die deutsche Mystik im Spannungsbereich von Theologie und Spiritualität. In: Literatur und Laienbildung im Spätmittelalter und in der Reformationszeit. Symposion Wolfenbüttel 1981. Hrsg. von Ludger Grenzmann / Karl Stackmann (Germanistische Symposien, Berichtsbände 5). Stuttgart 1984(b), S. 604–639.

Haas, Alois Maria: Sinn und Tragweite von Heinrich Seuses Passionsmystik. In: Die Passion Christi in Literatur und Kunst des Spätmittelalters. Hrsg. von Walter Haug / Burghart Wachinger. Tübingen 1993, S. 94–112.

Haas, Alois Maria: Die Verständlichkeit mystischer Erfahrung. In: Deutsche Mystik im abendländischen Zusammenhang. Neu erschlossene Texte, neue methodische Ansätze, neue theoretische Konzepte. Kolloquium Kloster Fischingen 1998. Hrsg. von Walter Haug/Wolfram Schneider-Lastin. Tübingen 2000, S. 9–29.

Haas, Alois Maria: Fülle der Zeit. Ein Durchblick durch die Mystik. In: Mystik – Überlieferung – Naturkunde. Gegenstände und Methoden mediävistischer Forschungspraxis. Tagung in Eichstätt am 15. und 17. April 1999, anlässlich der Begründung der ›Forschungsstelle für Geistliche Literatur des Mittelalters‹ an der Katholischen Universität Eichstätt. Hrsg. von Robert Luff/Rudolf Kilian Weigand (Germanistische Texte und Studien 70). Hildesheim/Zürich/New York 2002, S. 179–195.

Hadot, Pierre: Apophatisme et théologie négative. In: Hadot, Exercices spirituels et philosophie antique. Paris 1981, S. 185–193.

Haesli, Christa M.: Sprachpragmatische Texte des Clm 536 (11./12. Jahrhundert). In: Literarische Performativität. Lektüren vormoderner Texte. Hrsg. von Cornelia Herberichs/Christian Kiening (Medienwandel – Medienwechsel – Medienwissen 3). Zürich 2008, S. 62–81.

Hagby, Maryvonne/Hüpper, Dagmar: Die Gebete als dialogische Reden. Die ›Königstochter von Frankreich‹ (1400) und die ›Belle Hélène de Constantinople‹ (14. Jahrhundert). In: Sprechen mit Gott. Redeszenen in mittelalterlicher Bibeldichtung und Legende. Hrsg. von Nine Miedema/Angela Schrott/Monika Unzeitig (Historische Dialogforschung 2). Berlin 2012, S. 191–216.

Hahn, Alois: Rede- und Schweigeverbote. In: Kölner Zeitschrift für Soziologie und Sozialpsychologie 43 (1991), S. 86–105.

Hahn, Reinhard/Fasbender, Christoph (Hrsg.): ›Brandan‹. Die mitteldeutsche ›Reise‹-Fassung (Jenaer germanistische Forschungen NF 14). Heidelberg 2002.

Hale, Rosemary Drage: Rocking the Cradle. Margaretha Ebner Be(holds) the Divine. In: Performance and Transformation. New Approaches to Late Medieval Spirituality. Hrsg. von Mary A. Suydam/Joanna E. Ziegler. Basingstoke 1999, S. 211–239.

Hall, Kira: Performativity. In: Journal of Linguistic Anthropology 9 (2000), S. 184–187.

Hallensleben, Markus: Performance of Metaphor: The Body as Text – Text Implantation in Body Images. In: Performance and Performativity in German Cultural Studies. Hrsg. von Carolin Duttlinger/Lucia Ruprecht/Andrew Webber (German Linguistic and Cultural Studies 14). Oxford 2003, S. 241–255.

Hamburger, Jeffrey F.: The Rothschild Canticles. Art and Mysticism in Flanders and the Rhineland Circa 1300. New Haven/London 1990.

Hamburger, Jeffrey F.: The Visual and the Visionary. Art and Female Spirituality in Late Medieval Germany. New York 1998.

Hamburger, Jeffrey F.: Speculations on Speculation. Vision and Perception in the Theory and Practice of Mystical Devotion. In: Deutsche Mystik im abendländischen Zusammenhang. Neu erschlossene Texte, neue methodische Ansätze, neue theoretische Konzepte. Kolloquium Kloster Fischingen 1998. Hrsg. von Walter Haug/Wolfram Schneider-Lastin. Tübingen 2000, S. 353–408.

Hamburger, Jeffrey F.: St John the Divine. The Deified Evangelist in Medieval Art and Theology. Berkeley/London 2002.

Hamburger, Jeffrey F.: Another Perspective. The Book of Hours in Germany. In: Books of Hours Reconsidered. Hrsg. von Sandra Hindman/James Marrow. Turnhout 2013, S. 97–152, Anm. auf S. 505–510.

Hamburger, Jeffrey F./Marti, Susan (Hrsg.): Crown and Veil. Female Monasticism from the Fifth to the Fifteenth Century. New York/Chichester 2008.

Hamburger, Jeffrey F. / Palmer, Nigel (Hrsg.): The Prayer Book of Ursula Begerin. 2 Bde. Dietikon 2015.

Hamm, Berndt: Wollen und Nicht-Können als Thema der spätmittelalterlichen Bußseelsorge. In: Spätmittelalterliche Frömmigkeit zwischen Ideal und Praxis. Hrsg. von Berndt Hamm / Thomas Lentes (Spätmittelalter und Reformation, Neue Reihe 15). Tübingen 2001, S. 111–146.

Hamm, Berndt: ›Gott berühren‹. Mystische Erfahrung im ausgehenden Mittelalter. Zugleich ein Beitrag zur Klärung des Mystikbegriffs. In: Religiosität im späten Mittelalter. Spannungspole, Neuaufbrüche, Normierungen. Hrsg. von Reinhold Friedrich / Wolfgang Simon (Spätmittelalter, Humanismus, Reformation 54). Tübingen 2011, S. 449–472.

Hansel, Hans: Die Maria-Magdalena-Legende. Eine Quellen-Untersuchung. Bottrop 1937 (Diss. Greifswald 1931).

Harrison, Anna: ›I Am Wholly Your Own‹. Liturgical Piety and Community among the Nuns of Helfta. In: Church History. Studies in Christianity and Culture 78 (2009), S. 549–583.

Hasebrink, Burkhard: Das Predigtverfahren Meister Eckharts. Beobachtungen zur thematischen und pragmatischen Kohärenz der Predigt Q 12. In: Die deutsche Predigt im Mittelalter. Internationales Symposium am Fachbereich Germanistik der Freien Universität Berlin vom 3.–6. Oktober 1989. Hrsg. von Volker Mertens / Hans-Jochen Schiewer. Tübingen 1992, S. 150–168.

Hasebrink, Burkhard: Formen inizitativer Rede bei Meister Eckhard. Untersuchungen zur literarischen Konzeption der deutschen Predigt (Texte und Textgeschichte 32). Tübingen 1992(b).

Hasebrink, Burkhard: Spiegel und Spiegelung im ›Fließenden Licht der Gottheit‹. In: Deutsche Mystik im abendländischen Zusammenhang. Neu erschlossene Texte, neue methodische Ansätze, neue theoretische Konzepte. Kolloquium Kloster Fischingen 1998. Hrsg. von Walter Haug / Wolfram Schneider-Lastin. Tübingen 2000, S. 157–174.

Hasebrink, Burkhard: ›ein einic ein‹. Zur Darstellbarkeit der Liebeseinheit in mittelhochdeutscher Literatur. In: PBB 124 (2002), S. 442–465.

Hasebrink, Burkhard: ›Ich kann nicht ruhen, ich brenne‹. Überlegungen zur Ästhetik der Klage im ›Fließenden Licht der Gottheit‹. In: Das fremde Schöne. Dimensionen des Ästhetischen in der Literatur des Mittelalters. Hrsg. von Manuel Braun / Christopher Young (Trends in Medieval Philology 12). New York 2007, S. 91–107.

Hasebrink, Burkhard: Elsbeth von Oye. Offenbarungen (um 1340). In: Literarische Performativität. Lektüren vormoderner Texte. Hrsg. von Cornelia Herberichs / Christian Kiening (Medienwandel – Medienwechsel – Medienwissen 3). Zürich 2008, S. 259–279.

Hasebrink, Burkhard: Erecs Wunde. Zur Performativität der Freundschaft im höfischen Roman. In: Oxford German Studies 38 (2009[a]), S. 1–11.

Hasebrink, Burkhard: ›mitewürker gotes‹. Zur Performativität der Umdeutung in den deutschen Schriften Meister Eckharts. In: Literarische und religiöse Kommunikation in Mittelalter und Früher Neuzeit. DFG-Symposium 2006. Hrsg. von Peter Strohschneider. Berlin / New York 2009(b), S. 62–88.

Hasebrink, Burkhard: Koreferat zum Referat ›Saintly Writing and Writing Saints‹ von Racha Kirakosian. Public Final Meeting Marie Curie Network MITT, Freiburg 11.04.2013 (unveröffentlicht).

Hasebrink, Burkhard / Strohschneider, Peter: Religiöse Schriftkultur und säkulare Textwissenschaft. Germanistische Mediävistik in postsäkularem Kontext. In: Poetica 46 (2014), S. 277–292.

Haug, Walter: Das Gespräch mit dem unvergleichlichen Partner. Der mystische Dialog bei
 Mechthild von Magdeburg als Paradigma für eine personale Gesprächsstruktur. In: Das
 Gespräch. Hrsg. von Karlheinz Stierle / Rainer Warning (Poetik und Hermeneutik 11).
 München 1984, S. 251–279.

Haug, Walter: Literaturtheorie im deutschen Mittelalter. Von den Anfängen bis zum Ende des
 13. Jahrhunderts, 2. überarb. und erw. Aufl. Darmstadt 1992(a).

Haug, Walter: Grundformen religiöser Erfahrung als epochale Positionen. Vom frühmittel-
 alterlichen Analogiemodell zum hoch- und spätmittelalterlichen Differenzmodell. In:
 Religiöse Erfahrung. Historische Modelle in christlicher Tradition. Hrsg. von Walter
 Haug / Dietmar Mieth. München 1992(b), S. 75–108.

Haug, Walter: Gotteserfahrung und Du-Begegnung. Korrespondenzen in der Geschichte der
 Mystik und der Liebeslyrik. In: Geistliches in weltlicher und Weltliches in geistlicher
 Literatur des Mittelalters. Hrsg. von Christoph Huber / Burghart Wachinger / Hans-Joachim
 Ziegeler. Tübingen 2000, S. 195–212.

Haug, Walter: Die Wahrheit der Fiktion. Studien zur weltlichen und geistlichen Literatur des
 Mittelalters und der frühen Neuzeit. Tübingen 2003.

Haug, Walter: Gotteserfahrungen im abendländischen Mittelalter. In: Positivierung von
 Negativität. Letzte kleine Schriften. Hrsg. von Ulrich Barton. Tübingen 2008(a),
 S. 225–250.

Haug, Walter: Transzendenzerfahrung in Bildern des Abschieds. In: Positivierung von
 Negativität. Letzte kleine Schriften. Hrsg. von Ulrich Barton. Tübingen 2008, S. 354–370.

Heiler, Friedrich: Das Gebet. Eine religionsgeschichtliche und religionspsychologische
 Untersuchung. 5. Aufl. mit Nachträgen. München 1923.

Heim, Manfred: Prämonstratenserinnen. In: Mönchtum, Orden, Klöster. Von den Anfängen
 bis zur Gegenwart. Ein Lexikon. Hrsg. von Georg Schwaiger. 2. Aufl. München 1994,
 S. 366–367.

Heinemann, Wolfgang: Textsorten. Zur Diskussion um Basisklassen des Kommunizierens.
 Rückschau und Ausblick. In: Textsorten. Reflexionen und Analysen. Hrsg. von Kirsten
 Adamzik (Textsorten 1). Tübingen 2000, S. 9–29.

Heinz, Andreas: Die Zisterzienser und die Anfänge des Rosenkranzes. Das bisher
 unveröffentlichte älteste Zeugnis für den Leben-Jesu-Rosenkranz in einem Zisterzienserinnengebetbuch aus St. Thomas a. d. Kyll (um 1300). In: Analecta Cisterciensia 33 (1977),
 S. 262–309.

Heinzer, Felix: Imaginierte Passion – Vision im Spannungsfeld zwischen liturgischer Matrix
 und religiöser Erfahrung bei Elisabeth von Schönau. In: Nova de veteribus. Mittel-
 und neulateinische Studien für Paul Gerhard Schmidt. Hrsg. von Andreas Bihrer.
 München / Leipzig 2004, S. 463–475.

Heinzer, Felix: Die ›heilige Königstochter‹ in der Liturgie. Zur Inszenierung Elisabeths im
 Festoffizium ›Laetare Germania‹. In: Elisabeth von Thüringen – eine europäische Heilige.
 Hrsg. von Dieter Blume / Matthias Werner. Petersberg 2007, S. 215–225.

Hemptinne, Thérèse de: Reading, Writing and Devotional Practices. Lay and Religious Women
 and the Written Word in the Low Countries (1350–1550). In: The Voice of Silence. Women's
 Literacy in a Men's Church. Hrsg. von Thérèse de Hemptinne / María Eugenia Góngora
 (Medieval Church Studies 9). Turnhout 2004, S. 111–126.

Herberichs, Cornelia / Kiening, Christian: Einleitung. In: Literarische Performativität. Lektüren
 vormoderner Texte. Hrsg. von Cornelia Herberichs / Christian Kiening (Medienwandel –
 Medienwechsel – Medienwissen 3). Zürich 2008, S. 9–21.

Herbers, Klaus: Hagiographie im Kontext. Konzeption und Zielvorstellung. In: Hagiographie im Kontext. Wirkungsweisen und Möglichkeiten historischer Auswertung. Hrsg. von Dieter R. Bauer / Klaus Herbers (Beiträge zur Hagiographie 1). Stuttgart 2000, S. IX–XXVIII.

Hoenen, Maarten J. F. M.: Translating Mystical Texts from the Vernacular into Latin. The Intentions and Strategies behind Laurentius Surius' edition of John Ruusbroec's Complete Works (Cologne 1552). In: Per perscrutationem philosophicam. Neue Perspektiven der mittelalterlichen Forschung. Loris Sturlese zum 60. Geburtstag gewidmet. Hrsg. von Alessandra Beccarisi / Ruedi Imbach / Pasquale Porro (Corpus philosophorum Teutonicorum Medii Aevi. Beihefte 4). Hamburg 2008, S. 348–374.

Hollywood, Amy: The Soul as Virgin Wife. Mechthild of Magdeburg, Marguerite Porete, and Meister Eckhart, Notre Dame (Studies in Spirituality and Theology 1). London 1995.

Hollywood, Amy: Rezension zu Mary A. Suydam / Joanna E. Ziegler: Performance and Transformation. New Approaches to Late Medieval Spirituality (1999). In: Hypatia 16 (2001), S. 106–108.

Hollywood, Amy: Sensible Ecstasy. Mysticism, Sexual Difference and the Demands of History. Chicago 2002.

Huber, Augustinus Kurt: Hermann Joseph von Steinfeld. In: Neue Deutsche Biographie. Hrsg. von von der Historischen Kommission bei der Bayerischen Akademie der Wissenschaften. 25 Bde. Berlin 1953–2013, Bd. 8 (1969), S. 651 f.

Hübner, Gert: Erzählformen im höfischen Roman. Studien zur Fokalisierung im ›Eneas‹, im ›Iwein‹ und im ›Tristan‹ (Bibliotheca Germanica 44). Tübingen 2003.

Hübner, Gert: ›evidentia‹. Erzählformen und ihre Funktion. In: Historische Narratologie. Mediävistische Perspektiven. Hrsg. von Harald Haferland / Matthias Meyer (Trends in Medieval Philology 19). New York 2010, S. 119–147.

Huot, Sylvia: Polytextual Reading. The Meditative Reading of Real and Metaphorical Books. In: Orality and Literacy in the Middle Ages. Essays on a Conjunction and its Consequences in Honour of D.H. Green. Hrsg. von Mark Chinca / Christopher Young (Utrecht Studies in Medieval Literacy 12). Turnhout 2005, S. 203–222.

Ingarden, Roman: Das Literarische Kunstwerk. Mit einem Anhang von den Funktionen der Sprache im Theaterschauspiel. 2. verb. u. erw. Aufl. Tübingen 1960.

Iser, Wolfgang: Der implizite Leser. Kommunikationsformen des Romans von Bunyan bis Beckett. München 1972.

Janota, Johannes: Freundschaft auf Erden und im Himmel. Die Mystikerin Margareta Ebner und der Gottesfreund Heinrich von Nördlingen. In: Impulse und Resonanzen. Tübinger mediävistische Beiträge zum 80. Geburtstag von Walter Haug. Hrsg. von Gisela Vollmann-Profe u.a. Tübingen 2007, S. 275–300.

Jansen, Katherine Ludwig: The Making of the Magdalen. Preaching and Popular Devotion in the Later Middle Ages. Princeton / Chichester 2000.

Jantzen, Grace M.: Power, Gender and Christian Mysticism (Cambridge Studies in Ideology and Religion 8). Cambridge 1995.

Jones, Claire Taylor: ›Hostia jubilationis‹. Psalm Citation, Eucharistic Prayer, and Mystical Union in Gertrude of Helfta's ›Exercitia spiritualia‹. In: Speculum 89 (2014), S. 1005–1039.

Johnson, Ella: To Taste (›Sapere‹) Wisdom (›Sapientia‹). Eucharistic Devotion in the Writings of Gertrude of Helfta. In: Viator 44 (2013), S. 175–200.

Jolles, André: Einfache Formen. Legende, Sage, Mythe, Rätsel, Spruch, Kasus, Memorabile, Märchen, Witz (Konzepte der Sprach-und Literaturwissenschaft 15). 5. Aufl. Tübingen 1974 (Originalausgabe Tübingen 1930).

Jung, Jacqueline Elaine: The Tactile and the Visionary. Notes on the Place of Sculpture in the Medieval Religious Imagination. In: Looking Beyond. Visions, Dreams and Insights in Medieval Art and History. Hrsg. von Colum Hourihane (Occasional Papers Princeton University. Department of Art and Archaeology. Index of Christian Art 11). Princeton 2010, S. 203–240.

Jungandreas, Wolfgang: Ein moselfränkisches Zisterzienserinnengebetbuch im Trierer Raum um 1300. In: Archiv für mittelrheinische Kirchengeschichte 9 (1957), S. 195–213.

Kablitz, Andreas: Inkarnation, Überlegungen zur Konstitution eines Kulturmusters (›Novum Testamentum‹ – Dante. ›Vita nova, Commedia‹). In: Transgressionen, Literatur als Ethnographie. Hrsg. von Gerhard Neumann / Rainer Warning (Rombach Wissenschaften Litterae 98). Freiburg i. Br. 2003, S. 39–79.

Karnes, Michelle: Imagination, Meditation, and Cognition in the Middle Ages. Chicago 2011.

Kasten, Ingrid / Fischer-Lichte, Erika (Hrsg.): Transformationen des Religiösen. Performativität und Textualität im geistlichen Spiel. Berlin 2007.

Keller, Hildegard Elisabeth: ›înlougen‹. Blicke in symbolische Räume an Beispielen aus der mystischen Literatur des 12. bis 14. Jahrhunderts. In: Symbolik von Ort und Raum. Hrsg. von Paul Michel (Schriften zur Symbolforschung 11). Bern 1997. S. 353–376.

Keller, Hildegard Elisabeth: Absonderungen. Mystische Texte als literarische Inszenierung von Geheimnis. In: Deutsche Mystik im abendländischen Zusammenhang. Neu erschlossene Texte, neue methodische Ansätze, neue theoretische Konzepte. Kolloquium Kloster Fischingen 1998. Hrsg. von Walter Haug / Wolfram Schneider-Lastin. Tübingen 2000(a), S. 195–221.

Keller, Hildegard Elisabeth: My Secret is Mine. Studies on Religion and Eros in the German Middle Ages (Studies in Spirituality Supplements 4). Leuven 2000(b).

Kellermann, Karina: ›Exemplum‹ und ›historia‹. Zu poetologischen Traditionen in Hartmanns ›Iwein‹. In: Germanisch-Romanische Monatsschrift 42 (1992), S. 1–27.

Kellner, Beate: Wort Gottes – Stimme des Menschen. Textstatus und Profile von Autorschaft in Otfrids von Weißenburg ›Evangelienbuch‹. In: Geltung der Literatur. Formen ihrer Autorisierung und Legitimierung im Mittelalter. Hrsg. von Beate Kellner / Peter Strohschneider / Franziska Wenzel (Philologische Studien und Quellen 190). Berlin 2005, S. 139–162.

Kemper, Hans-Georg: Allegorische Allegorese. Zur Bildlichkeit und Struktur mystischer Literatur. In: Formen und Funktionen der Allegorie. Symposium Wolfenbüttel 1978. Hrsg. von Walter Haug (Germanistische Symposien, Berichtsbände 3). Stuttgart 1979, S. 90–125.

Kemper, Tobias A.: Die Kreuzigung Christi. Motivgeschichtliche Studien zu lateinischen und deutschen Passionstraktaten des Spätmittelalters (MTU 131). Tübingen 2006.

Kerby-Fulton, Kathryn: Prophet and Reformer. Smoke in the Vineyard. In: Voice of the Living Light. Hildegard of Bingen and Her World. Hrsg. von Barbara Newman. Berkeley 1998, S. 70–90.

Kern, Manfred: ›Lyrische Verwilderung‹. Texttypen und Ästhetik in der Liebeslyrik des 15. Jahrhunderts. In: Texttyp und Textproduktion in der Literatur des deutschen Mittelalters. Hrsg. von Elizabeth A. Andersen / Manfred Eikelmann / Anne Simon (Trends in Medieval Philology 7). Berlin / New York 2005, S. 371–393.

Kern, Udo: Wir sind ein Gespräch. Existential-ontologische theologische Überlegungen. In: Unerwartete Theologie. Festschrift für Bernd Hildebrandt. Hrsg. von Tilman Beyrich (Theologie. Forschung und Wissenschaft 17). Münster 2005, S. 135–154.

Kertscher, Jens / Mersch, Dieter: Einleitung der Herausgeber. In: Performativität und Praxis. Hrsg. von Jens Kertscher / Dieter Mersch. München 2003, S. 7–15.

Kesting, Peter: Maria-frouwe. Über den Einfluss der Marienverehrung auf den Minnesang bis Walther von der Vogelweide (Medium Aevum 5). München 1965.

Kieckhefer, Richard: ›Ihesus ist unser!‹ The Christ Child in the German Sister Books. In: The Christ Child in Medieval Culture: Alpha es et O! Hrsg. von Mary Dzon / Theresa M. Kenney. Toronto 2012, S. 380–399.

Kiening, Christian: Zwischen Körper und Schrift. Texte vor dem Zeitalter der Literatur. Frankfurt a. M. 2003.

Kiening, Christian: Gebete und Benediktionen von Muri (um 1150/1180). In: Literarische Performativität. Lektüren vormoderner Texte. Hrsg. von Cornelia Herberichs / Christian Kiening (Medienwandel – Medienwechsel – Medienwissen 3). Zürich 2008, S. 101–118.

Kiening, Christian: Mystische Bücher (Mediävistische Perspektiven 2). Zürich 2011 (nochmals erschienen in: Codex im Diskurs. Hrsg. von Thomas Haye / Johannes Heimrath. Wiesbaden 2014, S. 59–86).

Beverly Mayne Kienzle / Pamela J. Walker (Hrsg.): Women Preachers and Prophets through Two Millennia of Christianity. Berkeley 1998.

Kinsley, David: The Goddesses' Mirror. Visions of the Divine from East to West. Albany 1989.

Kirakosian, Racha: Which is the Greatest? Knowledge, Love or Enjoyment of God? The Mystic Christina of Hane in Comparison to Meister Eckhart. In: Mystical Theology 23/1 (2014[a]), S. 20–33.

Kirakosian, Racha: Rhetorics of Sanctity. Christina of Hane in the Early Modern Period – with a Comparison to a Mary Magdalene Legend. In: Oxford German Studies 43 (2014[b]), S. 380–399.

Kirakosian, Racha: Penitential Punishment and Purgatory. Christina of Hane and the Drama of Purification through Pain. In: Punishment and Penitential Practices in Medieval German Writing. Hrsg. von Sarah Bowden / Annette Volfing. London 2017(a).

Kirakosian, Racha: L'expérience transcendante dans l'espace immanent et le rôle du language performatif dans la biographie mystique de Christina de Hane. In: Le Moyen Âge 123 (2017[b]).

Kirakosian, Racha: Musical Heaven and Heavenly Music. At the Crossroads of Liturgical Music and Mystical Texts. In: Viator 48 (2017[c]).

Kirakosian, Racha: Das göttliche Herz im ›Fließenden Licht der Gottheit‹ Mechthilds von Magdeburg. Eine motivgeschichtliche Verortung. In: Euphorion 112 (2017[d]).

Kleinjung, Christine: Die Herren von Bolanden als Klostergründer. In: Alzeyer Geschichtsblätter 33 (2001), S. 17–33.

Köbele, Susanne: ›Primo aspectu monstruosa‹. Schriftauslegung bei Meister Eckhart. In: ZfdA 122 (1993[a]), S. 62–81.

Köbele, Susanne: Bilder der unbegriffenen Wahrheit. Zur Struktur mystischer Rede im Spannungsfeld von Latein und Volkssprache (Bibliotheca Germanica 30). Tübingen / Basel 1993(b).

Köbele, Susanne: Umbesetzungen. Zur Liebessprache in Liedern Frauenlobs. In: Geistliches in weltlicher und Weltliches in geistlicher Literatur des Mittelalters. Hrsg. von Christoph Huber / Burghart Wachinger / Hans-Joachim Ziegeler. Tübingen 2000, S. 213–235.

Köbele, Susanne: Frauenlobs Lieder. Parameter einer literarhistorischen Standortbestimmung. Tübingen / Basel 2003.

Köbele, Susanne: ›heilicheit durchbrechen‹. Grenzfälle von Heiligkeit in der mittelalterlichen Mystik. In: Sakralität zwischen Antike und Neuzeit. Hrsg. von Berndt Hamm / Klaus Herbers / Heidrun Stein-Kecks (Beiträge zur Hagiographie 6). Stuttgart 2007, S. 147–169.

Köbele, Susanne: Bonaventura. ›Itinerarium mentis in Deum‹ (1259). In: Literarische Perfor-
    mativität. Lektüren vormoderner Texte. Hrsg. von Cornelia Herberichs/Christian Kiening
    (Medienwandel – Medienwechsel – Medienwissen 3). Zürich 2008, S. 157–178.
Köbele, Susanne: Die Illusion der ›einfachen Form‹. Über das ästhetische und religiöse Risiko
    der Legende. In: PBB 134 (2012), S. 365–404.
Köbele, Susanne: Rhetorik und Erotik – Minnesang als ›süßer Klang‹. In: Poetica 45 (2013),
    S. 299–332.
Köbele, Susanne: Verheißung als Erfüllung. Zur Transformation prophetischer Autorschaft um
    1300. In: Prophetie und Autorschaft. Charisma, Heilversprechen und Gefährdung. Hrsg.
    von Christel Meier/Martina Wagner-Egelhaaf. Berlin 2014, S. 169–196.
Koch, Karl/Hegel, Eduard: Die Vita des Prämonstratensers Hermann Joseph von Steinfeld. Ein
    Beitrag zur Hagiographie und zur Frömmigkeitsgeschichte des Hochmittelalters (Colonia
    sacra 3). Köln 1958.
Koch, Peter/Oesterreicher, Wulf: Gesprochene Sprache in der Romania. Französisch,
    Italienisch, Spanisch (Romanistische Arbeitshefte 31). Tübingen 1990.
Koch, Peter/Oesterreicher, Wulf: Mündlichkeit und Schriftlichkeit von Texten. In: Textlinguistik.
    15 Einführungen. Hrsg. von Nina Janich. Tübingen 2008, S. 199–215.
König, Eberhard/Bartz, Gabriele: Das Stundenbuch. Perlen der Buchkunst. Die Gattung in
    Handschriften der Vaticana. Stuttgart/Zürich 1998.
Köster, Kurt: Leben und Gesichte der Christina von Retters (1269 bis 1291). In: Archiv für Mittel-
    rheinische Kirchengeschichte 8 (1956), S. 241–269.
Köster, Kurt: Christina von Hane (Hagen), gen. Retters. In: ²VL 1 (1978), Sp. 1225–1228.
Krämer, Sybille: Einleitung. In: Performativität und Medialität. Hrsg. von Krämer, Sybille.
    München 2004, S. 13–31.
Krämer, Sybille: Operationsraum Schrift. Über einen Perspektivenwechsel in der Betrachtung
    der Schrift. In: Schrift. Kulturtechnik zwischen Auge, Hand und Maschine. Hrsg. von Gernot
    Grube/Werner Kogge/Sybille Krämer. München 2005, S. 23–57.
Kraß, Andreas: ›Ich gruess dich gerne‹. Aspekte historischer Intertextualität am Beispiel von
    gereimten deutschen Übersetzungen der Mariensequenz ›Ave praeclara maris stella‹ in
    Mittelalter und Früher Neuzeit. In: Grundlagen: Forschungen, Editionen und Materialien
    zur deutschen Literatur und Sprache des Mittelalters und der Frühen Neuzeit. Hrsg. von
    Rudolf Bentzinger/Ulrich-Dieter Oppitz/Jürgen Wolf (ZdfA, Beiheft 18). Stuttgart 2013,
    S. 301–314.
Krings, Bruno: Die Prämonstratenser und ihr weiblicher Zweig. In: Studien zum Prämonstraten-
    serorden. Hrsg. von Irene Crusius/Lemut Flachenecker (Studien zur Germania Sacra 25).
    Göttingen 2003, S. 75–105.
Krings, Bruno: Die Frauenklöster in der Pfalz. In: Jahrbuch für westdeutsche Landesgeschichte
    35 (2009), S. 113–202.
Kroll, Jerome/Bachrach, Bernard: The Mystic Mind. The Psychology of Medieval Mystics and
    Ascetics. New York/London 2005.
Kuder, Ulrich: Mittelalterlicher Bildgebrauch: Überlegungen zum ersten Blatt eines Psalters aus
    der Zeit um 1200. In: Die Schönheit des Sichtbaren und Hörbaren. Festschrift für Norbert
    Knopp zum 65. Geburtstag. Hrsg. von Matthias Bunge. Wolznach 2001, S. 61–85.
Küenzlen, Franziska: Sprechen und Sprecher in ›Das Leben der Heiligen Dorothea des Johannes
    Marienwerder‹. In: Oxford German Studies 39, 2 (2010), S. 160–180.
Kugler, Hermann Josef: Hermann Josef von Steinfeld (um 1160–1241) im Kontext christlicher
    Mystik. St. Ottilien 1992.

Kunze, Konrad: ›Arnsteiner Mariengebet‹. In: ²VL 1 (1978), Sp. 498–500.

Kunze, Konrad: Deutschsprachige Hagiographie von den Anfängen bis 1350. In: Hagiographies. Histoire internationale de la littérature hagiographique, latine et vernaculaire, en Occident, des origines á 1550. Bd. 2. Hrsg. von Guy Philippart (Corpus Christianorum Hagiographies 2). Turnhout 1996, S. 211–238.

Kurras, Lotte: Die deutschen mittelalterlichen Handschriften, Erster Teil: Die literarischen und religiösen Handschriften. Anhang: Die Hardenbergschen Fragmente (Kataloge des Germanischen Nationalmuseums Nürnberg 1,1). Wiesbaden 1974.

Küsters, Urban: Der verschlossene Garten. Volkssprachliche Hohelied-Auslegung und monastische Lebensform im 12. Jahrhundert (Studia humaniora 2). Düsseldorf 1985.

Lachance, Paul: Introduction. In: Angela of Foligno. Complete Works. Hrsg. von Paul Lachance. Mahwa 1993, S. 15–119.

Laird, Martin S.: Gregory of Nyssa and the Grasp of Faith. Union, Knowledge, and Divine Presence (Oxford early Christian studies). Oxford 2004.

Landesarchiv Baden-Württemberg: Wasserzeichen-Informationssystem, DE3285-PO-82651, URL: http://www.wasserzeichen-online.de/wzis/?ref=DE3285-PO-82651 [10.08.2017].

Landesarchiv Baden-Württemberg: Wasserzeichen-Informationssystem, DE4440-PO-82652, URL: http://www.wasserzeichen-online.de/wzis/?ref=DE4440-PO-82652 [10.08.2017].

Landesarchiv Baden-Württemberg: Wasserzeichen-Informationssystem, DE8100-HBVI52_999, URL: http://www.wasserzeichen-online.de/wzis/?ref=DE8100-HBVI52_999 [10.08.2017].

Landesarchiv Baden-Württemberg: Wasserzeichen-Informationssystem, DE4200-Ettenheimmünster44_999a, onliner unter: www.wasserzeichen-online.de/?ref=DE4200-Ettenheimm%C3%BCnster44_999 [10.08.2017].

Langer, Otto: Affekt und Ratio. Rationalitätskritische Aspekte in der Mystik Bernhards von Clairvaux. In: Zisterziensische Spiritualität. Theologische Grundlagen, funktionale Voraussetzungen und bildhafte Ausprägungen im Mittelalter. 1. Himmelroder Kolloquium. Hrsg. von Clemens S. Kasper (Studien und Mitteilungen zur Geschichte des Benediktinerordens und seiner Zweige. Ergänzungsband 34). St. Ottilien 1994, S. 33–52.

Largier, Niklaus: ›Anima mea liquefacta est‹. Der Dialog der Seele mit Gott bei Mechthild von Magdeburg und Heinrich Seuse. In: Internationale katholische Zeitschrift Communio 16 (1987), S. 227–237.

Largier, Niklaus: Rhetorik des Begehrens. Die ›Unterscheidung der Geister‹ als Paradigma mittelalterlicher Subjektivität. In: Inszenierungen von Subjektivität in der Literatur des Mittelalters. Hrsg. von Martin Baisch u. a. Königstein im Taunus 2005, S. 249–270.

Largier, Niklaus: Die Kunst des Begehrens. Dekadenz, Sinnlichkeit und Askese. München 2007.

Largier, Niklaus: Medieval Mysticism. In: The Oxford Handbook of Religion and Emotion. Hrsg. von John Corrigan. Oxford 2008, S. 364–379.

Lechtermann, Christina: Funktionen des Unsagbarkeitstopos bei der Darstellung von Schmerz. In: Schmerz in der Literatur des Mittelalters und der Frühen Neuzeit. Hrsg. von Hans-Jochen Schiewer / Stefan Seeber / Markus Stock (Transatlantische Studien zu Mittelalter und Früher Neuzeit – Transatlantic Studies on Medieval and Early Modern Literature and Culture 4). Göttingen 2010, S. 85–104.

Leinsle, Ulrich G.: Zur rechtlichen Ordnung prämonstratensischer Seelsorge im Mittelalter. In: Rottenburger Jahrbuch für Kirchengeschichte 22 (2003), S. 31–46.

Lefèvre, Placide F.: les Statuts de Prémontré réformés sur les ordres de Grégoire IX et d'Innocent IV au XIIIᵉ siècle Louvain 1946 (Bibliothèque de la Revue d'histoire ecclésiastique 23), S. 146–151.

Lentes, Thomas: Textus Evangelii. Materialität und Inszenierung des textus in der Liturgie. In: ›Textus‹ im Mittelalter. Komponenten und Situationen des Wortgebrauchs im schriftsemantischen Feld. Hrsg. von Ludolf Kuchenbuch / Uta Kleine (Veröffentlichungen des Max Planck Instituts für Geschichte 216). Göttingen 2006, 133–148.

Lenz-Kemper, Barbara: Die hessischen Reimpredigten. 2 Bde. (DTM 89). Berlin 2008–2009. Bd. 1: Untersuchungen zu Überlieferung, Sprache und Herkunft (2008). Bd. 2: Texte (2009).

Leuchter, Christoph: Dichten im Uneigentlichen. Zur Metaphorik und Poetik Heinrichs von Morungen. Frankfurt a. M. 2003.

Lexer, Matthias: Mittelhochdeutsches Handwörterbuch. Zugleich als Supplement und alphabetischer Index zum Mittelhochdeutschen Wörterbuche von Benecke-Müller-Zarncke. Nachdruck der Ausgabe Leipzig 1872–1878 mit einer Einleitung von Kurt Gärtner. 3 Bde. Stuttgart 1992.

Lieb, Ludger / Müller, Stephan: Situationen literarischen Erzählens, Systematische Skizzen am Beispiel von ›Kaiserchronik‹ und Konrad Flecks ›Flore und Blanscheflur‹. In: Erzähltechnik und Erzählstrategien in der deutschen Literatur des Mittelalters. Hrsg. von Wolfgang Haubrichs / Eckart Conrad Lutz / Klaus Ridder (Wolfram-Studien 18). Berlin 2004, S. 33–57.

Linardou, Kallirroe: The Couch of Solomon, a Monk, a Byzantine Lady and the Song of Songs. In: The Church and Mary. Papers Read at the 2002 Summer Meeting and the 2002 Winter Meeting of the Ecclesiastical History Society. Hrsg. von Robert Norman Swanson. Suffolk / New York 2004, S. 73–85.

Lohmer, Christian: Rezension zu Bruno Krings: Die Statuten des Prämonstratenserordens von 1244/46 und ihre Überarbeitung im Jahr 1279 (2007). In: Deutsches Archiv für Erforschung des Mittelalters 65 (2009), S. 214.

Löser, Freimut: ›Schriftmystik‹. Schreibprozesse in Texten der deutschen Mystik. In: Finden – Gestalten – Vermitteln. Schreibprozesse und ihre Brechungen in der mittelalterlichen Überlieferung. Freiburger Colloquium 2010. Hrsg. von Eckart Conrad Lutz (Wolfram-Studien 22). Berlin 2012, S. 155–201.

Lot, Ferdinand: Étude sur le Lancelot en prose. Paris 1918.

Lutz, Eckart Conrad: Schreibprozesse? Zur Einleitung. In: Finden – Gestalten – Vermitteln. Schreibprozesse und ihre Brechungen in der mittelalterlichen Überlieferung. Freiburger Colloquium 2010. Hrsg. von Eckart Conrad Lutz (Wolfram-Studien 22). Berlin 2012, S. 9–22.

MacCulloch, Diarmaid: Silence. A Christian History. New York 2013.

Marielle Macé: Façons de lire, manières d'être. Mayenne 2011.

Marin, Louis: Des pouvoirs de l'image. Gloses. Paris 1993.

Martin, Roland: Untersuchungen zur rhein-moselfränkischen Dialektgrenze (Deutsche Dialektgeographie 11a). Marburg 1992.

Martinez, Matias / Scheffel, Michael: Einführung in die Erzähltheorie. 6. Aufl. München 2005.

Matter, E. Ann: The Voice of my Beloved. The Song of Songs in Western Medieval Christianity. Philadelphia 1990.

Matthews, Alastair: The Kaiserchronik. A Medieval Narrative. Oxford 2012.

Mazzoni, Cristina: Angela of Foligno. In: Medieval Holy Women in the Christian Tradition, c. 1100 – c. 1500. Hrsg. von Alastair J. Minnis / Rosalynn Voaden (Brepols Essays in European Culture 1). Turnhout 2010, S. 581–600.

McDevitt, Mary: ›The Ink of Our Mortality‹. The Late-Medieval Image of the Writing Christ Child. In: The Christ Child in Medieval Culture: Alpha es et O! Hrsg. von Mary Dzon / Theresa M. Kenney. Toronto 2012, S. 224–253.

McGinn, Bernard: Meister Eckhart and the Beguines in the Context of Vernacular Theology. In: Meister Eckhart and the Beguine Mystics. Hadewijch of Brabant, Mechthild of Magdeburg, and Margerite Porete. Hrsg. von Bernard McGinn. New York 1994(a), S. 1–14.

McGinn, Bernard: The Growth of Mysticism. Gregory the Great Through the Twelfth Century (The Presence of God 2). New York 1994(b).

McGinn, Bernard: The Flowering of Mysticism. Men and Women in the New Mysticism, 1200–1350. New York 1998.

McGinn, Bernard: The Mystical Thought of Meister Eckhart. The Man from Whom God Hid Nothing. New York 2001(a).

McGinn, Bernard: The Language of Inner Experience in Christian Mysticism. In: Spiritus. A Journal of Christian Spirituality 1 (2001[b]), S. 156–171.

McGinn, Bernard: The Harvest of Mysticism in Medieval Germany (1300–1500) (The Presence of God 4). New York 2005.

McNamer, Sarah: Affective Meditation and the Invention of Medieval Compassion. Philadelphia 2010.

Meier, Christel: Prophetentum als literarische Existenz. Hildegard von Bingen (1098–1179). Ein Porträt. In: Deutsche Literatur von Frauen. Hrsg. von Gisela Brinker-Gabler. 2 Bde. München 1988, Bd. 1: Vom Mittelalter bis zum Ende des 18. Jahrhunderts, S. 76–87.

Meier, Christel: Autorschaft im 12. Jahrhundert. Persönliche Identität und Rollenkonstrukt. In: Unverwechselbarkeit. Persönliche Identität und Identifikation in der vormodernen Gesellschaft. Hrsg. von Peter von Moos (Norm und Struktur 23). Köln/Weimar/Wien 2004. S. 207–266.

Mellon, Joelle: The Virgin Mary in the Perception of Women. Mother, Protector and Queen. Since the Middle Ages. Jefferson 2008.

Menne, Karl: Deutsche und niederländische Handschriften. Mitteilungen aus dem Stadtarchiv von Köln. Die Handschriften des Archivs. Heft 10, Abt. 1, Teil 2. Köln 1937.

Mertens, Thom: Mystieke cultuur en literatuur in de Late Middelleeuwen. In: Grote lijnen. Syntheses over Middelnederlandse letterkunde Rijksuniversiteit Te Leiden. Hrsg. Frits van von Oostrom (Nederlandse literatuur en cultuur in de middeleeuwen 11). Amsterdam 1995, S. 117–135.

Mertens, Volker: Sprechen mit Gott – Sprechen über Gott. Predigt und Legendendichtung im frühen 13. Jahrhundert (Rudolf von Ems, ›Barlaam und Josaphat‹). In: Sprechen mit Gott. Redeszenen in mittelalrerlicher Bibeldichtung und Legende. Hrsg. von Nine Miedema/Angela Schrott/Monika Unzeitig (Historische Dialogforschung 2). Berlin 2012, S. 269–283.

Michel, Paul: Alieniloquium. Elemente einer Grammatik der Bildrede (Zürcher germanistische Studien 3). Bern 1987.

Michel, Paul: Übergangsformen zwischen Typologie und anderen Gestalten des Textbezugs. In: Bildhafte Rede im Mittelalter und früher Neuzeit. Probleme ihrer Legitimation und ihrer Funktion. Hrsg. von Wolfgang Harms/Klaus Speckenbach. Tübingen 1992, S. 43–72.

Miedema, Nine: Zur historischen Narratologie am Beispiel der Dialoganalyse. In: Historische Narratologie. Mediävistische Perspektiven. Hrsg. von Harald Haferland/Matthias Meyer (Trends in Medieval Philology 19). New York 2010, S. 35–67.

Miedema, Nine: Gesprächsnormen. Höfische Kommunikation in didaktischen und erzählenden Texten des Hochmittelalters. In: Text und Normativität. XX. Anglo-German Colloquium. Hrsg. von Elke Brüggen u. a. Berlin/Boston 2012, S. 251–278.

Millem, Bruce: The Unspoken Word. Negative Theology in Meister Eckhart's German Sermons. Washington D.C. 2002.

Miller, Julie B.: Eroticized Violence in Medieval Women's Mystical Literature. A Call for a Feminist Critique. In: Journal of Feminist Studies in Religion 15 (1999), S. 25–49.

Mittermaier, Franz Paul: Ein bislang verschollener Hymnus auf die sel. Christina gen. von Retters. In: Archiv für mittelrheinische Kirchengeschichte 10 (1958), S. 353–355.

Mittermaier, Franz Paul: Das Verhältnis des Altenberger Priors Petrus Diederich (1643/55) zu den Prämonstratenserstiften Ober- und Nieder-Ilbenstadt in der Wetterau. In: Wetterauer Geschichtsblätter 7/8 (1959), S. 117–131.

Mittermaier, Franz Paul: Wo lebte die selige Christina, in Retters oder in Hane? In: Archiv für Mittelrheinische Kirchengeschichte 12 (1960), S. 75–97.

Mittermaier, Franz Paul: Lebensbeschreibung der sel. Christina, gen. von Retters. In: Archiv für Mittelrheinische Kirchengeschichte 17 (1965), S. 209–251.

Mohr, Wolfgang: Darbietungsform der Mystik bei Mechthild von Magdeburg. In: Märchen, Mythos, Dichtung. Festschrift zum 90. Geburtstag Friedrich von der Leyens. Hrsg. von Hugo Kuhn / Kurt Schier. München 1963, S. 375–399.

Mooney, Catherine M. (Hrsg.): Gendered Voices. Medieval Saints and their Interpreters. Philadelphia 1999.

Mooney, Catherine M.: Voice, Gender, and the Portrayal of Sanctity. In: Gendered Voices. Medieval Saints and Their Interpreters. Hrsg. von Catherine M. Mooney. Philadelphia 1999a, S. 1–15.

Mooney, Catherine M.: Imitatio Christi or Imitatio Mariae? Clare of Assisi and her interpreters In: Gendered Voices. Medieval Saints and Their Interpreters. Hrsg. von Catherine M. Mooney. Philadelphia 1999(b), S. 52–77.

Moos, Peter von: Was galt im lateinischen Mittelalter als das Literarische an der Literatur? Eine theologisch-rhetorische Antwort des 12. Jahrhunderts. In: Literarische Interessenbildung im Mittelalter. DFG-Symposion 1991. Hrsg. von Joachim Heinzle (Germanistische Symposien, Berichtsbände 14). Stuttgart / Weimar 1993, S. 431–451.

Moser, Virgil: Frühneuhochdeutsche Grammatik. Bd. 3: Lautlehre. Heidelberg 1951.

Mossman, Stephen: Marquard von Lindau and the Challenges of Religious Life in Late Medieval Germany. Oxford 2010.

Muessig, Carolyn: Prophecy and Song: Teaching and Preaching by Medieval Women. In: Women Preachers and Prophets through Two Millennia of Christianity. Hrsg. von Beverly Mayne Kienzle / Pamela J. Walker. Berkeley 1998, S. 146–158.

Müller, Catherine: How to Do Things with Mystical Language. Marguerite d'Oingt's Performative Writing. In: Performance and Transformation. New Approaches to Late Medieval Spirituality. Hrsg. von Mary A. Suydam / Joanna E. Ziegler. Basingstoke 1999, S. 27–45.

Müller, Jan-Dirk: Spielregeln für den Untergang. Die Welt des Nibelungenliedes. Tübingen 1998.

Müller, Jan-Dirk: Höfische Kompromisse. Acht Kapitel zur höfischen Epik. Tübingen 2007.

Müller, Maria E.: Die heilige Margarete, der Teufel und André Jolles. In: Sprechen mit Gott. Redeszenen in mittelalterlicher Bibeldichtung und Legende. Hrsg. von Nine Miedema / Angela Schrott / Monika Unzeitig (Historische Dialogforschung 2). Berlin 2012. S. 127–144.

Muir, Carolyn Diskant: Bride or Bridegroom? Masculine Identity in Mystic Marriages. In: Holiness and Masculinity in the Middle Ages. Hrsg. von P. H. Cullum / Katherine J. Lewis (Religion & Culture in the Middle Ages). Cardiff 2004, S. 58–78.

Neff, Amy: The Pain of ›Compassio‹. Mary's Labor at the Foot of the Cross. In: Art Bulletin 80 (1998), S. 254–273.

Nelstrop, Louise: Christian Mysticism. An Introduction to Contemporary Theoretical Approaches. Farnham / Burlington 2009.

Nellmann, Eberhard: Wolframs Erzähltechnik. Untersuchungen zur Funktion des Erzählers. Wiesbaden 1973.

Nemes, Balázs J.: Jutta von Sangerhausen (13. Jahrhundert). Eine ›neue Heilige‹ im Gefolge der heiligen Elisabeth von Thüringen? In: Zeitschrift für Thüringische Geschichte 63 (2009), S. 39–73.

Nemes, Balázs J.: Von der Schrift zum Buch – vom Ich zum Autor. Zur Text- und Autorkonstitution in Überlieferung und Rezeption des ›Fließenden Lichts der Gottheit‹ Mechthilds von Magdeburg (Bibliotheca Germanica 55). Tübingen / Basel 2010.

Nemes, Balázs J.: Rezension zu Urban Federer: Mystische Erfahrung im literarischen Dialog. Die Briefe Heinrichs von Nördlingen an Margaretha Ebner (2011). In: ZfdPh 132 (2013), S. 454–469.

Nemes, Balázs J.: Meister Eckhart auf der Wartburg. Fundbericht anlässlich der Wiederentdeckung einer frühen Eckhart-Handschrift aus dem Prämonstratenserinnenstift Altenberg im Bestand der Wartburg-Stiftung. In: Wartburg-Jahrbuch 15 (2017), S. 176–202.

Nemes, Balázs J./Märker, Almut: ›Hunc tercium conscripsi cum maximo labore occultandi‹. Schwester N von Helfta und ihre ›Sonderausgabe‹ des ›Legatus divinae pietatis‹ Gertruds von Helfta in der Leipziger Handschrift Ms 827. In: PBB 137 (2015), S. 248–296.

Nemes, Balázs J./Vinzent, Markus: Neue Texte aus dem Kreis der Kölner Eckhartisten? Eine wieder entdeckte Handschrift auf der Wartburg bei Eisenach mit Übersetzungen aus Meister Eckharts Bibelkommentaren und ihre Bedeutung für die Eckhart-Philologie (in Vorbereitung).

Neumann, Hans: Beiträge zur Textgeschichte des ›Fließenden Licht der Gottheit‹ und zur Lebensgeschichte Mechthilds von Magdeburg. In: Altdeutsche und altniederländische Mystik. Hrsg. von Kurt Ruh (Wege der Forschung 23). Darmstadt 1964, S. 175–239.

Neumann, Gerhard / Warning, Rainer: Einleitung. In: Transgressionen, Literatur als Ethnographie. Hrsg. von Gerhard Neumann / Rainer Warning (Rombach Wissenschaften Litterae 98). Freiburg i. Br. 2003, S. 7–16.

Newman, Barbara: Some Medieval Theologians and the Sophia Tradition. In: Downside Review 108 (1990), S. 111–130.

Newman, Barbara: Hildegard and Her Hagiographers. The Remaking of Female Sainthood. In: Gendered Voices: Medieval Saints and their Interpreters. Hrsg. von Catherine M. Mooney. Philadelphia 1999(a). S. 16–34.

Newman, Barbara: Intimate Pietis. Holy Trinity and Holy Family in the Late Middle Ages. In: Religion and Literature 31 (1999[b]), S. 77–101.

Newman, Barbara: Henry Suso and the Medieval Devotion to Christ the Goddess. In: Spiritus. A Journal of Christian Spirituality 2 (2002), S. 1–14.

Newman, Barbara: God and the Goddesses. Vision, Poetry, and Belief in the Middle Ages. Philadelphia 2003.

Newman, Barbara: What Did it Mean to Say ›I saw‹? The Clash Between Theory and Practice in Medieval Visionary Culture. In: Speculum 80 (2005), S. 1–43.

Newman, Barbara: Liminalities. Literate Women in the Long Twelfth Century. In: European Transformation. The Long Twelfth Century. Hrsg. von Thomas F. X. Noble / John Van Engen. Notre Dame 2012, S. 354–402.

Nichols, Stephen G.: Philology in a manuscript culture. In: Speculum 75 (1990), S. 1–10.

Nichols, Stephen G.: Philology and Its Discontents. In: The Future of the Middle Ages. Medieval Literature in the 1990s. Hrsg. von William D. Paden. Gainesville 1994, S. 113–141.

Nichols, Stephen G.: Why material philology? Some Thoughts. In: Philologie als Textwissenschaft. Alte und neue Horizonte. Hrsg. von Helmut Tervooren / Horst Wenzel (ZfdPh 116, Sonderheft). Berlin 1997, S. 10–30.

Oesterreicher, Wulf: ›Verschriftung‹ und ›Verschriftlichung‹ im Kontext medialer und konzeptioneller Schriftlichkeit. In: Schriftlichkeit im frühen Mittelalter. Hrsg. von Ursula Schaefer (ScriptOralia 53). Tübingen 1993, S. 267–292.

Ohly, Friedrich: Du bist mein, ich bin dein. Du in mir, ich in dir. Ich du, du ich. In: Kritische Bewahrung. Beiträge zur deutschen Philologie. Festschrift für Werner Schröder zum 60. Geburtstag. Hrsg. von Ernst-Joachim Schmidt. Berlin 1974, S. 371–415.

Ohly, Friedrich: Halbbiblische und außerbiblische Typologie. In: Simboli e simbologia nell'alto medioevo. Settimane di studio del centro italiano di studi sull'alto medioevo XXIII. 3–9 aprile 1975. Hrsg. von Centro italiano di studi sull'alto medioevo. 2 Bde. Spoleto 1976, Bd. 2, S. 429–472.

Ohly, Friedrich: Süße Nägel der Passion. Ein Beitrag zur theologischen Semantik. In: Collectanea philologica. Festschrift für Helmut Gipper zum 65. Geburtstag. Hrsg. von Günter Heintz / Peter Schmitte. 2 Bde. (Saecula spiritualia 14–15). Baden-Baden 1985, Bd. 2, S. 403–613.

Ohly, Friedrich: Eine Lehre der liebenden Gotteserkenntnis. Zum Titel des St. Trudperter Hohelieds. In: ZfdA 121 (1992), S. 399–404.

Ohly, Friedrich: Gebärden der Liebe zwischen Gott und Mensch im St. Trudperter Hohelied. In: Literaturwissenschaftliches Jahrbuch 34 (1993), S. 9–31.

Palazzo, Éric: Visions and Liturgical Experience in the Early Middle Ages. In: Looking Beyond. Visions, Dreams and Insights in Medieval Art and History. Hrsg. von Colum Hourihane (Occasional papers Princeton University. Department of Art and Archaeology. Index of Christian Art 11). Princeton 2010, S. 15–29.

Palmer, Nigel F.: Kapitel und Buch. Zu den Gliederungsprinzipien mittelalterlicher Bücher. In: Frühmittelalterliche Studien 23 (1989), S. 43–88.

Palmer, Nigel F.: Das Buch als Bedeutungsträger bei Mechthild von Magdeburg. In: Bildhafte Rede in Mittelalter und früher Neuzeit. Probleme ihrer Legitimation und ihrer Funktion. Hrsg. von Wolfgang Harms. Tübingen 1992, S. 217–235.

Palmer, Nigel F.: Manuscripts for Reading. The Material Evidence for the Use of Manuscripts Containing Middle High German Narrative Verse. In: Orality and Literacy in the Middle Ages. Essays on a Conjunction and its Consequences in Honour of D.H. Green. Hrsg. von Mark Chinca / Christopher Young (Utrecht Studies in Medieval Literacy 12). Turnhout 2005, S. 67–102.

Palmer, Nigel F.: Herzeliebe, weltlich und geistlich. Zur Metaphorik vom ›Einwohnen im Herzen‹ bei Wolfram von Eschenbach, Juliana von Cornillon, Hugo von Langenstein und Gertrud von Helfta. In: Innenräume in der Literatur des deutschen Mittelalters. XIX. Anglo-German Colloquium Oxford 2005. Hrsg. von Burkhard Hasebrink u. a. Tübingen 2008, S. 197–224.

Palmer, Nigel F.: ›In kaffin in got‹. Zur Rezeption des ›Paradisus anime intelligentis‹ in der Oxforder Handschrift MS. Laud. Misc. 479. In: ›Paradisus anime intelligentis‹. Studien zu einer dominikanischen Predigtsammlung aus dem Umkreis Meister Eckharts. Hrsg. von Burkhard Hasebrink / Nigel F. Palmer / Hans-Jochen Schiewer. Tübingen 2009, S. 69–131.

Palmer, Nigel F.: The German Prayers in their Literary and Historical Context. In: The Prayer Book of Ursula Begerin. Hrsg. von Jeffrey F. Hamburger / Nigel F. Palmer. 2 Bde. Dietikon 2015, Bd. 1: Art-historical and literary introduction; with a conservation report by Ulrike Bürger, S. 377–488.

Palmer, Nigel F.: Manuscripts of the Earliest Middle High German Prayers, ca. 1150–1250. In: Vernacular Manuscript Culture. Hrsg. von Erik Kwakkel (Studies in Medieval and Renaissance Book Culture). Leiden 2017.

Parkes, Malcolm Beckwith: Pause and Effect. An Introduction to the History of Punctuation in the West. Aldershot 1992.

Parkes, Malcolm Beckwith: Punctuation and the Medieval History of Texts. In: La Filologia testuale e le scienze umane. Atti del convengo internazionale. Roma, 19–22 aprile 1993. Hrsg. von Accademia Nazionale dei Lincei (Atti dei Convegni 111). Rom 1994, S. 265–277.

Parkes, Malcolm Beckwith: Medieval Punctuation and the Modern Editor. In: Filologia classica e filologia romanza. Esperienze ecdotiche a confronto. Atti del Convegno. Roma, 25–27 maggio 1995. Hrsg. von Anna Ferrari (Incontri di studio 2). Spoleto 1998, S. 337–349.

Parkes, Malcolm Beckwith: Their Hands Before our Eyes. A Closer Look at Scribes. The Lyell Lectures Delivered in the University of Oxford 1999. Aldershot 2008.

Paul, Hermann u. a. (Hrsg.): Mittelhochdeutsche Grammatik. 24. Aufl. überarb. von Peter Wiehl/Siegfried Grosse. Tübingen 1998.

Pauphilet, Albert: Études sur la Queste del Saint Graal attribuées à Gautier Map. Paris 1921.

Pelikan, Jaroslav: Mary through the Centuries. Her Place in the History of Culture. New Haven/London 1996.

›Performance‹. In: Duden-Online, URL: http://www.duden.de/suchen/dudenonline/Performance [10.08.2017].

Peters, Ursula: Das ›Leben‹ der Christine Ebner. Textanalyse und kulturhistorischer Kommentar. In: Abendländische Mystik im Mittelalter. Symposium Kloster Engelberg 1984. Hrsg. von Kurt Ruh (Germanistische Symposien, Berichtsbände 7). Stuttgart 1986, S. 402–422.

Peters, Ursula: Religiöse Erfahrung als literarisches Faktum. Zur Vorgeschichte und Genese frauenmystischer Texte des 13. und 14. Jahrhunderts. Tübingen 1988.

Peters, Ursula: Hofkleriker – Stadtschreiber – Mystikerin. Zum literarischen Status dreier Autorentypen. In: Autorentypen. Hrsg. von Walter Haug/Burghart Wachinger (Fortuna Vitrae 6). Tübingen 1991, S. 29–49.

Peters, Ursula: Mittelalterliche Literatur am Hof und im Kloster. Ergebnisse und Perspektiven eines historisch-anthropologischen Verständnisses. In: Mittelalterliche Literatur und Kunst im Spannungsfeld von Hof und Kloster. Ergebnisse der Berliner Tagung, 9.–11. Oktober 1997. Hrsg. von Nigel F. Palmer/Hans-Jochen Schiewer. Tübingen 1999, S. 167–192.

Peters, Ursula: Werkauftrag und Buchübergabe. Textentstehungsgeschichten in Autorbildern volkssprachiger Handschriften des 12. bis 15. Jahrhunderts. In: Autorbilder. Zur Medialität literarischer Kommunikation in Mittelalter und Früher Neuzeit. Hrsg. von Gerald Kapfhammer/Wolf-Dietrich Löhr/Barbara Nitsche (Tholos Kunsthistorische Studien 2). Münster 2007, S. 25–62.

Petersen, Jürgen H.: Kategorien des Erzählens. In: Poetica 9 (1977), S. 167–195.

Petit, François: La spiritualité des Prémontrés aux XXᵉ et XIIIᵉ siècles (Études de thélogie de d'histoire de la spiritualité 10). Paris 1947.

Petroff, Elizabeth Alvilda: Medieval Women's Visionary Literature. New York/Oxford 1986.

Petroff, Elizabeth Alvilda: Body and Soul. Essays on Medieval Women and Mysticism. New York/Oxford 1994.

Pfeiffer, K. Ludwig: Struktur- und Funktionsprobleme der Allegorie. In: Von der Materialität der Kommunikation zur Medienanthropologie. Aufsätze zur Methodologie der Literatur- und Kulturwissenschaften 1977–2009. Hrsg. von Ingo Berensmeyer/Nicola Glaubitz (Reihe Siegen 161). Heidelberg 2009, S. 159–187.

Pfister, Manfred: Konzepte der Intertextualität. In: Intertextualität. Formen, Funktionen, anglistische Fallstudien. Hrsg. von Manfred Pfister / Ulrich Broich. Tübingen 1985, S. 1–30.

Poor, Sara S.: Mechthild von Magdeburg, Gender, and the ›Unlearned Tongue‹. In: Journal of Medieval and Early Modern Studies 31 (2001), S. 213–250.

Poor, Sara S.: Mechthild of Magdeburg and Her Book. Gender and the Making of Textual Authority. Philadelphia 2004.

Powell, Morgan: ›Vox ex negativo‹. Hildegard of Bingen, Rupert of Deutz and Authorial Identity in the Twelfth Century. In: Unverwechselbarkeit. Persönliche Identität und Identifikation in der vormodernen Gesellschaft. Hrsg. von Peter von Moos (Norm und Struktur 23). Wien 2004, S. 267–295.

Prica, Aleksandra: Frau Ava. ›Johannes‹ und ›Leben Jesu‹ (um 1120). In: Literarische Performativität. Lektüren vormoderner Texte. Hrsg. von Cornelia Herberichs / Christian Kiening (Medienwandel – Medienwechsel – Medienwissen 3). Zürich 2008, S. 82–99.

Primus, Beatrice: Performanz und Grammatik. In: Oberfläche und Performanz. Untersuchungen zur Sprache als dynamischer Gestalt. Hrsg. von Angelika Linke / Helmuth Feilke (Germanistische Linguistik 283). Tübingen 2009, S. 99–116.

Quast, Bruno: ›drücken und schreiben‹. Passionsmystische Frömmigkeit in den Offenbarungen der Margarethe Ebner. In: Gewalt im Mittelalter. Realitäten – Imaginationen. Hrsg. von Manuel Braun / Cornelia Herberichs. München 2005, S. 293–306.

Rapp, Claudia: Storytelling as Spiritual Communication in Early Greek Hagiography. The Use of Diegesis. In: Journal of Early Christian Studies 6 (1998), S. 431–448.

Reed, Teresa: Shadows of Mary. Reading the Virgin Mary in Medieval Texts. Cardiff 2003.

Reinle, Christine: Adolf von Nassau (1292–1298). In: Die deutschen Herrscher des Mittelalters. Historische Portraits von Heinrich I. bis Maximilian I. (919–1519). Hrsg. von Bernd Schneidmüller / Stefan Weinfurter. München 2003, S. 360–371.

Ringler, Siegfried: Viten- und Offenbarungsliteratur in Frauenklöstern des Mittelalters. Quellen und Studien (MTU 72). Zürich / München 1980.

Ringler, Siegfried: Die Rezeption mittelalterlicher Frauenmystik als wissenschaftliches Problem, dargestellt am Werk der Christine Ebner. In Frauenmystik im Mittelalter. Hrsg. von Peter Dinzelbacher / Dieter R. Bauer. Ostfildern 1985, S. 178–200.

Robinson, Douglas: Introducing Performative Pragmatics. New York 2006.

Röckelein, Hedwig: Das Gewebe der Schriften. Historiographische Aspekte der karolingerzeitlichen Hagiographie Sachsens. In: Hagiographie im Kontext. Wirkungsweisen und Möglichkeiten historischer Auswertung. Hrsg. von Dieter R. Bauer / Klaus Herbers (Beiträge zur Hagiographie 1). Stuttgart 2000, S. 1–25.

Roloff, Volker: Reden und Schweigen. Zur Tradition und Gestaltung eines mittelalterlichen Themas in der französischen Literatur (Münchener Romanistische Arbeiten 34). München 1973.

Rubin, Miri: Mother of God. A History of the Virgin Mary. London 2010.

Ruh, Kurt: Hester. In: ²VL 3 (1981), Sp. 1201–1203.

Ruh, Kurt: Geschichte der abendländischen Mystik. Bd. 1: Die Grundlegung durch die Kirchenväter und die Mönchstheologie des 12. Jahrhunderts. München 1990.

Ruh, Kurt: Geschichte der abendländischen Mystik. Bd. 2: Frauenmystik und Franziskanische Mystik der Frühneuzeit. München 1993.

Ruberg, Uwe: Beredtes Schweigen. In lehrhafter und erzählender deutscher Literatur des Mittelalters (Münstersche Mittelalter-Schriften 32). München 1978.

Ruhrberg, Christine: Der literarische Körper der Heiligen. Leben und Viten der Christina von Stommeln (1242–1312) (Bibliotheca Germanica 35). Tübingen / Basel 1995.

Sahlin, Claire L.: His Heart was my Heart. Birgitta of Sweden's Devotion to the Heart of Mary. In: Heliga Birgitta – budskapet och förebilden. Hrsg. von Alf Härdelin / Mereth Lindgren. Stockholm 1993, S. 213–227.

Sahlin, Claire L.: The Virgin Mary and Birgitta of Sweden's Prophetic Vocation. In: Maria i Sverige under Tusen År. Hrsg. von Sven-Erik Brodd / Alf Härdelin. Skellefteå 1996, S. 227–254.

Sahlin, Claire L.: Birgitta of Sweden and the Voice of Prophecy. Woodbridge 2001.

Sand, Alexa: Vindictive Virgins. Animate Images and Theories of Art in some Thirteenth-Century Miracle Stories. In: Word & Image. A Journal of Verbal / Visual Enquiry 26 (2010), S. 150–159.

Sansterre, Jean-Marie: ›Omnes qui coram hac imagine genua flexerint …‹ La vénération d'images de saints et de la Vierge d'après les textes écrits en Angleterre du milieu du XIᵉ aux premières décennies du XIIIᵉ siècle. In: Cahiers de civilisation médiévale 49 (2006), S. 257–294.

Sansterre, Jean-Marie: La Vierge Marie et ses images chez Gautier de Coinci et Césaire de Heisterbach. In: Viator 41 (2010), S. 147–178.

Sauerwein, Friederike: Religiöse Identität oder ›Heiliger Schein‹? Weibliche Lebensgestaltung und hagiographische Überlieferung am Beispiel der hl. Lioba. In: Hagiographie im Kontext. Wirkungsweisen und Möglichkeiten historischer Auswertung. Hrsg. von Dieter R. Bauer / Klaus Herbers (Beiträge zur Hagiographie 1). Stuttgart 2000 S. 46–57.

Scarry, Elaine: On Vivacity. The Difference between Daydreaming and Imagining-Under-Authorial-Instruction. In: Representations 52 (1995), S. 1–26.

Schaefer, Ursula: Vokalität. Altenglische Dichtung zwischen Mündlichkeit und Schriftlichkeit (ScriptOralia 39). Tübingen 1992.

Scharbert, Josef: Weisheitsbücher. In: Marienlexikon. Hrsg. von Remigius Bäumer / Leo Scheffczyk. 6 Bde. St. Ottilien 1988–1994, Bd. 6 (1994), S. 702 f.

Scharloth, Joachim: Performanz als Modus des Sprechens und Interaktionsmodalität. Linguistische Fundierung eines kulturwissenschaftlichen Konzepts. In: Oberfläche und Performanz. Untersuchungen zur Sprache als dynamischer Gestalt. Hrsg. von Angelika Linke / Helmuth Feilke (Germanistische Linguistik 283). Tübingen 2009, S. 233–254.

Schechner, Richard: Performance Studies. An Introduction. 2. Aufl. New York / London 2006.

Scheepsma, Wybren: Check and Double-check. An Unknown Vision Cycle by a Religious Woman from the Low Countries. In: The Voice of Silence. Women's Literacy in a Men's Church. Hrsg. von Thérèse de Hemptinne / María Eugenia Góngora (Medieval Church Studies 9). Turnhout 2004, S. 207–221.

Schlotheuber, Eva: Klostereintritt und Übergangsriten. Die Bedeutung der Jungfräulichkeit für das Selbstverständnis der Nonnen der alten Orden. In: Frauen – Kloster – Kunst. Neue Forschungen zur Kulturgeschichte des Mittelalters. Beiträge zum internationalen Kolloquium vom 13. bis 16. Mai 2005 anlässlich der Ausstellung ›Krone und Schleier‹. Hrsg. von Jeffrey F. Hamburger / Carola Jäggi. Turnhout 2007, S. 43–55.

Schmidt, Margot (Hrsg.): Rudolf von Biberach. ›Die siben strassen zu got‹. Die hochalemannische Übertragung nach der Handschrift Einsiedeln 278. Quaracchi, Florentiae 1969.

Schmitt, Jean-Claude: L'exception corporelle. À propos de l'assomption de Marie. In: The Mind's Eye. Art and Theological Argument in the Middle Ages. Hrsg. von Jeffrey F. Hamburger / Anne-Marie Bouché. Princeton 2006, S. 151–185.

Schneider, Almut: ›er liez ze himel tougen erhellen sîner stimme dôn‹. Sprachklang als poetische Fundierung normativen Sprechens. In: Text und Normativität. XX. Anglo-German Colloquium. Hrsg. von Elke Brüggen u. a. Berlin / Boston 2012, S. 199–216.

Schneider, Karin: Gotische Schriften in deutscher Sprache I. Vom späten 12. Jahrhundert bis um 1300, Text- und Tafelband. Wiesbaden 1987.

Schneider, Wolfgang Christian: Durch Sinnbilder zur Schau. Performative Momente in Allegorie, Typos-Bezug und Mystagogie des spätantiken Christentums. In: Performativität und Praxis. Hrsg. von Jens Kertscher / Dieter Mersch. München 2003, S. 175–194.

Schnell, Rüdiger: Gender und Rhetorik in Mittelalter und früher Neuzeit. Zur Kommunikation der Geschlechter. In: Rhetorik 29 (2010), S. 1–18.

Schnyder, Marijke: Geschlechtsspezifisches Gesprächsverhalten. Höraktivitäten und Unterbrechungen in Radiogesprächsrunden (Sprach- und Literaturwissenschaft 36). Pfaffenweiler 1997 (Diss. Fribourg 1994).

Schnyder, Mireille: Topographie des Schweigens. Untersuchungen zum deutschen höfischen Roman um 1200 (Historische Semantik 3). Göttingen 2003.

Scholz, Manfred Günther: Zur Hörerfiktion in der Literatur des Spätmittelalters und der frühen Neuzeit. In: Literatur und Leser. Theorien und Modelle zur Rezeption literarischer Werke. Hrsg. von Gunter Grimm. Stuttgart 1975, S. 135–147.

Schotes, Paul: Reformbasilika Hane Bolanden. Bolanden 2009.

Schreiner, Klaus: ›wie Maria geleicht einem puch‹. Beiträge zur Buchmetaphorik des hohen und späten Mittelalters. In: Archiv für Geschichte des Buchwesens 11 (1971), S. 1437–1464.

Schreiner, Klaus: Marienverehrung, Lesekultur, Schriftlichkeit. Bildungs- und frömmigkeitsgeschichtliche Studien zur Auslegung und Darstellung von Mariä Verkündigung. In: Frühmittelalterliche Studien 24 (1990), S. 314–368.

Schreiner, Klaus: Maria: Jungfrau, Mutter, Herrscherin. München 1994.

Schroeder, Joy A.: The Feast of the Purification in the Liturgical Mysticism of Angela of Foligno. In: Mystics Quarterly 32 (2006), S. 35–67.

Schrott, Angela: Heiligenrede in altspanischen Texten. Dialogprofile und Techniken der Redeinszenierungen bei Gonzalo de Berceo. In: Sprechen mit Gott. Redeszenen in mittelalterlicher Bibeldichtung und Legende. Hrsg. von Nine Miedema / Angela Schrott / Monika Unzeitig (Historische Dialogforschung 2). Berlin 2012, S. 107–126.

Schuhmann, Martin: Reden und Erzählen. Figurenrede in Wolframs ›Parzival‹ und ›Titurel‹ (Frankfurter Beiträge zur Germanistik 49). Heidelberg 2008.

Schünemann, Silke: Florio und Bianceffora (1499). Studien zu einer literarischen Übersetzung (Frühe Neuzeit 106). Tübingen 2005 (Diss. Göttingen 2003).

Schützeichel, Rudolf: Mundart, Urkundensprache und Schriftsprache. Studien zur Sprachgeschichte am Mittelrhein (Rheinisches Archiv 54). Bonn 1960.

Schwitalla, Johannes: Gesprochenes Deutsch. Eine Einführung. 2. überarb. Aufl. (Grundlagen der Germanistik 33). Berlin 2003.

Searle, John Rogers: Expression and Meaning. Studies in the Theory of Speech Acts. Cambridge 1979.

Seebald, Christian: Hermeneutischer Dialog. Rudolfs von Ems ›Barlaam und Josaphat‹ und die Lehre von der ›bezeichenunge‹. In: Sprechen mit Gott. Redeszenen in mittelalterlicher Bibeldichtung und Legende. Hrsg. von Nine Miedema / Angela Schrott / Monika Unzeitig (Historische Dialogforschung 2). Berlin 2012, S. 285–303.

Seeber, Stefan: Freud und die Mediävistik. Witztheoretische Überlegungen anhand von Wolframs ›Parzival‹. In: Oxford German Studies 41 (2012), S. 129–147.

Seelhorst, Jörg: Autoreferentialität und Transformation. Zur Funktion mystischen Sprechens bei Mechthild von Magdeburg, Meister Eckhart und Heinrich Seuse (Bibliotheca Germanica 46). Tübingen/Basel 2003.

Sells, Michael A.: Mystical Languages of Unsaying. Chicago/London 1994.

Simons, Walter: ›Staining the Speech of Things Divine‹. The Use of Literacy in Medieval Beguine Communities. In: The Voice of Silence. Women's Literacy in a Men's Church. Hrsg. von Thérèse de Hemptinne/María Eugenia Góngora (Medieval Church Studies 9). Turnhout 2004, S. 85–110.

Smith, Katherine Allen: Bodies of Unsurpassed Beauty. ›Living‹ Images of the Virgin in the High Middle Ages. In: Viator 37 (2006), S. 168–187.

Söll, Ludwig: Gesprochenes und geschriebenes Französisch (Grundlagen der Romanistik 6). Berlin 1985.

Staub, Kurt Hans/Sänger, Thomas: Deutsche und niederländische Handschriften. Mit Ausnahme der Gebetbuchhandschriften (Die Handschriften der Hessischen Landes- und Hochschulbibliothek Darmstadt 6). Wiesbaden 1991.

Steinmetz, Ralf-Henning: Bearbeitungstypen in der Literatur des Mittelalters. Vorschläge für eine Klärung der Begriffe. In: Texttyp und Textproduktion in der deutschen Literatur des Mittelalters. Hrsg. von Elizabeth A. Andersen/Manfred Eikelmann/Anne Simon (Trends in Medieval Philology 7). Berlin/New York 2005, S. 41–61.

Stock, Markus: Figur. Zu einem Kernproblem historischer Narratologie. In: Historische Narratologie. Mediävistische Perspektiven. Hrsg. von Harald Haferland/Matthias Meyer (Trends in Medieval Philology 19). Berlin/New York 2010, S. 187–203.

Stolz, Michael: Maria und die Artes liberales. Aspekte einer mittelalterlichen Zuordnung. In: Maria in der Welt. Marienverehrung im Kontext der Sozialgeschichte 10.–18. Jahrhundert. Hrsg. von Claudia Opitz u. a. (Clio Lucdenensis 2). Zürich 1993, S. 95–120.

Stolz, Michael: Artes-liberales-Zyklen. Formationen des Wissens im Mittelalter (Bibliotheca Germanica 47). Tübingen/Basel 2004.

Stolz, Michael: Medieval Canonicity and Rewriting. A Case Study of the Sigune-Figure in Wolfram's ›Parzival‹. In: Textual Scholarship and the Canon. Hrsg. von Hans Walter Gabler/Peter Robinson/Paulius V. Subačius (Variants 7). Amsterdam/New York 2008, S. 75–94.

Stridde, Christine: Heinrich Wittenwiler: ›Der Ring‹ (um 1410). In: Literarische Performativität. Lektüren vormoderner Texte. Hrsg. von Cornelia Herberichs/Christian Kiening (Medienwandel – Medienwechsel – Medienwissen 3). Zürich 2008, S. 299–315.

Stridde, Christine: Verbalpräsenz und göttlicher Sprechakt. Zur Pragmatik spiritueller Kommunikation ›zwischen‹ St. Trudperter Hohelied und Mechthilds von Magdeburg ›Das Fliessende Licht der Gottheit‹. Stuttgart 2009.

Strohschneider, Peter: Textualität der mittelalterlichen Literatur. Eine Problemskizze am Beispiel des ›Wartburgkrieges‹. In: Mittelalter. Neue Wege durch einen alten Kontinent. Hrsg. von Jan-Dirk Müller/Horst Wenzel. Stuttgart/Leipzig 1999, S. 19–41.

Strohschneider, Peter: Textheiligung. Geltungsstrategien legendarischen Erzählens im Mittelalter am Beispiel von Konrads von Würzburg ›Alexius‹. In: Über die Stabilisierung und Legitimierung institutioneller Ordnungen. Hrsg. von Gert Melville/Hans Vorländer. Köln/Weimar/Wien 2002, S. 109–147.

Strohschneider, Peter: Höfische Textgeschichten. Über Selbstentwürfe vormoderner Literatur (Germanisch-Romanische Monatsschrift 55). Heidelberg 2014.

Strowick, Elisabeth: Sprechende Körper – Poetik der Ansteckung. Performativa in Literatur und Rhetorik. München 2009.

Studer, Monika: Im Schatten der Gottesbraut. Engel in Mechthilds ›Fliessendem Licht der Gottheit‹. In: Euphorion 103 (2009), S. 225–251.

Suerbaum, Almut: Dialogische Identitätskonzeption bei Mechthild von Magdeburg. In: Dialoge. Sprachliche Kommunikation in und zwischen Texten im deutschen Mittelalter. Hamburger Colloquium 1999. Hrsg. von Nikolaus Henkel / Martin H. Jones / Nigel F. Palmer. Tübingen 2003, S. 239–255.

Suerbaum, Almut: Entrelacement? Narrative Technique in Heinrich von dem Türlîn's ›Diu Crône‹. In: Oxford German Studies 34 (2005), S. 5–18.

Suerbaum, Almut: Die Paradoxie mystischer Lehre im ›St. Trudperter Hohenlied‹ und im ›Fließenden Licht der Gottheit‹. In: Dichtung und Didaxe. Lehrhaftes Sprechen in der deutschen Literatur des Mittelalters. Hrsg. von Henrike Lähnemann / Sandra Linden. Berlin / New York 2009, S. 27–40.

Suerbaum, Almut: ›O wie gar wundirbar ist dis wibes sterke!‹ Discourses of Sex, Gender, and Desire in Johannes Marienwerder's Life of Dorothea von Montau. In: Oxford German Studies 39 (2010), S. 181–197.

Suerbaum, Almut: Between Unio and Alienation. Expressions of Desire in the Strophic Poems of Hadewijch. In: Desire and Dante and the Middle Ages. Hrsg. von Manuele Gragnolati u.a. London 2012(a), S. 152–163.

Suerbaum, Almut: Sprachliche Interferenz bei Begriffen des Lassens. ›Lux Divinitatis‹ und das ›Fließende Licht der Gottheit‹. In: Semantik der Gelassenheit. Generierung, Etablierung, Transformation. Hrsg. von Burkhard Hasebrink / Susanne Bernhardt / Imke Früh (Historische Semantik 17). Göttingen 2012(b), S. 33–47.

Suydam, Mary A.: Beguine Textuality, Sacred Performances. In: Performance and Transformation. New Approaches to Late Medieval Spirituality. Hrsg. von Mary A. Suydam / Joanna E. Ziegler. Basingstoke 1999(a), S. 169–210.

Suydam, Mary A.: Background. An Introduction to Performance Studies. In: Performance and Transformation. New Approaches to Late Medieval Spirituality. Hrsg. von Mary A. Suydam / Joanna E. Ziegler. Basingstoke 1999(b), S. 1–25.

Suydam, Mary A./Ziegler, Joanna E. (Hrsg.): Performance and Transformation. New Approaches to Late Medieval Spirituality. Basingstoke 1999.

Swarzenski, Hanns: Die lateinischen illuminierten Handschriften des XIII. Jahrhunderts. In den Ländern am Rhein, Main und Donau. Berlin 1936.

Tavard, George H.: The Genesis of Mariology. In: A Feminist Companion to Mariology. Hrsg. von Amy-Jill Levine. London / New York 2005, S. 106–120.

Tax, Petrus W.: Die große Himmelsschau Mechthilds von Magdeburg. In: ZfdA 108 (1979), S. 112–137.

Tervooren, Helmut: Minnesang, Maria und das Hohe Lied. Bemerkungen zu einem vernachlässigten Thema. In: Vom Mittelalter zur Neuzeit. Festschrift für Horst Brunner. Hrsg. von Dorothea Klein. Wiesbaden 2000, S. 15–47.

Thali, Johanna: Beten – Schreiben – Lesen. Literarisches Leben und Marienspiritualität im Kloster Engelthal (Bibliotheca Germanica 42). Tübingen 2003.

Thali, Johanna: ›andaht‹ und ›betrachtung‹. Zur Semantik zweier Leitvokabeln der spätmittelalterlichen Frömmigkeitskultur. In: Semantik der Gelassenheit. Generierung, Etablierung, Transformation. Hrsg. von Burkhard Hasebrink / Susanne Bernhardt / Imke Früh (Historische Semantik 17). Göttingen 2012, S. 226–267.

Tkacz, Catherine Brown: Singing Women's Words as Sacramental Mimesis. In: Recherches de théologie ancienne et médiévale 70 (2003), S. 275–328.

Tobin, Frank J.: Mechthild von Magdeburg. A Medieval Mystic in Modern Eyes. Columbia, SC 1995.

Tobin, Frank J.: German Mystical Literature to 1350. In: A Companion to Middle High German Literature to the 14th century. Hrsg. von Francis G. Gentry. Leiden / Boston / Köln 2002, S. 345–377.

Unger, Helga: Interaktion von Gott und Mensch im ›Legatus divinae pietatis‹ (Buch II) Gertruds der Großen von Helfta. Liturgie – mystische Erfahrung – Seelsorge. In: Literatur und Liturgie. Historische Fallstudien. Hrsg. von Cornelia Herberichs / Norbert Kössinger / Stephanie Seidl (Lingua Historica Germanica 10). Berlin / Boston 2015, S. 133–165.

Valvekens, Emile: Le chapitre général de Prémontré et les nouveaux statuts de 1505. In: Analecta Praemonstratensia 14 (1938), S. 53–94.

Valvekens, Emile: Textes relatifs à la réforme des status Prémontrés en 1505. In: Analecta Praemonstratensia 15 (1939), S. 25–41.

Vejdovsky, Boris: The Act of Reading as Performance. In: Performance. Hrsg. von Peter Halter (SPELL 11). Tübingen 1999, S. 55–61.

Vinaver, Eugène: A la recherche d'une poétique médiévale. Paris 1970.

Voaden, Rosalynn: God's Words, Women's Voices. The Discernment of Spirits in the Writing of Late-Medieval Women Visionaries. Woodbridge / Rochester 1999.

Volfing, Annette: John the Evangelist in Medieval German Writing. Imitating the Inimitable. Oxford 2001.

Volfing, Annette: Dialog und Brautmystik bei Mechthild von Magdeburg. In: Dialoge. Sprachliche Kommunikation in und zwischen Texten im deutschen Mittelalter. Hamburger Colloquium 1999. Hrsg. von Nikolaus Henkel / Martin H. Jones / Nigel F. Palmer. Tübingen 2003, S. 257–266.

Volfing, Annette: Medieval Literacy and Textuality in Middle High German. Reading and Writing in Albrecht's Jüngerer Titurel. New York 2007.

Volfing, Annette: ›der sin was âne sinne‹. Zum Verhältnis von Rationalität und Allegorie in philosophischen und mystischen Texten. In: Relation und Inszenierung von Rationalität in der mittelalterlichen Literatur. Blaubeurer Kolloquium 2006. Hrsg. von Klaus Ridder (Wolfram-Studien 20). Berlin 2008, S. 329–350.

Volfing, Annette: ›Du bist selben eyn himmel‹. Textualization and Transformation in the Life of Dorothea von Montau. In: Oxford German Studies 39 (2010), S. 147–159.

Volfing, Annette: Ever-growing Desire. Spiritual Pregnancy in Hadewijch and in Middle High German Mystics. In: Desire and Dante and the Middle Ages. Hrsg. von Manuele Gragnolati u. a. London 2012, S. 45–57.

Volfing, Annette: Verdoppelung und Verdrängung. Simultane Diskurse in der mystischen Literatur. In: Stimme und Performanz in der mittelalterlichen Literatur. Hrsg. von Nine Miedema / Angela Schrott / Monika Unzeitig (Historische Dialogforschung 4). Berlin 2017(a).

Volfing, Annette: ›Daughter Zion‹ in Medieval German Literature. Abingdon 2017(b).

Vollmann, Benedikt Konrad: Vita. In: Lexikon des Mittelalters. 9 Bde. und Registerband. München 1980–1999. Bd. 8 (1997), Sp. 1751–1752.

Vollmann-Profe, Gisela: Mechthild in der Provinz. ›Das fließende Licht der Gottheit‹ und ›Das Leben der heiligen Dorothea‹. In: Impulse und Resonanzen. Tübinger mediävistische

Beiträge zum 80. Geburtstag von Walter Haug. Hrsg. von Gisela Vollmann-Profe u.a. Tübingen 2007, S. 265–274.

De Vooys, C. G. N.: De legende ›van sunte maria magdalena bekeringhe‹. In: Tijdschrift voor nederlandsche Taal- en Letterkunde 24 (1905), S. 16–44.

Vreese, Willem de: De handschriften van Jan Ruusbroec's werken (Vlaamsche academie voor taal- & letterkunde. Uitgaven. VI. reeks. Bekroonde werken 24). Gent 1900.

Vrudny, Kimberly: Friars, Scribes, and Corpses. A Marian Confraternal Reading of ›The Mirror of Human Salvation‹ (›Speculum humanae salvationis‹) (Mediaevalia Groningana New Series 12). Paris/Leuven 2010.

Vulic, Kathryn: Prayer and Vernacular Writing in Late-Medieval England (unveröffentlicht Diss. University of California 2004).

Warnar, Geert: ›Ex levitate mulierum‹. Masculine Mysticism and Jan van Ruusbroec's Perception of Religious Women. In: The Voice of Silence. Women's Literacy in a Men's Church. Hrsg. von Thérèse de Hemptinne/María Eugenia Góngora (Medieval Church Studies 9). Turnhout 2004, S. 193–206.

Watson, Nicholas: Richard Rolle and the Invention of Authority. Cambridge 1991.

Wehrli-Johns, Martina: Maria und Martha in der religiösen Frauenbewegung. In: Abendländische Mystik im Mittelalter. Symposium Kloster Engelberg 1984. Hrsg. von Kurt Ruh (Germanistische Symposien, Berichtsbände 7). Stuttgart 1986, S. 354–367.

Weidner, Daniel: Ein Beispielfall nach der Reformation. Sakrament, Rhetorik und Repräsentation bei Théodore de Bèze. In: Sakramentale Repräsentation. Substanz, Zeichen und Präsenz in der Frühen Neuzeit. Hrsg. von Stefanie Ertz/Heike Schlie. München 2012, S. 29–48.

Weimann, Britta: Moselfränkisch. Der Konsonantismus anhand der frühesten Urkunden (Rheinisches Archiv 157). Wien/Köln/Weimar 2012.

Weimann, Britta: Überlegungen zur Entwicklung der Mündlichkeit und Schriftlichkeit in Luxemburg. In: Vielfalt der Sprachen, Varianz der Perspektiven. Zur Geschichte und Gegenwart der Luxemburger Mehrsprachigkeit. Hrsg. von Heinz Sieburg (Interkulturalität. Studien zu Sprache, Literautr und Gesellschaft 3). Bielefeld 2013, S. 251–262.

Weinfurter, Stefan: Reformkanoniker und Reichsepiskopat im Hochmittelalter. In: Historisches Jahrbuch 97/98 (1978), S. 158–193.

Weiß, Bardo: Ekstase und Liebe. Die Unio mystica bei den deutschen Mystikerinnen des 12. und 13. Jahrhunderts. Paderborn 2000.

Weiß, Bardo: Die deutschen Mystikerinnen und ihr Gottesbild. Das Gottesbild der deutschen Mystikerinnen auf dem Hintergrund der Mönchstheologie. 3 Bde. Paderborn 2004.

Wells, David A.: Allegorie als Interpretationsmittel mittelalterlicher Texte. Möglichkeiten und Grenzen. In: Bildhafte Rede im Mittelalter und früher Neuzeit. Probleme ihrer Legitimation und ihrer Funktion. Hrsg. von Wolfgang Harms/Klaus Speckenbach. Tübingen 1992, S. 1–23.

Wentzlaff-Eggebert, Friedrich-Wilhelm: Deutsche Mystik zwischen Mittelalter und Neuzeit. Einheit und Wandlung ihrer Erscheinungsform. Berlin 1969.

Wenzel, Horst: Die Verkündigung an Maria. Zur Visualisierung des Wortes in der Szene oder: Schriftgeschichte im Bild. In: Maria in der Welt. Marienverehrung im Kontext der Sozialgeschichte 10.–18. Jahrhundert. Hrsg. von Claudia Opitz u.a. (Clio Lucdenensis 2). Zürich 1993, S. 23–52.

Wenzel, Horst: Die Schrift und das Heilige. In: Die Verschriftlichung der Welt. Bild, Text und Zahl in der Kultur des Mittelalters und der Frühen Neuzeit. Hrsg. von Horst Wenzel/Wilfried

Seipel/Gotthart Wunberg (Schriften des Kunsthistorischen Museums 5). Wien 2000,
S. 15–57.

Wenzel, Horst/Lechtermann, Christina: Repräsentation und Kinästhetik. Teilhabe am Text oder
die Verlebendigung der Worte. In: Paragrana 10 (2001), S. 191–213.

Wickersheimer, Ernest: Strasbourg (Catalogue Général des Manuscrits des Bibliothèques
Publiques de France, Départements 47). Paris 1923.

Wiederkehr, Ruth: Das Hermetschwiler Gebetbuch. Studien zu deutschsprachiger Gebetbuchliteratur der Nord- und Zentralschweiz im Spätmittelalter (Kulturtopographie des
alemannischen Raums 5). Berlin/ Boston 2013.

Wilhelm, Friedrich: Denkmäler deutscher Prosa des 11. und 12. Jahrhunderts. Abteilung A: Text;
Abteilung B: Kommentar (Münchener Texte 8). München 1914/1916 (Nachdruck in einem
Band [Germanistische Bücherei 3]. München 1960).

Williams-Krapp, Werner: Maria Magdalena. In: ²VL 5 (1985), Sp. 1258–1264.

Williams-Krapp, Werner: Die deutschen und niederländischen Legendare des Mittelalters.
Studien zu ihrer Überlieferungs-, Text- und Wirkungsgeschichte (Texte und Textgeschichte
20). Tübingen 1986.

Williams-Krapp, Werner: Frauenmystik und Ordensreform im 15. Jahrhundert. In: Literarische
Interessenbildung im Mittelalter. DFG-Symposion 1991. Hrsg. von Joachim Heinzle
(Germanistische Symposien, Berichtsbände 14). Stuttgart/Weimar 1993, S. 301–313.

Williams-Krapp, Werner: Deutschsprachige Hagiographie von ca. 1350 bis ca. 1550. In:
Hagiographies. Histoire internationale de la littérature hagiographique, latine et
vernaculaire, en Occident, des origines á 1550. Bd. 1. Hrsg. von Guy Philippart (Corpus
Christianorum Hagiographies 1). Turnhout 1994, S. 267–288.

Williams-Krapp, Werner: Maria Magdalena. In: ²VL 11 (2004), Sp. 967–977.

Williams-Krapp, Werner: ›Wir lesent daz vil sölichen sachen swerlich betrogen werdent‹. Zur
monastischen Rezeption von mystischer Literatur im 14. und 15. Jahrhundert. In: Nonnen,
Kanonissen und Mystikerinnen. Religiöse Frauengemeinschaften in Süddeutschland.
Beiträge zur interdisziplinären Tagung vom 21. bis 23. September 2005 in Frauenchiemsee.
Hrsg. von Eva Schlotheuber/Helmut Flachenecker/Ingrid Gardill (Veröffentlichungen des
Max-Planck-Instituts für Geschichte 235, Studien zur Germania Sacra 31). Göttingen 2008,
S. 263–278.

Williams-Krapp, Werner: Mystikdiskurse und mystische Literatur im 15. Jahrhundert. In: Neuere
Aspekte germanistischer Spätmittelalterforschung. Hrsg. von Freimut Löser u.a. (Imagines
Medii Aevi 29). Wiesbaden 2012, S. 261–285.

Williams-Krapp, Werner: ›Frauenmystik‹ in Nürnberg. Zu einem bisher unbekannten Werk des
Kartäusers Erhart Groß. In: Grundlagen. Forschungen, Editionen und Materialien zur
deutschen Literatur und Sprache des Mittelalters und der Frühen Neuzeit. Hrsg. von Rudolf
Bentzinger/Ulrich-Dieter Oppitz/Jürgen Wolf. Stuttgart 2013, S. 181–195.

Wirth, Uwe: Der Performanzbegriff im Spannungsfeld von Illokution, Iteration und Indexikalität.
In: Performanz. Zwischen Sprachphilosophie und Kulturwissenschaften. Hrsg. von Uwe
Wirth. Frankfurt a.M. 2002, S. 9–60.

Wirth, Uwe: Zwischenräumliche Bewegungspraktiken. In: Bewegen im Zwischenraum. Hrsg. von
Uwe Wirth (Wege der Kulturforschung 3). Berlin 2012, S. 7–34.

Wolf, Jürgen: Narrative Historisierungsstrategien in Heldenepos und Chronik – vorgestellt am
Beispiel von ›Kaiserchronik‹ und ›Klage‹. In: Erzähltechnik und Erzählstrategien in der
deutschen Literatur des Mittelalters. Hrsg. von Wolfgang Haubrichs/Eckart Conrad Lutz/
Klaus Ridder (Wolfram-Studien 18). Berlin 2004, S. 323–346.

Wolf, Jürgen: Psalter und Gebetbuch am Hof. Bindeglieder zwischen klerikal-literater und laikal-mündlicher Welt. In: Orality and Literacy in the Middle Ages. Essays on a Conjunction and its Consequences in Honour of D.H. Green. Hrsg. von Mark Chinca / Christopher Young (Utrecht Studies in Medieval Literacy 12). Turnhout 2005, S. 139–179.

Worstbrock, Franz Josef: Hermann Josef von Steinfeld. In: ²VL 3 (1981), Sp. 1062–1066.

Worstbrock, Franz Josef: Wiedererzählen und Übersetzen. In: Mittelalter und Frühe Neuzeit. Übergänge, Umbrüche und Neuansätze. Hrsg. von Walter Haug (Fortuna vitrea 16). Tübingen 1999, S. 128–142.

Wortham, Simon Morgan: The Derrida Dictionary. London / New York 2010.

Wronski-Mayersak, Corey: Dialogic Melting: Representing Mystical Union and Its Instability in Marguerite Porete's ›Mirror of Simple Souls‹. In: Viator 42 (2011), S. 157–182.

Wulf, Christoph / Göhlich, Michael / Zirfas, Jörg (Hrsg.): Grundlagen des Performativen. Eine Einführung in die Zusammenhänge von Sprache, Macht und Handeln. Weinheim / München 2001.

Wünsche, Gregor: Imitatio Ioannis oder Elsbeths Apokalypse. Die ›Offenbarungen‹ Elsbeths im Kontext der dominikanischen Johannesfrömmigkeit im 14. Jahrhundert. In: Schmerz in der Literatur des Mittelalters und der Frühen Neuzeit. Hrsg. von Hans-Jochen Schiewer / Stefan Seeber / Markus Stock (Transatlantische Studien zu Mittelalter und früher Neuzeit 4). Göttingen 2010, S. 167–190.

Ziegeler, Hans-Joachim: Erzählen im Spätmittelalter. Mären im Kontext von Minnereden, Bispeln und Romanen (MTU 87). München 1985.

Zimmermann, Béatrice W. Acklin: Gott im Denken berühren. Die theologischen Implikationen der Nonnenviten (Dokimion 14). Fribourg 1993.

Zimmermann, Béatrice W. Acklin (Hrsg.): Denkmodelle von Frauen im Mittelalter (Dokimion 15). Fribourg 1994.

Zech, Andrea: Spielarten des Gottes-Genusses. Semantiken des Genießens in der europäischen Frauenmystik des 13. Jahrhunderts (Historische Semantik 25). Göttingen 2015.

Zenck, Martin: Erzeugen und Nachvollziehen von Sinn. Rationale, performative und mimetische Verstehensbegriffe in den Kulturwissenschaften. Eine Einleitung zu den drei Sektionen. In: Erzeugen und Nachvollziehen von Sinn. Rationale, performative und mimetische Verstehensbegriffe in den Kulturwissenschaften. Hrsg. von Martin Zenck / Markus Jüngling. München 2011, S. 13–26.

Zotz, Nicola: Otfrid von Weißenburg. ›Evangelienbuch‹ (863/71). In: Literarische Performativität. Lektüren vormoderner Texte. Hrsg. von Cornelia Herberichs / Christian Kiening (Medienwandel – Medienwechsel – Medienwissen 3). Zürich 2008, S. 44–61.

Zumthor, Paul: La Poésie et la voix dans la littérature médiévale. Paris 1987.

Register

Namen-, Orts-, Sach- und Werkverzeichnis

Adolf von Nassau (König) 5 f., 6

Agnes von Rom 274

Altenberg (Prämonstratenserinnenkloster) 127 f., 131, 216

Ambrosius 74, 143

Amsterdam
– St. Maria Magdalena (Bethanië) (Reuerin-
nenkloster) 267

Angela von Foligno (Franziskaner-
terziarin) 55, 67, 78, 142, 171, 200, 218
– ›Instructiones‹ 55, 141, 198
– ›Memoriale‹ 55, 79, 143, 158, 235

Angelus Silesius
– ›Cherubinischer Wandersmann‹ 242, 245

Antonius von Florenz (OP) 245

›Der Arnsteiner Marienleich‹ 199, 204 f.,
211 f., 234

Augustinus 27, 43, 127, 134, 138, 148, 150,
151, 155, 173, 183, 232, 237, 240

›Ave Maria‹ 133, 135 f., 136, 203 f. 225, 227

›Ave praeclara‹ 73, 161, 203, 225

Beatrijz von Nazareth (Zisterzi-
ensierin) 238 f.

Begerin, Ursula (Reuerin) 139

Bernhard von Clairvaux (OCist) 3, 126, 134,
148, 171, 184, 189, 215, 234 f., 237, 240

Berthold von Regensburg (OFM) 75, 148

Birgitta von Schweden 12, 36, 55, 95, 152,
154, 158 f., 174, 196, 200, 206–208,
214 f., 219, 253

Blannbekin, Agnes (Begine) 55, 143, 174,
206 f., 215, 238 f., 251

Boethius 230

Bolanden
– Hane (Prämonstratenserinnenkloster) 5,
48–50, 61, 129–131, 203 f., 223, 227,
261 f., 275
– Herren von 5, 128, 130
– Werner I. von 5

Bonaventura (OFM) 78, 91, 191, 243

›Brandan‹ 77, 125

Caesarius von Heisterbach (OCist) 3

Christina von Stommeln (Begine) 55, 66 f.

Clara von Assisi (Franziskanerin) 218

Cod. Vat. lat. 4763, siehe ›Vatikanische
Gebete‹

Daniel
– Buch der Bibel 81

Diederich, Petrus (OPraem) 260 f.

Dionysius Areopagita 16, 40, 42, 90, 173,
229 f.

Dorothea von Montau (Rekluse) 14 f., 23, 53,
82, 86, 107, 173 f., 247

Ebner, Christine (Dominikanerin) 66, 68,
218

Ebner, Margareta (Dominikanerin) 7, 56, 57,
65 f., 82, 147, 162, 175, 200, 206, 218 f.,
226, 241, 244, 249, 251 f.

Ecclesia 133, 169, 188, 195

Meister Eckhart (OP) 12 f., 16, 91, 96 f., 108,
114 f., 127 f., 175, 217, 222, 230–235,
239, 248 f., 255

Ekbert von Schönau (OSB) 65 f.

Elisabeth (Zisterzienserin in Hove) 3

Elisabeth von Schönau (Benediktinerin) 3,
65 f., 157, 162, 191–193, 203, 211

Elisabeth von Thüringen (Landgräfin von
Thüringen) 46, 130 f., 161, 216

Elsass 131

Elsbeth von Oye (Dominikanerin) 54, 79

Elsbeth Achler von Reute (Franziskaner-
terziarin) 142 f.

Emmaus 85

Engelport (Prämonstratenserinnenkloster) 260, 262

Engelthal (Dominikanerinnenkloster) 203

Eriugena, Johannes Scottus 16, 183

Esther
– Buch der Bibel 73–75, 83, 211–216
– ›Hester‹ 75–77

https://doi.org/10.1515/9783110536324-016

Fegefeuer 57 f., 75, 132 f., 140, 154, 189 f.,
   193, 211, 213
Frauenlob (Heinrich von Meissen) 26
– ›Marienleich‹ 215, 234, 239
Freiburg i. Br.
– Adelhausen (Dominikanerinnenkloster) 174

Gebetbuch von Muri 140
Gerson, Jean 54 f., 218
Gertrud von Altenberg (Prämonstratenserin) 131, 261, 268
Gertrud (die Große) von Helfta (Zisterzienserin) 13, 18, 55, 70, 83, 142, 158,
   162, 175, 183, 207, 219, 237 f., 244
– ›ein botte der götlichen miltekeit‹ 53, 82 f.,
   150, 176, 216, 236, 241, 244
– ›Legatus divinae pietatis‹ 18, 53, 55, 109 f.,
   175, 181, 183, 206, 216, 236, 238
Gertrud von Nivelles 131
Gregor I., der Große (Papst) 77, 91, 148, 153,
   183
Gregor von Nyssa 172, 235

Haas, Johannes (OPraem) 4, 261
Hadewijch 13, 96 f., 160, 162 f., 185, 238 f.
Hagenau (Prämonstratenserkloster) 131
Hane, *siehe* Bolanden
Heinrich von Mügeln
– ›Der Tum‹ 74, 114, 215, 234, 239
Heinrich von Nördlingen (Weltpriester) 65 f.,
   70, 175, 252
Heinrich von St. Gallen
– ›Marienleben‹ 212
Helfta (Zisterzienserinnenkloster) 251
Hermann von Reichenau (OSB) 203
Hermann Josef von Steinfeld (OPraem) 3 f.,
   184, 211, 219
›Hester‹, *siehe* Esther
Hildegard von Bingen (Benediktinerin) 11–13,
   42, 53, 56, 65 f., 152 f., 156–158, 162,
   206, 224
Hrabanus Maurus 138

Ida von Gorsleeuw (Zisterzienserin) 238 f.
Ida von Löwen (Begine, Zisterzienserin) 238 f.
Ida von Nijvel (Zisterzienserin) 238 f.
Ivette von Huy (Rekluse) 238 f.

Jacob (OPraem?) 58, 116
Jan van Ruusbroec (CanR) 89
Joannes Ludolphus van Craywinckel
   (OPraem) 8, 50
Johannesoffenbarung 125, 190, 215, 225,
   236, 239, 243, 245
Judith
– Buch der Bibel 73 f.
Juliana von Norwich (Rekluse) 12
Jutta von Sangerhausen (Rekluse) 46
Jutta von Sponheim (Rekluse) 56

›Kaiserchronik‹ 63
Kana 188
Katharina von Alexandrien 130 f.
Katherina von Siena (Dominikanerin) 65 f.
Kempe, Margery 200, 207
Köln
– St. Barbara (Kartause) 266
– St. Maria Magdalena (Augustinerinnen-
   kloster) 266
Konrad von Megenberg
– ›Das Buch der Natur‹ 77, 161
Konrad von Würzburg
– ›Die Goldene Schmiede‹ 198 f., 201, 207,
   210, 212 f., 215, 217, 234 f., 239, 241

Lamprecht von Regensburg (OFM)
– ›Tochter Syon‹ 189
Langmann, Adelheid (Dominikanerin) 15, 17,
   58, 79, 81–83, 85 f., 89, 101, 110, 113,
   124, 126, 139 f., 149 f., 162, 174, 176,
   182 f., 188, 207 f., 215, 218 f., 226, 228 f.,
   236–238, 240, 247, 249, 251.
Lauer, Caspar OPraem 8, 260 f.
Lazarus 88, 91

Mainz 128–131
Margareta Contracta (Rekluse) 93
Margareta Cratz von Scharfenstein (Prämon-
   stratenserin) 261 f.
Margaretha von Antiochien 130 f.
Margarita von Ypern (Dominikannerin) 238 f.
Marguerite d'Oingt (Kartäuserin) 35 f., 226
Maria von Bethanien 88, 91
Maria Magdalena 88–91
Maria von Oignies 238 f.

Marquard von Lindau (OFM) 107

Martha 88 f., 91

Mechthild von Hackeborn (Zisterzienserin) 55, 70, 142, 175, 200 f.
– ›Liber specialis gratiae‹ 55, 82, 125, 200 f.,
   238 f.

Mechthild von Magdeburg 13 f., 15, 18, 45,
   54 f., 69 f., 95–97, 157 f., 188, 200, 214
– ›Das fließende Licht der Gottheit‹ 13, 37,
   44 f., 55, 57 f., 68 f., 71, 73, 79, 82, 98,
   108, 113, 123, 127, 136, 141–145, 151–153,
   155 f., 158 f., 161–163, 169, 173–175, 177,
   180, 183, 185–195, 207, 216–219, 222,
   224, 226, 236, 238–241, 244, 246 f.,
   252 f.
– ›Lux divinitatis‹ 55, 125, 136, 241

Meyer, Johannes (OP) 49 f.

Neidhart 148, 269 f.

Nikolaus von Myra 130 f.

Nikolauskapelle (Hane?) 116, 131

Notker von St. Gallen 211 f.

Origines 172

›Palmbaumtraktat‹ 181 f.

›Pater noster‹ 111, 134–136, 225–227

Paulus, Apostel 79

Petrus, Apostel 130 f.

Petrus von Celle (OSB) 245

Petrus von Dacien (OP) 66 f.

Pieter de Waghenare (OPraem)

Platon 172 f.

Plotin 172 f.

Porete, Margareta 12 f., 16, 194

Radegund 56, 78

Randecke, Herren von 128, 130

Richard von St. Viktor (CanR) 74, 237

Rommersdorf (Prämonstratenserkloster) 131,
   260 f.

Rothenkirchen (Prämonstratenserkloster) 67 f., 223, 262

Rudolf von Biberach (OFM) 237
– ›Die siben strassen zu got‹ 114, 235

Rupert von Deutz (OSB) 199, 237

Satan 77–79, 149

›St. Georgener Predigten‹ 74 f., 80, 83, 200

St. Thomas an der Kyll (Zisterzienserinnenkloster) 136

›Das St. Trudperter Hohelied‹ 81, 107, 112,
   148, 153, 182, 185, 190, 217–219, 237 f.

Sayn (Prämonstratenserkloster) 262

Schutzmantelmadonna 174

Seuse, Heinrich (OP) 12 f., 18, 70, 108, 133,
   175, 212, 242–244
– ›Büchlein der ewigen Weisheit‹ 82, 247 f.
– ›Das grosse Briefbuch‹ 175
– ›Leben‹ 241

›Speculum Virginum‹ 229

Speyer 128

Stagel, Elsbeth (Dominikanerin) 13

Sunder, Friedrich (OP) 13, 201

Susanna
– Buch der Bibel 73 f.

Tauler, Johannes (OP) 12 f., 108, 124, 153, 255
– ›Die Predigten Taulers‹ 74, 175, 231 f.

Thomas von Aquin (OP) 153

Thomasin von Zerklaere
– ›Der Welsche Gast‹ 149

Tobias (Tobit)
– Buch der Bibel 80

Trier 136

Ulrich III. Niblung (OCist) 113

›Vatikanische Gebete‹ 132–135

Weiler (Dominikanerinnenkloster) 174

Wernher, Priester
– ›Marienleben‹ 205, 246 f.

Wildgrafen, Grafen von 130

›Zeitglöcklein‹ 64

Stellenverzeichnis der Christina von Hane-Vita

Kap. 1 51, 74–76, 86, 89 f., 122, 170, 213 f., 216, 271

Kap. 2 82, 102, 214, 271

Kap. 3 83, 85, 103, 120, 146, 174, 185

Kap. 4 83, 103, 238, 272

Kap. 5 84, 103, 109, 111, 121, 136, 138, 147, 269–271

Kap. 6 103 f., 111, 119 f., 135, 141, 176, 186, 225, 238, 244, 271 f.

Kap. 7 85, 105, 109, 113, 115 f., 122, 135, 139, 142, 165, 183, 210, 269, 271, 275

Kap. 8 105, 113, 121, 123 f., 141, 147, 150, 223 f., 271–273

Kap. 9 5, 77 f., 80, 105, 112, 122, 124

Kap. 10 56, 79 f., 83, 103, 106 f., 113, 121 f., 139 f., 146 f., 149, 199, 224, 228, 269, 271

Kap. 12 123, 147, 271

Kap. 13 78, 91, 216, 273

Kap. 14 56, 113

Kap. 15 57, 81, 119, 122 f., 127, 139, 141, 177, 269–271, 273

Kap. 16 78 f., 99, 206

Kap. 17 109, 116, 123, 131, 141, 146, 170, 190, 206, 241, 269

Kap. 18 91, 155, 228, 273

Kap. 19 269

Kap. 20 116, 143, 162, 185, 224 f., 227, 269, 272

Kap. 21 85, 158, 160, 162, 175, 192 f., 225, 229, 269

Kap. 22 97, 109, 143, 160, 162, 178, 185, 225, 270

Kap. 23 5 f., 76, 122, 133, 139, 153–156, 228, 271, 273

Kap. 24 124, 139, 154 f., 180, 193, 272

Kap. 25 153 f., 156

Kap. 26 6, 153–155, 277

Kap. 27 133, 140 f., 161, 197, 203, 210, 213, 225

Kap. 28 116, 131, 207, 209, 277

Kap. 29 103 f., 121, 201 f., 277

Kap. 30 57, 97, 123, 170, 181, 202, 206, 225, 272 f.

Kap. 31 97, 100, 143, 158, 162, 164, 190, 213, 225, 270

Kap. 32 57, 64, 116, 122, 162, 179, 185, 213, 226 f., 269

Kap. 33 143 f., 241, 269 f.

Kap. 34 104, 174, 178, 208 f., 213

Kap. 35 152, 161, 185, 217

Kap. 36 109, 116, 131

Kap. 37 109, 174 f., 186, 212 f., 273

Kap. 38 57, 119, 122, 153, 206, 269, 271

Kap. 39 57, 77, 105, 119, 122 f., 125, 135, 243, 274, 277

Kap. 40 277

Kap. 41 124, 198, 277

Kap. 42 140, 236, 277

Kap. 43 187, 198, 277

Kap. 44 277

Kap. 45 187, 192, 277

Kap. 46 277

Kap. 47 177, 277

Kap. 48 241, 277

Kap. 49 184, 277

Kap. 50 277

Kap. 51 140, 277

Kap. 52 171, 201, 269, 277

Kap. 53 171, 177, 193, 202, 277

Kap. 54 213, 277

Kap. 55 277

Kap. 56 57, 76, 97, 140, 158, 188 f., 225, 229, 240, 271

Kap. 57 58, 70, 76, 100, 103, 108, 116, 122 f., 140, 152, 159, 177, 189, 206, 228, 269

Kap. 58 122, 140

Kap. 59 124, 203, 217, 249

Kap. 60 131, 185

Kap. 61 249

Kap. 62 123, 159, 177 f., 193, 237

Kap. 63 100, 103, 140, 161, 179, 206, 213–215, 241, 269

Kap. 64 123, 184 f., 200, 206, 217, 269, 277

Kap. 65 81, 103, 138, 159, 190 f., 206, 213, 216, 273, 277

Kap. 66 277

Kap. 67 187, 198, 200, 277

Kap. 68 98, 277

Kap. 69 76, 277

Kap. 70 140, 192, 238 f.

Kap. 71 186

Kap. 72 152 f., 236, 242, 269

Kap. 73 184, 214, 239

Kap. 74 123, 217

Kap. 75 201, 214

Kap. 76 141, 174, 269, 273

Kap. 78 105, 113 f., 155, 185, 228

Kap. 79 269, 272

Kap. 80 100, 103, 120, 159, 228, 239 f., 249, 270 f.

Kap. 81 109, 192, 214 f., 217, 240, 270, 273

Kap. 82 98, 192, 269

Kap. 83 140 f.

Kap. 84 58, 123, 241–243, 248, 269

Kap. 85 213

Kap. 87 76, 201

Kap. 88 202, 270

Kap. 89 76, 238

Kap. 91 140, 240, 248

Kap. 92 153, 187

Kap. 93 76

Kap. 94 165, 198, 236, 248, 269

Kap. 95 140, 165 f., 228, 248, 269 f., 273, 277

Kap. 96 140, 165, 274

Kap. 97 76, 97, 159, 164 f., 177, 193, 214 f., 238, 269, 277

Kap. 98 96, 164–166, 180, 228, 272

Kap. 99 122, 165, 234, 239 f., 280

Kap. 100 97, 160, 164–166, 191, 196, 201, 217, 229–233, 240, 249, 269